PSYCHOLOGY

Second Edition

PSYCHOLOGY

Douglas A. Bernstein

Edward J. Roy

Thomas K. Srull

Christopher D. Wickens

**UNIVERSITY OF ILLINOIS AT
URBANA-CHAMPAIGN**

HOUGHTON MIFFLIN COMPANY   BOSTON
DALLAS   GENEVA, ILLINOIS   PALO ALTO   PRINCETON, NEW JERSEY

To the researchers, past and present,

whose work embodies psychology today,

and to the students who will follow

in their footsteps to shape the psychology

of tomorrow.

Cover photograph by Ralph Mercer Photography

Anatomical illustrations by Joel Ito

Charts and Graphs by Boston Graphics, Inc.

Illustrations by Steven Moore on pages 35, 47, 85, 95 (top), 106, 139 (bottom), 145, 166, 194, 206, 209, 258, 268, 277, 292 (left), 346, 351, 358, 361, 373, 442, 477, 481, and 484.

Credits

Chapter opening photos: p. 1: Jean-Francois Podevin/The Image Bank **p. 31:** Michael Quackenbush/The Image Bank **p. 83:** Mieke Maas/The Image Bank **p. 125:** Lawrence Manning/West Light **p. 171:** Peter Hendrie/The Image Bank **p. 215:** John Wagner, Jr./The Image Bank **p. 255:** Don Klumpp/The Image Bank **p. 299:** Louis Jawitz/The Image Bank **p. 341:** Garry Gay/The Image Bank **p. 389:** Bill Varie/The Image Bank **p. 431:** John P. Kelly/The Image Bank **p. 469:** Owen Franken/Stock, Boston **p. 499:** Jack Elness/ Comstock **p. 535:** Cary Wolinsky/Stock, Boston **p. 575:** Rene Burri/Magnum **p. 623:** Michael deCamp/The Image Bank **p. 665:** Dag Sundberg/The Image Bank **p. 701:** Joe Viesti/Viesti Associates.

(Credits continue following references.)

Printed in the U.S.A.

Library of Congress Catalog Card Number: 90-83278

ISBN: 0-395-43246-4

ABCDEFGHIJ—VH—9876543210

BRIEF CONTENTS

C O N T E N T S

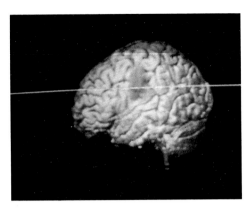

3

*Biological Aspects of
Psychology*   83

4

Sensation   125

6

Consciousness

5

Perception

7

Learning

8

Memory   299

9

Thought and Language   341

12

Emotion 469

13

Stress, Coping, and Health 499

14

Personality 535

10
Mental Abilities   389

11
Motivation

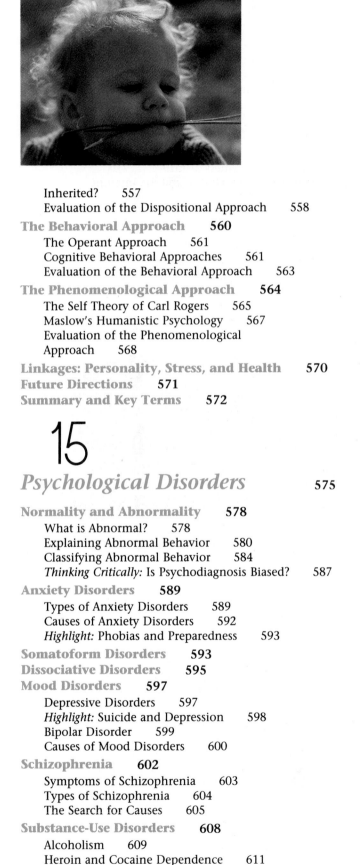

15

Psychological Disorders 575

16

Treatment of Psychological Disorders 623

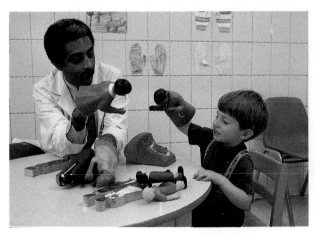

17

Social Cognition   665

18

Interpersonal Behavior and Group Influences   701

In revising *Psychology* we have rededicated ourselves to the goals we pursued when we wrote the First Edition:

■ To explore the full range of psychology, from cell to society, in an eclectic manner as free as possible from theoretical bias.

■ To balance our need to explain the content of psychology with an emphasis on the doing of psychology, through a blend of conceptual discussion and description of research studies.

■ To foster scientific attitudes and to help our readers learn to think critically by examining the ways that psychologists have solved, or failed to solve, fascinating puzzles of behavior and mental processes.

■ To produce a text that, without oversimplifying psychology, is clear, accessible, and enjoyable for students to read—even spiced now and again with humor.

■ To demonstrate that, in spite of its diversity, psychology is a notably integrated discipline in which each subfield is linked to other subfields by common interests and overarching research questions. The productive cross-fertilization among social, clinical, and biological psychologists in researching health and illness is just one recent example of how different types of psychologists benefit from and build on one another's work.

Responses from faculty and students who used the First Edition indicate that we achieved what we set out to do. In preparing the Second Edition we sought new ways to do justice to our goals.

We sought to respond to the needs of instructors who wanted us to reduce or expand coverage of various topics. For example, many instructors asked us to expand our coverage of adolescent and adult development in Chapter 2. We did so, and a more rounded picture of life-span development was the result.

We also sought to strike an ideal balance between classic and current research. The important historic findings of psychological research are here, but so is coverage of much recent work. More than a third of the research citations are new to the Second Edition, and we have added the latest information on such topics as:

- Day care (Chapter 2)

- Alzheimer's disease, Parkinson's disease, and mood disorders (Chapter 3)

- Biological effects of alcohol (Chapter 5)

- The role of emotion in forgetting, and the biological bases of memory (Chapter 8)

- Artificial intelligence (Chapter 9)

- Neural networks (Chapter 9)

- Creativity (Chapter 10)

- Panic and fear (Chapter 11)

- The "big five" theory of personality (Chapter 14)

- Cognitive behavior therapy (Chapter 16)

- The cognitive bases of prejudice (Chapter 17)

We wanted as well to present research findings as conclusions drawn from studies that are not infallible. Part of teaching students to think critically is to have them examine the limitations and flaws in the studies presented to them by authorities, and on this point we did not compromise.

We have also taken pains to draw attention to ethical considerations in psychology. These considerations are introduced in Chapter 1, and examined at other points throughout the text. One example occurs in Chapter 16, on Treatment of Psychological Disorders, where we discuss patients' rights; another is found in Chapter 18, in relation to Milgram's obedience research.

We have incorporated in the text frequent references to practical applications of psychological research. For example, in Chapter 5, on perception, we discuss psychology's contribution to aviation safety and present new material on the design of traffic circles. In a new discussion in Chapter 7 we examine the learning of everyday skills, such as driving a car or operating a computer. Chapter 8, Memory, proved an appropriate context for the discussion of courtroom behavior as well as an opportunity for students to improve their study skills and exam-taking techniques.

As in the First Edition, we have placed most of our discussion of historical events and trends into the chapter contexts where they are relevant, rather than attempting detailed coverage of psychology's history in Chapter 1.

Organization of the Text

No consensus exists on exactly what chapter sequence will present psychology to students in the most logical and comprehensible manner. Like other teachers, we have a preferred outline, and it is reflected in our table of contents. Rather than impose our sequence on your teaching, however, we have refrained from grouping the chapters into sections. Indeed, we designed each chapter to be a freestanding unit so that you may assign chapters in any order you wish.

We begin in Chapter 1 with an overview of the nature of psychology, a summary of the research and other activities associated with the various subfields within psychology, and a description of some of the research methods psychologists use. Then, to begin surveying the field, we move to Chapter 2, Human Development, where we show the reader how the principles and processes studied in each subfield come together across the human being's life span. Many instructors who followed our chapter organization in the First Edition found, as we have, that preceding physiology with human development had a salutary effect on their students. Again, however, if you wish to assign the development chapter out of sequence you may do so comfortably.

Other notable aspects of the text's organization:

- Unlike some other texts, we devote separate chapters to motivation; emotion; and stress, coping, and health (Chapters 11, 12, and 13). This enables us to cover these areas in the depth they deserve and, in particular, to present a detailed discussion of stress, one of the major subjects of psychological research during the past decade.

- We devote two separate but related chapters to social psychology (Chapters 17 and 18).

- We cover the methods of psychological research initially in Chapter 1, and we deepen that coverage with a statistics appendix that covers inferential as well as descriptive statistics. The appendix facilitates the learning of difficult concepts by focusing on a single research study throughout.

Users of the First Edition may wish to note that we have not changed the sequencing of chapters, or added or deleted chapters, in this revision. We have, however, improved the internal organization of several chapters in the book, including

- Chapter 2 on human development, where, for example, we have presented Piaget's developmental stages in a more coherent form.

- Chapter 7 on learning, in which we have added a new section on teaching and training of human skills.

- Chapters 17 and 18, the first of which is now focused on social cognition and the second on social interaction.

Special Features

Psychology contains a number of special features designed to promote efficient learning and students' mastery of the material. Some of the features from the First Edition have been revised and enhanced in the Second Edition, and some are new.

Linkages

We have built into the book an integrating tool called Linkages, which highlights some of the relationships among the various subfields in psychology. In the Second Edition, this tool has been considerably improved for ease and efficiency of use. It consists of four parts:

1. In the first few pages of each chapter, a linkage diagram (Linkages: An Overview), reconceived for the Second Edition, illustrates ways that the chapter sheds light on questions arising in other chapters and how material in other chapters helps illuminate questions raised in the current one. Each diagram carries a caption that discusses some of these linkages. The page numbers following each linking question direct the student to pages that carry further discussion of that question. (An appendix that carried these page numbers in the First Edition has been dropped from this edition.)

2. To further reinforce the linkages concept as the student reads through each chapter, each linking question is repeated in the margin of the page where the discussion appears.
3. One such discussion always appears near the end of the chapter in a linkages section that addresses at length a particularly timely or provocative question previously raised in that chapter's linkage diagram.
4. Also new to the Second Edition, each chapter contains at least one captioned photo that illustrates how the content of the chapter is related to that of another chapter.

By establishing ties between chapters, the Linkages material combines with the text narrative to highlight the network of relationships among psychology's subareas. However, the Linkages program does not require that you follow our text's chapter sequence.

Highlights

We have chosen not to employ any "boxed" material in the text. When we wish to emphasize a topic, we have placed it in a Highlight, a section that follows logically and directly from the narrative. These Highlights, analogous to a magnifying glass placed over particular topics in each chapter, allow the reader to examine selected topics in detail without being distracted from the chapter's narrative flow.

Thinking Critically

A new section in each chapter is called Thinking Critically. We try throughout the book to describe research on psychological phenomena in a way that reveals the logic of the scientific enterprise, that identifies possible flaws in design or interpretation, and that leaves room for more questions and further research. In other words, we try to display critical thinking processes. The Thinking Critically sections are designed to make these processes more explicit and accessible by providing a framework for analyzing evidence before drawing conclusions. The framework is built around five questions that the reader should find useful in analyzing not only studies in psychology but other forms of communication as well. These questions, first introduced when we discuss the importance of critical thinking in Chapter 1, are

1. What am I being asked to believe or accept?
2. What evidence is available to support the assertion?
3. Are there alternative ways of interpreting the evidence?
4. What additional evidence would help to evaluate the alternatives?
5. What conclusions are most reasonable?

Thinking Critically sections examine, for example, whether day care harms the emotional development of infants (Chapter 2), whether people can perceive what cannot be sensed (Chapter 5), whether IQ tests are unfairly biased against certain groups (Chapter 10), and other controversial issues. Like the Highlights, these sections are not boxed off from the main narrative.

In Review Charts

Also new to the Second Edition, In Review charts summarize key information in a convenient tabular format. We have placed two or three In Review charts strategically in each chapter to help students synthesize and assimilate large chunks of information—for example, on drug effects, key elements of personality theories, and stress responses and mediators.

Future Directions

Each chapter concludes with Future Directions, a section intended to excite and inform students about new trends. Here we offer our views on the directions that theory, research, and applications will take in future years. We also suggest courses that an interested student could take in psychology and other disciplines to learn more about the chapter's topic.

Chapter Summaries

These summaries have been reconfigured in the Second Edition to reflect more clearly the heading structure of each chapter. The chapters' key terms are now integrated into the summaries rather than set off as a separate list. These terms are defined in the glossary.

Ancillary Package

Accompanying this book are, among other ancillaries, a *Test Bank*, an *Instructor's Resource Manual*, and a *Study Guide*. Because these items were prepared by the lead author and his colleagues in the University of Illinois psychology department, you will find an especially high level of coordination between the textbook and these supplements. All three are additionally unified in the Second Edition by a shared set of learning objectives.

Test Bank (by Graeme McGufficke, Sandra S. Goss, and Douglas A. Bernstein)

The *Test Bank* contains more than 3,000 multiple-choice items (165 per chapter plus 35 on statistics) and three to five essay questions for each chapter of the text. All multiple-choice items are keyed to the learning objectives listed in the Instructor's Resource Manual and Study Guide. Approximately 1,000 questions have already been class-tested and are accompanied by graphs indicating the question's discriminative power, level of difficulty, the percentage of students who chose each response, and the relationship between students' performance on a given item and their overall performance on the test in which the item appeared.

Instructor's Resource Manual (by Sandra S. Goss and Douglas A. Bernstein)

The *Instructor's Resource Manual* contains a complete set of lecture outlines and learning objectives. The revised version of this manual contains nearly one hundred specific teaching aids—most of them new to the Second Edition—including handouts, demonstrations, and classroom exercises. It also contains other material that will be useful to teachers of large introductory courses, such as a section on classroom management and administration of large multisection courses, and a discussion of careers in psychology that instructors may want to distribute to students.

Study Guide (by Bridget Schoppert, Marcia Graber, and Douglas A. Bernstein)

The *Study Guide* employs numerous techniques that help students to learn. Each chapter contains a detailed outline, a key terms section that presents fresh examples and aids to remembering, learning objectives, and a "Concepts and Exercises" section that shows students how to apply their knowledge of psychology to everyday issues and concerns. In addition, each chapter concludes with a two-part self-quiz consisting of thirty multiple-choice questions. An answer key tells the student not only which response is correct but also why each of the other choices is wrong. The revised *Study Guide* also includes a write-in quiz for each chapter.

Other Ancillaries Available to Adopters

The *Test Bank, Instructor's Resource Manual,* and *Study Guide* are also available to adopters on disk for use on microcomputers.

The computerized *Test Bank* allows instructors to generate exams and to integrate their own test items with those on the disk.

The detailed lecture outlines that appear in the *Instructor's Resource Manual* are also available on disk in a generic ASCII-code version. This format allows instructors to use standard word-processing software to integrate their own lecture notes and ideas into the text lectures.

The computerized *Study Guide* is an interactive program that gives students feedback on incorrect as well as on correct answers.

These additional software items are available to adopters:

- Computer simulations that illustrate intriguing phenomena and recreate important experiments

- *Linkages*, HyperCard-based software that allows students to explore the linked sections of the textbook systematically and efficiently

- *Flash Card*, a new ancillary that helps students to master the technical vocabulary of psychology

Also offered to adopters are two sets of transparencies, available as well in slide form. One set contains more than 100 images from the text, most in full color; the other set provides 50 images from outside the text. Finally, a range of videocassettes containing films on topics in psychology is available on adoption of a minimum number of books.

Acknowledgments

Many people provided us with the help, criticism, and encouragement we needed, first to write, and then to revise, this book.

We first wish to thank Alison Clarke-Stewart (University of California, Irvine) for revising her chapter on human development. Professor Clarke-Stewart's skills as a writer are evident throughout the chapter, as is her command of the important themes and issues in development.

We are indebted to Michael T. Neitzel (University of Kentucky) for his expert assistance in the revision of Chapters 14, 15, and 16, on personality, psychological disorders, and treatment of psychological disorders.

Thanks are also due to the Department of Psychology at the University of Illinois at Urbana-Champaign, especially to its head, Emanuel Donchin, who has continued to provide us with a firm base of support. We are especially grateful to Diane Weidner for coordinating communication between the authors and Houghton Mifflin. Her unselfish devotion to helping us assumed heroic proportions at times; we thank you very much, Diane. Thanks also go to Helen Watson and Pattsie Petrie, of the Susan Stout Memorial Library, for their unfailing help and endless patience in response to our many complex and obscure requests for references. Cathy Stein contributed material on psychological testing to the chapter on mental abilities, and we appreciate her help. Illinois students, friends, and associates who evaluated parts of the Second Edition manuscript include Adriana Alcantara, Marie Banich, May Berenbaum, George M. McConkie, Richard Rowlison, and Ellen Wartella.

We owe a special debt to the colleagues listed below, who provided prerevision evaluations of or reviewed the manuscript for the Second Edition as it was being developed. Their advice and suggestions for improvements were responsible for many of the good qualities you will find in the book. If you have any criticisms, they probably involve areas these people warned us about.

C. Berkeley Adams, Jamestown Community College
Lewis R. Aiken, Pepperdine University
Judith Allen, Drake University
Eileen Astor-Stetson, Bloomsburg University
James Averill, University of Massachusetts, Amherst
Gregory F. Ball, Boston College
William A. Barnard, University of Northern Colorado
Byron L. Barrington, University of Wisconsin, Marathon Center
Lt. Col. Johnston Beach, The United States Military Academy
Kenneth A. Benson, Hinds Junior College
Terry D. Blumenthal, Wake Forest University
James F. Calhoun, University of Georgia
Paul Concepcion, Chemeketa Community College
Vernon R. Dorschner, Brainerd Community College
Karen Grover Duffy, State University of New York, Geneseo
William O. Dwyer, Memphis State University
Linda E. Flickinger, St. Clair County Community College
Robert E. Franken, University of Calgary
David Funder, University of California, Riverside
Theodore Gessner, George Mason University
William C. Gordon, University of New Mexico
Albrecht Werner Inhoff, State University of New York, Binghamton
Thomas T. Jackson, Fort Hays State University
Timothy D. Johnston, University of North Carolina, Greensboro
Kevin Jordan, San Jose State University
Andrew Kinney, Mohawk Community College
Jack Kirschenbaum, Fullerton College
John S. Klein, Castleton State University
Stephen B. Klein, Fort Hays State University
Ronald A. Kleinknecht, Western Washington University
Juliana Rasic Lachenmeyer, Fairleigh Dickinson University
Janet Landman, University of Michigan
S. David Leonard, University of Georgia
Bradley Lown, Buffalo State College
Hamish Macleod, University of Edinburgh

James Martinez, Mercy College of Detroit
Dale McAdam, University of Rochester
W. Hugh McGinley, University of Wyoming
Peter Moshein, University of Pittsburgh
Carol Pandey, Los Angeles Pierce College
Denis Parker, University of Aberdeen
Jim H. Patton, Baylor University
Patricia L. Phillips, Illinois State University
Robert R. Prochnow, St. Cloud State University
David A. Schroeder, University of Arkansas, Fayetteville
David Shwalb, Westminster College of Salt Lake City
Mark Siegel, University of the District of Columbia
Frank Sjursen, Shoreline Community College
Chris Spatz, Hendrix College
Linda Spear, State University of New York at Binghamton
A. H. Teich, University of Pittsburgh, Johnstown
Rod T. Todorovich, Honolulu Community College
Michael Trout, Champaign, Illinois
Benjamin Wallace, Cleveland State University
Janet Weigel-Bruno, Black Hawk College
Paul J. Wellman, Texas A & M University

We thank once again the reviewers of the First Edition, who helped us to shape and refine the foundation on which the Second Edition was built:

Paul Abramson, University of California, Los Angeles
Elizabeth Allgeier, Bowling Green State University
Craig A. Anderson, University of Missouri
Ruth L. Ault, Davidson College
James R. Averill, University of Massachusetts, Amherst
Lewis M. Barker, Baylor University
Deborah Belle, Boston University
Michael Best, Southern Methodist University
Robert C. Bolles, University of Washington
Nathan Brody, Wesleyan University
Rosalind Dymond Cartwright, Rush Medical College
Charles Cofer, University of North Carolina, Chapel Hill
Ellen Marie Cooper, Pennsylvania State University, University Park
Paul Cornwell, Pennsylvania State University, University Park
Xenia Coulter, Empire State College
Frank DaPolito, University of Dayton
Richard B. Day, McMaster University
Randy L. Diehl, University of Texas, Austin
Halford H. Fairchild, Association of Black Psychologists
J. Gregor Fetterman, Arizona State University
Jeffrey D. Fisher, University of Connecticut, Storrs
Randy D. Fisher, University of Central Florida
Robert A. Frank, University of Cincinnati
Irene Hanson Frieze, University of Pittsburgh
Adrienne Gans, New York University
Don Gawley, Indiana University, Bloomington
Sandra S. Goss, University of Illinois, Urbana-Champaign
Richard A. Griggs, University of Florida
Carlos V. Grijalva, University of California, Los Angeles

Robert W. Grossman, Kalamazoo College
Ruben C. Gur, University of Pennsylvania
Anne Harris, Arizona State University
Robert B. Hays, George Washington University
Steven R. Heyman, University of Wyoming
Deborah L. Holmes, Loyola University of Chicago
Ralph W. Hood, Jr., University of Tennessee, Chattanooga
Jeffrey A. Howard, Eckerd College
Earl Hunt, University of Washington
Janet Shibley Hyde, University of Wisconsin, Madison
Cynthia E. Jayne, Temple University School of Medicine
James D. Kestenbaum, Rochester Institute of Technology
David L. Kohfield, Southern Illinois University, Edwardsville
Marcy Lansman, University of North Carolina, Chapel Hill
Arnold A. Lazarus, Rutgers, The State University
Richard L. Leavy, Ohio Wesleyan University
Marc S. Lewis, University of Texas, Austin
Lewis R. Lieberman, Columbus College
Sanford Lopater, Christopher Newport College
Steven Lopez, University of Southern California
James Luginbuhl, North Carolina State University
Joseph G. Malpeli, University of Illinois, Urbana-Champaign
Margaret W. Matlin, State University of New York, Geneseo
Donald H. McBurney, University of Pittsburgh
Gerald A. Mendelsohn, University of California, Berkeley
Donald H. Mershon, North Carolina State University
Lawrence S. Meyers, California State University, Sacramento
Peter M. Milner, McGill University
James S. Nairne, University of Texas, Arlington
Patricia Parmelee, Philadelphia Geriatric Center
Anne C. Petersen, Pennsylvania State University, University Park
Terry F. Pettijohn, The Ohio State University, Marion
James O. Prochaska, University of Rhode Island
Kathryn Quina, University of Rhode Island
Stephen K. Reed, Florida Atlantic University
Janet Morgan Riggs, Gettysburg College
Richard J. Sanders, University of North Carolina, Wilmington
Timothy Schallert, University of Texas, Austin
Janet Ward Schofield, University of Pittsburgh
Bridget Schoppert, University of Illinois, Urbana-Champaign
David A. Schroeder, University of Arkansas, Fayetteville
Marian Schwartz, University of Wisconsin, Madison
Michael B. Sewall, Mohawk Valley Community College
Michael D. Spiegler, Providence College
Charles D. Spielberger, University of South Florida
Valerie N. Stratton, Pennsylvania State University, Altoona
Thomas K. Tutko, San Jose State University
Ryan D. Tweney, Bowling Green State University
Benjamin Wallace, Cleveland State University
Michael J. Watkins, Rice University
Paul J. Wellman, Texas A & M University
Ben A. Williams, University of Southern California
Sharon Wolf, California State University, Long Beach
William R. Wooten, Brown University

We also want to thank Katie Steele, who got this project off the ground by encouraging us to stop talking about this book and start writing it. We were consistently delighted by the caring, the enthusiasm, and the professionalism of everyone we had dealings with in Houghton Mifflin's College Division. The debt of gratitude we owe for their unwavering support and their commitment to this project can never be repaid.

Finally, we want to express our deepest appreciation to our families and friends. Their love saw us through an exhilarating but demanding period of our lives. They endured our hours at the computer, missed meals, postponed vacations, and occasional irritability during the creation of the first edition of this book, and they had to suffer all over again during the lengthy process of revision. Their faith in us is more important than they realize, and it will be cherished forever.

Left to right: Christopher D. Wickens,
Edward J. Roy, Thomas K. Srull,
Douglas A. Bernstein

PSYCHOLOGY

O UTLINE

The World of Psychology

Does watching violent television programs make a person more aggressive? Can cram courses help students do better on the SAT? How does day care affect infants' relationships with their parents? Can hypnosis help eye-witnesses recall forgotten details of a crime? We discuss all of these questions in this book, because they all relate to psychology.

Psychology is the science of behavior and mental processes. This means that psychologists use the methods of science to investigate all kinds of behavior and mental processes, from the activity of a single nerve cell to the social conflicts in a complex society. In this opening chapter we offer an overview of the field, including a description of what topics and approaches psychology encompasses, what psychologists do, and how psychologists go about their work. In later chapters we focus on the results of psychological research and how those results are being applied to improve the quality of life for many people.

From Cell to Society: The Scope of Psychology

As an illustration of the scope of psychology, consider the case of Allen DePrez, a thirty-eight-year-old air-traffic controller. Allen began drinking alcohol in high school, mostly as a way of fitting in at social occasions. He continued to drink mainly on weekends in college, where he met his wife. Allen's father and two brothers were known to drink heavily, but not until flight traffic at his airport doubled did Allen begin to have a drinking problem. As he became more anxious about his work, he began to drink during the week, often excessively. During the next twelve months he became increasingly irritable at home and dangerously error-prone at work. In fact, his mistakes prompted Allen's supervisors to place him on sick leave so that he could get professional help. But Allen was afraid that being labeled an alcoholic would hurt his chances for promotion. Instead of seeking help, he abruptly quit drinking, causing a physical and psychological reaction so severe that he was placed in a hospital detoxification unit (Meyer & Hardaway-Osborne, 1982).

Why did drinking become such a problem for Allen? Is problem drinking an inherited tendency, a learned habit, an addiction maintained by biological forces, or the result of all these factors? Why do people start drinking in the first place? Despite warnings about the dangers of alcohol abuse in the media and in the schools, about 18 million adults in the United States have serious drinking problems that result in everything from ill health and unemployment to violent aggression and fatal traffic accidents (Secretary of Health and Human Services, 1987). Why don't people heed warnings about the grave dangers of alcohol abuse? What can be done to motivate alcoholics to change and to influence everyone to use alcohol responsibly?

These are just a few of the questions that psychologists have asked about drinking. There are lists at least as long for other phenomena. The questions that particular psychologists choose to address and the places they look for answers depend on their area of specialization and on the theoretical approach they prefer.

Subfields of Psychology

In 1879, in Leipzig, Germany, Wilhelm Wundt established the first formal psychology laboratory. Wundt, a physician and physiologist, hoped to identify the basic elements of human consciousness. Over time, psychologists expanded the range of their research to encompass hundreds of other phenomena—from colorblindness and racial prejudice to severe depression, the structure of intelligence, and job satisfaction. As a result, even the most ambitious psychologist must make choices about what to study and what to leave to others. Thus, psychology today has numerous areas of specialization, or *subfields* (see Table 1.1).

Psychology's subfields are defined only in part by which phenomena psychologists choose to study. Many psychologists study memory, for example; but some are interested in its biological aspect (such as where memories are stored in the brain), while others prefer to study developmental aspects of memory (such as how it changes with age) or social aspects (such as how the presence of others influences what people remember). As the following sections illustrate, psychology's subfields are defined in part by the phenomena studied and in part by which aspects of the phenomena are emphasized.

Experimental Psychology   Wundt and other early psychologists, such as Edward Titchener and Hermann Ebbinghaus, used the term *experimental psychology* to distinguish their laboratory work from the endeavors of philosophers and others who thought and speculated about consciousness, memory, and other psychological matters but performed no experiments. As psychologists followed their interests and explored a widening range of topics, they took the experimental tradition with them. Thus, experimental methods (which we discuss later in this chapter) are the foundation of every subfield of psychology. What, then, is the special area known as experimental psychology?

Experimental psychologists study some of the most basic components of behavior and mental processes—including perception, learning, and memory—in animals and humans. They use scientific, experimental methods to ask questions such as why people continue to punish themselves with alcohol when they know that painful hangovers will appear the morning after a bout of heavy drinking. Work by experimental psychologists has shown that repeated

Wilhelm Wundt founded the first European psychology laboratory at the University of Leipzig in 1879. As described in Chapter 6, he was interested in identifying the basic sensations that underlie conscious experience. Wundt and other early psychologists, such as Hermann Ebbinghaus, whose work on memory we shall discuss in Chapter 8, were the founders of experimental psychology.

Table 1.1
Subfields of Psychology

Researchers in each of the subfields of psychology approach their work from a characteristic perspective. These perspectives are reflected in this sample of general questions and issues typically of interest to psychologists in each subfield.

Subfield	Typical Questions
Experimental psychology	What rules govern what people perceive, how they learn, what they remember, and what they forget? How are judgments and decisions made?
Biological psychology	How do the electrical and chemical activities in nerve cells influence behavior? Which parts of the brain control which kinds of behavior? What happens in the brain when people think or become emotional?
Personality psychology	How can personality differences be measured? Is personality inherited or learned? Can it be changed?
Social psychology	How can a person or a group influence the attitudes, actions, emotions, and mental processes of other people? What determines whether two people will be attracted to each other?
Clinical and counseling psychology	How do behavior and mental processes become disordered? What causes abnormalities, and how can they be treated?
Developmental psychology	How do attributes such as thinking, social skills, intelligence, language, and personality change over time? What factors facilitate or distort their growth?
Quantitative psychology	What mathematical tools can measure and predict personality, intelligence, judgment, and emotions? How can research data be best analyzed?

overindulgence in alcohol occurs partly because its immediate, rewarding effects (feeling "high") have more control over the behavior than its unpleasant, but delayed, consequences (feeling sick) (Mowrer & Ullman, 1945). Research by experimental psychologists has also helped educators advise students how to remember more of what they study. You may find some of the research described in Chapter 8, on memory, especially valuable as you prepare for tests. (Be sure to read about memory improvement and SQ3R study methods on pages 332–333.)

In recent years, some experimental psychologists have come to be called **cognitive psychologists** because they explore the mental activities involved in judgment, decision making, problem solving, imagination, and other aspects of complex thought, or *cognition*. What, for example, do you do when you take in information about alcohol abuse? How is that information represented internally, and how is it mentally processed to form an impression about alcohol use? These are questions examined by cognitive psychologists.

Experimental psychologists are also contributing to the field of engineering. For example, studies of how people perceive the world and handle information have allowed psychologists to suggest ways of arranging an airliner's vast array of instruments and warning lights so that the pilot can react to them quickly. *Engineering psychologists,* also known as *human-factors psychologists,* are helping to design everything from telephone equipment and computer keyboards to the control panels for nuclear power plants.

Biological Psychology   Psychologists who analyze how biology shapes behavior and mental processes are called **biological** or **physiological psychologists.** They might study, for example, where and how alcohol acts on the brain to impair the drinker's ability to think or talk or walk. They might also look for particular substances—biological "markers"—in the blood that might identify people who are especially likely to develop alcoholism (Schuckit & Gold, 1988).

Some biological psychologists explore how cells in the brain and the spinal cord interact. Experiences, perceptions, actions, and emotions all depend on how these cells communicate. Other researchers focus on the relationships between behavior and activity in the brain. They ask, for example, what parts of the brain become activated when people confront an unexpected event. Still others unravel the puzzle of how certain groups of nerve cells allow people to translate energy from the outside world into the experiences of seeing and hearing.

Personality Psychology   Whereas some psychologists seek laws that govern the behavior of people in general, **personality psychologists** focus on the characteristics that make each person unique. They also try to identify the specific ways people differ and to explore the relationships between people's personalities and their tendency to think, act, and feel in certain ways. For example, some people tend to attribute their success or failure to external forces, such as luck; other people believe that success or failure depends mostly on their own efforts. Personality researchers have found that differences like these are linked to many behaviors, from the tendency to drink to the risk of becoming ill (Eysenck, 1980; Strickland, 1989).

Social Psychology   Junior high school students do not simply wake up one morning and decide to start drinking alcohol. Social influences over time

Monitoring brain activity during sleep. The relationship between dreams and brain functions is just one of the many research topics pursued by biological psychologists.

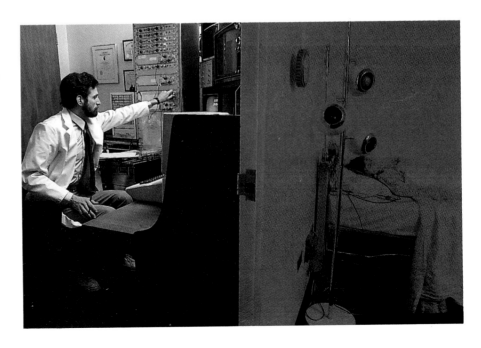

shape their behavior. They may see their parents, and especially their friends, drinking. They cannot help seeing movies, television shows, and, of course, ads that portray drinking as fun, adventurous, sexy, and glamorous.

Influences like these are the special interest of **social psychologists.** They study how people influence one another, especially in groups. How, for example, do people come to dislike or demean people from a particular ethnic group? How does the personality of a group's leader affect the group's ability to work together happily or to solve problems? *Industrial-organizational psychologists* often conduct and apply research on such questions in the business world. They help select the people most likely to work well in a specific setting, train supervisors to improve their leadership skills, and suggest other steps to increase productivity and job satisfaction.

Clinical Psychology   Most psychologists explore normal behavior and mental processes, but **clinical psychologists** try to understand and correct abnormal functioning. Using tests, interviews, and observations, they study the causes and symptoms of mental and behavioral disorders, including alcoholism and other forms of drug abuse. In the consulting room they use similar methods to pinpoint individuals' problems, and they offer therapy to help solve those problems.

Clinical psychology is closely related to *counseling psychology.* Psychologists in both areas study and seek to alleviate human problems. But compared with counseling psychologists, clinical psychologists tend to deal with a wider range of disorders, and they often focus on more severe problems. Counseling psychologists tend to work with people who have less intense difficulties, such as conflicts in choosing a career or problems adjusting to a job or college life.

Preventing disorders is another concern of clinical psychologists, especially those called **community psychologists.** Their emphasis on prevention has inspired programs to head off psychological problems among groups who face a high risk of developing mental disorders, such as teenage parents and other people under heavy stress.

Developmental Psychology   Behavior and mental processes are ever-changing phenomena taking place in an ever-changing environment. **Developmental psychologists** describe these changes and try to understand their causes and their effects throughout the life span. Included in this domain are questions about how the health of a fetus is affected when a pregnant woman drinks alcohol and how the social challenges teenagers face during adolescence alter the chances that they will abuse alcohol or other drugs.

Research by developmental psychologists has increased understanding of how people can best meet the challenges of old age, as well as how conditions early in life affect subsequent behavior and thought. For example, developmental researchers compared inner-city children whose families accepted and supported them with children from less supportive families. They found that ten years later the children from the supportive families were less disruptive in school and better able to handle stress (Garmezy, 1988).

Quantitative Psychology   The rules of science require that the topic studied—whether chemical reactions, planetary movements, memory, or stress—be measured accurately and analyzed carefully. Only then will the results of research be as free from error as possible. Many phenomena, however, are difficult to measure and analyze in a quantitative way. **Quantitative psychologists** develop and apply mathematical methods to summarize and analyze data from virtually every area of psychology. For example, they have helped biological psychologists find precise mathematical ways of describing how brain waves change when alcohol is consumed.

Whether they are studying excessive alcohol use, intelligence, sexual preferences, or depression, psychologists' research is guided by the general assumptions of particular theoretical approaches. For example, those who assume that alcohol abuse is essentially a biological problem are likely to search for genetic or biochemical causes; those who see the problem as developing mainly through learning might examine alcoholics' early experiences with drinking.

Sigmund Freud established the psychodynamic approach to the study of behavior and mental processes. Freud emphasized the role of constant unconscious conflicts in the creation and alteration of human personality.

The most fundamental methods of quantitative psychology are **statistical analyses,** which are mathematical tools for summarizing and analyzing data. They allow researchers to describe efficiently the average performance of a large group of subjects, to make educated guesses about how similar subjects might perform, and to make confident statements about whether, say, an observed difference between the problem-solving skills of men and women is significant or not. Some of these statistical methods are discussed in the appendix.

Quantitative psychologists also help construct and evaluate paper-and-pencil tests that are used in diagnosing people's problems and in choosing individuals for admission to everything from college to jobs in the military. In other studies, quantitative psychologists create mathematical formulas, or *models,* to describe and even predict complex behavior such as decision making. In diagnosing a patient's physical problems, for example, doctors consider physical examinations, medical histories, blood tests, brain scans, and many other sources of information. How do they combine all this information to reach a diagnosis? A quantitative psychologist might try to describe the process in mathematical terms, creating a model to predict diagnoses by other doctors.

Approaches to Psychology

Suppose you were a psychologist trying to understand why a certain group of people had failed when they tried to quit drinking alcohol. Where would you look for an answer? Would you search for events that might have prompted the relapse? Would you blame the physical discomfort created by quitting?

Many approaches like these are possible and useful. The one you would choose would most likely depend on your assumptions about the most important factors determining behavior and mental processes in general and excessive drinking in particular. These assumptions would lead you to prefer different theoretical approaches. Among the most significant approaches in psychology today are those known as the biological, psychodynamic, behavioral, humanistic, and cognitive approaches.

The Biological Approach   One way to approach problem drinking is to explore how alcohol affects the body and how physiological changes affect the need or desire for alcohol. This exploration reflects the biological approach, whose roots can be traced back to Wilhelm Wundt. Wundt, however, studied biological processes only indirectly, exploring, for example, how long it took people to react to a stimulus.

Today, the **biological approach** studies biological processes more directly, with a special emphasis on the electrical and chemical activity of the brain and on the actions of hormones. Thus, biological psychologists study emotions, mental disorders, memory, and other behavior and mental processes by learning about the biological components that underlie them.

The Psychodynamic Approach   About fifteen years after Wundt founded his laboratory, an alternative to Wundt's experimental psychology was offered by the Viennese physician Sigmund Freud. He began with a biological approach to psychology, assuming that normal and abnormal behavior and mental processes have a physical cause somewhere in the nervous system. But eventually Freud's work with people whose physical ailments had no apparent physical cause led him to a new approach. He created both a theory to explain personality and mental disorders and a form of therapy called *psychoanalysis.* His ideas form the foundation of the **psychodynamic approach,** which holds

John B. Watson, founder of the behavioral approach to psychology, believed that patterns of reward and punishment form the basis for all human behavior. B. F. Skinner's research mapped out some of the ways in which these rewards and punishments shape, maintain, and change behavior.

that all behavior and mental processes reflect constant and often unconscious struggles within each person. Usually, these struggles involve conflict between the impulse to satisfy instincts or wishes (for food, sex, or aggression, for example) and the restrictions imposed by society.

Not all those who take the psychodynamic approach embrace all of Freud's original ideas. But many take his perspective, viewing abnormal or problematic behavior as reflecting a failure to resolve conflicts adequately. Problem drinking might thus be seen as an attempt to reduce feelings of guilt over unacceptable impulses. It might also be seen as a way of manipulating other people, or even as slow-motion suicide (Connelly, 1980). A psychodynamic psychologist would expect therapy aimed at resolving inner conflicts to enhance a person's ability to quit drinking.

The Behavioral Approach In the early 1900s, at about the same time that Freud was developing his psychodynamic approach in Europe, John Watson, an American psychology professor, was urging psychologists to study only what they could observe directly, not unobservable mental events (Watson, 1913). If they focused only on observable actions, said Watson, psychologists would not have to rely on people's possibly distorted reports about their thoughts and feelings. Furthermore, if they concentrated on what they could observe, psychologists could begin to understand behavior whether it occurs in adults, children, the mentally ill, or animals.

Watson's views gave birth to the **behavioral approach** to psychology, whose most notable contemporary champion was Harvard psychologist B. F. Skinner. One key assumption of this approach is that most behaviors and ways of thinking depend on the pattern of rewards and punishments that each person has experienced. In this view, biological factors merely provide the raw material on which rewards, punishments, and other experiences act, molding each person.

Watson's views, like Freud's, were very controversial when first proposed. Most people were not ready to have their thoughts discounted and their behavior chalked up entirely to the effect of rewards and punishments—any more than they immediately embraced the notion of being controlled by dark, unconscious impulses. In fact, few behaviorists today endorse a version of the behavioral approach as radical as Watson's; many include thoughts, beliefs, and other cognitive activity in the theoretical picture. But contemporary behaviorists do suggest that most problematic behaviors can be changed by helping people to unlearn old habits and develop better ones. Thus, problem drinking might be viewed as a habit learned by watching others and maintained because it is associated with pleasant social occasions, relief from stress, or other rewards. According to this point of view, even once-addicted alcoholics might break the habit permanently if they learn to develop alternative responses in specific situations.

The Humanistic Approach In the early 1940s the choice of theoretical approaches open to psychologists was limited mainly to the biological, the psychoanalytic, and the behavioral. A psychotherapist and professor named Carl Rogers suggested a new alternative, one that would be reinforced by other theorists such as Abraham Maslow and Viktor Frankl. Though trained in the psychoanalytic tradition, Rogers gradually rejected its assumptions that people are controlled by instincts, just as he rejected the notion that people are controlled by biological forces or rewards and punishments. He proposed, in contrast, what is called the **humanistic approach.** Its fundamental assumption is that people control themselves. Furthermore, according to this approach, each person has an innate tendency to grow toward his or her own potential,

Carl Rogers was the most famous proponent of what has become the humanistic approach to psychology. Rogers deemphasized biological, psychodynamic, and behavioral factors in shaping human behavior because he believed that people's perceptions of the world and their innate tendency toward growth within that world were more important.

although the environment (including other people) may block this growth (Rogers, 1942).

According to the humanistic perspective, behavior is determined primarily by each person's capacity to *choose* how to think and act. These choices are dictated, say humanistic psychologists, by each individual's unique perception of the world. If you perceive the world as a friendly place, you are likely to feel happy and secure. If you view it as dangerous and hostile, you will probably be defensive and anxious. Seen from the humanistic perspective, the decision to drink or not, or to quit or not, will involve a decision that cannot be predicted by clearly specified, lawful principles of behavior. Rather, the choice will depend on uniquely individual perceptions that can be fully experienced only by the person involved. Thus, until the problem drinker decides to change, any effort by outsiders to hurry the process is likely to fail.

The Cognitive Approach We have noted that nineteenth-century psychologists such as Wundt were interested in analyzing the basic elements of consciousness, much as chemists of the time were determining the basic elements of physical matter. Other psychologists, such as William James (1890), worked to understand how mental processes such as learning and memory function to help people get along in the world. But from the 1920s to the mid-1970s, research focusing on consciousness and cognitive activity all but ceased as behaviorism, with its deemphasis of conscious experience, held sway. Then, dissatisfaction with the limitations of behaviorism led to a renewed emphasis on mental processes and to a cognitive approach that has become as influential now as behaviorism once was.

Like the humanistic approach, the cognitive approach emphasizes the importance of thoughts and other mental processes, but this approach depends far more than the humanistic approach on research into how mental processes operate. In other words, the **cognitive approach** focuses on how the brain takes in information, creates perceptions, processes information, and generates integrated patterns of behavior. If you were to examine a person's problem drinking from the cognitive perspective, you might look at how cognitive principles affect what that person recalls about the dangers of drinking, how that person perceives those dangers (are they personally threatening or are they categorized as only affecting "other people"?), and how he or she judges the effects of quitting (would it reduce the risks significantly?). Answers to these questions, according to the cognitive approach, should tell you whether the person will try to moderate his or her drinking.

An Eclectic Approach Which of these approaches is right? The question cannot be answered, because "rightness" or "wrongness" is not at issue. No one approach needs to be chosen and adhered to. Many psychologists choose an *eclectic* position, which means that they adopt a combination of attractive features from more than one approach. In studying problem drinking, for example, numerous researchers consider biological, cognitive, and behavioral variables. Each approach emphasizes a set of factors that tells part of the story of behavior and mental processes. ("In Review: Approaches to Psychology" summarizes the approaches.) You will see throughout this book that each approach has contributed to psychological theory, research, and applications.

Unity Within Diversity

Psychology's many subfields and approaches have led psychologists into a wide variety of interests and activities. They conduct research; they apply the results of research to solve and prevent human problems; they teach and write

In Review: Approaches to Psychology

Approach	Basic Assumptions
Biological	Behavior and mental processes are ultimately explained by genetics, the activity of the nervous system—especially the brain—and the action of hormones and other chemicals.
Psychodynamic	Behavior and mental processes are largely determined by internal mental and emotional conflicts. These conflicts usually pit desires for sex, aggression, security, and power against environmental obstacles to those desires.
Behavioral	Psychology can be studied scientifically only by examining the overt behavior of humans and animals. Behavior is largely shaped by the pattern of rewards and punishments that each person has experienced.
Humanistic	Behavior and mental processes are influenced primarily by an individual's innate potential for healthy growth and choices based on subjective perceptions of the world.
Cognitive	Behavior is determined largely by how information is stored, retrieved, and otherwise processed by the brain. Understanding behavior thus requires laboratory research on the principles that govern these processes, especially those that guide perception, memory, thought, judgment, and decision making.

about research findings and psychological knowledge (see Table 1.2). In spite of this diversity, however, at least two characteristics unify psychologists' activities and values.

First, because they are all interested in behavior and mental processes, psychologists in every subfield draw on and contribute to knowledge from other subfields. For example, the biological psychologist's finding that chemical imbalances in the brain can produce disordered thinking may provide the clinical psychologist with clues to the cause of certain mental disorders. Research by developmental psychologists may help cognitive psychologists better understand how the ability to use language, solve problems, or think logically is built up over time.

Research on how differing floor-plans and other building features affect the behavior, mood, and stress of occupants helps environmental psychologists advise architects on optimal designs for nursing homes, schools, prisons, dormitories, and other structures. Psychology's many subspecialties offer a remarkably wide range of opportunities for careers in research and service relating to all stages of the life span and to all aspects of behavior.

Table 1.2
Typical Activities and Work Settings for Psychologists
The fact that psychologists can work in a wide variety of settings and perform a wide range of functions accounts for the popularity of psychology as an undergraduate major. The facts, concepts, theories, and methods studied in psychology have proven valuable to many students, whether they pursue graduate work in psychology or enter medicine, law, business, or other fields.

Work Setting	Percentage of Psychologists	Typical Activities
Colleges and universities	33.9	Teaching and research in all psychological subfields
Mental health facilities (e.g., hospitals, clinics, and counseling centers)	24.5	Testing and treatment of children and adults
Private practice (an individual or a group of psychologists)	22.0	Psychological testing and treatment; consulting to business and industry
Business and industry	3.1	Testing potential employees; assessing employee satisfaction; identifying and resolving conflicts; improving leadership skills; offering stress-management and other training programs; improving equipment design to maximize efficiency and prevent accidents
Schools including schoolsforretarded and emotionally disturbedchildren)	3.7	Testing students' mental abilities and other characteristics; identifying children who have problems; designing and implementing programs to improve academic performance
Other	12.8	Teaching prison inmates; research in private institutes; advising members of legislatures on educational, research, or public policy matters; administration of research funds; research on improving the effectiveness of military personnel; etc.

Source: Adapted from Pion et al., 1986.

Second, because psychology is a science, all of its subfields emphasize *empirical research*—going beyond speculation to carefully gather and systematically analyze information about psychological phenomena. Thus, psychologists not only wonder about the causes of problem drinking but also gather information, or *data,* about it. Even psychologists who do not conduct research themselves depend on research discoveries to teach or write knowledgeably, provide up-to-date treatment, and solve the endless variety of problems they confront every day. Without its grounding in research, psychology might merge with philosophy, or psychologists might issue proclamations with no more credibility than those of astrologers or the *National Enquirer.*

To make it easier to appreciate and evaluate the research described in later chapters, we turn now to a general review of the goals of scientific research and the rules and methods that help psychologists make progress toward those goals. More detailed coverage of data analysis is offered in the appendix.

The Goals of Research

A graduate student in psychology had a bad case of the flu but recovered enough to attend a New Year's Eve party at which beer flowed freely. His medication prevented him from drinking alcohol, but he had a good time anyway. In fact he had such a good time that he felt drunk, his friends assumed he was drunk, and, in a photo of the party, he looked drunk. All this made him curious about whether just being around drinkers could create drunken behavior. He began to study the interaction between the chemical effects of alcohol and the social situation in which it is consumed. (Research related to this question is discussed in Chapter 6, on consciousness.) This story is not unusual. The research adventure in psychology, as in all other sciences, often begins simply—with curiosity.

Curiosity frequently provokes very interesting, very stimulating questions, but often these questions are phrased in terms that are too general to be investigated scientifically. Suppose, for example, that a rerun of "The Odd Couple" gets you wondering if it is true that people pair up as friends, even as spouses, with people who are very different from themselves. You might ask questions such as, Do opposites attract? Do people have better relationships if they are similar or if they are different? As the discussion of similar questions in Chapter 17 illustrates, the scientist must be more specific—asking: What kinds of relationships are involved? (The same rules might not apply to friendships and intimate relationships.) What do we mean by "opposites" and "similar"? (In every way or just, say, in personal characteristics or political beliefs or interests or values or financial background or physical attractiveness?) And how is the quality of a relationship measured? (Just staying together may

Curiosity about important everyday phenomena, such as what determines whether two people will be attracted to each other, is often the basis for psychological research. Often, the results not only contribute to knowledge about the phenomenon originally studied, but by provoking additional questions, help clarify principles governing other aspects of human behavior as well.

not signal happiness, and frequent arguing does not necessarily indicate lack of caring.) These more precise questions might seem less interesting than those you first posed, but you are more likely to be able to answer them with some confidence. Only by putting together the answers to many small questions will you begin to find answers to larger ones.

To find these answers, scientists depend on the accumulation of knowledge over many years by many people. They also rely on several levels of research guided by four basic goals: description, prediction, control, and explanation.

Description

In order to answer any research question, the scientist must first describe the phenomenon of interest. Suppose, for example, you decided to study inter-personal attraction by looking at social dating. You would first have to gather some detailed information about dating behavior. What criteria do single people use to decide whether to offer or accept a date? How do they evaluate the quality of a date? Do men use the same criteria as women?

These are just a few of the characteristics of the dating process that you would measure and summarize before trying to, say, predict the outcome of a date. Such descriptive data are usually collected through surveys, case studies, and observations, each of which we describe shortly.

Prediction

As you examine your data about dating, you might begin to see some interesting patterns. Contrary to the notion that "opposites attract," it might appear that people often seem to enjoy first dates more when both participants hold similar views on politics and religion than when their opinions differ. Noticing this apparent relationship, you might aim for a more ambitious research goal: prediction. You might, for example, predict that if a couple is similar in political and religious orientation, their enjoyment of the date will be higher than if their views conflict. A prediction that is stated as a specific, testable proposition about a phenomenon is called a **hypothesis.**

To test a hypothesis, scientists first gather additional data, looking not only for evidence that supports the hypothesis but also for evidence that refutes it. Then, typically, they analyze the data in order to detect relationships between **variables,** which are specific factors or characteristics that can vary in some way. Here, individual reactions to a dating experience can vary from utter disgust to unbounded joy, and belief similarity can range from very high to very low.

Suppose you are ready to begin gathering data to test the hypothesis about the role of belief similarity in dating enjoyment. But what does "enjoyment" mean? Tastes differ, and people may often find that a dating experience falls somewhere between the extremes of ecstatic and dreadful. To avoid definitional problems like this, scientists give each variable an **operational definition,** which is a statement of the operations or methods used to measure the variable. In this case, "dating enjoyment" might be operationally defined by how people rate their dates on a 10-point scale (where 1 = "total boredom" and 10 = "best date ever"). Belief similarity might be defined in terms of the percentage of matching answers given by each member of a dating couple to a questionnaire about politics and religion.

In prediction-oriented research, relationships between operationally defined variables usually appear as correlations. **Correlation** means just what it says:

Analysis of the correlations between variables such as the alcohol-drinking habits of parents and their teenage children can help researchers evaluate the effects of family influences on alcoholism.

"co-relation," the degree to which one variable is related to another. For example, you could test the hypothesis that belief similarity creates greater enjoyment than dissimilarity does by analyzing descriptive data to see whether similarity scores and enjoyment ratings are correlated, or related to one another. If similarity and enjoyment are related, then knowing the degree to which a couple shares certain beliefs should allow you to predict something about how much the couple would enjoy their date.

To confirm a hypothesis, however, you need to know more than the simple fact that two variables are correlated. You also need to know (1) how strong the correlation is, and (2) what its direction is. The correlation may be so weak that knowing something about one variable tells you very little about the other. Or the direction of the correlation may differ from the predicted relationship; it may turn out that similarity is associated with less rather than more enjoyment. The strength and direction of correlations can be summarized precisely by calculating a statistic called the **correlation coefficient**. We will not discuss how to calculate the coefficient here, but understanding its underlying logic clarifies the meaning of many research findings.

HIGHLIGHT

Correlation: The Foundation of Prediction

The correlation coefficient is given the symbol r for short. It can vary from 0.00 to +1.00 or −1.00. Thus, the coefficient includes (1) an absolute value, such as 0, .20, or .50, and (2) either a plus sign or a minus sign.

The absolute value of r indicates the strength of the relationship. An r of 0 between people's hat size and the age of their cars, for example, indicates that there is no correlation between the variables. A correlation of +1.00 or −1.00 indicates a perfect correlation, which means that if you know the value of one variable, you can predict the value of the other variable with certainty. An r of +.50 or −.50 suggests a relationship of intermediate strength.

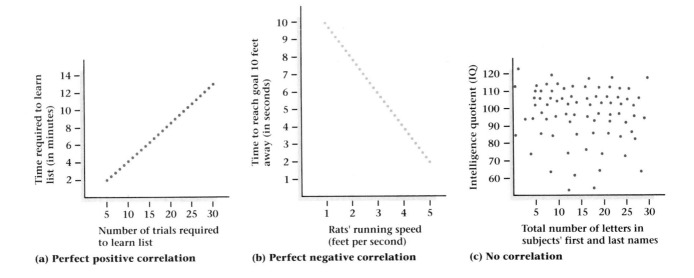

(a) **Perfect positive correlation**   (b) **Perfect negative correlation**   (c) **No correlation**

Figure 1.1
Three Correlations
The strength and direction of the correlation between variables can be pictured in a graph called a *scatterplot*. Here are three examples. In part (a), we have plotted the number of thirty-second trials that subjects took to learn a list of meaningless words against the number of minutes the subjects participated in the experiment. Since time in the lab and the number of trials are positively and perfectly correlated, the scatterplot appears as a straight line; you can predict the value of either variable once the value of the other is known. Part (b) shows the scatterplot representing the perfect negative correlation between rats' running speeds and the time it took the rats to reach a goal ten feet away. The higher the animals' speeds, the lower were their running times; again, one variable can be predicted perfectly from the other. Part (c) illustrates the scatterplot of the zero correlation (no relationship) between IQ and the length of people's names. Higher and higher correlations create ever tighter patterns of dots that begin to approximate straight lines.

The sign of a correlation coefficient indicates its direction. A plus sign means that the relationship between variables is *positive*—that is, as one variable changes, the other variable changes in the same direction. For example, the correlation between the cost of a particular gasoline purchase and the number of gallons pumped is positive; as gallons increase or decrease, so does the cost. A minus sign in the correlation coefficient indicates that the relationship is *negative,* which means that as one variable increases or decreases, the other changes in the opposite direction. If the time that people want to spend with a person decreases as the person's hostility increases, then hostility and popularity are negatively correlated (see Figure 1.1).

The variables of interest in psychology are seldom perfectly correlated or totally uncorrelated. In testing the hypothesis that belief similarity creates more dating enjoyment than dissimilarity does, suppose you find the correlation between similarity scores and enjoyment ratings to be −.60. This coefficient suggests that there is a reasonably strong, but imperfect, relationship between the variables. As a result, knowing how similar the couple's beliefs are would allow you to predict enjoyment better than you could by random guessing, but the predictions would not be perfectly accurate.

Notice that, in this case, even though the correlation is high, it actually weakens your hypothesis, because the correlation is negative. It indicates that as similarity increases, enjoyment decreases, exactly the opposite of what you predicted. A coefficient of +.60—the more similarity, the higher the enjoyment rating—would have supported the hypothesis (and is, indeed, what research actually shows; see Chapter 17).

How high or low must a correlation be to support or undermine a hypothesis? As we discuss in the appendix, the answer depends both on the probability that the correlation could have resulted simply by chance and on certain conventional rules. A correlation that is higher than would be expected by chance alone is said to be **statistically significant.** Traditionally, scientists do not consider correlations or other research results to be worthy of much attention if they are not statistically significant. Thus, before you accept the idea that the results of a study are important, be careful to note whether, at the very least, the researcher has shown those results to be statistically significant. Requiring evidence of significance is but one example of the kind of healthy skepticism that helps people to think critically about the world. ▪

The Limits of Correlational Research Researchers sometimes claim to find meaning in statistically nonsignificant coefficients, and even statistically significant coefficients are sometimes rather low. To many psychologists the fact that a correlation can be interpreted by different people in varying ways is a major weakness of correlational research.

Correlations have other weaknesses as well. Although a correlation indicates the *degree* of relationship between two variables, it does not indicate *why* they are related. You can identify the strong positive correlation between the amount of alcohol consumed and the intensity of the hangover the next morning, but that measurement gives no information about the biochemical processes driving the relationship. Moreover, the fact that two variables are correlated cannot tell you whether there is a *cause-and-effect* relationship between them—that is, whether one variable actually influences the other.

For example, data show that people with athletic physiques tend to be more confident and aggressive than those who are very thin or very fat. Does this mean that body structure determines personality? Chances are good that the answer is no. Arguing that certain body shapes cause certain psychological characteristics fails to take into account other important factors. These other factors provide alternative hypotheses that can account for the observed correlation. The relationship between body type and personality may stem from the fact that as children, people with well-proportioned bodies are less likely to be bullied, more likely to excel at sports, and more readily accepted into social groups. They may also have other experiences that increase their self-confidence beyond that of many less physically robust or classically shaped individuals.

Despite their limitations, correlational methods are valuable. They greatly enhance psychologists' ability to describe and predict phenomena; they help in the evaluation of existing hypotheses; and they often lead to new hypotheses. In some situations, they are the only methods available. For example, suppose a psychologist hypothesizes that fighting between parents causes children to develop mental disorders. An ideal way to test this hypothesis might be to take one hundred newborns, put some in conflict-filled homes and others in conflict-free homes, and observe which children develop problems. Since this manipulation of families would be unethical, however, the investigator must instead test the hypothesis by using sophisticated correlational methods.

Control

After observing 4,500 people in sixty-five bars, a team of researchers found a negative correlation between the tempo of jukebox music and the speed at which people drank alcohol: the slower the music, the faster the drinking (Schaefer et al., 1988). These observations led the researchers to hypothesize that slow music causes sadder moods and, in turn, faster drinking than does fast music. This is an interesting hypothesis, but is it accurate? Perhaps the differences were caused by something other than differing moods. For example, perhaps people clap their hands more to fast music, making it difficult to drink at the same time, and then make up for the missed drinks by drinking more during slow songs.

Using only correlational methods, a researcher might find it difficult to choose between these hypotheses. To rule out rival hypotheses, the psychologist

A strong correlation between variables does not guarantee that one actually caused the other. In order to support a claim that the rate of people's alcohol consumption in a bar is caused by, rather than merely being correlated with, the pace of background music, one would have to exert some control over the situation. Usually, this means conducting an experiment, using methods described in this chapter.

might aim for the scientific goal of control. He or she would try to establish a situation which eliminates factors that might interfere with an understanding of the cause-and-effect relationship. Instead of merely observing people who happen to come into view, the experimenter might ask social drinkers to serve as volunteers for a study in which they would drink alcohol in a barlike laboratory and repeatedly report on their mood. The experimenter would play music for the drinkers and systematically vary the tempo while keeping everything else constant—the age and sex of the subjects, how much they typically drink per day, and so on. Under these controlled conditions, if mood as well as drinking speed varied with musical tempos, the researcher would have strong evidence that tempo causes changes in emotion and in alcohol consumption.

When a researcher can manipulate one variable and observe its effect on another variable, the result is called *controlled research.* Controlled research uses experimental methods, which we discuss shortly. In our drinking example, the need to exert control over many aspects of the environment forced the experimenter to work in a laboratory, but controlled experiments can also be conducted in the "real world" if precautions are taken against unwanted external influences.

Explanation

After examining data from descriptive, predictive, or controlled research (usually from all three), scientists can begin to suggest explanations. For example, evidence that alcohol consumption increases under stress might be used to help explain why people drink alcohol. Explanations often include or lead to the formation of general rules about a category of behavior or mental processes, such as that alcoholism, overeating, smoking, and other apparently self-abusive actions may *all* be ways of escaping the discomforts of stress.

Sometimes general rules are organized into a **theory**, which is an integrated set of principles that can be used to account for, predict, and even control certain phenomena. In devising his theory of evolution, for example, Charles Darwin formed a set of principles that accounts for the development of all life on Earth, explains why there is so much variability in animal life, and allows predictions about the future of our planet. Sigmund Freud's theory of psychoanalysis provides an example of a psychological theory whose scope is almost as broad; it seeks to explain virtually all aspects of why people behave as they do. Other psychological theories focus on explaining more specific phenomena, such as color vision, memory, or sleep.

Theories are tentative explanations that must be evaluated scientifically. Predictions flowing from a theory proposed by one psychologist will be tested in correlational and experimental research by many other psychologists. If research supports a theory, that theory usually becomes a prominent explanation of some aspect of psychology. If not, the theory is revised or, sometimes, abandoned. Some explanations in science are so well established by constant reconfirmation and fit so well with other knowledge that they are called *laws*.

The constant formulation, evaluation, reformulation, and abandonment of theories generates many explanations of behavior and mental processes. In later chapters we discuss competing theories for many phenomena, and in so doing, we may give you the impression that psychology is in a state of confusion. Actually, *ferment* better describes the situation. The existence of conflicting theories helps motivate psychologists to expand their knowledge through creative research.

There is no fixed sequence that must be followed in working toward the goals of description, prediction, control, and explanation. Figure 1.2 shows how these goals interact. Sometimes explanatory theories spark the curiosity that begins new research and guides researchers in their choice of which variables to explore. Or the first step might come from observation. Seeing children playing together, for example, might inspire research that generates predictions or explanations that in turn might lead to a new theory of human relations. Without data, there would be nothing to explain; without explanatory theories, the data might never be organized in a usable way. The continuing interaction of theory and data lies at the heart of the process that has created the knowledge generated in psychology over the past century.

Methods of Research

Now that we have discussed the goals of psychological research, we will describe the primary methods that psychologists use to conduct this research. These methods include surveys, case studies, naturalistic observation, and experiments.

Figure 1.2
Goals and Methods of Psychological Research
Notice that all four research goals interact. Predictions lead not only to the collection of additional descriptive data but also to controlled experiments, all of which help to confirm or disconfirm predictions. In turn, controlled research leads to explanatory theories, which themselves generate new predictions about behavior and mental processes. This cycle is endless and endlessly productive in expanding psychological knowledge.

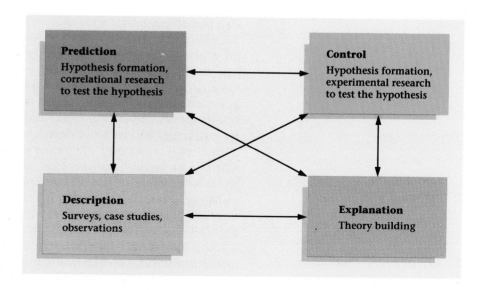

Prediction
Hypothesis formation, correlational research to test the hypothesis

Control
Hypothesis formation, experimental research to test the hypothesis

Description
Surveys, case studies, observations

Explanation
Theory building

Psychologists use surveys to gather information about the attitudes and behaviors of large numbers of people. Careful analysis of data collected through the survey method can provide useful descriptions of behavior patterns, not to mention valuable predictions about the outcome of an election.

Surveys

A **survey** involves asking people questions, in interviews or questionnaires, in order to obtain descriptions of their behavior, attitudes, beliefs, opinions, and intentions. To conduct a useful survey, researchers must phrase the questions and select the respondents carefully. Consider a survey conducted several years ago by Ann Landers. She asked her female readers whether they would prefer to have sexual relations with their partners or just to be held and cuddled. The results showed a preference for cuddling. Does this mean that sex is going out of style? Very unlikely. Several other explanations are possible. Perhaps the preference for cuddling emerged because the question was phrased in either-or terms, leaving no room for the respondent to indicate that she liked both cuddling and sex. Or perhaps the women who answered the question were not representative of the population as a whole; perhaps only those with insensitive or overly demanding partners bothered to respond. A different picture might have emerged if a different set of women had been asked a more carefully thought-out question.

Other problems that may lurk within the survey method are more difficult to avoid. People may be reluctant to admit undesirable or embarrassing things about themselves or may say what they feel they should say about an issue. For example, people may be reluctant to admit negative attitudes toward minorities or may understate the strength of those attitudes (Riggle et al., 1989).

In spite of these problems, surveys provide an excellent way of gathering large amounts of data from a large number of people at relatively low cost. Usually, survey data lead psychologists to formulate predictions and hypotheses and to test those hypotheses through additional correlational and experimental research.

Case Studies

Surveys give broad portraits; sometimes, the close-up view provided by a case study is more helpful. A **case study** is an intensive examination of a phenomenon in a particular individual, group, or situation. Case studies are especially useful when a phenomenon is complex or relatively rare, and they have long been used in clinical work. Freud's development of psychoanalysis, for example, was based on case studies of people whose paralysis or other physical symptoms disappeared when they were hypnotized or asleep.

Case studies have also played a special role in *neuropsychology*, the study of the relationships among brain activity, thinking, and behavior. Consider the case of Dr. P, a patient described by Oliver Sacks (1985). A distinguished musician with superior intelligence, Dr. P began to display such odd symptoms as the inability to recognize familiar people and to distinguish between people and inanimate objects. During a visit to a neurologist, Dr. P mistook his foot for his shoe. When he rose to leave, he tried to lift off his wife's head and put it, like a hat, on his own. He could not name even the most common objects when he looked at them, although he could describe them. When handed a glove, for example, he said, "A continuous surface, infolded on itself. It appears to have . . . five outpouchings, if this is the word. . . . A container of some sort." Only later, when he put it on his hand, did he exclaim, "My God, it's a glove!" (Sacks, 1985, p. 13).

Using case studies like this one, pioneers in neuropsychology noted the deficits suffered by people with particular kinds of brain damage or disease.

Eventually, neuropsychologists classified the brain disorders produced by injuries, tumors, poisoning, and other causes. (The cause of Dr. P's symptoms was apparently a large brain tumor.)

Case studies have one major limitation, however: cases are not necessarily representative. Just as visitors from another galaxy would err wildly if they tried to describe the typical earthling after meeting Arsenio Hall, Bette Midler, and Roseanne Barr, psychologists can wander astray if they do not have access to a representative sample. Furthermore, the reasons for behavior in one case may not apply in all others. Some brain-damaged patients, for example, may suffer psychological as well as physical traumas, so that some of their unusual behavior may not be a direct result of the brain injury.

Still, like surveys, case studies provide raw material for controlled research. They can be valuable sources of information about particular people, and they serve as the testing ground for new treatments, training programs, and other applications of research.

Naturalistic Observation

Sometimes the best way to gather descriptive data about a psychological phenomenon is to observe it as it occurs in the natural environment. This is especially true when other approaches are likely to be disruptive or misleading. For example, if you studied animals only by observing them in laboratory experiments, you probably would not see how cues in their natural environment normally affect them, and you might conclude that learning alone determines most of what they do. In contrast, **ethologists**—scientists who study animal behavior in its natural environment—have found that many behaviors of lower animals consist of inherited patterns that are predictable, stereotyped, and triggered automatically by environmental events.

Konrad Lorenz, one of the founders of ethology, provided many demonstrations of inborn but environmentally triggered behaviors. One of the most delightful showed that baby geese follow their mother because her movement and honking provide signals that are naturally attractive. To prove that any moving, honking object would provide the same "follow me" signal, Lorenz squatted and made mother-goose noises in front of newborn geese whose real mother was not present. Soon the goslings were following him wherever he went, much to the amusement of his neighbors.

Naturalistic observation of people can also be revealing. John Gottman, for example, observed children's play groups and watched how newcomers tried to join in. Popular children, he found, tended to blend gradually into the flow of activities; unpopular youngsters typically entered by disrupting the group in some way (Gottman, 1987; Putallaz & Gottman, 1981). Sometimes, psychologists use naturalistic observation to gather information about problematic behavior in preparation for changing it. For example, to help computer programmers design a better word-processing system, a psychologist might first observe how people use (and misuse) existing systems (Black, Carroll & McGuigan, 1987).

Naturalistic observation can provide large amounts of rich information, but it is not problem-free (Nietzel, Bernstein & Milich, 1991). For one thing, when people know they are being observed (and research ethics usually require that they do know), they tend to act differently than they otherwise would, at least for a while. Researchers typically combat this problem by observing long enough for subjects to get used to the situation and begin behaving more naturally. Observations can also be distorted if observers expect to see certain

The research of ethologist Konrad Lorenz helped demonstrate the automatic nature of much animal behavior. Here, he shows that baby geese will follow the first creature, including him, from whom they hear mother goose sounds.

behaviors. Researchers observing children playing together, for example, must have no prior information about the children's popularity. To get the most out of naturalistic observation, psychologists must counteract potential problems such as these.

Experiments

Suppose you read that a positive correlation exists between time spent in an alcoholism treatment program and success in giving up drinking. Is abstinence *caused* by the treatment? Surveys, case studies, or naturalistic observations are not likely to give a satisfactory answer. To determine whether a cause-and-effect relationship exists, a psychologist would want to conduct an experiment.

The Structure of Experiments Experiments are situations in which the researcher manipulates one variable and then observes the effect of that manipulation on another variable. The variable manipulated by the experimenter is called the **independent variable.** The variable to be observed is called the **dependent variable** because it is affected by, or *depends on*, the independent variable.

As an example, suppose a psychologist wants to test the hypothesis that a program of group discussions and social support causes alcoholics to alter their drinking behavior. As illustrated in Figure 1.3, the psychologist could conduct an experiment in which both treated and untreated alcoholics try to quit. The experimenter controls whether treatment is administered to each subject, so the presence or absence of treatment is the independent variable. Whether and how much the subjects drink after treatment is the dependent variable.

The group that receives the experimental treatment is called, naturally enough, the **experimental group.** The people who receive no treatment are called the **control group.** Control groups provide base lines against which to compare the performance of others. In this case, the no-treatment control group allows the experimenter to measure how much change in drinking behavior can be expected even without treatment. If everything about the two groups is exactly the same except for the exposure to treatment, then any difference in drinking behavior should be caused by (not merely correlated with) that treatment.

Selecting the Subjects The process of selecting subjects for any experiment (or survey, for that matter) is called **sampling.** Sampling should not be taken lightly. If the subjects chosen come from a particular subgroup (say, white male construction workers), the results of the experiment might apply, or *generalize,* only to people like them.

Ideally, in order for the results of an experiment to reveal something about people in general, the researcher chooses subjects who are representative of people in general. When every member of the population has an equal chance of being chosen for study, the individuals selected constitute a **random sample.** If not everyone in a population has an equal chance of being selected, the sample is said to be a **biased sample.**

It is important to understand that a random sample of the entire population is not always necessary or even desirable. For example, if you *want* to learn about the behavior of white male construction workers, all your subjects should be randomly selected from that group. Or, you might begin by conducting experiments on a particular population, such as college students,

Experiments are used in an endless variety of psychological specialties. In one study, for example, sport psychologists found that experimental groups of varsity women softball players who rode an exercycle or imagined batting during the time between pregame warmup and batting got significantly more hits than control groups who read magazines or imagined catching fly balls (Anshel & Wrisberg, 1988).

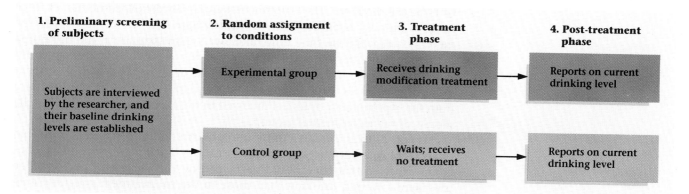

1. Preliminary screening of subjects

Subjects are interviewed by the researcher, and their baseline drinking levels are established

2. Random assignment to conditions

Experimental group

Control group

3. Treatment phase

Receives drinking modification treatment

Waits; receives no treatment

4. Post-treatment phase

Reports on current drinking level

Reports on current drinking level

Figure 1.3
Design of a Simple Treatment Versus No-Treatment Experiment
Ideally, the only difference between treated and untreated subjects in experiments like this one is whether the subjects receive the treatment that the researcher wishes to evaluate. Under such ideal circumstances, any difference in the results should be attributable to the treatment.

and then repeat the experiments on broader, more representative samples to determine if the same results appear. If results are fairly consistent regardless of the subjects' age, sex, race, social status, intelligence, and the like, then you could confidently draw your next sample from whatever willing group is at hand.

Flaws in Experimental Control   Once the hypothesis has been established, the independent and dependent variables have been chosen and operationally defined, the subjects selected, and the experiment conducted, you can collect and summarize the results. For our example, the data show that almost all treated subjects quit drinking completely and that no control subjects did so. At this point, you might be ready to believe that the treatment caused the difference in quitting rates. Before coming to that conclusion, however, you must consider other factors that might account for the results, especially confounding variables.

Confounding variables confuse, or confound, interpretation of the results of an experiment. Any factor that might have affected the dependent variable, along with or instead of the independent variable, may be a confounding variable. When confounding variables are present, you cannot know whether the independent or the confounding variable produced the results. Here we examine four sources of confounding variables: random variables, flaws in the design of the experiment, the subjects' expectations, and experimenter bias.

In an ideal research world, the only difference between the experimental and the control conditions would involve different amounts of the independent variable, such as the presence or absence of treatment. In reality, however, there are always other differences, especially in **random variables.** These are uncontrolled, sometimes uncontrollable, factors such as differences in the subjects—in their backgrounds, personalities, physical health, or vulnerability to stress, for example—as well as differences in the experimental conditions such as the time of day and noise level.

Random variables are so numerous that no experimenter can create groups that are equivalent on all of them. The next best thing is to distribute the effects of these variables randomly across groups. To do so, researchers often flip a coin or use some other random process to assign each subject to either the experimental or the control group. Procedures like this balance and minimize the effects of uncontrolled variables on the results of an experiment.

The basic design of an experiment is a second source of confounding variables. To take just one example, suppose that the experimental and control groups in a study of treatment for alcoholism had different amounts of contact with the experimenter. The experimental group saw the experimenter for three weekly sessions; people in the control group had no contact with the experimenter from the time they filled out a questionnaire at the beginning of the study until they reported on their drinking at the end of the experiment. Would the people in the control group have done better if they had spent more time with the experimenter? Did the opportunity to gain confidence from the experimenter or to feel involved in the experiment contribute to the success of the experimental group?

This possibility illustrates a third source of confounding: differences in what subjects think about the experimental situation. If alcoholics in the treatment group expected that they would be helped by the treatment, perhaps they tried harder to quit drinking than those in the no-treatment control group. In medical and psychological treatments, improvements created by the subjects' knowledge and expectations are called the *placebo effect*. A **placebo** (pronounced "pla-see-bow") is a treatment that contains no active ingredient but nevertheless produces an effect because a person *believes* it will have that effect. Patients may improve after they are given a drug, not because the drug contains an effective treatment for their illness, but because they believe that the drug will help them.

How can researchers determine the extent to which a result is caused by the independent variable or by a placebo effect? Often they include a special control group that receives only a placebo. Then they compare results for the experimental group, the placebo group, and those receiving no treatment. In one smoking-cessation study (Bernstein, 1970), for example, subjects in a placebo group took sugar pills described by the experimenter as "fast-acting tranquilizers" that would help them learn to endure the stress of giving up cigarettes. These subjects did as well at quitting as those in the experimental group, who received extensive treatment. This result suggests that the success of the experimental group may have been due largely to the subjects' expectations, not to the treatment methods.

A fourth potential confounding variable comes from **experimenter bias,** the unintentional effect that experimenters may exert on results. Robert Rosenthal (1966) demonstrated the power of experimenter bias. His subjects were laboratory assistants who were asked to run rats in a maze. Rosenthal told some of the assistants that their rats were bred to be particularly "maze-bright"; he told the others that their rats were "maze-dull." In fact, both groups of rats were randomly drawn from the same population and had equal maze-learning capabilities. But the maze-bright animals learned the maze significantly faster than the maze-dull rats. How was this possible? Rosenthal concluded that the result had nothing to do with the rats and everything to do with the experimenters. He suggested that the assistants' expectations about their rats' supposedly superior (or inferior) capabilities caused them to subtly bias or alter their training techniques, which in turn speeded or slowed the animals' learning.

To prevent experimenter bias from confounding results, experimenters often use a **double-blind design**, an arrangement in which the subjects as well as those giving the treatments are unaware of, or "blind" to, who is receiving a placebo and what results are to be expected. Only the director of the study—a person with no direct contact with the subjects—knows the hypotheses, who is in the experimental group, and who is in the placebo group.

In short, experiments are vital tools for examining cause-and-effect relationships between variables, but like the other methods we have described, they are vulnerable to error. (For a review of the methods we have discussed, see "In Review: Methods of Psychological Research.") Scientists maximize the

In Review: Methods of Psychological Research

Method	Features	Strengths	Pitfalls
Survey	A standard set of questions asked of a large number of subjects	Gathers large amounts of data relatively quickly and inexpensively	Sampling errors, poorly phrased questions, and response biases can distort results
Case study	Intensive examination of the behavior and mental processes associated with a specific person or situation	Provides detailed descriptive analysis of interesting, complex, or rare phenomena	May not provide representative samples of phenomena or their causes; can be expensive and time-consuming
Naturalistic observation	Observation of human or animal behavior in the environment where it typically occurs	Provides description of behavior presumably uncontaminated by outside influences	Observer bias and subject self-consciousness can distort results
Experiment	Manipulation of an independent variable and measurement of its effects on a dependent variable	Can establish a cause-and-effect relationship between independent and dependent variables	Sampling problems may restrict the generality of results; confounding variables may prevent valid conclusions

value of experimental methods by designing experiments to eliminate as many confounding variables as possible, repeating their studies to ensure consistent results, then tempering their interpretation of the results to take into account the limitations or problems that remain. They must also consider the welfare of their human or animal subjects.

HIGHLIGHT

Ethical Guidelines for Psychologists

Researchers might study severe anxiety by putting a gun to people's heads, or they might measure the influence of heredity and the environment on intelligence by taking newborn children away from intelligent and not-so-intelligent parents and randomly assigning half of each group to live in intellectually barren homes. They *might* do these things, but such potentially harmful methods are unethical.

In each of these examples, the ethical course of action is obvious: the psychologist must find another way to conduct the research. Psychologists often face complex ethical questions that force them to decide how to balance conflicting values. Many experiments reflect a compromise between the need to protect subjects from harm and the need to know about the unknown. In finding ways to help people cope with anxiety, for example, researchers may ask them to try new coping skills while enduring an anxiety-provoking, but not traumatic, situation.

When research does create discomfort for the subjects, researchers must determine that the potential benefits of the work in terms of new knowledge and human welfare outweigh any risks or discomfort to the subjects. They must also minimize the discomfort and risk involved, and they must act to prevent subjects from suffering any long-term negative consequences from participation. When people are the research subjects, researchers must inform them about every aspect of the study that might influence their decision to participate, and researchers must ensure that subjects' involvement is voluntary. If a researcher deceives people about an experiment because full disclosure beforehand would bias their behavior, the researcher must also reveal and justify the deception afterward.

The obligation to protect subjects' welfare also extends to animals, which are used as subjects in about 7 percent of psychological research (American Psychological Association, 1984). Psychologists study animals partly because their behavior is interesting in and of itself and partly because studies of animals can yield information relevant to human behavior that would be impossible or unethical to collect from humans.

Contrary to the allegations of some animal-rights activists, animals used in psychological research are not routinely subjected to extreme pain, starvation, or other inhumane conditions (Coile & Miller, 1984). Even in the small proportion of studies that require the use of electric shock, the discomfort created is mild, brief, and not harmful. In fact, psychologists are highly motivated to protect the welfare of animal subjects for several reasons. First, like most of us, they are humane individuals who take no pleasure in animals' suffering. Second, the Animal Welfare Act, the National Institutes of Health *Guide for the Care and Use of Laboratory Animals*, the American Psychological Association's Principles on Animal Use, and other laws and regulations set standards for the care and treatment of animal subjects. Third, inflicting undue stress on animal subjects is likely to create reactions that can act as confounding variables. For example, in an experiment on how the amount of food offered as a reward affects learning in rats, the researcher might reduce the animals' food intake in order to make them hungry enough to want the experimental rewards. But starving the subjects would introduce discomfort that would make it impossible to separate the effects of the reward from the effects of starvation.

In those relatively rare studies that require animals to undergo short-lived pain or other forms of moderate stress, legal and ethical standards require the psychologist to persuade funding agencies—as well as local committees charged with monitoring animal research—that the discomfort is justified by the expected benefits to human welfare. Sometimes, the proposed research is not permitted, but there are many cases in which the cost-benefit balance favors conducting the experiments. For example, many of the drugs that help alleviate the symptoms of severe mental disorders are available only because researchers were able to test their effects first on animals.

The responsibility for conducting research in the most humane fashion possible forms just one aspect of the ethical guidelines for psychologists that have been formulated by the American Psychological Association (APA). These standards begin as follows:

Psychologists respect the dignity and worth of the individual and strive for the preservation and protection of fundamental human rights. They are committed to increasing knowledge of human behavior and of people's understanding of themselves and others and to the utilization of such knowledge for the promotion of human welfare. . . . They use their skills only for purposes consistent with these values and do not knowingly permit their misuse by others. (APA, 1981, p. 633)

The APA then spells out the implications of this statement (APA, 1981, 1987, 1989). For example, as teachers, psychologists should strive to give students a complete, accurate, and up-to-date view of each topic rather than a narrow, biased point of view. Psychologists should perform only those services and use those techniques for which they are adequately trained; a biological psychologist untrained in clinical methods should not try to offer psychotherapy. Except in the most unusual circumstances (to be discussed in Chapter 16, on therapy), psychologists should not reveal information obtained from clients or students, and they should avoid situations in which a conflict of interest might impair their judgment or harm someone else. They should not, for example, have sexual relations with their clients, their students, or the employees they supervise.

Despite these guidelines, doubt arises in some cases about whether a particular practice or proposed experiment is ethical. Indeed, ethical principles for psychologists will continue to evolve as psychologists face new and more complex ethical issues in their work. ■

Thinking Critically About Psychology (or Anything Else)

Whether and how animals should be used in research are controversial questions about which many people hold strong opinions. Some people form their opinions on this and other issues by uncritically accepting what they are told. Indeed, there are politicians, advertisers, TV evangelists, and activists of all kinds who seek your votes, money, or allegiance and hope you will accept their promises, claims, and point of view without careful thought.

As an example, consider the following computer-generated form letter that recently arrived in the mail: "You have been approved by our Award Manager to receive a fun-filled vacation in Florida, consisting of a 5-day stay in Key West, Florida, plus a weekend at Disney World, in Orlando. All you have to do to receive this fabulous, once-in-a-lifetime dream trip is call us—today!" A non-toll-free phone number was provided.

At first glance, this letter suggests that the recipient has won a free trip. Before packing your bags, however, you should ask yourself some questions that are vital to the rational consideration of any issue, whether it be an advertising claim, the ethics of animal research, the risks of offshore oil drilling, or the wisdom of a government policy. Among the most basic of these questions are

1. *What am I being asked to believe or accept?* In this case, you are asked to believe that you have won a free trip.
2. *What evidence is available to support the assertion?* There is no evidence in the letter to support the notion that you won a free trip. Although the

Why should we buy beer recommended to us by a dog? Advertisers commonly depend on our uncritical acceptance of the associations they create between their products and qualities, such as status and success. When people buy a product they purchase the image associated with it—an image sometimes considered more important than the product itself.

"Award Manager" has "approved" the recipient to "receive" a vacation, the word *free* is never used.

3. *Are there alternative ways of interpreting the evidence?* Yes, the sender is trying to make money by somehow charging for the trip.

4. *What additional evidence would help to evaluate the alternatives?* You might call the company for information about hidden charges. (There was a large fee, it turned out.)

5. *What conclusions are most reasonable?* After this analysis, drawing a reasonable conclusion about the letter and what to do with it should be easy.

These questions provide one strategy for *critical thinking*—the process of assessing claims and making judgments on the basis of well-supported evidence (Wade, 1988).

Topics ranging from astrology and extrasensory perception (ESP) to abortion and gun control elicit a knee-jerk opinion from many people, often based on what they want to believe rather than on what rational analysis through critical thinking might support (Lamal, 1989). Abandoning uncritical acceptance of stated "facts" and even long-held beliefs for the more laborious but vital task of critically evaluating evidence can open the way to a fuller understanding of these and other topics. The same critical-thinking skills should be brought to bear when you read about research in psychology (and other fields). Before accepting assertions, ask yourself the five questions we listed.

To help you develop skill at evaluating issues, we include in each chapter of this book a special section called "Thinking Critically" in which we invite you to examine a particular issue by considering those five questions. This emphasis on critical thinking is grounded in our belief that blind acceptance of unsubstantiated information merely because it is cleverly stated, comes from prominent people, or is endorsed by many others can be dangerous— not just for the individual who gets stuck paying for a "free" vacation but also for citizens of a nation at large, who may get stuck with a ravaged environment, corrupt or unwise elected officials, or tyranny.

Future Directions

Before you begin what we hope will be an exciting tour of the discipline called psychology, we would like to point out a few things about how this book is organized and why. We move next to a chapter on developmental psychology, describing how a single cell develops into the complex and fascinating organism known as a human being. Examining developmental psychology first provides both a preview of the many aspects of behavior and mental processes to be discussed in later chapters and a portrait of the human being as a unified whole—a creature who can act and react, feel and think, plan and imagine, learn and remember, and, above all, be consciously aware of the world and communicate with it. Through the rest of the book, we examine in more detail each of the major components of behavior and mental processes that ultimately come together in the whole human being.

This process of piecing together behavior and mental processes begins with cells and other biological structures. Thus, in Chapter 3 we examine biological aspects of psychology, showing how nerve cells communicate with one another to create behavior and mental activity. Next, in Chapter 4, on sensation, we consider how special groups of cells detect sound, light, and other forms of energy and how they convert this energy into the sensations of hearing, vision, taste, smell, and touch. How we organize, interpret, and attend to these sensations is the subject of Chapter 5, on perception. The analysis of how we experience the world is continued in Chapter 6, where we focus on consciousness and how it is affected by sleep, hypnosis, meditation, and drugs.

Having brought the complexities of consciousness into the picture, we next consider learning, memory, decision making, thinking, and the use of language, all of which are covered in Chapters 7 through 9. Of course, some people are better at these processes than others; in Chapter 10, we discuss individual differences in mental ability.

Because psychology involves not only the study of what people do but also why they do it, we turn to the topic of motivation in Chapter 11. Few motivated behaviors occur in a neutral state. Most are accompanied by anger, joy, fear, hope, desperation, or any number of other emotions, the topic of Chapter 12.

At that point, we are ready to begin looking at how all the processes considered so far are integrated in functioning individuals and how those individuals relate to their environments. We begin this phase of study by considering in Chapter 13 how people's reactions to various forms of stress affect their health. We see that there are clear individual differences in people's responses to stress and that some of these differences seem to be related to personality, the topic of Chapter 14. There we consider what personality is and how it relates to behavior and mental processes. In Chapter 15, on psychological disorders, we review some of the many ways in which human behavior and mental processes can go awry. In Chapter 16 we describe the major approaches and methods used in treating psychological problems. In Chapters 17 and 18 we examine social psychology—the ways in which one person's actions, thoughts, attitudes, emotions, and other processes influence and are influenced by other people.

You might be wondering about the image on the cover. It is the Greek letter psi, the international symbol for psychology. In each chapter within the cover you will see that research in each subfield of psychology draws on and contributes to work in other psychological subfields. This interconnection reflects the fact that psychology's subfields are not isolated areas of inquiry. Their theories, methods, research findings, and applications to daily life are inextricably linked to form a unified discipline. We illustrate just a few of these linkages at the beginning of each chapter in a "Linkages" diagram, similar to the one shown on the next page. Each question in the diagram illustrates a linkage between the topics of two chapters; the page numbers indicate where the question is discussed. To help you keep these linkages in mind as you read the book we have also placed each linking question in the margin next to the major discussion of that question (see, for example, p. 38). By examining the diagram in each chapter, you can see how the topic of that chapter is related to other subfields of psychology and how the chapter is related to what you have studied or will study in other chapters. One of these relationships is given special attention at the end of each chapter in a section entitled "Linkages."

Of course, there are many more linkages within psychology than could be included in the diagrams. We hope that the diagrams will prompt you to look for other linkages. This kind of detective work can be enjoyable and useful as well. You may find it easier to remember material in one chapter by relating it to linked material in other chapters. Most of all, by staying alert to additional linkages as you read this book, you will come away not only with threads of knowledge about each subfield but with an appreciation of the interwoven fabric of psychology as a whole.

LINKAGES

The World of

Psychology

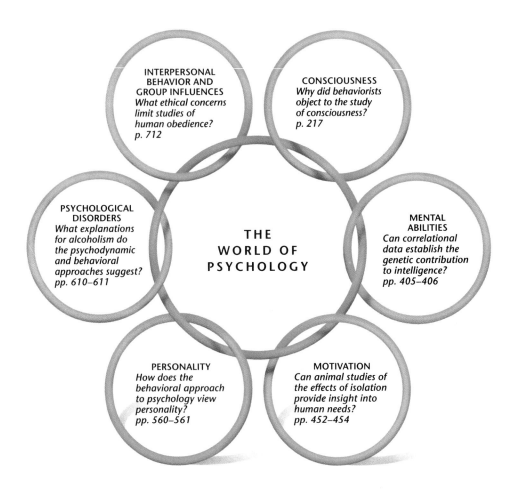

INTERPERSONAL
BEHAVIOR AND
GROUP INFLUENCES
*What ethical concerns
limit studies of
human obedience?*
p. 712

CONSCIOUSNESS
*Why did behaviorists
object to the study
of consciousness?*
p. 217

PSYCHOLOGICAL
DISORDERS
*What explanations
for alcoholism do
the psychodynamic
and behavioral
approaches suggest?*
pp. 610–611

THE
WORLD OF
PSYCHOLOGY

MENTAL
ABILITIES
*Can correlational
data establish the
genetic contribution
to intelligence?*
pp. 405–406

PERSONALITY
*How does the
behavioral approach
to psychology view
personality?*
pp. 560–561

MOTIVATION
*Can animal studies of
the effects of isolation
provide insight into
human needs?*
pp. 452–454

■ Look at the diagram above, which illustrates some of the relationships between the topics discussed in this chapter and other chapter topics. Time and again throughout this book, you will see how psychologists have applied the approaches and methods described in this chapter.

Diagrams like this one appear near the beginning of each chapter. Some of the questions in each diagram are discussed in other, "linked" chapters. The page numbers where the questions are discussed follow the questions. These diagrams are designed to help you understand some of the ways in which the subfields of psychology are related. Reading and thinking about the questions should help you pull facts together and to consider their implications. In some cases, reading the questions should help you recall ideas considered in other chapters that will help you understand the current chapter. You might also want to use the questions as a self-testing device when studying for quizzes and exams. Or you might want to read the discussions of some questions listed in a diagram before reading the chapter—to preview some of the chapter's content or to clarify its relevance to psychology as a whole. Exploring the Linkages questions might also give you ideas for term papers or, we hope, prove to be a pleasurable intellectual exercise. ■

Summary and Key Terms

Psychology is the science of behavior and mental processes. The topics included in this field range from the study of nerve cells to the interaction of people in families and other groups.

From Cell to Society: The Scope of Psychology

Subfields of Psychology

Because the subject matter of psychology is so diverse, most psychologists work in particular subfields within the discipline. *Experimental psychologists* focus on basic psychological processes such as learning, memory, and perception in both animals and humans. *Cognitive psychologists* study complex phenomena such as thinking, judgment, decision making, problem solving, language, and imagination. *Biological psychologists,* also called *physiological psychologists,* study topics such as how nerve cells communicate with one another and the role played by the nervous system in regulating behavior. *Personality psychologists* focus on the unique characteristics that determine individuals' behavior. *Social psychologists* examine questions regarding how people influence one another, especially in groups. *Clinical psychologists* provide direct service to troubled people and conduct research on abnormal behavior. *Community psychologists* emphasize the prevention of psychological disorders. *Developmental psychologists* specialize in trying to understand the development of behavior and mental processes over a lifetime. *Quantitative psychologists* find ways of measuring and analyzing the processes explored by psychologists in other subfields; among their fundamental methods are *statistical analyses.*

Approaches to Psychology

Psychologists also differ in their theoretical approaches. Those adopting a *biological approach* tend to view behavior and mental processes as the result of physiological processes. The *psychodynamic approach* sees behavior and mental processes as a struggle to resolve conflicts between impulses and the demands made by society to control those impulses. Psychologists who take the *behavioral approach* see behavior as determined primarily by learning based on past experiences with rewards and punishments. The *humanistic approach* views behavior as controlled by the decisions that people make about their lives based on their perceptions of the world. The *cognitive approach* advocates the idea that behavior cannot be understood until the basic mental processes that underlie it are understood.

Unity Within Diversity

In spite of the diversity of its subfields and theoretical approaches, psychology is unified both by the interaction and sharing of knowledge among researchers in every subfield and by their emphasis on empirical research.

The Goals of Research

Research in psychology, as in other sciences, focuses on four main goals: description, prediction, control, and explanation.

Description

Description involves the careful recording of mental and behavioral processes.

Prediction

Prediction typically involves research designed to evaluate hy-

potheses about the strength and direction of *correlations* between the *variables* found in descriptive research.

Control

To test hypotheses about whether the relationships between correlated variables reflect cause and effect, some measure of control must be introduced. The goal of control is sought through experimental research.

Explanation

The goal of explanation is approached by building on descriptive, predictive, and controlled research to create *theories* of behavior and mental processes. These theories generate additional descriptions and hypotheses, prompt predictions, and suggest new experiments.

Other Key Terms in This Section: operational definition, correlation coefficient, statistically significant.

Methods of Research

Psychologists use numerous research methods in their work. Most prominent among these are surveys, case studies, naturalistic observation, and experiments.

Surveys

Surveys are used to collect large amounts of information from many people at relatively low cost. They also may reveal issues to be investigated by other methods. To be most useful, surveys should be based on a large and representative sample of the people to be studied.

Case Studies

Case studies focus on a single individual or event. Researchers must be careful not to depend too heavily on case study data, because they typically do not reflect the behavior and mental processes of people in general.

Naturalistic Observation

Observation of people or animals outside of a laboratory, in their natural environment, is a way of gathering data about behavior without altering that behavior.

Experiments

In an *experiment* an investigator manipulates one variable, the *independent variable*, and watches for an effect on a second variable, the *dependent variable*. The main advantage of experiments is that they allow the researcher to eliminate systematically factors that might be causing some phenomenon and ultimately to establish with reasonable certainty what factor is the main cause. But experimental results can be distorted in several ways, especially by the action of uncontrolled factors, or *random variables*; flaws in the basic design of the experiment; subjects' perceptions of the experiment (*placebo* effects); and *experimenter bias*. In doing research, teaching, therapy, writing, consulting, or other tasks, psychologists are bound by the ethical standards of the American Psychological Association.

Other Key Terms in This Section: ethologist, experimental group, control group, sampling, random sample, biased sample, confounding variable, double-blind design.

O U T L I N E

Human Development

For several years in the late 1700s, people living in and around the Caune Woods of Aveyron, France, reported sighting a wild boy running naked with the animals. Supposedly, he had been lost or abandoned by his parents at a very early age and had grown up with only animals. Eventually, when this Wild Boy of Aveyron was about eleven, hunters captured him, and he was sent to Paris.

The scientists in Paris expected to observe what philosopher Jean-Jacques Rousseau had called the "noble savage." After all, here was a human being who had grown up uncontaminated by the evils and arbitrary rules of society. But what the scientists found was a dirty, frightened creature who crawled and trotted like a wild animal, who would eat the filthiest of garbage, and who preferred raw to cooked meat. He spent most of his time silently rocking back and forth. He would snarl at and attack anyone who tried to touch him. Though the scientists worked with the boy for more than ten years, they produced only minor changes in his behavior. He never learned to speak. His social behavior remained so backward that he was never able to live unguarded among other people.

If a child like the Wild Boy were found today, could modern psychologists "cure" him? Probably not. In recent times there have been children who were rescued after having been confined for years in closets and other environments that cut them off from other people. Invariably, these children find it extremely difficult to interact with others. Often they are unable to learn language. These cases highlight the importance of early contacts with other people for normal human development. They also underscore the need to know as much as possible about early development and what can help or hinder it.

Developmental psychology is the psychological specialty that documents the course of physical, social, emotional, moral, and intellectual development over a person's life span. *Development* refers to age-related changes that are systematic, sequential, and long-lasting. Developmental psychologists study when certain skills first

LINKAGES

Human

Development

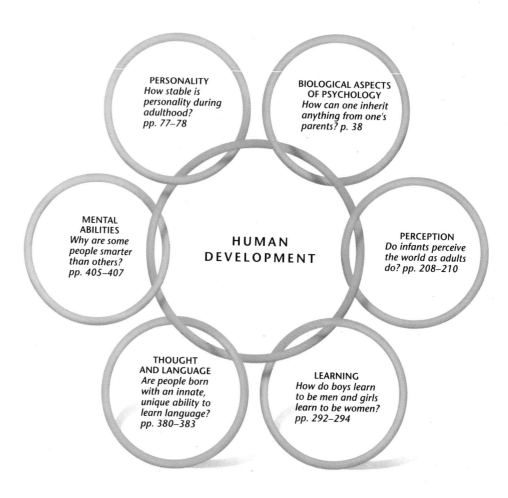

PERSONALITY
How stable is personality during adulthood?
pp. 77–78

BIOLOGICAL ASPECTS OF PSYCHOLOGY
How can one inherit anything from one's parents? p. 38

MENTAL ABILITIES
Why are some people smarter than others?
pp. 405–407

HUMAN DEVELOPMENT

PERCEPTION
Do infants perceive the world as adults do? pp. 208–210

THOUGHT AND LANGUAGE
Are people born with an innate, unique ability to learn language?
pp. 380–383

LEARNING
How do boys learn to be men and girls learn to be women?
pp. 292–294

■ Look at the diagram above, which illustrates some of the relationships between the topic of this chapter, human development, and other chapter topics. In order to understand a phenomenon, people often look to its origins. In physics, cosmologists try to decipher how the universe began and evolved. In biology, paleontologists try to uncover and understand the varied forms that life has taken over the ages. In psychology, developmental psychologists study how people change with age. They describe and analyze the changes that are likely to occur with age in each domain of psychology—perception, personality, and so on. The study of developmental psychology is interesting in its own right, but it also illuminates other areas of psychology, as this diagram suggests.

Differences between men and women are one example. Studies by developmental psychologists shed light on what these differences are, when they emerge, and how variable they are. Research by specialists in other subfields gives a deeper picture of the mechanisms behind these differences—showing how some differences might be inherited, how some might be learned.

Remember that some of the questions in the diagram are examined in this chapter and some are answered in other chapters; the page numbers indicate where the questions are discussed. We repeat each Linkage question in the margin as it is discussed in the text. ■

appear, how they change with age, and whether they change in a sudden spurt or gradually. They look at how development in one domain, say physical growth, is related to development in another domain, such as social relations. They want to know if everyone develops skills at the same rate or if slow starters sometimes end up ahead. They are interested in the processes of development. How do transitions from lower to higher levels of skill occur? How much of development is determined by children's inheritance of abilities from their parents? How much can the environment alter development?

In this chapter, you will read about how a person develops from a fertilized egg into a mature adult and how adults, too, change with time. We describe the milestones of growth in sensation, emotion, thinking, social behavior, and other domains that are examined in the book (see the Linkages diagram). We begin by considering how human development is studied; then we review development in various domains, from the moment of conception on.

The Study of Development

Today, most infants and children are cherished, nurtured, taught, and studied; but it was not always so. In most Western cultures, no special allowances were made for the fragility or limitations of youth until the nineteenth century. Today, parents await children's advances—the first tooth, the first step, the first word—with bated breath. Before the nineteenth century, such milestones were scorned or ignored. Children were neither encouraged nor expected to be happy, cheerful, or playful. Instead, parents tried to integrate their offspring as quickly as possible into the adult world of hard work and serious pursuits. What happened to bring about both the belief that children are worth watching and nurturing and the rise of developmental psychology?

Philosophical Roots

The change in thinking about children stemmed from many influences, but its roots may be traced to the work of two philosophers. The first was British philosopher John Locke. In essays published in the 1690s, Locke suggested that what happens during childhood has a profound and permanent effect on the individual. He proposed that the newborn infant is like a blank slate, or *tabula rasa,* on which experience writes its story. If parents take advantage of the early years to reason with and teach their children desirable habits, he believed, the children will grow into rational, responsible members of society.

Some seventy years later, French philosopher Jean-Jacques Rousseau argued that children are capable of discovering how the world operates without adult teaching. They should be allowed to grow as nature dictates, he said, with little guidance or pressure from parents. Rousseau also suggested that childhood is a unique period, a stage that is qualitatively different from later life.

Out of the arguments of Locke and Rousseau came two central questions that have intrigued students of development to this day. First, how much of a person's development is attributable to *nurture*—to teaching and other influences from the external environment—and how much comes from within the individual's *nature*, or genetic makeup? Second, does development occur in distinct *stages* over the life span? Psychologists generally agree that there are orderly sequences in development from infancy to adulthood, but a stage is more than just a step in a sequence. A stage involves a *qualitative* change

Observation of children as they explore their environment and interact with others has provided psychologists with a rich source of data for understanding human development.

from whatever preceded it. Furthermore, each stage builds on the preceding stages, and the order of stages cannot change. Both the question of whether such stages exist in human development and questions about the roles of nature and nurture remain important issues for developmental psychologists.

Scientific Approaches

The issues of developmental psychology are rooted in philosophy, but its methods are grounded in science. One of the first people to treat the study of development scientifically was G. Stanley Hall. From 1890 to 1910, Hall explored children's and adolescents' intellectual development, using interviews and questionnaires. Other psychologists preferred more precise measurements, such as the first intelligence test, developed by Alfred Binet and Theophile Simon in France. Because their test provided uniform standards for evaluating children, it created a quantitative yardstick of children's mental development. Still other psychologists advocated using observation to study development. Arnold Lucius Gesell, for example, designed the first observation room, a dome-shaped structure in which he could observe and photograph children without disturbing them.

Throughout the twentieth century, these three techniques of asking, testing, and observing children have been used to support or to disconfirm different theories of how development occurs. Especially significant were theories proposed by Arnold Gesell, John Watson, Sigmund Freud, and Jean Piaget.

Early in this century Gesell used his observations to support his theory that development is simply the natural unfolding of abilities with age. He demonstrated, for example, that motor skills, such as standing and walking, picking up a cube, and throwing a ball, develop in a fixed sequence of stages in all children, as Figure 2.1 illustrates. The order of the stages and the age at which they develop is determined by nature and is relatively unaffected by nurture. Only under extreme environmental conditions—such as famine, war, or poverty—are children thrown off this biologically programmed timetable. This type of natural growth or change, which unfolds in a fixed sequence relatively independent of the environment, is called **maturation.**

The environment, not nature, was the key to development in the view of John Watson. As we mentioned in Chapter 1, Watson was the founder of behaviorism. In 1918 he began conducting experiments with children. In one experiment he first showed that nine-month-old Albert was not afraid of a white rat, a rabbit, and other white objects. Then Watson banged a steel bar near Albert's head every time a white rat appeared. After several bangs, Albert began to draw back at the sight of the rat, cry, and try to crawl away. He reacted similarly when Watson showed him other white objects. Watson had demonstrated that an infant could learn to fear a previously innocuous object and come to fear similar objects. Childhood learning experiences, Watson showed, can have lasting effects.

From his experiments Watson inferred that children learn everything, from skills to fears. "Give me a dozen healthy infants," he wrote,

well formed, and my own specified world to bring them up in and I'll guarantee to take any one at random and train him to become any type of specialist I might select—doctor, lawyer, artist, merchant chief, and, yes, even beggar-man and thief, regardless of his talents, penchants, tendencies, abilities, vocations, and race of his ancestors. (Watson, 1930, p. 104)

This view stimulated much debate and much research, which is examined in later chapters.

Figure 2.1
Motor Development: An Example of Maturation
The left end of each bar indicates the age at which 25 percent of the infants tested were able to perform the stated behavior; 50 percent of the babies were performing the behavior at the age indicated by the vertical line in the bars; and the right end indicates the age at which 90 percent could do so (Frankenberg & Dodds, 1967). Although different infants achieve milestones of motor development at slightly different ages, all infants—regardless of their ethnicity, social class, or temperament—achieve them in the same order. Thus, motor development during infancy is maturational.

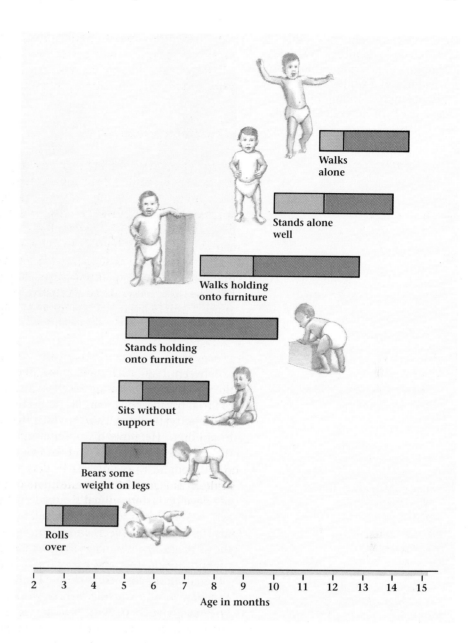

In Sigmund Freud's theory, development was not simply the result of benign growth toward maturity, as Gesell suggested, nor was it due solely to environmental experiences, as Watson claimed. Instead, said Freud, it was the product of both internal urges and external conditions, particularly children's sexual and aggressive urges and how parents handled them. His theory incorporated both nature and nurture.

Like Gesell's theory, Freud's theory was based on stages. According to Freud, as children grow older, their sexual urges become focused on different zones of the body: first the mouth, then the anal zone, then the genitals. In the school years, children experience a period of latency, during which explicit sexual urges are suspended. Finally, adolescents begin to express mature sexual urges through heterosexual contact. What happens during these stages of development, according to Freud, dramatically affects a person's later well-being. If too much of the child's sexual energy is *fixated* on an early stage, he or she will suffer psychological problems later. Freud's theory is discussed further in Chapter 14, on personality.

Here, in a classic photo, is John Watson and Little Albert. Watson is attempting to determine if Albert's learned fear of a white rat extends to other unfamiliar stimuli, in this case, a mask. (Courtesy of Dr. Benjamin Harris)

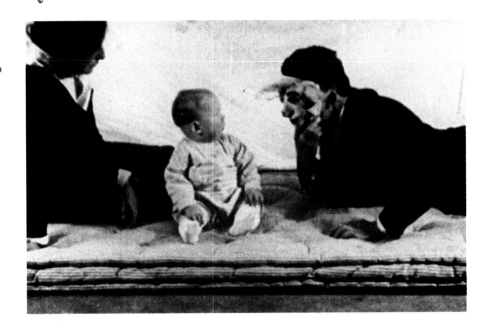

Between 1930 and 1960, most developmental psychologists adopted the theoretical approaches of Gesell, Watson, or Freud. In the 1970s, the influence of Swiss psychologist Jean Piaget dominated the field. Piaget used his remarkable observational skills to investigate the nuances of thinking and behavior in children. He wove his observations and inferences into a comprehensive theory of how thought and knowledge develop in stages from infancy to adulthood.

Piaget suggested that the influences of nature—what's inside the person's head—and nurture—what's outside in the world—are inseparable and interactive. As children actively manipulate and explore their surroundings, internal mental images of objects and actions guide them; experience, in turn, modifies these images. These images Piaget called schemas. **Schemas** are the basic units of knowledge, the building blocks of intellectual development. They are generalizations formed as people experience the world. Schemas organize past experiences and provide a framework for understanding future experiences. They may involve patterns of action, simple thoughts about objects, or complex ideas. At first, infants form simple schemas, such as a sucking schema, by which they consolidate their experiences of sucking into images of what objects can be sucked on—bottles, fingers, pacifiers. Later, children form more complex schemas like a schema for tying a knot or making a bed. Still later, adolescents form schemas about what it is to be in love. According to Piaget, different types of schemas appear in distinct stages that are marked by increasingly sophisticated modes of thought. We describe these stages later in this chapter.

Nature and Nurture

Today, developmental psychologists accept as given the notion that both internal and external conditions—both heredity and environment—contribute to development. The questions that interest them are *how much* and *how* each contributes to specific characteristics.

How much nature and nurture contribute varies from one characteristic to another. Heredity shapes some characteristics, such as physical size and appearance, so strongly that only extreme environmental conditions can affect them. Motor development is also, to a large extent, under genetic control. The sequence of motor development illustrated in Figure 2.1 appears in the same order in all infants, if at slightly different ages. Then during childhood, motor skills develop according to a maturational timetable that is helped along by experience. Six-year-olds are inevitably taller, stronger, and better coordinated than four-year-olds, and six-year-olds can more gracefully catch a ball, climb a ladder, and hold a pencil. Later, after children have acquired all the basic motor skills, the environment—lessons in soccer and piano, for example—plays an increasing role in children's motor abilities. Other characteristics, like intelligence and social skills, may be more easily affected from the very beginning by the environment than physical and motor development.

Although some human characteristics are more influenced by the environment and others more influenced by heredity, nature and nurture are inextricably intertwined. The environment encourages or discourages the expression of an individual's genetic potential; at the same time, inherited characteristics affect environments. For example, giving children plenty of stimulation increases the chances that they will develop their inherited intellectual potential, but children simultaneously affect their environments. Intelligent children are likely to seek out stimulating environments and evoke attention from adults.

If nature and nurture both contribute to human psychology, is there any reason to continue to probe the influence of each? Practical as well as intellectual goals make the effort worthwhile. If a community has very limited resources but wants to encourage its children's intellectual ability, how much effort should go into improving prenatal care and how much into helping preschool children? Developmental research can help people make such choices. Based on their research, developmental psychologists have encouraged the replacement of large, impersonal orphanages with small group and foster homes. They have supported programs for premature infants in newborn nurseries and children with learning disabilities. They have designed treatments for keeping elderly citizens physically and mentally fit. All these efforts were the result of research suggesting that in human development nurture can complement nature.

An environment full of new and interesting stimuli provides the ideal circumstances for the fullest development of a child's intellectual potential.

Beginnings

Nowhere are the complementary contributions of heredity and environment clearer than during the eventful nine months before birth. How does a single fertilized egg become a functioning newborn? For centuries, it was thought that a miniature human being was carried, preformed, in one parent or the other. This idea persisted until 1759, when a medical student named Kaspar Friedrich Wolff made two startling, but sound, suggestions. He said, first, that the infant is not preformed at conception but is assembled out of small structures, and second, that mother and father contribute equally to their offspring. Since Wolff's time, technical advances have permitted scientists to discover and record how conception and prenatal development occur.

Genetic Building Blocks

The process of development begins when a sperm from the father-to-be penetrates, or *fertilizes,* the ovum of the mother-to-be and forms a brand-new cell. This new cell carries a heritage from both mother and father through structures known as chromosomes.

The **chromosomes** are long, thin structures within each cell that are made up of more than a thousand genes. The **genes** are composed of **deoxyribonucleic acid (DNA)**—strands of sugar, phosphate, and nitrogen-containing molecules twisted around each other in a double spiral. The particular order in which the nitrogen-containing molecules are arranged in the DNA determines which protein each gene will produce. Proteins, in turn, direct a cell's activities. Thus, DNA within the chromosomes provides the individual's genetic code, a blueprint for constructing the human being, including eye color, height, blood type, inherited disorders, and the like.

How is the message in this code maintained through the years, as a person grows and ages, and from generation to generation? New cells are produced by the division of existing cells. In most human cells, there are twenty-three *pairs* of chromosomes that carry the genetic code. When these cells divide, the chromosomes duplicate themselves, so that each of the new cells also contains twenty-three pairs of chromosomes. However, the sperm and ova that join to produce a new human being are an exception. When sperm and ova are produced by cell division, the chromosome pairs are split and rearranged, leaving each sperm and ovum cell with just *one* member of each pair of chromosomes, or twenty-three *single* chromosomes. (Figure 2.2 shows how this process works.) Then, when sperm and ovum unite at conception to form a new cell, that cell has twenty-three pairs of chromosomes, half from the mother and half from the father.

These forty-six chromosomes contain the individual's **genotype**, the set of genes inherited from both parents. How the individual actually looks and acts is his or her **phenotype**. *Dominant* genes in the genotype are those that are expressed in the phenotype whenever they are present; *recessive* genes are expressed outwardly only when they are paired with a similar gene from the other parent. Few human characteristics are controlled by just one gene, however. Most traits in which heredity plays a role, such as intelligence and emotionality, are affected by more than one gene; in other words, they are *polygenic*. The phenotype reflects the influence of both the genotype (nature) and the environment in which the person lives and grows (nurture).

Linkages: How can one inherit anything from one's parents? (a link to Biological Aspects of Behavior)

Figure 2.2
Cell Division and the Genetic Code

Cell division in the sperm and ova is called *meiosis*. Shown here is a simplified view of meiosis in a hypothetical cell with only two pairs of chromosomes. Before meiosis begins, the chromosomes in each cell line up in pairs. The pairs are made of *homologous* chromosomes, which means that the chromosome from the father and the one from the mother contain variants of genes for the same trait. Next, the chromosomes double, then separate and separate again. The process has two especially significant results. First, in humans it produces cells that have only twenty-three chromosomes each. Second, it reshuffles genes and chromosomes, resulting in the infinite variation in characteristics seen from one individual to the next.

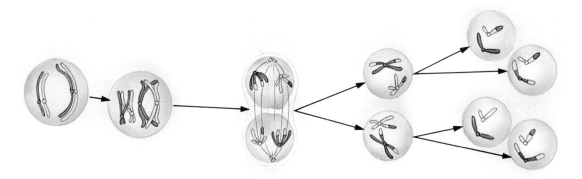

During the first stage of meiosis pairs of homologous chromosomes line up together and double. Homologous chromosomes exchange segments, thus creating new combinations of genes.

The paired chromosomes separate randomly, moving to opposite ends of the cell.

The cell divides. The resulting cells then go through several stages and divide again.

The result is four daughter cells, each of which has only half as many chromosomes as the original cell.

Prenatal Development

The union of sperm and ovum takes place in the woman's Fallopian tube. The new cell, called a *zygote,* then begins the rapid process of cell division that some nine months later will result in a multimillion-celled infant.

Stages of Prenatal Development   The first two weeks after fertilization are called the *germinal stage.* During this time the zygote divides, forming a sphere of many cells. Within six days the cells have separated into sections that will become the **embryo** (the developing individual), the *placenta* (which transmits nutrients from the mother and carries away wastes from the infant), the *amnion* (or "bag of waters" surrounding the embryo), and the *yolk sac* (which will produce blood). This little ball of cells floats freely for a day or two; then on about the seventh day after fertilization, it starts to attach itself to the lining of the uterine wall.

When attachment is complete, by about the fourteenth day after fertilization, the *embryonic stage* begins. During this stage the basic plan for the body emerges, and all the organs are created. The placenta begins to "breathe," digest, and excrete for the embryo. By the end of the second month after fertilization, the inch-long embryo, weighing less than one-tenth of an ounce, has a heart, nervous system, stomach, esophagus, and ovaries or testes (see Figure 2.3). It looks decidedly human, with eyes, ears, and nose, jaw, mouth, and lips. The tiny arms have elbows, hands, and stubby fingers; the legs have knees, ankles, and toes.

The embryo becomes a **fetus** in the third prenatal stage, when the cartilage in the bones starts to harden. In the *fetal stage,* which extends until birth, the various organs grow and function more efficiently. By the end of the third month after conception, the fetus can kick its legs, curl its toes, twist its feet, make a fist, turn its head, frown, open its mouth, swallow, and take a few practice "breaths" of amniotic fluid. By the end of the fifth month, the fetus is a foot long and weighs a pound. In the sixth month, the eyelids, which have been sealed, open. The fetus now has a well-developed grasp and abundant taste buds and can breathe regularly for as long as twenty-four hours at a time. This ability gives the fetus some chance of surviving in an incubator if born prematurely.

By the end of the seventh month, the fetus weighs about two pounds. If born prematurely, it has a 50-50 chance of survival. Its organ systems, although immature, are all functional. In the eighth and ninth months, the fetus becomes sensitive to a variety of outside sounds and responds to light and touch. It can lift its head, and it may even be able to learn. In one study, for example, Anthony DeCasper demonstrated that infants whose mothers repeatedly read them a Dr. Seuss story before they were born preferred the sound of this story to the sound of other conversation after they were born (Spence & DeCasper, 1982).

Prenatal Risks   In the embryonic period the placenta is selective. It allows beneficial materials such as nutrients in and screens out many potentially harmful substances, including most bacteria. But this screening is imperfect. Gases, viruses, nicotine, alcohol, and other drugs can pass through to the embryo. Severe damage can occur if the baby's mother takes certain drugs or has certain illnesses during the embryonic period. A baby whose mother has rubella (German measles) during the third or fourth week after conception has a 50 percent chance of being blind, deaf, or mentally retarded or of having

Figure 2.3
Prenatal Development:
The First Weeks
These drawings show the ovum, zygote, and embryo only slightly smaller than their actual sizes during the first seven weeks after conception.

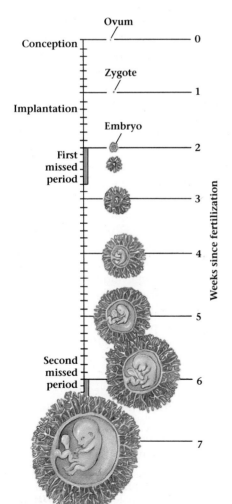

A fetus at twelve weeks. At this point of prenatal development, the fetus can kick its legs, make a fist, turn its head, squint, open its mouth, swallow, and take a few ''breaths'' of amniotic fluid.

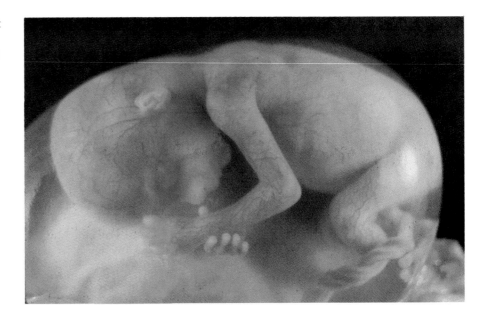

a heart malformation. If the mother has rubella later in the pregnancy, the likelihood that the baby will have one of these defects drops substantially.

Harmful external substances that invade the womb and result in birth defects are called **teratogens**. Teratogens are especially damaging in the embryonic stage because it is a **critical period** in prenatal development, an interval during which certain kinds of growth must occur if development is to proceed normally. Specific physical developments must take place during the embryonic stage, or they never will. If the heart, eyes, ears, hands, and feet do not appear in the embryonic period, they cannot form later on. And if they form incorrectly, the defects will be permanent.

During the fetal stage, the environment provided by the mother affects the baby's size, behavior, intelligence, and health, rather than the formation of organs and limbs. The mother's health and age, her nutrition before and during pregnancy, the emotional stresses she undergoes, and the drugs, nicotine, and alcohol she consumes all make a difference to the infant.

Of special concern today are the effects of alcohol and cocaine on prenatal development. Babies born to women who are alcoholics have a 44 percent chance of suffering from **fetal alcohol syndrome**, a pattern of defects that includes physical malformations of the face and mental retardation. Fetal alcohol syndrome is linked to heavy drinking, but even moderate drinking can harm infants' intellectual functioning (Streissguth et al., 1989). Mothers addicted to drugs like cocaine also put their infants at risk. They pass on their addiction to the fetus, and their babies are born premature, underweight, tense, and fussy, and have trouble sleeping (Jeremy & Hans, 1985). They are often brain damaged. A little drug for the mother is a lot for the fetus, who does not even have the enzymes necessary to break it down.

The likelihood that these potentially harmful factors in the environment will affect a particular infant depends on three things: the infant's inherited constitution, the stage of prenatal development during which the infant is exposed, and the intensity of the factor. A strong dose of a damaging factor during a critical period in a genetically susceptible infant is most likely to cause malformations or deficiencies.

Despite these vulnerabilities, mental or physical problems resulting from all harmful factors affect fewer than 5 percent of the babies born in the United

States. Mechanisms built into the human organism maintain normal development under all but the most adverse conditions. The vast majority of fetuses arrive at the end of their nine-month gestation averaging a healthy seven pounds and ready to continue a normal course of development in the world.

Birth

Today, the birth of an infant may take place at home, in a hospital delivery room or birthing room, or on an operating table. It may involve anesthesia, pain-killing drugs, Lamaze training, doctors, family, and friends. The options are many; there is no one right way to have a baby.

During the first hour or so after birth, babies are usually awake and gaze at the mother's face while the mother gazes at and touches the infant. Psychologists now believe that the mother's emotional *bond* to her infant begins at this point, develops slowly over the first three months, and is affected by the infant's increasing responsiveness.

Regardless of the procedure at birth, what happens during the first month is extremely important. Some infants have physical defects, such as heart malformations, that lead to death. Some fail at one of the four tasks that must be accomplished in the first few hours after birth: breathing, circulating blood and stabilizing blood pressure, controlling body temperature, and ingesting food and excreting waste. In the United States, one out of every hundred babies does not make it through the critical first month. In fact, more deaths occur during the first month after birth than at any other time except old age. This rate is better than that in underdeveloped countries, but it lags behind the rates of other technologically advanced nations like Japan, Sweden, and Canada—countries with more widely available health services.

Capacities of the Newborn

Even newborn infants actively use their senses to explore the world around them. At first they can attend to sights and sounds for only short periods, but gradually their attention lengthens and their exploration becomes more focused and systematic. Determining what they see and hear, however, is a tough challenge.

All newborns are extremely difficult to study. If they are held upright, their heads fall forward or backward; if they are lying down, they are likely to fall asleep. If the lights are too bright, they shut their eyes; if the lights are too dim, back to sleep they go. About 70 percent of the time, newborns are asleep. When they are not sleeping, they are drowsy, crying, awake and active, or awake and inactive. It is only when they are in this last state, which occurs infrequently in segments only a few minutes long, that infants observe their surroundings and seem most capable of learning. This is the time when researchers must assess infants' abilities.

To conduct these assessments, psychologists have shown infants objects or pictures and watched where they look and for how long. More sophisticated technology is used to film infants' eye movements as they scan objects or pictures. Psychologists also record changes in infants' heart rates, sucking rates, brain waves, movements, and skin conductance (a measure of perspiration associated with emotion) when objects are shown or sounds are made. From research using all these techniques, researchers have gleaned a fair picture of what infants can sense at birth and soon after.

Vision   At birth, the infant's vision is quite limited. A very rough estimate is that the newborn has 20:600 sight; that is, an object 20 feet away looks as clear as it would if it were viewed from 600 feet away by an adult with normal vision. This limitation in what infants can see is the result of immaturities in both the eye and the brain.

Although their vision is seriously limited, infants are by no means blind. The contrast between a mother's hair and face, for instance, is visible to the young infant. Although infants cannot see small objects on the other side of the room, they can see large objects close up—the distance at which most interaction with parents takes place. They particularly seem to enjoy looking at faces. This is not because faces have an innate attractiveness for infants but because faces contain highly visible elements, such as contour, contrast, complexity, and movement (Olson & Sherman, 1983). Infants, it seems, look longest at what they can see best: patterns with the largest visible elements, the most movement, and the greatest amount of contrast (Banks & Salapatek, 1983).

Newborns do more than take in visual sensations. They scan visual objects systematically, moving their eyes back and forth, looking for lines and corners (Banks & Salapatek, 1983). They get all the information they can out of an object before going on to something new (Hunter & Ames, 1988). They perceive that something is an object if they see connected surfaces that remain connected while the object moves (Spelke, 1982), and they perceive something as two objects if there are two parts that move separately (Spelke, van Hofsten & Kestenbaum, 1989). Can they tell if something is near or far, steep or shallow? We consider these questions in Chapter 5 after examining the principles that guide these perceptions.

Other Senses   What can the newborn hear? At birth, hearing is somewhat impaired by amniotic fluid left in the ear, but this fluid is soon gone. At two or three days of age, newborns can hear soft voices and can notice the difference between tones about one note apart on the musical scale (Aslin, Pisoni & Jusczyk, 1983). They can also locate sounds.

Interestingly, newborns are more sensitive to sounds that are in the range of speech than to other sounds. When they hear speech, babies open their eyes wider, look around for the sound, grimace, cry, or stop crying. Judging from where infants look or how fast they suck in order to hear recordings of different voices, researchers have concluded that infants also prefer certain *kinds* of speech. They like rising tones, spoken by women or children (Sullivan & Horowitz, 1983). They also like speech that is high-pitched, exaggerated, and expressive. In short, they like to hear the *baby talk* used by nearly all adults talking to babies (Fernald, 1981; Glenn & Cunningham, 1983).

Newborns also like certain smells and tastes better than others. They turn away from a noxious odor like ammonia and toward a sweet smell like flowers. Within a few days after birth, breast-fed babies prefer the odor of their own mother's milk to that of another mother's (Russell, 1976). Newborns can also taste the difference between water, sugar water, and milk, and they react differently depending on the concentration of sweet and bitter solutions (Ganchrow, Steiner & Daher, 1983). They suck longer and slower, pause for shorter periods, and smile and lick their upper lips when given a sweet solution.

Reflexes   In the first few weeks and months of life, babies' actions are dominated by involuntary, unlearned reactions called **reflexes**. These are swift, automatic movements in response to external stimuli; Figure 2.4 shows an example of the *grasping reflex*. More than twenty other reflexes have been observed in newborn infants. For example, the *rooting reflex* causes the infant

Figure 2.4
Reflexes in the Newborn
When a finger is pressed into the newborn's palm, the *palmar grasp reflex* causes the infant to hold on tightly enough to suspend its entire weight. The *Moro reflex* is a response to the sudden sensation of falling: the arms and legs are flung to the sides, hands open and fingers spread, then the arms are brought in toward the body in a hugging motion, hands now fisted, back arched, and legs fully extended. Other reflexes include the *stepping reflex,* also called the *automatic walking reflex,* and the *swimming reflex.*

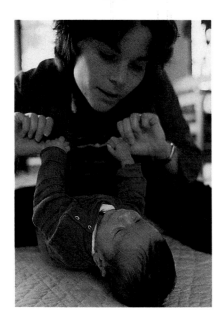

to turn its mouth toward a finger or nipple that touches its cheek. The *sucking reflex* makes the newborn suck on anything that touches its lips.

Most reflexes disappear within three or four months. If reflexes are absent in the newborn or fail to disappear within a few months, this may signal problems in brain development.

Infancy and Childhood: Cognitive Development

From conception through childhood, children's bodies and brains increase in size, complexity, and efficiency. These changes are related to advances in behavior and in *cognitive development*—the development of thinking, knowing, and remembering. Scientists have not proven whether the changes in the brain cause the advances in thinking or vice versa. But psychologists have documented, analyzed, and tried to explain the radical developments in cognition that occur from infancy through childhood, changes that take the child from an infant struggling to figure out how to reach the bottle that is just beyond her grasp to the competent creature who can read a book, write a poem, and compose an argument for going to computer camp.

One explanation of cognitive development, *learning theory*, grew out of Watson's behaviorism. Some learning theorists explain the development of children's thought in terms of the consequences of performing particular behaviors (Bijou & Baer, 1961). They suggest that if children are rewarded for speaking in long sentences, for learning the alphabet, or for saying that tulips are flowers, they will be more inclined to repeat those behaviors and will thus learn cognitive skills. This explanation of cognitive development has important weaknesses, however. For one thing, learning is not always tied to the obvious consequences of behavior. In addition, this theory does not make specific predictions of how learning would change with age. As discussed in other chapters, learning theory has value for understanding many aspects of behavior; but for understanding cognitive development, Piaget's work and the study of information processing have been more useful.

The Development of Knowledge: Piaget's Theory

The fascinating journey of cognitive development, from the simple reflexes of the newborn to the complex understanding of the adult, was charted most carefully by Piaget. As we mentioned earlier, Piaget proposed that this journey proceeds in a series of distinct stages (see Table 2.1). The thinking of infants, he said, is qualitatively different from the thinking of children, and the thinking of children is qualitatively different from that of adolescents—because they are at different stages of development. Younger children are not dumber than older ones, just different. With age and experience, all children's thinking goes through these stages—in the same order, without skipping, building upon previous stages and moving to a higher stage when new information won't fit the mental schemas of the old stage.

Two processes guide the development of schemas: organization and adaptation. *Organization* is the combination and integration of separate schemas into more complex patterns. The infant, for example, combines schemas of looking, reaching, holding, sucking, and swallowing to form a schema of drinking from the bottle. *Adaptation* is the modification of schemas that occurs with experience. It consists of two complementary processes: assimilation and accommodation.

Table 2.1
Piaget's Periods of Cognitive Development

According to Piaget, a predictable set of features characterizes each period of children's cognitive development.

Period	Activities and Achievements
Sensorimotor Birth–2 years	Infants discover aspects of the world through their sensory impressions, motor activities, and coordination of the two. They learn to differentiate themselves from the external world. They learn that objects exist even when they are not visible and that they are independent of the infant's own actions. They gain some appreciation of cause and effect.
Preoperational 2–7 years	Children cannot yet manipulate and transform information in logical ways, but they now can think in images and symbols. They become able to represent something with something else, acquire language, and play games of pretend. Intelligence at this stage is said to be intuitive, because children cannot make general, logical statements.
Concrete operational 7–11 years	Children can understand logical principles that apply to concrete external objects. They can appreciate that certain properties of an object remain the same, despite changes in appearance, and sort objects into categories. They can appreciate the perspective of another viewer. They can think about two concepts, such as longer and wider, at the same time.
Formal operational Over 11 years	Adolescents and adults can think logically about abstractions, can speculate, and can consider what might or what ought to be. They can work in probabilities and possibilities. They can imagine other worlds, especially ideal ones. They can reason about purely verbal or logical statements. They can relate any element or statement to any other, manipulate variables in a scientific experiment, and deal with proportions and analogies. They reflect on their own activity of thinking.

In **assimilation**, people take in information about new objects by trying out existing schemas and finding that the new objects fit those schemas. They *assimilate* new objects into their existing schemas. A baby boy is given a new toy. He examines it, sucks on it, waves it, and throws it—and discovers that this rattle, like others, is suckable, wavable, and throwable. Sometimes, like Cinderella's sisters squeezing their oversized feet into the glass slipper, people distort the information about the new object to make it fit their existing schemas. When squeezing won't work, people are forced to change, or *accommodate*, their schemas to the new objects.

In **accommodation,** the person tries out familiar schemas on new objects, finds that the schemas cannot be made to fit the objects, and changes the schemas. The baby is given a cup. He examines it, sucks on it, waves it, and throws it. He discovers that to suck on it, he can put only the edge in his mouth; to wave it, he must hold onto the handle; and throwing it will not work at all, because Mother removes the cup from his playpen. Similarly, the toddler refines her "doggie" schema when she meets a goat and discovers that her original schema does not extend to all four-legged creatures.

Sensorimotor Development   Piaget (1952) called the first stage of cognitive development the **sensorimotor period,** because the infant's mental activity is confined to sensory functions, like seeing and hearing, and motor skills, like grasping and sucking. At first, the infant's schemas are of simple sensory and motor functions such as these. As motor skills develop and voluntary actions come to replace reflexes, babies elaborate these simple schemas into complex ones of waving or shaking and later of inserting or building.

At first infants repeat these actions for the sheer pleasure of it. Only later do they begin to use their schemas to achieve a goal—to get a toy that is out of reach, to put two objects together. By the end of the sensorimotor period, they begin to experiment, repeating and modifying actions to see the effects. The toddler picks up a spoon full of grape jelly. She holds it flat, she tips it one way, she tips it the other way, she slowly turns it upside down. She stirs the jelly on the tray. She smears it on her hands, in her hair, and on everything else within reach.

According to Piaget, while infants are exploring and experimenting like this, they come to form *mental representations* of objects and actions. The sensorimotor period ends when they can form mental representations so that they can think about objects and actions even while the objects are not visible or the actions are not occurring. One sign that children have reached this milestone occurs when they find a hidden object. This behavior was of particular interest to Piaget. For him, it reflected infants' knowledge that they do not have to look at, touch, or suck an object to know that it exists; it exists even when out of sight. Piaget called this knowledge **object permanence.**

The first evidence that object permanence is developing, according to Piaget, appears when infants are four to eight months old. At this age, for the first time, they can recognize a familiar object even if part of it is hidden from view. This shows that infants have some primitive mental representation of objects. If an object is completely hidden, however, they will not search for it. Out of sight, said Piaget, is literally out of mind for infants at this stage.

Several months later, infants will search briefly for a hidden object, but their search is haphazard and ineffective. Even if the infant watches an object being moved from one hiding place to another, he or she may search for it in the first place it was hidden. Not until they are eighteen to twenty-four months old do infants apparently become able to picture and follow events in their minds. They look for the object in places other than where they saw it last, sometimes in completely new places. They have a mental representation of the object that is completely separate from their immediate perception of it. Their concept of objects as permanent, according to Piaget, is now fully developed.

Preoperational Development   For Piaget, the ability to form mental representations marks the end of the sensorimotor period and the beginning of the second major stage of cognitive development. In this **preoperational period,** children begin to understand, create, and use *symbols* to represent things that are not present; they can draw, pretend, and talk. (How children learn to talk is described in Chapter 9, on thought and language.)

The ability to symbolize opens up vast new domains for two- to four-year-olds. Two-year-olds might use a finger for a horse, or pretend to be Mommy or Daddy. They watch a television show and a day later playfully imitate what they saw. At the age of three or four, children symbolize intricate roles and events as they play school, house, doctor, and Star Wars.

In the second half of the preoperational stage, from ages four to seven, children's thinking is dominated not by logical thought but by intuition, by guesses. They know many things about people, toys, animals, vehicles, and food—but only what can be seen and touched. Their reasoning about things unseen is often wrong or even bizarre by adult standards. They assume, for instance, that dreams are real and take place outside of themselves as "pictures on the window," "a circus in the room," or "something from the sky." They believe that inanimate objects are alive and have intentions, feelings, and consciousness. The clouds go slowly because they have no paws or legs. Flowers grow because they want to. Empty cars feel lonely.

According to Piaget, children with preoperational thought are not only intuitive but also *egocentric.* They cannot understand that other people have different perspectives from their own. When their eyes are closed, they think that no one can see them. They assume that others see, hear, feel, and think exactly what they do. They believe that rivers are for *them* to swim in. The clouds do not just bring rain; they bring rain to *their* own garden.

As evidence that children's thinking at this stage is in many ways illogical (by adult standards, at least), Piaget noted that children are unable to figure out that the amount of something is the same even if you change its shape. The ability to recognize that important properties of a substance—such as number, volume, length, or weight—remain constant despite changes in shape or position Piaget called **conservation.** It was the focus of much of his research (see Figure 2.5).

In one test of conservation, Piaget showed children water from two equal-sized glasses being poured into a tall, thin glass and a short, wide one and asked them if one glass contained more. Children at this stage of development guessed that one glass (usually the taller one) contained more. They were dominated by the evidence of their eyes. If the glass looked bigger, then it contained more. Children at this stage did not understand the logic of *reversibility* (you just poured the water from one container to another, so you can pour it back and it will still be the same amount) or *complementarity* (one glass is taller but it also is narrower; the other is shorter but it also is fatter). They focused on only one dimension at a time—the most salient one—and made their best intuitive guess. Indeed, Piaget named this stage "preoperational" because children at this stage do not understand logical mental *operations* like reversibility and complementarity.

Concrete Operational Thought   Sometime around the age of six or seven, children do develop the ability to conserve number and amount. When they do so, they enter what Piaget called the stage of **concrete operations.** Now they can count, measure, add, and subtract; their thinking is no longer dominated by visual appearances. They can use simple logic and perform simple mental manipulations and operations. They can sort objects into classes (such as tools, fruit, and vehicles) or series (such as largest to smallest) by systematic searching and ordering. They realize that if A is larger than B and B is larger than C, then A is larger than C. In the preoperational period, if children are shown a picture of eight tulips and four daisies and are asked, "Are there more tulips or more flowers?" they will answer, "More tulips."

According to Piaget (in the beret in this photo), an infant's mental activities focus initially on the most basic sensory and motor skills, such as grasping or waving objects. He saw babies' mental representations of their own actions and of objects they encounter as forming the basis for increasingly complex modes of thought as they progress through childhood, then adolescence.

Type of conservation	First display	Second display	Child is asked
Length	 The child sees two sticks of equal length and agrees that they are of equal length.	 The experimenter moves one stick over.	Is one stick longer? Preconserving child will say that one of the sticks is longer. Conserving child will say that they are both the same length.
Liquid quantity	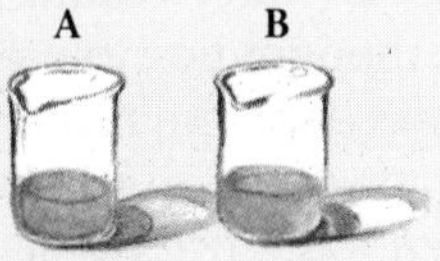 The child sees two beakers filled with water and says that they both contain the same amount of water.	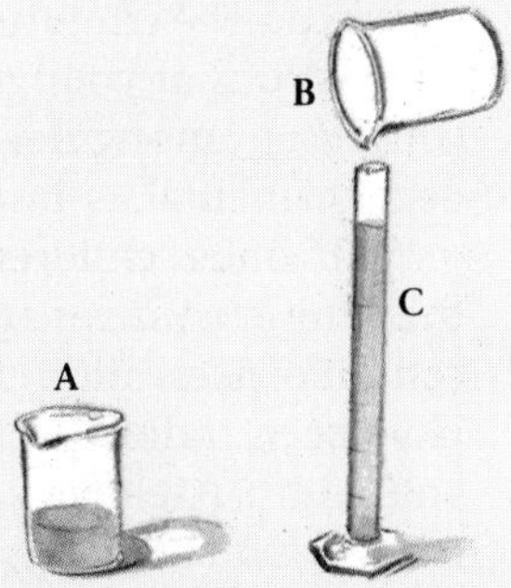 The experimenter pours water from B into a tall, thin beaker C, so that water level in C is higher than in A.	Does one beaker have more water? Preconserving child will say that C has more water: "See, it's higher." Conserving child will say that they have the same amount of water: "You only poured it!"
Substance amount	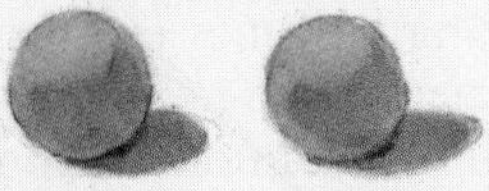 The child sees two identical clay balls and acknowledges that the two have equal amounts of clay.	 The experimenter rolls out one of the balls.	Do the two pieces have the same amount of clay? Preconserving child will say that the long piece has more clay. Conserving child will say that the two pieces have the same amount of clay.

Figure 2.5
Conservation
Here are some of the procedures that have been used to test children's ability to conserve length, liquid quantity, and substance amount. Conservation of area and conservation of volume may be tested in a similar way. The ability to conserve makes it possible for children to begin thinking logically about the world and to mentally manipulate numbers and other objects.

They are apparently unable to think beyond the fact that there are more tulips than daisies. In the concrete operational period, however, children have outgrown this difficulty in understanding classes and subclasses.

Still, concrete operational children can perform their logical operations only on real, concrete objects—tulips and glasses, not justice and freedom. The ability to think logically about abstract ideas comes in the next stage of cognitive development. This *formal operational period* occurs during adolescence, which we discuss later in this chapter.

Modifying Piaget's Theory

Piaget's observations and demonstrations of children's cognitive development are vivid and fascinating. Many psychologists have tested his findings and theory with experiments of their own. On the basis of these experiments, it appears that just as children accommodate their schemas to take account of new information, Piaget's theory needs some modification.

What needs to be modified most is Piaget's description of developmental stages. When Piaget's tests of infants' object permanence have been changed slightly, for example, infants' responses have changed, too. If toys are hidden under smaller, lighter covers than Piaget used, infants are more likely to remove the covers to find the hidden toys (Rader, Spiro & Firestone, 1979). If the experimenter simply turns the light out and does not use a cover to hide the object, infants as young as five months old have been observed to reach for the object in the dark (Bower & Wishart, 1972).

Why do these results differ from Piaget's? Finding a hidden object requires two things: (1) mentally representing the hidden object, and (2) figuring out where it might be (Harris, 1974). Piaget's tests did not allow for the possibility that an infant might know that an object exists but not have adequate strategies for finding it. Other researchers have found that even infants under one year old can recall some past experiences and events, such as peekaboo and bedtime routines, and they can find familiar household objects and toys at home (Ashmead & Perlmutter, 1980). Furthermore, children can imitate previously seen actions at younger ages than Piaget found (Meltzoff, 1988). The general consensus among developmental psychologists now seems to be that infants develop mental representations earlier than Piaget's demonstrations suggested.

With older children, too, researchers have found evidence of advanced thinking at younger ages than Piaget thought possible. Preoperational children can do conservation tasks if they can count the number of objects or if they have been trained to focus on relevant dimensions, such as number, height, and width (Gelman, 1969). Children can correctly answer questions about classes and subclasses if the questions are phrased to emphasize the general class rather than the subclass (Siegel et al., 1978)—if they are asked, for example, "Are there more tulips or more of all the flowers?" rather than "Are there more tulips or more flowers?"

Piaget was right in pointing out that there are significant shifts with age in children's thinking and that thinking becomes more systematic, consistent, and integrated. His descriptions of assimilation and accommodation as mechanisms by which development occurs remain one of the strong, if untestable, contributions of his theory. But today, developmental psychologists generally believe that cognitive abilities appear gradually and in particular areas and that children do not suddenly jump from one stage of global understanding to another. Their reasoning in any situation is based on how easy the task is, how familiar they are with the objects involved, how well they understand the language the adult uses, and what kind of experiences they have previously had in similar situations.

Information Processing

An alternative to Piaget's approach is to describe children's cognitive activities in terms of **information processing**, examining how information is taken in, remembered or forgotten, and used. Like Piaget, developmental psychologists taking this approach attempt to describe the processes that go on inside the child's head. But unlike Piaget, they focus on gradual quantitative changes in children's mental capacities, rather than on sudden qualitative advances or stages. This type of research has shown that children gradually get better at taking in and remembering information as they get older.

For one thing, children's attention spans lengthen with age. Very young infants pay attention to their surroundings for only short periods and then they doze off. Toddlers can pay attention for longer periods but are easily distracted. By school age, children can work, watch, or listen for long periods.

As their attention spans increase, children can also take in sensations and shift their attention more rapidly (Manis, Keating & Morrison, 1980). With age, children's exploration of the world also becomes more selective; they learn to focus on the relevant parts of incoming information and ignore the rest. This allows them to select round pegs to put into round holes, regardless of the color or length of the pegs. In short, for the first five or six years, children's ability to absorb information improves.

As cognitive development advances, children can explore and interact with their world in ever more complex ways.

There are also marked improvements in memory. Preschoolers can hold only two or three pieces of information in their immediate memories; children older than seven years can hold about seven pieces of information (Morrison, Holmes & Haith, 1974). These older children are also better at remembering more complex and abstract information, such as the gist of what several people have said during a conversation. Their memories are more accurate, extensive, and well organized. The knowledge they have accumulated allows them to draw more inferences and to integrate new information into a more complete network of facts, a more complete mental filing system.

During the school years, with the help of teachers, children also learn how and when to memorize. They learn strategies for remembering and studying. For example, they learn to rehearse or repeat information over and over to help fix it in memory. They learn to place information into categories or, as discussed in Chapter 8, to use mnemonics like "*i* before *e* except after *c*" to help them remember. They learn what situations call for deliberate memorization and what factors affect memory.

Variations in the Pace of Cognitive Development

You have seen that children get better at looking, listening, thinking, and remembering over the years from infancy to twelve. (To review the course of cognitive development through these years, see "In Review: Milestones of Cognitive Development in Infancy and Childhood.") Within this general trend, however, there are large individual differences; some children are mentally precocious, while others lag behind their peers. Why?

First of all, heredity plays an important role (Plomin, 1989). From the beginning, infants show differences in their mental abilities. Infants who spend less time gazing at a checkerboard, because they process the information it contains faster and then turn away ("I've seen this. What else is new?"), are advanced on later tests of cognitive development (Rose, Feldman & Wallace, 1988; Sigman, Cohen, Beckwith & Parmelee, 1986). They are also likely to have more intelligent parents (Plomin, 1989; Weinberg, 1989). As discussed in Chapter 10, on mental ability, genes do not *fix* the child's cognitive development, but they do set some general limits on it.

Within those limits, experience plays a role. Children in especially barren residential institutions—deprived of the everyday sights, sounds, and feelings provided by conversation and loving interaction, by pictures and books, even by television and radio—develop more slowly than children in normal family environments (Dennis, 1960, 1973). Such severe deprivation can impair intellectual development noticeably by the time children are two or three years old. If the deprivation continues, it may permanently harm the child. Even in their own homes, children's development may be impaired by deprivation and despair. In one study, children were observed and repeatedly tested from the time they were born until they were adolescents (Seifer & Sameroff, 1989). Cognitive development was below normal among those children who faced an abundance of negative experiences—for example, having a mother who was mentally ill, anxious, uneducated, unmarried, poor, and did not interact much with the child.

In average homes, too, children's cognitive development is related to their surroundings and experiences—but not to such an extreme degree. Probably the most that average parents can do for their children is to make the difference between the child's getting A's and getting C's. To achieve those A's, parents can expose the child, from the early years, to a variety of interesting materials and experiences—though not so many that the child is overwhelmed (Clarke-Stewart, 1988a; Wachs & Gruen, 1982). One set of crayons, some blocks, an

In Review: Milestones of Cognitive Development in Infancy and Childhood

Age*	Achievement	Description
3–4 months	Maturation of senses	Immaturities that limit the newborn's vision and hearing are overcome.
	Voluntary movement	Reflexes disappear and infants begin to gain voluntary control over their movements.
12–18 months	Mental representation	Infants can form images of objects and actions in their minds.
	Object permanence	Infants understand that objects exist even when out of sight.
18–24 months	Symbolic thought	Young children use symbols to represent things that are not present in their pretend play, drawing, and talk.
4 years	Intuitive thought	Children reason about events, real and imagined, by guessing rather than by logical analysis.
6–7 years	Conservation	Children recognize that important properties of a substance, such as number or amount, remain constant despite changes in shape or position.
	Concrete operations	Children can apply simple logical operations to real objects.
7–8 years	Information processing	Children can remember about seven pieces of information; they begin to learn strategies for memorization.

* These ages are approximate; they indicate the order in which children first reach these milestones of cognitive development rather than the exact ages.

electric train, a doll, a tea set, a puzzle or two, and some books will do more for the child's cognitive development than *all* the dolls *or* puzzles *or* trains at the toy store.

Parents can also be stimulating and supportive themselves. Children need to know that their actions have predictable consequences. They learn this from parents who smile at their smiles, respond to their cries, and pay attention to their gestures. They benefit from parents who read and talk to them, who encourage and help them to explore, and who actively teach them.

To improve the cognitive skills of children who lack these advantages, developmental psychologists have provided some children with extra lessons, stimulating materials, and educational contact with sensitive adults. In the

United States, the most substantial effort to provide this kind of help is Project Head Start, a preschool program for poor children.

Though experiences in the early years of childhood are important for cognitive development, they are not absolutely critical in the same way that the embryonic period of prenatal development is critical for organ formation. The effects of negative *or* positive early experience on cognitive development are, to a large extent, reversible, so that later gains—or losses—are possible (Clarke & Clarke, 1976a; Kagan, 1984). In Chapter 10, on mental abilities, we examine more closely how heredity, the environment, and efforts like Head Start affect cognitive development.

Infancy and Childhood: Social and Emotional Development

Life for the child is more than learning about physical objects. There is also a social world to be explored and experienced. From the first months of life, infants are attracted by the faces, voices, and actions of people. Most babies are also immensely attractive creatures themselves, with their tiny bodies, large eyes, chubby cheeks, rosebud mouths, and soft gurgles. These qualities exert a powerful pull on people around them, especially parents.

Early Social Interaction

Parents respond to their infants' expressions. When infants smile, mothers stay nearby and respond to the smile, usually with a return smile (Clarke-Stewart, 1973). When infants cry, mothers' hearts beat faster (Donovan, Leavitt & Balling, 1978; Wiesenfeld & Klorman, 1978), and they often try to soothe the crying. From an early age, infants communicate goals to their parents (Tronick, 1989). Infants signal the mother when they want to interact, by looking at her and smiling; they indicate that they do not want to interact by turning away and sucking their thumb. Infants are part of a mutual communication system in which their attempts to achieve a goal are aided by their parents.

Infants also respond to their parents' expressions of emotion. They gaze at their mother's beaming face (Malatesta & Izard, 1984) and look angry when the mother does (Lelwica & Haviland, 1983). They may even imitate the parent's expressions of surprise, fear, or sadness (Field et al., 1983). In one study (Cohn & Tronick, 1983) researchers tested the ability of three-month-olds to respond to emotional cues from their mothers. Some mothers acted normally, whereas others were asked to act depressed. Babies of the "depressed" mothers spent more time protesting, reacting warily, looking away, or giving only fleeting smiles. If mothers actually are depressed, their infants also turn away or protest (Cohn & Tronick, 1989). By this age, infants' emotional expressions are strongly related to mothers' reports of their own angry or sad feelings (Hamilton, 1989), and the infants can match happy, sad, and angry voices with pictures of the appropriate facial expressions (Walker-Andrews, 1988).

Although infants respond to their parents' emotions, these reactions do not mean that the infants recognize those emotions or understand their meaning. When researchers showed four-month-old infants various kinds of faces, as in Figure 2.6, the infants did smile at noticeable facial expressions—like toothy smiles of the sort that mothers usually give their infants—but they generally could not distinguish among subtle facial expressions of emotion (Oster, 1981).

Mutual eye contact, exaggerated facial expressions, and shared baby talk are an important part of the early social interactions that promote an enduring bond of attachment between parent and child.

Figure 2.6
Infants and Emotions

Do young infants react to the emotions expressed in faces or to facial features alone? The faces pictured here were part of an experiment on this question. Infants were shown pairs of photographs. One group of infants saw a sad face (right) paired with a face with an open-mouthed, toothy smile (left); another group saw a sad face and a face with a closed-mouthed smile; a third saw the sad face and a face with the toothy smile upside down. Infants looked longer at the upright toothy grin than at the sad face, but they did *not* look at the upside-down toothy grin or at the closed-mouth smile longer than at the sad face. Thus, it appears that, at four months of age, infants respond more to facial expressions (like toothy smiles) than to the emotions (such as happiness or sadness) those faces convey.

 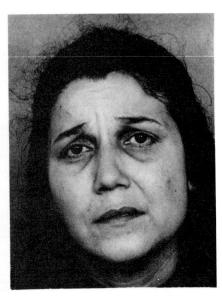

Source: Copyright Paul Ekman 1975. Ekman, P. & Friesen, M.V. *Unmasking the Face,* reprint edition. Palo Alto, CA: Consulting Psychologists Press, 1984.

Individual Temperament

From the moment they are born, infants differ from one another in the emotions that they express and the goals that they have. Some infants are active and vigorous; they splash, thrash, and wriggle. Others lie still most of the time. Some infants approach a new object with enthusiasm; others turn away or fuss. Some are acutely aware of every sight and sound; others are oblivious to loud noises or wet diapers. Some infants whimper; others kick, scream, and wail. These characteristics make up the infant's **temperament,** which is the basic, natural disposition of an individual.

In some of the most extensive research ever done on infant temperament, Alexander Thomas and Stella Chess (1977) found three main temperament patterns. *Easy babies,* the most common kind, get hungry and sleepy at predictable times, react to new situations cheerfully, and seldom fuss. *Difficult babies* are irregular and irritable. Those in the third group, *slow-to-warm-up babies,* react warily to new situations but eventually come to enjoy them.

Temperament is the beginning of an individual's personality, and traces of early temperamental characteristics weave their way throughout childhood (McNeil & Persson-Blennow, 1988). Easy infants usually stay easy, and difficult infants remain difficult (Guerin & Gottfried, 1986; Riese, 1986). Timid toddlers tend to become shy preschoolers and are restrained and inhibited as eight-year-olds (Kagan et al., 1988).

However, not every cautious infant ends up painfully shy, not every difficult baby becomes an elderly curmudgeon, nor does each easy baby develop into Miss Congeniality. In temperament, as in cognitive development, nature interacts with nurture. Many events take place between infancy and adulthood to shift the individual's development in one direction or another.

One possibly influential factor is the "goodness of fit," or match, between the infant's temperament and the parents' expectations, desires, and personal styles. When a mother believes she is responsible for her infant's behavior, an easy child might reassure her. If the mother is looking for signs of assertiveness, perhaps because she herself was victimized as a child and needs reassurance that her baby is "tough," a difficult child might prove welcome.

If parent and infant are in tune, chances increase that temperamental qualities will be stable.

Consider, for example, Chinese-American and Caucasian-American children. At birth, Chinese-American infants are calmer, less changeable, less perturbable, and more easily consoled when upset than Caucasian infants, suggesting that there may be an inherited predisposition toward self-control in the Chinese. This inherited tendency is then powerfully reinforced by the Chinese culture. Compared with Caucasian parents, Chinese parents are less likely to reward and stimulate babbling and smiling, and more likely to maintain close control of their young children (Kagan, Kearsley & Zelazo, 1978; Kriger & Kroes, 1972; Smith & Freedman, 1983). The children, in turn, are more dependent on their mothers and less likely to play by themselves; they are less vocal, noisy, and active than Caucasian children. These temperamental differences between children in different ethnic groups illustrate the combined contributions of nature and nurture.

The Infant Grows Attached

Over the first year of life, while the mother is responding to the infant and the infant is responding to the mother, the infant begins to form a deep and enduring tie to this caregiver and playmate. It is the infant's first love affair, with all the joy of togetherness and pain of separation that mark love affairs at any age.

The relationship develops in phases (Ainsworth, 1973). At first, the infant responds to anyone: all faces are beautiful, all arms can give comfort. This phase lasts only a few weeks or months and ends when the infant can discriminate among people and pick out parents from the crowd. In the second phase, infants respond differently to familiar and unfamiliar people, smiling or vocalizing to those whom they recognize, crying when those people leave, and finding comfort in their soothing. The third phase begins sometime around six or seven months, when the baby shows evidence of forming a true **attachment**—an affectionate, close, and enduring relationship—with the single person with whom the baby has shared many experiences. The baby seeks contact with this person—usually the mother—crawling after her, calling her, embracing her, clambering up into her lap, or protesting when she leaves. This phase continues through the second and third years.

Infants also develop attachments to their fathers, but often this occurs a little later than the attachment to the mother (Kotelchuck, 1976; Lamb, 1976). Not only is father-infant interaction less frequent than mother-infant interaction, but most studies show that it has a somewhat different nature. Mothers tend to feed, bathe, dress, cuddle, and talk to their infants, whereas fathers are more likely to play with, jiggle, and toss them, especially sons (Clarke-Stewart, 1978, 1980; Lamb, 1977). Fathers are usually just as sensitive and responsive to their infant's expressions while things are going well, but when the baby gets bored or distressed, fathers may not do as well as mothers (Frodi et al., 1978; Power & Parke, 1983). After the attachment to the father has formed, though, the father often becomes the toddler's preferred play partner (Clarke-Stewart, 1980; Lynn & Cross, 1974).

The amount of closeness and contact the infant seeks with mother or father depends to some extent on the infant. Those who are ill or tired or slow-to-warm-up may require more closeness. Closeness also depends on the parent. An infant whose mother has been absent, aloof, or unresponsive is likely to need more closeness with her than one whose mother has been accessible and responsive.

Most infants, with loving and sensitive mothers, form a **secure attachment** to her (Clarke-Stewart, 1988a). The urge to be close is balanced by an urge to explore the environment. The infant uses the mother as a home base, sallying forth to explore and play, but returning to her periodically for comfort and contact. Securely attached children can tolerate brief separations from their mother, but they are always happy to see her return and always receptive to her overtures of contact. These mother-child pairs have harmonious interactions from the earliest months (Isabella, Belsky & von Eye, 1989).

Some infants, however, form an **anxious insecure attachment.** They may avoid or ignore the mother when she approaches or when she returns after a brief separation. Or they are upset when their mother leaves, but when she returns, they act angry and reject her efforts at contact; when picked up, they squirm to get down. The mothers of these children are likely to be rejecting, abusive, or neglectful.

The security of a child's attachment to parents has far-reaching implications. Compared with children who are insecurely attached, children who are securely attached tend to be more socially and emotionally competent; more cooperative, enthusiastic, and persistent; better at solving problems; more compliant and controlled; and more popular and playful (Clarke-Stewart, 1988a). But attachment is just one of a number of factors—including stressful events and family characteristics—that affect the course of development. A secure attachment does not guarantee confidence and competence, and an insecure attachment does not ensure pathology.

T H I N K I N G   C R I T I C A L L Y

Does Day Care Harm the Emotional Development of Infants?

With the mothers of half the infants in the United States working outside the home, concern has been expressed about how daily separations from their mothers affect infants. Some have argued that putting infants in day care, with a babysitter or in a day-care center, damages the quality of the mother-infant relationship and increases the babies' risk for psychological problems later on (Belsky, 1988). The steps for critical thinking presented in Chapter 1 offer a strategy for evaluating this issue.

What am I being asked to believe or accept?
The claim to be evaluated here is that the daily separations created by day care damage the formation of an attachment between the mother and infant and harm the infant's emotional development.

What evidence is available to support the assertion?
There is clear evidence that separation from the mother is painful for young children. Furthermore, if separation lasts a week or more, young children who have formed an attachment to their mother protest, then become apathetic and mournful, and finally seem to lose interest in the missing mother (Robertson & Robertson, 1971). But day care does not involve such lasting separations, and research has shown that infants who are in day care *do* form attachments to their mothers. In fact, they prefer their mothers to their babysitters or daytime caregivers (Clarke-Stewart & Fein, 1983).

The question is, are these attachments as secure as the attachments formed by infants who are raised at home? Researchers have examined this question by comparing how infants react to brief separations from their mother in an unfamiliar room with an unfamiliar woman. Infants who are relatively unperturbed and ignore or avoid their mothers after the separations are rated as insecurely attached. Combining data from about twenty studies reveals that infants in full-time day care are somewhat more likely to be classified as insecurely attached. About 36 percent of them are classified as insecure in this assessment of attachment; only 29 percent of the infants who were not in full-time day care were counted as insecure (Clarke-Stewart, 1989a). These results appear to support the suggestion that day care harms infants' attachments to their mothers.

Are there alternative ways of interpreting the evidence?

Perhaps factors other than day care are at work, and the difference between infants in day care and at home with their mothers is only apparent, not real. What could these other factors be?

One factor is the method that was used to assess attachment. Recall that infants in these studies were judged insecure if they were relatively unperturbed by a brief separation from their mother in an unfamiliar room with an unfamiliar woman. It may be that infants who experienced routine separations from their mothers when they were left in day care felt more comfortable in this situation and therefore sought out less closeness with their mothers. Maybe they were expressing their independence, not their insecurity. A second factor is possible differences between the infants' mothers. Perhaps mothers who value independence in themselves and in their children are more likely to be working and to place their children in day care, whereas mothers who value closeness with their children are more likely to stay home. This *self-selection* could have led more children to be classified as insecure among the infants of working mothers.

What additional evidence would help to evaluate the alternatives?

Finding a heightened rate of insecure attachment among the infants of working mothers does not, by itself, demonstrate that day care is harmful. To judge the effects of day care, other measures of emotional adjustment are necessary. If infants in day care showed consistent signs of impaired emotional relations in other situations (for example, at home) and with other caregivers (for example, with the father), this evidence would support the argument that day care harms children's emotional development. Investigation of the behavior and attitudes of parents who use day care for their infants and those who do not would also be useful. If both groups of parents were comparable in every measurable way except for their use of day care, this too would support the argument.

What conclusions are most reasonable?

Psychologists cannot yet say whether day care, *per se*, is harmless or harmful. The most reasonable conclusions at present are that there is an increased likelihood that infants in day care will ignore or avoid their mothers after a brief separation, and that, until we have figured out why, we should study the development of infants in day care with great care. Some day-care situations may be more harmful than others, and some infants may be more vulnerable than others to negative effects. For example, it seems likely that infants would be harmed if they were in unstable or low-quality day care, if they spent more than eight hours a day in the day-care setting, if they were temperamentally difficult, and if their parents were insensitive.

Relationships with Parents

From the age of two on, the nature of children's relationships with their parents changes. From two to four years, children become more self-reliant and autonomous (Mahler, Pine & Bergman, 1975). They are no longer distressed by brief separations from parents, and they are willing to tolerate being farther

Linkages: Research in developmental psychology on the relationship between parents' socialization styles and behavior patterns appearing in their children has helped shape some of the parent-training programs described in Chapter 14 on personality. These programs are designed to help the parents of unruly children, for example, adopt more systematic and authoritative methods that can minimize the frequency of scenes like this.

away (Rheingold & Eckerman, 1971). They assert their independence by turning their backs, ignoring their parents' wishes (Clarke-Stewart & Hevey, 1981; Maccoby & Feldman, 1972).

Parents react to their children's new independence in various ways. In part, the variations arise because parents differ in the outcomes they want most for their children and in the methods they use to convey their values. These differences are reflected in **socialization,** which is the process by which parents and others in authority teach children the skills and rules needed to function in their society.

Socialization Styles   Differences in styles of socialization depend in part on the parents—their cultural backgrounds, personalities, financial and psychological circumstances, levels of education, and occupations. In American society, parents with high levels of education, high status, and professional occupations are likely to encourage self-direction in their children. They do so by letting children make their own decisions about, say, how their rooms look, and considering, if not always accepting, their children's ideas and wishes. They tend to request that clothes be picked up and to explain why rather than to set down arbitrary rules. In contrast, parents with lower levels of education and less-skilled occupations are more likely to value conformity to rules and authority. They are usually stricter and more likely to enforce rules about room cleaning or ''talking back'' with spankings or other punishments.

These differences in socialization style may be rooted in the different living and working conditions of the two groups (Kohn, 1977). Educated parents tend to assume that their children will also be educated, so they are more likely to try to prepare them to make decisions for themselves. Less-privileged adults, who usually must follow someone else's orders, tend to prepare their youngsters to do the same. External stress is important as well. Financial difficulties, lack of job security, and the like can make parents more neglectful or more likely to punish their children (Patterson, 1982).

In addition, socialization styles are shaped by children and the temperaments with which they are born. Mothers of very active children tend to get into power struggles with them and have difficulty controlling them (Buss, 1981). Mothers of difficult or aggressive children do more controlling, warning, prohibiting, and removing of objects than mothers of children with easy dispositions (Bates, 1980; Lytton, 1987). Difficult children persist in their troublesome actions longer and ignore, protest, or fuss at their mothers' attempts to control them.

Together, all these factors create complex socialization patterns. Although each family is unique, the patterns can be grouped into broad categories. Using a sample of parents in Berkeley, California, Diana Baumrind found three distinct patterns (Baumrind, 1971). **Authoritarian parents** were firm, punitive, and unsympathetic. They valued obedience from their children and authority for themselves. They tried to shape their children's behavior to meet a set standard and to curb the children's wills. They did not encourage independence. They were detached and seldom praised their youngsters. In contrast, **permissive parents** gave their children complete freedom, and their discipline was lax. The third group, **authoritative parents**, reasoned with their children, encouraging give and take. They allowed children increasing responsibility as they got older and better at making decisions. They were firm but understanding. They set limits but also encouraged independence. Their demands were reasonable, rational, and consistent.

Socialization Outcomes   Baumrind found that these three socialization styles were consistently related to children's behavior. Authoritarian parents

Linkages: How do children's re-lationships with their parents affect their personality? (a link to Personality)

had children who were unfriendly, distrustful, and withdrawn. The children of permissive parents were immature, dependent, and unhappy; they were likely to have tantrums or to ask for help when they encountered even slight difficulties. Children raised by authoritative parents were friendly, cooperative, self-reliant, and socially responsible.

Baumrind's study, along with others, suggests that socialization patterns affect children's social and emotional development. Strict, heavy-handed discipline is associated with children who are well-controlled but also fearful, dependent, and submissive. Extreme permissiveness appears to foster outgoing, sociable behavior and intellectual striving, but it may make children less persistent and more aggressive. The effects of discipline, however, depend on how affectionate the parents are. A restrictive and hostile parent may raise a withdrawn, anxious, quarrelsome child. A restrictive but affectionate parent is more likely to raise a child who is polite, obedient, and dependent.

Socialization styles may also help mold children's moral behavior. Children who are given orders, threats, and punishments are more likely than others to cheat and less likely to experience guilt or to accept blame after doing something wrong (Hoffman, 1970). Children are more likely to behave morally and generously when their parents are authoritative. These parents prohibit immoral actions but also explain why the child should act in particular ways. Still, you cannot predict whether children, or adults, will help or hurt someone just by knowing how they were raised. In Chapter 18 we look at other factors that help determine whether people will obey the law or break it, help someone or turn their backs.

HIGHLIGHT

Child Abuse: Socialization Gone Awry

Unfortunately, some parents cannot provide consistent and reasonable so-cialization. Many of these parents abuse their children—physically, sexually, or emotionally. Each year about 500,000 children in the United States are beaten, burned, thrown, kicked, and battered by their parents; more than 200,000 others are threatened, ridiculed, or terrorized.

Most abusive parents say that they love their children. Few have any specific psychiatric illness. Nevertheless, abusive parents generally have psy-chological problems (Kempe & Helfer, 1972; Kochanek, 1986). They are impatient, immature, and ignorant of child development. They have little self-esteem. They often consider severe physical punishment necessary for the children to behave "properly." They respond angrily to infants' crying and may be violent toward their spouse as well. Many of these parents are plagued with stress—unemployment, poverty, violence, chaos—yet lack the psychological or social resources for dealing effectively with that stress.

In *some* cases, qualities in the child trigger abuse (Kochanek, 1986). All children put stress on their parents, but overburdened or psychologically disturbed parents may abuse a troublesome child. Children who are under-weight, handicapped, or difficult at birth, who cry often, mature slowly, and need special care in infancy, and who are annoying and aggressive as toddlers are more likely to be victims of abuse. Abused children begin hitting their peers and caregivers in day care as early as one or two years of age (Main & George, 1985). As children, they are difficult to manage and have emotional and psychological problems like extreme dependency, low self-esteem, and depression. These characteristics of abused children are likely to be both effects of abuse and triggers for further abuse.

As adolescents, children who have been abused may turn to stealing, suicide, or homicide (Hart & Brassard, 1987). Temper tantrums, acting out in school, hitting other children—these significantly predict adolescent and adult offenses. In one study, nearly one-quarter of aggressive eight-year-old boys were convicted of crimes before they reached thirty (Eron et al., 1983).

Abuse is part of a vicious cycle that is perpetuated across generations. Unless there are compensating conditions, children who are abused grow up distrustful and chronically angry. They have seen their parents set an example of abusive behavior and have formed a mental image of "parenting" as bad, neglectful, abusive. As adults, they are psychologically distressed and remember their childhoods as filled with severe punishment and abuse (Hart & Brassard, 1987; Main & Goldwyn, 1984).

Psychological help aimed at raising low self-esteem and improving child-care skills can break the vicious cycle of abusive parents raising children who later abuse their own children. With therapy and training most parents can learn gentler and more responsible means of discipline, and they can break out of their self-imposed isolation from family and friends (Egeland, Jacobvitz & Sroufe, 1988). ■

Relationships with Other Children

The saga of social development over the years of childhood is the story of an enlarging social world, which broadens to include brothers and sisters, playmates and classmates. (For an overview of this period, see "In Review: Social and Emotional Development During Infancy and Childhood.") Social relationships with other children are different from relationships with parents. Relationships with other children are relations with equals, and they are based on common interests, feelings, and skills, not just on the child's need for security or proximity.

Though relationships with peers may not always be cordial, they are often among the closest and most positive in a child's life. In our culture, children's friendships are almost always with children of the same sex. The reasons, presumably, are that children of the same sex share the same play interests and that children are attracted to others who are like themselves and want to avoid those who are different. Friends are more interactive than nonfriends; they smile and laugh together more, pay closer atttention to equality in their conversations, and talk about mutual rather than their own idiosyncratic ends.

Toddlers use what they have learned playing with Mom and Dad, though, in their interactions with peers, playing games like peekaboo, give-and-take, and roll-the-ball (Mueller, 1989). For very young children, interactions with other children usually involve toys. For two-year-olds, it is the toy itself, not the other child, that is the focus of interest (Mueller & Lucas, 1975). Two-year-olds spend most of their play time simply watching their peers play with toys, taking toys away from their peers, or playing alongside them in *parallel play;* that is, using the same toys but not interacting (Mueller & Vandell, 1979).

For three-year-olds, toys are no longer ends in themselves; they help children elicit responses from their peers. This is the age when children also begin to use objects symbolically and to make believe. By age four, children begin to converse about their common activities and to borrow and lend toys. This play is still an egocentric, "me-first" affair, however. By the end of the preschool period, play reaches a new level of maturity. Children begin to cooperate, to divide roles, and to share goals (Parten, 1932, 1971).

In the school years, peer interaction becomes more complex and structured. School children play games with rules, such as marbles, jacks, and Simon Says. They play on teams. They tutor each other. They continue to cooperate in achieving goals, but they also begin to compete—sometimes at the expense of cooperation.

The school years are also the time when friends become important and friendships become long-lasting. A sibling may be a special kind of friend. By the time they are five, siblings spend twice as much time together as they spend with both parents combined (Bank & Kahn, 1975). During the school years children begin to understand that feelings, not things, keep friends together. By the end of this period most children have formed intimate friendships that can survive minor disputes because they are based on commitment, trust, and loyalty (Berndt, 1978a; Selman, 1981).

Friendships differ from other relationships because they are marked by more equality. Because of this equality as well as their intensity, friendships appear to be the best contexts for learning social skills like cooperation and intimacy. Children who have supportive friends become more popular with other kids as well (Berndt & Hawkins, 1987). Children who do not have friends usually have problems in later life (Parker & Asher, 1987).

Social Skills and Understanding

The changes in peer relationships over the years from two to twelve can be traced in part to children's increasing social competence. As children get older, they are less apt to stare, cry, point, suck their thumbs, or flee; they play, smile, and laugh more (Blurton-Jones, 1972; Mueller, 1972; Smith & Connolly, 1972). They become better able to follow the rules in games and to act in harmony in groups. They grow increasingly sensitive to the rights of minorities (Selman et al., 1983). They learn more elaborate and appropriate ways of helping and comforting each other (Zahn-Waxler, Iannotti & Chapman, 1982). They learn the rules that govern social interactions and society at large. For example, they learn to be polite. By six years of age, children begin to say "Can I swing?" or "Please may I swing?" instead of "Let me swing" (Bates, 1976; Garvey, 1975). They also learn to control their emotional expressions to conform to social norms (Ekman, 1980); they smile when greeting Grandmother and try not to cry when hurt or angry. Through the school years, children become aware of subtle distinctions between types of rules and become more flexible in complying with arbitrary ones.

Understanding Other People and Social Roles Children's increased social competence is due in part to their growing ability to detect and interpret emotional signals and social situations. At three or four, children can name typical facial expressions of happiness, sadness, anger, and fear (Camras, 1977). As they get older, they learn to recognize a wider range of emotions and to predict how a person will feel in emotion-provoking situations.

Over the school years, children's understanding of people deepens. For one thing, they learn that people do not always express what they feel (Gnepp, 1983; Selman, 1980). They also come to realize that individuals have abiding personal dispositions, or personalities. By the end of elementary school, they begin to describe people in terms of inferred, stable psychological attributes, such as "really conceited; he thinks he's great," or "real sensitive, a lot more than most people" (Barenboim, 1981; Rholes & Ruble, 1984). Children's understanding of people and their feelings parallels the development of their understanding of the nonsocial world (Marini & Case, 1989).

Part of understanding people is knowing about social roles. Toddlers pretend to perform imaginary acts such as bathing the baby or hosing the fire, but they are not aware that these acts are part of social roles. Later, they begin to understand that parents buy things, make phone calls, and clean house; that doctors wear white coats, ask to look at your tongue, and give injections. At age four, children understand how two or three roles fit together, and they can play family. By age six, children understand whole networks of roles, such as teachers, students, principal, and janitor, allowing them to play school (Watson, 1981).

Gender Roles Many of the roles children learn about are linked to gender. In Western civilization, some roles, like firefighter, have traditionally been masculine, whereas others, like nurse, have traditionally been feminine. These traditions are not nearly as strong as they once were, but there are still **gender roles** in our society. These are the general patterns of work, appearance, and behavior that are associated with being male or female. They persist because their roots are deep.

Even before children are able to learn gender roles, there are differences between the sexes (Feingold, 1988; Jacklin, 1989; Maccoby & Jacklin, 1974; Shepherd-Look, 1982). From conception there are physical differences between boys and girls. Girls are, on the average, physically more mature than boys and less susceptible to illness. Girls suffer less from speech, learning, and behavior disorders, mental retardation, emotional problems, and sleep disorders.

Through childhood many other differences between boys and girls become apparent. As a group, girls speak and write earlier and more fluently, are better at grammar and spelling. At the same time, girls are less skilled at manipulating objects, constructing three-dimensional forms, and mentally manipulating figures and pictures. They are worse at high school math (Hyde, Fennema & Lamon, 1990). Girls are also less physically aggressive, are less inclined to hit an obstacle or a person, and tend to be more nurturant and emotionally empathic. Boys play in larger groups and spaces, enjoying noisier, more strenuous physical games like soccer and football. All-boy play tends to be vigorous; all-girl play tends to be more orderly (DiPietro, 1981).

These differences between boys and girls may have a foundation in biology, but many of the differences stem from socialization. Parents, teachers, and other authorities (including influential figures on television) consciously or inadvertently pass on their ideas about "appropriate" behaviors for boys and girls. This teaching tends to bolster and amplify any biological predispositions that distinguish boys and girls. From an early age, most boys prefer and are

Linkages: How does a child's social perception differ from an adult's? (a link to Social Cognition)

Socialization by parents and others typically encourages interests and activities traditionally associated with a child's own gender.

In Review: Social and Emotional Development During Infancy and Childhood

Age	Relationships with Parents	Relationships with Other Children	Social Understanding
Birth–2 years	Infants form an attachment to the primary caregiver.	Play focuses on toys, not on other children.	Infants respond to emotional expressions of others.
2–4 years	Children become more autonomous and no longer need their parents' constant attention.	Toys are a way of eliciting responses from other children.	Young children can recognize emotions of others.
4–10 years	Parents actively socialize their children.	Children begin to cooperate, compete, play games, and form friendships with peers.	Children learn social rules, like politeness, and roles, like being a male or female; they learn to control their emotions.

given cars, trucks, balls, and guns. Girls are more likely to like and to be given dolls, irons, flowers, and pretty clothes. Boys are encouraged to achieve, compete, control their feelings, act independent, and assume personal responsibility. Girls are encouraged to be expressive, nurturant, reflective, dependent, obedient, and unselfish (Block, 1983; Hoffman, 1977; Shepherd-Look, 1982). Children also pick up notions of what is appropriate behavior simply by watching what peers and adults do. How they learn these behaviors is a topic we explore in Chapter 7, on learning.

The mixture of biological makeup and learning makes it impossible to say exactly how gender roles are acquired. Still, parents can, if they wish, avoid obvious gender typing. They can encourage girls to be independent and boys to be nurturant. Nevertheless, teachers, neighbors, casual acquaintances, even strangers typically react to children on the basis of their sex (Frisch, 1977), and gender stereotypes are still rampant in textbooks and on television.

Adolescence

The years of middle childhood usually pass smoothly, as children busy themselves with schoolwork, hobbies, friends, and clubs. Adolescence changes things drastically. All adolescents undergo significant changes in size, shape, and physical capacities. In Western societies many adolescents also experience substantial changes in their social life, reasoning abilities, and views of themselves.

The Big Shakeup

The first and most visible sign that adolescence has begun is a sudden spurt in physical growth. Beginning at about ten and a half for girls and at about twelve for boys, weight and height increase dramatically (see Figure 2.7). Suddenly, adolescents find themselves in new bodies. At the end of the growth spurt, menstruation begins in females and live sperm are produced in males.

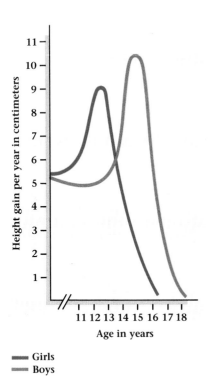

Source: Adapted from Tanner, Whitehouse &
Takaishi, 1966

Figure 2.7
Adolescent Growth
At about age ten and a half, girls
begin their growth spurt and are
temporarily taller than their male
peers. When boys, at about age
twelve, begin their growth spurt,
they usually grow faster and for a
longer period of time than girls. Adolescents may grow as much as five
inches a year.

Puberty—the condition of being able for the first time to reproduce—is also
characterized by changes such as fuller breasts and rounder curves in females,
broad shoulders and narrow hips in males.

There are psychological changes as well. Young adolescents begin to realize
that they are no longer children; yet they are far from adult. In Western
cultures, *early adolescence*—the years from twelve to sixteen or so—is fraught
with ups and downs. Moods often swing wildly from one extreme to the other:
from elation at a girlfriend's kiss to dejection at a failed exam (Csikszentmihalyi
& Larson, 1984). Sexual interest stirs, and there are opportunities to smoke,
drink alcohol, and take other drugs. All of this can be very disorienting. For
adolescents, this is their first big shakeup; it changes how they act, how they
feel, and how they think.

Early adolescence challenges self-esteem, especially if other stresses occur.
For example, self-esteem usually drops among girls who reach puberty, begin
dating, and shift from elementary to junior high school all at the same time
(Simmons, Rosenberg & Rosenberg, 1973). They suffer from combined uncer-
tainties about their bodies, boys, and books. Uncertainty about their physical
appearance is particularly devastating to adolescents. They desperately want
to be attractive, and their self-esteem depends in large measure on whether
they think they are. Some of them, especially girls who already have shaky
self-esteem, develop eating disorders, which we discuss in Chapter 11, on
motivation.

Still another factor affecting self-esteem is physical maturity. Boys who go
through puberty early are accepted by their peers and teachers as mature; they
have higher status, become leaders, and tend to be happy, poised, and relaxed.
Those who reach puberty late feel rejected, dependent, and dominated by
others (Duke et al., 1982; Peterson, 1987). For girls, maturing early is likely to
lead to embarrassment, to sexual activity, and to increased distance between
the girls and their parents (Brooks-Gunn, 1988; Peterson, 1987). These differences between early and late maturers may persist into adulthood (Jones,
1957).

Although adolescence was once considered to be a period of inevitable
storm and stress, recent research suggests that over half of today's teens find
early adolescence relatively trouble free; only about 15 percent of the adolescents studied experience serious turmoil (Peterson, 1987). For girls, the turmoil
typically results in depression; for boys, rebellion.

Parents and Peers

The changes and pressures of adolescence are often reflected in family conflicts.
Teenagers express the need to experience life on their own terms; they are no
longer content to accept all their parents' rules and values. This can lead to
bickering over everything from taking out the garbage to who left the gallon
of milk on top of the refrigerator. In one study, college students described the
typical relationship between parent and adolescent as most like that between
guard and prisoner (Wish, Deutsch & Kaplan, 1976). Serious conflicts often
lead to serious problems, including running away, pregnancy, stealing, even
suicide (Montemayor, 1983). Fortunately, conflicts are less severe than this in
most families and usually diminish by late adolescence, particularly if the
adolescent leaves home (Sullivan & Sullivan, 1980).

In early adolescence, though, conflict with families or a desire for the
company of people with common interests leads many teenagers to "hang
out" with other teenagers. Adolescents influence one another to look and act
alike in many ways, from musical tastes and dancing to smoking and skipping

Adolescence tends to be a time of emotional highs and lows as teenagers mature physically, discover the opposite sex, and worry about being accepted by their peer group.

school (Condry & Siman, 1974; Krosnick & Judd, 1982). By ninth grade, adolescents say that their relationships with their peers are closer than those with their parents (Bowerman & Kinch, 1956; Hunter & Youniss, 1982).

HIGHLIGHT

Sex and Babies

For as long as people have been keeping track, sexual activity among adolescents has been on the rise. Today, about half of America's youth has had sexual intercourse by age sixteen, compared with fewer than 10 percent fifty years ago (Brooks-Gunn & Furstenberg, 1989). Teens who have sex differ from those who do not in a number of ways. They hold less conventional attitudes and values, and they are more likely to smoke, drink, and use drugs. Their parents are less educated, exert less control over them, and are less likely to talk openly with them. A substantial number of sexually active girls were sexually abused as children (Musick, 1987). Perhaps most important, sexual activity is promoted by peers and older brothers and sisters (Rodgers & Rowe, 1988).

Too often, sexual activity leads to declining school achievement and interest, sexually transmitted diseases, and, of course, unplanned and unwanted pregnancies. Teenagers have the highest rates of sexually transmitted diseases (such as gonorrhea, chlamydia, and pelvic inflammatory disease) of any age group (Brooks-Gunn & Furstenberg, 1989). One-fifth of all AIDS (Acquired Immune Deficiency Syndrome) cases start in adolescence. Nearly one-quarter of all teenage girls in the United States get pregnant before they reach age eighteen (Furstenberg, Brooks-Gunn & Chase-Lansdale, 1989).

In fact, the United States has the highest rate of teenage pregnancy in the industrialized world. This is not because American adolescents are more sexually active than other teenagers but because they do not use effective contraception. Countries in which attitudes toward sex are more liberal, sex education more thorough, and contraceptives more readily available have lower rates of teenage pregnancy (Furstenberg et al., 1989).

About 40 percent of American adolescents who become pregnant have an abortion, 12 percent get married, and 4 percent give up their baby for adoption. The largest number of pregnant teens become single mothers. Adolescents who have their babies face serious risks. First, there are physical risks. The medical risks of pregnancy for teenagers are twice those for women who get pregnant in their twenties. Second, there are social and economic risks. When teenagers marry because the girl is pregnant, the marriage is likely to break up within six years (Alan Guttmacher Institute, 1981). When the girl raises the child alone, she ends up with less education, poorer economic opportunities, and, usually, more children than she wants or can afford to support (Furstenberg et al., 1989). She feels sadder and more tense than her peers who are not parents (Brown, Adams & Kellam, 1981). Teenage mothers are less positive and stimulating with their children than older mothers (Garcia Coll, Oh & Hoffman, 1987); they more often abuse them. The children of teenage mothers, in turn, are likely to develop behavior problems and to do poorly in school (Furstenberg et al., 1989). Clearly, sexual activity in adolescence can start a vicious chain reaction that echoes through the generations. ■

Identity

In many Third World cultures today and in the United States in earlier times, the end of early adolescence, around the age of sixteen, marked the beginning of adulthood: work, parenting, and grown-up responsibilities. In modern America, the transition from childhood to adulthood often lasts into the early twenties. Adolescents spend a substantial amount of time being students, trainees, and apprentices. This lengthened adolescence has created special problems—among them, finding or forming an identity. The journey through early adolescence behind them, adolescents' major psychological task is to answer the critical question: Who am I?

Most adolescents have not thought about this question before. As young children, their self-concepts were based on fleeting, sometimes inaccurate, perceptions. When preschool children are asked to describe themselves, they often mention a favorite or habitual activity: "I watch TV," "I walk to school," or "I do the dishes" (Keller, Ford & Meacham, 1978). At eight or nine, children identify themselves by giving facts such as their sex, age, name, physical appearance, likes, and dislikes. They may still describe themselves in terms of what they do, but they now include how well they do it compared with other children (Secord & Peevers, 1974). By age eleven, many children, especially girls, begin to describe themselves in terms of social relationships and personality characteristics. A sense of a unique self develops gradually over the years of middle childhood, then erupts during adolescence in the form of dramatically increased self-consciousness and self-awareness. Adolescents begin to think of themselves in terms of general, stable psychological characteristics (Damon & Hart, 1982).

Identity formation is a central task of adolescence according to Erik Erikson (1968). In his theory of development, there are eight stages of psychosocial development over the life span; they are outlined in Table 2.2. Each stage focuses on one issue or crisis that is especially important at that time of life. How the person resolves these issues shapes his or her personality and social

Table 2.2
Erikson's Stages of Psychosocial Development

In each of Erikson's stages of development, interest is focused on a different psychological issue. The issue is resolved by finding a balance between two extreme outcomes. We discuss the stages after adolescence later in this chapter.

Age	Central Psychological Issue or Crisis
First year	**Trust versus mistrust** Infants learn to trust or mistrust that their needs will be met by the world, especially by the mother.
Second year	**Autonomy versus shame and doubt** Children learn to exercise will, to make choices, and to control themselves, or they become uncertain and doubt that they can do things by themselves.
Third to fifth year	**Initiative versus guilt** Children learn to initiate activities and enjoy their accomplishments, acquiring direction and purpose. If they are not allowed initiative, they feel guilty for their attempts at independence.
Sixth year through puberty	**Industry versus inferiority** Children develop a sense of industry and curiosity and are eager to learn, or they feel inferior and lose interest in the tasks before them.
Adolescence	**Identity versus role confusion** Adolescents come to see themselves as unique and integrated persons with an ideology, or they become confused about what they want out of life.
Early adulthood	**Intimacy versus isolation** Young people become able to commit themselves to another person, or they develop a sense of isolation and feel they have no one in the world but themselves.
Middle age	**Generativity versus stagnation** Adults are willing to have and care for children and to devote themselves to their work and the common good, or they become self-centered and inactive.
Old age	**Integrity versus despair** Older people enter a period of reflection, becoming assured that their lives have been meaningful and ready to face death with acceptance and dignity. Or they are in despair for their unaccomplished goals, failures, and ill-spent lives.

relationships. If an issue is resolved positively, Erikson claimed, this will be reflected in positive characteristics, such as trust, autonomy, initiative, and industry. If the crisis is not resolved positively, the person will be psychologically troubled and cope less effectively with later crises.

According to Erikson, events of late adolescence—graduating from high school, going to college, and forging new relationships—challenge the adolescent's self-concept, precipitating an **identity crisis**. In this crisis, the adolescent must develop an integrated image of himself or herself as a unique person. This is done by pulling together self-knowledge acquired during childhood. If infancy and childhood brought trust, autonomy, and initiative, according to Erikson, the adolescent will resolve the identity crisis positively, feeling self-confident and competent. If infancy and childhood resulted in feelings of mistrust, shame, guilt, and inferiority, the adolescent will be confused about his or her identity and goals.

There is some limited empirical support for Erikson's ideas about the identity crisis. In this phase of adolescence, young people do consider alternative identities (Waterman, 1982). They "try out" being rebellious, studious, or detached, as they try to resolve questions about sexuality, self-worth, industriousness, and independence. By the time they are twenty-one, most adolescents have resolved the identity crisis in a way that is consistent with their self-image and the historical era in which they are living. They are ready to enter adulthood with self-confidence. Basically the same people who entered adolescence, they have more mature attitudes and behavior, more consistent goals and values, and a clearer idea of who they are (Adams & Jones, 1983; Dusek & Flaherty, 1981; Savin-Williams & Demo, 1984).

Abstract Thought and Moral Reasoning

One reason that adolescents can develop a conscious identity is that at this age it is possible for the first time to think and reason about abstract concepts. For many young people in this society, adolescence begins a stage of cognitive development that Piaget called the **formal operational period**, a stage marked by the ability to engage in hypothetical thinking, including the imagination of logical consequences. For example, adolescents who have reached the level of formal operations can consider various strategies for finding a part-time job and recognize that some methods are more likely to lead to success than others. They can form general concepts and understand the impact of the past on the present and the present on the future. They can question social institutions; think about the world as it might be and ought to be; and consider the ramifications of love, morality, work, politics, philosophy, and religion. They can think logically and systematically about symbols and propositions, regardless of whether the propositions are true. For example, they might evaluate the idea "Suppose there were no money in the world" logically to determine the possible consequences. They can reflect on and analyze their own mental processes, recognizing that, for example, they tend to be too optimistic or trusting. They can focus on form and symbolism in art and literature, going beyond the content of a painting or a book to see what the artist or author was trying to say about the world.

Kohlberg's Stages of Moral Reasoning   One domain in which adolescents can apply their advanced cognitive skills is morality. To examine how people think about morality, psychologists have presented subjects with hypothetical moral dilemmas. Perhaps the most famous of these is the "Heinz dilemma":

In Europe, a woman was near death from a special kind of cancer. There was one drug that the doctors thought might save her. It was a form of radium that a druggist in the same town had recently discovered. The drug was expensive to make, but the druggist was charging ten times what the drug cost him to make. He paid $200 for the radium and charged $2000 for a small dose of the drug. The sick woman's husband, Heinz, went to everyone he knew to borrow the money, but could only get together about $1000, which was half of what it cost. He told the druggist that his wife was dying and asked him to sell it cheaper or let him pay later. But the druggist said, "No, I discovered the drug and I'm going to make money from it." So Heinz got desperate and considered breaking into the man's store to steal the drug for his wife. Should Heinz steal the radium? (Kohlberg & Gilligan, 1971, pp. 1072–1073).

Using moral dilemmas like this one, Lawrence Kohlberg found that the reasons given for moral choices change systematically and consistently over time. He proposed that moral reasoning develops in six stages (see Table 2.3).

- Stage 1 and Stage 2 moral judgments are selfish. People at these stages are concerned with avoiding punishment or following rules when it is to their own advantage.
- In Stage 3 and Stage 4 people are concerned about other people; they think that morality consists of following rules and conventions such as duty to the family, to marriage vows, to the country.

Table 2.3
Kohlberg's Stages of Moral Development

Kohlberg's stages of moral reasoning reveal developmental differences in how people think about moral issues. More important than whether they say Heinz should or should not steal the drug is the reasoning behind their decision. Here are some examples of answers that might be given at different stages of development.

Stage	What Is Right?	Should Heinz Steal the Drug?
1	Obeying and avoiding punishment from a superior authority	Heinz should not steal the drug because he will be jailed.
2	Making a fair exchange, a good deal	Heinz should steal the drug because his wife will repay him later.
3	Pleasing others and getting their approval	Heinz should steal the drug because he loves his wife and because she and the rest of the family will approve.
4	Doing your duty, following rules and social order	Heinz should steal the drug for his wife because he has a duty to care for her, or he should not steal the drug because stealing is illegal.
5	Respecting rules and laws, but recognizing that they may have limits	Heinz should steal the drug because life is more important than property.
6	Following universal ethical principles, such as justice, reciprocity, equality, and respect for human life and rights	Heinz should steal the drug because of the principle of preserving and respecting life.

▪ Stages 5 and 6 represent the highest level of moral reasoning. Moral judgments at this level are based on personal standards or on universal principles of justice, equality, and respect for human life, not on the dictates of authority figures or society. People who have reached this level view rules and laws as arbitrary but respect them because they protect human welfare. They believe that individual rights can sometimes supersede these laws if the laws become destructive.

What makes people advance from one stage to another? Hearing moral reasoning that is one stage higher than their own or encountering a situation that requires more advanced reasoning seems to push people into reasoning at a higher level (Enright, Lapsley & Levy, 1983; Turiel, 1966; Walker, 1982).

Evaluating Kohlberg's Stages   To test this outline of moral development, Kohlberg and his associates studied the moral reasoning of males from ten to thirty years of age (Colby et al., 1983). The subjects proceeded through the stages in the order Kohlberg proposed. None of them skipped a stage; only rarely did any seem to move back a stage. But the subjects moved through the stages at different rates and reached different levels. Most adolescents reasoned at a Stage 3 level. Some of those tested never rose above Stage 2; only about 20 percent of the adults tested reached Stage 5; none reached Stage 6. Stage 6 is seen only rarely in extraordinary individuals, such as Mahatma Gandhi and Martin Luther King, Jr. Moral development is apparently an adaptation to the moral world in which one finds oneself. It is not a milestone like puberty or an achievement like graduation.

Other tests of Kohlberg's stages (e.g., Walker, 1989) generally support the sequence of stages he proposed. In forty-five studies in twenty-seven cultures from Alaska to Zambia, all researchers found that their subjects make upward progress, without reversals (Snarey, 1987). Up to the final level of reasoning, all stages were present in all of these cultures. Some moral judgments, however, did not fit into Kohlberg's stages. In Papua–New Guinea, Taiwan, and Israeli kibbutzim, people explained their answers to the moral dilemmas by pointing to the importance of the community. This kind of reasoning did not appear in the American males studied by Kohlberg, but it is similar to the reasoning sometimes expressed by American females.

Carol Gilligan (1982; Gilligan & Wiggins, 1987) has suggested that for girls and women the moral ideal is not the abstract, impersonal concept of justice that Kohlberg documented in his male subjects, but one of caring and relationships. For example, when one girl, Amy, was asked whether Heinz should steal the drug, she replied:

Well, I don't think so. . . . He really shouldn't steal the drug—but his wife shouldn't die either. If he stole the drug, he might save his wife then, but if he did, he might have to go to jail, and then his wife might get sicker again, and he couldn't get more of the drug. . . . So, they should really just talk it out and find some other way to make the money. (Gilligan, 1982, p. 28)

In Amy's eyes, the central issue in determining what is moral is not the rules that prevail in a world of people standing alone but the need to protect enduring relationships and fulfill human needs. Gilligan called into question Kohlberg's assumption that the highest level of morality is based on justice. When she asked people about moral conflicts, she found that although men generally focused on justice, only half of the women did so. The other half focused on caring. Taken together, the results of research in different countries and with women subjects as well as men suggest that moral ideals are not absolute and universal. To some extent, at the highest levels, moral reasoning is a product of culture and history.

An international gathering of students at the United Nations. According to Piaget, when children reach adolescence, they begin to show the abstract thought processes that will allow them to consider life's most complex issues, problems, and dilemmas.

Moral Reasoning and Moral Action   How is a person's level of moral reasoning related to the way he or she behaves? In one study, 120 junior high school students were given the opportunity to cheat on tests and games (Krebs & Kohlberg, 1973). Of the children whose reasoning was at Stage 1 or 2, 75 percent cheated at least once. Of those who reasoned at Stage 3 or 4, 65 percent cheated. Of those who had reached Stage 5, only 20 percent cheated.

These results suggest that there is indeed a relationship between moral reasoning and moral behavior. In another study, however, higher scores on moral dilemmas were tied to less cheating *only* if the subjects were asked about the dilemmas before they were tempted to cheat. If they were interviewed after the tests, higher moral reasoning seemed to be associated with more cheating (Krebs, 1967). It may be that interviewing people about their moral judgments before a test made them suspicious about the situation and so they acted at the highest level of moral reasoning of which they were capable. Otherwise, their decision to cheat or not was determined by things like how much they wanted to pass the test and how likely they thought they were to get caught.

Thus the relationship between moral reasoning and moral action is not a simple one. Children and adolescents can be encouraged to move to a higher level of reasoning by exposing them to arguments at a higher stage, perhaps as they argue issues out with each other. But the development of moral behavior involves more than cognitive knowledge. Children and adolescents need vivid emotional experiences in solving real moral problems (Haan, Aerts, & Cooper, 1985). They need to see consistent models of moral reasoning and behavior in the acts of their parents and peers. They need parents who promote their moral behavior with authoritative socialization, as we discussed earlier. Finally, as we discuss in Chapter 18, the situation itself may have a large effect on whether a person decides to act morally.

Adulthood

Development does not end with adolescence. Adults, too, go through transitions and experience physical and cognitive changes. (The changes associated with both eras are summarized in ''In Review: Milestones of Adolescence and

Adulthood," see p. 76.) For our purposes, adulthood can be divided into three periods: *early adulthood* (ages twenty to forty), *middle adulthood* (ages forty to sixty-five), and *late adulthood* (from age sixty-five on).

The Aging Body

In early adulthood, physical growth continues. Shoulder width, height, and chest size increase. People continue to develop their athletic abilities. By their mid-thirties nearly everyone shows some hearing impairment but, for most people, these years are the prime of life.

Middle adulthood starts the downhill slide of the aging body. The first place most people notice the change is in the mirror. They see sagging skin under the chin, crows' feet, dryness, and flabbiness. It helps to have stayed out of the sun or to have used sunscreens and moisturizers religiously. But this just slows the process; gravity works relentlessly on facial skin. Meanwhile, shoulder width, height, and chest size decrease. Muscle, too, decreases, and fat increases, especially around the midriff. The body of the average sixty-year-old woman is 42 percent fat, compared to about 26 percent fat when she was twenty (Henig, 1988).

With any luck, the impact of these images in the mirror is softened because the senses begin to lose acuity in middle adulthood (Fozard et al., 1977). People become less sensitive to light, less accurate at perceiving differences in distance, and slower and less acute at seeing details. Increased farsightedness is an inevitable change that begins around age forty. You know you're getting older when you find yourself reading in the position your parents once did, holding books farther and farther from your face.

Inside the body, bone mass is dwindling. The risk of heart disease increases, ultimately affecting one of every three men and one of every four women. In the reproductive system, fertility declines quickly during a woman's forties, as menstrual periods get shorter and more irregular. Eventually, menstruation stops altogether, and a woman has reached **menopause**. Despite the widespread belief that all women suffer through menopause with hot flashes and night sweats, bursts of temper and crying, only one-quarter of the women in one survey said that they were uncomfortable during menopause (Corby & Solnick, 1980). In men, the middle years see sexual responsiveness slowing and the number of sperm produced in the testes dropping to about half. The orgasms of both men and women become weaker, and the frequency of intercourse typically declines.

Despite these signs of an aging body, most people are well into late adulthood before their bodily functions are noticeably impaired. Most organs of the body have so great a reserve capacity that middle-aged adults feel the physical changes of aging only when they are under stress. Most people do not have major health problems until they pass the age of seventy-five.

In late adulthood people develop "age spots" and wrinkles. Men shrink about an inch, and women about two inches, as their posture changes and cartilage disks between the spinal vertebra become thinner. Hearts beat more slowly. Hardening of the arteries and a build-up of fat deposits on the artery walls may lead to heart disease. The digestive system slows down and becomes less efficient. Both digestive disorders and heart disease sometimes result from problems of diet—too little fluid, too little fiber—and inactivity.

In addition, the brain shrinks during late adulthood. Reflexes (such as the knee jerk reflex) grow weak or disappear. The blood flow to the brain slows.

The Experienced Mind

Despite the aging of the brain, cognition undergoes little change for the worse until late adulthood. Alert older people can think just as quickly as alert younger people. In fact, older people may function as well as or better than younger adults in everyday situations that tap their memories and learning skills. The experienced teacher may deal with an unruly child more skillfully than the novice, and the senior lawyer may understand the implications of a new law more quickly and thoroughly than the recent graduate. Their years of accumulating and organizing information can make older adults practiced, skillful, learned, and wise.

Linkages: How do mental abilities change over the life span? (a link to Mental Abilities)

Early and Middle Adulthood Cognitive changes in early and middle adulthood are generally improvements. During this period, adults improve performance on tests of vocabulary, comprehension, and general knowledge, especially if they use these abilities in their daily lives or engage in enriching activities such as travel or reading (Botwinick, 1977; Eichorn et al., 1981). Young and middle-aged adults learn new information and new skills; they remember old information and hone old skills.

Some psychologists suggest that the nature of thought may also change during adulthood. Adult thought is often more complex and adaptive than adolescent thought (Labouvie-Vief, 1982). For some adults, a stage of *problem-finding* occurs in adulthood, following the problem-solving level of Piaget's formal operational period (Arlin, 1980). In this stage, the rules of logic that are intellectual toys for adolescents come to be applied to the real world. Further, adults can understand, as adolescents cannot, the contradictions inherent in thinking. They see the possibilities and problems in every course of action (Riegel, 1975)—in deciding whether to start a new business or back a political candidate, whether to move to a new place, change jobs, and so on. Middle-aged adults are more expert than adolescents or young adults at making rational decisions and at relating logic and abstractions to actions, emotions, social issues, and personal relationships (Tversky & Kahneman, 1981). As they draw these relationships, their thought becomes more global, concerned with broad moral and practical concerns (Labouvie-Vief, 1982).

Late Adulthood It is not until late in adulthood—after sixty-five or so—that some intellectual abilities decline in some people. Psychologists who specialize in the study of cognitive abilities have analyzed why this decline occurs; we examine their findings in Chapter 10, on mental abilities. They have found that for some cognitive tasks, old age is usually not a hindrance. Which mental abilities tend to suffer during late adulthood?

In one long-term study, reasoning, mathematical ability, and verbal comprehension began to decline after age sixty-seven (Schaie, 1979; Schaie & Labouvie-Vief, 1974). This is also the time when the brain may begin to register new information at a slower speed (Kline & Szafran, 1975). Like young children, older adults are more likely to be distracted (Hoyer & Plude, 1980). If they are asked to do something they know how to do well—like naming familiar objects—older adults do just as well as younger ones (Poon & Fozard, 1978). But they are slower and less effective when asked to perform an unfamiliar task or to solve a complex problem they have not seen before (Craik & Rabinowitz, 1984).

Memory also declines with age. For some unfortunate people, this decline is dramatically hastened and intensified by organic brain disorders such as Alzheimer's disease; but in most cases, the loss of memory is slower and need not produce severe senility. Most older adults can repeat information they have just heard, but they may have difficulty if they must think about the information as well as remember it. For example, it is difficult for many older people to repeat a series of numbers backward or to do a mathematical calculation in their heads (Fozard, 1980).

When facing complex problems, older people apparently suffer from having too much information to sift through (Arenberg, 1982). They have trouble going over the possible choices and planning and executing their next choice. As people age, they grow less efficient at organizing the elements of a problem and at holding and manipulating more than one idea at a time (Hebb, 1978).

Although remembering verbal material and solving complex problems become more difficult in old age, the picture is not entirely bleak. Just as physical exercise can maintain a fit body, continued mental exercise can help people think and remember effectively and creatively. This fact is exemplified by historians and philosophers who reach a peak of creative production when they are in their sixties, by composers in their seventies who continue to write beautiful music, and by poets who produce their best work while in their eighties (Lehman, 1968). With mental abilities, as with muscles, the principle is "use it or lose it," or, as one psychologist has said, "He who lives by his wits, dies with his wits" (Krech, 1978). If they have kept in touch with their inspiring passions and kept them up to date, people continue to be creative thinkers. If they spend their old age achieving a new understanding of the self and the world, they grow in wisdom. Only when old age is fraught with unresolved conflicts does inspiration die and creativity wither.

Social and Psychological Changes

Changes in social relationships and positions also occur in adulthood. Do these changes occur in systematic stages? This notion was popularized in Gail Sheehy's 1977 best-seller *Passages*. Her book was based on research, such as that by Daniel Levinson, that suggested that men go through progressive, predictable, age-linked stages, each offering challenges that must be met before moving on to the next stage (see Figure 2.8). The timetable proposed for these stages was quite rigid, allowing no more than four years' leeway for each transition. Other researchers, however, found that development in adulthood does not fall neatly into stages; instead, people follow any of several developmental paths (Schlossberg, 1987). What seems to matter most is the individual's experiences—being dumped by a husband, fired from a job, going back to school, getting remarried.

Even the differences between early, middle, and late adulthood are blurring in today's society (Neugarten & Neugarten, 1987). Only a few decades ago middle age was thought to begin when children grew up and left the parents' home, and old age was seen as beginning after retirement. Now, children leave home (and often return) when their parents are anywhere from thirty-five to sixty-five, and people retire at ages from fifty-five to eighty-five. Consequently, developmental periods in adulthood cannot be defined in terms of such events. They also cannot be divided according to people's physical health or activities. Now, many retirees and their spouses are healthy and vigorous, financially well off, and integrated into the lives of their families and communities. The line between middle age and old age is no longer clear.

The Social Clock   The blurring of periods in adulthood is also seen in the rhythm and timing of more particular events. Traditionally, many milestones were expected to occur within particular age ranges, according to the beat of

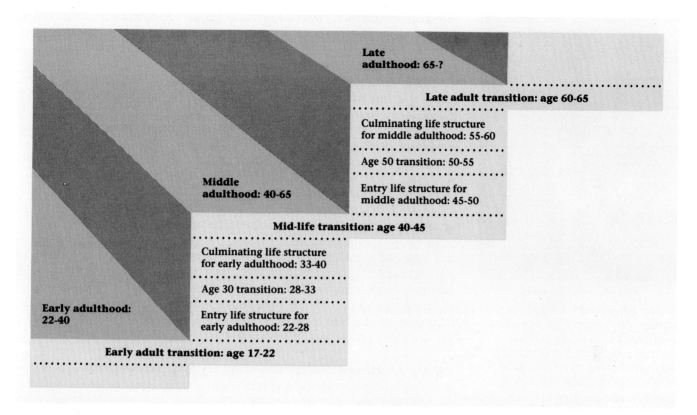

Source: Levinson et al., 1978

Figure 2.8
Levinson's Ladder of Adult Transitions
Adulthood for men is conceived of as stages of relative calm surrounded by more tumultuous transition periods. At each age a man faces specific tasks and challenges, such as choosing a career and a mate, which he must meet if he is to proceed successfully up the ladder.

a social clock (Neugarten, 1968). The markers on the social clock included completing school, leaving home, getting married, having a child, and becoming a grandparent. There were never absolute ages on the social clock; it ticked at different rates in different classes and cultures and for men and women. These events tended to occur earlier in traditional than in unconventional or "sophisticated" groups, for example (Olsen, 1969). But whatever age was considered normal, being "on time" in achieving these milestones was less stressful than being either early or late (Neugarten & Neugarten, 1987). Getting married early, for example, could create problems with peers if they were not also getting married.

Today, the ticking of the social clock is quieter than in the past (Neugarten & Neugarten, 1987). More men and women marry, divorce, remarry, and divorce again up through their seventies. More stay single. More women have their first child before they are fifteen, and more do so after thirty-five. More men and women exit and re-enter school, enter and re-enter the work force, and begin second and third careers through their seventies. All across adulthood, age has become a poor predictor of the timing of life events.

Nevertheless, the influence of traditional timetables has not disappeared. Today, as in the past, most people have expectations about major life events and turning points and when they should occur. If their lives are noticeably out of sync—as when a parent dies during one's adolescence rather than middle age, when marriage is long delayed, or when the birth of a child comes in the early teens—people (or those around them) often feel discomfort. Consequently, it still makes sense to discuss adults' social and psychological development in terms of broad age periods.

Early Adulthood   In their twenties, men and women enter the adult world. They decide on an occupation, or at least take a job, and often become

Middle adulthood tends to be a time during which people become deeply committed to building personal monuments through childrearing, occupational achievements, or as shown here, political office. Some people find it possible to do all these things and more.

preoccupied with their careers. They also become concerned with love. Having resolved their identity crisis, they develop a capacity for and concern with intimacy (Erikson, 1968; Vaillant, 1977), appreciating more fully the uniqueness and separateness of others. This intimacy may include sexual intimacy, friendship, or mutual intellectual stimulation. It may lead to marriage. All this comes at a time when, having separated from their parents and become more independent, young adults may be experiencing isolation and loneliness. They may view the future with a mixture of anticipation, fear, and insecurity (Levinson, 1978).

In their thirties, adults settle down and decide what is important in life (Levinson, 1978). According to Erikson, this is when people become concerned with producing something that will outlast them, usually through parenthood or job achievements (see Table 2.2). Erikson called this concern the **crisis of generativity.** If people do not resolve it, he suggested, they stagnate.

For many American adults, however, the greatest tension occurs between two types of generativity—parenthood versus achievement. Especially for women, the demands of children and career often pull in opposite directions. Devotion to a job may lead to guilt about depriving children of attention; too much emphasis on home life may impair productivity at work. This stressful balancing act can lead to anxiety, frustration, and conflicts at home and on the job, leaving some parents feeling and performing below par in both places.

Middle Adulthood   Sometime around age forty, between early and middle adulthood, people experience a **midlife transition.** They reappraise and may modify their lives and relationships. They may shift away from an earlier emphasis on a career or switch to a new career. Some feel invigorated and liberated; others may feel upset and have a midlife crisis (Levinson, 1978; Vaillant, 1977).

No one knows how many people experience a crisis during the midlife transition. The contrast between youth and middle age may be especially upsetting for men who matured early in adolescence and were sociable and athletic rather than intellectual (Block, 1971). Women who have chosen a career over a family now hear the biological clock ticking out their last childbearing years. Women who have had children, however, become more independent and confident, oriented toward achievement and events outside the family (Helson & Moane, 1987). For both men and women, the emerging sexuality of teenage children, the emptiness of the nest as children leave home, or the declining health or death of an elderly parent may precipitate a crisis. People in the midlife transition may feel caught between the generations, pressured by the expenses of college on one side and of nursing homes on the other.

After the midlife transition, the middle years of adulthood are often a time of satisfaction and happiness. Most people feel the pleasure of progress, embodied in grandchildren, career promotions, regained privacy, and the opportunity to pursue gratifying interests.

HIGHLIGHT

Love, Marriage, and Divorce

American society idealizes marriage as a relationship between two people who feel intense romantic love for each other. The reality, though, is that people tend to marry those who are similar to themselves in education, economic status, religion, race, and ethnic group (Murstein, 1980). They also tend to choose mates who are essentially their equals in physical attractiveness, intelligence, and sexual interest.

Neither age nor income seems to determine whether a couple will be satisfied with their marriage (Spanier & Lewis, 1980). What matters most to women is intimacy and emotional security; what matters most to men is loyalty and commitment to the future of the marriage (Reedy, Birren & Schaie, 1981). Although most young adults say that a marriage of equals is their ideal, few actually live such a marriage. Among a hundred couples participating in one study, 80 percent said that their marriages were cooperative, with power equally shared, but the researchers rated only 12 percent of the marriages as cooperative (Miller & Olson, 1978). About four marriages in ten now end in divorce.

Divorce may free people from a bad relationship, but it is also likely to make them feel anxious, guilty, incompetent, depressed, and lonely; it may lead to health problems (Brody, 1983; Cargan & Melko, 1982). Furthermore, 70 percent of divorces in the United States involve couples with children. When parents divorce, the effect on children may be even more dramatic than the effect on the adults. The likelihood that a person will get divorced is significantly increased if his or her parents are divorced (Levinger & Moles, 1979).

Divorce can be a traumatic experience for everyone involved. The good news is that the negative effects are not inevitable, and they do not have to be long-lasting. By two or three years after the divorce, in most families, routines are back to normal, physical symptoms have disappeared, the intense psychological stress is over, and adults and children have improved self-esteem and are functioning competently (Clarke-Stewart, 1989b).

Most people who divorce remarry within three years (Glick, 1980). In these marriages, partners are older, more mature, more experienced. Their marriages tend to be more egalitarian, to have better communication, and to engender more trust and good will (Furstenberg, 1982). Most seem to be about as satisfying, happy, and worrisome as first marriages (Furstenberg, 1982). They are just as likely to end in divorce. ■

Late Adulthood From fifty-five to seventy-five, most people think of themselves as middle-aged, not old (Neugarten, 1977). Most of the men and more than half of the women are married, and they see their children frequently. Many have a living parent. They are active and influential politically and socially; they often are physically vigorous.

Men and women who have been employed usually retire from their jobs in this period. Those with an adequate income, good health, and little investment in their work retire with joyful anticipation of good times at leisure. Those forced to retire with insufficient funds face it with dread. Still others retire in name only and go right on working. Which of these paths is followed makes all the difference in how people react to retirement. They adjust most easily to retirement if they view it as a choice (Neugarten, Havighurst & Tobin, 1968).

People make psychological as well as social changes during late adulthood. They generally become more inward looking, cautious, and conforming (Neugarten, 1977; Reedy, 1983). Many also become more *androgynous,* showing some of the characteristics of the other sex as well as of their own. Women become more assertive, men more nurturant, especially if they are grandparents (Fiske, 1980; Hyde & Phillis, 1979).

Death and Dying

With the onset of old age, people become aware that death is approaching. They watch as their friends disappear. They feel their health deteriorating, their strength waning, and their intellectual capabilities declining. A few years or a few months before death, people experience a sharp decline in mental functioning known as **terminal drop** (Berkowitz, 1965).

The awareness of impending death brings about the last psychological crisis, according to Erikson, in which people evaluate their lives and accomplishments and affirm them as meaningful or meaningless. They tend to become more philosophical and reflective. They attempt to put their lives into perspective. They reminisce, resolve past conflicts, and integrate past events. They may also become more interested in the religious and spiritual side of life (Butler, 1963). This "life review" may trigger anxiety, regret, guilt, and despair, or it may allow people to face their own death and the deaths of friends and relatives with a feeling of peace and acceptance (Butler, 1975; Erikson, 1968; Lieberman & Tobin, 1983).

The elderly can be helped to feel better physically and psychologically if they continue to be socially active and useful. For example, old people who are given parties, plants, or pets are happier and more alert and do not die as soon as those who receive less attention (Kastenbaum, 1965; Rodin & Langer, 1977). Withdrawing care, control, and social contact from people who are sick is likely to make them sicker.

Even the actual confrontation with death does not have to bring despair and depression. People generally want to be told if they are dying (Hinton,

In Review: Milestones of Adolescence and Adulthood

Age	Physical Changes	Cognitive Changes	Social Events and Psychological Changes
Early adolescence (11–15 years)	Puberty brings reproductive capacity and marked bodily changes.	Formal operations and principled moral reasoning become possible for the first time (this occurs only for some people).	A social and emotional shakeup results from growing sexual awareness, mood swings, physical changes, conflicts with parents.
Late adolescence (16–20 years)	Physical growth continues.	Formal operations and principled moral reasoning become more likely.	An identity crisis accompanies graduation from high school.
Early adulthood (20–39 years)	Physical growth continues; hearing impairment begins.	Increases continue in knowledge, problem-finding ability, and moral reasoning.	People choose a job and often a mate; they may become parents.
Middle adulthood (40–65 years)	Size and muscle mass decrease, fat increases, eyesight declines, reproductive capacity in women ends.	Thought becomes more complex, adaptive, and global.	Midlife transition may lead to change; for most, the middle years are satisfying.
Late adulthood (over 65 years)	Size decreases; organs become less efficient.	Reasoning, mathematical ability, comprehension, novel problem solving, and memory may decline.	Retirement requires adjustments; people look inward; awareness of death precipitates life review.

1967). When death finally is imminent, old people strive for a death with dignity, love, affection, physical contact, and no pain (Schulz, 1978). As they think about death, they are comforted by their religious faith, their achievements, and the love of their friends and family (Kastenbaum, Kastenbaum & Morris, 1989). Interestingly, very few take comfort from the thought that their children and grandchildren will survive and carry on their name and tradition.

Linkages: Human Development and Personality

How stable is personality during adulthood?

Marriage, childbirth, divorce, promotion, firing, illness, the death of loved ones—these events and others mark the lives of adults. We have described how people tend to change during their lives. But how are the people sitting in class with you going to be the *same* ten years from now? Will the young man who is sociable at parties also seek out people in his old age? Will the woman who was apprehensive before getting married at age forty feel nervous before she retires at seventy? Twenty years from now, are you likely to be much the same person you are today?

These questions interest both developmental and personality psychologists. One way to answer them is to examine a person's distinguishing characteristics, or *traits,* over the years. Personality psychologists have developed important tools for doing this, including personality tests such as the Personality Research Form (PRF) and The California Psychological Inventory (CPI). These tests consist of questions or statements like "I am often very tense on the job," to which the test taker answers *true, false,* or *cannot say.* Analysis of the answers allows the tester to compile an inventory of how one person compares with other people—whether, for example, compared with other people you tend to be hostile or trusting, confident or anxious, and so on.

To examine the stability of personality, developmental psychologists have tested individuals repeatedly over many years. The results indicate that some basic personality traits—shyness, sociability, aggressiveness—change very little

In some ways, each of us changes greatly during our lives, but in other ways, we stay essentially the same.

during adulthood (Costa & McCrae, 1988; McCrae & Costa, 1982). However, these data might reflect stable self-portraits, not stable traits. Perhaps people's *views* of their personalities stay the same even when their personalities change. To test this hypothesis, researchers asked spouses to rate the personality of subjects. If people really change and only their ideas about themselves stay stable, then their self-ratings and their spouse's ratings of them should become more and more dissimilar over time. This divergence, however, does not occur (McCrae & Costa, 1983).

Thus, there is good evidence that shyness, sociability, and aggressiveness remain quite stable during the adult years, just as they did across childhood and as they do from childhood into adulthood (Caspi, Elder & Bem, 1988; Dubow, Huesmann & Eron, 1987; West & Graziano, 1989). The woman who, at thirty, was more outgoing than other thirty-year-olds is likely to be more outgoing at seventy-five than others her age, although she may not be as sociable as she was at thirty. The boy who was painfully shy may delay, or even avoid, marriage and parenthood. The altruistic adolescent probably becomes a compassionate adult.

Other aspects of personality, however, seem to be less stable than these basic traits. A confident seventy-five-year-old woman may have been insecure twenty years ago. She may be anxious with teenagers but relaxed with everyone else. Whether you see a particular personality as stable may depend both on what aspects of personality you look at and whether you consider stability through the years or stability in different situations. Furthermore, different people show varying degrees of stability (Bem & Allen, 1974). This variation depends in part on events. An unexpected crisis—a spouse leaving, a child dying—may change an adult's outlook on life.

When personalities do change, it is often in response to such events (Moss & Susman, 1980). More often, however, personality is not permanently altered by major stressors, especially when people live in stable environments. Indeed, among the majority of people who remain healthy and socially involved, most aspects of personality do not change markedly from early to later adulthood (Thomae, 1980; West & Graziano, 1989). Why? One theory is that certain basic traits, such as aggressiveness or emotionality, appear to be inherited and less likely to be altered by life experiences. Other possible explanations come from psychodynamic, behavioral, and humanistic theories of personality, which suggest that recurring psychological defense mechanisms, well-entrenched behavior patterns, and consistent ways of perceiving even a changing world create relatively unchanging personalities (see Chapter 14).

In the details behind these generalizations lie some of the most interesting questions and findings about personality and its development. Why, for example, would a man who was apparently happy and involved with his work at thirty sink into a deep depression and consider life to be meaningless at age fifty? If you are generous and cheerful and confident with acquaintances but anxious and angry at home, is there a "real you"? If you want to become less anxious when you meet strangers, can you? In Chapters 14 through 16 we examine theories and research that provide a closer look at adult personality, at what it is and why and how it may change, for better or worse.

Future Directions

We have traced the journey of human development from conception to death. It is a complex and convoluted journey. Researchers over the past eighty years have charted this developmental journey and some of its variations. Psychologists now know what newborns can see and hear, when babies start to walk and talk, whether preschoolers can run and read, what changes puberty brings, and which mental faculties are the first to fail. They are getting better at predicting the direction that an individual will take on the developmental journey: whether he or she will do well in school, cheat on tests, feel insecure in a strange situation, or beat up the teacher. They are learning more and more about the processes of development, about how people learn new habits, incorporate new information, and form new relationships, and about how these processes depend on inherited traits and past experiences. They have replaced the notion of global developmental stages with a looser notion of developmental levels in particular areas of development.

Still, there is much to learn. Future research will probe beneath the surface of the developmental landscape with the help of better methods, more precise measures, more refined theories, and increased knowledge gained both from other areas of psychology and from other fields, such as genetics, physiology, neurology, and anthropology. Developmental psychologists will continue to probe the connections between brain and behavior, inheritance and intelligence, culture and child rearing. A few of the many questions they will investigate are the following: Do infants have mental images or mental models of their mothers that form the basis for their attachment to these caregivers? Do young children have a theory of how the mind works and, if so, how does it affect their own reasoning? What is the effect of infant day care on children's emotional adjustment? How accurate are children as eyewitnesses? Can they reliably testify about abuse they have experienced? Is joint custody after divorce the best arrangement for young children?

You will be able to follow the progress of research in this fascinating field by taking courses in infancy, child development, adolescence, life-span development, language acquisition, cognitive development, and social development.

Summary and Key Terms

The Study of Development

Developmental psychology is the study of systematic, sequential age-related changes in mental abilities, social relationships, emotions, and moral understanding over the life span.

Philosophical Roots

A central question in developmental psychology is the relative influences of nature and nurture, a theme that had its origins in the philosophies of John Locke and Jean-Jacques Rousseau. Another central question is whether skills and abilities develop gradually or in distinct stages.

Scientific Approaches

In the early part of the twentieth century, Arnold Gesell stressed nature in his theory of development, proposing that development is *maturation*—the natural unfolding of abilities with age. John Watson took the opposite view, claiming that development is learning—shaped by the external environment. Sigmund Freud began to bring nature and nurture together by suggesting that development depends on both internal forces (children's sexual and aggressive urges) and external conditions (how parents handle the children's urges). Jean Piaget fully integrated the influences of nature and nurture in his theory of cognitive development. According to Piaget, knowledge develops as chil-

dren actively explore the environment guided by internal mental images, or *schemas*.

Nature and Nurture

Today we accept as given the notion that both heredity and environment affect development and ask not whether but how much and how each contributes.

Beginnings

Genetic Building Blocks

The basic units through which nature contributes to development are *chromosomes*, cellular structures made up of *genes* constituted of *deoxyribonucleic acid (DNA)*. These provide the individual's genetic code, or *genotype*; how the person actually looks and acts is his or her *phenotype*. The phenotype reflects both the genotype (nature) and the environment (nurture).

Prenatal Development

Development begins with the union of an ovum and a sperm. In the first two weeks after fertilization, the new cell develops into an *embryo*. The embryo develops into a *fetus* in the embryonic stage of prenatal development. This is a *critical period* for development, a time when certain organs must develop properly, or they never will. Development of organs at this stage is markedly and irrevocably affected by harmful *teratogens* like drugs and alcohol. In the fetal stage of prenatal development, adverse conditions may harm the infant's size, behavior, intelligence, or health. Babies born to women who drink heavily have a strong chance of suffering from *fetal alcohol syndrome*.

Birth

In the hours immediately after birth, the infant must begin breathing air, circulating blood, controlling body temperature, ingesting food, and excreting waste—critical tasks for survival.

Capacities of the Newborn

Newborn infants have limited but effective senses of vision, hearing, and smell. Motor behavior in the first few months of life is dominated by *reflexes*: swift, automatic responses to external stimuli.

Infancy and Childhood: Cognitive Development

The Development of Knowledge: Piaget's Theory

According to Piaget, with experience, schemas are modified through the complementary processes of *assimilation* (fitting new objects or events into existing schemas) and *accommodation* (changing schemas when new objects will not fit the existing schemas). Cognitive development occurs in a fixed sequence of stages. During the first stage, the *sensorimotor period*, infants progress from simple senses and reflexes to complex mental representations of objects and actions. This allows the child to think about objects that are not immediately present. The ability to recognize that objects continue to exist even when they are hidden from view Piaget called *object permanence*. Once children have developed this knowledge, they move to the second stage of cognitive development, the *preoperational period*. During this period, children can use symbols, but they do not have the ability to think logically and rationally. Their understanding of the world is intuitive and often egocentric. When children develop the ability to think logically about concrete objects, they enter the period of *concrete operations*. They can solve simple problems and have a knowledge of *conservation*, recognizing that, for example, the amount of a substance does not change even when its shape changes.

Modifying Piaget's Theory

Recent research has led to a modification of Piaget's proposal that cognitive development progresses in sharply marked stages of global understanding. Developmental psychologists now believe that levels of understanding are reached more gradually, in specific areas rather than across the board, and that children's reasoning in any situation is affected by how easy the task is and how familiar the child is with the objects and language.

Information Processing

Psychologists who explain cognitive development in terms of *information processing* have documented age-related improvements in children's attention spans, their abilities to explore and focus on features of the environment, and their memories.

Variations in the Pace of Cognitive Development

How fast children develop cognitive abilities depends to a certain extent on how stimulating and supportive their environments are.

Infancy and Childhood: Social and Emotional Development

Early Social Interaction

Infants and their caregivers, from the early months, respond to each other's emotional expressions.

Individual Temperament

Most infants can be classified as having easy, difficult, or slow-to-warm-up *temperaments*. Whether they retain these traits may depend to some extent on the mesh of the traits with the parents' expectations and demands.

The Infant Grows Attached

Over the first six or seven months of life, infants form deep and abiding emotional *attachments* to their parents. These attachments may be *secure* or *insecure*, depending to a large extent on whether the parents are rejecting or responsive and loving.

Relationships with Parents

From age two on, children seek and are given more autonomy from their parents. Parents begin to teach their children the skills and rules needed in their society using styles of *socialization* that are *authoritarian, permissive*, or *authoritative*. Authoritative parents tend to have more competent and cooperative children.

Relationships with Other Children

Over the childhood years, interactions with siblings and peers increase in cooperation and competition. Children come to base their friendships on feelings, not things.

Social Skills and Understanding

The changes in children's social relationships grow in part from their increasing social competence. They learn to interpret and understand social situations and emotional signals. They learn social rules and roles, including those related to gender. *Gender roles* are based on both biological differences between the sexes and, to a larger extent, on implicit and explicit socialization by parents, teachers, peers, and the media.

Adolescence

The Big Shakeup

Puberty brings about physical changes that lead to psychological changes. Early adolescence is a period of wide mood swings and shaky self-esteem.

Parents and Peers

Adolescence is also a period of conflict with parents and closeness and conformity to friends.

Identity

Later adolescence focuses on finding an answer to the question: Who am I? Events like graduating from high school and going to college challenge the adolescent's self-concept, precipitating an *identity crisis*. To resolve this crisis the adolescent must develop an integrated image of himself or herself as a unique person.

Abstract Thought and Moral Reasoning

For many people, adolescence begins a stage of cognitive development that Piaget called the *formal operational period*.

Formal abstract reasoning now becomes more sophisticated, and principled moral judgment becomes possible for the first time. Such advanced understanding may be reflected in moral action—if there are no other more compelling circumstances.

Adulthood

The Aging Body

Middle adulthood starts a downhill slide that includes decreased acuity of the senses, increased risk of heart disease, and the end of fertility in women, signaled by *menopause*. Nevertheless, most people do not have major health problems until they pass the age of seventy-five.

The Experienced Mind

In early and middle adulthood, cognitive changes are generally positive, including advanced reasoning and problem-finding ability. In late adulthood, some intellectual abilities decline. This is particularly true for tasks that are unfamiliar, complex, or difficult, and for people who have not kept mentally active.

Social and Psychological Changes

Although the ticking of the *social clock* is quieter now than it was in past generations, there are still social and psychological changes associated with different periods of adulthood. In their twenties, young adults make occupational choices and form intimate commitments. In their thirties, they settle down, and decide what is important. They become concerned with producing something that will outlast them in a *crisis of generativity*. Sometime around age forty, adults experience a *midlife transition,* which may or may not be a crisis. The forties and fifties are often times of satisfaction. In their sixties, people contend with the issue of retirement. They generally become more inward looking, cautious, and conforming.

Death and Dying

In their seventies and eighties, people confront their own mortality. They may become more philosophical and reflective as they review their lives. A few years or months before death, they experience a sharp decline in mental functioning known as *terminal drop*. Still, they strive for a death with dignity, love, and no pain.

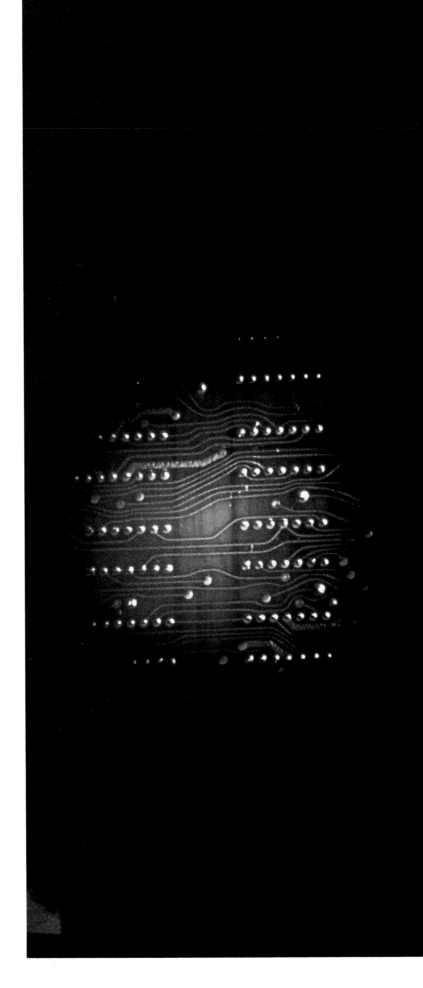

CHAPTER 3

Biological Aspects of Psychology

One evening in 1983 a man whom we will call Arthur had a mild stroke. A *stroke* is a disruption of blood flow to part of the brain; the result is tissue damage. If the damage is severe, a stroke can cause death. If the damage is less severe, part of the victim's brain does not work as it should. Many stroke victims are paralyzed or unable to remember things. Some experience more specific problems, such as an inability to recognize faces or use numbers. In Arthur's case the damage was very specific: he lost the ability to name fruits and vegetables. His other verbal abilities were perfectly normal. In fact, he could name an abacus or a sphinx; he could even look at the word *apple* and then pick an apple out of a group of objects and describe it. But when presented with an apple or an orange and asked to name it, Arthur was dumbfounded (Hart, Berndt & Caramazza, 1985). His condition must have been exasperating, but it was not debilitating; he returned to work at a federal agency (fortunately, not the Department of Agriculture).

The story of Arthur vividly illustrates the fact that normal behavior depends on normal brain functioning. Indeed, no behavior or mental activity could occur were it not for biological processes. **Biological psychology** focuses on these processes—on cells and organs and how they work. Thus, biological psychologists ask questions about the nature of the physical and chemical changes that occur when, for example, you learn, forget, see, think, worry, or fall asleep.

This attempt to understand the biological factors in behavior and mental processes is important to virtually every area of psychology, as the Linkages diagram suggests. In fact, a full understanding of psychology requires at least some familiarity with biological structures and mechanisms. In this chapter we provide an introduction to some of the most important of those structures and mechanisms.

But let's begin at the beginning. A human being can develop from a single cell into a functioning individual in part because various cells in the body specialize to become different tissues, such as skin, bones, and hair.

LINKAGES

Biological Aspects

of Psychology

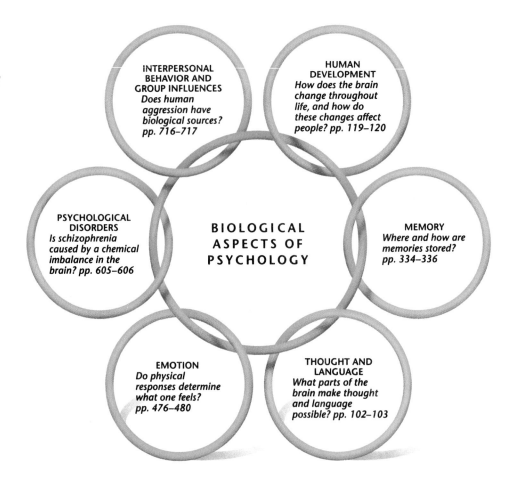

INTERPERSONAL
BEHAVIOR AND
GROUP INFLUENCES
*Does human
aggression have
biological sources?*
pp. 716–717

HUMAN
DEVELOPMENT
*How does the brain
change throughout
life, and how do
these changes affect
people? pp. 119–120*

PSYCHOLOGICAL
DISORDERS
*Is schizophrenia
caused by a chemical
imbalance in the
brain? pp. 605–606*

BIOLOGICAL
ASPECTS OF
PSYCHOLOGY

MEMORY
*Where and how are
memories stored?
pp. 334–336*

EMOTION
*Do physical
responses determine
what one feels?
pp. 476–480*

THOUGHT AND
LANGUAGE
*What parts of the
brain make thought
and language
possible? pp. 102–103*

■ Look at the diagram above, which illustrates some of the relationships between the topic of this chapter, biological aspects of psychology, and other chapter topics. All thoughts, feelings, and actions take place through the body, making biological structures and processes important to all aspects of psychology. Whether you are examining the bond between a mother and child or the distress of a person suffering from a psychological disorder, it is useful to ask what part might be played by biological phenomena. In this chapter we introduce some basic facts about biological structures and processes that underlie behavior and mental processes. In later chapters we build on this information to examine more specifically how biological factors influence psychological processes.

The chemistry of the brain is one important example. We do not attempt to cover biochemistry, but we do describe some important chemical substances and outline key ways in which they act on pathways in the brain to influence behavior and mental processes. Later we discuss how knowledge about these substances has helped researchers to propose explanations for many psychological phenomena—from how memory works to how psychological disorders arise. The page numbers in the diagram indicate where these and other questions are discussed in the text. ■

For psychology, the most interesting specializations are those that allow cells to communicate with one another. When cells communicate, a body becomes an integrated whole that detects what is in the world and responds to that world. The body contains several systems that are specialized for communication. Foremost among them is the nervous system.

The Nervous System: An Overview

The **nervous system** is a complex combination of cells that allows an organism to gain information about what is going on inside and outside the body and to respond appropriately. Thus, the nervous system has three basic functions: receiving information, or *input;* integrating that input with previous information to generate choices and decisions (*processing*); and guiding actions, or *output.* The parts of the nervous system that provide input about the environment are known as senses, or **sensory systems**. These include hearing, vision, taste, smell, and touch, each of which we describe in the next chapter. Output flows through **motor systems**, which are parts of the nervous system that influence muscles and other organs to respond to the environment.

Figure 3.1 illustrates the three basic functions. In this example, light reflected from an object stimulates cells in the eyes to send signals to the brain. The brain interprets this input, based on previous experience, as either an appealing snack or a dog biscuit and then sends signals to the arm and hand muscles to either grasp the object or wave it away with a smile. Either way, information has been taken in, processed, and acted on.

Figure 3.1
Functions of the Nervous System
The three main functions of the nervous system are to receive information, to integrate or process that information, and to guide actions. Here, the visual information received—a small object offered by a friend—is integrated with what the person knows about the appearance of hors d'oeuvres and dog biscuits and about the friend's liking for practical jokes. The result of this information processing will be a decision to refuse the object or to reach out for it while preparing the mouth and stomach to eat.

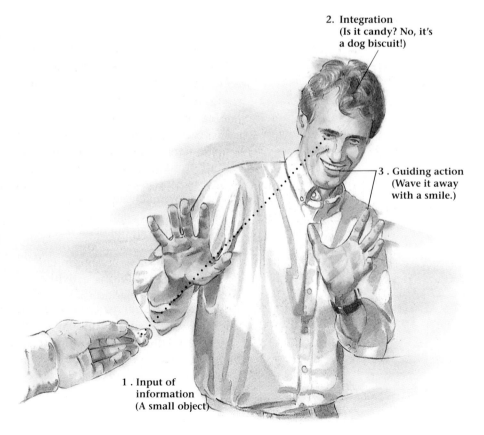

2. Integration
(Is it candy? No, it's
a dog biscuit!)

3. Guiding action
(Wave it away
with a smile.)

1. Input of
information
(A small object)

Figure 3.2
Organization of the Nervous System

The bone-encased central nervous system (CNS) is made up of the brain and spinal cord and acts as the body's central information processor, decision maker, and director of actions. The peripheral nervous system includes all nerves not housed in bone and functions mainly to carry messages. The somatic subsystem of the peripheral nervous system transmits sensory information to the CNS from the outside world and conveys instructions from the CNS to the muscles. The autonomic subsystem conveys messages from the CNS that alter the activity of organs and glands and sends information about that activity back to the brain.

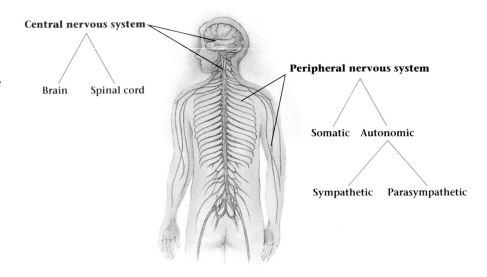

This sequence of input, processing, and output might remind you of the functions of a computer. Like the nervous system, computers have input and output functions and a central processor. As this and other chapters will show, however, the nervous system is much more complex and flexible in its functioning than any computer yet constructed. Furthermore, unlike today's computers, it has capacities for creativity, emotion, and judgment.

The nervous system has two major divisions, which work together: the central nervous system and the peripheral nervous system (see Figure 3.2). The **central nervous system (CNS)** is the part encased in bone. It includes the brain, which is inside the skull, and the spinal cord, which is inside the spinal column (backbone). The CNS is the "central executive" of the body; in other words, information is usually sent to the CNS to be processed and acted on.

The **peripheral nervous system** includes all of the nervous system that is not housed in bone. It has two main subsystems. The first is the **somatic nervous system**, which transmits information from the senses to the CNS and carries signals from the CNS to the muscles that move the skeleton. The somatic nervous system is involved, for example, in sending sensations of warmth from the skin to the brain when you lie in the sun at the beach. The second subsystem is the **autonomic nervous system (ANS)**; it carries messages back and forth between the CNS and the heart, lungs, and other organs and glands. These messages increase or decrease the activity of the organs and glands to meet varying demands placed on the body.

The name *autonomic* means "autonomous" and suggests independent operation. The name is appropriate because although the ANS is influenced by the brain, it controls activities that are normally outside of conscious control, such as digestion and perspiration. The ANS has two divisions to exercise this control: the *sympathetic* and *parasympathetic* branches. Generally, the sympathetic system mobilizes the body for action; the parasympathetic system regulates the body's functions to conserve energy. Thus, these two branches often create opposite effects. For example, the sympathetic nervous system can make the heart beat faster, whereas the parasympathetic nervous system can slow it down.

These functions may seem mundane, but they are vital for life. The autonomic nervous system controls processes that the somatic nervous system requires to perform its own functions. For example, when you want to move your muscles, you create a demand for energy; the autonomic nervous system fills the bill by increasing sugar in the bloodstream. If you decide to stand up, you need increased blood pressure so that your blood does not flow out of your brain and toward your feet. Again, the autonomic nervous system makes the adjustment. Disorders of the autonomic nervous system can produce people who sweat uncontrollably, faint whenever they stand up, or are unable to have sex. We examine the ANS in more detail in Chapter 12, on emotion. For now, we will consider how these and other components of the nervous system communicate with one another and with the rest of the body.

Communication in the Nervous System

The hallmark of the nervous system is its role in carrying messages from one part of the body to another. This function is possible because the fundamental units of the nervous system are special cells called **neurons**, which have the remarkable ability to communicate with one another.

Neurons: The Basic Units of the Nervous System

Neurons share many characteristics with every other kind of cell in the body. First, as Figure 3.3 illustrates, they have an *outer membrane* that, like a fine screen, lets some substances pass in and out while blocking others. Second, each neuron has a *cell body*, which contains a *nucleus*. The nucleus carries the genetic information that determines how a cell will function; it controls, for example, whether the cell will be a liver cell or a brain cell. Third, neurons contain *mitochondria*, which are structures that turn oxygen and glucose into energy. This process is especially vital to brain cells. Although the brain

Figure 3.3
The Neuron
Part (a) shows the cell body of a neuron, enlarged from one of the neurons shown in part (b). The cell body has typical cell elements, including an outer membrane and mitochondria. Some of the shapes characteristic of neurons are depicted in part (b). Notice the fibers extending outward from each cell body. These fibers, the axons and dendrites, are among the features that make neurons unique.

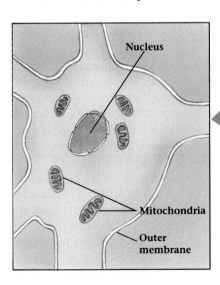

(a) Cell body of a neuron

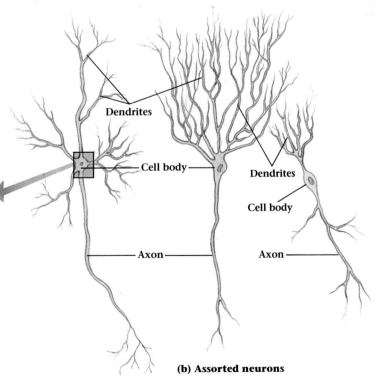

(b) Assorted neurons

accounts for only 2 percent of the body's weight, it consumes more than 20 percent of the body's oxygen (Sokoloff, 1981).

All of this energy is required to perform the special function of the nervous system: transmitting signals between cells. Three special features enable neurons to perform this feat. The first is their structure. Although neurons come in many shapes and sizes, all have long, thin fibers that extend outward from the cell body (see Figure 3.3). When these fibers get close to other neurons, communication between the cells can occur. Second, some of these fibers have an excitable surface membrane that allows a signal to be sent from one end of the neuron to the other. The third specialization involves **synapses**, which are minute gaps between neurons; signals are sent from one neuron to another across synapses.

The Structure of Neurons: Axons and Dendrites   The fibers extending from a neuron's cell body fall into two categories: axons and dendrites. **Axons** are the fibers that carry signals away from the cell body, out to where communication occurs with other neurons. Each neuron generally has only one axon leaving the cell body, but that one axon may have many branches. Axons can be very short or several feet long, like the axon that sends signals from the spinal cord all the way down to the big toe. **Dendrites** are the fibers that receive signals from the axons of other neurons and carry those signals to the cell body. A neuron can have dozens or hundreds of dendrites. Usually dendrites have many branches. (*Dendrite* means "of a tree" in Greek.) Remember that *a*xons carry signals *a*way from the cell body, whereas *d*endrites *d*etect those signals.

As a rule, the axon delivers its signals to the dendrites of a second cell; those dendrites in turn transmit the signal to their cell body, which may relay the signal down its axon and thus on to a third cell, and so on. These communication patterns permit the brain to conduct extremely complex information processing. A single neuron may influence anywhere from 1,000 to 100,000 other neurons (Guroff, 1980).

Like the cables connecting parts of a computer, however, axons and dendrites are not of much use unless there is a signal to be sent and received. Such signals can occur in the nervous system because of two other special features of neurons: the membrane of their axons and the synapses between them.

Membranes and Action Potentials   To understand the signals in the nervous system, you first need to know something about molecules and membranes. Many molecules carry a positive or a negative electrical charge. The cell membrane is *selectively permeable,* which means that it lets some molecules pass through yet excludes others. Normally, it keeps the distribution of positively and negatively charged molecules inside and outside the cell uneven. The result is that the inside of the cell is slightly negative compared with the outside, and the membrane is said to be *polarized.* Because molecules with a positive charge are attracted to those with a negative charge, a force called an *electrical potential* drives positively charged molecules toward the inside of the cell, but many are kept outside by the membrane.

For communication in the nervous system the most important "excluded" molecule is sodium (the same sodium found in table salt), which is symbolized Na^+ when it is positively charged. Sodium is highly concentrated on the outside of the cell and is strongly attracted to negatively charged molecules inside the cell. However, sodium can pass through the membrane only by going through special *channels,* or holes, in the membrane. These channels, which are distributed along the axon, act as *gates* that can be opened or closed.

Figure 3.4
The Beginning of an Action Potential

This is a very diagrammatic view of a polarized axon. Much of the negative charge inside the axon is produced by proteins, P⁻. Notice that most of the sodium gates in the cell membrane are closed in this polarized axon. If stimulation of the cell causes depolarization near a particular sodium gate, that gate may swing open, allowing sodium (Na⁺) to rush into the axon, stimulating the next gate to open, and so on down the axon. This spread of depolarization and the consequent progressive entry of sodium into the cell is called an action potential; when it occurs, the cell is said to have fired. The cell is repolarized when the Na⁺ gates are closed and gates are opened for potassium, K⁺, to flow out.

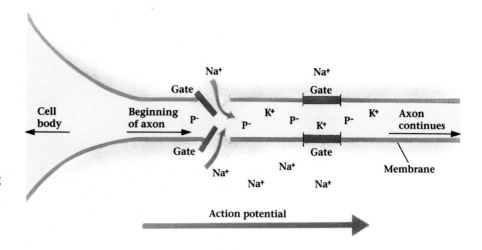

Normally these sodium channels are closed, but changes in the environment of the cell can *depolarize* the membrane, making the area inside the membrane less negative. If the membrane is depolarized to a point called the *threshold*, then the gate swings open (see Figure 3.4). As Na⁺ then rushes into the cell, the adjacent area of the axon becomes more depolarized, which causes the neighboring gate to open. This sequence continues, and the change in electrical potential spreads like a wild rumor all the way down the axon.

This abrupt change in the potential of an axon is called an **action potential**, and its contagious nature is referred to as its *self-propagating* property. When the neuron shoots an action potential down its axon, the neuron is said to have *fired*. This is an *all-or-none* type of communication: the cell either fires at full strength or does not fire at all.

The speed of the action potential as it moves down an axon is constant for a particular cell, but in different cells the speed ranges from 0.2 meters per second to 120 meters per second (about 260 miles per hour). The speed depends on the diameter of the axon—larger ones are faster—and on whether myelin is present. **Myelin** is a fatty substance that wraps around some axons and speeds action potentials. Larger, myelinated cells usually occur in the parts of the nervous system that carry the most urgently needed information. For example, the sensory neurons that receive information from the environment about onrushing trains, hot irons, and other dangers are fast-acting, myelinated cells.

Although each neuron fires or does not fire in an "all-or-none" fashion, its *rate* of firing varies. It can fire over and over because the sodium gates open only briefly and then close. Between firings there is a brief rest, called a **refractory period**. During this time, gates for positively charged potassium molecules (K⁺) open briefly; they flow out of the axon, and the membrane becomes polarized again. Then the neuron can fire again. Because the refractory period is quite short, a neuron can send action potentials down its axon at rates of up to one thousand per second. The *pattern* of repeated action potentials amounts to a coded message. (We describe some of the codes used by the nervous system in Chapter 4, on sensation.)

Synapses and Communication Between Cells How does the action potential in one neuron have an effect on the next neuron? For communication to occur *between* cells, the signal must be transferred across the synapse between neurons. Usually synapses occur between the axon of one neuron and a dendrite of another.

Figure 3.5
A Synapse
This photograph taken through an electron microscope shows part of a neural synapse magnified 50,000 times. Clearly visible are the mitochondria; the neurotransmitter-containing vesicles in the ending of the axon of the presynaptic cell; the synapse itself, which is the narrow gap between the cells; and the dendrite of the postsynaptic cell.

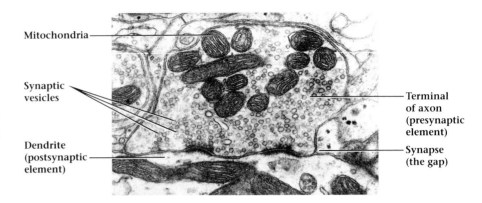

Mitochondria

Synaptic
vesicles

Dendrite
(postsynaptic
element)

Terminal
of axon
(presynaptic
element)

Synapse
(the gap)

Unlike the communication down the axon within a neuron, which uses electrical signals, communication at the synapse between neurons is chemical in nature. The transfer of information across a synapse is accomplished by chemicals called **neurotransmitters.** They are stored in many little bags, called *vesicles,* at the tips of axons (see Figure 3.5). When an action potential reaches a synapse, the axon of the *presynaptic* neuron releases a neurotransmitter.

The neurotransmitter then spreads across the synapse to reach the next, or *postsynaptic,* cell (see Figure 3.6). There the neurotransmitter triggers a change in the membrane potential, thus creating an electrical signal once again. This

Figure 3.6
Communication Between Neurons
When a neuron fires, a self-propagating action potential shoots to the end of its axon, triggering the release of a neurotransmitter into the synapse. This stimulates the neighboring cell. One type of stimulation is excitatory, causing depolarization of the postsynaptic cell, which will cause that neuron to fire an action potential if threshold is reached.

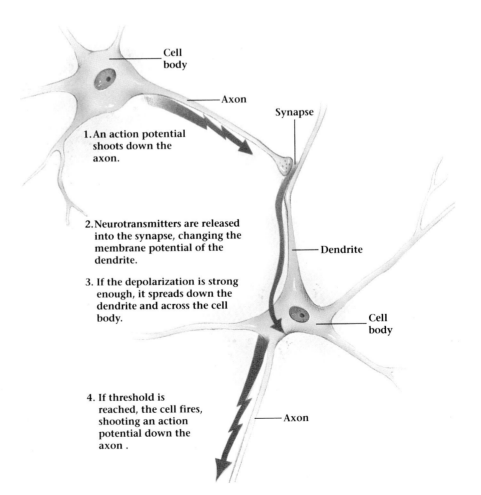

Cell
body

Axon

Synapse

1. An action potential
   shoots down the
   axon.

2. Neurotransmitters are released
   into the synapse, changing the
   membrane potential of the
   dendrite.

3. If the depolarization is strong
   enough, it spreads down the
   dendrite and across the cell
   body.

Dendrite

Cell
body

4. If threshold is
   reached, the cell fires,
   shooting an action
   potential down the
   axon.

Axon

change in the membrane potential of the dendrite of the postsynaptic cell is called the **postsynaptic potential.** It spreads toward the postsynaptic cell body.

Unlike the action potential in an axon, which remains at a constant strength, the postsynaptic potential fades as it goes along. Usually, it is not strong enough to pass all the way along the dendrite and through the cell body. However, other postsynaptic potentials may appear in the dendrite in a short time, and other postsynaptic potentials may be generated at nearby synapses on the same dendrite. These potentials may be added together, creating a signal strong enough to reach and pass through the cell body, where the signal can trigger a new action potential in the axon of the postsynaptic cell.

Even when a signal reaches the cell body, however, it may not tell the cell to fire. Unlike the action potential, the postsynaptic potential may make the postsynaptic membrane either more or less polarized. Thus, the postsynaptic potential may be either *excitatory,* making the postsynaptic cell more likely to fire, or *inhibitory,* making the cell less likely to fire. The signal sent and its result depend on several factors, including the type of neurotransmitter released, the postsynaptic sites it stimulates, and what other messages also reach the postsynaptic cell.

Interactions Between Neurons

Neurotransmitters can stimulate a postsynaptic neuron only at specialized sites in the membrane, called **receptors.** Receptors are usually located on the dendrites, sometimes on the cell body. The receptors "recognize" only one type of neurotransmitter. Like a puzzle piece fitting into its proper place, a neurotransmitter fits snugly into its own receptors but not into receptors for other neurotransmitters. Only when a neurotransmitter fits precisely into a receptor does it produce the postsynaptic potential that passes on a signal from one neuron to another (see Figure 3.7 and "In Review: Neurons").

Figure 3.7
Neurotransmitters and Receptors
Neurotransmitters influence postsynaptic cells by stimulating special receptors on the surface of their membranes. Each receptor receives only one type of neurotransmitter; the two fit together like puzzle pieces or like a key in a lock. Stimulation of these receptors by their neurotransmitters causes them, in turn, to either help or hinder the generation of a wave of depolarization in their cell's dendrites.

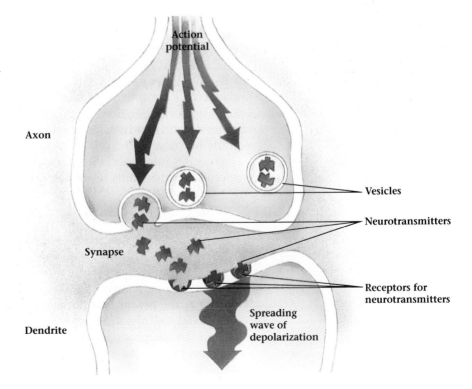

In Review: Neurons

Part	Function	Type of Signal Carried
Axon	Carries signals away from the cell body	The action potential, an all-or-none electrical signal, shoots down the axon to vesicles at the tip of the axon, releasing neurotransmitters.
Synapse	Provides an area for the transfer of signals between axon and dendrite	The neurotransmitters released by the axon cross the synapse to reach receptors on the dendrite.
Dendrite	Receives signals from axons and carries signals to the cell body	The interaction between neurotransmitters and receptors triggers an electrical signal, the postsynaptic potential. It may be excitatory or inhibitory, and it fades as it passes along the dendrite.

What that signal will be depends in part on what type of receptor the neurotransmitter contacts. Stimulation of *excitatory receptors* makes the cell more likely to fire; stimulation of *inhibitory receptors,* in contrast, makes the cell less likely to fire. Though a receptor recognizes only one type of neurotransmitter, a neurotransmitter can stimulate both inhibitory and excitatory receptors. As a result, the same neurotransmitter may produce both excitatory and inhibitory effects in different locations.

Normally, a neurotransmitter stays at the receptor site for only a brief time before it is removed in one of two ways. An *enzyme,* which is a substance that can change the structure of molecules, may break down the neurotransmitter. More commonly, the neurotransmitter is transported back into its presynaptic area, a process called *reuptake.*

Because a neuron may have synapses with thousands of other neurons, it may receive a conflicting pattern of excitatory ("fire") and inhibitory ("don't fire") signals (see Figure 3.8). Whether or not the neuron fires and how rapidly it fires depend on which kind of signal predominates from moment to moment at the junction of the cell body and the axon. Thus, each neuron integrates or processes information from many other neurons, and the behavior of each neuron depends on its relationship to other neurons.

The Central Nervous System: Organization and Functions

Impressive as individual neurons are, understanding their functions requires looking at the organization of groups of neurons. Neurons in the brain and spinal cord are organized into groups called *networks.* Many neurons in a network are reciprocally connected, sending axons to the dendrites of each other neuron in the network. Signals from one network also go to other networks, and small networks are organized into bigger collections. Within

Figure 3.8
Integration of Neural Signals
The signals that a neuron receives can arrive at its dendrites or at its cell body. These signals, which typically come from many cells, can be conflicting. Some are excitatory, stimulating the cell to fire; others are inhibitory signals that tell the cell not to fire. Whether the cell actually fires or not at any given moment depends on a number of factors, including whether excitatory or inhibitory messages predominate at the junction of the cell body and the axon.

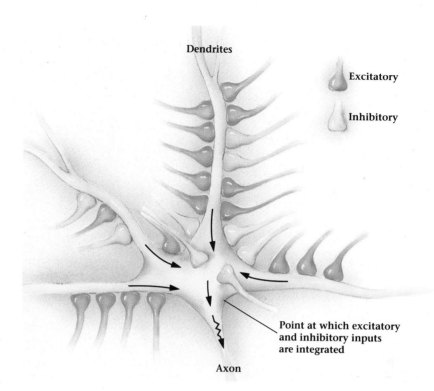

Dendrites

Excitatory

Inhibitory

Point at which excitatory and inhibitory inputs are integrated

Axon

all of these collections, the units integrate excitation and inhibition signals from each other. Using computer modeling, scientists have made progress in understanding how this organization of networks works. This new field, called *computational neuroscience* (Sejnowski, Koch & Churchland, 1988), is involved, for example, in exploring how people recognize objects in the world, a process we examine in Chapter 5, on perception.

Although computers are used to model brain function, the central nervous system is not neatly laid out like computer circuits or the carefully planned streets of a new suburb. In fact, the central nervous system looks more like Boston, with distinct neighborhoods, winding back streets, and multilaned expressways. The "neighborhoods" of the nervous system are collections of neuronal cell bodies called **nuclei**. The "highways" of the nervous system are made up of axons that travel together in bundles called **fiber tracts** or **pathways**. Like a freeway ramp, the axon from a given cell may merge with and leave fiber tracts, and it may send branches into other tracts.

Are particular "neighborhoods" or "highways" of the brain responsible for specific functions? One psychologist, Karl Lashley, spent years trying to locate specific sites where particular memories are stored in the rat brain. He taught rats to perform a certain task, then removed part of their brains. Much to Lashley's dismay, the rats continued to remember how to do the task, even after large segments of their brains had been removed. He eventually gave up looking for the location of memories, concluding in exasperation that they must be stored diffusely throughout the brain (Lashley, 1929).

Was Lashley right, or are memories localized? And is there a "hunger center," which is active when you are hungry, or a vision region, where you experience sight? Yes and no. Functions are localized in particular regions, but each function may take place in many areas. We explain this idea further in later chapters as we examine specific processes such as memory and sensation. Here we will introduce the major structures of the central nervous system and their functions. First, however, we examine how scientists go about studying the brain to try to relate its structures to its functions.

Many major nuclei and fiber tracts in the nervous system are visible to the naked eye. The cell bodies in this slice of brain tissue, for example, appear gray and are referred to as "gray matter." Bundles of axons are known as fiber tracts, or "white matter." They appear white because larger axons are coated with fatty myelin.

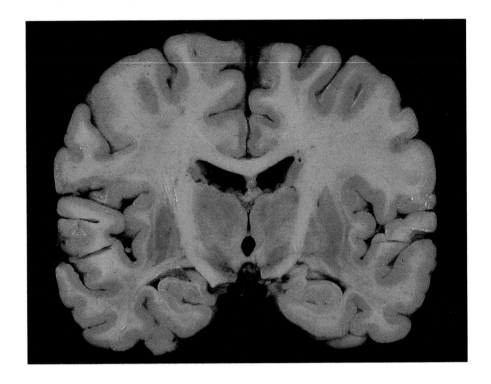

Relating Structure to Function

Most methods for studying the living brain employ special devices that can detect the brain's electrical activity or the consequences of that activity. The "microphones" of these devices can be so small and sensitive that they can detect the activity of an individual neuron. This *single-unit recording* is done by implanting an electrode into the brain. Animals are the subjects for most of this research, but recordings of humans are sometimes made in the course of brain surgery. After recording the signals that neurons send to one another, researchers try to decipher the codes that they use.

Smooth movements require the coordination of neural activity in both the brain and the spinal cord. Without this coordination, walking would be a difficult and jerky affair, similar to the reflexive movements created in paralyzed people by computer-controlled electrical stimulation of the legs.

Electrical stimulation is another technique for studying the brain. Stimulation of a set of neurons causes action potentials to travel down their axons and release neurotransmitters, just as if they were stimulated by other neurons. This technique is used extensively in animal studies. In addition, patients who need brain surgery sometimes volunteer to have an electrode lowered into the brain during the operation, so that the effects can be observed when neurons in specific areas are made to fire. This painless electrical stimulation can cause the patient to move a particular body part or report a sound, a smell, or other sensory experience.

The collective electrical activity of the brain's many neurons can be measured by electrodes attached to the skin over the skull. The resulting recordings are called **electroencephalograms,** or **EEGs.** EEG patterns may be related to certain mental disorders, brain damage, and even particular thought processes in normal people (see Figure 3.9). EEGs can show second-to-second changes in brain activity, but they do have a disadvantage: they cannot indicate the precise source of the activity.

A new technique called *positron emission tomography*, or **PET scanning**, allows scientists to monitor brain activity and locate functions without surgery. This technique relies on the fact that actively firing neurons must increase their oxygen and glucose (sugar) consumption, and they need an increased supply of blood to do so. Thus, areas of increased activity can be detected by marking blood, oxygen, or glucose with harmless radioactive substances and then

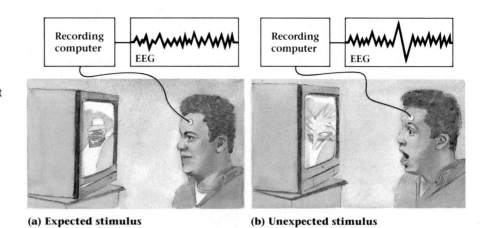

(a) Expected stimulus　　　　**(b) Unexpected stimulus**

Figure 3.9
Eavesdropping on the Brain
EEG, or "brain wave," tracings provide one way to gather clues about what happens in the brain during various kinds of mental activity. Part (a): the EEG pattern summarized by a computer as a subject watches stimuli that occur in an expected and predictable way. Part (b): the pattern that typically appears when the subject encounters unexpected and surprising stimuli. The large drop in the EEG tracing usually occurs about 0.3 seconds after an unexpected stimulus.

measuring where the radioactivity becomes concentrated. To detect the radioactivity, a person's head is placed at the center of an array of radiation detectors. The signals are then fed to a special computer that can use the signals to develop a "picture" of a cross-section of the brain. For example, Figure 3.10 shows PET scans of a person suffering from cycles of deep depression and wild elation (Baxter et al., 1985). Indeed, PET scans and related techniques are now being used to refine the diagnosis of numerous disorders.

Another new, nonsurgical technique is called *magnetic resonance imaging,* or **MRI.** It does not use radioactive isotopes; instead, it detects the magnetic fields that surround the atoms in brain tissue. As you can see in Figure 3.11, MRI produces much clearer pictures of brain structures than PET scans. It has helped in the detection of abnormalities in the brain structure of people who suffer from *Alzheimer's disease,* a severe brain disorder seen mostly in the elderly that causes a progressive loss of memory and degeneration of personality. MRI has found in Alzheimer's patients a 40 percent reduction in the size of the hippocampus, a brain structure involved in the formation of new memories (Seab et al., 1988). MRI detects structure, whereas PET scans detect neuronal activity, and recently the two techniques have been combined to produce a picture of structure and activity in the same brain (see Figure 3.12).

Remarkable as these new techniques are, much of what psychologists know about the brain has come from studying animals and the victims of strokes and other localized brain damage. Examining these patients and, sometimes,

Figure 3.10
PET Scans of One Patient
Activity in a particular "slice," or level, of the brain can be precisely located when positron-emitting radioactive isotopes are used, because when these isotopes decay, they emit simultaneous signals in two exactly opposite directions. Here, the three sets of ovals represent overhead views of what was going on at three different levels of a patient's brain on three different days. Glucose consumption associated with intense brain activity shows up red on these scans. There was an abnormally low amount of activity on the seventeenth and the twenty-seventh of May, when the patient was depressed, but the scan shows about a 40 percent increase in activity (essentially normal) on the eighteenth, when the patient was in a more upbeat, almost elated, mood. Scans like these help to detect abnormal brain activity and to begin to trace its location.

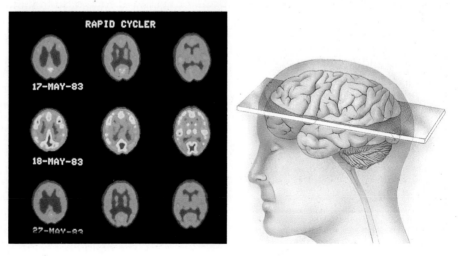

Source: Baxter et al., 1985.

Figure 3.11
Magnetic Resonance Image
of the Brain
Magnetic resonance imaging provided these views of particular "slices" of the living brains of a normal person (top) and a patient with Alzheimer's disease (bottom). They show that the hippocampus (H) has degenerated in the Alzheimer's patient. On average, the hippocampus of Alzheimer's patients was found to be 40 percent smaller than in normals. Damage to the hippocampus may be responsible for the severe memory impairments in Alzheimer's disease.

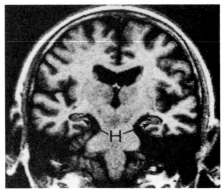
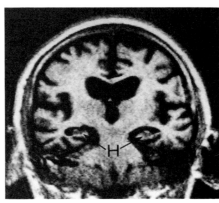
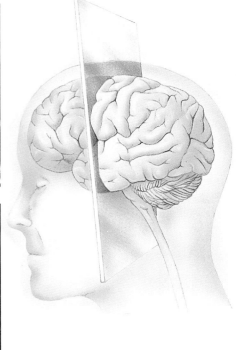

Source: Seab et al., (1988).

studying their brains after death can reveal a relationship between damage to a specific part of the brain and loss of a particular ability.

HIGHLIGHT

Recovery from Brain Damage

"Whoa! *That* was a good one! Try it, Hobbs — just poke his brain right where my finger is."

Source: The Far Side. Copyright 1986 Universal Press Syndicate. Reprinted with permission.

Analysis of the consequences of brain damage has greatly increased understanding of how the brain works, but it is often a study of tragedy. There are heroic recoveries from brain damage, but more often the victim is permanently enfeebled in some way. Why is recovery so rare and difficult? If a damaged arm heals itself, why doesn't a damaged brain?

There are several reasons. First, the brain of an adult animal generally cannot make new neurons. During development, neurons divide and multiply as other cells do, but in maturity the neurons stop dividing and cannot produce more cells in response to injury. *Glial cells,* which provide support for neurons, continue to divide; neurons do not.

A second problem arises because the brain's axons and dendrites form dense networks, with interwoven fibers making connections near and far. Even if new neurons could be grown, their axons and dendrites would have to re-establish all their former communication links. In the peripheral nervous system the glial cells form "tunnels" that guide the regrowth of the axons. But in the central nervous system, re-establishing communication links is almost impossible, because glial cells "clean up" after brain damage, consuming injured neurons and forming a barrier to new connections.

Nevertheless, the brain does try to heal itself. Undamaged tissue tries to take over for lost tissue, partly by changing its function and partly by

Figure 3.12
Combining PET Scans and Magnetic Resonance Imaging
PET scans provide information about the brain's activity but very little structural information; MRI shows structure but no activity. Recently researchers have been able to superimpose images from both techniques, and even construct a three-dimensional view of the living brain. This reconstruction shows the brain of a seven-year-old girl with epilepsy. The detailed picture of the convolutions of the cortex is from the MRI; the pink area of unusual activity is from PET, showing the source of the epileptic activity along the motor cortex. The images at the right are the PET image and the MRI image at one plane, or "slice," through the brain. With this information, surgeons were able to remove the damaged part of the brain and eliminate the girl's seizures (Levin et al., 1989). In the future such techniques will also be applied to the study of normal brains.

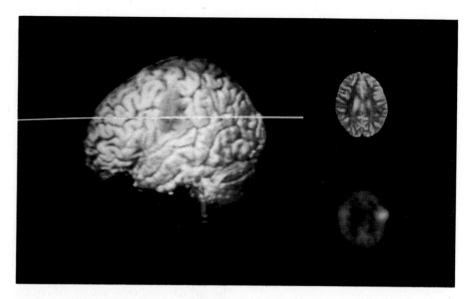

Source: D. N. Levin, H. Xiaoping, K. K. Tan, S. Galhotra, C. A. Pelizzari, G. T. Y. Chen, R. N. Beck, C-T. Chen, M. D. Cooper, J. F. Mullan, J. Hekmatpanah (1989). The brain: Integrated three-dimensional display of MR and PET images. *Radiology, 172,* 783–789. By permission of the author.

sprouting new axons and dendrites to make new connections. Unfortunately, these changes rarely result in total restoration of lost functions.

Scientists are trying several new methods for helping people recover from brain damage. One approach is to replace lost tissue with tissue from another brain. Scientists have transplanted tissue from a still-developing fetal brain into the brain of an adult animal. If the receiving animal does not reject the graft, the graft sends axons out into the brain and makes some functional connections. In experimental animals this treatment has reversed learning difficulties, impaired movement, and other results of brain damage. In humans the technique has been used, with very promising results, to treat people with Parkinson's disease, a disorder that creates shakiness and difficulties in moving (Lindvall et al., 1990).

If scientists succeed in transplanting brain tissue so that tissue and lost functions can be regained, they will face a dilemma: who gives up the brain tissue to be transplanted? One possibility is to use tissue from aborted fetuses, but this procedure would not be acceptable to some people. Another alternative is cross-species transplant. Scientists have already transplanted tissue from a mouse into a rat (Brundin et al., 1985). In the case of Parkinson's disease, a person might be both donor and recipient of transplanted tissue, because cells of the adrenal gland may become neurons when placed in the brain, and people can live with just one adrenal gland. Two Parkinson's patients who received a grafted adrenal dramatically improved their ability to walk and produce fine movements, such as handwriting (Madrazo et al., 1987). However, studies with animals suggest that these gains resulted from surgical manipulation that prompted the brain's own regenerative powers (Fiandaca et al., 1988). This is a controversy that must be resolved.

Another approach seeks to find ways to guide newly sprouted axons in the central nervous system. Recently researchers have "engineered" cells from rats to produce *nerve growth factor,* a substance that helps stimulate and guide the growth of axons. The cells were then implanted into the brain of rats with brain damage, where they secreted nerve growth factor; in many cases the brain damage was prevented or reversed, with surviving neurons sprouting axons that grew toward the graft (Rosenberg et al., 1988). The technique has not yet been tried in humans.

Yet another prospect is suggested by studies of bird brains (Nottebohm, 1985). Each year, the male canary learns new songs and then forgets many of the songs at the end of the breeding season. Each year, a part of the brain related to the learning of songs grows by neuronal cell division. Later the neurons die, and the cycle repeats during the next season. If scientists could discover what is different about this part of the bird brain, perhaps the same processes could be generated in the human brain, allowing it to produce new neurons and heal itself. ■

We return now to an overview of the anatomy of the central nervous system and the functions of its structures. Our exploration begins at the spinal cord and progresses upward, toward the skull.

The Spinal Cord

The **spinal cord** receives signals from peripheral senses, such as the sense of touch from the fingertips, and relays the signals upward to the brain through fibers within the cord. Neurons in the spinal cord also carry signals downward. For example, axons from neurons in the brain stimulate cells in the spinal cord that, in turn, cause muscles to contract and move the body. In addition, cells of the spinal cord direct some simple behaviors by themselves, without instructions from the brain. These behaviors are called **reflexes** because the response to an incoming signal is directly "reflected" back out.

Reflexes   The cells controlling a reflex are called a *reflex pathway,* or *reflex arc.* The pathway consists of a sensory neuron; a minimal number of connecting neurons, called *interneurons;* and a motor neuron (see Figure 3.13). The sensory neuron is often called an *afferent* neuron and the motor neuron an *efferent* neuron, because *afferent* means "coming toward" and *efferent,* "going away." (To remember these terms, notice that *afferent* and *approach* both begin with *a*; *efferent* and *exit* both begin with *e*.)

Because spinal reflexes include few time-consuming synapses, they are very fast. And because they do not involve the brain, spinal reflexes are considered involuntary. For example, suppose you sleepily reach for a pot of hot water to make your morning coffee and touch the hot burner instead. The incoming nerve impulses from sensory neurons in your hand quickly stimulate the fibers that operate your arm muscles, and you withdraw your hand. Although information about the pain does go on to the brain for analysis, your muscles respond without waiting for instructions from the brain.

Principles of Central Nervous System Functioning   Although the spinal cord is far simpler than the brain, its functioning demonstrates principles that govern the entire central nervous system. One of these principles is coordination of opposing actions. When a simple spinal reflex set off by touching a hot burner causes one set of arm muscles to contract, another reflex makes an opposing set of muscles relax. If this did not happen, the arm would go rigid.

A second principle is that complicated behaviors are built up from simpler ones. For example, the complex movements involved in walking are built up of reflexes that prompt repeated cycles of contraction and relaxation in the muscles of each arm and leg. These reflexes work even without input from your brain. Of course, your brain directs where you walk, but it adjusts, rather than overrides, the reflex connections in the spinal cord.

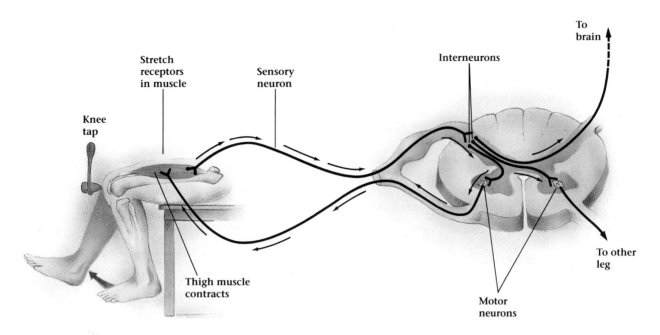

Figure 3.13
A Reflex Pathway
A tap on the knee sets off an almost instantaneous sequence of events, beginning with the stimulation of sensory neurons that respond to stretch. When those neurons fire, their axons, which end within the spinal cord, cause interneurons to fire. This in turn stimulates the firing of motor neurons with axons ending in the thigh muscles. The result is a contraction of the thigh muscles and a kicking of the lower leg and foot. Information about the knee tap and about what the leg has done also ascends to the cerebral cortex, but the reflex is completed without waiting for guidance from the brain.

Third, smooth functioning depends on feedback systems. In a **feedback system** information about the consequences of an action goes back to the source of the action, so that adjustments can be made. A thermostat is the classic example of a feedback system. You set the thermostat to the desired temperature and the furnace generates heat, while the thermostat monitors the room temperature. When the desired temperature has been reached, that information is fed back to the thermostat, which turns off the furnace. When the temperature drops below the desired level, the furnace goes on again. When feedback keeps a bodily function such as temperature within a steady range, the result is called **homeostasis.**

The spinal cord does not have a thermostat, but muscles have stretch receptors that send impulses to the spinal cord to let it know how extended they are. A reflex pathway then adjusts the muscle contraction. This feedback stabilizes the position of the body and allows smooth movements. This reflexive feedback also causes the knee-jerk response when the knee is tapped. The tapping causes the thigh muscle to stretch. Information about the stretching goes into the spinal cord, which reflexively causes thigh muscles to contract, as Figure 3.13 shows.

The Brain

The brain has three major subdivisions: the hindbrain, midbrain, and forebrain. Opening the skull and removing the brain's protective wrapping reveals the outer surface of the forebrain, a wrinkled surface called the **cerebral cortex.** (Cortex means "bark.") Beneath the forebrain is the midbrain; under that lies the hindbrain.

The Hindbrain   As you can see in Figure 3.14, the **hindbrain** is an extension of the spinal cord, but it lies inside the skull. Blood pressure, heart rate, breathing, and many other vital functions are controlled by nuclei in the hindbrain, particularly in an area called the **medulla.** The **cerebellum** is also part of the hindbrain. Its primary function is to control finely coordinated movements, such as threading a needle. The cerebellum may also be the

Figure 3.14
Major Structures of the Brain
This view from the side of a section cut down the middle of the brain reveals the forebrain, midbrain, hindbrain, and spinal cord. Many of these subdivisions do not have clear-cut borders, since they are all interconnected by fiber tracts. Indeed, though beautifully adapted to its functions, the brain was not the work of a city planner. Its anatomy reflects the fact that it evolved over millions of years. Newer structures (such as the cerebral cortex, which is the outer surface of the forebrain) that handle higher mental functions were built on older ones (like the medulla) that coordinate heart rate, breathing, and other more basic functions.

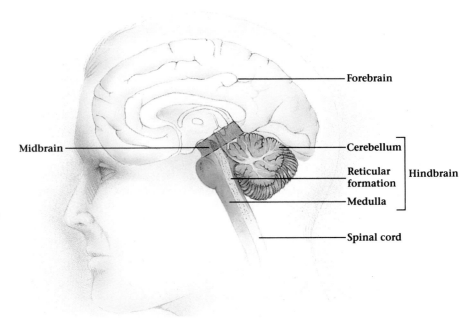

storehouse for well-rehearsed movements, such as those associated with ballet, piano playing, and athletics (McCormick & Thompson, 1984).

Reflexes and feedback systems are important to the functioning of the hindbrain, as they are in the spinal cord. For example, if blood pressure drops, heart action increases reflexively to compensate for that drop. If you stand up very quickly, your blood pressure can drop so suddenly that it produces lightheadedness until the hindbrain reflex "catches up." If the hindbrain does not activate mechanisms to increase blood pressure, you will faint.

The Midbrain   As its name implies, the **midbrain** lies between the hindbrain and the forebrain. In humans it is a small structure, but it serves some very important functions. Information from the eyes, ears, and skin is relayed through the midbrain, and certain types of automatic behaviors are controlled there. For example, when you move your head, midbrain circuits allow you to move your eyes smoothly in the opposite direction, so that you can keep your eyes focused sharply on an object despite the movement of your head. And when a loud noise causes you to turn your head reflexively and look in the direction of the sound, your midbrain circuits are at work.

One vital midbrain nucleus is the **substantia nigra**, meaning "black substance." This small area and its connections to other areas are necessary for the smooth initiation of movement. Without it, you would find it difficult, if not impossible, to get up out of a chair, lift your hand to swat a fly, or move your mouth to form words.

The Reticular Formation   Threading throughout the hindbrain and midbrain is a collection of cells that are not arranged in any well-defined nucleus (see Figure 3.14). Because the collection looks like a net, it is called the **reticular formation.** (*Reticular* means "netlike.") This network is very important in altering the activity of the rest of the brain. It is involved, for example, in arousal and attention. Stimulating an animal's reticular formation will rouse the animal from sleep.

The Forebrain   The **forebrain** is the most highly developed part of the brain. It is responsible for the most complex aspects of behavior and mental life.

One part of the forebrain is called the *diencephalon* (see Figure 3.15). It includes two structures deep within the brain, the hypothalamus and the thalamus, that are involved in emotion, basic drives, and sensation. The **thalamus** relays signals from the eyes and other sense organs to upper levels in the brain, and it plays an important role in processing and making sense out of this information. Under the thalamus lies the hypothalamus. (*Hypo-* means "under.") Hunger, thirst, and sex drives are regulated in part by the **hypothalamus**. It has many connections to and from the autonomic nervous system and the endocrine system (described later in this chapter), as well as to other parts of the brain. Destruction of one section of the hypothalamus results in an overwhelming urge to eat. Damage to another area of the male's hypothalamus causes the sex organs to degenerate and the sex drive to decrease drastically. We discuss these and other functions of the hypothalamus in more detail in Chapters 11 and 12, on motivation and emotion.

The largest part of the forebrain is the **cerebrum.** Two important structures within it are the striatum and hippocampus. Along with the substantia nigra, the **striatum** is responsible for smooth initiation of movement. Damage to the **hippocampus** results in the inability to form new memories. In one case, a patient known as R.B. suffered a stroke that damaged only his hippocampus. Although tests indicated that his intelligence was above average and he could recall old memories, he was almost totally unable to build new ones (Squire, 1986).

The hippocampus is also considered part of the **limbic system**, which is a set of structures that play important roles in regulating emotion and memory. Among the other structures in the limbic system are the hypothalamus, the septum, and the amygdala (see Figure 3.15). The limbic system is a "system" because its components have major interconnections and influence related functions.

The outermost part of the cerebrum appears rather round and has right and left halves that are similar in appearance. These halves are called the **cerebral hemispheres.** The outer surface of the cerebral hemispheres, the **cerebral cortex,** has a surface area of one to two square feet—an area that is larger than it looks because of the folds that allow the cortex to fit compactly inside the skull. The cerebral cortex is much larger in humans than in other animals (with a few exceptions, such as dolphins). Because it is associated with the analysis of information from all the senses, control of voluntary movements, higher-order thought, and other complex aspects of human behavior and mental processes, we will describe the cerebral cortex in more detail than the other areas.

Figure 3.15
Some Structures of the Forebrain
The forebrain is divided into the cerebrum and the diencephalon. Many of the structures of the cerebrum are covered by the outer "bark" of the cerebral cortex. This diagram shows some of the structures that lie deep within the cerebrum, including the striatum, septum, and hippocampus. The diencephalon includes the hypothalamus and thalamus.

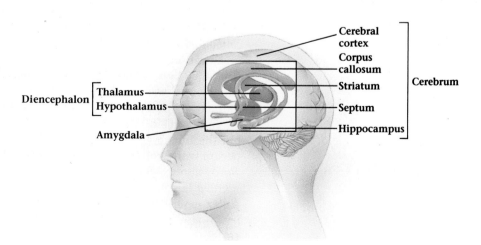

The Cerebral Cortex

The folds of the cerebral cortex give the surface of the human brain its wrinkled appearance, its ridges and valleys. The ridges are called *gyri* and the valleys, *sulci* or *fissures.* As you can see in Figure 3.16, several deep sulci divide the cortex into four areas: the *frontal, parietal, occipital,* and *temporal lobes.* Thus, the gyri and sulci provide landmarks for describing the cortex, although the functions of the cortex do not follow these boundaries. Divided according to functions, the cortex includes areas called the sensory cortex, association cortex, and motor cortex.

Sensory and Motor Cortex   Different regions of the **sensory cortex** receive information about different senses. As Figure 3.16 shows, the sensory cortex lies in the parietal, occipital, and temporal lobes. Cells in the occipital lobe receive visual information; information from the ears reaches cells in the temporal lobe. Cells in the parietal lobe take in information from the skin about touch, pain, and temperature; these areas are called the *somatosensory cortex.* Information about skin sensations from neighboring parts of the body comes to neighboring parts of the somatosensory cortex, as Figure 3.17 illustrates. It is as if the outline of a tiny person, dangling upside down, determined the location of the information. This pattern is called the *homunculus,* which means "little man."

Neurons in specific areas of the **motor cortex**, which is in the frontal lobe, initiate voluntary movements in specific parts of the body. Some control movement of the hand; others stimulate movement of the foot, the knee, the head, and so on. The motor cortex is arranged in a way that mirrors the somatosensory cortex. For example, as you can see in Figure 3.17, the parts of the motor cortex that control the hands are near parts of the sensory cortex that receive sensory information from the hands.

Linkages: What parts of the brain make thought and language possible? (a link to Thought and Language)

Association Cortex   Parts of the cerebral cortex that are not directly involved with receiving specific sensory information or initiating movement are called the **association cortex**. The term *association* is appropriate because these areas receive information from more than one sense or combine sensory and motor information. These are the areas that perform such complex cognitive tasks as associating words with images and other abstract thinking.

Association cortex occurs in all of the lobes and forms a large part of the cerebral cortex in human beings. This is one reason why damage to association areas can create severe deficits in all kinds of mental abilities. One of the most devastating, called *aphasia,* involves difficulty in producing or understanding speech. In the 1860s, Paul Broca described the difficulties that result from damage to the association cortex in the frontal lobe near motor areas that control facial muscles. This part of the cortex on the left side of the brain is called *Broca's area* (see Figure 3.16). When Broca's area is damaged, the mental organization of speech suffers. Victims have great difficulty speaking, and what they say is often grammatically incorrect. Each word comes slowly. One patient who was asked about a dental appointment said haltingly, "Yes . . . Monday . . . Dad and Dick . . . Wednesday 9 o'clock . . . 10 o'clock . . . doctors . . . and . . . teeth" (Geschwind, 1979). The ideas—dentists and teeth—are right, but the fluency is gone. A fascinating aspect of the disorder is that when a person with Broca's aphasia sings, the words come fluently and correctly. The words to music presumably are handled by a different part of the brain.

Other language problems result from damage to a portion of the association cortex described in the 1870s by Carl Wernicke. Like Broca's area, *Wernicke's area* is also on the left side; it is in the temporal lobe, near the area of sensory cortex that receives information from the ears, as Figure 3.16 shows. Wernicke's

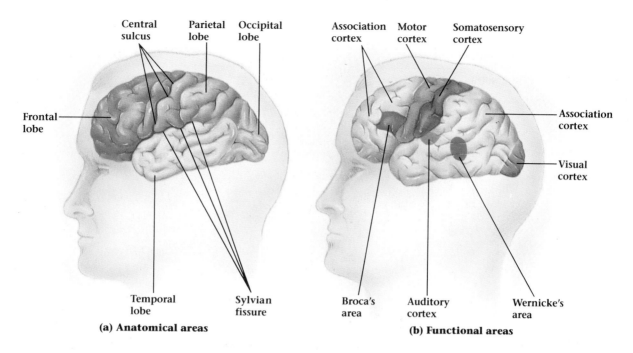

Figure 3.16
The Cerebral Cortex (viewed from the left side)
The ridges and valleys of the cortex are landmarks that divide the cortex into four lobes: the frontal, parietal, occipital, and temporal. These terms describe anatomical regions, but the cortex is also divided in terms of function. These functional areas include visual, auditory, and soma-tosensory cortex (which receive information from the senses); association cortex (which integrates information); and motor cortex (which controls movement). Also illustrated are Wernicke's area, which is involved in the interpretation of speech, and Broca's area, a region vital to the production of speech. (These two areas are usually found only on the left side of the cortex.)

area also receives input from the visual cortex. It is involved in the interpretation of both speech and written words. Damage to Wernicke's area produces complicated symptoms. It can leave fluency intact but disrupt the ability to understand the meaning of words or to speak comprehensibly. One patient who was asked to describe a picture of two boys stealing cookies behind a woman's back said, "Mother is away here working her work to get her better, but when she's looking the two boys looking in the other part. She's working another time" (Geschwind, 1979).

In the normal person with no brain damage, Broca's and Wernicke's areas participate in producing and understanding language. Language information reaches Wernicke's area from the auditory cortex (for spoken language) or from the visual cortex (for written language). In Wernicke's area, the words are interpreted and the structure of a verbal response is formed. The output from Wernicke's area goes to Broca's area, where a detailed program for vocalization is formed. This program is relayed to adjacent areas of the motor cortex to produce speech (Geschwind, 1979). Thus, the complex function known as language involves activity in the sensory, association, and motor cortices.

The Divided Brain in a Unified Self

Linkages: Are spatial and verbal abilities controlled by different parts of the brain? (a link to Mental Abilities)

A striking idea emerged from observations of people with damage to the language areas of the brain. It was noticed that damage to limited areas of the left hemisphere impaired the ability to use or comprehend language, while damage to corresponding parts of the right hemisphere usually did not. Perhaps, then, the right and left halves of the brain serve different functions.

This concept was not entirely new. It had long been understood, for example, that most sensory and motor pathways cross over as they enter or leave the brain. As a result, the left hemisphere receives information from and controls movements of the right side of the body, while the right hemisphere receives input from and controls the left side of the body. However, these functions, although divided, are performed by *both* sides of the brain. In contrast, the

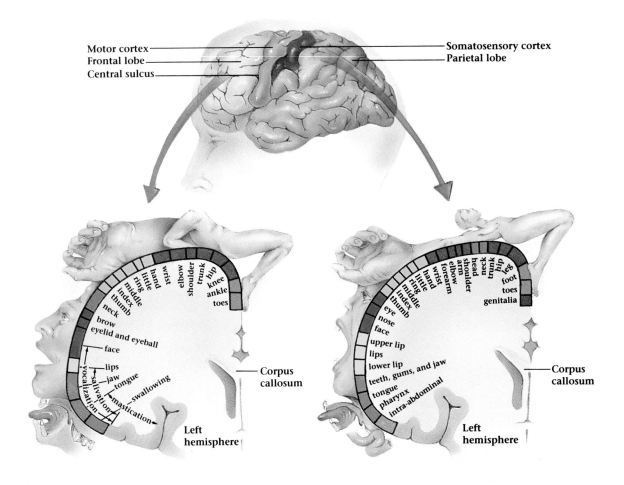

(a) Motor areas (end view)   **(b) Sensory areas (end view)**

Source: Penfield & Rasmussen, 1978.

Figure 3.17
Motor and Somatosensory Cortex
The areas of cortex that move parts of the body (motor cortex) and receive sensory input from body parts (somatosensory cortex) occupy neighboring regions on each side of the central sulcus. These regions appear in both hemispheres; here we show only those on the left side, looking from the back of the brain toward the front. Areas controlling movement of neighboring parts of the body, like the foot and leg, occupy neighboring parts of motor cortex. Areas receiving input from neighboring body parts, like the lips and tongue, are near one another in the somatosensory cortex. Can you find the error in this classic drawing? (The figure shows the right side of the body but shows the left hand and left side of the face.)

fact that language centers, such as Broca's area and Wernicke's area, are almost exclusively on the left side of the brain, suggested that each hemisphere might be specialized to perform some functions almost independently of the other hemisphere.

In the late 1800s there was much interest in this idea that the hemispheres might be specialized, but techniques were not available to test it. Renewed interest in this issue grew out of studies during the 1960s by Roger Sperry, Michael Gazzaniga, and their colleagues.

Split-Brain Studies   Sperry and his colleagues studied *split-brain* patients— people who had undergone a radical surgical procedure in an attempt to control severe epilepsy. Before surgery their seizures began in one hemisphere and then spread to engulf the whole brain. As a last resort, the two hemispheres in these people were isolated from each other by severing the **corpus callosum,** a massive bundle of more than a million fibers that connects the two hemispheres (see Figure 3.18).

After the surgery, researchers used a special apparatus to present visual images to only *one* side of these patients' split brains (see Figure 3.19). They found that severing the tie between the hemispheres dramatically affected the

Figure 3.18
The Brain's Left and Right Hemispheres
The brain's two hemispheres are joined by a core bundle of nerve fibers known as the corpus callosum; in this figure the corpus callosum has been cut so that the two hemispheres can be separated. Though they look nearly the same, the two cerebral hemispheres perform somewhat different tasks. For one thing, the left hemisphere receives sensory input from and controls movement on the right side of the body. The right hemisphere senses and controls the left side of the body.

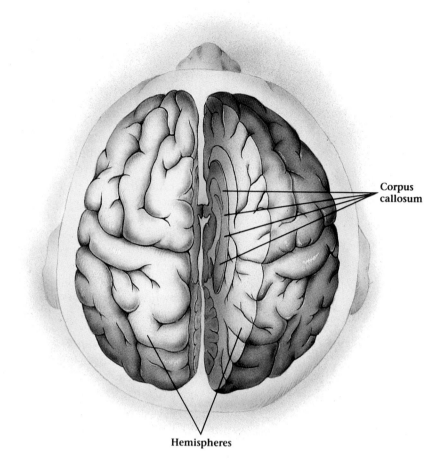

Corpus callosum

Hemispheres

way these people thought and dealt with the world. For example, when the image of a spoon was presented to the left, language-oriented side of patient N.G.'s brain, she could say what the spoon was, but she could not describe the spoon in words when it was presented to the right side of her brain. Her right hemisphere knew what the object was, however. Using her left hand (controlled by the right hemisphere), N.G. could pick out the spoon from a group of other objects by its shape. When asked what she had just grasped, she replied, "A pencil." The right hemisphere recognized the object, but the patient could not describe it because the left (language) half of her brain did not see or feel it (Sperry, 1968).

Though the right hemisphere has no control over spoken language in split-brain patients, it does have important capabilities, including some related to nonspoken language. For example, a split-brain patient's right hemisphere can guide the left hand in spelling out words with Scrabble tiles (Gazzaniga & LeDoux, 1978). Thanks to this ability, researchers discovered that the right hemisphere of split-brain patients has self-awareness and normal learning abilities. It is also superior to the left on tasks dealing with spatial relations, especially drawing three-dimensional shapes and at recognizing human faces.

Lateralization of Normal Brains   Sperry concluded from his studies that each hemisphere in the split-brain patient has its own "private sensations, perceptions, thoughts, and ideas all of which are cut off from the corresponding experiences in the opposite hemisphere. . . . In many respects each disconnected hemisphere appears to have a separate mind of its own" (Sperry, 1974).

But when the hemispheres are *not* disconnected, are their functions different? Are certain functions, such as mathematical reasoning or language skills, lateralized? A **lateralized** task is one that is performed more efficiently by one hemisphere than by the other hemisphere.

To find out, researchers presented images to just one hemisphere of people with normal brains and then measured how fast they could analyze information. If information is presented to one side of the brain and that side is specialized to analyze that type of information, a person's responses will be faster than if the information must first be transferred to the other hemisphere for analysis. These studies have confirmed that the left hemisphere has better logical and language abilities than the right, whereas the right hemisphere has better spatial, artistic, and musical abilities (Springer & Deutsch, 1985). PET scans of normal people receiving varying kinds of auditory stimulation also demonstrate these asymmetries of function (see Figure 3.20).

The precise nature and degree of lateralization vary quite a bit among individuals. Among about a third of left-handed people, either the right hemisphere or both hemispheres control language functions (Springer & Deutsch, 1989). Only about 5 percent of right-handed people have language controlled by the right hemisphere.

Although the two hemispheres are somewhat specialized, the differences between them should not be exaggerated. People are probably not "left-brained" or "right-brained" in the same way that they are left- or right-handed. Normally the corpus callosum integrates the functions of the two hemispheres so that people are not aware of their "two brains." The hemispheres work so closely together, and each makes up so well for whatever lack of ability the other may have, that people are normally unaware that their brains are made up of two partially independent, somewhat specialized halves. Furthermore, there is no evidence that programs designed to train one hemisphere or to synchronize the two hemispheres can enhance performance (Druckman & Swets, 1988).

Figure 3.19
Apparatus for Studying Split-Brain Subjects.
When the subject stares at the dot on the screen, images briefly presented on one side of the dot go to only one side of the brain. For example, a picture of a spoon presented on the left side of the screen goes to the right side of the brain; thus, the right side of the brain could direct the left hand to identify the spoon, but the language areas on the left side of the brain would not know what it was, and the subject would not be able to identify the object verbally.

Figure 3.20
Lateralization of the Cerebral Hemispheres: Evidence from PET Scans

These PET scans show overhead views of a section of a person's brain that was receiving different kinds of stimulation. At the upper left, the subject was resting, with eyes open and ears plugged. Note that the greatest brain activity, as indicated by the red color, is in the visual cortex, which is receiving input from the eyes. As shown at the lower left, when the subject listened to spoken language, the left (more language oriented) side of the brain, especially the auditory cortex in the temporal lobe, became more active, but the right temporal lobe did not; the visual and frontal areas were also active. However, when listening to music (lower right), there is intense activity in the right temporal lobe, but little in the left. When the subject heard both words and music, (upper right) temporal cortex on both sides of the brain became activated. Here is visual evidence of the involvement of each side of the brain in processing different kinds of information (Phelps & Mazziotta, 1985).

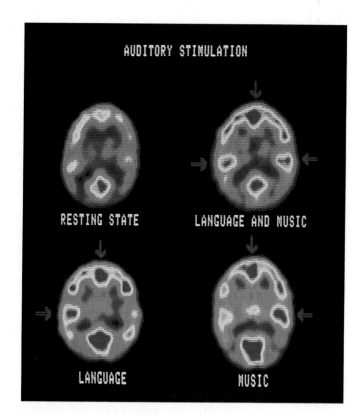

Source: Mazziotta & Phelps, 1982.

The Chemistry of Psychology

So far, we have described how the cells of the nervous system communicate by releasing neurotransmitters at their synapses, and we have outlined some of the basic structures of the nervous system and their functions. Now we pull these topics together by examining two questions. First, which neurotransmitters occur in these structures? Different sets of neurons use different neurotransmitters; a group of neurons that communicates using the same neurotransmitter is called a **neurotransmitter system**. Second, how do these systems affect behavior? Certain neurotransmitter systems seem to play a dominant role in particular behaviors. There is good evidence, for example, that malfunctions of one neurotransmitter system plays a major role in some types of senility.

Seven Major Neurotransmitters

At least fifty chemicals that occur naturally in the brain act as neurotransmitters, and new ones are discovered every year. Most of the neurotransmitters discovered in the last several years, however, have two special properties. First, chemically they are *peptides,* which are essentially small proteins. Second, these peptide neurotransmitters work in a way somewhat different from straightforward neurotransmitters, which transfer information across a synapse from one cell to another. Peptide neurotransmitters are usually released into synapses along with other neurotransmitters and prolong the other neurotransmitters' actions or modulate their effects in some other way. Hence, substances like this are sometimes called *neuromodulators.* However, we will use only the term *neurotransmitter,* because the distinction between "neurotransmitter" and "neuromodulator" is not a clear one. Depending on the type of receptor, some traditional neurotransmitters can act as either a neuromodulator or a straightforward neurotransmitter.

In the following sections we describe seven of the most important neurotransmitters: acetylcholine, norepinephrine, serotonin, dopamine, GABA, glutamate, and endorphins. Usually the suffix *-ergic* is added to the name of a neurotransmitter to make the word an adjective. Thus, a group of neurons using dopamine as a neurotransmitter is called a *dopaminergic system* and a group using acetylcholine is called *cholinergic.*

Acetylcholine   The first compound to be identified as a neurotransmitter was **acetylcholine,** which is used by neurons in both the peripheral and the central nervous systems. In the peripheral nervous system, cholinergic neurons control the contraction of muscles by releasing acetylcholine onto muscle tissues. In the brain, cholinergic neurons are especially plentiful in the striatum, where they occur in circuits that are important for movement (see Figure 3.21). Axons of cholinergic neurons also make up major pathways in the limbic system, including the hippocampus, and other areas of the cerebrum that are involved in memory (Bartus et al., 1982). Drugs that interfere with acetylcholine prevent the formation of new memories.

Indeed, cholinergic neurons may hold the key to Alzheimer's disease, which causes a devastating loss of memory. Some estimates suggest that as many as 10 percent of people over the age of sixty-five and 47 percent over the age of eighty-five have Alzheimer's disease (Evans et al., 1989). In at least 40 percent of the cases, the disease appears to be inherited (Fitch, Becker & Heller, 1988). The problem stems in part from a nearly complete loss of cholinergic neurons from a nucleus in the forebrain that sends fibers to the cerebral cortex and hippocampus (Whitehouse et al., 1983).

Norepinephrine   Neurons that use **norepinephrine** are called *adrenergic.* (Norepinephrine is also called *noradrenaline.*) Like acetylcholine, norepinephrine occurs in both the central and the peripheral nervous systems; in both places, it contributes to arousal. Approximately half of the norepinephrine in the brain is contained in cells of the *locus coeruleus* ("blue spot"), which is near the reticular formation in the hindbrain (see Figure 3.21). There are relatively few cells in the locus coeruleus, but each sends out an axon that branches extensively, making contact with as many as 100,000 other cells (Moore & Bloom, 1979; Swanson, 1976).

Figure 3.21
Examples of Neurotransmitter Pathways
Neurons that release a certain neurotransmitter may be concentrated in one particular region (indicated by dots) and send fibers into other regions, to which they communicate across synapses (arrows). Four examples are shown here.

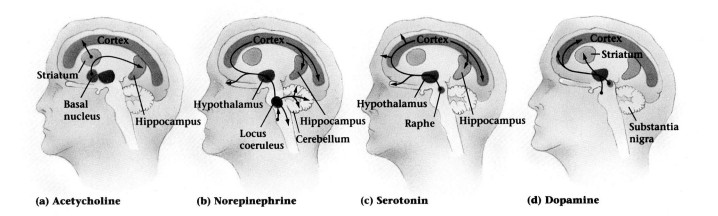

(a) Acetycholine   (b) Norepinephrine   (c) Serotonin   (d) Dopamine

Because adrenergic systems cover a lot of territory, it is logical that norepinephrine shapes several broad categories of behavior. Indeed, norepinephrine is involved in the appearance of wakefulness and sleep, in learning, and in the regulation of mood. In particular, abnormalities in norepinephrine systems have been linked to depression, but the exact nature of the link is still not clear. Some researchers have tied depression to abnormally low levels of norepinephrine (Bunney, Goodwin & Murphy, 1972; Crow et al., 1984), but others have found evidence that depressed people have elevated levels of norepinephrine (Gold, Goodwin & Chrousos, 1988). We look at this puzzle more closely in Chapter 15, on psychological disorders.

Serotonin The neurotransmitter **serotonin** is similar to norepinephrine in several ways. First, most of the cells that use it as a neurotransmitter occur in an area along the midline of the hindbrain; for serotonin the region is the *raphe nuclei* (see Figure 3.21). Second, serotonergic axons send branches throughout the forebrain, including the hypothalamus, the hippocampus, and the cerebral cortex. Third, serotonin affects sleep and mood.

Serotonin differs from norepinephrine, however, in that the brain can use one of the substances from which it is made, *tryptophan,* directly from food. As a result, what you eat can affect the amount of serotonin in your brain. Carbohydrates increase the amount of tryptophan getting into the brain, and therefore how much serotonin is made; so a meal high in carbohydrates produces increased levels of serotonin. Serotonin, in turn, normally causes a reduction in the desire for carbohydrates. In some people this feedback system is apparently disrupted. According to some researchers (Wurtman & Wurtman, 1989), disturbances of mood and appetite that occur in certain types of obesity, premenstrual tension, and some types of depression are tied to malfunctioning of the serotonin system.

Dopamine Figure 3.21 shows that **dopamine** is the neurotransmitter used in the substantia nigra and striatum, which are important for movement. Indeed, malfunctioning of the dopamine system in these regions contributes to movement disorders, including Parkinson's disease. In *Parkinson's disease* dopamine cells in the substantia nigra completely degenerate; the victim experiences severe shakiness and has difficulty beginning any movement. Parkinson's is most common in elderly people. Scientists are looking for possible environmental causes of the disease (Tanner, 1989).

Other dopaminergic systems send axons from the midbrain to the forebrain, including the cerebral cortex. Some of these neurons are important in the experience of reward, or pleasure, which is vital in shaping and motivating behavior (Wise & Rompre, 1989). Animals will work intensively to receive a direct infusion of dopamine into the forebrain. These dopaminergic systems play a role in the rewarding properties of many drugs, including cocaine (Wise, 1988). Malfunctioning of other dopaminergic neurons that go to the cortex may be partly responsible for *schizophrenia,* a psychological disorder in which perception, emotional expression, and thought are severely distorted (Weinberger, 1988).

GABA Neurons in widespread regions of the brain use **GABA**, which stands for ''gamma-amino butyric acid.'' GABA reduces the likelihood that the postsynaptic neuron will fire an action potential; in fact, it is the major inhibitory neurotransmitter in the central nervous system. When you fall asleep, neurons that use GABA deserve part of the credit.

Malfunctioning of GABA systems has been implicated in a variety of disorders, including severe anxiety and Huntington's disease. *Huntington's disease* is an inherited disorder that results in the loss of many GABA-containing neurons in the striatum. Normally these GABA systems inhibit dopamine systems. When they are lost through Huntington's disease, the dopamine systems may run wild, with effects that are in some ways the opposite of those of Parkinson's disease. Instead of being unable to begin movements, the victim is plagued by uncontrollable movement of the arms and legs, along with a progressive loss of cognitive abilities.

Because drugs that block GABA receptors produce intense repetitive electrical discharges, known as *seizures,* researchers suspect that a malfunctioning in GABA systems probably also contributes to *epilepsy,* a brain disorder that produces seizures, often with convulsive movements. Repeated or sustained seizures can result in permanent brain damage; drug treatments can reduce their frequency and severity, but completely effective drugs are not yet available.

Glutamate   The major excitatory neurotransmitter in the central nervous system is **glutamate.** Glutamate is used by more neurons than any other neurotransmitter; its synapses are especially plentiful in the cerebral cortex and the hippocampus.

Glutamate is particularly important because it plays a major role in the ability of the brain to "strengthen" its synaptic connections—that is, to allow messages to cross the synapse more efficiently. This process is necessary for normal development and may be at the root of learning. According to one theory, learning takes place when repeated use of particular synapses allows them to communicate more efficiently than before (Hebb, 1949). Glutamate appears to be involved in this process because one type of receptor for glutamate is initially activated only if the postsynaptic membrane is stimulated by more than one neuron at the same time (Cotman, Monaghan & Ganong, 1988). Somehow—the precise mechanism is still unknown—this combined stimulation makes it easier to stimulate these glutamate receptors on future occasions, even by just one neuron. The increased sensitivity of these receptors means that, in a sense, the postsynaptic cell has "learned."

Overactivity of glutamate synapses can cause neurons to die. In fact, this overactivity is the main cause of the brain damage that occurs when oxygen is cut off from neurons during a stroke. Glutamate can "excite neurons to death," so blocking glutamate receptors immediately after a brain trauma can prevent permanent brain damage (Faden et al., 1989). It has also been suggested that glutamate may contribute to the loss of cells from the hippocampus that occurs in Alzheimer's disease (Cotman et al., 1988).

Endorphins   One family of neurotransmitters was discovered in the 1970s by scientists who were interested in opiates. *Opiates,* which are derived from poppy flowers, can relieve pain, produce euphoria, and in high doses, bring on sleep; morphine and heroin are examples. After marking morphine with a radioactive substance, researchers traced where it became concentrated in the brain. They found that the opiates bind to receptors that were not associated with any then-known neurotransmitter. Since it was extremely unlikely that the brain had developed opiate receptors just in case a person might want to use morphine or heroin, researchers reasoned that the body must contain a substance similar to opiates. This hypothesis led to the search for a naturally occurring, or endogenous, morphine, which was called *endorphin,* a contraction of "endogenous morphine."

It turned out that there are many natural opiatelike compounds. Thus, the term **endorphin** now refers to any neurotransmitter that can bind to the same receptors stimulated by opiates. Neurons in several parts of the brain use endorphins, including pathways that modify pain signals to the brain.

Drugs, Neurotransmitters, and Behavior

Like naturally occurring neurotransmitters, **psychoactive drugs** are chemicals that may affect behavior, mental processes, and conscious experience. Some of these drugs, like cocaine, are used mainly for pleasure or escape; others are used to treat mental disorders. The study of both kinds of psychoactive drugs is called **psychopharmacology.**

Predicting the overall response to a drug is difficult. Sometimes a single drug produces more than one kind of effect on neurotransmitters or their receptors. In addition, a particular drug may interact with more than one type of receptor or with more than one neurotransmitter system. Furthermore, the nervous system usually compensates for any disturbance, including drug stimulation. For example, repeated exposure to a drug that blocks receptors for a certain neurotransmitter leads to a compensatory increase in the number of receptors available to respond to that neurotransmitter. As a result, the drug's effect may change after several weeks or years of use.

Nevertheless, scientists have learned a lot about psychoactive drugs and how they produce their effects. Most psychoactive drugs act by (1) altering the amount of neurotransmitter released by a neuron, (2) mimicking the neurotransmitter at the receptor site, (3) blocking receptors for certain neurotransmitters, or (4) blocking inactivation of the neurotransmitter in the synapse.

Altering the Amount of Neurotransmitter Released   Some drugs act by causing neurotransmitters to be released from the presynaptic endings into a synapse. For example, amphetamine triggers the release of neurotransmitters such as norepinephrine and dopamine. This release creates signals similar to those that would occur if rapidly firing neurons were flooding the synapses with these neurotransmitters.

The treatment for Parkinson's disease illustrates another way that a drug may alter the amount of neurotransmitter available for release. Recall that Parkinson's disease involves the death of many dopamine cells in the substantia nigra, making movement very difficult. The search for a drug to combat the disease began with the assumption that increasing the amount of dopamine

Linkages: In Chapter 16 we discuss some of the drugs used in the treatment of mental disorders, ranging from anxiety and depression to schizophrenia. Research in biological psychology on the role of neurotransmitters in emotion and behavior has helped explain how these drugs work and why they sometimes create undesirable side effects.

Figure 3.22
Agonists and Antagonists
Part (a) depicts a molecule of neuro-transmitter interacting with a recep-tor on a neuron's dendrites. Note that it fits into the receptor and stimulates it, starting a wave of de-polarization if the receptor is excita-tory. If, as shown in part (b), a drug molecule is similar enough to the neurotransmitter that normally stim-ulates the receptor, the drug will act as an *agonist,* changing the mem-brane potential of the receptor in the same way the neurotransmitter would. An *antagonist* is a drug mole-cule that is similar enough to oc-cupy a receptor site but not similar enough to stimulate it. The drug blocks the natural neurotransmitter from reaching and acting on the re-ceptor, as part (c) shows. Certain snake venoms, for example, para-lyze prey by blocking acetylcholine receptors in the peripheral ner-vous system that normally produce muscle movement.

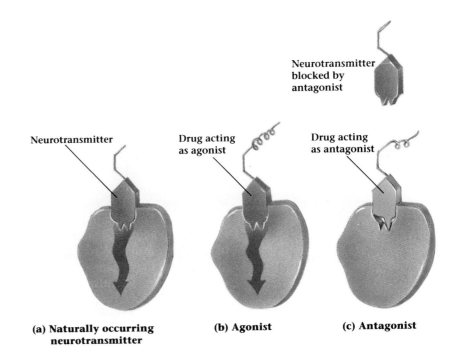

(a) Naturally occurring   (b) Agonist   (c) Antagonist
    neurotransmitter

in remaining neurons might partially compensate for the dead cells. To increase the dopamine available, researchers used the knowledge that the brain makes dopamine from a compound called *L-dopa;* once L-dopa is in the brain, dopaminergic neurons take it up and convert it to dopamine. Giving L-dopa to victims of Parkinson's disease turned out to be an effective treatment. For some unknown reason, however, the treatment is effective only for several years. Something about the dopaminergic system adjusts, so that L-dopa no longer relieves Parkinsonian symptoms. Thus, the search for effective treat-ments for Parkinson's disease continues.

Mimicking Neurotransmitters   If a molecule is very similar to a certain neurotransmitter, it may fool that transmitter's receptors and occupy them itself. Many drugs, called **receptor agonists**, mimic neurotransmitters in this way, fitting snugly into the receptors and changing the membrane potential of a cell just as the neurotransmitter would (see Figure 3.22). LSD, a reality-distorting drug discussed in Chapter 6, is one example; it produces its effects by acting as an agonist on one type of serotonin receptor (Jacobs, 1987).

Blocking Receptors   Some drugs, called **receptor antagonists**, are similar enough to a neurotransmitter to occupy its receptors, but they differ enough from that neurotransmitter so that they fail to change the membrane potential of the neuron. As long as they are attached to the receptors, however, antagonists block neurotransmitters from occupying and acting on them (see Figure 3.22). Thus, the neurotransmitters cannot have their normal effects. (For a summary of these effects, see "In Review: Major Neurotransmitters.")

One prominent application of antagonists is in the treatment of schizo-phrenia. No one has a "cure" for schizophrenia, but the drugs that partially relieve its symptoms have one feature in common: they are all antagonists that occupy dopamine receptors and prevent dopamine from producing its normal effects. The fact that this result is helpful suggests that schizophrenia is a result of overactivity of dopaminergic neurons that send axons to the cerebral cortex (Weinberger, 1988). Unfortunately, the drugs that relieve schizophrenia also prevent dopamine from reaching receptors in other parts of the brain and therefore create some very troublesome side effects, which we discuss in Chapter 16, on treatment of psychological disorders.

HIGHLIGHT

Naloxone and the Placebo Effect

One important receptor antagonist is **naloxone**, a drug that can block the actions of both opiates and endorphins. Because it blocks opiate receptors, naloxone has proved valuable in saving the lives of people who have taken overdoses of heroin. It has also been a valuable tool for studying endorphins and the puzzling phenomenon called the *placebo effect.*

We noted in Chapter 1 that a placebo contains no active ingredient but creates an effect because people receiving it expect the effect to occur. For example, researchers have found that many individuals who receive a placebo can tolerate electrical current applied to a tooth without feeling pain, as if they had been given morphine. About a third of people tested respond

In Review: Major Neurotransmitters

Neurotransmitter	Normal Function	Disorder Associated with Malfunctioning	Effects of Blocking or Enhancing Neurotransmitter
Acetylcholine	Movement, memory	Alzheimer's disease	Blocking cholinergic receptors prevents memory formation.
Norepinephrine	Sleep, learning, mood	Depression	Cocaine and some drugs used to treat depression enhance norepinephrine by blocking inactivation.
Serotonin	Mood, appetite	Depression	Some drugs used to treat depression enhance serotonin by blocking inactivation.
Dopamine	Movement, reward	Parkinson's disease, schizophrenia	Drugs used to treat schizophrenia block dopamine receptors; cocaine enhances dopamine by blocking inactivation.
GABA	Movement	Huntington's disease; epilepsy	Blocking GABA receptors causes seizures; antiepilepsy drugs enhance GABA's effects.
Glutamate	Memory	Neuron loss after stroke	Drugs that block glutamate receptors reduce brain damage after stroke.
Endorphin	Modulation of pain	No established disorder	Endorphins are blocked by naloxone and mimicked by opiates.

this way to placebos. A truly remarkable result was found when people were also given naloxone. Those who were less sensitive to pain after receiving a placebo became *more* sensitive when they were given both the placebo and naloxone (Levine, Gordon & Fields, 1979). Naloxone had reversed the placebo effect. Thus, people's *belief* that they are getting an effective drug appears to activate the endorphin system, releasing the body's own painkillers; when naloxone blocks the endorphin system, no relief occurs. Subsequent research has shown that the strength of the naloxone-reversible placebo response is correlated with a person's opinions about his or her ability to withstand pain (Bandura et al., 1987).

This work with naloxone made it clear that beliefs can have concrete effects on physiology. Recent studies suggest that attitudes can also influence the immune system. As we discuss in Chapter 13, on stress, coping, and health, researchers are attempting to ascertain under what conditions attitudes and beliefs may influence disease processes (Rodin & Salovey, 1989). ■

Blocking Inactivation   Many drugs act by interfering with the removal of a neurotransmitter. The result is an increase in the concentration of neurotransmitter remaining in a synapse and an enhancement of the normal actions of the neurotransmitter (see Figure 3.23).

Many drugs that are used to treat depression, for example, seem to work by blocking the reuptake of norepinephrine and serotonin, thus making more of these chemicals available and in turn improving mood. The mechanism by which these drugs relieve depression is not clear, however, because some drugs that block the removal of norepinephrine do not combat depression.

Endocrine Systems

Neurons are not the only cells that can communicate with one another in ways that affect behavior and mental processes. Another class of cells with this ability occurs in **endocrine systems.** The cells in these systems group together in special organs, called *endocrine glands,* which communicate, much as neurons do, by secreting chemicals. In this case, the chemicals are called

Figure 3.23
Drug Effects on Reuptake
Neurotransmitters normally remain in the synapse for only a short time; most are reabsorbed by the axons that secreted them by a process called reuptake, depicted in part (a). However, as part (b) illustrates, drugs that block the sites on the axon where reuptake occurs can temporarily stop the process, keeping the neurotransmitter in the synapse and thereby intensifying its effects. Cocaine is one drug that acts in this way.

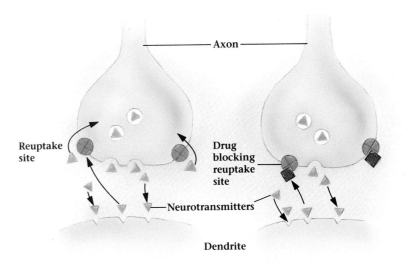

(a) **Normal reuptake**   (b) **Drug blocking reuptake**

hormones. Figure 3.24 shows the location and functions of some of the major endocrine glands.

Hormones from the endocrine organs are similar to neurotransmitters. In fact, some chemicals, such as norepinephrine and endorphin, act both as hormones and as neurotransmitters. However, whereas neurons secrete neurotransmitters into synapses, endocrine organs put their chemicals into the bloodstream, which carries them throughout the body. In this way, endocrine glands can stimulate cells with which they have no direct connection.

Not all cells receive the hormonal message. Only cells with receptors for the hormone are able to respond. These cells in target organs typically form a coordinated system. For example, when the sex hormone estrogen is secreted by a woman's ovaries, it activates her reproductive system. It causes the uterus to grow in preparation for nurturing an embryo; it enlarges the breasts to prepare them for nursing; at the same time, it stimulates the brain to enhance interest in sexual activity and the pituitary gland to release another hormone that causes a mature egg to be released by the ovary for fertilization.

Each hormone is controlled by a feedback system. This system usually has four elements: the brain, the pituitary gland, the endocrine organ, and the target organs, with the brain being one of the target organs that completes the loop. Each element in the system uses hormones to signal the next element. Our analysis of the chain of events begins with the brain:

1. The brain controls the pituitary gland by signaling the hypothalamus to release hormones that stimulate receptors of the pituitary gland. (The hypothalamus thus functions as an endocrine gland.)

Figure 3.24
Some Major Glands of the Endocrine System
Each of the glands shown releases its hormones into the bloodstream. Even the hypothalamus, a part of the brain, regulates the adjacent pituitary gland by secreting hormones. Each hormone acts on many organs, including the brain, producing coordinated effects throughout the body; for example, hormones from the adrenal gland produce the fight-or-flight syndrome.

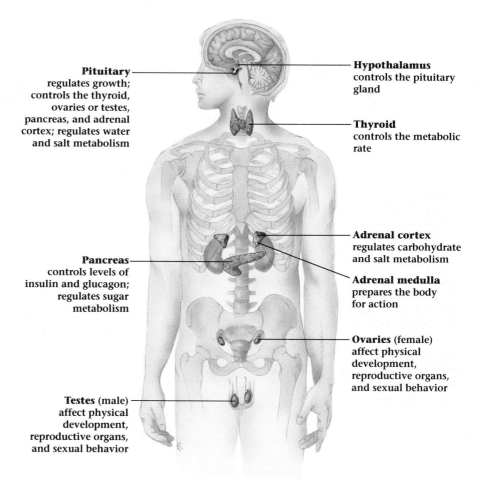

Pituitary
regulates growth; controls the thyroid, ovaries or testes, pancreas, and adrenal cortex; regulates water and salt metabolism

Hypothalamus
controls the pituitary gland

Thyroid
controls the metabolic rate

Adrenal cortex
regulates carbohydrate and salt metabolism

Adrenal medulla
prepares the body for action

Pancreas
controls levels of insulin and glucagon; regulates sugar metabolism

Ovaries (female)
affect physical development, reproductive organs, and sexual behavior

Testes (male)
affect physical development, reproductive organs, and sexual behavior

2. The pituitary gland then secretes one of its many different hormones, which stimulates another endocrine gland to secrete its hormones. For example, when the brain interprets a situation as threatening, the pituitary causes the adrenal glands to release the hormone cortisol into the bloodstream. Adrenaline is also released by the adrenal gland, but the nervous system directly controls its release.

3. These hormones in turn act on cells in the body. In the case of the adrenal hormones, the result is a set of responses called the **fight-or-flight syndrome**, which prepares the animal or person for action in response to danger: the heart beats faster, the liver releases glucose into the bloodstream, fuels are mobilized from fat stores, and the organism is generally placed in a state of high arousal.

4. Feedback regarding the hormones is sent to the brain and the pituitary gland. Just as a thermostat and furnace regulate heat, this feedback system regulates hormone secretion within a certain range. If the output of the final gland in the sequence falls below some level, feedback causes the brain and pituitary to stimulate increased secretion. When the hormone rises above a certain level, feedback signals the brain and pituitary to stop stimulating its secretion.

As another example of the effect of hormones, consider the male sex hormones, the androgens. Pituitary hormones cause the male sex organs to secrete androgens, increase a male's motivation for sexual activity, stimulate the maturation of sperm (Davidson, Camargo & Smith, 1979), and increase males' aggressiveness. (The relationship between androgens and aggressiveness in humans is complicated and controversial; we discuss it again in Chapter 18.) Androgens also have muscle-mass enhancing (*anabolic*) effects, which are responsible for the abuse of synthetic androgens, called *anabolic steroids*. The dangers of synthetic anabolic steroids are many, including liver damage, increased risk of cancer, and sterility. Excessive doses may also be related to increased aggressiveness, extreme mood swings, and bizarre symptoms of severe mental disorder (Pope & Katz, 1988). Unfortunately, researchers have not yet determined whether the steroids are actually causing these behavioral changes. It may be that steroids tend to be taken by individuals already prone to aggressiveness, emotional instability, and other problems.

The relationship among hormones, the brain, and behavior is complex. As illustrated by the feedback systems we have described, the brain has ultimate control over the secretion of hormones, and hormones in turn modify brain function and behavior. The secretion of almost all hormones is also affected by psychological processes such as stress.

T H I N K I N G   C R I T I C A L L Y

Is PMS a Hormonal Problem?

When people are in a bad mood or irritable, they and other people around them look for a cause. If an easily identifiable physiological change has occurred, they may attribute the change in mood to a biological cause. So when women experience negative moods before the onset of their menstrual period, they or others may attribute the negative moods to this biological event. However, too readily attributing a negative consequence to a biological process that is experienced by a whole class of individuals may foster false stereotypes. So the issue of menstrually related mood changes must be carefully evaluated.

What am I being asked to believe or accept?

During the menstrual cycle, estrogen levels in blood increase, then progesterone increases, and then both hormones drop before menstruation. These fluctuations of sex hormones could conceivably be responsible for **premenstrual syndrome (PMS)**, a monthly experience of depressed mood and irritability in some women. The assertion is that PMS is a biological problem caused by hormones.

What evidence is available to support the assertion?

There is some evidence that female sex hormones can affect mood. In one study women who had their ovaries removed for medical reasons (thus eliminating the natural source of estrogen) were given estrogen or a placebo. The women receiving estrogen showed a more positive mood than those who received a placebo (Sherwin, 1988).

PMS is more than the absence of positive mood, however. Is there something abnormal about hormone levels in PMS sufferers that might cause negative moods? Some studies have found either high or low levels of estrogen or progesterone in PMS sufferers relative to non-PMS women (Backstrom & Carstensen, 1974; Halbreich et al., 1986; Hammarback et al., 1989). Other studies have found no such difference (Rubinow et al., 1988; Smith, 1975).

Another proposed biological explanation of PMS suggests that the levels of sex hormones in PMS women are normal but that they respond to the hormones abnormally. For example, sex hormones affect endorphins, and one study found that PMS women have an unusual reduction in blood endorphins before menstruation (Facchinetti et al., 1987). Studies with animals show that sex hormones affect a number of neurotransmitter systems in the brain, such as serotonin and GABA (Majewska et al., 1986; Wilson, Dwyer & Roy, 1989), but relating this information to human PMS will be difficult, because the neurotransmitters are not easily measured in living humans.

Other evidence is based on the idea that if PMS results from hormonal deficiencies, it should respond to estrogen or progesterone supplements. In one study of estrogen and PMS, estrogen treatment produced more long-lasting improvement than did a placebo (Magos, Brincat & Shedd, 1986). Some placebo-controlled studies have also found progesterone to be beneficial (Dennerstein et al., 1985). But the improvement could be related to the sedative properties of progesterone and does not necessarily imply that progesterone deficiency caused the original symptoms.

Are there alternative ways of interpreting the evidence?

Some people argue that the results of hormonal research on PMS are confusing because PMS is an illusion that both reflects and fosters the societal belief that women are unstable. The symptoms labeled as PMS could reflect the internalization of cultural expectations. For American women these expectations reflect a lifetime of hearing that menstruation is a difficult time. One experiment found that women who are misled into believing that they are at the premenstrual point in their cycle (when they are actually in the middle of their cycle) report increased negative feelings (Ruble, 1977). Additional evidence for the view that premenstrual mood changes reflect cultural expectations comes from cross-cultural research showing that women in some societies are unfamiliar with the symptoms of PMS (Gottlieb, 1988).

How is it possible that women who believe that their emotions change with the menstrual cycle could be wrong? People can be biased when they recall their feelings. In one study women kept daily ratings of their feelings;

later, some of the women were asked to recall the ratings that they made when they were menstruating. To the extent that the women believed PMS to be real, their recall exaggerated their negative symptoms during their last period. Their memories were consistent with their theories about PMS, but not with their own ratings of daily feelings (McFarland, Ross & DeCourville, 1989). Interestingly, these daily ratings of emotional experiences did not vary with the women's menstrual cycle. Thus, they could continue to have the theory of PMS in the absence of an actual increase in negative symptoms, because their memories of previous menstrual periods remained biased. This study demonstrates how a cultural myth can be maintained in the absence of substantiating experience.

However, the fact that the women in the study failed to describe menstrually related negative experiences in their diaries is at variance with some studies of women who seek help for PMS (Rubinow & Roy-Byrne, 1984). In other words, it might explain how women without PMS mistakenly think that they experience mood cycles, but it does not mean that the symptoms of women with PMS verified by daily ratings can be explained in the same way.

What additional evidence would help to evaluate the alternatives?

Many studies on PMS have been conducted, but the number of well-controlled studies is quite small. More studies that use daily descriptions of symptoms and consistent definitions of the syndrome may help to clarify the syndrome. The American Psychiatric Association included the disorder in its diagnostic manual (DSM-III-R; APA, 1987), in an appendix titled "Proposed Diagnostic Categories Needing Further Study." The disorder was termed *late luteal phase dysphoric disorder* (LLPDD) rather than premenstrual syndrome. Symptoms that are consistent with the diagnosis of LLPDD include sudden changes in mood, irritability, anxiety or tension, depression, fatigue, and food cravings.

The inclusion of LLPDD in the manual was a matter of much debate and was opposed by the American Psychiatric Association's Committee on Women. However, the committee that proposed the inclusion of the disorder, which included a majority of women, argued that many women are already being treated for "PMS" and that research on PMS cannot be accomplished until consistent diagnostic criteria are applied. Responding to criticisms that LLPDD reinforces myths about hormones and women's emotionality, the committee noted that recognizing LLPDD as a disorder implies that the vast majority of women do *not* have mood disturbances in relation to the menstrual cycle (Spitzer et al., 1989).

More studies also need to be conducted on possible nonbiological causes of PMS, including those derived from principles of social psychology that reveal how people attribute causes to other people's behavior (see Chapter 17). For example, a person's irritability is more likely to be attributed to biological causes if the observer thinks the person is a premenstrual woman, rather than a male or a nonpremenstrual woman (Koeske, 1987). There may also be very subtle changes caused by hormones, such as an increase in arousability, that interact with cultural beliefs about the menstrual cycle and, together, determine mood. Thus, the hormonal effects may not be inherently negative (Koeske, 1987).

What conclusions are most reasonable?

At this point, no conclusions about a biological cause of PMS are warranted. As with most controversies about biological versus environmental determinants of behavior, the issues are complex and will be resolved only after much careful study. ▪

Linkages: Biological Psychology and Human Development

How does the brain change throughout life, and how do these changes affect people?

We have described in this chapter how certain pathological changes in the brain produce severe disorders, such as Parkinson's disease and Alzheimer's disease. But even in the absence of disease, the brain changes throughout life. What are these changes, and what are their effects? How are they related to developments in sensory and motor capabilities, mental ability, and other characteristics that we described in Chapter 2?

PET scans are one technique that researchers have used to begin to answer these questions. They have uncovered some interesting correlations between changes in neural activity and the behavior of human newborns and young infants. Among newborns, activity is relatively high in the thalamus but low in the striatum. This pattern may be related to the way newborns move: they make nonpurposeful, sweeping movements of the arms and legs, much like patients with Huntington's disease, who have a hyperactive thalamus and a degenerated striatum (Chugani & Phelps, 1986). During the second and third months of life, activity increases in many regions of the cortex, a change that is correlated with the loss of subcortically controlled reflexes such as the grasping reflex. When infants are around eight or nine months old, activity in the frontal cortex increases, a development that correlates well with the apparent beginnings of cognitive activity in infants (Chugani & Phelps, 1986).

These changes do not reflect the appearance of new cells: essentially all the neurons the brain will ever have are present at birth. What does increase after birth is the number of dendrites and synapses. In one area of the cortex the number of synapses increases tenfold from birth to twelve months of age (Huttenlocher, 1979). In fact, by the time children are six or seven years old, their brains have more dendrites and use twice as much metabolic fuel as those of adults (Chugani & Phelps, 1986; Huttenlocher, 1979). In early adolescence, there is actually a reduction in the number of dendrites and neural connections, so that the adult level is reached by about the age of fourteen (see Figure 3.25).

Figure 3.25
Changes in Neurons of the Cerebral Cortex During Development
Neurons generate an overabundance of dendrites during childhood. During adolescence, extra dendrites are "pruned" until they reach a level characteristic of the adult.

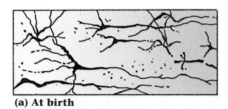

(a) At birth

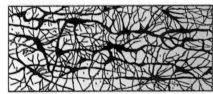

(b) Six years old

(c) Fourteen years old

This general pattern is found not only in humans but in all animals: the brain overproduces neural connections, establishes the usefulness of certain connections, and then "prunes" the extra connections (Cowan, 1979). Thus, we cannot determine mental ability simply by counting the number of dendrites and synapses. One possible explanation for this overproduction is that when there are many neural connections, development can take many paths. Overproduction of synapses, especially in the frontal cortex, may be essential for infants to develop certain intellectual abilities (Goldman-Rakic, 1987). Surgically produced lesions of an adult monkey cortex cause the monkey to revert to infant-level performance on some tasks. Some scientists believe that the pruning of connections may reflect a process whereby those connections that are used survive, while others die.

Even as dendrites are pruned, the brain retains the ability to "rewire" itself—to form new connections—throughout life. The genes apparently determine the basic pattern of growth and the major lines of connections, the "highways" of the brain and its general architecture. The details seem to depend on extragenetic factors such as the complexity and interest of the environment. For example, researchers have compared the brains of rats raised in individual cages with only a boring view of the side of the cage (and no intellectually stimulating reading material) and the brains of rats raised with interesting toys and stimulating playmates. The cerebral cortex of those from the enriched environment had more and longer dendrites and more synapses than the cortex of animals from barren, individual housing (Turner & Greenough, 1985; Volkmar & Greenough, 1972). Furthermore, the number of cortical synapses increased when old animals who had always lived in boring individual cages were moved to an enriched environment (Green, Greenough & Schlumpf, 1983). Researchers have not yet determined whether an enriched environment stimulates the development of new connections or slows down normal pruning; it is also not known whether animals will lose synaptic complexity if they are moved from an enriched to a barren environment.

In any event, this line of research highlights the interaction of environmental and genetic factors. Within constraints set by genetics, interactions with the world appear to mold the brain itself. Some of the overproduced synapses may reflect genetically directed preparation for certain types of experiences. Generation of these synapses is an "experience-expectant" process, and accounts for sensitive periods during development when certain things can be most easily learned. Overproduction of synapses also occurs in response to totally new experiences; this process is "experience dependent" (Greenough, Black & Wallace, 1987). To the extent that these ideas and research findings apply to humans, they hold obvious implications for how people raise children and treat the elderly. These findings may someday help explain why, as discussed in Chapter 2, children raised in stimulating environments tend to show faster and more extensive cognitive development that those from barren backgrounds.

Future Directions

Today, information about the brain is increasing at an explosive rate as people from many disciplines apply their techniques to the study of the nervous system. Medical researchers, biochemists, physiologists, and psychologists are all beginning to see themselves as neuroscientists.

Technical breakthroughs have allowed an enormous amount of information to be gathered in a short time. PET scans, MRI, techniques from molecular biology, and advances in computer technology have been invaluable in efforts to understand the biological bases of behavior. New techniques, such as monitoring the brain's magnetic fields (Hari & Lounasmaa, 1989), will allow more rapid, more detailed, monitoring of brain activity.

Some of the most exciting work in coming years is likely to focus on biological factors in diseases. Scientists may soon be able to answer confidently questions such as: What specific biological processes occur in Alzheimer's disease and schizophrenia? Can genetic differences be used to predict who is susceptible to alcoholism or other disorders (Blum et al., 1990)? Better ways of treating or even preventing many disorders may well be found. Research on gene therapy for some genetic disorders such as Alzheimer's disease is progressing, with the possibility of new genes being inserted into brain cells by virus carriers (Friedmann, 1989). Some degenerative diseases might be reversed by aiding the body's own restorative powers.

There are also exciting new developments that show that the inevitable progressive degeneration in some diseases can be greatly slowed by drug treatments. In the case of Parkinson's disease, the clues came from drug addicts: a chemistry graduate student who was synthesizing his own heroinlike compounds made one with a contaminant that caused the substantia nigra to degenerate. A number of drug users developed Parkinson's disease in their early twenties, normally a very rare occurrence. Researchers isolated the contaminant and found it caused Parkinson's symptoms in animals. They then discovered that the contaminant was only active when it was converted to a toxic metabolite; drugs that blocked the conversion prevented the Parkinson's symptoms in animals. Recent trials show that the same drug slows the progression of Parkinson's disease in humans (Tetrud & Langston, 1989). Interestingly, when the drug is given to normal rats, it dramatically extends their life span, suggesting that the drug may more generally slow the aging process (Knoll, Dallo & Yen, 1989).

The future also holds greater understanding of biological aspects of cognitive functions, such as learning and memory. The ways that complex neural networks allow the brain to solve complicated problems will be unraveled, and the principles derived will allow computers to enter human domains such as the understanding of language. Already some "neural network" computers have been taught some spoken language. In learning the language, the computers went through babbling and other stages similar to those found in the development of normal human language (Sejnowski & Rosenberg, 1987).

The larger question of how the functioning of the nervous system translates into what people experience as mind will be more difficult to answer. How do all the details fit together? More information than any individual can master is being generated about such questions. It will take some great minds, probably working with great computers, to synthesize this information into a vision of how the brain generates experience and behavior.

If you are interested in taking part in this collective adventure, either as a participant scientist or as an informed spectator, you can prepare yourself by learning more about both physical and psychological sciences. Relevant courses offered by psychology departments include physiological psychology, sensation and perception, learning and memory, motivation and emotion, abnormal psychology, and drugs and behavior. Courses in chemistry, physiology, anatomy, and computer science are also relevant. Studying the relationships between body and mind is an interdisciplinary adventure, so having a broad background will help you greatly.

Summary and Key Terms

The Nervous System: An Overview

The *nervous system* allows an organism to take in information from the environment, integrate the information with previous experiences, and act. The major parts of the nervous system are the *central nervous system* (*CNS*), which consists of the spinal cord and the brain, and the *peripheral nervous system*, which consists of the *somatic nervous system* (sensory and motor nerves) and the *autonomic nervous system*, or *ANS* (sympathetic and parasympathetic divisions).

Other Key Terms in This Section: biological psychology, sensory systems, motor systems.

Communication in the Nervous System

The fundamental units of the nervous system are cells called *neurons*. Signals in the nervous system are transmitted from one end of a neuron to the other end and from one neuron to another.

Neurons: The Basic Units of the Nervous System

Characteristics of the neurons that permit them to transmit signals include their structure of fibers, the excitable surface of some of these fibers, and the *synapses*, or gaps, between cells.

Neurons have cell bodies and two types of fibers, called *axons* and *dendrites*. Axons carry signals away from the cell body; dendrites carry signals to the cell body. The selectively permeable membrane of neurons normally keeps the distribution of electrically charged molecules uneven between the inside of cells and the outside, creating an electrical force called a *potential*. The membrane surface of the axon can transmit a disturbance in this potential, called an *action potential,* from one end of the axon to the other. When an action potential reaches the end of an axon, the axon releases a chemical called a *neurotransmitter.* It crosses the synapse and interacts with the postsynaptic cell, creating a *postsynaptic potential* that makes the postsynaptic cell more or less likely to fire an action potential. Thus, communication within a neuron is electrical, whereas communication between neurons is chemical. Because the fibers of neurons have many branches, each neuron can interact with thousands of other neurons.

Interactions Between Neurons

Neurotransmitters stimulate postsynaptic cells only at special sites called *receptors*. This interaction creates a signal that can make the postsynaptic cell either more or less likely to fire its action potential. Each neuron constantly integrates signals received at its many synapses; the result of this integration determines how often the neuron will fire an action potential.

Other Key Terms in This Section: myelin, refractory period, postsynaptic potential.

The Central Nervous System: Organization and Functions

Neurons are organized in networks of reciprocally connected cells. A group of neuron cell bodies is called a *nucleus*. A collection of axons is a *fiber tract* or *pathway.*

Relating Structure to Function

Researchers monitor brain activity and attempt to relate brain activity to behavior using single-unit recording, electrical stimulation, *EEGs, PET scans,* and *MRI.*

The Spinal Cord

The *spinal cord* receives information from the peripheral senses and sends it to the brain; it also relays messages from the brain to the periphery. Within the spinal cord and throughout the central nervous system, opposing actions are coordinated; complex behaviors can be built up from simple components, such as *reflexes*; and *feedback systems* adjust output.

The Brain

The brain's major subdivisions are the *hindbrain, midbrain,* and *forebrain.* The hindbrain includes the *medulla* and *cerebellum.* The midbrain includes the *substantia nigra.* The *reticular formation* is found in both the hindbrain and midbrain. The forebrain is the largest and most highly developed part of the brain; it includes the *cerebrum* and *diencephalon.* The outer surface of the *cerebral hemispheres* is called the *cerebral cortex.* Deeper structures include the *striatum* and *hippocampus.* The diencephalon includes the *hypothalamus* and *thalamus.* Several of these structures form the *limbic system.*

The Cerebral Cortex

The cerebral cortex is responsible for much of the higher functions of the brain, such as speech and reasoning. The functional areas of the cortex consist of *sensory cortex, motor cortex,* and *association cortex.* Specific functions, such as language production and comprehension, are coordinated by particular regions within these areas.

The Divided Brain in a Unified Self

The right and left cerebral hemispheres of the cerebral cortex are specialized to some degree in their functions. In most people, the left hemisphere is more active in linguistic and logical tasks; the right hemisphere in spatial, musical, and artistic tasks. The hemispheres are connected through the *corpus callosum*, allowing them to operate in a coordinated fashion.

Other Key Terms in This Section: homeostasis, lateralized.

The Chemistry of Psychology

Neurons that use the same neurotransmitter form a *neurotransmitter system.*

Seven Major Neurotransmitters

Acetylcholine systems in the brain influence memory processes and movement. *Norepinephrine* is released by a small number of neurons with axons that spread widely throughout the brain; it is involved in arousal, mood, and learning. *Serotonin* is another pervasive neurotransmitter; it is active in systems regulating mood, attention, and appetite. *Dopamine* systems are involved in movement and higher cognitive activities; Parkinson's disease and schizophrenia both involve a disturbance of dopaminergic function. *GABA* is an inhibitory neurotransmitter involved in anxiety and epilepsy. *Glutamate* is the most common excitatory neurotransmitter; it is involved in learning and, in excess, may cause neuronal death. *Endorphins* are peptide neurotransmitters that modulate pain pathways.

Drugs, Neurotransmitters, and Behavior

Many *psychoactive drugs* affect behavior and mental processes by altering neurotransmission, especially by competing for neurotransmitter receptors as either *receptor agonists* or *receptor antagonists*. Because neurotransmitter systems adjust to pharmacological influences, the long-term responses to continuing drug treatments are difficult to predict.

Other Key Term in This Section: *psychopharmacology.*

Endocrine Systems

Like nervous system cells, cells of the *endocrine system* communicate by releasing a chemical that is a signal to other cells. However, the chemicals of the endocrine system, called *hormones*, are carried by the bloodstream to remote target organs. Feedback processes are involved in the control of most endocrine systems. The brain is the main controller: through the hypothalamus, it controls the pituitary gland, which in turn controls endocrine organs in the body. The brain is also a target organ for most endocrine systems. The target organs often produce a coordinated response to hormonal stimulation. One of these is the *fight-or-flight syndrome*, which is set off by adrenal hormones that prepare for action in times of stress.

O U T L I N E

Sensation

A recurring controversy in tabloids across the country poses a rather bizarre question: is Elvis Presley really dead? The controversy has been fueled by people who say they have seen him alive and well and, in one case, ordering lunch at a Burger King in Michigan. Similarly, many of the staunchest believers in flying saucers base their claims on what they have seen with their own eyes. There are also some mentally disturbed people who hear voices that tell them to hurt other people. To these individuals, a living Elvis, an alien spacecraft, or an evil voice are as real as anything they sense. Should they trust their eyes and ears to report reality?

What, exactly, *is* reality? The seventeenth-century British philosopher John Locke held that people can gain knowledge about the reality of the outside world *only* through the senses. The senses, however, do not simply mirror the world outside. They actively shape information about the outside world, rather than passively receiving unedited reports about an objective reality. The senses of each individual help to create his or her own reality, which may or may not always be in synchrony with that of others.

A **sense** is a system that translates information from outside the nervous system into neural activity. For example, vision is the system through which the eyes convert light into neural activity. This neural activity tells the brain something about the source of the light (for example, that it is bright) or about objects from which it is reflected (for example, that a round, red object is out there). These messages from the senses are called **sensations.** Since they provide the link between the self and the world outside the brain, sensations help shape many kinds of behavior and mental processes (see the Linkages diagram).

Traditionally, psychologists have distinguished between sensation—the initial message from the senses—and *perception,* which is an interpreted message from the senses, a message that has been given meaning in terms of previous experiences. Thus, you do not actually "sense" a cat lying on the sofa; you see shapes and colors—visual sensations. Because of your knowledge of the world, you

LINKAGES

Sensation

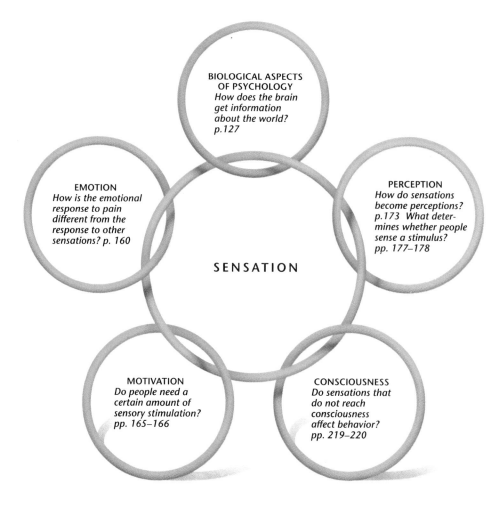

BIOLOGICAL ASPECTS
OF PSYCHOLOGY
*How does the brain
get information
about the world?
p.127*

PERCEPTION
*How do sensations
become perceptions?
p.173 What deter-
mines whether people
sense a stimulus?
pp. 177–178*

EMOTION
*How is the emotional
response to pain
different from the
response to other
sensations? p. 160*

SENSATION

MOTIVATION
*Do people need a
certain amount of
sensory stimulation?
pp. 165–166*

CONSCIOUSNESS
*Do sensations that
do not reach
consciousness
affect behavior?
pp. 219–220*

■ Look at the diagram above, which illustrates some of the relationships between the topic of this chapter, sensation, and other chapter topics. Consider pain. In Chapter 3 we described chemicals in the brain that can relieve pain; in this chapter we examine how information about pain reaches your brain in the first place. To do so, we discuss many of the structures introduced in Chapter 3, but our focus now is on the senses, which put people in touch with the reality of the world beyond the brain.

What happens if people are denied this contact, if they are deprived of stimulation from the senses? Research into this question ties the study of sensation to motivation and personality, because people differ in how they react to sensory stimulation, and these differences affect what people are motivated to do. The page numbers in the diagram indicate where this and other linkages are discussed; we repeat each Linkage question in the margin next to where it is discussed in the text. But keep in mind that the diagram shows only a sampling of the linkages between sensation and other aspects of psychology. ■

interpret, or perceive, these sensations as a cat (or Elvis). However, recent research has made it more difficult to draw a clear line between sensation and perception. That research shows that the process of interpreting sensations begins in the sense organs themselves and continues into the brain. Even previous experience can shape what you sense, causing you not to notice, for example, the familiar chiming of the living room clock, but leaving you sensitive to the slightest sound when you walk down a dark alley at midnight.

In this chapter we cover the first steps of the sensation-perception process, examining the ways in which the senses pick up information and convert it into forms the brain can use. In the next chapter we will discuss the later phases of the sensation-perception process, along with *psychophysics,* the laws that govern how physical energy is converted into psychological experience. Together, these chapters illustrate how human beings create, with the sense organs and the brain, their own worlds and their own realities.

Sensory Systems

Linkages: How does the brain get information about the world? (a link to Biological Aspects of Psychology)

The senses gather information about the world by detecting various forms of *energy,* such as sound, light, heat, and physical pressure. For example, the eyes detect light energy, the ears detect the energy of sound, and the skin detects the energy of heat and pressure. Humans depend primarily on vision, hearing, and the skin senses to gain information about the world; they depend less than other animals on smell and taste. There are also senses that provide information to the brain from the rest of the body. All of these senses must detect stimuli, encode them into neural activity, and transfer this coded information to the brain.

Steps in Sensation

Figure 4.1 illustrates the basic steps in sensation. At each step, sensory information is processed in some way: the information that arrives at one point in the system is not the same as the information that goes to the next step.

In some sensory systems, the first step in sensation involves **accessory structures,** which modify the stimulus. The lens of the eye is an accessory structure that changes incoming light by focusing it; the outer part of the ear is an accessory structure that collects sound.

The second step in sensation is **transduction,** which is the process of converting incoming energy into neural activity. Just as a radio receives energy and transduces it into sounds, the ears receive sound energy and transduce it into neural activity that people recognize as voices, music, and other auditory experiences. Transduction takes place at structures called **receptors,** cells that are specialized to detect certain forms of energy. These sensory receptors are distinct from neurotransmitter receptors, which were discussed in Chapter 3, but both types of receptors translate one kind of signal into a different kind of signal. Sensory receptors respond best to *changes* in energy. A constant level of stimulation usually produces **adaptation,** a process through which responsiveness to an unchanging stimulus decreases over time.

Next, the output from receptors is transferred to the brain via sensory nerves. For all the senses but smell, the information is taken first to the thalamus, which relays it to the cerebral cortex. It is in the cortex that the most complex processing occurs, and sensation becomes perception.

Figure 4.1
Elements of a Sensory System
Sensory systems have many features in common. Objects generate energy that is focused by accessory structures and detected by sensory receptors, which convert the energy into neural signals. As the signals are transferred through parts of the brain, information is extracted and analyzed. In the cerebral cortex, the information is further analyzed and compared with sensory experiences stored in memory.

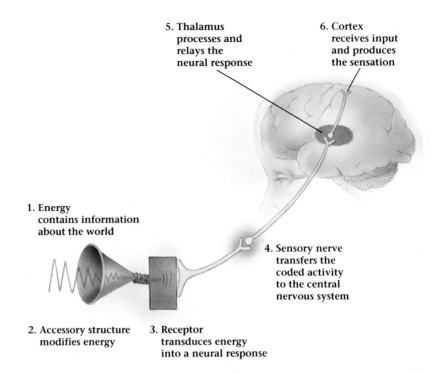

5. Thalamus processes and relays the neural response

6. Cortex receives input and produces the sensation

1. Energy contains information about the world

4. Sensory nerve transfers the coded activity to the central nervous system

2. Accessory structure modifies energy

3. Receptor transduces energy into a neural response

The Problem of Coding

When receptors transduce energy, they must somehow code the physical properties of the stimulus into firing patterns that, when organized by the brain, allow you to make sense of the stimulus—to tell, for example, whether you are looking at a dog or a cat. Each psychological dimension of a sensation, such as the brightness or color of light, must have a corresponding physical dimension that is coded by sensory receptors.

As a way of thinking about the problem of coding, suppose that, for your birthday, you are given a Pet Brain, a new product inspired by the people who brought us Pet Rocks and Teenage Mutant Ninja Turtles. Your Pet Brain is definitely alive (the guarantee says so), but it does not seem to respond when you talk to it. You show it an ice cream sundae; no response. You show it pictures of other highly attractive brains; no response. You are about to deposit your Pet Brain in the garbage disposal when you suddenly realize that you two are not talking the same language. You should be buzzing the brain's sensory nerves to send it messages and recording from its motor nerves to discern its responses.

After having this brilliant insight and setting up a little electric stimulator, you are faced with an even more awesome problem. How do you describe a hot-fudge sundae in terms of action potentials? This is the problem of coding. **Coding** is the translation of the physical properties of a stimulus into a pattern of neural activity that specifically identifies those physical properties.

Now you realize that if you want the brain to see the sundae, you should probably stimulate its optic nerve (the nerve from the eye to the brain) rather than its auditory nerve (the nerve from the ear to the brain). This idea is based on the doctrine of **specific nerve energies:** stimulation of a particular sensory nerve provides codes for that one sense, no matter how the stimulation takes place. For example, if you apply gentle pressure to your eyeball, you will produce activity in the optic nerve and sense little spots of light. Similarly, electrical stimulation of the optic nerve is coded and sensed as light.

Having chosen the optic nerve to convey visual information, you must next code the specific attributes of the sundae stimulus: the soft white curves of the vanilla ice cream, the dark richness of the chocolate, the bright redness of the cherry on top. These dimensions must be coded in the language of neural activity. As described in the previous chapter, this language is made up of membrane potentials in dendrites and cell bodies and action potentials in axons.

Some attributes of a stimulus are coded fairly simply. For example, stimulus intensity is often coded by a neuron's rate of firing. A bright light will cause some neurons in the visual system to fire faster than will a dim light. But the codes can also be very complex, and information can be recoded at each of several relay points as it makes its way through the brain. Sensory psychologists are still working on deciphering the codes that the brain uses; your Pet Brain may have to wait a while to appreciate the beauty of that sundae.

Representing Stimuli

As sensory systems transfer information to the brain, they also organize that information. This organized information is called a *representation*. If you have read Chapter 3, you are already familiar with some characteristics of sensory representations. In humans, representations of vision, hearing, and the skin senses in the cerebral cortex share the following features:

1. The information from each of these senses reaches the cortex via the thalamus. (Figure 3.16 shows where these areas of the brain are.)
2. The representation of the sensory world in the cortex is *contralateral* to the part of the world being sensed. For example, the left side of the primary visual cortex "sees" the right side of the world, and the right side of the somatosensory cortex "feels" the left side of the body. This happens because nerve fibers from each side of the body cross on their way to the thalamus.
3. The cortex contains maps, or **topographical representations,** of each sense. This means that any two points that are next to each other in the stimulus are represented next to each other in the brain. There are multiple maps of each sense, but the area that receives the input directly from the thalamus is called the **primary cortex** for that sense.
4. The density of nerve fibers at any particular part of a sense organ determines the extent of its representation in the cortex. For example, the fingertips, which have a higher density of receptors for touch than the skin on the back does, have a larger area of cortex representing them than does the skin on the back.
5. Each region of primary sensory cortex is divided into columns of cells that have similar properties. For example, some columns of cells in the visual cortex respond most to diagonal lines; other columns respond most to edges.
6. For each of the senses, regions of cortex other than the primary areas do more complex processing of sensory information. Called **association cortex,** some of these areas contain representations of more than one sense; others provide additional representations for a given sense.

In short, sensory systems convert some form of energy into neural activity. Often the energy is first modified by accessory structures; then a sensory receptor converts the energy to neural activity. The pattern of neural activity encodes physical properties of the energy. The codes are modified as the information is transferred to the brain and processed further. In the rest of this chapter we describe these processes in specific sensory systems.

Hearing

When Neil Armstrong stepped onto the moon in 1969, he proclaimed, ''That's one small step for a man, one giant leap for mankind.'' Many people heard him because the words were transferred back to earth by radio. But if Armstrong had taken off his space helmet, thrown it high over his head, and shouted, ''Whoo-ee! I can moonwalk!'' not even an astronaut three feet away could have heard him. Why? Because he would have been speaking into airless, empty space. **Sound** is a repetitive fluctuation in the pressure of a medium like air, and it cannot exist in a place like the moon, which has almost no atmosphere.

Sound

The fluctuations in pressure that constitute sound are produced by the vibrations of an object. Each time the object moves outward, it increases the pressure in the medium around it. As the object moves back, the pressure drops. In speech, for example, the vibrating object is the vocal cord, and the medium is air. When you speak, your vocal cords vibrate, producing fluctuations in air pressure that spread as waves. A *wave* is a repetitive variation in pressure that spreads out in three dimensions. The wave can move great distances, but the air itself barely moves. Imagine a jam-packed line of people waiting for a movie. If someone at the rear of the line violently shoves the next person, a wave of people jostling against people may spread all the way to the front of the line, but the person who shoved first is still no closer to getting into the theater.

The Physical Characteristics of Sound Sound is represented graphically by **waveforms** like those in Figure 4.2. A waveform represents in two dimensions the wave that moves through the air in three dimensions.

Three characteristics of the waveform are important in understanding sounds. First, the difference in the air pressure from the baseline to the peak of the waveform is the **amplitude** of the sound. Second, the distance from one peak

Figure 4.2
Sound Waves and Waveforms
The molecules of air around a sound source are unevenly distributed. Regions of greater compression of air molecules alternate with regions of lesser compression because of the to-and-fro vibrations of the object generating the sound. These variations in compression can be represented as a *waveform.* The point where the air is compressed the most is the peak of the graph. The lowest point, or trough, is where the air pressure is lowest.

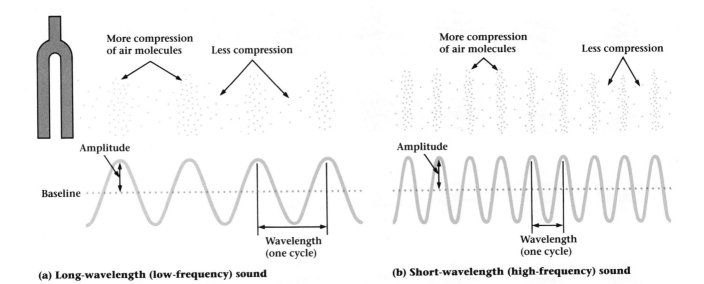

(a) Long-wavelength (low-frequency) sound   **(b) Short-wavelength (high-frequency) sound**

A musical synthesizer can produce the sounds of different instruments—say a piano and a trumpet—by combining sine waves in various ways. The auditory system takes the opposite approach: it can analyze the mixture that makes up a sound into its component sine waves.

to the next is the **wavelength.** Third, **frequency** is the number of complete waves, or cycles, that pass by a given point in space every second. Frequency is described in a unit called *hertz,* abbreviated Hz (for Heinrich Hertz, a nineteenth-century physicist who studied energy waves). One cycle per second is 1 hertz. Because the speed of sound is constant in a given medium, frequency and wavelength are inversely related; that is, the longer the wavelength, the lower the frequency. Likewise, high-frequency sound is short-wavelength sound.

Most sounds are mixtures of many frequencies and amplitudes. In contrast, a *pure tone* is made up of only one frequency and can be represented by what is known in mathematics as a *sine wave.* The waveforms in Figure 4.2 are sine waves; each has just one frequency. A complex sound can be analyzed into its component, simple sine waves by a mathematical process called *Fourier analysis.* This technique can be used to eliminate noises that are regular, like engine noises: after the waveforms are analyzed, a sound synthesizer produces the *opposite* waveforms. The opposing waves cancel each other out, and the amazing result is silence.

Psychological Dimensions of Sound   The frequency and amplitude of sound waves determine the sounds that you hear. These *physical* characteristics of the waves produce the *psychological* dimensions of sound known as pitch, loudness, and timbre.

Pitch—how high or low a tone sounds—depends on the frequency of sound waves. High-frequency waves are sensed as sounds of high pitch. The highest note on a piano has a frequency of about 4,000 hertz; the lowest note has a frequency of about 50 hertz. Humans can hear sounds from about 20 hertz to about 20,000 hertz.

Loudness is determined by the amplitude of the sound wave; waves with greater amplitude produce sensations of louder sounds. Loudness is described in units called *decibels,* abbreviated dB. By definition, 0 decibels is the minimal detectable sound for normal hearing. Table 4.1 gives examples of the loudness of some common sounds.

Timbre is the quality of sound; it is determined by complex wave patterns that are added on to the lowest, or *fundamental,* frequency of a sound. The extra waves allow you to tell, for example, the difference between a middle C

Table 4.1
Intensity of Sound Sources

Because sound intensity varies across an extremely wide range, an unusual scale is used to describe it. A barely audible sound is, by definition, 0 decibels; every increase of 20 decibels reflects a tenfold multiplication of the amplitude of the sound waves. Thus at 20 decibels a whisper is 10 times as intense as a barely audible sound, and the noise of a subway train (100 decibels) is 10,000 times as intense as a whisper.

Source	Sound Level (dB)
Spacecraft launch (from 45 m)	180
Loudest rock band on record	160
Pain threshold (approximate)	140
Large jet motor (at 22 m)	120
Loudest human shout on record	111
Heavy auto traffic	100
Conversation (at about 1 m)	60
Quiet office	40
Soft whisper	20
Threshold of hearing	0

Source: Levine & Shefner, 1981.

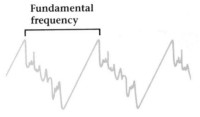

(a) One note played on a piano

(b) Explosion (noise)

Source: (Part b) Boring et al., 1948.

Figure 4.3
Timbre
Because most sounds are not pure tones, they have complex waveforms. Even when a single note is played, musical instruments produce complex waveforms. Part (a) shows the waveform produced by one note played on a piano, C below middle C. The fundamental frequency is 130 hertz; multiples of this fundamental frequency determine the sound's timbre. Because the components of this complex wave have a systematic relationship to the fundamental frequency, the sound is musical. Part (b) shows the waveform produced by an explosion. Explosions are normally considered noise rather than music, because their waveforms are very irregular.

played on the piano and a middle C played on a trumpet. Figure 4.3(a) shows that a musical note played on a piano has one fundamental frequency as well as other added waves; the other waves give the tone its timbre. Because the added waves are multiples of the fundamental frequency of the note, the sound is musical. In contrast, the component waves of a noise do not have a systematic relationship, as Figure 4.3(b) illustrates; a *noise* is a sum of unrelated waveforms.

The Ear

Sharks can ''hear'' underwater sounds through simple nerve endings in their skin. Their ''hearing'' is good enough to get by in the sea, but hardly adequate to appreciate Mozart or the Rolling Stones. By contrast, humans have very sophisticated ears that detect sounds with great sensitivity and precision. The ear converts sound into neural activity through its accessory structures and a fascinating series of transduction mechanisms.

Auditory Accessory Structures   Sound waves are collected in the outer ear, beginning with the **pinna**, the crumpled, oddly shaped part of the ear on the side of the head. The pinna funnels sound down through the ear canal (see Figure 4.4). At the end of the ear canal, the sound waves reach the middle ear, where they strike a tightly stretched membrane known as the eardrum, or **tympanic membrane.** The sound waves set up vibrations in the tympanic membrane that match the waves in amplitude and frequency.

Next the vibrations of the tympanic membrane are transferred through a chain of three tiny bones named for their shapes: the *malleus,* or *hammer;* the *incus,* or *anvil;* and the *stapes,* or *stirrup* (see Figure 4.4). Each bone passes on whatever vibration it receives to its nearest neighbor. At the end of this chain of bones is another membrane, the *oval window.* The bones focus the vibrations of the tympanic membrane onto the smaller oval window, thereby amplifying the changes in pressure produced by the original sound waves.

Auditory Transduction   When sound vibrations pass from the stapes through the oval window, they enter the inner ear, a world of fluid-filled spirals. They are now in the **cochlea**, the structure in which transduction actually occurs.

The cochlea is wrapped into a coiled spiral. (*Cochlea* is derived from the Greek word for ''snail.'') If you unwrapped it, you would see that a fluid-filled duct runs down its length. The **basilar membrane** forms the floor of this long duct (see Figure 4.5). Whenever a sound wave passes through the fluid in the duct, it moves the basilar membrane, and this movement deforms *hair cells* near the membrane. These hair cells, which are exquisitely sensitive to any change in their shape, make connections with fibers from the **auditory nerve,** a bundle of axons that go into the brain. Mechanical deformation of the hair cells stimulates the auditory nerve, changing the electrical activity of some of its neurons and thus sending a coded signal to the brain about the amplitude and frequency of sound waves, which you sense as loudness and pitch.

Deafness   Problems with the bones of the middle ear are one cause of deafness. Sometimes the bones of the middle ear fuse together, preventing accurate reproduction of vibrations. This is called *conduction deafness*. It may be treated by breaking the bones apart or replacing the natural bones with plastic ones; a hearing aid that amplifies the input can also be helpful.

Figure 4.4
Structures of the Ear
The outer ear (pinna and ear canal) channel sound waves into the middle ear, where the vibrations of the tympanic membrane are amplified by the delicate bones that stimulate the cochlea. In the cochlea the vibrations are transduced into changes in neural activity, which are sent along the auditory nerve to the brain.

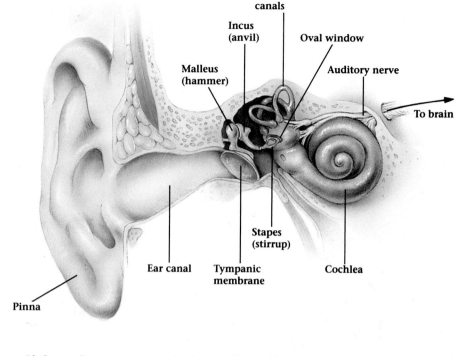

The pinna, or outer ear, gathers sound waves and funnels them into the middle ear. Some animals have a large pinna that can be directed to help localize the source of a sound.

If the auditory nerve or the hair cells are damaged, an impairment called *nerve deafness* results. Hair cells are destroyed by loud noises (including intense rock music); they can be regenerated in some animals, but the damage may be permanent in humans (Corwin & Cotanche, 1988). Nerve deafness cannot be improved by conventional hearing aids, though it can be alleviated by *cochlear implants.* These electronic devices have a tiny microphone that transduces sounds into electronic signals; the electronic signals activate an electrode implanted in the cochlea, and the resulting firing of the auditory nerve sends signals to the brain.

Coding of Intensity and Frequency

The auditory system can respond to an incredibly wide range of sound intensities. On the low end, the faintest sound that can be heard moves the hair cells less than the diameter of a single hydrogen atom (Hudspeth, 1983). On the high end, sounds more than a trillion times more intense can also be heard. Between these extremes, the auditory system codes intensity in a generally straightforward way: the more intense the sound, the more rapid the firing of a given neuron.

How do people tell the difference between one musical note and another? Recall that the pitch of a sound depends on its frequency. Differences in frequency appear to be coded in two ways, which are described by the place theory and the frequency-matching theory.

Place Theory   Georg von Békésy did some pioneering experiments to figure out how frequency is coded. He opened the skulls of human cadavers, exposed the cochlea, and made a hole in the cochlear wall to observe the basilar membrane. He then presented his "volunteers" with sounds of different frequencies by mechanically vibrating a rubber membrane that was installed in place of the oval window. With sensitive optical instruments, von Békésy

Figure 4.5
The Cochlea
The vibrations of the stirrup set up vibrations in the fluid inside the cochlea. The coils of the cochlea are unfolded in this illustration to show the path of the fluid waves along the basilar membrane. Movements of the basilar membrane stimulate the hair cells, which transduce the vibrations into changes in neural firing patterns.

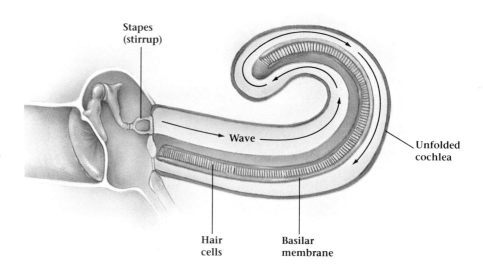

Stapes
(stirrup)

Wave

Unfolded
cochlea

Hair
cells

Basilar
membrane

observed ripples of waves moving down the basilar membrane. He noticed something very important. The outline of the waves, called the *envelope,* grows and reaches a peak; then it quickly tapers off to smaller and smaller fluctuations, much like an ocean wave that crests and then dissolves.

Figure 4.6 illustrates this wave. The critical feature of this wave is that the place on the basilar membrane where the envelope peaks depends on the frequency of the sound. High-frequency sounds produce a wave that peaks soon after it starts down the basilar membrane. Lower-frequency sounds produce a wave that peaks farther along the basilar membrane, farther from the stirrup.

How does the location of the peak affect the coding of frequency? According to the **place theory**, also called the *traveling wave theory,* the greatest response by hair cells occurs at the peak of the wave. In other words, hair cells at a particular place on the basilar membrane respond most to a particular frequency of sound and signal that frequency to the auditory nerve. Each neuron in the auditory nerve is also most sensitive to a specific frequency, which is called its **characteristic frequency** (see Figure 4.7). So if neurons with a certain characteristic frequency are firing within the auditory nerve, you will sense the sound that stimulated them as being of a certain pitch.

An important consequence of this arrangement is that exposure to a very loud noise of a particular frequency for a long time causes the loss of hair cells at one spot on the basilar membrane, as well as the ability to hear sounds of that frequency (see Figure 4.8). Interestingly, loud noise does more damage to hair cells when it is combined with a smoky atmosphere, as in a bar, apparently because the reduced oxygen available makes the hair cells more vulnerable (Fechter, Young & Carlisle, 1988).

Frequency-Matching Theory   Though the place theory accounts for a great deal of experimental data on hearing, it cannot provide a complete explanation of how frequency is coded. In particular, it cannot account for the coding of very low frequencies, such as that of a deep bass note, because there are no auditory nerve fibers that have very low characteristic frequencies. Since humans can hear frequencies as low as 20 hertz, however, they must be coded somehow. How?

Figure 4.6
Movements of the Basilar Membrane

As vibrations of the cochlear fluid spread along the basilar membrane, the membrane is deflected and then recovers. The point at which the bending of the basilar membrane reaches a maximum is different for each sound frequency. This graph shows the deflections that occur in response to sounds of three frequencies. The arrows indicate the location of greatest deflection in each case; according to place theory, these are the locations at which the hair cells receive the greatest stimulation.

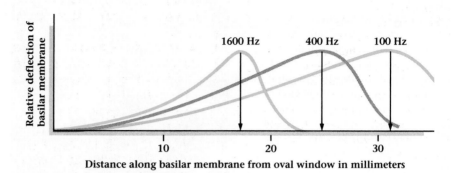

Source: Rasmussen & Windle, 1960.

Frequency matching seems to be the answer. **Frequency matching** means that the firing *rate* of a neuron in the auditory nerve matches the frequency of a sound wave. For example, one neuron might fire at every peak of a wave. Thus, a sound of 20 hertz could be coded by a neuron that fires twenty times per second. When certain auditory nerve fibers fire at twenty times per second, you sense a very low-pitched sound; when fibers fire at 100 times per second you sense a slightly higher-pitched sound.

In this simple form, however, frequency matching would apply to few sounds, because no neuron can fire faster than 1,000 times per second. A slightly more complicated process can account for the coding of moderate frequencies above 1,000 hertz. These frequencies can be matched, not by a single neuron but by the summed activity of a group of neurons firing in concert. Some neurons in the group might fire, for example, at every other wave peak, others at every fifth peak, and so on, producing a *volley* of firing at a combined frequency higher than any could manage alone. Indeed, the frequency-matching theory is sometimes called the **volley theory** of frequency coding.

In summary, the nervous system apparently uses more than one way to code the range of audible frequencies. The lowest sound frequencies are coded by matching the frequency with the firing rate of auditory nerve fibers (frequency matching). Low to moderate frequencies are coded by both frequency matching and the place on the basilar membrane where the wave peaks. High frequencies are coded exclusively by the place where the wave peaks.

Auditory Pathways and Representations

Before sounds can be heard, the information coded in the activity of auditory nerve fibers must be conveyed to the brain and processed further. (For a review of how changes in air pressure become signals in the brain that are perceived as sounds, see "In Review: Hearing.") The auditory nerve, the bundle of axons that conveys this information, makes one or two synapses and crosses the midline before reaching the thalamus. From there, the information is relayed to the **primary auditory cortex**. This area in the temporal lobe is connected to areas of the brain involved in language perception and production.

Cells in the auditory cortex have preferred frequencies, just as neurons in the auditory nerve do. Neighboring cells in the cortex have similar preferred

Figure 4.7
Determination of Characteristic Frequencies

Each curve represents a different nerve fiber and shows the minimum intensity of a sound at each frequency that is needed to stimulate that nerve. The bottom point on each curve corresponds to the frequency to which the nerve is most sensitive; even a very faint sound at that frequency will cause that fiber to fire. Here the characteristic frequency of one fiber is about 3,000 hertz, whereas the characteristic frequency of the other fiber is about 10,000 hertz.

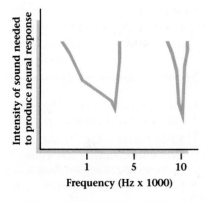

Figure 4.8
Effects of Loud Sounds
High-intensity sounds can actually rip off the hair cells normally attached to the basilar membrane. Generally, any sound that is loud enough to produce a ringing sensation in the ears causes some damage. Small amounts of damage can accumulate over many years to produce a significant hearing loss. These scanning electron micrographs illustrate the effect of intense sound on the inner ear. Part (a): cochlea of a normal guinea pig, showing three rows of outer hair cells and one row of inner hair cells. Part (b): cochlea of a guinea pig after twenty-four-hour exposure to a sound level approached by loud rock music (2,000 hertz at 120 decibels).

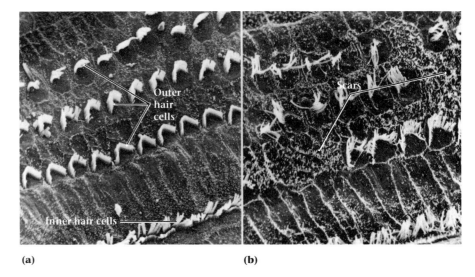

(a)   (b)

frequencies; thus, the auditory cortex provides a map of sound frequencies. However, although each neuron in the auditory nerve has a "favorite," or characteristic, frequency, each responds to some extent to a range of frequencies. Therefore, the cortex must examine the pattern of activity of a number of neurons in order to determine the frequency of a sound. The cortex is thus not just a passive warehouse of coded information; it must process the information before sounds can be heard.

In Review: Hearing

Aspect of Sensory System	Elements	Key Characteristics
Energy	Sound—pressure fluctuations of air produced by vibrations	Amplitude, frequency, and complexity of the sound waves determine the loudness, pitch, and timbre of sounds.
Accessory structures	Ear—pinna, tympanic membrane, malleus, incus, stapes, oval window, basilar membrane	Changes in pressure produced by the original wave are amplified.
Transduction mechanism	Hair cells of the basilar membrane	Frequencies are coded by the location of the hair cells receiving the greatest stimulation (place theory) and by the firing rate of neurons (frequency matching).
Pathways and representations	Auditory nerve to thalamus to primary auditory cortex	Neighboring cells in auditory cortex have similar preferred frequencies, thus providing a map of sound frequencies.

Vision

Nature has provided each species with a visual system uniquely adapted to its way of life. Eagles who soar high in the sky have the incredible ability to see a mouse move in the grass from a mile away. Frogs have eyes that are specialized to identify flies, the mainstay of their diet. Cats have special "reflectors" at the back of their eyes that help them to see even in very dim light. The human visual system is adapted to do many things well: it combines great sensitivity and great sharpness, enabling people to see objects near and far, during the day and night. Our night vision is not as acute as that of some animals, but our color vision is excellent. This is not a bad tradeoff, since the ability to experience the colorful splendor of a sunset seems worth an occasional stumble in the dark. In this section, we consider our visual sense and how it responds to light.

Light

Light is a form of energy known as *electromagnetic radiation.* Most electromagnetic radiation—including x-rays, radio waves, television signals, and radar—passes through space undetected by the human eye. As Figure 4.9 shows, **visible light** is electromagnetic radiation that has a wavelength from just under 400 nanometers to about 750 nanometers. (A *nanometer* is one-billionth of a meter.) Unlike sound, light does not need a medium to pass through; it has some properties of waves and some properties of particles. Light waves are like particles that pass through space, but they vibrate with a certain wavelength. Therefore, it is correct to refer to light as either *light waves* or *light rays.*

Sensations of light depend on two physical dimensions of light waves: intensity and wavelength. **Light intensity** refers to how much energy the light contains; it determines the brightness of light. What color you sense depends mainly on **light wavelength.** At a given intensity, different wavelengths produce sensations of different colors. For instance, 440-nanometer light appears violet-blue, and 600-nanometer light appears orangish-red.

Even with the aid of modern high beam headlights, limitations of the human visual system dangerously reduce drivers' ability to see road hazards at night or in other low-light situations.

Figure 4.9
The Spectrum of
Electromagnetic Energy
The eye is sensitive to a very limited range of wavelengths.   Electronic instruments have detectors for other ranges of wavelengths and, in effect, "see" their own kind of light, just as the eye sees visible light.

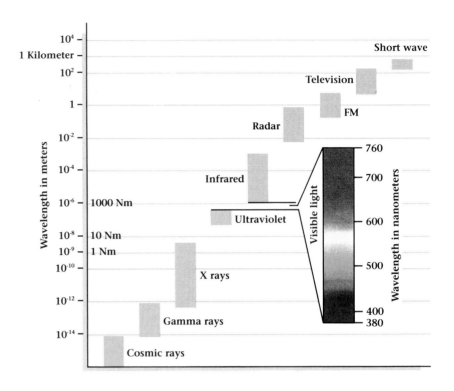

Focusing Light: Accessory Structures of the Eye

Light energy is transduced into neural activity in the eye. First, the accessory structures of the eye focus light rays into a sharp image. The light rays enter the eye by passing through the curved, transparent protective layer called the **cornea** (see Figure 4.10). Then the light passes through the **pupil,** the opening just behind the cornea. The **iris,** which gives the eyes their color, adjusts the amount of light allowed into the eye by constricting to reduce the size of the pupil or relaxing to enlarge it. Directly behind the pupil is the **lens.** The cornea and the lens of the eye are both curved so that, like the lens of a camera, they bend light rays. The light rays are focused on the surface at the back of the eye; this surface is called the **retina.**

Figure 4.11 illustrates how the lens bends light rays from a point source so that they meet at a point on the retina. If the rays meet either in front of the retina or behind it, the image will be out of focus. The muscles that hold the lens adjust its shape so that either near or far objects can be focused on the retina. If you peer at something very close, for example, your muscles must tighten the lens, making it more curved, to obtain a focused image. This ability to change the shape of the lens to bend light rays is called **accommodation.** Over time, the lens loses some of its flexibility, and accommodation becomes more difficult. This is why most older people need glasses for reading or close work.

Converting Light into Images: Visual Transduction

Visual transduction, the conversion of light energy into neural activity, takes place in the retina. The word *retina* is Latin for "net," and the retina is an intricate network of cells. Before transduction can occur, light rays must

Figure 4.10
Major Structures of the Eye
As shown in this top view of the eye, light rays are bent by the combined actions of the cornea and the lens and focused on the retina at the back of the eye. Transduction of light energy into neural activity takes place in the retina. Nerve fibers known as the optic nerve pass out the back of the eye and continue to the brain.

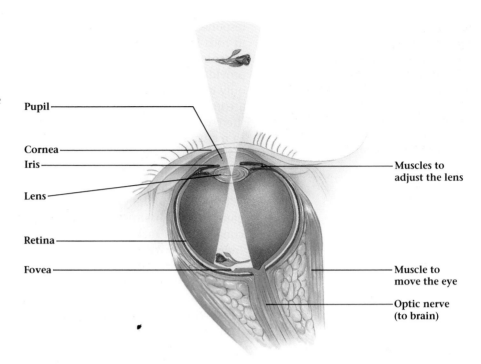

actually pass *through* several layers in this network to reach photoreceptor cells. First we will describe how the photoreceptors work; then we will explain how other cells in the retina operate.

Photoreceptors   The **photoreceptors** are specialized cells in the retina that convert light energy into neural activity. They contain **photopigments**, which are chemicals that respond to light. When light strikes a photopigment, the photopigment breaks apart, changing the membrane potential of the photoreceptor cell. As we noted in Chapter 3, this change in membrane potential provides a signal that can be transferred to the brain.

The retina has two basic types of photoreceptors: **rods** and **cones**. As their names imply, these cells differ in shape, but they also differ in composition,

Figure 4.11
The Lens and the Retinal Image
Objects in the world can be thought of as consisting of many point sources of light. Light rays from the top of an object are focused at the bottom of the image on the retinal surface. Similarly, rays from the right side of the object end up on the left side of the retinal image. The brain rearranges this upside down and reversed image so that people see the object as it is. To be in focus, rays from each point of the object must converge at a point on the retinal surface.

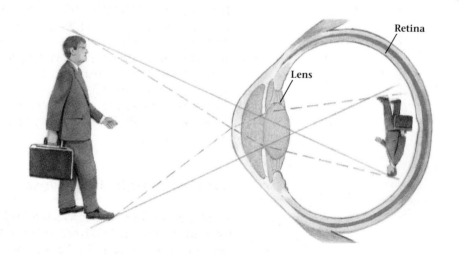

response to light, and location in the eye. For one thing, the photopigment in rods includes a substance called *rhodopsin,* whereas the photopigment in cones includes one of three varieties of *iodopsin.* The multiple forms of iodopsin provide the basis for color vision, which is explained later. Because rods have only one pigment, they are unable to discriminate colors. However, the rods are more sensitive to light than cones. Thus, rods allow you to see even when there is very little light, as on a moonlit night. But if you have trouble trying to match a pair of socks in a darkened bedroom, you now know the reason: because the light is dim, you are seeing with your rods, which cannot discriminate colors. At higher light intensities, the cones, with their ability to detect colors, become most active in vision.

The rods and cones also differ in their distribution in the eye. Cones are concentrated in the center of the retina, a region called the **fovea.** This concentration makes spatial discrimination, or **acuity,** greatest in the fovea. Indeed, the fovea is precisely where the eye focuses the light coming from objects you look at. Variations in the density of cones in the fovea probably account for individual differences in visual acuity (Curcio et al., 1987). There are no rods in the fovea. With increasing distance from the fovea, the number of cones gradually decreases and the proportion of rods gradually increases. Thus, if you are trying to detect a small amount of light, such as that from a faint star, it is better to look slightly away from where you expect to see it. This focuses the weak light on the very light-sensitive rods outside the fovea. Because cones do not work well in low light, looking directly at the star will make it seem to disappear.

Visual experience can modify the retina. For example, large amounts of reading may lead to nearsightedness (Young et al., 1969). Why? In studies with chickens, the birds were outfitted with special goggles that presented part of their retinas with an unpatterned image; that part of the eyeball became elongated, or myopic (Wallman et al., 1987). The researchers suggested that when humans read, the areas around the fovea are constantly presented with a relatively unpatterned image, causing the eyeball to elongate. (We urge you to continue reading this chapter, but perhaps rest your eyes now and then.)

Dark Adaptation   After a photopigment has broken down in response to light, new photopigment molecules are put together. This takes a little time, however. When you first come from bright sunshine into a dark place like a

Cone cells in the retina allow people to see color, but they do not operate well in low-light conditions. This is why it is so difficult to see colors in dim light.

Figure 4.12
Cells in the Retina
Light rays actually pass through several layers of cells before striking the photoreceptive rods and cones. Signals generated by the rods and cones then go back toward the surface of the retina, passing through the bipolar cells and on to the ganglion cells. Axons from the ganglion cells form the optic nerve that sends signals to the brain. Interconnections among the interneurons, the bipolar cells, and the ganglion cells allow the eye to begin analyzing visual information even before that information leaves the retina. In effect, the cells of the retina are outposts of the brain.

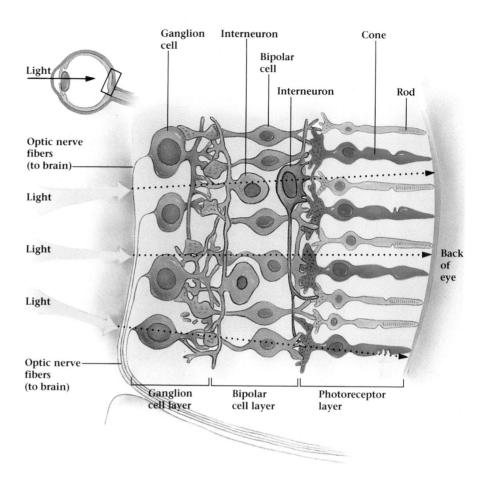

theater, you cannot see because your photoreceptors, especially your rods, do not yet have enough photopigment. In the dark, your photoreceptors synthesize more photopigments, and your ability to see gradually increases. This increasing ability to see in the dark as time passes is called **dark adaptation.**

The different properties of rods and cones shape the course of dark adaptation. Cones adapt to the dark more quickly than rods, but even when they are completely dark-adapted, the cones are not nearly as sensitive to light. The rods take about forty-five minutes to adapt completely to darkness. Thus, when you enter a dark theater, sensitivity to light increases somewhat as your cones adapt; then sensitivity rises more slowly as your rods adapt. Overall, your sensitivity to light increases some ten thousandfold after half an hour or so in a darkened room. This may be too slow to avoid tripping over someone in a theater, but helps immensely if you are working for a long time in a photographic darkroom.

A fully dark-adapted rod is incredibly sensitive to light; it can even respond to a single photon, the smallest division of light energy. Vision is not accurate at this low level of light, however, because rods occasionally are activated by the warmth of the body (Schnapf & Baylor, 1987). This thermal activation of rods is sensed as light, so you sense some light even in complete darkness.

Interactions in the Retina   If the eye simply transferred to the brain the stimuli that are focused on the retina, the images would appear like a somewhat blurred TV image. Instead, the eye actually sharpens visual images. How? The key lies in the interactions among the cells of the retina, which are illustrated in Figure 4.12. The most direct connections from the photoreceptor cells to the brain go first to **bipolar cells** and then to *ganglion cells;* the axons of

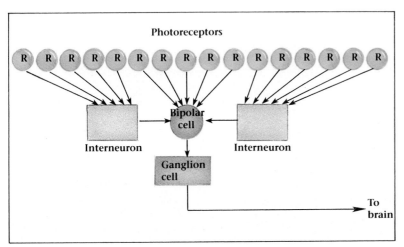

(a) Convergence

Figure 4.13
Convergence and Lateral Inhibition Among Retinal Cells
Input from many photoreceptors converges onto bipolar cells in the retina. Many receptors feed directly into a given bipolar cell, as part (a) shows, and many receptors have indirect input to bipolar cells by influencing interneurons. As part (b) illustrates, this influence is often inhibitory. The bipolar cell of photoreceptor A makes a lateral connection to an interneuron that synapses on the bipolar cell of photoreceptor B. When A is stimulated, it excites the interneuron, which inhibits the bipolar cell of B. Thus, light shining on photoreceptor A actually inhibits the signal that photoreceptor B sends to the brain. Light striking photoreceptor A both sends a signal to the brain that there is light at point A and makes it appear that there is less light at point B than there really is.

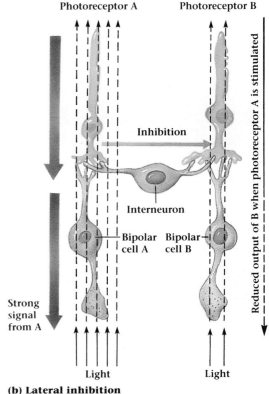

(b) Lateral inhibition

ganglion cells form the optic nerve that extends out of the eye and into the brain. However, interactions with other cells modify this direct path. Two types of interactions are especially important.

First, most bipolar cells receive input from many photoreceptors, as illustrated in Figure 4.13(a); this arrangement is called **convergence**. Convergence increases the sensitivity of each bipolar cell, because light striking any of the photoreceptors to which the cell is connected will stimulate it. However, convergence reduces acuity, because information about exactly *which* photoreceptor was stimulated is lost. Thus, it is not surprising that that there is little convergence among the cones of the fovea, an area that is good at detecting fine details but is not very sensitive to light.

Second, photoreceptor cells make connections to other types of cells in the retina, *interneurons*, which make lateral (sideways) connections between bipolar cells. Through these lateral connections, the response to light by one cell can excite or inhibit the response of a neighboring cell. Figure 4.13(b) illustrates **lateral inhibition**.

Lateral interactions have the important result of enhancing the sensation of contrast. Why? Most of the time, the amounts of light reaching two photoreceptors will differ. As Figure 4.13(b) illustrates, through its lateral connections the photoreceptor receiving more light inhibits the output to the brain from the photoreceptor receiving less light, making it seem as if there is less light at that cell than there really is. Therefore, the brain actually receives a *comparison* of the light hitting two neighboring points, and whatever difference exists between the light reaching the two photoreceptors is exaggerated. This exaggeration is important, because specific features of objects can create differences in amounts of incoming light. For example, the visual image of the edge of an object contains a transition from a lighter region to

Figure 4.14
Center-Surround Fields of Ganglion Cells

Light falling on photoreceptors in the center of the receptive field of a center-on ganglion cell increases its firing activity, whereas light falling on photoreceptors in the area surrounding the center (the surround) decreases that activity. As part (a) shows, the arrangement is just the opposite in a center-off ganglion cell, where light falling on photoreceptors in the center of the receptive field decreases the activity of the cell. Part (b) shows that these center-surround receptive fields allow ganglion cells to act as edge detectors. An edge is a region of light next to a region of relative darkness. If an edge is outside the receptive field of a center-on ganglion cell, there will be a uniform amount of light on both the excitatory center and the inhibitory surround, thus creating a moderate amount of activity. If, as shown in the middle drawing, the dark side of an edge covers a large portion of the inhibitory surround but leaves light on the excitatory center, the output of the cell will be high, signaling an edge in its receptive field. When, as shown at right, the dark area covers both the center and the surround of the ganglion cell, its activity will be lower, because neither segment of the receptive field of the cell is receiving much stimulation.

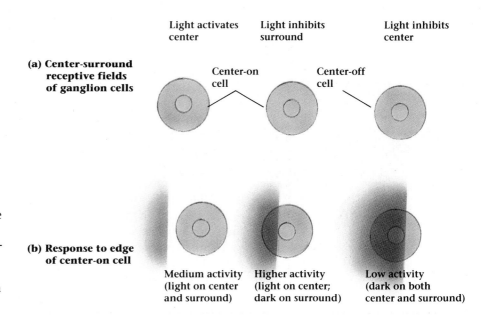

(a) Center-surround receptive fields of ganglion cells

Light activates center   Light inhibits surround   Light inhibits center

Center-on cell   Center-off cell

(b) Response to edge of center-on cell

Medium activity (light on center and surround)   Higher activity (light on center; dark on surround)   Low activity (dark on both center and surround)

a darker region. Lateral inhibition in the retina enhances this difference, creating contrast that sharpens the edge and makes it more noticeable.

Ganglion Cells and Their Receptive Fields   Photoreceptors, bipolar cells, and interneurons communicate by releasing neurotransmitters. But, as discussed in Chapter 3, neurotransmitters cause only small, graded changes in the membrane potential of the next cell, which cannot travel the distance from eye to brain. **Ganglion cells** are the cells in the retina that generate action potentials capable of traveling that distance. Ganglion cells are stimulated by bipolar cells, and their axons extend out of the retina to the brain.

What message do ganglion cells send on to the brain? The answer depends on the **receptive field** of each cell, which is that part of the retina *and* the corresponding part of the visual world to which a cell responds. Most ganglion cells have what is called a *center-surround receptive field.* That is, most ganglion cells compare the amount of light stimulating the photoreceptors in the center of their receptive fields with the amount of light stimulating the photoreceptors in the area surrounding the center. This comparison results from the lateral interactions in the retina that enhance contrast. As Figure 4.14 illustrates, some center-surround ganglion cells (center-on cells) are activated by light in the center of their receptive field; light in the regions surrounding the center inhibits their activity. Other center-surround ganglion cells (center-off cells) work in just the opposite way. They are inhibited by light in the center and activated by light in the surrounding area.

The result of the center-surround receptive fields, as Figure 4.14(b) illustrates, is to optimize the detection of variations, such as edges and small spots of light or dark. In fact, as Figure 4.15 demonstrates, people see a sharper contrast between darker and lighter areas than actually exists. By enhancing the sensation of edges and other important features, the retina reports to the brain an ''improved'' version of the visual world.

Seeing Color

Perhaps the most salient feature of visual sensation is color. An advertising agent might tell you about the impact of color on buying preferences, a poet

Figure 4.15
Visual Effects of Lateral
Inhibition
One effect of lateral inhibition
among retinal cells is the appearance of dark spots at the intersec-
tions of the black boxes in this
figure, called the Hermann grid.
When you look directly at an intersection, the dark spot disappears,
because ganglion cells in the fovea
have smaller receptive fields than
those elsewhere in the retina. The
receptive fields of two ganglion cells
projected onto the pattern show
how, at the intersection, the ganglion cell on the left has more
whiteness shining on the inhibitory
surround. Thus, the output of the
cell is reduced compared to that of
the one on the right, and the spot
on the left appears darker.

might tell you about the beauty of color, but we will tell you about how it works—which is itself a thing of elegance and beauty.

Wavelengths and Color Sensations We noted earlier that, at a given intensity, each wavelength of light is sensed as a certain color (look again at Figure 4.9). However, the eye is seldom if ever presented with pure light of a single wavelength. Sunlight, for example, is a mixture of all wavelengths of light. When sunlight passes through a droplet of water, the different wavelengths of light are bent to different degrees, separating into a colorful rainbow. The spectrum of color found in the rainbow illustrates an important concept: the sensation produced by a mixture of different wavelengths of light is not the same as the sensations produced by separate wavelengths.

Characteristics of the mixture of wavelengths striking the eyes determine the color sensation. There are three separate aspects of this sensation: hue, saturation, and brightness. These are *psychological* dimensions that correspond roughly to the physical properties of light. **Hue** is the essential "color," determined by the dominant wavelength in the mixture of the light. Black, white, and gray are not considered hues because no wavelength predominates in them. **Saturation** is related to the purity of a color. A color is more saturated and more pure if a single wavelength is relatively more intense—contains more energy—than other wavelengths. If a broad variety of wavelengths is added to a pure hue, the color is said to be *desaturated*. For example, pastels are colors that have been desaturated by the addition of whiteness. **Brightness** refers to the overall intensity of all of the wavelengths making up light. However, as we discuss in Chapter 5, the perceived brightness of an object also depends on the brightness and hue of other objects nearby.

The color circle shown in Figure 4.16 arranges hues according to their perceived similarities. If light of two different wavelengths but equal intensity is mixed, the color that is at the midpoint of a line drawn between the two original colors on the color circle is produced. You are probably familiar with a different form of color mixing in which paints are combined. Like other physical objects, paints reflect certain wavelengths and absorb all others. For example, grass is green because it absorbs all wavelengths *except* green light. Mixing paints is *subtractive color mixing;* the two paints absorb, or subtract, more wavelengths of light than either one does alone. Because of this subtraction, mixing two paints produces a color darker than the lighter of the two colors being mixed. In fact, if you keep combining different colored paints, all of the wavelengths will eventually be subtracted, resulting in black.

In contrast, mixing two *lights* of different wavelengths is *additive color mixing,* because the effects of the wavelengths from each light are added together, stimulating more cones. Mixing lights produces a color lighter than the darker of the two starting colors. Thus, if you keep adding different colored lights, you eventually get white (the combination of all wavelengths).

By mixing lights of just a few wavelengths, different color sensations can be produced. How many wavelengths are needed to create any color? Figure 4.17 illustrates an experiment that addresses this question. The answer helped lead scientists to an important theory of how people sense color.

The Trichromatic Theory of Color Vision Early in the nineteenth century, Thomas Young and, later, Hermann von Helmholtz established that any color could be matched by mixing pure lights of just three wavelengths of light. For example, by mixing blue light (about 440 nanometers), green light (about 510 nanometers), and red light (about 600 nanometers) in different ratios, any other color can be produced. Young and Helmholtz interpreted this evidence to mean that there must be three types of visual elements, each of which is most sensitive to different wavelengths, and that information from these three elements combines to produce the sensation of color. This theory of color vision is called the *Young-Helmholtz theory,* or the **trichromatic theory.**

Support for the trichromatic theory has come from recordings of the responses of individual photoreceptors to particular wavelengths of light, from indirect measures of absorption of light, and from electrical recordings from human cones (Schnapf, Kraft & Baylor, 1987). This research reveals that there are three types of cones. Although each type responds to a broad range of wavelengths, each is most sensitive to particular wavelengths. *Short-wavelength cones* respond most to light of about 440 nanometers (a shade of blue). *Medium-wavelength cones* are most sensitive to light of about 530 nanometers (a shade of green). Finally, *long-wavelength cones* respond best to light of about 560 nanometers (a shade of red).

Note that no single cone, by itself, can signal the color of a light. It is the *ratio* of the activities of the three types of cones that indicates what color will be sensed. Color vision is therefore coded by the pattern of activity of the different cones. For example, a light is sensed as yellow if it has a pure wavelength of 570 nanometers; this light stimulates both medium- and long-wavelength cones, as illustrated by arrow A in Figure 4.18. But this is not the only way to sense yellow; it is also sensed whenever any mixture of other lights stimulates the same pattern of activity in these two types of cones.

The Opponent-Process Theory of Color Vision   Brilliant as it is, the trichromatic theory in its simplest form cannot explain some aspects of color

The many colors of the rainbow are created as sunlight passes through water droplets in the air and is separated into light of different wavelengths.

Figure 4.16
The Color Circle
Ordering the colors according to their psychological similarities results in a circle that reveals some interesting things about color vision. For example, although there are pure wavelengths that are sensed as red or green, there is no single wavelength that corresponds to purple. The color circle also allows one to predict the result of additive mixing of two colored lights. The resulting color will be on a line between the two starting colors, the exact location on the line depending on the relative proportions of the two colors. For example, mixing equal amounts of pure green and pure red will produce yellow, the color that lies at the midpoint of the line connecting red and green. This circle also reveals how purple can be generated: by mixing red and blue light.

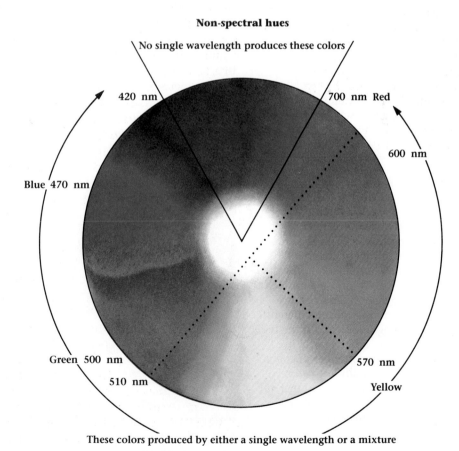

Non-spectral hues

No single wavelength produces these colors

420 nm   700 nm Red

                                                            600 nm

Blue 470 nm

Green 500 nm   570 nm

510 nm   Yellow

These colors produced by either a single wavelength or a mixture

Spectral hues

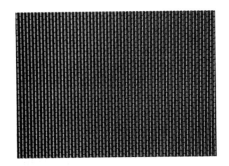

The discovery of three types of cones and how their activity can combine was put to use in color television. Color television screens, like the one above, have microscopic dots, or elements, that are either red, green, or blue. The television broadcast excites these elements to varying degrees, mixing their colors to produce many other colors. You see these color mixtures rather than patterns of red, green, and blue because the dots are too small and close together to be seen individually.

vision. For example, it cannot account for color afterimages. If you stare at Figure 4.19 for thirty seconds and then look at the blank white space below it, you will see an afterimage. What was yellow in the original image will be blue in the afterimage, what was green before will appear red, and what was black will now appear white.

This type of observation led Ewald Hering to offer an alternative to the trichromatic theory of color vision, called the **opponent-process theory.** It holds that the visual elements sensitive to color are grouped into three pairs and that the members of each pair oppose, or inhibit, each other. The three pairs are a *red-green* element, a *blue-yellow* element, and a *black-white* element. Each element signals one color or the other—red or green, for example—but never both. This explains color afterimages. When one part of an opponent pair is no longer stimulated, the other is automatically activated. Thus, if the original image you looked at were green, the afterimage would be red (see Figure 4.19).

The opponent-process theory also explains the phenomenon of complementary colors. Two colors are **complementary** if gray results when lights of the two colors are mixed together. On the color circle (see Figure 4.16), complementary colors are roughly opposite. Red and green are complementary, as are yellow and blue. Notice that complementary colors are *opponent* colors in Hering's theory. According to opponent-process theory, complementary colors stimulate the same visual element (for example, red-green) in opposite directions, canceling each other out. Thus, the theory helps explain why mixing complementary colors produces gray.

A Synthesis The trichromatic and opponent-process theories seem quite different, but both are correct to some extent, and together, they can explain most of what is now known about color vision. Electrical recordings made from different types of cells in the retina paved the way for a synthesis of the two theories.

At the level of the photoreceptors, the trichromatic theory is right: as we said, there are three types of cones. However, we also noted that output from many photoreceptors feeds into each ganglion cell, and the output from the ganglion cell goes to the brain. Recall that the receptive fields of most ganglion

Figure 4.17
Matching a Color by Mixing Lights of Pure Wavelengths
Experiments like this generated the information that led Young to propose the trichromatic theory of color vision. The subject is presented with a target color on the left side of the display; the subject's task is to adjust the intensity of the different pure-wavelength lights until the resultant mixture looks exactly like the target. A large number of colors can be matched with just two mixing lights, but Young found that *any* color can be matched by mixing *three* pure wavelength lights.

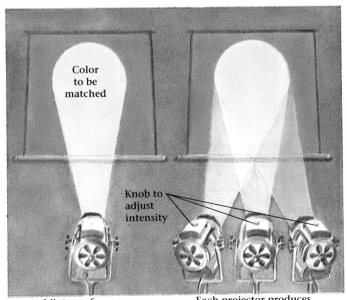

Figure 4.18
Relative Responses of Three Cone Types to Different Wavelengths of Light

Each type of cone responds to a range of wavelengths but responds more to some wavelengths than to others. Because each cone type responds to a range of wavelengths, it is possible to generate the same pattern of output—and hence the same sensation of color—by more than one combination of wavelengths. For example, a pure light of 570 nanometers (A in the figure) stimulates long-wavelength cones at 1.0 relative units and medium-wavelength cones at 0.7 relative units. This ratio of cone activity (1/0.7 = 1.4) yields the sensation of yellow. Any combination of wavelengths at the proper intensity that generates the same ratio of activity in these cone types will produce the sensation of yellow.

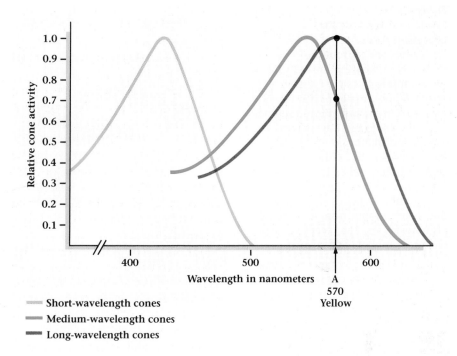

Figure 4.19
Afterimages Produced by the Opponent-Process Nature of Color Vision

Stare at the dot in the figure for at least thirty seconds, then fixate on the dot in the white space below it.

cells are arranged in center-surround patterns. The center and the surround are color coded, as illustrated in Figure 4.20. The center responds best to one color, and the surround responds best to a different color. This color coding arises because varying proportions of the three cone types feed into the center and surround of the ganglion cell.

When either the center or the surround of the ganglion cell is stimulated, the other area is inhibited. In other words, the colors to which the center and the surround of a given ganglion cell are most responsive are opponent colors. Recordings from many ganglion cells show that three very common pairs of opponent colors are those predicted by Hering's opponent-process theory: red-green, blue-yellow, and white-black. Stimulating both the center and the surround cancels the effects of either light, producing gray. White-black cells receive input from all types of cones, so it does not matter what color stimulates them.

In summary, color vision is possible because the three types of cones have different sensitivities to different wavelengths, as the trichromatic theory suggests. The sensation of different colors results from stimulating the three cone types in different ratios. Because there are three types of cones, any color can be produced by mixing three different wavelengths of light. But the story does not end there. The output from cones is fed into ganglion cells, and the center and surround of the ganglion cells respond to different colors and inhibit each other. This activity provides the basis for the phenomena of complementary colors (which produce gray when mixed) and afterimages. Therefore, the trichromatic theory embodies the properties of the photoreceptors, while the opponent-process theory embodies the properties of the ganglion cells. Both theories are needed to account for the complexity of visual sensations of color.

Colorblindness What kind of color vision would a person have if he or she had cones containing only two of the three color-sensitive pigments mentioned earlier? Many people do have this condition, and they are described as *colorblind.* They are not actually blind to all color; they simply discriminate

Figure 4.20
Color Coding and the Ganglion Cells

The center and surround of the receptive fields of ganglion cells form the anatomical basis for opponent colors. Some ganglion cells, like G₂, have a center whose photoreceptors respond best to red wavelengths and a surround that responds best to green wavelengths. Other ganglion cells pair blue and yellow. Some ganglion cells have receptive fields that are not particular about color; they receive input from all types of photoreceptors. The receptive fields of some ganglion cells overlap.

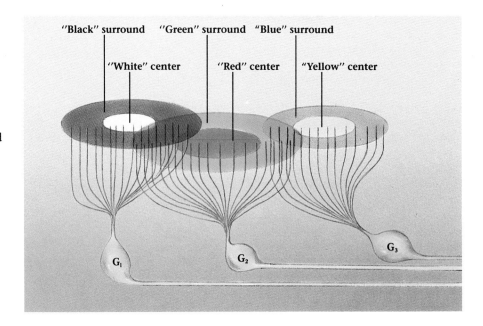

Figure 4.21
A Test for Red-Green Colorblindness

Because people with red-green colorblindness do not discriminate red from green, they do not see the red 48 embedded in the green dots. However, they are still able to discriminate red from blue.

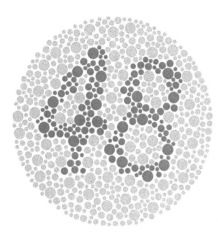

fewer colors than other people. Scientists have found the genes that direct different cones to produce pigments sensitive to blue, green, or red; colorblind people do not have the genes that code one or more of the pigments (Nathans, Thomas & Hogness, 1986).

The most common form of colorblindness involves red and green. To people with red-green colorblindness, red and green look the same; they probably appear much like brown does to people with normal vision. Examine Figure 4.21 to determine whether you might be colorblind. If you have three types of cone pigments, you should be able to see a 48 embedded in the figure; if you are red-green colorblind, the 48 will not be apparent.

Visual Pathways and Representations

In addition to all the processing by the retina that we have described, even more elaborate processing takes place within the brain. Information is brought there by axons from ganglion cells. These axons, which are several inches long, leave the eye as a bundle of fibers called the **optic nerve**. The axons from all of the ganglion cells converge and exit the eyeball at one point (see Figure 4.12). This exit point has no photoreceptors and is therefore insensitive to light, creating a **blind spot**, as Figure 4.22 demonstrates.

After leaving the retina, about half the fibers of the optic nerve cross over to the opposite side of the brain at a structure called the **optic chiasm**. (*Chiasm* means "cross.") Fibers from the inside half of each eye, nearest to the nose, cross over; fibers from the outside half of each eye do not, as Figure 4.23 shows. This arrangement makes sense when you realize that the same half of each eye is looking at the same part of the visual field. Thus, the crossing at the optic chiasm brings all the visual information about the right half of the visual world to the left hemisphere of the brain and information from the left half of the visual world to the right hemisphere of the brain.

The optic chiasm is part of the bottom surface of the brain; beyond the chiasm, the fibers ascend into the brain itself. The axons from most of the ganglion cells in the retina finally end and form synapses in the thalamus, in a specific region called the **lateral geniculate nucleus (LGN)**. Neurons of the

Figure 4.22
The Blind Spot
The blind spot occurs in the region of the retina where the axons from the ganglion cells leave the eye as the optic nerve; the area is devoid of photoreceptors. To "see" your blind spot, cover your left eye and stare at the cross. Move the page closer and farther away, and at some point (less than one foot from your face), the dot to the right should disappear from view. When this happens, the vertical lines around the dot will probably look as if they are continuous, since the brain tends to fill in visual information at the blind spot. We are not normally aware of the blind spot, because the blind spot of one eye is in the normal visual field of the other eye.

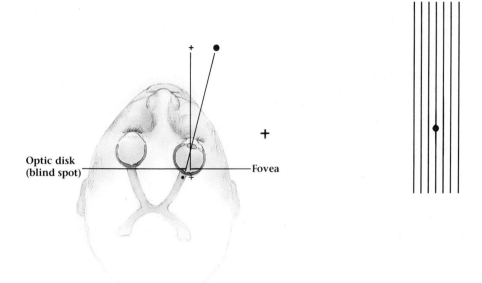

LGN have center-surround receptive fields similar to those of ganglion cells. The LGN is organized in layers of neurons. Each layer contains a whole map of one side of the visual field, but neurons of different layers respond to particular aspects of visual stimuli: the form of objects, their color, their movement, and depth cues are each handled separately, like unassembled parts of a jigsaw puzzle (Livingstone & Hubel, 1988). Neurons in the LGN then relay the visual input to the **primary visual cortex**, which lies in the occipital lobe at the back of the brain.

Organization of the Visual Cortex   As in the LGN, visual elements such as form, color, movement, and depth are handled separately by the first cortical areas they reach; even in later stages of cortical processing, these aspects of visual sensation appear to remain segregated (Livingstone & Hubel, 1988). Somewhere in the cortex the puzzle of these separate visual sensations is finally assembled to become an integrated conscious experience. There is evidence, however, that even conscious visual experience may not be completely unitary. The brain continues to process separately the "what is it?" and "where is it?" of a visual image. In fact, some patients with brain damage can recall parts of a visual image, but not their correct spatial relationship. For example, they may be able to "see" a mental image of the parts of a cow's head, its horn and ears, but not be able to assemble them mentally in their respective places (Kosslyn, 1988).

The retina's topographical map of the visual world is maintained all the way to the brain. That is, neighboring points in the retina are represented in neighboring cells in the primary visual cortex. The map is a distorted one, however. A larger area of cortex is devoted to the areas of the retina that have many photoreceptors. For example, the fovea, which is densely packed with photoreceptors, is represented in an especially large segment of cortex.

In areas neighboring primary visual cortex there are additional complete visual maps. In fact, there are more than ten complete representations of the visual world on primates' visual cortex (Merzenich & Kaas, 1980).

Each point of the topographical maps is made up of columns of cells that share a function, such as responding to one type of visual stimulus. The

Figure 4.23
Pathways from the Ganglion Cells into the Brain
Light rays from the right side of the visual field (everything on the right side of what you are looking at) end up on the left half of the retina. In order to unite information from both eyes about the right visual field in the same part of the brain, one of the pathways must cross over to the other side of the brain. From the right eye, the axons from the nasal side of the retina (the side nearer the nose, which receives input from the right visual field) cross over the midline and travel with those fibers from the left eye which also receive input from the right side of the visual world. A similar arrangement unites left visual field information from both eyes in the right side of the brain. Fibers from the nasal side of the retina of the left eye cross the midline, while fibers from the part of it toward the ear remain uncrossed. The axons have a synapse in the thalamus, in the lateral geniculate nucleus. From there, neurons send axons to the visual cortex in the occipital lobe.

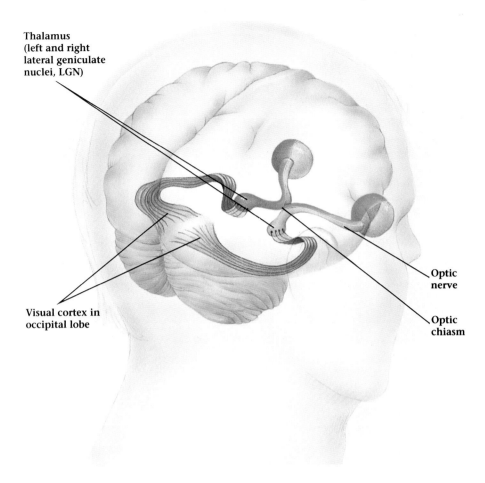

Thalamus
(left and right
lateral geniculate
nuclei, LGN)

Optic
nerve

Optic
chiasm

Visual cortex in
occipital lobe

columns are arranged perpendicular to the surface of the cortex. For example, if a cell that responds to diagonal lines in a particular spot in the visual field is located, most of the cells in a column extending above and below it will also respond to diagonal lines. Other properties are represented by whole columns of cells, so, for example, there are columns in which all of the cells are most sensitive to a particular color.

Feature Detectors Unlike the cells of the retina or the LGN, few cells in the cortex have center-surround receptive fields. They respond, as just mentioned, to certain features of objects in the visual field (Hubel & Wiesel, 1979). For example, a specific cell in the cortex might respond only to vertical edges. No matter where in the receptive field a vertical edge is presented, this cell increases its firing rate. Another class of cells might respond only to moving objects; a third might respond only to objects with corners. These cells in the cortex that respond to specific features of objects are called **feature detectors.** How do they work? No one yet knows for sure, but feature detectors might function by combining the input from a number of center-surround ganglion cells, as illustrated in Figure 4.24.

One theory of how the cortex puts together information from the ganglion cells to produce feature detectors is called the *hierarchical feature-detection model.* This model holds that any object seen is a compilation of features and that complex feature detectors are built up out of more and more complex connections of simpler feature detectors (Hubel & Wiesel, 1979). For example, several center-surround cells might feed into one cortical cell to make a line detector, and several line detectors might feed into another cortical cell to

Figure 4.24
Construction of a Feature Detector

The cortical cell in this case responds best to a bar-shaped light stimulus. The output from several ganglion cells that have receptive fields in a row and have excitatory centers goes to the lateral geniculate nucleus (LGN). The output from those LGN cells feeds into one cell in the cortex. This cortical cell responds best when all of the LGN cells are excited, and the LGN cells are excited when light falls on the center of the receptive fields of the ganglion cells—in other words, when a bar-shaped light is oriented so that it stimulates the centers of the receptive fields. Rotating the bar to a different orientation would no longer stimulate this particular cortical cell.

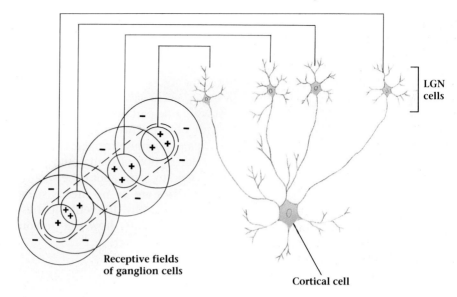

Receptive fields
of ganglion cells

LGN cells

Cortical cell

Source: Hubel & Wiesel, 1965; Kuffler & Nicholls, 1976.

make a cell that responds to a particular spatial orientation, such as the vertical. With further connections, a more complex detector, such as a "box detector," might be built from the simpler line and corner detectors.

The problem with using this model to explain how people see patterns and objects is that they would need a complex feature detector corresponding to each recognized object. For example, to recognize your grandmother, you would need a "grandmother cell," a complex feature detector that fires whenever you see your grandmother, from any angle, no matter what she is wearing. The question of whether people actually have the immense number of specific feature detectors needed to sense each of the vast array of visual stimuli is still unanswered, but most scientists think it is unlikely.

Spatial Frequency Analysis   One alternative to the feature-detection model is the *spatial frequency filter model.* Unlike the feature-detection model, this view does not require a specific cell for every type of visual sensation. According to the spatial frequency filter model, the brain analyzes patterns not by putting together information about lines, edges, and other features, but by analyzing gradual changes in brightness over broad areas.

This model points out, first, that *any* pattern, no matter how complex, can be decomposed into regions of light and dark, which can in turn be represented by sine waves, as Figure 4.25(a) illustrates. The pattern of bars in the figure is called a *sine-wave grating.* Narrow areas of light and dark are represented by a high-frequency sine wave, and broader areas of light and dark are represented by a lower-frequency sine wave.

If many gratings like those in Figure 4.25(a) are combined with different frequencies and different orientations, a complex pattern results. The spatial frequency filter model suggests that the brain does the opposite. This theory suggests that the brain analyzes the visual world into patterns of alternating light and dark of different frequencies and, in effect, represents those patterns as a collection of many sine waves. Large areas of uniform light or dark correspond to low-frequency components; areas of detailed pattern correspond to high-frequency components. The theory says that the brain, in effect, does complex Fourier analysis (see page 131) and decomposes a complicated waveform into simple sine waves. Even if a pattern of light and dark did not start out as sine waves, it can be *represented* in the brain as a collection of many sine waves.

What evidence is there that the visual cortex might do these complicated mathematics? If a series of gratings like those in Figure 4.25(a) is shined on the retina, each neuron responds best to a grating with a particular frequency; in effect, each has a preferred sine wave (Kelly & Burbeck, 1984). Further, removing one part of the cortex does not eliminate the ability to see a certain type of object. This suggests that a large part of the visual cortex might participate, possibly through Fourier analysis, in sensing each object.

Our description of spatial frequency analysis demonstrates that there is still a great deal to learn about the way the brain makes use of its sensory input. The mysteries are by no means solved, and there is evidence to support at least two drastically different theories of how people see things. ("In Review: Seeing" summarizes how the nervous system gathers the information that allows people to see.)

Figure 4.25
Spatial Frequency
The gratings in part (a) illustrate two different "pure" spatial frequencies, analogous to two pure tones. The one on the left is of low spatial frequency and high amplitude; the one on the right is of higher spatial frequency and low amplitude. By adding together appropriate sine waves representing pure spatial frequencies, it is possible to represent images that do not initially appear anything like sine waves. Part (b) illustrates how the visual system can extract information based on a spatial frequency analysis of a visual pattern. The image on the right was generated by a computer, which took an average of the light-dark level within each block of the figure on the left. The blocks are a low spatial frequency analysis of the figure, but the edges of the blocks are a high spatial frequency component that interferes with "seeing" the figure. To see just the low spatial frequency components, take off your glasses (if you wear them), and blur your vision by squinting. The right-hand figure will now look like Lincoln.

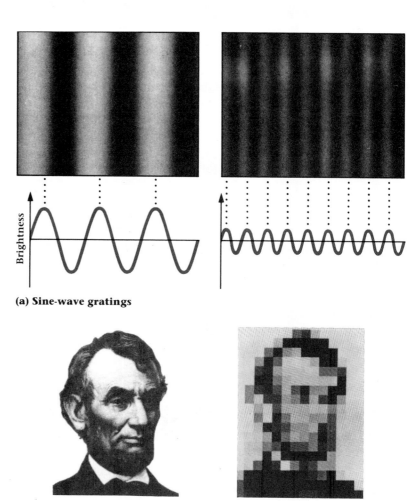

(a) Sine-wave gratings

(b) Spatial frequency analysis of a pattern

Source: (Part a) From *Fundamentals of Sensation and Perception* by M.W. Levine and J.M. Shefner, Addison Wesley, 1981; (Part b) Leon B. Harmon and Bela Julesz (1973). *Science,* 180: 1194–97. Copyright 1973 by the AAAs.

In Review: Seeing

Aspect of Sensory System	Elements	Key Characteristics
Energy	Light—electromagnetic radiation from almost 400 nm to about 750 nm	The intensity, wavelength, and complexity of light waves determine the brightness, hue, and saturation of visual sensations.
Accessory structures	Eye—cornea, pupil, iris, lens	Light rays are bent to focus on the retina.
Transduction mechanism	Photoreceptors (rods and cones) in the retina	Rods are more sensitive to light than cones, but cones discriminate among colors. Sensations of color depend first on the cones, which respond differently to different light wavelengths, and then on processing by ganglion cells. Interactions among cells of the retina exaggerate differences in the light stimuli reaching the photoreceptors, enhancing the sensation of contrast.
Pathways and representations	Optic nerve to optic chiasm to LGN of thalamus to primary visual cortex	Neighboring points in the visual world are represented at neighboring points in the LGN and primary visual cortex. Neurons there respond to particular aspects of the visual stimulus—such as color, movement, or form.

The Chemical Senses: Smell and Taste

There are animals without vision, and there are animals without hearing, but there are no animals without some form of chemical sense, some sense that arises from the interaction of chemicals and receptors. **Olfaction** (smell) detects chemicals that are airborne, or *volatile*. **Gustation** (taste) detects chemicals in solution that come into contact with receptors inside the mouth.

Olfaction

People sense odors in the upper part of the nose (see Figure 4.26). Receptors there detect molecules that pass into the moisture of the lining of the nose. Odor molecules bind to the receptors and cause depolarization of the membrane, leading to an action potential in the olfactory nerve (Firestein & Werblin, 1989). Molecules can reach these receptors either through the nose

Figure 4.26
The Olfactory System: The Nose and the Rose
Airborne chemicals from the rose reach the olfactory area through the nostrils and the back of the mouth. Fibers pass directly from the olfactory area to the olfactory bulb in the brain, and from there signals pass to areas such as the hypothalamus and amygdala, which are involved in emotion.

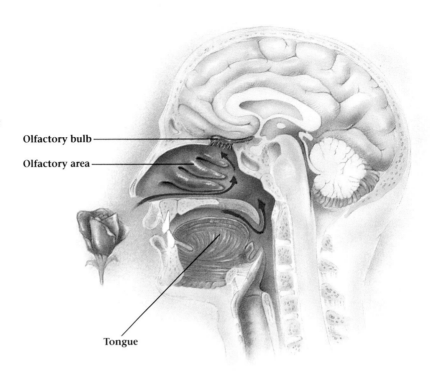

Olfactory bulb

Olfactory area

Tongue

or through an opening in the palate at the back of the mouth. Thus, the olfactory sense is a dual sense: unlike the other senses, it detects objects that are either internal, in the mouth, or external, entering through the nose (Rozin, 1982). Substances that have similar chemical structures tend to have similar odors, but how olfactory receptors in the nose discriminate various smells and code them in ways the brain can interpret is still unknown.

Almost everyone is incapable of sensing at least a few odors. For example, about 33 percent of people are unable to smell the odor of camphor (mothballs), and about 3 percent cannot detect sweat. People in these categories may count themselves lucky.

Olfaction is the only sense that does not send its messages through the thalamus. Instead, the axons from the nose extend directly into the brain, where they have a synapse in a structure called the **olfactory bulb.** Connections from the olfactory bulb spread diffusely through the brain, but they are especially plentiful in the amygdala, a part of the brain involved in emotional experience.

HIGHLIGHT

The Special Significance of Smells

The unique anatomical features of the olfactory system may account for some unique aspects in the relationship of olfaction to emotion and memory. Smells are emotionally very powerful. For example, catching a whiff of the cologne once worn by a lost loved one can reactivate intense feelings of love, anger, or sadness associated with that person. Odors can also bring back very accurate memories of significant experiences associated with them; sights, sounds, and other sensory experiences are far less capable of doing this (Engen, 1987). On the other hand, smells are relatively disconnected from verbal learning. People have a curious difficulty in associating a

"Hold it right there, young lady! Before you go out, you take off some of that makeup and wash off that gallon of pheromones!"

Source: The Far Side. Copyright 1988 Universal Press Syndicate. Reprinted with permission.

name with a particular odor. Odors are recognized as familiar but cannot be named, a phenomenon called the "tip-of-the-nose" state (Engen, 1987).

For many animals, olfaction plays an important role in communication and other social behavior. Chemicals called **pheromones** that are released by one animal and detected by another can shape that second animal's behavior or physiology. For example, male snakes detect a chemical exuded on the skin of female snakes that causes them to "court" the female (Mason et al., 1989). Literally hundreds of male snakes wrap themselves around a single female, forming a "mating ball." Strictly speaking, a pheromone produces a response that is not learned.

There is no solid evidence that humans give off or can smell pheromones that act as sexual attractants, but learned associations between certain odors and emotional experiences, including sexual activity, may enhance a person's readiness for sex. People also use olfactory information in other social situations. For example, after just a few hours of contact, mothers can usually identify their newborn babies by the infants' smell or the smell of their clothing (Porter, Cernich & McLaughlin, 1983). And adults can tell males from females on the basis of smell, although the discrimination is based mainly on the strength of the odor (male odors are stronger) rather than on a specific smell (Doty, 1981). ▪

Gustation

The chemical sense system in the mouth is gustation, or taste. The receptors for taste are in the taste buds, which are grouped together in structures called **papillae.** There are about ten thousand taste buds in the normal person's mouth, most of them on the tongue. Others are located at the back of the throat.

The human taste system detects only a very few elementary sensations: sweet, sour, bitter, and salty. Each taste bud responds best to one or two of these categories, but it also responds weakly to other categories. The sensation of a particular substance results from the coded *pattern* of responses by many taste buds. However, different regions of the tongue are more sensitive to different tastes. For example, the back of the tongue is most sensitive to bitterness, and the front of the tongue is most sensitive to sweetness.

Scientists are still trying to determine the properties that allow chemicals to stimulate specific types of taste receptors. They do know that sweetness is signaled when a chemical fits into receptor sites at three points (Raloff, 1985). This knowledge has allowed chemists to design new chemicals that fit receptors just that way, making a substance taste sweet. Saccharin and aspartame (NutraSweet) are two such chemicals.

There is another way to produce sweet sensations without sugar: use chemicals to modify the taste receptors so that they send coded signals for sweetness to the brain. For example, "miracle fruit," native to Africa, contains a substance that modifies sweetness receptors so that they respond to acids like vinegar, which normally taste sour (Bartoshuk et al., 1974). If you first eat miracle fruit, anything that normally tastes sour will instead taste sweet.

Salty is another important dimension of taste. Most people like a certain degree of saltiness in their food, but excessive salt intake can contribute to high blood pressure and heart disease. At least in animals, taste responses to salt are determined in part during prenatal development. If the mother is put on a low-salt diet, the offspring are less likely to prefer salt (Hill & Przekop, 1988). No information is yet available about whether taste responsiveness to salt is similarly determined in humans.

Smell, Taste, and Flavor

There are some reasons to believe that smell and taste sometimes act as two components of just one system, known as *flavor* (Rozin, 1982). Most of the properties that make food taste good are actually odors detected by the olfactory system, not activities of the taste system. (This is why everything tastes like cardboard when you have a stuffy nose.) There is also some evidence that the olfactory and gustatory pathways converge in some areas of the brain (Van Buskirk & Erickson, 1977). Still, no one knows yet how smell and taste come to seem like one sensation.

Some aspects of flavor are also affected by other characteristics of food, especially temperature. Warm foods are experienced as sweeter, although temperature does not alter saltiness (Frankmann & Green, 1987). Also, warming releases aromas that rise from the mouth into the nose and create more flavor sensations. This is why many people find hot pizza delicious and cold pizza disgusting. Even the texture of food can alter its flavor. The texture and the heat of food are sensed through nerve endings in the mouth that are sensitive to temperature, touch, and pain—sensations that we examine in the next section.

Somatic Senses and the Vestibular System

Some senses are not located in a specific organ, such as the eye or the ear. These are the **somatic senses**, also called **somatosensory systems**, which are spread throughout the body. The somatic senses include the skin senses of touch, temperature, and pain as well as kinesthesia, the sense that tells the brain where the parts of the body are. The vestibular system will also be considered in this section, even though it is not strictly a somatosensory system, because its function—telling the brain about the position and movements of the head—is closely related to kinesthesia.

The sense of touch provides information about the world that is vital to survival. Its importance is revealed in many other aspects of behavior as well. For example, this sculptor can create without his sight, but not without touch.

Touch and Temperature

Touch is vitally important. Blind people survive and prosper, as do deaf people and people who cannot taste or smell. But a person without touch would have difficulty surviving. Without a sense of touch, you could not even swallow food.

The Stimulus and Receptors for Touch   The energy detected by the sense of touch is a mechanical deformation of tissue, usually of the skin. The skin covers nearly two square yards of surface and weighs more than twenty pounds. The hairs distributed virtually everywhere on the skin do not sense anything directly, but when hairs are bent, they deform the skin beneath them. The receptors that transduce this deformation into neural activity are in or somewhere near the skin.

Many nerve endings in the skin are candidates for the role of touch receptor. Some neurons come from the spinal cord, enter the skin and simply end; these are called *free nerve endings.* Many other neurons end in a variety of elaborate, specialized structures. However, there is generally little relationship between the type of nerve ending and the type of sensory information carried by the neuron. Many types of nerve endings respond to mechanical stimuli, but the exact process through which they transduce mechanical energy is still unknown.

People do more than just passively respond to whatever happens to come in contact with their bodies; jellyfish can do that much. For humans, touch is also an active sense that is used to get specific information. Much as you can look as well as just see, you can also touch as well as feel. When people are involved in active sensing, they usually use the part of the sensory apparatus that has the greatest sensitivity. For vision, this is the fovea; for touch, the fingertips. (The area of primary sensory cortex devoted to the fingertips is correspondingly large, as you can see in Figure 3.17.) Fingertip touch is the main way people explore the textures of surfaces. It can be extremely sensitive, as is evident not only in sensual caresses but also in the speed with which blind people can read Braille. The mouth, especially the lips, also has many touch receptors, which is one reason why kissing is so popular.

Adaptation of Touch Receptors Constant input from all the touch neurons would provide an abundance of unnecessary information. Once you get dressed, for example, you do not need to be constantly reminded that you are wearing clothes and in fact do not continue to feel your clothes against your skin. *Changes* in touch (for example, if your jeans suddenly drop to your knees) constitute the most important sensory information.

The touch sense emphasizes changes and filters out excess information partly through adaptation, which, as mentioned earlier, results in reduced responding to constant stimulation. Typically, a touch neuron responds with a burst of firing when a stimulus is applied, then quickly returns to baseline firing rates, even though the stimulus may still be in contact with the skin. If the touch pressure increases, the neuron again responds with an increase in firing rate, but then it again slows down. A few neurons adapt more slowly, continuing to fire at an elevated rate as long as pressure is applied to the skin. By attending to this input, you can sense a constant stimulus.

Coding and Representation of Touch Information The sense of touch codes information about three aspects of an object in contact with the skin: How heavy is it? Is it vibrating? Where is it? The *intensity* of the stimulus—how heavy it is—is coded by both the firing rate of individual neurons and the number of neurons stimulated. A heavy object produces a higher rate of firing and stimulates more neurons than a light object. *Vibrations* are simply rapid fluctuations in pressure, and information about them is also coded by changes in the firing rate. *Location* is coded much as it is for vision: by the spatial organization of the information.

Basically, the information is organized so that signals from neighboring points on the skin stay next to each other, even as they ascend from the skin through the spinal cord to the thalamus and on to an area called *somatosensory cortex*. Consequently, just as there is a topographical map of the visual field in the brain, the area of cortex that receives touch information resembles a map of the surface of the body. (To confirm this, look again at Figure 3.17.) As with the other senses, these representations are contralateral; input from the left side of the body goes to the right side of the brain.

Temperature When you lie on a beach in the summer and dig your toes in the sand, you experience a pleasant stimulation, part of which comes from the sensation of the warmth of the sand. Touch and temperature seem to be separate senses, and to some extent they are, but the difference between the two senses is not always clear.

Some sensory neurons of the skin clearly respond to a change in temperature, but not to simple contact by a thermally neutral stimulus. There are "warm fibers" that increase their firing rates when the temperature changes in the range of about 95° to 115° F (35° to 47° C). Temperatures above this range are painful and stimulate different fibers. Other fibers are "cold fibers"; they respond to a broad range of cool temperatures.

However, many of the fibers that respond to temperature also respond to touch. Different patterns of activity in a single nerve fiber can code different stimuli. For example, in one neuron a brief, smooth increase in firing might signal touch; a sustained, regular increase in the same neuron might signal warmth; and variable, high-frequency activity could signal pain (Wall & Cronly-Dillon, 1960). But because no one knows how the different stimuli set up different patterns of firing, scientists have so far been unable to resolve whether each of the skin senses has a separate existence or whether they are just aspects of the touch sense.

Because the same neurons sometimes respond to both touch and temperature, you might expect that these sensations sometimes interact. This does, in fact, happen. For example, warm and cold objects feel much heavier than thermally neutral objects—up to 250 percent heavier (Stevens & Hooper, 1982).

Pain

The skin senses can convey a great deal of pleasure, but a change in the intensity of the same kind of stimulation can create a distinctly different sensation: pain. Pain provides you with information about the impact of the

If pain were based only on the nature of incoming stimuli, this Hindu fakir (religious mendicant) would be hurting. However, the experience of pain is a complex phenomenon that is affected by psychological and biological variables that can make it more or, as in this case, less intense.

world on your body; it can tell you, "You have just crushed your left thumb with a hammer." Pain also has a distinctly aversive emotional component. Researchers trying to understand pain have focused on the information-carrying aspects of pain, its emotional components, and the various ways that the brain can adjust the amount of pain that reaches consciousness.

Pain as an Information Sense   The information-carrying aspect of pain is very similar to touch and temperature. The receptors for pain are free nerve endings, but no one knows how the free nerve endings that signal pain differ from other free nerve endings. Much is also still unknown about just how pain is created, but it appears that some painful stimuli damage tissue and cause the release of *bradykinin,* a chemical that fits into specialized receptors in pain neurons, causing them to fire.

Two types of nerve fibers carry pain signals from the skin to the spinal cord. *A-delta fibers* carry sharp, pricking pain; they are myelinated to carry the sharp pain message quickly. *C fibers* carry several types of pain, including chronic, dull aches and burning sensations. Some of these same C fibers also respond to nonpainful touch, but with a different pattern of firing.

Both A-delta and C fibers carry the pain impulses into the spinal cord, where they form synapses with neurons that carry the pain signals to the thalamus and other parts of the brain (see Figure 4.27). Different pain neurons respond to different degrees of painful stimuli, but each neuron will respond to many

Figure 4.27
Pain Pathways
Pain messages are carried from the periphery to the brain by way of the spinal cord. A-delta fibers carry information about sharp pain. C fibers are unmyelinated fibers that carry several types of pain, including chronic, dull aches. Pain fibers make synapses in the reticular formation, causing arousal. They also project to the thalamus and from there to the cortex. Incoming pain messages can be "gated," or blocked, in several ways, including by signals that descend from the brain to the spinal cord.

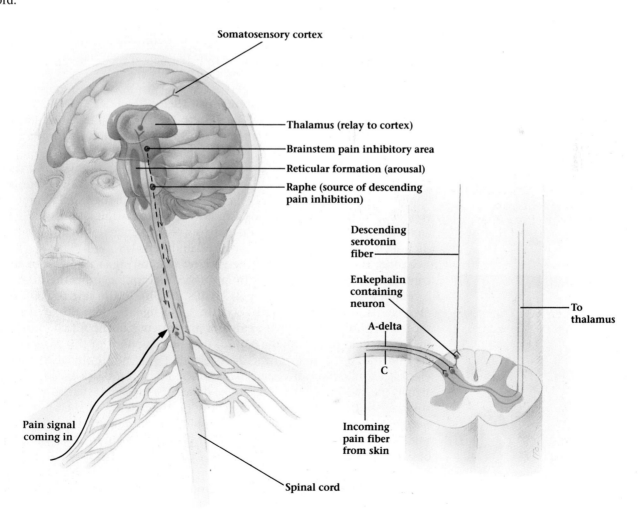

Somatosensory cortex

Thalamus (relay to cortex)

Brainstem pain inhibitory area

Reticular formation (arousal)

Raphe (source of descending pain inhibition)

Descending serotonin fiber

Enkephalin containing neuron

A-delta

C

To thalamus

Pain signal coming in

Incoming pain fiber from skin

Spinal cord

types of stimuli, such as noxious heat, intense mechanical pressure, or chemical irritation. Numerous types of neurotransmitters are used by different pain neurons, which suggests that scientists may find a variety of ways to alter pain sensations (Willis, 1988a).

Emotional Aspects of Pain   All senses can have emotional components, most of which are learned responses. For example, the smell of baking cookies may make you feel happy because it has been associated with happy childhood times. The emotional response to pain is more direct. Specific pathways carry an emotional component of the painful stimulus to areas of the hindbrain and reticular formation (see Figure 4.27), activating aversion.

Nevertheless, the overall emotional response to pain depends greatly on cognitive factors. For example, experimenters compared responses to a precise, painful stimulus by (1) people who were informed about the nature of the stimulus and when to expect it, and (2) people who were not informed. Knowing about pain seemed to make it less aversive, even though the sensation was reported to be just as intense (Mayer & Price, 1982). Other factors that affect the impact of pain sensations include whether people use pain-reducing strategies (such as distracting thoughts or mental images of pleasant stimuli) and whether they expect these strategies to succeed (Marino, Gwynn & Spanos, 1989). Further examples of how cognitive factors can influence people's reaction to aversive stimuli are contained in Chapters 12 and 13, on emotion and stress.

Modulation of Pain: The Gate Control Theory   Pain is extremely useful, because in the long run it protects you from harm. However, there are times when enough is enough. Fortunately, the nervous system has several mechanisms for controlling the experience of pain.

One explanation of how the nervous system controls the amount of pain that reaches the brain is the **gate control theory** (Melzack & Wall, 1965). It holds that there is a functional "gate" in the spinal cord that either lets pain impulses travel upward to the brain or blocks their progress. According to the theory, this gate can be closed by two mechanisms.

First, input from other skin senses can come into the spinal cord at the same time the pain gets there and "take over" the pathways that the pain impulses would have used. This appears to be why rubbing the skin around a wound reduces the pain that is felt, why electrical stimulation of the skin around a painful spot relieves the pain, and why scratching relieves itching. (Itching is actually low-level activity in pain fibers.)

Second, the brain can close the gate by sending signals down the spinal cord. The control of sensation by messages descending from the brain is a common aspect of sensory systems (Willis, 1988b). In the case of pain, these messages from the brain block incoming pain signals when they synapse in the spinal cord. The result is **analgesia,** the absence of the sensation of pain in the presence of a normally painful stimulus. Support for this aspect of the gate theory has come from the discovery that descending signals created by electrical stimulation of certain parts of the brain can block ascending pain signals (Reynolds, 1969). For example, if part of a rat's brainstem is electrically stimulated, the pain signal generated by heating the tip of the animal's tail never reaches the brain. Permanently implanting stimulating electrodes in the same region of the human brain has reduced severe pain in about 60 percent of patients (Barbaro, 1988).

Natural Analgesics   How messages from the brain block pain signals is not entirely clear, but two classes of substances seem to play a role: (1) the

Linkages: How is the emotional response to pain different from the response to other sensations? (a link to Emotion)

Bruno

Little Endorphin Annie

Linkages: As described in Chapter 13, hypnosis can create circumstances in which a person is temporarily insensitive to pain. This patient's only anesthesia during the surgical removal of her appendix consisted of tape-recorded hypnotic suggestions that she would feel no pain.

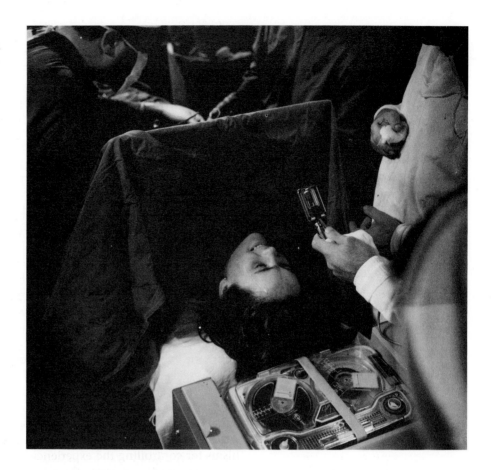

neurotransmitter *serotonin,* which is released by neurons descending from the brain, and (2) natural opiates called *endorphins.* These natural painkillers act at many levels of the pain pathway, including the spinal cord, where they block the synapses of the fibers that carry pain signals. Endorphins may also relieve pain when the adrenal and pituitary glands secrete them into the bloodstream as hormones.

Most of the time, the endorphin system is not active as an analgesic. This makes sense; chronic analgesia would defeat the purpose of pain, which is to prompt you to escape or avoid damaging stimuli. Constant activity of the endorphin system would not solve the problem of pain anyway, since, as with the opiate drugs discussed in Chapter 6, tolerance and addiction can also develop with endorphins. That is, chronically high levels of endorphins would lose their effectiveness.

What conditions cause the body to ease its own pain? Again, scientists do not have all the answers, but they do know that certain conditions can activate natural analgesic systems. For example, there is evidence that an endorphin system operates during the late stages of pregnancy to reduce the mother's labor pains somewhat (Facchinetti et al., 1982). Further, as we discussed in Chapter 3, an endorphin system is activated when people *believe* they are receiving a painkiller, even when they get only a placebo. Physical or psychological stress can also activate natural analgesic systems. Different types of stress apparently bring different analgesic systems into action (Watkins & Mayer, 1982). For example, ridiculous as it may seem, shocking a rat's front feet activates a different system than shocking its hind feet. Stress-induced release of endorphins may account for instances in which severely injured soldiers and athletes continue to perform with no apparent pain.

T H I N K I N G   C R I T I C A L L Y

Does Acupuncture

Relieve Pain Through

Physical Effects?

One way to activate the natural analgesic systems and thus control pain may be through acupuncture. *Acupuncture* is an ancient and still widely used treatment in Oriental medicine that is alleged to relieve pain and many other maladies. The method is based on the idea that body energy flows along lines called *channels* or *meridians* (Vincent & Richardson, 1986). There are fourteen main channels, and a person's health supposedly depends on the balance of energy flowing in them. Stimulating the channels by inserting very fine needles into the skin and twirling them is said to restore a balanced flow of energy. The important spots to stimulate are called Ho-Ku points. Modern practitioners of acupuncture also use electrical stimulation through needles at the same points. The needles produce an aching and tingling sensation called Teh-ch'i at the site of stimulation, but they relieve pain at distant, seemingly unrelated parts of the body.

What am I being asked to believe or accept?
Acupuncturists assert that twirling a needle in the skin can relieve pain caused by everything from tooth extraction to cancer and even "phantom pain," the experience of excruciating discomfort from a limb even though the limb has been removed. The relief from pain is said to occur as a result of the physical effects of acupuncture.

What evidence is available to support the assertion?
There is no scientific evidence to verify the theory underlying acupuncture regarding the existence of channels of energy. However, there is evidence regarding the more specific assertions that acupuncture relieves pain and that it does so through physical, not purely psychological, mechanisms.

In studying acupuncture, it is very difficult to control for the placebo effect, especially in double-blind fashion. (How could a therapist not know whether the treatment he or she is giving is acupuncture or not? From the patient's perspective, what placebo treatment could look and feel like having a needle inserted and twirled in the skin?) Nevertheless, researchers have tried to separate the psychological and physical effects of acupuncture by, for example, inserting needles but not twirling them; placing the needles in spots on the body where, unknown to the patient, they should have no beneficial effects; or using mock electrical nerve stimulation, in which no current is actually delivered.

In one such controlled study of headache pain, 33 percent of the patients in a placebo group improved following mock electrical nerve stimulation (which is about the usual proportion of the general population that responds to a placebo), but 53 percent reported reduced pain following real acupuncture (Dowson, Lewith & Machin, 1985). Acupuncture was superior to the placebo, but the best pain relief came from a combination of codeine and acupuncture. Overall, controlled studies like this usually find acupuncture to be superior to placebo treatments; 50 to 80 percent of patients reporting various forms of clinical pain are helped by acupuncture (Richardson & Vincent, 1986).

Western scientists' confidence that a physical mechanism is responsible for these effects was greatly enhanced by the discovery that acupuncture activates the endorphin system. For example, acupuncture is associated with the release of endorphins into the fluid surrounding the brain, and drugs that slow the breakdown of opiates also prolong the analgesia produced by acupuncture (He, 1987). Furthermore, the pain-reducing effects of acupuncture during electrical stimulation of a tooth can be reversed by naloxone, a substance that also blocks the painkilling effects of opiate drugs (see Chapter 3). This suggests that acupuncture somehow activates the body's natural painkilling system. However, not all studies have found that naloxone reverses acupuncture analgesia (e.g., Chapman et al., 1983). In the cases where acupuncuture activates endorphins, is this activation brought about through the placebo effect? Probably not entirely, because acupuncture produces naloxone-reversible analgesia in monkeys, who are much less likely than humans to have developed positive expectancies by reading about acupuncture (Ha et al., 1981).

Are there alternative ways of interpreting the evidence?

Yes. This evidence might be interpreted as simply confirming that the body's painkilling system can be stimulated by external means. Acupuncture may merely provide one activating method; there may be other, even more efficient methods for doing so. We already know, for example, that successful placebo treatments for pain appear to operate by activating the endorphin system. Perhaps acupuncture is no more than an especially effective placebo.

What additional evidence would be helpful to evaluate the alternatives?

Researchers need to focus not just on the effects of acupuncture but on the general relationship between internal painkilling systems and external methods for stimulating them. Regarding acupuncture itself, scientists do not know what factors govern whether it will activate the endorphin system. Other important unknowns include the types of pain for which acupuncture is most effective, the types of patients who respond best, and the precise procedures that are most effective.

What conclusions are most reasonable?

There seems little doubt that, in some circumstances, acupuncture relieves pain. It is even effective for some types of pain that resist other forms of treatment (Terenius, 1988). Acupuncture is not a panacea, however. For example, acupuncture does not appear to be useful for relieving the pain of major surgery (He, 1987).

Part of the value of acupuncture surely lies in placebo and other psychological effects that, to some extent, accompany virtually all forms of medical and psychological treatment. These effects apparently do not tell the whole acupuncture story, however. The rest of the story may indeed involve activation of an endorphin mechanism, though there is still some controversy about this.

If scientists can determine how natural analgesic systems are brought into play by acupuncture and other means, it may someday be possible to use these methods in an alternating sequence with painkilling drugs. Thus, the total amount of medication necessary to relieve pain would be reduced, along with the risk of creating drug tolerance and addiction (Watkins & Mayer, 1982). There is certainly a crying need for better methods of pain control. Despite all the modern therapies available, the pain of arthritis, migraine headaches, back disorders, cancer, and other physical ailments imposes a heavy burden, causing suffering and disability for millions and costing more than $70 billion a year in medical costs, lost working days, and worker compensation (Bonica, 1984).

Proprioception

Most sensory systems receive information from the external world, such as the light reflected off green grass or the feeling of cool water. But as far as the brain is concerned, the rest of the body is "out there" too, and you know about the position of your body and what each part of your body is doing only because sensory systems provide this information to the brain. These sensory systems are called **proprioceptive** ("received from one's own").

Kinesthesia   The sense that tells you where the parts of your body are with respect to each other is **kinesthesia**. You probably do not think much about kinesthetic information, but you definitely use it. For example, even with your eyes closed, you can usually do a decent job of touching two fingers together in front of you. To do this, you must know where each finger is with respect to your body. You also depend on kinesthetic information to guide all your movements. Otherwise, it would be impossible to develop or improve any motor skill, from basic walking to complex athletic movements. These movement patterns become simple and fluid because, with practice, the brain uses kinesthetic information automatically.

Kinesthesia also plays an important role in a person's sense of self. Consider the case of Christina. Christina has a rare neurological disease that, for unknown reasons, causes degeneration of the spinal neurons that provide kinesthetic information (Sacks, 1985). When the disorder began, Christina had difficulty holding onto objects; she would either grab them too tightly or let them slip out of her hands. Then she had trouble moving; she would rise from bed and flop onto the ground like a rag doll. Soon she began to feel she was losing her body; she was becoming disembodied, like a ghost. One time she became annoyed when she thought her roommate was tapping her fingers on a table top. Then Christina saw that it was not her roommate but she herself who was tapping. Her hands were on their own, and her body was doing things she did not know about. The disease progressed until Christina had no sense of where her body was or what it was doing, even though all of her other senses were intact. With practice she learned to guide the movements of her hands and feet, by watching them closely and concentrating very hard. But she had a permanent loss of her sense of self. She became permanently separated from herself, a stranger in her own body.

Normally, kinesthetic information comes from both muscles and joints. Receptors in muscle fibers send information to the brain about the stretching of muscles, although their main role is to control muscle contraction (McCloskey, 1978). The primary source of kinesthetic information comes from receptors in the joints. When the position of the bones changes, these receptors transduce this mechanical energy into neural activity, providing information about both the rate of change and the angle of the bones. This coded information goes to the spinal cord and is sent from there to the thalamus along with sensory information from the skin. Eventually it goes to the somatosensory cortex and to the cerebellum (see Figure 3.14), which is involved in the coordination of movements.

Vestibular Sense   Whereas kinesthesia tells the brain about where body parts are in relation to one another, the **vestibular sense** tells the brain about the position of the head (and hence the body) in space and about its general movements. It is often thought of as the sense of balance. People usually become aware of the vestibular sense only when they overstimulate it and become dizzy.

The smooth coordination of all physical movement, from scratching your nose to complex dance steps, depends on kinesthesia, the sense that provides information about where each part of the body is in relation to all the others.

Two vestibular sacs and three semicircular canals that are part of the inner ear are the organs for the vestibular sense. (You can see the semicircular canals in Figure 4.4; the vestibular sacs connect these canals and the cochlea.) The **vestibular sacs** are filled with fluid and contain small crystals called **otoliths** ("ear stones") that rest on hair endings. Because gravity pulls the otoliths toward the earth, they shift when the head tilts, stimulating the hair endings and providing information to the brain about the position of the head with respect to the earth. Astronauts beyond the pull of the earth's gravity do not receive this information, which may contribute to "space sickness."

The **semicircular canals** give information that is independent of gravity. They are fluid-filled, arc-shaped tubes; tiny hairs extend into the fluid in the canals. Whenever the head moves or changes its rate of movement, in any direction, the fluid in at least one of the canals moves, bending the hairs. This bending stimulates neurons that travel with the auditory nerve, signaling to the brain the amount and direction of head movement.

The vestibular system has neural connections to the cerebellum, to the part of the autonomic nervous system (ANS) that affects the digestive system, and to the muscles of the eyes. The connections to the cerebellum help coordinate bodily movements. The connections to the ANS help create the nausea that sometimes follows overstimulation of the vestibular system by amusement park rides, for example. The connections to the eye muscles create *vestibular-ocular reflexes*. For example, when your head moves in one direction, your eyes reflexively move in the opposite direction. This reflex allows your eyes to fixate on a point in space even when the head is moving around. You can demonstrate it by having a friend spin you around on a stool for a while; when you stop, try to fix your gaze on one point in the room. You will be unable to do so, because the excitation of the vestibular system will cause your eyes to move repeatedly in the direction opposite to that in which you were spinning. The vestibular-ocular reflexes allow remarkable feats of coordination. Consider, for example, a professional baseball player chasing a fly ball. Despite the fact that his body and eyes are moving up and down as he runs, he can continue to fixate on the ball (which is also moving) well enough to judge its exact trajectory and catch it.

Linkages: Sensation and Motivation

Do people need a certain amount of sensory stimulation?

So far, we have described particular types of sensation—sights and sounds, smells and tastes, and so on—but the overall *amount* of sensory stimulation available also has strong motivational properties. Prisoners in dark, solitary confinement, for example, commonly say that the lack of sensory stimulation is in itself extremely unpleasant. In the laboratory, psychologists have found that *sensory deprivation,* a prolonged reduction in exposure to sensory stimuli, has wide-ranging effects.

One of the first experiments on sensory deprivation took place in the early 1950s at McGill University in Montreal. Student volunteers were told that they would be paid the equivalent of about one hundred of today's U.S. dollars for every day they remained in a small room that was soundproofed and dimly lighted (Bexton, Heron & Scott, 1954). Food, water, and toilet facilities were available on request, but the subjects spent most of their time on a cot, seeing, hearing, and doing almost nothing (see Figure 4.28). How did the students react? The first day was usually easy; they slept most of the time. But it did not take long for the volunteers to become extremely bored and restless; many

Figure 4.28
A Sensory Deprivation Chamber
Subjects in early sensory deprivation
experiments were asked to lie for
days at a time on a soft cot while
wearing translucent, vision-blurring
goggles as well as gloves and padded
arm tubes that minimized touch
sensations. Their heads were surrounded by U-shaped pillows and an
air conditioner provided constant,
dull background noise.

experienced irritability and dramatic mood shifts. In spite of the large monetary
incentive, few students remained in sensory deprivation for more than two or
three days.

Subjects in similar experiments almost always terminate sensory deprivation
sooner than they think they will (Goldberger, 1982). An extended period of
sensory deprivation seems to temporarily impair some people's ability to react
quickly to visual or auditory signals, to solve mental problems efficiently, and
to perform other complex tasks (Suedfeld, 1980; Zubek, 1969). Some people
seem to react to sensory deprivation by creating their own sensations in the
form of imagined sights and sounds (Heron, 1957; Suedfeld, 1980; Zubek,
1969). Indeed, while they are deprived of normal levels of sensory stimulation,
subjects seem to be motivated to obtain any kind of stimulation they can get.
Deprived subjects will gladly listen to a monotonous recording of old stock
market price reports; they will even ask that it be played repeatedly (Bexton,
1953).

These findings regarding the effects of sensory deprivation suggest that
everyone is motivated to obtain at least some sensory stimulation most of the
time. Why? Sensory stimulation produces not only specific information about
stimuli but also an increase in *arousal,* which is general activation of physiological systems. According to one prominent theory of motivation, discussed
in Chapter 11, people are motivated to behave in ways that keep the level of
arousal within an optimal range. When arousal is too high, people seek to
reduce it; when arousal is too low, they seek to increase it.

Thus, too much sensory input, as well as the deprivation of sensory
stimulation, may be aversive. Too much stimulation may produce overarousal,
which, like underarousal, creates discomfort and can interfere with the ability
to perform physical or mental tasks. In fact, a form of sensory deprivation
known as restricted environmental stimulation (REST) is used to reduce
overarousal and some of the problems it may cause. Many people find REST
pleasant and relaxing, especially when it consists of floating for a few hours
in a large, dark, soundproof tank of body-temperature water (Suedfeld, 1980).
For some people, periods of REST appear to create long-term reductions in
high blood pressure and other stress-related problems (Fine & Turner, 1982;
Kristeller, Schwartz & Black, 1982; Suedfeld, 1980; Suedfeld, Roy & Landon,
1982; McGrady et al., 1987). REST has also been used to modify smoking
behavior and alcohol abuse (Suedfeld & Baker-Brown, 1986; Cooper, Adams
& Scott, 1988). Some of the evidence suggests that REST may provide effective
treatment beyond placebo effects (Cooper et al., 1988).

How much stimulation is enough and how much is too much? Research
on motivation and on the links between sensation and motivation indicates
that the answer varies from person to person. People differ in their optimal
level of arousal. Furthermore, there are individual differences in sensitivity to
sensory stimulation; the same sensory input therefore produces different levels
of arousal in different people. People whose nervous systems are particularly
sensitive to sensory stimulation may find that it does not take much input to
keep their arousal at an optimal level, so they usually prefer relatively quiet,
solitary activities.

In short, people do seem to need some sensory stimulation, but the amount
varies from person to person, and this difference helps shape motivation.
Whether people are motivated to increase stimulation through social contacts
or skydiving or to reduce stimulation by seeking solitude, quiet activities, or
rest depends to some extent on their optimal level of arousal and their
sensitivity to sensory stimulation. Thus, the constant regulation of arousal
and the stimulation underlying it helps account for the endless decisions that
people make about how to spend their time.

Future Directions

In this chapter we have described how sensory systems allow people to make contact with the outside world as well as with what is going on within their own bodies. The study of these systems has been somewhat unusual. On one hand, it is tied up with very abstract issues, with questions at the core of philosophy, such as: What is reality? How can we know what it is? On the other hand, the study of sensory systems has led to some of the most concrete, down-to-earth research in psychology. This work focuses on learning more about just how sensory systems detect energy, transduce it, and send it to the brain in a usable form. As we will describe in the next chapter, on perception, there has also been intense research on how people interpret sensations to build reality.

Psychologists have accumulated a vast body of knowledge in these areas, but much remains unknown or poorly understood, and the research goes on. For some senses, such as olfaction, we still need to learn more about transduction. For other senses, the major questions concern how the brain processes the information it receives. When it comes to the transition from sensation to perception, to how the pathways and connections give rise to perception and subjective reality, we still know very little. For the major senses, the task is to learn what the relevant "features" are—if the brain indeed codes features—and to describe how connections in the cortex generate feature detectors.

This task has practical applications: researchers would like to build computers that can see and recognize objects. But building a computer that can extract the relevant features of an image and recognize objects from any angle has turned out to be difficult (Waldrop, 1984). If we knew how the brain does it, perhaps we could construct computers that could do it. Some recently understood principles, such as the independent processing of several dimensions of visual sensation (for example, edge detection, movement, and color), are being applied in supercomputer modeling of vision (Poggio, Gamble & Little, 1988). These principles have also been applied in the development of artificial sensory organs that are integrated into the nervous system. For example, as noted earlier, an artificial cochlea has been developed that stimulates the auditory nerve, and an artificial eye has been developed that sends signals directly to the visual cortex (Loeb, 1989). The sensations derived from these devices are still crude, but the possibilities are exciting.

There are many as-yet-unsolved mysteries of sensation and many practical applications of the information to come. For more detailed information on sensory systems and how they work, consider taking courses on sensation and perception, biological psychology, vision, or speech and hearing.

Summary and Key Terms

Sensory Systems

A *sense* is a system that translates information from outside the nervous system into neural activity. Messages from the senses are called *sensations*.

Steps in Sensation

Accessory structures first collect and modify sensory stimuli. *Transduction* is the process of converting incoming energy into neural activity; it is accomplished by sensory *receptors*, neural cells specialized to detect energy of some type. *Adaptation* takes place when receptors receive unchanging stimulation. Neural activity is transferred through the thalamus (except in the case of olfaction) and on to the cortex.

The Problem of Coding

Coding is the translation of physical properties of a stimulus into a pattern of neural activity that specifically identifies those physical properties. It is the language the brain uses to describe sensations. Coding is characterized by *specific nerve energies:* stimulation of a particular sensory nerve provides codes for that one sense no matter how the stimulation takes place.

Representing Stimuli

The *representations* of sensory information in the central nervous system maintain the *topographical relationships* of the stimuli. Information from the left side of the sensory world is represented in the right side of the cerebral cortex, and vice versa. The region of cerebral cortex in which a sense is first represented is called the *primary cortex* for that sense. Neurons in primary cortex are organized in columns that have similar response properties. The density of sensory receptors in an area determines how much of the cortex is devoted to representing that part of the sensory world. There are multiple topographical representations of the sensory world, as well as areas of cortex, called *association cortex*, that integrate information from more than one sense.

Hearing

Sound

Sound is a repetitive fluctuation in the pressure of a medium like air; it travels in waves that can be represented as *waveforms*. The *frequency* (which is inversely related to *wavelength*) and *amplitude* of sound waves produce the psychological dimensions of *pitch* and *loudness*, respectively. *Timbre*, the quality of sound, depends on complex wave patterns that are added on to the basic frequency of the sound.

The Ear

The energy from sound waves is collected and transmitted to the *cochlea* through a series of accessory structures, including the *pinna, tympanic membrane,* malleus (hammer), incus (anvil), stapes (stirrup), and oval window. Transduction occurs when sound energy stimulates hair cells in the *basilar membrane* of the cochlea, which in turn stimulate the *auditory nerve.*

Coding of Intensity and Frequency

The intensity of a sound stimulus is coded by the firing rate of auditory neurons. *Place theory* describes the coding of high frequencies: they are coded by the place on the basilar membrane where the wave envelope peaks. Each neuron in the auditory nerve is most sensitive to a specific frequency (its *characteristic frequency*). Very low frequencies are coded by *frequency matching,* which means that the firing rate of a neuron matches the frequency of a sound wave; according to *volley theory,* some frequencies may be matched by the firing rate of a group of neurons. Low to moderate frequencies are coded through a combination of these methods.

Auditory Pathways and Representations

Auditory information is relayed through the thalamus to the *primary auditory cortex* and to other areas of auditory cortex. Sounds of similar frequency activate neighboring cells in the cortex.

Vision

Light

Visible light is electromagnetic radiation with a wavelength from about 400 to about 750 nanometers. *Light intensity,* or the amount of energy in light, determines its brightness. Differing *light wavelengths* are sensed as different colors.

Focusing Light: Accessory Structures of the Eye

Accessory structures of the eye include the *cornea, pupil, iris,* and *lens.* Through *accommodation* and other means, these structures focus light rays on the *retina,* the netlike structure of cells at the back of the eye.

Converting Light into Images: Visual Transduction

Photoreceptors in the retina—*cones* and *rods*—have *photopigments* and can transduce light into neural activity. Rods and cones differ in their shape, their sensitivity to light, their ability to discriminate colors, and their distribution across the retina. The *fovea,* the area of highest *acuity,* has only cones, which are color-sensitive. Rods are more sensitive to light but do not discriminate colors; they are distributed in areas around the fovea. Both types of photoreceptors contribute to *dark adaptation.* From the photoreceptors, energy transduced from light is transferred to *bipolar* cells and to *ganglion* cells, with *interneurons* making lateral connections between the bipolar cells and ganglion cells. As a result of *convergence* and *lateral inhibition,* most ganglion cells in effect compare the amount of light falling on the center of their *receptive fields* with that falling on the surrounding area. The result is that the retina enhances the contrast between dark and light areas.

Seeing Color

The color of an object depends on which of the wavelengths striking it are absorbed and which are reflected. The sensation of color has three psychological dimensions: *hue,* which is determined by the dominant wavelength in the mixture of light; *saturation,* which depends on the relative intensity of a single wavelength; and *brightness,* which is a function of the overall intensity of all the wavelengths. According to the *trichromatic* (or Young-Helmholtz) *theory,* color vision results from the fact that the eye includes three types of cones, each of which is most sensitive to short, medium, or long wavelengths; information from the three types combines to produce the sensation of color. According to the *opponent-process* (or Hering) *theory,* there are red-green, blue-yellow, and black-white visual elements; the members of each pair inhibit each other so that only one member of a pair may produce a signal at a time. This theory explains color afterimages as well as the fact that *complementary colors* cancel each other out and produce gray when mixed together.

Visual Pathways and Representations

The ganglion cells send action potentials out of the eye, at a point that creates a *blind spot.* Axons of ganglion cells travel in the *optic nerve* through the *optic chiasm* and terminate in the *lateral geniculate nucleus (LGN)* of the thalamus. Neurons in the LGN send visual information on to the *primary visual cortex,* where cells detect and respond to features such as lines, edges, certain orientations, certain colors, and so on. One theory suggests that increasingly complex *feature detectors* are hierarchically built out of simpler feature detectors. Another theory suggests that the visual system analyzes input into spatial frequencies of light and dark.

The Chemical Senses: Smell and Taste

Olfaction

Olfaction detects volatile chemicals that come into contact with olfactory receptors in the nose. Olfactory signals are sent to the *olfactory bulb* in the brain without passing through the thalamus. *Pheromones* are odors from one animal that change the physiology or behavior of another animal.

Gustation

Gustation detects chemicals that come into contact with taste receptors in *papillae* on the tongue and in other parts of the mouth. Elementary taste sensations are limited to sweet, sour, bitter, and salty. The pattern of responses by many taste buds determines a taste sensation.

Smell, Taste, and Flavor

The senses of smell (olfaction) and taste (gustation) both detect chemicals, and the two senses interact as *flavor.*

Somatic Senses and the Vestibular System

The *somatic senses,* or *somatosensory systems,* include skin senses and proprioceptive senses. The skin senses include touch, temperature, and pain.

Touch and Temperature

Nerve endings in the skin generate touch sensations when they are mechanically stimulated. Some nerve endings are sensitive to temperature and some respond to both temperature and touch. Signals from neighboring points on the skin stay next to each other even in the cortex.

Pain

Pain protects the body from damaging stimuli. Sharp pain and dull, chronic pain are carried by different fibers (*A-delta* and *C fibers,* respectively). The emotional response to pain depends on how the painful stimulus is interpreted. According to the *gate control theory,* pain signals can be blocked by competing signals from other skin senses and by messages sent from the brain down the spinal cord. These messages produce natural *analgesia.*

Proprioception

Proprioceptive senses provide information about the body. *Kinesthesia* provides information about the positions of body parts with respect to each other, and the *vestibular sense* provides information about the position of the head in space, through the *otoliths* in *vestibular sacs* and the *semicircular canals.*

OUTLINE

Perception

A pilot making an approach to an airport must perceive very accurately the distance to the runway and the angle of approach in order to control the plane's landing. For the pilots of four Boeing 727s in 1966, this perception failed disastrously, causing plane crashes in Chicago, Salt Lake City, Cincinnati, and Tokyo. The incidents had several factors in common. They all took place on clear nights, with the runway well in sight; the pilots did not have to rely on instruments. They flew in over dark water toward runways with upward-sloping city lights in the distance. And all of the planes crashed short of the runway.

Conrad Kraft, an engineering psychologist at Boeing Aircraft Corporation, gathered these findings. Kraft believed that the key to the crashes lay in the combination of dark water below the aircraft and upward-sloping, lighted terrain beyond. He theorized that the pilots had assumed that the airport and city lights lay on a flat rather than an upward-sloping surface, believed they were flying at a higher altitude than they were, and therefore tried to "correct" their altitudes, bringing the planes down too low and crashing.

In fact, this was what happened. How did Kraft reach his correct diagnosis? It could not come solely from the principles of sensation described in the previous chapter; those principles govern how receptors in the eyes and other senses receive energy and convert it into signals that are sent to the brain. Sensations provide raw information about the environment but do not give much meaning to that information. It was Kraft's knowledge of the principles of *perception* that led him to a correct diagnosis.

Perception is the process through which sensations are interpreted, using knowledge and understanding of the world, so that they become meaningful experiences. Thus, perception is not a passive process of simply absorbing and decoding incoming sensations. If it were, people's understanding of the environment would be poor indeed. The visual scene would be a constantly changing, confusing mosaic of lights and color. The auditory world would be a din of buzzing, humming, and shrieking

LINKAGES

Perception

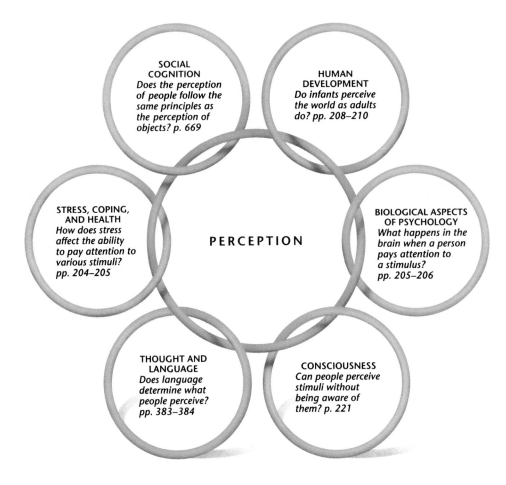

SOCIAL COGNITION
Does the perception of people follow the same principles as the perception of objects? p. 669

HUMAN DEVELOPMENT
Do infants perceive the world as adults do? pp. 208–210

STRESS, COPING, AND HEALTH
How does stress affect the ability to pay attention to various stimuli? pp. 204–205

BIOLOGICAL ASPECTS OF PSYCHOLOGY
What happens in the brain when a person pays attention to a stimulus? pp. 205–206

PERCEPTION

THOUGHT AND LANGUAGE
Does language determine what people perceive? pp. 383–384

CONSCIOUSNESS
Can people perceive stimuli without being aware of them? p. 221

■ Look at the diagram above, which illustrates some of the relationships between the topic of this chapter, perception, and other chapter topics. (The page numbers in the diagram indicate where the questions in the diagram are discussed.) The closest relationship exists between sensation and perception, which is the process of interpreting the stimulation from the senses. In fact, many pioneers of psychology thought that perception was no more than the sum of sensations, but researchers soon found that perception is more complicated than that. How you perceive the world, it turns out, depends not just on what comes to you from the senses but also on your knowledge and expectations and what you pay attention to. Thus research on perception has ties to the study of thought and consciousness as well as to the study of sensation.

To examine perception, we introduce many concepts that are also applied in later chapters—in particular, the concepts of schema, feature analysis, and attention. These concepts are fundamental to attempts to explain how people remember and think, topics we examine closely in Chapters 8 and 9. ■

Figure 5.1
What Do You See?

Linkages: How do sensations become perceptions? (a link to Sensation)

noises. Instead, human brains take sensations and create a coherent world. People fill in missing information and draw on past experiences to give meaning to what they see, hear, or touch. For example, the sensations coming from the stimuli in Figure 5.1 tell you only that there are four straight lines that contact one another at ninety-degree angles. Yet you instantly see this pattern as a meaningful object: a square.

Later in this chapter we describe many other examples of how perception creates people's experience of the world as an organized, recognizable place. By shaping experience, perceptions influence thoughts, feelings, and actions (see the Linkages diagram). As a preview, imagine you are spending the night in a strange, isolated old house. Groans and creaks in the old structure keep you awake. You look out the window and see a shrouded figure. This sight could set off an anxiety attack, but not until your perceptual processes organize the visual stimuli into a distinct shape that is located at a particular distance, stands out from the woods in the background, and is moving toward you. Fear would also depend on your recognizing this visual pattern as an approaching stranger who might mean you harm, not a bush swaying in the wind.

This imaginary experience illustrates three components of perception: detecting stimuli, organizing them into a distinct pattern, and recognizing the pattern. We examine each of these processes in this chapter, but first we take a closer look at the characteristics of perception.

From Sensing to Perceiving: An Overview

The senses create a physical code from a stimulus; perception goes beyond this code to draw on knowledge of the world and interpret what is out there. As we noted in the previous chapter, however, sensation and perception overlap. The sensory processes themselves do some preliminary interpretation of the outside world, highlighting certain features by registering them with greater emphasis than others. For example, cells of the retina emphasize edges and changes, so that you see more contrast than the physical stimulus actually contains. And when you look at the sky on a rainy day, the stimuli reaching your eyes include several wavelengths of light, but your eyes combine data about those wavelengths and ''tell'' the brain that it is seeing one color: gray.

Thus, interpretation of a stimulus begins even before information about the stimulus reaches the brain. Perception appears to add information, based on prior knowledge, to what comes from the sensory systems. In this sense, perception may be a primitive version of the knowledge-based processes, discussed in Chapter 9, that allow people to learn concepts, make judgments, and reach decisions. Suppose, for example, that your retinas transmit signals to your brain indicating that a stimulus below and just in front of you is brown in color and long, narrow, and wavy in shape. Is the stimulus a snake or a rope? The answer, in the form of an interpretation of the stimulus by your perceptual apparatus, will prompt you to ignore the object, run from it, or pick it up.

Six Features of Perception

The snake example helps illustrate six characteristics of perception. First, perception is generally *knowledge based*. If you do not know what snakes or ropes look like, especially if you do not know how to tell the difference between them, your chances of avoiding snakes in the woods are poor.

Second, perception is often *inferential.* People do not always have complete sensory information at hand, but their perceptual systems make *perceptual hypotheses,* which are inferences about what they may not be able to hear, see, or feel. Thus, if you know what a snake looks like, you will perceive the long, narrow stimulus as a snake even though the underbrush conceals its last few inches. You will not say, "Wow, if that thing had a tail, I'd swear it was a snake." Or consider the blind spot discussed in Chapter 4. The blind spot has no light receptors, but you do not perceive the resulting "hole" in the visual world because your perceptual apparatus fills it in.

Third, perception is *categorical;* it places sensations into categories based on common features. Thus, if what you are looking at has enough snakelike characteristics (long, round, scales, tapered tail, forked tongue, beady little eyes), you place the stimulus in the snake category, even if it does not look exactly like any other snake. Similarly, you place certain sounds in a category called "human voice," even if they sound unlike any other voice you have ever heard.

Fourth, perception is *relational.* You perceive a stimulus pattern as a snake not only because it has snakelike features but also because these features are related to one another in a coherent and consistent way. The tapered tail appears at the end of the body, not in the middle; there is a beady little eye on each side of the head, which is at the end opposite the tail. In the same way, your ability to perceive that someone is unusually tall requires that you see that person in relation to other people.

Fifth, much of perception is *adaptive,* allowing you to focus on the most important information needed to handle a particular situation. For example, your perceptual apparatus focuses first on whether the stimulus you suddenly encounter is a snake or a rope, not on whether it is a king snake or a python. The details will be filled in later, perhaps from a safer distance. Similarly, people quickly identify stimuli associated with food or other desirable goals, as well as those that are likely to be dangerous.

Finally, many perceptual processes operate *automatically.* You do not have to stop and consciously ask yourself, "Is that a rope or a snake?" The question is asked and answered much more quickly—so quickly, in fact, that you are unaware of having done it.

Approaches to Perception

How does perception work, and which of its six features are most important? Researchers like Irving Rock (1983) emphasize the knowledge-based, inferential characteristics of perception. Called **constructionists,** they argue that the perceptual system must often construct an image of reality from fragments of sensory information, much as a paleontologist reconstructs an entire dinosaur from a few bits of bone. This reconstruction process explains how the mind can perceive the images in Figure 5.2 as a triangle and a face, even though the sensory information is incomplete.

In contrast, James Gibson (1979) and others have argued that the incoming stimuli themselves provide most of the cues people need in order to get along in the natural world, and these cues are usually registered *directly* by the senses. Because of his emphasis on the rich sources of information available in the natural environment, Gibson's approach to perception is often called **ecological.** In his view, stimuli that need reconstruction, like those in Figure 5.2, occur only in the artificial world of the laboratory. When people perceive depth, for example, they do not first sense stimuli as two-dimensional and then construct a three-dimensional version of the world. Instead, as Figure

Figure 5.2
The Constructionist View of Perception
These stimuli demonstrate the constructionist view of perception: when you look at them, you perceive more than is actually in the sensory information.

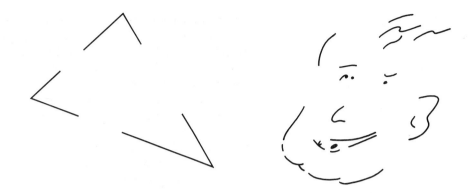

5.3 illustrates, the stimuli that reach the eye tell people automatically about depth.

The debate over the constructionist and ecological views remains unresolved, partly because each seems to do a good job of explaining certain aspects of perceptual experience. There is very good evidence, for example, that much of the information needed to interpret position in and movement through space can be perceived directly, without inference. But suppose your view of a face is fleeting and incomplete, or suppose you hear only the fragment of a conversation. How much of these sensory experiences do you perceive directly and how much must be reconstructed, either automatically or through conscious effort, using past knowledge and experience? Psychologists of the ecological school might say that these are rather infrequent situations and that most of the interesting issues of perception involve the way people tune in so well to the rich sources of information provided by the natural environment. Constructionists, however, might point to important perceptual errors that people make when the sensory world is impoverished and ambiguous and note that these errors reveal the inferential nature of perception.

Much in this debate between the ecological and constructionist approaches recalls questions about the roles of nature and nurture that were introduced

Figure 5.3
The Ecological View of Perception
Seen in three dimensions, the texture of this surface appears rougher up close and finer as it recedes into the distance. The ecological approach to perception suggests that the visual system has adapted so that this change in texture, known as a textural gradient, automatically cues people to distance and depth, with no reasoning required.

in Chapter 2, on development. How much of perception depends on the sensory equipment that people are born with, and how much of it is learned? This issue is addressed at the end of this chapter, as we consider how infants perceive the world. You will also recognize principles from both the ecological and the constructionist schools in the following sections, as we discuss how people detect stimuli, organize them into patterns, and recognize those patterns.

Psychophysics

Human perceptual processes range from the very simple, such as listening for a faint sound in a quiet house, to the very complex, such as evaluating and appreciating an architect's design. The most basic perceptual processes involve ascertaining whether a stimulus is present and, if present, how strong or intense it is.

Absolute Thresholds: Is Something Out There?

If you are lost in the woods on a moonless night, your safety may depend on detecting a faint glimmer of light or hearing the distant call of a search party. This process of deciding whether a stimulus is present begins with the sensory receptors and raw sensations.

Determining Thresholds   The minimum detectable amount of light, sound, pressure, or other physical energy is called the *absolute threshold*. This threshold can be amazingly low. Normal human vision, for example, can detect light that is equivalent to a single candle flame burning in the dark thirty miles away! Table 5.1 lists thresholds for vision, hearing, taste, smell, and touch.

The information in Table 5.1 was compiled by psychologists whose specialty is **psychophysics**, an area that focuses on the relationship between the *physical* characteristics of environmental stimuli and the *psychological* experience those stimuli produce. Psychophysical research involves asking not only what stimuli people can detect but also what changes in intensity or other qualities of those stimuli they can perceive. These questions seek to understand how people make contact with and become conscious of the world; it is thus not surprising

Table 5.1
Value of the Absolute Threshold

Examples of stimuli at the absolute threshold for the five primary senses.

Sense	Absolute Threshold
Vision	A candle flame seen at 30 miles on a clear night
Hearing	The tick of a watch under quiet conditions at 20 feet
Taste	1 teaspoon of sugar in 2 gallons of water
Smell	1 drop of perfume diffused into the entire volume of air in a 6-room apartment
Touch	The wing of a fly falling on your cheek from a distance of 1 centimeter

Source: Galanter, 1962.

that the earliest psychologists concerned themselves primarily with psychophysical research.

To get an idea of how psychophysical research is done, suppose you are a subject in a typical experiment on the absolute threshold for vision. You are brought into a laboratory, and the lights are turned out. After your eyes have adapted to the darkness, many brief flashes of light are presented one at a time at varying intensities. Each time, you are asked if you saw the stimulus.

The pattern of yes or no responses in such an experiment usually forms a curve similar to that shown in Figure 5.4. As you can see, the "absolute" threshold is actually not absolute. Sometimes a stimulus of a particular intensity will be perceived; at other times, it will not. Because of this variability, the *exact* amount of energy corresponding to a person's absolute threshold cannot be determined. To get around this problem, psychophysicists have redefined the **absolute threshold** as the minimum amount of energy that can be detected 50 percent of the time.

Sources of Threshold Variation   Why should there be variability in an "absolute" threshold? Psychologists have long been aware of two reasons: internal noise and response bias.

Internal noise is the spontaneous, random firing of neurons. It occurs because the nervous system is never inactive. Thus, a person trying to detect a faint ray of light in an otherwise dark environment does so against a background of spontaneously firing neurons. This firing is a little like "snow" on a television screen or static on a radio. If the level of internal noise happens to be high at a particular moment, it may be mistaken for an external light or sound. If the level of internal noise is extremely low, the energy added by a faint light or sound may not create enough total neural activity to make that stimulus noticeable (see Figure 5.5).

The second source of variation in absolute threshold, **response bias**, is a person's willingness or reluctance to respond to a stimulus. It reflects *motivation*—wants and needs—and expectancies. For example, people who are penalized if they incorrectly report seeing a faint light may not report detected

Linkages: What determines whether people sense a stimulus? (a link to Sensation)

Figure 5.4
The Absolute Threshold
This graph shows the relationship between the percentage of times that a signal is detected and the physical intensity of that stimulus. If the absolute threshold were indeed absolute, a signal of a particular intensity would always be detected, and any signal below that intensity would never be detected. In that case, the red line would represent the relationship, with no reports when the stimulus is below the threshold and 100 percent of the reports above it. Instead, the absolute threshold is defined as the intensity at which the signal is detected with 50 percent accuracy.

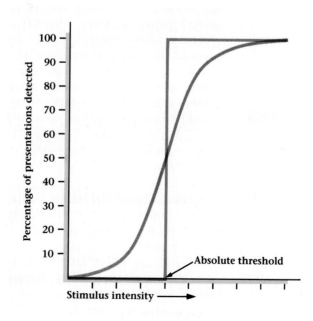

Figure 5.5
Neural Noise and Its Effects
This graph shows an example of the randomly changing neural noise in the part of the brain where detection of, say, sound takes place and the added energy caused by two signals, marked A and B. Because the random activity is already high when signal A occurs, the signal and noise together generate enough total activity to stand out from the average activity level; therefore, signal A will probably be detected. But signal B occurs when the momentary level of noise happens to be low, and the total energy of the signal plus noise is no greater than the average noise level alone. Thus, signal B will probably not be detected.

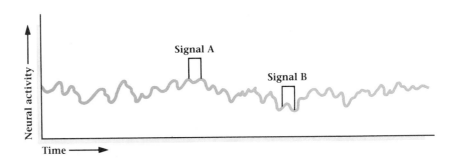

signals unless they are very confident about them. People who expect a stimulus to occur will be more likely to detect it than people who do not.

Going Beyond the Threshold: Signal-Detection Theory

Obviously, detection of a stimulus is not determined by the intensity or other characteristics of the stimulus alone. The effects of neural noise and response bias can never be entirely eliminated. As a result, researchers have gone beyond trying to determine thresholds. They have turned to **signal-detection theory** (Green & Swets, 1965), which is a mathematical model of what determines people's reports that a near-threshold stimulus has or has not occurred. This theory permits psychologists to identify the effects of response bias and to compare people's ability to detect stimuli.

Signal-detection theory is concerned not only with how people detect faint lights and sounds but with their response to events of any kind. How good are you at finding typing errors in your term paper? How likely is a basketball official to see a player's foul? Will an airport security guard spot the weapon in a hijacker's x-rayed luggage? What causes "false alarms" that lead the guard to "see" weapons where there are none? Signal-detection theory provides a way to understand and predict correct responses, missed signals, and false alarms in these and many other situations.

Signal-detection theory begins by doing away with the notion of an absolute threshold. It assumes instead that detection of a faint signal depends on two factors: sensitivity and response criterion. **Sensitivity** refers to the ability to detect a stimulus; it is influenced by neural noise, the intensity of the stimulus, and the capacity of the sensory system. The **response criterion** sets the amount of stimulus energy required for a person to justify reporting that a signal has occurred. It is the internal rule, also known as bias, that influences a person's decision about whether to report a signal; it reflects the person's motivation and expectations.

Analyzing Signal Detection   To separate the effects of sensitivity and the response criterion so that each can be measured, researchers use a special set of methods that has two key features.

First, researchers present signals on some trials but not on others. The no-signal trials are called *catch trials,* because they are designed to catch the subject's tendency to respond (perhaps because of sensory noise or bias) when nothing is there. Figure 5.6(a) shows the possible outcomes of this procedure. When a signal is presented and the subject detects it, the response is called a *hit.* If the subject fails to detect the signal, the error is called a *miss.* A *false*

(a) Possible outcomes

	Signal presented?	
	Yes	No
Subject's response — Yes	Hit	False alarm
Subject's response — No	Miss	Correct rejection

(a) Possible outcomes

	Signal presented?	
	Yes	No
Subject's response — Yes	Hit 60%	False alarm 40%
Subject's response — No	Miss 40%	Correct rejection 60%

(b) Signal presented on 50% of the trials

	Signal presented?	
	Yes	No
Subject's response — Yes	Hit 90%	False alarm 50%
Subject's response — No	Miss 10%	Correct rejection 50%

(c) Signal presented on 90% of the trials

Figure 5.6
Signal Detection

Part (a) shows the possible outcomes during a typical signal-detection task. One way in which experimenters examine sensitivity is to manipulate the response bias by altering the percentage of trials on which a signal is presented. Parts (b) and (c) compare the outcomes when a signal is presented on 50 percent of the trials and on 90 percent of the trials.

alarm occurs if the subject reports a signal when no signal was presented. Reporting no signal when none was given is called a *correct rejection*.

Second, instead of letting the response bias vary in unknown ways, signal-detection researchers *manipulate* the bias. For example, they might alter the person's motivation by offering money, or they might alter the person's expectations by changing the percentage of trials on which the stimulus occurs. Then they look at what happens to the person's responses.

Suppose a signal is presented on 50 percent of the trials, and the subject responds as in Figure 5.6(b). The same subject might then be given trials on which he or she is told that signals will occur, say, 90 percent of the time, as in Figure 5.6(c). This change *increases* the subject's expectancy of a stimulus, which *lowers* the subject's response criterion. Under these circumstances, subjects report detecting a signal more often—even when they are unsure about its occurrence—than they do in trials on which the signal occurs only rarely. Thus, the percentage of hits goes up, but so too does the percentage of false alarms.

Researchers estimate subjects' sensitivity by examining the overall pattern of hits and false alarms that occurs as the experimenter manipulates the response bias. When performance on the trials is plotted, the resulting curve is called a *receiver operating characteristic (ROC)* curve, and its shape provides a measure of a subject's sensitivity. As shown in Figure 5.7, the more bowed the curve, the greater the sensitivity.

Some Applications Signal-detection theory has given psychologists an important tool for analyzing why people sometimes fail to detect important signals, such as why an airport security guard might overlook a concealed weapon. The problem might be inadequate sensitivity. After hours on duty, the guard might nod off briefly just as a signal occurs (a miss). Another possibility relates to response criteria. Perhaps no one has ever tried to conceal a weapon at the guard's airport; knowing this, the guard's expectancy level is low. Or perhaps the guard wants to avoid a false alarm that might unnecessarily upset the crowd in the terminal. In either case, the guard's response criterion is high; thus, mildly weaponlike images on the x-ray screen are not likely to provoke a warning from the guard.

Recognition of these possibilities has led psychologists to recommend ways of improving the accuracy of those working at signal-detection tasks (Warm, 1984; Wickens, 1991). For example, setting the pace and complexity of a detection task so that it challenges workers enough to keep them alert without overwhelming them can improve their vigilance and accuracy by keeping their sensitivity high. Inserting "false signals" into the stream of things to be inspected will also make true signals more likely to be detected, since these extra signals will increase the expectation of a signal and so will lead the person to set a lower response criterion.

Signal-detection theory also has applications to eyewitness testimony. When a witness tries to identify a suspect in a police line-up, justice demands that the detection process be as sensitive as possible, producing the fewest possible misses and false alarms. Typically, a line-up consists of people who are somewhat similar in appearance to the suspect, so that none will be automatically ruled out. But even when this precaution is taken, several factors can distort a witness's response to a line-up.

For one thing, witnesses bring with them a response bias. Some witnesses may want to see someone, anyone, convicted when a crime has been committed; their response criterion may be so low that they are likely to identify someone in any line-up as the criminal. These people have what is called a *risky bias*. On the basis of signal-detection theory, psychologists have

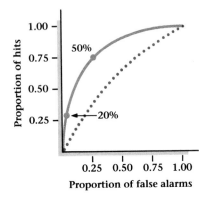

Figure 5.7
Receiver Operating
Characteristic (ROC) Curves
These two curves compare the signal-detection performance of two
subjects. Each curve shows the proportion of hits and false alarms
given by a subject as the expectancy
for a stimulus is changed by changing the percentage of trials on which
a signal is presented. For example,
when a signal is presented only 20
percent of the time, there are few
hits but almost no false alarms. The
bowed shape of the solid curve indicates that this subject is quite sensitive to the signal. The "flatter" dotted curve illustrates the performance
of an observer with lower sensitivity
in discriminating signals from non-
signals. Lower sensitivity may occur
either because the observer is trying
to detect signals that are fainter or
because the observer's eyes or ears
are less keen.

Table 5.2
Weber Constants (K) for
Different Sensory Inputs

The value of Weber's constant
fraction differs from one sense to
another. Senses that are most important for survival tend to be
the most sensitive.

Pitch	.003
Brightness	.017
Weight	.020
Loudness	.100
Pressure on skin	.140
Saltiness of taste	.200

recommended that officers remind witnesses that the criminal might *not* be
in the line-up. This reminder tends to lower the witness's expectation of seeing
the criminal and, in turn, raises the response criterion. Researchers have also
suggested that the suspect and others in the line-up should look equally
dissimilar from one another. If the suspect is markedly different in appearance
from the others in the line-up, an eyewitness with a risky bias—likely to find
a culprit in any group—might select the suspect merely by guessing (Ellison
& Buckhout, 1981).

Judging Differences Between Stimuli: Weber's Law

Often people must not only detect a stimulus but also determine whether two
stimuli are the same or different. For example, when tuning up, musicians
must decide if notes played by two instruments have the same pitch. When
repainting part of a wall, a painter may need to decide if the new paint matches
the old.

It turns out that people's ability to judge differences in the amount of a
stimulus depends on how much of that stimulus there is. More specifically,
the ability to detect differences declines as the magnitude of the stimulus
increases. For example, when comparing the weights of two envelopes, you
will be able to detect a difference of as little as a fraction of an ounce, but
when comparing two boxes weighing around fifty pounds, you may not notice
a difference unless it is a pound or more. This characteristic of perception
illustrates its adaptive nature. People rarely need to make fine discriminations
between large quantities (such as the brightness of a flash bulb versus that of
a spotlight), but such judgments are often required between small quantities,
such as the subtle differences in the shading of an x-ray that might indicate
a tumor.

One of the oldest laws in psychology gives a precise description of this
relationship between the intensity of a stimulus and the ability to detect a
change in its magnitude. Named after the nineteenth-century German physiologist Ernst Weber (pronounced "vayber"), **Weber's law** states that the
smallest detectable difference in stimulus energy is a constant fraction of the
intensity of the stimulus. The smallest detectable difference in the stimulus is
called the **difference threshold** or **just-noticeable difference (JND)**. The
constant fraction, which is different for different types of sensory input, is
given the symbol K.

In algebraic terms, Weber's law is $JND = KI$, where K is the constant fraction
and I is the amount, or intensity, of the stimulus. For example, the value of
K for weight is .02. If an object weighs 25 pounds (I), the JND is half a pound
(.02 × 25 pounds). In other words, for 25 pounds of luggage, barbell, or other
liftable object, a half-pound increase in weight is necessary before a change
can be detected.

Table 5.2 lists the value of K for a variety of sensory inputs. The value of K
represents the ability to detect differences. The smaller the value of K, the
more sensitive a sense is to stimulus differences. For example, K for vision is
0.017, which indicates a high degree of sensitivity; only a small change in the
intensity of light is needed to notice a difference in its brightness.

Differences in K demonstrate again the adaptive nature of perception.
Humans, who depend more heavily on vision than on taste for survival, have
a greater sensitivity (smaller K) for vision than for taste. Bats are highly
sensitive to sound, upon which they depend to navigate and find food in their
nocturnal world.

Though Weber's law does not hold when stimuli are very intense or very
weak, it does apply to complex as well as simple stimuli. Thus, you would

When a stereo is playing very softly, it takes only a very small increase in volume to notice the change. If the music is already blaring, it takes a much larger increase in volume before the music sounds louder. This relationship between the initial amount of a stimulus and the amount of energy that must be added to notice a change is described by Weber's law.

surely notice a twenty-cent increase in a forty-cent bus fare; this 50 percent increase (20/40) is well above the JND for noticing changes in cost. But the same twenty-cent increase in your monthly rent would be less than a JND and thus unlikely to cause notice, let alone concern.

Judging Stimulus Magnitude: Fechner's and Stevens's Laws

According to Weber's law the more there is of some stimulus, the more the amount must change in order for any change to be noticed. In 1860, Gustav Fechner proposed that Weber's law could also be used to understand the psychological experience, or perception, of stimulus magnitude. That is, it can help answer such questions as: how much brighter must a lightbulb be to appear twice as bright as a 100-watt bulb?

Fechner reasoned that since the JND is the smallest detectable *change* in the perceived magnitude of a stimulus, adding JNDs should give a measurement of the perceived magnitude of the stimulus. Furthermore, since more stimulus energy is required to produce a JND as a stimulus becomes more intense, the perceived magnitude increases more slowly as the physical magnitude grows. Thus, as physical magnitude increases, larger and larger increases in physical energy will be necessary to obtain equal changes in *perceived* magnitude. In other words, constant increases in physical energy will produce progressively smaller increases in perceived magnitude. The perceived difference in brightness between a 75-watt bulb and a 100-watt bulb will be greater than the difference between a 100-watt bulb and a 125-watt bulb. More precisely, **Fechner's law** states that the perceived magnitude of a stimulus is the product of *K* for the particular sensory system involved and the logarithm of the stimulus intensity. Figure 5.8 depicts this relationship.

Although Fechner's law describes fairly well how people judge the loudness of sounds, the brightness of lights, and the intensity of many other sensations, it does not apply to some stimuli. For example, contrary to Fechner's law, each successive increase in the perceived intensity of electric shock takes *less and less* of an increase in physical energy. S. S. Stevens found a way around this problem. By asking subjects to estimate the relative magnitude of stimuli of varying intensities, he found that their responses followed a formula that became known as **Stevens's power law** (S. S. Stevens, 1957). It is somewhat more complex than Fechner's law and beyond the scope of this book, but it also works better to explain perceived magnitude for all of the different senses.

T H I N K I N G   C R I T I C A L L Y

Can People Perceive What Cannot Be Sensed?

The laws of Weber, Fechner, and Stevens are all based on the assumption that people experience the world through the sensory systems. Throughout history, however, various people have claimed *extrasensory perception,* the ability to perceive stimuli from the past, the present, and the future through a mechanism beyond that of vision, hearing, touch, taste, and smell. The study of these claims is often called *parapsychology,* meaning an area that alters or "goes beyond" psychology.

What am I being asked to believe or accept?
Three main classes of extrasensory perception (ESP) have been investigated by parapsychologists: clairvoyance, telepathy, and psychokinesis. *Clairvoyance* involves perceiving signals from objects obscured from view or out of

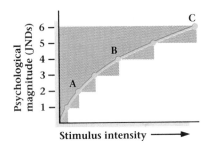

Figure 5.8
Fechner's Law Applied to a Visual Stimulus
Larger and larger increases in physical energy (the horizontal axis) are required to produce equal increases in psychological perception (JNDs, on the vertical axis). The difference between points A and B is perceived as equal to the difference between points B and C, since in each case the difference is two JNDs. But note that the increase in energy required to make a light appear two JNDs brighter is much greater when going from the fourth to the sixth JND (point B to point C) than from the second to the fourth JND (point A to point B). Another way of saying this is that as perceptual experience increases arithmetically (from 1 to 2 to 3), the stimulus energy involved increases geometrically (from, say, 1 to 4 to 9). The smooth curve shows what this function looks like. In mathematical terms, this curve is said to describe a *logarithmic* relation between perceived magnitude and stimulus intensity.

earshot; for example, being able to "see" the face of a card that is face-down in another room. Reading another person's thoughts is an example of *telepathy*, which is communication between individuals using extrasensory signals. *Psychokinesis* refers to the use of mental processes to move or control objects; for example, bending a spoon merely by looking at it or influencing the roll of dice (Swets & Druckman, 1988). Believers in ESP argue that none of these phenomena can be accounted for by our current knowledge of human sensory processes, nor can they be explained away as a magician's trick or a quirk of statistical analysis.

What evidence is available to support the assertion?
Several experiments have apparently demonstrated clairvoyance, psychokinesis, or telepathy in laboratory environments. In a typical ESP experiment on clairvoyance, for example, a subject is blindfolded and asked to report the colors of a stack of cards by feeling them with his or her fingertips (Youtz, 1968). Some subjects do far better at color naming than would be expected by the laws of chance alone.

Are there alternative ways of interpreting the evidence?
It turns out that different colors give off different amounts of radiant energy. Is it possible that certain subjects' sense of touch is particularly sensitive to differences in heat? Some evidence for this possibility comes from experiments in which color-guessing performance drops to chance levels after heat-blocking filters are placed over the cards. In addition, studies of blind readers of Braille reveal that their reading speed is affected by the color of the paper on which the Braille is printed (Duplessis, 1979). Thus, the claims made about color guessing, at least, can be accounted for by extra*sensitive* rather than extrasensory perception.

Other apparent feats of clairvoyance, telepathy, and psychokinesis have failed to hold up under the scrutiny of careful scientific investigation. These demonstrations have been found to rest not on psychic power but on magicians' skills (Randi, 1980, 1987). Indeed, since 1964, James Randi, an expert magician and ESP skeptic, has carried a $10,000 check that he will give to anyone who can perform a genuine act of ESP under scientific conditions; after hundreds of challenges, he still has his money.

Why might honest researchers be deceived about parapsychological phenomena? As you will see later in this chapter, people—including scientists—sometimes perceive what they want to perceive.

What additional evidence would help to evaluate the alternatives?
Even serious claims for small ESP effects have found a cool reception in the scientific community, first because the statistical evidence offered to support these claims is sometimes flawed (Hansel, 1968), but also because many scientists demand more conclusive evidence from ESP researchers than from other researchers. For example, many psychologists will not accept the results of parapsychologists' experiments until these experiments are repeated by psychologists who are neutral or skeptical about ESP. This is certainly not a standard they would apply to research in, say, psychophysics.

The more stringent standard applied to ESP research has at least two justifications. First, in rare cases researchers have tampered with their equipment and measurements. Second, many apparent parapsychological phenomena *are* difficult to replicate. Under close scrutiny by outside observers in the researcher's own laboratory, the phenomena often fail to occur. Clearly, additional results collected in precisely controlled settings will be necessary to satisfy the scientific community regarding the status of ESP phenomena.

What conclusions are most reasonable?

If it is to be a science, parapsychology must be based on scientific principles. Yet parapsychologists do not always assume that ESP is even based on the known physics of energy. In explaining how telepathy might work, for example, some have argued that distance has no effect on the strength of "mental signals." This argument flies in the face of the inverse square law of physics, which says that the strength of a communications signal decreases at a rate proportional to the square of the distance from its source.

Do all these criticisms mean that parapsychology has been disproven? No. In the first place, scientists in the past have been surprised by the existence of phenomena, like subatomic particles, that they once believed impossible. Furthermore, reputable and honest researchers continue to report phenomena that are not easily explainable by alternative mechanisms. Recently, a distinguished panel of scientists reviewed much of the literature in this area and visited the most respected laboratories (Swets & Druckman, 1988). The panel concluded that the data offered were not convincing enough to warrant efforts to use ESP to improve human performance in, say, air traffic control, but they did recognize the possible value of additional research. Until such research identifies plausible, scientifically respectable mechanisms through which ESP signals might be transmitted, the majority of the scientific community is likely to remain skeptical. ■

Organizing the Perceptual World

Suppose for a moment that you are driving down a busy road while searching for Barney's Diner, an unfamiliar restaurant where you are to meet a friend. The roadside is crammed with signs of all shapes and colors, some flashing, some rotating, and some standing still. If you are ever to recognize the one sign that says "Barney's Diner," you must impose some sort of organization on this overwhelming smorgasbord of visual information.

How do you do this? How do you know where one sign ends and another begins? And how do you know that an apparently tiny sign is not too small to read but is just far away? In this section, we describe some of the organizational processes that allow people to understand which parts of the smorgasbord of visual information are objects and which are not, how far away these objects are, how bright or colorful they are, which ones are moving, and which are still. These are the perceptual processes that allow people to understand the world.

Principles of Perceptual Organization

Before you can recognize the "Barney's Diner" sign, your perceptual system must first separate that sign from its background of lights, colors, letters, and other competing stimuli. Two basic principles of perceptual organization—*figure-ground perception* and *grouping*—guide this initial organization.

Figure and Ground   When you look at a complex visual scene or listen to a noisy environment, your perceptual apparatus automatically picks out certain objects or sounds to be figures (that is, the features to be emphasized) and relegates others to be **ground**—the meaningless, contourless background. For example, as you drive up to an intersection, a stop sign becomes a figure, standing out clearly against the background of trees, houses, and cars. A **figure**

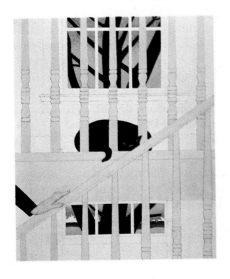

The fact that you perceive a cat behind the railing and a tree outside the window—even though neither object can be seen in its entirety—illustrates the perceptual tendency known as closure. Without it, the world would appear to be a confusing array of fragmented images.

is the part of the visual field that has meaning, stands in front of the rest, and always seems to include the contours or borders that separate it from the relatively meaningless background (Rubin, 1915).

The relationship between figure and ground is usually, but not always, clear cut. Consider Figure 5.9. What do you see? You can repeatedly reverse figure and ground to see faces, then a vase, then faces again. Figure 5.9 illustrates that perception is not only an active process but also a categorical one. People usually assign sensory stimulation to one perceptual category or another, rarely to both or to something in between. You cannot, for instance, easily perceive Figure 5.9 as both a vase and two faces at the same time.

Grouping   Why is it that certain parts of the world become figure and others become background, even when nothing in particular stands out in the physical pattern of light that falls on the retina? The answer is that certain inherent properties of stimuli lead people to group them together, more or less automatically.

Early in this century, German psychologists described the principles behind this grouping of stimuli. They argued that people perceive sights and sounds as organized wholes. These wholes, they said, are different from and more than just the sum of the individual sensations, much as water becomes something more than just an assortment of hydrogen and oxygen atoms. Thus, the drawing in Figure 5.1 is perceived as a square (an organized whole) and not just four lines and four angles. Because the German word meaning (roughly) "whole figure" is *Gestalt,* these researchers became known as **Gestalt psychologists.** They proposed a number of principles or properties that lead the perceptual system to "glue" raw sensations together in particular ways, organizing stimuli into a world of shapes and patterns. These grouping principles include:

1. **Proximity**   The closer objects are to one another, the more likely they are to be perceived as belonging together, as in Figure 5.10(a).
2. **Similarity**   Similar elements are perceived to be part of a group, as in Figure 5.10(b). People wearing the same school colors at a stadium will be perceived as belonging together even if they are not seated close together. A flute and a tuba that are both playing a rising scale will be perceived together even though the pitch of their notes is quite distinct.
3. **Continuity**   Sensations that appear to create a continuous form are perceived as belonging together, as in Figure 5.10(c).
4. **Closure**   People tend to fill in missing contours to form a complete object, as in Figure 5.10(d).
5. **Orientation**   When basic features of stimuli have the same orientation (such as horizontal or vertical), people tend to group those stimuli together (Beck, 1966; Olson & Attneave, 1970). Thus, you group the vertical lines of a grove of standing trees together and see those trees separately from their fallen neighbors in the undergrowth. Figure 5.10(e) provides another example. Feature-detecting cells in the visual cortex, described in Chapter 4, appear to be responsible for this aspect of perceptual grouping.
6. **Simplicity**   People tend to group features of a stimulus in a way that provides the simplest interpretation of the world (Hatfield & Epstein, 1986; Hochberg & McAlister, 1955). Consider, for example, what it takes to describe each pattern in Figure 5.10(f). To describe the figure on the left in two dimensions, you need only say that it is a hexagon. To describe it as a three-dimensional figure, you would have to say that it is a cube with sides of equal length, which is being viewed from a certain unusual angle. The

Figure 5.9
Figure-Ground Perception
What do you see? At first, you may perceive two faces staring at each other. If so, the space between the two faces is the ground—the background behind the faces that form the figure. But look again. You may also perceive the figure as a vase or candleholder. Now the spaces on each side, which formerly had been meaningful figures, take on the meaningless properties of ground.

Figure 5.10
Gestalt Principles of Perceptual Grouping
You probably perceive (a) as being made up of two groups of two dots plus two single dots, rather than as three groups of two dots or some other arrangement. In (b), you see two columns of X's and two columns of O's, rather than four rows of XOXO, illustrating the principle of similarity. You see the symbol in (c) as consisting of two continuous lines—one straight and one curved—not one of the other discontinuous forms shown in the figure. You immediately perceive the disconnected line segments of (d) as a triangle and a circle. In (e), the different orientation of the lines in one quadrant of the rectangle makes that quadrant stand out from the others. In (f), both figures are the same three-dimensional cube viewed from different angles, but the one on the left is normally perceived as a two-dimensional hexagon with lines running through it; the other, as a three-dimensional cube.

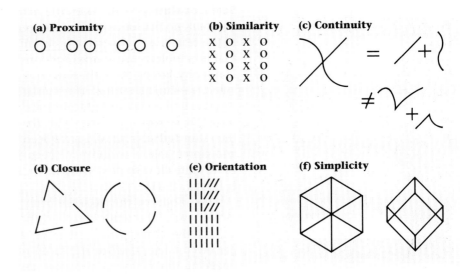

simpler, more economical, two-dimensional perception will prevail. For the second figure, on the other hand, the two-dimensional interpretation is not nearly as simple to describe, because the shape is no longer a simple hexagon. You would have to describe it as "two overlapping squares with lines connecting their corresponding corners." The three-dimensional interpretation (a cube) is now simpler and more naturally perceived.

7. **Common fate** Sets of objects that are moving in the same direction at the same speed are perceived together. Thus, a flock of birds, although separated in space, is perceived as a group. Marching band directors often use this principle, arranging for groups of musicians to move identically, causing the audience to perceive waves of motion (see Figure 5.11).

These Gestalt principles allow people to organize the world into identifiable shapes and patterns. The sensations change from moment to moment, however, whereas people interpret the patterns as being stable. This interpretation depends on perceptual constancy, to which we turn next.

Perceptual Constancy

Suppose that one sunny day you are watching a friend walking toward you along a tree-lined sidewalk. The sensations produced by this movement are actually rather bizarre. For one thing, the size of the image on your retinas keeps getting larger as your friend gets closer. To demonstrate this effect to yourself, look at a distant person and hold your hand out at arm's length in front of your eyes. The image of your hand will completely block your view of the person, because the retinal image of the person is so small. Try the same thing when the person is three feet away. Your retinal image of the person will now be so much larger that your hand can no longer cover all of it. But you perceive the person as being closer now, not bigger.

This example illustrates **perceptual constancy**, the perception of objects as constant in size, shape, color, and other properties despite changes in their retinal image. Without this aspect of perception, the world would be an Alice-in-Wonderland kind of place in which objects seemed continuously to change their properties.

Figure 5.11
Principle of Common Fate
This principle is illustrated by the common direction and form of motion of the two ballet dancers.

Size Constancy   Why does the perceived size of objects stay more or less constant, no matter what changes occur in the size of their retinal image? Part of the reason is that perception is knowledge based, and experience tells you that most objects (aside from balloons) do not suddenly change size. However, familiarity is not the only source of size constancy. Years ago, people were asked to estimate the size of an unfamiliar object viewed at varying distances by adjusting a disk of light until the disk seemed to be the same size as the object. If lack of familiarity with the objects had eliminated size constancy, the estimated sizes should have been similar to the size of the retinal image, and closer objects would have been judged to be larger. In fact, the people came quite close to perceiving the true size of the unfamiliar objects (Holway & Boring, 1941).

What produced this accurate perception of size? As objects move closer or farther away, the brain perceives the change in distance and automatically adjusts the perception. (Later we describe how changes in distance are perceived.) The *perceived size* of an object is equal to the size of the retinal image multiplied by the perceived distance (Holway & Boring, 1941).

Here again, it is clear that perception is relational: the retinal image is interpreted in relation to perceived distance. As an object moves closer, its retinal image increases, but the perceived distance decreases at the same rate, and the perceived size remains constant. If, instead, a balloon is inflated in front of your eyes, perceived distance remains constant, and the perceived size (correctly) increases as the retinal image increases.

As another example, fix your eyes on a bar of light (a bright fluorescent light is a good choice) and stare at it for thirty seconds or so, in order to form a good afterimage. This afterimage represents a retinal image of a constant size. Now shift your gaze from the light to a distant wall. The perceived size of the afterimage will now be larger because the retinal image is being multiplied by a larger perceived distance.

The relationships among retinal size, perceived size, and perceived distance can have unfortunate effects. People may perceive objects with smaller retinal images to be farther away than those with larger images, even when the distance is in fact the same. This error may explain why small cars have higher accident rates than large ones (Eberts & MacMillan, 1985). A small car produces a smaller retinal image at a given distance than a larger car, possibly causing the driver of a following vehicle to overestimate the distance to the small car and therefore fail to brake in time to avoid a rear-end collision. This misjudgment illustrates the inferential aspect of perception. People make logical inferences or hypotheses about the world based on the available cues. If the cues are imperfect, the inferences may be wrong.

If you were to trace the outline of this floating object, you would see that its image is oval-shaped. However, the perceptual principle of shape constancy causes you to perceive it as the perfectly circular life ring that it is.

Shape Constancy   The principles of shape constancy are closely related to those of size constancy. To see shape constancy at work, remember what page you are on, close this book, and tilt it toward and away from you several times. The book will continue to look rectangular, even though the shape of its retinal image changed dramatically as you moved it. The brain automatically integrates information about retinal images and distance as movement occurs. In this case, the distance information involved the difference in distance between the near and the far edges of the book.

Brightness Constancy   No matter how the amount of light striking an object changes, its perceived brightness remains relatively constant. You could demonstrate this constancy by placing a lump of coal in sunlight and a piece of white paper in some shade nearby. The coal would still look very dark and

Figure 5.12
Brightness Constancy
You probably perceive the inner ring on the left to be brighter than the inner ring on the right. But if you carefully examine the inner circles alone, by covering the surround, you will see that the two are of equal intensity. The brighter surround in the right-hand ring leads you to perceive its inner ring as relatively darker.

the paper very bright, even though much more light energy is reflected to the eyes from the sun-bathed coal than from the shaded paper.

Of course, one reason the coal would continue to look dark, no matter what the illumination, is that you know that coal is black, illustrating once again the knowledge-based nature of perception. Another reason is that the coal is still the darkest object *relative to* its background in the sunlight, and the paper is the brightest object *relative to* its background in the shade. The brightness of an object is perceived in relation to its background (see Figure 5.12).

Depth Perception

Thanks to the constancies of perception, people perceive coherent, stable objects. Imagine trying to deal with a world in which objects changed their form as often as their images changed on your retinas. Figure 5.13 shows a case in which perceptual constancy fails. Why does the nearer baseball player seem larger? Why does size constancy fail here?

The answer lies in perceived distance, one of the most important factors underlying size and shape constancy. Perception of distance, or **depth perception**, allows people to experience the world in three-dimensional depth. How can this occur, when all visual information comes through two-dimensional retinal images? There are two reasons: cues provided by the environment, sometimes described as *stimulus cues,* and properties of the visual system itself.

Stimulus Cues To some extent, people perceive depth through the same cues that an artist uses to create the impression of depth and distance on a two-dimensional canvas. These cues are actually specific characteristics of visual stimuli. Figure 5.14 illustrates several of them.

■ Look first at the two men at the far left of Figure 5.14. They illustrate the principle of **relative size:** if two objects are assumed to be the same size, the object producing a larger image on the retina is perceived as closer than the one producing a smaller image.

■ Another cue comes from *height in the visual field:* more distant objects are usually higher in the visual field than those nearby. The woman near the man at the front of Figure 5.14 therefore appears to be farther away.

■ The woman walking by the car in the middle of the picture illustrates another depth cue called **interposition.** Closer objects block the view of

Figure 5.13
A Violation of Size Constancy
The two baseball players in the picture appear to be very different sizes, even though you know that their heights are probably much the same. The discussion of stimulus cues for depth explains why.

Figure 5.14
Stimulus Cues for Depth Perception
See if you can identify how cues of relative size, interposition, linear perspective, height in the visual field, textural gradient, and shadows combine to create a sense of three-dimensionality.

things farther away. (Misleading cues from both height in the visual field and interposition account for the violation of size constancy in Figure 5.13. The more distant ballplayer is lower, not higher in the visual field; also the stocking on the pitcher's leg is in a position such that it appears that the runner's leg is in front of, not behind the pitcher's leg, thereby providing a misleading interposition cue.)

▪ The figure at the far right of Figure 5.14 is seen as farther away in part because she is standing near a point in the road where its edges, like all parallel lines that recede into the distance, appear to converge toward a single point. This apparent convergence provides a cue called **linear perspective.** The closer together two converging lines are, the greater the perceived distance.

Parallel lines seem to converge as they extend into the distance. This illusion provides linear perspective cues for distance; objects near where the lines "meet" are perceived as farther away than those located where the lines appear farther apart.

■ Notice that the road in the picture disappears into a hazy background. Since greater distances usually produce less clarity, **reduced clarity** is interpreted as a cue for greater distance. The effect of clarity on perceived distance explains why a mountain viewed on a hazy day appears to loom larger than the same mountain on a clear day. The haze acts as a cue for greater distance and a greater perceived distance produces a larger perceived size.

■ *Light and shadow* also contribute to the perception of three dimensions (Ramanchandran, 1988). Hence the buildings in the background of Figure 5.14 are seen as three-dimensional cubes, not flat billboards, because of the shadows on their right faces. Figure 5.15 gives another example of the effect of shading on depth perception.

Sometimes motion provides a cue to depth, a phenomenon called *structure through motion* (Braunstein, 1989). Hold a twisted wire behind a paper illuminated from behind and look at the two-dimensional shadow cast by the wire. Now slowly twist the wire and watch the three-dimensional properties of the image come to life. You "see" the figure rotating in depth.

Two additional stimulus cues for depth come from **gradients,** which are continuous changes across the visual field. A **textural gradient** is a graduated change in the texture of the visual field, as you can see from the sidewalk and the centerline of the road in Figure 5.14. (It was also illustrated in Figure 5.3, as an example of Gibson's ecological approach.) Texture appears less detailed as distance increases; so as the texture of a surface changes across the retinal image, people perceive a change in distance.

The second gradient cue is the **movement gradient,** which is the graduated difference in the apparent movement of objects. The next time you are riding in a car in an open area, look out the side window at an object of intermediate distance (for example, a house). The telephone poles and other objects closest to you will appear to fly rapidly across your visual field; in contrast, distant trees may seem motionless or even appear to move along with you. This difference in relative movement, sometimes called *motion parallax,* provides cues to the difference in distance. Faster relative movement indicates less distance.

Cues Based on Properties of the Visual System   Several cues to depth result from the way human eyes are built and positioned. One of these cues

Figure 5.15
Light, Shadow, and Depth Perception
Here you perceive the three-dimensionality of a series of protruding rivets. Now hold the book upside down and look again. The rivets look like dents, and the dents look like bumps. This reversal occurs because people normally assume that illumination comes from above and interpret the pattern of light and shadows from the perspective of this assumption. When the picture is turned upside down, light coming from the top would produce the observed pattern of shadows only if the circles were dents, not rivets.

is related to facts discussed in Chapter 4. To bring an image into focus on the retina, the lens of the eyeball changes shape, or *accommodates.* To accomplish this feat, muscles surrounding the lens must either tighten, to make the lens more curved for focusing on close objects, or relax, to flatten the lens for focusing on more distant objects. Information about the activity of the muscles is relayed to the brain, and this accommodation cue helps create the perception of distance.

The location of each eye at a different spot on the head produces two other depth cues. One is **convergence:** because each eye is located at a slightly different place, the eyes must converge, or rotate inward, in order to project the image of an object on each retina. As Figure 5.16 shows, the closer the object is, the more "cross-eyed" the viewer must become in order to achieve a focused image. The brain receives and processes neural information from the eye muscles about this activity; the greater the activity, the closer the object is perceived to be.

Second, because of their differing locations, each eye receives a slightly different view of the world, as Figure 5.17 illustrates. The difference between the two retinal images of an object is called **binocular disparity.** For any particular object, this disparity decreases with increasing distance. The brain combines the two images, processes information about the amount of disparity, and generates the impression of a single object having its correct depth, as well as height and width. Thus, Viewmaster slide viewers and 3-D movies can create the appearance of depth by displaying to each eye a separate photograph of an object or scene, each taken from a slightly different angle.

What binocular disparity does for depth perception, the placement of the ears does for sound localization; that is, it provides a cue for the directions from which sounds arise. If a sound is continuous, the peak of sound waves coming toward the right side of the head will reach the right ear before reaching the left ear. Similarly, a sound coming from the right side of the

Figure 5.16
Convergence
The strength of proprioceptive information going to the brain depends on the closeness of objects. The closer an object, the more the eyes must converge, and the greater the proprioceptive information.

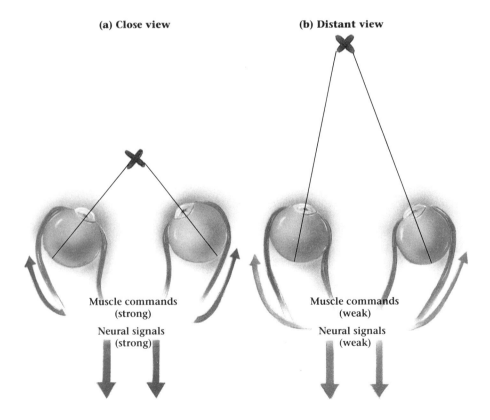

(a) Close view

(b) Distant view

Muscle commands (strong)

Neural signals (strong)

Muscle commands (weak)

Neural signals (weak)

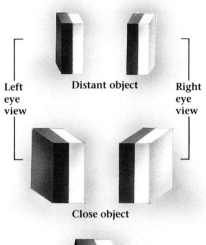

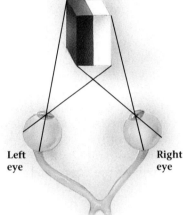

Images go to brain
where they are compared

Figure 5.17
Binocular Disparity
Each eye has a slightly different view of the cube. The difference between views is greater when the cube is close than when it is far away. For a quick demonstration, hold a pencil up vertically about six inches in front of you. Close one eye and take note of where the pencil is relative to the objects in the background. Now open that eye and close the other one. Notice how the pencil seems to shift slightly and how it obscures slightly different parts of the background. These are the two views your eyes have of that pencil. If you now hold the pencil at arm's length or look at some other narrow vertical object some distance away, there is less difference in the angles at which the two eyes see the object, and the amount of disparity (or shift) decreases.

head will be a little bit louder to the right ear than to the left ear, because the head blocks some of the sound from the left ear. Thus, the nervous system uses both timing and intensity cues to locate sounds. This ability to localize sounds requires sophisticated analysis of auditory input by the brain.

The Perception of Motion

Sometimes, the critical property of an object is not its size or shape or distance but its motion—how fast it is going and where it is heading. The perception of moving form is quite different from the perception of still form. For example, a still photograph of twelve points of light attached to the hands, elbows, shoulders, ankles, knees, and hips of a person in a dark room cannot be recognized as a human form. However, the moment these same points of light are viewed in a movie of the person walking or jogging, they are instantly recognized as human movement; even the sex of the figure can be identified (Johansson, Hofsten & Jansson, 1980). In other words, people often get a lot of additional information about the world from seeing it in motion.

Usually the perception of motion occurs as visual patterns from objects move across the surface of the retina. Like distance perception, the perception of motion requires translating this two-dimensional retinal image into a three-dimensional experience. People make this translation automatically.

Looming, which is a rapid expansion in the size of an image so that it fills the available space on the retina, is a good example. When an image looms, there is an automatic tendency to perceive it as an approaching stimulus, not an expanding object viewed at a constant distance. Furthermore, if the rate of expansion is as fast to the right as to the left, and as fast above as below, this information signals that the object is directly approaching the eyes. In other words: duck! (Regan, Kaufman & Lincoln, 1986).

If movement of the retinal image were the only factor contributing to motion perception, however, swinging your head around or even rotating your eyeballs should create the perception that everything in the visual field is moving in the opposite direction. This does not happen because as discussed in Chapter 4, the brain also receives information about the motion of the eyes and head. If the brain determines that all of the movement of light on the retina is due to bodily movement, the outside world is perceived as stable. To demonstrate this, close one eye and wiggle your open eyeball by gently pushing your lower eyelid. Now the brain no longer receives the usual signals that the eye is moved by its own muscles, and the world is perceived as the moving element.

When you *are* moving, the movement gradient discussed in the section on depth perception can provide another cue to this fact. Imagine you are in a car riding forward toward the horizon. As you look forward, objects appear to diverge from the point where the road disappears into the horizon and to move faster as they move away from this vanishing point. This pattern is automatically perceived as the forward movement of your own body toward and past unmoving objects.

Normally, as you move through an environment, the flow of visual information across the retina is also combined with information from the vestibular and tactile senses discussed in Chapter 4. For example, if you accelerate in a car, you feel pressure from the back of the seat and you feel your head tilt backward. When visual flow is perceived without appropriate sensations from other parts of the body, motion sickness may be the result. This explains why people sometimes feel sick in flight and driving simulators (including some video games); the moving images suggest that they are in motion when there is no real motion (Andersen, 1986).

Thus, the perception that you or the world is moving may depend on a combination of information from the retinal image, gradients, head and eye movements, and the vestibular and tactile senses. British psychologist Gordon Denton used an understanding of motion perception to suggest a clever solution to a serious problem in the British highway system. Drivers were not slowing down enough as they approached traffic circles. Denton suggested that a series of lines be painted across the highway at progressively closer intervals as the required stopping point was approached. When traversed at a constant speed, the lines appear to go by at an increasing rate, creating the perception of acceleration and prompting drivers to slow down. When this technique was introduced at a particularly hazardous traffic circle in Scotland, approach speeds dropped significantly, and the traffic accident rate declined from fourteen in the twelve months prior to the innovation to only two in the fourteen months following (Denton, 1980).

Perceptual Illusions

The perceptual cues we have described convey precise information, continuously and automatically, about a multitude of objects and surfaces. As a result, you can walk downstairs, toss a wad of paper into a distant trash can, avoid collisions while driving, and accomplish a thousand other everyday acts with little hesitation and without a second thought. In fact, you are unlikely to become aware of perceptual cues at all unless you read about them or unless they create an inaccurate or distorted view of reality. In Chapter 6, on consciousness, we describe how distorted perceptions can come about through sleep, hypnosis, drugs, and other circumstances; here we are concerned with those distortions of reality known as *perceptual illusions.*

A Sampling of Illusions Motion pictures depend on one perceptual illusion: *stroboscopic motion,* the perception of motion produced when a series of images, each slightly different from the next, are presented one after the other. Illusory movement may also occur if you adopt the wrong frame of reference or the wrong hypothesis. Normally, when there is relative movement between figure and ground, the figure is more likely to be perceived as moving and the background as stable. If you therefore perceive a figure to be moving when it is not, the illusion is called *induced motion.*

You may experience induced motion when you sit in a stationary car in a parking lot, and the vehicle next to you begins to move slowly backward. You are likely to perceive your own car as drifting forward—even though cues from the vestibular senses tell you that you are not moving, and your kinesthetic senses say that your foot is planted firmly on the brake. Why are these vestibular and kinesthetic cues temporarily ignored? The answer lies in **visual dominance.** When information received by the visual system conflicts with information coming from other senses, the sense of vision normally wins the battle and is perceived as accurate (Posner, Nissen & Klein, 1976).

Figure 5.18 presents six other perceptual illusions. Parts (a) through (c) involve distortions of shape; they support the Gestalt principle that the whole is different from the sum of its parts. Part (d) shows an illusion called the *Poggendorf illusion;* it occurs when a diagonal line intersects a horizontal or vertical one. The eye "bends" the angular line away from the vertical one. Thus, it appears that lines A and B in the figure will not connect, even though they do.

The *Ebbinghaus illusion* is shown in Figure 5.18(e). Look at the circles in the center of each pattern. The one on the left probably looks smaller to you than the one on the right, though both are in fact the same size. This illusion

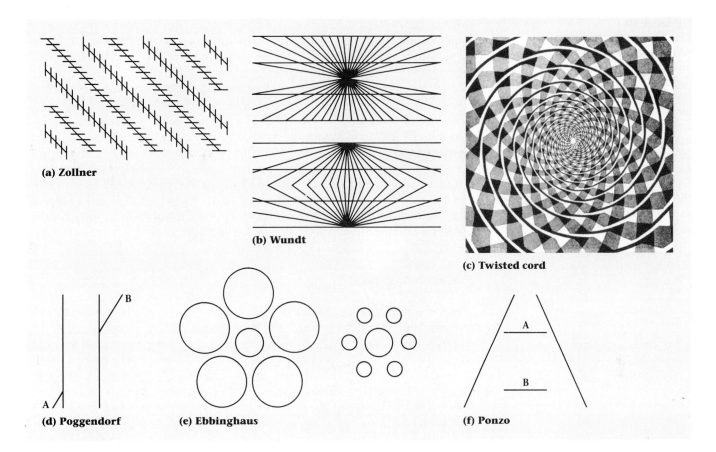

(a) Zollner

(b) Wundt

(c) Twisted cord

(d) Poggendorf

(e) Ebbinghaus

(f) Ponzo

Figure 5.18
Six Perceptual Illusions
In the Zollner illusion (a), you can focus attention directly on a pair of parallel lines to establish that they are in fact parallel, but if you draw back to consider the entire figure, you get the clear impression that they are not parallel. The horizontal lines in the Wundt illusion (b) are actually parallel, and the twisted cord (c) is actually made up of concentric circles. The distortions of directions in the Zollner and Wundt illusions appear to be related to the Poggendorf illusion (d). The lines in the Poggendorf illusion will actually connect behind the obstruction. The Ebbinghaus illusion (e) is a direct analogy to the misjudgment of brightness shown in Figure 5.12. The Ponzo illusion (f) uses converging lines to create the impression that the top horizontal line is at a greater distance than the bottom one. This greater perceived distance, multiplied by the retinal size of the top line, gives it a larger perceived size (length) than the bottom line, even though the two are identical.

illustrates again that perceptual judgments take place *relative to* some context. In the left-hand pattern, the context (or background) for the center, which consists of larger objects, creates the perception that the center circle is relatively small. The right-hand center circle appears in a context of smaller objects, making you perceive it as larger. Dieters should keep this in mind: a small meal looks more substantial if served on a small plate. Advertisers use this fact to make their products look more filling.

Other illusions involving size result from the way in which the perceptual system automatically grabs onto any cue to depth in order to provide a three-dimensional interpretation of a stimulus. The *Ponzo illusion* is a perfect example. In Figure 5.18(f), line segment A looks longer than segment B, yet they are the same length. You misperceive their lengths because the perceptual system uses the converging lines as its primary depth cue (recall linear perspective, discussed earlier). Thus, you view the region where the lines are closer together as more distant. Recall that when two objects have retinal images of the same size, the one perceived as farther away is seen as larger. As a result, the line seen as more distant here is also seen as longer. (See Figure 5.19 for another fascinating, and common, illusion.)

Analyzing Illusions   Illusions are more than just perceptual curiosities. They tell a great deal about factors like linear perspective that underlie normal perception. (For an overview of normal perception, see "In Review: Features of Perception.") Sometimes they produce perceptual distortions that can have consequences outside of the laboratory, as Figure 5.20 illustrates.

Probably the best-known and most studied perceptual illusion is the *Müller-Lyer illusion,* shown in Figure 5.21(a). The arrow shaft on the left seems shorter, even though the two shafts are actually of equal length. Richard Gregory

Figure 5.19
The Moon Illusion
Why does the moon appear larger on the horizon than overhead? Experiments by Kaufman and Rock (1962) suggest that it is because the moon on the horizon, seen across an intervening space filled with houses, trees, and terrain, appears to be farther away. Since the horizon moon has nearly the same size retinal image as the moon overhead, the greater perceived distance causes us to experience the horizon moon as larger.

Figure 5.20
A Practical Example of the Poggendorf Illusion
Here a surgeon has inserted a diagonal probe to contact a bullet embedded on the far side of the bone. The distortion caused by the Poggendorf illusion will cause the surgeon to misjudge the required point of entry if the probe goes in at an angle (Coren & Girgus, 1978). The probe will miss the bullet.

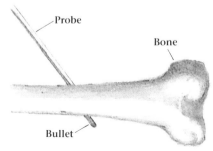

Source: Matlin, 1988.

(1968, 1973) has argued that this illusion, like the Ponzo illusion, represents a misapplication of the depth cue of linear perspective. The convergence of the arrowheads on each side of the shaft on the left makes the shaft appear to be the closest part of the scene—like the outside corner of the house in Figure 5.21(b)—whereas the divergence of the arrowheads on the right makes that shaft seem to be toward the back. By the logic applied to the Ponzo illusion, the more "distant" shaft appears to be larger.

The idea that depth cues underlie the Müller-Lyer illusion is supported by the fact that increasing the amount of three-dimensional information in the drawing increases the magnitude of the illusion (Leibowitz et al., 1969). Furthermore, the illusion is stronger among subjects who have more experience making depth and distance judgments using parallel lines and corners (Gregory, 1968; Leibowitz, 1971). For example, Pedersen and Wheeler (1983) found that the illusion was experienced more strongly by Navajo Indians who had been raised in rectangular frame dwellings, and therefore were used to seeing the converging lines and corners shown in Figure 5.21(b), than by those raised in the traditional circular hogans.

Attractive as the depth perception theory of the Müller-Lyer illusion may seem, it cannot account for some phenomena. A striking example is shown in Figure 5.21(c). The figure has no converging lines to suggest distance, and the figure does not give a feeling of three-dimensionality, yet it still creates a misjudgment like that in the Müller-Lyer illusion. Why? One proposed explanation is that the perceived length of an object is based on its "frame." When the frame is perceived as larger, as it is in the right side of Figure 5.21(c), so is the line segment within it (Rock, 1978).

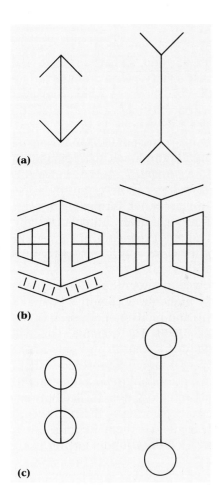

(a)

(b)

(c)

Figure 5.21
Variations on the Müller-Lyer Illusion
Part (a) shows the Müller-Lyer illusion. In part (b) the illusion is placed in a three-dimensional context, in which the vertical line is used to form the outside corner of a house and the inside corner of a room. The inside corner looks taller. Part (c) shows a demonstration of the illusion that does not involve perception of three dimensions.

Perhaps the best conclusion to offer at this point is that illusions such as the Müller-Lyer are multiply determined. After all, since perception is based on many principles, it seems reasonable that illusions could reflect the violation of more than one of them.

Distortions of perception may even be created by the same factors that create response bias in detecting stimuli: motivation, experience, and expectancy. In one classic study, children were asked to estimate the size of poker chips by adjusting a disk of light to match a displayed chip. Children who had been told they could use the poker chip to buy candy estimated the chip to be larger than other children did, suggesting that objects that are more important may be perceived as larger (Lambert, Solomon & Watson, 1949). In the next section we examine how motivation, expectations, and other factors highlighted by signal-detection theory can also affect the speed and accuracy with which people recognize objects in the world.

In Review: *Features of Perception*

Feature	Description	Example
Knowledge-based	Perception matches incoming stimuli with previously learned information.	You perceive words in a language you know well faster than those in a less familiar language.
Inferential	People do not always perceive stimuli exactly as they are, but infer what should be there.	You perceive the incomplete shape in Figure 5.2 as a triangle.
Categorical	Many different stimuli may be experienced as belonging to a single perceptual category.	The shapes A, a, and *a* are all perceived as the letter *A*.
Relational	Perception is influenced by the relationships between one stimulus and the other stimuli around it.	A 5'8" person will be perceived as short when standing among college basketball players, but as tall when near a junior high school team.
Adaptive	Perception allows people to focus on the most important aspects of the environment.	You are most likely to perceive the speed of a car if it is approaching you in a crosswalk; you would be more likely to perceive its color if you are looking at it in a showroom.
Automatic	Many perceptual processes operate very rapidly, without conscious awareness.	You can recognize common objects, including your friends, without being aware of the categorical, knowledge-based operations involved in doing so.

Recognizing the Perceptual World

In discussing how people organize the perceptual world, we have so far ignored one vital question: how do people recognize what objects are? If you are driving in search of Barney's Diner, exactly what happens when your eyes finally locate the pattern of light that spells out "Barney's Diner"? How do you recognize it as the place you are seeking?

Basically, the brain must analyze the incoming pattern of light and compare that pattern to information stored in memory. If it finds a match, recognition takes place and the stimulus is placed into a *perceptual category*. Once this recognition occurs, your perception of a stimulus may never be the same. Look at Figure 5.22. Do you see anything familiar? If not, turn to Figure 5.23. Now look at Figure 5.22 again. You should now see it in an entirely new light. The difference between your "before" and "after" experience of Figure 5.22 is the difference between the sensory world before and after a perceptual match occurs and recognition takes place.

Two types of processing appear to be involved in recognition. Some aspects of recognition begin at the "top," guided by higher-level cognitive processes and by psychological factors like expectations and motivation; these make up **top-down processing** (Lindsay & Norman, 1977). For example, you will recognize the Barney's Diner sign more easily if it appears precisely at the corner where your map says you should expect it rather than a block earlier. Other aspects of recognition depend first on the information about the stimulus that comes "up" to the brain from the sensory receptors; this is called **bottom-up processing**. When people inspect an abstract painting or listen to speech in an unfamiliar language, with little knowledge to help them interpret either, they are using primarily bottom-up processing. How does bottom-up processing work?

Feature Analysis

In Chapter 4 we described one way in which bottom-up processing might produce recognition. Recall that specific neurons in the brain called *feature detectors* fire in response to certain features of stimuli, such as lines, edges, corners, and angles (Hubel & Wiesel, 1979). And there are cells in the auditory cortex that fire only in response to features corresponding to different pitches, loudnesses, and timbres of sounds.

The presence of feature detectors in the visual and auditory cortex supports the view that recognition occurs by means of **feature analysis** (Biederman, 1987). According to this view, any stimulus or object can be described as a combination of features. The letter *A*, for example, can be described as consisting of one horizontal and two angular lines connected at an acute angle. The sensory system analyzes a stimulus into a set of such features. Then the brain compares this set against information stored in memory. (How memories are stored is discussed in Chapter 8.) If there is a match, recognition occurs.

Feature analysis not only explains how people recognize stimuli that are exactly like familiar ones but also provides a plausible explanation for how different stimuli can be given the same interpretation. When you look at, say, a dachshund, Saint Bernard, or poodle, you recognize each animal as a dog, because each presents a pattern of features that corresponds to a stored category you know as *dog*. But what happens when a combination of features does not quite match a stored perceptual category—if you see a three-legged dog, for example? Here, the recognition process places the stimulus in the closest

Figure 5.22
Perceptual Categorization
For the identity of this figure, turn the page.

category, while also noting the features that do not fit that category. Thus, you say, "That's a dog with three legs"; you do not say, "That's a milking stool."

Models of Object Recognition

Feature analysis is critically important to object recognition, but the precise way in which features in a stimulus become associated with a recognized object or perceptual category remains a matter of considerable debate (Hasher & Johnson, 1987).

According to the *hierarchical feature-detection model,* feature detectors are organized so that specific sets of neurons in the brain fire only when they find their match in the perceptual world, much as only one fork in a row of tuning forks will vibrate when its matching pitch is played; the result is recognition (Lindsay & Norman, 1977). However, we noted in Chapter 4 that this model has at least one serious problem: you would need a different feature detector for every one of the seemingly infinite number of specific sights, sounds, smells, and other stimuli that you recognize. Remember the "grandmother cell"? (We also noted in Chapter 4 that the spatial frequency filter model may also describe how the brain analyzes patterns, but we do not yet know whether this model can produce a better explanation of how recognition occurs.)

Do people maintain mental lists of features about each category and recognize a stimulus as belonging to the category with which it matches the most features? Do they match the stimulus to a specific instance or memorable example of a category and then associate the stimulus with that category (Hintzman, 1986)? Or do they match the stimulus to a *schema,* a mental representation of the category that preserves the *average* characteristics of all of its members, without maintaining the details of any specific example (Hasher & Johnson, 1987)?

Possibilities like these are being explored by psychologists and computer scientists working together to develop computer programs that can classify objects rapidly and effectively. Such programs are required for teaching

Figure 5.23
Another Version of Figure 5.22
Now that you can identify the figure clearly, look back to the previous figure, which should be much easier to recognize.

Figure 5.24
Recognizing a Word
Each letter in the word shown here is ambiguous. The first could be *R* or *P,* the second *E* or *F,* and the third *D* or *B.* Yet *together* the letters are easily perceived as *RED.* According to PDP models, recognition occurs because the letters together excite each other's appropriate and correct interpretation. For example, the interpretation of the first letter as *R* and not *P* is excited, while incorrect interpretations are inhibited. Simultaneously, the interpretation of the last letter as *D* and not *B* is excited because only *D* is consistent with an *R* as the first letter. Recognition thus occurs in parallel.

Source: McClelland & Rumelhart, 1986.

computers to read handwriting and for teaching industrial robots to recognize objects that they must grasp and manipulate.

One explanation of object recognition has developed from research on the neurophysiology of the human brain. As discussed in Chapter 3, neurons in the brain are organized into units called networks, and there is a constant interplay between excitation and inhibition within and between networks. This concept provides the basic elements for **parallel distributed processing (PDP) models** of recognition, also called *neural networks* or *connectionist models* (McClelland & Rumelhart, 1986).

According to PDP models, recognition does not depend on one neural unit in just one place but on the parallel operation of connected units that may be widely distributed. Recognition occurs as a result of the parallel (simultaneous) operation of connected units that are activated when matched by features in the stimulus. The *connections* between units either excite or inhibit other units. Each connection has a different weight or strength, which is formed on the basis of past experience in classifying patterns. Figure 5.24 provides an example. PDP models are run on computers as a means of imitating human perception.

Top-Down Processing

Bottom-up feature analysis, whether accomplished by schemas, PDP operations, or some other process, can nicely explain how a set of diverse stimuli (a dachshund and a Saint Bernard, for example) can be assigned to one category as long as the stimuli share many of the same features. But bottom-up feature analysis cannot easily explain how people handle *ambiguous* stimuli, assigning a stimulus sometimes to one category and sometimes to another. In Figure 5.9, for example, you can recognize the stimulus either as a vase or as two faces. In Figure 5.25, one stimulus pattern can be recognized as either the number *13* or the letter *B*; another pattern can be perceived as either a lowercase

130Y   413467

Figure 5.25
Limitations of Bottom-Up
Processing
Because the same physical stimulus can be recognized in different ways from time to time, perceptual processing must depend in part on internal factors, not just on the stimulus itself.

b or a baseball cap. Since these shifting recognitions are based on the same stimulus pattern, the differences cannot be attributed to feature analysis or some other bottom-up process.

Expectancy The shifting perceptions of the patterns in Figure 5.25 must have something to do with the *context* in which these stimuli are embedded. An ambiguous pattern is perceived as a number when next to other numbers, as a letter when accompanied by other letters, as a hat when on top of a head. The context creates an *expectancy* about what will be perceived.

Along with motivation, expectancy is a major factor that influences perception through top-down processing. As an example, look at Figure 5.26(a). How old is the woman you see? Look again, because like the vase-face example in Figure 5.9, this is an ambiguous figure. Some people immediately see an attractive young woman wearing a feathered hat and turning her head away. Others see an old woman with a large nose and a protruding chin (Boring, 1930). Which one you recognize first can be influenced by what you expect to see. Robert Leeper (1935) showed people either Figure 5.26(b), in which the young woman is strongly emphasized, or Figure 5.26(c), which makes the old woman stand out. Then he showed Figure 5.26(a), the ambiguous drawing, to everyone. Most of those who had first seen the "young woman" version continued to see her in the ambiguous figure, whereas the old woman was more often identified by those who had seen the version emphasizing her. Thus, past experience, like context, can create expectancy.

Expectancy, in turn, can bias perception toward one recognition or another by creating a *perceptual set,* a readiness or predisposition to perceive a stimulus in a certain way. This effect of expectancy applies to sounds as well as to sights. The raw sound "eye scream" takes on two very different meanings when heard in the context of "I scream whenever I am angry" as opposed to "I love ice cream."

The expectancy created by a familiar context can make recognition easier. For example, in one experiment, people were shown a familiar scene, like a kitchen. Then they were given a very brief glimpse of an object that would be expected in that context (for example, a loaf of bread) or one that would be unexpected (for example, a rural mailbox). Although the two objects were roughly the same size and shape, the subjects recognized the object that fit the context more readily than the object that did not (Palmer, 1975). Similarly, people have a more difficult time recognizing objects when certain expected properties are violated, as Figure 5.27 illustrates (Biederman et al., 1981).

Just as the perception of objects and words is guided by top-down processes, the perception of people can also be influenced by expectancies. Thus, you may initially categorize someone as a certain type of person because he or she belongs to a certain fraternity or sorority. Then you may interpret that person's behavior in the light of your initial perception. In the chapter on social cognition we explore some of the consequences of this process.

Motivation Suppose you are very hungry as you drive down the street of an unfamiliar city. You don't care if you find Barney's Diner or not; you'll eat anywhere. In this state of mind, you are likely to experience many false alarms, slamming on the brakes and salivating at the sight of "Eaton's Furniture," "Burger's Body Shop," "Cherry Hill Estates," or any other sign that even hints at food.

Many motives can alter perceptions. If you have ever watched an athletic contest, you probably remember a time when an obviously demented referee incorrectly called a foul on the team you wanted to win. You knew the call was wrong because you clearly saw the other team's player at fault. But suppose

(a)

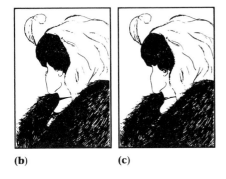

(b)   **(c)**

Figure 5.26
An Ambiguous Figure
Which face do you see in part (a)?
Unambiguous portraits of the young
and old women are shown in parts
(b) and (c).

you had been cheering for the other team. The chances are good that you
would have seen the referee's call as the right one.

The effect of motivation on the categorization of ambiguous stimuli was
demonstrated in a classic laboratory study (Schafer & Murphy, 1943). Figure
5.28 explains the experiment. The results of the experiment indicated that
people are biased toward recognizing stimuli that fall in a category that is
associated with reward.

Top-Down and Bottom-Up Processes Together

Though we have discussed them separately, bottom-up and top-down processing work together in a constant interaction that creates the experience of
a recognizable world. (For a summary of both, see "In Review: Mechanisms
of Pattern Recognition.") In fact, one kind of processing will "fill in" when
the other becomes impaired. (We described this phenomenon as closure when
we discussed the perception of objects.) In Figure 5.10(d), for example, top-
down processing took over to allow recognition of an object, even though the
poor quality of an incomplete drawing made bottom-up processing difficult.
Similarly, if you have had only a brief encounter with someone, you tend to
"fill in the gaps" about that person's personality by using your knowledge of
other people whose appearance or actions or interests remind you of this
person, even though the result may be an incorrect inference about the person.

Reading illustrates the interaction of bottom-up and top-down processing
beautifully. Even when the quality of the raw stimulus on the printed page
becomes quite poor, as in Figure 5.29, top-down processes compensate to
make continued reading possible. They allow you to fill in where words are
not well perceived and processed, thus giving a general idea of the meaning
of the text.

You can fill in the gaps left by stimuli because the world is *redundant,* giving
multiple clues about what is going on. If you lose or miss one stimulus in a
pattern, others can fill in the gaps so that you can still recognize the total
pattern. There is so much redundancy in written language, for example, that
many of the words and letters you see are not needed. Fo- ex-mp-e y-u c-n
r-ad -hi- se-te-ce -it- ev-ry -hi-d l-tt-r m-ss-ng. Similarly, vision in three
dimensions normally provides multiple redundant cues to depth, and perception is unambiguous. It is only when many of the cues are eliminated that
ambiguous stimuli, allowing multiple interpretations, create the sort of depth
illusions discussed earlier in the chapter.

Figure 5.27
Context and Recognition
These are examples of stimuli used
by Biederman et al. (1981). On the
left, the fire hydrant is harder to perceive because it is in the wrong location and unsupported. On the right,
the car is harder to see because of its
inappropriate size and location.

Source: Human Factors Society, Inc., 1981.

For the spoken word, too, top-down processing can compensate for ambiguous stimuli. This fact was nicely illustrated in an experiment in which strings of five words in meaningless order, such as "wet brought who socks some," were read to subjects. The background was so noisy that an average of only 75 percent of the words could be recognized (Miller, Heise & Lichten, 1951). Under these conditions, bottom-up processing was difficult, because the quality of the raw stimuli was poor. But when the same words, presented under the same noisy conditions, were reordered to make a meaningful sentence (for example, "who brought some wet socks"), a second group of subjects was able to recognize almost every word. In fact, in order to reduce their performance to that of the first group, the noise level had to be doubled! Why? When the words were in meaningless order, only bottom-up processing was available, and recognizing one word was no help in identifying the next. The meaningful sentence provided a more familiar context, allowing for some top-down processing in which hearing one word helped the listener make a reasonable guess (based on knowledge and experience) about the others.

Research on the effects of top-down processing also shows how much truth there is in such sayings as "beauty is in the eye of the beholder." Perhaps you have come to perceive someone as physically more attractive or less attractive as you got to know him or her better. Assuming no cosmetic surgery, this change in perception occurs largely because the new information comes to alter, in top-down fashion, your interpretation of the raw sensations provided by the person's "real" appearance. Indeed, reality is actually somewhat different for each person. In Chapters 14 and 15, we consider how these differences help form the basis of individual personalities and behavior disorders.

In Review: Mechanisms of Pattern Recognition

Mechanism or Model	Description	Example
Hierarchical feature detection	Physical patterns are recognized because the set of features stored in memory of the perceptual category are present in the stimulus.	You categorize a dog as a dog because it has the physical features that characterize dogs (e.g., four legs, hair, size, a bark, panting tongue).
Schema	Physical patterns are recognized because they match most closely the "average" physical appearance of all examples of that class of stimuli as experienced in the past.	You categorize a dog as a dog because the creature you see has a size, shape, and color similar to the average experience of these features in dogs you have seen in the past.
Neural networks	Physical patterns are recognized because features that have appeared together in the past excited each other's representation in the brain when they were perceived. Thus, excitement spreads across connections that form neural networks.	A dog is perceived because the neural unit activated by "panting tongue," excites the unit activated by a "barking sound" and by a "wagging tail." The more these neural units are experienced together, the stronger their connections become.
Top-down processing	Physical patterns are recognized because they appear in a *context* in which they are expected or because the perceiver is motivated to perceive them.	A small dark blob straining against a leash is perceived as a dog because that is a context in which a dog would logically be expected.

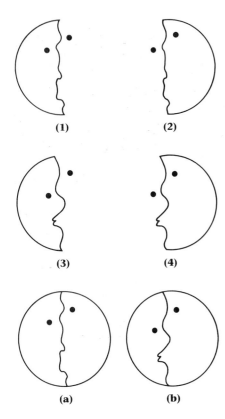

(1)   (2)

(3)   (4)

(a)   (b)

Figure 5.28
Motivation and Recognition
Schafer and Murphy (1943) trained people to associate names with profiles 1, 2, 3, and 4. The people received money when two of the profiles were presented and lost money when the other two appeared. After training, the people were shown brief glimpses of ambiguous figures created by combining one rewarded and one punished profile, as in sections (a) and (b), and were asked to name the face they perceived. The people reported seeing the rewarded face significantly more than half the time.

Figure 5.29
Interaction of Top-Down and Bottom-Up Processing
Top-down processing assists in reading the obscured text on the top line. However, in the bottom line, the words are not meaningfully related, so top-down processing cannot operate.

Attention

Believe it or not, you still haven't found Barney's Diner. As you continue driving, you turn on the radio and catch a particularly interesting story about aliens who have landed in the parking lot of a Columbus, Ohio, shopping center. After listening intently to the story, you realize that you have not been paying attention to your search for Barney's. Did you miss it? Your not being sure demonstrates that it is often necessary to pay attention to something in order to perceive it.

Attention is the process of directing and focusing certain psychological resources, usually by voluntary control, to enhance perception, performance, and mental experience. For example, in order to read this page you focused a psychological resource when you shifted your attention from the television, the newspaper, or whatever else you were paying attention to earlier. And you will do it again, should you shift from reading to listening to a nearby conversation.

Selective Attention

Part of the reason everyone experiences a somewhat different reality is that everyone pays attention to somewhat different aspects of the environment. Like a spotlight on a dark night, the beam of attention is too narrow to illuminate the entire world at once (Eriksen & Yeh, 1985; Wachtel, 1967). It must scan the environment sequentially. In other words, attention is *selective*, focusing on some stimuli while ignoring others.

What determines where the attentional spotlight moves—which things are attended to and which are not? For one thing, attention can be automatically attracted to very familiar stimuli, like the sound of your own name (Moray, 1960). More generally, events or stimuli that have certain properties tend to attract attention. Characteristics that may attract attention include large size, high intensity, contrast, motion, and novelty. Advertisers use these characteristics, creating ads containing large, bright, colorful images; high volume; lots of novelty; and unexpected contrasts. Magicians capitalize on selective attention by creating compelling visual events that pull the audience's attention away from the actions that lie behind their tricks.

The focus of attention (like the ability to detect signals) is also determined by motivation and expectancy. Thus, compared with someone who has just eaten, a hungry person's attention will be more readily attracted to the smell of food.

Focused and Divided Attention

Although attention is selective, people can also *divide* attention, devoting psychological resources to more than one task or stimulus at a time. In fact,

it is very easy to read this redundant sentence
BUT NOT
better resist reading past grammar &/or word string

A three-ringed circus makes spectators aware of how difficult it is to pay attention to many different events at once. Whether we are at the circus or not, limitations on our attentional resources force us to be selective, attending at any given moment to some aspects of the environment while ignoring others.

people sometimes have difficulty *focusing* attention, keeping the attentional spotlight on just one task or stimulus.

Look at the list of words in Figure 5.30. Now read the list and say aloud, as fast as you can, the color of the ink in which each word is printed. You probably went through a good deal of fumbling and confusion as you performed this exercise, known as the *Stroop task* (Keele, 1973; Stroop, 1935). Why? You were trying to keep your attention focused on one aspect of the stimuli (color) when another very powerful aspect (the meaning of the words) was competing for your attention. Further, these two aspects of the stimuli called for *incompatible* responses (for example, saying "red" when reading the word *green*).

This simple task illustrates two facts about attention. First, it is difficult to maintain the *focus* of attention on just one stimulus or one aspect of a stimulus when another aspect is also attention-getting. In this case, the two competing stimulus aspects are the color and the meaning of a single word. Second, it may be very easy to *divide* attention between two stimuli or aspects of stimuli, especially if they are physically close or similar. Thus, the difficulty of the Stroop task lies in the fact that it requires you to focus on just one stimulus aspect and ignore others, when you are instead dividing attention between the two, perceiving both the word's meaning and color at the same time.

Under other circumstances, people can focus attention very narrowly. For example, Colin Cherry (1953) asked subjects to perform a **dichotic listening task,** in which different messages are played into each ear. To force the subjects to focus attention on only one of the messages, Cherry asked them to *shadow* one of the messages; that is, to repeat immediately, word for word, everything heard in one ear. After performing this task for a while, the people could say almost nothing about what had been presented to the nonattended ear. They could not even report if the message played to that ear had remained in English, had been replaced by a string of foreign language words, or had become a string of nonsense syllables. Similarly, in another experiment people watched a screen on which two video games were superimposed. When they were told to focus attention on the stimuli in one of the games, they became totally unaware of events in the other game (Neisser & Becklan, 1975).

Figure 5.30
Stroop Task
The task here is to say the color of the ink in which each word is printed.

BLUE	**GREEN**
GREEN	**ORANGE**
PURPLE	ORANGE
GREEN	BLUE
RED	**RED**
GRAY	GRAY
RED	**BLUE**
BLUE	**PURPLE**

This ability to focus attention can be a blessing, allowing you, for example, to "tune out" a boring lecture and focus attention on something more enjoyable. But limitations on the ability to divide attention can also be inconvenient, as when you try to watch television and have a conversation at the same time.

What determines whether you can divide attention, performing more than a few actions at a time, for example, or listening to more than one voice? The ability depends in part on how much you practice doing it, what other tasks are performed, the difficulty of the tasks, and the amount of stress involved.

Practice People who are experienced at dividing their attention do better at it than novices. Experience helps because extensive practice allows a person to process and act on perceptual information so automatically that the practiced task requires little attention, making it possible for other tasks to be carried out at the same time, with no loss in performance (Detweiller & Schneider, 1988). For example, skilled typists can transcribe a written message and perform an auditory shadowing task simultaneously just as well as they can perform either task alone (Shaffer, 1975). Obviously, it is easier to divide attention between two sets of stimuli when one of them no longer requires much attention in order to be perceived and processed.

Nature of the Stimuli In general, the closer together in space two stimuli are, the more easily they can be perceived at the same time. Dividing attention is also easier when the stimuli do not compete for attention through the same sensory system; for example, people can perceive a light and a sound at the same time more easily than two lights or two sounds. Why? Apparently, the human brain has more than one pool of attentional resources and more than one spotlight of attention (Navon & Gopher, 1979; Wickens, 1989). Each spotlight of attention tends to focus on a particular information-processing channel.

This is one reason why skilled secretaries can type and shadow efficiently at the same time: typing requires visual perception (and movement of the fingers and hands), whereas shadowing requires auditory perception and vocal responses (Shaffer, 1975). Somewhat different attentional resources are used in each task (Tsang & Wickens, 1988). This notion of different attentional pools also helps explain why a driver can listen to the radio while steering safely and why voice control can be an effective way of interacting with a computer while your hands are busy on the keyboard (Martin, 1989).

Difficulty of the Task If you drive a car down an open road, you probably have no trouble conversing with passengers. But if the traffic becomes heavy, your conversation will probably become less fluent and may stop altogether, because the driving task is now more difficult and takes more attentional resources. Similarly, remembering a seven-digit phone number you have just heard demands attention and can be disrupted by other attention-getting tasks, such as being asked what time it is. The more difficult a task, the more it interferes with other tasks (Wickens, 1989).

Linkages: How does stress affect the ability to pay attention to various stimuli? (a link to Stress, Coping, and Health)

Stress Suppose your job is to operate the controls of a modern, automated power plant. You face a vast array of dials, meters, graphs, charts, and warning lights. Should a serious problem occur, all of these stimuli will compete for your attention. To perceive all of them correctly, your beam of attention must be divided as widely as possible. However, the stress of emergency situations tends to narrow attention, not broaden it (Easterbrook, 1959; Hockey, 1984).

Nowhere have the limits of the ability to divide attention under stress been more clearly and tragically demonstrated than just prior to the crash of an

Linkages: Stress tends to narrow the focus of our attention, as was clearly demonstrated in the 1979 accident at the Three Mile Island nuclear power plant. A loss of coolant flowing to one of the reactors threatened to expose the radioactive fuel core and trigger a meltdown. During the first few minutes of coolant loss, the plant operators paid attention only to certain indicators, which, as it turned out, gave them incorrect information. These faulty indicators suggested that the coolant pressure was too high, not too low. Under the stress of the emergency, the operators' attention was not wide enough to perceive information from other displays, which were showing the true status of the reactor. As a result, the operators shut off a pump that would have restored badly needed coolant, an error that made the situation far worse than it might have been (Rubinstein & Mason, 1979; Wickens, 1984b).

Eastern Airlines L1011 into the Florida Everglades in 1972 (Wiener, 1977). The plane was approaching the Miami airport at night when the crew became aware of a warning light indicating that the landing gear was malfunctioning. They set the autopilot for level flight and then directed their attention to diagnosing the cause of the warning light. Somehow the autopilot setting was moved so that it produced a gradual descent. As the plane came closer to the ground, air traffic controllers, as well as auditory and visual signals in the cockpit, warned the crew of their situation. But their attention was so intently focused on the landing gear problem that they did not pay attention to these signals until it was too late to avoid disaster.

Decreases in the ability to divide attention is only one of many consequences of stress, which will be discussed in Chapter 13. Exactly why this ability is impaired under stress is not fully understood, but engineering psychologists are recommending steps to counteract it. They have suggested that instrument displays be arranged so that, as attention narrows, critical information is less likely to be ignored (Hanes & Woods, 1986). At the same time, other psychologists are pursuing clues about the basis of attentional narrowing at the biological level.

HIGHLIGHT

Attention and the Brain

Linkages: What happens in the brain when a person pays attention to a stimulus? (a link to Biological Aspects of Psychology)

Unlike brain structures and chemicals, attention cannot be seen. Psychologists in the past studied it only indirectly, by examining its effects. Today, psychologists look at physiological changes that occur as people focus and divide their attention.

For example, subjects in one study were asked to hold a series of digits in memory while their pupil diameters were measured (Beatty, 1982; Kahneman, Beatty & Pollack, 1967). Pupil enlargement usually accompanies stress, excitement, and other emotions. As the subjects attempted to place each new digit in memory, their pupils grew larger and larger. As the subjects "emptied" their memory by recalling the items they had been holding,

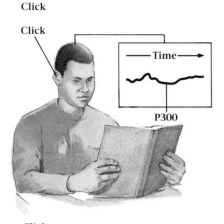

Click

Click

Time →

P300

Click

Click

Time →

P300

Figure 5.31
The P300 and Attention
Note the larger P300 when attention
is focused on the tones as opposed
to the book (Squires et al., 1977).

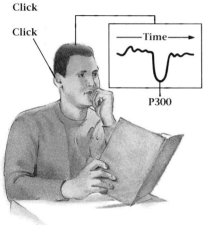

their pupils gradually returned to their original diameter. Thus, this study suggests that pupil diameter can serve as a measure of the attentional resources being mobilized as a person performs a task.

The electroencephalograph (EEG), which measures the electrical activity of the brain, provides another window on attention (see Chapter 3). One EEG measure has been especially useful: the evoked brain potential. The **evoked potential**, or **EP**, is a small, temporary change in EEG voltage that is evoked by a stimulus. One of these changes is called the *P300* because it is a positive swing in electrical voltage that occurs about 300 milliseconds after a stimulus. The presence of a large P300 seems to indicate that a particular stimulus is attended to (Donchin, Kramer & Wickens, 1986; Pritchard, 1981). For example, in one experiment (Squires et al., 1977) when subjects were engrossed in a book, a series of clicking sounds occurring about every two seconds evoked only a very small P300, but if attention was directed away from the book to the clicks, the P300s were large (see Figure 5.31). Thus, the P300 provides a way of tracing where a person's attention is being directed from moment to moment.

Another experiment monitored the allocation of attention in a more complex visual environment. Subjects viewed a display similar to what air traffic controllers see on their radar screens (Wickens et al., 1980). The subjects were told that half of the aircraft on the screen were important and must be monitored; these appeared on the screen as squares. They were told that the other aircraft, represented by circles, could be ignored. They were also told that they should be careful to notice when an "important" aircraft began to flash on the screen. Clear P300s occurred only when "important" aircraft flashed. Later, after a simple instruction to switch attention to the circles, the EP pattern was reversed completely: P300s occurred only when the previously "unimportant" aircraft flashed.

Although neither pupil size nor EPs can take experimenters inside the head to show exactly what attention is, they have brought psychologists a step closer to identifying attention as something that might be measured independently, apart from the performance that it generates. ▪

Applications of Research on Perception

Throughout this chapter we have mentioned ways in which the perceptual system shapes people's ability to handle a variety of tasks, from recognizing restaurant signs to detecting weapons at an airport security checkpoint. In this section we examine the application of perception research to two areas in which perception is particularly important: aviation and reading.

Aviation Psychology

Much of the impetus for research on perception in aviation has come from accidents caused in part by failures of perception (Hurst & Hurst, 1982; Wiener, 1977, Wiener & Nagel, 1988). As described at the opening of this chapter, four Boeing crashes in 1966 resulted from pilots' misperceptions of their altitude. The pilots expected the airport and city lights to lie on a flat surface, but the surface sloped upward. Their assumption that terrain is usually flat led them to make a false perceptual hypothesis about their environment and then to crash. When Conrad Kraft (1978) designed a simulator that recreated the conditions surrounding the crashes, he found that eleven of twelve experienced flight instructors made the same errors while "flying" the simulator.

The pilot of a modern commercial jetliner is faced with a potentially overwhelming array of visual and auditory signals that must be correctly perceived and interpreted to ensure a safe landing.

Kraft's research showed dramatically that estimations of size and distance can be distorted when the physical world does not conform to people's expectations. The research led to the simple but effective recommendation that pilots rely on their instruments extensively during night flight, even in clear weather, and recognize the extent to which the human perceptual system can be tricked.

Top-Down Processing in the Cockpit   Nowhere is the need for clear communications more vital than in the aircraft cockpit, especially as the skies become ever more crowded with commercial air traffic (Office of Technology Assessment, 1988; Wiener & Nagel, 1988). Indeed, air traffic control communications use a restricted vocabulary and standardized phrases in order to avoid ambiguity. Yet two characteristics of the cockpit environment make it possible for top-down processing to take over, allowing pilots to hear what they expect or want to hear. First, the radio signal is sometimes muddled by static or "clipped" by the microphone switch. Second, because aviation communications are standardized, the messages are usually short, with little of the built-in redundancy that, in normal conversation, allows people to perceive correctly even if some words are missing.

In 1979 an aircraft accident in the Canary Islands in which two jumbo jets collided on the runway was blamed largely on faulty communications arising from these factors. The pilot of one jet, in a hurry to depart because of worsening weather, perceived the air traffic controller's message as "take off" when the controller had actually instructed the pilot *not* to take off because the other aircraft was still on the runway. Hundreds of people were killed in the resulting collision (Hawkins, 1987).

Divided Attention   Restrictions on the ability to divide attention between two visual events can present a major problem to pilots. Often they must watch both their instruments and the world outside the plane, a feat requiring a constant shifting of head and eyes from the instrument panel to a window and back again. Technology known as the *head-up display* is intended to make simultaneous observation possible. It projects an image of the instrument panel onto the window of the cockpit, allowing the pilot to see the outside world while watching the flight instruments. Head-up displays are also being introduced in some automobiles to allow drivers to see their fuel gauge, speedometer, or even an electronic map without taking their eyes away from the road (Swift & Freeman, 1986).

Does it work? Some research has indicated that the head-up display is not always effective. In a simulation experiment, pilots were actually slower and less accurate in detecting another aircraft on the runway when they were using the head-up display than when they flew without it (Fischer, Haines & Price, 1980). Just because two visual stimuli are in the same location in space (and thus on the retina), there is no guarantee that both will be perceived. The head-up display is not a cure-all for the problem of divided visual attention.

Reading

Few would disagree that reading is one of the most important abilities in the human repertoire. Visual perception plays a vital role in making this skill possible.

Normally when a person reads, his or her eyes scan across the page, stopping to fixate at various points, then making short jumps from one position to the next. Two factors place physical limits on how fast people can read coherent text: (1) how rapidly they can shift from one fixation to the next (that is, the minimum time they can spend on one fixation before moving on), and (2) how much print they can take in at a single fixation.

The minimum time people can spend on one fixation and then move to the next is fairly well defined at around 250 milliseconds, meaning that humans can make no more than about four fixations per second. The amount people can perceive during one fixation, the maximum visual "window," is roughly ten characters to the left and right of the fixation point for each eye. Thus, if we assume that people can make no more than four eye fixations per second, that they have a twenty-character window, and that twenty characters is roughly three words, the maximum possible reading speed would be around seven hundred words per minute.

Actually, this estimate is somewhat optimistic, because fixations are usually longer than 250 milliseconds when words are less familiar. Also, people rarely if ever move their eyes a full twenty characters. In any event, a normal reader typically reads only about three hundred words per minute, although there is great variation among individuals and among different kinds of reading material. (Most people read novels faster than technical journal articles or textbooks.)

To read faster than six to seven hundred words per minute, people must *skim,* skipping some letters and words altogether. This technique works because of the redundancy of language and top-down processing. Still, skimming disrupts comprehension, especially if the material is difficult and its information content is high (that is, not very redundant). This is not to suggest that skimming and speed-reading are bad habits. In fact, one of the most important reading skills is **adaptive reading** (Anderson, 1979), which means speeding up and slowing down according to the content of the material and the level of comprehension required.

Problems in comprehending and integrating word meaning often account for the limited speed of slow readers (Carver, 1972; Wickelgren, 1979). An extreme example of these problems is **dyslexia,** a condition in which a person with normal intelligence and full comprehension of spoken words has difficulty understanding written words. A dyslexic child can follow a spoken instruction to "Go over to the table and take the apples out of the bag" but might be mystified by the same request made in writing. Obviously, this disruption in the perceptual process of translating letters on the page into meaningful interpretations can create major obstacles to learning.

There is now strong evidence that dyslexia is not the result of a single breakdown in the perceptual process, so the term actually refers to a number of different reading deficiencies (Tyler & Elliott, 1988). One possible factor involves *sensory memory,* which is the extremely brief impression that sensory information makes before it is transferred to the perceptual centers of the brain for further processing. The sensory memory for visual stimuli appears to persist *longer* for dyslexic people than for other readers (DiLollo, Hanson & McIntyre, 1983; Stanley & Hall, 1973). As a result, for dyslexic people, physical images of letters or words from one eye fixation may not disappear quickly enough to avoid interfering with the perception of images in the next fixation. Despite intense study, psychologists are not yet sure what causes dyslexia.

Linkages: Perception and Human Development

Do infants perceive the world as adults do?

We have said that perception is knowledge based, and we have seen the important role that knowledge plays in recognition. But what evidence is there that knowledge, or experience with the world, is in fact necessary for basic

Figure 5.32
The Visual Cliff
The infant readily crosses the shallow side of the test apparatus but hesitates to crawl over what appears to be a cliff.

aspects of perception, such as perceptual constancy? If perception is knowledge based, does that mean that heredity is not important or that infants perceive the world much differently from adults? Philosophers have long debated whether babies are born with perceptual abilities or whether they acquire them by seeing, hearing, smelling, touching, and tasting things. Developmental psychologists have provided some answers, thereby also shaping understanding of the nature of perception. For example, we mentioned in Chapter 2 that infants use movement cues to distinguish objects as separate from each other. Researchers have also focused special attention on whether infants can perceive depth and distance.

One of the most popular techniques for studying infants' depth perception uses the *visual cliff,* a glass-topped table shown in Figure 5.32. A pattern is placed beneath the table in a way that makes one side of the table seem to be a high cliff. A ten-month-old infant placed in the middle of the apparatus will calmly crawl across the shallow side to reach the parent but will hesitate and cry rather than crawl over what appears to be a cliff (Gibson & Walk, 1960).

This behavior does not tell us whether depth perception is innate, however, because infants old enough to crawl have already had considerable experience with the visual world. They may have learned to perceive depth after birth but before participating in visual-cliff research. Other researchers therefore placed even younger infants on the deep side of a visual cliff and compared their behavior and heart rates to the same measures taken while they were on the shallow side (Campos, Langer & Krowitz, 1970). On the deep side, the infants' heart rates slowed significantly, they cried less, and they were more attentive to what was below them.

These results suggest that even very young babies perceived the depth beneath them, but that they were not frightened by it. Here is a fascinating interaction of nature and nurture. It appears that depth perception is present at birth, but that fear and avoidance of the danger sometimes associated with depth do not develop until an infant is old enough to crawl into trouble.

We have seen that adults use many cues to perceive depth. Which ones do infants use? The use of motion cues to discriminate depth appears to be present as early as three months (Yonas, Arterberry & Granrud, 1987). Can infants also use linear perspective and recognize that the place where two straight lines appear to converge is farther away?

To find out, one study used a trapezoid window like the one shown in Figure 5.33 (Kaufmann, Maland & Yonas, 1981). When adults look at such a window with one eye closed (so that binocular depth cues are not available), the trapezoidal shape and the depth cue of linear perspective produces the illusion that the window is rectangular, with the wide side closer than the narrow side. The researchers reasoned that if infants have the same perception,

Figure 5.33
Development of Linear Perspective Cues
The trapezoid window used by Kaufman et al. (1981) looks as though it is slanted away from you at the right even though the right end is closer. A five-month-old will reach for the side of the display that is physically closer (at the right), even though it is the side that linear cues indicate—to older children and adults—is farther away.

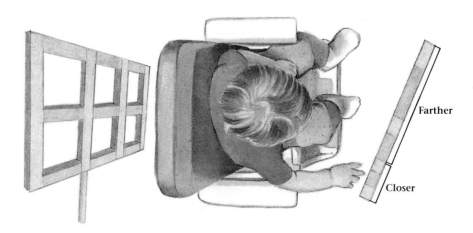

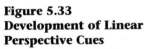

they should reach for the side of the window that appears closest to them—the wide side (see Figure 5.33). A patch was placed over one eye (babies are notoriously poor at keeping one eye closed on command), and the window was displayed so that the wide end was actually farther from the baby than the narrow end. Five-month-old infants reached for the narrow (actually closer) end of the window, suggesting that linear perspective cues were not controlling their perception. But seven-month-olds consistently reached for the wider (actually more distant) end of the window. Linear perspective cues caused them, like adults, to perceive it as closer.

Other research has outlined the development of the ability to use binocular disparity—the difference between the images seen by each eye—to perceive depth and distance. Only when infants are around three to five months of age can they use this cue, and the ability to do so depends on both biological maturation and experience. The brain cells that integrate the two images to create the experience of three-dimensionality, called *binocular cells,* can develop only during a critical period very early in life. If they do not appear then, they never will. Further, for these cells to develop (and, with them, depth perception) each eye must focus on the same object at the same time during the critical period (Blakemore & Van Slayters, 1974).

In summary, there is little doubt that some of the basic building blocks of perception are present at birth or within the first few months of life, thus making it possible for infants to perceive many aspects of their surroundings in ways that approximate adult perception. These building blocks include such organ-based cues to depth as accommodation, convergence, and binocular disparity, as well as the stimulus cue of relative motion. But these cues alone are not enough to produce full perceptual capabilities. Experience with the world is necessary to acquire most stimulus cues, such as linear perspective, and to learn to interpret cues: to recognize objects and know which objects are closer and which are farther away, to know that falls of greater distance are more dangerous, and to use depth and distance cues to move effectively through the world. Like so many aspects of human psychology, perception is the result of a blending of heredity and environment.

Future Directions

We have outlined how perception translates raw sensations into information that is meaningful and useful to the perceiver. The process is elaborate, involving numerous components and operations, many of which depend on both bottom-up and top-down processing. Because perception is one of the oldest specialties in psychology, dating back to the psychophysical research of Weber and Fechner, knowledge about perception is extensive.

Yet questions and debates remain. One of the most enduring controversies involves the conflict between the constructionist view that perception involves mainly knowledge-based inferences about fragmentary sensations and the ecological view that much of perception results from processing well-developed and rich sensations offered by the natural world. Research based on the ecological position has begun to identify cues in the natural environment that are important to the perception of complex events and actions, such as the perception of a running human form or the visual sensations that a pilot experiences as an aircraft descends toward the runway (Cutting, 1988).

Researchers are also addressing the question of how people recognize the shape and identity of objects in a cluttered dynamic world. How well can this be done by bottom-up processing, using only the information in the stimulus, and how much does this process depend on top-down processing, using knowledge and expectancies of what objects should look like (Biederman, 1988; Braunstein, 1989)?

These efforts are relevant both to human perception and to the design of computers that can hear and see. Programming a computer to imitate even the simplest perceptual processes—such as understanding words or recognizing a cup on a cluttered desk—often results in a process that takes more time than human perception. More complex but still commonplace processes—such as understanding the continuous flow of rapid speech or recognizing a cup being tossed in the air—tax the capabilities of today's most advanced computers. Why? It may be that until researchers more fully understand perception, the methods for programming a computer to perceive may be too inefficient and cumbersome even for supercomputers. Better understanding of basic perceptual processes might lead to programs that will allow computers to rival people in their perceptual abilities. It is also possible that no machine will ever be able to perceive the world as smoothly and automatically as humans do.

Two rapidly developing areas of perceptual research have grown from efforts to use computers to perform visual tasks. We described the first of these in the section on pattern recognition: PDP models. These models are represented by computer simulations that can recognize patterns, like a signature or a spoken word. The second area is the field of *computational vision,* which describes how computers should reconstruct a three-dimensional world from computations performed on two-dimensional images of light, shadow, and contours. Psychologists are trying to understand how far these mathematical formulas will go in describing how humans recognize objects and discriminate their own motion from the motion of objects (Biederman, 1988; Marr, 1982).

Finally, as in many other fields of psychology, research in perception is moving toward a better understanding of the mechanisms of the brain. In the field of attention, physiological psychologists are studying how blood flow and metabolic activity in the brain may define attentional resources (Posner, 1989).

If you want to learn more about these and other aspects of perception, consider taking the basic course in the area, which is usually called sensation and perception. Many psychology departments also offer advanced courses in perception. If the idea of programming computers to perceive intrigues you, look for courses in artificial intelligence; they are commonly offered by computer science departments.

Summary and Key Terms

From Sensing to Perceiving: An Overview

Perception is the active process through which people use knowledge and understanding of the world to interpret sensations as meaningful experiences.

Six Features of Perception

Perception has six main characteristics. It is: (1) knowledge based, (2) inferential, (3) categorical, (4) relational, (5) adaptive, and (6) often automatic, operating without our awareness.

Approaches to Perception

The *constructionist* view of perception suggests that the perceptual system constructs the experience of reality by interpreting raw sensations on the basis of what people have learned. The *ecological* approach emphasizes the natural features of percep-

tion, suggesting that the cues people use to form perceptions lie in the environment itself.

Psychophysics

Absolute Thresholds: Is Something Out There?

Psychophysics is the study of the relationship between the physical characteristics of stimuli and the psychological experience of those stimuli. It has traditionally been concerned with matters such as determining *absolute thresholds* for the detection of stimuli. *Internal noise* and *response bias* cause variation in the absolute threshold.

Going Beyond the Threshold: Signal-Detection Theory

Signal-detection theory describes how detection is affected by *sensitivity* and the *response criterion,* or bias. Sensitivity and response bias can be graphed as the receiver operating characteristic curve. Signal-detection theory has been applied to problems in areas, such as improving airport security and minimizing bias in eyewitness testimony.

Judging Differences Between Stimuli: Weber's Law

Weber's law states that the minimum detectable amount of change in a stimulus, the *difference threshold* or *just-noticeable difference (JND),* increases in proportion to the initial amount of the stimulus. The less the initial stimulation, the smaller the change has to be in order to be detected.

Judging Stimulus Magnitude: Fechner's and Stevens's Laws

Fechner's and Stevens's laws relate the perceived magnitude of a stimulus to its physical intensity. *Fechner's law* describes this relation for most stimuli: constant increases in physical energy produce smaller increases in perceived magnitude. Fechner's law, however, does not apply to some stimuli. *Stevens's power law* provides a better description of perceived magnitude for all the senses.

Organizing the Perceptual World

Principles of Perceptual Organization

When people perceive objects or sounds, they automatically discriminate *figure* from *ground.* In addition, the perceptual system automatically groups stimuli into patterns on the basis of the *Gestalt* principles of *proximity, similarity, continuity, closure, orientation, simplicity,* and *common fate.*

Perceptual Constancy

Because of *perceptual constancy,* the brightness, size, and shape of objects can be seen as constant even though the sensations received from those objects may change. Size and shape constancy depend on the relationship between the retinal image of the object and the knowledge-based perception of its distance. Brightness constancy depends on the perceived relationship between the brightness of an object and its background.

Depth Perception

The perception of distance, or *depth perception,* depends partly on stimulus cues and partly on the physical structure of the visual system. Some of the stimulus cues are *relative size, height in the visual field, interposition, linear perspective, reduced clarity, shadows,* and *textural gradients* and *movement gradients.* Cues based on the structure of the visual system include *binocular disparity* (the fact that the eyes are set apart), *convergence* of the eyes (the fact that the eyes must move to focus on the same object), and accommodation (the change in the shape of the lenses as objects are brought into focus).

The Perception of Motion

The perception of motion results, in part, from the movement of stimuli across the retina. Expanding, or *looming,* stimulation of the retina is perceived as an approaching object. Stimulation of the retina by moving objects is interpreted along with information about movement of the head, eyes, and other parts of the body. In this way, retinal stimulation resulting from one's own movement can be distinguished from motion resulting from the movement of external objects.

Perceptual Illusions

Perceptual illusions are distortions of reality that result when principles of perception are applied inappropriately. For example, induced motion results when the perceptual system misinterprets which parts of the environment are stable and which are moving. Illusions of motion may result from *visual dominance.* Many illusions are caused by misreading depth cues and by evaluating stimuli in the context of their surroundings.

Recognizing the Perceptual World

The ability to recognize objects in the world is based on finding a match between the pattern of sensations organized by the perceptual system and a pattern already stored in memory. Recognition depends in part on *bottom-up processing,* which is the analysis of the sensory information coming from the basic features of the stimulus, and in part on *top-down processing,* which is guided by cognitive processes and other psychological factors.

Feature Analysis

Bottom-up processing seems to be accomplished by *feature analysis.*

Models of Object Recognition

Feature analysis may involve matching the sensory input to mental lists of features, to mental representations of specific examples, or to schemas. Recent research has focused on *parallel distributed processing (PDP) models* of pattern recognition.

Top-Down Processing

Top-down processing is influenced by expectancy, memories, and motivation. Expectancy produces a perceptual set to make a particular categorization. Top-down processing helps people recognize objects and both spoken and printed words.

Top-Down and Bottom-Up Processes Together

Bottom-up and top-down processing commonly work together to create recognition of stimulus patterns. Top-down processing can fill in missing gaps in the physical stimuli, in part because redundant stimuli are provided.

Attention

Attention is the process of focusing psychological resources to selectively enhance information processing.

Selective Attention

Stimuli that attract attention (or distract it from other stimuli) tend to be high in intensity, novelty, and contrast. People are also more likely to attend to stimuli in which they are especially interested.

Focused and Divided Attention

People can sometimes attend to two sets of stimuli at once, especially with practice, if the tasks are easy or if different senses are involved. However, there are limits to how well people can divide attention, as has been shown by *dichotic listening task* experiments. These limits are particularly great under stressful conditions, when the focus of attention tends to narrow. The allocation of attentional resources can be monitored in the laboratory by observing changes in pupillary dilation and in *evoked potentials (EP)*.

Applications of Research on Perception

Aviation Psychology

In aviation, accurate size and distance judgments, top-down processing, and attention are all important to safety.

Reading

The number of letters or words perceived during a fixation and the minimum time spent on each fixation put physical limitations on reading speed. Skimming usually results in some loss of comprehension; *adaptive reading* maximizes both overall speed and comprehension. Reading problems such as *dyslexia* may result from several different, not fully understood, causes.

OUTLINE

Consciousness

Consider your best friend, whom, for the sake of discussion, we will call Chris. Chris looks and acts reasonably normal, but is Chris fully human? Does Chris experience consciousness? How would you know? You can ask, and Chris can tell you: "Of course!" But is there any way to confirm or deny Chris's claims to consciousness? What is consciousness anyway?

Psychologist William James once said about consciousness: "Its meaning we know as long as no one asks us to define it." For our purposes, **consciousness** can be defined as the mental process of being aware of one's own thoughts, feelings, or perceptions. Thus, consciousness involves thinking about thinking, a self aware of itself; its essential property is *self-reference*.

The elusiveness of consciousness is evident in the case of people suffering from *prosopagnosia*, a condition that can be brought on by a stroke or herpes-related encephalitis. People with prosopagnosia show an emotional response (measurable through a change in skin conductance) when they see their own face or the faces of familiar people. (Tranel & Damasio, 1985). Thus, at some level, their nervous systems "recognize" the faces. But they cannot report this recognition. At the level of conscious awareness, they lose the ability to recognize faces—including their own face in a mirror.

The study of consciousness sometimes gets lost in the shuffle as psychologists focus on perception, memory, cognition, and other specific aspects of mental life. Like a melody playing softly in the background, however, consciousness remains at the heart of psychology (see the Linkages diagram). Consciousness is a property of many mental processes rather than a unique mental process; thus, memories can be conscious, but consciousness is not memory; perceptions can be conscious, but consciousness is not perception. In this chapter we consider how several varieties of mental activity are related to consciousness. Then we explore the variations in consciousness that occur as people daydream, sleep, and dream and as they modify their consciousness through hypnosis, meditation, or drugs.

LINKAGES

Consciousness

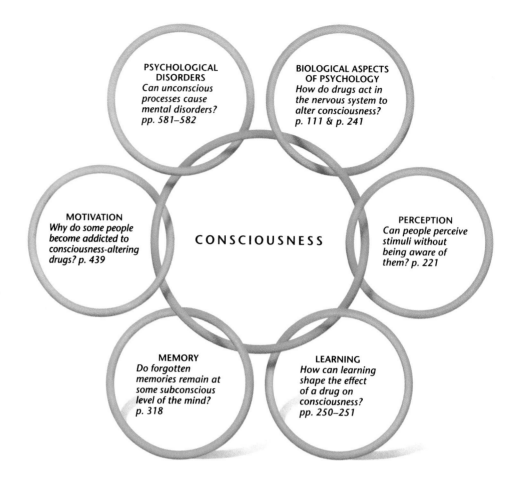

PSYCHOLOGICAL
DISORDERS
*Can unconscious
processes cause
mental disorders?
pp. 581–582*

BIOLOGICAL ASPECTS
OF PSYCHOLOGY
*How do drugs act in
the nervous system to
alter consciousness?
p. 111 & p. 241*

MOTIVATION
*Why do some people
become addicted to
consciousness-altering
drugs? p. 439*

CONSCIOUSNESS

PERCEPTION
*Can people perceive
stimuli without
being aware of
them? p. 221*

MEMORY
*Do forgotten
memories remain at
some subconscious
level of the mind?
p. 318*

LEARNING
*How can learning
shape the effect
of a drug on
consciousness?
pp. 250–251*

■ Look at the diagram above, which illustrates some of the relationships between the topic of this chapter, consciousness, and other chapter topics. Research in biological psychology, for example, provides a wealth of information about what your brain is doing while you sleep and how chemicals in the brain change if you drink alcohol or coffee. These activities alter your consciousness, your subjective experience of internal and external stimuli. The experience has often been compared to a flowing stream, that changes constantly. Many of the changes reflect variations in attention, discussed in Chapter 5, on perception.

By learning more about how subjective experience varies, psychologists are deepening their understanding of many facets of life. By penetrating the mystery of dreams and the causes of sleep disorders, for example, some psychologists hope to create new methods of helping people with psychological disorders. And understanding how learning can shape the effects of drugs on consciousness may lead to better ways of treating addictions.

These and other linkages between consciousness and other aspects of psychology are discussed in the text. The diagram shows a sampling of these links; the page numbers indicate where the questions are discussed. ■

Analyzing Consciousness

The early history of psychology is actually the history of the study of consciousness. Wilhelm Wundt, the man whose research founded European psychology in the 1870s, sought to understand the *structure* of consciousness. He hoped to define basic building blocks of consciousness by carefully observing conscious experience. At about the same time, William James, an American, began research aimed at defining how consciousness *functions* to help people adapt to their environments (James, 1890, 1892). James's approach, which became known as *functionalism,* focused on the ongoing "stream" of consciousness—the ever-changing pattern of images, sensations, memories, and other mental events. He wanted to know how the whole process works. Why, for example, do people remember recent events better than things that happened in the distant past?

Over the years, the concept of consciousness underwent large fluctuations in respectability. In the early 1900s, John B. Watson argued that psychologists could more profitably study behavior instead of consciousness. He did not deny the existence of consciousness, but he argued that attempts to study it had not produced any knowledge that scientists could agree on, because consciousness cannot be observed directly. Watson's approach, known as *behaviorism,* was to study only observable stimuli and responses, and it dominated psychological research for most of this century. By the 1950s, however, some psychologists began to feel that behaviorism was too confining. Eventually, the mainstream of American psychology widened to include again the study of consciousness. In this section we examine how it is studied, how it is related to various mental activities, and how consciousness itself varies.

Linkages: Why did behaviorists object to the study of consciousness? (a link to the World of Psychology)

The Study of Consciousness

The behaviorists' argument that consciousness cannot be directly observed is still valid. No one can directly observe anyone else's conscious experiences. Wundt and other *structuralist psychologists* tried to study consciousness through *introspection.* They presented a stimulus—say, a bright red object—to highly trained subjects (including themselves) who attempted to identify individual sensations, such as redness or brightness, that they believed were combined to create the total conscious experience of the stimulus. Introspection by itself, however, can give false impressions about perceptions and the experience of consciousness. For example, you probably experience reading as a continuous flow of information as your eyes smoothly scan across lines of words. But as we discussed in the chapter on perception, your eyes actually make jerky movements as they fixate on each successive spot. Furthermore, between the quick jumps (saccades) to the next fixation spot, your eyes do not actually take in any information (McConkie et al., 1988).

If introspection is not reliable, how can psychologists examine consciousness? Modern technology has allowed psychologists to obtain objective observations of what the brain is doing while some conscious activity is going on. For example, studies of conscious cognitive activities can be combined with EEG recordings or PET scans, as described in Chapter 3. Still, these are records of the activity of the brain, not of conscious experience.

To study consciousness, psychologists have had to devise ingenious ways of externalizing what is an internal process. For example, consider one of America's favorite dogs, Lassie. Does Lassie experience consciousness? To find out whether animals have consciousness, some scientists have studied animals' responses to seeing themselves in a mirror. If an animal demonstrates that it knows that the animal in the mirror is itself, then it must be aware of that self; hence, it must have consciousness. Indeed, chimpanzees raised in the wild can recognize themselves in mirrors, but chimpanzees raised in captive isolation cannot, implying that consciousness arises out of social interactions (Gallup et al., 1971).

H I G H L I G H T

Time and Consciousness

As another example of the difficulties and the potential in studying consciousness, consider time. You certainly experience time; it is part of your consciousness. The continuously flowing stream that makes up your moment-to-moment consciousness is experienced as "now." But just what do you experience when you experience time? And how long is "now"?

Philosophers and psychologists have offered varying answers. The philosophers Heidegger and Kant argued that the present time barely exists; it is merely a window through which the future becomes the past. On the other hand, St. Augustine argued in *Confessions* that the present is all there is:

This much is now clear and obvious, however: neither past nor future exist, and we may not speak of three times, past, present, and future; rather, ought we properly to speak of three times . . . the present of things past, namely, memory; the present of things present, namely, perception; the present of things to come, namely, expectation.

Psychologists have long tried to understand the relationship between consciousness and time through experimental analysis. According to Ernst Poppel (1988), for example, every experience of time falls into one of four basic categories: the experience of simultaneity (things happening at the same time), the experience of sequential relations (one thing happening after another), the experience of the present, and the experience of duration. Here we take a brief look at the experimental analysis of the first three of these categories.

First, how can the subjective experience of "simultaneous" be distinguished from "sequential" in an experimental setting? Headphones can be placed on a subject, and a click lasting only 1 millisecond can be presented to each ear separately. If the clicks are presented simultaneously (no measurable interval between them), they will be experienced as one click rather than two and will seem to come from inside the head rather than from either ear. If the experimenter separates the two clicks by 1 millisecond, they will still be experienced as a single click, but the subjective location of the sound moves to the left or right inside the head. If the interval is increased to 2 milliseconds, the experience of the single click moves still further to one side, still inside the head. Thus, two stimuli are experienced as simultaneous even if they are not, as long as they appear within a "window of simultaneity" (Poppel, 1988).

How long does the window of simultaneity stay open? Experiments with normal people suggest that it lasts between 4 and 5 milliseconds. Clicks separated by longer intervals are experienced as two clicks. As sense organs differ, so do the windows of simultaneity for different senses. For touch, the stimuli must be separated by about 10 milliseconds to feel sequential, and for vision, the stimuli must be separated by about 20 to 30 milliseconds.

Once you know that two events are separate, are you also conscious of the order in which they occurred? Not necessarily. The clicks must be separated by 30 to 40 milliseconds before you can tell which came first. Interestingly,

Figure 6.1
The Necker Cube
Each of the two squares in the Necker cube can be perceived as either the front or rear surface of the cube. Take a few seconds and try to make the cube switch back and forth between the two perspectives. Now try to hold one perspective in view and prevent the cube from switching to the other perspective. How long can you hold one perspective? If the whole cube is maintained in consciousness, one perspective cannot be held for longer than about 3 seconds before it flips to the other.

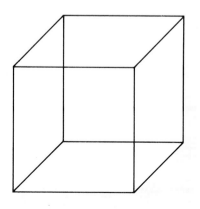

Source: Poppel, 1985.

Figure 6.2
The Mouse and the Man
Although you can organize this stimulus as either a mouse or as a man's face, the organization tends to shift after about 3 seconds, suggesting that "the present" lasts about that long in human consciousness.

Linkages: Do sensations that do not reach consciousness affect behavior? (a link to Sensation)

Activity in this young man's frontalis (upper facial) muscles is not directly accessible to consciousness. However, with the help of a biofeedback device which monitors and displays moment to moment tension readings on a screen, he can become aware of, and perhaps even learn to control, this nonconscious activity.

the interval required for events to be experienced in a temporal order is the same for auditory, tactile, and visual stimuli. This fact suggests that the timing function occurs centrally in the brain rather than in the various sensory organs.

Finally, what is "the present"? How long is it? Several lines of evidence suggest that the experience of "now" lasts about 3 seconds, much longer than "simultaneous." For example, the Necker cube shown in Figure 6.1 can be held in consciousness as a given configuration for only about 3 seconds at most, suggesting that, in the visual domain, "now" lasts at most about 3 seconds. Likewise, the perception of Figure 6.2 can be flipped back and forth between two meanings, revealing a mouse or a man. It too cannot be held in consciousness for more than about 3 seconds before the other perception appears.

Using stimuli similar to the Necker cube, experimenters have taught monkeys to report which perception they are subjectively experiencing in their "now" while the researchers record electrical impulses from neurons in the cerebral cortex. Particular neurons respond when one subjective perception is being experienced but not the other (Logothetis & Schall, 1989). Thus, it is becoming possible to study the physiology of an internal perceptual state in monkeys that may correspond to conscious perception in humans. ■

Consciousness and the Cognitive Unconscious

If our discussion of time and consciousness introduced some new ideas, it is probably because you may not have previously been aware of perceiving "now" or of how long it lasts for you. Indeed, much mental activity occurs outside of consciousness. In Chapter 5 we discussed how well-rehearsed mental processes can become automatic, occurring without your attention. If you are a skilled typist, you can read handwriting and type the words without ever becoming aware of the content of the writing. But you can also direct your attention to the writing and make it conscious if you choose.

Some events, however, simply cannot be experienced consciously. You can try to focus your attention on the modulation of blood pressure by your brain, for example, but you can't do it. The process occurs at the **nonconscious level**, meaning that it is totally inaccessible to conscious experience. Becoming even indirectly aware of nonconscious events usually requires special methods. In *biofeedback*, for example, a person connected to a measuring device can watch a meter that keeps track of the output of nonconscious events, such as blood pressure. With this information some people can learn to control the nonconscious process, but the process itself remains outside of conscious experience.

Many other mental activities are not conscious but can either become conscious or can influence conscious experience, thought, and action; these activities have been called the *cognitive unconscious* (Kihlstrom, 1987). In fact, psychologists have created many ways of charting the territories outside of consciousness. According to one approach, besides the nonconscious level, these regions can be divided into the preconscious and the unconscious/subconscious levels.

Mental activity and information that is outside of awareness but can be easily brought into awareness is **preconscious**. Focus for a moment on the way your tongue feels as it rests or moves around inside your mouth. You are now probably much more aware of your tongue than you were a few seconds ago. Where were those perceptions before you focused on them? They were there all the time, but they were outside your awareness, at the preconscious level. The amount of material at this level far surpasses what is present at the

Evidence for the operation of sub-conscious mental processing includes research showing that surgery patients may be able to hear and later comply with instructions or suggestions given while they are under anesthesia and of which they have no memory (Bennett, 1984). In another study, people showed physiological arousal to emotionally charged words even when they were not paying attention to them (Von Wright, Anderson & Stenman, 1975).

Source: © 1986, Washington Post Writers Group. Reprinted with permission.

conscious level at any moment. Thus, in a trivia game you may come up with obscure information that you did not even know you knew by drawing on your large storehouse of memories that exists at the preconscious level.

Many of the basic assumptions and inferences people make about the world also appear to operate at the preconscious level. Consider the following sentence: "When the bell rang, Jim waited until the others had left before he approached the professor." You can easily understand the sentence and picture the situation, because you presume or infer that professors teach classes, Jim is a male's name, students leave the room at the end of classes, and students may talk to professors after class.

Other kinds of mental activity and information are more difficult than preconscious material to bring into consciousness, but they can nevertheless alter thoughts, feelings, and behavior. Sigmund Freud, founder of psychoanalysis, suggested that there is an **unconscious** level of mental processing, which contains sexual, aggressive, and other impulses, as well as once-conscious but unacceptable thoughts, feelings, and memories. Material at this level, he said, is the main determinant of human behavior and the source of all mental disorder. (We examine Freud's ideas in Chapter 14, on personality.) Those who do not accept Freud's theory sometimes use the term **subconscious** to describe the mental level at which important, but normally inaccessible, mental processes take place.

One example of people's ability to process information at a subconscious level is the *cocktail party phenomenon*. While paying close attention to a conversation with someone in a noisy, crowded room, you might suddenly be distracted by something—perhaps your name or an obscene word—in another conversation. Though you were not consciously focused on that other discussion, your brain perceives something significant and redirects your attention to it (Moray, 1960).

THINKING CRITICALLY

Can You Be

Influenced by

Subliminal

Perceptions?

Clearly, a great deal of what your mind accomplishes occurs outside of conscious awareness, and subconscious mental activity can affect conscious activity. These notions suggest another possibility: can your thoughts, emotions, and actions be influenced by information that is perceived at a *subliminal* level, below your threshold of conscious awareness? If, for example, a message flashes on your television too fast for you to notice it, can it influence you anyway? In the 1950s some advertisers allegedly used subliminal messages. For example, theater owners supposedly embedded the subliminal message "buy popcorn" in films in an effort to boost sales at the refreshment stand. People are outraged by even the idea of such attempts at subtle "mind control," but open attempts to use subliminal perception find acceptance in the self-improvement field. People buy tapes containing statements like "I always get the results I want" or "I don't need to eat" at a subliminal level; they hope that by listening to the tapes they will effortlessly change attitudes and appetites and, in turn, make a million dollars or lose those unwanted pounds.

What am I being asked to believe or accept?

Attempts to use subliminal perception assume that stimuli presented too briefly or softly to be consciously seen or heard can nevertheless be sensed and their meaning perceived. Some even argue that information perceived without awareness will be especially influential, making you unusually likely to remember it, be persuaded by it, or act on it. One implication of this view is that others might be able to influence you without your knowledge or consent.

What evidence is available to support the assertion?

Linkages: Can people perceive stimuli without being aware of them? (a link to Perception)

Some evidence that subliminal perceptions can affect conscious judgments and reactions comes from research using the *tachistoscope,* an instrument that presents visual stimuli for such short intervals—say, 5 milliseconds—that they cannot be perceived consciously. For example, subliminal perception is thought to be operating in the *priming task.* In this experiment subjects are shown a target stimulus long enough for them to perceive it, but too briefly to be sure if it is a meaningful word or nonsense letters. It turns out that subjects' accuracy at detecting meaningful words improves if the target is preceded by a "priming" stimulus that is also a meaningful word. The priming word improves subjects' performance even though it is presented too fast to be consciously perceived (Balota, 1983). Priming appears to involve the interaction of perception and a memory system that acts at the subconscious level (Tulving & Schacter, 1990).

Subliminal perceptions can also affect emotional responses to a stimulus. Sheldon Bach and George Klein (1957) showed slides of people's faces along with brief flashes of slides of the words *happy* or *sad.* The words were not perceived, but when the subjects were asked to describe the faces, they described those that had been randomly associated with the word *sad* as sadder than those that had been paired with *happy.* In other studies the mere repetition of an unfamiliar stimulus at a subliminal level increased the attractiveness of the stimulus when it was later perceived consciously. This result is consistent with the fact that, in general, familiarity increases attractiveness (a process described in Chapter 17, on social cognition). The effect can take place even when familiarization occurs below the threshold for conscious recognition (Kunst-Wilson & Zajonc, 1980).

Evidence for the effectiveness of subliminal stimulation in promoting self-esteem, motivation, weight loss, or other self-improvement goals comes not from experimental research but mainly from anecdotal reports by satisfied customers, tape developers, and advertisers (e.g., McGarvey, 1989).

Are there alternative ways of interpreting the evidence?

Over the years, evidence for subliminal perception has been criticized on the grounds that it is not actually subliminal (Holender, 1986). Some argue, for example, that traces of supposedly subliminal stimuli last long enough in the sensory system to make them more noticeable than intended. However, these criticisms have been countered by experiments showing that a subliminal stimulus has an impact even if it is "masked" by another stimulus coming immediately afterward, effectively erasing the trace of the preceding stimulus (Marcel, 1983).

On the other hand, consumers' reports that subliminal perception tapes produce dramatic self-improvement are wide open to alternative interpretations. For one thing, these reports may stem not from real change but from a tendency (discussed in Chapter 17) for people to keep their attitudes consistent with their behavior, and vice versa. If you spend a bundle on subliminal tapes, it is far more comfortable to believe and to report that they worked than that you wasted money. Even when changes occur, the placebo effect (discussed in Chapter 1), not subliminal influences, may be responsible. The motivation a person needs to quit smoking, for example, might be supplied not by subliminal stimulation itself but by the *belief* that a subliminal tape will work.

What additional evidence would help to evaluate the alternatives?
The value of subliminal stimulation for producing self-improvement must be assessed through controlled experiments of the sort described in Chapter 1. For example, people with a particular, measurable problem (such as being overweight) could be randomly assigned (1) to hear tapes containing subliminal messages, (2) to hear the same tapes without the messages, or (3) to hear no tapes at all. If the tapes-with-messages group does better at losing weight than the no-treatment group, subliminal stimulation might be responsible. However, if the tapes-without-messages group does as well as the one getting the messages, placebo effects, not subliminal perception, could be the ingredient producing behavioral change.

Producers of subliminal tapes have not conducted studies like these. A few scientists have reported experimental evidence supporting the value of subliminal messages for self-improvement (Silverman, 1983). But flaws in the design and methods of these studies, along with negative evidence from better-controlled studies, leave little confidence in this evidence (Vitiello et al., 1989).

What conclusions are most reasonable?
The evidence available so far suggests that subliminal perception does take place but that it has virtually no potential for "mind control." Subliminal perception will not create needs or goals that do not already exist. In fact, the effects of subconscious perception are relatively short-lived and probably cannot control very much behavior for very long (Cherry, 1953; Vokey & Read, 1985). Thus, if you are already thirsty, have some money, and don't mind missing a few minutes of a movie, a subliminal message *might* influence you to buy a soft drink at the refreshment stand. But ads that you can see consciously will probably have an even greater effect. ▪

States of Consciousness

Mental activity is constantly changing. The characteristics of consciousness at any particular moment—for example, what reaches awareness, how efficiently you are thinking—are usually referred to as the **state of consciousness.** Possible states range from deep sleep to alert wakefulness, with many gradations in between. Imagine for a moment that you know everything that is going on in an airplane en route from New York to Los Angeles. In the cockpit, the pilot calmly scans the instruments while talking to an air-traffic controller on the ground. In seat 37B, a sales representative has just polished off her second Scotch as she works on plans for the next day's sales meeting. Nearby, a young mother gazes out the window, daydreaming, while her small son sleeps in her lap, dreaming dreams of his own.

Each of these people is experiencing a different state of consciousness. Some states are active and some passive (Hilgard, 1980). The daydreaming mother is simply letting her mind wander, passively observing the images, memories, and other mental events that come unbidden to mind. In contrast, the sales representative is actively manipulating her mental activity, considering various courses of action and speculating about their likely outcomes. States of consciousness can also be classified according to whether they are brought on, like sleep, by natural processes or by choice, through activities like drug-taking.

Like the pilot, most people spend most of their time in what is called the *normal waking* state of consciousness. The mental processes in this familiar condition vary considerably. These variations in normal waking consciousness often reflect variations in attention and arousal. While focused on what you are reading, you may temporarily ignore the rest of your world. If you are very upset or very bored, you may not notice important things in the environment, making it dangerous for you to be behind the wheel of a car.

When changes in your mental processes are extensive enough for you or others to notice significant differences in how you are functioning, you are said to have entered an **altered state of consciousness** (Ludwig, 1969; Zinberg, 1974). Though the borderline between normal and altered states is often fuzzy, altered states tend to have a few general characteristics (Martindale, 1981).

1. Cognitive processes may become shallow, careless, or uncritical. Many hypnotized subjects, for example, readily accept the truth of a statement like ''You are an English sheepdog.''
2. Self-perceptions and perceptions of the world may change. Dreams, drugs, hypnosis, and meditation, for example, may make people see, hear, smell, taste, or feel things that are not really there; become more intensely aware of what *is* there; or misperceive reality in strange or frightening ways.
3. Normal inhibitions or self-control may weaken. A hypnotized person may not only believe that he or she is an English sheepdog but also begin acting like one.

In the sections that follow we take a look at some of the most interesting and important altered states of consciousness, beginning with the most common and natural ones.

Daydreaming

In normal waking consciousness, attention shifts repeatedly back and forth between the external and internal world. Usually attention gravitates toward the external world and toward experiencing it in a clear, organized, and realistic way. In daydreams, however, this balance of attention is reversed. **Daydreaming** is an altered state of consciousness in which attention shifts away from external stimuli to dwell on internal events, sometimes in a fantasy-oriented, unrealistic way (Singer, 1976). It is the altered state closest to the normal waking state of consciousness.

Daydreaming can interfere with daily living, but usually it is harmless and may even be helpful. It can bring relief from mental work or from unpleasant or boring situations. And because the mind may wander freely during day-dreams, they sometimes stimulate creative ideas.

Why do people daydream? No one knows for sure. Freud suggested that daydreams, like night dreams, provide a way of expressing unconscious feelings, wishes, and impulses. Or perhaps daydreaming is a constant part of mental life, a part that other processes usually obscure but that appears when pressing demands for mental activity subside. Daydreaming may even maintain mental activity at some desirable level when the outside world offers too little stimulation.

Evidence for these last two notions comes from an experiment in which the mental demands on subjects were reduced. They spent forty-five to sixty minutes of their day lying on a bed in a dimly lit room, relaxed but fully awake (Foulkes & Fleisher, 1975). (Their experience resembled that of people placed in sensory deprivation chambers, which were discussed in Chapter 4.) At six randomly selected times, an experimenter asked the subjects to describe their current mental experience. Only 38 percent of the responses suggested that the subjects were in full waking consciousness. The rest indicated some degree of daydreaming, from "mind wandering" and lack of awareness of the laboratory to uncontrolled thoughts and the perception of imaginary sights and sounds. Just over half of the subjects reported at least one visual or auditory hallucination.

Research of this type demonstrates that the boundaries between states of consciousness are not sharply defined. Fragments from one state may appear when they are least expected. In daydreams, mental activities associated with the waking state and with sleep sometimes appear together.

Sleeping and Dreaming

According to ancient myths, to sleep is to take leave of your senses, to lose control, and to flirt with death by letting the soul wander freely. Early psychologists thought that most mental activity stopped when people slept. In fact, research has revealed that sleep is a very active, complex state.

Stages of Sleep

Probably the most important technological step toward expanding research on sleep came in 1919 when Hans Berger, a German psychiatrist, developed the *electroencephalogram,* or *EEG.* As discussed in previous chapters, the EEG provides a record of the electrical activity of the brain. The recordings, often called *brain waves,* can be characterized by variations in height (amplitude) and speed (frequency). The brain waves of an awake, alert individual show high frequency and low amplitude; they appear as small, closely spaced, irregular spikes on the EEG tracing. As an individual relaxes, with eyes closed, **alpha waves** may appear; these are rhythmic brain waves that occur at a speed of about 8 to 12 cycles per second.

When researchers used EEGs to measure brain activity during sleep, they found several distinctive patterns of brain waves (Loomis, Harvey & Hobart, 1937). The amplitude and frequency of these waves changed systematically throughout the night. William Dement and Nathaniel Kleitman (1957) used these systematic changes in brain waves, combined with activity of muscles and the eyes, to identify six stages of sleep: stage 0, which is a prelude to sleep, four stages of quiet sleep, and rapid eye movement sleep.

Stage 0 and Quiet Sleep   During stage 0, you are relaxed, with eyes closed, but awake. The EEG at this stage shows a mixture of brain waves, including some alpha waves. During stage 0, there may be considerable tension in the body, and your eyes move normally. The next stages, stages 1 through 4, are

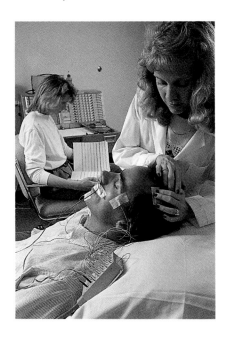

The electroencephalogram (EEG) allows scientists to record brain activity through electrodes attached to the skull. The advent of this technology opened the door to the scientific study of sleep. This subject's brain waves will be monitored throughout the night in a sleep laboratory.

called **quiet sleep,** or **slow-wave sleep,** because all of them are accompanied by slow brain waves, deep breathing, a calm and regular heartbeat, and reduced blood pressure.

As you drift from stage 0 into stage 1 sleep, your eyes move more slowly and begin to roll. The EEG frequency becomes irregular, and alpha waves begin to disappear (see Figure 6.3). This EEG pattern is actually very similar to the one that occurs when you are fully awake and mentally active. After a few minutes in stage 1, you enter stage 2 sleep. In this stage, the EEG shows sharply pointed waves called *sleep spindles.* There are also occasional *K complexes,* which are special waves with high peaks and deep valleys. As you gradually enter stage 3 sleep, spindles and K complexes continue to appear, but they are now mixed with **delta waves,** which are much slower (0.5 to 0.3 cycle per second) and have much higher amplitude. When delta waves occur more than 50 percent of the time, you have entered stage 4, the deepest level of sleep, from which it is most difficult to be roused. It takes about half an hour to reach stage 4 from stage 1 sleep.

REM Sleep   After thirty to forty minutes in stage 4, a sleeper begins to retrace the journey, returning through stages 3 and 2 to stage 1. Then begins an extraordinary stage known as **REM** (for rapid-eye-movement) **sleep,** or **active sleep.** As in stage 1, the EEG during REM resembles that when you are active and awake, but now your heart rate, respiration, blood pressure, and other physiological patterns also resemble those occurring during the day. At the same time, you begin rapid eye movements beneath closed lids (Aserinsky & Kleitman, 1953). Paradoxically, while the brain waves and other measures resemble those of a person awake, muscle tone decreases to the point of virtual paralysis. Sudden, twitchy spasms appear, especially in your face and hands.

What is going on during this *paradoxical sleep?* Because of the rapid eye movements, it looks as if the sleeper is scanning some private, internal world, so researchers began waking people up during REM. In about 80 percent of these awakenings, the people said they had been dreaming. In contrast, reports of dreams occurred only 7 percent of the time when non-REM sleep was interrupted (Dement & Kleitman, 1957).

A Night's Sleep   During the night, most people travel up and down through these stages of sleep four to six times. Each complete circuit takes about ninety

Figure 6.3
EEGs During Sleep
Notice the regular patterns of alpha waves in stage 0 (relaxed wakefulness), the sleep spindles and K complexes in stage 2, and the slower delta waves in stages 3 and 4 (Webb, 1968, p. 15).

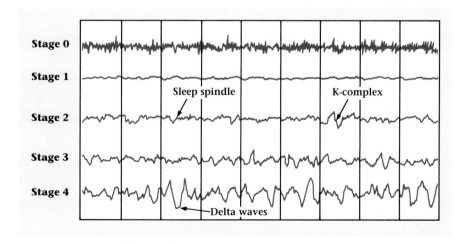

Source: Webb, 1968.

minutes and has a somewhat different itinerary, as Figure 6.4 shows. During the first half of the night most of the time is spent in deeper sleep (stages 3 and 4) and only a few minutes in REM. The last half of the night is dominated by stage 2 and REM sleep, from which sleepers finally wake up.

Over the life span, the pattern of sleep changes. An average infant spends about sixteen hours a day asleep; after age seventy, the average person sleeps only about six hours a day (Roffwarg, Muzio & Dement, 1966). Most of the decrease in total sleeping time comes out of REM sleep. As Figure 6.5 illustrates, REM accounts for half of total sleep at birth, but less than 15 percent in later life.

Of course, each sleeper may deviate from this pattern in many ways. There are light sleepers and deep sleepers, as well as long sleepers (who sleep for nine or ten hours a night and more on weekends) and short sleepers (who average only five or six hours). Good sleepers fall asleep within ten minutes of getting into bed and remain asleep until morning. Poor sleepers may take an hour or more to get to sleep and usually wake up at least once during the night. In other words, most people develop their own style of sleep which, barring such conditions as unusual stress, does not vary much from one night to the next (Clausen, Sersen & Lidsky, 1974).

Sleep Disorders

Almost everyone has trouble sleeping sometimes, especially during times of stress. Sleep disorders can be a temporary annoyance or a long-term, even life-threatening, problem.

The most common sleeping problem is **insomnia,** a general term for conditions in which a person feels tired during the day because of trouble falling asleep or staying asleep. About 25 to 30 million Americans are chronic insomniacs (Coates & Thoreson, 1977). Besides being tiring, insomnia is tied to mental distress. In one study, people with insomnia were three times as likely to display a mental disorder as those who had no sleep complaints (Ford

Figure 6.4
A Night's Sleep
During a typical night a sleeper goes through this sequence of EEG stages. Notice that sleep is deepest during the first part of the night and more shallow later on, when REM sleep becomes more prominent.

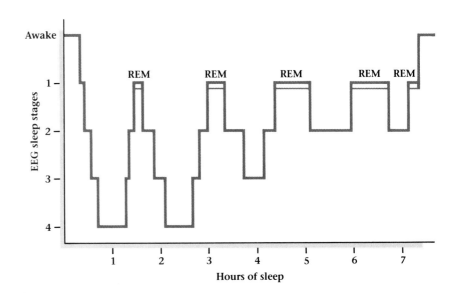

Source: Cartwright, 1978.

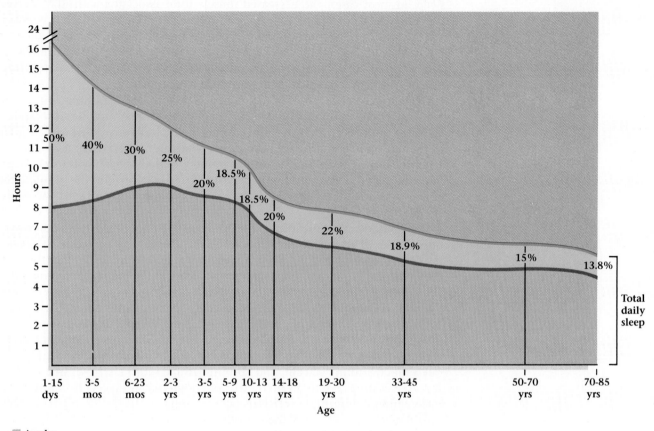

Awake

REM sleep

Non-REM sleep

Figure 6.5
Sleep and Dreaming over the Life Span
Certain changes typically occur in total daily sleep, non-REM sleep, REM sleep, and the percentage of REM sleep from infancy to old age. Notice first that people tend to sleep less as they get older. Notice also the sharp reduction in the percentage of REM sleep, from about eight hours per day in infancy to less than an hour per day by age seventy. Non-REM sleep time also decreases somewhat but, compared to the drop in REM, remains relatively stable. After age twenty, however, non-REM sleep contains less and less of the deepest, or stage 4, sleep.

Note: Percentages indicate portion of total sleep time spent in REM.
Source: Roffwarg et al., 1966.

& Kamerow, 1989). Insomnia lasting at least one year also predicted the development of depression and anxiety disorders, problems described in Chapter 15, on psychological disorders. Notice, however, that these data do not indicate whether insomnia contributes directly to mental disorders or whether factors that eventually lead to disorders also disrupt sleep.

Sleeping pills or alcohol may relieve insomnia temporarily, but they can also be dangerous, especially if taken together, and sleeping pills are highly addictive. Several psychological approaches can help insomniacs—including biofeedback, relaxation training, stress management, and psychotherapy, which we describe in later chapters (Bootzin & Nicassio, 1978; Woolfolk & McNulty, 1983). Insomniacs may also be able to alleviate their problem by going to bed only when they are sleepy and getting out of bed whenever they cannot sleep (Lacks et al., 1983). This helps them to associate being in bed with sleeping rather than with wakefulness. Skipping caffeine late in the day and keeping a regular schedule also help in many cases.

Sleeping too much can be a problem, too. People suffering from **hypersomnia** not only sleep longer than most people at night but also feel tired and take one or more naps during the day. More disturbing, however, is a daytime disorder called **narcolepsy.** Its victims switch abruptly and without warning from an active, often emotional waking state into several minutes of REM sleep. In most cases, the decreased muscle tone associated with REM causes the narcoleptic to collapse on the spot and remain briefly immobilized even after awakening. The exact causes of hypersomnia and narcolepsy are unknown, but narcolepsy appears to have a genetic basis (Parkes & Lock, 1989). Stimulants can be used to treat these problems, but the drugs can be dangerous. Scheduling one or two naps a day may help minimize the problem.

Sleep apnea is a disorder in which people briefly stop breathing while they are asleep. This awakens them, and they resume breathing. Because apnea episodes can occur hundreds of times per night, sufferers do not feel rested in the morning. Usually they have no recollection of their night awakenings. The problem is much more common in men. It seems to be a disorder of the brainstem and of the autonomic nervous system's control of breathing. One effective treatment is to wear a mask over the nose that provides a steady stream of air.

Some infants stop breathing during sleep but do not awaken and consequently die. This tragic occurrence is called *sudden infant death syndrome (SIDS)*. Its relationship to sleep apnea in adults is unknown, but there is evidence that SIDS may be due to abnormalities in the brainstem regions that control breathing (Kinney & Filiano, 1988).

Other less dangerous sleep disorders include nightmares and night terrors. **Nightmares** are frightening, sometimes recurring dreams that apparently take place during REM sleep. **Night terrors** occur in quiet sleep; they are often accompanied by a horrific dream that makes the dreamer sit up staring, let out a bloodcurdling scream, and abruptly awaken into a state of intense fear that may last up to half an hour. This phenomenon is especially common in male children, but milder versions occur among adults. In the morning they may remember nothing of the episode.

Like night terrors, **sleepwalking** starts primarily in non-REM sleep, especially in stage 4, and is most common during childhood (Jacobson, Kales & Kales, 1969). In the morning, sleepwalkers usually have no memory of their travels. Sleepwalking itself is not dangerous, but accidents can happen. Contrary to popular belief, awakening a sleepwalker is not harmful. Drugs are sometimes used to treat sleepwalking, but parents can simply protect most children from the dangers of sleepwalking until they outgrow the problem. One adult sleepwalker was cured by his wife, who blew a whistle whenever her husband began one of his nocturnal strolls (Meyer, 1975).

A condition similar to sleepwalking, but occurring during REM sleep, is called **REM behavior disorder** (Schenck et al., 1987). Brain recordings indicate that the person is in REM sleep, but the near paralysis that normally accompanies REM sleep is not present. The person appears to be acting out dreams. If the dreams are violent, the condition can be dangerous to the dreamer or those nearby. Forty-four percent of REM behavior disorder patients have attacked their sleeping partners during the episodes. One sixty-seven-year-old man grabbed his wife's neck with both hands while dreaming that he was trying to break the neck of a deer; his wife now sleeps in a separate bed. REM behavior disorder is most common in men over sixty, and it is often associated with a neurological disorder such as a stroke.

Why Do People Sleep?

No one knows exactly why people sleep. Psychologists have tried to find out both how brain mechanisms might explain why people fall asleep and what functions sleep serves.

Figure 6.6
Sleep, Dreaming, and the Brain
This diagram shows the location of some of the brain structures thought to be involved in sleep and dreaming (and in other altered states discussed later).

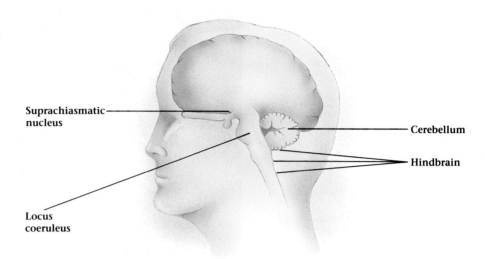

Suprachiasmatic nucleus

Cerebellum

Hindbrain

Locus coeruleus

Sleep as a Circadian Rhythm The cycle of waking and sleeping is one example of the rhythmic character of life. Many physiological processes exhibit a rhythm of approximately twenty-four hours and are thus called **circadian rhythms** (from the Latin *circa dies,* or "about a day"). Longer and shorter rhythms also occur, but twenty-four-hour rhythms are especially prominent.

What controls these rhythms? They are linked, or *entrained,* to environmental signals such as the light and dark of day and night, but rhythms continue even in the absence of all external time cues. Volunteers have lived for weeks or months without external cues (in a deep cave, for example), and their daily rhythms, including sleep and wakefulness, continued. When the rhythm is not entrained by light and dark cues, most people maintain an approximately twenty-five-hour day.

The maintenance of circadian rhythms in the absence of external signals suggests that there must be a built-in biological clock. This clock appears to be located in an area of the hypothalamus called the *suprachiasmatic nucleus* (see Figure 6.6). Neurons in this area exhibit a twenty-four- to twenty-five-hour rhythm in firing even when they are removed from the brain and put in a dish (Gillette, 1986). Signals from the eyes to the suprachiasmatic nucleus tell the brain whether it is day or night and keep the brain entrained to a twenty-four-hour day. Signals from the suprachiasmatic nucleus then drive other parts of the brain that function rhythmically. For example, signals from the suprachiasmatic nucleus reach the hindbrain, and this area in turn activates sleep or wakefulness (McCarley, 1987).

H I G H L I G H T

Confusing the Biological Clock

What happens if the sleep-wake cycle is disrupted? Depression, which is discussed in Chapter 15, on psychological disorders, may be one result. Another is *jet lag*—the fatigue, irritability, and sleeping problems that often follow a long airplane trip. While travelers' bodies are preparing for a night's sleep at their normal bedtime, the clock at their new location says it

The speed of long distance air travel has effectively shrunk the world, but rapid travel across time zones can confuse our biological clocks and bring on the symptoms of jet lag.

is time for lunch. Related problems plague nurses, police officers, and others who must change their work shifts, and thus their sleeping hours, from daytime to all night to evening. For several days after moving to a new shift, many have a hard time getting to sleep and feel tired and grouchy. Even nine days after a shift in sleep time, the circadian rhythm of body temperature is not fully realigned with the sleep-wake cycle (Monk, Moline & Graeber, 1988).

People do not work at top efficiency under such conditions. The problem can become constant if shift changes occur frequently and randomly. Those who work variable shifts experience significantly more alcohol-related problems, job stress, and emotional problems than people on less erratic schedules (Gordon et al., 1986). The effects may be dangerous in other ways as well. The accident at the Three Mile Island nuclear power plant (described in Chapter 9) appears to have been caused in part by inattention and confusion among employees, all of whom had just been put on the night shift (Moore-Ede, Sulzman & Fuller, 1982).

Rhythms readjust more readily when the sleep portion of the cycle is shifted to a later rather than an earlier point, because the underlying rhythm (without entrainment) is longer than twenty-four hours. (It is therefore less disruptive to travel across time zones to the west than to the east.) Also, exposure to properly timed bright light (equivalent to daylight) can rapidly reset the biological clock (Czeisler et al., 1989, 1990). Consequently, world travelers who spend a lot of time outdoors after arrival tend to adjust to their new schedule more rapidly than those who do not. The Philadelphia police department used these principles to plan its shift changes, with beneficial results: after eleven months with the new, research-guided scheduling, sleep problems among officers had decreased, on-the-job automobile accidents declined 40 percent, and alcohol usage dropped 50 percent (Czeisler, 1988). ■

The Functions of Sleep   Why does disrupting the sleep-wake cycle cause such problems? Examining people deprived of sleep provides another approach to understanding why people sleep at all. People who go without sleep for as long as a week usually do not display serious effects. But they do become very sleepy, and they may become irritable or report not being alert. The performance of sleep-deprived individuals on interesting tasks does not deteriorate greatly (Webb, 1975), but boring tasks are performed poorly. Perhaps because they tend to sleep somewhat less anyway, the performance of sleep-deprived elderly people suffers less than that of similarly deprived young people (Bonnet & Arand, 1989).

Some researchers argue that sleep, especially non-REM sleep, allows the body to rest and restore itself for future activity (Adam & Oswald, 1977). This notion is supported by the facts that the amount of non-REM sleep remains fairly stable over the life span and that both short and long sleepers get their deep, non-REM sleep first and in about the same amounts (Hartmann, Baekeland & Zwilling, 1972). Animal studies also support a restorative role for sleep (e.g., Rechtschaffen et al., 1983; see Figure 6.7).

People who are totally sleep deprived do not make up all the sleep they lost, hour for hour. Instead, they get about twice a normal night's sleep, then wake up with no notable aftereffects. In contrast, if people are awakened every time an EEG shows them entering REM, so that they are deprived only of REM sleep, they compensate for the loss more directly. Dement (1960) found that the more nights subjects were kept from REM sleep, the more they tended to enter it. Eventually, instead of having the usual five or six REM episodes each night, they had dozens. Further, when they were allowed to sleep normally on subsequent nights, they tended to "rebound" by spending about twice the normal amount of time in REM, apparently recovering much of what they had lost.

Why should people have such a strong need for REM sleep? One theory says that REM sleep helps maintain the function of norepinephrine neurons in the locus coeruleus (Siegel & Rogawski, 1988; see Figure 6.6). As described in Chapter 3, norepinephrine is one of the brain's major chemical messengers, or *neurotransmitters,* and the locus coeruleus is important in maintaining alertness and mood. Its cells are continually active during waking, but receptors for norepinephrine become less sensitive if they are continuously stimulated

Figure 6.7
Evidence for the Restorative Effects of Sleep
In one study, rats were placed on a platform that rotated whenever their EEG showed they were beginning to sleep; if they failed to walk when the platform moved, a plexiglas barrier pushed them into a pan of water. Another group of rats was subjected to these same stressful conditions for the same number of days, but the movements of the platform were not tied to their sleep state; thus, they were not sleep-deprived. All of the sleep-deprived rats suffered severe physical disorders and some died, whereas the control rats did not (Rechtschaffen et al., 1983).

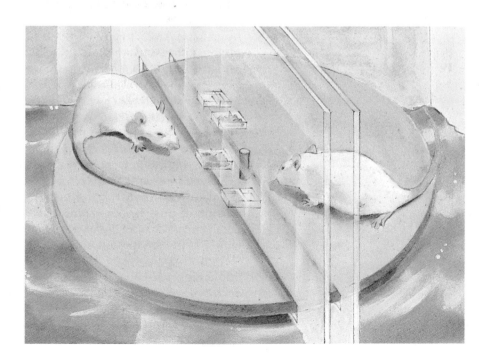

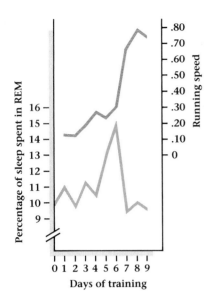

Source: Drucker-Colin & McGaugh, 1977.

Figure 6.8
REM Sleep and Learning
The upper curve shows rats' average running speed as they learned their way around a maze over several days. The lower curve shows the average percentage of REM sleep during the nights between practice sessions. Notice that the rats spent more time in REM on nights during the learning phase than after learning was complete.

for too long. During REM sleep, the activity of the locus coeruleus is almost completely shut down, allowing postsynaptic norepinephrine cells to restore the sensitivity of their receptors. Thus, REM sleep may be vital to maintaining alertness during waking hours. This theory implies that other neural and mental activities during REM sleep (including dreams) are merely by-products of the cell-restoring function of REM sleep.

Other researchers suggest that the brain's activity during REM sleep is far more purposeful. One hypothesis is that REM time is spent developing, checking, and expanding nerve connections in the brain (Roffwarg, Muzio & Dement, 1966). The fact that people get much more REM sleep during infancy and childhood, when the brain is still developing rather rapidly, is consistent with this view. Before birth, when their brains are growing fastest, babies spend over 80 percent of their time in REM sleep. In contrast, animals whose brains and behavior are already well developed at birth (such as guinea pigs) spend very little of their early sleep in REM (Cartwright, 1978).

A related function of REM sleep may be to help imprint what people have learned during the day. Thus, there may be more REM sleep in the early years because every day is crammed with new experiences. REM may also increase temporarily after intense mental efforts. Animals spend an unusually long time in REM sleep after sessions of maze learning; but as Figure 6.8 illustrates, they go back to their normal time in REM once they have mastered the task (Block, Hennevin & LeConte, 1977). An alternative explanation of the same data is that during REM sleep the brain prunes the extraneous connections it has made during the day, keeping only those connections important for useful memories (Crick & Mitchison, 1983).

REM sleep may also be a time of thinking about and adjusting to the day's events or problems. For example, when people in an experiment wore glasses that distorted or restricted their vision, their amount of REM sleep increased at first. But once they became accustomed to their new view of the world, the amount of REM sleep returned to normal (Herman & Roffwarg, 1983; Luce, 1971).

Dreams and Dreaming

Some have argued that the need for REM sleep might be related to the reason for dreaming, since the two so often occur together. However, we cannot be certain that REM sleep and dreaming are identical, since dreaming is a subjective experience. Also, people have reported dreaming when they are awakened from non-REM as well as from REM sleep.

Most researchers agree that the mind is active during all stages of sleep, not just during dreams. **Dreams** differ from other mental activity during sleep because they are storylike sequences of images, sensations, and perceptions that last anywhere from several seconds to many minutes. Dreams may be organized or chaotic, realistic or bizarre, and contain anything from a boring replay of yesterday's trip to the laundry room to a dazzling journey through a world of pure fantasy. Sometimes they even provide creative solutions to perplexing problems. For example, after racking his brain for days to come up with a story about good and evil in the same person, author Robert Louis Stevenson had a dream in which a man drank a substance that turned him into a monster (Hill, 1968). The dream inspired *The Strange Case of Dr. Jekyll and Mr. Hyde*. The history of science is full of similar examples; the benzene ring and the double-helix shape of the DNA molecule apparently also came to their discoverers in dreams.

This 1931 painting by Thomas Hart Benton illustrates the fact that the content of dreams often relates to the events and concerns of the dreamer's life. Why dreams occur and what they might mean are subjects of continuing research and debate.

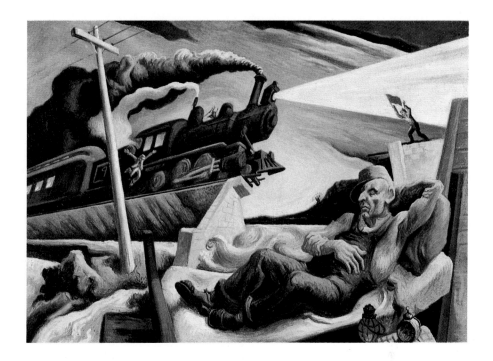

Research has left little doubt that everyone dreams during every night of normal sleep. Whether you remember a dream depends on how you sleep and wake up (Cartwright, 1978). Recall is also more likely if you wake up abruptly and lie quietly while writing or tape-recording your recollections.

Why do you dream? Over thousands of years of speculation, dreams have been characterized as supernatural, psychological, or physiological events. Dreams have been considered messages from the gods, the dead, or other spiritual sources that give instructions or glimpses into the future (Lewin, 1983). As you might expect, psychologists tend to view dreams as psychological events that contain information about the dreamer's mental processes. Freud (1900) called dreams the "royal road to a knowledge of the unconscious mind." He theorized that when people sleep, they allow normally unconscious impulses and wishes to appear in dreams, usually in disguised form. In Chapter 16 we discuss these ideas and how the interpretation of dreams is used to understand and treat mental disorders.

Some theorists see dreams as a meaningless by-product of REM sleep. One hypothesis holds that when neural circuits using the neurotransmitters norepinephrine and serotonin are shut down, acetylcholine circuits transport essentially random messages from a "dream-state generator" in the hindbrain to the cortex (Quattrochi et al., 1989). Dreams result as the cortex tries to make sense of these messages in light of memories and feelings. This view suggests that dreams are meaning imposed on random input, much like looking at cloud formations and seeing faces in them. Similarly, Christopher Evans (1984) proposed that, like a computer running a test of its programs, the brain must regularly check its neural circuits when the system is "down" or "off line"—that is, asleep. Dreams, he said, are the by-product of that process—a temporary, perhaps accidental, glimpse into the material that the brain is scanning, sorting, and reorganizing.

Do these theories mean that dreams have no psychological significance? Not at all. For one thing, whatever the physiological explanation for dreams, psychological factors may still be important. One study investigated the dreams of twenty-nine divorcing or recently divorced women (Cartwright et al., 1984). Nineteen of the women were depressed; the rest were not. The patterns of dreaming differed in the two groups. The depressed women dreamed repeatedly of the past, whereas the nondepressed women more often had problem-solving dreams and dreams containing elements of the distant and recent past, the present, and the future. Thus, even if the raw material of dreams comes strictly from physiological activity and has no inherent meaning, the mental style or current concerns of the dreamer may still determine how that activity is organized and recalled.

Some investigators believe that people can even learn to direct the content of their dreams and use them to work through their problems. Evidence that sleep does not involve a total loss of self-awareness or mental functioning and is thus open to conscious direction comes from reports of **lucid dreaming**, in which the sleeper is aware of dreaming *while a dream is happening* (Laberge et al., 1981). Other researchers contend that people who are lucid dreaming are not actually asleep. Like questions about why people sleep and dream at all, a resolution of this issue awaits further research.

Hypnosis

The word *hypnosis* comes from the Greek word *hypnos,* which means "sleep," but hypnotized people are not truly asleep. **Hypnosis** is commonly defined as an altered state of consciousness brought on by special techniques and characterized by responsiveness to suggestions for changes in experience and behavior (Orne, 1977, 1980).

What does it feel like to be hypnotized? The only way to know for sure is to try it. People often report that their bodies feel "asleep" while their minds remain active and alert. Many are fully aware of being hypnotized. Some report sensations of spinning, floating, dizziness, or apparent changes in the size of their bodies. Most hypnotized people do not feel forced to follow the hypnotist's instructions; they simply see no reason to refuse (Gill & Brenman, 1959; Hilgard, 1965).

Standing-room-only audiences love to watch hypnotized people forget their own names or act like chickens. Few leave these demonstrations disappointed; but many leave with questions about what hypnosis is, who is susceptible to it and why, and what it can accomplish. Although there are still no final answers to these questions, there are some useful theories and research.

Experiencing Hypnosis

In the late eighteenth century, Franz Anton Mesmer, an Austrian physician, popularized *mesmerism*—what we now call hypnosis—in order to cure patients of paralysis and other disorders. He hypnotized people by bringing them in contact with magnetized objects and substances that supposedly redistributed a magnetic fluid in their bodies. Around 1860, A. A. Liebeault, director of a French medical clinic, induced hypnosis by suggesting to his subjects that they were relaxed and sleepy; this is the procedure that is most common today. Whatever the specifics, all procedures for inducing hypnosis focus people's attention on a restricted, often monotonous set of stimuli (usually including the hypnotist's voice) while asking them to shut out everything else as they imagine certain feelings.

Source: Hilgard, 1965.

Figure 6.9
Hypnotic Age Regression
Here are the signatures of a male and female before hypnotically induced age regression (top) and while age-regressed (bottom). Notice that the lower signatures look less mature; one is even printed rather than written. In spite of such changes in behavior, the things people "recall" during age regression are not especially accurate and are subject to the usual distortions associated with attempts to retrieve old memories (Nash et al., 1986).

The results can be fascinating. Hypnotized people may show changes in movement, sensation, perception, memory, motivation, emotion, thinking, and other dimensions. For example, people told that their eyes will not open may struggle fruitlessly to open them. They can be made to appear deaf, blind, or unable to smell; they may become less sensitive to pain. Hypnotized people may forget their own telephone numbers; sometimes they can recall memories they were unable to retrieve before hypnosis. Some people seem to display **age regression**, in which they not only recall but seem to re-enact behaviors from childhood. (Figure 6.9 provides an example.) Sometimes the influence of hypnosis can be extended for hours or days by **posthypnotic suggestions**— instructions about experiences or behavior to take place after hypnosis has ended (say, whistling "Dixie" whenever someone coughs).

Ernest Hilgard (1965) has summarized the ways people change when they are hypnotized.

1. Hypnotized people show *reduced planfulness*. In other words, they tend not to initiate actions, preferring to wait for the hypnotist's instructions. One subject said, "At one point I was trying to decide if my legs were crossed, but I couldn't tell, and didn't quite have the initiative to move to find out" (Hilgard, 1965, p. 6).
2. Hypnotized people ignore everything except the hypnotist's voice and whatever it points out; their *attention is redistributed*. One person described the experience this way: "Your voice came in my ear and *filled* my head" (Hilgard, 1965, p. 13). This is an extreme form of selective attention, which is described in Chapter 5.
3. The ability to *fantasize* is enhanced, so that people can easily put themselves into various scenes or vividly relive old memories.
4. The willingness to accept apparent distortions of reality increases. This willingness is part of *reduced reality testing*, a tendency not to question whether stated facts are true. Thus, a hypnotized person might begin to shiver in a very warm room because the hypnotist says it has just begun to snow. However, even though the experiences seem vivid and real, hypnotized subjects are still able to discriminate reality from nonreality (Lynn, Weekes & Milano, 1989).
5. Hypnotized people are especially good at *role-taking*, easily behaving as if they are, say, a different age or a member of the opposite sex.
6. Many hypnotized people experience **posthypnotic amnesia**. That is, they cannot remember what happened while they were hypnotized. For some, recall fails even when they are told what went on.

Who Can Be Hypnotized?

Not everyone can be hypnotized. Special tests can measure hypnotic **susceptibility**, the degree to which people respond to hypnotic suggestions. Examples include the Stanford Hypnotic Susceptibility Scales, or SHSS (Weitzenhoffer & Hilgard, 1962), and the Harvard Group Scale of Hypnotic Susceptibility (Shor & Orne, 1963). These tests begin with a standard hypnotic induction, followed by suggestions that the person cannot speak or that the person's arm is rigid; points are awarded for each suggestion followed. These tests show that about 10 to 15 percent of adults are excellent hypnotic subjects. Another 10 percent or so are difficult or impossible to hypnotize and display few, if any, hypnotic behaviors. Most people fall somewhere between these extremes (Hilgard, 1982).

We know that hypnosis can be induced by staring at an object or in
other ways that are much simpler
than Mesmer's elaborate rituals.

Is there something different about susceptible individuals? About the only
traits that set susceptible people apart from others are a more active imagination
(Wilson & Barber, 1978), proneness to fantasy (Lynn & Rhue, 1986), and an
ability to concentrate on a single activity for a long time (Graham & Evans,
1977). People can improve their susceptibility by learning to think more
favorably about hypnosis and to accept hypnotic suggestions, by watching
what good hypnotic subjects do, or by practicing (Gfeller, Lynn & Pribble,
1987; Spanos, Lush, & Gwynn, 1989; Wickless & Kirsch, 1990). At any particular
time, a person's *willingness* to be hypnotized may be more important than
general hypnotic susceptibility in determining responsiveness. The idea that
one person can hypnotize another against his or her will is a myth.

Explaining Hypnosis

Hypnotized people often look and act differently from those who are not
hypnotized (Hilgard, 1965), but do the differences signal an altered state of
consciousness? Role theory, state theory, and dissociation theory offer different
answers to this question.

Role Theory   According to **role theory**, hypnosis does not create a special
state of consciousness; hypnotized subjects merely act in accordance with a
special social role, which demands compliance (Sarbin, 1950). The procedures
for inducing hypnosis, this theory suggests, provide a socially acceptable reason
to follow the hypnotist's suggestions, much as a nurse's uniform or the title
of doctor provide good reasons for medical patients to remove their clothing
on command.

Support for role theory comes from both everyday life and experiments.
Every day, unhypnotized people behave in the bizarre fashion normally
associated with hypnosis. On television game shows you will see apparently
normal, certainly unhypnotized individuals scream, jump around, hug and
kiss total strangers, and generally make fools of themselves. In the laboratory,
motivated but unhypnotized volunteers can duplicate virtually every aspect

Figure 6.10
Can Hypnosis Produce Blindness?
The top row in this figure looks like gibberish, but it can be read as the numbers and letters in the lower row if viewed through special glasses with one eye closed. Frank Pattie (1935) found that hypnotized subjects who had been given suggestions for blindness in one eye were unable to read the numbers and letters while wearing the special glasses, a result indicating that both eyes were in fact working normally.

Source: Pattie, 1935.

of hypnotic behavior, from arm rigidity to pain tolerance to age regression (Barber, 1969; Orne, 1970; Orne & Evans, 1965). In one experiment decades ago, Frank Pattie (1935) showed that people whom hypnosis had made deaf or insensitive to touch could actually hear and feel, in spite of the fact that they otherwise behaved (and believed) that they could not. Figure 6.10 illustrates how Pattie demonstrated that one person who thought she was blind while hypnotized could in fact see. Pattie's conclusions have been confirmed in more recent studies (e.g., Bryant & McConkey, 1989).

State Theory   Does all this evidence mean that hypnosis involves nothing more than providing a good reason to do things that people might have done for other reasons? **State theorists** say no; hypnosis does create an altered state of consciousness. They point to subtle differences between hypnotized and nonhypnotized people, which usually involve the *way* they carry out suggestions. For example, in one experiment hypnotized people and people who had been asked to simulate hypnosis were told that they would run their hands through their hair whenever they heard the word *experiment* (Orne, Sheehan & Evans, 1968). Simulators did so only when the hypnotist said the cue word; hypnotized subjects complied no matter who said it.

State theorists hold that such differences between hypnotized and nonhypnotized people indicate that hypnotized people are not just role-playing; they are experiencing a special state of consciousness. In their view, even if people enter hypnosis in response to the demands of a social role or other external influences, once hypnotized their basic mental processes change significantly, and in ways that do not occur in unhypnotized people (Orne, 1980).

Dissociation Theory   To explain these changes in mental processes, Hilgard (1977, 1979) proposed a blending of role and state theories. He suggested that hypnosis is not one specific state but a general condition in which people reorganize the ways in which their behavior is controlled. Usually, the ego, or self, determines what people pay attention to, what they perceive and remember, how they act, and so on. This central control can be temporarily broken up, however, by a process called *dissociation*. Dissociation occurs when two or more thoughts or perceptions take place simultaneously and independently, even though the person may be aware of only one (Hilgard, 1979). Hypnosis, said Hilgard, creates a dissociation, a split in consciousness. As a result, body movements that are normally under voluntary control can take place on their own, and normally involuntary processes, such as overt reactions to sound or pain, can become voluntary.

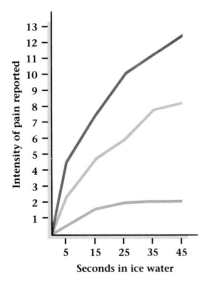

Source: Hilgard, 1977.

Figure 6.11
Reports of Pain in Hypnosis
This graph compares the average reports of pain while a hand was immersed in ice water under three conditions: (1) reports by non-hypnotized subjects (red line); (2) verbal reports of pain given by hypnotized subjects who were told they would experience no pain (orange line); and (3) reports indicated by key pressing when hypnotized subjects were told they would experience no pain but were asked to press a key if "any part of them" felt pain (green line). The nonverbal reports by this "hidden observer" suggest that under hypnosis the experience of pain was dissociated from conscious awareness.

Evidence for dissociation during hypnosis comes from an experiment in which hypnotized subjects were asked to immerse one hand in ice-cold water after being told that they would feel no pain (Hilgard, Morgan & MacDonald, 1975). With the other, nonimmersed hand, the subjects were asked to press a key to indicate if "any part of them" experienced pain. The subjects' oral reports indicated almost no pain, but their key pressing told a different story, as Figure 6.11 shows. Hilgard concluded that a "hidden observer" was reporting on pain that was reaching the person but had been separated, or dissociated, from conscious awareness (Hilgard, 1977).

According to Hilgard's **dissociation theory** of hypnosis, the relaxation of central control within the hypnotized person is accompanied by a *social agreement* to share some of that control with the hypnotist. For a time, the hypnotist is allowed to determine what the subject will experience and do. Thus, hypnosis is a socially agreed-upon opportunity to display the ability to let mental functions become dissociated. If only a limited degree of dissociation occurs in a hypnotic situation, the person may not experience a change in consciousness. But if profound dissociation takes place, the hypnotized person may enter an altered state. (For a comparison of hypnosis and the other altered states we have discussed, see "In Review: Some Altered States of Consciousness.") In short, according to Hilgard, compliance with a social role may account for part of the story, but hypnosis also creates significant changes in mental processes.

Appealing as dissociation theory may be, further research will be necessary to establish its validity and to explore the roles of social and cognitive factors in hypnotic phenomena. In summary, there is much left to learn about the nature of hypnosis.

Some Uses of Hypnosis

Despite debate about what hypnosis is, it has been put to many good uses, especially in the control of pain. Hypnosis seems to be the only anesthetic some people need to protect them from the pain of dental work, childbirth, burns, abdominal surgery, and spinal taps (Finer, 1980). For other people hypnosis has relieved the chronic pain of arthritis, nerve damage, migraine headaches, and cancer (Hilgard, 1980; Long, 1986). Hypnotic suggestion can reduce nausea and vomiting produced by chemotherapy (Redd, 1984), and it has helped minimize bleeding during surgery (Gerschman, Reade & Burrows, 1980). Some therapists have had moderate success helping clients to stop using cigarettes, alcohol, or other drugs by offering posthypnotic suggestions that those substances will produce nausea or disgust.

Other applications of hypnosis are controversial, especially attempts to use hypnosis to enhance a person's memory. Certainly, when hypnotized people show age regression, they are not actually becoming younger. Instead, they are probably recalling or reconstructing early memories as well as imagining and acting out past actions (Foenander & Burrows, 1980). Similarly, researchers have questioned whether hypnotizing witnesses actually helps them recall the events of a crime. Instead, people's confidence in hypnosis may prompt them unintentionally to distort information or inaccurately reconstruct events (Loftus & Loftus, 1980; McCann & Sheehan, 1988; Orne, 1979). In fact, the American Medical Association and the American Psychological Association oppose using hypnosis to obtain reports about crimes from victims and witnesses. Courts in several states disqualify testimony from people who have been hypnotized.

In Review: Some Altered States of Consciousness

State	Characteristics	Postulated Benefits
Daydreaming	Attention directed toward internal events; fantasy-oriented	Maintains adequate level of mental activity
Sleeping		Restores body and brain
Stage 1	Irregular EEG, rolling eyes	
Stage 2	Sleep spindles, K complexes in EEG	
Stage 3	Addition of delta waves to EEG	
Stage 4	More than 50% delta waves in EEG	
REM sleep	EEG, heart rate, and other physiological patterns characteristic of the waking state combined with rapid eye movements and reduced muscle tone	Allows dreams to occur; allows norepinephrine sensitivity to restore itself; allows new connections between neurons to be consolidated or unused connections to be pruned
Hypnotized state	Increased susceptibility to suggestions for changes in experience or behavior	Pain control, for example
Meditative state	Passive mental processes with alpha activity in brain waves	Reduces stress and anxiety

Meditation

Separation of mind and body, a sense of timelessness, a feeling of oneness with the universe, increased self-knowledge, ecstasy—all these effects sometimes accompany hypnosis (Hilgard, 1979). Similar effects can be sought through **meditation**, which is a set of techniques designed to create an altered state of consciousness characterized by inner peace and tranquillity (Shapiro & Walsh, 1984). Many people believe that meditation helps them gain awareness of their relationship to the universe, understand themselves more clearly, decrease stress and anxiety, and even improve performance in everything from work to tennis.

There is no single "right" way to create a meditative state. Most common are *focusing* methods (Ornstein, 1977). These methods aim at narrowing attention to just one thing—a word, a sound, or an object—long enough for the meditator to stop thinking about *anything* and to experience nothing but pure awareness. They call for the meditator to (1) find a quiet environment, (2) assume a comfortable position, (3) use a mental device to organize attention, and (4) take a passive attitude (Benson, 1975).

What the meditator focuses on is far less important than doing so with a passive attitude. To organize attention, meditators may, for example, inwardly name every sound or thought that reaches consciousness, focus on the sound of their own breathing, or slowly repeat a *mantra,* which is a soothing word or phrase such as *om* (meaning "I am"). If attention begins to wander, there is a natural tendency to try to refocus it, but these active efforts block the way to the meditative state (Shapiro, 1980). Instead, new meditators are encouraged to observe any distractions but to make no effort to get rid of them, instead letting them fall away on their own. In other words, you achieve a passive attitude by not trying to achieve it.

Linkages: Can meditation help people deal with psychological problems? (a link to Treatment of Psychological Disorders)

During a typical meditation session, respiration, heart rate, muscle tension, blood pressure, and oxygen consumption decrease (Shapiro & Giber, 1978; Wallace & Benson, 1972). Most forms of meditation are also accompanied by a considerable amount of alpha wave activity, the brain-wave pattern commonly found during a relaxed, eyes-closed, waking state (see Figure 6.3). Meditators may also experience significant reductions in stress-related problems such as general anxiety, high blood pressure, and insomnia (Carrington, 1986; Smith, 1975). More generally, meditators' scores on personality tests indicate increases in general mental health, self-esteem, and social openness (Shapiro & Giber, 1978). As with most things, meditation should be used in moderation. Meditating for very long periods may produce dizziness, anxiety, confusion, depression, and restlessness (Otis, 1984), not to mention interference with work and other activities.

Exactly how meditation produces its effects is unclear. Most of them can be achieved by other means, including biofeedback, hypnosis, and just relaxing (Holmes, 1984). Still, proponents of meditation claim that it alone can create the uplifting altered state that can lead to true enlightenment (Deikman, 1982). Unfortunately, this condition cannot at present be measured objectively and scientifically.

Psychoactive Drugs

Alterations in consciousness are frequently brought about by **psychoactive drugs,** chemical substances that act on the brain to create psychological effects. Some psychoactive drugs—particularly caffeine, nicotine, and alcohol—are so much a part of American life that many people may not think of them as drugs that change their states of consciousness. But they are and they do.

The Varying Effects of Drugs

The enjoyable or medically beneficial effects of psychoactive drugs are often marred by undesirable effects. The most insidious effects occur when drug use becomes drug abuse. *Drug abuse* is the self-administration of drugs in ways that deviate from either the medical or social norms of a society (Gilman et al., 1985); in other words, using drugs too often, for longer than medically necessary, or in excessive doses. The definitions of what is "too often," "too long," or "excessive" vary from one society to another and over time in a given society. For example, cigarette smoking was once socially acceptable in America. As its health hazards became well known, however, smoking became socially unacceptable in most segments of American society. Indeed, during the 1980s American society became increasingly intolerant toward many psychoactive drugs, mainly because of their health risks or their potential for creating dependence.

Dependence may be psychological or physiological or both. *Psychological dependence* occurs when drug use continues despite adverse consequences, when a person acts as if the drug is needed for a sense of well-being, and when a person becomes preoccupied with obtaining the drug if it becomes unavailable. Psychological dependence can occur with or without *physical dependence,* or *addiction,* which is an altered physiological state in which continued use of the drug is required to prevent the onset of a *withdrawal syndrome.* Withdrawal syndromes vary with different drugs but often include nausea, headache, chills, or other physical discomfort, in addition to craving for the drug. Physical dependence can develop gradually, without the user's awareness. As addiction develops over time, drug tolerance often does, too. *Tolerance* is a condition in which increasingly large amounts of a drug are required to produce a given effect. For addicts, drug use commonly becomes a compulsive, uncontrollable act that pervades their lives and leaves them very likely to resume drug use even if they stop for a time (Gilman et al., 1985).

The causes of drug use and drug abuse are not the same (Newcomb & Bentler, 1989). The switch from casual, social use of drugs to drug abuse is tied to individual psychological processes, such as the desire to protect oneself from emotional distress (Newcomb & Bentler, 1989). In contrast, the roots of casual drug use in the United States are primarily social. For example, pressure to conform with peers (a process explored in Chapter 18) is one reason for casual use. In one survey of high school seniors, 92 percent had tried alcohol and 57 percent had tried an illegal drug such as marijuana (Johnston et al., 1987). During the 1980s, however, drug use declined nationally as the dangers of drug abuse became more prominent (Johnston et al., 1989).

The potential for "normal" individuals to become dependent on drugs should not be underestimated. All drugs with the potential for creating dependence affect parts of the brain that activate pleasant feelings or suppress distress (Wise, 1978). Normally, these areas are activated and produce pleasure when people eat or drink or engage in other important survival behaviors. Drugs short-circuit this connection by *directly* stimulating the brain's pleasure centers. Animals that have become addicted to cocaine will choose cocaine over food to the point of starvation (Bozarth & Wise, 1985).

In Chapter 15, on psychological disorders, we look more closely at the causes of drug abuse. In this chapter, we focus on how some commonly used psychoactive drugs affect consciousness.

Linkages: How do drugs act in the nervous system to alter consciousness? (a link to Biological Aspects of Psychology)

What changes in consciousness do drugs produce? The effects vary widely, from racing thoughts to feelings of euphoria, from hallucinations to anxiety reduction, from sleep to coma, or even death. This range of effects reflects the equally wide range of effects on neurotransmitters, the chemical messengers between neurons. (You might find it useful to review the summary of neurotransmitters in Chapter 3.) Psychoactive drugs generally compete with or alter the availability of neurotransmitters, distorting the balance of those neurotransmitters. For example, cocaine blocks the removal of dopamine from synapses, thus increasing the amount of that neurotransmitter that reaches the postsynaptic receptors. Often, drugs affect several neurotransmitters, and assigning a critical role to just one change can be difficult.

Understanding the effects of drugs is further complicated by the fact that more than biochemistry is involved in determining a drug's effects. *Learned* expectations and responses also play a role. Their importance was demonstrated in a study in which male social drinkers were given either tonic water or a vodka-and-tonic mixture in which the alcohol could not be tasted (Lang et al., 1975). The vodka mixture brought the drinkers' blood-alcohol content to 0.1 percent, the level at which most states define a person as legally drunk. Half the people drinking each beverage were told what they were drinking. But the other half were misinformed: they thought either that they were drinking alcohol when they were not or that they were consuming no alcohol when they were. Then a research assistant, posing as an obnoxious fellow subject, angered the subjects. Later they were allowed to hurt him by administering electric shocks as part of an experiment. (The assistant appeared to be shocked, but no electricity actually reached him.) What happened? Legally

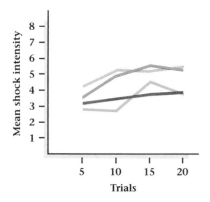

Source: Lang et al., 1975.

Figure 6.12
Expectancy and the Effects of Alcohol on Aggressiveness
In this experiment, aggression was measured by the intensity of shocks that subjects delivered to another person over several trials. Shocks given by people who thought they had been drinking (brown and blue lines) were significantly more intense, whether the subjects actually had alcohol or not, than those given by subjects who were sober or at least thought they were (red and green lines). Thus, aggression was influenced more by the subjects' expectancies than by alcohol itself.

drunk subjects who did not think they had been drinking did not perceive themselves as drunk and tended to be less aggressive than sober people who perceived themselves to be drunk, as Figure 6.12 shows. The effect of alcohol on aggressiveness, as measured by the strength of the shocks, depended not on whether the people were drunk or sober but on their expectations.

In short, the effects of psychoactive drugs are complex and variable. In the sections that follow we consider several major categories of psychoactive drugs, including depressants, stimulants, narcotics, and hallucinogens. We discuss what is known about their biochemical effects and their typical effects on consciousness.

Depressants

Drugs that depress functioning of the central nervous system are called **depressants**. The most familiar depressants are alcohol, sedatives, and anxiolytics. All three enhance neurotransmission at GABA synapses. Because GABA reduces the likelihood that postsynaptic neurons will fire, enhancing GABA function reduces the excitability of many neural circuits.

Alcohol   Alcohol is one of the oldest and most widely used drugs in the world. In the United States alone, over 100 million people drink it in an endless variety of beverages.

Reactions to alcohol vary considerably from person to person. In our culture, some drinkers begin talking too loudly, acting silly, or telling others exactly what they think of them. Emotional reactions range from euphoria to deep sadness. Those who have been inhibiting aggression may become unpredictably impulsive or even violent (Steele, 1986).

What causes these effects of alcohol? Several neurotransmitters seem to be involved, including dopamine, norepinephrine, serotonin, endorphins, and GABA (Koob & Bloom, 1988). The GABA effect is particularly interesting, because drugs that interact with GABA receptors in a different way can reverse the intoxicating effects of alcohol, as Figure 6.13 illustrates (Suzdak et al., 1986). Some of the effects of alcohol—such as happiness, sadness, adventurousness, lust, or anger—depend on both the biological consequences of alcohol and a person's learned expectations (Keane, Lisman & Kreutzer, 1980; Marlatt & Rohsenow, 1980). Many other effects—such as disruptions of muscular coordination, balance, speech, and thought—tend to occur whether or not the drinker expects them (Vuchinich & Sobell, 1978).

The biological consequences depend on the amount of alcohol carried by the blood to the brain. Since alcohol is broken down by the liver at the rate of about one ounce per hour, it has little effect on the brain if consumed that slowly. But most people drink faster, and the consequences differ somewhat for men and women. Recent research suggests that, even after allowing for differences in size, men's bodies are more efficient at beginning to break alcohol down even before it reaches the liver. As a result, women may have higher blood alcohol levels than men following equal doses of alcohol (Frezza et al., 1990).

About two ounces of alcohol may cause feelings of relaxation, happiness, and well-being. Inhibitions may be reduced, perhaps because the drug depresses activity in parts of the cerebral cortex that normally keep people from doing things they know they should not do. Alcohol especially affects the locus coeruleus, which normally activates the cortex (Koob & Bloom, 1988; see Figure 6.6). As the dose of alcohol increases, more and more of the brain's activity is impaired, resulting in confused or disorganized thinking, slurred

Figure 6.13
GABA Receptors and Alcohol
Both rats in this photograph received the same amount of alcohol, enough to incapacitate them with drunkenness. But the rat on the right also received a drug that reverses the intoxicating effect of alcohol, and within two minutes it was acting completely sober. The drug, Ro15-4513, binds to part of the brain's GABA receptor complex, blocking the ability of alcohol to stimulate the GABA receptor. The company that developed Ro15-4513 decided to discontinue work on the drug because of ethical and legal concerns. Before lamenting this decision, note that the drug does not reverse the effects of alcohol on the hindbrain's breathing centers. So if you were drinking to become intoxicated and Ro was frustrating your attempts, you could more easily ingest a lethal overdose.

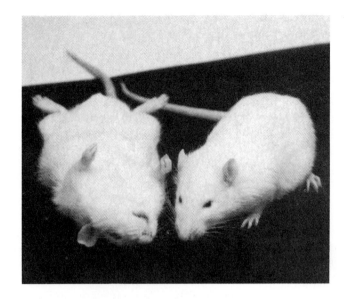

Source: Kolata, 1986.

speech, and disruptions in coordination and balance, due to effects of the drug on the cerebellum (Rogers et al., 1986). Further increases in alcohol produce sleep. Rapid consumption of more than thirty ounces of alcohol inhibits the hindbrain, where breathing and heart action are controlled, until sleep becomes death.

Counting ounces can be misleading, however, because the actual amount of alcohol in the blood depends not only on how fast a person drinks but also on what a person drinks and how rapidly it is absorbed. Straight whiskey and cocktails high in alcohol content generally have stronger effects than wine or beer, which contain lower concentrations of alcohol. Alcohol also enters the bloodstream more rapidly if the drinker's stomach is empty and more slowly if the stomach is full. Filling up on food before drinking delays

Though practice may make it seem easy, driving a car is actually a rather complex task that requires the driver to be constantly alert to a wide range of incoming stimuli, to make fast and accurate decisions about how to respond, and to execute those responses in a skillful, coordinated fashion. Alcohol can impair all these processes (as well as our ability to judge the degree of impairment) thus making drinking and driving a deadly combination.

the effects of excessive drinking, but does not prevent them. And nothing developed so far can protect the overindulgent drinker from the next morning's hangover, which is the result of the metabolism of alcohol into toxic compounds (Gilman et al., 1985).

Sedatives Sometimes called "downers" or sleeping pills, *sedatives* are another group of depressants that can create physical dependence. The most common sedatives are *barbiturates*, which carry trade names such as Seconal and Nembutal. (Methaqualone, or Quaalude, has effects similar to those of barbiturates.) Small doses of sedatives bring relaxation and mild euphoria but can also disrupt muscle coordination, mental concentration, and the ability to work. Sedatives also cause very deep sleep; overdoses can be fatal. Addicts who try to give up barbiturates may experience withdrawal symptoms more severe than those created by any other drug. The symptoms can include intense agitation, violent outbursts, convulsions, hallucinations, and even sudden death.

Anxiolytics As their name suggests, *anxiolytics* are prescribed by physicians to help patients feel free from anxiety. They were formerly known as *tranquilizers*. Although anxiolytics relieve anxiety, they also have sedative properties, and they can be addictive. One type of anxiolytic, meprobamate (sold as Miltown), can be taken in small daily doses for anxiety, but its effects resemble those of barbiturates; overdoses can bring on sleep, and very large doses can cause death. Another group of anxiolytics, called *benzodiazepines*, also relieves anxiety but does not create as much sleepiness as meprobamate. It is very difficult to commit suicide by taking an overdose of benzodiazepines. They are sold under such trade names as Librium and Valium. Like alcohol, benzodiazepines affect the GABA receptor system, but they do not bind directly to GABA receptors (Squires & Braestrup, 1977). Instead, benzodiazepines enhance the binding of GABA to its receptors, resulting in increased inhibition whenever GABA is released.

The widespread use of anxiolytics—over 100 million prescriptions per year in the United States alone—has led to misuse. Many patients become psychologically and physically dependent on anxiolytics and suffer symptoms similar to barbiturate withdrawal when they discontinue using them (Gilman et al., 1985). Many long-term users experience confusion, disorientation, uncontrolled anger, loss of memory, and other undesirable symptoms. Worse still, some people combine alcohol with anxiolytics. The effects of this combination on mental functioning and motor coordination can be fatal, especially if a person is foolish enough to drive a car under its influence.

Stimulants

Chemicals that can increase behavioral and mental activity are known as **stimulants.** Two of those discussed here, amphetamines and cocaine, do so mainly by augmenting the action of the neurotransmitters dopamine and norepinephrine.

Amphetamines Benzedrine, Dexedrine, and Methadrine are some of the trade names for *amphetamines*; they are also called "uppers" or "speed." The rewarding properties of amphetamine are due to its ability to release dopamine. Blocking dopamine receptors reduces the consumption of amphetamines (see Wise, 1978).

Linkages: Through neurotransmitter mechanisms described in Chapter 3, cocaine produces euphoria and increased physiological activation, but its users run a high risk of ruining their lives by becoming psychologically or physically dependent on the drug.

Amphetamines were first synthesized to relieve asthma and nasal congestion. They stimulate both the brain and the sympathetic branch of the autonomic nervous system. Arousal of the sympathetic system produces increased heart rate and blood pressure, constriction of blood vessels and shrinking of mucous membranes (thus relieving stuffy noses), suppression of appetite, and alertness.

The desire to lose weight, to stay awake, or to experience a "high" has led many people to abuse amphetamines. Continued use can produce severe restlessness, sleeplessness, heart problems, mental confusion, suspiciousness, nonstop talking, and in extreme cases, symptoms similar to those of paranoid schizophrenia; as described in Chapter 15, these often include false beliefs about being watched or persecuted by hostile forces. Like the symptoms of schizophrenia, these symptoms are often relieved by antipsychotic drugs.

Cocaine   The leaves of the coca plant are the source of cocaine, which has many similarities to amphetamine. Like amphetamine, cocaine acts on dopamine synapses, but cocaine mainly blocks the inactivation of dopamine. In a laboratory study that controlled for the numbing of the nose from cocaine, the psychological effects of cocaine and amphetamine were indistinguishable (Van Dyke & Byck, 1982). Furthermore, the psychological problems caused by cocaine and amphetamine abuse are virtually indistinguishable (Gawin & Ellinwood, 1988).

The various forms of cocaine and amphetamine differ primarily in the time-course of their effects. Time-course is very important, because it can influence the addictiveness of a drug. Animal studies show that drugs with rapid onset and short duration are more highly addictive than others (Kato, Wakasa & Yanagita, 1987). This fact may help explain why *crack*—a purified, especially potent, and smokable form of cocaine—is particularly addictive. Crack has a fast onset and short duration. It causes a rapid "rush," followed quickly by a depressed mood that can be relieved by more crack.

Like many other now-outlawed drugs, cocaine was once sold legally as medicine; Sigmund Freud once recommended it for relieving depression. It even appeared in the original recipe for Coca-Cola. It stimulates self-confidence, well-being, and optimism. Continued use of cocaine, however, can lead to nausea, overactivity, sleeplessness, paranoid thinking, a sudden depressive "crash," and hallucinations. Overdoses, especially of crack, can be fatal (Kozel, Grider & Adams, 1982). Even small doses can result in death from heart attack or stroke. Cocaine can lead to physical addiction as well as strong psychological dependence (Jones, 1984).

Because of the strong effects of cocaine on the brain's pleasure centers, it has been exceedingly difficult to devise effective ways of helping cocaine addicts quit permanently. Antidepressant drugs show some potential as a treatment for cocaine abuse, but more promising candidates are drugs like *buprenorphine.* Acting on opiate receptors, buprenorphine can suppress the self-administration of cocaine by addicted monkeys (Mello et al., 1989).

Caffeine   The most widely used psychoactive drug in the world, caffeine is regularly consumed by 82 to 92 percent of North American adults (Gilbert, 1984). It occurs in coffee, tea, chocolate, and many soft drinks. Tolerance develops to caffeine's stimulant properties, and caffeine can induce physical dependence (Griffiths & Woodson, 1988). Withdrawal symptoms may include headaches, fatigue, anxiety, shakiness, and craving. The withdrawal syndrome begins to appear twelve to twenty-four hours after abstinence, peaks at about forty-eight hours, and lasts about a week.

Caffeine is a psychoactive drug that appears in so many forms that people are not always aware of consuming it.

Narcotics

The ability to induce sleep and relieve pain distinguishes the **narcotics**—particularly opium, morphine, and heroin (Julien, 1988). They are also called *opiates*. *Opium,* which means "plant of joy," comes from the poppy plant. Raw opium can relieve pain while bringing feelings of well-being and dreamy relaxation. One of the most active ingredients in opium is *morphine,* a drug isolated in the early 1800s and used throughout the world for the relief of pain. Percodan and Demoral are both trade names for drugs similar to morphine. *Heroin* is derived from morphine but is three times more powerful, producing a particularly intense pleasurable reaction.

Narcotics have complex effects on consciousness. Drowsy, cloudy feelings occur because the opiates, somewhat like alcohol and barbiturates, depress the activity of some parts of the cerebral cortex. But they can also create excitation in other parts, causing some users to experience euphoria (Wise & Bozarth, 1984). Recent evidence suggests that narcotics kill pain because they are chemically similar to the body's own "natural opiates" (discussed in Chapters 3 and 4). As a result, opiates can occupy receptors for these natural painkillers and mimic their effects, blocking pain from reaching the brain or reducing the person's awareness of it (Julien, 1988).

Until the early part of this century, opium and morphine were as available as aspirin is today. Stores sold them for pain, diarrhea, coughs, and many other physical ills. But because they are highly addictive, narcotics have been outlawed for nonprescription use in the United States since 1914. Still, heroin addicts number in the hundreds of thousands, risking death through overdoses, contaminated drugs, or AIDS (acquired immune deficiency syndrome) contracted by sharing drug-injection needles.

Psychedelics

Drugs that alter consciousness by producing a temporary loss of contact with reality and changes in emotion, perception, and thought are called **psychedelics.** The changes often include gross distortions in body image (one may feel gigantic or very tiny), loss of identity (confusion about who you are), dreamlike fantasies, and hallucinations. The effects can resemble the most severe forms of mental disorder described in Chapter 15. For this reason, psychedelic drugs are also called *hallucinogens* or *psychotomimetics* (mimicking psychosis). Some, including mescaline and psilocybin, have been used for centuries in magical or religious rituals. Here we discuss three psychedelics: LSD, PCP, and marijuana.

LSD *Lysergic acid diethylamide (LSD)* is one of the most powerful psychedelics. It was first synthesized in 1938 by Swiss chemist Albert Hofmann from a fungus growing on rye grain. One day he accidentally ingested a minuscule amount of the substance and experienced some strange effects. He tried another dose and later described the experience:

I lost all count of time . . . everything appeared deformed as in a faulty mirror. Space and time became more and more disorganized and I was overcome by a fear that I was going out of my mind. The worst part of it being that I was clearly aware of my condition. . . . Occasionally, I felt as if I were out of my body. I thought I had died. My ego seemed suspended somewhere in space, from where I saw my dead body lying on the sofa. . . . Acoustic perceptions, such as the noise of water gushing from a tap or the spoken word, were transformed into optical illusions (quoted in Julien, 1988, pp. 179–180).

The hallucinogenic effects of LSD may result from its ability to occupy one kind of receptor for serotonin, mimicking that neurotransmitter (Jacobs, 1987). If a drug that blocks serotonin receptors is administered with LSD, these effects are greatly reduced (Appel & Rosencrans, 1984).

The exact effects of LSD in humans depend on who takes it and why, where it is taken, and who else is present. "Bad trips" can produce psychotic episodes, especially in unstable people. Sometimes "flashbacks" occur, in which the person is suddenly returned to an LSD-like state of consciousness weeks, months, or years after using the drug. Distortions in visual sensations can remain even two years after cessation of heavy use of LSD (Abraham & Wolf, 1988). Tolerance develops to the psychological effects of LSD after several days of use, but the potential for psychological or physical dependence is lower than for other psychoactive drugs.

PCP *Phencyclidine* is an anesthetic often called "angel dust." PCP attaches to specific binding sites in the brain that are not related to any known neurotransmitter (Vincent et al., 1979).

PCP's effects when swallowed, smoked, or snorted include agitated excitement, disorientation, and hallucinations. It is very dangerous. Even relatively small doses create insensitivity to pain, psychological separation from the world and from one's own body, rigidity, a blank stare, and an inability to speak. The drug also kills neurons in the cerebral cortex (Olney, Labruyere & Price, 1989). Higher doses bring stupor and mental confusion that may last from a few hours to a few days. PCP users have been known to jump off buildings because they do not recognize danger or feel pain. The drug can also cause the user to injure or kill others.

Marijuana A mixture of crushed leaves, flowers, and stems from the hemp plant (*Cannabis sativa*) makes up marijuana. The active ingredient is tetrahydrocannabinol, or THC. When inhaled from a marijuana cigarette, or "joint," THC enters the bloodstream through the lungs and reaches peak concentrations within ten to thirty minutes. It is absorbed by many organs, including the brain, where it continues to affect consciousness for two to three hours. The action of THC has not been tied to any particular neurotransmitter system.

Marijuana is a popular, but illegal, psychoactive drug whose potential for harm is still a matter of uncertainty and debate.

At low or moderate doses, marijuana produces relaxation and reduces anxiety. It may bring initial restlessness and hilarity followed by a dreamy, carefree state of relaxation; expansion of space and time; a more vivid sense of touch, sight, smell, taste, and hearing; hunger, especially a craving for sweets; and subtle changes in thought formation and expression (National Commission on Marijuana and Drug Abuse, 1972). Marijuana may also interfere with the ability to remember what happened just a few seconds ago, making it difficult to carry out complex mental or physical tasks (Jaffe, 1975). These effects become more intense at larger doses (the equivalent of several joints). At very high levels, a person may occasionally experience vivid phenomena similar to those associated with LSD. Unlike depressants, excessive doses of marijuana do not produce the downward spiral to anesthesia, coma, or death.

Since the late 1800s, marijuana has been controversial. Some see it as a recreational drug that is not addictive and has fewer harmful effects than alcohol. It ranks second in popularity among young drug users, surpassed only by alcohol (Johnston, O'Malley & Bachman, 1989). Critics see marijuana as a menace that leads to abuse of more dangerous drugs and to criminal behavior. Currently, the laws (though not always the facts) reflect this view; growing, selling, or possessing marijuana has been outlawed in most of the United States since the 1930s and has been illegal under U.S. federal law since 1970. Numerous government groups that have summarized research on marijuana have reached remarkably similar conclusions (Commission of Inquiry into the Non-medical Use of Drugs, 1970, 1972, 1973; Marijuana and Health, 1980; National Academy of Sciences, 1982; National Commission on Marijuana and Drug Abuse, 1972; Report of the British Advisory Committee on Drug Dependence, 1968). They can be summarized as follows:

1. In and of itself, marijuana use does not cause aggressiveness, juvenile delinquency, or violent crime. Indeed, criminal behavior by marijuana users is more likely due to their abuse of alcohol, amphetamines, or opiates.
2. Marijuana is the least potent of all psychoactive drugs. (For a summary of our discussion of these drugs, see ''In Review: Major Classes of Psychoactive Drugs.'') Moderate use presents few, if any, significant health hazards. However, like all psychoactive drugs, marijuana easily reaches a developing fetus and thus should not be used by pregnant women.

3. Marijuana's interference with muscular coordination is a significant contributor to automobile accidents. People should not drive after using it. Some motor impairment continues well after the subjective effects of the drug have worn off. In one study pilots had impaired ability to land a simulated aircraft even twenty-four hours after smoking one joint (Yesavage et al., 1985).

4. Marijuana may have medical uses. Because it expands breathing passages, reduces the pressure of fluid within the eye, and inhibits nausea and epileptic seizures, it is sometimes helpful in treating asthma, glaucoma, epilepsy, and the nausea brought on by cancer chemotherapy.

5. Significant hazards may be associated with smoking large amounts of marijuana for long periods of time. These include (a) the closing of breathing passages, creating a risk of bronchitis and asthma; (b) suppression of the body's immune system, possibly leaving it unusually vulnerable to infection; (c) possible reductions in the male sex hormone testosterone and a corresponding reduction in sperm count; and (d) stress on the heart, especially in people with cardiovascular problems. The existence of an "amotivational syndrome," characterized by lethargy and apathy, is possible but not well established (Gilman et al., 1985).

So is marijuana a simple pleasure that should be legalized or a menace to be stamped out? The evidence available so far tells a reasonably benign story,

In Review: Major Classes of Psychoactive Drugs

Drug	Trade/Street Name	Main Effects	Potential for Physical/ Psychological Dependence
Depressants			
Alcohol	"booze"	Relaxation, anxiety reduction, sleep	High/High
Sedatives (barbiturates)	Seconal, Tuinal, ("downers") Nembutal		High/High
Anxiolytics (meprobamate, benzodiazepines)	Miltown, Equanil, Librium, Valium		Moderate to high/High
Stimulants			
Amphetamines	Benzedrine, Dexedrine, Methadrine ("speed," "uppers," "ice")	Alertness, euphoria	Moderate/High
Cocaine	"coke"		Moderate to high/High
Caffeine		Alertness	Moderate/Moderate
Narcotics			
Opium		Euphoria	High/High
Morphine	Percodan, Demoral	Euphoria, pain control	High/High
Heroin	"junk," "smack"	Euphoria, pain control	High/High
Psychedelics			
LSD	"acid"	Mind expansion, hallucinations	Low/Low
Phencyclidine	"PCP," "angel dust"	Exhilaration	Unknown/High
Marijuana (cannabis)	"pot," "dope," "reefer"	Euphoria, relaxation	Low/Moderate

but the physical, psychological, and social dangers of marijuana, like the hazards of tobacco and alcohol, might take many years to detect (Kandel et al., 1986). Perhaps it is best for now to echo Robert Julien's (1981) reminder of what Saint Thomas Aquinas wrote seven centuries ago: "Nothing is intrinsically good or evil, but its manner of usage may make it so."

Linkages: Consciousness and Learning

How can learning shape the effect of a drug on consciousness?

More is involved in the effects of a drug than biochemistry. As we noted in the case of alcohol, the learning that comes with experience also plays an important role. Two types of learning may shape how a person feels and acts after taking a drug.

First, experience with a drug creates learned responses, called *conditioned responses,* to that drug. This type of learning occurs outside of awareness and depends on the pairing of stimuli and responses. The development of tolerance to a drug seems to reflect this type of learning. Over time, people tend to need larger and larger doses of morphine, for example, to maintain its original painkilling effects. Why? One reason is that with continued use morphine tends to clear more rapidly from the bloodstream, but learning also plays a role (Baker & Tiffany, 1985). The features of the room in which the injection is usually given, the sight of the needle, or other environmental stimuli may become associated with the response to the drug. As a result of this association, these stimuli come to elicit a response of their own. Paradoxically, this conditioned response can be the *opposite* of the response to the drug. So in the case of morphine, the environmental stimuli that have been associated with the drug come to elicit an *increase* in sensitivity to pain, the opposite of the usual effect of morphine (Siegel & Ellsworth, 1986). Larger and larger doses are required to overcome these conditioned responses and obtain the desired reduction in pain. An experienced drug user is likely to develop other conditioned responses to environmental cues as well. Before a heroin addict injects the drug, for example, his or her breathing rate may increase in anticipation of the drug's tendency to depress breathing.

This kind of learning may make experienced drug users especially vulnerable to accidental overdoses. Each year, about 1 percent of all heroin addicts die from overdoses (Maurer & Vogel, 1973). The fatal dosage, however, is often no greater than the dose that has been tolerated many times in the past (Reed, 1980). How can this be? To find out, Shepard Siegel (1984) interviewed heroin addicts who had received emergency treatment for overdoses. He found that 70 percent of them had *not* taken an unusually large dose, but they *had* injected themselves in unfamiliar surroundings when the overdose occurred. In other words, they had injected themselves in surroundings that did not provide the stimuli that had come to elicit conditioned responses opposite to those produced by the drug. As a result, they were not physiologically "ready" for the drug, and it had stronger effects than usual, becoming in some cases an overdose. Studies with animals show the same effects.

The smell of alcohol, the sight of bottles and glasses, and the camaraderie of social occasions are all stimuli commonly associated with alcohol drinking. Through the principles of learning described in Chapter 7, these stimuli can become cues that lead some people to feel and act "drunk," whether they have been drinking or not. This is why party hosts sometimes act "high" after merely serving alcohol to their guests.

Learned responses to drugs may also play a role in the return to drug abuse by those attempting to kick their habit. Sometimes the conditioned response to a drug is the *same* as the response normally produced by the drug. In this case, people, places, and other cues associated with drug-taking remind the addict of the pleasurable effects of the drug and promote drug-taking (Eikelboom & Stewart, 1982). What determines whether learning produces the same response as the drug or the opposite response? Scientists are still trying to decipher this complex mystery, but the answer may be related to where in the nervous system a drug has its main effects (Eikelboom & Stewart, 1982).

In the next chapter we examine what researchers have learned about how conditioned responses are learned. But as we discuss there, people also learn just by watching other people. These observations represent a second way in which learning influences the effects of drugs: people look to those around them for information about what to expect from a drug and how to behave while under its influence. What they see can vary. Anthropological studies demonstrate that alcohol-induced changes in behavior are different in different cultures (MacAndrew & Edgerton, 1969). In particular, the increased aggressiveness and sexual promiscuity that Americans associate with alcohol probably reflect customs more than they represent biochemical effects. For example, members of the Camba society in Bolivia drink a potent brew that is 89 percent alcohol. During their revels, these people repeatedly pass out, wake up, and then start drinking again, but all the while maintain tranquil social relations.

The learned nature of some responses to alcohol is also demonstrated by cases in which the model for "drunken comportment" has changed. When Europeans brought alcohol to Tahiti in the 1700s, the Tahitians at first became relaxed and slightly befuddled when drinking it. But after several years of watching the drunken violence of European sailors, Tahitian drinkers became violent themselves. Fortunately, subsequent learning experiences have once again made their response to alcohol more pacific (MacAndrew & Edgerton, 1969).

These experiments and examples show that when psychologists attempt to analyze how drugs affect consciousness, they find that the roles of biology and learning are tightly interwoven. Understanding the complex roles of learning in determining the effects of drugs may lead to more effective therapies for drug addiction (Turkhan, 1989).

Future Directions

The most influential psychological theories today view human behavior as guided by both conscious and subconscious mental events and processes; these mediate the effects of rewards, punishment, and other external consequences of behavior. As a result, the study of consciousness provides a kind of conceptual meeting place for ideas and findings from many areas of psychology. In fact, investigators and researchers from disciplines as diverse as biology, psychology, linguistics, electrical engineering, and computer science—all interested in the broad field called *cognitive science*—work together in special programs to pursue the common goal of better understanding human consciousness.

There is a long way to go. Psychologists still do not know where or how self-referent properties occur in the human brain. Some have suggested that the left hemisphere plays a special role as the "interpreter" of mental activity from both hemispheres, and perhaps this special role is related to consciousness (Gazzaniga, 1989).

The shifts from one state of consciousness to another, like waking and sleep, can be studied directly. If sleep disorders predict the appearance of psychological disorders, perhaps this link provides opportunities for early intervention, assuming better sleep therapies can be developed. And if people can intentionally alter their dreams, this may aid the course of psychotherapy. The broader field of circadian rhythms is also promising new therapies for mental disorders, such as bipolar disorder, that may be caused by disruptions of these rhythms.

Intense research is under way to understand how drugs affect consciousness. For example, investigators are trying to find the natural substance that normally fits into the binding site of the benzodiazepines (De Robertis et al., 1988); it will most certainly lead to a better understanding of the chemistry of anxiety. New drugs will be developed to treat drug abuse by reducing craving without, themselves, producing addiction. Earlier we noted that drugs like buprenorphine show potential as treatments for cocaine abuse. Another drug, *buspirone*, has also shown promise in treating both cocaine abuse and alcoholism. Buspirone is an anxiolytic drug that affects some serotonin receptors (Jann, 1988). The fact that drugs like buspirone appear to block the craving for more than one type of abused drug supports the notion that there may be common (and perhaps treatable) mechanisms underlying all drugs of abuse (Koob & Bloom, 1988).

Future research will also help answer questions about the possibility of undiscovered potential in human consciousness. For example, we already know that peaceful mental images can block the perception of pain (Elton, Burrows & Stanley, 1980; Turk, 1978). In one experiment, cancer patients who used self-hypnosis to reduce their pain and group psychotherapy to reduce their anxiety about death lived an average of 18 months longer than patients receiving only conventional therapy (Spiegel et al., 1989). The author of this study has emphasized that *all* of the patients received conventional radiation and drug therapy and that this work in no way implies that one can "wish away your cancer." But the work does suggest that it will be valuable to learn how psychological processes can affect the course of the disease.

In this chapter we have barely scratched the surface of the study of consciousness. For more detailed information, consider taking courses in cognitive psychology, psychopharmacology, and sleep. Also look for courses that offer lectures and direct experience with meditation and hypnosis.

Summary and Key Terms

Consciousness can be defined as the mental process of being aware of one's own thoughts, feelings, and perceptions. Its essential property is self-reference, a self aware of itself.

Analyzing Consciousness

Consciousness has been a major focus of psychology since the field first took shape in the late 1800s. Early psychologists were interested in trying to understand the structure of consciousness, to find mental building blocks that create mental life. Later, behaviorists focused on studying only overt behavior. Recently, however, the study of consciousness has made a comeback.

The Study of Consciousness

Structuralist psychologists attempted to study consciousness through introspection, but introspection can produce misleading reports. Today psychologists study consciousness by making inferences not only from self-reports but also from observable behaviors and physiological measures.

Consciousness and the Cognitive Unconscious

Psychologists typically divide the areas of mental activity that are outside of conscious awareness into several categories. The *preconscious* includes mental activities that are outside of awareness (like perception of the ticking of a clock) but can be easily brought into awareness. *Subconscious* or *unconscious* mental activity contains thoughts, memories, and processes that are

more difficult to bring into awareness. Those processes that cannot be brought into awareness are called *nonconscious*.

States of Consciousness

A person's *state of consciousness* is constantly changing, like the varying flow of a stream. When the changes are particularly noticeable, they are called *altered states of consciousness*. Some of these, such as daydreaming and sleep, occur naturally; others are brought on by special means, such as hypnosis, meditation, or drugs.

Daydreaming

Daydreaming is the altered state of consciousness closest to the waking state. During daydreams, attention tends to shift from its normal focus on external stimuli to dwell more on internal events, including fantasy. Daydreaming may "take over" as a substitute when the outside world offers too little stimulation.

Sleeping and Dreaming

Sleep is a very active and complex state that normally occurs each night.

Stages of Sleep

Sleep normally begins with the lightest stage (stage 1 sleep) and progresses gradually to the deepest (stage 4 sleep). People travel up and down through these stages—known as *quiet sleep* or *slow-wave sleep*—several times each night. Gradually, they spend more time in the lighter stages, particularly in a special stage called *rapid-eye-movement (REM sleep,* or *active sleep).* This is where most dreaming is reported to occur.

Sleep Disorders

Sleep disorders can disrupt the natural rhythm of sleep. Among the most common is *insomnia,* in which a person feels tired because of trouble falling or staying asleep. *Hypersomnia* involves too much sleep, and *narcolepsy* is sudden daytime sleeping. In *sleep apnea,* people briefly stop breathing while they are asleep. *Sudden infant death syndrome (SIDS)* may be due to brainstem abnormalities. *Nightmares* and *night terrors* are different kinds of frightening dreams. *Sleepwalking* happens most frequently during childhood. *REM behavior disorder* is potentially dangerous because the decrease in muscle tone that normally prevents people from acting out REM dreams is absent.

Why Do People Sleep?

The cycle of waking and sleeping is a natural *circadian rhythm,* but the purpose of sleep is not entirely understood. Non-REM sleep may provide a time for rest and repair of the body. REM sleep may help maintain areas of the brain that keep people alert during the day, or it may allow the brain to "check its circuits," eliminate useless information, and imprint what people have learned during the day.

Dreams and Dreaming

Dreams are storylike sequences of images, sensations, and perceptions that last anywhere from several seconds to many minutes. Even though dreams themselves may be no more than the meaningless by-products of brain activity, the way people recall and organize them may still tell us something about their mental style and current concerns. Evidence for *lucid dreaming* suggests that people may be able to control their own dreams.

Other Key Terms in This Section: alpha waves, delta waves

Hypnosis

Hypnosis is a well-known but still poorly understood phenomenon.

Experiencing Hypnosis

Hypnotized people tend to focus all their attention on the hypnotist and then passively follow his or her instructions and suggestions. They become very good at fantasizing and role-taking and often act as if unlikely or impossible events have taken place. They may exhibit apparent *age regression,* and they often experience *posthypnotic amnesia* and obey *posthypnotic suggestions.*

Who Can Be Hypnotized?

Some people are excellent hypnotic subjects, whereas some cannot be hypnotized. Tests of hypnotic *susceptibility* indicate that most people fall between these extremes.

Explaining Hypnosis

Hypnotic phenomena have been explained in several ways. *Role theory* suggests that hypnosis creates a special social role that gives people permission to act in unusual ways. *State theory* sees hypnosis as a special state of consciousness. Hilgard's *dissociation theory* combines aspects of role and state theories. It says that

hypnotic subjects enter into an implicit social contract with the hypnotist in which they agree to allow normally well-integrated mental processes to become disorganized, or dissociated, and to share control over their mental processes. From this perspective, hypnosis does involve social role-taking, but if enough dissociation takes place, there is an altered state of consciousness as well.

Some Uses of Hypnosis

Hypnosis has been put to many good uses, especially in the control of pain. Hypnotic suggestions can also reduce the discomfort associated with cancer chemotherapy and help minimize bleeding during surgery.

Meditation

Meditation brings about an altered state characterized by feelings of inner peace and tranquillity. The meditative state can be reached by several techniques, but it usually requires a quiet place, a comfortable position, a device for organizing attention, and a passive attitude. Proponents emphasize the physical, psychological, and behavioral benefits of meditation, but exactly how it works is unclear.

Psychoactive Drugs

Psychoactive drugs bring about a wide variety of changes in consciousness, from relaxation and drowsiness to confident optimism, wild excitement, or flights of bizarre fantasy.

The Varying Effects of Drugs

Adverse effects frequently accompany the use of psychoactive drugs, especially when use becomes abuse. Psychological and physical dependence, tolerance, and a withdrawal syndrome may result. Drugs that produce dependence share the property of directly stimulating the brain's pleasure centers. The particular consequences of using a psychoactive drug depend both on how the drug affects neurotransmitters and on the user's learned expectations and responses.

Depressants

Alcohol, sedatives, and anxiolytics are all *depressants.* They reduce activity in the central nervous system, often by enhancing the action of inhibitory neurotransmitters. They have considerable potential for producing both psychological and physical dependence.

Stimulants

Stimulants such as amphetamines and cocaine increase behavioral and mental activity primarily by augmenting the action of the neurotransmitters dopamine and norepinephrine. These drugs can also produce both psychological and physical dependency. Caffeine, the world's most popular stimulant, may also create dependency.

Narcotics

Narcotics such as opium, morphine, and heroin are highly addictive drugs that induce sleep and relieve pain.

Psychedelics

LSD, PCP, and marijuana are examples of *psychedelics,* or *hallucinogens.* Psychedelics alter consciousness by producing a temporary loss of contact with reality and changes in emotion, perception, and thought. PCP is particularly dangerous.

O U T L I N E

Learning

In the spring, shortly after they emerge from their chrysalis, male black swallowtail butterflies engage in "hilltopping." They fly to the top of the nearest hill or rise; then the first to arrive vigorously defends the territory against all other male black swallowtails while he waits for the chance to mate with females of the species. Indeed, these amorous males will attack any fluttering black object—moths, bumblebees, grasshoppers, blackbirds, even humans who happen to wear black T-shirts (Lederhouse, 1982). Some of these fights are obviously ill-advised, but the butterflies' actions are not governed by thought or experience. They are inherited, or *instinctual,* behaviors.

Instinctual behavior patterns such as this abound in the animal world. Different species of birds build nests of varying sizes, shapes, and locations, while different types of spiders spin webs with characteristic shapes. Evidence that these behaviors are inherited comes in two forms. First, individual animals perform the behavior successfully, often perfectly, the first time. Second, even when they are separated from their species at birth, many animals display these behaviors without ever having seen them. These instinctual behavior patterns are called *species-specific.*

How did species acquire their differing instinctive behaviors? Charles Darwin's theory of evolution (1859) says that *natural selection* over millions of years holds the answer. That is, those individuals in a species whose appearance and patterns of action allow them to elude predators, withstand the elements, find food, and mate successfully survive and produce offspring with similar characteristics. Other, less adaptive attributes die out of the species along with the unfortunate creatures who carry them.

Natural selection produces instinctual responses that are adaptive under many circumstances, but these responses have an important limitation: they change only very slowly, over generations. As a result, individual organisms may be unable to survive large and sudden environmental changes—a habitat-destroying volcanic

LINKAGES

Learning

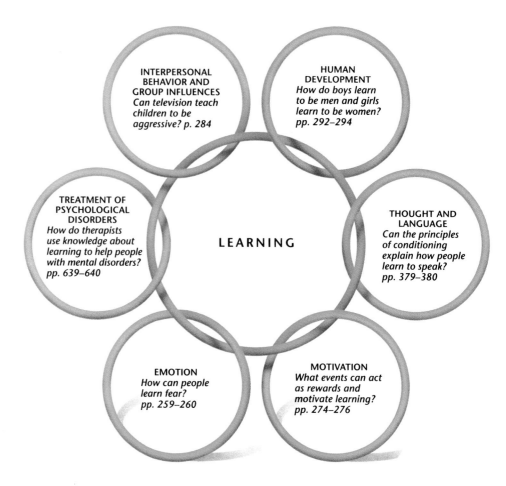

INTERPERSONAL
BEHAVIOR AND
GROUP INFLUENCES
*Can television teach
children to be
aggressive? p. 284*

HUMAN
DEVELOPMENT
*How do boys learn
to be men and girls
learn to be women?
pp. 292–294*

TREATMENT OF
PSYCHOLOGICAL
DISORDERS
*How do therapists
use knowledge about
learning to help people
with mental disorders?
pp. 639–640*

LEARNING

THOUGHT AND
LANGUAGE
*Can the principles
of conditioning
explain how people
learn to speak?
pp. 379–380*

EMOTION
*How can people
learn fear?
pp. 259–260*

MOTIVATION
*What events can act
as rewards and
motivate learning?
pp. 274–276*

■ Look at the diagram above, which illustrates some of the relationships between the topic of this chapter, learning, and other chapter topics. In psychology, *learning* means far more than acquiring academic information or skills. When boys and girls begin to act in ways that their culture considers right for men and women, that, too, is called learning; so is the change that occurs if a toddler begins fighting every day with his or her playmates. Thus the principles of learning discussed in this chapter have very broad application.

Among the most interesting applications are attempts to use the principles of learning to understand normal and abnormal personalities and to treat psychological disorders. To what extent do people learn to be shy or aggressive, obedient or rebellious? Do they learn to have irrational fears, depressions, or hallucinations? Can they "learn" their way out of psychological disorders? These are questions explored by researchers in personality and psychological disorders, and we discuss them in Chapters 14 through 16.

Like other Linkages diagrams, this one shows just a sampling of the links with other topics. For example, our examination (in Chapter 8) of the physiology of memory also sheds light on the biological basis of learning. The page numbers following the questions indicate where the questions in the diagram are addressed; each linking question is repeated in the margin when it is discussed. ■

eruption, for example—unless they can rapidly adjust their behavior through learning. Learning, for example, allows people to radically change their "nest-building" behavior, producing sprawling, airy ranch homes or peaked-roof bungalows, depending on whether they decide to live in Hawaii or Alaska.

Psychologists traditionally defined learning as any relatively permanent change in behavior that results from past experience. However, learned responses are not always performed. For example, you might not know that a friend has learned to speak German unless you observed the person in situations calling for that skill. As a result, some psychologists now define **learning** as any relatively permanent change in behavior or mental processes that results from past experience.

The kinds of changes that constitute learning range from the simple to the complex. For example, the sound of your new chiming clock, though quite noticeable at first, soon fades into the background. This fading is known as *habituation,* a form of learning so basic that it occurs even in organisms as rudimentary as the sea slug *aplysia* (Kandel, 1976). More elaborate forms of learning occur when a toddler learns to fear a doctor's white coat because it has been associated with the pain of an injection, when a child learns to read, or when you acquire facts, concepts, and values that help you solve problems or think logically about ethical issues.

Among all organisms, human beings are the least controlled by instincts, and in humans the ability to learn has reached a remarkably high level. Indeed, learning is central to being human. The Linkages diagram shows just a few of the ways in which learning plays a role in other areas of psychology.

People learn primarily by identifying relationships between events and noting the regularity in the world around them. When two things occur together regularly, people can predict the occurrence of one from knowledge of the other. People learn that a clear blue sky means dry weather, that too little sleep makes them irritable, that they can reach someone on the telephone by dialing a certain number, that screaming orders motivates some people and just angers others.

Which relationships do people identify, and how do they do it? What determines whether and how people learn? These and other basic questions about learning are among the most frequently and intensively studied topics in psychology. For several decades, much of the research on learning was guided by the behaviorist approach discussed in Chapter 1, which stresses the importance of reward and punishment in altering the frequency of different forms of observable behavior. That approach was inspired by the hope that all behavior could be explained by a few basic principles of learning and by the idea that all learning amounted to the automatic formation of associations. Research eventually showed that these ideas about learning were oversimplified, but understanding how associations are formed is still basic to an understanding of learning. Thus, to begin, we consider two models of how associations develop; these models are called classical and instrumental conditioning.

Classical Conditioning

At the opening bars of the national anthem, a young ballplayer's heart may begin pounding; those sounds signal that the game is about to begin. A small flashing light on a control panel may make an airplane pilot's adrenaline flow, because it means that something has gone seriously wrong. These people were not born with these reactions; they learned them from associations between stimuli. The experimental study of this kind of learning was begun, almost by accident, by Ivan Petrovich Pavlov.

Pavlov's Discovery

Pavlov is one of the best-known figures in psychology, but he was not a psychologist. A Russian physiologist, Pavlov won a Nobel Prize in 1904 for his work on the physiology of dogs' digestive systems. During his research, Pavlov noticed a strange phenomenon: his dogs sometimes salivated when no food was present—for example, when they saw the assistant who normally brought their food.

Pavlov devised a simple experiment to determine how salivation could occur in the absence of an obvious physical cause. First he performed an operation to divert a dog's saliva into a container, so that the amount secreted could be measured precisely. He then confined the dog in the apparatus shown in Figure 7.1. The experiment had three phases.

In the first phase Pavlov confirmed that when meat powder was placed on the dog's tongue, the dog salivated, but that it did not salivate in response to the sound of a buzzer. Thus, Pavlov established the existence of the two basic components for his experiment: a natural reflex (the dog's salivation when food was placed on its tongue) and a neutral stimulus (the sound of the buzzer). A *reflex* is the swift, automatic response to a stimulus, such as shivering in the cold or jumping when you are jabbed with a needle. A *neutral stimulus* is one that initially does not elicit the reflex being studied, although it may elicit other responses. For example, when the buzzer was first sounded in Pavlov's experiment, the dog displayed an orienting response of pricking up its ears, turning toward the sound, and sniffing around, but it did not salivate.

It was the second and third phases of the experiment that showed how one type of learning can occur. In the second phase, Pavlov sounded the buzzer and then quickly placed meat powder in the dog's mouth. The dog salivated. This *pairing*—the buzzer followed immediately by meat powder—was repeated several times. In the third phase of the experiment the buzzer was sounded

Figure 7.1
Apparatus Used in Pavlov's Experiments
Dogs were surgically prepared and then restrained in a harness. Saliva flowed into a tube inserted in the dog's cheek. The amount of saliva secreted was then recorded by a pen attached to a slowly moving drum of paper.

Pen recording on cylinder

Figure 7.2
Classical Conditioning
Before classical conditioning has occurred, meat powder on a dog's tongue produces salivation, but the sound of a buzzer—a neutral stimulus—does not. During the process of conditioning, the buzzer is paired on numerous trials with the meat powder. After classical conditioning has taken place, the sound of the buzzer alone acts as a conditioned stimulus, producing salivation.

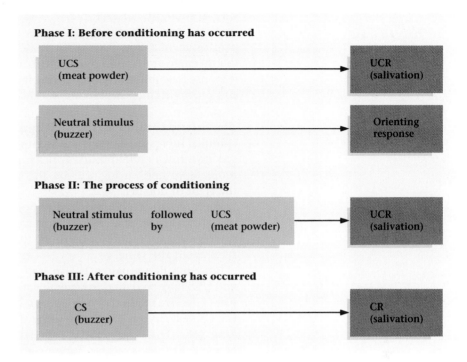

alone, and the dog again salivated even though no meat powder was presented. In other words, the buzzer by itself now elicited salivation.

Pavlov's experiment was the first demonstration of what today is called **classical conditioning**—a procedure in which a neutral stimulus is paired with a stimulus that triggers a reflexive response until the neutral stimulus alone provokes a similar response. Figure 7.2 shows the basic elements of classical conditioning. The stimulus that elicits a response without conditioning, like the meat powder in Pavlov's experiment, is called the **unconditioned stimulus (UCS)**. The automatic, unlearned reaction to this stimulus is called the **unconditioned response (UCR)**. The previously neutral stimulus, after being paired with the unconditioned stimulus, is called the **conditioned stimulus (CS)**, and the response it comes to elicit is a **conditioned response (CR)**.

Thus it is that a person feels a ripple of emotion—a conditioned response—when hearing the song or smelling the cologne associated with a long-lost lover. Through its association with that person, the song or fragrance, which once had no particular significance, has become a conditioned stimulus that can provoke emotional reactions experienced in the past.

Establishing a Conditioned Response

Linkages: How can people learn fear? (a link to Emotion)

What if conditioned responses were always as intense, enduring, and easily formed as responses to love songs and old lovers? Life would be difficult, that's what. You might feel weak-kneed and nostalgic at the sight of cars, trees, beds, glasses, or anything else you ever saw while the loved one was present. How would you like to get angry on every bright day because you associate sunshine with a parking ticket you received two years ago?

Fortunately, classical conditioning is not this general or inevitable. Some conditioned responses are easier to acquire than others, and the responses can vary in strength. For example, a toddler might learn to react with fear (CR) at the sight of a doctor (CS), if doctors have been consistently paired with the pain of an injection (UCS). But the child's conditioned response to doctors might range from mild agitation to intense fear. How easily a conditioned response is acquired and how strong it is depend on both what the conditioned and unconditioned stimuli are and how they are paired.

The Intensity and Pairing of Stimuli   As the intensity of an unconditioned stimulus increases, so does the strength of the conditioned response and the speed with which it appears. For example, the more painful the injection, the more rapid and strong will be the toddler's conditioned fear response to the sight of doctors.

The strength of a conditioned response also tends to increase as the number of CS-UCS pairings increases. However, this rule is true only up to a point. After a critical number of pairings, the strength of the conditioned response stays about the same.

How stimuli are paired is also important. Figure 7.3 illustrates that the CS and UCS may be paired in several ways in order to produce conditioning. The most effective method of producing a strong conditioned response is to present the CS, leave it on while presenting the UCS, and then terminate both at the same time. This arrangement, called **delayed conditioning**, is diagrammed in Figure 7.3(b). For example, for efficient conditioning of fear (CR) to the sound of a buzzer (CS), the buzzer would be sounded for a total of, say, three seconds. One second after the buzzer (CS) is turned on, shock (UCS) would begin and continue for two seconds; then both the buzzer and the shock would be turned off at the same time.

The optimal interval between the onset of the CS and the onset of the UCS is very short, typically between one-half and one second (Ross & Ross, 1971). As this interval increases, the conditioned response usually weakens. In general, a conditioned response does not develop if the delay between the CS and UCS is more than several seconds. However, this rule does not apply in one case: the learning of aversions to certain tastes.

Figure 7.3
Pairing of Stimuli in Various Types of Classical Conditioning
In simultaneous conditioning, the CS and the UCS come on and go off at the same time, as shown in part (a). Part (b) outlines delayed conditioning, in which the CS comes on before the UCS, but both go off at the same time. In trace conditioning, the CS comes on and goes off before the UCS comes on, as shown in part (c). In backward conditioning, part (d), the UCS comes on first and, just as it is terminated, the CS comes on. Backward conditioning is less effective than trace, simultaneous, or delayed conditioning because in backward conditioning the CS does not predict the UCS.

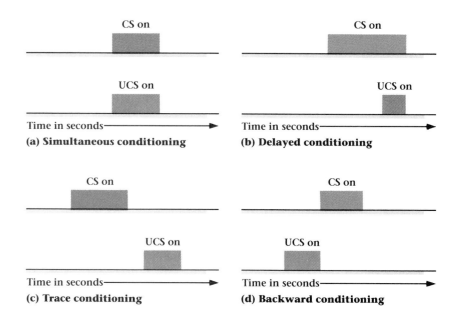

H I G H L I G H T

The Special Case of Taste-Aversion Learning

In a strange twist of history, the study of taste aversion began with the advent of the atomic bomb. Once the bomb had become a reality, scientists in many disciplines began trying to understand the effects of prolonged exposure to radiation. Psychologist John Garcia was one of them. While investigating the effects of radiation, he discovered a phenomenon that led to the study of taste-aversion learning.

In one of Garcia's studies, rats were exposed to radiation once a week for about eight hours (Garcia et al., 1956). The radiation caused nausea in the rats. As the weeks passed, the rats drank almost no water inside the radiation chamber, but they drank their normal amount as soon as they were returned to their home cage. Why? The most obvious hypothesis was that something about the radiation was leading the rats to drink less. To test this idea, the animals were placed inside the radiation chamber, but no radiation was administered. They still refused to drink.

The researchers began to understand the cause of the rats' behavior when they noticed that the water bottles in the radiation chamber were plastic, whereas those in the home cage were glass. The plastic bottles changed the taste of the water, and this unique taste had been repeatedly paired with the nausea caused by radiation. Thus, the rats' refusal to drink was a result of classical conditioning: the plastic-tasting water had become a conditioned stimulus, and the rats had learned to avoid it.

To test this conclusion, rats were given water that had a unique flavor and that eventually made them ill. As before, the rats developed a classically conditioned aversion to the water. The surprise was how easily this conditioning could occur. Even if the rats did not become ill until seven or eight hours after drinking the water, the taste aversion still developed and persisted for a very long time. In one experiment, rats refused to drink salt-flavored water after just one pairing with illness, and their aversion persisted for a month (Garcia, Hankins & Rusiniak, 1974).

Using the principles of taste aversion conditioning, some Western ranchers have set out lithium-laced mutton for marauding wolves and coyotes to eat. The nausea created by the lithium becomes associated with the mutton taste, thus making sheep an undesirable meal for these predators.

The power of taste-aversion learning has been put to work to help western ranchers plagued by wolves and coyotes that kill and eat their sheep. To alleviate this problem without killing the wolves and coyotes, chopped mutton laced with a small dose of lithium chloride, the UCS, was given to wolves (Garcia, Rusiniak & Brett, 1977; Gustavson et al., 1974). After digesting this substance, the wolves suffered dizziness and severe nausea, the UCR. Later, they were placed in a pen with live sheep (mutton on the hoof; the CS). At first they started their usual attack, but after biting and smelling the sheep several times, the wolves withdrew (the CR). Later, the doors of the pen were opened, and a dramatic role reversal occurred: the wolves were literally chased away by the sheep! Now ranchers often lace a carcass with enough lithium chloride to make wolves and coyotes ill, thus "teaching" them not to kill sheep.

People, too, develop classically conditioned taste aversions, as Ilene Bernstein (1978) demonstrated. She gave one group of cancer patients a unique flavor of ice cream, Mapletoff, one hour before they received chemotherapy, which produces nausea as a side effect. A second group was given the same ice cream on a day they did not receive chemotherapy. A third group was not given any ice cream. Approximately five months later, all three groups were asked to taste several flavors of ice cream and select their favorite. Two groups chose the Mapletoff: those who had not previously tasted it and those who had eaten it when they did not receive chemotherapy. In contrast, those who had eaten Mapletoff before receiving chemotherapy found the flavor very distasteful. Similarly, people who experience food poisoning may never again eat the type of food that made them so ill—even though they may not feel the effects of the poisoning until hours after eating the food. ■

Classical conditioning principles might suggest that the illness often experienced by contestants (especially the winners) in overeating competitions would leave them with a strong and lasting aversion to the food consumed. This may not happen, however. For one thing, if the contestant has eaten and enjoyed the food in the past, its taste has not been a reliable predictor of illness, thus weakening the aversion. Further, the circumstances under which the overeating occurred may have been so unusual that the person may not expect to become ill when eating smaller amounts under normal circumstances. These mitigating factors highlight the role of predictive value and cognitive factors in human classical conditioning.

Biological Preparedness for Conditioning   Why can taste aversion be conditioned so easily even when there is a long delay between the CS and UCS? No one yet knows for sure. One hypothesis is that organisms are *biologically prepared* to learn some associations more readily than others and that the associations involved in taste-aversion learning are among these (Seligman, 1970; Staddon & Ettinger, 1989).

Evidence that organisms are innately "prepared" to learn associations between certain stimuli and certain responses comes from several sources. People, for example, are much more likely to develop a conditioned fear of harmless dogs, snakes, and rats than of equally harmless doorknobs or stereos (Cook, Hodes & Lang, 1986; Kleinknecht, 1986). Experiments with animals suggest that they are prone to learn the type of associations that are most common in or most relevant to their environment (Best, Best & Henggeler, 1977; Staddon & Ettinger, 1989).

One example comes from a study in which rats were either shocked or made nauseous in the combined presence of a bright light, a loud buzzer, and saccharin-flavored water. Only certain conditioned associations were formed. Specifically, the animals that had been shocked developed a conditioned fear response to the light and the buzzer, but not to the flavored water. Those who had been made nauseous developed a conditioned avoidance of the flavored water, but no particular response to the light or buzzer (Garcia & Koelling, 1966). Notice that these results are adaptive: nausea is more likely to be produced by something that is eaten or drunk than by an external stimulus like noise. Accordingly, nausea is more likely to become a conditioned response to an internal stimulus, such as a saccharin flavor, than to an external stimulus, such as a sound.

Predictive Value There is another possible reason why tastes can be conditioned after one trial despite a long delay between CS and UCS. Perhaps the delay between the CS and UCS is not as critical as the **predictive value** of the CS; that is, the ability of the CS *reliably* to predict or signal the UCS. Note that in Garcia's research *every time* the rats drank the water, they became ill; in the Bernstein study the *only* time the cancer patients ate the Mapletoff ice cream, they became ill. Thus, learning in these experiments may have been facilitated despite long delays between the CS and UCS because the CS was an extremely reliable predictor of the UCS (Revusky, 1971, 1977). Similarly, if you experience pain every time you visit your dentist, you are more likely to develop a conditioned response of anxiety to the dental office than if pain occurs only during certain especially difficult appointments. In the first case but not the second, the CS (the dentist's office) is regularly associated with pain (the UCS) and thus has predictive value.

To investigate the effect of predictive value on conditioning, Robert Rescorla (1968) gave several groups of rats the same *number* of pairings of a buzzer with electric shocks, but some of the rats were also given shocks when they did *not* hear the buzzer. For that group, the CS did not have high predictive value, and compared with the other rats, these animals developed much weaker conditioned responses to the buzzer. Even though the number of CS-UCS pairings was identical, the strength of the conditioned response dropped as predictive value decreased.

What Is Learned in Classical Conditioning?

Pavlov believed that during classical conditioning the conditioned and unconditioned stimuli are associated because of their *contiguity*, or close proximity in time and space. Early researchers also thought that just about any association could be created through classical conditioning. But our discussion has shown that these ideas are oversimplified. For one thing, nature seems to prepare organisms to learn certain associations more easily than others. Furthermore, research on taste-aversion learning indicates that stimulus contiguity is neither necessary nor sufficient to produce classical conditioning.

What is learned in classical conditioning seems to be whether the unconditioned stimulus can be predicted by the conditioned stimulus (Dickinson & Mackintosh, 1978; Rescorla, 1988). The idea that classical conditioning involves learning to predict future events highlights the role that cognitive factors such as expectations may play in learning (Turkkan, 1989); we discuss these factors later in this chapter.

Pavlov also thought that, through conditioning, the conditioned stimulus comes to substitute for the unconditioned stimulus. If this were so, the conditioned response ought to be identical to the unconditioned response. However, the two responses do not always take exactly the same form. In one study, for example, people were classically conditioned to lift a finger from an electrode at the sound of a bell, thereby avoiding a mild electric shock. Because the subject's hand was placed palm downward, the conditioned response involved lifting the finger by straightening it. When the hand was placed palm upward, however, the conditioned response remained strong, even though the muscular response required to lift the finger now involved a curling motion, the opposite of the motion required earlier (Wickens, 1938). Thus, the specific form of the conditioned response may change, but the function remains the same.

In some cases, the conditioned and unconditioned responses may even be opposite physiological reactions. For example, when a person is given insulin

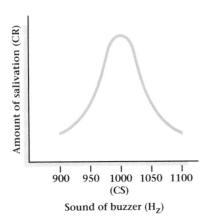

Figure 7.4
Stimulus Generalization
The strength of a response is greatest when a new stimulus closely resembles the CS. Here, the CS is the sound of a buzzer at 1,000 hertz, and the CR is salivation. As the new stimulus becomes less similar to the CS, or farther away from 1,000 hertz, the strength of the CR—in this case, amount of salivation—is reduced.

Figure 7.5
Extinction
Pavlov found that the amount of saliva secreted in response to a buzzer decreased steadily as progressively more trials were presented without the UCS. Eventually the dog no longer showed a CR to the buzzer at all. Extinction had taken place (Pavlov, 1927).

(UCS), the typical reaction is lowered blood sugar (UCR). If a buzzer is sounded immediately before the injections, classical conditioning will occur. The buzzer becomes a conditioned stimulus, but the conditioned response elicited by the sound of the buzzer is an *increase* in blood sugar—the opposite of the UCR (Flaherty et al., 1980). The buzzer seems to act as a signal to the body to prepare for the insulin, and the body begins to produce more blood sugar to counteract the drop in blood sugar that insulin has produced in the past. Similarly, we described in the chapter on consciousness how counteracting responses may be conditioned to drugs like heroin and morphine and help create tolerance to these drugs.

Obviously, classical conditioning does not merely promote the substitution of the CS for the UCS or the CR for the UCR. Rather, classical conditioning seems to accomplish a useful purpose for the organism. That purpose is to produce an adaptive, automatic response when a signal predictably forecasts an important event.

Conditioned Responses over Time

In natural environments classically conditioned responses usually have some adaptive value. The rat that learns to avoid salt-flavored water after becoming violently ill, for example, is adapting to its environment. Environmental conditions change, however, and it is important to learn to react differently when they do. In this section, we discuss how conditioned responses change over time.

Stimulus Generalization and Discrimination   Once a conditioned response is acquired, stimuli that are similar but not identical to the conditioned stimulus also elicit it. This phenomenon is called **stimulus generalization.** Usually the greater the similarity between a new stimulus and the conditioned stimulus, the stronger the conditioned response will be. Figure 7.4 shows an example.

Stimulus generalization has obvious advantages. It is adaptive, for example, for a person who becomes sick after drinking sour-smelling milk to avoid other dairy products that give off an odor resembling the smell associated with the illness. However, generalization would be dangerous if it had no limits. Most people would be frightened to see a real lion in their home, but imagine the inconvenience if you became fearful every time you saw a cat or a picture of a lion.

Stimulus generalization does not run amok because it is balanced by a complementary process called stimulus discrimination. Through **stimulus discrimination,** organisms learn to differentiate among similar stimuli. An infant's crying commonly becomes a conditioned stimulus for its mother, whose conditioned response might include waking out of a deep sleep at the baby's slightest fussing. Yet the same mother might sleep soundly while someone else's baby cries.

Extinction   In general, a CS continues to elicit the conditioned response only if the UCS continues to appear, at least periodically. For example, dogs in one experiment were conditioned to salivate at the sound of a buzzer (Pavlov, 1927). Then the buzzer was repeatedly sounded, but no meat powder was presented. As the CS was presented repeatedly *without* the UCS, the strength of the conditioned response decreased. As Figure 7.5 shows, salivation was almost completely eliminated by the sixth trial. This gradual disappearance of a conditioned response by eliminating the association between conditioned and unconditioned stimuli is called **extinction.**

Figure 7.6
Changes over Time in the Strength of a CR
As the CS and UCS are repeatedly paired during the initial conditioning of the CR, the strength of the CR increases. During extinction, the strength drops as more trials occur in which the CS is presented without the UCS; eventually the CR disappears completely. However, after a brief period of time, the CR reappears when the CS is again presented. In general, the longer the period of time before the new presentation of the CS, the stronger the CR.

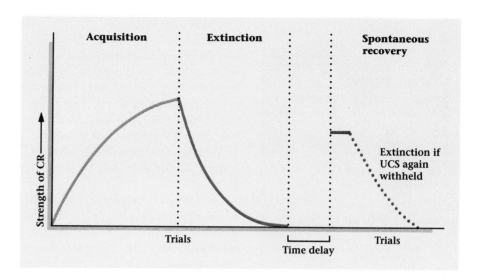

Extinction does not simply erase learning, however. If the CS and the UCS are again paired after the conditioned response has been extinguished, the conditioned response returns to its original strength very quickly, often after only one or two trials. This quick relearning of a conditioned response after extinction is called **reconditioning.** Because reconditioning takes much less time than the original conditioning, some change in the organism must persist even after extinction.

Additional evidence for this conclusion comes from the phenomenon illustrated in Figure 7.6. Suppose that after extinction the CS does not appear for a while and then again recurs without the UCS. What will happen? As Figure 7.6 shows, the conditioned response temporarily reappears. This reappearance of the conditioned response after extinction (and without further CS-UCS pairings) is called **spontaneous recovery.** In general, the longer the time between extinction and the reappearance of the CS, the stronger the recovered conditioned response. However, unless the UCS is again paired with the CS, extinction rapidly occurs again.

Higher-Order Conditioning If a CS is paired with a new neutral stimulus, the new stimulus can itself elicit the CR. This process of forming an association between a neutral stimulus and a conditioned (rather than an unconditioned) stimulus is called **higher-order conditioning.** In Pavlov's research a tone that had become a CS for salivation was paired with a light, and eventually the light alone elicited the CR, salivation. Higher-order conditioning, however, tends to be weaker than the initial conditioning, which involved a UCS, and is more rapidly extinguished.

Classical Conditioning of Human Behavior

Several decades ago, Watson and other behaviorists believed that all behavior could be explained by the principles of classical conditioning. Their faith was misplaced, but these principles do operate in many domains of both human and animal behavior. ("In Review: Basic Processes of Classical Conditioning" summarizes key aspects of classical conditioning.) Classical conditioning of emotional reactions has received the most study, because these quick physiological reactions are the easiest unconditioned responses to analyze. The following are just a few applications of classical conditioning to emotions and to physical and mental health.

Linkages: As discussed in Chapter 15 on psychological disorders, phobias related to small animals and other harmless objects and situations can greatly interfere with people's lives. Clinical as well as laboratory research suggests that these strong, irrational fears often develop as a classically conditioned response (CR) following unfortunate, sometimes repeated, associations between, say, pain (a UCS) and the originally neutral, but now feared stimulus object (CS).

Phobias and Anxiety   **Phobias** are strong fears of objects or situations that either are not objectively dangerous—public speaking, for example—or are less dangerous than the phobic person's reaction suggests. Many fears are the result of classical conditioning (Kalish, 1981). For example, a child who is frightened by a large dog may learn a dog phobia that is so intense and generalized that he or she might refuse to go near *any* dog. A truly dangerous situation can also produce classical conditioning of very long-lasting fears. In one study, fifteen years after combat, military veterans responded to simulated battle sounds with elevated *galvanic skin responses*—changes in the electrical activity of the skin that accompany emotional arousal (Edwards & Acker, 1972).

Can classical conditioning also produce a general state of anxiety or more severe psychological disorders? Pavlov thought so. He studied the development of such disturbances in animals, hoping that the results might apply to fear-related disorders in human beings. In one experiment he taught a dog to salivate in response to a circle but not in response to an oval. Then he put the dog through many trials in which the oval was changed to look more and more like a circle. As the discrimination became more and more difficult, the dog did not know how to respond. The animal began to make mistakes; its behavior became very erratic; it began to bark and snarl; and it tried to escape. Pavlov called the dog's behavior an *experimental neurosis*. Such "neuroses" seem to result whenever an animal is placed in conflict. If animals face such conflicts long enough, their life expectancy is greatly reduced (Liddell, 1950).

Are there human parallels to these neurotic animals? Possibly. As we discuss in Chapter 13, on stress, continued work at difficult tasks, internal conflicts, and an inability to control the environment may have harmful, even life-threatening, consequences for people's health.

Promoting Health and Treating Illness   Fortunately, the fears, anxiety, and other difficulties sometimes created or intensified by classical conditioning can also be relieved by classical conditioning procedures. Joseph Wolpe (1958) pioneered the development of these procedures. Using techniques that had helped laboratory animals with experimental neuroses, Wolpe showed that irrational fears could be relieved through *systematic desensitization,* a procedure that associates a new response, such as relaxation, with a feared stimulus. For example, to treat a thunderstorm phobia, a therapist might first teach the client to relax deeply and then associate that relaxation with gradually more intense sights and sounds of thunderstorms (presented on videotape). Desensitization is discussed in more detail in Chapter 16, on treatment of psychological disorders.

Researchers are constantly looking for medical applications of classical conditioning. Its principles are already being used to ease reactions to hay fever and other allergies (Russell et al., 1984; Sampson & Jolie, 1984). Of course, there are drugs that control allergic reactions, but the drugs usually have unwanted side effects such as severe drowsiness. By pairing a drug with a unique stimulus such as a strange odor, researchers have tried to teach people a conditioned response that will, by itself, alleviate the allergic reaction. The results of this line of research are still only preliminary, but they suggest that a response that reduces allergy symptoms can be conditioned.

Other exciting work in this area suggests that decreases in the body's *immune response*—the biological activity that protects the body from infection—can be classically conditioned (Ader & Cohen, 1985; Cohen & Ader, 1988). This research raises the possibility that *increases* in the immune response could also be conditioned, thus making it possible to fight disease with less medication and fewer harmful side effects.

In Review: Basic Processes of Classical Conditioning

Process	Description	Example
Acquisition	A neutral stimulus and a UCS are paired. The neutral stimulus becomes a CS, eliciting the CR.	A child learns to fear (CR) the doctor's office (CS) by associating it with the reflexive emotional reaction (UCR) to a painful injection (UCS).
Stimulus generalization	A CR is elicited not only by the CS but also by stimuli similar to the CS.	A child fears all doctors' offices and places that smell like them.
Stimulus discrimination	Generalization is limited so that some stimuli similar to the CS do not elicit the CR.	A child learns that his mother's doctor's office is not associated with UCS.
Extinction	The CS is presented alone, without the UCS. Eventually the CS no longer elicits the CR.	A child visits the doctor's office several times for a checkup, but does not receive a shot. Fear may eventually cease.

Instrumental and Operant Conditioning

Much of what people learn cannot be described as classical conditioning. In classical conditioning, neutral and unconditioned stimuli are paired, and the result is that the previously neutral stimulus becomes a conditioned stimulus, eliciting a conditioned response. Notice that both stimuli occur before or along with the conditioned response. However, people also learn associations between responses and the stimuli that *follow* them—in other words, between behavior and its consequences. A child learns to say "please" in order to get a piece of candy; a headache sufferer learns to take a pill in order to escape pain; a dog learns to "shake hands" in order to get a treat. All of these responses are *instrumental* in obtaining something rewarding for the person or animal. **Instrumental conditioning** is a process through which responses are learned that help produce some rewarding or desired effect.

From the Puzzle Box to the Skinner Box

At just about the time that Pavlov was conducting his experiments in Russia, American psychologist Edward L. Thorndike was discovering the principles of instrumental learning. To study whether animals can think and reason, Thorndike devised an elaborate cage called a *puzzle box* (see Figure 7.7). An animal, usually a hungry cat, was placed in the puzzle box and had to learn some response—say, stepping on a small lever—in order to unlock the door and get out. When the cat succeeded, it was rewarded with food and then placed back inside the box. After several trials, the cat walked calmly to the lever, pushed it down with its paw, strolled through the opened door, and ate.

It is clear that cats in this situation learned something, because over the course of the trials they took less time to get out of the cage. But did they understand the task? During the first few trials the cats took a long time to discover the secret of opening the door. Thorndike thought that at some point a cat would suddenly understand, or gain *insight* about, the task and perform

Figure 7.7
Thorndike's Puzzle Box
A sample "puzzle box," as used in
Thorndike's research. Because a rope
is connected to both the door latch
and the pedal, a cat can open the
door by pressing down on the pedal.

the response very quickly. In fact, however, he found no such quick change
(Thorndike, 1898). Instead, the amount of time a cat took to open the door
declined very gradually over the trials. In some cases, a cat actually took longer
on one trial than it did on the previous trial. In other words, there was no
evidence that the cats suddenly understood the task.

The Law of Effect   What, then, were Thorndike's cats learning? On the first
few trials, the cats performed a great many responses, almost at random. They
might run back and forth, scratch at the bars, meow, rub their faces, and so
on. Eventually, they stepped on the lever, and the door opened. Thorndike
argued that bonds were formed between the stimuli in the cage and all of
these responses. However, any response that did not produce a rewarding
effect (opening the door) became weaker over time, and any response that
did have the rewarding effect became stronger over time, so that eventually
the cat required less time to open the door.

What was happening, said Thorndike, was analogous to Darwin's law of
natural selection. Much as Darwin said that, over generations, those characteristics of species that best fit the environment ultimately survive, so too it
appeared that those responses of individuals that best fit the environment
survive. Learning, said Thorndike, is governed by the **law of effect.** According
to this law, if a response made in the presence of a particular stimulus is
followed by a reward, that response is more likely to be made the next time
the stimulus is encountered. Responses that are not rewarded are less likely
to be performed again.

Thorndike believed that the law of effect changes behavior as automatically
as plants turn toward light, whether or not a person or an animal understands
the relationship. The mere *association* of stimuli, responses, and effects,
Thorndike argued, produces learning.

Operant Conditioning   Decades after Thorndike published his work, another American psychologist, B. F. Skinner, extended and formalized many of
Thorndike's ideas. Skinner emphasized that during instrumental conditioning
an organism learns a response by *operating on* the environment, so he called

Figure 7.8
Skinner Boxes
Shown here are two common forms of the Skinner box. In frame (a), a rat presses a bar to obtain food from a tube. In frame (b), a pigeon pecks a plastic key; this briefly opens a door that gives the pigeon access to a tray of food.

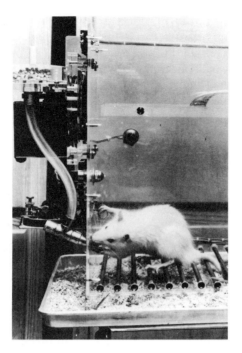

a   b

the process of learning these responses **operant conditioning.** His primary aim was to analyze how behavior is changed by its consequences.

To study operant conditioning, Skinner devised some new tools. One was a chamber known as a *Skinner box.* The experimenter can control it completely. Usually it is soundproof and kept at a constant temperature. It contains a device that the animal can operate in order to get a reward. For example, rats are usually placed in a box like the one shown in Figure 7.8, which has a lever; when the lever is pressed, a food pellet drops through a thin tube. Skinner also developed the *cumulative recorder,* a device that monitors the rate at which a particular response is made, producing a graph like the one in Figure 7.9. The graph shows both the total number of relevant responses (for example, the number of times the rat pressed the lever) and when each response occurred. Thus, it provides a precise picture of how the rate of some action changes over time.

Figure 7.9
A Cumulative Record
Graphs like this one, produced by a cumulative recorder, allow researchers to see how much time has elapsed between one response and the next. Notice that responses 1 and 2 were separated by a considerable amount of time, but little time passed between responses 3, 4, 5, and 6. The record shows exactly how the pattern of responses changed over time.

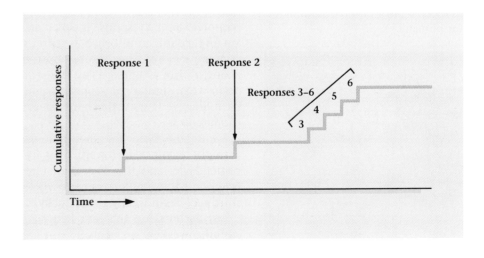

Instrumental and operant conditioning differ from each other in one important respect. In instrumental conditioning, the experimenter defines each opportunity for the subject to produce a response, and conditioning is usually measured by how long it takes for the response to appear (for example, how long it takes the cat to get out of the puzzle box). In operant conditioning, the subject is free to make responses at any time, so conditioning is measured by the *rate* of responding. In most other ways, these forms of learning are essentially the same, and the principles that apply to one also apply to the other. Thus, in the following sections, the term *operant conditioning* refers to both.

Basic Components of Operant Conditioning

The tools Skinner devised allowed him and other researchers to choose an arbitrary response, arrange relationships between that response and its consequences, and then analyze how those consequences affected behavior. They found that the basic phenomena of classical conditioning—stimulus generalization, stimulus discrimination, extinction, and spontaneous recovery—also occur in operant conditioning. In operant conditioning, however, the basic components are operants, reinforcers, and discriminative stimuli.

Operants and Reinforcers   Skinner introduced the term *operant* or *operant response* to distinguish the responses in operant conditioning from those in classical conditioning. Recall that in classical conditioning the conditioned response does not affect whether or when the stimulus occurs. Pavlov's dogs salivated when a buzzer sounded, but the salivation had no effect on the buzzer or on whether food was presented. In contrast, an **operant** is a response that has some effect on the world; it is a response that *operates on* the environment. For example, when a child says, "Momma, I'm hungry" and is then fed, the child has made an operant response that determines when food will appear. A further distinction is that, in classical conditioning, the conditioned response is typically an automatic response to stimuli; in operant conditioning, the learned response is under voluntary control.

A **reinforcer** increases the probability that an operant behavior will occur again. There are two main types of reinforcers: positive and negative. **Positive reinforcers** are stimuli that strengthen a response if they are *presented* after that response occurs. They are roughly equivalent to rewards. The food given to a hungry pigeon after it pecks a key is a positive reinforcer; its presentation increases the pigeon's key pecking. Smiles, food, money, and many other desirable outcomes act as positive reinforcers for people. Presenting a positive reinforcer after a response is called *positive reinforcement*. **Negative reinforcers** are unpleasant stimuli such as pain or boredom that strengthen a response if they are *removed* after the response occurs. For example, if the response of taking aspirin is followed by the removal of pain, aspirin taking is likely to occur when similar pain appears again. The process of strengthening behavior by following it with the removal of an aversive stimulus is called *negative reinforcement*.

Events sometimes reinforce actions even if those actions had nothing to do with the event. The reward may follow the action through sheer luck or coincidence, and this "accidental reinforcement" can lead to *superstitious behavior*. For example, someone who wins a lottery while wearing a particular shirt may begin wearing the "lucky shirt" more often.

Just as breaking the link between a conditioned and an unconditioned stimulus weakens a classically conditioned response, ending the relationship between an operant response and its consequences weakens that response. In

A touch, a smile, and a look of love are among the many social stimuli that can serve as positive reinforcers for humans.

Figure 7.10
Stimulus Discrimination
In this experiment the rat could jump from the stand through any one of the three doors, but it was reinforced only if it jumped through the door that differed from the other two. As you can see, the rat learned to do this quite well. For example, in the left-hand panel, it learned to discriminate diagonal from horizontal stripes, and in the middle panel, it learned to discriminate vertical from horizontal stripes.

other words, failure to reinforce a response *extinguishes* that response; the response occurs less often and eventually may disappear. If bar pressing no longer brings food, a rat stops pressing; if repeated phone calls to a friend bring nothing but ringing, you eventually stop phoning. The process of weakening behavior by not reinforcing it is called *extinction.*

Discriminative Stimuli and Stimulus Control Even if you have been reinforced for telling jokes at parties, you are not likely to do so at funerals. Pigeons show similar wisdom. If they are reinforced for pecking a key when a red light is on but are not reinforced for pecking when a green light is on, they will eventually peck only when they see a red light. Their behavior demonstrates the effect of **discriminative stimuli**, which are stimuli that signal whether reinforcement is available if a certain response is made. When an organism learns to make a particular response in the presence of one stimulus but not another, *stimulus discrimination* has occurred (see Figure 7.10). Another way to say this is that the response is now under *stimulus control.* In general, stimulus discrimination allows people or animals to learn what is appropriate (reinforced) and inappropriate (not reinforced) in particular situations.

Stimulus generalization also occurs in operant conditioning; that is, organisms often perform a response in the presence of a stimulus that is similar, but not identical, to the one that previously signaled the availability of reinforcement. As in classical conditioning, the more similar the new stimulus is to the old, the more likely it is that the response will be performed. So, for example, a day-care worker who has successfully entertained one toddler with a Godzilla imitation might try the same stunt with other children of a similar age, but would be less likely to do so with newborn infants or the day-care center director.

Forming and Strengthening Operant Behavior

Daily life is full of examples of operant conditioning. People go to movies, parties, classes, and jobs primarily because doing so brings reinforcement. Their behavior may seem far removed from that of key-pecking pigeons, door-opening cats, and lever-pressing rats. By studying simple animal behaviors, however, psychologists have painstakingly described how various contingencies between responses and their consequences can govern human actions, establishing new behaviors and altering the frequency of others. They have addressed such questions as: What is the effect of the type or timing of a reinforcer? How are established behaviors eliminated? How can new responses be established through operant conditioning?

Teaching new behavior patterns through operant conditioning is much easier when the teacher shapes the desired behavior by requiring, then reinforcing, gradually improved versions rather than waiting for a perfect performance to occur spontaneously. Indeed, without shaping, that perfect performance might never occur.

Shaping   Imagine that you want to train your dog, Moxie, to sit and to "shake hands." The basic method using positive reinforcement is obvious: every time Moxie sits and shakes hands, you give her a treat. But the problem is also obvious: smart as Moxie is, she may never spontaneously make the desired response, so you will never be able to give the reward. Instead of your teaching and Moxie's learning, the two of you will just stare at each other.

The way around this problem is to shape Moxie's behavior. **Shaping** is accomplished by reinforcing **successive approximations**—that is, responses that come successively closer to the desired response. For example, you might first give Moxie a dog treat whenever she sits down. Then you might reward her only when she sits and partially lifts a paw. Next, you might reward more complete paw lifting. Eventually, you would require that Moxie perform the entire sit-lift-shake sequence before offering the reward. Shaping is an extremely powerful, widely used tool. Animal trainers have used it to teach wild beasts to roller-skate and jump through hoops and to teach pigeons to play Ping-Pong (Breland & Breland, 1966).

Delay and Size of Reinforcement   Much of human behavior is learned and maintained because it is regularly reinforced. But many people overeat, smoke, drink too much, or procrastinate, even though they know these behaviors are bad for them and even though they want to eliminate them. They just cannot seem to change; they seem to lack "self-control." If behavior is controlled by its consequences, why do people perform acts that are ultimately self-defeating?

An answer lies in the timing of reinforcers. The good feelings (positive reinforcers) that follow, say, drinking too much are immediate; hangovers and other negative consequences are usually delayed. Recall that in classical conditioning, increasing the delay between the conditioned stimulus and the unconditioned stimulus usually weakens the conditioned response. Similarly, operant conditioning is stronger when the delay in receiving a reinforcer is short (Kalish, 1981). Immediate consequences of a behavior affect the behavior more strongly than delayed consequences. Thus, under some conditions, delaying reward for even a few seconds can decrease the effectiveness of positive reinforcement. The size of a reinforcement is also important. In general, conditioning proceeds faster when the reinforcer is large than when it is small.

Schedules of Reinforcement   So far, we have talked as if a reinforcer is delivered every time a particular response occurs. Sometimes it is, and this arrangement is called a **continuous reinforcement schedule**. Very often, however, reinforcement is administered only some of the time; the result is a **partial**, or **intermittent, reinforcement schedule.**

Most intermittent schedules can be classified according to (1) whether the delivery of reinforcers is determined by the number of responses made or by the time that has elapsed since the last reinforcer, and (2) whether the delivery schedule is fixed or variable. This way of classifying schedules produces four basic types of intermittent reinforcement.

1. **Fixed-ratio (FR) schedules** provide reinforcement following a fixed number of responses. A rat might receive food after every tenth bar press (FR 10) or after every twentieth one (FR 20); a factory worker might be paid ten dollars for every ten widgets he or she assembles.
2. **Variable-ratio (VR) schedules** also call for reinforcement after a given number of responses, but that number varies from one reinforcement to the next. On a VR 30 schedule, a rat might sometimes be reinforced after

ten bar presses, sometimes after fifty bar presses, but an *average* of thirty responses would occur before reinforcement was given. Gambling also offers a variable-ratio schedule; a slot machine, for example, pays off only after a frustratingly unpredictable number of lever pulls.

3. **Fixed-interval (FI) schedules** provide reinforcement for the first response that occurs after some fixed time has passed since the last reward, regardless of how many responses have been made during that interval. For example, on an FI 60 schedule, the first response after 60 seconds have passed will be rewarded. Employers often use fixed-interval schedules, paying people once a week regardless of how much work they have done since their last paycheck.

4. **Variable-interval (VI) schedules** reinforce the first response after some period of time, but the amount of time varies. In a VI 60 schedule, for example, the first response to occur after an *average* of one minute is reinforced, but the actual time between reinforcements might vary from, say, 1 second to 120 seconds. Teachers use VI schedules when they give "points" or other rewards—at unpredictably varying time intervals—to those children who are in their seats and working productively. A VI schedule has also been successfully used to encourage seat-belt use: during a ten-week test in Illinois, police stopped drivers at random and awarded prizes to those who were buckled up (Mortimer et al., 1988).

Different schedules of reinforcement produce different patterns of responding, as Figure 7.11 shows (Skinner, 1961). The figure illustrates two important points. First, both fixed- and variable-ratio schedules produce very high rates of behavior, because in both cases the frequency of reward depends directly on the rate of responding. Thus, manufacturers who want to maintain high production rates often use fixed-ratio schedules, paying factory workers on a *piecework* basis, according to the number of items they produce. Similarly, gamblers reinforced on a variable-ratio schedule for pulling the slot machine's handle tend to maintain a high rate of responding.

The second important aspect of Figure 7.11 involves the "scallops" shown in the FI schedule. Under an FI schedule, it does not matter how many responses are made during the time between rewards. As a result, the rate of responding typically drops dramatically immediately after reinforcement and then increases as the time for another reward approaches. When teachers schedule quizzes on the same day each week, for example, most students will study just before each quiz and then almost cease studying. Behavior rewarded by a variable-interval schedule looks quite different. The unpredictable timing of rewards typically generates slow but steady responding. Thus, when students know that a "pop quiz" may occur at any time during the week, their studying is likely to be relatively steady from day to day.

Schedules and Extinction In general, behaviors learned under a partial reinforcement schedule are far more difficult to extinguish than those learned on a continuous reinforcement schedule. This phenomenon—called the **partial reinforcement extinction effect**—is easy to understand if you imagine yourself in a hotel lobby with a broken candy machine and a broken slot machine. If you deposit money in the broken candy machine, you will probably extinguish (stop putting money in) very quickly. Because the machine usually delivers its goodies on a continuous reinforcement schedule, it is easy to tell that it is not going to provide a reinforcer. But because slot machines are known to offer rewards on an intermittent and unpredictable schedule, you might put in coin after coin, unsure of whether the machine is broken or is simply not paying off at the moment.

Figure 7.11
Schedules of Reinforcement
These curves show the patterns of
behavior that typically occur when
different types of schedules are in
effect. The steepness of each curve
indicates the rate of responding; the
thin diagonal lines crossing the
curves show when reinforcement
was given. In general, the rate of
responding is higher under ratio
schedules than under interval
schedules.

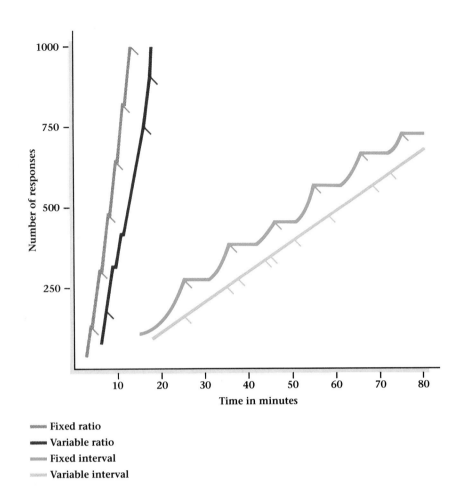

Fixed ratio
Variable ratio
Fixed interval
Variable interval

Source: Adapted from "Teaching Machines" by B. F. Skinner. Copyright © 1961 by Scientific American,
Inc. All rights reserved.

In short, distinguishing between partial reinforcement and extinction is
more difficult than distinguishing between continuous reinforcement and
extinction. As a result, responses reinforced on a partial schedule are likely to
resist extinction longer than those reinforced on a continuous reinforcement
schedule. Consider the toddler who cries and screams after being lovingly
tucked into bed for the night. If the parents ignore this behavior whenever it
occurs, it is likely to extinguish quite rapidly (Williams, 1959). However, if
they give up and cuddle the child after varying intervals each night, they risk
reinforcing the crying on a VI schedule. The crying will become ever more
difficult to eliminate because, from the child's point of view, it takes an
unpredictably varying amount of fussing to get attention. Partial reinforcement
also helps to explain why superstitious behavior is so resistant to extinction
(Chance, 1988). The laws of chance dictate that if, for example, you wear a
"lucky shirt" often enough, a rewarding event will follow now and then.

Analyzing Reinforcers

Linkages: What events can act as re-
wards and motivate learning? (a link
to Motivation)

We have described the powerful effect of reinforcement, but what makes
something a reinforcer? The easy answer is that almost anything can become
a reinforcer if it is properly paired with a stimulus that is already reinforcing.
Psychologists use the term **primary reinforcer** to describe stimuli that are

already reinforcing—things like food, water, or the relief of pain, all of which are inherently rewarding. Previously neutral stimuli that acquire reinforcing power after being paired with a primary reinforcer are called secondary reinforcers. In other words, **secondary reinforcers** are rewards that people or animals *learn* to like.

Secondary reinforcement greatly expands the power of operant and instrumental conditioning. Money is the most obvious secondary reinforcer; some people will do anything for it, even though it tastes terrible. Its reinforcing power lies in its association with the many rewards it can buy. Smiles and other forms of social approval (like the words "good job!") are also important secondary reinforcers for human beings.

What makes primary reinforcers inherently reinforcing? One view is that primary reinforcers satisfy hunger, thirst, and other physiological needs basic to survival. This explanation is incomplete, however, because stimuli like saccharin, which have no nutritional value, can wield as much reinforcing power as sugar, which is nutritious.

Another possibility is that all primary reinforcers exert a particular effect on the brain. James Olds and Peter Milner (1954; Olds, 1973) discovered that mild electrical stimulation of certain areas of the hypothalamus of rats can be such a powerful reinforcer that even a hungry rat in a Skinner box will ignore food, preferring to press for hours a lever that activates stimulation of the "pleasure centers" of the brain. Can primary reinforcers be defined in terms of their ability to stimulate the brain's "pleasure centers"? An important difference between brain stimulation and conventional primary reinforcers like food and drink suggests otherwise. Specifically, reinforcement with food or water can create resistance to extinction. In contrast, when stimulation of the pleasure centers is stopped, animals show rapid extinction of the lever-pressing response, even when the stimulation had been given on a partial reinforcement schedule (Olds & Fobes, 1981). Recent research suggests that stimulation of "pleasure centers" in the brain produces activity of the neurotransmitter dopamine (Wise & Rompre, 1989), which has been tied to the pleasurable effects of cocaine and certain other drugs of abuse.

A much different approach to understanding reinforcement has been proposed by David Premack (1965). Instead of trying to define what makes a

Parents and teachers often use secondary reinforcers, such as praise, privileges, "points," or even money to develop and maintain children's behavior in areas ranging from household chores to studying. The convenience and seemingly endless variety of secondary reinforcers make it possible to use the rewards that each individual finds desirable or (when money or tokens are used) to let each person choose which rewards to buy later.

stimulus a primary or secondary reinforcer, he focuses on the activities people engage in and on the variability of reinforcing power. According to Premack, at any moment each person has a hierarchy of behavioral preferences, ranked from most to least desirable, like a kind of psychological Top 40. The higher on the hierarchy an activity is, the greater its power as a reinforcer, and any activity will serve as a reinforcer for any other activity that is less preferred at the moment. Thus, when parents use car keys or shopping trips to reward teenagers for studying or mowing the lawn, they are offering activities high on the teenagers' preference hierarchies to reinforce activities lower on the hierarchy.

Preference hierarchies differ from one person to the next and from one occasion to the next. To a hungry person, eating is such a preferred activity that the opportunity to eat will reinforce almost any behavior, from putting money in a vending machine to begging from strangers. But once hunger is satisfied, eating drops so low on the preference hierarchy that it temporarily loses virtually all power as a reinforcer; there is almost nothing the person will bother to do for food. Because money can be exchanged for whatever a person finds reinforcing at the moment, it is almost always a powerful reinforcer. But not always. To an infant, cash has far less reinforcing power than, say, the chance to play with a colorful toy.

What makes something a reinforcer? Survival value? Activation of pleasure centers in the brain? Constantly shifting preference patterns based on these? Researchers cannot say for sure, but this has not stopped them from effectively using reinforcers to strengthen a wide variety of behaviors.

Negative Reinforcement

Positive reinforcement alone, whether based on food, love, money, or even Superbowl tickets, does not make the world go around. Often, people are more interested in acting to escape or prevent some unpleasantness than in obtaining something pleasant. In other words, behavior is often molded by negative reinforcement.

The effects of negative reinforcement can be studied through either escape conditioning or avoidance conditioning. **Escape conditioning** takes place when an organism learns to make a response in order to end an aversive stimulus, or negative reinforcer. Dogs learn to jump over the barrier in a shuttle box to escape shock (see Figure 7.12); parents often learn to give in to children's demands for snacks because doing so stops their whining. Now imagine that a signal—say, a buzzer or blinking light—occurs just a few seconds before the grid in one side of a shuttle box is electrified. If the animal jumps over the barrier very quickly after hearing or seeing the signal, it can avoid the shock altogether. When an animal or person responds to a signal in a way that avoids exposure to an aversive stimulus, **avoidance conditioning** has occurred.

This example illustrates that avoidance conditioning often represents a marriage of classical and instrumental conditioning. Because of its value in predicting shock, the buzzer or blinking light becomes a conditioned stimulus that, through classical conditioning, elicits a conditioned fear response. The dog then acquires an instrumental response—jumping the barrier—which is reinforced because it terminates the fear stimulus.

Along with positive reinforcement, avoidance conditioning is one of the most important influences on everyday behavior. Most people go to work or school even when they would rather stay in bed, and they stop at red lights even when they are in a hurry. Each of these behaviors reflects avoidance

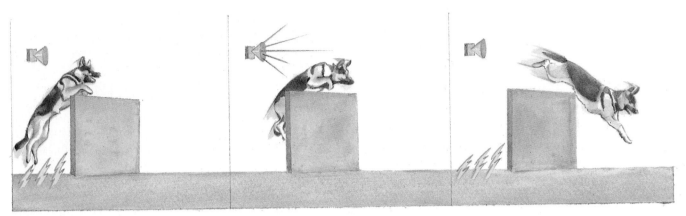

Source: From *The Psychology of Learning and Memory,* by Douglas L. Hintzman. Copyright © 1978 by W. H. Freeman and Company. Reprinted with permission.

Figure 7.12
A Shuttle Box

Studies of negative reinforcement frequently use a shuttle box. It has two compartments, usually separated by a barrier, and its floor is an electric grid. Shock can be administered through the grid to each compartment independently. In the first panel, escape conditioning, the animal can escape shock by jumping over the barrier to the next compartment (second panel). In the third panel, avoidance conditioning, a buzzer signals the imminent onset of shock; the animal can thus avoid the shock entirely if it jumps quickly enough after the buzzer sounds.

conditioning, because each behavior allows people to avoid a negative consequence, such as going on welfare or getting a traffic ticket.

Avoidance is a very difficult habit to break. In one demonstration of its persistence, dogs were trained to jump over the barrier of a shuttle box when a signal for shock was given. After just ten trials, the shock was permanently shut off. But the dogs continued to jump over the barrier whenever the signal was given, for the next five hundred trials, at which time the experiment was terminated (Solomon, Kamin & Wynne, 1953). Why? Every jumping response was still reinforced because it reduced fear, an aversive internal stimulus over which the experimenter has little control.

Notice, too, that the avoidance responses prevented the animal from learning that an alternative behavior such as doing nothing would have been easier and more adaptive. Phobias are often preserved in the same way. If you fear elevators and therefore avoid them, you will never discover that they are safe and comfortable. Unfortunately, avoidance conditioning may prevent people from learning new, more desirable behaviors. For example, fear of doing something embarrassing may cause people with limited social skills to learn to shy away from social situations.

Punishment

Both positive and negative reinforcement *increase* the frequency of a response. In contrast, **punishment** is the presentation of an aversive stimulus or the removal of a pleasant stimulus; it *decreases* the frequency of the immediately preceding response. Shouting "No!" and swatting your dog when it begins chewing on the rug is punishment that presents a negative stimulus following a response. Confiscating a teenager's concert tickets because of rude behavior is punishment that removes a positive stimulus.

Punishment and negative reinforcement are often confused, but they are quite different. Reinforcement *strengthens* behavior; punishment *weakens* it. If shock is *turned off* when a rat presses a lever, that is negative reinforcement; it increases the probability that the rat will press the lever when shock occurs again. But if shock is *turned on* when the rat presses the lever, that is punishment; the rat will be less likely to press the lever again.

Many people object to using punishment because it seems cruel. Others advocate punishment because it works. Both views are partly correct. If misused or overused, punishment can be cruel; when used properly and within limits, it can be very effective, as Fig. 7.13 illustrates.

Figure 7.13
The Uses of Punishment
This infant boy suffered from chronic ruminative disorder, a relatively common condition in which an infant regurgitates all food. The picture on the left was taken when the boy was approximately one year old and had been vomiting for four months. Drugs, surgery, and physical restraints all failed to help him. As a last resort, intense electric shock was applied to the boy's leg at the first sign of after-meal vomiting; shock was continued at one-second intervals until the signs of vomiting had stopped. Six treatments eliminated the boy's vomiting response to food. The picture on the right shows the boy thirteen days after punishment with electric shock had eliminated the vomiting response. His body weight increased 26 percent in two weeks. He was physically and psychologically healthy when tested six months, one year, and two years later (Lang & Melamed, 1969).

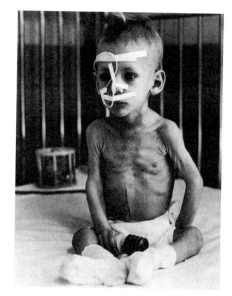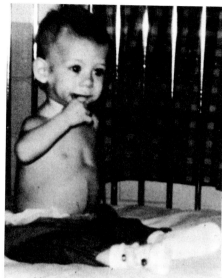

Source: Lang & Melamed, 1969.

HIGHLIGHT

Using Punishment Wisely

Although punishment can change behavior, it has several drawbacks. First, it often produces undesirable side effects. For example, if a parent punishes a child for saying a vulgar word, the child may associate the punisher with the punishment and end up fearing the parent. Second, punishment is often ineffective, especially with animals or young children, unless it is administered immediately after the response and each time the response is made. If a child gets into the cookie jar and enjoys eating a few cookies before being discovered and punished, the effect of punishment will be greatly reduced. If a child confesses to wrongdoing and is then punished, the punishment may discourage honest confession rather than eliminating undesirable behavior. Third, punishment is often an aggressive act, and children often learn through imitation. Hence, a punished child may learn to imitate the parent's punishing behavior when relating to others. Finally, even when punishment is effective, it often works only in a very particular environment. After punishment, a child might stop using a particular word in front of a parent—but continue using it in the presence of other people. Punishment may even produce misunderstanding. A young boy asks his mother at breakfast to "pass the damn milk over here." She slaps him, whereupon he says, "Okay, okay, can I have the damn butter?"

For these reasons, punishment is most effective when several guidelines are followed. First, to prevent development of a general fear of the punisher, the punisher should specify why punishment is being given and that the behavior is being punished, not the person. Second, the punishment should be immediate and sufficiently severe to eliminate the undesirable response. Mild words of annoyance may actually reinforce a child's pranks, because adult attention of almost any kind can be reinforcing to some children. Finally, more appropriate responses should be identified and positively reinforced. As the frequency of appropriate behavior is increased through reinforcement, the frequency of the undesirable response decreases, as does the need for punishment.

When these guidelines are not followed, the beneficial effects of punishment may be wiped out or only temporary. American prisons provide one of the most obvious examples. Prisons are notoriously ineffective at producing long-term improvement in criminals' behavior, in part because punishment is often delayed by lengthy court proceedings. For example, of 108,580 prisoners released from prisons in 11 states during 1983, 62.5 percent were arrested again within three years, and 41.4 percent were imprisoned again (Beck & Shipley, 1989). ■

Operant Conditioning of Human Behavior

The principles of operant conditioning were originally worked out with animals in the laboratory, but they are most valuable for understanding and guiding human behavior in an endless variety of everyday situations. ("In Review: Reinforcement and Punishment" summarizes some key concepts of operant conditioning.) The importance of operant conditioning in human life is perhaps best demonstrated by the unscientific but very effective use of rewards and punishments by parents, teachers, and peers. These consequences are vital to helping children learn what is and is not appropriate behavior at the dinner table, in the classroom, at a birthday party. Indeed, people learn how to be "civilized" partly through the positive ("good!") and negative ("stop that!") responses from others. In addition, the scientific study of operant conditioning has led to numerous specialized procedures for developing or altering behavior.

Treating Problematic Behavior Treatment programs that combine the use of rewards for appropriate behaviors and extinction (or carefully administered punishment) for inappropriate behaviors have helped countless mental patients, mentally retarded individuals, and hard-to-manage children to develop the behavior patterns they need to live happier and more productive lives. Some of these procedures are discussed in Chapter 16, on treatment of psychological disorders. Many self-help books for people trying to lose weight, stop smoking, avoid procrastination, or reach other goals incorporate positive reinforcement principles, recommending self-reward following each successive achievement in the self-improvement program.

When people cannot do anything about the consequences of a behavior, discriminative stimuli may hold the key to changing the behavior. For example, overeaters cannot easily eliminate the reward value of food, but they can alter environmental discriminative stimuli that engender overeating. Often this means replacing cues for eating with cues for other behaviors. Many overeaters tend to sit at the dinner table long after finishing a meal. During this time, they may munch on candies and dessert. By leaving the table immediately after a meal and taking a walk, they can eliminate a significant amount of excessive eating. Similarly, people trying to quit smoking often find initial abstinence easier if they stay away from bars and other places that contain discriminative stimuli for smoking.

Stimulus control can also help insomniacs (Bootzin & Nicassio, 1978; Lichstein & Fischer, 1985; Morawitz, 1989). Much more so than average, insomniacs tend to use their beds for nonsleeping activities such as watching television, writing letters, reading magazines, worrying, and so on. Soon the bedroom becomes a discriminative stimulus for so many activities that relaxation and sleep become less and less likely. But if insomniacs begin to

Learned helplessness stemming from a sense of lost control over the environment can be especially acute among the elderly and has been associated with depression and the intensification of physical problems. In recent years, some nursing homes have developed programs aimed at restoring this sense of control and, in turn, promoting the psychological and physical well-being of their residents.

use their beds only for sleeping, there is a good chance that their insomnia can be eliminated (Hill, 1982).

Learned Helplessness   One of the most important things people learn through operant conditioning is that in most situations, they have at least some control over their environment. Babies learn that cries attract attention, children learn how to make the TV louder, adults learn what it takes to succeed in the workplace. In short, people learn to expect that certain actions on their part predict certain consequences. If this learning is disrupted or does not occur, however, problems may result. One is **learned helplessness,** a tendency to give up any effort to control the environment (Seligman, 1975).

An experiment with dogs provided one of the most powerful demonstrations of learned helplessness. Each dog stood in a harness over an electric grid. At random intervals, a strong electric shock was administered. The dogs in group A could maintain some control over their environment, because the shock was turned off whenever they pushed a button with their nose. Each dog in group B was paired with one in group A. Group B animals could not themselves control the shock; whenever it came on, they had to wait until their partner pushed the button to shut it off. Thus, both groups received an identical amount of shock. The only difference was that those in group A could control it and those in group B could not.

An interesting thing happened when these dogs were moved to a new environment, a shuttle box similar to that in Figure 7.12. A signal was given and, after a ten-second interval, one side of the box was electrified. The dogs in group A quickly learned to jump over the barrier into the safe compartment. The dogs in group B behaved very differently. At first they barked and cried, but then they simply stood still and endured whatever shock was administered. Even though there was an obvious way to avoid the shock, these dogs never tried to find it. Because of their prior experience with uncontrollable shock, they had learned to be helpless (Mineka & Hendersen, 1985; Seligman & Maier, 1967).

Related studies suggest that lack of operant control over the environment can lead to helplessness in humans as well (Kofta & Sedek, 1989). In one experiment, people were given a set of problems to solve. There were no correct solutions, so no matter how hard they tried, these people were doomed to failure. Later, when these same people were given a new set of problems that could be solved quite easily, they failed again—this time because they did not *try* to find the correct solutions. Apparently they did not try because they believed that the task was beyond their abilities (Dweck & Repucci, 1973).

These results appear to reflect a general phenomenon. When people begin to *believe* that nothing they can do will change their lives or control their destiny, they generally stop trying to improve their lot (Dweck & Licht, 1980). Instead, they tend to endure painful situations passively (Seligman, Klein & Miller, 1976). Especially in humans, helplessness often results in severe depression and other stress-related problems described in Chapters 13 and 15 (Abramson, Metalsky & Alloy, 1989; Peterson, Seligman & Vaillant, 1988).

Improving Education   The study of how people learn is crucial to understanding how best to teach them (Glaser, 1990). Recent studies conclude that the most successful educational techniques rely on basic principles of operant conditioning, offering positive reinforcement for correct performance and immediate corrective feedback following mistakes (e.g., Walberg, 1987). An emphasis on positive reinforcement (rather than punishment), along with an emphasis on group cooperation and family involvement, appears to be responsible for the great success of Japanese education (Simons, 1987).

In Review: Reinforcement and Punishment

Concept	Description	Example or Comment
Positive reinforcement	Increasing the frequency of behavior by following it with the presentation of a positive reinforcer—a pleasant, positive stimulus or experience.	Saying "good job" after someone works hard to perform a task.
Negative reinforcement	Increasing the frequency of behavior by following it with the removal of a negative reinforcer—an unpleasant stimulus or experience.	Parents restore driving privileges to a teenager after a semester of improved grades.
Escape conditioning	A subject is conditioned to make a response that ends a negative reinforcer.	A little boy learns that crying will cut short the time that he must stay in his room.
Avoidance conditioning	A subject is conditioned to make a response that avoids a negative reinforcer.	You slow your car to the speed limit as soon as you spot a policecar, thus avoiding arrest and reducing the fear of arrest. Very resistant to extinction.
Punishment	Decreasing the frequency of behavior (usually undesirable behavior) by either presenting an unpleasant stimulus or removing a pleasant one.	Swatting the dog after she steals food off the table. A number of cautions should be kept in mind before using punishment.

Social Learning

Much but not all of human learning follows the principles of classical and operant conditioning. According to traditional accounts of conditioning, learning requires direct, personal experience with stimulus pairings or the consequences of responses. But imagine what life would be like if you had to suffer burns or be hit by a car before learning to use a potholder or to cross streets carefully. In fact, most human learning occurs when people are with other people, and **social learning** theorists highlight the fact that people can learn from the experience of others.

Lessons of the Bobo Doll

A series of experiments by Albert Bandura and his colleagues provided dramatic demonstrations of social learning. In one study nursery school children watched a film starring an adult and a large, inflatable, bottom-heavy "Bobo" doll (Bandura, 1965). The adult in the film punched the Bobo doll in the nose, kicked it, threw objects at it, and hit its head with a hammer while saying things like "Sockeroo!" There were different endings to the film. Some children saw an ending in which the aggressive adult was called a "champion" by a second adult and rewarded with candy and soft drinks. Some saw the aggressor scolded, spanked, and called a "bad person." Some saw an ending in which there was neither reward nor punishment. After the film each child was allowed to play alone with a Bobo doll. How the children played in this and similar studies led to some important conclusions about learning.

First, those children who had seen the adult rewarded imitated the aggressive adult the most. Thus, the reinforcement that the children saw in the film— but did not directly experience—influenced their behavior. They learned through **vicarious conditioning**, which is the process of learning by seeing or hearing about the consequences of other people's actions. A child who sees a friend sent to the principal's office for throwing mud will learn not to do the same; the child who sees a playmate rewarded after picking up scattered toys may later do likewise. Many people fear flying although they have never experienced an air crash, because they have heard about the disastrous experiences of others and imagined crashing.

What about the children who saw the adult punished for Bobo abuse? They played with the doll much less than any other group. However, when the researcher offered these children a piece of candy for every behavior from the film that they could perform, they performed just as many aggressive behaviors as the other children (Bandura, 1965). Seeing the adult punished had originally produced a vicariously conditioned tendency not to *perform* aggressive behaviors, but the children still *learned* those behaviors. They demonstrated that learning may occur even when there is no immediate change in performance.

A third conclusion is based on the behavior of children who saw films in which the adults were neither rewarded nor punished. Although there was no vicarious reward, the children learned and imitated behavior. For example, in one study preschool children watched films in which adults either sat quietly beside a Bobo doll or viciously attacked it. Later, the children were left in a room with the same doll. Those who had seen aggressive behavior were the most aggressive. Furthermore, as Figure 7.14 shows, these children often imitated the adult's attack blow for blow and kick for kick (Bandura, Ross & Ross, 1963). Learning, said Bandura, may occur by observation even though *neither* the person observed nor the observer is reinforced.

Figure 7.14
Observational Learning
After children have observed a
model, they often reproduce many
of the model's acts precisely.

Source: Bandura, Ross & Ross, 1963.

Observational Learning

The process of learning by watching others is called **observational learning;**
the person who is watched is called the *model*. Through observational learning
people can profit from other people's experiences rather than "learning the
hard way," by personally repeating those experiences. However, the fact that
people *can* learn by watching the behavior of others does not mean that they
will. At one time or another, most people ignore the experience of others and
must find out for themselves that it is not a good idea to wait until the last
minute to study for an exam, to drink and drive, or to invest in get-rich-quick
schemes.

What determines whether observational learning will occur? According to
Bandura, there are four requirements.

1. *Attention.* You cannot learn unless you pay reasonably close attention to
   what is happening around you.
2. *Retention.* You must not only attend to the observed behavior but also
   remember it at some later time.
3. *Ability to reproduce the behavior.* You must be capable of performing the act.
4. *Motivation.* In general, you will perform the act only if there is some
   motivation or reason to do so. People are most likely to imitate those whom
   they see *rewarded* for their behavior (as in the Bobo doll studies) and whom
   they *like.* Liking, in turn, tends to be enhanced if the model is attractive or
   powerful (this is why advertisers use movie or sports stars, not street people,
   to endorse their products), or similar to the observer in gender, age, or
   other characteristics (Bandura, 1977).

Observational learning seems to be a powerful source of the subtle socialization discussed in Chapter 2, on development. Observational learning helps
youngsters to become cooperative, productive members of society. Experiments
show, for example, that children are more willing to help and share after
seeing a demonstration of helping by a warm, powerful model—even after
some months have elapsed (Bryan, 1975; Mussen & Eisenberg-Berg, 1977). But
observational learning can also override attempts to teach "civilized" behaviors.
Some young people are drawn into drug use and drug-dealing, for example,
because their parents' rewards and punishments are far less influential than
the sight of successful drug dealers flaunting their money, power, and status.
(In recent years, some children have begun to play "drug dealer" the way
earlier generations played "cowboys.") More commonly, parents who, say,
drink too much or tell white lies may find their children imitating these
actions in spite of punishment for doing so. The "do as I say, not as I do"
approach usually doesn't work.

*Linkages: How can people learn from
other people? (a link to Interpersonal
Behavior and Group Influences)*

THINKING CRITICALLY

Does Watching

Violence on Television

Make People More

Violent?

Linkages: Can television teach children to be aggressive? (a link to Interpersonal Behavior and Group Influences)

If observational learning is important, then surely television—and televised violence—must teach American children a great deal. It is estimated that the average child in the United States has spent more time watching television than attending school (Liebert & Sprafkin, 1988). It is further estimated that prime-time TV programs present an average of 5 violent acts per hour; Saturday morning cartoons include nearly 20 per hour (Gerbner et al., 1986). By the time the average American child is fifteen years old, he or she will have watched approximately 24,000 televised shootings (Greene, 1985).

What is the effect of watching so much violence? Psychologists have speculated that watching televised violence might be emotionally arousing, making it more likely that viewers will react violently to frustration in the environment (Huston & Wright, 1989). Televised violence might also provide models that viewers imitate, particularly if the violence is carried out by attractive, powerful models—the "good guys," for example (Bandura, 1983). Finally, prolonged viewing of violent TV programs may "desensitize" viewers, making them less emotionally moved when they see others suffer and, as a result, less disturbed by inflicting pain on others (Cline, Croft & Courrier, 1973).

What am I being asked to believe or accept?

Many have argued that, through one of these mechanisms or another, watching violence on television causes violent behavior in viewers (Eron, 1987; Hearold, 1986). Indeed in 1985, the American Psychological Association affirmed the conclusion of a National Institute of Mental Health study, which stated, "The consensus among most of the research community is that violence on television does lead to aggressive behavior by children and teenagers who watch the programs."

What evidence is available to support the assertion?

Three types of evidence back up the claim that watching violent television programs increases violent behavior. First, some evidence comes from anecdotes and case studies. Children have poked each other's eyes out after watching the Three Stooges appear to do so on television (Associated Press, 1984). Adults have claimed that watching TV shows prompted them to commit murders or other violent acts matching those seen on the shows. In 1984 a wave of teen suicides followed broadcast of a program depicting a suicide pact between two high school students.

Second, many correlational studies have found a strong link between watching violent television programs and later acts of aggression and violence. One study tracked people from the age of eight (in 1960) until thirty (in 1982). Those who watched more television violence as children were significantly more likely to be convicted of violent crimes as adults. These same people were also more likely to rely on physical punishment of their own children, and their children tended to be much more aggressive than average. These results were found in the United States, Israel, Australia, Poland, and the Netherlands. A significant positive correlation between television violence and violent behavior was even observed in countries such as Finland where the number of violent shows is very small (Centerwall, 1989; Eron, 1987).

Finally, experiments have supported the view that TV violence increases aggression among viewers (Centerwall, 1989). In one study, groups of boys watched violent or nonviolent programs in a controlled setting and then played floor hockey (Josephson, 1987). Boys who had watched the violent shows were more likely than those who had watched nonviolent programs to behave aggressively on the hockey floor. This effect was greatest for those boys who had the most aggressive tendencies to begin with. More extensive experiments in which children are exposed for long periods to carefully controlled types of television programs also suggest that exposure to large amounts of violent activity on television results in aggressive behavior (Huesmann, Laperspetz & Eron, 1984; Leyens et al., 1975; Parke et al., 1977). For example, compared with children who watched an equal number of nonviolent movies, children who were exposed to several violent movies became more aggressive in their interactions with other children (Leyens et al., 1975).

Are there alternative ways of interpreting the evidence?

Anecdotal reports and case studies are certainly open to different interpretations. If people face imprisonment or worse for their violent acts, how much credibility do you give to their claims that their actions were triggered by television programs? If anyone bothered to ask them, how many other people might say that the same programs made them *less* likely to be violent? Even if suicides follow a TV broadcast about suicide, close study of the phenomenon suggests several reasons to believe that depression or other factors besides the show itself may be more influential causal agents. First, not all teens who watched are affected; second, audience size is often unrelated to the size of the suicide increase; and third, some shows are followed by decreases in suicide (Kessler et al., 1988).

What about the correlational evidence? Recall from Chapter 1 that a correlation between two variables does not necessarily imply that one caused the other; both might be caused by a third factor. Why, for example, are certain people watching so much television violence in the first place? This question suggests two possible "third factors" that might account for the observed relationship between watching TV violence and acting aggressively.

For one thing, people who tend to be aggressive may prefer to watch more violent TV programs *and* behave aggressively toward others. Thus, personality traits or disposition, which we discuss in Chapter 14, may account for the observed correlations. Second, perhaps poverty, unemployment, or the effects of drugs and alcohol leave certain people with both more time to watch television *and* frustration or other stressors that trigger aggressive behavior. One study tested this possibility by comparing the childhood television-viewing habits of forty-eight inmates imprisoned for violent crimes to those of forty-five noncriminals with similar socioeconomic backgrounds (Heath, Kruttschnitt & Ward, 1986). There was no significant difference between the groups' reported television-watching as children, suggesting that early viewing habits did not create the difference in aggressiveness.

Finally, the results of controlled experiments on the effects of televised violence may lack generality (Freedman, 1988). Who is to say, for example, whether an increase in aggressive acts in a hockey game has any later bearing on a child's tendency to commit an act of violence?

What additional evidence would be helpful to evaluate the alternatives?

By their nature, correlational studies of observed violence and violent behavior can never be totally conclusive because a third, unidentified causal variable might be responsible for the results. More important would be further evidence from controlled experiments (e.g., Bryant, Carveth &

Brown, 1981) in which equivalent groups of people are given different "doses" of TV violence, and its effects on their subsequent behavior are observed. However, studies like this create a potential ethical dilemma. If watching violent television programs does cause violent behavior, are psychologists justified in creating conditions that might lead some people to a higher level of violent behavior? If such violence occurred, would the researchers be partly responsible to the victims and to society? If some subjects commit violent acts, should the researchers continue the experiment to establish a pattern, or should they terminate these subjects' participation? Difficulty in answering questions like these is partly responsible for the prevalence of correlational research in this area and for some of the remaining uncertainty about the effects of television violence.

It will also be important to have a better understanding of how observed violence relates to other causes of aggressive behavior, some of which are discussed in Chapter 18.

What conclusions are most reasonable?
The preponderance of evidence collected so far makes it reasonable to conclude that watching TV violence may be one cause of violent behavior. But any cause-effect relationship between watching TV violence and acting violently is not an inevitable one, and there are many circumstances in which the effect does not occur (Widom, 1989). Parents, peers, and other environmental influences, along with personality factors, may dampen or amplify the effect of watching televised violence. Not every viewer is equally vulnerable. Those most vulnerable may be those who are most aggressive or violence-prone in the first place. ▪

Skill Learning

Despite its occasional hazards, observational learning is vital to human development. It not only protects people from danger but saves an enormous amount of time that might be wasted on trial and error. You can "get the idea" of how to perform all sorts of complex action sequences known as *skills* by watching other people demonstrate them. Indeed, many of the skills that people learn to perform in everyday life—tying a shoe, opening doors, riding a bike, operating a computer, shooting a basketball, playing the piano, driving a car—can all be learned, at least in part, without direct reinforcement or punishment. Instead, learning a skill depends mainly on imitation or on following instructions about what to do, plus—as musicians and athletes know especially well—a lot of practice.

Psychological research (e.g., Glaser & Bassok, 1989; Holding, 1989) has led to six important conclusions about the kind of training and practice that leads to the most rapid development of a variety of skills.

1. Distributing practice sessions over a long time, rather than massing them together, leads to more efficient learning during each session (Dempster, 1988; see Figure 7.15). The advantage of distributed over massed practice also holds for learning academic material; this is one reason why "cramming" for exams is not an efficient way to learn.
2. Learning very complicated skills is made easier by *part-task training*, which means practicing each component of the skill separately, then putting them all together (Mane, Adams & Donchin, 1989). Training to drive a manual-shift car, for example, might involve separate sessions of practice at shifting gears and then steering through traffic, rather than sessions of gear-shifting in city traffic. Part-task training also makes sense when practicing the whole

Figure 7.15
Massed Versus Distributed
Practice

Subjects in the distributed practice group work on learning their task for four one-hour sessions, each separated by a one-hour rest period. The massed practice group works for four hours straight. As you can see, although each group spends the same amount of time practicing the task, distributed practice produces significantly better results. Although a program of distributed practice may take more time from beginning to end, the practice sessions can be shorter, leaving time between sessions for doing (or learning) other things.

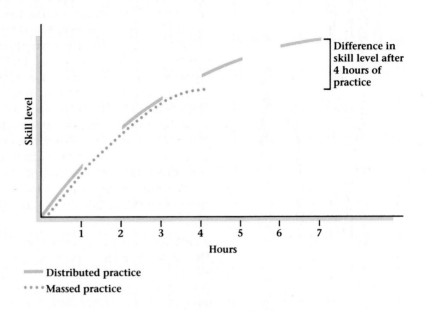

task means spending a lot of time performing already-mastered components of the skill (Wightman & Lintern, 1985). If most of a lengthy piano piece is well learned, for example, it makes sense to spend the most time practicing the troublesome arpeggios rather than repeating easy sections just to get to those arpeggios. Of course, when components of a complex skill are intimately coordinated, it may not be a good idea to practice them separately (Wightman & Lintern, 1985). In learning to use a manual transmission, it would not be efficient to practice moving the gear-shift lever in some sessions and pressing the clutch and accelerator pedals in others; the driver must be able to do these at the same time (Gopher, Weil & Siegal, 1989).

3. Skill development can be aided by two closely related techniques known as adaptive training and guided training. In *adaptive training* the student begins with very easy versions of a skill and then attempts gradually more difficult versions (Lintern & Gopher, 1978). *Guided training* provides supports—like "training wheels"—that prevent the learner from making disruptive or dangerous mistakes as skill develops (Carroll & Carrithers, 1984). Both techniques have drawbacks. Adaptive training can teach low-level skills that must be unlearned once more advanced levels are reached, and guided training can make some students so dependent on the "training wheels" that they may fail to learn the skills needed to perform without them.

4. It is not necessary to avoid making errors, but immediate feedback about which responses are right and wrong, plus the opportunity to correct errors, is vital to efficient skill development (Glaser & Bassok, 1989). Although some psychologists view feedback as reinforcement or punishment, researchers in skill learning see it as information that helps the learner remain aware of success and identify sources of error (Holding, 1989). Feedback should be given as soon as possible, but only when the student can give it full attention. A frightened driving student who has stalled midway through a left turn and faces oncoming traffic will not be helped much by being told, just then, why the car stalled.

5. The surest way to maintain a skill is to practice it well beyond initial mastery. This practice is called *overlearning*, and it allows the skill to operate automatically. A skill that is practiced only until it is performed perfectly once will be easily forgotten, but a skill that is practiced time and again after perfection is reached—like bike riding or roller-skating—is usually maintained, or at least easily recovered, for a lifetime.

6. Skills learned on one kind of task can sometimes aid performance of a second, but only if the second task is procedurally similar to the first (Holding, 1976; Singley & Anderson, 1989). This *positive transfer* of a skill is likely to occur as long as the tasks require similar responses. A person who knows how to use the manual transmission in one car will easily learn to drive another manual shift car, even if the two cars look physically different.

Cognitive Processes in Learning

Pioneers in the study of conditioning hoped to explain all learning as the result of reinforcement and the automatic, unthinking formation of simple associations. Research on skill learning, vicarious conditioning, and observational learning has undermined this view. There is also the phenomenon of language learning. When children learn to speak, they learn more than a chain of associations, since they learn to create new sentences. Furthermore, learning a language requires learning abstract rules that reflect the structure of the language. This kind of learning requires the use of symbols. It requires thinking, ideas, images, and other forms of mental representation described in the chapters on development and thought. In other words, *cognitive processes*—how people represent, store, and use information—play an important role in learning.

Cognition and Conditioning

Even classical and operant conditioning may involve more than automatic associations and reinforcement. As discussed earlier, what is learned during classical conditioning may be a cognitive expectancy. That is, the conditioned stimulus leads the organism to expect the unconditioned stimulus. The learner forms a mental representation of stimuli in the environment and can recognize what goes with what (Rescorla, 1988).

Support for this view includes evidence, discussed earlier, that a conditioned response is best formed when the CS becomes, through pairing, a *reliable predictor* of the UCS. Further support comes from studies of *blocking*. To understand this phenomenon, suppose a CS always occurs along with a UCS and then, after some period of time, another stimulus is also paired with the UCS. Will the new stimulus also come to elicit a conditioned response?

To find out, Leon Kamin (1969) used the procedure illustrated in Figure 7.16. To take a human example, consider a child who develops a conditioned fear response (CR) by repeatedly associating the smell of the doctor's office (CS) with the pain of injections (UCS). After this conditioned fear response has been formed, the child visits the doctor again, and this time the office has new wallpaper. Will the wallpaper become a CS as the smell did? No, its conditioning power has been *blocked*. In general, once a CS is linked to a UCS, pairing a second stimulus with the UCS will not create a conditioned response

Figure 7.16
Blocking

In Kamin's study of blocking, one group of rats learned a fear response to both light and noise; they later showed a conditioned fear response to either the light or the noise. A second group of rats first learned a conditioned fear response to noise, then the light was added as an additional potential CS. Even though the light was repeatedly paired with shock, these rats later showed no fear response to the light. The training with one CS apparently *blocked* the rats from learning another CS that was subsequently added.

	Phase 1	Phase 2	Test phase	Result
Group 1	(no treatment)	CS = light and noise UCS = shock	light ⟶ CR? noise ⟶ CR?	Yes Yes
Group 2	CS = noise UCS = shock	CS = light and noise UCS = shock	noise ⟶ CR? light ⟶ CR?	Yes No

to the new stimulus. It thus appears that once people (and animals) have one useful predictor of a UCS, they ignore others that may be just as good.

Similarly, cognitive factors influence operant conditioning. For example, why is it that winning the lottery can make the shirt worn that day "lucky," while having no effect on the status of the winner's shoes, socks, cologne, underwear, car, or dog? The answer lies partly in cognitive factors such as attention, memory, and expectancy. Perhaps because it was particularly distinctive (even ugly), the shirt was probably the item of clothing the person *attended to* and *remembered* best from that day; if a distinctive tie or scarf had been worn, it might have become "lucky" instead. No "lucky" car or dog was created because people tend to *expect* that good or bad events will be related to things they choose to do, not to things they own. Furthermore, people focus more attention on (and remember better) occasions when rewards follow their actions than occasions when nothing significant occurs. In short, cognitive factors are often important in altering the impact of reinforcement.

Thus, much as the Gestalt psychologists argued that the whole of a perception is greater than the sum of its parts, cognitive views of learning hold that learning is more than the sum of reinforcement effects and stimulus-response associations. Much as we showed in Chapter 5 that perception may depend on the meaning attached to sensations, so, too, some forms of learning require higher mental processes and depend on how the learner attaches meaning to events. In Chapters 8 and 9, we examine memory, language, and other cognitive processes in some detail, including how language and concepts are learned. Here we look at two important cognitive processes—insight and latent learning.

Insight

Wolfgang Köhler was a Gestalt psychologist whose work on learning happened almost by accident. A German, he was visiting the island of Tenerife when World War I broke out. The British confined Köhler to the island for the duration of the war, and he devoted his time there to studying a colony of chimpanzees. In 1925 he published his findings in *The Mentality of Apes*, a book that remains a classic treatise on cognitive processes in learning.

Köhler began his work only a decade or so after Thorndike published his research on how cats learn in a puzzle box. Recall that Thorndike's results supported the view that the gradual formation of associations is the bedrock of learning—a view disputed by Gestalt psychologists like Köhler. Köhler argued that the problem Thorndike set for his cats determined the type of learning they demonstrated. Thorndike's puzzle box, he said, forced animals to use a trial-and-error strategy in which they had to happen on an answer through associations. Perhaps pushing a lever would open the door, but how could the cat possibly know in advance? Even a Nobel laureate put in such a puzzle box would have to start pushing and pulling things until he or she discovered what worked.

Köhler's approach was quite different. He put a chimpanzee in a cage and placed a piece of fruit so that it was visible but out of the animal's reach. He sometimes hung the fruit from a string too high to reach, or on the ground too far outside the cage to be retrieved. Many of the chimps overcame these obstacles easily. For example, if the fruit was on the ground outside the cage, the animal might thrust its arm through the cage. When this strategy was unsuccessful, some chimps looked around the cage and, finding a long stick, used it to rake in the fruit. Surprised that the chimpanzees could solve these problems, Köhler tried more difficult tasks. Again, the chimps proved very adept, as Figures 7.17 and 7.18 illustrate.

Were the chimps simply demonstrating the results of previously formed associations? Köhler thought not, and three observations buttressed his claim that something more than automatic associations was involved. First, once a chimpanzee solved a particular problem, it would immediately do the same thing if faced with a similar situation. In other words, it acted as if it understood the problem precisely. Second, Köhler's chimpanzees rarely tried a solution that did not work. Third, they often reached a solution quite suddenly. When confronted with a piece of fruit hanging from a string, for example, a chimp might jump for it several times. Then it would stop jumping, look up, and pace back and forth. Finally it would run over to a wooden crate, place it directly under the fruit, and climb on top of it to reach the fruit. Once, when there were no boxes—or any other objects—in the room, a chimp went over to Köhler, dragged him by the arm until he stood beneath the fruit, and then started climbing up his back!

Köhler believed that the only explanation for these results was that the chimpanzees suddenly saw new relationships that were never learned in the

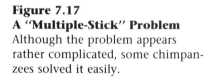

Figure 7.17
A "Multiple-Stick" Problem
Although the problem appears rather complicated, some chimpanzees solved it easily.

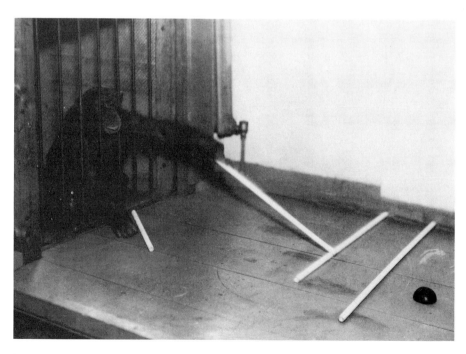

Source: Yerkes Regional Primate Research Center of Emory University.

Figure 7.18
Insight
Shown here are three examples of impressive problem solving by chimpanzees. Frame (a): A chimpanzee has taken a fifteen-foot pole, fixed it in the ground, and climbed all the way to the top; the chimp dropped to the ground after grabbing the fruit. Frame (b): After retrieving two wooden boxes from different areas of the compound, this chimp stacked them on top of one another, climbed to the top with a long pole, and then knocked down the fruit. Frame (c): A chimpanzee stacked three boxes on top of one another and climbed to the top of all three to reach the fruit.

a   b   c

Source: Köhler, 1976.

past; in other words, they had **insight** into the problem as a whole, not just specific stimulus-response associations between its specific elements. The chimpanzees, he argued, perceived the global organization of the problem and used whatever specifics were available in order to solve it. In any case, Köhler's results showed that learning does not always proceed at the painfully slow pace dictated by trial and error.

Latent Learning and Cognitive Maps

Edward Tolman's research on rats' ability to find their way through a maze also shed light on cognitive factors in learning. When he began his investigations in the 1920s, hundreds of experiments had been conducted in which rats were placed in mazes like the one shown in Figure 7.19. The rats' task was to go from the start box to the goal box, where they were rewarded with food. The rats typically took many wrong turns but over the course of many trials made successively fewer mistakes. The standard interpretation was that the rats learned a long chain of turning responses that were reinforced by the food. Tolman disagreed and offered evidence for an alternative interpretation.

In one of his studies, for example, three groups of rats were placed in the same maze once a day for twelve consecutive days (Tolman & Honzik, 1930). For group A, food was placed in the goal box on each trial. These rats gradually improved their performance so that, by the end of the experiment, they made only one or two mistakes as they ran through the maze (see Figure 7.19). Group B also ran the maze once a day, but there was never any food in their goal box. These animals continued to make many errors throughout the experiment. Neither of these results is surprising, and each is consistent with a reinforcement view of learning.

The third group of rats, group C, was the critical one. For the first ten days, they received no reinforcement for running the maze and continued to make many mistakes. But on the eleventh day, food was placed in their goal box for the first time. Then a very surprising thing happened: on the day after receiving reinforcement, these rats made almost no mistakes. In fact, their performance was just as good as that of the rats who had been reinforced

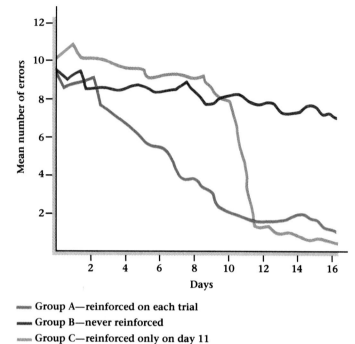

— Group A—reinforced on each trial
— Group B—never reinforced
— Group C—reinforced only on day 11

Figure 7.19
Latent Learning
When rats are put in the same maze for several days, they make many wrong turns if no reinforcement is provided for correct turns. However, notice that the performance of group C improved dramatically the day after it first received reinforcement. The reinforcement, argued Tolman, affected the rats' performance, but they must have learned the maze earlier, before receiving the reinforcement. Results like this led Tolman to argue that animals develop a cognitive map of the maze even in the absence of reward (Tolman & Honzik, 1930).

every day. In other words, the single reinforcement trial on day 11 produced a dramatic change in their performance the next day.

Tolman argued that these results supported two conclusions. First, notice that the rats in group C improved their performance the *first* time they ran the maze after being reinforced. The reinforcement on day 11 could not have significantly affected the rats' learning of the maze itself; it simply changed their subsequent performance. They must have learned the maze earlier. Therefore, the rats (like the children in Bandura's experiment who did not imitate the model until they were rewarded for doing so) demonstrated **latent learning**—learning that is not evident when it first occurs. Second, because the rats' performance changed immediately after the first reinforcement trial, Tolman argued that the results he obtained could occur only if the rats had earlier developed a **cognitive map**—that is, a mental representation of the particular spatial arrangement, the maze.

Tolman concluded that cognitive maps are developed naturally through experience, even in the absence of any response or reinforcement. Research on learning in the natural environment has supported these views. Humans develop mental maps of shopping malls and city streets, even when they receive no direct reward for doing so (Chase, 1986).

How do boys learn to be men and girls learn to be women?

Linkages: Learning and Human Development

Some human learning involves automatic associations and some involves rational thought, but most requires a blending of the two. Research into these different forms of learning is helping to illuminate some basic processes of human life, such as the formation of gender roles.

Work by developmental psychologists has outlined the story of how children gradually learn their roles. By the age of two or three, children usually develop a *gender identity*; that is, they begin to comprehend that they are boys or girls and that they are different from children of the opposite sex (Thompson, 1975). Both boys and girls at this age believe that girls "like to play with dolls," "talk a lot," and the like, and that boys prefer to play with cars, help their fathers, build things, and so on (Kuhn, Nash & Brucken, 1978). By the third year, behavioral differences between boys and girls are evident, and sex-typed choices in toys and play activities become more and more apparent as children grow. Especially around the age of five or six, after they have figured out that they are either boys or girls and are beginning to realize that sex is based on anatomy and cannot be changed, children watch, prefer, and imitate people of their own sex (Bryan & Luria, 1978; Slaby & Frey, 1975). They organize the world into masculine and feminine categories (Bem, 1987). Gender *stereotypes* tend to be especially rigid around this age, as children state confidently that women cannot be firefighters, men are never nurses, boys do not play with dolls, and girls do not like trucks (Marantz & Mansfield, 1977).

What processes account for these developments? Parents are central. Their influence on children's gender identity seems to begin with the way parents view their newborn children. Newborn boys and girls are virtually indistinguishable, yet adults who think they are looking at a boy tend to describe the child as strong, robust, and active; those who think they are looking at a girl tend to describe the child as soft, delicate, and passive (Luria & Rubin, 1974). Similarly, adults who see an infant startle in response to a jack-in-the-box tend to label the reaction as anger when they think the child is a boy, but as fear when they think the baby is a girl (Condry & Condry, 1976).

Not surprisingly, parents also treat boys and girls differently. They tend to label and reinforce children in ways that are likely to increase the probability of one set of behaviors in girls and another in boys. From infancy on, parents

As children grow, the combination of modeling and reinforcement by parents, peers, and others tends to create an environment that shapes behaviors and preferences traditionally associated with either a male or a female gender identity.

dress boys and girls differently and provide them with different toys. Parents tend to emphasize independence, achievement, and competition in boys and sensitivity, empathy, and trustworthiness in girls (Block, 1980). In general, both mothers and fathers reinforce sons for being physical, engaging in independent acts, and playing with objects. Daughters are more likely to be reinforced for both helping and requesting help from others (Huston, 1983).

Behaviors not consistent with the child's gender role often are discouraged, although the range of acceptable behaviors for girls tends to be somewhat wider than that for boys. Parents seem to be more tolerant when a daughter engages in masculine behaviors than when a son engages in feminine ones. The same is true of peers in nursery school and kindergarten: girls tend not to chastise other girls who play with "boys'" toys or engage in other masculine behaviors, but boys often make disparaging remarks to other boys who play with "girls'" toys or otherwise display feminine actions (Langlois & Downs, 1980). Thus, it appears that boys are subject to stronger sanctions against sex-inappropriate behaviors than are girls.

Once children begin to form a gender identity, they look for appropriate models (Kohlberg, 1966). The most obvious models are, of course, their parents, but children's books and television also offer gender-role models. Content analyses of written material for children indicate that females in these media are often fearful, frequently give up easily, and ask others for help. Males are portrayed as active and goal oriented. A similar pattern of differences appears in television programming (Sternglanz & Serbin, 1974). Children who watch the most television also have the most rigid assumptions about what is appropriate behavior for each gender (Greer, 1980).

In short, children's development of gender roles demonstrates the importance of various learning processes—including direct reinforcement and punishment, observation, and cognitive expectancies (Hoffman & Hurst, 1990).

Future Directions

Because learning is so basic to human life, it has been the subject of intense research for over a hundred years. As a result, many important laws of learning have been discovered. Today, researchers seek to expand on this earlier work. Psychologists are working to determine the similarities and differences between the most automatic, stimulus-bound, often subconscious learning and learning that involves interpretation, reasoning, insight, and other cognitive processes.

There is renewed interest in classical conditioning, as psychologists recognize its importance in a very broad range of human and animal experience (Rescorla, 1988; Turkkan, 1989). Research suggests that the operation of the body's immune system (Cohen & Ader, 1988), the activation of internal pain-control mechanisms (Wickramasekera, 1985), and even aspects of the understanding of language (Turkkan, 1989) may be responses that can be brought about when needed through classical conditioning. Future years will undoubtedly see additional experimentation on these possibilities.

The relationship between learning and memory has also inspired new study. Much of this research is taking place at the level of the nerve cell. Working with simple organisms, psychologists are beginning to unravel the mystery of how synaptic transmissions are modified as learning progresses (Mathies, 1989) and to understand the neural changes that take place as more complex organisms learn more complex tasks (Greenough, 1985). Some of this research is described in Chapter 3, on biological aspects of psychology, and in Chapter 8, on memory. Meanwhile, as discussed in Chapter 5, on perception, other psychologists are tackling the problem from a different direction, simulating neural networks by attempting to program sophisticated computers to "learn" the kinds of skills that humans learn (Rumelhart & McClelland, 1986). Some of this work involves attempts to understand and create a computer model of the changes in neural connections that occur when experts practice a skill until it becomes automatic (Schneider & Detweiller, 1988).

Up until the mid 1970s, researchers focused on the learning of relatively simple overt behaviors, and animals were the primary subjects. Very little attention was paid to the more complex knowledge that people acquire through everyday experience. More recently, as psychologists turned away from the assumption that all learning can be explained by the formation of associations, they began to examine complex, everyday tasks. For example, college students must learn the spatial relationships among the various buildings on campus; only recently have psychologists begun to understand how this is possible (Hirtle & Jonides, 1985). Future research is bound to include detailed examinations of how people acquire such complex skills in the natural environment. Already, researchers have examined how people learn to understand speech (Massaro, 1989), solve arithmetic problems (Greeno, Riley & Gelman, 1984; Stigler, 1984; Wilkinson, 1984), understand stories (Myers et al., 1984), recognize music (Bharucha, 1984; Pollard-Gott, 1983), use computer programs (Ross, 1984), and analyze X-rays (Lesgold, 1984).

One result of the growing emphasis on cognitive factors in learning is that research on learning has become more closely related to studies of the thinking, reasoning, and problem-solving processes covered in Chapter 9. Researchers are particularly interested in knowing more about how *experts* learn cognitive skills (Glaser & Bassok, 1989; Singley & Anderson, 1989). Experts are usually better than novices, but *how* are they better? Does the expert chess player, physicist, waiter, or racetrack bettor simply know more than amateurs? Or do they also think and reason in a qualitatively different way? Understanding how expertise develops, and thus how people can more rapidly learn to become experts, represents an important new direction in psychology, which is considered in the next three chapters.

The desire to understand how skills are developed will also be reflected in the never-ending quest for improved education. The effectiveness of some principles—positive reinforcement and feedback, for example—are well established. New applications of these methods and the development of better ones remain a challenge for educational psychologists. How, for example, can educators take better advantage of the wealth of technology offered by modern computer science? What is the best use for features of computers such as three-dimensional graphics, animation, and artificial intelligence? These and other questions will be addressed by psychologists who wish to put laboratory studies of learning to practical use (Glaser, 1990).

To learn more about the field of learning, consider taking a course or two in the area. Some learning courses include laboratory sections that allow you to gain firsthand experience with the principles of human and animal learning.

Summary and Key Terms

Individuals adapt to changes in the environment through the process of learning. Traditionally, learning has been defined as any relatively permanent change in behavior that results from past experience. However, because learned responses are not always performed, some psychologists prefer to define *learning* as any relatively permanent change in behavior or mental processes that results from past experience.

Classical Conditioning

Pavlov's Discovery

One form of learning is *classical conditioning*. It occurs when a *conditioned stimulus*, or *CS* (such as a buzzer), is repeatedly paired with an *unconditioned stimulus*, or *UCS* (such as meat powder on a dog's tongue), which naturally brings about an *unconditioned response*, or *UCR* (such as salivation). Eventually the conditioned stimulus will elicit a response, known as the *conditioned response*, or *CR*, even when the unconditioned stimulus is not presented.

Establishing a Conditioned Response

In general, the strength of a conditioned response and the speed with which it is acquired increase as the intensity of the UCS increases. Some stimuli, however, are easier to associate than others; organisms seem to be biologically prepared to learn certain associations. The way stimuli are paired also determines the speed and strength of conditioning. Up to a point, the strength of the conditioned response increases as the number of CS-UCS pairings increases. *Delayed conditioning,* which means presenting the CS shortly before the UCS but removing both stimuli at the same time, is the most effective method of pairing the stimuli. In general, a conditioned response will fail to develop if the interval between the conditioned and the unconditioned stimulus is more than several seconds. In some cases, however, such as learning an aversion to certain tastes, the interval can be quite long. This phenomenon indicates that the *predictive value* of the conditioned stimulus may determine whether conditioning occurs.

What Is Learned in Classical Conditioning?

Classical conditioning involves learning that the CS predicts the occurrence of the UCS. The conditioned response that follows is not just an automatic, unvarying reflex but a response that accomplishes a function. Thus, classical conditioning produces an adaptive, automatic response to a signal that predicts an event.

Conditioned Responses Over Time

Because of *stimulus generalization,* conditioned responses occur after stimuli that are similar but not identical to conditioned stimuli. Generalization is limited by *stimulus discrimination,* prompting conditioned responses to some stimuli but not others. If the UCS is no longer paired with the CS, the conditioned response eventually disappears; this is *extinction.* After extinction has occurred, the conditioned response often reappears if the CS is presented after some time; this is *spontaneous recovery.* In addition, if the conditioned and unconditioned stimuli are paired once or twice after extinction, *reconditioning* occurs; that is, the conditioned response reverts to its original strength. *Higher-order conditioning* occurs when a new neutral stimulus is associated with a CS, and itself comes to produce the CR.

Classical Conditioning of Human Behavior

Classical conditioning plays a role in emotional disturbances, certain illnesses, and *phobias.* Classical conditioning principles also underlie techniques developed to treat cases of anxiety, allergies, and other common problems.

Instrumental and Operant Conditioning

Instrumental conditioning is the process through which an organism learns to emit a response in order to obtain a reward or avoid an aversive stimulus.

From the Puzzle Box to the Skinner Box

The *law of effect,* postulated by Edward Thorndike, holds that any response that produces a reward becomes more likely over

time and any response that does not produce a reward becomes less likely over time. Skinner called this process *operant conditioning,* rather than instrumental conditioning. In operant conditioning the organism is free to respond at any time, and conditioning is measured by the rate of responding. In most respects, instrumental and operant conditioning are alike.

Basic Components of Operant Conditioning

An *operant* is a response that has some effect on the world. A *reinforcer* increases the probability that the operant preceding it will occur again; in other words, reinforcers strengthen behavior. There are two types of reinforcers: *positive reinforcers,* which strengthen a response if they are presented after that response occurs, and *negative reinforcers,* which strengthen a response if they are removed after it occurs. Superstitious behavior results when a response is coincidentally followed by a reinforcer, although that response did not actually cause the reinforcer to appear. *Discriminative stimuli* indicate whether reinforcement is available for a particular behavior.

Forming and Strengthening Operant Behavior

Complex responses can be learned through *shaping*; this process involves reinforcing *successive approximations* of the desired response. In general, operant conditioning proceeds more quickly when the delay in receiving reinforcement is short than when it is long, and when the reinforcement is large than when it is small. Reinforcement may be delivered on a *continuous reinforcement schedule* or on one of four basic types of *partial* or *intermittent reinforcement schedules: fixed ratio (FR), variable ratio (VR), fixed interval (FI),* and *variable interval (VI).* Ratio schedules lead to a rapid rate of responding. Behavior learned through partial reinforcement, particularly through variable schedules, is very resistant to extinction; this phenomenon is called the *partial reinforcement extinction effect.*

Analyzing Reinforcers

Psychologists do not know for sure what makes certain reinforcers, called *primary reinforcers,* inherently rewarding. *Secondary reinforcers* are rewards that people or animals learn to like because of their association with primary reinforcers.

Negative Reinforcement

Both escape conditioning and avoidance conditioning are the result of negative reinforcement. *Escape conditioning* results when behavior terminates a negative reinforcer. *Avoidance conditioning* results when behavior avoids a negative reinforcer; it reflects both classical and operant conditioning. Behaviors learned through avoidance conditioning are very resistant to extinction.

Punishment

Punishment decreases the frequency of a behavior by following it with an unpleasant stimulus or removal of a pleasant one. Punishment modifies behavior but has several drawbacks. Fear of punishment may generalize to the person doing the punishing; it is ineffective when delayed; it can be situation specific; and it teaches only what not to do, not what should be done to obtain reward.

Operant Conditioning of Human Behavior

The principles of operant conditioning have been used in many spheres of life, from the teaching of everyday social skills to treatment of overeating and sleep disorders to classroom education. *Learned helplessness* appears to result when behavior has no influence over its consequences.

Social Learning

Lessons of the Bobo Doll

Studies of *social learning* indicate that learning can occur (a) through *vicarious conditioning*, (b) even when performance does not change, and (c) without any reinforcement, through *observational learning*.

Observational Learning

Observational learning is more likely to occur when the person observed is rewarded and is attractive and similar to the observer. Although it is vital to human development, observational learning can be a source of socially harmful behaviors. There is evidence, for example, that watching violent television programs may be a cause of violent behavior.

Skill Learning

Observational learning along with practice plays an important role in the learning of *skills*. Strategies for learning skills efficiently include distributed practice and part-task training. Adaptive training can also be helpful if it prevents serious errors and doesn't teach the wrong skills. Continued practice after a skill is learned is important to prevent forgetting. The learning of one skill can transfer to aid performance of a similar skill.

Cognitive Processes in Learning

Cognitive processes play an important role in many types of learning.

Cognition and Conditioning

Even classical and operant conditioning may be influenced by cognitive processes. In classical conditioning, for example, an expectancy seems to be learned. Studies of predictive value and of blocking indicate that a conditioned response is best formed when the conditioned stimulus is both a reliable and a useful predictor of the unconditioned stimulus. In operant conditioning, attention, memory, and expectations can all shape the impact of reinforcers.

Insight

Experiments on *insight* also suggest that cognitive processes play an important role in learning, even by animals. Insights are formed suddenly and immediately transfer to other problems.

Latent Learning and Cognitive Maps

Both animals and humans also display *latent learning*. They also form *cognitive maps* of their environments, even in the absence of any reinforcement for doing so.

OUTLINE

CHAPTER 8

Memory

In 1989 a thirty-year-old man in Manhattan, Kansas memorized 35,000 digits of *pi* (the ratio of the circumference of a circle to its diameter). The man's current goal is to memorize the first 100,000 digits of *pi*. He is challenged, he says, by the fact that his father could recite each of William Shakespeare's 37 plays and 150 sonnets. In the past twenty years, however, only three people have managed to memorize 100,000 digits. One of them was ultimately confined to a mental hospital. Unable to control his memory, his mind was so continuously flooded with old facts that he could not function normally (Associated Press, 1989).

Such rare cases aside, memory allows people to learn and to survive. As the Linkages diagram suggests, memory is intimately tied to many other aspects of psychology. Without memory, you would not know how to shut off the alarm, take a shower, get dressed, or find your way home. You would be unable to communicate with other people because you would not remember what words mean or even what you had just said. You would be unaware of your own likes and dislikes, and you would have no idea of who you were in any meaningful sense.

Memory is full of paradoxes. It is not unusual, for example, for people to remember the name of their first-grade teacher but not the name of someone they met just a minute ago. Remarkable as it is, the memory system is far from perfect. Like perception, memory is selective; people retain some information but also lose some. And what people recall can be shaped by a surprisingly large number of factors, including the tendency to embellish or simplify what they report.

In this chapter we describe what is known about both memory and forgetting. Much of the research we discuss concerns how people remember verbal material, so some of the material here may be of immediate use to you in learning and studying for exams.

LINKAGES

Memory

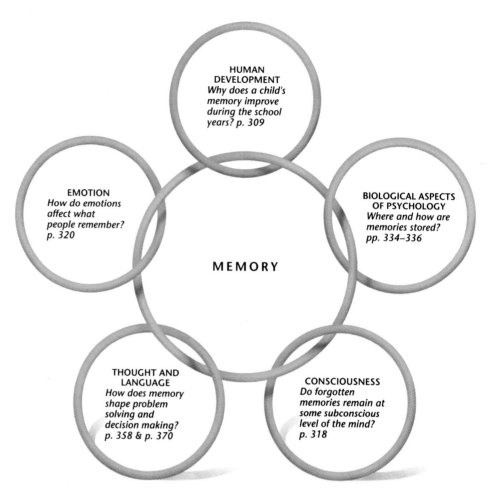

HUMAN DEVELOPMENT
Why does a child's memory improve during the school years? p. 309

EMOTION
How do emotions affect what people remember? p. 320

BIOLOGICAL ASPECTS OF PSYCHOLOGY
Where and how are memories stored? pp. 334–336

MEMORY

THOUGHT AND LANGUAGE
How does memory shape problem solving and decision making? p. 358 & p. 370

CONSCIOUSNESS
Do forgotten memories remain at some subconscious level of the mind? p. 318

■ Look at the diagram above, which illustrates some of the relationships between the topic of this chapter, memory, and other chapter topics. The scientific study of memory began with Hermann Ebbinghaus, who tried to study pure memory, uncontaminated by feelings and thoughts associated with whatever is being remembered. But in the real world, these associations shape what people remember. People who are happy and people who are sad are likely to do better at remembering different types of material, for example. Thus, research on memory is increasingly linked with the study of other topics in psychology such as emotion.

A particularly interesting link occurs between the study of memory and the study of thought. As we discuss in this chapter, how you think about something affects whether and how you remember it. In addition, limitations on your memory affect what you can think about and thus how you can solve problems and make decisions. If you forget most of the suspects in a detective story, for example, you are not likely to be able to solve the mystery. If a doctor does not remember the side effects of a drug, his or her decision to prescribe it might be disastrous. Researchers are exploring both how experts differ from nonexperts in how they remember their area of expertise and how these differences affect their ability to solve problems.

The diagram shows just a sampling of the links between the study of memory and other aspects of psychology. The page numbers indicate where the questions in the diagram are discussed. ■

The Memory System: An Overview

Mathematician John Griffith estimated that by the time the average person dies, he or she will have stored five hundred times as much information as can be found in the *Encyclopaedia Britannica* (Hunt, 1982). The impressive capacity of human memory depends on a complex mental system. Our exploration of this system begins with a look at the kinds of information it can handle. Then we describe the processes involved in memory and the stages through which information passes in order to become permanent memories.

Three Types of Memory

In which hand does the Statue of Liberty hold her torch? When was the last time you spent cash for something? What part of speech is used to modify a noun? The first question is likely to elicit a visual image; to answer the second, you must recall a particular event in your life; and the third requires general knowledge unlikely to be tied to a specific event. Some theorists argue that answering each of these questions requires a different type of memory (Brewer & Pani, 1984). How many types of memory are there? No one is sure, but most research suggests that there are at least three basic types. Each is named for the kind of information it handles: episodic, semantic, and procedural (Tulving, 1985).

Any memory of a specific event that happened while you were present is an **episodic memory**—such as what you had for dinner yesterday or where you were last Friday night. **Semantic memory** contains generalized knowledge of the world that does not involve memory of a specific event. For example, you can answer a question like "Are wrenches pets or tools?" without remembering any specific episode in which you learned that wrenches are tools. As a general rule, people convey episodic memories by saying, "I remember when . . . ," whereas they convey semantic memories by saying, "I know that . . ." (Tulving, 1972, 1982). **Procedural memory**, also called *skill memory*, involves how to do things—how to ride a bicycle, read a map, swim. Often, a procedural memory consists of a complicated sequence of movements that cannot be described adequately in words. A gymnast, for example, might find it impossible to describe the exact motions required for a particular routine; an automobile mechanic might not be able to say exactly how to set an engine's timing correctly.

Many activities require all three types of memory. Consider a game of tennis. Knowing the rules of the game or how many sets are needed to win a match involves semantic memory. Remembering which side served last requires episodic memory. Knowing how to lob or volley involves procedural memory.

Basic Memory Processes

Episodic, semantic, and procedural memory all rely on the same basic memory processes. Usually these processes operate so effortlessly that people are not aware of them. Occasionally, however, something goes wrong. For example, one of the authors sometimes drives to work and sometimes walks. On one occasion, he drove, forgot that he had driven, and walked home. When he failed to find his car in its normal spot the next morning, he called the police to report the car stolen. After about twenty-four hours, the police called to let

Procedural memories involve skills that can usually be learned only through repetition. This is why parents not only tell children how to tie a shoe but also show them the steps and then let them practice.

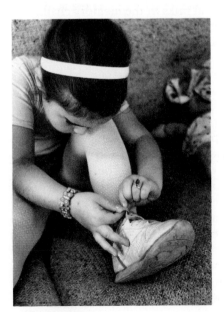

him know that they had found the car parked next to the psychology building on campus and that it had been towed to a storage area. When he went to retrieve the car, he was once again stranded because he had forgotten to bring his car keys.

What went wrong? There are several possibilities, because remembering requires the flawless operation of three fundamental processes—encoding, storage, and retrieval (see Figure 8.1). A breakdown of any one of these processes produces some degree of forgetting.

First, information must be put into memory, a step that requires **encoding**. Just as incoming sensory information must be coded so that it can be communicated to the brain, information to be remembered must be put in a form that the memory system can accept and use. In the memory system, sensory information is put into various *memory codes,* which are mental representations of physical stimuli. For example, **acoustic codes** represent information as sequences of sounds. **Visual codes** represent stimuli as pictures. **Semantic codes** represent an experience by its general meaning. Thus, if you see a billboard that reads "Huey's Going Out of Business Sale—50% Off Everything in Stock," you might encode the sound of the words as if they had been spoken (acoustic coding), the image of the letters as they were arranged on the sign (visual coding), or the fact that you saw an ad for Huey's (semantic coding). The way stimuli are coded can influence what is remembered. For example, semantic coding might allow you to remember seeing a car parked in your neighbors' driveway just before their house was robbed. But if there was little or no other coding, you might not be able to remember the make, model, or color of the car (Bahrick & Boucher, 1968).

The second basic memory process is **storage**, which simply means maintaining information over time. Episodic, semantic, and procedural memories can be stored for a very long time. When you find it possible to use a pogo stick or recall a party from many years ago, you are depending on the storage capacity of your memory.

The third process, **retrieval**, occurs when you find information stored in memory and bring it into consciousness. Retrieving stored information like your address or telephone number is usually so fast and effortless as to seem automatic. Only when you try to retrieve other kinds of information—such as the answer to a quiz question that you know but cannot quite recall—do you become aware of the searching process.

Encoding, storage, and retrieval are all vital links in the memory chain. The author's forgetfulness might thus be traced to the fact that the location of his car was (a) never properly encoded, (b) encoded but never stored, or (c) stored but not retrieved.

Three Stages of Memory

Any memory, whatever its content, is the result of encoding, storage, and retrieval. Why, then, do people remember some information far better and far longer than other information? For example, suppose your friends throw a surprise party for you. On entering the room, you might barely notice, and later fail to recall, the flash from a camera. And you might forget in a few seconds the name of a person you met at the party. But if you live to be a hundred, you will never forget where the party took place or how surprised and pleased you were.

Why do some stimuli leave no more than a fleeting impression and others remain in memory forever? There are a number of reasons, but the most important involves how extensively information is processed. The most

Figure 8.1
Basic Memory Processes
Remembering something requires
three basic processes. First, the item
must be encoded—put in a form
that can be placed in memory. Second, it must be stored, or maintained, in memory. Finally, it must
be retrieved, or recovered from
memory. If any of these processes
fails to operate properly, forgetting
will occur.

| **Encoding** Code and put into memory | → | **Storage** Maintain in memory | → | **Retrieval** Recover from memory |

influential theories of memory suggest that in order for information to become
firmly embedded in memory, it must pass through three stages of processing:
sensory memory, short-term memory, and long-term memory (Atkinson &
Shiffrin, 1968).

Figure 8.2 outlines these stages. In the first stage, known as *sensory memory,*
information from the senses—sights or sounds, for example—is held in *sensory
registers* for a fraction of a second. Information in the sensory registers may
be attended to, analyzed, and encoded as a meaningful pattern; this is the
process of *perception* discussed in Chapter 5. If the information in sensory
memory is perceived, it can enter the second stage, *short-term memory.* If
nothing further is done, the information will disappear in twenty seconds or
so. But if the information in short-term memory is further processed, it may
be encoded into *long-term memory,* where it may remain indefinitely.

Your reading of this sentence illustrates all three stages of memory at work.
As you read, light energy reflected from the page is converted to neural activity
and registered in sensory memory. If you pay attention to these stimuli, your
perception of the patterns of light can be held in short-term memory. This
stage of memory holds the early parts of the sentence so that they can be
integrated and understood as you read the rest of the sentence. As you read,
you are constantly recognizing words by matching your perceptions of them
with the patterns and meanings you have stored in long-term memory. Thus,
all three memory stages are necessary for you to understand a sentence.

The human memory system allows
us to encode, store, and retrieve a
lifetime of experiences. Without it,
we would have no sense of who
we are.

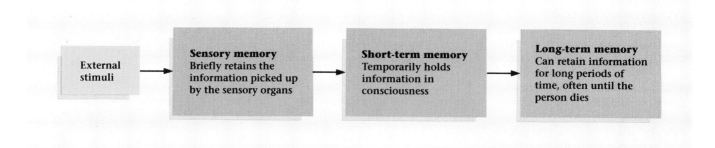

Figure 8.2
The Three Stages of Memory
Here is a very basic overview of the human memory system. The first stage captures information that the eyes, ears, and other sense organs pick up from the environment. In the second stage distinct patterns of energy, such as recognizable images or understandable words, are briefly held in consciousness. The third stage allows information to be retained for use hours, days, or even years later.

In the following sections, we describe the three stages of memory one by one, along with the encoding, storage, and retrieval processes associated with each. Some of the words and methods we use may seem to suggest that the memory system is a chain of fancy recorders and that each stage of memory is a box that passively receives information from the preceding stage. But in fact, memory (like perception) is an active process, and the three stages interact (Cowan, 1988). What is already in long-term memory constantly influences how new experiences are encoded.

As a demonstration of this interaction, read the passage in Figure 8.3, then turn away and try to recall as much of it as possible. To find out the title of the paragraph, read the footnote at the bottom of page 306; then read the passage again. During this second reading, the passage should make a lot more sense and be much easier to remember (Bransford & Johnson, 1972). Reading the title of the passage allowed you to retrieve from long-term memory your knowledge about the topic. On the second reading, this knowledge created new expectations about the passage, which allowed you to process the passage more efficiently. In general, as you gain more knowledge in an area, it becomes easier and easier to remember new things about it.

Sensory Memory

We have said that in order to recognize incoming stimuli, the brain must analyze and compare them to what is already stored in long-term memory. This process is nearly, but not quite, instantaneous. As a result, the impression that stimuli make on the senses must be maintained for a short time. This maintenance is the job of the **sensory registers**, which hold incoming information long enough for it to be processed further; there is a separate register for each of the five sensory modalities. This type of memory, called **sensory memory**, is very primitive and very brief. But sensory memories last long enough to connect one impression to the next, so that people experience a smooth flow of information.

Capacity of the Sensory Registers

Most of what is known about sensory memory comes from studies of the sensory register for visual information. For many years, researchers puzzled over how much information this register could hold and for how long. Several answers came out of experiments on how the eyes look at the world.

When you look around, it seems as if your eyes are moving slowly but smoothly, like a movie camera scanning a scene. In fact, they are not. As

Figure 8.3
The Role of Memory in Comprehension
What is already stored in long-term memory affects the ability to comprehend and remember new information.

The procedure is actually quite simple. First you arrange items into different groups. Of course one pile may be sufficient depending on how much there is to do. If you have to go somewhere else due to lack of facilities that is the next step; otherwise, you are pretty well set. It is important not to overdo things. That is, it is better to do too few things at once than too many. In the short run this may not seem important but complications can easily arise. A mistake can be expensive as well. At first, the whole procedure will seem complicated. Soon, however, it will become just another facet of life. It is difficult to foresee any end to the necessity for this task in the immediate future, but then, one never can tell. After the procedure is completed one arranges the materials into different groups again. Then they can be put into their appropriate places. Eventually they will be used once more and the whole cycle will then have to be repeated. However, that is part of life.

Source: Bransford & Johnson, 1972.

noted in earlier chapters, your eyes fixate at one point for about one-fourth of a second and then rapidly jump to a new position. This rapid jumping from one fixation point to another is called *saccadic eye movement*.

How much information can a person glean from just one eye fixation? Several experiments addressed this question by showing people displays that showed from one to twelve different letters arranged in rows. Each display was presented for such a short time (for example, one-tenth of a second) that the subjects did not have a chance to move their eyes while it was visible; they saw the display in only one fixation. Then, with the display removed, they were asked to report as many letters as possible (McDougall, 1904). People typically reported only up to four or five items, even when the display included more than five. In other words, it appeared that there is a limit to how much information people can glean in a single fixation and that the limit is about four or five items. This limit is called the *span of apprehension*.

George Sperling (1960) was working on his doctoral dissertation when he noticed something very important about these experiments. The subjects often claimed that although they could report only four or five items, they had in fact *seen* the entire display. Why was this important? If the subjects were correct, then the span of apprehension indicated not a limit on how much they could *see* but a limit on how much they could *remember and report*.

How could these two types of limitations be disentangled? Recall that the subjects were shown a display for a very brief time and then were asked to report all of the letters in the display; this is called the *whole-report procedure*. Sperling devised a *partial-report procedure*, outlined in Figure 8.4. A person was shown a display of three rows of letters and, just after it was shut off, heard a tone. If the tone was high pitched, the subject was supposed to report only the top row of letters. If the tone was medium pitched, only the middle row was to be reported. And if the subjects heard a low-pitched tone, only the bottom row was to be reported. Notice that the subjects did not know which row was to be reported until after the display had been shut off. As a result, they had to pay attention to the entire display and then retrieve the requested items from memory.

With this procedure, Sperling believed he could distinguish limitations on what people can see from limitations on what they can remember. To understand why, consider the trials in which subjects were shown twelve letters, as in Figure 8.4. How many letters must a person have available in memory in order to report all four letters in any row, regardless of which tone is sounded? Since subjects did not know which tone would sound until after the display was removed, perfect performance could occur only if the person had all twelve letters stored in memory.

Figure 8.4
Studying Sensory Memory with the Partial-Report Procedure

Sperling devised the partial-report procedure to determine the limits of sensory memory. For 50 milliseconds (one-twentieth of a second), subjects are presented with an array containing from three to twelve letters. The display disappears, a signal sounds, and subjects are asked to report some of what they saw. Because they do not know which row they are to recall until after the display has disappeared, they must keep all the letters in memory to complete the task successfully.

1. An array with a varying number of letters is displayed for 50 milliseconds.

2. Immediately after the display is turned off, a tone is sounded that tells the subject which row to report.

3. The subject tries to report the letters in the appropriate row.

A	D	J	E	← High tone (top row)
X	P	S	B	← Medium tone (middle row)
N	L	B	H	← Low tone (bottom row)

?

Source: Loftus & Loftus, 1976.

Figure 8.5
Results of a Sensory Memory Experiment

When the whole-report procedure is used, by the time people report about four letters, they have already forgotten the rest of the display. By using the partial-report procedure, Sperling found that subjects can retain nine or ten letters out of a twelve-letter display. However, forgetting usually takes place within a second or two.

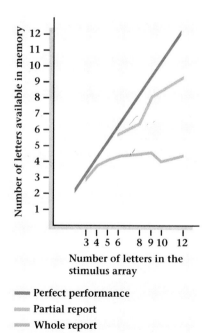

— Perfect performance
— Partial report
— Whole report

Source: Sperling, 1960.

By using the partial-report procedure in this way, Sperling estimated the number of items that were both seen and available in memory. Figure 8.5 shows the results. Clearly, many more items were available in people's memory than had been thought. Why, then, could subjects *report* only four or five letters? By increasing the time between the presentation of the letters and the tone, Sperling found that subjects' memory of the display faded continuously and decayed completely after about one second. Thus, by the time the subjects in the whole-report condition could report four or five items, the memory of the other items was lost. In other words, what subjects had been claiming all along was correct: they were able to see more items than they could report. The span of apprehension reflected a limit not on how much they could see but on how long information could be held in the sensory register.

Properties of Sensory Memory

Experiments like Sperling's helped establish the fact that the sensory registers retain mental representations of visual images for only a very brief time. These representations are called **icons**, and the sensory register holding them is called **iconic memory**. Most icons last no more than one second, but there are conditions in which an icon can last a bit longer. The major determinant of how long an icon lasts is the strength of the visual stimulus (for example, its brightness). The stronger the visual stimulus, the more slowly the icon fades (Long & Beaton, 1982). As noted in the chapter on perception, unusual persistence of an icon may play a role in the reading disorder known as dyslexia.

Thanks to iconic memory, people do not notice their saccadic eye movements, and the flow of information does not stop with every blink. The image from each fixation lasts long enough to give the perception of a continuous flow of visual information. Thus, iconic memory allows people to see a smooth flow of images when watching a movie (Loftus, 1983) or when one object passes in front of another (Mace & Turvey, 1983). Another interesting property of iconic memory is that it can lay one image on top of another, so that information is *summed,* as in Figure 8.6. This summation is most successful when the first image is seen for a relatively long period before it is removed (Loftus & Hanna, 1989) and when the time between the two images is not too long (Loftus & Hogden, 1988).

Note: The title of the passage on page 305 is "Washing Clothes."

Source: Ericksen & Collins, 1967.

Figure 8.6
Summation of Information in Iconic Memory
Researchers showed subjects the top panel for 6 milliseconds, shut it off, and then presented the middle panel for 6 milliseconds. Subjects were able to identify the nonsense syllable (VOH) because the two iconic images, or mental representations, became superimposed. The superimposed image is shown in the lower panel.

Each of the other senses also has its own sensory register, but, besides iconic memory, only echoic memory has received much study so far. **Echoic memory** is the sensory register for auditory sensations; an **echo** in this context is the mental representation of a sound in sensory memory. Experiments like Sperling's indicate that iconic and echoic memory have essentially the same properties, with one exception. Unlike an icon, an echo characteristically lasts up to several seconds, probably because of the physiology of the ear.

For both the echo and the icon, research suggests that encoding is minimal. That is, icons and echoes are faithful reproductions of the physical stimulus, virtual copies of the information provided by the senses (Sakitt & Long, 1979).

Without further processing, icons, echoes, and other sensory memories simply fade away. *Selective attention,* the focusing of mental resources on only part of the stimulus field, controls what information is processed further. Thus, perception is responsible for capturing the elusive impressions of sensory memory and transferring them to short-term memory.

Short-Term Memory

Sensory registers typically store information for only a second or so; the information in **short-term memory** typically lasts less than half a minute. When you look up a phone number and then dial the phone or check the *TV Guide* and then change the channel, you are using short-term memory, which is also called *working memory*. In a sense, people live in short-term memory, because it provides much of their consciousness of the present. As its name implies, however, short-term memory can be fragile. For instance, you might forget the number you just looked up before you can dial it. In the following sections, we discuss how information in short-term memory is encoded, stored, and retrieved.

Encoding

If you attend to and perceive a stimulus, it enters short-term memory. Information is much more elaborately encoded in short-term memory than in the sensory registers. Various types of memory codes can be used, but acoustic coding seems to dominate, especially for the encoding of verbal information (Ellis & Hunt, 1989).

How do psychologists know this? One convincing piece of evidence comes from an analysis of the mistakes people make when encoding information in short-term memory. The mistakes tend to be *acoustically related,* which means that they involve the substitution of similar sounds. For example, R. Conrad (1964) showed people strings of letters and asked them to repeat the letters immediately. Their mistakes tended to involve replacing the correct letter, say, *C,* with something that sounded like it, such as *D, P,* or *T.* This result was obtained even though the letters were presented visually, without any sound.

Storage

You can easily determine the capacity of short-term memory by conducting the simple experiment, designed by Darlene Howard (1983), that is shown in Figure 8.7. The maximum number of items you can recall perfectly after one presentation is called the **immediate memory span.** If your memory span is like most people's, you can repeat about six or seven items from the test in

Figure 8.7
Capacity of Short-Term Memory
These materials can be used to test your immediate, or short-term, memory span. Have a friend read the items in the top row at the rate of about one per second; then try to repeat them back in exactly the same order. If you are able to do this perfectly, have your friend read the next row. Each row contains one additional item. Continue until you make a mistake. Most people are perfect at this task until they reach six or seven items. The maximum number of items you can repeat back perfectly is your immediate memory span.

```
9  2  5                            G  M  N
8  6  4  2                         S  L  R  R
3  7  6  5  4                      V  O  E  P  G
6  2  7  4  1  8                   X  W  D  X  Q  O
0  4  0  1  4  7  3                E  P  H  H  J  A  E
1  9  2  2  3  5  3  0             Z  D  O  F  W  D  S  V
4  8  6  8  5  4  3  3  2          D  T  Y  N  R  H  E  H  Q
2  5  3  1  9  7  1  7  6  8       K  H  W  D  A  G  R  O  F  Z
8  5  1  2  9  6  1  9  4  5  0    U  D  F  F  W  H  D  Q  D  G  E
9  1  8  5  4  6  9  4  2  9  3  7 Q  M  R  H  X  Z  D  P  R  R  E  H
```

CAT BOAT RUG
RUN BEACH PLANT LIGHT
SUIT WATCH CUT STAIRS CAR
JUNK LONE GAME CALL WOOD HEART
FRAME PATCH CROSS DRUG DESK HORSE LAW
CLOTHES CHOOSE GIFT DRIVE BOOK TREE HAIR THIS
DRESS CLERK FILM BASE SPEND SERVE BOOK LOW TIME
STONE ALL NAIL DOOR HOPE EARL FEEL BUY COPE GRAPE
AGE SOFT FALL STORE PUT TRUE SMALL FREE CHECK MAIL LEAF
LOG DAY TIME CHESS LAKE CUT BIRD SHEET YOUR SEE STREET WHEEL

Source: Howard, 1983.

Information such as a new phone number is placed in short-term, or working, memory, where it tends to disappear rapidly unless we take steps to prevent its loss.

Figure 8.7. The interesting thing is that you should come up with about the same number whether you estimate your immediate memory span with digits, letters, words, or virtually any type of unit (Hayes, 1952; Pollack, 1953). When George Miller (1956) noticed that studies of a wide variety of tasks showed the same limit on the ability to process information, he pointed out that the limit seems to be a "magic number" of seven plus or minus two. This is the capacity of short-term memory. The "magic number" applies, however, not to a certain number of discrete elements but to the number of *meaningful groupings* of information, called **chunks.**

To see the difference between discrete elements and chunks, read the following letters to a friend, pausing at each dash: FB-ITW-AC-IAI-BMB-MW. The chances are very good that your friend will not be able to repeat this string of letters perfectly. Why? There are fifteen letters, which is more than most people's immediate memory span. But if you change the pauses when you read the letters so that they are grouped as FBI-TWA-CIA-IBM-BMW, the chances are very good that your friend will repeat the string easily (Bower, 1975). They are the same fifteen letters, but they will be processed *not* as fifteen separate letters but as five meaningful chunks of information. The capacity of short-term memory is almost always between five and nine chunks.

The Power of Chunking   Chunks of information can become very complex. If someone read to you, "The boy in the red shirt kicked his mother in the shin," you could probably repeat the sentence very easily. Yet it contains twelve words and forty-three letters. How can you repeat the sentence so effortlessly? The answer is that people can build bigger and bigger chunks of information (Simon, 1974). In this case, you might represent "the boy in the red shirt" as one chunk of information rather than as six words or nineteen letters. Similarly, "kicked his mother" and "in the shin" represent separate chunks of information.

Linkages: Why does a child's memory improve during the school years? (a link to Human Development)

Learning to use bigger and bigger chunks of information can noticeably improve short-term memory. For example, children's memories improve in part because they gradually become able to hold as many as seven chunks in memory, but also because they become better able to group information into chunks. A notable demonstration of the power of chunking comes from an experiment with a college student of average intelligence who had no unusual memory skills (Chase & Ericsson, 1979). At the beginning of the experiment, his immediate memory span was seven digits. For an hour a day about four days a week, the experimenters gave the student a set of digits and asked him to repeat them. If he was correct, they increased the number of items by one and repeated the procedure. If he made a mistake, the number of items was decreased by one and the procedure was repeated. After six months, the student's immediate memory span had increased to thirty-eight items (Ericsson, Chase & Faloon, 1980). After two years, it had increased to approximately two hundred items (Chase & Ericsson, 1981).

How was this achievement possible? Hours of practice were not the sole answer; the student learned to use an elaborate method of chunking. A runner, he encoded long sequences of digits as times in a race. If the first four digits were 3-2-7-8, he thought of it as "3 minutes, 27.8 seconds, close to a world's record for the mile." Similarly, one waiter taught himself to remember up to twenty complete dinner orders without taking notes (Ericsson & Polson, 1988).

In short, although the capacity of short-term memory is more or less constant—at seven plus or minus two chunks of meaningful information—the size of those chunks can vary. Learn to group more items into a meaningful chunk, and you can greatly increase your memory span. We discuss some simple methods for improving memory later in the chapter.

Integrating Short- and Long-Term Memory   Notice that chunking demonstrates the interaction of short-term and long-term memory. You cannot come up with a meaningful grouping of information if you do no more than passively take it in. Chunking requires that you relate the information in short-term memory to information in long-term memory, encoding and

The person who provides simultaneous translation of a diplomat's speech must, among other things, store long, often complicated segments of the speech in short-term memory while searching long-term memory for the equivalent second-language expressions. This complex task is made easier by grouping and storing the speaker's words as phrases, sentences, or other large chunks, thus expanding the total amount of information that can be held in short-term memory at any one time.

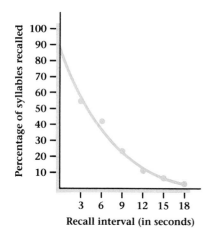

Source: Peterson & Peterson, 1959.

Figure 8.8
Forgetting in Short-Term Memory
The graph shows the percentage of nonsense syllables recalled after various intervals during which rehearsal was prevented. Notice that there was virtually complete forgetting after a delay of 18 seconds.

organizing the new information in terms of what you already know. Thus, in these situations semantic as well as acoustic codes will be used.

Effective chunking requires the ability to move information rapidly back and forth between short- and long-term memory. Chess masters who can play and win several games at once, even when blindfolded, have learned to chunk visual images of each game and to use prior knowledge to encode new information quickly into both short-term and long-term memory. Many daily tasks also involve the simultaneous use of short- and long-term memory. For example, imagine that you are buying something for 83 cents, so you go through your change and pick out two quarters, two dimes, two nickels, and three pennies. To do this you must retrieve the rules of addition from long-term memory *and* keep a running count in short-term memory of how much you have so far.

Duration   Imagine what life would be like if you kept remembering every phone number you ever dialed or every conversation you ever heard. It is an unlikely prospect because most people usually forget information in short-term memory quickly unless they continue to **rehearse** it, repeating it to themselves. You have undoubtedly experienced this yourself. In order to hold a telephone number in short-term memory while you walk across the room to dial the phone, you continue to rehearse the number. If a friend comes in and interrupts you, even for a few seconds, you may forget the number. By rehearsing information, however, you can maintain it in short-term memory for as long as you want.

How long does unrehearsed information stay in short-term memory? To answer this question, researchers needed a way to prevent rehearsal. In two famous experiments John Brown (1958) and Lloyd and Margaret Peterson (1959) devised a method for doing so, which is called the **Brown-Peterson procedure.** A subject is presented with a group of three letters, such as GRB. Then the subject counts backward by threes from an arbitrarily selected number until a signal is given. Counting prevents the subject from rehearsing the letters. On the signal, the subject stops counting and tries to recall the letters. By varying the number of seconds that the subject counts backward, the experimenter can determine how much forgetting takes place over a certain amount of time. As you can see in Figure 8.8, information in short-term memory is forgotten gradually but rapidly: after eighteen seconds, subjects can remember almost nothing (Peterson & Peterson, 1959).

Evidence from these and other experiments suggests that *unrehearsed* information can be maintained in short-term memory for no more than about twenty seconds. This time limit can be a blessing, but it can sometimes be dangerous. For example, on May 17, 1986, an air traffic controller at Chicago's O'Hare Field forgot that he had just instructed an aircraft to land on one runway and allowed another plane to take off on an intersecting runway. The two aircraft missed each other by only twenty feet.

Causes of Forgetting   Why do people forget information in short-term memory so rapidly? Either of two processes can be the cause (Reitman, 1971, 1974; Shiffrin, 1973). One process is *decay*. The mental representation of a stimulus may simply disappear gradually, much as letters on a piece of steel are eaten away by rust and become less distinct over time. Forgetting also occurs because of *interference* from other information. New information, for example, can produce interference by *displacing* information already in short-term memory. Like a workbench, short-term memory can hold only a limited number of items; when additional items are added, the old ones tend to "fall off" (Klatzky, 1980). Displacement is one reason why the phone number you just looked up is likely to drop out of short-term memory if you read another

Table 8.1
An Experiment to Explore How Information Is Stored in Short-Term Memory
Control subjects were given the names of three fruits on each of four trials. Experimental groups were given lists of vegetables, flowers, or professions on the first three trials, then a list of fruits on the fourth trial.

Group	Trial 1	Trial 2	Trial 3	Trial 4
Fruit (control)	Fruits	Fruits	Fruits	Fruits
Vegetable	Vegetables	Vegetables	Vegetables	Fruits
Flower	Flowers	Flowers	Flowers	Fruits
Profession	Professions	Professions	Professions	Fruits

number before dialing. Rehearsal prevents displacement by re-entering the same information into short-term memory.

What Is Stored? So far, we have said that information is often encoded into short-term memory acoustically (by how it sounds); that how much is remembered depends on how the information is grouped; and that unless it is rehearsed, information is very quickly forgotten. There is yet another question to consider about the storage of information in short-term memory: how is the information represented mentally when it is stored?

To find out, Delos Wickens (1973) used a variation of the Brown-Peterson procedure and came up with a surprising answer. Each of four groups of subjects was given four recall trials. Table 8.1 lists the types of items given to each group. One group, the "fruit group," was given the names of three kinds of fruit on all four trials. The vegetable group received the names of vegetables on the first three trials, but on the fourth trial it was given the names of fruits. As Table 8.1 shows, the flower and profession groups were also given a new type of word on the fourth trial.

The results are shown in Figure 8.9. The performance of the fruit group declined steadily across trials because of increasing interference from the previously learned words. The other groups showed a similar decline over the first three trials. However, their performance *improved* on the fourth trial, when the category of the words they tried to remember was shifted.

Notice that the amount of improvement depended on the degree of similarity between word categories. When the words to be learned shifted from vegetables to fruits, the improvement was small. Improvement was intermediate for the shift from flowers to fruits and large for the shift from professions to fruits. Old information interfered less with new information if the new information was very different from the old.

Why did similarity have this effect? One possibility is that lists of fruits and vegetables interfere with each other because they have many *features* in common—what the item looks like, what it tastes like, where it is found, and so on. The shift from professions to fruits brought almost complete release from interference because these categories have virtually no common features (Wickens, 1972). Thus, this study suggests that stimuli are represented in memory not as single units but as *collections of features*.

Retrieval

Imagine that you are holding certain information in short-term memory—for example, the digits 4-2-6. When asked for this information, you can give it, but the process is not as instantaneous as it may seem. Your ability to report what is in short-term memory depends on a process of search and retrieval. How does this process work? Do people examine all of the information in

Figure 8.9
Release from Interference
When subjects had to recall lists of fruits on four trials, performance declined steadily. This result reflects a buildup of interference from one list of fruits to the next. For other groups, the type of words to be recalled was shifted on the fourth trial, and the result was a release from interference; in other words, recall improved. The release from interference was complete when the category changed from professions to fruits, because professions share virtually no features with fruits.

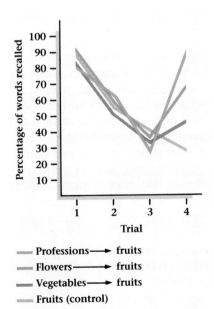

Source: Wickens, 1973.

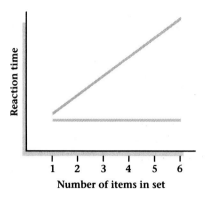

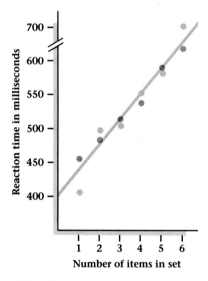

Source: Sternberg, 1966.

Figure 8.10
Short-Term Memory Scanning
How does the time needed to retrieve an item from short-term memory change as the number of items changes? The answer depends on whether the information is retrieved through a serial or a parallel search of short-term memory. Predictions for a serial search model and a parallel search model are shown in part (a); typical empirical data are shown in part (b). Researchers have concluded from results like these that the search process in short-term memory is serial.

short-term memory at once, in a **parallel search,** or do they use a **serial search,** examining one piece at a time?

To determine which type of search is used, Saul Sternberg (1966, 1969) gave people several digits to remember and then gave them a probe number. The subjects' task was to determine whether the probe number had been part of the original set of digits. In order to answer, subjects had to compare the probe number to the numbers in memory. Sternberg reasoned that if items in memory are examined all at once (a parallel search), the number of digits presented in the original set should have no effect on the time it takes to respond to the probe number. However, if items in memory are examined one at a time (a serial search), the time needed to respond to the probe should increase as the length of the original list increases. Sternberg found that for each item added to the list, there is a corresponding increase in the time taken for the search (see Figure 8.10). To be precise, it takes about 1/25 of a second to scan a single item in short-term memory.

Sternberg found another interesting result by comparing the time taken for yes and no responses. Obviously, a person would need to search all the items in order to determine that a probe number was not in the set. But you would think that, in order to say yes, subjects would search only long enough to find the probe number; this should take less time. In fact, this is not what happened. People took the same amount of time to make a positive or a negative response. In other words, the search does not stop when a match is found but continues through the entire set. In short, the evidence indicates that people retrieve information from short-term memory through an *exhaustive serial search.* Figure 8.11 summarizes much of what we have said about short-term memory.

Long-Term Memory

Short-term memory holds information so briefly that it is not what people usually have in mind when they talk about memory. Usually, they are thinking about long-term memory. To understand long-term memory, we look again at the processes of encoding, storage, and retrieval.

Encoding

Some information seems to be encoded into long-term memory automatically (Watkins, 1989). Automatic encoding is most common when people are engaged in other tasks that are well practiced. People learn and remember many things while driving, for example, even though they do not consciously attempt to memorize them. People are also exceptionally good at remembering, without conscious effort, the frequency and context of certain events (Hintzman, 1988; Humphreys, Bain & Pike, 1989). At other times, however, encoding requires effort and conscious strategies. Probably the most frequent strategy for encoding new information is rehearsal.

H I G H L I G H T

Rehearsal and Levels of Processing

There appear to be two basic types of rehearsal: maintenance and elaborative. **Maintenance rehearsal** involves repeating an item over and over, as

"Hey, good buddy! How you doin'?"   "Can't kick, big fella. What's shakin'?"

Source: Drawing by Lorenz; © 1988 The New Yorker Magazine, Inc.

you might do to use a new phone number. This method can keep an item active in short-term memory, but it is ineffective for encoding information into long-term memory. Far more effective is **elaborative rehearsal**, which involves thinking about how new material relates to information already stored in long-term memory. For example, just repeating a new person's name to yourself is not a very effective strategy for memorizing it. Instead, if you have difficulty remembering new names, try thinking for a moment about how the new person's name is related to something you already know. If you are introduced to a man named Jim Crews, you might think, "He reminds me of my Uncle Jim, who always wears a crew cut."

A key way of viewing the difference between maintenance rehearsal and elaborative rehearsal involves the degree or depth to which incoming information is mentally processed. The more you think about and organize new information and relate it to existing knowledge, the "deeper" the processing. Maintenance rehearsal reflects shallow processing; elaborative rehearsal involves deeper processing. According to Fergus Craik and Robert Lockhart (1972), how long you remember something depends on the level of processing.

In one experiment, for example, college students were allowed to look for one minute at a picture of a living room. One group was told only that several small x's had been embedded in the picture and that they should try to locate them by scanning the picture vertically and horizontally. This procedure required only a relatively shallow level of processing, because the subjects could complete the task without ever thinking about the objects. A second group was told that the x's had been placed at the edges of objects in the picture and that they should direct their attention to the contours of the objects. A third group was told to look at the picture and think about what they would do with the objects if they owned them. As a result, they had to relate the new information in the picture to other information stored in long-term memory. Following this relatively deep level of processing, these people recalled about thirty objects from the picture—roughly eight times as many as the other two groups (Bransford, Nitsch & Franks, 1977).

Figure 8.11
Another View of the Memory System
We have now seen that information that is attended to and perceived is encoded into short-term memory. If it is not rehearsed or if it is displaced by new information, this information will be lost. Chunking, using information already in long-term memory, can help hold more information in short-term memory.

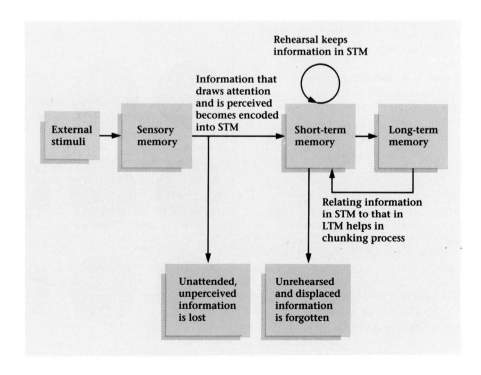

The most important conclusion to be drawn from research like this is that memory is much more strongly determined by internal than by external factors. External factors, such as how the information is displayed and how long you are exposed to it, are not nearly as important as how you think about the information in relation to existing knowledge. For example, noticing *distinctive features*—attributes that are noticeably different from what you already know or expect—makes information more memorable (Graesser & Nakamura, 1982). ■

Semantic Coding   The successful encoding of information into long-term memory is the result of a relatively deep level of processing. In doing this deep processing, people often ignore physical features and other details about the information and concentrate on its underlying meaning. Thus, whereas short-term memory often involves acoustic coding, long-term memory normally involves *semantic* coding. In other words, in long-term memory people are more likely to encode general meanings or general ideas than specific details.

The dominance of semantic coding in long-term memory was demonstrated in a classic study by Jacqueline Sachs (1967). First, people listened to tape-recorded passages. Then Sachs gave them sentences and asked whether each exact sentence had been in the taped passage. People did very well when they were tested immediately (using mainly short-term memory). After only twenty-seven seconds, however, at which point the information had to be retrieved from long-term memory, they could not determine which of two sentences they had heard if both sentences expressed the same meaning. For example, they could not determine whether they had heard "He sent a letter about it to Galileo, the great Italian scientist" or "A letter about it was sent to Galileo, the great Italian scientist." In other words, they remembered the general meaning of what they had heard, but not the exact wording.

Counterfeiters depend on the fact that people encode the general meaning of visual stimuli. For example, most people shown the display in Figure 8.12

Figure 8.12
Encoding into Long-Term Memory
Shown a display like this, most subjects were unable to identify the correct image of a penny. The answer is A.

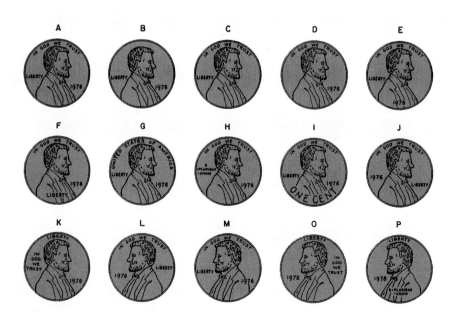

Source: Nickerson & Adams, 1979.

are unable to choose the correct picture of a penny (Nickerson & Adams, 1979).

Visual Coding Although long-term memory normally involves semantic coding, people can also encode images into long-term memory. In one study, for example, people viewed 2,500 pictures. It took sixteen hours just to present the stimuli. Still, the subjects later correctly recognized more than 90 percent of the pictures tested (Standing, Conezio & Haber, 1970).

One reason why pictures are remembered so well is that they have many distinctive features, which are likely to attract attention and to be perceived and encoded. Another reason is that these stimuli may be represented in terms of both a visual code and a semantic code. *Dual coding theory* suggests that information is remembered better when it is represented in both codes rather than in only one (Paivio, 1986).

Individuals with **eidetic imagery**, commonly called *photographic memory*, go far beyond recognizing recently seen pictures; they have automatic, long-term, detailed, and vivid images of virtually everything they have seen. About 5 percent of all school-age children have eidetic imagery, but almost no adults have it (Haber, 1979; Leask, Haber & Haber, 1969; Merritt, 1979). Why the ability to store detailed images disappears with age is not known.

Storage

Whereas the capacity of short-term memory is limited, the capacity of long-term memory is extremely large, and possibly even unlimited (Tulving, 1974). People remember details of the region in which they grew up just as well as they remember the region in which they currently live (Beatty, 1985), even when they do not make periodic visits back home (Beatty & Spangenberger, 1988). People can remember aspects of a foreign language even when they have not spoken it for over fifty years (Bahrick, 1984).

Despite the impressive capacity of long-term memory, you are more likely to be aware of the frustrations of forgetting. Drama critic and humorist Robert Benchley offered an extreme, if facetious, example. He claimed that several years after graduating, he tried to recall everything he had learned in college—and came up with just thirty-nine items. They included statements like "Charlemagne either died or was born or did something with the Holy Roman Empire in 800" and "Marcus Aurelius had a son who turned out to be a bad boy." Is that all he learned in four years? Not at all. The typical college student will learn literally thousands of things, and many of them will be represented in memory until death. But people do forget. Why? Does forgetting indicate that there is a limit to the storage capacity of long-term memory? To answer this question, it is necessary first to look more closely at the nature of forgetting.

The Course of Forgetting Hermann Ebbinghaus, a German psychologist, began the systematic study of long-term memory and forgetting about a hundred years ago. Today, Ebbinghaus's methods seem rather quaint. He used only himself as a subject. To time his experiments, he used a metronome, a mechanical device that makes a sound at constant intervals. His aim was to study memory in its "pure" form, uncontaminated by emotional reactions and other pre-existing associations between new material and what was already in memory. To eliminate such associations, Ebbinghaus created the *nonsense syllable*, a meaningless set of two consonants and a vowel, such as POF, XEM, and QAL. He read aloud, to the beat of the metronome, a list of nonsense syllables. Then he tried to recall the syllables.

This man has not used a pogo stick since he was ten. Because his memory of how to do it is not entirely gone, he will take less time to relearn the skill than he needed to learn it initially. In other words, his memory will display some savings.

To measure forgetting, Ebbinghaus devised the *method of savings,* which involves computing the difference between the number of repetitions needed to learn a list of words and the number of repetitions needed to relearn it after some time has elapsed. This difference is called the **savings.** If it took Ebbinghaus ten trials to learn a list and ten more trials to relearn it, there would be no savings, and forgetting would have been complete. If it took him ten trials to learn the list and only five trials to relearn it, there would be a savings of 50 percent.

As you can see in Figure 8.13, Ebbinghaus found that savings declines (and forgetting increases) as time passes. However, the most dramatic drop in what people retain in long-term memory occurs during the first nine hours, especially in the first hour. After this initial decline, the rate of forgetting slows down considerably. In Ebbinghaus's study, some savings existed even thirty-one days after the original learning.

Ebbinghaus's research had some important limitations, but it produced two lasting discoveries. One is the shape of the forgetting curve depicted in Figure 8.13. Psychologists have subsequently substituted words, sentences, and even stories for nonsense syllables. In virtually all cases the forgetting curve shows the same strong initial drop in memory, followed by a much more moderate decrease over time (Slamecka & McElree, 1983). Of course, people remember sensible stories better than nonsense syllables, but the *shape* of the curve is the same no matter what type of material is involved (Davis & Moore, 1935).

The second of Ebbinghaus's important discoveries is just how long-lasting "savings" in long-term memory can be. Psychologists now know from the method of savings that information is often retained for decades (Ellis & Hunt, 1983). People who have not used a foreign language for many years are often able to relearn it very quickly. The same is true of academic subjects like algebra and motor skills such as learning to ride a bicycle. You may forget something you have learned if you do not use the information, but it is very easy to relearn the material if the need arises (MacLeod, 1988) indicating that the forgetting was not complete.

Causes of Forgetting   Although Ebbinghaus's work described the course of forgetting, it did not reveal why forgetting occurs. In our discussion of short-term memory, we noted the two main causes of forgetting: decay and interference. **Decay theory** suggests that if people do not use information

Figure 8.13
Ebbinghaus's Curve of Forgetting
Ebbinghaus found that most forgetting occurs during the first nine hours after learning, especially during the first hour. After that, forgetting continues, but at a much slower rate (Ebbinghaus, 1885).

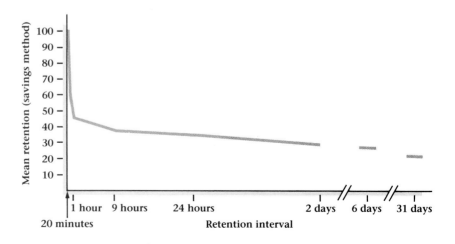

**Table 8.2
Procedures for Studying Interference**

Proactive interference occurs when previously learned material interferes with the learning of new material. Retroactive interference occurs when learning new information inhibits the recall of previously learned information.

Proactive Interference

Group	Time 1	Time 2	Time 3	Result
Experimental	Learn list A	Learn list B	Recall list B	The experimental group will suffer from proactive interference, and the control group will be able to recall more material from list B.
Control	– – –	Learn list B	Recall list B	

Retroactive Interference

Group	Time 1	Time 2	Time 3	Result
Experimental	Learn list A	Learn list B	Recall list A	The experimental group will suffer from retroactive interference, and the control group will be able to recall more of the material from list A.
Control	Learn list A	– – –	Recall list A	

stored in long-term memory, it gradually fades until it is lost. In contrast, **interference theory** holds that the forgetting of information in long-term memory is due to the influence of other learning. The interference can be **retroactive**, in which learning new information interferes with recall of older information, or **proactive**, in which old information interferes with learning new information. Table 8.2 outlines the types of experiments used to study the influence of each form of interference on long-term memory.

Suppose a person learns something, and then, when tested on it after various intervals, remembers less and less as the delays become longer. Is this forgetting due to decay or to interference? It is not easy to tell, because longer delays produce both more decay and more retroactive interference as the subject is exposed to further information while waiting. To separate the effects of decay from those of interference, Karl Dallenbach sought to create situations in which time passed but there was no accompanying interference. Evidence of forgetting in such a situation would suggest that decay, not interference, was operating.

The subjects in one such experiment were, of all things, cockroaches (Minimi & Dallenbach, 1946). Cockroaches avoid light, but the researchers conditioned them to avoid a dark area of their cage by shocking them there. After learning to stay in the light, some roaches were returned to their normal laboratory environment. Members of another group were placed individually in small cotton-lined boxes, in which they could breathe but not move. The researchers reasoned that this group would not experience the interference associated with normal physical activity. Later, each group of cockroaches was again taught to avoid the dark area. Figure 8.14a shows their savings scores (see p. 319). As the delay in reconditioning lengthened, the difference between the groups grew. Savings declined only slightly for the immobilized cockroaches but dropped dramatically for those that had been normally active. These results strongly support the notion that forgetting, at least in this situation, was due to interference, not to decay.

So much for cockroaches, what about humans? In another of Dallenbach's studies, college students learned a list of nonsense syllables and then either continued with their waking routine or were sheltered from interference by going to sleep. While the delay (and thus the decay) was held constant for both groups, the greater interference associated with being awake produced much more forgetting, as Figure 8.14b shows (Jenkins & Dallenbach, 1924). Results like these suggest that though it is possible that decay sometimes occurs, interference is the major cause of forgetting in long-term memory.

Linkages: Do forgotten memories remain at some subconscious level of the mind? (a link to Consciousness)

Duration and Capacity If interference causes forgetting from long-term memory, what does that say about the storage capacity of long-term memory? The answer depends on how interference produces forgetting. Does it push the information out of memory, or does it merely hinder the ability to retrieve the information?

To find out, Endel Tulving and Joseph Psotka (1971) presented people with different numbers of word lists. Each list contained words from six semantic categories, such as types of buildings (hut, cottage, tent, hotel) and earth formations (cliff, river, hill, volcano). Some people learned a list and then recalled as many of the words as possible. Other groups learned the first list and then learned different numbers of other lists before trying to recall the first one. The results were dramatic. As the number of intervening lists increased, the number of words that people could recall from the original list declined consistently (Tulving & Psotka, 1971). These results reflected strong retroactive interference. Then the researchers gave a second test, in which they provided people with a cue by telling them the category of the words (such as types of buildings) to be recalled. Now the number of intervening lists had almost no effect on the number of words recalled from the original list, as Figure 8.15 shows (see p. 320). This result indicated that the words were still represented in long-term memory; they had not been pushed out, but the people were unable to retrieve them without appropriate cues. In other words, the original forgetting was due to a failure in retrieval.

Findings like these have led some theorists to conclude that all forgetting from long-term memory is due to some form of retrieval failure (Ratcliff & McKoon, 1989). Does this theory mean that everything in long-term memory remains there until death, even if people cannot always, or ever, recall it? Some theorists say yes, others say no, arguing that interference may also cause information to be displaced from long-term memory. No one yet knows for sure. What we do know is that a great deal of information remains in the system for years or even decades (Pillemer et al., 1988).

Forms of Representation We have seen that, in sensory memory, information is typically represented as sounds or visual images, while information in short-term memory appears to be represented as unique collections, or bundles, of features (Jones, 1989). In long-term memory, too, it seems that individual words, as well as some other types of information, are represented as unique collections of features. As discussed in the chapter on perception, it is the process of matching these stored features to those present in patterns of incoming stimuli that allows us to recognize objects. Features stored in long-term memory are part of the "raw material" that people manipulate in the process of thinking. (Chapter 9 discusses the relationship between long-term memory and thought.) Much of the evidence about how information is represented in long-term memory comes from studies of how people retrieve that information.

Retrieval

Stimuli that help people retrieve information from long-term memory, like the category cues given in the Tulving and Psotka (1971) experiment, are

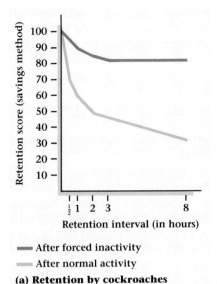

(a) Retention by cockroaches

■■■ After forced inactivity
■■■ After normal activity

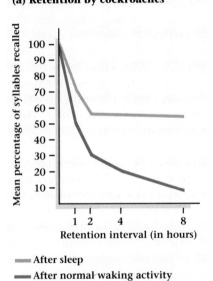

■■■ After sleep
■■■ After normal waking activity

(b) Retention by college students

(Source: Minimi & Dallenbach, 1946.)

Figure 8.14
Interference and Forgetting
Forgetting occurs much more rapidly if (a) cockroaches or (b) college students engage in normal activity after learning than if they spend the time immobilized or asleep. These results suggest that interference is much more important in forgetting than is the passage of time.

called **retrieval cues.** They allow people to recall things that were once forgotten and help them to recognize information stored in memory. In general, recognition tasks are easier than recall tasks because they contain more retrieval cues. For example, it is usually easier to recognize the correct alternative on a multiple-choice exam than to recall material "cold" on an essay test.

Which cues are most effective at aiding retrieval depends on the degree to which they tap into information that was encoded at the time of learning (Tulving, 1979; Tulving & Thomson, 1973). This rule is known as the **encoding specificity principle.** Because long-term memories are often encoded semantically, cues that evoke the meaning of the stored information tend to work best. For example, imagine you have learned a long list of sentences, one of which is either (1) "The man lifted the piano" or (2) "The man tuned the piano." Having the cue "something heavy" during a recall test would probably help you remember the first sentence, because you probably encoded something about the weight of a piano, but "something heavy" would probably not help you recall the second sentence. The cue "makes nice sounds" would be likely to help you recall the second sentence, but not the first (Barclay et al., 1974).

Context and State Dependence   In general, people remember more when their efforts at recall take place in the same environment in which they learned, because they tend to encode features of the environment where the learning occurred. These features later act as effective retrieval cues.

Members of a university diving club provided one demonstration of this principle. They first learned lists of words while they were either on shore or submerged twenty feet underwater. Then they tried to recall as many of the words as possible, again either on shore or underwater. Those who originally learned underwater scored much better when they were tested underwater than when they were tested on shore. Similarly, those who had learned the words on shore did better when tested on shore (Godden & Baddeley, 1975).

When memory can be helped or hindered by such similarities in context, it is called *context-dependent.* One study found that students remember better when tested in the classroom in which they learned material than when tested in a different classroom (Smith, Glenberg & Bjork, 1978). This context dependency effect is not always strong (Saufley, Otaka & Bavaresco, 1985; Smith, Vela & Williamson, 1988), but some students do find it helpful to study for a test in the classroom where the test will be given.

Like the external environment, your internal psychological environment can be encoded when you learn, and it, too, can act as a retrieval cue. When a person's internal state can aid or impede retrieval, memory is called *state-dependent.* For example, if people learn new material while under the influence of marijuana, they tend to recall it better if they are also tested under the influence of marijuana (Eich et al., 1975). Similar effects have been found with alcohol (Overton, 1984), other drugs (Eich, 1989), and mood states. College students remember more positive incidents from their diaries or from their earlier life when they are in a positive mood at the time of recall (Bower, 1981; Ehrlichman & Halpern, 1988). More negative events tend to be recalled when people are in a negative mood (Lewinsohn & Rosenbaum, 1987). These differences are strongest when people try to recall personally meaningful episodes, because these events were most likely to be colored by their own mood (Eich & Metcalfe, 1989). State-dependent memory effects are particularly noticeable in people with bipolar disorder, a condition characterized by dramatic changes in mood (see Chapter 15).

Linkages: How do emotions affect what people remember? (a link to Emotion)

Figure 8.15
Retrieval Failure and Forgetting
These two curves show the results of the two stages in Tulving and Psotka's experiment. On the initial recall test, the ability to recall a list of items was strongly influenced by the number of other lists learned before the test, reflecting the effect of retroactive interference. On the second recall test, retrieval cues were provided, and the interfering effect of the intervening lists was negligible. In other words, information that could not be retrieved without cues could be recalled with cues.

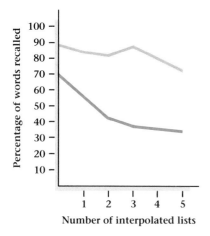

Recall when given item categories as retrieval cues

Initial recall

Source: Tulving & Psotka, 1971.

The Role of Emotion   Notice that state-dependent memory reflects a match in a person's emotional state at two different times. The match between a person's emotional state and the content of information to be learned also affects memory. When people in one study read a story that contained both happy and sad events, for example, they recalled more happy incidents if they were made to feel happy rather than sad (Bower, Gilligan & Monteiro, 1981). Their emotional state facilitated the processing of information that was similar in tone to that state. Preliminary evidence suggests that both the way information is encoded and the way it is retrieved are involved in this *mood congruency effect* (Leventhal & Tomarken, 1986).

The strength of the effect of emotions on memory depends on both the type of emotion and the information to be remembered. In general, positive emotions can do more than negative ones to facilitate memory. Negative emotions tend to interfere with memory (Ellis & Ashbrook, 1988), perhaps because they are often accompanied by angry or panicky thoughts that distract attention from retrieval. The impact of emotions on memory is greatest for information that does not have many links with what is already known (Leventhal & Tomarken, 1986). This is partly because retrieving information from long-term memory is easier when the material is well integrated with existing knowledge. When there is little integration, the emotion associated with the information may be one of the only retrieval cues available.

Intense emotional experiences tend to produce memories that are unusually vivid, detailed, and long-lasting (Reisberg et al., 1988). In fact, these memories are called *flashbulb memories* because they preserve particular experiences in such great detail (Brown & Kulik, 1977; Thompson & Cowan, 1986). Thus, people may recall exactly where they were and what they were doing when they learned of a relative's death.

Some theorists have suggested that there may be a special biological mechanism for flashbulb memories, complete with special storage areas in the brain, and that flashbulb memories are virtually perfect (Brown & Kulik, 1977; Mishkin & Appenzeller, 1987; Schmidt & Bohannon, 1988). However, recent research has shown that the accuracy of flashbulb memories decreases over time (Christianson, 1989). It appears that flashbulb memories occur primarily because the remembered event has many consequences for the person's life (McCloskey et al., 1988). When people get married or learn that a parent has died, they know that their life will change, often dramatically. As a result, they think about the event and form an elaborate network of associations with other areas of knowledge, thus making accurate retrieval of the event more likely (Cohen et al., 1988).

A very different effect can occur as a result of negative emotions. People may be motivated *not* to recall particularly painful events, or to distort them in ways that make them less upsetting (Erdelyi, 1985; Erdelyi & Goldberg, 1979), a phenomenon known as *motivated forgetting*. In fact, some people dwell on positive memories in order to make themselves feel better (Clark & Isen, 1982). These tendencies may serve as the basis for some of the defense mechanisms discussed in the chapters on stress and personality. People may also direct their attention away from upsetting situations (such as a bloody accident scene) with the result that information about them is never encoded.

Retrieving Incomplete Knowledge   One other important characteristic of retrieval is exemplified by the *feeling-of-knowing experience* (Hart, 1967; Nelson et al., 1982; Nelson & Narens, 1980). In a typical experiment, subjects are asked trivia questions. When they cannot answer a question, they are asked

The memory of some experiences, especially those accompanied by intense emotion, can be intense and durable. This victim of the 1989 earthquake in San Francisco will probably never forget where she was or what she was doing when the quake hit. However, though most people in the area will retain vivid "flashbulb memories" of that day, some of the most emotionally affected victims may distort or even fail to recall details of the disaster.

to estimate the probability that they could recognize the correct answer if they were given several options. People are surprisingly accurate at this task; the correlation between their predictions and their actual ability to recognize the items is as high as .70. Apparently people have incomplete knowledge of some answers—they know that they know the answer but cannot recall it.

In another example of incomplete knowledge, dictionary definitions of certain words were read to people (Brown & McNeill, 1966). If they could not recall a defined word, they were asked whether they could identify particular features of the word such as how many syllables it has, what letter it begins with, or what words it rhymes with. Again, people proved to be quite good. This is often called the *tip-of-the-tongue phenomenon*.

How is it possible to have incomplete knowledge? As discussed earlier, it seems that individual words, as well as answers to trivia questions and other information, are represented in long-term memory as unique collections of features. Often people can retrieve some of the features (how many syllables a word has, what it rhymes with, and so on) but not enough features to identify the word.

Constructing Memories

We have described how information is encoded, stored, and retrieved through sensory, short-term, and long-term memory processes. (Figure 8.16 summarizes key aspects of these processes.) As noted earlier, this remarkable system is not just an automatic record-and-playback machine. What gets encoded, stored, and retrieved is shaped by factors such as what information is already in the system and how people perceive and think about incoming information. In other words, to some extent people construct their memories.

Memory is constantly affected by the generalized knowledge about the world that each person has stored in long-term semantic memory (Harris, Sardarpoor-Bascom & Meyer, 1989). Much of this knowledge is represented in terms of *schemas,* which are mental representations of general categories of objects, events, or people. For example, most people have a schema for *baseball game,*

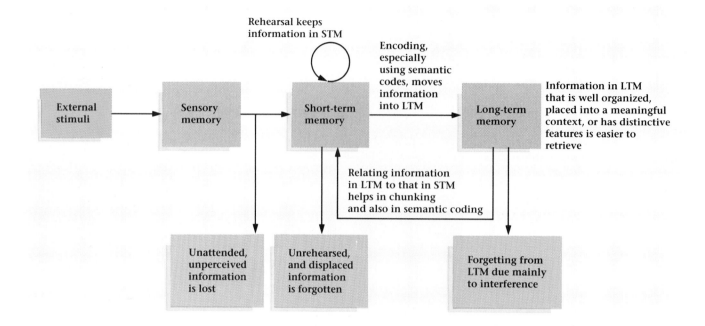

Figure 8.16
A Final Overview of the Memory System
Sensory memory, short-term memory, and long-term memory relate to one another to create a complex, highly organized system for encoding, storing, and retrieving information.

so simply hearing these words is likely to activate whole clusters of information in long-term memory. Thus, *baseball game* immediately brings to mind information about the rules along with images of players, bats, balls, a green field, summer days, and, perhaps, hot dogs and stadiums.

Schemas can affect memory in at least two important ways. First, the generalized knowledge they contain provides a basis for making inferences about incoming information during the encoding stage. So if you hear that "the baseball player was injured," your schema about baseball might prompt you to encode the player as a male even though no information about gender was given.

Second, generalized knowledge also affects recall, as shown in Figure 8.17. Another example is provided by an experiment in which undergraduates waited for several minutes in the small, cluttered office of a graduate student (Brewer & Treyens, 1981). When later asked to recall everything that was in the office, most of the students mistakenly "remembered" that books were present, even though there were none. Apparently, the general knowledge that graduate students read many books influenced the subjects' memory of what was in the room.

The concept of constructive memory suggests that what we remember is determined in part by our perceptual biases and by what we find convenient or comfortable to remember.

Doonesbury   BY GARRY TRUDEAU

Source: © Copyright 1986, G. B. Trudeau. Reprinted with permission of Universal Press Syndicate. All rights reserved.

Figure 8.17
Constructive Memory
Carmichael, Hogan, and Walter (1932) showed people figures like these, along with various labels. In the first case, for example, the experimenter might comment, ''This tends to resemble eyeglasses'' or ''This tends to resemble a dumbbell.'' When the subjects were later asked to reproduce the figures, their drawings were likely to resemble the items mentioned by the experimenter. In other words, the labels given to ambiguous items altered the subjects' memory of them.

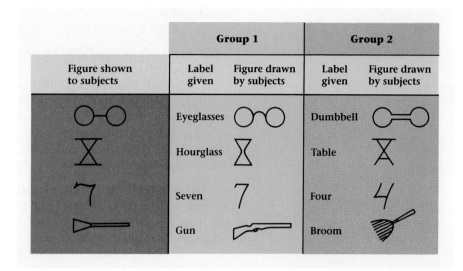

Figure shown to subjects	Group 1		Group 2	
	Label given	Figure drawn by subjects	Label given	Figure drawn by subjects
⚬—⚬	Eyeglasses	⚬⚬	Dumbbell	⚬—⚬
⋈	Hourglass	⋈	Table	⋈
⅂	Seven	7	Four	4
⊐—	Gun	🔫	Broom	🧹

In short, people use their existing knowledge to organize new information as they receive it and to fill in gaps in the information they encode and retrieve. In this way, memories are constructed. To study this process, sometimes called *constructive memory,* Rebecca Sulin and D. James Dooling (1974) asked their subjects to read a long passage about a dictator. In one case, the dictator was a fictitious character named Gerald Martin; in another, Adolf Hitler. Later, subjects were asked if the passage contained the statement ''He hated the Jews particularly and so persecuted them.'' This statement was not in the passage, but those who had been told that they were reading about Hitler ''remembered'' the statement more often than subjects who had read about Gerald Martin.

T H I N K I N G   C R I T I C A L L Y

Is the Memory of Eyewitnesses and Jurors Adequate to Produce Just Verdicts?

The courtroom is a place where memory processes play a vital role and where errors in memory can have tragic consequences. For example, in 1985 two Vietnamese men happened to be held in the same Georgia jail—one was being held for murder and the other for theft. Unfortunately, the wrong man was taken to the murder trial. For days, he sat in a courtroom claiming that a mistake had been made, but the trial proceeded and two eyewitnesses testified under oath that he was the murderer. Only an alert jailer and a fingerprint check prevented a miscarriage of justice.

There is a peculiar irony in the court system in the United States. Lawyers use notes to ask their questions in just the right way and in a particular order; judges use notes to deliver their instructions in an unbiased manner; and even defendants can use notes to aid in their own defense. But witnesses and jurors must often rely entirely on their memories; they are forbidden by many judges from using any external memory aids, a tradition that most trial lawyers strongly support (Jacoby & Padgett, 1989).

What am I being asked to believe or accept?
The general assumption underlying court proceedings is that witnesses can accurately report what they have seen or heard; that jurors can accurately

encode, store, and retrieve information about the evidence presented; and that jurors can then make a just decision.

What evidence is available to support the assertion?

There is actually very little scientific evidence to suggest that justice is most likely to prevail in a typical court proceeding. Judges and legislators rely instead on tradition and experience, interpreting the outcome of court proceedings as evidence that justice has been done in most cases. It is simply assumed that the motivation of witnesses and jurors to be accurate and to do the right thing renders them capable of playing their respective roles without significant error.

Are there alternative ways of interpreting the evidence?

The assumption that witnesses and jurors are highly motivated is probably a safe one; at least there is little evidence to suggest otherwise. But the same outcomes that many interpret as supportive of the present court system can also be viewed in other, less optimistic ways. For example, there are many reasons to doubt that witnesses and jurors are capable of accurately remembering everything they see and hear, regardless of how motivated they may be.

Consider first the role of witnesses. The most compelling evidence a lawyer can provide is that of eyewitnesses, but eyewitnesses can make mistakes (Loftus, 1984). In real-life contexts, all memory processes operate in concert. Witnesses can remember only what is perceived, and they can perceive only what is attended to. The witnesses' task is to report as accurately as possible what they saw or heard; but no matter how highly motivated they are, there are limits to how faithful their reports can be. Experiments indicate that even the form of a question can alter a witness's memory (Loftus, 1979). If a witness is asked, "How fast was the blue car going when it slammed into the truck?" he or she is likely to recall a higher speed than if asked "How fast was the blue car going when it hit the truck?" And when a situation is violent, the overall accuracy of eyewitness testimony is reduced.

There is also evidence that an object mentioned after the fact is often mistakenly remembered as having been at a site. If a lawyer says that a screwdriver was lying on the ground (when it was not), witnesses often report that they saw it. Some theorists believe that when objects are subsequently mentioned, they are integrated into the old memory representation (Loftus & Hoffman, 1989). Others believe that mentioning an object creates retroactive interference, making the original memory more difficult to retrieve (Tversky & Tuchin, 1989). Still others believe that witnesses are actually aware that they did not see the object themselves (Zaragoza & Koshmider, 1989).

Now consider the role of jurors. Their task is not only to remember all the evidence (a tall order, in most cases), but to evaluate its accuracy. This means making judgments about the credibility of each witness, weighing the testimony of apparently reliable witnesses more heavily than that of apparently unreliable ones (Schum, 1975). In making these judgments, jurors often rely as much (or even more) on *how* the witness presents evidence as on the content or relevance of that evidence.

Many jurors are impressed, for example, when a witness can recall a large number of details. In fact, extremely detailed testimony from prosecution witnesses is especially likely to lead to guilty verdicts, even when the details reported are irrelevant (Bell & Loftus, 1989). Apparently, when a witness gives very detailed testimony, jurors infer that the witness paid especially close attention or has a particularly accurate memory, and thus is highly credible. At first glance, these inferences might seem reasonable. However, as discussed in Chapter 5, on perception, the ability to divide attention is limited. As a result, a witness might focus attention on the crime and the criminal or on the surrounding details, but probably not on both. Hence, research suggests that witnesses who accurately remember unimportant details of a crime scene are not likely to recall accurately the criminal's facial features, height, hair color, and other identifying characteristics (Wells & Leippe, 1981).

Even witnesses' confidence about their testimony is not always a reliable guide to their credibility. In several experiments, investigators have staged crimes for subjects who then both report details of the crime and rate their confidence in the accuracy of their own reports. Frequently, their expressions of confidence are much greater than the accuracy of their reports (Hosch & Cooper, 1982). (Explanations for this overconfidence are discussed in Chapter 9, on thought.) In fact, a witness's asserted confidence is often unrelated to accuracy, particularly if violent incidents are involved (Clifford & Hollin, 1981).

What additional evidence would help to evaluate the alternatives?
Several lines of evidence should be especially helpful to judges, legislators, and voters as they decide whether to alter the rules of judicial proceedings. Which jury instructions are easily remembered and which are not? What happens when a particular juror remembers something incorrectly? Do the other jurors correct the error during the deliberations? There is evidence that they may, but not always (Hastie, Penrod, & Pennington, 1983). Can careful instructions improve the memories of witnesses? Some recent research has indicated that when witnesses are told to think very carefully about the source of their memories, they can distinguish between whether they actually saw an object or someone else mentioned it to them at a later time (Lindsay & Johnson, 1989). If these types of warnings and instructions can be perfected, an important source of memory bias in court might be eliminated.

What conclusions are most reasonable?
Many safeguards are built into the judicial system to minimize the chances that an innocent person will be falsely convicted. Nevertheless, experimental evidence does suggest that the system is far from perfect and might be improved by changes that take into account the limitations of human memory. Research on the role that memory plays in criminal proceedings may eventually lead to a court system that improves the protection of the rights and welfare of all citizens. ■

Distinguishing Between Short-Term and Long-Term Memory

Is it necessary to draw a distinction between short-term and long-term memory? Fergus Craik and Robert Lockhart (1972) have proposed that it is not. According to their **levels-of-processing model,** which we discussed earlier, how well something is remembered reflects a single dimension: the degree or depth to which incoming information is processed. From this perspective, most incoming information disappears immediately from memory because it is not attended to or processed enough to create anything more than a brief impression. However, the icons, echoes, and other sensory representations that are perceived and processed further stay in memory longer and are encoded better. Exactly how long they stay in memory depends on how elaborate the mental processing and encoding becomes—how much it is

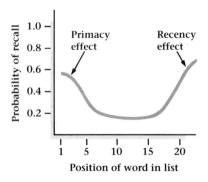

Figure 8.18
A Serial-Position Curve
The probability of recalling an item
is plotted here as a function of its
serial position in a list of items.
Generally, the first several items are
likely to be recalled (the primacy effect); items in the middle of the list
are much less likely to be recalled;
and the last several items are recalled very well (the recency effect).

thought about, organized, and related to existing knowledge. Thus, there is
no reason to distinguish between short-term and long-term memory. What
most people call short-term memory is simply that part of memory that people
happen to be thinking about at any particular time. Long-term memory is
that part of memory that people are not thinking about at any given moment.

However, other psychologists believe that it is necessary to distinguish short-
term from long-term memory. They argue that the two are qualitatively
different in the sense that they obey different laws (Cowan, 1988). For example,
we have seen that there are good reasons for believing that short-term and
long-term memory differ from each other (and from sensory memory) in
terms of encoding methods, duration, and storage capacity. ("In Review: Three
Stages of Memory" summarizes these differences. See p. 328.) Evidence that
information is transferred from short-term memory to another type of storage
also supports the view that short- and long-term memory should be considered
distinct. This evidence comes from experiments on recall and from research
on the biology of memory.

Serial-Position Curves   Look at the following list of words for thirty seconds,
then look away and try to recall as many words as you can, in any order: *bed,
rest, quilt, dream, sheet, mattress, pillow, night, snore, pajamas.* Which words you
recall depends in part on their *serial position;* that is, on where the words were
in the list, as Figure 8.18 shows. Figure 8.18 is a *serial-position curve,* which is
a plot of the chances of recalling the words in each position in a list. For the
first two or three words in a list, recall is very good, a characteristic that is
called the **primacy effect.** The probability of recall decreases for words in the
middle of the list and then rises dramatically for the last few words. The ease
of recalling words near the end of a list is called the **recency effect.**

The primacy effect occurs because the words at the beginning of a list are
rehearsed much more often than any of the other words on the list (Rundus,
1971). But why does the recency effect occur? If short-term and long-term
memory are indeed distinct, then one possibility is that, when the test is given
immediately after the list is read, the last four or five words in the list are still
in short-term memory and thus are easily recalled. On the other hand, the
beginning and the middle of the list must be retrieved from long-term memory.

To test this hypothesis, Murray Glanzer and Anita Cunitz (1966) gave a list
of words to two groups of people. They asked one group to recall the list
immediately after it was given. The second group was given a list, immediately
performed a mental arithmetic task for thirty seconds, and then tried to recall
as many words as possible. As Figure 8.19 shows, no recency effect occurred
among those in the second group. Performing the arithmetic task before
recalling the list displaced the last several words from short-term memory,
making them no more likely to be recalled than those in the middle of the
list. Since the performance of the two groups was otherwise very similar, the
normal recency effect appears to be the result of keeping the last several words
in short-term memory until the test is administered.

Biological Research   Evidence that information is transferred from short-
term memory to another, distinct system also comes from observations of
how certain brain injuries and drugs affect memory. For example, damage to
the hippocampus, which is part of the limbic system described in Chapter 3,
on biological aspects of psychology, often results in **anterograde amnesia,** a
loss of memory for any event occurring after the injury.

A striking example is the case of a man with the initials HM (Milner, 1966).
Part of his hippocampus had been removed in order to end severe epileptic

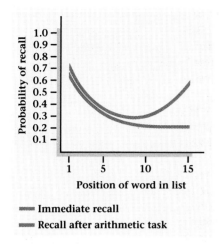

Immediate recall

Recall after arithmetic task

Source: Glanzer & Cunitz, 1966.

Figure 8.19
Separating Short-Term from Long-Term Memory
Both a primacy and a recency effect occur when subjects must recall a list immediately after the last item is presented. But when subjects perform an arithmetic task after hearing the last item, the recency effect disappears. The arithmetic task apparently displaces the words in short-term memory, leaving only those in long-term memory available for retrieval. Thus, it appears that the recency effect is based on retrieving the last several items from short-term memory.

seizures. Afterward, both his long-term memory and his short-term memory appeared normal, but he had a severe problem. He had had the operation when he was twenty-seven years old. Two years later, he still believed that he was twenty-seven. When his family moved into a new house, HM could not remember the new address or even how to get there. When he was told that his uncle had died, he grieved in a normal way. But soon afterward, he began to ask why his uncle had not visited him. Each time he was told of his uncle's death, HM became just as upset as when he was first told. In short, the surgery had apparently destroyed the mechanism that transfers information from short-term to long-term memory. HM could not learn anything new.

Another condition, **retrograde amnesia**, involves a loss of memory for events *prior to* some critical injury. Often, a person with this condition is unable to remember anything that took place in the months, or even years, before the injury. In most cases, the memories return gradually. The most distant events are recalled first, and the person gradually regains better and better memory for events leading up to the injury. Recovery is seldom complete, however, and the person may never remember the last few seconds before the injury. For example, one man received a severe blow to the head after being thrown from his motorcycle. After regaining consciousness, he claimed that he was eleven years old. Over the next three months, he gradually recalled more and more of his life. He remembered when he was twelve, thirteen, and so on—right up until the time he was riding his motorcycle the day of the accident. But he was never able to remember what happened just before the accident (Baddeley, 1982). Those final events must have been encoded into short-term memory, but apparently they were never successfully transferred into long-term memory.

Drugs, too, can disrupt the transfer of information from short-term to long-term memory. Smoking marijuana, for example, does not appear to affect the retrieval of information from short-term memory (Darley et al., 1973a). Nor does it affect retrieval from long-term memory (Darley et al., 1973b). But marijuana does inhibit the transfer of information from short-term to long-term memory.

The damage to memory in all these cases is consistent with the view that short-term and long-term memory are distinct systems; the problems are tied to an inability to transfer information from one system to the other. Psychologists do not yet know exactly how, physiologically, this transfer occurs. One view is that it involves *trace consolidation*. In other words, some physiological trace that codes the experience must be gradually transformed and stabilized if the memory is to endure.

It seems likely that trace consolidation depends primarily on the movement of electrical impulses within clusters of neurons in the brain. Information in short-term memory is erased by any event that suppresses neural activity in the brain. Physical blows to the head, anesthetics, and various types of poisoning—such as that from carbon monoxide—all suppress neural activity, and all disrupt the transfer of information from short-term to long-term memory. Similarly, transfer of information from short-term to long-term memory is often disrupted by strong but random sets of electrical impulses, such as in the electroshock treatments described in Chapter 16, on the treatment of psychological disorders. The information being transferred from short-term to long-term memory seems to be vulnerable to destruction for only a minute or so (Chorover, 1965).

Taken together, this research prompts most theorists to continue thinking of short-term memory and long-term memory as distinct systems (e.g. Crowder, 1989). They also recognize, however, that the levels-of-processing view is

A severe blow to the head can wipe out information held in short-term memory or prevent its transfer to long-term storage. Thus, after the fight, this boxer may not recall the punch that knocked him out.

relatively new and that it has inspired important lines of experimentation (Anderson, 1989). It remains to be seen whether levels-of-processing theory will ultimately provide a single, integrated view of the memory system (Nilsson, 1989).

In Review: Three Stages of Memory

Stage of Memory	Encoding	Storage	Retrieval
Sensory	Minimal; has a pure sensory quality	Great capacity, but decays after a second or so	Automatic
Short-term	Primarily acoustic	Capacity limited to 7 plus or minus 2 chunks; duration about 20 seconds unless rehearsed	Serial search
Long-term	Primarily semantic	Appears to have no limitations on capacity or duration	Strongly affected by how well new information is integrated with existing knowledge

Improving Your Memory

In psychology, as in medicine, physics, and other sciences, practical progress does not always require theoretical certainty. Even though some basic questions about what memory is and how it works resist final answers, psychologists know a great deal about how memory changes over the years and how people can improve their memories. The two keys are metamemory and mnemonics (pronounced "knee-monics").

Metamemory

How people try to remember something, and consequently how well they perform, is shaped to a great extent by what they know about memory (Cavanaugh, 1988). **Metamemory** is the name for knowledge about how your own memory works. It consists of three types of knowledge (Flavell, 1985; Flavell & Wellman, 1977).

First, metamemory involves understanding the abilities and limitations of your own memory. Preschool children are notoriously weak in this kind of understanding. They know that the way people look does not affect their memory, that noise interferes with remembering, and that it is harder to remember many items than a few. But they deny that they ever forget anything and claim that they can remember quantities of information beyond their own (or anyone else's) capacity (Flavell, Friedrichs & Hoyt, 1970). Only in the school years do children learn the limits—and the strengths—of their memories.

Second, metamemory involves knowledge about different types of tasks. For example, children learn to use different strategies for memorization when they know they will face a short-answer test, which requires recall, rather than a multiple-choice test, which for the most part requires only recognition (Horowitz & Horowitz, 1975).

Third, metamemory involves knowledge of what types of strategies are most effective in remembering new information. This aspect of metamemory is the most likely to change dramatically with age and experience (Fabricius &

Linkages: It is easy to think of the mentally retarded people described in Chapter 10, on mental ability, as utterly different from people of normal intelligence, but it is important to realize that part of the difference lies in metamemory, or the knowledge of how one's memory works. Retarded children are not as good as normal children of the same age at using mental strategies such as chunking or elaborative rehearsal to help them learn, make decisions, or solve problems. Teaching retarded children when and how to use some of these strategies can help these youngsters reach their maximum level of functioning, which may be higher than expected.

Wellman, 1983). Consider the use of rehearsal. Children as young as five *may* rehearse items when they are asked to remember something (Flavell, Beach & Chinsky, 1966; Istomina, 1975). But most five-year-olds do not use rehearsal to help them remember. They learn to rehearse in elementary school, and they refine their rehearsal strategies over the school years.

For example, suppose a group of five-year-olds and a group of ten-year-olds are asked to memorize lists of words. The two groups will probably do equally well if the word lists are short, but the older group will do much better than the younger on a long list. Why? Rote rehearsal, the younger children's main strategy, is very effective for recalling short lists. But when the older children are given a long list, they tend to combine rote rehearsal with more elaborate strategies, such as stringing the words into meaningful sentences or fitting them into different categories. Young children do not realize that rote rehearsal is ineffective with a longer list, and they continue to use it. In this sense, their metamemory is not as good as that of older children; as a result, their performance is much poorer. We know that the difference in performance is due to the strategy used, not ability, because it can be largely eliminated by teaching younger children to use a different strategy (Brown, 1975).

Investigations of metamemory have pointed out differences between retarded and normal children that are similar to those between younger and older normal children. For example, normal ten-year-olds use rote rehearsal to remember a short list of items, but elaborative rehearsal when given a long list. Retarded ten-year-olds, however, like normal five-year-olds, tend to use rote rehearsal regardless of the length of the list. Again, the difference between groups can be eliminated or substantially reduced by teaching retarded children to use a more effective strategy (Schneider, 1984). Teaching them to do so, however, is difficult, as we describe in Chapter 10, on mental abilities.

Mnemonics

People with normal memory skills (Harris & Morris, 1984) as well as brain-damaged individuals (Wilson, 1987) can benefit from **mnemonics**, which are strategies for placing information in an organized context in order to remember it. For example, to remember the names of the Great Lakes, you might remember the acronym HOMES, and the lake names will follow easily: Huron, Ontario, Michigan, Erie, and Superior. Verbal organization is the basis for many mnemonics. You can link items by weaving them into a story or a sentence or a rhyme. To help customers remember where they have parked their cars, some large garages have replaced section designations such as "A1" or "A2" with labels such as color names or months. Customers can then tie the location of their cars to information already in long-term memory—for example, "I parked in the month of my mother's birthday."

Classical Mnemonics One simple but powerful method that can be used to remember almost anything is the *peg-word system*. The first step in using this method is to learn a list of words to serve as memory "pegs." One popular list is: one is a bun, two is a shoe, three is a tree, four is a door, five is a hive, six is a stick, seven is heaven, eight is a gate, nine is a line, and ten is a hen. Once you learn such a list, you can use it to help you remember anything. For each item to be remembered, create an image or association between it and a peg word. Figure 8.20 illustrates an example suggested by Gordon Bower (1973). In general, the more novel and vivid you make the images and the better they interrelate the objects involved, the more effective they will be (Zoller et al., 1989).

Figure 8.20
The Peg-Word Technique
Suppose you want to remember to pick up milk, bread, bananas, carrots, and coffee at the store. If you use this sample list of peg words, then the first word (number one) is bun. Since milk is the first item to be remembered, you might imagine milk being poured onto a bun. For the bread, you might imagine a shoe (number two) kicking a loaf of bread.

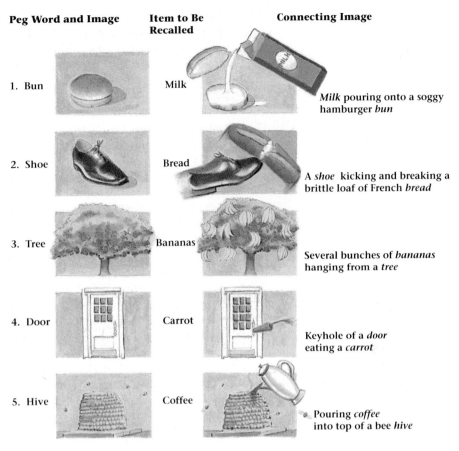

Peg Word and Image	Item to Be Recalled	Connecting Image
1. Bun	Milk	*Milk* pouring onto a soggy hamburger *bun*
2. Shoe	Bread	A *shoe* kicking and breaking a brittle loaf of French *bread*
3. Tree	Bananas	Several bunches of *bananas* hanging from a *tree*
4. Door	Carrot	Keyhole of a *door* eating a *carrot*
5. Hive	Coffee	Pouring *coffee* into top of a bee *hive*

Source: American Psychological Association, 1973.

One of the authors was introduced as a college student to another popular mnemonic. His roommate, who was known to brag a bit, said that he could remember any one hundred words if he had enough time to think about them. A bet of $100 was made, the words were read, and the author lost. It was, as they say, a real learning experience. The author's friend had used a powerful and ancient mnemonic called the *method of loci* (pronounced "low-sigh"), or the method of places. To use this method, first think about a set of familiar geographic locations. For example, if you use your home, you might imagine walking along the sidewalk, up the steps, through the front door, around all four corners of the living room, and through each of the other rooms. Next, imagine each item to be remembered in one of these locations. Whenever you want to remember a list, use the same locations, in the same order. As with the peg-word system, particularly vivid images seem to be particularly effective (Bower, 1970). For example, tomatoes smashed against the front door or bananas hanging from the bedroom ceiling might be helpful in recalling items from a grocery list.

These and other mnemonic systems share one characteristic: each requires that you have a well-learned body of knowledge (such as peg words or geographical locations) that can be used to provide a *context* for organizing incoming information (Hilton, 1986). Thus, the success of these strategies provides yet another demonstration of the importance of relating new information to knowledge already stored in memory.

Guidelines for Studying Most of the procedures discussed so far were devised for remembering arbitrary lists. When you want to remember more organized material, such as a chapter in a textbook, the same principles apply. In other words, create a context in which to organize the information. Resist the urge simply to read and reread the material. Such repetition may seem effective, because maintenance rehearsal keeps material in short-term memory. But it is not effective, no matter how much time you spend on it, for retaining information over long periods. Don't be subject to the "labor in vain effect" (Nelson & Leonesio, 1988). Instead, think about the material and elaborate it into an organized, meaningful context. What you learn will then be less subject to both proactive and retroactive interference (Reder & Anderson, 1980).

One way to create a context for new knowledge is to take the role of an instructor and try explaining to a friend the information you are learning. The lecture you create will establish an outline or framework into which you can place new information (Kellogg, 1988). In addition, your friend's questions may reveal any gaps in your memory of the material.

In addition, plan ahead and spend your time wisely. As discussed in the chapter on learning, *distributed practice* is much more effective than *massed practice* for learning new information. If you are going to spend ten hours studying for a test, you will be much better off studying for ten one-hour blocks (separated by periods of sleep and other activity) than "cramming" for one ten-hour block. By scheduling more study sessions, you will stay fresh and tend to think about the material from a new perspective at each session. This method will help you elaborate the material and remember it.

Reading a Textbook More specific advice for remembering textbook material comes from a study that examined how successful and unsuccessful college students approach their reading (Whimbey, 1976). Unsuccessful students tend to read the material straight through; they do not slow down when they reach a difficult section; and they keep going even when they do not understand what they are reading. In contrast, successful college students monitor their own performance, reread difficult sections, and periodically stop to review what they have learned before going on.

In short, effective learners engage in a very deep level of processing. They are active learners, thinking of each new fact in relation to other material. As a result, they learn to see similarities and differences among facts and ideas, and they create a context in which many new facts can be organized effectively.

Based on what is known about memory, we suggest two specific guidelines for reading a textbook. First, make sure that you understand what you are reading before moving on. Second, use the *SQ3R method,* which is one of the most successful strategies for remembering textbook material (Anderson, 1978; Frase, 1975; Rickards, 1976; Thomas & Robinson, 1972). SQ3R stands for the five activities that should be followed when you read a chapter: survey, question, read, recite, and review. These activities are designed to increase the depth to which you process the information you read.

1. **Survey** One of the best ways to begin a new chapter is by *not* reading it. Instead, take a few minutes to skim the chapter. Look at the section headings and any boldface or italicized terms. Obtain a general idea of what material will be discussed, how it is organized, and how its topics relate to one another and to what you already know. Some people find it useful to survey the entire chapter once and then survey each major section in a little more detail before reading it.

2. **Question**   Before reading each section, stop and ask yourself what content will be covered and what information should be extracted from it.
3. **Read**   Read the text, but think about the material as you read. Are the questions you raised earlier being answered? Do you see the connections between the topics?
4. **Recite**   At the end of each section, stop and recite the major points. Resist the temptation to be passive by mumbling something like, "Oh, I remember that." Put the ideas into your own words.
5. **Review**   Finally, at the end of the chapter, review all the material. You should see connections not only within a section but also among the sections. The objective is to see how the author has organized the material. Once you grasp the organization, the individual facts will be far easier to remember.

At the end, take a break. Relax. Approach each chapter fresh. Following these procedures will not only allow you to learn and remember the material better but also save you considerable time.

Lecture Notes   Lectures are very common in colleges and universities, but they are far from an ideal method for conveying information. Important details in lectures are usually remembered no better than unimportant ones (Cohen, 1989). In fact, jokes and parenthetical remarks in a lecture seem to be remembered far better than major topic statements (Kintsch & Bates, 1977).

Taking notes does help people remember what was said in a lecture (Peper & Mayer, 1978). Unfortunately, effective note-taking is not an easily acquired skill. By using what you know about memory, however, you can devise some simple strategies for taking and using notes effectively. ("In Review: Improving Your Memory" summarizes these tips for studying.)

A first step is to realize that, in note-taking, more is not necessarily better; it may be worse. Taking detailed notes of everything requires that you pay attention to everything that is said—the unimportant as well as the important—and leaves little time for thinking about the material. In fact, the thinking involved in note-taking is often more important than the writing, because it provides a framework for the facts. (This is why borrowing notes from other people is not nearly as effective as taking your own. It is difficult to read notes if you do not have the general framework of the lecture already stored in memory.) Notetakers who concentrate on expressing the major ideas in relatively few words remember more than those who try to catch every detail (Howe, 1970). In short, the best way to take notes is to think about what is being said, draw connections with other material in the lecture, and then summarize the major points clearly and concisely.

Once you have a set of lecture notes, what should you do with them? Review the notes as soon as possible after the lecture so that you can fill in missing details and decipher your scribbles. Do not wait until a few days before an exam. As discussed earlier, most forgetting from long-term memory occurs within the first few hours after learning.

When the time comes for serious study, resist the urge to read your notes passively. Use them actively, as if they were a chapter in a textbook. Look for the "big picture." Write a detailed outline. Think about how various points are related to one another and how the topics themselves are interrelated. Once you have organized the material, the details will make more sense and will be much easier to remember. Go slowly and do it well. In the end, you will save yourself considerable time by being organized and efficient the first time you go through your notes.

In Review: Improving Your Memory

Domain	Helpful Techniques
Metamemory	Analyze your strengths and weaknesses (e.g., in using rehearsal strategies). Analyze the task (e.g., does it require recall or recognition?). Choose the appropriate memory strategies.
Lists of items	Use mnemonics: Look for meaningful acronyms. Try the peg-word technique. Use the method of loci.
Textbook material	Follow the SQ3R system. Allocate your time to allow for distributed practice. Read actively, not passively.
Lectures	Take notes, but record only the main points. Think about the overall organization of the material. Review your notes as soon after the lecture as possible in order to fill in missing points.
Studying for Exams	Write a detailed outline of your lecture notes rather than passively reading them.

Linkages: Biological Bases of Memory

Where and how are memories stored?

All of our tips for improving memory will not do very much for victims of Alzheimer's disease or other people suffering from severe biological disturbances of the memory system. To understand their problems, we need to supplement the study of the mental processes involved in memory with a different level of analysis—an analysis of the physical changes that take place in the brain when people encode, store, and retrieve information.

Many scientists assume that each new experience leaves in the brain a physical representation, which is often called an *engram* or *memory trace,* but little is known about these theoretical traces. What scientists have uncovered is information about how brain cells change when memories are formed and stored during learning, and which parts of the brain are involved in the formation of memories. Recall from Chapter 3 that communication between brain cells takes place at the synapses between axons and dendrites and that this communication depends on chemicals, called neurotransmitters, released at the synapses. There is evidence that memories are embodied in at least two kinds of changes in synapses.

First, as discussed in Chapter 3, new synapses may be formed. In animals that have been exposed to a complicated environment or required to learn a new motor task, neurons in certain parts of the brain develop more synapses, which not only increase communication to other neurons but, through longer dendrites with more branches, also receive more communication from other neurons (Rosenzweig, Bennett & Diamond, 1972; Turner & Greenough, 1985). It is likely that the new synapses are involved in the storage of new memories.

Second, when a memory is stored, communication at existing synapses is improved. Evidence for this improvement comes from experiments with simple marine snails, such as *aplysia* and *hermissenda*. Rudimentary as they are, these snails can learn and have memory. By studying individual synapses in these animals while a memory is being formed, scientists discovered that simultaneously activating two inputs to a synapse makes it easier for a signal from a single input to cross the synapse later (Farley & Alkon, 1985; Goelet et al., 1986). Recent experiments indicate that similar strengthening, or *potentiation,* of synapses occurs in the hippocampus of rats (Cotman, 1988).

In the hippocampus, this strengthening occurs at synapses that use glutamate as a neurotransmitter. As discussed in Chapter 3, one type of glutamate receptor is initially activated only if the postsynaptic neuron is being stimulated by input from more than one neuron. After these multiple stimulations are repeated a number of times, this type of glutamate receptor appears to become "sensitized" so that it will respond to input from just one neuron.

Though the role of glutamate in memory formation has been most clearly demonstrated experimentally, other neurotransmitters are probably involved as well. Acetylcholine, for example, also plays a prominent role in memory, though the mechanisms are less well understood. The memory problems of Alzheimer's patients appear related to a deficiency in neurons that use acetylcholine and send fibers to the hippocampus and cortex (Coyle, Price & DeLong, 1983). Drugs that interfere with acetylcholine neurotransmission impair memory, and drugs or dietary supplements that increase the amount of acetylcholine in the brain sometimes improve memory in aging experimental animals and humans (Bartus et al., 1982). However, increasing acetylcholine levels is by no means a certain way to improve memory. Intense research is under way to better understand cholinergic systems and their relationship to memory.

Other biochemical mechanisms also appear to be involved in the storage of long-term memories in mammals. One of these mechanisms appears to involve changes in protein synthesis, because blocking synthesis of new proteins prevents the formation of new memories (Matthies, 1989).

Some of the biochemical mechanisms of memory storage used in complicated brains like those of mammals are also used by simple organisms like fruit flies. The difference is that the more complicated brains appear to have more of these mechanisms, thus giving them many more ways of accomplishing the important task of forming memories.

Where in the human brain do these changes related to memory occur? Do synapses develop and grow stronger only in special regions that store memories, or are memories distributed throughout the brain? It appears that memory involves both specialized regions for memory formation and widespread areas for storage.

In the formation of new memories, several brain regions are vital, including the hippocampus and nearby parts of the cortex, the amygdala, and the thalamus (see Figure 8.21). Damage to these subcortical areas results in anterograde amnesia (the inability to form new memories), as we described in the case of HM, who had damage in the hippocampus and surrounding areas. It is clear that the hippocampus does not actually store the memories, however, since HM retained most of his memories from the years before part of his hippocampus had been removed.

Interestingly, although patients cannot form new memories of events following hippocampal damage, they can learn *how* to do things. For example, people with hippocampal damage can learn the new skill of reading words backward in a mirror, but they do not remember the practice sessions. This suggests that various brain regions may play different roles in the formation of episodic and procedural memory.

The thalamus is also important in the early stages of the formation of new memories, although this area is less well understood than the hippocampus.

Figure 8.21
Some Brain Structures Involved
in Memory

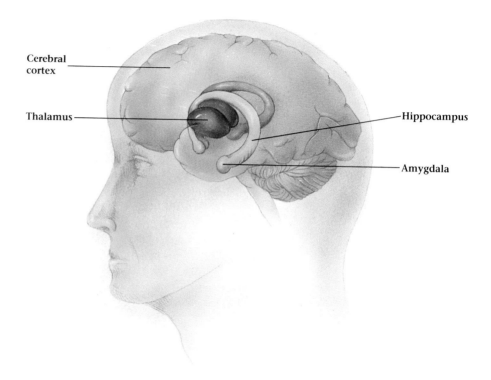

Cerebral
cortex

Thalamus

Hippocampus

Amygdala

One patient, NA, had very restricted damage to part of the thalamus because of a bizarre accident. His roommate at an air force flight school was practicing fencing when NA accidentally stepped into the path of one of his thrusts. The foil entered his right nostril and went straight into his brain. After the accident, NA no longer had any ability to form verbal memories, but there was no impairment in his formation of visual memories (Squire, 1986).

The hippocampus, amygdala, and thalamus all send nerve fibers to the cerebral cortex, and it is in the cortex that memories are probably stored. As described in Chapters 3 and 4, messages from different senses are represented in different regions of the cortex; specific aspects of an experience are probably stored near these regions. For example, short-term memory for sounds is disrupted by damage to auditory association cortex (Colombo et al., 1990). A memory, however, involves more than one sensory system. Even in the simple case of a rat remembering a maze, the experience of the maze involves visual experience, olfactory experience, specific movements, and the like. Thus, memories are both localized and distributed: certain brain areas store specific aspects of each remembered event, but many brain systems are involved in experiencing a whole event (Squire, 1986).

The more scientists learn about the physiology of memory, the more they see that no single explanation will account for all types of memory. No single structure or neurotransmitter is exclusively involved in memory formation or storage.

Future Directions

The understanding of memory has advanced considerably since Ebbinghaus began experimental investigations of the topic a hundred years ago. During the 1990s, prominent topics of debate and research are likely to include the controversy about how many types of memory there are, the value of levels-of-processing theory, and questions about how memory works in everyday life. For example, it is sensory memory that allows people to "see" many more objects from a scene than is possible from a single visual fixation (Loftus, 1985). These overlapping images, in turn, allow people to build up a mental model of the environment and of the various surrounding objects (Loftus & Hanna, 1989). Research on how this process works, and on whether disrupting it causes such disorders as dyslexia, may be important for understanding how it is that people experience and interact with the world.

Researchers are also studying the enormously elaborate autobiographical records that each individual retains over a lifetime. How people develop a memory representation of themselves, how they relate this knowledge to memories of their early childhood, and how they use knowledge about themselves as guides to choosing a mate or deciding on other actions are all questions being studied (Cohen, 1989; Klein et al., 1989; Ross, 1989).

Researchers are also investigating the causes and consequences of becoming an expert (Chi, Glaser & Farr, 1988). For example, how do physicians learn to understand the relationships between anatomical structure and the patterns seen on x-ray plates (Myles-Worsley, Johnston & Simons, 1989)? Experts store huge bodies of organized information in memory and can read x-rays easily, but students tend to make certain systematic and predictable errors. Why? Experts' mental representations of information in their field tend to change over the course of several years. Individual facts are integrated with one another, and the entire body of knowledge is organized more effectively. As a result, experts suffer less than nonexperts from both proactive and retroactive interference. Exactly how this improvement occurs remains something of a mystery. In the next chapter we look more closely at the thought processes of experts, as well as at efforts to "teach" computers to perform like experts.

Finally, there is enormous excitement about relating what is known about normal and abnormal memory. For example, if patients suffering from anterograde amnesia play a complicated game, they later have no recollection of having played the game. But some of them play the game better the next time, improving their performance at the same rate expected from a person with normal memory. One interpretation is that although these patients have no *episodic memory* of ever having played the game, their *semantic knowledge* of the game has increased (Cermak, 1989). Another possibility is that whatever caused the amnesia leaves the procedural memory system unaffected, even though it is divorced from any episodic memory. How the episodic experience is translated into semantic or procedural knowledge, and how they can become completely disassociated in memory, are unanswered questions (Shimamura & Squire, 1988).

There are, of course, many other unresolved issues. Courses on learning and memory provide an excellent starting place for learning more about the latest research, as well as for studying the basic principles of memory in more detail. Other relevant courses include cognitive psychology and experimental psychology.

Summary and Key Terms

The Memory System: An Overview

Three Types of Memory

Most psychologists agree that there are at least three basic types of memory. *Episodic memory* contains information about specific events in a person's life. *Semantic memory* contains generalized knowledge about the world. *Procedural memory* (also called skill memory) contains information about how to do various things.

Basic Memory Processes

There are three basic memory processes. *Encoding* transforms stimulus information into some type of mental representation.

Storage maintains information in the memory system over time. *Retrieval* is the process of accessing previously stored information from memory.

Other Key Terms in This Section: *acoustic codes, visual codes, semantic codes*

Three Stages of Memory

In order for information to be retained over a long time, it must pass through three stages of processing: sensory memory, short-term memory, and long-term memory. However, some information will be processed to one stage without being passed on to the next.

Sensory Memory

Capacity of the Sensory Registers

Sensory memory holds incoming stimulus information in *sensory registers* for a very brief time. It appears that sensory memory has the capacity to retain any information that can be picked up by the sense organs.

Properties of Sensory Memory

Encoding is minimal in sensory memory; sensory memories are relatively faithful representations of external stimuli. *Icons,* the representations of visual images in *iconic memory,* usually fade after about one second. *Echos,* the representations of sounds in *echoic memory,* can last up to several seconds.

Short-Term Memory

Perception transfers information from sensory memory to *short-term memory,* which is also known as working memory.

Encoding

Different memory codes can be used to encode information into short-term memory, but acoustic codes appear to dominate in most verbal tasks.

Storage

It has been found by examining people's *immediate memory span* that the capacity of short-term memory is approximately seven *chunks,* or meaningful groupings of information. Forgetting can occur because of decay or interference. Studies using the *Brown-Peterson procedure* show that information appears to decay within twenty seconds or fall prey to interference if it is not *rehearsed.* Many stimuli are represented in short-term memory not as single units but as collections of features.

Retrieval

The retrieval of information from short-term memory appears to involve an exhaustive *serial search* rather than a *parallel search.* Nevertheless, retrieval is extremely fast. For example, it takes about 1/25 of a second to retrieve a single letter from short-term memory.

Long-Term Memory

Encoding

Elaborative rehearsal is much more effective than *maintenance rehearsal* in encoding information into long-term memory. Elaborative rehearsal represents a deep level of processing, in

which the person thinks about new information, relating it to existing knowledge. Long-term memory normally involves semantic coding; that is, people tend to encode general meanings into long-term memory, not specific details. *Eidetic imagery,* or photographic memory, is found in about 5 percent of all school-age children but almost never in adults.

Storage

Hermann Ebbinghaus began investigating long-term memory and forgetting about a hundred years ago and introduced the method of *savings.* He found that (1) the rate of forgetting from long-term memory is fastest during the first several hours after learning and then slows down considerably, and (2) savings can be long-lasting. Several studies that have contrasted *decay theory* and *interference theory* suggest that most forgetting from long-term memory is due to either *retroactive interference* or *proactive interference.* Interference seems to produce forgetting not by displacing information but by impairing the ability to retrieve information from long-term memory. Thus, long-term memory appears to have virtually unlimited capacity and duration.

Retrieval

Retrieval cues help people remember things that they would otherwise not be able to recall. Their effectiveness follows the *encoding specificity principle:* cues help retrieval only if they match some feature of the information that was originally encoded. Context-dependent and state-dependent memory and the mood-congruency effect are phenomena that illustrate the role of retrieval cues.

Constructing Memories

Much prior knowledge is represented in terms of schemas. Schemas provide a basis for making inferences at the time of encoding, and they affect the way events are later recalled. Thus, people do not simply play back memories; they construct them. Partly because of these constructive processes, the memories of eyewitnesses are often distorted.

Distinguishing Between Short-Term and Long-Term Memory

The *levels-of-processing model* holds that how well information is remembered depends on how deeply it is processed and that the distinction between short- and long-term memory is unnecessary. However, several pieces of evidence suggest that short-term and long-term memory represent distinct systems. For example, although serial-position curves show both *primacy effects* and *recency effects* after immediate recall, the recency effect is eliminated if a distracting task is administered just before recall. Further evidence that information is transferred from short-term to long-term memory comes from clinical cases of *anterograde* and *retrograde amnesia.*

Improving Your Memory

Metamemory

Metamemory is knowledge about one's own memory system. This knowledge often determines the strategies people use for remembering new information. Many differences in memory performance (such as those between young and old children or between normal and retarded children) are due to the strategies used, not ability. With training, many of these differences can be eliminated.

Mnemonics

Mnemonics are devices that are used to remember things better. Two of the simplest but most powerful mnemonics are the peg-word system and the method of loci. They are useful because they provide a context for organizing material more effectively. The key to remembering textbook material is to read actively rather than passively. One of the most effective ways to do this is to follow the SQ3R method: survey, question, read, recite, and review. Similarly, to take lecture notes or to study them effectively, organize the points into a meaningful framework and think about how each main point relates to others.

OUTLINE

Thought and Language

Dr. Joyce Wallace, a New York City internist, was having trouble figuring out what was the matter with "Laura McBride," a forty-three-year-old woman. Laura reported pains in her stomach and abdomen, aching muscles, irritability, occasional dizzy spells, and general tiredness (Roueche, 1986). The doctor's initial hypothesis was iron-deficiency anemia, a condition in which the level of oxygen-carrying hemoglobin in the blood is too low. There was some evidence to support that hypothesis. A physical examination revealed that Laura's spleen was somewhat enlarged, and blood tests showed low hemoglobin and high production of red blood cells, suggesting that her body was attempting to compensate for the loss of hemoglobin. However, other tests revealed normal iron levels. Perhaps she was losing blood through internal bleeding, but a stool test ruled that out. Had Laura been vomiting blood? She said no. Blood in the urine? No. How about abnormally heavy menstrual flow? No. During the next week, as Dr. Wallace puzzled over the problem, tests showed a worsening hemoglobin situation and Laura reported more intense pain, now accompanied by cramps, shortness of breath, and severe loss of energy. Clearly, this woman's blood was becoming less and less capable of sustaining her. But if it was not actually being lost, what was happening to it? Finally, the doctor decided to look at a smear of Laura's blood on a microscope slide. What she saw—a condition called *basophilic stippling*—indicated that some poison was destroying Laura's red blood cells. What could be poisoning her? Laura spent most of her time at home, but her teenage daughters, who lived with her, were not affected at all. Wallace asked herself, "What does Laura do that the girls do not?" Well, she works with paintings, repairing and restoring them. Paint. Lead! She might be suffering from lead poisoning! When the next blood test showed a lead level seven times higher than normal, Dr. Wallace knew she was right at last.

To solve this medical mystery, Dr. Wallace relied on her ability to think, solve problems, and make judgments and decisions. She used these higher mental processes to

LINKAGES

Thought and

Language

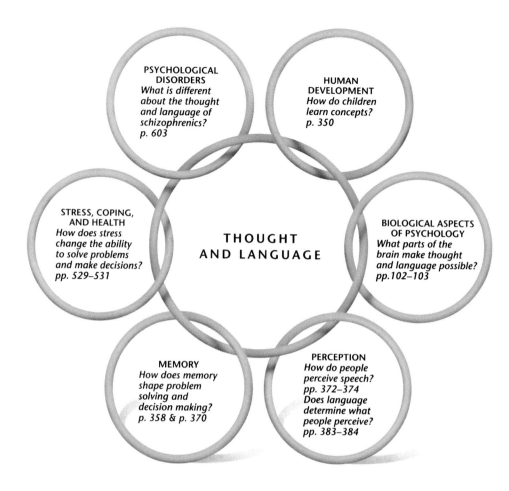

PSYCHOLOGICAL DISORDERS
What is different about the thought and language of schizophrenics?
p. 603

HUMAN DEVELOPMENT
How do children learn concepts?
p. 350

STRESS, COPING, AND HEALTH
How does stress change the ability to solve problems and make decisions?
pp. 529–531

THOUGHT AND LANGUAGE

BIOLOGICAL ASPECTS OF PSYCHOLOGY
What parts of the brain make thought and language possible?
pp. 102–103

MEMORY
How does memory shape problem solving and decision making?
p. 358 & p. 370

PERCEPTION
How do people perceive speech?
pp. 372–374
Does language determine what people perceive?
pp. 383–384

■ Look at the diagram above, which illustrates some of the relationships between the topics of this chapter, thought and language, and other chapter topics. Sensation, perception, consciousness, and memory all provide the raw materials for thinking. Thus, in this chapter we encounter again concepts introduced in the chapters on those topics—including schemas, features, and attention—and examine the role they play in thinking.

The page numbers indicate where the questions in the diagram are discussed. The diagram shows just a sampling of the linkages among topics; other linkages to the study of thought and language are noted in the diagrams in other chapters. For example, language holds particular interest to psychologists studying human development and learning. What roles are played by nature and by nurture? Is the ability to learn to speak unique to children? Do the principles of conditioning explain how children learn to speak? These and other Linkages questions are repeated in the margin near where they are discussed. ■

weigh the pros and cons of hypotheses and to reach decisions about what tests to order and how to interpret them. She also consulted with the patient and other physicians using that remarkable human capability known as language.

The work of a physician is but one example of the thinking, decision making, problem solving, and linguistic communication that occurs in an unending stream in human beings all the time. These processes are involved in everything from a restaurant customer's choice between shrimp and roast beef to a national leader's decisions about actions that could lead to nuclear war. How good are human judgments and decisions? What factors influence them? How are thoughts transformed into language? Psychologists have been studying these questions for many years. In this chapter, we introduce some of their findings and highlight the importance of their research (see the Linkages diagram). We first examine a general framework for understanding human cognition and then look at specific cognitive processes.

From Stimulus to Action: An Overview

If you think that Dr. Wallace had a difficult time diagnosing Laura's illness, consider the situation faced by the astronauts on *Apollo 13*. As they approached the moon on April 17, 1970, they heard an explosion. An oxygen tank had ruptured. Faced with potential catastrophe, the crew had to take immediate action and answer some crucial questions. Was the damage so extensive that the mission should be aborted? Which systems still operated normally? How would the damage affect the crew's ability to return to earth? The crew needed to figure out how to survive with the depleted oxygen supply and how to navigate despite the damage. To solve these problems, they relied on extensive communication with ground control. As it turned out, the moon landing had to be scrubbed, but ways were found to conserve enough oxygen to sustain the crew until they could get back to earth.

The physician's task may appear far removed from the concerns of astronauts, but the mental processes involved are surprisingly similar. In both situations, people perceive a complex pattern of incoming stimuli, evaluate that pattern, and make decisions about it. Often these processes occur so quickly and appear so complicated that the task of analyzing them may seem like trying to nail Jell-O to a tree. To understand what happens between the presentation of stimuli and the execution of responses, many psychologists study people as if they were information-processing systems.

The Human Information-Processing System

An **information-processing system** receives information, represents the information with symbols, and manipulates those representations. According to this model, information from a stimulus is passed through several stages before a response is made, and at each stage, the information is transformed (Wickens, 1991). Figure 9.1 shows these stages.

In the first stage, information about the stimulus reaches the brain by way of the sensory receptors. This stage does not require attention. In the second stage, the information must be perceived and recognized. Recall from the chapter on perception that to recognize a stimulus, people match the perceived pattern to a pattern in long-term memory. In addition, various kinds of encoding are used to hold new information in memory; thus, information is further transformed at this stage, which demands relatively little attention. In

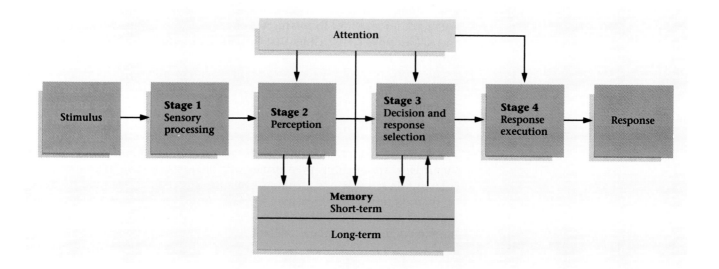

Figure 9.1
An Information-Processing Model
Information is transformed during the operations of each stage of information processing, each requiring some minimum amount of time for execution. Certain stages depend heavily on both short-term and long-term memory, and require some attention—that limited supply of mental energy that is required for information processing to be carried out efficiently.

the third stage, once the stimulus has been recognized, it is necessary to decide what to do with it. This stage demands more attention than does perception. The information may simply be stored in memory. If, however, the decision is made to take some action, a response must also be selected before the fourth stage—execution of the response—can occur. The response usually affects some part of the environment, providing new information that is "fed back" to the system to be processed.

When all goes well in this sequence, human behavior is a model of smooth efficiency. However, the complexity of information processing is apparent in the errors that can occur at various points in the sequence, for various reasons. *Mistakes* involve errors of perception and interpretation, which occur at the second stage of information processing (see Figure 9.1). When you make a mistake, you have not correctly interpreted incoming data. Even when incoming information is interpreted correctly, another type of error can occur, called a slip. *Slips* are errors in selecting and executing a response, which occur at the third and fourth stages (Norman, 1981, 1988; Reason, 1990). If you do not study enough for a test (and thus do not correctly perceive the meaning of the lectures and the textbook), most of the incorrect answers you give would be classified as mistakes. But it would be a slip if you accidentally marked (*b*) on your answer sheet when you intended to mark the nearby (*c*).

Unlike mistakes, slips usually occur when people are so highly practiced at a task that much of their behavior is being carried out automatically, without conscious thought. Under these circumstances, one stimulus may be similar enough to another to "capture" the stream of ongoing actions, producing a slip. Suppose you are about to pour syrup on a stack of pancakes, a task that requires little attention. If your orange juice pitcher is very similar to the one holding the syrup, you may slip and pour orange juice, not syrup, on your pancakes. Unfortunately, people also make far more serious slips, especially when operating equipment, with results ranging from a deleted computer file to a serious automobile, industrial, or aviation accident (Nagel, 1988).

The information-processing model points to ways of preventing different kinds of errors (Reason, 1990). For example, if a power plant is plagued by stage 1 mistakes because the amount of information coming from a vast array of instruments exceeds technicians' ability to correctly perceive all of it, the solution may be to reduce the information load or to increase the number of operators. What if the problem involves stage 3 slips such as moving the wrong control handle? In that case the best course of action may be to redesign the instruments so that controls with different functions are located farther apart, have more distinctively shaped handles, or move in opposite directions (Norman, 1988).

High-Speed Decision Making

To see what psychologists know about human information processing and how they know it, let's first consider the relatively simple case in which all four stages of information processing occur so rapidly that people may not even be conscious of making a decision. Imagine you are driving a little too fast late at night and approach a green traffic light that suddenly turns yellow. In an instant you must decide whether to apply the brakes or floor the accelerator. Here is a situation in which a stimulus is presented, a decision must be made under extreme time pressure, and then the decision must be translated into action.

Reaction Times   Psychologists have studied how people make decisions like this by examining **reaction time**, the time elapsing between the presentation of a stimulus and an overt response. Reaction time is the total time needed for all the stages shown in Figure 9.1. In fact, the study of reaction time helped generate the information-processing approach. If cognition involves distinct stages, as the information-processing approach holds, then each stage must take some time. Therefore, one should be able to infer what stages exist by examining changes in **mental chronometry**, the timing of mental events (Posner, 1978).

In a typical reaction-time task in the laboratory, a subject must rapidly say a particular word or push a certain button in response to a stimulus. Even in such simple situations, several factors influence reaction times (Wickens, 1991).

One important factor is the *complexity* of the decision. The larger the number of possible actions that might be carried out in response to a set of stimuli, the longer the reaction time. The tennis player who knows that her opponent

The sensory-perceptual, response selection, and response execution stages of information processing sometimes take place so rapidly that people are not aware of having completed them. This is especially true when, as in skilled video-game players, the task is well practiced.

Figure 9.2
Stimulus-Response
Compatibility

Suppose a cook is standing in front of the stove when a pot starts to boil over (a stimulus). The cook must rapidly adjust the appropriate dial to reduce the heat (the response). How fast the cook reacts may depend in part on the design of the stove. In the stove shown in (a), the dials are placed next to the burners, and a clear and visually compatible association determines which stimulus belongs to which response. In (b), however, this compatibility does not exist, and reaction time will be much slower. Designers of automobiles, photocopiers, and appliances pay a lot of attention to the relationship between buttons, levers, and dials and the actions that users want to accomplish with them.

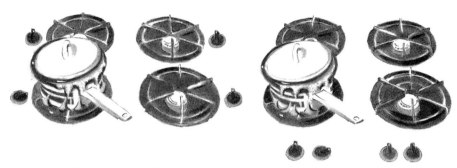

(a) A compatible relationship   **(b) An incompatible relationship**

usually serves to the same spot on the court will have a simple decision to make when the serve is made and will react rapidly. In contrast, when she faces an opponent whose serve is less predictable, her reaction will be slower because a more complex decision about which way to move is now required.

Reaction time is also influenced by *stimulus-response compatibility*. If the relationship between a set of possible stimuli and possible responses is a natural or compatible one, reaction time will be fast. If it is not, reaction time will be slower. Figure 9.2 illustrates compatible and incompatible relationships. Incompatible stimulus-response relationships are major culprits in causing slips in the use of all kinds of equipment (Norman, 1988).

Expectancy, too, affects reaction time. As noted in Chapter 5, expected stimuli are perceived more quickly than those that are surprising. Expectancy has the same effect on response time: people respond faster to stimuli that they anticipate and more slowly to those that surprise them. For example, the times that sprinters achieve in a track meet depend in part on their expectancy of the starting gun, since this affects their reaction time in getting off the starting block.

Finally, in any reaction-time task there is a *speed-accuracy tradeoff*. If you try to respond quickly, errors increase; if you try for an error-free performance, reaction time increases (Pachella, 1974). Sprinters who try too hard to anticipate the gun may have especially fast running times but may also have especially frequent false starts—errors—that disqualify them from the race.

Evoked Brain Potentials Research on reaction time has expanded understanding of decision making under time pressure, but reaction times cannot directly measure the details of what goes on between the presentation of a stimulus and the execution of a response. For example, reaction times alone cannot indicate how long it takes for response selection to begin, although there have been many ingenious efforts to make inferences about such things (Coles, 1989; Pachella, 1974). To analyze mental events and their timing more directly, psychologists turned to other methods, such as the electroencephalogram (EEG), described in Chapter 3, to detect evoked brain potentials.

The **evoked brain potential** is the small, temporary change in voltage that occurs in response to discrete events. By recording a series of responses to the same event, researchers can determine the **average evoked potential**. Figure 9.3 shows an example. Each peak reflects the firing of large groups of neurons, within different regions of the brain, at different times during the information-processing sequence. Thus, the pattern of the peaks provides information that is more precise than overall reaction time.

The first negative peak, called N100, occurs around 100 milliseconds after the stimulus. It reflects the initial, sensory, stage of information processing,

Figure 9.3
Average Evoked Potentials
The average EEG tracing produced from several trials on which a subject's name is presented. Evoked potentials are averaged in this way so that the random variations in the EEG tracings are eliminated. The result is the appearance of a negative peak (N100) followed by a large positive peak (P300).

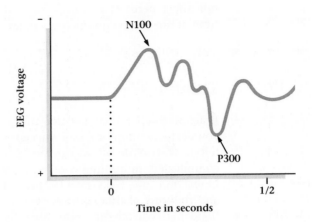

and its voltage comes directly from the primary sensory cortex (shown in Figure 3.16) that processes the stimulus. The positive peak called P300 occurs roughly 300 to 500 milliseconds after a stimulus. As described in the chapter on perception, P300 seems to signal the time at which the second, perceptual, stage of information processing is completed and the significance of a stimulus has been evaluated. Stimuli that are quite surprising, and therefore significant, produce large P300s compared to stimuli that are routine and expected (Donchin, 1981; Pritchard, 1981).

Once researchers had established the meaning of the P300, they were able to use it to study the timing of mental events (Coles, 1989). For example, Greg McCarthy and Emanuel Donchin (1979) asked people to press one of two buttons when they saw the word *right* or *left*. Sometimes the subjects were told to give a compatible response—pressing the right button in response to the word *right* and the left button in response to the word *left*. At other times, the assignment was incompatible: to press the left button in response to the word *right* and vice versa. As Figure 9.4 shows, variation in compatibility had a strong effect on reaction time, but it did not affect the timing of the P300. Therefore, the researchers concluded that stimulus-response compatibility does

Figure 9.4
Effects of Stimulus-Response Compatibility
The McCarthy and Donchin (1979) experiment on the effects of stimulus-response compatibility shows that compatibility alters the speed of response selection (stage 3 of the information-processing sequence) but does not seem to alter the timing of perception (stage 2).

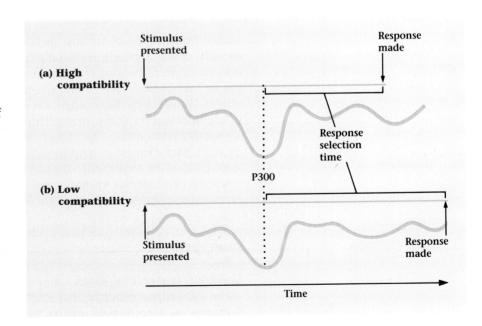

not affect perceptual processing. When incompatibility lengthens reaction time, it does so by producing a delay in *selecting* the response.

Thinking

Reaction times and evoked potentials yield clues about what is going on when you decide to stop or speed through that yellow traffic light, but they do not tell how you do it. Moreover, day after day you make decisions more complicated, more time consuming, and less well practiced than those made in reaction-time tasks. Like Dr. Joyce Wallace, the astronauts aboard *Apollo 13*, and millions of other people, you consider situations, imagine what might happen, daydream, and reminisce. In short, you think.

Decades ago, American behaviorist John Watson argued that thought is nothing more than covert speech. If thought and speech are identical, however, why do people often have such a difficult time translating their thoughts into words? This intuitive case against Watson's view was bolstered in 1947 by a rather heroic experiment by Scott Smith (Smith et al., 1947). If Watson's view were correct, Smith reasoned that paralyzing the speech muscles should disrupt thinking. Smith took a dose of curare, a potentially lethal drug that temporarily paralyzes the peripheral nervous system, including the vocal apparatus. The paralysis was so complete that Smith needed respirators to help him breathe. But despite the devastating effect of the drug on the speech system, Smith reported that he had lucid thoughts, could perform mental arithmetic, and understood what was going on around him just as well as before taking the drug. This and other experiments have made a convincing case that thought is more than covert speech.

Another way of looking at thought is to consider it as part of the information-processing model. In this view, cognitive processes involve a transformation and manipulation of information that has been encoded and stored in short-term and long-term memory. Thus, **thinking** can be defined as the manipulation of mental representations. Sometimes people perform these manipulations consciously, in order to reason, understand a situation, solve a problem, or make a decision. At other times, such as when people daydream, the manipulations are less goal-directed.

What do people have in mind—what do they manipulate—when they think? What are the mental representations used in thought? A definitive answer has eluded both philosophers and psychologists. But as its definition suggests, thought depends greatly on the memory capacities discussed in the previous chapter. Indeed, because it occurs on a moment-to-moment basis, thought can be said to take place in short-term memory, where, like rehearsal, it takes attention and effort. But thought also depends on long-term memory for most of the information that it manipulates. This information is stored in at least six forms that, together, constitute the "raw material," or basic elements, of thought. Each element is used by different people in different ways in various kinds of thinking. In the following sections we discuss these six basic elements—concepts, propositions, mental models, scripts, words, and images—and how people manipulate them in thought.

Concepts

Think about anything—dogs, happiness, sex, movies, fame, pizza—and you are manipulating concepts, one of the most basic ingredients of thought. **Concepts** are categories of objects, events, or ideas with common properties.

Concepts may be concrete and visual, such as the concepts *round* or *red*, but they may also be abstract, such as the concepts *truth* and *justice*. To "have a concept" is to recognize the properties or relationships that are shared by and define members of the category. For example, the concept *bird* includes such properties as having feathers, laying eggs, and being able to fly.

Concepts are vital to thought because they allow you to address each object or event you encounter not as something new and unique but as related to a category that is already known. Concepts make logical thought possible. If you have the concepts *whale* and *bird*, you can decide whether a whale is a bird without actually having either creature in the room with you.

Types of Concepts   Some concepts (called **artificial concepts**) can be clearly defined by a set of rules or properties such that each member of the concept has all of the defining properties and no nonmember does. For example, the concept *square* can be defined as "a shape with four equal sides and four right-angle corners." Any object that does not contain all of these features simply is not a square. To study concept learning in the laboratory, psychologists often use artificial concepts because the members of the concept can be neatly defined (Trabasso & Bower, 1968).

In contrast, try to define the concept *home* or *game*. These are examples of **natural concepts**, concepts that have no fixed set of *defining* features but instead share a set of *characteristic* features. Members of a natural concept need not possess all of the characteristic features. One characteristic feature of the natural concept *bird*, for example, is the ability to fly; but an ostrich is a bird even though it cannot fly, because it possesses enough other characteristic features of bird (feathers, wings, and the like). Having just one bird property is not enough; snakes lay eggs and bats can fly, but neither are birds. It is usually the *combination* of properties that defines a concept. Outside the laboratory, most of the concepts people use seem to be natural rather than artificial.

The boundaries of a natural concept are fuzzy, and some members of the concept are better examples of the concept than others. The more characteristic features a particular example shares, the greater its degree of belongingness

Both a space shuttle and a hot air balloon are examples of the natural concept "aircraft," but most people would probably think of the space shuttle, with its wings, as the better example. A prototype of the concept is probably an airplane.

to the concept (Rosch, 1975). A robin, a chicken, an ostrich, and a penguin are all birds. But a robin is a better example than the other three, because a robin can fly and is closer to the size and proportion of what most people, through experience, think of as a typical bird. A member of a natural concept that possesses all or most of its characteristic features is called a **prototype** or is said to be *prototypical*. Thus, the robin is a prototypical bird. Prototypes are often embodied in the *schemas*, or clusters of information that are stored in long-term memory.

Linkages: How do children learn concepts? (a link to Human Development)

Learning Concepts   Prototypes play a role in one of the most important cognitive tasks a child faces: learning the concepts he or she will need in order to think as an adult. Even adults continue to refine and elaborate concepts through experience. For example, the dimensions of the concepts *right* and *wrong* become quite complex as moral development progresses. As we suggested in the chapter on development, people learn that it is sometimes wrong to follow orders and that disobedience in the face of injustice is sometimes right.

Some natural concepts are learned by identifying prototypes and then adding less typical examples as one learns more about the concept. This *prototype-matching strategy* is reflected in the illustrations in books for very young children. The concept *house*, for example, is usually accompanied by a drawing of a square structure with windows and a chimney. An igloo is also a house, but it will take some time and experience for children to learn that.

Children also learn concepts by forming and testing hypotheses about the rules defining them. For example, a child who sees a small, square grocery store might, on the basis of its size and shape, hypothesize that the grocery store is a house. This hypothesis will be disproven when he or she calls it a house and is corrected by a parent who explains the differences between houses and stores.

The ease of concept learning can be predicted in part by the complexity of the concept and the kinds of rules involved in defining it (Bourne, 1967). The simplest classification rule is called the **affirmation**, or **one-feature**, **rule**, in which only one attribute defines the concept. A club that admits only women, for example, would be using a one-feature rule to define the concept *member*. The next easiest classification rule to learn is the **conjunctive rule**, which is based on two or more attributes and requires that all of them be present. Thus, a club might allow entry only to those who are over eighteen *and* owners of Jaguar automobiles. The **disjunctive rule** is slightly more difficult to learn. It holds that members of a concept must have one feature *or* another. Here, club membership might be restricted to those who are either over eighteen *or* know the manager.

Other Elements of Thought

Although concepts are vital to nearly all aspects of thought, several other elements are important in one kind of thinking or another.

Propositions   Thinking often involves relating concepts to one another, and these relationships are usually represented by propositions. A **proposition** is the smallest unit of knowledge that can stand as a separate assertion. Propositions, which usually take the form of a sentence, may be true or false. They may represent the relationship between a concept and a property of that concept ("Birds have wings" or "The organization is not corrupt"), or they may relate two or more concepts to each other ("Dogs chase cats" or "Rob cheated on the test").

Figure 9.5
Applying a Mental Model
Subjects looked at this figure and tried to imagine the path the marble would follow as it exited the curved tube. A majority of subjects drew the incorrect (curved) path indicated by the dotted line, rather than the correct (straight) path indicated by the dashed line (McClosky, 1983).

Mental Models   Especially when people think about physical processes and devices, the information to be manipulated may take the form of mental models. **Mental models** are clusters of propositions that represent people's understanding of how things (usually physical things) work; these models then guide their interaction with those things (Gentner & Stevens, 1983; Johnson-Laird, 1983, Norman, 1988; Rouse & Morris, 1986). For example, people may use their mental model of a computer to understand the correct sequence of commands necessary to edit, save, then retrieve a text file. This model might consist of propositions such as "Each file must have its own name," "Pressing the F10 key stores the file in a place on the disk," and the like.

Sometimes, mental models are incorrect, in spite of a lifetime of experience with the objects or devices involved. For example, look at Figure 9.5. Which path do you think the marble will take after it leaves the tube? In one study over half of the subjects, who were college students, incorrectly stated that it would follow the curved path rather than the straight one (McCloskie, 1983). The propositions that made up their mental model of how bodies move had the past motion of the ball influencing its current motion and denied one of Newton's basic laws of physics. Erroneous mental models about wind currents are also at work when people throw things out the window of a speeding car, only to have them re-enter the car through another window.

Scripts   Whereas mental models are representations in long-term memory about how physical things work, **scripts** are representations of familiar patterns or sequences of activity, usually involving people's behavior (Shank & Abelson, 1977). For example, you might have a script of the events that occur when you enter a restaurant to order dinner. Mentally reviewing that script would help you think about what you should do in a particular situation.

People also use scripts to interpret new information and events, putting them into the familiar framework of the script. Events that violate scripts may be misinterpreted or even ignored. You might, for example, step over a heart attack victim on the sidewalk because your script for walking down a city street tells you that someone lying on a sidewalk is drunk. Indeed, scripts are involved in the top-down processing (discussed in Chapter 5) that prompts people to recognize and react to expected events more quickly than to unexpected ones. If a bank customer pulls a gun and demands money, the script-violating aspect of the event—though attention-getting—may slow observers' perception of the situation and interfere with decisions on a course of action.

Words   In the everyday process of thinking, people often translate concepts, propositions, mental models, and scripts into specific words. For example, if you must figure out how long it would take three people to complete a job and you know how long it takes two people to finish it, you might find yourself silently restating the problem's concepts and their relationships into words. Much of human thought seems to be language-bound. As discussed earlier, thought can be carried out without using the muscular structures involved in language (Smith et al., 1947), but are the cognitive structures of language necessary to allow thought?

Hans Furth (1964) looked for an answer to this question by studying the cognitive abilities of deaf children. Most American deaf children are taught American Sign Language (ASL) quite early. Furth, however, studied children who were not taught any language, because their parents felt that learning ASL might retard their eventual acquisition of vocal speech and lip reading. Therefore, these children were language-deficient. Were they also deficient in thinking ability? Furth carefully tested their ability to solve problems that did not involve language, and he found no cognitive deficits. At the very least, his experiment suggests that there can be thought without language.

Furth himself offered a stronger conclusion. Thought, he said, is unhampered by the loss of language. Many psychologists dispute this view, because language seems to provide an effective organizing tool for guiding people's thinking, as well as a rich vocabulary to help give meaning to concepts (Bruner, 1964). The precise relationship between thought and language may never be fully established, mainly because there is probably no single relationship involved. The importance of language for thought varies from person to person. Thinking sometimes requires language. But in other cases, as when you think about how an acquaintance would look in glasses, thinking is based on the manipulation of images, the subject of the next section.

Using Images

Scientists have long described the importance of visual imagery in thinking about the problems they try to solve and, sometimes, these images provide critical insights (Arnheim, 1969). We mentioned in Chapter 6, for example, that a dreamed image helped solve the puzzle of how the DNA molecule is constructed. Like concepts, propositions, mental models, and scripts, visual images can be manipulated in thought (Kosslyn, 1983).

Manipulating Images   To get a better visual image of an object, you might move closer or use binoculars or a zoom lens. Do people do the same thing with mental images, and if so, how are mental images manipulated?

In the last twenty years, some very clever investigations have addressed this question. For example, Steven Kosslyn (1976) asked people to form a mental image of an object such as a cat and then asked questions about it, such as "Does it have a head?" and "Does it have claws?" The smaller the detail in question, the longer people took to answer the question, as if they were indeed mentally zooming in to the level of detail necessary to answer the question. The finer the detail required by the question, the greater the zoom and the longer the response time.

Similarly, Roger Shepard and Jacqueline Metzler (1971) found evidence that people can imagine the rotation of objects in their minds. Their subjects viewed pairs of objects like those shown in Figure 9.6. Their task was to decide if the two objects were identical or mirror images of each other. Each addition to the difference in the angular orientation of the two objects added a constant amount to the time they took to make the decision. Thus, it looked as if the subjects imagined the rotation of one of the objects at a constant rate until it was lined up in the same orientation as the other.

The need for mental rotation contributes to the problems people sometimes have if they are using a map and driving south in an unfamiliar city. Their visual image of the north-up map must be mentally rotated—like the objects in Shepard and Metzler's study—so that left and right on the map correspond with left and right as they look forward at the road. Designers of electronic maps for automobiles and aircraft are considering ways of allowing the map to rotate so that the direction one is heading is always "up" on the map (Wickens, Aretz & Harwood, 1989).

Though we cannot yet say exactly what goes on when people think by manipulating images, the information obtained so far suggests that, like other mental events, imagining involves its own systematic chronometry. Moreover, the manipulations performed on images are very similar to those that would be performed on the objects themselves (Kosslyn, 1983).

Figure 9.6
Imagining the Rotation of Objects
Subjects were asked to decide if two objects in pairs like these were identical or not. The time needed to decide about each pair increased with the amount of rotation necessary to put one object in the same orientation as the other. Apparently, to answer the question, the subjects imagined the rotation of the objects. Here, the objects in (a) are identical; those in (b) are different.

(a)

(b)

Source: Shepard, 1971.

Maps and Spatial Thinking Even people who do not usually use images in most of their thinking may employ them to navigate through a particular environment. Especially when that environment is new, people tend to imagine specific objects and landmarks as they try to go from one place to another. Finally, after gaining a lot of experience in the environment, people acquire an overall *cognitive map* of it.

Useful as they are, cognitive maps are not accurate copies of the environment; they include systematic distortions. One distortion results from *rectangular bias*, a tendency to impose a rectangular north-south-east-west grid on the environment. For example, when asked to draw a map of Paris, most Parisians straighten out the bends of the Seine River in an effort to make it conform more closely to an east-west flow (Milgram & Jodelet, 1976). The rectangular bias also distorts the sense of relative locations. If you were asked where Reno, Nevada, is with respect to San Diego, California, you would probably answer, northeast (Stevens & Coupe, 1978). After all, Nevada is east of California, and Reno is north of San Diego. But because southern California ''bends'' to the east, Reno is in fact northwest of San Diego.

In other words, people tend to mentally simplify complex material in the world. Most of the time, this simplification is efficient and useful. But the costs humans must pay are certain systematic biases, such as false perceptions guided by top-down processes and expectancies, distortions of memory, and distortions of spatial thinking.

Reasoning

Whatever the elements of thought, the degree to which people achieve the goals of thinking depends on how they manipulate those elements. If they manipulate them to reach a valid conclusion, then they are said to be rational. If someone tells you that negotiating with terrorists only leads to more terrorism, would you agree? To determine your response, you would want to collect some evidence, but you would also need to exercise your powers of reasoning. **Reasoning** is the process by which people evaluate and generate arguments and reach conclusions. (The ''Thinking Critically'' section in each chapter of this book is designed to highlight this vital process.)

Rules of Logic The mental procedures that yield a valid conclusion are known as **logic**. At the core of the study of logic lie the rules for evaluating **syllogisms**, which are arguments made up of two propositions, called *premises*, and a conclusion based on those premises. For example:

All bats are mammals. No mammals lay eggs. Therefore, bats do not lay eggs.

A syllogism like this is valid because both the premises and the rules of logic are correct. Consider in contrast the syllogism:

All gun owners are people. All criminals are people. Therefore, all gun owners are criminals.

This syllogism illustrates a violation of a general principle of logic, namely, that if ''All A's are B'' and ''All C's are B,'' it does *not* follow that ''All A's are C.''

Now consider the following syllogism:

All psychologists are brilliant. The authors of this text are psychologists. Therefore, the authors of this text are brilliant.

Do you agree? The conclusion does follow logically from the premises, but you are probably a little uncertain about our brilliance. In other words, although the logic of these statements is impeccable, the conclusion remains at odds with your general knowledge of the world, because the first premise is false. Obviously, reasoning depends on both knowledge of the world and an understanding of what is logical. If premises are false, you should reject a conclusion flowing from them as invalid, even if the logic of the argument is sound.

In addition to the rules of logic, scholars have also defined rules for determining the probability of events and procedures for determining which of several possible courses of action will yield the result most satisfying to the decision maker. All of these rules amount to prescriptions for how people *should* think, but they don't always describe how people actually do think. Instead, people's thoughts may be biased by beliefs, or follow mental heuristics.

Beliefs and Wishes   People often accept a conclusion even when an argument is illogical if the conclusion agrees with their attitudes. For example, consider the following syllogism:

America is a free country. In a free country, all people have equal opportunity. Therefore, in America all people have equal opportunity.

William McGuire (1960) found that people's belief in the validity of conclusions like this was based only in part on logical thinking. To a large extent, their reaction was influenced by the degree to which they believed that the conclusion was true, independent of the truth of the premises or the logic that followed from those premises. In court, prosecutors may be frustrated by this tendency when the defendant is a member of the clergy or a sweet elderly person. The jury may remain unpersuaded by the prosecution's logically sound arguments based on true premises, because the logical conclusion (that a sweet old woman poisoned her sister) is at odds with the jury members' schemas about such people and their scripted beliefs about how the world operates. In other words, the conclusions that people reach are based on both logical and wishful thinking (Evans, Barston & Pollard, 1983).

"No woman can be an effective combat soldier; this person is a woman, therefore, she should not be a combatant." The logic of this syllogism is correct, but because the first premise is wrong, legislators and military policymakers who base their decisions on this logic alone will reach erroneous conclusions. Indeed, women are excluded by law and regulation from military units likely to see combat, but Captain Linda Bray, commander of a military police unit that participated in the 1989 invasion of Panama unexpectedly found herself in a firefight with Panamanian defense forces. She acquitted herself well, thus raising anew the debate over the role of women in combat.

Heuristics Even when people are not swayed by specific wishes, beliefs, or needs, the laws of logical thinking do not always provide a good description of how they actually think. However intelligent, expert, or objective people are, they sometimes violate these laws in their everyday thinking. Much thinking seems to be based instead on **heuristics**, which are mental shortcuts or rules of thumb (Kahneman, Slovic & Tversky, 1982; Tversky & Kahneman, 1974).

Suppose, for example, that you are about to leave home in the morning but cannot find your watch. You might search for the watch in every possible location, room by room. This approach involves using an **algorithm**, which is a systematic procedure that cannot fail to produce a solution. To obtain the same outcome more quickly, however, you are likely to search first in the places where your past experience suggests the watch might be; this approach is a heuristic. Similarly, in deciding which political candidates to vote for, your rule of thumb might be to support all those in a particular party—a heuristic—rather than researching the views of each individual. People use heuristics like these because they are easy and frequently work well. However, heuristics can also bias cognitive processes and cause errors. For example, many who vote for everyone on the election ticket of a particular party may later discover that they got the president they wanted, but they also got a local sheriff whose views they despise.

Heuristics often guide people's judgments about what events are probable or what hypotheses are likely to be true. Amos Tversky and Daniel Kahneman have described three heuristics that people seem to use intuitively to make many of these judgments (Kahneman, Slovic & Tversky, 1982).

1. *The anchoring heuristic* People use the **anchoring heuristic** when they estimate the probability of an event not by starting from scratch but by adjusting an earlier estimate. In other words, people judge how likely it is that, say, they will be mugged in a given city by using new information to alter their initial impression. This strategy sounds reasonable, but the starting value biases the final estimate. Once people have fixed a starting point, their adjustments of the initial judgment tend to be insufficient. It is as if they drop a mental anchor at one hypothesis or estimate and then cannot move very far from that original judgment. Thus, if a person assumes that the probability of being mugged in New York is 90 percent and is then told that the figure is closer to 1 percent, he or she may only reduce the estimate to 80 percent. Similarly, impressions of a new acquaintance (or of a suspect in a trial) are molded by the effect of anchoring. As we discuss in Chapter 17, on social cognition, initial impressions—whether good or bad—are not easily shifted by later evidence.

2. *The representativeness heuristic* The **representativeness heuristic** involves judging the probability that a hypothesis is true or that an example belongs to a certain class of items by focusing on the similarities between the example and a larger class of items and then determining whether the example represents essential features of the class. For example, suppose you encounter a man who is tidy, small in stature, wears glasses, speaks quietly, and is somewhat shy. If asked whether this person is likely to be a librarian or a farmer, what would you say? Tversky and Kahneman (1974) found that most of their subjects chose *librarian*. But the chances are that this answer would be wrong. It is true that the description is more similar to the prototypical librarian than to the prototypical farmer. But because there are many more farmers in the world than librarians, there are probably more farmers than librarians who match this description; therefore, a man matching this description is more likely to be a farmer than a librarian. In

In Review: Tools of Thought

Tool	Definition	How It Is Used
Concepts	Categories of objects, events, or ideas with common properties	Concepts are related to each other through propositions.
Propositions	Smallest unit of knowledge that can stand as a separate assertion	Propositions are usually evaluated as to truth or falsity.
Syllogisms	Combination of two propositions (premises) and a conclusion	The conclusion is valid if it is logically consistent with correct premises.
Mental Models	Clusters of propositions that represent people's understanding of how things work	Mental models guide people's interactions with things; they may be correct or biased.
Scripts	Mental representations of a typical sequence of activity, usually involving people's behavior	Scripts may be used to interpret what will happen or is happening in familiar situations; a component of top-down processing.
Words	Basic unit of language involved in much of our thinking	Words can be used to express concepts, propositions, syllogisms, mental models, and scripts.
Images	Visual mental representations of physical objects, events, and scenes	Images can be manipulated—rotated, expanded, and examined—to help thinking about spatial problems like those involved in navigation. Cognitive maps are images and may be biased.
Heuristics	Mental shortcuts or rules of thumb that help solve problems and reduce mental effort	Anchoring, representativeness, or availability heuristics can provide quick answers that are often correct, but may sometimes be biased.
Algorithms	Formal procedures that will eventually offer a solution to a problem if enough time and effort are spent	Algorithms are often avoided in thinking because they are inefficient.

fact, almost any set of male physical features is more likely to belong to a farmer than a librarian.

Similarly, one study found that if a patient has symptoms that are similar to a common disease but are even more representative of a very rare one, physicians are likely to diagnose the rare disease (Christenssen-Szalanski &

Bushyhead, 1981). On the basis of probability alone, it is more likely that the patient has the common disease, but the physicians used the representativeness heuristic in reaching a diagnosis. When using this heuristic, people ignore the overall probabilities and focus instead on what is representative or typical of the available evidence.

3. *The availability heuristic* Even when people use probability information to help them judge group membership or to assess a hypothesis, they may employ a third heuristic that can bias their thinking. The **availability heuristic** involves judging the probability of an event or hypothesis by how easily the hypothesis or examples of the event can be brought to mind. Thus, people tend to choose the hypothesis or alternative that is most mentally "available," much as you might choose which sweater to wear on the basis of which is on top in the drawer.

This shortcut tends to work well because, among other reasons, what people remember most easily *are* frequent events or hypotheses. However, the availability heuristic can lead to biased judgments, especially when mental availability and actual frequency fail to correspond. For example, television news reports showing the grisly aftermath of gangland shootings and airline crashes may make these relatively rare events so memorable that people avoid certain cities or refuse to fly because they overestimate the frequency of crime or the probability of a crash (Slovic, 1984).

These three heuristics represent only some of the strategies that people use intuitively, and they create only some of the biases and limitations evident in human reasoning. (See "In Review: Tools of Thought" for a summary of the structures and transformations involved in thinking.) We discuss other biases and limitations in the following sections, as we take a closer look at two common goals of thinking: problem solving and decision making.

Problem Solving

Four characteristics describe problem solving: (1) where you are (the problem) is not where you would like to be (the solution); (2) the path between the problem and its solution is not obvious; (3) often you must spend considerable effort to understand, or *diagnose*, the problem; and (4) to diagnose or eliminate the problem, you may need to form several hypotheses about which path is correct and then test those hypotheses. A physician like the one described at the beginning of this chapter, for example, must relate information about a patient's symptoms to knowledge about the patient's medical history and possible diseases, generate hypotheses about the patient's illness, review test results, try various treatments, and observe the effects on the patient. The many unnecessary replacements of automobile parts, unnecessary tests performed in hospitals, and all-too-frequent misdiagnoses testify to the fact that people's problem-solving skills often leave much to be desired.

Problems in Problem Solving

Problem solving involves understanding the problem (diagnosis), devising a plan to solve the problem, executing the plan, and evaluating the results (Polya, 1957). Many problem-solving difficulties occur at the start, with diagnosis. There are many strategies for diagnosis. In the case at the beginning of the chapter, for example, Dr. Wallace systematically formulated hypotheses, tested them, and used the results to reject incorrect options until a correct diagnosis was reached. This algorithm may sound simple and foolproof, but people who follow it may encounter frustrating difficulties that push them to adopt heuristic approaches that may be little better than trial and error. In the following sections we describe four of these pitfalls in problem solving.

Multiple Hypotheses   Often, people begin to solve a problem with only a vague notion of which hypothesis to test. For example, there may be a dozen reasons why a car will not start. Which of these hypotheses should be tested and in what order?

People seem to have a difficult time entertaining more than two or three hypotheses at one time (Mehle, 1982). The limited capacity of short-term memory, discussed in Chapter 8, may be part of the reason. As a result, the correct hypothesis is often neglected. Which hypothesis a person considers may depend not on which is most likely but on the availability heuristic. In other words, the particular hypothesis considered may be one that is remembered most readily, which may not be the best hypothesis at all. Several characteristics might make one hypothesis easier to remember than others—for example, its simplicity, emotional content, and how recently it was experienced (Tversky & Kahneman, 1974). Thus, the auto mechanic troubleshooting your car might diagnose the problem as the same as one encountered the day before, simply because that hypothesis is most easily brought to mind.

Mental Sets   Sometimes people are so blinded by one hypothesis or strategy that they continue to apply it even when better alternatives should be obvious (a clear case of the anchoring heuristic at work). An example devised by Abraham Luchins (1942) is shown in Figure 9.7. The object of each problem in the figure is to use three jars with specified capacities to obtain a certain amount of liquid. For example, in the first problem you are to obtain 21 quarts by using three jars that have capacities of 8, 35, and 3 quarts, respectively. The solution is to fill jar B to its capacity, 35 quarts, and then use its contents to fill jar A to its capacity of 8 quarts, leaving 27 quarts in jar B. Then pour liquid from jar B to fill jar C to its capacity twice, leaving 21 quarts in jar B [$27 - (2 \times 3) = 21$]. In other words, the solution is to apply the equation $B - A - 2C$. Now solve the remaining problems.

If you went through the problems in Figure 9.7, you found that a similar solution worked each time. But what happened with problem 7? If you are like most people, you did not notice that it has a simpler solution (namely, $A + C$). Instead, you succumbed to a **mental set**, the tendency for old patterns of problem solving to persist (Sweller & Gee, 1978). In the Luchins jar problem, the mental set consists of a tendency to stick with a strategy or solution that worked in the past. Figures 9.8 and 9.9 show that a mental set may also restrict your perception of the problem itself.

Yet another restriction on problem solving may come from experience with objects. Once people become accustomed to using an object for one type of function, they may be blinded to other ways of using it. Thus, experience may produce **functional fixedness**, a tendency to avoid using familiar objects in creative but useful ways. Figure 9.10 illustrates an example.

The Confirmation Bias   Anyone who has suffered through a series of medical tests knows that diagnosis is not a one-shot decision. Instead, like Dr. Wallace, the physician chooses an initial hypothesis on the basis of observed symptoms and then orders further tests or evaluates additional symptoms to confirm or refute the hypothesis. This process may be distorted by the *confirmation bias:* humans have a strong bias to confirm rather than to refute

---

Linkages: How does memory shape problem solving? (a link to Memory)

Figure 9.7
The Luchins Jar Problem
The problem is to obtain the volume of liquid shown in the first column by filling jars with the capacities shown in the next three columns. Each line represents a different problem. Such problems have been used to show that people often fall prey to mental sets that prevent them from using the most efficient solution.

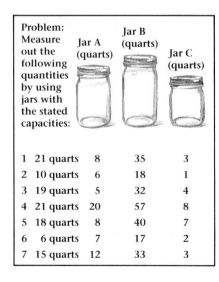

Problem: Measure out the following quantities by using jars with the stated capacities:	Jar A (quarts)	Jar B (quarts)	Jar C (quarts)
1 21 quarts	8	35	3
2 10 quarts	6	18	1
3 19 quarts	5	32	4
4 21 quarts	20	57	8
5 18 quarts	8	40	7
6 6 quarts	7	17	2
7 15 quarts	12	33	3

Figure 9.8
The Nine-Dot Problem
The task is to draw no more than four lines that run through all nine dots on the page without lifting your pencil from the paper. Figure 9.9 shows two ways of going beyond constraints to solve the problem.

the hypothesis they have chosen, even in the face of strong evidence against that hypothesis. In other words, people are quite willing to perceive and interpret data that support a hypothesis, but they tend to ignore information that is inconsistent with it (Gorman, 1986; Levine, 1966). Thus, the confirmation bias may be seen as a form of the anchoring heuristic, in that it involves reluctance to abandon an initial hypothesis.

The 1979 accident at a nuclear reactor at Three Mile Island, in Pennsylvania, provides a dramatic example of confirmation bias (Adams, 1989; Rubinstein & Mason, 1979). A loss of coolant flowing to one of the reactors threatened to expose the radioactive fuel core and trigger a meltdown. The control-room operators could have formed either of two hypotheses about what was wrong inside the reactor. Either the water pressure in the reactor core was too high, creating the danger of an explosion, or it was too low, a condition that could lead to a meltdown. Several symptoms supported the correct hypothesis (the pressure was indeed low), but one defective meter indicated that the pressure was too high. During the first few minutes of the crisis, the operators paid attention only to the faulty indicator. Because they had used that meter to establish their original hypothesis of high pressure, they failed to appreciate symptoms of low pressure until after they had shut down an emergency pump that would have restored badly needed coolant. Their error made the situation far worse than it might have been (Adams, 1989; Rubinstein & Mason, 1979; Wickens, 1991).

What is the cause of the confirmation bias? One possibility is that mental effort is required to abandon old hypotheses and construct new ones and that people tend to avoid complex mental operations (Rasmussen, 1981; Shugan, 1980). This *cognitive laziness* may discourage attention to alternative hypotheses. Furthermore, to admit that one is wrong may threaten self-esteem. This *cognitive conceit* (Fischoff, 1977) may lead people to search for and find confirming evidence and ignore contradictory evidence.

Ignoring Negative Evidence   Often, what does not happen can be as important as what does happen. For example, when troubleshooting a car, a symptom of headlight failure might lead you to hypothesize that the battery is low. But if this were the case, other battery-powered equipment should also have failed. The fact that these symptoms are not present is important in disconfirming your original hypothesis. The absence of symptoms can provide important evidence for or against a hypothesis. Compared with symptoms that are *present*, however, symptoms or events that do not occur are less likely to be noticed and observed (Hunt & Rouse, 1981). People have a difficult time using the absence of symptoms to help eliminate hypotheses from consideration (Ashcraft, 1989).

Improving Problem-Solving Skills

How can you improve your ability to solve problems? Are there any easily taught techniques that will give you the problem-solving skill of an expert? In the following sections, we try to answer these questions.

Avoiding Pitfalls in Reasoning   Perhaps the most obvious step that you can take to improve your problem solving is to avoid errors in syllogistic reasoning. Imagery can help (Levine, 1988). The pictures shown in Figure 9.11, called *Venn diagrams*, are one example. To solve a syllogism, you can draw the Venn representation of the two premises and see whether the conclusion is consistent with both. Suppose you had to figure out the truth

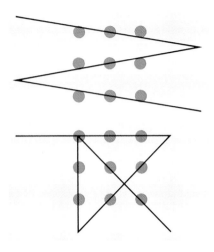

Figure 9.9
Two Creative Solutions to the Nine-Dot Problem
Many people find such puzzles difficult because they fail to break out of mental sets that create artificial constraints on the range of solutions: here, the mental sets involve the tendency to draw within the frame laid out by the dots and to draw through the middle of each dot.

of the following syllogism: All artists are beekeepers. Some beekeepers are chemists. Therefore, all artists are chemists. Venn diagrams would show that this conclusion is false. More concrete images may also be used. Phillip Johnson-Laird and Mark Steedman (1978) found that subjects improved their performance on such problems by imagining sets of people who were dressed as beekeepers, artists, chemists, or some combination (e.g., people wearing berets and holding a brush, with bees flying around them). Another study found that syllogisms were easier to solve if their premises involved concepts that could be visualized easily (like beekeepers) rather than those that could not (like truth) (Clemant & Falmagne, 1986).

Other weaknesses in problem solving are more difficult to remedy. Psychologists have reasoned that it should be possible to train people not to fall prey to the biases that impair problem solving—to *debias* people, as Baruch Fischoff (1982) put it. Attempts to do this have produced some modest improvements in problem solving. For example, in one study, cautioning people against their tendency to anchor on a hypothesis reduced the magnitude of the confirmation bias and increased their openness to alternative evidence (Lopes, 1982).

Adopting Better Strategies   Many anecdotal reports over the years have suggested that an incubation strategy may aid problem solving. **Incubation** involves putting the problem aside for a while and turning to some other mental activity while the problem "incubates," perhaps at a subconscious level, as described in the chapter on consciousness. For example, French mathematician J. H. Poincaré claimed that his insights into Fuchsian functions occurred suddenly as he was stepping onto a bus (Poincaré, 1913). However, it appears that incubation aids problem solving only if the incubation period is preceded by lengthy preparation (Silviera, 1971). Incubation may help mainly by allowing mental sets and other biases to dissipate, permitting a fresh approach.

Life is full of problems, but the chances of solving them efficiently improve when people adopt systematic and logical approaches.

Figure 9.10
An Example of Functional Fixedness
The task is to fasten together two strings that are hanging from the ceiling but are out of reach of each other. Several tools are available in the room. The solution is to take a heavy tool, such as a pair of pliers, attach it to one of the strings, and swing it like a pendulum until that string can be reached while holding the other. The solution is not easily arrived at, however, because most people fixate on the usual function of the pliers as a hand tool rather than hypothesizing their role as a pendulum weight. Moreover, people are more likely to use the pliers if the tools are scattered around the room rather than neatly contained in a toolbox. Apparently, when the pliers are in a toolbox, their function as a tool is emphasized, and the mental set becomes nearly impossible to break.

A heuristic known as decomposition may also help problem solving. **Decomposition** consists of breaking a problem into smaller elements. If you must write a long term paper, for example, you might decompose the problem into a series of smaller, more manageable subproblems, such as finding appropriate references, writing an outline, creating a first draft, and so on.

Finally, if a problem seems unsolvable, it may be worthwhile to go back and reformulate it (Ashcraft, 1989). You might convert the problem into different forms—mental movies, pictures, or arithmetic statements.

Imitating the Expert Scientists, engineers, physicians, maintenance technicians, auto mechanics, and labor negotiators, to name just a few, are well-paid because of their expertise in solving problems. It is amazing how quickly a computer expert, for example, can find and solve a programming problem that has stumped us for hours. What do these experts bring to a situation that a novice does not? Experience and knowledge, for one thing. As a result, experts frequently proceed by looking for similarities between current and past problems. More than novices, they can relate new information and new

Figure 9.11
Venn Diagrams
These diagrams represent three different but logically correct interpretations of the statement "Some A's are not B's." This statement is an equally valid description of "Some Democrats are not New Yorkers," which is represented by syllogism 1; "Some federal employees are not senators," which is represented by syllogism 2; or "Some Albanians are not Chinese," which is represented by syllogism 3. Typically, however, people assume that only a diagram like the one illustrating syllogism 1 represents the statement and therefore assume that the statement also implies "Some B's are not A's."

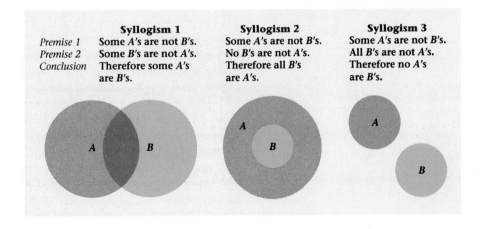

	Syllogism 1	Syllogism 2	Syllogism 3
Premise 1	Some A's are not B's.	Some A's are not B's.	Some A's are not B's.
Premise 2	Some B's are not A's.	No B's are not A's.	All B's are not A's.
Conclusion	Therefore some A's are B's.	Therefore all B's are A's.	Therefore no A's are B's.

experiences to past experiences and existing knowledge (Larkin et al., 1981; Ortega, 1989). This strategy produces one of the most important general differences between the expert and the novice: the ability to use existing knowledge to organize new information into chunks, as described in the chapter on memory.

By chunking many elements of information into a smaller number of more meaningful units, experts apparently can visualize problems more clearly and efficiently than novices. Experts can use their experience as a guide because they tend to perceive the similarity between new and old problems more deeply than novices (Chi, Feltovitch & Glaser, 1981; Hardimann, Dufresne & Mestre, 1989). Specifically, experts see the similarity of underlying principles, while novices perceive similarity only in superficial features. As a result, experts can more quickly and easily apply these principles to solve the new problem.

In one study, for example, expert physicists and novice physics students sorted physics problems into groups (Chi et al., 1981). The novices grouped together problems that looked similar (such as those involving blocks lying on an inclined plane), while the experts grouped together problems that could be solved by the same principle (such as Newton's second law of motion). Similar differences were found in how experienced versus novice mathematics students sorted word problems (Novick, 1988).

Are there shortcuts to achieving expertise? After carefully reviewing the literature, Richard Mayer (1983) concluded that claims of "instant" shortcuts to expertise must be viewed with some skepticism. The most important characteristic of any expert problem solver, he noted, is extensive knowledge in the problem area. Knowledge allows the expert to perceive the elements of a problem as a chunk, to understand the relations between problem elements, and to draw on past experience. In one study, teaching students to use general strategies, such as diagrams, did improve their ability to solve mathematical problems—but only after the students had mastered a good deal of mathematical knowledge (Schoenfeld, 1979). In short, there seems to be no substitute for putting in the hard work needed to acquire knowledge. Once you possess this knowledge, however, you can learn shortcuts that will allow you to take maximum advantage of it.

Limitations of Expertise   Although experts are often better problem solvers than novices, expertise also carries a danger: using analogies to past experience can lead to the traps of functional fixedness and mental sets. As a Zen proverb says, "In the mind of the beginner there are many possibilities; in the mind of the expert, few." The top-down, knowledge-driven processes, described in the chapter on perception, can bias you toward seeing what you expect or want to see. Thus, these processes can prevent you from seeing a problem in new and different ways. Indeed, there is a thin line between using past experience and being trapped by it.

The benefits of experience may also be limited because feedback about a solution is delayed (Brehmer, 1981; Dawes, Faust & Meehl, 1988). Often, experts receive information about the correctness of a proposed solution only long after they have forgotten how they came to that answer. As a result, they cannot use the feedback to improve problem-solving methods. Furthermore, the confirmation bias may prevent them from appreciating that a proposed solution was incorrect (Fischoff & Slovic, 1980).

In short, experience alone does not ensure excellence at problem solving, and practice may not make perfect. A book by Christopher Cerf (1984) gives further reason for skepticism; it details fantastically erroneous predictions by experts. Table 9.1 shows a few of them.

Table 9.1
Some Expert Opinions

Experts typically have a larger store of knowledge about their realm of expertise, but even confidently stated opinions based on this knowledge can turn out to be incorrect, as these examples from Christopher Cerf's *The Experts Speak* (1984) clearly show.

On the possibility of painless surgery through anesthesia:
"'Knife' and 'pain' are two words in surgery that must forever be associated. . . . To this compulsory combination we shall have to adjust ourselves." (Dr. Alfred Velpeau, professor of surgery, Paris Faculty of Medicine, 1839)

On the hazards of cigarette smoking:
"If excessive smoking actually plays a role in the production of lung cancer, it seems to be a minor one." (Dr. W. C. Heuper, National Cancer Institute, 1954)

On the stock market (one week before the disastrous 1929 crash that wiped out over $50 billion in investments):
"Stocks have reached what looks like a permanently high plateau." (Irving Fisher, professor of economics, Yale University, 1929)

On the prospects of war with Japan (three years before the December 1941 Japanese attack on Pearl Harbor):
"A Japanese attack on Pearl Harbor is a strategic impossibility." (Major George F. Eliot, military science writer, 1938)

On the value of personal computers:
"There is no reason for any individual to have a computer in their home." (Ken Olson, president, Digital Equipment Corporation, 1977)

On the concept of the airplane:
"Heavier-than-air flying machines are impossible." (Lord Kelvin, mathematician, physicist, and president of the British Royal Society, 1895)

Problem Solving by Computer

In view of all of the weaknesses of human problem solving, some people hope that computers can take over some of the thinking for humans. (For a summary of our discussion of human problem solving, see "In Review: Solving Problems.") Already, some problems are being solved by **expert systems**, which are computer programs that solve very specific problems, like diagnosing infectious diseases (Shortcliffe, 1983) or reasoning about the location of mineral deposits in the earth or the wisdom of an investment. Some of the most effective expert systems being developed today are in the area of medical diagnosis. These systems are designed as "consultants" that ask questions about the patient and, by sharing their reasoning, help physicians to correctly diagnose infectious diseases.

How do expert systems work? A problem-solving computer needs two basic elements: (1) an extensive knowledge base about the area in which problems are to be solved; and (2) an *inference engine*, a set of procedures for using the facts in the knowledge base to solve problems (Madni, 1988). Computers, like people, can use two main types of procedures for problem solving: algorithms and heuristics. As noted earlier, algorithms are precise, step-by-step statements of logical and computational operations that guarantee a solution; heuristics provide mental rules of thumb that work often, but not always.

Computers are good at following algorithms, because algorithms do not require much flexibility. Indeed, many problems, like computing statistical tests, are best handled by algorithms, and therefore by computers. Algorithms are not terribly efficient, however. For example, an algorithm for a chess-playing computer might first consider all possible moves, then all possible

In Review: Solving Problems

Steps	Pitfalls	Remedies
Define the problem	Inexperience: the tendency to see each problem as unique.	Gain experience and practice in seeing the similarity between present problems and previous problems.
Form hypotheses about solutions	Availability heuristic: the tendency to recall the hypothesis or solution that is most available to memory, most recently experienced, or the simplest.	Force yourself to entertain different hypothesis.
	Anchoring heuristic, or mental set: the tendency to anchor on the first solution or hypothesis and not adjust your beliefs in light of new evidence or failures of the current approach.	Break the mental set, stop, and try a fresh approach.
Test hypotheses	The tendency to ignore negative evidence.	In evaluating a hypothesis, consider the things you should see (but don't) if the hypothesis were true.
	Confirmation bias: the tendency to seek only evidence that confirms your hypothesis.	Look for disconfirming evidence that, if found, would show your hypothesis to be false.

countermoves by the opponent, then all possible counter-countermoves, and so on, until the "best" move is determined. After each move by the opponent, the computer could determine which move would produce a sequence of moves that would result in victory the greatest number of times, and in defeat the fewest possible times. The problem is that this algorithm is impossibly complex even for the fastest supercomputer; it would need to consider around 10^{120} possible sequences of moves, an astronomically large number that could occupy much of the world's computer power for years (Solso, 1988).

Chess-playing computers programmed to use humanlike heuristics rather than impossibly time-consuming algorithms can best any human opponent. Almost. In October of 1989, world chess champion Gary Kasparov defeated a highly advanced computer program known as Deep Thought in thirty-six moves.

Many researchers have concluded that the most effective procedures in computerized problem solving are humanlike heuristics. As research has shed light on how people use heuristics, it has become possible to translate heuristics into computer programs (Dreyfus & Dreyfus, 1986). A heuristic for problem solving might specify the most logical place to start looking for a solution, or the rules under which different algorithms should be used, or the most relevant kind of information about a problem. For example, a computer can be given the rule of thumb that "if the Dow-Jones stock price index drops below x, and company y has quarterly revenues greater than z, then buy stock in that company." For chess playing, a heuristic might immediately eliminate a number of potentially absurd moves, such as moving one's queen to a position where it will be taken. Heuristic-based computer programs play chess as effectively as their algorithmic competitors (Best, 1989).

THINKING CRITICALLY

Can Computers Improve on Human Problem Solving?

Expert systems represent just one application of **artificial intelligence (AI)**, which is the study of how to program computers to imitate the products of human perception, understanding, and thought. One approach to AI began in the 1950s and focuses on programming computers to manipulate symbols in a logical way. A second very different approach appeared in the mid-1980s: the AI subfield known as *connectionism*, or *neural networks*, which we discussed in Chapter 5, on perception (Cowan & Sharp, 1988). Researchers in this area program computers to imitate not the symbolic operations of logic but the communications among neurons in the brain. Some neural network programs can recognize a particular handwriting style or discriminate one person's face from another. Advances in both areas have created high expectations regarding what artificial intelligence may ultimately accomplish.

What am I being asked to believe or accept?
Some scientists assert that someday, with increasingly powerful machines and new insights into human mental processes, computers will be able to take over much of the job of thinking, much as the HAL device aboard the spaceship did in the film *2001: A Space Odyssey*. Computers, they assert, will be able to match people's ability to perceive the environment and solve problems.

What evidence is available to support the assertion?
Programmers have had modest success in demonstrating problem-solving abilities by computers. The greatest successes have come in expert systems, which deal with a very specific type of problem. There are chess programs that can beat all but the world's grand masters (Best, 1989), medical problem-solving programs that can compete closely with physicians in the accuracy of their recommendations (Goldman, 1988), and computerized devices that can read and understand speech. In addition, computerized neural networks, like humans, can train themselves to recognize patterns by looking at examples; they do not need formal rules for recognition built into them by programmers.

Are there alternative ways of interpreting the evidence?
Some scientists argue that the partial successes of AI systems to date do not prove that computers will ever achieve anything resembling the full breadth

of human perception and thought (Dreyfus & Dreyfus, 1986, 1988; Graubard, 1988). Alternative interpretations of the evidence focus on what the machines and programs *cannot* do.

First, AI systems fail to function with anywhere near the capacity or speed of the human brain. The brain is estimated to have one million times the computation rate of even the most advanced supercomputers, and its storage capacity is estimated to be ten million times greater (Schwartz, 1988). Such capacity and speed seem critical for achieving insights and drawing analogies between one domain of thought and another.

Second, AI systems are successful only in very narrowly defined fields, like diagnosis of infectious disease or chess playing. In spite of efforts to develop general problem-solving computers (Newell & Simon, 1972), the ability demonstrated in one domain (say, disease diagnosis) does not easily transfer to a different domain, such as locating mineral deposits. In other words, computer "intelligence" seems to be very specific and narrow in scope. One reason for this narrowness is that success in each domain depends on a lot of "common-sense know-how" and on special heuristics that cannot be translated into general symbolic rules that the computer can transfer from domain to domain. Indeed, the specialized rules and information must be gathered from human experts in each domain, through a process known as knowledge engineering (Chignell & Peterson, 1988).

Even within a domain, there are a number of reasons why computers show limited ability. For one thing, there are no effective ways of putting into computer code all aspects of the reasoning of human experts. Sometimes, the experts can only say, "I know it when I see it, but I can't put it into words" (Dreyfus & Dreyfus, 1988). In addition, part of being an expert is knowing about cases in which standard rules don't apply. Computers still aren't very good at this, or at realizing that the solutions arrived at just don't make sense and that a new approach should be tried. Finally, humans are particularly good at drawing analogies and making associations among different domains. For example, applying knowledge about the behavior of fluids and other physical systems that exist within a state of apparent chaos has recently generated insights regarding economic trends (Gleick, 1988). In the medical case presented at the beginning of the chapter, it was knowledge of Laura's contact with paintings, which on the surface has nothing to do with her internal body chemistry, that led to Dr. Wallace's insightful diagnosis. Making these connections among remote knowledge domains is far beyond the grasp of AI systems, partly because the builders of the systems seldom know ahead of time what other areas may lead to insight. (If they did, they might not need the computer.) Thus, they can't tell computers where to look for new ideas or how to use them.

A fourth limitation of AI systems based on symbolic manipulations comes from their dependence on "if-then" rules of the following sort: "If the patient reports a fever, then look for an infection." Although thousands of such rules can be built into a program, major problems are encountered in telling the computer how to recognize the "if" condition in the real world (Dreyfus & Dreyfus, 1988). Consider two such rules: "If it's a dog, then feed it" and "If it's a clock, then set it." Humans can recognize patterns like clocks and dogs with ease, but computers are very poor at this task. This is true partly because identifying, say, a clock, requires having a concept of a clock. And as discussed earlier in this chapter, forming natural concepts requires people to perform the amazing task of putting into the same category many examples that may have very different physical features (from digital alarm clocks to Big Ben). Indeed, the success of pattern-recognition programs has generally involved artificial concepts and simple, well-defined patterns, like circles and squares. Many scientists believe that computerized neural networks will do a much better job of recognizing ill-defined patterns than will the rule-based logic typical of the original AI efforts (Cowan & Sharp, 1988; Rummelhart & McClelland, 1986). The neural networks developed so far, however, still fall well short of the capacities of the human perceptual system. For example, they are incredibly slow to learn how to classify patterns, and unlike humans, they don't show sudden insights when a key feature is suddenly discovered.

What additional evidence would help to evaluate the alternatives?
Clearly, the most important new evidence will come from examining the successes and failures of the best AI systems in their efforts to mimic human perception and thought. This evidence should emerge as computer scientists begin to use techniques that are more similar to processes in the human brain. These include programming neural networks and the use of multiple computers that can work together, just as the many neural and chemical elements of the brain are active at once.

Furthermore, linking together more and more computers may begin to reduce the gap between the capacities of computers and that of the human brain (Waltz, 1988). Finally, more and better psychological theory regarding human ideas, intention, and insight will provide more useful information to the computer scientist about how these cognitive processes are actually carried out.

What conclusions are most reasonable?
Perhaps the most reasonable conclusion about whether computers can improve on human problem solving is that it is premature to draw any firm conclusions. Though today's most sophisticated computers cannot perceive and think about the world at large anywhere near as well as humans can, the field of AI is likely to see dramatic breakthroughs. ▪

Decision Making

Once you diagnose a problem or analyze a situation, the next step is usually to do something about it. This step requires deciding on a course of action (stage 3 of the information-processing model shown in Figure 9.1). The physician described in the opening of this chapter faced a simple decision: to recommend either that the patient stop working with lead paint or that she protect herself against it. However, decisions are often far more difficult: A patient must decide whether to undergo a dangerous operation; a young adult must choose a career; a corporate executive must decide whether to shut down a factory. Unlike the high-speed decisions discussed earlier, these decisions require considerable time and mental effort.

Even the "right" decision sometimes leads to the "wrong" outcome, because the world is uncertain; chance is fickle. Decisions made when the outcome is uncertain are called *risky decisions* or *decisions under uncertainty*. Chance aside, psychologists have discovered many other reasons why human decisions may lead to unsatisfactory outcomes, and we describe some of them here.

Evaluating Options

If someone asked you to choose a gift of $5 or $10, no strings attached, you would probably decide to take the gift of greater value. But now suppose that the choice is between taking (1) a course that is taught by an excellent professor at a convenient time but does not count toward your major, or (2) a course that is required for your major but is taught by a mediocre instructor at an inconvenient time. Each option has both positive and negative features, or *attributes*, a fact that greatly complicates decision making. Deciding which car to buy, which college to attend, or even how to spend the evening are all examples of this kind of *multiattribute decision making* (Edwards, 1987).

Multiattribute decisions can be difficult in part because the limited storage capacity of short-term memory does not permit people to easily keep in mind, combine, and compare all of the attributes of all of the options (Fischoff, Slovic & Lichtenstein, 1977). Instead, people tend to focus on the one attribute that is most important to them. If learning from stimulating lectures is most important to you, then you might choose the course with the better professor, without giving much consideration to curriculum requirements (Tversky, 1972). Often multiattribute decisions are also complicated by difficulties in weighing the options and estimating the probabilities of the outcomes.

Utility and Value   In most important decisions, the attributes of the options cannot be measured in dollars or other relatively objective terms. Instead, people are forced to compare ''apples and oranges.'' Psychologists use the term **utility** to describe the subjective, personal value of each attribute. In deciding which course to take, for example, you would have to think about the positive and negative utilities of each attribute of each course—the value for the major, quality of instruction, and convenience. These must then somehow be weighed and combined. Will the positive utility of completing a required course be higher than the negative utility of sitting through pointless lectures first thing in the morning? Will the positive utility of listening to a great instructor outweigh the negative utility of losing the opportunity to fulfill a requirement? The outcome of all this thought will be a decision.

Expected Value   Multiattribute decisions are difficult enough when you know a lot about the consequences associated with each option, but often decisions must be made in the face of uncertainty. That required class at 8 AM might be taught by someone you do not know. One or both of the cars you are considering could have serious mechanical problems. Uncertainty adds new difficulties to the decision-making process: to make a good decision, you should take into account not only the attributes of the options but also the probabilities and risks of their possible outcomes.

In studying risky decision making, psychologists begin by assuming that the best decision is the one that maximizes **expected value**, or the total amount of benefit you could expect to receive if the decision (even if not always correct) were repeated on several occasions. Suppose someone asks you to enter a raffle. You know that it costs $2 to enter and that the probability of winning the $100 prize is one in ten (.10). Should you enter? The expected value of entering is computed by multiplying the probability of gain (.10) by the size of the gain ($100); this is the average benefit you would receive if you entered the raffle many times. From this product you would then subtract the probability of loss (which is 1.0; the entry fee is a certain loss) multiplied by the amount of the loss ($2). That is, $(0.10 \times \$100) - (1.0 \times \$2) = +\$8$. Since this eight-dollar expected value is greater than the expected value of not entering (which is zero), you should enter. However if the odds of winning the raffle were one in a hundred (.01), then the expected value of entering would be $(.01 \times \$100) - (1.0 \times \$2) = -\$1$. In this case, since the expected value is negative, you should not enter the raffle.

Biases and Flaws in Decision Making

In fact, people do not always behave so as to maximize their expected values, and it is important to consider some of the reasons why.

For one thing, positive utilities are not mirror images of negative utilities. Instead, people feel worse about losing a certain amount than they feel good about gaining the same amount (Edwards, Lindman & Phillips, 1965). Thus, they may be willing to expend more effort to try collecting a $100 debt than to try winning a $100 prize.

Further, large losses are seen as *disproportionately* more serious than small losses (Kahneman & Tversky, 1984). Though the prospect of losing $10,000 should, objectively, be seen as twice as bad as a $5,000 loss, people may do more than twice as much to avoid the larger loss. It is this reasoning in part that leads people to buy insurance—to avoid large losses, even though such losses are very unlikely.

It also appears that the utility of a specific gain depends not on the absolute increase in value but on what the starting point was. Suppose you can take some action to receive a coupon for a free dinner worth $10. Does this gain have the same utility as having an extra $10 added to a paycheck? The dollar amount is the same, but people tend to behave as if the difference in utility between $0 and $10 is much greater than the difference between $200 and $210. Thus, they may refuse to drive across town after work to earn a $10 bonus but would gladly make the same trip to pick up a $10 coupon. This tendency calls to mind Weber's law of psychophysics, discussed in Chapter 5, on perception. How much a difference in value means depends on how much you already have (Edwards, Lindman & Phillips, 1965).

Biases in the perception of probability are also a source of less than optimal decisions. Two such biases are especially interesting. The first is the tendency to overestimate rare probabilities—and underestimate very frequent ones (Kahneman & Tversky, 1984). This bias not only helps explain why people buy insurance but why they gamble and enter lotteries, even though the odds are against them and the decision to do so has a negative expected value. According to the formula for expected value, buying a $1 lottery ticket—when the probability of winning $4,000,000 is one in ten million—yields an expected

The disastrous decision to launch the space shuttle Challenger in thirty-eight degree weather exemplifies a risky decision apparently flawed by biases in the decision makers' processing of information about the pros and cons of the options.

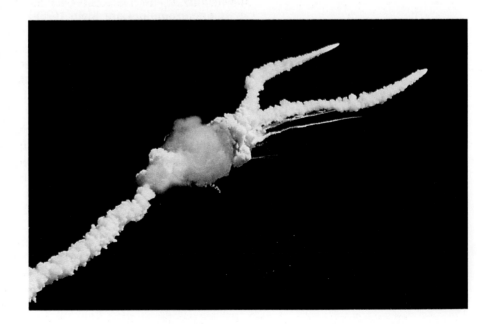

value of $-60¢$. But because people overestimate the probability of winning, they think there is a positive expected value. The tendency to overestimate the likelihood of unlikely events is amplified by the availability heuristic: both vivid memories of rare gambling successes and the publicity given to lottery winners help people recall gains rather than losses when deciding about future gambles (Waagenaar, 1989).

Bias relating to probability is called the *gambler's fallacy*: people believe that events in a random process will correct themselves. This belief is false. For example, if you flip a coin and it comes up heads ten times in a row, the chance that it will come up heads on the eleventh try is still 50 percent. Some gamblers, however, will continue feeding a slot machine that hasn't paid off much for hours, assuming it is "due."

Yet another factor underlying flaws in human decision making is the tendency for people to be unrealistically confident in the accuracy of their predictions. Baruch Fischoff and Donald MacGregor (1982) used an ingenious approach to study this bias. They asked people whether they believed that a certain event would occur—for example, that a certain sports team would win—and how confident they were about this prediction. After the events in question, the accuracy of the forecasts was computed and compared with the confidence assigned to the predictions. Sure enough, people's confidence in their predictions was consistently greater than their accuracy. This overconfidence operates even when people make predictions concerning the accuracy of their own memory (Fischoff, 1980). The moral of the story is to be wary when people express confidence that a forecast or decision is correct. They will be wrong more often than they think.

Expertise in Decision Making

Linkages: How does memory shape decision making? (a link to Memory)

People's decisions can be flawed in many ways besides those we have discussed (Kahneman, Slovic & Tversky, 1982; Wickens, 1991). Indeed, it sometimes seems surprising that decisions are made correctly at all. Judges, physicians, stockbrokers, and other professional decision makers are vulnerable to many of the same limitations as the rest of us (Shurman, 1988). Still, many experts make decisions in ways that avoid some of the biases in mentally estimating probability and calculating utility (Barnett, 1989).

As one example, Gary Klein (1989) studied the decisions fire chiefs made about how to attack a fire. Through many observations and interviews, he found that fire chiefs use their experience first to recognize and categorize a fire as a particular type. Then they search their long-term memory for a plan of attack that worked in the past with that type of fire. To the extent that their memory is accurate, the decision will probably be the right one. Here, the information available in the expert's long-term memory reduces the need to hold and evaluate numerous alternatives in short-term memory, where many of the biases shown by less expert decision makers operate.

Language

So far, our discussion of thinking has assumed that people have a crucial skill: the ability to use language. This ability provides both a vehicle for the mind's communication with itself and the most important means of communicating with others. Other animals can communicate, but none appears to have the means to do so with the systematic rules, precision, and infinite range of creative expression that human language allows. And only humans pass communication through the ages, so that generation after generation can learn from and enjoy the heritage of its ancestors. In this section we describe the elements that make up a language, how people use language to communicate, and how language is learned.

The Elements of Language

A **language** has two basic elements: symbols, such as words, and a set of rules, called **grammar**, for combining those symbols. These two components allow human language to be at once rule-bound and creative. With no more than 50,000 to 100,000 words (the vocabulary of the typical college student), humans can create and understand an infinite number of sentences. All of the sentences ever articulated are created from just a few dozen categories of sounds. The power of language comes from the way these rather unimpressive raw materials are organized according to rules. This organization occurs at several levels.

From Sounds to Sentences   Organization occurs first at the level of sounds. A **phoneme** is the smallest unit of sound that affects the meaning of speech. Changing a phoneme changes the meaning of a word, much as changing a letter in a printed word changes its meaning. *Tea* has a meaning different from *sea*, and *sight* is different from *sit*.

Each spoken language consists of roughly thirty to fifty phonemes. English has twenty-six letters, but it has about forty phonemes. The *a* in *cat* and the *a* in *cake*, for example, are different English phonemes. Many of the letter sounds are phonemes (including *ell*, *aitch*, and *em*), but so are the sounds *th* and *sh*. Sounds that are considered one phoneme in English are different phonemes in other languages, and sounds that are different phonemes in English may be just one phoneme in another language. In Spanish, for example, *s* and *z* are considered the same phoneme.

Although changing a phoneme affects meaning, phonemes themselves are not meaningful. They are combined to form the second level of organization: morphemes. A **morpheme** is the smallest unit of language that has meaning. Word stems like *dog* and *run* are morphemes, but so are prefixes like *un-* and suffixes like *-ed,* because they have meaning even though they cannot stand alone.

Words are made up of one or more morphemes. Words, in turn, are combined to form phrases and sentences according to a set of rules called **syntax**. For example, according to English syntax, a subject and a verb must be combined in a sentence, adjectives typically appear before the noun that they modify, and so forth. Compare the following sentences:

Fatal accidents deter careful drivers. Snows sudden floods melting cause.

The first sentence makes sense, but the second sentence violates English syntax. If the words were reordered, however, they would produce the perfectly acceptable sentence "Melting snows cause sudden floods."

Even if you use English phonemes combined in proper ways to form morphemes strung together according to the laws of English syntax, you may not end up with an acceptable English sentence. Consider the sentence "Rapid bouquets deter sudden neighbors." It somehow sounds right, but it is nonsense. Why? It has syntax, but it ignores the set of rules, called **semantics**, that govern the meaning of words and sentences. For example, the meaning of the noun *bouquets* is not one that can be logically modified by the word *rapid*.

Surface Structure and Deep Structure   So far, we have discussed elements of language that are apparent in the sentences people produce. These elements were the focus of study for linguists and *psycholinguists* (psychologists who deal with language) for many decades. Then, in 1957, linguist Noam Chomsky started a revolution in the study of language. He argued that if linguists studied only the language that people produced, they would never uncover the principles that account for all the sentences that people create. They could not explain, for example, how one sentence, such as "This is my old friend" has more than one meaning (*old* can mean "aged" or "long-standing"). And by looking only at sentences produced, linguists could not account for the close relationships between the meanings of such apparently different sentences as "Don't give up just because things look bad" and "It ain't over 'til it's over."

To take these aspects of language into account, Chomsky proposed a more abstract level of analysis. Behind the word strings that people produce, called **surface structures**, there is, he said, a **deep structure**, an abstract representation of the relationships expressed in a sentence. For example, the surface structure "The shooting of the psychologist was terrible" may represent either of two deep structures: (1) that the psychologist had terrible aim, or (2) that it was terrible that someone shot the psychologist. Chomsky developed rules for transforming deep structures into surface structures and for relating sentences to each other.

Since Chomsky proposed his first analysis of deep and surface structures, he and others have proposed many revisions of those ideas. The debates go well beyond what we can consider here. For our purposes, what is important about Chomsky's ideas is that they encouraged psychologists to analyze not just people's verbal behavior or the rules of grammar but also the possible mental representations that verbal behavior reflects.

Understanding Words and Sentences

When you speak, you have an idea or proposition to be conveyed, but sounds are transmitted. How is your idea translated into those sounds? If your communication is successful, your listener ends up not simply with the sounds you transmitted but with an idea or proposition that matches, or approximates, the one with which you began. How?

Figure 9.12 illustrates an analysis of these processes. The speaker starts with an idea, which is translated, modified, and elaborated into a specific set of phrases, which are encoded into sounds by mechanisms of the throat and mouth. The listener must take this string of sounds and go through the reverse process in order to "decode" the message. If the encoding and decoding processes are error free, the ideas of speaker and listeners will match, and the communication will be successful. As discussed in the chapter on memory, it is the underlying meaning, not the specific word string, that the listener is likely to encode and remember. The process by which speech is "decoded" by the listener into meaning usually happens so rapidly and automatically that people take it for granted, but in the following sections we describe how this process depends on the combination of bottom-up and top-down processing.

Perceiving Words   When you listen to someone speak, what you perceive is a series of words. It sounds as if there is a distinct pause between each word, while the phonemes within a word are heard as a continuous string. However, this is not the case, as Figure 9.13 demonstrates. It shows a *speech spectrograph*,

Linkages: How do people perceive speech? (a link to Perception)

Figure 9.12
Producing and Comprehending Speech

The listener on the right has interpreted the speaker's message in a way that differs from the speaker's intended deep structure. Obviously, identical surface structures can correspond to distinctly different deep structures.

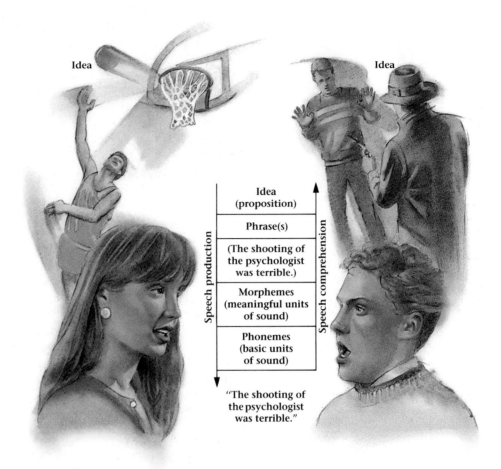

which is a visual representation of the frequencies of speech sounds as they unfold over time. The spectrograph shows that breaks occur not between words but within the words. You hear the breaks between, instead of within, words because of the top-down processing discussed in Chapter 5, on perception. Because you know what the word should sound like, you recognize the sounds when they occur, and you perceive them as separate units, even if the physical stimuli are not separated.

Understanding Sentences   Suppose you are asked to memorize two meaningless strings of sounds: "Haky deeb um flut recile pav togert disen" and "A hyaky deeb reciled the dison togently um flutests pav." You might predict that it would be easier to learn the shorter first string, because it should put a lighter burden on short-term memory. Surprisingly, William Epstein (1961) found that people learned the second string more easily. It is longer than the first, but it is also more sentencelike and more grammatical. Apparently, the organization of the sounds into a sentencelike structure, with the function words *the* and *a* and endings like *-ed*, allowed Epstein's subjects to chunk the sounds into more easily memorized units. Thus, the extra sounds added to the second sentence actually reduced the burden on short-term memory.

Experiments like Epstein's have demonstrated that syntax plays a crucial role in the comprehension of sentences. Instead of simply decoding speech word by word, people treat grammatical constituents, such as phrases, as separate units, or chunks (Fodor, Bever & Garrett, 1974).

Although both syntax and word meanings are important to comprehension, they still do not tell the whole story. For example, knowing the meaning of words and proper word order does not explain why people understand that

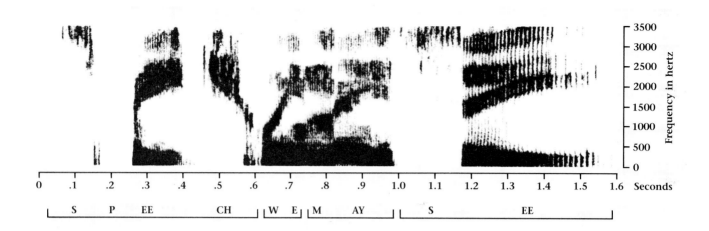

Source: Lachman, Lachman & Butterfield, 1979.

Figure 9.13
A Speech Spectrograph
This is the visual representation of the speech sounds in the phrase "Speech we may see." The vertical axis shows the frequencies of the speech sounds; the horizontal axis shows the passage of time. You would hear the phrase as four distinct words. Notice, however, that the pauses actually occur not between the words but between the *p* and *ee* in *speech* and again between *ee* and *ch* in the same word.

only one of the phrases "Ruth eats fruit" and "Fruit eats Ruth" is semantically correct. For this understanding, people also rely on knowledge of the world. Although both phrases are syntactically correct, you should have greater trouble reading the second string. If you read the strings in a hurry, your mind will probably automatically "reorganize" the second sentence to another form, such as "The fruit was eaten by Ruth" (Fillenbaum, 1974). In other words, through top-down processing, people use their vast store of knowledge to find and impose meaning and organization, as well as grammatical structure, on words.

Understanding Conversations

Suppose you have been able to program a computer with all the rules and knowledge discussed so far—with rules for decoding spoken phonemes and written letters into words, rules of syntax, a dictionary of the meanings of words, and an encyclopedia of knowledge of the world. Now you ask your unfortunate computer to make sense of the following conversation:

A: You goin' to the gym today to work out?
B: Well I *am* flabby, but only if I can hook a ride with Jim. It's a long way.
A: I'm afraid I heard his transmission's conked out, and it's at the shop.
B: Oh [pause], then I guess it won't work out.

You probably had little trouble understanding this conversation, but the computer would be at a loss. The first problem is that the grammar is not complete. For example, the fact that the first sentence is a question would be indicated only by a rising tone of voice. Second, because both participants understand the general gist of the dialogue, certain ambiguous terms take on different meanings in different sentences (for example, *it* in lines 2, 3, and 4; *work out* in lines 1 and 4; and *gym* versus *Jim* in lines 1 and 2). Third, having the gist allows you to understand the meaning of words or phrases like *hook*, *I'm afraid*, and *conked out*, and to know that the transmission is actually part of Jim's car, not a part of Jim. These are things that the computer could not easily "understand."

The Role of Context Difficulties in programming a computer to understand conversations arise first because the use of language is knowledge-driven and

Linkages: In Chapter 5 on perception, we noted that familiarity, expectancy, and other aspects of top-down processing can alter your perception of a variety of incoming stimuli. The top-down processing of speech helps explain why speech in a language you do not understand sounds like a continuous stream and seems to be uttered at a much faster rate than speech in your own language. Because your brain does not know where each word in an unfamiliar language starts and stops, you do not hear the gaps between words; as shown in Figure 9.13, the gaps, after all, are not physically there. And because you do not perceive gaps between words, the sounds run together at what seems to be a faster-than-normal rate.

relies on the *context* in which words are spoken or written. This use of context creates one of the greatest challenges in the development of artificial intelligence for speech recognition. As noted in Chapter 5, people use context to interpret and impose meaning on stimuli—including language. A statement like "Wow, are you smart!" can be interpreted as "I think you're an idiot," depending on the context (and perhaps the tone of voice). Thus, understanding language involves constructing meaning out of sounds, just as recalling stored memories sometimes involves constructing information based partly on the context in which that information is encoded or retrieved.

The context for understanding language may be created by the situation. Richard Mayer (1983) reported seeing a sign in a laundromat in Santa Barbara, California, that said, "Not responsible for clothes you may have stolen." The words themselves could easily mean "The owner is not responsible if you steal someone else's clothes." But the context created by the situation indicates that the sign was meant to warn people not to leave their belongings unattended.

An individual's personal history also forms part of the context of a situation. Thus, people's educational and cultural backgrounds help shape their understanding of a communication. As an example, read the following:

Every Saturday night, four good friends get together. When Jerry, Mike, and Pat arrived, Karen was sitting in her living room writing some notes. She quickly gathered the cards and stood up to greet her friends at the door. They followed her into the living room but as usual they couldn't agree on exactly what to play. Jerry eventually took a stand and set things up. Finally, they began to play. Karen's recorder filled the room with soft and pleasant music. Early in the evening, Mike noticed Pat's hand and the many diamonds. As the night progressed the tempo of play increased. Finally, a lull in the activities occurred. Taking advantage of this, Jerry pondered the arrangement in front of him. Mike interrupted Jerry's reverie and said, "Let's hear the score." They listened carefully and commented on their performance. When the comments were all heard, exhausted but happy, Karen's friends went home (Anderson et al., 1977).

In a laboratory study, music majors tended to interpret this passage as describing a music practice session, whereas other students typically read it as the description of a card game (Anderson et al., 1977). The interpretations are vastly different because of the role played by scripts (Shank & Abelson, 1977). The script that each listener has—of the typical musical rehearsal or the typical bridge game—serves as a framework for interpreting ambiguous words like *stand* and *diamonds*.

One application of artificial intelligence, a system called SAM (Script Applier Mechanism), takes the importance of context and the usefulness of scripts into account. The program first tries to understand the gist of a conversation and then "loads" the appropriate script (Shank & Abelson, 1977). This script-based knowledge improves the ability of the computer to interpret ambiguous words and sentences. Of course, the whole knowledge base related to the various scripts must be programmmed into the computer in the first place. There is no replacement for human experience.

Beyond Syntax and Semantics: Conventions The use of scripts and context demonstrates that much of the meaning of conversations is not transmitted directly by the words themselves. In fact, the words by themselves may mean something quite different from what is intended and understood by a conversation. For example, the question "Do you know what time it is?" literally asks for a yes or no answer, not a statement of the correct time, which is both the intended meaning and likely response. "I think you should clean up your room" is intended (and perceived) as a request, not a report of a parent's thought processes. In these and other cases, *conventions*, built up over years of experience, govern conversation and how the listener understands it.

Conventions dictate subtle changes in sentences that neither semantic nor syntactic rules describe. Consider the difference between "It is at the LIBRARY that we will meet at 4:00" and "It is at FOUR O'CLOCK that we will meet at the library." Using the rules of both syntax and semantics, the two sentences mean the same thing; but the two messages are spoken with very different assumptions about what the listener knows. In the first sentence, the speaker

Though we are often unaware of it, our ability to understand what others say in conversation depends heavily on factors such as context and commonly accepted, or conventional, usages. Thus, though the words alone do not say so, "Will you join me in a cup of coffee?" conveys to most people an invitation to drink some coffee, not to climb into a giant cup of coffee with the speaker.

assumes that the listener knows the time of the meeting but is confused about the place. In the second example just the opposite is assumed. These distinctions are between known or "given" information and new or "asserted" information (Haviland & Clark, 1974). Conventions of conversation call for asserted information to be highlighted, by placing it early in the sentence and often by giving it inflection and emphasis.

Finally, people are often guided to an understanding of conversations by nonverbal cues. The frown, the enthusiastic nod, the bored yawn—all signal differences in understanding or interest that have an important bearing on the exchange of information. Studies showing the greater efficiency of face-to-face conversations compared with, say, telephone exchanges (Chapanis et al., 1977) have provided much of the impetus for the development of TV telephones, which allow speakers to see each other's faces.

Stages of Language Development

Once people have learned to speak, they use the many rules of language naturally and automatically to generate correct sentences and to reject incorrect ones, even though most people would have a difficult time stating the rules. For example, in an instant you know that the words "Bei mir bist du schoen" are not English and that the string of words "Quickly peaches sheep deserve" is not an acceptable sentence. Children the world over learn language with impressive speed and regularity. Developmental psychologists have painstakingly detailed the steps in this process.

From Babbling to Words   **Babblings** are the first sounds infants make that resemble speech. These repetitions of syllables ("bababa," "mamama," "dadada") begin at about four months of age and, although meaningless to the baby, are a delight to parents. During much of the first year, infants the world over make the same babbling sounds. At about nine months, however, babies who hear only English start to lose their German gutturals and French nasals. Beginning at this time, too, they begin to shorten some of their vocalizations to "da," "duh," and "ma." These sounds, which soon replace babbling, seem very much like language. Babies use them in specific contexts and with obvious purpose (Dore, 1978). Accompanied by appropriate gestures, they may be used to express joy ("oohwow") or anger ("uh-uh-uh"), to get something that is out of reach ("engh-engh"), or to point out something interesting ("dah!").

A mother will often claim of her year-old infant, "She doesn't talk, but she understands everything I say." This is not quite true. A twelve-month-old may understand some of the mother's words, but he or she is likely to rely on cues other than words to figure out what the mother means. Mother may be pointing to the ball while she says, "Where is the ball?" But ten- to twelve-month-olds can understand a few words—certainly more words than they can say (Huttenlocher, 1974). Proper names and object words are among the first words they understand. Often the very first word they understand is a pet's name.

Proper names and object words—words like *cookie, doggy, shoe, truck,* and *mama*—are also among the first words children are likely to say when, at around twelve to eighteen months of age, they begin to talk. Nouns for simple object categories (*dog, flower*) are acquired first, rather than either more general nouns (*animal, plant*) or more specific names (*collie, rose*) (Rosch et al., 1976).

Of course, these early words do not sound exactly like adult language. Babies usually reduce them to a shorter, easier form, like "duh" for *duck* or "mih" for *milk*. Children make themselves understood, however, by using gestures,

The delightful babblings of infants may be meaningless at first, but they represent the beginning of the remarkable process of language development.

intonations, facial expressions, and interminable repetitions. If they have a word for an object, they "overextend" it to cover more ground. Thus, they might use *fly* for all insects and perhaps for other small things like raisins and M&Ms; they might use *dog* for cats, bears, and horses (Clark & Clark, 1977; Rosch, 1975). Children make these "errors" because their vocabularies are limited, not because they fail to notice the difference between dogs and cats or because they want to eat a fly (Fremgen & Fay, 1980; Rescorla, 1981).

Until they can say the conventional words for objects, children overextend the words they have, use all-purpose sounds (like "dat" or "dis"), and coin new words (like *pepping* for "shaking the pepper shaker"). This **one-word stage** of speech lasts for about six months. During this period, children build up their vocabularies a word at a time and tend to use words one at a time.

First Sentences   By eighteen to twenty-four months of age, children usually have a vocabulary of some fifty words. Then their language undergoes an explosion; it is not uncommon at this point for children to learn several new words a day and to begin to put words together. At first, children's sentences consist of two-word pairs. These are more elaborate, less ambiguous, and somewhat less tied to gestures than children's one-word expressions. For example, to call attention to a dog, which was once done by pointing and saying, "Doggy," the child now says, "See doggy." Still, children's two-word utterances are **telegraphic**. Brief and to the point, they leave out any word that is not absolutely essential. If she wants her mother to give her a book, the twenty-month-old might first say, "Give book," then, "Mommy give," and, if that does not work, "Mommy book." The child also uses rising intonation to indicate a question ("Go out?") and word stress to indicate location ("Play *park*") or asserted information ("*Big* car").

Three-word sentences come next in the development of language. They are still telegraphic, but more nearly complete: "Mommy give book." The child can speak in sentences that have the usual subject-verb-object form of adult sentences. Other words and word endings begin appearing, too, such as the suffix *-ing*, prepositions *in* and *on*, the plural *s*, and irregular past tenses ("It broke," "I ate") (Brown, 1973; Dale, 1976).   Later, children learn to use the suffix *-ed* for the past tense ("I walked"). But once they have mastered the rule for using *-ed* to express past events, they overapply the rule to irregular verbs that they previously used correctly, saying, for example, "It breaked" or "It broked" or "I eated."

Children also expand their vocabularies with adjectives, although at first, they do not always get the antonyms straight. For example, they are likely to use both *less* and *more* to mean "more" or *tall* and *short* to mean "tall" (Donaldson & Balfour, 1968). After acquiring some adjectives, children begin to use auxiliary verbs ("Adam is going") and to ask questions using *wh-* words (*what, where, whose, who, why, when,* in roughly this order). They begin to put ideas together in sentences ("Here's the ball I was looking for"). Until they are about five years old, however, children join events in the order in which they occur ("We went to the zoo and had ice cream") and understand sentences better if they follow this order (Clark, 1978; Kavanaugh & Jirkovsky, 1982). By age five, children have acquired most of the syntax of their native language.

How Is Language Learned?

Despite all that has been learned in recent years about the steps children follow in learning language, mystery still surrounds the question of just how they learn it. We know a great deal about what happens, but why and how it happens is still open to debate. Obviously, children pick up the specific content of language from the speech they hear around them; English children learn English, French children learn French. As parents and children share meals, playtime, and conversations, children learn that words refer to objects and actions and what the labels for them are. But how do they learn syntax?

Linkages: Can the principles of conditioning explain how people learn to speak? (a link to Learning)

Conditioning and Imitation   Our discussion of conditioning in Chapter 7, on learning, suggests one possibility: perhaps children learn syntax because of the way their parents reinforce them. In fact, however, observations suggest that reinforcement cannot fully explain the learning of syntax. Usually parents are more concerned about *what* is said than about its form (Hirsch-Pasek, Treiman & Schneiderman, 1984). When the little boy with chocolate crumbs on his face says, "I not eat cookie," the mother is more likely to respond "Yes, you did eat it" rather than asking the child to say, "I did not eat the cookie," and then reinforcing him for using a grammatically correct form.

Although adults do not give lessons on grammar, they do greatly modify their speech when talking to their language-learning children. They shorten their sentences and use concrete, basic nouns and active verbs—not pronouns, adjectives, conjunctions, or past tenses. They exaggerate, repeat, enunciate clearly, and stick to the here-and-now, in grammatically correct utterances. This kind of talk, which parallels children's own, has been called **motherese**—although fathers, aunts, uncles, and older siblings also speak it.

Parents seem to use motherese to help children understand what is being said. But does it help children acquire language? Apparently not. Children do not learn to speak correctly earlier if their mothers speak down to their level (Chesnic et al., 1983; Nelson et al., 1983). In fact, within the range of language spoken by most mothers to their children, the more complex the mother's language, the earlier and more rapidly their children learn to speak in complex sentences (Clarke-Stewart & Hevey, 1981; Gleitman, Newport & Gleitman, 1984).

If the aim is to help a child learn syntax, expanding the child's utterances is more helpful than speaking motherese. Children learn syntax most rapidly when adults offer simple revisions of their sentences, implicitly correcting their syntax, and continue with the topic they are discussing. For example,

Child: Mommy fix.

Mother: Okay, Mommy will fix the truck.

Child: It breaked.

Mother: Yes, it broke.

Child: It broke.

Mother: Let's see if we can fix it.

This recasting obviously involves modeling correct speech forms, and as noted in Chapter 7, modeling, or imitation, is an important source of learning. Especially if the child is given approval for imitating recast forms, adults' recasting of language cannot help but shape language development.

But if children learned syntax by imitation, why would they overgeneralize rules for plurals and past tenses? Why, for example, do children who at one time said "I went" later say "I goed"? Adults never use this form of speech. Its sudden appearance cannot be explained by either imitation or reinforcement but, rather, by the mastery of rules. Neither conditioning nor imitation seems entirely adequate to explain how children learn language. Children must still analyze for themselves the underlying patterns in the welter of language examples they hear around them.

Linkages: Are people born with an innate, unique ability to learn language? (a link to Human Development)

Nature and Nurture The ease with which children everywhere discover these patterns and learn language has encouraged some to argue that humans are "prewired," or biologically programmed, to learn language. This biological preparedness is reflected in the unique speech-generating properties of the human mouth and throat (Aitchison, 1983), as well as in such brain regions as Broca's area and Wernicke's area, discussed in Chapter 3 and illustrated in Figure 3.16.

Chomsky (1957) has suggested that human beings possess an innate *language acquisition device*—a *LAD* for short—that processes speech and allows children to understand the regularities of speech and fundamental relationships among words. The LAD permits youngsters to gather ideas about the rules of language without even being aware of doing so. They then use these ideas to understand and construct their native language.

Evidence to support this hypothesis is hard to come by, however. One suggestive finding is that there is some similarity in the syntax of all languages. Another is the fact that children born deaf and never exposed to language make up gestural systems that have several properties of natural spoken language, including placement of subjects before verbs and agent-action-object sequences, such as "June saw Bob" (Goldin-Meadow & Feldman, 1977).

Even if there is a LAD, it has a limited warranty. One unfortunate child was confined by her father to isolation and abuse in a small room until she was rescued at age thirteen and a half (Curtiss, 1977). Like the Wild Boy of Aveyron, whom we described in Chapter 2, she had not heard any language, and she could not speak at all when she was discovered. After six years of therapy and language training, she still had not learned to use possessive forms, auxiliary verbs, or *what*, *which*, and *that*. She could not combine ideas into a single sentence. Her speech was the equivalent of a two- or three-year-old's. Such cases suggest that to acquire complex features of language a person must be exposed to speech before a certain age. That is, there appears to be a *critical period* for learning language similar to the critical periods for capacities such as binocular depth perception, discussed in Chapter 5. This suggestion is supported by research showing that people who learn a second language after the age of thirteen or fourteen are less efficient than younger learners in acquiring that language (Johnson & Newport, 1989) and are unlikely ever to speak it without an accent (Lenneberg, 1967). These results indicate that though genetic factors are largely responsible for the appearance and pace of language learning, certain major environmental variables, like delayed exposure to a first or second language, can alter the process significantly.

HIGHLIGHT

Is Language Unique to Humans?

Language, some say, is qualitatively different from all other forms of communication and sets humans apart from other creatures. Yet animals do use symbols to communicate. Bees dance in a way that indicates the direction and distance of sources of nectar; the grunts and gestures of chimpanzees signify various attitudes and emotions. This is certainly communication, but is it language? Does the child's ability to learn language reflect an innate ability unique to humans?

Some researchers have examined this question by trying to teach non-human species to use language. Chimps and gorillas have been the most popular subjects, because at maturity they are estimated to have the intelligence of two- or three-year-old children, who are usually well on their way to learning language. Hence, if these animals cannot learn language, their intelligence cannot be blamed. Instead, failure would be attributed to the absence of an appropriate genetic makeup.

Can nonhuman primates learn to use language? This question is not simple, for at least two reasons. First, language is more than just communication, but defining just when animals are exhibiting that "something more" is a source of debate. What seems to set human language apart from

Several chimpanzees and gorillas have been taught to use American Sign Language (ASL). Here, Nim signs "toothbrush" when his teacher shows one and signs "play" upon seeing the teacher sign "out." These animals' accomplishments with ASL are remarkable, but there is considerable controversy about whether they have actually learned language.

the gestures, grunts, chirps, or cries of other animals is grammar, a set of formal rules for combining words. Using the rules of grammar, people can take a relatively small number of words and create with them an almost infinite number of unique sentences. Second, because of their muscular structures, nonhuman primates will never be able to "speak" in the same way that humans do (Aitchison, 1983). To test these animals' ability to learn language, investigators therefore must devise novel ways for them to communicate.

David and Ann Premack taught their chimp, Sarah, to communicate by placing different-shaped chips, symbolizing words, on a magnetic board (Premack, 1971). Lana, a chimpanzee studied by Duane Rumbaugh (1977), learned to communicate by pressing keys on a specially designed computer. Probably the most successful medium, however, has been American Sign Language (ASL), the language of the deaf based on hand gestures. It was used by Beatrice and Allen Gardner with the chimp Washoe, by Herbert Terrace with a chimp named Nim, and by Penny Patterson with a gorilla named Koko.

All five of these studies produced certain common findings. First, Washoe, Lana, Sarah, Nim, and Koko all mastered from 130 up to 500 words (a fairly extensive vocabulary, although modest in comparison to the at least 2,000-word vocabulary of the average three-year-old human). Their vocabulary included names for concrete objects, such as *apple* or *me*; verbs, such as *tickle* and *eat*; adjectives, such as *happy* and *big*; and adverbs, such as *again*. Second, the animals combined the words in sentences, expressing wishes like "You tickle me" or "If Sarah good, then apple." Finally, all these animals seemed to enjoy their communication tools and used them spontaneously to interact with their caretakers.

In spite of these findings, controversy still surrounds the critical question: Did these animals really learn language? The Gardners, who have spent years observing not only Washoe but also several of her companions, concluded that the chimps made humanlike efforts to communicate with each other and, more importantly, combined words in systematic order. For example, if Washoe wanted to be tickled, she would gesture, "You tickle Washoe." But if she wanted to do the tickling, she would gesture, "Washoe tickle you." The correct placement of object and subject in these sentences suggested that Washoe was following a set of rules for word combination—in other words, a grammar (Gardner & Gardner, 1978). The Premacks and Patterson drew similar conclusions regarding the language skills of Sarah and Koko (Patterson, 1978; Premack, 1971).

Indeed, for a time, many felt that there really was not much that is qualitatively different about humans' language skills. But this line of thinking was challenged by the conclusions of Terrace and his colleagues in their investigation of Nim (Terrace et al., 1979). Terrace noticed many subtle characteristics of Nim's communications that seemed quite different from a child's use of language, and he argued that chimps in other studies demonstrated these same characteristics.

First, consider the size of sentences. A child progresses from single-word utterances to two-word "sentences" ("Me hungry," "Nice kitty") and then gradually produces longer and longer utterances. Nim, in contrast, started with the ability to combine gestures into strings of two or three but never used longer strings that conveyed more sophisticated messages. Thus, the ape was never able to say anything equivalent to a three-year-old child's "I want to go to Wendy's for a hamburger, OK?"

Second, children use language spontaneously and creatively. They use it not only to communicate their wishes but also to express ideas and to guide their own activities. Terrace questioned whether the animals' use of language demonstrated these characteristics. Many of their sentences were requests for food, tickling, baths, pets, and other pleasurable objects and experiences. Is such behavior qualitatively different from the behavior of rats who run a maze to get food, or the family dog, who learns to sit up and beg at the dinner table for a scrap of food? The apes are certainly intelligent, and their ability to string gestures together is impressive. However, argued Terrace, they lack the tendency to communicate in the spontaneous and expanding fashion of the two- or three-year-old child. Other researchers also concluded that chimps are not naturally predisposed to associate seen objects with heard words, as human infants are (Savage-Rumbaugh et al., 1983).

Finally, Terrace questioned whether experimenter bias influenced the reports of the chimps' communications. Consciously or not, experimenters who hope to conclude that chimps learn language might tend to ignore strings that violate grammatical order or to reinterpret ambiguous strings so that they make grammatical sense. If Nim sees someone holding a banana and signs, "Nim banana," the experimenter might assume the word order is correct and means "Nim wants the banana" rather than, for example, "That banana belongs to Nim," in which case the word order would be wrong. Furthermore, although the reports of the experiments indicate that the chimps formed sentences spontaneously, Terrace argued that videotapes revealed that the chimps may have been responding to subtle prompts from the experimenters.

Psychologists are still not in full agreement about whether chimps can learn language. Two things are clear, however. First, whatever the chimp and gorilla do learn is a much more primitive and limited form of communication than that learned by children. And second, in chimps, unlike humans, the level of communication does not do justice to their overall intelligence; that is, these animals are smarter than their "language" production suggests. The evidence to date favors the view that genetics provides humans with language abilities that are unique and that no nonhuman species consistently and naturally orders symbols according to specific rules like the grammar that governs human language. ■

Linkages: Perception and Language

Does language determine what people perceive?

The language that people speak forms part of their knowledge of the world, and that knowledge, as noted in Chapter 5, guides perceptions. This relationship raises the question of whether there is an even closer relationship between the two. Do differences among the languages of the world create differences in how people perceive the world?

Benjamin Whorf thought that the answer was yes (Whorf, 1956). He noted, for example, that Eskimos have some twenty names for snow, whereas most Americans have only a few. Whorf proposed that this difference in language should lead to a greater ability to discriminate between varieties of snow—a perceptual ability. When the discrimination abilities of Americans and Eskimos are compared, there are indeed significant differences. However, these results leave another question unanswered: are the differences in perception the *result* of differences in language?

One of the most interesting tests of Whorf's ideas was conducted by Eleanor Rosch (1972). She compared the perception of colors by Americans with that by members of the Dani tribe of New Guinea. In the language of the Dani,

The Eskimo language has many more words than English does for describing various types of snow. Eskimos are also far better than native English speakers at visually perceiving snow's differing varieties. Does this mean that language shapes perception or that perception shapes language?

there are only two color names, one for dark, "cold" colors and one for lighter, "warm" ones. In contrast, English speakers have names for a vast number of different hues. Of these, it is possible to identify eleven *focal* colors; these are prototypes, the particular wavelengths of light that are the best examples of the eleven major color categories (red, yellow, green, blue, black, gray, white, purple, orange, pink, and brown). Thus, fire-engine red is the focal color for red. Rosch reasoned that, if Whorf's views were correct, then English speakers, who have verbal labels for focal colors, should recognize them better than nonfocal colors, but that for the Dani, the focal-nonfocal distinction should make no difference. In fact, however, Rosch found that both the Dani and the Americans perceived focal colors more efficiently than nonfocal ones (Heider, 1972).

Thus, the fact that Eskimos recognize and have verbal labels for subtle but important differences among snow textures that Americans don't even perceive suggests a *correlation* between language and perception in various cultures. But it appears doubtful that language *causes* such differences in perception, as Whorf claimed. It seems far more likely that, beneath the differences in both language and perception, there is a third variable: frequency of use and the society's need for certain objects. Eskimos, for example, live in a snowy world. Their lives depend on making fine discriminations about the snow—between the snow bridge that is old and the one that will collapse, between the snowfield that can be crossed easily and the one that must be avoided. Hence, they learn to discriminate differences that are unimportant to people in warmer climates, and they attach names to those discriminated differences.

Future Directions

As some of the simpler, easily observed phenomena of cognition yield their secrets, the challenge grows to understand the most complex mental phenomena, including thought, decision making, and problem solving. Techniques such as brain-wave recording, verbal reports of thought processes, and computer simulations of thought have all been enlisted in this effort. For example, researchers are studying how well-established findings regarding reaction time can be used to build better computers, airplanes, automobiles, and other systems. (This is the field of engineering psychology, which was discussed in Chapter 1.) Verbal narratives, spoken by expert problem solvers while they solve problems, are used to help create computer programs that will solve new problems in the same way the experts do. The information-processing approach is helping to create a better understanding of the sources of human errors and of ways of preventing them (Norman, 1988; Reason, 1990).

Numerous questions about problem solving and decision making are on the research agenda for coming years (Wickens, 1991). How good or bad is human decision making? To what extent do decision-making heuristics save work and produce good results? How often and to what extent do they get people into trouble? Does laboratory research on decision making by, say, mock juries have applications in the real world? Can debiasing procedures be used to improve decision making outside the laboratory? Several companies have marketed products that are supposed to help people make decisions, but it is extremely difficult to evaluate the effectiveness of these aids. Their true value remains questionable (Wickens, 1991).

Finally, the study of artificial intelligence is one of the most rapidly expanding interdisciplinary areas in science. Drawing on concepts from psychology, engineering, computer science, and many other fields, researchers will continue to try teaching computers to think, reason, and communicate effectively. Although many remain skeptical that computers will ever be able to match human mental abilities (Dreyfus & Dreyfus, 1986; Graubard, 1988), efforts to achieve this goal have helped scientists to learn more about the human mind and to design computer-based expert systems that can help solve problems. Research on neural networks and connectionism has also linked the psychological study of perception and cognition with studies of electrophysiology and computer science. Psychologists' involvement in future research in this area will lead not only to more sophisticated computers but also to a fuller understanding of complex mental processes in humans.

Indeed, cognitive psychology is rapidly becoming one of the most exciting areas in psychology. To learn more about the research explosion taking place in the areas of thought, decision making, problem solving, and language, consider taking courses in experimental psychology, cognitive psychology (sometimes called *higher processes* or *thinking*), psycholinguistics, or engineering psychology (which is sometimes called *human factors*).

Summary and Key Terms

From Stimulus to Action: An Overview

The Human Information-Processing System

The *information-processing* approach offers a general model of human cognition. According to this model, between the presentation of a stimulus and the execution of a response, information is received, transformed, and manipulated through a series of stages. Errors occur because of failures at different stages of information processing. Mistakes occur when perception is incorrect. Slips, which are often associated with highly practiced skills, occur when the wrong response is selected.

High-Speed Decision Making

The minimum time needed to process information through the information-processing stages is the *reaction time*. Among the factors affecting reaction times are the complexity of the choice

of a response, stimulus-response compatibility, expectancy, and the tradeoff between speed and accuracy. *Evoked brain potentials* and *average evoked potentials* provide another way of measuring *mental chronometry*, the timing of mental events.

Thinking

Thinking involves the mental manipulation of information represented in long-term and short-term memory. This information may be stored in at least six forms: concepts, propositions, mental models, scripts, words, and images.

Concepts

Concepts are basic units of thought. They are categories of objects, events, or ideas with common properties. They may be natural or artificial. *Artificial concepts* are precisely defined by the presence or absence of certain features. *Natural concepts* are fuzzy; there is no fixed set of defining properties determining membership in a natural concept, as there is for artificial concepts. Concepts are learned by building up a memory of a *prototype* or by testing hypotheses about what defines membership in them. The ease of concept learning is affected by the complexity of rules defining a concept—such as the *affirmation*, or *one-feature rule*, the *conjunctive rule*, and the *disjunctive rule*.

Other Elements of Thought

The raw material of thought may also take the form of *propositions*, which are assertions that state how two or more concepts are related. Propositions can be true or false. *Mental models* are essentially large clusters of propositions describing people's understanding (accurate or inaccurate) of physical devices or processes. *Scripts* are mental representations of familiar patterns or sequences, usually involving human activities; they help people think about those activities and interpret new events. People often mentally translate concepts, propositions, mental models, and scripts into words and images; thus, words and images are other basic elements that may be manipulated when people think. Words are important, but not necessary, for thought.

Using Images

Mental images can be mentally inspected, expanded, and rotated. Mental representations of real environments are often distorted and simplified in systematic ways.

Reasoning

Reasoning is the process by which people evaluate and generate arguments and reach conclusions. *Syllogisms* are sets of propositions that include premises and conclusions based on the premises. To reach a sound conclusion, people should consider both the empirical truth or falsity of the premises and the *logic* of the argument itself. But in fact, people's belief in a conclusion is often based on whether the conclusions are consistent with their attitudes and on *heuristics*, mental shortcuts or rules of thumb. Whereas *algorithms* are systematic procedures that always produce a solution, heuristics work most of the time but sometimes produce errors. Three important heuristics are the *anchoring heuristic* (estimating the probability of an event by adjusting a starting value), the *representativeness heuristic* (categorizing an event by how representative it is of a category of events, regardless of how probable the category is), and the *availability heuristic* (estimating probability by how available an event is in memory).

Problem Solving

Problems in Problem Solving

Many of the difficulties that people experience in solving problems arise when dealing with hypotheses. People do not easily entertain multiple hypotheses about what is wrong. Because of *mental sets* they may persevere in applying one hypothesis even when it is obviously unsuccessful and, through *functional fixedness*, tend to miss opportunities to use familiar objects in unusual ways. People are reluctant to revise or change hypotheses on the basis of new data. People also fail to use the absence of symptoms as evidence in solving problems.

Improving Problem-Solving Skills

Limitations in problem solving can be addressed in various ways. Pictures or Venn diagrams help solve syllogistic reasoning problems. Training can eliminate some biases. *Incubation* and *decomposition* are two strategies that can aid problem solving. Experts are superior to novices in problem solving because of their knowledge and experience. They can draw on knowledge of similar problems, visualize related components of a problem as a single chunk, and perceive relations among problems in terms of underlying principles rather than surface features. There is no shortcut to obtaining the extensive knowledge that is the main component of expertise. However, expertise can also prevent the expert from seeing problems in new ways.

Problem Solving by Computer

Some specific problems can be solved by computer programs known as *expert systems*. These systems are one application of *artificial intelligence* (AI). There are two approaches to AI: one focuses on programming computers to imitate the logical manipulation of symbols that occurs in human thought; the other (connectionism) attempts to imitate the connections among neurons in the human brain. However, current problem-solving computer systems have far less capacity and speed than the human brain, and they deal successfully only with specific domains. They cannot draw insight from different areas and don't show common sense.

Decision Making

Evaluating Options

Decisions are sometimes difficult because there are too many alternatives and too many attributes of each alternative to consider at one time. Furthermore, decisions often involve comparisons of *utility*, not of simple objective value. Decision making is also complicated by the fact that the world is unpredictable, which makes decisions risky. People should act in ways that maximize the *expected value* of their decisions.

Biases and Flaws in Decision Making

People often fail to maximize expected value in their decisions because losses are perceived differently from gains of equal size and because they tend to overestimate the probability of rare events, underestimate the probability of very frequent events, and feel overconfident in the accuracy of their forecasts. The *gambler's fallacy* leads people to believe that outcomes in a random process, such as slot machine operation, are affected by previous outcomes.

Expertise in Decision Making

Experts tend to avoid some of the problems of decision making by relying on long-term memory to recognize familiar situations and choose the right course of action.

Language

The Elements of Language

Language consists of *words* or word symbols and rules for their combination—a *grammar*. Spoken words are made up of *phonemes*, which are combined to make *morphemes*. Combinations of words must have both *syntax* (grammar) and *semantics* (meaning). Behind the word strings, or *surface structures*, is an underlying representation, or *deep structure*, that expresses the relationship among the ideas in a sentence. Ambiguous sentences occur when one surface structure reflects two or more deep structures.

Understanding Words and Sentences

When people listen to speech, the perceptual system allows them to perceive gaps between words, even where these gaps are not physically present in the stream of sound. Syntax and semantics also help people understand spoken messages.

Understanding Conversations

To understand language generally and conversations in particular, people use their knowledge of the world and the context. This knowledge is often described by scripts. In addition, communication in conversations is shaped by conventions regarding the difference between new and given information and by nonverbal cues.

Stages of Language Development

Children develop grammar according to an orderly pattern. *Babblings* and the *one-word stage* of speech come first, then *telegraphic* two-word sentences. Next come three-word sentences and certain grammatical forms that appear in a somewhat predictable order. Once children learn certain regular verb forms and plural endings, they overgeneralize rules. Children acquire most of the syntax of their native language by the time they are five years old.

How Is Language Learned?

Conditioning and imitation both play a role in a child's acquisition of language, but neither can provide a complete explanation of how children acquire syntax. Adults tend to speak *motherese* to children, but expanding children's utterances is more helpful than motherese in teaching syntax. Humans may be biologically programmed to learn language, perhaps through an inborn *language acquisition device*, or *LAD*. In any event, it appears that language must be learned during a certain critical period if normal language is to occur. Although other animals also communicate, humans seem to be born with unique language abilities.

O U T L I N E

Mental Abilities

Janice, an elementary school student, had a serious problem. She was distracted in class and seldom settled down to work. When she did, she made many mistakes, and she rarely completed a task. Was Janice not smart enough to succeed in school, was she just lazy, or was something else wrong? A series of tests revealed that Janice suffered from a mild form of dyslexia, a reading disorder discussed in the chapter on perception. Her difficulty in interpreting the shapes of numbers and letters had blocked development of her reading and arithmetic skills, created frustration, and left her easily distracted from schoolwork, which she found unrewarding at best. As a result of the tests, Janice was placed in a specialized program of reading instruction. As her reading skills improved, she was finally able to display the excellent abilities that her reading problems had hidden.

A test had a very different result for Daryl, a high school student with a good academic record who was eager to attend college. Daryl took a college entrance examination the day after he had starred in his high school play. Tired after weeks of intensive rehearsals, he was also anxious because those rehearsals had caused him to fail a calculus exam. The fatigue and anxiety made it difficult for Daryl to read the entrance examination, to understand it, and to think clearly, and he did not perform at his best. His low score on the entrance exam dented his self-esteem and may have contributed to his rejection by the college he had most wanted to attend.

Fortunately, Daryl's case is an exception. Most people's scores on college entrance examinations are a better reflection of their ability. Still, the cases of Janice and Daryl demonstrate the importance of tests of **mental ability**—the capacity to perform the higher mental processes of reasoning, remembering, understanding, problem solving, and decision making. Performance on these tests can shape what classes children attend, what jobs they can obtain as adults, and generally what opportunities are opened or closed to them.

The activities involved in tests of mental ability—remembering, reasoning, and so on—were examined in

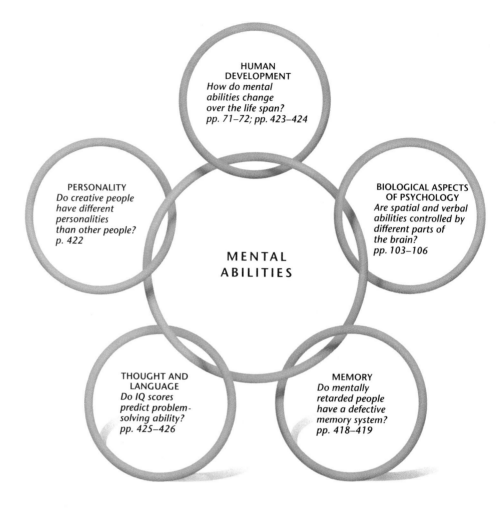

HUMAN
DEVELOPMENT
*How do mental
abilities change
over the life span?*
pp. 71–72; pp. 423–424

PERSONALITY
*Do creative people
have different
personalities
than other people?*
p. 422

BIOLOGICAL ASPECTS
OF PSYCHOLOGY
*Are spatial and verbal
abilities controlled by
different parts of
the brain?*
pp. 103–106

MENTAL
ABILITIES

THOUGHT AND
LANGUAGE
*Do IQ scores
predict problem-
solving ability?*
pp. 425–426

MEMORY
*Do mentally
retarded people
have a defective
memory system?*
pp. 418–419

■ Look at the diagram above, which illustrates some of the relationships between the topic of this chapter, mental abilities, and other chapter topics. In chapters so far we have examined processes and capabilities that are basic to human psychology. With this chapter we take up another perspective, one that emphasizes the differences among people. In the chapters on perception and thought, for example, we discussed attention and its role in information processing; in this chapter we examine whether differences in the ability to mobilize attention are related to differences in intelligence or other mental abilities. Exploring these differences provides another avenue for understanding how the brain works and what processes are involved in cognitive activities.

Much of the research on mental abilities has involved attempts to measure and predict those abilities through tests. As a result, the research has helped spur procedures for determining whether tests give consistent, unbiased results and whether they measure what they are intended to measure. As you will see, these same procedures are critical in other areas of psychology, especially in attempts to understand differences in personality.

These and other topics that link the study of mental abilities and other aspects of psychology are discussed in this and other chapters of the text. The diagram shows just a sampling of these links. The page numbers indicate where the questions are discussed in the text. ■

Chapters 8 and 9. There, we discussed similarities in how people carry out these activities whether they are plumbers in New York or physicists in Moscow. In contrast, we focus in this chapter on how people such as Janice and Daryl *differ* in their ability to perform these activities. (The Linkages diagram shows relationships to other chapters.)

Western society places special emphasis on one mental ability: intelligence. We begin by discussing how psychologists have tried to measure intelligence through standardized tests. This discussion leads to a consideration of the fundamentals of psychological testing. What characteristics make a test good or bad, and how do intelligence tests measure up to these criteria? Next, we discuss what the test scores mean and how they are used. Finally, we look beyond the tests to consider theories of intelligence and its relationship to other mental abilities.

Testing for Intelligence

Usually, it helps to begin the study of a concept by defining it, but defining intelligence has proved to be a difficult task, and psychologists do not agree on a single definition. E. G. Boring (1923) defined intelligence as "whatever an intelligence test measures." More specific definitions have ranged from the ability to think abstractly to the ability to deal effectively with the environment. Robert Sternberg (1985) conceived of **intelligence** in terms of three characteristics: the possession of knowledge, the ability to use information processing to reason about the world, and the ability to employ that reasoning adaptively in different environments. Pioneers in the study of intelligence focused on efforts to measure rather than define it, so we begin by examining those efforts.

A Brief History of IQ Tests

In the late 1800s, Sir Francis Galton tried, unsuccessfully, to test intellectual ability by measuring perceptual and motor abilities, such as how fast people responded to simple stimuli and how sensitive they were to pain. Other researchers soon concluded that these abilities had very little to do with intelligent behavior (Wissler, 1901). Alfred Binet, a French psychologist, took a more successful path; his test provided the model for today's intelligence tests.

The Stanford-Binet Test   In 1904 the French government commissioned Binet to find a way to identify children who might need special instruction. Two assumptions guided Binet when he created his set, or *battery*, of items. First, he assumed that intelligence is involved in many reasoning, thinking, and problem-solving activities. Therefore, instead of looking at performance on perceptual and motor tasks, as Galton had, Binet looked for items that would highlight differences in children's ability to judge, reason, and solve problems (Binet & Simon, 1905). His test included tasks such as unwrapping a piece of candy, repeating numbers or sentences from memory, and identifying familiar objects (Frank, 1976). Second, Binet assumed that children's intelligence increases with age. If certain children do better on a test than other children their own age, he reasoned, those children are mentally "older" and thus more intelligent.

To select the items for his test, Binet administered potential questions to children of various ages and then categorized the questions according to the age at which the average child could answer them correctly. For example, a "six-year-old item" was one that a substantial majority of the six-year-olds could answer. Thus, Binet's test included a series of *age-graded tasks*. By determining the number of items a child answered correctly at different age levels, the tester identified the child's *mental age*. Children whose mental age equaled their actual, or *chronological*, age were considered of "regular" intelligence. Those whose mental age was higher than their actual age were known as "advanced." Those with a lower mental than actual age were labeled "retarded" and in need of special education (Reisman, 1976).

About a decade after Binet published his test, Lewis Terman at Stanford University developed an English version known as the **Stanford-Binet** (Terman, 1916). Terman added items to measure the intelligence of adults and, applying an idea suggested by William Stern, revised the method of scoring. A child's mental age was divided by his or her chronological age, and the quotient was multiplied by 100; the result was called the *intelligence quotient*, or *IQ*. Thus, a child whose mental age and chronological age were equal would have an IQ of 100, which is considered "average" intelligence. A child who was ten years old but scored at the mental age of a twelve-year-old would have an IQ of $12/10 \times 100 = 120$.

From this method of scoring came the term **IQ tests**, a name that is widely used for any test designed to measure intelligence on an objective, standardized scale. The Stanford-Binet became the model for IQ tests. Table 10.1 gives examples of the kinds of items included on the test.

Early Testing in America   The scoring method used on the Stanford-Binet reflected important differences between Binet and the pioneers of IQ testing in the United States. To Binet, his test was simply a useful tool for determining which children needed special help in school. He did not believe he was measuring some fixed trait. In contrast, the method used to score the Stanford-Binet allowed testers to rank everyone who took the test. That goal was important to Terman and others who popularized the test in the United States because of their beliefs about what it was they were testing. Unlike Binet, they held that intelligence was a fixed and inherited entity; that different groups were favored with varying amounts of this thing called intelligence; and that IQ tests could pinpoint who did and who did not have the right genes to produce a suitable amount of intelligence. These beliefs led to some unfortunate outcomes, as enthusiasm for testing outpaced understanding of what was being tested.

Even before Terman developed the Stanford-Binet, psychologist Henry Goddard had translated Binet's test. In 1912 the U.S. immigration office asked Goddard to identify immigrants who were mentally defective. Goddard's test included questions that required familiarity not only with writing skills but also with American culture, such as what a tennis court looks like. Today it is painfully obvious that the test was not a fair measure of the intelligence of immigrants or anyone else unfamiliar with the English language or with American culture. But Goddard concluded from the test results that 83 percent of Jews, 80 percent of Hungarians, 87 percent of Russians, and 79 percent of Italians immigrating to America were "feeble-minded" (Goddard, 1917)!

The government also used mental tests to deal with another problem: how to screen out army recruits of low mental ability and to assign appropriate jobs to new soldiers. When the United States entered World War I, a team of psychologists was commissioned to develop a test for these purposes. Altogether, 1,726,966 men were tested. Again, the test favored people who were familiar with a particular culture. For example, one test item was "Five hundred is played with (*rackets, pins, cards, dice*)." Furthermore, the men were under

Table 10.1
The Stanford-Binet

These are samples of the type of items included on the Stanford-Binet test. In both Binet's original test and Terman's revision of it, an age level was assigned to each item.

Age	Task
2	Place geometric shapes into corresponding openings; identify body parts; stack blocks; identify common objects.
4	Name objects from memory; complete analogies (e.g., fire is hot; ice is _____); identify objects of similar shape; answer simple questions (e.g., "Why do we have schools?").
6	Define simple words; explain differences (e.g., between a fish and a horse); identify missing parts of a picture; count out objects.
8	Answer questions about a simple story; identify absurdities (e.g., in statements like "John had to walk on crutches because he hurt his arm"); explain similarities and differences among objects; tell how to handle certain situations (e.g., finding a stray puppy).
10	Define more difficult words; give explanations (e.g., about why people should be quiet in a library); list as many words as possible; repeat 6-digit numbers.
12	Identify more difficult verbal and pictured absurdities; repeat 5-digit numbers in reverse order; define abstract words (e.g., *sorrow*); fill in a missing word in a sentence.
14	Solve reasoning problems; identify relationships among points of the compass; find similarities in apparently opposite concepts (e.g., *high* and *low*); predict the number of holes that will appear when folded paper is cut and then opened.
Adult	Supply several missing words for incomplete sentences; repeat 6-digit numbers in reverse order; create a sentence using several unrelated words (e.g., *forest, businesslike*, and *dismayed*); describe similarities between concepts (e.g., *teaching* and *business*).

Source: Nietzel & Bernstein, 1987.

stress and were tested in crowded rooms where instructions were not always audible. It is thus not surprising that test scores were low. In fact, 47 percent of those tested showed a mental age of thirteen or lower (Yerkes, 1921). From the test results Canadian psychologist C. C. Brigham (1923) incorrectly concluded that (1) from 1890 to 1915 the mental age of immigrants to America had declined from 13.8 to 11.4, and (2) the main source of this decline was the increase in immigration from southern and eastern Europe.

Brigham's conclusions, along with the results of Goddard's tests, became part of the "scientific" evidence that was used to justify the Immigration Act of 1924, which established quotas limiting immigration from various nations. The quotas were especially low for countries whose immigrants had tested poorly. Some people also used the test results to argue for segregation of African-Americans. And in some states people whose low IQ scores earned them the label of "imbecile" could be sterilized against their wishes or even without their knowledge (Gould, 1983).

In 1930 Brigham repudiated his statements about the army test results. The methods used to reach conclusions about the intelligence of national groups were wrong, he acknowledged, and the tests themselves measured not innate intelligence but familiarity with American language and culture (Gould, 1983). Soon other psychologists recognized weaknesses in existing tests of mental abilities. Some worried that the tests gave too much emphasis to vocabulary, and many concluded that intelligence could not be assessed by testing only verbal skills or by any one test.

A new test developed by David Wechsler (1949) addressed these concerns. Wechsler's test was made up of several subtests and improved on earlier tests in at least two ways. First, some of Wechsler's subtests had little or no verbal content and reduced the extent to which answers depended on a particular culture. Second, Wechsler's test allowed the tester to develop a profile describing an individual's performance on each subtest and to compute more than one score. Thus, with Wechsler's approach a test can indicate a child's specific strengths and weaknesses. Wechsler's approach also acknowledged that describing intelligence by just one number is misleading.

IQ Tests Today

Since Wechsler introduced his test, psychologists have continued to improve IQ tests. One innovation has been the creation of tests that can be given to groups rather than being administered to one individual at a time. In addition, the method of scoring IQ tests has been changed.

Individual and Group Tests   Today, the Wechsler scales and the Stanford-Binet are the most widely used individually administered IQ tests in schools. Both are given by specially trained people to one individual at a time.

The Wechsler includes eleven subtests. Six require verbal skills and make up the **verbal scale** of the test. These include such items as remembering a series of digits, performing arithmetic problems, defining vocabulary words, and understanding and answering questions (e.g., "What did Shakespeare do?"). The remaining five tests have little or no verbal content and make up

Comparison of verbal and performance scores on the Wechsler scale can provide useful information. For example, a high score on the performance scale and a low verbal score could mean that the child has a language deficiency that prevents the verbal scale from accurately measuring that child's mental abilities.

Figure 10.1
Sample Items from the
Performance Section of the
Wechsler Test
Items like these tap aspects of intelligence but require little or no verbal ability.

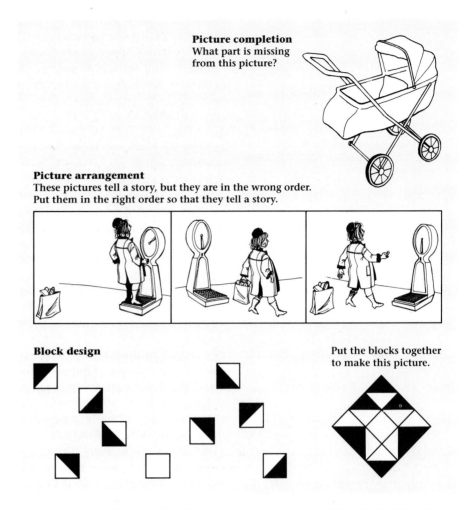

Picture completion
What part is missing from this picture?

Picture arrangement
These pictures tell a story, but they are in the wrong order. Put them in the right order so that they tell a story.

Block design

Put the blocks together to make this picture.

the **performance scale.** They include tasks that require understanding the relations of objects in space and manipulation of materials—for example, assembling blocks, solving mazes, and completing pictures. Figure 10.1 gives examples of items from one section of the performance scale. The tester can compute a score for verbal IQ, performance IQ, and overall IQ. Different forms of Wechsler's tests have been developed for different age ranges. For example, the *Wechsler Adult Intelligence Scale—Revised (WAIS-R)* is a test for adults; the *Wechsler Intelligence Scale for Children—Revised (WISC-R)* is for children five to fifteen, and the *Wechsler Preschool and Primary Scale of Intelligence—Revised. (WPPSI-R)* is for preschoolers (Aiken, 1987).

Like the Wechsler scales, the latest edition of the Stanford-Binet also uses subtests. It provides scores on verbal reasoning (for example, "What is similar about an orange, apple, and grape?"), quantitative reasoning (e.g., math problems), abstract/visual reasoning (e.g., explaining why one should wear a coat in winter; identifying absurdities in drawings), and short-term memory, along with a composite IQ (Thorndike, Hagan & Sattler, 1986).

Tests similar to the Stanford-Binet and Wechsler scales have been designed for administration to groups; examples include the Miller Analogies Test and the Wonderlick Personnel test. Group tests allow more data to be collected in less time, while also allowing test takers to work at their own pace. But group tests also have drawbacks. The tester has little chance to assure that everyone is adequately motivated and has understood and followed instructions. These issues may be particularly important when testing children or anyone who is physically handicapped or emotionally disturbed (Aiken, 1987). Furthermore, compared with tests administered individually, group tests contain a larger proportion of multiple-choice questions and fewer questions that are performance based or open-ended. Thus, group tests generally sample a narrower range of behaviors.

Scoring IQ Tests   IQ scores are no longer calculated by dividing mental age by chronological age. If you take an IQ test today, the points you earn for each correct subtest or age-level answer are summed. Then the summed raw scores are compared to the raw scores earned by other people. The average raw score obtained by people at each age level is *assigned* the IQ score of 100. Other raw scores are assigned IQ values that reflect how far each score deviates from the average for that person's age group. This procedure may sound arbitrary, but it is based on a well-documented assumption about many characteristics: most people's scores fall in the middle of the range of possible scores and, more specifically, follow a bell-shaped distribution known as the *normal distribution*, as Figure 10.2 illustrates. (The appendix on statistics provides a fuller explanation of the normal distribution and how IQ tests are scored.)

As a result of this scoring method, your **intelligence quotient**, or **IQ score**, reflects your **relative** standing within a population of your age. If you do better on the test than the average person in your age group, you will receive an IQ score above 100; how far above depends on how much better than average you do. Similarly, a person scoring well below the age-group average will have an IQ well below 100.

Our review of the early history of intelligence testing in the United States suggests an obvious question: are these tests fair? Some early IQ tests contained vocabulary items that would be unfamiliar to lower-income youths even if they were not foreign-born. For example, consider the question "Which is most similar to a xylophone? (*violin, tuba, drum, marimba, piano*)." No matter how intelligent children are, if they have never had a chance to see an orchestra or to have any experience with these instruments, they may easily miss the answer. Test makers today try to avoid such culturally problematic

Figure 10.2
The Distribution of IQ Scores in a Population
This distribution is typical of the normal curve, which is described in the statistics appendix. Each raw score is given an IQ value that reflects how far it deviates from the average performance of a given age group, which is assigned an IQ of 100. As a result, half the population ends up with an IQ below 100 and half above 100; about two-thirds of the IQ scores of an age group fall between 85 and 115; about one-sixth fall below 85 and one-sixth fall above 115.

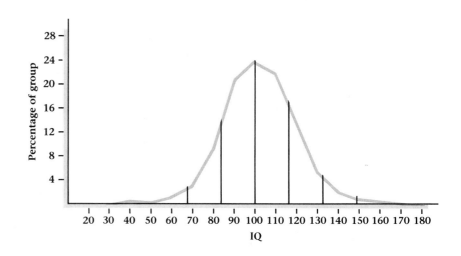

Note: Curve represents distribution of IQ scores in the standardized group for the 1937 version of the Stanford-Binet.

questions, but before assessing whether their efforts have produced tests that are fair to all groups, it is necessary to examine some principles of psychological testing and some criteria for evaluating tests.

Principles of Psychological Testing

Unless you are very unusual, you have taken innumerable tests in your life—IQ tests, school examinations, tests for a driver's license, perhaps even some of the personality tests described in Chapter 14. Why are tests so widely used? Any **test** is a systematic procedure for observing behavior in a standard situation and describing it with the help of a numerical scale or a system of categories (Cronbach, 1970). A test has three major advantages over interviews and other means of evaluation.

First, the administration, scoring, and interpretation of tests are *standardized;* that is, the conditions are as similar as possible for everyone who takes the test. Standardization helps ensure that no matter who gives and scores the test, the results are comparable; it reduces the chance that extraneous factors will distort the results. Insofar as the biases of those giving the test do not influence the results, a test is said to be *objective.*

Second, tests use *quantifiable* terms—scores—to summarize the test taker's performance. This characteristic allows testers to calculate **norms**, which are descriptions of the frequency of particular scores. Norms tell test administrators, for example, what percentage of high school students obtained each possible score on a college entrance exam. (The distribution shown in Figure 10.2 represents the norms for an IQ test.) Norms allow scores to be compared statistically. As a result, it is possible to tell, for example, whether a particular IQ score or entrance exam score is above or below the average score obtained by people of the same age.

Third, tests are *economical* and *efficient.* Once a test has been developed, it can often be given to many people in less time and for less money than other ways of obtaining information.

Of course, some tests are better than others. Two characteristics are important in determining how good a test is: reliability and validity. Both are expressed in terms of a *correlation*, which is a measure of the relationship between two variables. (For example, a high positive correlation between two variables, like age and year in school, suggests that as one variable increases, so does the other. Chapter 1 provides a fuller explanation of correlations.)

Reliability   If you stepped on a scale, checked your weight, stepped off, stepped immediately back on, and found that your weight had increased by twenty pounds, you would be wise to try a different scale. A good scale, or a good test, must have **reliability**; in other words, the results must be repeatable or stable. If a person receives a very high score on a reasoning test the first time it is given but gets a very low score when the test is given again, the test is probably unreliable. The higher the reliability of a test, the less susceptible its scores are to insignificant or random changes in the test taker or the testing environment, such as the temperature of the room.

To estimate reliability, researchers obtain two sets of scores on the same test from the same people and compute the correlation coefficient between the scores. When the correlation is high and positive (usually above +.80 or so), the test is considered reliable. The two sets of scores can be obtained in several ways.

Perhaps the most obvious method of obtaining two scores to measure reliability is to give the same test to the same people on two occasions. This method is called *test-retest reliability*. Of course, the test-retest method can

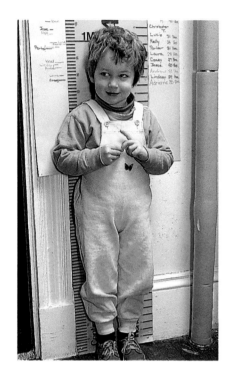

If a yardstick yields the same reading on two occasions on the same day, it is said to be a reliable measure of height. Tests that yield similar results on repeated occasions are also said to be reliable.

measure reliability only if the trait itself does not change during the time between the two tests. If a test measures short-term memory capacity and you learn how to chunk material in the period between the tests, your second score will be higher than the first, but not because the test is unreliable.

The test-retest method has an obvious problem: some people may benefit more than others from the experience of the first test, thus improving their scores on the second testing and making the test look unreliable. Other methods of calculating reliability alleviate this problem. One method uses an *alternate form* of the test on the second testing. Still another method is to use *split halves*. Just one test is given, but when it is scored, the test is divided into two comparable halves. Each half is scored separately, and then the correlation between the two scores is calculated.

Validity   A test may be reliable and still not be valid. The **validity** of a test is the degree to which it measures what it is supposed to measure (Anastasi, 1976). No test has "high" or "low" validity in an absolute sense; its validity depends on how the test is being used. For example, Galton administered a test that was good at measuring an individual's threshold for pain, but it turned out to be an invalid measure of intelligence. In contrast, if people who score high on a test of creativity also produce award-winning artistic work, the test has high validity as a test of creativity.

Most forms of validity, like reliability, can be measured with a correlation coefficient, but determining what the test scores should be correlated with may be troublesome. The answer depends on what the test is supposed to measure. There are three basic approaches.

One method is to analyze how much the content of a test covers a representative sample of the domain to be measured; the resulting measure is called *content validity*. If an instructor spends only five minutes out of twenty lectures discussing the mating behavior of the tree frog and then focuses half the items of the midterm on this topic, you might want to question the content validity of the exam. Similarly, a test that measures only verbal fluency would not have acceptable content validity as an intelligence test because it ignores other aspects of intelligence. A content-valid test includes items relating to the entire area of interest, not just a narrow slice of it. Some researchers measure content validity by calculating an index representing the percentage of experts who rate each of the items on a test as essential for measuring a particular trait or ability (Lawshe, 1975).

Another way of assessing validity measures *construct validity*, the extent to which scores on a test "behave" in accordance with a theory about the trait or construct of interest. For example, if your theory holds that an intelligent person is very good at solving problems, people who score high on an intelligence test should also score high on tests of problem-solving ability. If they do not, the test has low construct validity with regard to this particular theory of intelligence. Because psychologists disagree about how to define intelligence, they also disagree about how to measure the construct validity of intelligence tests.

A third approach is to measure *criterion validity*, the extent to which test scores correlate with another direct and independent measure of what the test is supposed to assess. To assess the criterion validity of a test of eye-hand coordination, you might calculate its correlation with a test of skill at video games. This independent measure is called the *criterion*.

When the goal is to predict future behavior, the criterion is some measure of future performance; criterion-related validity is then called *predictive validity*. For example, one way to measure the validity of the Scholastic Aptitude Test (SAT) is to determine its ability to predict the grade-point average (GPA) of first-year college students. These grade-point averages, then, are the criterion, and the SAT is valid insofar as it is correlated with them. By this measure, the SAT does its job reasonably well. If the mathematical and verbal portions of the SAT are combined, the correlation with first-year grade-point averages is about $+.42$ (Donlon, 1984).

HIGHLIGHT

The Case of the SAT

Controversies over the SAT test indicate some of the difficulties of constructing a good test and determining its validity. The name of the test—Scholastic Aptitude Test—suggests that it assesses *aptitude*, or the potential for success. The purpose of the test (and its equivalent, the American College Testing program, or ACT) is to predict a student's potential for success in college. Admission committees at colleges around the country use the test to help them decide which students to accept and which to reject—a practice that has stimulated considerable debate.

One criticism is that the SAT may not measure potential, because students can in a sense "cheat" the test, raising their scores by taking special courses or by taking the test several times. If these ploys work, then the test is measuring factors other than academic potential, and those who can afford multiple tests or special courses have a distinct advantage.

Do these extra aids work? It depends. Merely taking the test again is not likely to improve a student's score very much, unless a particular event such as illness artificially lowered the first score. SAT courses may teach people how to distribute their time wisely, when to guess, and other test-taking strategies. However, this information is most likely to alter students' scores only if they are unfamiliar with standardized tests like the SAT. Courses may also provide information on the content covered by the test. This information may help people who have been out of touch with the content—for example, someone who has had no math courses during the previous year

The Scholastic Aptitude Test (SAT) and its equivalent, the American College Test (ACT), are used by thousands of colleges and universities to screen applicants for admission. The tests are supposed to predict academic success, but there is controversy over what they actually test and worry over their potential for misuse.

(Carroll, 1982; Messick, 1980). Courses may also help some test takers who are unfamiliar with questions that have complex instructions (Powers, 1986). Otherwise, cram courses do not seem to offer substantial advantages. Samuel Messick and Ann Jungeblut (1981) concluded that SAT-preparation courses can raise SAT scores by only ten to fifteen points, which is rarely enough to alter substantially the chances for admission into a college.

A second criticism is that the SAT is not an aptitude test at all but an achievement test. The verbal portion of the SAT, for example, depends greatly on vocabulary, which in turn depends on previous learning—in other words, on achievement. Whereas *aptitude tests* aim to measure a person's capability for mastering an area of knowledge, *achievement tests* try to assess the amount of knowledge that someone has already acquired in a specific area. (Examinations in academic courses are an obvious example of achievement tests.) Difficulty in separating aptitude from achievement is not unique to the SAT. In practice, the difference between aptitude and achievement tests is hazy at best (Angoff, 1988).

Whether the SAT is called an aptitude test or an achievement test, it has some predictive validity for academic success. The correlation between total SAT scores and first-year grade-point averages of about +.42 indicates that the test is reasonably, but not spectacularly, valid (Donlon, 1984). One reason the validity of the SAT is not higher is the criterion itself: the GPA. Certain areas of study have stricter grading standards than others; in other words, the mean grade-point averages in some courses are lower than in others (Ory, 1986; Williams, 1985). Furthermore, people with higher SAT scores tend to gravitate toward disciplines with tougher grading standards (Goldman & Widawski, 1976). Thus, the GPA for people in difficult courses is lower than it would be if uniform grading standards were applied, thus lowering the correlation of the GPA with SAT scores.

Actually, high school grade-point averages do a better job of predicting college success than SAT scores do; their correlation with first-year GPA is nearly +.50. Some conclude that the additional information provided by SAT scores is not worth the financial cost and emotional stress suffered by test takers (Gottfredson & Crouse, 1986). However, the best way to predict college grades involves using both high school GPA *and* SAT scores (Anastasi, 1982).

Finally, the SAT is controversial because it is sometimes used in ways not intended by its developers. For example, scholarships established for students who demonstrated academic achievement in high school have been awarded on the basis of SAT scores, even though the SAT itself is not designed to measure achievement (Landers, 1989a). Some colleges have publicized their mean SAT scores as a way of proving their quality (Landers, 1989b), and rankings of the mean scores of cities or states have been used to evaluate the relative quality of public schools. These rankings can be misleading, for several reasons. To take just one example, a state in which only good students tend to take the SAT will have a higher mean score than a state in which most high school seniors take the test. (See the appendix on statistics for more on how the mean can sometimes misrepresent a set of data.) Mean SAT scores alone say little about the quality of education at a school or in a state. ■

Evaluating IQ Tests

The measures of reliability and validity we have discussed provide a first step in judging IQ tests. Are IQ tests adequately reliable and valid? What do they predict, and are they equally good predictors no matter who is taking the test?

How Reliable Are IQ Tests? When IQ tests are administered to the same people several years apart, their scores are not very stable. For example, correlations between tests taken by people when they were around three years old and when they were teenagers are only about +.54 (Brody & Brody, 1976; Humphreys & Davey, 1988). This figure would be a respectable predictive validity coefficient, but standards for reliability are more stringent. These findings do not indicate that IQ tests are unreliable, but rather that the tests are measuring abilities that change over time. After all, as described in the chapter on development, many cognitive skills change rapidly during childhood.

IQ scores fluctuate most in childhood, up to the age of about twelve; then they usually become much more stable. When split-half reliability is computed, the reliability of IQ tests is high; the correlation between scores is generally about +.90. Of course, a person's score may vary from one test to another if factors such as motivation or anxiety change. In general, people do better when they try harder. Still, compared with most tests, IQ tests usually provide consistent results.

Are IQ Tests Valid? The validity of IQ tests depends on the criterion being used. One approach is to measure the predictive validity of IQ tests for academic success. In fact, IQ tests do a reasonably good job of predicting success in school; the correlation of IQ with high school grades is approximately +.50 (Cronbach, 1970).

Do these results mean that IQ tests are valid measures of *intelligence?* Not necessarily. Academic success, after all, may reflect intellectual behavior, but it does not define all aspects of intelligent behavior. Winston Churchill was a modest student at best. As children, Leonardo da Vinci and Thomas Edison had problems in reading, writing, or mathematics that would no doubt have resulted in low IQ scores. (Their problems were related to learning disabilities, which are mentioned in Chapter 15.) It is impossible to determine whether IQ tests are valid tests of "intelligence" without a definition or independent measure of intelligence. To date, as already noted, psychologists do not agree on a definition of intelligence.

In fact, IQ tests assess only a narrow range of the qualities that might be considered aspects of intelligence. For example, the multiple-choice format of some IQ tests requires people to identify *one* correct answer (Jones, 1989). This format may discriminate against those who excel at solving problems by exploring and generating alternative ways of thinking about a question. IQ tests seem best at assessing aspects of intelligence related to schoolwork, such as abstract reasoning and verbal comprehension.

There is evidence, however, that IQ tests can predict more than academic success. One study that kept track of people for over fifty years found that children with high IQs tended to grow up to be successful adults (Terman & Oden, 1947). This study identified more than a thousand children who had scored very high on IQ tests; most received IQ scores over 135 when they were ten years old. Few if any became truly creative geniuses—such as world-famous inventors, authors, artists, or composers, but only eleven failed to graduate from high school, and more than two-thirds graduated from college. Ninety-seven earned Ph.D.'s; ninety-two, law degrees; and fifty-seven, medical degrees. In 1955 their median family income was well above the national average. (Terman & Oden, 1959).

In addition, people scoring high on tests of such cognitive abilities as verbal and arithmetic reasoning tend to perform better in the workplace than those who earned lower scores (Ghiselli, 1973; Herrnstein, 1989). The predictive validity of IQ scores is especially good for managerial and other complex jobs (Hunter, 1986). High IQ scores apparently reflect the ability to learn job-

Many people who achieved great things in their lives did not always show childhood brilliance at academic tasks of the kind measured by intelligence tests. There is more to intelligence than IQ scores.

relevant information and to deal with unpredictable, changing aspects of the job environment (Hunter, 1986)—characteristics that are needed in complex jobs.

Conclusions   By the standard measures for judging psychological tests, IQ tests have good reliability and reasonably good predictive validity for certain criteria. Although they tap a limited range of mental abilities, IQ tests do provide some useful information about the likelihood that a person will succeed in school or work.

Still, a particular IQ score may give a distorted view of an individual. The conditions of testing, as well as variations in motivation or anxiety, may lead to a misleading score. For example, comfort and rapport with the tester may affect performance on individually administered tests. A child who is suspicious of strangers, who is not used to prolonged one-to-one interactions with adults, or who has not had a warm, trusting relationship with adults will be less likely to exert maximum effort on the test (Jones, 1989).

Our earlier discussion of the history of IQ tests suggests another of their possible limitations. Early IQ tests were biased against groups that were not familiar with the dominant culture of the day. Are some people's abilities still more likely than others to be underestimated by current IQ tests? (See Figure 10.3.) Test developers now devote special effort to eliminating obviously biased

Figure 10.3
Items from the Black Intelligence Test of Cultural Homogeneity
Here are some items from a test in which success depends heavily on familiarity with words, terms, and expressions from African-American culture. Robert L. Williams of the Black Studies Program at Washington University constructed this test not to compete with standard tests of intellectual ability but to show that poor performance on a culture-bound test is probably due more to lack of familiarity with the culture represented than to lack of mental ability. (For each item, choose the correct definition or answer from the alternatives given.)

1. Black draught:	(a) winter's cold wind
	(b) laxative
	(c) black soldier
	(d) dark beer

2. Clean:	(a) just out of the bathtub
	(b) very well dressed
	(c) very religious
	(d) has a great deal

3. Crib:	(a) an apartment
	(b) a game
	(c) a job
	(d) hot stuff

4. Do rag:	(a) the hair
	(b) the shoes
	(c) washing
	(d) tablecloth

5. Four corners:	(a) rapping
	(b) singing
	(c) the streets
	(d) dancing

6. Who wrote the Negro National Anthem?	(a) Langston Hughes
	(b) Paul Lawrence Dunbar
	(c) James Weldon Johnson
	(d) Frederick Douglass

Answers:
1. B   3. A   5. D
2. B   4. A   6. C

Source: Williams, 1972.

questions (Jones, 1989; Educational Testing Service, 1987). Furthermore, for years IQ tests have included more than one scale; as a result, areas that are most influenced by culture, such as vocabulary, can be assessed separately from dimensions that are less vulnerable to cultural bias. Still, controversy about the fairness of IQ tests continues.

T H I N K I N G   C R I T I C A L L Y

Are IQ Tests Unfairly Biased Against Certain Groups?

Despite numerous attempts to eliminate cultural bias from IQ tests, the mean scores of some minority groups are lower than the mean scores of white, middle-class individuals (Humphreys, 1988; Wainer, 1988). People have gone to court in an effort to halt the use of IQ tests as a guide for placing children in special education classes (*Larry P.* v. *Riles*, 1975), making hiring decisions (*Griggs* v. *Duke Power Company*, 1971), or granting state licenses to insurance agents. Plaintiffs in these cases argue that using IQ tests to make decisions about people creates unfair discrimination that deprives minorities of equal opportunities for employment, high-quality education, or job advancement.

What am I being asked to believe or accept?
Some critics of IQ tests argue that a disproportionately large number of people in minority groups score low on IQ tests for reasons that are un-related to intelligence, job potential, or other criteria that the tests are supposed to predict.

What evidence is available to support the assertion?
Careful evaluation of tests combined with the results of some experimental research reveals several possible sources of bias in the tests.

First, whatever the content of a test, noncognitive factors such as motivation and trust that influence performance on IQ tests may put certain groups at a disadvantage. Children from minority groups may be less likely to be motivated to try to perform well on standardized tests (Bradley-Johnson, Graham & Johnson, 1986). They may also be less likely than white children to trust or establish rapport with an adult tester (Jones, 1989).

Second, many test items require vocabulary and experience drawn from white, middle-class culture. As a result, these tests often measure *achievement* in acquiring knowledge of the dominant culture. Researchers have attempted to construct "culture-fair" tests that reduce, if not totally eliminate, this dependence on knowledge of a specific culture; Figure 10.4 shows an example. These tests do indeed produce smaller differences between majority and minority groups than more traditional measures.

Third, IQ tests may reward those who *interpret* questions as expected by the test designer's culture. Conventional IQ tests have clearly defined "right" and "wrong" answers. Yet experienced testers know that a child may interpret test questions in a manner that is "intelligent" or "correct" but still different from what the test designer had in mind; the different interpretation produces a "wrong" answer. Here is one interaction between a tester and a five-year-old minority child from a lower-middle-class home:

Tester: How are wood and coal alike? How are they the same?
Child: They're hard.
Tester: An apple and a peach?
Child: They taste good.
Tester: A ship and an automobile?
Child: They're hard. (Jones, 1989)

Figure 10.4
Culture-Fair Tests
These are items from the Learning Potential Assessment Device (LPAD). The task here is to outline the square and two triangles embedded in patterns of dots, using each dot only once. The LPAD not only measures children's ability to deal with such problems but also allows them to try solving problems again after receiving some training. Thus, a measure of baseline performance is supplemented by evidence of potential for learning (Feuerstein, 1980).

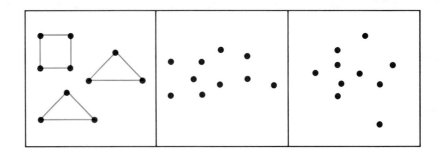

Source: Feuerstein, 1979.

The child correctly identified aspects of similarity, but not the ones the test designer had in mind. The fact that she didn't use the type of similarity that the designer was looking for (i.e., forms of fuel, fruit, transportation) does not mean that she can't. Perhaps various groups have ways of thinking about test items that differ from those of the culture reflected in the test designer's expectations. If so, members of these groups would end up with an artificially high number of answers scored as incorrect.

Are there alternative ways of interpreting the evidence?
The evidence might be interpreted as showing that although IQ tests do *not* provide an unbiased measure of mental ability in general, they still *do* provide a fair test of whether a person is likely to succeed in school or on the job. They may be biased—but not in a way that unfairly discriminates among groups. Perhaps performance on IQ tests does depend on cultural factors and familiarity with the dominant culture, but perhaps these factors are just as important for success at school or work as they are for success on the tests themselves. According to this view, it doesn't matter very much if IQ tests also measure achievement as long as the aspects of achievement measured are useful in predicting academic or occupational success, or whatever criterion is of interest.

Indeed, there is research showing that SAT scores predict academic success for minority students as well as they do for others (Humphreys & Davey, 1988). Furthermore, culture-fair tests do not predict academic achievement as well as conventional tests do (Aiken, 1987; Humphreys, 1988).

What additional evidence would help to evaluate the alternatives?
Evaluation of whether tests differentiate fairly or unfairly depends on whether the sources of test-score differences are relevant to predicting performance in the academic or job environment for which the test is intended. Unfortunately, in many cases, this question has not yet been satisfactorily answered. To take an extreme example, perhaps mean score differences between racial groups result entirely from differences on a certain group of test items that have nothing to do with how well the test as a whole predicts academic success. It is important to conduct research on this possibility.

Alternative tests must also be explored, particularly those based on problem-solving skills and more open-ended questions (Jones & Appfelbaum, 1989). These tests tap abilities different from those measured by most IQ tests. If new tests show less bias than traditional tests but equal or better predictive validity, many of the issues discussed in this section will have been resolved.

What conclusions are most reasonable?

The effort to reduce unfair cultural biases in test development is well founded, but "culture-fair" tests will do little good if they fail to predict success as well as conventional tests. Whether one considers it good or bad, fair or unfair, the fact is that having information and skills based on the values of the dominant culture is highly valued by that culture and influences both educational achievement and success in many jobs. As long as this is the case, it is reasonable that tests designed to predict success in these areas will measure a person's access to the information and skills valued by the dominant culture.

Stopping at that conclusion, however, would mean solidifying the status quo, in which members of certain groups are denied access to many educational and economic benefits because they do not meet the expectations of the dominant culture. Many psychologists urge that attention be focused on altering conditions such as poverty, poor schools, and inadequate nutrition and health care in order to raise IQ scores. As we discuss in the next section, improvements in these conditions might eliminate many of the reasons for concern about test bias. ■

Interpreting and Using IQ Scores

It is one thing to know that IQ tests predict academic or job success; it is something else to know what to make of particular test scores. If you receive a low IQ score, can you blame your parents' genes? How should teachers react if they are told that certain students have low IQ scores? This section examines questions like these regarding the meaning and use of IQ scores.

Do IQ Scores Measure Innate Ability?

Linkages: Why are some people smarter than others? (a link to Human Development)

Throughout the history of mental testing, people have argued about the importance of nature and nurture. Years of debate and research have brought psychologists to the conclusion that both heredity and the environment influence mental abilities. We outlined these conclusions in the chapter on development. Here we take a closer look at how psychologists examine the effects of heredity and environment on IQ scores and at their findings.

Studying Genetic and Environmental Influences It is unlikely that anyone will ever pinpoint the exact contributions of heredity and environment. For one thing, nature and nurture usually interact. For example, by asking many questions, bright children help generate an enriching environment for themselves; thus, innate abilities allow people to take better advantage of their environment (Scarr & Carter-Saltzman, 1982). In addition, in the real world the effects of heredity and environment are usually *confounded*. If bright parents give their children an environment favorable to the development of intelligence, for example, their children are favored by both heredity and environment.

Linkages: Can correlational data establish the genetic contribution to intelligence? (a link to the World of Psychology)

Correlational studies are one method psychologists use to try to untangle the influences of heredity and environment. To test the influence of genetics on individual differences in IQ scores, psychologists have compared the scores of people who have different degrees of genetic similarity, such as identical and nonidentical twins. Whereas identical twins have exactly the same genetic makeup, the genetic makeup of nonidentical twins is no more similar than

that of any other pair of siblings. Therefore, if genetic factors have an important influence on how well people perform on IQ tests, the correlation between the scores of identical twins should be higher than the correlation between the scores of nonidentical twins. Similarly, if genetic factors are important, correlations between biological parents and their children should be higher than correlations between adoptive parents and their children.

Notice, however, that the difference between correlations may reflect something besides the effect of heredity. Identical twins, for example, may share more than genetic makeup; they may experience a nearly identical environment. To distinguish genetic and environmental effects, psychologists have examined identical twins who were separated when very young and reared in different environments—perhaps in different orphanages or by different adoptive parents. Twins reared apart are likely to have less similar environments than twins reared together.

What do such studies find? First, heredity does have a strong effect on IQ scores. When identical twins who were separated at birth and adopted by different families are tested many years later, the correlation between scores is usually high and positive (at least +.60). If one sibling receives a high IQ score, the other probably will, too; if one is low, the other is likely to be low as well. However, studies of correlations between IQ scores also highlight the importance of the environment. Consider any two people—a set of identical twins, a set of nonidentical twins, siblings of different ages, or unrelated children brought together in a foster home. No matter what the degree of genetic similarity in these pairs, the correlation between their IQ scores is higher if they share the same home than if they are raised in different environments, as Figure 10.5 shows (Scarr & Carter-Saltzman, 1982).

In fact, one might wonder why the IQ scores of siblings do not correlate even more strongly than they do. The answer appears to be that even if they are raised together, their environments differ. First-borns may be treated differently from last-borns; having older or younger siblings creates differing pressures, opportunities, and responsibilities; and each child encounters different friends, school experiences, illnesses, and challenges. Indeed, any experience may be perceived differently by children of differing ages and thus have differing effects.

Figure 10.5
Correlations of IQ Scores
The correlation between pairs increases as hereditary or environmental similarity increases.

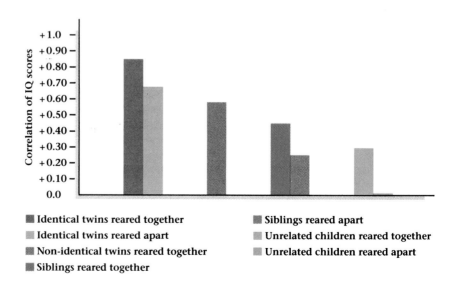

- Identical twins reared together
- Identical twins reared apart
- Non-identical twins reared together
- Siblings reared together
- Siblings reared apart
- Unrelated children reared together
- Unrelated children reared apart

Source: Bouchard et al., 1981.

The strength of environmental effects is highlighted by studies that compare children's IQ scores before and after environmental changes such as adoption. Generally, studies of children from relatively impoverished backgrounds who were adopted into homes with more enriching intellectual environments— environments with interesting materials and experiences, as well as a supportive, responsive adult—find modest increases in the children's IQ scores. In one study, for example, the IQ scores of adopted children were an average of fourteen points higher than those of siblings who remained with the biological parents in a poorer, less enriching environment (Schiff et al., 1978).

More recently, a study of French children who were adopted soon after birth demonstrated the importance of both genetic and environmental effects. When these children's IQs were measured after years of living in their adopted homes, those whose biological parents were from higher socioeconomic groups (where superior IQs are most common) had higher measured IQs than those whose biological parents were from low socioeconomic groups, regardless of the socioeconomic status of the adopted homes (Capron & Duyme, 1989). These findings suggest that a genetic component of the children's mental abilities continued to have an influence in the adopted environment. At the same time, the study found that the IQ scores of children from low socioeconomic backgrounds who were exposed to more academically enriched environments through adoption into high socioeconomic families increased by twelve to fifteen points (Capron & Duyme, 1989).

Conclusions   All in all, some researchers have concluded that the influence of heredity and environment on mental abilities appears to be about equal (Loehlin, 1989; Plomin, 1989). However, the relative contributions of heredity and environment may change from one individual to the next and from one time to another. At certain times, or for certain people, one factor may exert a greater influence than the other. Environmental influences, for example, seem to be greater at a younger age (Angoff, 1989) and tend to diminish over the years.

One way to express this relationship of heredity and environment uses the concept of **reaction range**: genetics roughly define a potential range of ability; the effects of environment can push a child up or down within this range. For any individual, however, the reaction range does not establish fixed, impenetrable boundaries; environmental factors might influence an individual's genetically based ability far more than would be expected for people in general (Platt & Sanislow, 1988; Zigler & Seitz, 1982).

What Conditions Can Raise IQ Scores?

In the chapter on human development, we outlined some of the environmental conditions that help or deter cognitive development. For example, a lack of caring attention or normal intellectual stimulation can stymie a child's mental growth. One study found that higher levels of chaos and noise in the home are associated with lower test scores (Wachs & Gruen, 1982). Low test scores are also linked with poverty, poor schools, and inadequate nutrition and health care (Humphreys & Davey, 1988; Weinberg, 1989). Efforts to improve these conditions are part of a movement known as community psychology, which is discussed in Chapter 16.

Can the effect of bad environments be reversed? Not always, but efforts to intervene in the lives of children and enrich their environments have had some success. Conditions for improving children's performance include rewards for progress, encouragement of effort, and creation of expectations for success. Even in college, establishing these conditions can be effective; in one

Project Head Start is designed to provide children from impoverished backgrounds with the preparation they will need to succeed in grade school. Such early enrichment programs have resulted in IQ gains of from five to fifteen points (Lazar et al. 1982; Zigler & Seitz, 1982).

study, doing so dramatically improved the success of minority students in passing a difficult college mathematics course and thus increased their access to science and engineering degrees (Watkins, 1989).

The best-known attempt to enrich children's environments is Project Head Start, a set of programs established by the federal government in the 1960s to help preschoolers from lower-income homes. In some of these programs teachers visit the home and work with the child and parents on cognitive skills. In others, the children attend group classes in nursery schools. Some programs emphasize health and nutrition.

Head Start has brought measurable benefits to children's health (Zigler & Seitz, 1982), as well as substantial improvements in their academic and intellectual skills. In general, the most consistently effective programs for poor preschoolers provide a moderate degree of structure. They offer an orderly physical setting, a predictable schedule, high-quality educational materials, and teachers who try to provide regular opportunities for learning (Zigler & Seitz, 1982). They provide a high teacher-to-student ratio and encourage parental involvement (Woodhead, 1988).

Do the gains achieved by preschool enrichment programs last? The effect on IQ scores often diminishes after a year or two (Woodhead, 1988). In one study, gains in cognitive development disappeared by the time the children were in high school, if not before (Lazar et al., 1982). However, this fadeout does not always occur (Seitz, Apfel & Rosenbaum, 1981; Zigler & Seitz, 1982). Furthermore, even when gains in IQ scores do fade, more general academic gains may remain. Children who have taken part in enrichment programs are less likely to be held back in school or to need special education programs (Palmer & Anderson, 1979), and they are more likely to complete high school and attend college (Jordan et al., 1985). When fadeout does occur, reduced motivation, not loss of mental ability, may be the cause (Zigler & Seitz, 1982). Children may lose motivation when they leave a special preschool program and enter the substandard schools that often serve poor children.

Martin Woodhead (1988) concluded that the primary benefits of early enrichment programs probably lie in their effect on children's attitudes toward school. Especially in borderline cases, it may be favorable attitudes toward school that help reduce the chances that children will be held back a grade or placed in special education classes. Children who avoid these experiences may retain positive attitudes about school and enter a cycle in which gains due to early enrichment are maintained and amplified on a long-term basis (Woodhead, 1988).

What Causes Group Differences in IQ Scores?

Much of the controversy about differences in IQ scores is not over differences among individuals but over differences in the mean scores of groups such as poor people and rich people or white people and black people. To interpret these differences correctly and analyze their sources, some pitfalls must be avoided.

First, group scores are just that; they do not tell about individuals. For example, the range of differences in IQ scores among whites and among blacks is far greater than the average difference between blacks and whites as groups. Although the mean score of whites is higher than the mean score of blacks, large numbers of blacks score well above the mean score of whites, and large numbers of whites score below the mean level of blacks (see Figure 10.6).

Second, remember that inherited characteristics are not necessarily fixed and that environmentally determined features are not necessarily changeable. A favorable environment may improve a child's performance, even if the inherited influences on that child's IQ are negative, while the effects of harmful environmental influences cannot always be corrected (Humphreys, 1984).

Socioeconomic Differences Upper-class American communities have shown mean IQ scores seventeen points higher than those of lower-class communities with the same racial-ethnic makeup (Vane, 1972). And the correlation between family income and children's IQ scores is +.30 (Cleary et al., 1975). Why?

The average IQ scores of different racial or socioeconomic groups may differ, but group differences say little or nothing about particular individuals. Many people from the lower-scoring group will have IQ scores that are higher than people from the group with the higher average score (see Figure 10.6).

Figure 10.6
A Representation of Black-White IQ Differences
Even though, on the average, whites have higher IQ scores than blacks, the variation around the averages for both groups is such that many individual blacks score higher than many individual whites.

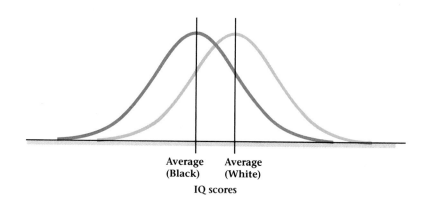

Average (Black)   Average (White)

IQ scores

The positive correlation between a child's IQ and the family's socioeconomic status appears to be the result of three factors. First, parents' jobs and status are determined by characteristics related to their own intelligence, and this intelligence is partly determined by a genetic component that in turn contributes to the child's IQ score. Second, the parents' jobs and education determine their income, which affects the child's environment in ways that can increase or decrease the child's IQ score (Cronbach, 1975; MacKenzie, 1984). Third, motivational differences may play a role. Upper- and middle-income families demonstrate greater motivation to succeed and excel in academic endeavors (Atkinson & Raynor, 1974). Perhaps these families instill in their children greater motivation to succeed on IQ tests. As a result, children from middle- and upper-class families perhaps make a greater effort and therefore obtain higher scores (Bradley-Johnson et al., 1986; Zigler & Seitz, 1982).

Racial Differences   The mean IQ score of African-Americans tends to be around fifteen points lower than the mean score of Caucasians, although this difference has been declining (Humphreys, 1988). Some have argued that this gap is due mostly to hereditary differences between blacks and whites. In support of this view, Arthur Jensen (1969) noted that heredity makes an important contribution to the differences in IQ scores within groups. Note, however, that the existence of hereditary differences among individuals *within* groups does not indicate whether differences *between* groups result from similar genetic causes (Lewontin, 1976). Your genes shape your height, but the difference in height between a group of ten-year-olds and a group of fifteen-year-olds is certainly not due to hereditary factors alone. Similarly, over the last fifty years, the average height of Japanese males has increased by 3.5 inches (Angoff, 1989), but this increase reflects improved environmental conditions, not a change in the genetic makeup.

Critics of Jensen's view also point to the very large differences between the environments in which the average black child and the average white child grow up. To take only the most blatant evidence, in 1986, 29.9 percent of black families in America lived at or below the poverty level compared to 8.2 percent of white families (Littman, 1989). Compared with whites, blacks are also more likely to have parents with poor educational backgrounds, as well as inferior nutrition, health care, and schools. All of these conditions are likely to pull down scores on IQ tests.

Evidence for the influence of environmental factors on the average black-white IQ difference comes, too, from adoption studies. In one of these, black children from disadvantaged homes were adopted by white middle- to upper-class families in the first years of their lives (Scarr & Weinberg, 1976). Within a few years, the mean IQ score of these children was 110. Using the scores of nonadopted children from similar backgrounds as a comparison suggests that adoption raised the children's IQ scores at least ten points.

In short, there appear to be important nongenetic factors working to decrease the mean score of black children. Given identical environments and educational advantages, the differences in the mean IQ scores of black and white children might be significantly reduced. Indeed, the recently narrowing gap between blacks and whites on tests of mathematical aptitude and intelligence may be related to improved environmental conditions for many black children. It is difficult to know whether the gap will ever be eliminated, but many psychologists have urged that research should focus not on the source of the racial differences in mean scores but on how children should be cared for and educated (Humphreys, 1984; Scarr & Carter-Saltzman, 1982; Zigler & Seitz, 1982). After all, whatever heredity might be contributing to children's performance, it may be possible for them to improve greatly, given the right conditions.

IQ Scores in the Classroom

Obviously, IQ scores are neither a crystal ball into some predestined future nor a measure of some fixed quantity. Consider the case of Philip R., an African-American man now in his forties. When Philip was two, a physician labeled him mentally retarded, and he was sent to a state institution. His Stanford-Binet IQ score of 60 confirmed the doctor's label, and Philip remained in the institution for fifteen years. Because he communicated mainly with grunts and gestures, Philip received no formal training in academic subjects, but he did become highly proficient at daily living skills. At fifteen, Philip began to work with a local shoemaker, who was impressed with how rapidly the youngster mastered tasks that were demonstrated for him. Through this man's efforts, Philip began to learn to speak a few words. At seventeen, Philip took an army physical; it revealed that he had a severe hearing loss in both ears. When surgery and dual hearing aids improved his hearing, Philip rapidly began to acquire expressive language. After spending years learning basic academic skills from the shoemaker, Philip entered a public high school at the age of twenty-three. He graduated in three years, went to college, and completed medical school at the age of thirty-three. Today he is a successful orthopedic surgeon (DeStefano, 1986).

Using IQ scores or other labels to categorize people may also have more subtle effects on how they are treated and how they behave. In a controversial study, Robert Rosenthal and Lenore Jacobson (1968) found that labels create *expectancies* that can have dramatic effects. Teachers were told that a test could indicate which grade-school students were about to enter a "blooming" period of rapid academic growth, and they were given the names of students who had supposedly scored high on the test. In fact, the experimenters *randomly* selected the "bloomers." But during the next year, the IQ scores of the bloomers dramatically increased; two-thirds showed an increase of at least twenty points. Only one-quarter of the children in the control group showed the same increase.

Apparently, the teachers' expectancies about the children influenced them in ways that showed up on IQ tests. How can expectancy become a self-fulfilling prophecy? To find out, Alan Chaiken and his colleagues (Chaiken, Sigler & Derlega, 1974) videotaped teacher-child interactions in a classroom in which teachers had been informed (falsely) that certain pupils were

There are differences in the average IQ scores of whites and blacks, but those who attribute these differences primarily to hereditary factors are ignoring a number of environmental, social, and other nongenetic factors that are important in creating (and may now be narrowing) this IQ gap.

particularly bright. They found that the teachers favored the "brighter" students in several ways. They smiled at these students more often than at others, made more eye contact, and generally reacted more positively to their comments. Children receiving this extra social reinforcement are not only getting more intense teaching but are also more likely to enjoy school, to have their mistakes corrected, and to continue trying to improve.

These results suggest that the "rich get richer": those perceived to be blessed with high mental abilities are given better opportunities to improve those abilities. Is there also a "poor get poorer" effect? Clearly, it would not be ethical to conduct an experiment in which children were falsely labeled stupid. However, there is evidence that teachers tend to be less patient, less encouraging, and less likely to try teaching as much material to students whom they do not consider bright (Cooper, 1979; Luce & Hoge, 1978; Trujillo, 1986). Thus, it is not hard to imagine that being tagged with a low IQ score or some other negative label may limit a person's educational opportunities.

Attempts to replicate Rosenthal and Jacobson's findings have not always been successful (Elashoff, 1979), and some researchers have found that the effect of inaccurate teacher expectancies, although significant, is small compared with the effect of a teacher's accurate perception of the child's abilities (Jussiam, 1989). It is probably safest to conclude that teacher expectancies may influence pupil performance under some circumstances but not others and that even when expectancies do not affect IQ scores, they may influence academic performance (Snow & Yallow, 1982).

Whenever people try to "summarize" other people with a label, a test score, or a profile, they run the risk of oversimplifying reality and making errors. ("In Review: Influences on IQ Scores" summarizes the factors that can shape IQ scores.) But intelligence tests can also prevent errors. Boredom or lack of motivation at school can make a child appear mentally slow, even retarded.

In Review: Influences on IQ Scores

Source of Effect	Description	Examples of Evidence for Effect
Genetic	Genes seem to establish an approximate range of performance on IQ tests.	The IQ scores of siblings who share no common environment are positively correlated. There is a greater correlation of scores of identical twins than of non-identical twins.
Environmental	Environmental conditions push people up or down within the range of their potential. Nutrition, medical care, sensory and intellectual stimulation, interpersonal relations, and motivation are all significant features of the environment.	IQ scores have risen among children who are adopted into homes that offer a stimulating, enriching environment.

An IQ test conducted under the right circumstances is likely to reveal the child's abilities. The test can highlight the motivational problem and prevent the mistake of moving a bright child to a class for the mentally handicapped. And, as Alfred Binet had hoped, IQ tests have been enormously helpful in identifying children who do need special educational attention.

Furthermore, the alternatives to IQ tests may not be very attractive. Should testing be replaced by teachers' judgments or some other subjective, potentially more biased assessment method (Weinberg, 1989)? Subjective assessment might lead some teachers to overemphasize classroom disruptiveness and thus place children who show conduct problems, not lack of mental ability, in special education classes, while leaving well-behaved children with special needs to struggle with work that is beyond their capabilities. Objective mental abilities tests minimize this possibility. In short, despite their limitations, IQ tests seem to provide a standardized and often helpful way of assessing and comparing some of the important mental abilities of large numbers of people.

Intelligence and the Diversity of Mental Abilities

If you are a teacher or administrator who cannot possibly know all your students well and you want one score to tell you something about their potential for academic success, then IQ tests are probably your answer. As we have said, IQ scores do a reasonable job of predicting academic and occupational success. However, differences in mental abilities extend well beyond those measured by IQ tests. Are any of these differences significant? Do IQ tests measure all important aspects of intelligence? Indeed, is there a single trait that can be called *intelligence?* To examine these questions, we first describe different ways of studying intelligence.

The Psychometric Approach

One method of studying intelligence, called the **psychometric approach**, analyzes test scores in order to describe the structure of intelligence. Much of the research using this approach has tried to answer one key question: is intelligence one general ability, or is it a label for a bundle of abilities? The answer has practical implications. For example, if intelligence is a single characteristic, a potential employer might assume that someone with a low IQ could not do any mental task well. But if intelligence is composed of many independent abilities, a poor showing in one area—say, spatial abilities— would not rule out good performance in understanding information or solving problems.

Spearman's *g* In the late 1920s, Charles Spearman, a statistician who helped develop methods for calculating the correlation coefficient, provided the cornerstone for recent debate about whether intelligence is a single, general characteristic. Spearman noted that scores on almost all tests of mental abilities were positively correlated (Spearman, 1927). That is, people who did well on one test tended to do better than average on all of the others. Spearman concluded that these correlations were created by a very general factor of mental ability, which was called **g**, or the **g-factor** of intelligence.

At first, Spearman held that people's scores on a test depended on just two things: the *g*-factor plus *s-factors*, which represented the specific information and skills needed for a particular test. Further examination of test scores, however, found correlations that could not be explained by either *g* or *s* and were called *group factors*. Spearman modified his theory to try to accommodate these factors, but he continued to maintain that *g* represented a controlling mental force (Gould, 1983).

L. L. Thurstone, in particular, disagreed with Spearman's theory. In 1938 he published a paper criticizing Spearman's mathematical methods and denying the significance of Spearman's *g*. Using a statistical technique called factor analysis, he analyzed the correlations among IQ tests. **Factor analysis** examines the correlations between all possible pairs of tests and identifies groups of tests that are more correlated with each other than they are with other tests. These differences in correlations may indicate that the tests within a group are all tapping one ability and that different groups of tests are measuring distinct abilities.

Instead of a dominating *g* factor, Thurstone's factor analysis revealed several independent *primary mental abilities*. He identified these as numerical ability, reasoning, verbal fluency, spatial visualization, perceptual ability, memory, and verbal comprehension. Thurstone said that Spearman's *g*-factor contributed little to the correlation among scores. It was, he argued, secondary to the primary mental abilities.

Decades later, Raymond B. Cattell (1971) contested Thurstone's analysis, reanalyzed data, and argued that *g* exists but that there are two kinds of *g*, which he labeled fluid and crystallized. **Fluid intelligence** is the basic power of reasoning and problem solving. It produces induction, deduction, and an understanding of relationships between ideas. **Crystallized intelligence**, in contrast, involves specific knowledge gained as a result of applying fluid intelligence. It produces, for example, a good vocabulary and familiarity with the multiplication tables. Since people with greater fluid intelligence are likely to gain more crystallized intelligence, measures of the two sorts of intelligence are positively correlated.

Conclusions Who is right? After decades of research and debate, most psychologists today agree that there *is* a positive correlation between several tests of mental ability, a correlation that can be described by one number, labeled *g*. However, the brain probably does not "contain" some unified "thing" corresponding to what people call intelligence, and *g* is likely to be a collection of subskills and mental abilities—such as reasoning ability, test-taking skill, reading ability, and so forth (Humphreys, 1984)—many of which are needed to succeed on any test of intelligence.

How important is *g?* Because *g* is the result of an analysis of correlations among scores, the answer depends on who is taking the tests. Any correlation coefficient is shaped by the range of data involved. Consider the correlation between height and weight. If you include all ages in the population—from infants to adults—the correlation between height and weight will be rather high, because infants are always much shorter and lighter than adults. But if you restrict the range of scores by studying only adults—a category that includes many short, heavy people and many tall, skinny people—the relationship between height and weight will be weaker and the correlation smaller. Similarly, if the range of mental abilities reflected by test scores is large, then there will generally be a positive correlation between most tests, and factor analysis will reveal the *g* factor. But when the range of ability is small, correlations decline, and factor analysis will give little evidence of the *g* factor.

In other words, the psychometric approach to the study of intelligence has important limitations (Fredericksen, 1986; Jones, 1989). The data it generates depend in part on which tests are used, which subjects take those tests and under what conditions, what methods of statistical analysis are chosen, and what labels are chosen to describe the factors that emerge. For these and other reasons, some scientists argue that the fundamental nature of mental abilities can be found only by turning to evidence other than the test scores used by the psychometric approach.

The Information-Processing Approach

IQ tests, the various analyses of *g*, and Thurstone's analysis of primary mental abilities all focus on the *products* of intelligence—the answers to a test. The **information-processing approach** looks instead at the *process* of intelligent behavior (Hunt, 1983; Sternberg, 1982; Vernon, 1987a). It asks: What mental operations are necessary to answer the questions on an IQ test or to perform other intellectual tasks? What aspects of this performance depend on past learning, and what aspects depend on attention, short-term memory, and processing speed? In short, intelligence can be examined by focusing on differences in information processing. This approach relates the basic mental processes discussed in the chapters on perception, memory, and thought to research on IQ tests. Are there individual differences in basic mental processes that correlate with differences in IQ scores or other measures of intelligence? More specifically, are differences in the attention given to basic mental processes or in the speed of these processes related to measures of intelligence?

The Role of Attention   The notion that intelligence is related to attention builds on the results of research by Earl Hunt and others (Eysenck, 1987; Hunt, 1980; Hunt & Lansman, 1983; Stankov, 1983). As we discussed in the chapter on perception, attention represents a pool of resources or mental energy. When people perform difficult tasks or perform more than one task at a time, they must call on greater amounts of these resources. Does intelligent behavior depend on how well people can mobilize and distribute the resources of attention?

Intelligent behavior might depend on flexibility or agility in shifting attention from one mental activity to another. So far researchers have found

Linkages: The information-processing model introduced in Chapter 9, on thought and language, suggests that human mental processes consist of an ongoing sequence of sensation, perception, decision making, and response selection and execution that allows us to recognize, think about, and respond to the world. Applying this model to intelligence might suggest that those with the most rapid information-processors (the ''fastest'' brains) would do best on mental ability tests, including those on TV game shows. Research suggests, however, that this is true only to an extent and that there is more to intelligent behavior than sheer processing speed. (Photo courtesy of Jeopardy!, hosted by Alex Trebek.)

small positive correlations between measures of intelligence and measures of attentional flexibility (Larson & Saccuzo, 1989).

Another possibility is that intelligent behavior depends on the amount of attention that can be mobilized (Eysenck, 1987; Weiss, 1986). To examine this view, Hunt (1980) had people take the Raven Progressive Matrices test twice (see Figure 10.7). The first time, he increased the difficulty of the problems until the subject made an error; the person's score on this version of the test provided a measure of intelligence. The second time the person took the test, Hunt kept the problems easy. However, while taking the test the second time, the subject also had to perform another task: pressing a switch whenever a particular tone was heard. People could perform this concurrent task well, Hunt reasoned, only if performing the easy spatial-ability task left extra attentional resources available. Thus, if intelligence depends on the availability of attentional resources, performance on this concurrent task should be related to performance on the first version of the spatial-ability test. And it was. Hunt concluded that people with greater intellectual ability had more attentional resources available. These abundant resources not only allowed better performance on the easy problems but also left sufficient resources for superior performance on the concurrent task. Thus, having more attentional resources appears valuable in carrying out the simultaneous mental operations that are often necessary for problem solving and other intelligent activities.

Processing Speed   Another possible link between differences in information processing and differences in intelligence has been under study at least since Sir Francis Galton's work in the nineteenth century. Perhaps, suggested Galton, intelligent people have "faster brains" than other people—perhaps they carry out basic mental processes more quickly. When a task is complex, having a "fast brain" might decrease the chance that information will be lost before it can be used (Carlson, Jensen & Widaman, 1983; Vernon, 1987b). A "fast brain" might allow people to do a better job of mastering material in everyday life and therefore allow them to build up a good knowledge base (Vernon, 1983).

These hypotheses sound reasonable, but research suggests that the speed of basic processing plays only a small role in determining intelligent behavior. In one study, Hunt and his colleagues measured the speed with which people could decide whether two letters (for example, *a* and *A*) shared the same name. This test provided a measure of speed of access to long-term memory. Speed on this test was positively correlated with scores on standardized tests of verbal fluency and comprehension, but the correlation was just +.33. Other correlations between measures of basic cognitive processes and measures of verbal intelligence are also rather modest. It appears that only a small portion of individual differences in performance on tests of reasoning or general comprehension can be tied to differences in any one type of mechanistic infor-

Figure 10.7
Items from the Raven Progressive Matrices Test
The task is to complete the patterns by choosing from a group of alternative patches. In the figure, patch 4 will complete the pattern.

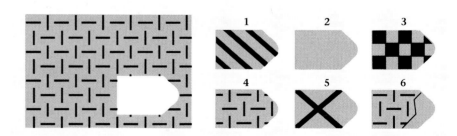

Source: Raven, 1948.

mation processing such as the speed of gaining access to memory (Hunt, 1983, 1987).

This is a modest conclusion, and it suggests many other questions. Are there "nonmechanistic" aspects of information processing that are correlated with performance on tests of reasoning? How is information processing related to other aspects of intelligence besides those measured by reasoning and comprehension tests? Robert Sternberg has integrated information-processing research into a broad theory of intelligence that addresses questions like these.

The Triarchical Theory of Intelligence   Sternberg's theory aims to explain a range of behavior that goes far beyond that measured by typical IQ tests. According to Sternberg (1988), most theories of intelligence are incomplete, because a complete theory must deal with three aspects of intelligence: its internal components, the relation of these components to experience, and its external effects. Sternberg deals with each of these in his *triarchical theory* of intelligence.

First, says Sternberg, the internal aspect of intelligence consists of the processes involved in thinking. According to him, there are three sets of processes, or *components:* performance components, knowledge-acquisition components, and metacomponents. *Performance components* are the processes of perceiving stimuli, holding information in short-term memory, comparing values, retrieving material from long-term memory, and calculating sums and differences. *Knowledge-acquisition components* are processes used in gaining and storing new information. *Metacomponents* are the processes that control performance and knowledge-acquisition components; they are involved in organizing and setting up a problem. Metacomponents determine the problem-solving strategies people use—how they decide on the nature of a problem, know what performance components to use, know what needs to be known before trying to solve a problem, and know how to evaluate a proposed solution. According to Sternberg, the metacomponents hold the greatest importance in intelligent cognitive activities such as solving analogies (of the form "A is to B as C is to . . ."). In fact, Sternberg found that although people with better reasoning ability end up solving analogies faster and more accurately than people with lower reasoning ability, they devote *more* time to understanding the analogy before coming up with the solution.

The second aspect of intelligence involves the relationship between the internal world of the components and the external world; it amounts to the ability to profit from experience by altering how the components are applied. According to Sternberg, intelligence involves being able both to deal with novelty and to make some processes automatic. When a task is familiar and well learned, good performance depends on the automatic manner in which performance components like encoding are carried out. When a task is unfamiliar, however, good performance depends on the way that metacomponents aid reasoning and problem solving (Sternberg & Gastel, 1989).

Finally, in everyday life intelligence is manifested by adapting to or shaping environments or by selecting new environments. This aspect of intelligence might be thought of as "street smarts." Intelligent people can use performance components, knowledge-acquisition components, and metacomponents to achieve goals. Thus, intelligent behavior varies with the context. The kinds of knowledge and metacomponents that are appropriate for solving a physics problem in the laboratory are not the same as those needed for explaining your way out of an embarrassing situation, settling a family dispute, or getting the best price on a used car.

Because it is so broad, many parts of Sternberg's theory are difficult to test. Exactly how should "street smarts" be measured, for example? Nevertheless,

As the limitations and the potential of mentally retarded individuals are better understood, their opportunities and their role in society will continue to expand. This young man, the first retarded senatorial page, was hired by Senator John Chaffee, of Rhode Island, in 1985.

Linkages: Do mentally retarded people have a defective memory system? (a link to Memory)

Sternberg's theory is important, because it extends the concept of intelligence into areas that most psychologists traditionally did not examine and emphasizes what intelligence means in everyday life.

H I G H L I G H T

Understanding and Treating Mental Retardation

The usefulness of both IQ tests and studies of information processing is evident in efforts to deal with mental retardation. IQ tests have long been used to help define and diagnose mental retardation. More recently, studies of information processing have provided useful information about how the cognitive skills of mentally retarded people are deficient and how these people can best be helped.

What is mental retardation? The label "mentally retarded" is applied to people whose measured IQ is less than about 70 *and* who fail to display the level of skill at daily living, communication, and other tasks that are normally expected of those their age. People within this very broad category differ greatly in their mental abilities, and in their ability to function independently in daily life. Table 10.2 shows a classification that divides the range of low IQ scores into categories that reflect these differences.

Mental retardation sometimes has a clearly identifiable cause. The best-known example is *Down syndrome*, which is caused by an extra chromosone in the genes. Children with Down syndrome typically have IQ scores in the 40 to 55 range. Intelligence may also be limited by environmental conditions or traumas such as meningitis or encephalitis contracted during infancy, birth traumas resulting from an oversupply or undersupply of oxygen, and excessive use of drugs or alcohol by a mother during pregnancy.

In most cases, however, no genetic or environmental cause of retardation is directly observed. These are usually cases of mild retardation and are known as **familial retardation** for two reasons: (1) most people in this group come from families of lower socioeconomic status, and (2) they are more likely than those suffering from a genetic defect to have a relative who is also retarded (Plomin, 1989). These facts have led psychologists to conclude that familial retardation results from a complex interaction between heredity and environment.

Exactly *how* are the mentally retarded deficient in their cognitive skills? Studies of information processing show that there are some significant ways in which the retarded do *not* differ from those with higher IQ scores. For example, they are just as proficient at recognizing simple stimuli, and their rate of forgetting information from short-term memory is no more rapid (Belmont & Butterfield, 1971). Mildly retarded children do, however, differ from other people in three important ways (Campione et al., 1982).

1. They perform certain mental operations, such as those involved in retrieving information from memory, more slowly.
2. They simply know fewer facts about the world. It is likely that this deficiency is a consequence of a third problem.
3. They are not very good at using particular mental *strategies* that may be important in learning and problem solving. For example, they do not spontaneously rehearse material that must be held in short-term memory.

What are the reasons for this deficiency in using strategies? As we discussed in Chapter 8, on memory, the differences between normal and

**Table 10.2
Categories of Mental
Retardation**

These are rough categories. Especially at the upper end of the scale, many retarded persons can be taught to handle tasks well beyond what their IQ score might suggest. Furthermore, IQ is not the only diagnostic criterion for retardation. Many people with IQs less than 70 can function adequately in their everyday environment and hence would not be classified as mentally retarded.

Level of Retardation	IQ Scores	Characteristics
Mild	50–70	A majority of all the mentally retarded. Usually show no physical symptoms of abnormality. Individuals with higher IQs can marry, maintain a family, and work in menial, unskilled jobs. Abstract reasoning is difficult for those with the lower IQs of this category. Capable of some academic learning to a sixth-grade level.
Moderate	35–49	Often lack physical coordination. Can be trained to take care of themselves and to acquire some reading and writing skills. Abilities of a 4- to 7-year-old. Capable of living outside an institution with their families.
Severe	20–34	Only a few can benefit from any schooling. Can communicate vocally after extensive training. Most require constant supervision.
Profound	Below 20	Mental age less than 3. Very limited communication. Require constant supervision. Can learn to walk, utter a few simple phrases, and feed themselves.

retarded children in some ways resemble differences between older and younger children. Both younger children and retarded children show deficiencies in *metamemory*—the knowledge of how their memory works. More generally, retarded children are deficient in **metacognition**: the knowledge of what strategies to apply, when to apply them, and how to deploy them in new situations so that new specific knowledge can be gained and different problems mastered.

It is deficiencies in metacognition that most limit the intellectual performance of the mildly retarded. If retarded children are simply taught a strategy, they are not likely to use it again on their own or to transfer the strategy to a different task. Because of this characteristic, it is important to teach retarded children to evaluate the appropriateness of strategies (Wong, 1986) and to monitor the success (or failure) of their strategies. Finally, like other children, retarded children must be made aware that effort, combined with effective strategies, is likely to pay off (Borkowski, Weyhing & Turner, 1986).

Despite the difficulties, the intellectual abilities of the retarded can be raised. For example, one program that emphasized positive parent-child communications and began when the children were as young as thirty months old helped children with Down syndrome to master reading skills at a second-grade level. These skills, in turn, provided the foundation for further intellectual and social achievement (Rynders & Horrobin, 1980; Turkington, 1987).

Designing effective programs for retarded children is complicated by the fact that how people learn depends not just on cognitive skills but also on social and emotional factors. Much debate has focused on *mainstreaming*, the policy of teaching handicapped children, including those who are retarded, in regular classrooms, along with those who are not handicapped. Is mainstreaming good for retarded children? Susan Harter and Edward Zigler (1974) concluded that retarded children who are taught in separate settings, especially in institutions, may demonstrate less curiosity and exploration than "mainstreamed" children, perhaps as a result of the sterile environments of many institutions. Yet these children also showed greater confidence in tackling problems than children who were "mainstreamed." Given a choice, the "mainstreamed" children tended to select tasks that they could be sure of doing well; the segregated children did not. Perhaps the confidence of "mainstreamed" children is damaged by the contrast they see with the brighter pupils around them (Kauffman, Gerber & Semmel, 1988).

Observations like this suggest that educators should not overemphasize training the retarded to learn specific cognitive skills and raising their IQ scores. Instead, educators should place greater emphasis on improving the children's motivation, confidence, emotional well-being, and general social competence (Zigler & Seitz, 1982). ∎

Multiple Intelligences

Despite low performance on IQ tests, some retarded people show incredible ability in narrowly defined skills (Treffert, 1988). One child whose IQ score was just 50 could correctly state the day of the week for any date between 1880 and 1950 (Scheerer, Rothman & Goldstein, 1945). He could play melodies on the piano by ear and sing Italian operatic pieces he had heard, although he had no understanding of what he was doing. He could spell forward or backward any word spoken to him and memorize long speeches.

In fact, many people who earn only average IQ scores show exceptional ability in one specific area. This phenomenon is one piece of evidence cited by Howard Gardner for his theory of *multiple intelligences* (Gardner, 1983). To study intelligence, Gardner focused on how people learn and use symbol systems such as language, mathematics, and music. He asked: do these systems all require the same abilities and processes, the same "intelligence"?

To find out, Gardner looked not just at test scores and information-processing experiments but also at how children develop, at the exceptional abilities of child prodigies and remarkable adults, at biological research, and at the values and traditions of various cultures. According to Gardner, all people possess a small number of intellectual potentials, or "intelligences," each of which involves a set of skills that allows them to solve problems. Biology provides raw capacities unique to each of these intelligences; cultures provide symbolic systems such as language to mobilize the raw capacities. Although normally the intelligences interact, they can function with some independence, and individuals may develop certain intelligences further than others.

The specific intelligences that Gardner proposed are (1) linguistic intelligence, (2) logical-mathematical intelligence, (3) spatial intelligence, (4) musical intelligence, (5) body-kinesthetic intelligence, which is demonstrated by the skills of dancers, athletes and neurosurgeons, and (6) personal intelligence, which refers to knowledge and understanding of oneself and of one's relations to others. Conventional IQ tests sample only the first three of these intelligences. Evidence for *g*, Gardner argued, comes from the fact that most IQ tests rely heavily on just linguistic and logical-mathematical intelligences. IQ tests predict academic success because schools value these particular intelligences. But conventional IQ tests, he claimed, fail to do justice to the diversity of intelligences.

If only measuring the multifaceted concept of intelligence were this easy!

Source: Drawing by McCallister; © 1990 The New Yorker Magazine, Inc.

Determination of the validity or usefulness of Gardner's theory must await further research. The theory does, however, highlight aspects of mental ability that are not measured by IQ tests but that may be important in certain kinds of human activity. Indeed, as we discuss in the following sections, some aspects of mental ability seem to be somewhat independent of intelligence. ("In Review: Analyzing Mental Abilities" summarizes Gardner's theory, along with the other views of intelligence we have discussed. See p. 424.)

Creativity

In each area of ability identified by Gardner, there are people who demonstrate **creativity**; in other words, they can produce novel but effective solutions to challenges. Corporate executives and homemakers, scientists and artists, all may be more or less creative. To measure creativity, some psychologists have generated tests of **divergent thinking**, the ability to think along many paths to generate many solutions to a problem (Guilford & Hoepfner, 1971). The Consequences Test is an example. It asks questions like "Imagine all of the things that might possibly happen if all national and local laws were suddenly abolished" (Guilford, 1959). Divergent thinking tests are scored by counting the number of *different* but plausible responses that a person can list for each item or by the extent to which a person's answers are different from those given by most test takers.

Of course, the ability to come up with different answers or different ways of looking at a situation does not guarantee that anything creative will be produced. Therisa Amabile has identified three components necessary for creativity (Amabile, 1989; Amabile, Hennesey & Grossman, 1986).

Creative people may share certain personality traits, but being creative says little about one's IQ. Indeed, because traditional mental ability tests measure convergent thinking, while creativity requires divergent thinking, researchers have found relatively low correlations between IQ and creativity test scores.

1. Expertise in the field of endeavor, which is directly tied to what a person has learned. For example, a painter or composer must know the paints, techniques, or instruments available.
2. A set of creative skills, including the ability to persist at problem solving, the use of divergent thinking, and the ability to break mental sets and take risks. Amabile believes that training can influence many of these skills, some of which are closely linked to the strategies for problem solving discussed in Chapter 9.
3. The motivation to pursue creative production for intrinsic (or internal) rewards such as satisfaction rather than for extrinsic (or external) rewards like prize money.

In fact, in several experiments Amabile and her colleagues found that external rewards can deter creativity. They asked groups of children or adults to create artistic products such as collages or stories. Some subjects were asked only to work on the project. Others were told in advance that the project was to be judged for its creativity and excellence and that rewards were to be given or winners announced. When the works were reviewed by experts (who had no idea which works were created by which group), those in the "reward" group were judged to be significantly less creative.

What determines whether a person is creative? Two possibilities can be ruled out.

First, creativity is not simply inherited. Notice that each of Amabile's components is affected by environmental factors. There is evidence that environmental influences on creative behavior are at least as strong as those on intelligence. Correlations on measures of creativity between identical twins raised in different homes are considerably lower than the correlations in their IQ scores (Nichols, 1978).

Linkages: Do creative people have different personalities than other people? (a link to Personality)

Second, although some popular stereotypes suggest that creative people are at least a bit odd, it is not necessary to be strange or to suffer from some psychological disorder to be creative. One study did show that a sample of British artists were more likely to be treated for mood disorders than British citizens of similar background who were not artists (Jamison, 1984). Other research, however, indicates that various kinds of mental disorders are no more likely to occur in the creative person than in the noncreative person (Carson, Butcher & Coleman, 1988). There is some evidence that creative people share certain personality traits. In particular, compared with less creative people, they tend to be more independent, rely more on intuitive thinking, and have higher self-acceptance and energy (Barron & Harrington, 1981).

Are creative people also intelligent people? Comparisons of people's scores on IQ tests and on tests of creativity have found only modest correlations, ranging between +.10 and +.30 (Anastasi, 1971; Barron & Harrington, 1981; Dellas & Gaier, 1970). This result is not surprising, because creativity requires divergent thinking, and traditional IQ tests test **convergent thinking**—the ability to apply logic and knowledge in order to narrow down the number of possible solutions to a problem. Thus, the questions on traditional IQ tests have only one or a small number of acceptable answers. The low correlation between IQ and creativity does not mean that the two are completely unrelated, however. Studies based on measures of creativity like the Consequences Test suggest that an average or above-average IQ is necessary (although not sufficient) for creative behavior to emerge (Barron & Harrington, 1981).

Creative behavior, in short, requires divergent thinking that is *appropriate* for a situation or problem. To be productive rather than bizarre, a creative person must be firmly anchored to reality, understand society's needs, and learn from the experience and knowledge of others. These are qualities that require some degree of intelligence.

Changes in Mental Abilities

Linkages: How do mental abilities change over the life span? (a link to Human Development)

If creativity is strongly influenced by the environment, can anyone learn to become creative? To some extent, perhaps, but early influences can set lifelong patterns. As a person gets older, the development of creativity may become more difficult.

The passage of time has consequences for other mental abilities as well, but findings regarding age-related changes depend to some extent on the method of study. One method is to use a **cross-sectional study**, which compares data collected simultaneously from people of different ages. However, cross-sectional studies contain a major confounding variable: because older subjects were born in a different year than younger ones, they may have had very different educational, cultural, nutritional, and medical experiences. These differences, and not just younger age, might account for higher IQ scores among younger people. Furthermore, because young adults are not as rusty when it comes to taking formal tests, their age group (or *cohort*) often outperforms their seniors in tests of cognition.

Changes associated with age can also be examined through **longitudinal studies**, in which a group of people is repeatedly tested as they grow older. Longitudinal studies, however, may be marred by another problem. As a group of people the same age is tested through the years, fewer members of the group can be tested, because some die or become incapacitated. The remaining people are likely to be the healthiest in the group and may also have retained better mental powers than the dropouts (Botwinick, 1977). Hence, longitudinal studies may *underestimate* the degree to which abilities decline with age.

In short, cross-sectional studies are likely to overestimate and longitudinal studies to underestimate the effects of age on ability. But the general picture painted by both types of studies is reasonably consistent: IQ scores usually remain fairly constant from early adulthood until about sixty to seventy years of age. Then—excluding cases of senility, Alzheimer's disease, and other organic disorders—some components of intelligence, but not others, begin to fail.

As noted in Chapter 2, on development, the classic pattern is that capacities related to numerical skills, speeded performance, and spatial processing decline and that little or no loss, and possibly even some improvement, occurs in verbal ability and general knowledge (Botwinick, 1977). In other words, different aspects of mental ability show a different developmental course over the life span. *Crystallized intelligence*, which depends on retrieving information and facts about the world from long-term memory, may continue to grow well into old age. *Fluid intelligence*, which involves rapid and flexible manipulations of ideas and symbols, remains stable during adulthood and then declines in late life (Hayslip & Sterns, 1979).

How and where does this decline show up? The decline in fluid intelligence is evident in somewhat slower processing of new information and the need for more time to solve unfamiliar problems. More specifically, among those over sixty-five or seventy, problems in four areas of information processing often seem to impair problem-solving ability.

1. *Short-term memory* The ability to hold and organize material in short-term memory declines beyond age fifty or sixty, particularly when attention must be redirected. This decline is seen when older people try to solve mathematical word problems that require that they attend to stimuli relevant for deciding how to solve the problem while also making computations (Fozard, 1980).

2. *Processing speed* There is a general slowing of all mental processes (Salthouse, 1985; Strayer, Wickens & Braune, 1987). For many tasks, this slowing may not create obstacles. However, when solving a problem that requires

manipulating material in short-term memory, quick processing of information is critical to success (Rabbit, 1977). To multiply two two-digit numbers mentally, for example, a person must combine the subsums before they decay.

3. *Organization*   Older people seem to be less likely to solve problems by adopting specific search strategies, or heuristics (Young, 1966, 1971). For example, a good heuristic for locating a problem in the wiring of a circuit is to perform a test that narrows down the regions where the problem might be. Marguerite Young (1966, 1971) found that the tests carried out by older people tended to be more random and haphazard. This result may occur partly because many older people are out of practice at solving such problems.

4. *Conservatism*   Older people tend to be more conservative in problem solving than their younger counterparts. They are less likely to abandon an incorrect hypothesis in favor of a new one (Offenback, 1974), and they require more information before making a tentative decision (Rabbitt, 1977). Laboratory studies suggest that older people are also more likely than younger ones to choose conservative, risk-free options over more radical, riskier ones (Botwinick, 1966).

In summary, in old age, as in earlier life, there is a gradual, continual accumulation of knowledge about the world; some systematic changes in the limits of mental processes; and qualitative changes in how those processes are carried out.

In Review: Analyzing Mental Abilities

Approach	Method	Key Findings or Propositions
Psychometric	Define the structure of intelligence by examining factor analysis of the correlations between scores on tests of mental abilities.	Performance on many tests of mental abilities is highly correlated, but this correlation, represented by *g*, reflects a bundle of abilities, not just one trait.
Information Processing	Understand intelligence by examining the mental operations involved in intelligent behavior.	The amount of attentional resources available makes a significant contribution to performance on IQ tests. The speed of basic processes is somewhat less important.
Sternberg's triarchical theory	Understand intelligence by examining the information processing involved in thinking, changes with experience, and effects in different environments.	Thinking involves three components. High intelligence is shown in the effective organization of these components, in altering their use to deal with novel or familiar problems, and in adapting problem-solving strategies to different environments.
Gardner's theory of multiple intelligences	Understand intelligence by examining test scores, information processing, biological and developmental research, the skills valued by different cultures, and exceptional people.	Biology provides the capacity for six distinct "intelligences" valued by society: linguistic, logical-mathematical, spatial, musical, body-kinesthetic, and personal.

Linkages: Mental Abilities and Thought

Do IQ scores predict problem-solving ability?

The outcome of a horserace depends on track conditions, temperature, the horses' training, the skill of the jockeys, and a multitude of other factors. People who display cognitive complexity, that is, who can keep in mind and mentally combine numerous interacting factors, tend to be especially successful at dealing with complicated situations, whether they involve betting, business decisions, or advanced scientific research.

About ten years ago, a certain "Mr. X" faced a lawsuit in Great Britain. He was accused of engaging in a number of complex but shady financial deals. In his defense, his lawyers claimed that because Mr. X had an IQ score of just 80 and minimal education, he simply could not have carried out the deals (Turnstall et al., 1982). That might sound reasonable, but there is evidence that a high IQ is not necessarily important for thinking through the kinds of financial problems that Mr. X was accused of handling.

Support for this argument comes from, of all places, the racetrack. Horse betting is, after all, a form of financial problem solving. To choose the winner consistently, a bettor needs a sophisticated mental model of all of the variables that can influence how fast certain horses will run at a specific track—age, conditioning, weather, jockey, trainer, and the like—*and* how these variables will interact. When thirty avid racetrack bettors in Delaware were studied, some were clearly better bettors than others (Ceci & Liker, 1986). The good bettors, or "experts," predicted very accurately the final handicap that each horse was assigned at race time, a skill closely related to the ability to predict the winner. Most important, the expert and nonexpert bettors did not differ at all in the IQ scores they received on the WAIS. Both groups had received a mean IQ of around 100. At least one expert bettor had a WAIS IQ of only 82!

This study is just one piece of the evidence that supports a general conclusion: IQ scores are not good predictors of problem-solving ability. Since IQ tests attempt to provide measures of ability free of knowledge about any particular domain, this result is not very surprising. As discussed in Chapter 9, effective problem solving requires knowledge about the domain associated with the problem (mechanics need to know about cars to diagnose automotive malfunctions correctly, for example). Furthermore, effective problem solving requires the ability to come up with multiple hypotheses and avoid mental sets or functional fixedness. In other words, good problem solving requires divergent thinking. As noted earlier, IQ tests stress convergent thinking.

If IQ scores do not predict problem-solving ability, are there other differences among individuals that do? Studies of mental abilities suggest two possible factors: cognitive complexity and the ability to devise a good strategy.

Cognitive complexity involves flexibility of thought and the ability to anticipate future events and to alter a course of action based on unexpected happenings. Most important, cognitively complex people can think *multidimensionally;* in other words, they can interpret the consequences of their actions in a variety of ways and appreciate several aspects of a problem. In the study of Delaware bettors, expert and nonexpert bettors reached their predictions in different ways. The experts used a more cognitively complex mental model to integrate fifteen variables about each of the horses described in the official racing program. That is, in making their predictions, they considered more variables and relied more on the interactions among variables than did the nonexperts.

To measure cognitive complexity, Siegried Streufert (1986) asked several business executives to play a game in which they managed a fictitious company, making decisions about investments, expansion, marketing, and so forth. Streufert rated the executives high on cognitive complexity if they simultaneously considered several factors and thought through the many implications of a decision. Two findings of Streufert's study were especially significant. First, cognitive complexity does not appear to be closely related to IQ scores. Second, cognitive complexity is *domain specific*. People who are cognitively complex in one domain, such as business decision making, may not show cognitive complexity in another area, such as family relations. An executive might react to a son or daughter in a rigid way, showing no appreciation for the child's point of view, even though the executive regularly considers all sides of business issues.

Other studies have highlighted the importance of strategies in distinguishing good from bad problem solvers. For example, Sternberg (1986) showed that differences in the ability to solve analogies can be traced to differences in problem-solving strategies. The importance of differing strategies was also demonstrated in the study discussed in Chapter 9 in which expert physicists used more sophisticated problem-solving methods than inexperienced students (Chi et al., 1981). The same results appeared in a study comparing physics problem solvers within a college physics class (Hardimann, Dufresne & Mestre, 1989). Poor problem solvers judged the similarity between physics problems in terms of surface features, such as whether the problems involved inclined planes; good problem solvers judged similarity in terms of the similarity of underlying principles, such as whether problems could be solved using the same physical law. The differences were not related to underlying mathematical ability as measured by a typical IQ test.

These results emphasize the importance of understanding that IQ tests do not measure all aspects of the abilities people commonly have in mind when they talk about intelligence. If the everyday concept of "intelligence" means anything after all, it surely includes the ability to think and solve problems. The relationship between scores on IQ tests and the capacity for intelligent thought is not necessarily strong or consistent, however. Good problem solvers in business, at home, or at the track depend to some extent on the mental abilities that IQ tests measure (Hunter, 1986), but they also employ knowledge and processes that are not measured by traditional IQ tests.

Future Directions

The study and testing of mental abilities have far-reaching implications for education; for who is hired, fired, or promoted; and for governmental policies for the disadvantaged. Because of this broad reach, these topics stir heated debates and biases that may have little to do with scientific findings. Yet some solid conclusions about intelligence and mental ability are emerging.

First, there seems to be a developing consensus that different definitions of intelligence are needed to serve different purposes. There are varying views, however, about how far beyond the academic domain psychologists should look for the characteristics of intelligent behavior. For example, there is disagreement about whether to follow Sternberg's suggestion to include adaptive changes in everyday life in measures of intelligence. Second, most psychologists agree that the brain does not contain some unified "thing" corresponding to intelligence and that the correlation between tests of mental ability, labeled *g*, is likely to reflect a bundle of abilities. Third, most psychologists agree that the mental abilities of a particular individual result from a complex interaction between heredity and environment.

The development of the Kaufman Assessment Battery for Children, or K-ABC (Kaufman & Kaufman, 1983) is one indication that the information-processing approach to mental abilities is here to stay. Like other IQ tests, the K-ABC assesses factual knowledge and academic skills, but it also contains subscales designed to assess information-processing abilities. One scale contains tasks (such as imitating a sequence of hand movements) that require the orderly use of one piece of information at a time, while another presents problems (such as identifying a picture from small glimpses) that can be solved only by integrating several sources of information.

Where is the field moving? Some insight is provided by a book compiled by most of the best researchers in the field (Sternberg & Detterman, 1986). From their thoughts and conclusions, it is apparent that much effort will be given to understanding the information-processing operations that underlie intelligent behavior and how they are related to traditional measures of intelligence. There will also be growing concern for evaluating mental abilities in the context of how an individual relates to society. This concern is likely to be reflected in studies of intelligent behavior in everyday problem-solving situations, in research on the role of intelligence in the ability to deal successfully with other people, and in continued interest in heredity-environment issues (Plomin, 1989).

Psychologists will also work to develop better and broader tests. Many tests will likely go beyond traditional formats in an effort to tap divergent thinking (Jones & Appfelbaum, 1989). At the same time, more sophisticated statistical analyses will produce better understanding of the correlations between intelligence measures of different groups (Loehlin, 1989). These techniques will begin to overcome the major fundamental limitation of correlations: they do not usually allow conclusions about what causes the correlation. Perhaps these new analytical methods will help to sort out the complex effects of heredity and environment on mental ability.

Finally, the information-processing approach to mental abilities will continue to increase understanding of how information-processing mechanisms are related to brain processes. Progress is likely to come through research on physiological measures such as the speed of evoked potentials and changes or differences in neurochemistry and metabolic activity during intelligent thought. These efforts will be paralleled by increasingly sophisticated approaches to understanding the structure of the genetic code and its relation to differences in cognitive functioning.

If you want to learn more about mental abilities, consider taking a course in tests and measurement, sometimes called psychometrics. Many courses in cognitive psychology also address the nature of individual differences in intelligent behavior. Advanced courses in behavioral genetics should also be of interest.

Summary and Key Terms

Mental ability refers to the capacity to perform the higher mental processes of reasoning, remembering, understanding, and problem solving.

Testing for Intelligence

Psychologists have not reached a consensus on how best to define *intelligence*. Proposed definitions often focus on the role of intelligence in reasoning, problem solving, and dealing with the environment.

A Brief History of IQ Tests

Binet developed a test of intelligence in order to identify children who needed special instruction. His test included questions that required reasoning and problem solving of varying levels of difficulty, graded by age. Terman developed a revision of Binet's test that became known as the *Stanford-Binet* test; it included items to assess the intelligence of adults as well as that of children and became the model for *IQ tests*. Pioneers in the use of IQ tests in the United States failed to acknowledge that performance on their tests reflected not just mental ability but also knowledge of the dominant culture of the time. The results were used to justify discrimination against certain groups. Wechsler tests remedied some of the deficiencies of the earlier IQ tests. Made up of subtests, some of which had little verbal content, these tests allowed testers to generate scores for different parts of the test.

IQ Tests Today

IQ tests today may be administered either to one person at a time or to an entire group. In schools the Stanford-Binet and the Wechsler tests are the most often used individually administered tests. Both include subtests and provide scores for parts of the test as well as an overall score. Currently, a person's *intelligence quotient*, or *IQ score*, reflects how far that person's performance on the test deviates from the average performance by people in his or her age group. An average performance produces an IQ of 100.

Principles of Psychological Testing

Tests have three key advantages over other techniques of evaluation. They are standardized, so that the performances of different people are comparable; they produce scores that can be compared with *norms*; and they are economical and efficient. A good test must be *reliable*, which means that the results for each person are stable, and *valid*, which means that the test measures what it is supposed to measure. Measures of reliability and validity are typically expressed as correlation coefficients. Reliability can be measured by the test-retest, alternate form, and split-halves methods. Validity can be evaluated by measuring content validity, construct validity, or predictive validity, which means measuring the correlation between the test score and a criterion that is another measure of the performance that the test is supposed to predict. The predictive validity of the SAT, for example, may be judged by measuring the correlation between SAT scores and grade-point averages. By this measure, the predictive validity of the SAT is reasonably good.

Evaluating IQ Tests

A person's IQ score is likely to change over the years of childhood, but this instability reflects changing abilities. Otherwise, IQ tests are reliable tests, and they do a good job of predicting academic success and success in complex jobs. However, IQ tests assess only some of the abilities that might be considered aspects of intelligence, and they may favor those most familiar with middle-class culture. Nonetheless, this familiarity is also important for academic and occupational success.

Other Key Terms in This Section: verbal scale, performance scale.

Interpreting and Using IQ Scores

Do IQ Scores Measure Innate Ability?

Both heredity and the environment influence IQ scores, and their effects interact. The influence of heredity is shown by the high correlation between IQ scores of identical twins raised in separate households and by the similarity in the IQ scores of children adopted at birth and their biological parents. The influence of the environment is revealed by the higher correlation of IQ between siblings who share the same environment than by those who do not and by the effects of environmental changes such as adoption. Some researchers have used the concept of *reaction range* to express the interaction between biological and environmental determinants of mental ability.

What Conditions Can Raise IQ Scores?

An enriched environment sometimes raises IQ scores. Initial large gains in cognitive performance that result from interventions like Head Start may decline over time, but the programs can produce lasting gains in other aspects of scholastic competence and may improve children's attitude toward school.

What Causes Group Differences in IQ Scores?

Different socioeconomic and racial groups have different mean IQ scores. These differences result from both environmental and genetic factors. Differences in motivation and environmental enrichment are major sources of differences in the mean IQ scores of these groups.

IQ Scores in the Classroom

Like any label, an IQ score can generate expectations that affect both how other people respond to a person and how that person behaves. Children labeled with low IQ scores may be offered fewer or lower-quality educational opportunities. If used properly, however, IQ scores may help educators to identify a student's strengths and weaknesses and to offer the curriculum that will best serve that student.

Intelligence and the Diversity of Mental Abilities

The Psychometric Approach

The *psychometric approach* attempts to analyze the structure of intelligence by examining correlations between tests of mental ability. Because scores on almost all tests of mental abilities are positively correlated, Spearman concluded that all of these tests measure a general factor of mental ability, called *g* or the *g-factor* of intelligence. As a result of *factor analysis*, other researchers have concluded that intelligence is not a single trait. It seems likely that *g* reflects a collection of subskills and mental abilities needed to succeed on any test of intelligence. Because *g* is the result of an analysis of correlations, its importance varies with the test, the test takers, and the test interpreters.

The Information-Processing Approach

The *information-processing approach* to intelligence focuses on the processes by which intelligent behavior is produced. Small positive correlations have been found between IQ scores and measures of the flexibility and capacity of attention, and between IQ scores and measures of the speed of information processing. According to Sternberg, intelligent thinking involves three types of mental processes, called performance components, knowledge-acquisition components, and metacomponents. Of these, the metacomponents are most important in cognitive activities such as solving analogies. Sternberg's triarchical theory also holds that intelligence depends on the ability to profit from experience and to deal with the environment.

Both IQ tests and the information-processing approach have helped psychologists understand mental retardation, a term applied to those who typically have an IQ score below about 70 and whose communication and daily living skills are less than expected of people their age. Compared to those of normal intelligence, retarded people process information more slowly, know fewer facts about the world, and are poorer at using strategies. However, strategies can be taught to the mentally retarded.

Multiple Intelligences

Gardner's approach to intelligence is based not only on the results of mental tests and information-processing research but also on studies of prodigies, human development, biology, and various cultures. He holds that biology equips humans with the raw capacities for several intelligences that can function with some independence—specifically, linguistic, logical-mathematical, spatial, musical, body-kinesthetic, and personal intelligences.

Creativity

Tests of *divergent thinking* are used to measure differences in *creativity*. In contrast, IQ tests require *convergent thinking*. Although creativity and IQ scores are not highly correlated, creative behavior requires intelligence. More specifically, the emergence of creativity requires expertise in a creative field, skills at problem solving and divergent thinking, and motivation to pursue a creative endeavor for its own sake.

Changes in Mental Abilities

Cross-sectional and *longitudinal studies* are used to examine age-related changes in mental abilities. IQ scores remain relatively constant throughout most of adulthood, until the age of sixty or seventy. In old age some aspects of *crystallized intelligence* continue to grow, but *fluid intelligence* may decline. Changes in several aspects of information processing may impair problem-solving ability.

Other Key Terms in This Section: familial retardation, meta-cognition.

O UTLINE

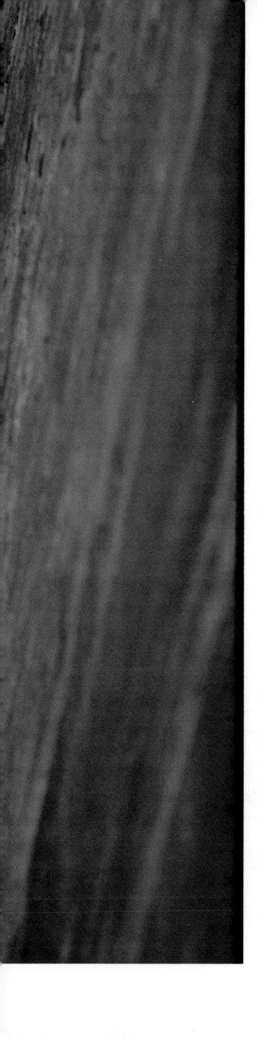

Motivation

One of the authors recently left his family for two weeks and spent a lot of money so that he could go halfway around the world to risk his life climbing Mt. Everest. Another author spent that time chasing an errant golf ball. Why did they do this? Why, for that matter, do people help others or ignore them, eat a lot or starve themselves, mow their lawns or let them grow wild, haunt art museums or sleazy bars, go to college or drop out of high school? These questions illustrate that it is not enough to know *how* people behave. We also need to know *why* they do what they do.

Like the question of how people behave and think, the puzzle of why they do so involves concepts and research from many areas of psychology (see the Linkages diagram). One way to approach this puzzle is to use concepts of motivation. In this chapter we provide an overview of those concepts and look at some important examples of motivated behavior.

Basic Concepts of Motivation

The word *motivation* comes from *movere*, the Latin word meaning "to move." Psychologists who study motivation focus on internal and external influences that might "move" a person. They ask questions such as: What starts a person acting in a particular way? What determines the direction, strength, and persistence of that action? In short, **motivation** refers to the influences that govern the initiation, direction, intensity, and persistence of behavior (Evans, 1989).

Finding Unity in Diversity and Change

Concepts of motivation help psychologists to accomplish what Albert Einstein once said was the whole purpose of science: to discover unity in diversity. Suppose that a man holds down two jobs, consistently turns down

LINKAGES
Motivation

INTERPERSONAL BEHAVIOR AND GROUP INFLUENCES
*What motivates people to be aggressive? pp. 715–718
How is motivation influenced by others? pp. 735–737*

BIOLOGICAL ASPECTS OF PSYCHOLOGY
*How does the brain affect eating? pp. 442–443
How do hormones affect human sexual behavior? pp. 447–448*

PERSONALITY
Can behavior be motivated by needs and drives of which people are unaware? pp. 542–543

MOTIVATION

SENSATION
Do people need a certain amount of sensory stimulation? pp. 165–166

STRESS, COPING, AND HEALTH
What happens when motives are in conflict? pp. 463–465

LEARNING
What events can act as rewards and motivate learning? pp. 274–276

■ Look at the diagram above, which illustrates some of the relationships between the topic of this chapter, motivation, and other chapter topics. One of the strongest links is that between motivation and biological psychology. When psychologists try to explain why certain behaviors begin or how they are governed, the biological structures and processes discussed in Chapter 3 are often an important part of the answer. To understand changes in sexual activity, for example, psychologists use information about how the brain and endocrine systems influence each other and how hormones influence behavior.

Almost any aspect of psychology might be discussed under the topic of motivation. Why, for example, are people aggressive or altruistic? What motivates them? Some psychologists tried to answer these questions by using concepts like instinct and drive, which we discuss in this chapter. But the answers also require (among other things) an understanding of how people influence one another, a subject examined by researchers in social psychology. Thus, we hold these topics for discussion in Chapter 18.

Many other questions about motivation are also addressed in other chapters; the diagram gives just a sampling of these links. The page numbers indicate where the questions in the diagram are discussed. ■

invitations to the movies, wears old clothes, drives an old car, eats food left behind from other people's lunches, refuses to give to charity, and keeps his furnace set at sixty degrees in the dead of winter. Why? Possibly he does so because he likes to work hard, hates movies, fears new clothes and new cars, enjoys other people's cold leftovers, does not care about the poor, and likes cold air. This set of statements certainly covers all of this man's behaviors. A far simpler way of accounting for those behaviors, however, is to suggest that the man is trying to save as much money as possible. In other words, by suggesting a **motive**, a reason or purpose for behavior, you can find unity beneath the apparent diversity of many behaviors.

In more formal terms, motivation can be described as an **intervening variable**, which is a variable that is not observed directly but that helps to account for relationships between various stimuli and responses. In other words, environmental stimuli and behavioral responses to them are often related because of some motivational factor that intervenes, or comes between them. Figure 11.1 shows one example. In this case, all the responses can be understood by viewing them as guided by the single unifying motive of thirst. As an intervening variable, motivation helps to explain why different stimuli can lead to the same response, and why the same stimulus can produce different responses.

Similarly, motivation provides a way to explain fluctuations in behavior over time. For example, some college students never become interested in their courses, and they do not respond to deadlines or failing grades. But once they are put on academic probation, these students often go to class more frequently, study harder, get better grades, and even become interested in the material. In other words, the same stimuli elicit different responses at different times. The idea that a person's motivation changes is useful in accounting for fluctuations in eating, drinking, smoking, or even the amount of effort people put into a marriage, a job, a tennis game, or other activities.

Sources of Motivation

Philosophers have assumed for centuries that reason and free will guide human behavior. However, research with humans and animals forced psychologists to conclude that not all human behavior is guided by reason, and they began

Figure 11.1
Motives as Intervening Variables
Motives can act as explanatory links between apparently unrelated stimuli and responses. In this example, seeing thirst as the common motive provides an explanation of why each stimulus elicits the responses shown.

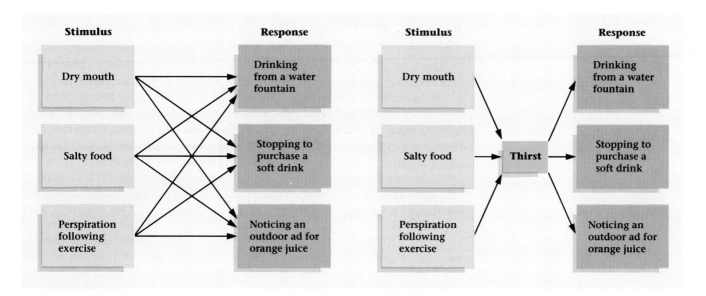

to study other factors that might serve as sources of motivation. These sources fall into four categories.

First, some human behavior, like most animal behavior, is motivated by basic *biological factors*, particularly the need for food, water, temperature regulation, and the like (Tinbergen, 1989). Second, *cognitive factors* motivate human behavior (Zimmerman & Schunk, 1989). People often behave in a certain way because of what they think is possible and because of how they anticipate others will react. *Emotional factors* provide a third source of motivation (Petri, 1986). A person who once nearly starved to death might later hoard food, not because there is any real danger of future famine, but because the thought of running out of food creates emotional distress. Panic, fear, anger, love, hatred, and many other emotions can be crucial to behavior ranging from selfless giving to brutal murder. Fourth, people react to parents, teachers, siblings, friends, television, and other forces. The combined influence of these *social factors* in motivation has a profound effect on virtually every aspect of human behavior (Geen, Beatty & Arkin, 1984). In one way or another, motivational theorists have recognized the importance of each of these factors.

Theoretical Perspectives

Some theorists have emphasized biological factors as the most important determinants of motivation; others have stressed the role of emotional, social, and cognitive factors. No single theory provides a complete explanation of why humans behave as they do. In the following section, we review five of the most prominent theoretical approaches to motivation, each of which offers an important perspective on that question.

Instinct Theory

The work of ethologists—researchers who observe animals in their natural habitat—has long emphasized the importance of instincts. **Instincts** are automatic, involuntary, and unlearned behavior patterns that are consistently "released" in the presence of particular stimuli (Tinbergen, 1989). For example, the male three-spined stickleback fish suddenly becomes aggressive when it spots the red underbelly of another male. Such behavior is not learned and is often referred to as a *fixed-action pattern*.

William McDougall was one of the earliest psychologists to postulate the existence of instincts in human behavior. But instinct theory faded as an explanation of human motivation because of three significant problems. First, theorists began to propose the existence of more and more instincts. In the early 1900s McDougall (1908) postulated eighteen human instincts, including self-assertion, reproduction, pugnacity, and gregariousness. Over the next twenty years, the list of human instincts reached 10,000, and one critic even suggested that his colleagues had "an instinct to produce instincts" (Bernard, 1924). Instincts had become meaningless labels that merely described behavior. Saying that someone gambles because of a gambling instinct, watches television because of a television-watching instinct, and works hard because of a work instinct explains nothing. Second, it is difficult to disprove the existence of an instinct. If Mary wears a watch, someone might claim that she does so because of an instinct to own gold, to know the correct time, or to look attractive. There is no clear-cut way to decide which of these possibilities should be ruled out. Third, far from being rigid and predetermined, much

The male greater frigate bird displays his red throat as part of a mating ritual. This behavior is instinctive; it does not have to be learned.

human behavior changes as a function of changing contingencies of reward and punishment. Instinct theory failed to accommodate the role of learning.

Although instinct theory fell short of fully explaining human behavior, evidence of the power of biology to shape human behavior remains. The strong, enduring, and widespread tendency for humans to be aggressive, to seek sexual gratification, and to fiercely protect their young suggests that some behaviors may be "wired-in" predispositions that cannot be suppressed. Further, as we saw in the chapter on learning, people, like animals, may be "biologically prepared" to learn certain fears or aversions. However, human predispositions can be modified by learning; civilization shapes "wired-in" human tendencies.

Drive Reduction Theory

The shortcomings of instinct theory eventually led to the drive reduction theory of motivation. Like instinct theory, drive reduction theory emphasizes the role of biological factors, but it is based on the concept of homeostasis. **Homeostasis** is the tendency for animals and humans to keep their physiological systems at a steady level, or *equilibrium*, by constantly adjusting themselves in response to change. We described a version of this concept in Chapter 3 when we discussed the feedback loops that allow smooth bodily movements and keep various hormones at desirable levels.

According to **drive reduction theory**, much motivation arises from imbalances in homeostasis. When an imbalance occurs, it creates a **need**—a biological requirement for well-being. This need, in turn, creates a **drive**—a psychological state of arousal that prompts the organism to take action to restore the balance and, in the process, to reduce the drive (Hull, 1943). For example, if you have had no water for some time, the chemical balance of your body fluids is disturbed, creating a biological need for water. The psychological consequence of this need is a drive—thirst—that motivates you to find and drink water. After drinking, the need for water is satisfied, and the drive to drink is reduced. In other words, drives push people to satisfy needs, thus leading to drive reduction and a return to homeostasis (see Figure 11.2).

Figure 11.2
Drive Reduction Theory and
Homeostasis
Internal homeostatic mechanisms, such as the regulation of body temperature or food and water intake, are often compared to thermostats. If the temperature in a house drops below the thermostat setting, the heat comes on and brings the temperature up to that preset level, achieving homeostasis. When the temperature reaches or exceeds the preset point, the furnace shuts off.

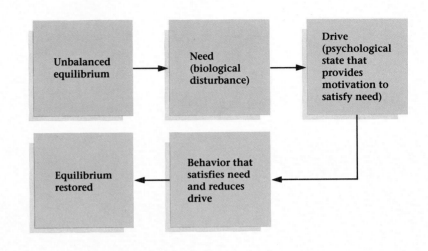

Drive reduction theory incorporates the influence of learning by distinguishing between primary and secondary drives. **Primary drives** are those that arise from basic biological needs, such as the need for food or water. (You may recall from Chapter 7, on learning, that food, water, and other things that satisfy primary drives are known as *primary reinforcers*.) Neither basic biological needs nor the primary drives to satisfy them require any learning (Hull, 1951). However, through classical conditioning or other learning mechanisms, people can acquire other drives. These learned drives are known as **secondary drives**. (Here, too, is a link with learning principles: we discussed in Chapter 7 how neutral stimuli can, through association with primary reinforcers, become learned, or secondary, reinforcers.) Once a secondary drive is learned, it motivates people to act *as if* they have an unmet basic need.

For example, coins, paper money, and checks cannot directly satisfy any primary drive. However, through classical and operant conditioning, modeling, and cognition, people learn that money can buy food, water, shelter, and other primary reinforcers. As having money becomes associated with the satisfaction of primary drives, it becomes a learned, or secondary, drive. Having too little money (a condition most people feel they are in most of the time) thus motivates a wide variety of behaviors, from hard work to thievery, designed to obtain more funds.

Thanks in part to the concept of secondary drives, drive reduction theory was able to account for far more behavior than instinct theory. Still, drive reduction theory has lost much of its influence, primarily because it cannot adequately explain certain aspects of behavior. Particularly puzzling are behaviors in which humans and animals go to great lengths to do things that do not obviously reduce any primary or secondary drive.

Consider curiosity. Animals frequently explore and manipulate what is around them, even though these activities do not lead to drive reduction. When new objects are placed in the environment, most animals smell, touch, and manipulate them in countless ways. Rats will carefully explore every inch of a maze they have never seen, but the time they spend investigating a second maze depends on how similar it is to the first. If it is identical, little additional exploration occurs; if, however, its appearance, smell, or layout is different, the animal will again cover every nook and cranny (Montgomery, 1953). Rats will also exert an extraordinary effort simply to enter a new environment, especially if it is complex and full of novel objects (Berlyne, 1960; Dember, Earl & Paradise, 1957; Myers & Miller, 1954). Monkeys are actually willing to "pay" for the opportunity to satisfy their curiosity (Bolles, 1975), as Figure 11.3 demonstrates. People are no less curious. Most find it difficult to resist checking out anything that is new or unusual. They go to the new mall or museum, read the newspaper, and travel around the world just to see what there is to see.

Other human behaviors are equally difficult to explain through drive reduction. People go out of their way to ride roller coasters, climb mountains, go to horror movies, and do countless other things that, like curiosity-motivated behaviors, fail to reduce any known drive (Csikszentmihalyi, 1975; Deci, 1980). Quite the opposite. These behaviors appear to *increase* people's levels of activation, or arousal. The realization that people are sometimes motivated to reduce arousal through drive reduction and sometimes seek to increase it (Smith & Dorfman, 1975) led to theories tying motivation to the regulation of arousal.

Arousal Theory

Most theorists think of **arousal** as a general level of activation reflected in the state of several physiological systems (Brehm & Self, 1989). Thus, one's level of arousal can be measured by electrical activity in the brain, by heart action, by muscle tension, and by the state of many other organ systems (Petri, 1986). Normally, arousal is lowest during deep, quiet sleep and highest during periods of panic or extreme excitement. Arousal is increased by hunger, thirst, or other biological drives. It is also elevated by very intense stimuli (bright lights or loud noises, for example), by unexpected or novel events, and by caffeine and other stimulant drugs.

People perform best, and often feel best, when arousal is moderate. Figure 11.4(a) depicts the general relationship between level of arousal and efficiency of performance. Overarousal can be particularly detrimental to performance. For example, it has been estimated that because of overarousal 75 to 85 percent

Figure 11.3
Curiosity
This monkey learned to perform a complicated task simply for the opportunity to look at a moving electric train.

Linkages: People who characteristically enjoy high levels of arousal are more likely to smoke, drink alcohol, engage in frequent sexual activity, listen to loud music, eat spicy foods, and do things that are novel and risky (Farley, 1986; Zuckerman, 1979). Those with a lower optimal arousal level tend to behave in ways that bring less intense stimulation and to take fewer risks. Most of the differences in optimal arousal have a strong biological basis and, as discussed in Chapter 14, help create each individual's personality.

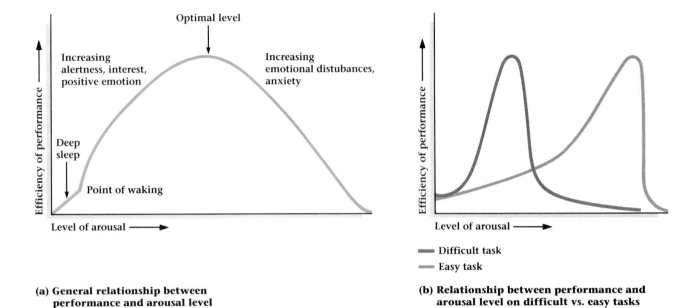

(a) **General relationship between performance and arousal level**

(b) **Relationship between performance and arousal level on difficult vs. easy tasks**

Source: Part (a): Hebb, 1955.

Figure 11.4
The Arousal-Performance Relationship
Notice in part (a) that performance is very poor when arousal is very low *or* very high and that it is best when arousal is at some intermediate level. When you are nearly asleep, for example, it is difficult to process information efficiently or to organize verbal or physical responses. Overexcitement can also interfere with attention, perception, thinking, and the smooth coordination of physical actions. In general, optimal performance comes at a lower level of arousal on difficult or complex tasks and at a higher level of arousal on easy tasks, as shown in part (b). Because animal research early in this century by Robert Yerkes and his colleagues provided supportive evidence, this arousal-performance relationship is sometimes referred to as the Yerkes-Dodson law, even though Yerkes never actually discussed performance as a function of arousal (Winton, 1987).

of soldiers in battle sometimes "freeze" and are unable to fire their weapons (Marshall, 1947). Overarousal can also interfere with performance on intellectual tasks (Ford, Wright & Haythornthwaite, 1985); this lower level of performance is just one of the consequences of stress discussed in Chapter 13.

Figure 11.4(b) shows that the point at which arousal begins to interfere with performance depends on the difficulty of the task. People can tolerate a high level of arousal if the task is easy. However, heightened levels of arousal begin to interfere with task performance more quickly when the task is difficult. Thus, overarousal can cause students to perform far below their potential on particularly difficult tests (Sarason, 1984).

Arousal theories of motivation suggest that people are motivated to behave in ways that maintain what is, for them, an *optimal level* of arousal (Fiske & Maddi, 1961; Hebb, 1955). In general, people are motivated to increase their arousal level when it is too low and to decrease it when it is too high. They seek excitement when they are bored and relaxation when they have had too much excitement. After listening to lectures in the morning and studying all afternoon, for example, you might feel the urge to see an exciting movie that evening. But if your day was spent playing baseball, engaging in a fierce political debate, and helping a friend move, an evening of quiet relaxation might seem ideal. If you do not think so, it may be because you have a very high optimal level of arousal.

Indeed, people differ substantially in the amount of arousal at which they are at their personal "peak" (Zuckerman, 1984). These differences in optimal arousal may shape broader differences in personality discussed in Chapter 14. Extraversion-introversion is an example. *Extraverts* are more likely than other people to prefer stimulating activities and experiences. (Farley, 1986). These preferences may amount to ways of increasing the internal level of arousal to compensate for the fact that extraverts generally have low levels of cortical arousal. *Introverts*, in contrast, have a naturally higher level of cortical arousal and prefer to behave in ways that involve less intense stimulation and risk taking. These differences in optimal arousal have a strong biological basis (Eysenck & Eysenck, 1985).

Arousal theory may also hold the key to better understanding the relationship between motivation and emotion. As we discuss in Chapter 12, on emotion, high degrees of arousal are present during emotional episodes, and emotionally aroused people are intensely motivated. The reciprocal influence of motivation and emotion is an issue that theorists in both areas are working to understand (Petri, 1986).

Incentive Theory

Instinct, drive, and arousal theories of motivation all have one thing in common: they focus on internal processes that push people to behave in certain ways. Incentive theory, in contrast, emphasizes that environmental stimuli may motivate behavior by pulling people toward them. According to **incentive theory**, behavior is goal-directed; actions are directed toward attaining positive incentives and avoiding negative incentives.

The two major constructs of incentive theory are expectancy and value. The theory says, in short, that if a person *expects* a particular behavior to lead to a positive outcome (one that has high *value*), the person will be motivated to engage in that behavior. Conversely, if a person expects a particular behavior to lead to a negative incentive, the person will be motivated not to perform that behavior. Thus, motivation is closely linked to the nature and availability of incentives in the environment.

The specific nature of incentives can vary from one person to another and from one situation to another. For example, the prospect of free tickets to see a movie about Mozart might motivate an adult to study but would probably have little effect on a severely retarded child. In addition, the value of an incentive often depends on a person's drive state. Food is a more motivating incentive when you are hungry than when you are satiated (Logue, 1986).

Along with arousal theory, incentive theory helps explain why people play chess, ride roller coasters, and engage in other activities that do not involve drive reduction. The mental and physical stimulation associated with these activities is enough to pull people toward them, at least for a while.

Opponent-Process Theory

Both the changing value of incentives and the regulation of arousal are combined in an approach to motivation called **opponent-process theory** (Solomon, 1980; Solomon & Corbit, 1974). This theory is based on two assumptions. First, any reaction to a stimulus is automatically followed by an opposite reaction, called the *opponent process*. For example, being startled by a sudden sound is typically followed by relaxation and relief. Second, after repeated exposure to the same stimulus, the initial reaction weakens, and the opponent process becomes stronger.

Opponent-process theory uses both assumptions to account for drug addiction. As Figure 11.5 shows, the first several exposures to heroin produce an intensely pleasurable rush, followed by a reduction in pleasure and a mild, unpleasant feeling of withdrawal associated with a craving for another dose. After continued drug use, however, the initial reaction becomes less intense, and the withdrawal reaction occurs more quickly, becomes more intense, and lasts longer (Marlatt et al., 1988). In fact, as people become addicted, withdrawal becomes so aversive that they are motivated to use the drug again to avoid the discomfort of *not* using it.

Linkages: Why do some people become addicted to consciousness-altering drugs? (a link to Consciousness)

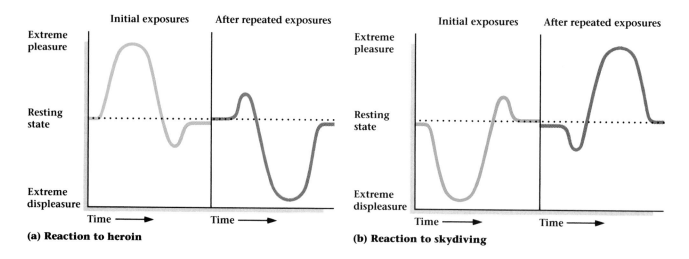

(a) Reaction to heroin

(b) Reaction to skydiving

Source: Solomon & Corbit, 1974.

Figure 11.5
Opponent Processes
Part (a) shows how experiences of pleasure and displeasure change over time as a person continues to use heroin. Part (b) shows the sequence of skydivers' emotional reactions to their sport. During the first few jumps, most novices are terrified. Once safely on the ground, however, they feel pleasure and relief. After repeated jumps, the initial terror becomes mild anxiety, and the pleasurable reaction becomes an intense euphoria that lasts longer with practice. According to Solomon (1980), people's motivation to repeat dangerous activities like these can get so strong that it becomes a special type of addiction.

Opponent-process theory can be especially useful for understanding changes in emotion that result from various activities and for explaining patterns of behavior like skydiving in which people appear motivated to put themselves in danger.

The five theoretical approaches we have outlined are complementary (see "In Review: Theories of Motivation"). Each emphasizes different sources of motivation, and each has helped to guide research into motivated behaviors such as eating, sex, attachment to others, and work, all of which are considered in the sections that follow.

In Review: Theories of Motivation

Theory	Main Points
Instinct	Innate biological instincts guide behavior.
Drive reduction	Behavior is guided by biological needs and learned ways of reducing drives arising from those needs.
Arousal	People seek to maintain an optimal level of physiological arousal, which differs from person to person. Maximum performance occurs at optimal arousal levels.
Incentive	Behavior is guided by the lure of available rewards. Cognitive factors influence expectations of the value of various rewards and the likelihood of attaining them.
Opponent process	Behavior is guided by sequential patterns of physical, psychological, and emotional pleasure and discomfort. Initial reactions to activities tend to weaken over time, while subsequent, opposite reactions get stronger.

Hunger and Eating

Hunger is deceptively simple; people get hungry when they do not eat. But trying to specify what causes hunger or what determines whether people eat and when they stop eating quickly leads to the conclusion that even this very basic motive can be complicated. Here we focus on the biological processes involved in hunger and eating, including the physical changes that make people experience hunger and the factors that start and stop eating. We also consider the role played by such nonbiological factors as learning and thought.

Biological Mechanisms

Clearly, hunger is based largely in biological makeup, but what, exactly, tells you that you are hungry or full?

The Role of Stomach Cues The stomach seems a logical place to look for mechanisms that control hunger and eating. After all, people often get "hunger pangs" in the stomach when they are hungry and complain of having a "full stomach" after eating a large meal.

To study the role of the stomach, physiologist Walter Cannon arranged for a subject to swallow a deflated balloon. Then the balloon was inflated and attached by a tube to a machine that measured the pressure that stomach contractions exerted against it. The subject reported strong hunger pangs when the contractions were strong and few pangs when the contractions were weak or absent (Cannon & Washburn, 1912). These results supported the idea that hunger pangs are related to stomach movements, but they did not clarify what caused hunger itself.

Other researchers placed a large amount of dry material with no nutritional value directly into dogs' stomachs. The animals ate very little; some stopped eating completely, even though nutritious food was easily available (Janowitz & Grossman, 1949, 1951). These experiments suggested that the stomach might control the hunger motive; but hunger, it turns out, is not that simple (Quartermain et al., 1971). For example, people who have had their stomachs removed because of illness still experience hunger pangs when they do not eat and still eat normal amounts of food (Janowitz, 1967). Thus, hunger and the regulation of eating must stem from somewhere other than the stomach alone.

The Role of Taste Cues There is another obvious candidate in the search for mechanisms that might control eating: the taste of food. Many experiments have demonstrated that taste exerts an important influence on eating. For example, when one group of animals was offered just one type of food while another group was offered a succession of distinctly different-tasting foods, the group receiving the varied menu ate nearly four times more than the one-food animals. As each new food was introduced, the animals began to eat voraciously, regardless of how much they had already eaten (LeMagnen, 1971; Peck, 1978).

Similar experiments with humans led to essentially the same conclusion (Cabanac, 1971). All things being equal, people consume more food during a multicourse meal than when only one type of food is served. This variation in consumption is due in part to the fact that the taste of a given food becomes less and less enjoyable as more of it is eaten (Woody et al., 1981).

Is taste, then, the controller of hunger and eating? If it were, animals without the ability to taste would not know when to stop eating. But somehow they do (Jordan, 1969; Snowdon, 1969). Similarly, when intravenous feeding prevents people from tasting their nutrients, they eat very little by mouth when allowed to do so and thus maintain a roughly constant body weight (Deutsch, Young & Kalogeris, 1978). In other words, though taste cues have some influence over eating, they do not appear to tell the whole story.

Linkages: How does the brain affect eating? (a link to Biological Aspects of Psychology)

The Role of the Brain   Other research into hunger and the regulation of eating has focused on the hypothalamus, a structure in the forebrain described in the chapter on biological aspects of psychology. Two regions of the hypothalamus in particular have been studied: the *lateral area* and the *ventromedial nucleus*, which are shown in Figure 11.6.

When fibers in the lateral area of the hypothalamus are *destroyed*, rats stop eating almost entirely. Most resume eating eventually, but they consume only small amounts of their most preferred foods and maintain a much-reduced weight (Keesey & Powley, 1975). In contrast, if the lateral hypothalamus is electrically *stimulated*, one result is that the rats begin to eat vast quantities, even if they have just consumed enough food to have stopped eating. In short, the lateral area of the hypothalamus seems to act as a "start-eating" center. When it is stimulated, it causes eating; when it is destroyed, the tendency to start eating is destroyed as well.

The story is the opposite for the ventromedial nucleus. If surgery *destroys* fibers in a rat's ventromedial nucleus, the animal will eat far more than usual, increasing its weight up to threefold. Then the rat begins to eat enough food to maintain itself at the higher weight it has reached (Teitelbaum, 1961). If the ventromedial nucleus is electrically *stimulated*, the rat stops eating. Thus, it appears that the ventromedial nucleus is a "stop-eating" center. Stimulate it and animals stop eating; destroy it and their tendency to stop eating is disrupted.

Other motivated behaviors are also affected by the lateral and ventromedial areas, so designating these areas as "hunger" and "satiety" areas is an oversimplification. A more complex explanation of how these regions of the hypothalamus affect hunger and eating comes from the **set-point concept**. It suggests that a homeostatic mechanism in the brain establishes a level, or *set point*, based on body weight or a related metabolic signal, much as a thermostat

Figure 11.6
The Hypothalamus and Hunger
Studies of the hypothalamus have concentrated on stimulating or destroying fibers that pass through the lateral area and the ventromedial nucleus. Here are some of the results of this research.

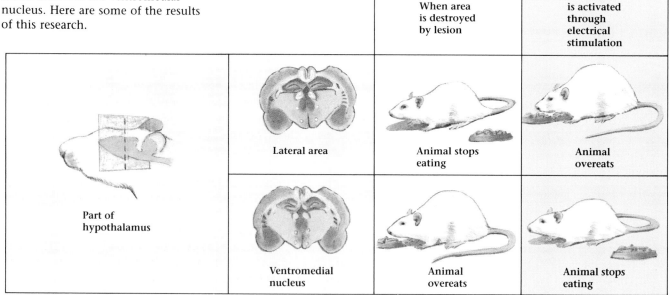

After surgical destruction of its ventromedial nucleus, this rat ate enough to triple its body weight. Interestingly, such animals become picky eaters, choosing only foods that taste good and ignoring all others (Miller, Bailey & Stevenson, 1930; Teitelbaum, 1957).

sets temperature (Keesey & Powley, 1975; Nisbett, 1972; Powley & Keesey, 1970). This view suggests that normal animals eat until their set point is reached, then stop until their brain senses a drop in desirable intake, at which time they eat again. Destruction or stimulation of the lateral or ventromedial areas may alter the set point. Thus, when animals with ventromedial damage eat more and maintain a higher weight, it may be because their set points have been raised. Similarly, damage to the lateral hypothalamus may lower the set point, causing less eating and maintenance of a lower weight.

Signals for Hunger How does a person's brain "know" when to signal "eat" and when to signal "stop eating"? It appears to gather its cues by constantly monitoring the contents of the blood. This fact was established years ago when researchers deprived rats of food for long periods of time and injected some of the deprived rats with the blood of rats that had just eaten. When finally given access to food, the injected rats ate very little, if anything (Davis et al., 1969). Apparently, these hungry animals' brains "read" something in the satiated animals' blood that told them there was little need to eat.

Exactly what the brain "reads" in the blood is not fully understood, but the level of glucose (sugar) is part of the story. When the level of blood sugar drops, eating increases dramatically (Friedman & Stricker, 1976; Mogenson, 1976). When large doses of glucose are injected into the blood of a food-deprived animal, it refuses to eat.

The suppression of eating after glucose injections is particularly strong when the injection is given in a vein that provides blood to the liver. Some researchers have suggested that the liver plays an important role in hunger and eating, by receiving information about the blood and then passing that information on to the brain through nerve connections (Russek, 1971). Even when these connections are severed, however, the brain still manages to regulate eating in relation to blood sugar. Thus, it appears that the brain directly monitors the blood passing through it (Granneman & Friedman, 1980).

Whatever their exact nature, the signals that prompt a person or animal to start eating (hunger cues) are probably different from those that cause eating to stop (satiety cues). One possible "stop-eating" signal is the hormone cholecystokinin, or CCK. During a meal, CCK is released from the gut and from neurons in the hypothalamus (Schick et al., 1986). When CCK is injected into animals' brains, they not only stop eating but also show other signs of being satiated, such as grooming and sleeping.

Nonbiological Factors

Biological processes do not by themselves explain when animals or people start or stop eating. For example, animals come to associate calorie-rich meals with satiety, and they stop eating sooner after a high-calorie meal than when eating a lower-calorie meal. In other words, satiation and the termination of eating also depend in part on learning, in this case on *conditioned satiation*, which is the tendency to stop eating because of the association of certain stimuli with satiety.

The influence of learning can also be more subtle. For example, eating can be triggered by sights and smells that have come to be associated with enjoyable food. Thus, seeing a pizza on television may suddenly make you hungry enough to order one, even though you had not been feeling hungry just a minute ago. Similarly, after stuffing themselves at Thanksgiving dinner, most people find that the sight of pumpkin pie is enough to make them want some (with whipped cream). Other social occasions provide other specific cues that, through learning, stimulate hunger for particular items. Eating popcorn at movies, pretzels with beer, and hot dogs at baseball games are just a few examples. In many social situations, what and how much you eat may depend on what others do rather than what you need biologically. The restraint shown by companions at an elegant dinner may cause you to refuse a second helping of prime rib, just as the gluttonous example set by friends at a picnic may lead you to gorge yourself, too.

Even general eating patterns can be modified by cognitive, social, and emotional factors. For example, family problems, overwork, and other stressors described in Chapter 13 stimulate some people to eat more than usual; others eat less. On hearing of the death of a loved one, even a hungry person may suddenly not feel like eating at all.

Eating Disorders

The role of learning, thought, emotion, and other nonbiological factors in hunger and eating has been of special interest to researchers in psychology, medicine, and other fields who seek to understand and treat eating disorders (Crandall, 1988). The most common and health-threatening of these disorders are obesity, anorexia nervosa, and bulimia.

Obesity About 12 percent of Americans between the ages of fourteen and sixty-one display **obesity**, a condition of severe overweight, often by as much as one hundred pounds (Stewart & Brook, 1983). Obesity threatens the health of millions of Americans, often contributing to diabetes, high blood pressure, and increased risk of heart attack (Wilson, 1984).

In most cases, obesity results when someone consumes more calories than the body can *metabolize*, or burn up; obese people usually eat more than those of normal weight. They are also finicky eaters; they eat larger-than-average amounts of foods they like and less-than-average amounts of less-preferred foods (Peck, 1978). Obese people are also less willing than those of normal weight to expend effort to obtain food. One study found that obese people will eat more shelled nuts than will people of normal weight, but they will eat *less* than normal people if they must remove the shells themselves (Schachter & Friedman, 1974).

It had long been thought that one reason obese people eat so much is that they have a higher-than-average sensitivity to environmental cues, including the sight, smell, and taste of food (Rodin, 1973; Schachter, 1971; Schachter & Rodin, 1974). This view suggests that a person of normal weight is less likely than an obese person to notice the goodies in a bakery window. But there is now some question about whether obese people are actually more sensitive to their environments (Rodin, 1980) and, even if they are, whether this sensitivity can fully account for obesity. For example, not all people who eat a lot become obese. Why?

Several physiological characteristics may make certain people prone to obesity. First, certain body types (for example, short limbs and barrel chests) may predispose people to obesity (Mayer, 1975). Second, the tendency to accumulate fat stems from the presence of more and larger fat cells in obese individuals than in normal-weight people, especially if they were overweight in childhood (Hirsch & Knittle, 1970; Knittle et al., 1979). Third, obese people may have a higher set point for body weight and therefore feel hungry more often than other people (Keesey, 1980; Nisbett, 1972). These higher set points may result from both genetics and early, even prenatal, nutrition that may have created particularly large and numerous fat cells (Foreyt & Kondo, 1984).

Differences in the rate at which people metabolize food may also play a role in obesity. The body maintains a set point for weight by changing both food intake and energy output (Keesey & Powley, 1986). If intake is lowered, the metabolic rate also drops, conserving energy and curbing weight loss. But when obese people reduce to a normal weight, their metabolic rate tends to drop *below* a normal level. As a result, they begin to gain weight again even if they eat an amount that would maintain a constant weight in a normal person. These facts suggest that long-term overeating can raise set points for weight (Keesey & Powley, 1986; Kolata, 1985). Thus, diet plans that focus on drastically reduced food intake can be counterproductive. In fact, animal studies suggest that losing and then regaining large amounts of weight can result in a slowly increasing average weight (Archambault et al., 1989; Brownell et al., 1986). To achieve gradual and permanent weight loss, increasing physical activity is also important, because it burns calories without slowing the metabolic rate (Donahoe et al., 1984).

Among the psychological factors associated with obesity may be a failure to develop conditioned satiety—associating the end of a normal-sized meal with feelings of satisfaction—that is strong enough to prevent overeating (Booth, 1980). Maladaptive reactions to stress may also be involved. As mentioned earlier, many people tend to eat more when under stress; this reaction may be particularly extreme among those who become obese (Herman & Polivy, 1975; McKenna, 1972).

Anorexia Nervosa Even more perplexing than obesity is **anorexia nervosa**, an eating disorder characterized by self-starvation and dramatic weight loss. Some anorexics are obsessed with food and its preparation but eat almost nothing. The self-starvation of anorexics creates serious, often irreversible, physical damage. Between 4 and 30 percent of these people actually starve themselves to death (Eisner et al., 1985; Szmukler & Russell, 1986). About 95 percent of the people who suffer from anorexia are female, and the incidence of the problem has increased greatly in the last few decades, affecting as many as 1 percent of American women between the ages of fifteen and thirty (Gilbert & DeBlassie, 1984).

The causes of anorexia are not known. It has been speculated that anorexics have an abnormally low set point or some physiological abnormality (Gwirtsman & Germer, 1981), but there is not much evidence for this view (Bemis, 1978). For one thing, no specific abnormalities have been found in the brains of anorexics. Further, anorexics often report strong hunger yet refuse to eat. Psychological factors that might contribute to the problem include the apparent obsession with thinness in America and young people's concern with appearing attractive. In other words, anorexics appear to develop a fear of being fat, which they take to dangerous extremes (Achenbach, 1982). Many anorexics continue to view themselves as too fat or misshapen even as they are wasting away (Davis, 1986).

Drugs, hospitalization, and psychotherapy are all used to treat anorexia. In about 70 percent of cases, some combination of treatment and the passage of time brings recovery and maintenance of normal weight (Hsu, 1980). (For a summary of the processes involved in hunger and the regulation of eating, see "In Review: Major Factors Controlling Hunger and Eating.")

Bulimia About half of all anorexics display another eating disorder: bulimia (Casper et al., 1980). **Bulimia** involves eating massive quantities of food (say, several boxes of cookies, a loaf of bread, a half gallon of ice cream, and a bucket of fried chicken) and then eliminating the food by self-induced vomiting or strong laxatives (Garfinkel, Moldofsky & Garner, 1980). These "binge-purge" episodes may occur once a week or several times a day (Fairburn, 1981; Pyle, Mitchell & Eckert, 1981). Informed guesses have placed the incidence of bulimia in the United States at about five million people.

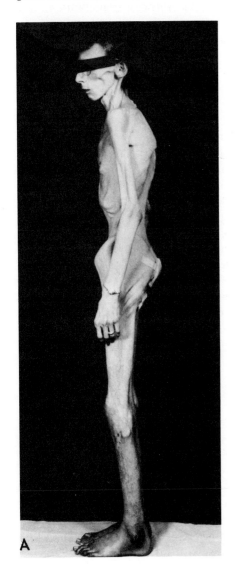

Some anorexics literally starve themselves to death. This woman weighed only forty-seven pounds when she began a treatment program that saved her life.

In Review: Major Factors Controlling Hunger and Eating

	Stimulate Eating	**Inhibit Eating**
Biological	Stomach contractions are associated with subjective feelings of hunger; taste becomes less enjoyable as more of a particular food is consumed, and thus varied tastes increase eating; the lateral area of hypothalamus serves as a start-eating center by monitoring reductions in blood sugar.	The ventromedial nucleus of the hypothalamus serves as a stop-eating center by monitoring blood; CCK, a hormone, is released during a meal and "read" by the ventromedial nucleus.
Nonbiological	Sights and smells of particular foods elicit eating because of prior associations; family customs and social occasions often include norms for eating in particular ways; stress is often associated with eating more.	Contemporary American society values thinness, and thus can inhibit eating; conditioned satiation occurs when certain foods are associated with satiety; negative emotional reactions sometimes result in a loss of hunger.

Like anorexics, bulimics are usually female; their eating problems usually begin when they are about fifteen years old; and they are obsessed with being slender. However, bulimia and anorexia are separate disorders. For one thing, most bulimics maintain a reasonably normal weight. Most of them also realize that their eating habits are problematic, while most anorexics do not.

Bulimia usually is not a life-threatening disorder (Fairburn, 1981; Schlesier-Stroop, 1984). There *are* consequences, however, including dehydration, nutritional imbalances, and intestinal damage. Many bulimics also develop raw throats from frequent vomiting and from the objects they insert to induce vomiting. More generally, their preoccupation with eating and with avoiding fatness prevents many bulimics from working productively (Herzog, 1982). Unfortunately, little is known about the causes of bulimia or about effective treatment (Rodin et al., 1990).

Sexual Behavior

Unlike food, sex is not necessary for individual survival, but a species without a strong motivation for reproduction would soon cease to exist. The determinants of sexual motivation vary widely from one species to the next. Typically they involve a complex interplay of the physical and social environment with the individual's physiology and learned behavior. For example, one species of bird that lives in the desert requires adequate sex hormones and a suitable mate before it engages in sexual behavior; however, it also requires a particular environment. As long as the dry season lasts it shows no

Although no one has ever died from a lack of sex, it is a strong source of motivation for most people.

Linkages: How do hormones affect human sexual behavior? (a link to Biological Aspects of Psychology)

interest in sex, but within ten minutes of the first rainfall the birds vigorously copulate.

Human sexual behavior is also shaped by both biological and environmental factors (although rainfall is not usually critical). Analyzing these factors is difficult. Because many people object to the frank exploration of sexual matters and because ethical concerns restrict the manipulations researchers can use, the ways in which human sexuality can be scientifically explored are limited (Money, 1987). The most common method for conducting research on human sexuality uses surveys.

Alfred Kinsey conducted the first major surveys of sexual behaviors (Kinsey, Pomeroy & Martin, 1948; Kinsey et al., 1953). His interviews covered many aspects of respondents' sex lives, desires, and fantasies. They indicated that sexual practices that were publicly considered immoral, such as homosexuality, were actually widespread. However, Kinsey's work suffered from methodological problems like those discussed in Chapter 1. Among other things, Kinsey's sample was far from random and representative; only Caucasian volunteers were included, for example (Hyman & Barmack, 1954; Terman, 1948). Still, no subsequent survey has superseded the breadth of Kinsey's work (Money, 1987), and it laid a foundation for other scientific studies of human sexuality.

Sources of Sexual Motivation

Sex serves the function of reproduction, but the strong positive reinforcement tied to human sexual activity takes it beyond this biological purpose. In humans, biological factors are less important in the regulation of sexual behavior than what people learn about how and when to express themselves sexually. Still, biological factors provide the raw material for sexual motivation.

The Role of Hormones The biological underpinnings of human sexual motivation are evident in the roles played by feminine and masculine hormones. The feminine hormones are **estrogens** and **progestins**; the main ones are **estradiol** and **progesterone**. The masculine hormones are **androgens**; the principal androgen is **testosterone**. Each of these hormones circulates in the bloodstream of members of *both* sexes, but relatively more androgens circulate in men and relatively more estrogens and progestins circulate in women.

The feminine and masculine hormones are secreted by the ovaries and testes. As discussed in Chapter 3, the secretion of hormones is controlled by feedback systems that involve the brain as well as glands. Figure 11.7 illustrates how the feedback system works in the case of the masculine and feminine hormones.

These hormones have both organizational and activational effects (Phoenix et al., 1959). The *organizational effects* of hormones are permanent changes in the brain and the way an individual thereafter responds to hormones. The *activational effects* are reversible changes in behavior that remain as long as the hormone levels are elevated.

The organizational effects of hormones occur during very early development (prenatal in humans), when either a "malelike" or a "femalelike" pattern of brain connections is laid down. In nonhuman mammals—a rat, for example—the male must be exposed to androgens during this time in order for normal male sexual behavior to occur in adulthood. If its testes are removed before the androgens have a chance to act, in adulthood the rat will behave exactly as a female. Information about organizational effects in humans is sketchier. (We discuss some of the controversies later.) It is clear, however, that there

Figure 11.7
The Regulation of Sex Hormones
Feedback loops involving the hypothalamus and pituitary gland as well
as the ovaries or testes control the
secretion of sex hormones. In males,
high levels of testosterone reduce activity in the hypothalamus, which
lowers secretion of luteinizing hormone (LH), which causes less testosterone to be secreted. This feedback
system tends to keep the secretion
of testosterone reasonably constant.
In females, the feedback loops are
more complex. High levels of estrogen increase hypothalamic activity,
causing more LH to be secreted,
which causes more estrogen to be
secreted. At some point the secretion
of LH increases very rapidly, and a
surge of hormone is released. This
increased LH not only prompts the
release of more estrogen but also
causes the ovary to release an egg.
Androgens fluctuate across the menstrual cycle as estrogens and progestins do, and peak around ovulation.

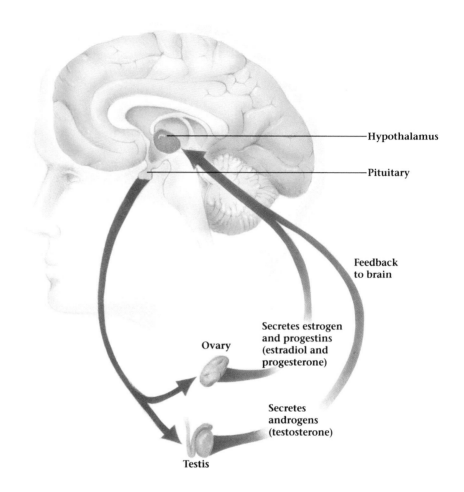

are regions of the human brain that are different in males and females, and
these are analogous to areas in animals that are affected by organizational
effects of hormones (Swaab & Fliers, 1985).

Once hormones have had their early organizational effects, they stay at low
levels until puberty, when hormone levels rise and the activational effects
occur. The rising hormone levels activate interest in sexual behavior. Although
sexual activity at puberty is determined by a complex interaction of physical
changes, social skills, and opportunity for sex, there is also a positive correlation
between sexual activity and levels of hormones in the blood (Udry et al.,
1985). There is evidence that androgens are the critical hormones for activating
sexual interest in *both* sexes, although estrogens may also activate sexual
interest in women (Davidson, Kwan & Greenleaf, 1982; Sherwin, Gelfand &
Brender, 1985; Stanislaw & Rice, 1988).

Further evidence of the activational effects of hormones comes from studies
in which hormone levels have been altered for medical reasons. People who
have had their hormone-secreting ovaries or testes removed show a decline
in sexual motivation and behavior on the average, although some individuals
are apparently not affected (Sherwin et al., 1985). If appropriate hormonal
treatments are given to people whose hormone levels have decreased as a
result of chemical imbalances or surgical removal of the ovaries or testes, their
sexual interest and behavior increase (Sherwin et al., 1985).

Nonbiological Factors Hormones generally activate interest in sexual
behavior, but the many forms this behavior takes are shaped more precisely

by a lifetime of learning. Some sexual behaviors are learned as part of the development of gender roles, described in Chapters 2 and 7. Other kinds of early social experiences may also be necessary for the development of sexual motivation and behavior. Studying this question experimentally in humans would be unethical because it would require manipulating children's early social experiences. However, research with monkeys (described later in this chapter) suggests that contact with a nurturing adult is important for the development of normal sexual behavior (Harlow, 1958). Other studies show that the opportunity to engage in physical play before puberty is important. Animals that are denied play periods during development never learn to copulate successfully (Goldfoot, 1977).

Furthermore, attitudes toward sexual behavior change as cultural expectations change. In a survey in the 1920s, most husbands wanted more frequent sexual contact with their wives, whereas the wives wanted less (Davis, 1929). In a similar survey in the 1970s, only 2 percent of wives said that intercourse was too frequent, and 32 percent thought it was too infrequent (Bell & Bell, 1972). This trend is also evident among unmarried women, especially those involved in a serious relationship (Sherwin & Sherry, 1985).

Human Sexual Activity

Across cultures, a consistent pattern of behavior leads up to copulation. Flirtatious behavior typically involves establishing eye contact and holding the gaze; talking with considerable animation about inconsequential things; gradually rotating to face each other; moving closer together; moistening the lips and smiling; displaying partially covered parts of the body; lightly touching each other as if by accident; and mirroring one another's postures and facial expressions (Perper, 1985).

What happens next? The first extensive laboratory research on human sexual behavior was conducted by William Masters and Virginia Johnson and reported in 1966 in *Human Sexual Response*. Their book contained detailed descriptions of the physical and psychological responses of more than six hundred males and females as they received natural or artificial sexual stimulation. Although their research examined sexual behavior in isolation from the contexts in which it normally occurs, it yielded important data about the **sexual response cycle**, which is the pattern of arousal during and after sexual activity (Masters & Johnson, 1966). Figure 11.8 illustrates the cycle.

Figure 11.8
The Sexual Response Cycle
Men show one primary pattern of sexual response, which is depicted in part (a). Women display at least three different patterns from time to time; these are labeled A, B, and C in part (b). In both men and women, the first, or *excitement*, phase of the sexual response cycle occurs in response to sexually stimulating input, either from the environment or from one's own thoughts. If this stimulation continues, it leads to intensification of the excitement in the second, or *plateau*, phase. Sexual tension becomes extreme in this phase. If stimulation continues, the person reaches the third, or *orgasmic* stage, which, though only lasting a few seconds, provides an intensely pleasurable release of physical and psychological tension. The *resolution* phase follows, during which the person returns to a state of relaxation. At this point men enter a *refractory period* during which they are temporarily insensitive to sexual stimulation. Women are capable of immediately repeating the cycle if stimulation continues.

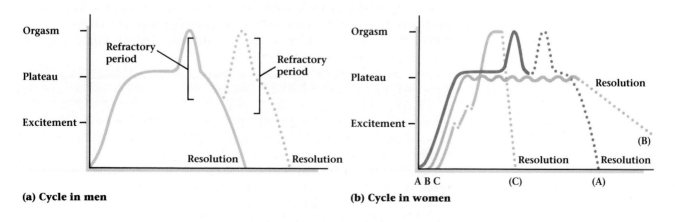

(a) Cycle in men   (b) Cycle in women

Source: Masters & Johnson, 1966.

Usually, human sexual activity is **heterosexual**, involving members of the opposite sex. People who engage in activities with partners of both sexes are called **bisexual**. Sometimes, sexual behavior is **homosexual**—that is, focused toward members of one's own sex. However, behavior is only one aspect of *sexual orientation*, which has three components: behavior, attraction, and identification. For example, in terms of behavior, homosexuality means engaging in sexual activity with a partner of one's own sex. Defined by sexual attraction, it means being attracted to or aroused by members of the same sex. And defined by sexual identification, homosexuality means a self-acknowledged preference for members of one's own sex. These three components of sexual orientation do not necessarily go together.

THINKING CRITICALLY

How Does Homosexuality Develop?

Over the years, homosexuality has been characterized as genetically determined, as the result of particular learning experiences, or merely as the result of personal choice. It seems likely that, as is so often the case, some combination of nature and nurture is at work.

What am I being asked to believe or accept?
Michael Storms has suggested that a particular blending of social, biological, learning, and emotional factors must come together to produce a homosexual orientation (Storms, 1980, 1981). His theory is based in part on the fact that children first form close friendships with same-sex peers. Storms suggests that children whose biologically based sex drive develops at an early age are thus likely to focus their sexual fantasies on members of their own sex. If these children begin to masturbate, their sexual arousal may be classically conditioned to the fantasized sights and sounds of members of the same sex. These individuals, the theory asserts, would be more likely to develop a homosexual orientation than those whose sex drives and masturbatory behaviors begin at a later age, and who thus associate features of the *opposite* sex with heightened sexual arousal.

What evidence is available to support the assertion?
For one thing, a person's earliest sexual fantasies, especially those accompanied by orgasm, appear to be extremely influential in development, for two reasons. First, subsequent fantasies are often built up from the initial ones (Sarnoff, 1976). Thus, if a young boy fantasizes about another boy while masturbating, he is likely to think about other males during subsequent experiences with masturbation. Second, people examine the content of their fantasies when they construct their sexual identity (Gagnon & Simon, 1973). Those who fantasize about same-sex partners might begin to think of themselves as homosexual.

Other evidence in support of Storms' theory consists of large differences in the age at which adult homosexuals and heterosexuals recall being aware of their own sexuality. About 60 to 80 percent of homosexual men report having sexual drives before the age of thirteen. In contrast, only 20 to 30 percent of heterosexual men report having sexual drives that early (Saghir & Robins, 1973).

Are there alternative ways of interpreting the evidence?
These findings are by no means definitive. People's retrospective reports about when their sex drives first appeared may be inaccurate or biased by constructive memory or other distorting factors described in Chapter 8. Because homosexuality is the exception rather than the rule, homosexuals

might be more aware than heterosexuals of early sexual feelings. In addition, which is the cause and which the effect? Even if sex drive appears earlier among homosexual men, its early appearance may be the *result* of homosexuality rather than its cause. In other words, it could be that some people are born with a biologically determined homosexual orientation, and their experience of sexual urges occurs at an earlier age because they are associating with same-sex children, whom they already find sexually attractive. If this is the case, there is no need to invoke learning-based explanations in which homosexuals come to associate a nonspecific sex drive with their same-sex playmates.

What additional evidence would help to evaluate the alternatives?

Several lines of evidence on the origins of homosexuality make it a bit easier to evaluate Storms' theory and the conflicting interpretations of data related to it.

Some evidence indicates that biological factors might indeed play an important role in homosexuality. For example, animal studies suggest that male homosexuality can arise from low levels of androgen during prenatal development. Conversely, female homosexuality can arise from the exposure of females to androgens prenatally. In humans, the exposure of females to androgens from *congenital adrenal hyperplasia*, a condition existing before birth, makes it much more likely that the woman will be bisexual or homosexual in adulthood (Money, Schwartz & Lewis, 1984). Also, the pattern of pituitary hormone control in male homosexuals is similar to that of females (see Figure 11.7), which is consistent with the idea that homosexuality has a biological basis (Gladue, Green & Hellman, 1984). Moreover, studies of identical twins reared apart indicate that there is a genetic component to homosexuality (Eckert et al., 1986; Ellis & Ames, 1987).

There is also evidence that family relationships affect the appearance of homosexuality. Male homosexuals report their fathers as being more rejecting and distant than male heterosexuals do (Siegelman, 1974). In one study 39 percent of lesbians—but only 5 percent of heterosexual women—had lost one or both parents, through divorce or death, before they were ten years old (Saghir & Robins, 1973). And only 23 percent of lesbian women but 83 percent of heterosexual women reported having a close relationship with their mothers.

Other evidence associates certain reactions to gender roles during early childhood with the development of homosexuality in adult males. People who do not fit gender-role stereotypes may be pressured into rejecting the role. In one survey, 67 percent of male homosexuals, as opposed to 3 percent of heterosexual males, considered themselves to be effeminate during preadolescence (Saghir & Robins, 1973). These males reported *gender nonconformity*, such as playing more with girls; as a result, they were called ''sissies'' by their male peers (Adams & Chioto, 1983; Bell, Weinberg & Hammersmith, 1983). Although those responses are retrospective, their validity is strengthened by a study that followed males from early childhood to young adulthood. Seventy-five percent of forty-four extremely effeminate boys became homosexual or bisexual; only one bisexual was identified in a comparison group of more masculine boys (Green, 1987). Lopsided as these findings are, there are still many homosexual males (25 percent in Green's study) who do not fit this developmental pattern.

What conclusions are most reasonable?

The evidence and analyses we have reviewed suggest that just as heterosexuals are very diverse, so, too, are homosexuals. There is no evidence that all homosexuals share a common developmental pattern, family history, or biological predisposition. In fact, it appears that a homosexual orientation

Young children's need for support may be particularly evident in a close attachment to the mother or other caregiver. To a lesser degree, teddy bears, "security blankets," and other cuddly objects sometimes become support symbols as well.

Linkages: Can animal studies of the effects of isolation provide insight into human needs? (a link to the World of Psychology)

stems from the interaction of many family, sociosexual, and biological factors (Money, 1987). This conclusion may be less conclusive than some would wish, but when scientific knowledge about a topic is limited, so too must be the conclusions drawn from it. ■

Social Motives

People are social animals. As such, their behavior is influenced by a variety of social motives, some of which are quite powerful. Three of the most important are the motive to develop emotional attachments to another, to become parents, and to affiliate in groups. Although there is no biological need to do any of these things, each of them can have a pervasive influence on human behavior.

Developing Attachments

In the chapter on development, we described how infants typically form a very special relationship with their primary caregiver, usually the mother. This is one form of psychological *attachment*, a strong emotional bond that is forged with another who is perceived as better able to cope with the world (Bowlby, 1989). Youngsters who are away from their mothers for prolonged periods (for example, during hospitalization) often become terrified and later cling to her, screaming at any hint that she might leave even for a moment. Observations like these suggest that the need to be physically and emotionally supported resembles a physiological drive like hunger or thirst, although children who grow up without such support do not die. Why is the motivation for attachment so strong?

According to one explanation, children may become fiercely attached to their mothers because it is the mother who provides the food and water vital for life (Gewirtz, 1972; Sears, 1972). Experiments by Harry Harlow, however, suggest that other factors may be involved as well. Harlow (1958) separated newborn monkeys from their mothers and then reared the monkeys in cages containing two artificial mothers (see Figure 11.9). One was made of wire, but it had a rubber nipple from which the infant could obtain milk. This "mother" provided food but no physical comfort. The other mother substitute had no food nipple, but it was made of soft, comfortable terrycloth. If attachment forms entirely because mothers provide food, the infants would be expected to prefer the wire mother. In fact, they spent most of their time with the terrycloth mother. And when they were frightened by a mechanical robot or an unfamiliar room, the infants immediately ran to their terrycloth mother and clung to it. Harlow concluded that the monkeys were motivated by the need for *contact comfort*. The terrycloth mother provided feelings of softness and cuddling, which were things the infants needed when their safety was in jeopardy.

What happens when attachments do not form normally? Harlow raised monkeys isolated from all social stimuli from birth. After a year of this isolation, they showed dramatic disturbances (see Figure 11.10). When visited by normally active, playful monkeys, they withdrew to a corner, huddling or rocking back and forth for hours. If one of the normal monkeys approached, those that had been isolated often bit themselves until left alone. These monkeys' problems continued into adulthood. Neither males nor females developed appropriate sexual relationships. Though the males sometimes tried

Figure 11.9
Wire and Terrycloth ''Mothers''
Here are the two types of artificial mothers used in Harlow's research. Although baby monkeys received milk from the wire mother, they spent most of their time with the terrycloth version and would cling to it when frightened.

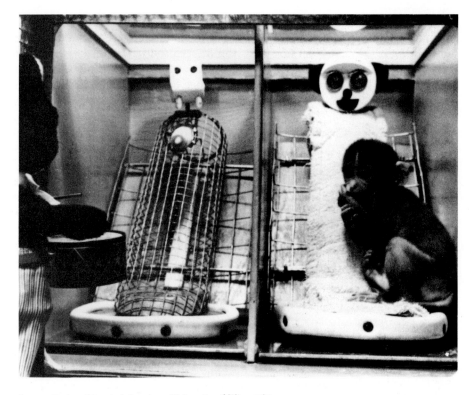

Source: Harlow Primate Laboratory, University of Wisconsin.

Figure 11.10
Monkeys Raised in Isolation
Monkeys reared without any social contact develop a variety of disorders. As shown at left, many of them spend most of their time huddled in a corner of the cage. At right, one of these animals began to bite himself when a stranger approached.

to mate with a female, they seldom got further than touching a potential partner. Isolated females quickly ran from any male who made a sexual advance. When some of the females were made pregnant through artificial insemination, their maternal behaviors were woefully inadequate. In most cases, these mothers totally ignored their infants. When the infants began to send distress signals, the mothers physically abused and sometimes even killed them. In short, it seems that when early attachment in monkeys is prevented by social isolation, the animals are permanently deficient, socially and emotionally.

Source: Harlow Primate Laboratory, University of Wisconsin.

Are there parallels to human development? It would be tempting to conclude that there are. Social, emotional, and intellectual deficits are common among children raised in institutions that offer little of the warmth or other social contacts associated with the development of attachment (Dennis, 1973; Provence & Lipton, 1962). Some of these children's behavior resembles that of Harlow's monkeys: they may be withdrawn and terrified of others, often failing to respond to any social contact. Though people do not die under conditions that impair attachment, they may develop social, emotional, and psychological problems (Ainsworth, 1989).

Still, it is important to recognize the limits of the analogy between Harlow's monkeys and human beings. For one thing, there is now considerable evidence that unfortunate early experiences may be less devastating and less permanent in humans than in lower animals (Clarke & Clarke, 1976b; Kagan, 1984; Lerner, 1984). Also, the total isolation suffered by Harlow's monkeys has almost no parallel in human experience. They were deprived not only of the comfort and contact of a mother but also the opportunity to learn anything about social interaction and behavior.

Parenting

Parents' devotion to the care and protection of their children is one of the world's strongest social forces (Bowlby, 1989). Infants' signals of discomfort or danger typically elicit an immediate helping response from the mother. Figure 11.11 shows the results of one study that examined the strength of this response in rats (Warden, 1931). Not all creatures, however, exhibit parental devotion. The treatment of offspring varies considerably from one species to another. Many types of fish and reptiles, for example, do nothing to care for their numerous young. Most of these newborns soon die, leaving only a minority to preserve the species. Mammals have far fewer babies but provide much more intense care (Brazelton & Tronick, 1983). Typically, the mother feeds the young, keeps them warm, cleans them, protects them, and teaches them skills needed for survival. This period of dependency can last from months in animals like dogs, to years in monkeys, to decades in humans.

What creates a parenting motive so intense that in some species it can overcome a parent's motive to survive? No one knows for sure. Some instinct-oriented theorists believe that nurturing, in humans and animals, involves automatic, unlearned responses to signals from the young such as smiling or crying (Ainsworth, 1989). A crying, lost child instantly attracts a crowd of concerned adults, for example. In some animals, parenting behavior is controlled to some extent by biological factors, especially hormones. In several studies when blood from a mother rat was injected into another rat, male or female, that rat immediately began to build a nest; lick, clean, and protect newborn rats; and even attempt to nurse them (Terkel & Rosenblatt, 1972).

In monkeys and other higher animals, however, parenting behaviors appear to require some learning. As illustrated in research by Harlow and others, parenting behaviors do not develop automatically. Monkeys separated from their parents at an early age often fail to care for their own offspring (Harlow, Harlow & Suomi, 1971; Rock, 1978). Similarly, children who are neglected or abused by their parents may grow up to neglect or abuse their own youngsters. In the United States, 700,000 children are subjected to some form of abuse each year. Fewer than 10 percent of abusing parents manifest symptoms of severe mental disorder, but 40 percent of them were themselves abused as children (Bowlby, 1989).

Figure 11.11
Parental Devotion
An early study examined parental devotion in rats by counting the number of electric shocks a female would tolerate in order to (1) have sex after being sexually deprived, (2) eat when very hungry, (3) drink when very thirsty, or (4) reach her distressed baby. It is easy to see that the strongest motivation was engendered by the sounds of a distressed infant.

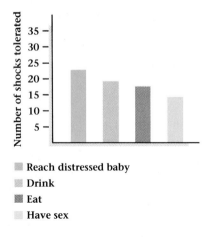

■ Reach distressed baby
■ Drink
■ Eat
■ Have sex

Source: Adapted from Warden, 1931.

Parents' motivation to protect their children can be strong enough to overcome concern for personal safety. Some animals will jeopardize their own lives in order to protect their young.

Unfortunately, all the reasons behind the wide range of parenting patterns, from overprotection to abuse, are still not fully understood. It is safe to conclude, however, that parenting involves an interaction of innate and learned behaviors whose proportions vary from one species to another.

Affiliation

Linkages: What needs do other people fulfill? (a link to Social Cognition)

The tendency for people to affiliate with others may come simply from a need to feel part of a group or to feel loved. It may also reflect the fact that people can help other people meet their needs. In fact, there are many things that people can do only with others.

For one thing, there are many situations in which it is difficult to evaluate your own decisions, opinions, abilities, and the like. If you just refused to let a classmate borrow your lecture notes and are not sure if you acted appropriately, you might ask friends for their opinions. People also routinely consult others before making major decisions, in an effort to avoid errors (Taylor & Lobel, 1989). In short, other people provide a source of *social comparison* (Wood, 1989), a topic we discuss in more detail in the chapter on social cognition.

Other people can also provide support and comfort in times of trouble (Rodin & Salovey, 1989). As described in the chapter on stress, having a network of friends helps people to cope with divorce, illness, a death in the family, and other negative events.

The existence of mutual-support groups for parents of retarded children, spouses or children of alcoholics, unwed mothers, AIDS patients, and people facing all kinds of serious adjustment problems suggests that people in trouble are especially motivated to affiliate with others (Taylor, Buunk & Aspinwall, 1990). Stanley Schachter (1959) found evidence of this tendency in a laboratory experiment. The subjects were two groups of female college students. Those in the high-anxiety group were told that the experiment for which they had volunteered would include very painful electric shocks. Those in the low-anxiety group were told that they would receive only mild, "tickling" shocks. Members of both groups had to wait several minutes before the experiment began and were given the option of waiting alone or with another volunteer. Those in the high-anxiety group were much more likely to wait with someone else, even though the other person was presumed to be just as worried about

Motivation for affiliation is sometimes reflected in a desire to become part of a national or global community, as illustrated by the success of such epic charitable efforts as Hands Across America, Farm Aid and USA for Africa.

the shocks. In fact, there is some evidence that the motive to affiliate when anxious is reduced if the other person is *not* anxious. In a follow-up study, Schachter (1959) gave high-anxiety subjects the choice of waiting alone or with another woman who was there merely to see an academic adviser. Given these options, the women preferred to be alone. The motivation to affiliate with others who are suffering from the same sort of anxiety is seen in young children as well (Carlson & Masters, 1986).

Success and Work Motivation

This sentence was written at 6 A.M. on a beautiful Sunday in June. Why would someone get up that early to work on a weekend? Why do people take their work seriously and do the best job they can? Most people work at least in part to receive financial compensation, but it would be a mistake to assume that the sole motivation for work is monetary.

The next time you visit someone's home or office, take a look at the mementos displayed there. There may be framed diplomas, photographs of memorable events, stuffed fish or game, photographs of children and grandchildren, or cases filled with trophies and ribbons. All of these are badges of worth, affirmations that the person deserves approval or admiration. That so many people proudly display such outward signs of their value serves as a reminder that much human behavior is motivated by the desire for approval, admiration, and other positive evaluations—in short, for *esteem*—from others and from themselves. In this section, we examine two of the most prominent avenues to esteem: achievement in general and a job in particular.

Achievement Motivation

Although many rewards come from others, some of the most pleasing come from within. Many athletes who hold world records continue to maintain extraordinarily rigorous training schedules; many people who have built small

For some people, the need to achieve is so strong that it helps them overcome even apparently insurmountable obstacles. Here, Mark Wellman, a climber who was partially paralyzed by a fall in 1982, ascends El Capitan with the help of climbing companion Mike Corbett. Wellman used only his arms to reach the 3,200-foot summit.

Figure 11.12
Assessment of Need Achievement
This picture is similar to those included in the Thematic Apperception Test, or TAT (Morgan & Murray, 1935). The strength of people's achievement motivation is inferred from the stories people tell about what has happened and will happen in TAT pictures. A response like "The young man is hoping that he will be able to make his grandmother proud of him" would reflect clear achievement motivation.

Source: Murray, 1971.

businesses into multimillion-dollar corporations continue to work eighty-hour weeks, overseeing every detail of the operation. What motivates such people?

Over the last few decades, a great deal of research has focused on the characteristics and consequences of **need achievement**, a specific motive first postulated by Henry Murray (1938). People with a high need for achievement are motivated to master tasks—be they sports, business operations, intellectual activities, artistic creations, hobbies, or virtually anything else—and they experience intense feelings of satisfaction from doing so. They expend considerable effort striving for excellence, they enjoy doing it, and they take great pride in achieving at a high level. An individual's need for achievement is often measured by the Thematic Apperception Test (TAT), a set of ambiguously drawn pictures like Figure 11.12.

Individual Differences How do people with strong motivation to achieve differ from other people? To find out, researchers gave children a test designed to measure their need for achievement and then asked them to play a ringtoss game. Children who scored low on the need-for-achievement test tended either to stand so close to the target that they never failed to score or so far away that it was impossible for them to succeed. In contrast, the children who scored high on the need-achievement test chose to stand at an intermediate distance from the target, making the game challenging but not impossible. These children were happy when they succeeded, and they saw the game as even more challenging when they failed (McClelland, 1958).

These and other experiments indicate that individuals with high achievement motivation tend to establish challenging and difficult—but realistic—goals. Perhaps most important, they actively pursue success and are willing to take risks in that pursuit. They experience intense satisfaction from success; in fact, one classic definition of high achievement motivation is the capacity to experience pride in success. But if they feel they have tried their best, individuals with high achievement motivation are not particularly bothered by failure. Those with low achievement motivation also prefer to succeed. For the most part, though, success brings them not joy but relief at having avoided failure (Atkinson & Birch, 1978).

In general, people who are very motivated to achieve tend to be preoccupied with their performance and level of ability. They prefer tasks that have clear outcomes, and they would rather receive feedback from a harsh but competent critic than from one who is friendlier but less competent (McClelland, 1985). They like to struggle with a problem rather than ask for help, they are able to delay gratification, and they make careful plans about the future (Raynor, 1970). In contrast, people less motivated to achieve do not enjoy or seek feedback, and they tend to respond to failure by quitting (Weiner, 1980).

Development of Achievement Motivation Achievement motivation appears to be largely learned in early childhood, much of it through interactions with one's parents. For example, one study found that ten-year-old boys who scored high on tests of achievement motivation had mothers who strongly encouraged independent thinking and rewarded success with hugs and other signs of affection (Winterbottom, 1953). In another study, young boys were given a very difficult task at which they were sure to fail. Fathers whose sons scored low on achievement motivation tests often became irritated, discouraged their boys from continuing to try, and often interfered or even completed the task themselves (Rosen & D'Andrade, 1959). More recently, David McClelland (1985) described the pattern of parenting that is typically associated with children who score high on achievement motivation tests. The parents of these children tend to (1) encourage the child to attempt difficult tasks, especially new ones; (2) offer praise and other rewards for success; (3) encourage the child to find ways to succeed, instead of merely complaining about failure; and (4) prompt the child to go on to the next, somewhat more difficult challenge.

The culture also shapes achievement motivation. The written material used to teach children to read provides one source of cultural influence. Reading primers do not contain statements like "You're no good if you don't do well in school" or "Success in life doesn't matter." Nonetheless, the events and themes in stories give children subtle messages about what their culture values. Is the hero or heroine someone who worked hard and overcame obstacles (thus modeling reinforcement of persistence and hard work) or someone who loafed and then won the lottery (suggesting that rewards come randomly and that commitment to achievement is irrelevant)? Does the description of living "happily ever after" include having a nice house and a big car? These are examples of differing *achievement themes* in children's stories; they are blueprints for the goals one should aspire to and how one reaches them.

It is not known whether differences in these messages actually *cause* differences in achievement motivation. However, a study by Richard de Charms and Gerald Moeller (1962) found a strong positive correlation between the number of high-achievement themes in children's reading material and the industrial achievements in these children's countries years later, when they became adults. For example, the number of industrial patents issued was much higher in countries in which children's books contained many high-achievement themes.

Achievement motivation can also be developed after childhood, even among people whose early backgrounds did not encourage it (McClelland, 1985). In one study high school and college students with low achievement motivation were helped to develop fantasies about their own success. They imagined setting goals that were difficult but not impossible. Then they imagined themselves concentrating on breaking a complicated problem into smaller, more manageable steps. (You might recall from Chapter 9 that this decomposition heuristic can be very useful in problem solving.) They fantasized about working intensely, failing but not being discouraged, continuing to work, and finally feeling elated at success. After the program, these students' grades and general academic performance improved, which suggested that their achievement motivation had been intensified (McClelland, 1985).

HIGHLIGHT

Gender Differences in Achievement Motivation

The behavior of women with a high level of achievement motivation is much more variable than that of men equally motivated by achievement. In particular, women who are highly motivated to achieve do not always establish challenging goals for themselves when given a choice, and they do not always persist when confronted with failure (Dweck, 1986). In fact, some of them withdraw from and even avoid situations in which their achievement could be evaluated.

Gender differences in achievement motivation begin to appear at a very early age. The question of why they occur is the subject of considerable debate (Koestner, Zuckerman & Koestner, 1989). One thing is clear: females are much more likely than males to attribute failure on school-related tasks to a lack of ability, and they tend to begin doing so when they are quite young (Dweck & Gilliard, 1975). Many continue to see themselves as incompetent even in the face of objective evidence that they do better academically than their male counterparts (Licht & Dweck, 1984).

Girls' readiness to deprecate their own abilities in school may stem in part from classroom experiences and become part of their identity (Kernis, Brockner & Frankel, 1989). For reasons that are not yet fully understood, elementary school teachers tend to use different styles of criticism for boys and girls. Girls are likely to be told what they did wrong and what they should do instead. Boys are also likely to hear this kind of criticism; but in addition, boys are often told that they are not concentrating or are not being careful enough (Dweck et al., 1978). Carol Dweck suggested that the feedback given to girls leads them to think of *themselves* as incompetent, whereas the boys conclude that any failure was due only to lack of effort or some other aspect of the *situation*. When Dweck and her colleagues arranged for girls who were very motivated to achieve to receive the type of criticism normally directed toward boys, the girls' behavior became more like that of boys with high achievement motivation. The girls tended to adopt challenging goals, to try hard, and to persist in the face of failure (Dweck et al., 1978).

It is thus becoming increasingly clear that many gender differences in achievement motivation and behavior are due to the way boys and girls learn to think of themselves and their performance (Burns & Seligman, 1989). Some children learn a short-term perspective in which they focus only on their performance of the task at hand. However, children can also be taught to adopt a long-term perspective in which they focus on constantly learning more (Elliott & Dweck, 1988). This perspective can motivate them not only to pass a test or receive a good grade but also to constantly improve and truly master the material. People who adopt this orientation toward mastery achieve at very high levels and experience intense pride in their accomplishments. This is true of both males and females (Bergen & Dweck, 1989).

Traditional gender-role stereotypes often make it difficult for women who have a high need for achievement. In analyzing this problem, Matina Horner (1970) suggested that such women are pulled in two directions. On the one hand, they are motivated to pursue excellence and achieve success. On the other hand, society gives them a variety of messages that it is "unfeminine" to be so "aggressive." Many of them learn that men are threatened by women who achieve at "too high" a level; some women actually hide some of their successes or act in ways that undermine their chances of success. This "fear of success" pattern is one of the most unfortunate consequences of long-entrenched cultural factors that produce gender differences in achievement motivation. ■

Jobs and Motivation

Employers are less likely to be interested in a worker's personal need to achieve than in whether their employees are motivated to work hard. One of the most influential approaches to motivation on the job was initiated by Frederick Herzberg.

Job Satisfaction and Dissatisfaction Herzberg suggested that the factors associated with job *satisfaction* are different from those linked to *dissatisfaction* (Herzberg, 1966, 1968). According to Herzberg's theory, dissatisfaction with a job comes primarily from its external, or *extrinsic*, characteristics, such as inadequate job security, salary and fringe benefits, working conditions, job status, and relationships with coworkers and supervisors. However, jobs with exemplary extrinsic characteristics do not necessarily bring job satisfaction. Satisfaction is tied to *intrinsic* aspects of the job, especially those that foster esteem. Important factors in satisfaction include being given individual responsibility, having opportunities for advancement, and doing work that is challenging, that allows unusual degrees of achievement, and that fosters personal growth. If these conditions are absent, workers may not be satisfied, but they probably will not be dissatisfied unless the extrinsic factors just described are also lacking.

There is substantial evidence for Herzberg's theoretical separation of satisfaction and dissatisfaction (Petri, 1986). Consider assembly-line workers. Their jobs are repetitive, often boring, and generally unrewarding. Employers typically try to improve performance on the assembly line by upgrading extrinsic aspects of the job such as pay, benefits, and job security. This approach can decrease dissatisfaction, but it does little to increase job satisfaction (Szilagyi & Wallace, 1980).

Designing Jobs That Motivate Intentionally or not, managers structure jobs in ways that reflect a theory about people and what motivates them (Riggio, 1989). Employers who see employees as basically lazy, untrustworthy, ambitionless creatures who have little creative insight and prefer to avoid responsibility tend to design jobs that are very structured and heavily supervised; they give employees very little say in deciding what to do and how to do it. The employees then tend not to be satisfied and show a lack of motivation to perform at peak efficiency (Wexley & Yukl, 1984).

In contrast, employers who view employees as creative, responsible individuals who enjoy a challenge and are capable of self-direction are likely to design jobs in which workers are (1) encouraged to participate in decisions about how work should be done; (2) given problems to solve, without being told how to solve them; (3) taught more than one skill; and (4) given lots of individual responsibility. For example, instead of requiring factory workers to perform just one small task over and over on an assembly line, some employers enhance assembly-line jobs by having workers rotate from one responsibility to another, or they have employees work in teams to discuss and solve

American companies have followed Japanese models in redesigning jobs to enhance responsibility and flexibility. The hope is to increase both employee productivity and job satisfaction.

problems and arrange for teams to produce a complete product. Workers in these "enhanced" jobs tend to be more satisfied and productive than their counterparts in more rigidly structured jobs (Deci, Connell, & Ryan, 1987).

Edward Deci and his colleagues have suggested that poor motivation among workers arises largely from the feeling of having little or no control over the work environment (Deci, Connell & Ryan, 1987). This view is consistent with evidence discussed in Chapter 13 that a sense of control over important aspects of life is an important buffer against stress and that lack of control can lead to many kinds of problems.

The Importance of Goals   Allowing people to set and achieve clear goals can increase their performance and satisfaction (Schneider, 1985). Increased performance produces more economic benefits for the company, and increased job satisfaction leads to lower absenteeism and lower turnover (Ilgen & Klein, 1989).

The goals that are most effective in maintaining work motivation have three characteristics (Katzell & Thompson, 1990). First, effective goals are personally meaningful. When employees are told in a memo from a faceless administrator that their goal should be an increase in production, they are likely to feel put upon and may not be motivated to meet the goal. Second, effective goals are specific and concrete. The goal of "doing better" is usually not a very effective motivator. A particular target, such as increasing sales by 10 percent, makes a far more motivating goal. It is there for all to see, and it is easy to know if the goal has been reached. Finally, the effectiveness of goals depends on how management treats them. Goals are likely to be very effective if management supports goal setting by employees themselves, offers special rewards for reaching goals, and provides encouragement after failure.

In short, jobs that offer personal challenges, independence, and rewards of many kinds provide enough satisfaction for people to feel excitement and pleasure in continuing hard work.

Relations Among Motives: Maslow's Hierarchy

At any time, many motives might guide a person's behavior. What determines which ones will? Abraham Maslow (1970) offered a perspective that addresses this question. He suggested that five basic classes of needs, or motives, influence human behavior. These motives are organized in a hierarchy, as illustrated in Figure 11.13. According to Maslow, needs at the lowest level of the hierarchy must be at least partially satisfied before people can be motivated by higher-level goals.

From the bottom to the top of the hierarchy, the five levels of motives, according to Maslow, are:

1. *Biological, or physiological*   These motives include the need for food, water, oxygen, activity, and sleep.
2. *Safety*   Being cared for as a child and having a secure source of income and a place to live as an adult are examples of safety needs. Many people spend most of their lives in an attempt to satisfy needs at this level.
3. *Belongingness and love*   Belongingness is integration into various kinds of social groups, such as clubs and other formal social organizations. By *love* Maslow meant affectionate relationships with others. Some of these relationships may have a sexual component; ideally, all of them are based on mutual respect, admiration, and trust.
4. *Esteem*   An honest, fundamental respect for a person as a useful, honorable human being constitutes esteem. Esteem brings feelings of competence and confidence and a sense of achievement and individuality. The effort to meet esteem needs can take infinitely varied forms. Some people pursue esteem through their careers; others through their relationships with family, friends, or the larger community.
5. *Self-actualization*   When people are motivated not so much by unmet needs as by the desire to become all they are capable of, then they are seeking self-actualization. This means, for example, exploring and enhancing relationships with others, following interests for pure pleasure rather than for status or esteem, and being concerned with issues affecting all people, not just oneself. Maslow viewed self-actualizing motives as the essence of mental health. Although he saw self-actualization as a motive inherent in all people, he recognized that very few people spend much time or effort seeking it. Only the rare individual, such as Mother Teresa or Martin Luther King, Jr., approaches full self-actualization.

Why does self-actualization apparently motivate so few people? Maslow's hierarchy suggests one possible reason. Most people are so oriented toward

Figure 11.13
Maslow's Hierarchy of Motives
According to Maslow, motives are organized in a hierarchy in which motives at lower levels take precedence over those at higher levels. Motives at lower levels must be at least partly satisfied before those above them can significantly influence an individual's behavior.

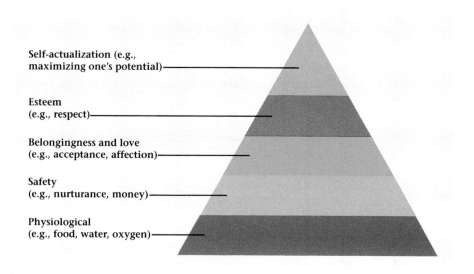

Source: Adapted from Maslow, 1943.

lower-level motives that they seldom concern themselves with self-actualization. Culturally reinforced gender roles are another factor inhibiting self-actualization. In American society, for example, women often feel constrained about expressing a desire for authority and power; men frequently find it difficult to display tenderness, fear, dependency, or other feelings stereotyped as unmanly. The emphasis in American society on esteem also inhibits self-actualization. It encourages people to spend their lives motivated by the desire to acquire more things, to show that they are somehow better than others.

One weakness of Maslow's system is that it is too simplistic (Williams & Page, 1989). People do not always act according to his hierarchy; even when lower-level needs are unmet, some people continue to be motivated by higher levels in the hierarchy. Examples of this inversion of Maslow's hierarchy abound in the history of political and moral causes. In 1981, for example, Bobby Sand, Kieran Doherty, and seven other imprisoned men starved themselves to death to protest continued British rule over Northern Ireland.

Nevertheless, Maslow's classification is useful for thinking about the relationships among human motives. Most researchers agree that his system includes the basic human motives and that his hierarchy provides an organized description of the basic sources of motivation referred to in other theories. It also appears that, *in general*, motives lower in Maslow's hierarchy do take precedence over those higher in the hierarchy. For example, people deprived of food may become completely dominated by it (Keys et al., 1950). Maslow's framework also makes it clear that differing motives can be in conflict, a topic we examine more closely next.

Linkages: Motivation and Stress

What happens when motives are in conflict?

If people's motivation were always clear and simple, human behavior would be relatively easy to understand. However, the motivation for people's actions is sometimes so obscure and complicated that their behavior appears to make no sense, even to them. The healthy and popular child of wealthy parents commits suicide; the abused former spouse of an alcoholic marries another alcoholic; a successful executive suddenly abandons job and family for a life of beachcombing with a new lover. Sometimes, actions like these are responses to stress, and stress, in turn, often reflects conflicting motives, such as the desire to live but to avoid the pain of life, or to have money as well as freedom. Anyone trying to understand human behavior must recognize not only that there are numerous sources of motivation but also that several motives often operate at the same time, thus provoking stress.

Suppose it's late on a Saturday night and you're bored, so you think about going to a convenience store for a snack. What are your motives? Hunger might play a role in sending you out, as might the prospect of the boredom-fighting stimulation (arousal) you will obtain from a trip to the store. Even sexual motivation might be involved, as you think about the possibility of meeting someone exciting in the frozen pizza aisle. But safety-related motives might make you hesitate. What if you should get mugged? And an esteem motive might prompt you to shrink from being seen without a companion on an evening seemingly filled with couples.

These are just a few of the motives that might be relevant to a trivial decision. When the decision is important, the number and strength of motivational pushes and pulls is likely to be even greater, creating stress through conflicting behavioral tendencies. Following the lead of Kurt Lewin (1931), Neal Miller (1959) identified four basic types of motivational conflict, each of which may play a role in stress.

Conflicting motives almost always create stress. For example, when one member of a dual-career couple is offered promotion to a new job in a distant city, there is likely to be stressful conflict within (and between) partners about whether to seize an opportunity that advances the progress of one at the expense of the other.

1. *Approach-approach conflicts*   When a person is motivated to engage in two desirable activities that cannot be pursued simultaneously, an *approach-approach conflict* exists. If you are trying to choose which of two movies to see or must decide between going to a prestigious law school versus accepting a lucrative job, you face an approach-approach conflict. As the importance of the decision increases, so does the difficulty of making it. Still, approach-approach conflicts are usually resolved with relative ease.

2. *Avoidance-avoidance conflicts*   An *avoidance-avoidance conflict* arises when a person faces two unattractive situations, and avoidance of one forces exposure to the other. For example, a woman with an unwanted pregnancy may be morally opposed to abortion. In this case, neither having the baby nor terminating the pregnancy is desirable. Like most avoidance-avoidance conflicts, this conflict is very difficult to resolve and creates intense emotions.

3. *Approach-avoidance conflicts*   When one event or activity has both attractive and unattractive features, an *approach-avoidance conflict* is created. Acting to attain the desirable features requires exposure to the undesirable ones as well; avoiding the negative features means giving up something desirable. Consider, for example, the dilemma of the student who is offered a stolen copy of an important exam. Cheating will bring guilt and reduced self-esteem, but also a good grade. Approach-avoidance conflicts are difficult to resolve (Weiner, 1972). As the person moves toward the situation or thinks about entering it, the negative aspects become more prominent, and the person begins to back away or decides to stay away. This makes the negative aspects of the situation more remote and highlights the positive side. The result is continuing vacillation between approach and avoidance, creating a great deal of emotional turmoil.

4. *Multiple approach-avoidance conflicts*   Suppose a person must choose between two jobs. One offers a high salary with a prestigious organization but requires long working hours and moving to a miserable climate. The other boasts plenty of opportunity for advancement and good fringe benefits, in a better climate, but offers lousy pay and an unpredictable schedule. This is an example of a *multiple approach-avoidance conflict*, a situation in which a choice must be made between two or more alternatives, each of which has both positive and negative features. Multiple approach-avoidance conflicts are the most difficult to resolve, partly because the features of each option are often difficult to compare. For example, how much is a good climate "worth" in terms of unpredictable working hours? To what extent will the chance for rapid advancement compensate for a low starting salary? As discussed in Chapter 9, such multiattribute comparisons are difficult to make with confidence. To make rational decisions, people should analyze the expected values of each course of action.

Unfortunately, people do not always choose rationally, partly because of the shortcomings and biases inherent in human thought processes but also because of stress. While in the midst of motivational conflicts, most people tend to be tense, irritable, and vulnerable to many other stress-related problems described in Chapter 13. These reactions are especially likely when the correct choices are not obvious, when varying motives have approximately equal strength, and when a choice can bring frightening or irrevocable consequences (as in decisions to marry, to divorce, or to approve disconnection of a life-support system). Resolution of such conflicts may be a long time in coming or may be made impulsively and thoughtlessly, just to end the discomfort of uncertainty. Even after the conflict is resolved, signs of stress may continue in the form of anxiety about the correctness of the decision or guilt over bad choices. Sometimes, these and other consequences of conflicting motives create depression and other serious disorders.

Since motivational conflicts are inevitable, it is important to understand their effect and to have some idea of how to resolve them effectively and with a minimum of residual distress. In Chapter 13, on stress, we discuss one approach to resolving motivational conflicts.

Future Directions

Because the concept of motivation centers around the initiation, persistence, and change of behavior, the study of motivation is intertwined with most other areas of psychology. For example, we reviewed biological psychology research in discussing hunger, social psychology research in examining affiliation and work motivation, and personality research in discussing the need for achievement. Indeed, most theorists today prefer not to think of motivation as a separate area of psychological research.

A recent trend in motivational research is to examine *personal strivings*, long-term goals that people pursue over a long period and try to achieve through their everyday actions (Emmons, 1989). Personal strivings might include developing a coherent philosophy of life, becoming a respected scholar in a certain area, contributing to a successful and happy family, or becoming a world-class chess player. People who report high levels of life satisfaction tend to be committed to at least one long-term life objective (Baumeister, 1989). They also perceive themselves as striving to attain that goal on a regular basis, and they see the goal as difficult, but not impossible, to reach (Pervin, 1989).

People's goals characteristically shift over the course of the life span, and everyone experiences temporary periods of confusion, anxiety, and dissatisfaction. Researchers are beginning to identify those situations that tend to elicit low levels of life satisfaction (Ruehlman & Wolchik, 1988). One such situation involves having a goal that is personally meaningful but not being sure of how to achieve it. This situation is most likely to occur during major transitions, as when college students who go off to live on their own for the first time want to be successful academically and socially but are confused about how to do so (Stewart, 1989). It is not surprising that these individuals often experience periods of anxiety and distress (Cantor & Kihlstrom, 1989). The same is true of parents who have their first child (Ruble et al., 1988).

Dissatisfaction with life can also occur when a person is preoccupied with avoiding negative results rather than achieving positive ones (Emmons, 1989). For example, instead of focusing on doing what it takes to become an outstanding criminal lawyer, a person might be constantly worried about making mistakes, losing a big case, or being embarrassed. Such fears can have both physiological and psychological consequences (Cantor & Langston, 1989; Smith et al., 1989), and they tend to be compounded by beliefs that attaining a goal might be impossible (Emmons & King, 1989).

Long-term personal strivings can lead to long-term conflict (Zirkel & Cantor, 1990). For example, if career and family concerns are perceived to be in conflict, there will be almost daily stress which, as we discuss in Chapter 13, can impair both physical and psychological health. In contrast, people who perceive the various aspects of their lives to be in balance and see their various goals as complementing one another tend to report very high levels of life satisfaction (Emmons & King, 1988).

In short, whereas motivational research has historically been concerned with short-term motives, researchers are increasingly turning their attention to those that are pursued over the long term. Personality, clinical, social, developmental, and biological psychologists are all contributing to this effort. If you are interested in studying motivation in more detail, you can expect to find motivational issues discussed in courses in all of these areas, as well as in a course usually labeled "motivation and emotion."

Summary and Key Terms

Basic Concepts of Motivation

Motivation can be defined as those processes that govern the initiation, direction, intensity, and persistence of behavior.

Finding Unity in Diversity and Change

Suggesting a *motive* for behavior identifies a theme underlying behaviors that otherwise appear to be quite different. Motivational concepts serve as *intervening variables* that explain both why one response may be given to very different stimuli and why the same stimulus may produce very different responses over time.

Sources of Motivation

Motivation has many sources, but they fall into four categories: biological, cognitive, emotional, and social.

Theoretical Perspectives

Instinct Theory

Instinct theory postulates innate, fixed-action patterns that are automatically elicited by the presence of some stimulus.

Drive Reduction Theory

Both biological factors and learning are important in *drive reduction theory*. This theory holds that when *homeostasis* is upset, a *need* is created, which produces a *drive* to restore homeostasis. Biology creates the *primary drives*, but people are also motivated by *secondary drives*, which are learned.

Arousal Theory

According to *arousal theory*, people are motivated to maintain an optimal level of *arousal*. People generally feel best and perform best when they are at their own optimal level.

Incentive Theory

The role of environmental incentives is highlighted by *incentive theory*. In general, people are motivated to perform behaviors when they expect those behaviors to have outcomes that they value highly.

Opponent-Process Theory

Two assumptions underlie *opponent-process theory:* first, any reaction to a stimulus is followed by an opposite reaction; second, with repeated exposure to a stimulus the initial reaction weakens and the opponent process becomes stronger.

Hunger and Eating

Biological Mechanisms

Cues from the stomach and the taste of food both play a part in regulating hunger, but the role of the brain appears central. The brain monitors glucose levels in the blood and, through the lateral area and the ventromedial nucleus of the hypothalamus, acts to start and stop eating. These mechanisms seem to act in a way that maintains a *set point*.

Nonbiological Factors

Eating is also influenced by nonbiological factors such as conditioned satiety, the sight of food, learned eating traditions, and cues from other people.

Eating Disorders

Obesity, anorexia nervosa, and bulimia are all health-threatening eating disorders. Among the factors that may contribute to *obesity* are body type, having more and larger fat cells, a higher-than-average set point for food intake, a lower-than-average metabolic rate, and a tendency to cope with stress by eating. *Anorexia nervosa* is marked by self-starvation, sometimes leading to death. *Bulimia* is characterized by eating large quantities of food and then purging with laxatives or self-induced vomiting.

Sexual Behavior

Though not essential for individual survival, sexual motivation is very strong in human beings.

Sources of Sexual Motivation

Social and cultural factors often outweigh biological determinants of human sexual behavior, but hormones have important organizational and activational effects. The masculine hormones are called *androgens*; the primary one is *testosterone*. The feminine hormones are called *estrogens* and *progestins*; the two primary ones are *estradiol* and *progesterone*.

Human Sexual Activity

The *sexual response cycle* differs for men and women. While men show one primary pattern of sexual response, women display at least three different patterns from time to time. Sexual activity may be *heterosexual, bisexual,* or *homosexual.* Sexual orientation has three components—behavior, attraction, and identification—which do not necessarily go together.

Social Motives

Developing Attachments

A psychological attachment is often formed between an infant and the primary caregiver, usually the mother. Harlow's research with monkeys suggests that the development of attachment is important for the later appearance of various kinds of social behavior.

Parenting

One of the strongest forms of motivation is parental devotion to the care and protection of the young. In humans, as well as in animals, responding to distress signals from the young appears to be automatic and unlearned. But parenting in higher animals reflects both innate and learned patterns of behavior.

Affiliation

People are motivated to affiliate with other people, who provide sources of information, social comparison, and social support.

Success and Work Motivation

Achievement Motivation

Need achievement is reflected in the capacity to experience pride in success. Individuals with high achievement motivation strive to achieve excellence, persist in the face of failure, and establish challenging but realistic goals. Gender differences in achievement behavior are pronounced and often appear at a young age. In particular, females are more likely than males to attribute failure on school-related tasks to a lack of ability. These differences appear to reflect early learning experiences.

Jobs and Motivation

The motivation to work comes from factors that produce job satisfaction and eliminate dissatisfaction. Workers are most satisfied, and tend to perform best, when they are working toward their own goals and receive concrete feedback. Jobs that include a variety of tasks and give workers individual responsibility are the most motivating.

Relations Among Motives: Maslow's Hierarchy

Maslow proposed that there are five classes of human motives and that these motives form a hierarchy, from meeting basic biological needs to attaining self-actualization. According to Maslow, motives at the lowest levels of the hierarchy must be at least partially satisfied before people can be motivated by higher-level goals.

Emotion

The alien race of Fungi from the twelfth moon of Nitswa in the galaxy Androgena recently prepared a subclone of humanoids to send to Earth to infiltrate the human race. The designers managed to get the product to look like the models in *GQ* and *Cosmopolitan*, and the humanoids were shipped via overnight timewarp to cities around the world. However, the Fungi were not successful at infiltrating human society because their clones, who were perfect reproductions of humans in every other way, had one major flaw: the humanoids had no emotions. This was because Fungi designers could not understand emotions. After all, humans "smile" when they are happy but also sometimes when they are nervous. And Fungi designers could not see the usefulness of emotions, which they considered mere disruptions of logical thought patterns. But Earthlings quickly recognized the Fungi "people" as nonhuman, mainly because it was so difficult to interact with them. Fungi could not share humans' joys and sorrows, did not respond to their anger, and returned their smiles only by saying, "I see you contracting your zygomatic muscles; thank you." Humans usually responded with "See you later, Fungi."

Our little science fiction story illustrates the importance of emotions to human experience and to social interactions. In other chapters we have mentioned their important effects on motivation, performance, and memory (see the Linkages diagram). In this chapter we describe what is known about the defining features of emotions and why they are valuable to human beings. We address three basic questions about emotions: (1) what is emotion? (2) where is emotion (in the heart or in the head)? and (3) how do people communicate emotions?

What Is Emotion?

It has been suggested (Stolar, unpublished manuscript) that psychologists examining emotion have been like the proverbial blind men who come upon an elephant and

LINKAGES

Emotion

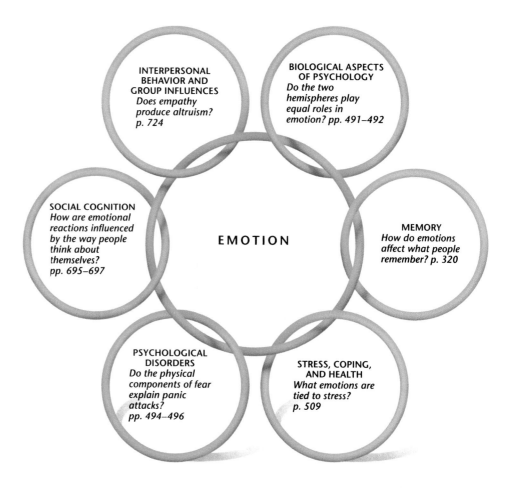

INTERPERSONAL BEHAVIOR AND GROUP INFLUENCES
Does empathy produce altruism?
p. 724

BIOLOGICAL ASPECTS OF PSYCHOLOGY
Do the two hemispheres play equal roles in emotion? pp. 491–492

SOCIAL COGNITION
How are emotional reactions influenced by the way people think about themselves? pp. 695–697

EMOTION

MEMORY
How do emotions affect what people remember? p. 320

PSYCHOLOGICAL DISORDERS
Do the physical components of fear explain panic attacks? pp. 494–496

STRESS, COPING, AND HEALTH
What emotions are tied to stress? p. 509

■ Look at the diagram above, which illustrates some of the relationships between the topic of this chapter, emotion, and other chapter topics. We mentioned another linkage in the previous chapter: emotionally aroused people are also intensely motivated people. Why? Pleasure and pain are often components of emotions, and people are strongly motivated to enhance pleasure and avoid pain.

The study of emotions is probably tied most strongly to biological psychology, because the bodily responses that accompany emotions provide a dimension that distinguishes emotions from other types of mental processes. Why do people get "cold feet" when they are afraid but not when they are angry? Can you be afraid even when your heart does not beat fast? Understanding emotion means exploring questions like these, and answering these questions depends on research in biological psychology. Thus, in this chapter we revisit topics introduced in Chapter 3 such as the autonomic nervous system and the lateralization of brain functions.

For years, many psychologists tried to avoid the study of emotional experiences, because emotions are not overt behaviors that can be easily measured. Today, however, investigators in many areas consider the role of emotions. The diagram provides a sampling of these additional linkages between emotions and other aspects of psychology; the page numbers indicate where these linkages are discussed. ■

try to decide what it is. In that proverb, one blind man bumps into the elephant's leg, wraps his arms around it, and says, "This is a large tree." Another grabs the trunk and says, "This is a snake." A third grasps the tail and says, "This is a rope." Similarly, some theorists say that the essential quality of emotion is the physiological response; some say that the relation of a feeling to one's goals is the important part; and some say that emotions exist only in a social context. Emotion is a multifaceted phenomenon, and its essential qualities are not easily defined. Joy, sorrow, anger, fear, anxiety, love, hate, mirth, and lust: what properties do all these experiences share that make them emotions? The definition of emotion we will give combines elements highlighted by several of psychology's best "elephant analysts" (Averill, 1980; James, 1890; Ortony, Clore & Collins, 1988).

Emotions are transitory states, characterized by six features. First, emotions are neither overt behaviors nor specific thoughts; they are experiences. As a result, emotions are often mixed and even contradictory; assigning specific labels to them may be difficult. For example, you might find it difficult to determine all of your feelings about a friend's serious illness. Certainly you feel sadness, but it may be mixed with guilty relief that you remain healthy.

Second, emotional experience has *valence*, which means it is either positive or negative, something you would like either to enhance or eliminate. Thus, changes in emotions can change your motivation. Most people tend to act in ways that bring about happiness, satisfaction, and other positive emotions and to avoid doing things that cause pain, anxiety, disgust, or sadness.

Third, emotions are passions, not actions. Eating, for example, is an action, but hunger is a passion. Actions are initiated by the actor, whereas passions happen to the actor. You eat, but hunger happens to you. Similarly, emotions happen to you. You cannot decide to experience joy or sorrow; instead, you "fall in love" or are "overcome by grief."

The passionate nature of emotions does not mean that you have no control over them, however, because of their fourth feature: emotions arise in part from a cognitive appraisal of a situation. Seeing a lion elicits different emotions depending on whether you think the animal is a tame pet or a wild, hungry beast; your *interpretation* of the situation can alter your emotional reaction to it. Emotions depend not just on situations but on what you *think* about those situations, such as how you interpret their potential for threat or pleasure.

Although you cannot consciously determine your emotions, part of the situation you interpret is your own emotions as they develop. Emotions are, therefore, experiences that are both triggered by the thinking self and experienced by the self as happening to the self. They reveal the individual as both agent and object, as both I and me, both the controller of thoughts and the recipient of passions. The extent to which you are a "victim" of your passions versus a rational designer of your emotions is one of the central dilemmas of human existence, and a subject of literature as much as of psychology.

Fifth, emotions are accompanied by bodily responses. When you are surprised, for example, you probably show a wide-eyed, open-mouthed expression and raise your hands to your face. The facial and bodily movements that accompany emotion are partly reflexive and partly learned, as we discuss later. In addition, internal, *visceral* responses—changes in heart rate, for example— also accompany emotion. These visceral responses are reflexive, occurring as automatically as salivation in response to food.

Finally, emotions vary in intensity, from the quiet satisfaction of a person watching a beautiful sunset to the raging fury of a wronged lover. The importance of this feature of emotion is evident in people whose emotional intensity is very low. Nothing seems to get them excited; they appear to take no real pleasure in anything, and they do not get very upset about anything.

An extreme lack of emotion may make it difficult or impossible to hold a job or to function normally in other ways. Too much emotional arousal can also cause problems, as we discussed in Chapter 11, on motivation. An overly emotional person may be unable to concentrate or to coordinate thoughts and actions efficiently. Stage fright—which brings sweaty palms, dry mouth, tremors, and other signs of strong physiological arousal—is one example; it can lead to forgotten lines, botched musical numbers, and other performance disasters.

In summary, an **emotion** is a valenced experience that is felt with some intensity as happening to the self, generated in part by a cognitive appraisal of the situation, and accompanied by both learned and reflexive physical responses.

Where Is Emotion: In the Heart or in the Head?

No other psychological process produces the kinds of bodily responses that emotions produce. Most thoughts do not arouse noticeable physiological changes, but if you think, for example, about what you should have said to that rude salesperson yesterday and become angry, then your pulse and breathing quicken and you become red in the face. How do these responses fit into the experience of emotion? This question has been the center of one of the major controversies in the study of emotion. Let's begin by looking at how visceral responses are controlled by the nervous system.

Emotions and the Autonomic Nervous System

If you get red in the face when you are angry or embarrassed, it is because the autonomic nervous system has increased the flow of blood to your face. Recall from Chapter 3 that the *autonomic nervous system*, or *ANS*, is the part of the peripheral nervous system that carries information between the brain and all organs of the body except the striated muscles (such as the arm and leg muscles). The ANS affects all of the organs—the heart and blood vessels, the digestive system, and so on. Each of these organs has ongoing activity independent of the autonomic nervous system, but input from the autonomic system *modulates* this activity, increasing or decreasing it. For example, your heart continues to beat even without input from the autonomic system, but input from the autonomic system may increase or decrease its rate.

By modulating the activity of organs, the autonomic system coordinates their functioning to meet the needs of the whole organism and prepares the body for changes. If you are aroused to increased activity—to run to catch the bus, for instance—more glucose is needed to fuel your muscles. The autonomic nervous system provides the needed energy by stimulating secretion of glucose-generating hormones and by promoting blood flow to the muscles. Much of the arousal discussed in the chapter on motivation involves the ANS.

Organization of the Autonomic Nervous System   Figure 12.1 illustrates the organization of the ANS. Notice that there are exactly two synapses between the central nervous system (the brain and spinal cord) and each target organ. First, a central nervous system cell connects to an ANS cell out in the body; the ANS cell then synapses on the target organ. For example, in order to increase heart rate, cells in the spinal cord stimulate a collection of ANS cells, which then transmit the message to the heart. A collection of ANS cells is called a *ganglion*.

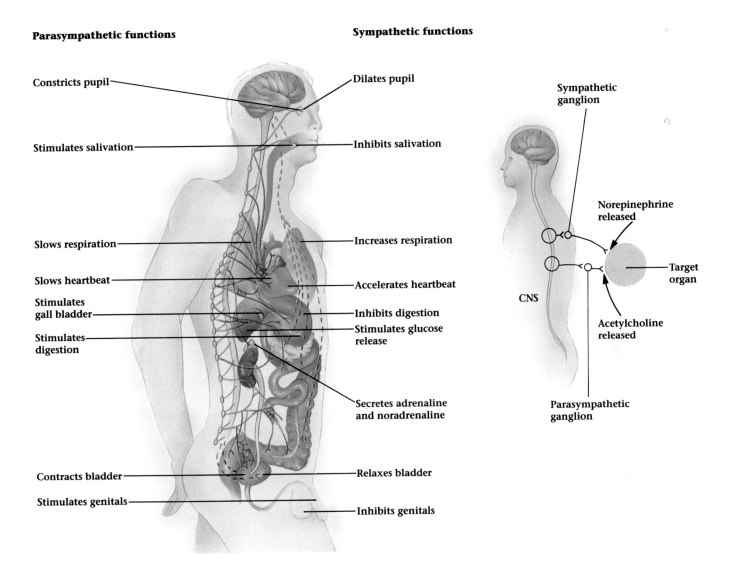

Parasympathetic functions

Constricts pupil

Stimulates salivation

Slows respiration

Slows heartbeat

Stimulates gall bladder

Stimulates digestion

Contracts bladder

Stimulates genitals

Sympathetic functions

Dilates pupil

Inhibits salivation

Increases respiration

Accelerates heartbeat

Inhibits digestion

Stimulates glucose release

Secretes adrenaline and noradrenaline

Relaxes bladder

Inhibits genitals

Sympathetic ganglion

Norepinephrine released

Target organ

CNS

Acetylcholine released

Parasympathetic ganglion

Figure 12.1
The Autonomic Nervous System
Emotional responses involve activation of the autonomic nervous system, which includes sympathetic and parasympathetic subsystems. Which of the bodily responses depicted do you associate with emotional experiences?

There are two divisions in the autonomic nervous system: the sympathetic nervous system and the parasympathetic nervous system. The **parasympathetic nervous system** typically influences activity related to the protection, nourishment, and growth of the body. Digestion is one example. The parasympathetic system increases movement of the intestinal system, allowing more nutrients to be extracted from food. The **sympathetic nervous system** usually prepares the organism for vigorous activity. When one part of the sympathetic system is stimulated, other parts are stimulated "in sympathy" with it (Gellhorn & Loofbourrow, 1963). Activation of the sympathetic nervous system usually produces increased heart rate and blood pressure, rapid or irregular breathing, dilated pupils, perspiration, dry mouth, increased blood sugar, piloerection ("goose bumps"), trembling, and other changes. You have probably experienced these reactions after a near-accident. They are sometimes called the **fight-or-flight syndrome**, because they prepare the body to combat or to run from a threatening situation. Either branch of the autonomic nervous system can be activated during an emotion. For example, the sympathetic nervous system increases your heart rate when you are angry; the parasympathetic nervous system causes tears to flow when you are grieving.

In both the parasympathetic and sympathetic systems, the neurotransmitter at the ganglia is always acetylcholine (see Figure 12.1). In the parasympathetic

These skydivers are likely to show notable changes in autonomic arousal just before a jump, but it would probably be unclear from their physiological activity alone whether the emotion they experience is fear or excitement.

system, the neurotransmitter at the target organ is also acetylcholine, but in the sympathetic system, the neurotransmitter at the target organ is almost always norepinephrine (also known as noradrenaline). Very often, the same organ is innervated by fibers of both the sympathetic and the parasympathetic system, each of which may produce opposite effects. For example, norepinephrine released by the sympathetic nerves on the heart speeds up the heart, whereas acetylcholine released by parasympathetic nerves slows it down.

One part of the sympathetic nervous system deserves special mention: the **adrenal gland**. There are two adrenal glands, one on each side of the body just above the kidney. Each adrenal gland has two parts. The outer *adrenal cortex* is part of the endocrine system; the inner *adrenal medulla* is part of the sympathetic nervous system. The adrenal cortex releases cortisol, a hormone important in the reactions of the body to stress. The adrenal medulla acts as a ganglion of the sympathetic system, since it links the brain and various sympathetic target organs. Like other ganglia, the adrenal medulla receives stimulation from the central nervous system via fibers that use the neurotransmitter acetylcholine. Unlike other ganglia, however, the cells of the adrenal gland do not have axons that travel to a target organ. Instead, its cells simply dump noradrenaline and adrenaline into the bloodstream, thereby activating all target organs of the sympathetic system. The release of adrenaline is responsible for the fight-or-flight syndrome, which we discuss further in Chapter 13, on stress.

The Autonomic System and Consciousness   The autonomic system and the parts of the brain involved in consciousness are connected, but only indirectly. The autonomic system does not, for example, provide direct feedback to the sensory areas of the cerebral cortex; the feedback that is available to consciousness is indirect. Thus, you are not immediately aware that your stomach has secreted gastric juices, but you may hear your stomach grumbling.

Similarly, the activities of the autonomic nervous system can be influenced only indirectly. Most people cannot consciously and directly create changes in the activity of the ANS, such as a rise in blood pressure or sweating, but they can decide to do certain things that will, in turn, alter the activities of the ANS. To arouse autonomic innervation of sex organs, you might imagine yourself in an erotic situation. To raise your blood pressure, you might hold your breath and strain your muscles. Through *biofeedback*, a procedure in which special monitoring equipment provides information about autonomic activity, people may eventually learn what it feels like to have lower blood pressure, for example, and may also learn to reproduce that feeling and decrease their blood pressure.

THINKING CRITICALLY

Can Lie Detectors Reliably Detect Lying?

The normally involuntary nature of the autonomic nervous system provides the basis for using polygraphs as lie detectors. *Polygraphs* are instruments that record several types of physiological activity. For lie detection, polygraphs record physiological responses governed by the autonomic nervous system—usually heart rate, respiration, and skin resistance (which is affected by slight changes in perspiration).

Use of the polygraph as a lie detector is based on the idea that emotional responses usually accompany lies, because people feel guilty or fear being found out. To identify the perpetrator of a crime, the polygraph tester asks questions that are specifically related to the crime, such as, "Did you stab anyone on October 23, 1990?" Responses to such *relevant questions* are then compared to responses to general inquiries, called *control questions*, such as, "Have you ever tried to hurt someone?" The assumption is that most innocent people may have tried to hurt someone at some time and will feel guilty when asked, but they should have no reason to feel guilty about what they did on October 23, 1990. Thus, an innocent person is expected to display a stronger emotional response to control than to relevant questions (Raskin & Podlesny, 1979).

What am I being asked to believe or accept?

People who run polygraph lie-detection services contend that polygraphs can save employers a great deal of money by identifying potential employees who might steal and that they can ascertain guilt or innocence in criminal investigations, because they can detect lies.

What evidence is available to support the assertion?

First, there is no evidence that the polygraph can predict behavior; it cannot. Second, most people do have some emotional response when they lie, but statistics about the accuracy of the polygraph in detecting deception are difficult to obtain. Estimates vary widely, from those finding that polygraphs can detect 90 percent of guilty, lying individuals (Raskin & Podlesny, 1979) to those saying that truthful, innocent persons are deemed guilty liars as often as 50 percent of the time (Lykken, 1979).

Are there alternative ways of interpreting the evidence?

The wide variance in the evidence suggests that the results reflect factors other than the alleged link between lying and emotion—in particular, cognitive interpretations. We have already noted that these interpretations influence emotional responses. A person who believes that lying is acceptable and that fooling the polygraph is possible would not generate a fear response while lying on the test. However, an innocent person convinced that "everything always goes wrong" might show a large fear response, which would wrongly suggest guilt.

The role of cognitive interpretations has another implication: for a polygraph test to be effective, the person being tested must believe that the machine is infallible in its ability to detect lies. Since this is not true, using the polygraph requires lying to the person being tested. In one case, police in a small Pennsylvania town reportedly concocted a "lie detector" made from a kitchen colander that was connected by wires to a copy machine containing a sheet of paper marked with the words "he's lying" (Shepard, Kohut & Sweet, 1989)! The colander was placed on a burglary suspect's head. Whenever the man was suspected of lying, interrogators pressed the copy button and showed the "result." Believing in the machine's power, the man confessed his crime.

Finally, even the most favorable evidence regarding the effectiveness of the lie detector has another damaging interpretation. When there are few liars and many innocent people, even if polygraph tests caught 90 percent of the liars and exonerated 90 percent of the innocent, they would still falsely accuse a large number of people of lying.

What additional evidence would help to evaluate the alternatives?

The factors that determine whether a polygraph will be effective in a specific case are not fully known. However, the use of the polygraph as a lie detector is based on the erroneous assumption that consistent patterns in the physiological arousal measured by the polygraph will distinguish true from false statements. Thus, new information on the accuracy of polygraphs will probably be as variant and vague as current data. More important would be evaluative data on lie-detecting devices that measure forms of physiological activity that might be related to lying but are not under direct or indirect voluntary control. One such device, which measures the brain waves emitted during certain cognitive operations, is now being developed (Farwell & Donchin, 1989). Such devices may be more accurate than polygraph tests because they do not depend on a connection between making false statements and emotional responses.

What conclusions are most reasonable?

Emotional responses detectable by polygraphs do accompany lying for most individuals, so polygraph testing can catch some liars. Most researchers, however, think that a guilty person can "fool" a polygraph lie detector. In fact, the American Psychological Association expressed "great reservations about the use of polygraph tests to detect deception" (Abeles, 1985).

Until recently, polygraph testing had been gaining popularity among criminal investigators, security agencies such as the CIA, and businesses hoping to weed out employees who might be thieves or drug abusers. However, the U.S. Congress recently paid heed to testimony about the fallibility of polygraph testing: it outlawed the use of polygraphs for pre-employment screening. Certain industries such as security agencies and defense industries were excluded from the ban, despite expert testimony that the use of polygraphs is not valid even in these cases. ■

The James-Lange Theory

Linkages: Do physical responses determine what one feels? (a link to Biological Aspects of Psychology)

Suppose you are walking in the woods and come upon a mean-looking bear. The encounter scares the daylights out of you, and you begin to run for dear life. Do you run because you are afraid, or are you afraid because you run? The example and the question come from the work of William James, one of the first psychologists to propose a formal answer to questions about how autonomic responses are related to the experience of emotion. James argued that you are afraid because you run. Your running and other physiological responses, he said, follow directly from the perception of the bear. Without some form of these responses, you would feel no fear.

Presented like this, in its simplest form, James's theory may sound preposterous. It goes against common sense, which says that it would be silly to run from something unless you are already afraid of it. How did James come to conclude otherwise? James's main method was to scrutinize his own mental processes. He decided that after stripping away all physiological responses, there was *nothing* left of the experience of an emotion (James, 1890). A similar view was proposed by Carl Lange, a Danish physician; as a result, James's formulation is usually called the *James-Lange theory*.

Figure 12.2 outlines James's view of the source of emotion. First, a perception affects the cerebral cortex, said James, then

quick as a flash, reflex currents pass down through their pre-ordained channels, alter the condition of muscle, skin, and viscus; and these alterations, perceived, like the original object, in as many portions of the cortex, combine with it in consciousness and transform it from an object-simply-apprehended into an object-emotionally-felt. (James, 1890, p. 759)

In other words, the brain interprets a situation in such a way that physiological responses are called for, but the interpretation is not necessarily conscious until the physical responses occur. This subsequent perception of peripheral responses, according to James, constitutes the experience of emotion. *Peripheral responses* are bodily responses—such as a palpitating heart, sinking stomach,

Figure 12.2
The James-Lange Theory of Emotion
This theory states that bodily responses are the core of the emotional experience. James argued that the conscious experience of emotion does not occur until the brain receives feedback about physiological responses.

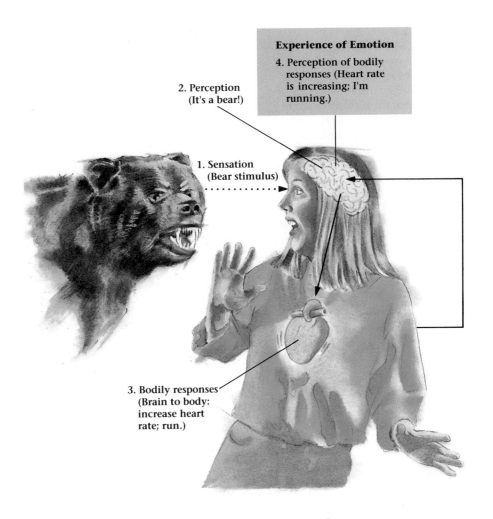

Experience of Emotion
4. Perception of bodily responses (Heart rate is increasing; I'm running.)

2. Perception (It's a bear!)

1. Sensation (Bear stimulus)

3. Bodily responses (Brain to body: increase heart rate; run.)

facial grimace, and perspiration—rather than neural responses confined to the central nervous system. Thus, the **James-Lange theory** holds that reflexive peripheral responses *precede* the experience of emotion. The conscious aspect of emotion arises later, when the brain observes these responses.

Notice that, according to James's view, there is no emotion generated solely by activity of the central nervous system. There is no direct central experience of emotion in a special "brain center." This theory, therefore, suggests one reason why you may have difficulty knowing your true feelings: you must interpret your feelings from your responses; there is no direct access to feelings from one part of the brain to another.

Evaluating James's Theory   James's theory has several implications. First, if the perception of peripheral physiological responses constitutes emotion, then each shade of emotion should stem from distinguishable patterns of physiological arousal. For example, fear should be tied to one pattern of bodily responses, and anger should arise from a different pattern. According to James's theory, if two patterns of responses are not different, then they cannot be distinguished as two emotions.

Contemporary research shows that the pattern of autonomic changes *does* vary with different emotional states. For example, Figure 12.3 shows that anger and fear both cause heart rate to rise; but anger *increases* blood flow to the hands and feet, whereas fear *reduces* blood flow to the hands and feet (Ekman, Levenson & Friesen, 1983; Levenson, Ekman & Friesen, 1990). Thus, fear

Figure 12.3
Patterns of Physiological Change Associated with Different Emotions

In one experiment, movements of the face characteristic of different emotions produced different patterns of change in (a) heart rate; (b) peripheral blood flow, as indexed by finger temperature; (c) skin conductance; and (d) muscle activity. For example, making an angry face caused heart rate and finger temperature to rise, whereas making a fearful face (as in Figure 12.4) raised heart rate but lowered finger temperature.

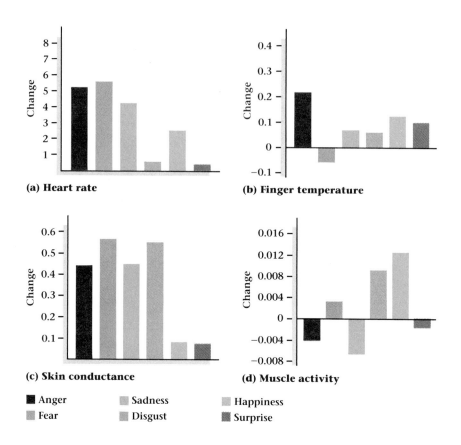

(a) Heart rate

(b) Finger temperature

(c) Skin conductance

(d) Muscle activity

■ Anger ▨ Sadness ▨ Happiness
▨ Fear ▨ Disgust ▨ Surprise

Source: Figure 3 from "Voluntary Facial Action Generates Emotion-Specific Autonomic Nervous System Activity," by R. W. Levenson, P. Ekman, and W. V. Friesen, *Psychophysiology*, 1990, 27, 363–384. Copyright 1990, The Society for Psychophysiological Research. Reprinted with permission of the author and the publisher from Levenson, Ekman, and Friesen, 1990.

produces "cold feet"; anger does not. Disgust is distinguished from other negative emotions because it causes an increase in muscle activity but no increase in heart rate. Also, when people mentally "relive" different emotional experiences, they show different patterns of autonomic activity (Ekman, Levenson & Friesen, 1983).

Furthermore, different patterns of autonomic activity are intimately associated with specific emotional facial expressions, and vice versa. When Paul Ekman and his colleagues (Ekman, Levenson & Friesen, 1983) instructed professional actors to move specific facial muscles or parts of the face, various facial configurations produced autonomic responses like those normally accompanying emotion. Furthermore, different facial configurations led to different patterns of responses (see Figures 12.3 and 12.4). A similar experiment used nonactors as subjects (Levenson, Ekman & Friesen, 1990). The patterns of autonomic activity produced when they made expressions of fear, anger, disgust, and sadness could be differentiated from one another and from happiness. Also, a large majority of the subjects reported feeling the emotion associated with the expression they had created, even though they did not realize that this specific emotion was being modeled. (They could not see the expression their face portrayed.)

Edgar Allan Poe noted this relationship between facial expressions and feelings more than a hundred years ago:

When I wish to find out how wise or how stupid or how good or how wicked is anyone, or what are his thoughts at the moment, I fashion the expression of my

Figure 12.4
Voluntary Facial Movements and Emotional Autonomic Responses
Without being asked to experience an emotion, this man was instructed to (left) "raise your brows and pull them together"; (center) "raise your upper eyelids"; and (right) "also stretch your lips horizontally, back toward your ears." Carrying out these instructions produced changes in heart rate characteristic of fear and the experience of fear.

Source: Copyright, Paul Ekman, 1983. Photos of actor Tom Harrison, from Ekman, P., Levenson, R. W. & Friesen, W. V. (1983). Autonomic nervous system distinguishes among emotions, *Science*, 221.

face, as accurately as possible, in accordance with the expression of his, and then wait to see what thoughts or sentiments arise in my mind or heart, as if to match or correspond with the expression. (Quoted in Levenson et al., 1990)

Mimicking the face of a person you are talking with may elicit in you the same feelings that person is having, including the autonomic responses, and may thus contribute to empathy and bonding.

These results support James's theory because they indicate that peripheral autonomic responses are sufficiently varied that at least basic emotions can be discriminated. Further, when people voluntarily produce peripheral responses (by contracting appropriate facial muscles), the emotions associated with those responses follow. James's theory correctly predicted that subjects who voluntarily produce the physiological responses associated with fear will feel fear even though there is nothing in the environment to be afraid of.

James's theory also implies that if a person cannot experience physiological changes in the body's periphery, he or she should not experience emotions. Walter Cannon, a distinguished physiologist of the 1920s, disagreed and demonstrated that animals show emotional behavior even after visceral sensory fibers have been disconnected from the brain. But Cannon's work left an important question unanswered: is the *experience* of emotion the same after surgery? Animals cannot tell us.

One approach with human subjects is to evaluate the emotional effects of drugs that modify the physiological responses produced during emotions. For example, drugs that reduce physiological arousal can reduce the intensity of emotional experience. When propranolol, a drug that blocks norepinephrine receptors, was given to music students at a recital, it reduced their experience of anxiety—and improved their piano playing (Brantigan, Brantigan & Joseph, 1978).

Another approach has addressed this question by studying people with spinal cord injuries. George Hohmann reasoned that if peripheral feedback is important to the experience of emotion, then the higher on the spinal cord damage occurs (and therefore the less feedback the brain receives), the less intense the experience of emotions should be. The results of Hohmann's study matched this prediction. However, Hohmann's work was conducted in the 1960s, when treatment of spinal cord injuries emphasized passive resignation to disability, and these people may have withdrawn from emotional situations. A more recent study examined students with spinal cord injuries who were actively coping and maintained important life goals (Chwalisz, Diener &

Gallagher, 1988). These people experienced the full range of emotions, including as much happiness as noninjured people. They showed at most a weak trend for some emotions to be felt less intensely.

These results appear to contradict James's theory because they suggest that emotions occur without extensive feedback from bodily responses. However, these studies ignore the importance of facial expressions as bodily responses. James included facial expressions as peripheral responses, and facial expressions can occur despite spinal cord damage. Thus, the James-Lange formulation is somewhat weakened but retains its credibility.

A variation on James's theory emphasizes facial expressions as the responses that are interpreted as emotions. According to this *facial feedback hypothesis*, movements of the face provide information about what emotion is being felt (Izard, 1971, 1990; Laird, 1984). Thus, if you find yourself frowning, you must be unhappy. The facial movement is involuntary, and the feedback from that movement directs further emotional responses. As discussed earlier, if you can control your facial muscles to reproduce the movements associated with specific emotions, you should to some extent experience those emotions.

The Cannon-Bard Theory

Could the activation of any part of the central nervous system produce an experience of emotion in the absence of facial or visceral responses? Walter Cannon thought so; he and Philip Bard suggested an alternative to James's theory. In their view, you feel fear at the sight of a wild bear without ever taking a step. The responses of the autonomic nervous system, they said, do not help generate emotion (Cannon, 1927). Instead, Cannon and Bard proposed that the experience of emotion originates in the central nervous system—specifically, in the thalamus, the structure in the brain that relays information from most sense organs to the cortex.

According to the **Cannon-Bard theory** of emotion, the brain interprets an emotional situation through the thalamus, which sends signals simultaneously to the autonomic nervous system and to the cerebral cortex, where the emotion becomes conscious. When you see that bear in the woods, the brain receives sensory information about it, interprets that information as a bear, and *directly* creates the experience of fear while *at the same time* sending messages to the heart, lungs, and legs to initiate a rapid departure. According to the Cannon-Bard theory, then, there is a direct, central experience of emotion, with or without feedback about peripheral responses, as Figure 12.5 shows.

Subsequent work suggests that the thalamus does not produce the direct central experience of emotion, as Cannon had theorized. Do other parts of the brain perhaps create this experience? Recent research points to several possibilities. Work with animals indicates that for one basic emotion, fear, connections from the thalamus go directly to the amygdala, which generates the emotional responses (LeDoux, Romanski & Xagoraris, 1989; see Figure 12.6). According to this evidence, strong emotions can sometimes by-pass the cortex and do not require conscious thought to activate them. This may explain why people find it so difficult to overcome a strong fear, or *phobia*, even though they may consciously know the fear is irrational.

Another updated version of the Cannon-Bard theory suggests that specific parts of the brain produce the feelings of pleasure or pain in emotion. This notion came about when scientists discovered by accident that electrical stimulation of certain parts of the brain is reinforcing. (These are the "pleasure centers" discussed in Chapter 7, on learning.) The scientists noticed that rats with stimulating electrodes in their brains kept returning to the place in the

Figure 12.5
The Cannon-Bard Theory of Emotion
Cannon argued that emotion is generated directly by the central nervous system and that peripheral responses occur independently of this central experience of emotion. The brain "knows" that fear is being experienced even before feedback from the autonomic nervous system reaches the brain.

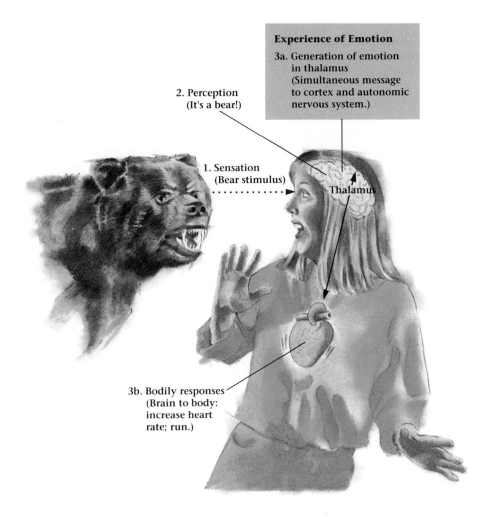

Experience of Emotion
3a. Generation of emotion in thalamus (Simultaneous message to cortex and autonomic nervous system.)

2. Perception (It's a bear!)

1. Sensation (Bear stimulus)

Thalamus

3b. Bodily responses (Brain to body: increase heart rate; run.)

cage where they received the stimulation. The investigators thought this was bizarre behavior, but they had the insight to revise the apparatus so the animals could control delivery of the stimulation by pressing a bar. Amazingly, rats pressed the bar incessantly to receive this electrical stimulation, even to the point of neglecting other bodily needs like food and water (Olds & Milner, 1954).

The brain areas in which stimulation is experienced as pleasurable include the locus coeruleus and other areas associated with the autonomic nervous system, as well as dopaminergic systems (described in Chapter 3) that are activated by drugs of abuse (Segal & Bloom, 1976; Wise, 1988). In contrast, there are other brain regions whose stimulation is so aversive that animals will work hard to avoid that stimulation. Presumably, part of the direct central experience of emotions involves areas of the brain whose activity is experienced as either reinforcing or aversive.

Some of the brain regions where stimulation is reinforcing appear to form a kind of "autonomic nervous system" within the brain (Hartman et al., 1986). Just as the autonomic nervous system modulates the activity of organs that can function without input from the ANS, several neurotransmitter systems in the brain appear to modulate the activity of other brain cells. Noradrenergic cells in the locus coeruleus play this "autonomic" role, releasing noradrenaline and modulating the activity of other brain cells, as well as sending signals to the peripheral autonomic nervous system (Olpe, Steinmann & Jones, 1985).

Figure 12.6
Parts of the Brain Involved in the Experience of Emotion
Sensory information comes into the brain to alert the individual to an emotion-evoking situation. Most sensory information goes through the thalamus; the cingulate cortex and hippocampus are involved in the interpretation of this sensory input. Output from these areas goes to the amygdala and hypothalamus, which control the autonomic nervous system via brainstem connections. There are also connections from the thalamus directly to the amygdala. The locus coeruleus is one area of the brainstem that causes both widespread arousal of cortical areas and changes in autonomic activity.

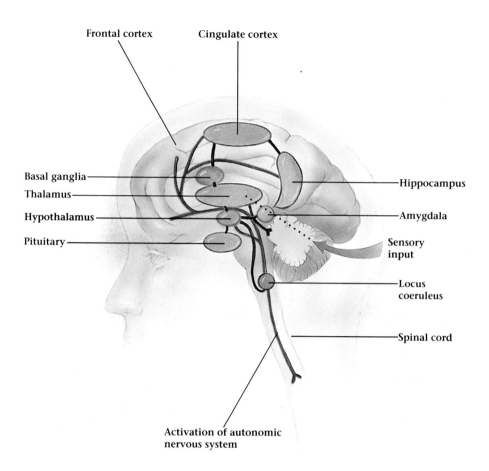

This variation on Cannon's theory, in which the brain contains its own "autonomic nervous system," unifies the picture of emotional responses. The same cells that project fibers down the spinal cord to activate the traditional autonomic nervous system also appear to send fibers into the rest of the brain, activating cells in areas such as the hypothalamus and the limbic system. Thus, an emotional situation energizes the entire body, including parts of the brain, creating changes in the central nervous system that are part of the same response that produces a racing heart or other symptoms of emotion in the peripheral autonomic system. A common neural system could activate emotional facial expressions and autonomic visceral responses (Levenson, Ekman & Friesen, 1990).

Thus, there is increasing evidence for the main thrust of Cannon's theory: that emotion occurs through the activation of specific parts of the central nervous system. However, different parts of the CNS may be activated for different emotions and for different aspects of the total emotional experience.

The Schachter-Singer Theory

The James-Lange and the Cannon-Bard theories of emotion both provide helpful guides to the study of emotion. However, although both recognized that the interpretation of autonomic feedback or situations is important in emotional experience, neither devoted much attention to how interpretation takes place. Modern research on this aspect of emotion was sparked largely by a creative proposition by Stanley Schachter and Jerome Singer.

Schachter's theory of emotion predicts that these sports fans would attribute their physiological arousal to the game they are watching and label their emotion "excitement."

Schachter agreed with James that the feeling of emotions arises from perceiving feedback from bodily responses, but he also believed, as Cannon did, that this feedback is not sufficiently varied to generate subtle emotional differences. After all, there are at least 558 different labels for emotions in the English language (Averill, 1980). To reconcile these views, Schachter and Singer proposed that emotions are produced by both feedback from peripheral responses *and* a cognitive appraisal of what caused those responses (Schachter & Singer, 1962). Thus, cognitive interpretation comes into play twice: once when you perceive the situation that leads to bodily responses and again when you identify feedback from those responses as a particular emotion.

Figure 12.7 outlines the **Schachter-Singer theory**. As in the James-Lange theory, the first step is the perception of a situation, followed by bodily responses. However, whereas James said that the brain perceives the responses as a particular emotion solely on the basis of the feedback, Schachter argued that the brain may interpret a particular pattern of feedback in many ways and give it many labels. According to Schachter and Singer (1962), the cognitive act of *labeling* an originally undifferentiated pattern of physiological arousal constitutes the core of emotion. The labeling depends on an **attribution**, which is the process of identifying the cause of some event. People may attribute their physiological arousal to different emotions depending on the information that is available about the situation. For example, if you are watching the final seconds of a close football game, you might attribute your racing heart, rapid breathing, and perspiration to excitement; but you might attribute the same physiological reactions to anxiety if you are waiting for an important exam to begin. Thus, the emotion you experience upon seeing a bear in the woods might be fear, excitement, astonishment, or surprise, depending on how you label your reaction.

Figure 12.7
The Schachter-Singer Theory of Emotion
A modification of the James-Lange theory, the Schachter theory adds the idea that peripheral feedback must be interpreted in light of knowledge about what might have caused autonomic responses.

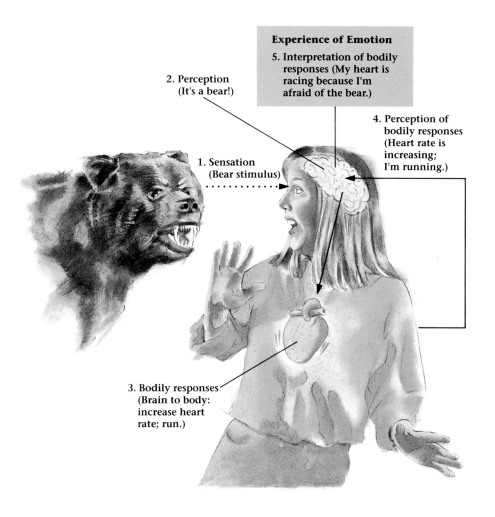

Experience of Emotion
5. Interpretation of bodily responses (My heart is racing because I'm afraid of the bear.)

2. Perception (It's a bear!)

4. Perception of bodily responses (Heart rate is increasing; I'm running.)

1. Sensation (Bear stimulus)

3. Bodily responses (Brain to body: increase heart rate; run.)

Evaluating the Schachter Theory Some experiments have supported Schachter's view that both physiological responses and the cognitive labeling of those responses play a role in emotion; other experiments have failed to support the theory. These mixed results are evident in research on three hypotheses generated by the Schachter theory.

First, like James's theory, Schachter's theory predicts that if physiological responses are reduced or eliminated, the experience of emotion should be reduced or eliminated as well. We have seen in evaluating James's theory that there are mixed results with respect to this prediction.

Second, Schachter's theory predicts that if emotional arousal is attributed to a *nonemotional* cause, the intensity of emotional experience should be reduced. So if you notice your heart pounding before an exam but say to yourself, "Sure my heart's pounding, but I'm not nervous—I just drank five cups of coffee!" then you should feel "wired" from caffeine rather than afraid or worried. This prediction has received some support (Schachter & Singer, 1962).

A third prediction from the Schachter theory is that if arousal is artificially induced—by drugs, for example—emotion will be experienced if there is a situation to which the drug-induced arousal can reasonably be attributed. By the same logic, artificially induced physiological responses should *intensify* emotion if the responses can be attributed to an emotion-producing situation. To test this prediction, Schachter and Singer (1962) attempted to separate the physiological and cognitive components of an emotional experience. To produce physiological arousal, they injected subjects with adrenaline. Some

Linkages: In line with the information-processing model described in Chapter 9, several theorists have expanded on Schachter's theory of emotion. They have suggested that the emotions people experience depend not just on their labeling of physiological activity but also on their cognitive interpretation of situations (Lazarus & Folkman, 1984). Because this man may have thought of the flood that devastated his neighborhood as an adventure and an opportunity to relax, he may have experienced positive emotions. Many of his neighbors, though, probably felt anger, anxiety, and other negative emotions as their thoughts focused on the flood's disastrous consequences for their homes and property.

of the people were told that they were receiving an injection of a new vitamin; the others were given accurate information about the injection and its likely arousing effects. Then the subjects were placed in a situation designed to generate emotion. With them was an actor who appeared to be another subject but was actually working for the experimenters. Some subjects were given a questionnaire containing insulting items about topics such as their mothers' extramarital sexual activity. In these cases, the actor-subject responded angrily to the questionnaire. With other subjects, who did not receive the questionnaire, the actor pretended to feel happy, even euphoric.

The Schachter theory predicts that those who were correctly informed about the injection and its effects would not be influenced much by social cues in the environment—that is, by the actor's anger or joy—because they would attribute any arousal to the injection, not to an emotion. In contrast, people who did not know that the injection could cause arousal should attribute their arousal to emotion. They should therefore experience stronger emotions and look to the environment for clues to what emotion they were experiencing. Thus, people who were misinformed about the injection and were with an apparently euphoric actor should attribute their otherwise unexplained arousal to euphoria (a cue provided by the actor) and therefore experience positive emotions. Those in the presence of an angry actor should label their physiological responses as anger, not only because of the actor's behavior but also because of the questionnaire.

The results matched these predictions (Schachter & Singer, 1962). Thus, key predictions of Schachter's theory were supported: attributing arousal to an emotion intensified the emotion, and social cues in the environment guided the labeling of emotional arousal. However, the magnitude of the effects was small. Indeed, some investigators have been unable to replicate Schachter's results (Leventhal & Tomarken, 1986; Marshall & Zimbardo, 1979; Maslach, 1979).

The Transfer of Excitation   In spite of its problems, the Schachter theory of emotion is still influential and has stimulated interesting research. Some of this research has shown that physiological arousal can be attributed to emotion and can intensify emotional experience *regardless* of the source of arousal (Zillmann, 1984). For example, people who have been aroused by physical exercise show greater anger when provoked than people who have been physically less active. The person attributes the exercise-produced arousal to anger, thus intensifying the emotion. Similarly, compared with a person at rest, exercise-aroused people experience stronger feelings of attraction or dislike when they meet an attractive or unattractive member of the opposite sex (White, Fishbein & Rutstein, 1981).

When arousal from one experience carries over to an independent situation, it is called **transferred excitation** (Reisenzein, 1983). People remain physiologically aroused longer than they think they do, which helps explain transfer of excitation. For the transfer to occur, there must be a period during which the overt signs of arousal subside but the sympathetic nervous system is still active. Because a person still activated from exercise may feel calm, it is easy to attribute any subsequently noticed arousal to emotion. If the person still felt aroused, he or she would accurately attribute the arousal to exercise (Zillmann, 1978a). The transfer of excitation is especially likely when the pattern of arousal from the nonemotional source is similar to the pattern associated with a particular emotion. Thus, a person is more likely to mistake the pounding heart, increased respiration, and facial redness created by exercise for anger rather than contentment.

Arousal created by one emotion can also transfer to intensify another. For example, arousal from fear, like arousal from exercise, can enhance sexual feelings. One study of this transfer took place in British Columbia over a deep gorge filled with roaring rapids. The gorge could be crossed either by a precarious swinging bridge or by a safe wooden structure across a quiet part of the river. A female experimenter asked men who had just crossed each bridge to fill out a questionnaire that included a measure of sexual imagery. The men who met the woman after crossing the dangerous bridge had much higher sexual imagery scores than the men who had crossed the safe bridge. Furthermore, they were more likely to rate her as attractive (Dutton & Aron, 1974). When the person giving out the questionnaire was a male, however, the type of bridge crossed had no impact on sexual imagery.

One interpretation of these results is that excitement from crossing the bridge was transferred to the men's interaction with the woman. However, you might have thought of another possibility: perhaps the men who crossed the dangerous bridge were simply more adventurous in both bridge crossing and sexual encounters. This possibility was tested by repeating the experiment, with one change. This time, the woman approached the men farther down the trail, long after the arousal from crossing the bridge had subsided. In this case, the apparently adventurous men were no more likely than others to rate the woman as attractive or to call her for a date, suggesting that it was indeed transfer of excitation, not just adventurousness, that produced the original difference between groups.

Conclusions It appears that both peripheral autonomic responses (including facial responses) and the cognitive interpretation of those responses play a role in the experience of emotion. ("In Review: Theories of Emotion" summarizes key elements of the three theories we have discussed.) In addition, there appears to be some direct experiencing of emotion by the central nervous system, independent of physiological arousal. So emotion is probably both in the heart and in the head (including the face). No theory has resolved the issue of which, if any, component of emotion is primary. However, the three theories we have discussed have all helped psychologists better understand how these components interact to produce emotional experience.

In Review: Theories of Emotion

Theory	Source of Emotions	Evidence for Theory
James-Lange	The CNS generates specific physical responses; observation of the physical responses constitutes emotion.	Different emotions are associated with different physical responses.
Cannon-Bard	Parts of the CNS directly generate emotions; physical responses are not necessary.	People with spinal cord damage experience a full range of emotions without feedback from peripheral responses.
Schachter-Singer	The CNS generates non-specific physical responses; interpretation of the physical responses in light of the situation constitutes emotions.	Excitation generated by physical activity can transfer to increase emotional intensity.

How Do People Communicate Emotions?

Imagine a normal American male sitting down to watch television. You can see his face, but you cannot see what he is watching. He might be involved in complex patterns of thought, perhaps comparing his investments with those of the experts on "Wall Street Week." Equally plausibly, his mind might be attaining the consistency of mashed potatoes while he watches reruns of "Gilligan's Island." There is very little you can observe that indicates the nature of his thought patterns. However, if the television program creates an *emotional* experience, you could make a reasonably accurate guess about what kind of emotion it is by watching his face (Patrick, Craig & Prkachin, 1986; Wagner, MacDonald & Manstead, 1986). Why should an emotional experience cause the muscles of the face to contract in a distinct pattern? So far, we have described emotion from the inside, as people experience their own emotions. In this section, we examine the communication of emotion; in other words, how people express and recognize emotions.

Different species have evolved a variety of ways to communicate emotions. For people, even movement and body positioning can convey a certain amount of emotional information. In conversation between members of the opposite sex, for example, leaning toward and looking directly at one another usually indicate liking and possibly even sexual interest; leaning back and looking away tend to suggest boredom or hostility. Such cues, however, are often complex and subtle. Contrary to the claims of popular books and articles on body language, there is no fixed set of signals in body movement or posture that always conveys a specific set of emotional messages (Goleman, 1986).

Indeed, in humans, *facial* movement and expression play the primary role in communicating emotions, and we focus our attention on them. The human face can generate six to seven thousand different expressions (Izard, 1971).

Observers can discriminate very small changes in facial patterns; a twitch of the mouth can carry a lot of information. Are facial expressions of emotion innate, or are they learned? And how are they controlled? How are they used in communicating emotion?

Innate Expressions of Emotion

Charles Darwin observed that certain facial expressions seem to be universal. He proposed that these expressions are biologically determined, passed on genetically from one generation to the next. The facial expressions seen today, Darwin argued, are those that have been most effective at telling others something about how a person is feeling and what he or she is about to do. If someone is red in the face and scowling, for example, you will probably assume that he or she is angry, and you will be unlikely to choose that particular moment to ask for a loan.

Darwin's theory about facial expressions is widely but not universally accepted. Some facial expressions that express emotions are learned, not innate. However, two types of evidence indicate that, as Darwin proposed, the basic facial expressions of emotions are innate.

One source of evidence comes from infants. They do not need to be taught to grimace in pain or to smile in pleasure; they show facial movements that are appropriately correlated with their well-being. Even blind infants, who cannot see adults in order to imitate them, show the same emotional expressions as do sighted infants (Goodenough, 1932).

Second, for the most basic emotions, people of all cultures show similar facial responses to similar emotional stimuli (Ekman, 1984; Ekman & Friesen, 1986). For example, the pattern of facial movements we call a smile is universally related to positive emotions. However, people may cover a lie with a smile or smile when faced with an awkward situation. If people smile when they are not happy, how do psychologists know that smiles are innate rather than learned signals? It turns out that smiles that express positive emotion can be distinguished from other smiles.

In fact, Ekman and colleagues categorized seventeen types of smiles, including "false smiles," which are aimed at convincing another person that

The innate origin of some emotional expressions is supported by the fact that the facial movement pattern we call a smile is related to happiness, pleasure, and other positive emotions in human cultures throughout the world.

enjoyment is occurring; "masking smiles," which hide unhappiness; and "miserable smiles," which indicate a willingness to endure unpleasantness. They called the smile that occurs with genuine happiness the *Duchenne smile*, after the French investigator who more than a hundred years ago first noticed the difference between spontaneous, happy smiles and posed smiles. A genuine, Duchenne smile includes contractions of the muscles around the eyes (which creates a distinctive wrinkling of the skin around the eyes) as well as the muscles that raise the lips and cheeks. Very few people can voluntarily contract the muscles around the eyes when they pose a fake smile, so this feature can often be used to discern "lying smiles" from genuine smiles (Ekman, Friesen & O'Sullivan, 1988). In a recent study of people watching films by themselves, the Duchenne smile was highly correlated with subjective reports of positive emotions, as well as with EEG recordings of a pattern of brain waves related to positive emotions. Other types of smiles were not (Ekman, Davidson & Friesen, 1990).

Just as genuine smiles are associated with positive emotion in all cultures, sadness is universally accompanied by slackened muscle tone and a "long" face. Likewise, in all cultures, people contort their faces in a similar way when presented with something disgusting. And a furrowed brow seems to be related to obstacles to goals or unpleasantness (Smith, 1989). Anger is also associated with a facial expression that is recognized by all cultures. One study on the expression of anger and threat examined the artwork—particularly ceremonial masks—of various Western and non-Western cultures (Aronoff, Barclay & Stevenson, 1988). The threatening masks of all eighteen cultures examined contained similar elements, such as triangular eyes and diagonal lines on the cheeks. In particular, angular and diagonal elements carry the impression of threat (see Figure 12.8), for unknown reasons.

Social Aspects of Emotional Expression

Although some basic emotional expressions are innate, many other expressions are neither innate nor universal. People in different cultures use different facial expressions to express some emotions. People learn how to express certain emotions in particular ways, as specified by cultural rules. For example, suppose you say, "I just bought a new car," and all your friends stick their tongues out at you. In North America, this probably would mean that they feel jealous or resentful. In China, this response would express surprise.

As noted earlier, people even learn to use facial expressions ironically or to miscommunicate their feelings. They can show a smile that communicates contempt or derision rather than friendliness. They may look mock-serious before revealing a happy surprise or smile a greeting that is not particularly joyful. And of course, even facial expressions that do arise from emotions can be controlled to some extent, as any poker player or politician knows.

The effects of learning are evident in a child's expanding repertoire of emotional expressions. Although infants begin with an innate set of emotional responses, they soon learn to imitate facial expressions and to use facial expressions to signal an ever-widening range of emotions. As they grow older, these expressions become more precise and somewhat more individualized, so that a particular expression conveys an unmistakable emotional message to anyone who knows that person well.

If facial expressions become too idiosyncratic, however, no one will know what the expressions mean, and they will fail to elicit the desired response from others. Operant shaping, described in Chapter 7, on learning, probably helps keep emotional expressions within certain limits. If you could not see

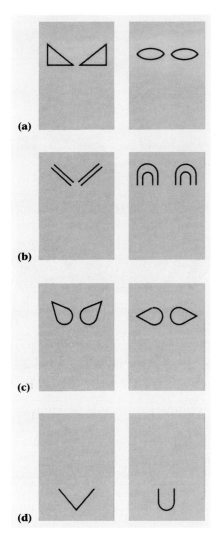

Source: Aronoff, Barclay & Stevenson, 1988.

Figure 12.8
Elements of Ceremonial Facial Masks That Convey Threat
Certain geometrical elements are common to the threatening ceremonial masks of all the cultures examined. People in various cultures were asked which member of each pair was more threatening. In these displays the triangular and diagonal elements in the left-hand member of each pair convey threat most clearly. Note that Halloween pumpkins carved to look "scary" tend to have these threatening elements as well.

The extent to which control of emotional expression is expected varies from one culture to another. This was illustrated in a study of Japanese and American students who were shown movies that contained distressing scenes. When the subjects viewed the movie with a group of peers, the Japanese students showed little facial expressiveness compared with the American students. But, as pictured here, when they viewed the movie by themselves, Japanese and American students showed the same facial expressions (Ekman, Friesen, and Ellsworth, 1972).

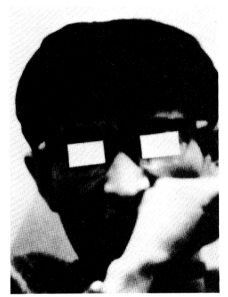

other people's facial expressions or observe their overt responses to yours, you might show fewer, or at least less intense, facial signs of emotion. Indeed, as congenitally blind people grow older, their facial expressions tend to become less animated (Izard, 1977).

The communicative value of emotional expressions depends on context. One of the most interesting examples is **social referencing** (Campos & Stenberg, 1981). In an uncertain situation, other people provide a *reference* that reduces uncertainty. People may look to the facial expressions, tone of voice, and bodily gestures of others for guidance about how to proceed. A novice chess player, for instance, might reach out to move the queen, catch sight of a spectator's grimace, and infer that another move would be better. The person providing the facial cues may or may not intend to communicate information. If a situation has no ambiguities, people may not pay attention even if the cues are present.

For infants, the visual-cliff experiments described in Chapter 5, on perception, provide an example of an uncertain situation. To reach its mother, an infant in these experiments must cross the visual cliff (see Figure 5.32). If there is no apparent dropoff or if the drop is very dramatic, like that of a four-foot cliff, there is no ambiguity, and a one-year-old knows what to do. It crawls across in the first case and stays put in the second case. However, if the apparent dropoff is shallow enough to create uncertainty (say, two feet), then the infant looks to its mother's emotional expressions to relieve uncertainty. In one study, mothers were asked to display either a fearful or a joyful face. When the mothers made a fearful face, no infant crossed the glass floor. But when they posed a joyful face, fifteen out of nineteen infants crossed (Sorce et al., 1981). Infants who cannot yet understand spoken language depend to a large degree on adults' emotional expressions for information (Campos & Barrett, 1984).

Communication through emotional expression may explain some behaviors that many have considered biologically "wired in." For example, infants' fear of strangers is greatly influenced by the mother's emotional expressions. If a stranger enters the room and the mother abruptly says "Hello" and frowns, an eight-month-old infant will have an increased heart rate and show distress when the stranger approaches. But if the mother says a cheery "Hello," the

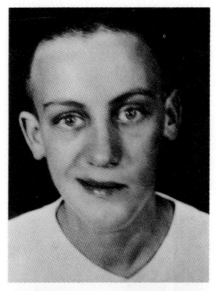

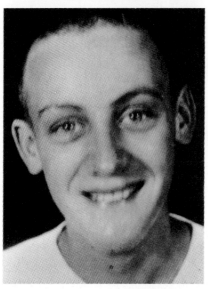

Source: From *The Neurological Examination*, 4th ed. by R. N. DeJong. New York: Lippincott/ Harper & Row, 1979.

Figure 12.9
Control of Voluntary and Emotional Facial Movements

This man has a tumor in the motor cortex that prevents him from voluntarily moving the muscles on the left side of his face to form a smile. In the top photograph he is trying to smile in response to a command from the examiner. Even though he cannot smile on command, he is perfectly capable of smiling with genuine happiness, as the bottom photograph shows, because these movements are controlled by the extrapyramidal motor system.

infant's heart rate actually slows down, and it shows less distress (Sorce et al., 1982). Thus, the emotional expression of one person can communicate values and shape the behavior of another person. This type of emotional communication is an important source of knowledge about the world, and it continues to influence people even in adulthood.

As children grow, they learn an *emotion culture*—rules that govern what emotions are appropriate in what circumstances and what emotional expressions are allowed. These rules vary from culture to culture and also within one culture over time. For example, child-rearing manuals, diaries, marriage manuals, and other sources indicate that the unspoken rules about anger in the United States have changed over the years. The emotion culture shifted from relative unconcern with anger to strict suppression of the expression of anger, which became the norm by the 1920s (Stearns & Stearns, 1986).

The emotion culture can also change within a lifetime. Students in medical school, for example, must learn new rules about expressing emotions during intimate contact with human bodies. As one medical student described the process:

How do I set aside 25 years of living? Experience which made close contact with someone's body a sensual event? Maybe it's attraction, maybe disgust. But it isn't supposed to be part of what I feel when I touch a patient. I feel some of those things, and I want to learn not to. (Quoted in Smith & Kleinman, 1989)

Thus, relearning the rules of emotion is part of an unofficial curriculum at medical school; by observing doctors, students learn how to modify and control these feelings (Smith & Kleinman, 1989). In Western medicine it is common to transform the patient into an analytical object or event, to avoid sensitive contact. If the process of resocialization is successful, the medical student emerges from medical school with affective neutrality toward patients, thus reflecting and perpetuating the rules of Western medicine. However, transforming the body into an impersonal object in one sphere sometimes makes it difficult to maintain normal emotions in intimate situations, such as at home with one's spouse.

Facial Expressions and the Brain

A posed, social smile and a smile that reflects real happiness not only look somewhat different but are controlled by different neurons in the brain (Rinn, 1984). Voluntary facial movements are controlled by a part of the motor cortex known as the *pyramidal motor system*. Involuntary facial movements accompanying emotions are governed by the *extrapyramidal motor system*, which is controlled by subcortical areas such as the basal ganglia (see Figure 12.6). People can partially suppress emotion-driven facial expressions because the pyramidal system can control the extrapyramidal system.

Neurological damage can disrupt these control systems, as Figures 12.9 and 12.10 illustrate. The man shown in Figure 12.9 can smile reflexively when he is happy, but he cannot force himself to smile. The woman shown in Figure 12.10 laughs uncontrollably but feels no mirth (Peck, 1969).

Studies of people with different kinds of brain damage have revealed another characteristic of emotional expression. Recall from Chapter 3, on biological psychology, that although the cerebral hemispheres normally operate together, the hemispheres play somewhat different roles in functions such as language. Similarly, the perception, experience, and expression of emotion are not controlled equally by each hemisphere. For example, some people with damage to the left hemisphere no longer laugh at jokes, even though they can still

Figure 12.10
Separation of Emotional
Experience from Emotional
Expression
This woman has a neurological disease (amyotrophic lateral sclerosis)
that causes involuntary nonemotional laughing. She reported that
the laughter was painful and she
was struggling to suppress it.

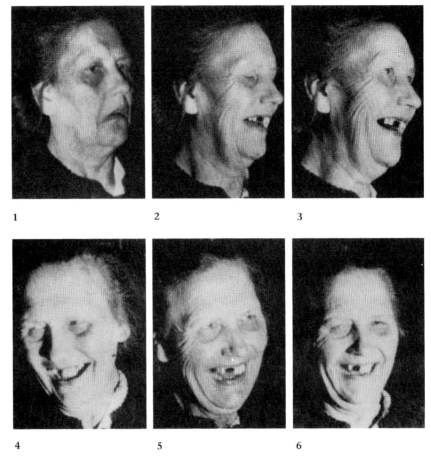

Source: From "Pathophysiology of emotional disorders associated with brain damage" by K. Poeck, in
P. J. Vinken and G. W. Bruyn (eds.) *Handbook of Clinical Neurology*, vol. 3. New York: American Elsevier,
1969.

*Linkages: Do the two hemispheres
play equal roles in emotion? (a link to
Biological Aspects of Psychology)*

understand the meaning of the words, the logic (or illogic) underlying them,
and the punch lines. And compared with normal individuals, depressed people
show greater electrical activity in the right frontal cortex (Schaffer, Davidson
& Saron, 1983).

In general, the right frontal hemisphere is activated during negative emotion,
whereas the left is more active in positive emotion. For example, EEG recordings
indicate that occurrence of the Duchenne smile (which accompanies positive
emotions) is correlated with activation of the left frontal cortex (Davidson et
al., 1990). This asymmetry of EEG activity during smiling is found even in
infants (Davidson, 1984).

However, for facial expressions in general, the right hemisphere contributes
more than the left to motor activation of facial muscles (Sackeim, Gur &
Saucy, 1978). Because the nerves controlling muscles cross over the midline
the contribution of the right hemisphere is observed in the left side of the
face; thus, the left side of the face is more expressive than the right. Surprisingly,
emotional facial expressions in infants are more pronounced on the right side
of the face (Best & Queen, 1989; see Figure 12.11). No one knows what change
in the brain causes the switch in expressiveness from the right side to the left
side of the face. In perceiving as well as expressing emotion, the brain's right
hemisphere is more active than the left. ("In Review: The Brain and the
Communication of Emotion" summarizes our discussion of the differing roles
of the two hemispheres in emotion.)

Figure 12.11
Asymmetry of Emotional Expressions in Babies
The right side of a baby's face shows more intense emotional expression than the left side. These are composite faces made up of mirror images of each side of the face. Both positive and negative emotional expression are more intense on the right-side composites. In contrast, adults show more intense facial expressions of emotions on the left side.

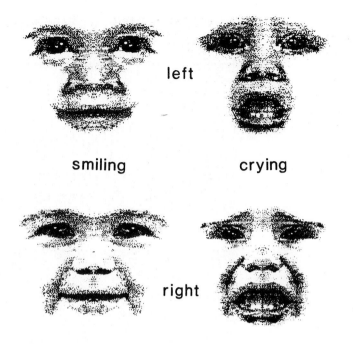

smiling   crying

right

Source: Best & Queen, 1989.

HIGHLIGHT

Suppressing Emotions

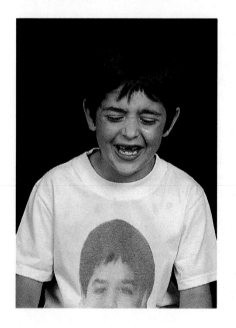

Young children's relative inability to suppress emotions, especially negative ones, may be related to the fact that neural pathways between their cerebral hemispheres are not yet fully developed or functional.

The relationship between the cerebral hemispheres may also be important in suppressing the expression of emotions. Specifically, Richard Davidson (1984) suggested that communication between the hemispheres may be important in the development of this ability.

Some evidence for this idea comes from observations of infants. Anyone with intact hearing will testify that infants do not inhibit emotional expressions, especially negative ones. Infants also have less well developed functional connections between the hemispheres (Rakic & Yaklovlev, 1968). In fact, until about the age of thirteen the corpus callosum (the structure connecting the hemispheres) is not fully myelinated; that is, its axons are not yet covered with the fatty sheath that speeds neural activity (Rakic & Yaklovlev, 1968). Perhaps the developing fibers of the corpus callosum speed interhemispheric cooperation in the inhibition of emotion and contribute to the child's ability to suppress negative emotional displays.

Among adults, too, individual differences in interhemispheric communication may be partly responsible for differences in the ability to suppress emotional expression. One possibility is that the suppression of negative emotions involves cutting off the communication of emotional information that normally goes from the right hemisphere (where negative emotions tend to be generated) to verbal areas in the left hemisphere (Galin, 1974). Therefore, among people who characteristically suppress emotions, the autonomic responses to emotion may be disconnected from the ability to report an emotional experience. In fact, when mildly stressful stimuli are presented to people who typically suppress emotion, their autonomic activity increases, even though they report feeling little or no anxiety (Weinberger, Schwartz & Davidson, 1979). ■

In Review: The Brain and the Communication of Emotion

Area of the Brain	Role
Pyramidal motor system	Controls voluntary facial movements used in culturally defined emotional communication.
Extrapyramidal motor system	Controls involuntary expression of genuine emotions.
Right hemisphere	Relatively more active in negative emotions and depression and, for adults, in facial expressions in general; also perceives emotions better than left hemisphere.
Left hemisphere	Relatively more active in positive emotions and, for infants, in facial expressions in general.
Corpus callosum	Allows cooperation between hemispheres that may be important in the suppression of emotional expression.

Linkages: Psychological Disorders and the Emotion of Fear

Do the physical components of fear explain panic attacks?

You are walking down the street, minding your own business, when out of nowhere it begins. First you feel lightheaded and disoriented, then anxious. Your heart starts to pound in your chest, your legs get rubbery, you become sick to your stomach, and you feel as if you are losing control. The emotional intensity builds rapidly until you feel pure fear, stark terror; you know you are going to die on the spot. But you don't die, the panic subsides, and you are left wondering what in the world is going on. Soon you begin to worry that whatever it was, it will happen again. Weeks later, the panic does strike a second time. You become very worried and spend much of your time dreading the possibility of yet another attack. If an attack occurs while you are driving or doing some other specific activity, you may develop an intense fear of that activity. What began as an apparently baseless emotional experience has come to dominate your life, and you do all you can to avoid a recurrence of that experience.

For millions of people, this scenario is all too familiar. These people suffer from **panic disorder**, the experience of intense fear in circumstances when there is nothing to fear. Panic disorder commonly has three components: the panic attack itself, chronic anxiety about whether an attack will strike, and avoidance behaviors aimed at preventing attacks. Together with other anxiety disorders described in Chapter 15, on psychological disorders, these are the most common psychiatric problems in the United States (Robins et al., 1984).

The physical symptoms of fear play a large part in patients' descriptions of panic attacks. But, as for other emotions we have discussed, it is not clear whether the experience of fear precedes the physical responses, or vice versa. This uncertainty helps keep alive controversy about the relative roles of biological and cognitive-behavioral factors in panic disorder. Does panic disorder reflect biological overreactivity or perhaps learned associations plus exaggerated interpretations of threat? The answer has implications for whether drug therapy or psychotherapy is the most appropriate treatment for panic disorder.

Evidence from studies with twins suggests that panic disorder does have a genetic component (Kendler et al., 1986). There is also clear evidence that there is something physically abnormal in panic-disorder patients (Gorman et al., 1989). The most striking finding is that a panic episode can be elicited in many of these patients by the injection of lactate, whereas normal subjects rarely respond to lactate with fear. Carbon dioxide, caffeine, yohimbine (a drug that blocks one type of norepinephrine receptor), and other laboratory stimuli can also induce an attack in panic-disorder patients. These treatments all stimulate brainstem areas that control the autonomic nervous system. Accordingly, one hypothesis is that panic-disorder patients have hypersensitive brainstem mechanisms that regulate autonomic responses that constitute part of the emotion of fear.

PET scans of the brain made both before and during a panic attack induced by the infusion of lactate offer additional information. *Before* panic occurred, panic-disorder patients had an abnormal asymmetry of blood flow (more to the right than to the left hemisphere; see Figure 12.12). But *during* the panic attack, the brain activity of these patients was indistinguishable from that which accompanies anxiety in normal people anticipating a painful experience (Reiman et al., 1989).

Indeed, though the appearance of unexplained symptoms of physical arousal may set the stage for a panic attack, the person's cognitive interpretation of those symptoms can determine whether or not the attack actually develops. In one study of panic attacks induced by breathing air rich in carbon dioxide, patients were told that they could control the amount of carbon dioxide they were inhaling by turning a dial on a control panel. In fact the dial had no effect. They were therefore under the illusion that they could control the development of the panic attack. Patients who had the illusion of control were less likely to have a full-blown panic attack (Sanderson, Rapee & Barlow,

Figure 12.12
Anxiety and the Brain
Positron emission tomography (PET) scans of a patient susceptible to panic attacks. The left half of this image represents cerebral blood flow, and the right half of the image represents the difference between the left hemisphere blood flow and the right hemisphere blood flow. The bright spot on the right side is an area called the parahippocampal gyrus, which had greater blood flow on the right side in all of the panic attack patients examined, but not in normal subjects. (From Reiman et al., 1984.

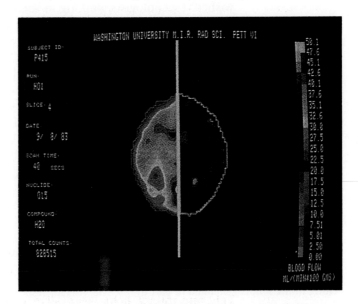

Source: Reprinted with permission from *Psychology Today Magazine*. Copyright © 1985 (PT Partners, L. P.)

1989). Thus, if catastrophic thoughts about embarrassment or death occur in response to initial symptoms, they may set off a snowball effect in which fear continues to grow. It is in the process of interpreting and coping with the symptoms that the cognitive aspects of emotion may play an important role in panic disorder.

Because both biological and cognitive factors contribute to panic disorder, treatment often focuses on both aspects. The anxiolytic benzodiazepine drugs (discussed in Chapter 6, on consciousness) can be effective, as can behavior therapy techniques discussed in Chapter 16.

Future Directions

The James-Lange, Cannon-Bard, and Schachter-Singer theories clearly state relatively simple relationships among physiological responses, cognitive activity, and the experience of emotion; but psychologists have still not pinpointed exactly how emotional experiences are produced. As PET scans, magnetic resonance imaging, EEG recordings, and other techniques for monitoring brain activity are refined, researchers may be able to observe brain activity more precisely and to relate that activity to subjective reports of emotional experience, as in the studies of panic that we just described. Determining the areas of the brain that generate emotions may also clarify how emotions and motivational systems interact.

Several of the recent studies discussed in this chapter have opened interesting lines of investigation. For example, observations that some aspects of emotional expression do not vary across cultures and that some of these expressions occur in infants provide evidence that biology plays an important role in determining emotional expressions. Yet social factors are critical in shaping the way emotions are expressed, in communicating values, and in shaping behavior. Future research will be needed to clarify the interactions of social and biological factors in emotional experience and expression.

Current knowledge suggests that future studies will find that thinking and feeling cannot be as neatly separated as psychologists in the past might have wished. Psychologists working in the field of artificial intelligence have even begun to attempt computer simulations of human thinking that include emotions.

In all of these areas, future research is likely to emphasize the adaptive functions of emotions, instead of portraying them as disruptions to smooth functioning. If you wish to study emotion in more detail, consider taking a course in motivation and emotion. You will also find that most courses in biological psychology deal with the physiological and anatomical bases of emotion. A course on stress and coping may offer valuable coverage of the negative effects of emotional overarousal.

Summary and Key Terms

What Is Emotion?

An *emotion* is a transitory, valenced experience that is felt with some intensity as happening to the self, is generated in part by a cognitive appraisal of a situation, and is accompanied by both learned and reflexive responses.

Where Is Emotion, In the Heart or in the Head?

Emotions and the Autonomic Nervous System
The visceral responses that are part of emotional experiences are produced by the *autonomic nervous system (ANS)*. This system modulates the activity of all the body's organs, allowing the body

to respond to demands from the environment in a coordinated fashion. The autonomic nervous system has two divisions: the *sympathetic* and the *parasympathetic* nervous systems. The parasympathetic system is involved mainly in the protection, nourishment, and growth of the body; the sympathetic system usually prepares the body for vigorous action. The *adrenal glands*, acting as specialized cells of the sympathetic nervous system, contribute to the *fight-or-flight* syndrome by releasing adrenaline into the bloodstream. Activity of the autonomic nervous system does not reach consciousness directly but can be detected indirectly, such as through biofeedback. Because of the involuntary nature of the autonomic responses which often accompany feelings of guilt, polygraphs—instruments that measure these responses—have been used as lie detectors; however, there is no specific physiological response pattern that reliably accompanies lying.

The James-Lange Theory

The *James-Lange theory* of emotion holds that peripheral responses are the primary source of emotion and that self-observation of these responses constitutes the emotional experience. The theory is supported by evidence that, at least for several basic emotions, the physiological responses are distinguishable enough for emotions to be generated this way. Distinct facial expressions are linked to these patterns of physiological change. Studies of people with spinal cord damage do not support an important role for autonomic activity in parts of the body beyond the face, except perhaps in affecting the intensity of some emotions.

The Cannon-Bard Theory

The *Cannon-Bard theory* of emotion proposes that emotional experience occurs independently of peripheral responses and that there is a direct experience of emotion based on activity of the central nervous system. Updated versions of this theory suggest that various parts of the central nervous system may be involved in different emotions and different aspects of emotional experience. Some pathways in the brain, such as from the thalamus to the amygdala, allow strong emotions to occur before conscious thought can take place. Specific parts of the brain appear to be responsible for the feelings of pleasure or pain in emotion. One updated version of the Cannon-Bard theory suggests that emotion depends on pathways in the brain, including those from the locus coeruleus, that constitute a kind of "autonomic nervous system" within the brain, modulating the activity of other areas of the brain.

The Schachter-Singer Theory

The *Schachter-Singer theory* of emotion suggests that peripheral responses are primary sources of emotion but that cognitive interpretations of the eliciting situation are required to label the emotion, a process that depends on *attribution*. Attributing arousal from one situation to stimuli in another situation can produce *transferred excitation*, intensifying the emotion experienced in the second situation.

How Do People Communicate Emotions?

In humans, facial movement and expression play the primary role in communicating emotions.

Innate Expressions of Emotion

Darwin suggested that certain facial expressions of emotion are innate and universal and that these expressions evolved because they communicate an animal's emotional condition to other animals. Some facial expressions of basic emotions do appear to be innate. Even blind infants smile when happy and cry when in discomfort. And certain facial movements are universally associated with certain emotions. The Duchenne smile and enjoyment is one example; a slackened face and sadness is another.

Social Aspects of Emotional Expression

Many expressions of emotion are learned. As a result, the same emotion may be expressed facially in different ways in different cultures. Especially in ambiguous situations, other people's facial expressions of emotion may be vital sources of information about what to do or what not to do, a phenomenon called *social referencing*. As children grow up, they learn the rules of emotional expression appropriate to their culture. These rules are called one's emotion culture. Even in adulthood, a change in social or professional role may require learning new ways of expressing emotion.

Facial Expressions and the Brain

Voluntary facial movements and involuntary facial expressions are controlled by different parts of the brain. The right and left cerebral hemispheres play somewhat different roles in emotional expression. The right frontal areas are activated in negative emotions; left frontal areas are activated in positive emotional expressions like the Duchenne smile. However, the right hemisphere seems to play the dominant role in both facial expressions of emotion (the left side of the face shows more expressiveness in adults) and the perception of emotion. Suppression of emotions in adults may involve reduced communication between the cerebral hemispheres.

O U T L I N E

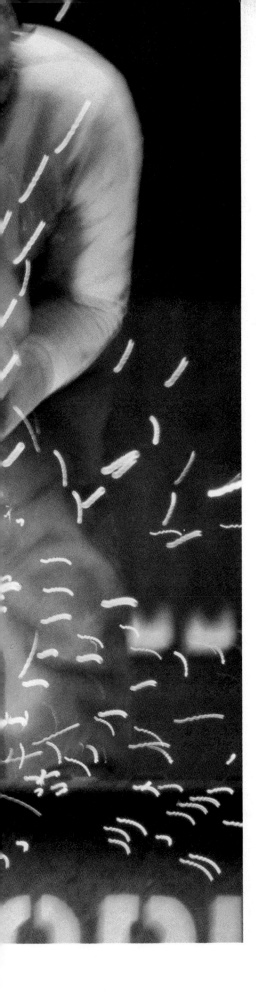

Stress, Coping, and Health

In trying to make the elderly happy and healthy, most nursing homes protect them from the bothersome details of life. Nutritionally balanced meals are planned for them and served at the same time each day in a particular room. A reliable schedule of sleeping, waking, bathing, recreation, medication, field trips, visits from relatives, and physical checkups is established for them. Even decisions about bedroom furniture are taken care of so that the residents have little to worry about. Why, then, are nursing home residents often unhappy, unhealthy, and much more likely to die than people who must cope with all of life's daily hassles?

According to some psychologists, these problems appear partly *because* of the efforts made on behalf of residents. Although death is inevitable, illness, unhappiness, and death are not due to age alone but are also related to psychological factors, especially to people's feeling of being in control of their lives. In one nursing home, some residents were allowed more control over what they ate, how their rooms were arranged, and whether their personal telephones were turned on or off. During the next eighteen months, these people were more active and alert, happier and healthier, and had a death rate 50 percent lower than residents who received equal attention from the staff but whose decision-making power was unchanged (Rodin, 1986a). Even among elderly people outside of nursing homes or other institutions, a sense of personal control and an optimistic outlook have been associated with resistance to disease (Rodin, 1986b). Attempts to protect the elderly from daily decision making may create a sense of lost control that is stressful—and, as we shall discuss in this chapter, stress can make people more vulnerable to illness.

You have probably heard that death and taxes are the only two things you can be sure of in life. If there is a third, it must surely be stress. Stress is basic to life—no matter how wealthy, powerful, good-looking, or happy you might be—and it is related to many areas of psychology (see the Linkages diagram). Mild stress can be stimulating, motivating, and sometimes even desirable.

LINKAGES

Stress, Coping,

and Health

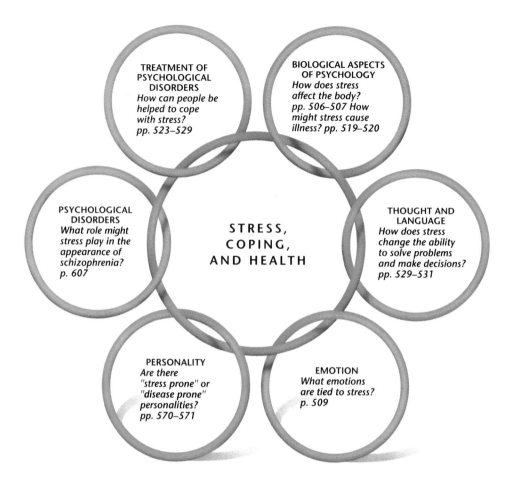

TREATMENT OF PSYCHOLOGICAL DISORDERS
How can people be helped to cope with stress?
pp. 523–529

BIOLOGICAL ASPECTS OF PSYCHOLOGY
How does stress affect the body?
pp. 506–507 How might stress cause illness? pp. 519–520

PSYCHOLOGICAL DISORDERS
What role might stress play in the appearance of schizophrenia?
p. 607

STRESS, COPING, AND HEALTH

THOUGHT AND LANGUAGE
How does stress change the ability to solve problems and make decisions?
pp. 529–531

PERSONALITY
Are there "stress prone" or "disease prone" personalities?
pp. 570–571

EMOTION
What emotions are tied to stress?
p. 509

■ Look at the diagram above, which illustrates some of the relationships between the topics of this chapter, stress, coping, and health, and other chapter topics. Stress is a process that affects and is affected by thoughts and feelings and physical reactions, so the ties between research on stress and other areas of psychology are numerous. Cognitive psychology, for example, assumes an important role in research on stress, because the way people think about stressful events can greatly alter the effect of those events.

Research on biological aspects of stress is particularly intriguing. This research involves study of the endocrine and autonomic nervous systems (discussed in Chapters 3 and 12). It shows that the body's vulnerability to disease is influenced by psychological as well as physical sources of stress. The precise mechanisms for this influence are not yet known, but we discuss several possibilities in this chapter.

The diagram shows just a sampling of links between stress and various areas of psychology; the page numbers indicate where the questions in the diagram are discussed. ■

But, as it becomes more severe, stress can bring on physical, psychological, and behavioral problems. In this chapter, we discuss what stress is, what its effects are, and how efforts to cope with it can prevent illness and promote health.

What Is Stress?

Stress is the process of adjusting to or dealing with circumstances that disrupt, or threaten to disrupt a person's physical or psychological functioning (Burchfield, 1979; Lazarus & Folkman, 1984; Selye, 1976). Here are two examples.

Marlene has spent ten hours of a sweltering August day on a crowded bus from Cleveland, Ohio, to Muncie, Indiana. The air conditioner is not working, and she discovers that the person next to her has apparently not had a bath since the beginning of the decade. By the time she reaches Muncie, Marlene is hot, dizzy, depressed, tired, and irritable.

Jack is waiting in a room full of other college seniors to interview for a job with a large accounting firm. His grades are not outstanding, but he hopes to get by on his personality. He feels that his parents and his fiancée expect him to land a high-prestige, high-paying position. He is very nervous. His mouth is dry, his stomach feels tight, his heart is pounding, and perspiration has begun to soak through his new suit.

These sketches illustrate that stress involves a relationship between people and their environments—more specifically, between stressors and stress reactions. **Stressors** are events and situations (such as bus rides or interviews) to which people must react. **Stress reactions** are the physical, psychological, and behavioral responses (such as nausea, nervousness, and fatigue) people display in the face of stressors. *Mediating factors*, such as the circumstances in which stressors occur and each person's characteristics, make people more or less sensitive to stressors and to stress responses. Thus, stress is not a specific event but a process (see Figure 13.1). We consider stressors and stress responses first and then examine some of the factors that influence the relationship between them.

Stressors

Many stressors involve physical demands such as invading viruses, extreme temperatures, or strenuous work. For humans, however, many of the most significant stressors are psychological. The person who must give a speech to

Figure 13.1
The Process of Stress
Stressful events, a person's reactions to those events, and interactions between the person and the situation are all important components of stress. The interactions are stress mediators; they moderate or intensify the impact of a stressful situation. For example, just one or two minor stressors might create extreme stress reactions if they are not controllable and are the latest of dozens of hassles in the life of a stress-prone individual with few coping skills. The same circumstances might not have much effect if that individual is more skilled or has more support from family or friends. Note the two-way relationships in the stress process. For example, as effective coping skills minimize stress reactions, the experience of having milder stress responses will solidify those skills. And as coping skills (such as refusing unreasonable demands) improve, some stressors (such as the boss's unreasonable demands) may decrease.

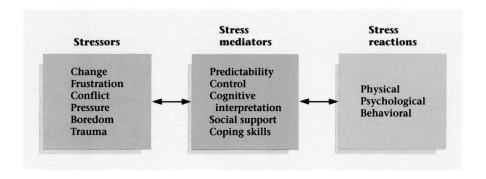

Long periods of boring, quiet unpredictability punctuated by episodes of intense pressure can create significant stress for firefighters and other emergency personnel.

impress a potential employer is facing stressors that can be just as demanding as a day of hard physical labor. Many, perhaps most, human stressors include both physical and psychological components. Athletes, for example, are challenged by the demands of physical exertion, as well as by the pressure of competition. In this section, we focus on the psychological stressors that, combined with the physical demands of life, contribute most significantly to the stress process.

Major Psychological Stressors

Even very pleasant events can be stressors (Brown & McGill, 1989). For example, the increased salary and status associated with a promotion may be desirable, but the upgrade also requires finding ways of handling new responsibilities and increased pressures. Similarly, it is not uncommon for people to feel exhausted after the travel and intense fun-seeking of a vacation and somewhat depressed by the ''real world'' when the excitement of a wedding is over. Still, the events and situations most likely to be associated with stress are unpleasant ones—those involving frustration, pressure, boredom, trauma, conflict, or change (DeLongis, Folkman & Lazarus, 1988; Rowlison & Felner, 1988).

Frustrating situations contain some obstacle that stands between a person and his or her goals. Waiting in a long line at the bank or being unable to find a phone to make an important call are simple examples of frustrating situations. More substantial illustrations include being unable to earn a decent living because of adverse economic conditions or job discrimination or failing in repeated attempts to find a love relationship.

Pressure situations require a person to do too much in too short a time. If you are trying to fix Thanksgiving dinner for twenty people on a day's notice, or if you are struggling to finish the last two questions on an essay test in ten minutes, you are under pressure. Many air-traffic controllers, physicians, nurses, and police officers face constant or long-lasting pressure. They must make many difficult decisions, sometimes involving life and death, under heavy time pressure. People under such pressure day after day sometimes begin to perform poorly and develop physical illness, alcoholism, anxiety, and many of the other stress-related problems described later in this chapter.

Boredom, or understimulation, is the opposite of pressure, but it, too, can be a stressor, especially if it continues for a long time. The agony of solitary confinement in prison or the tedium of a remote military post are probably the most extreme examples.

Trauma is a shocking physical or emotional experience. Catastrophes such as rape, military combat, fire, tornadoes, or torture are only a few examples. More common disasters, such as a divorce or the sudden death of someone close, can be equally devastating.

Conflict is almost always stressful. The most obvious examples are disputes in which friends, family members, or coworkers fight with, insult, or otherwise get nasty with each other. If you can recall the last time you experienced one of these interpersonal conflicts (even if you were just a spectator), you can probably also remember the discomfort you felt. Internal conflicts can be equally, if not more, distressing than those with other people. Imagine, for example, the stress that might result when a woman stays with a man she does not love only because she fears he will commit suicide if she leaves. In Chapter 11, on motivation, we described four types of internal conflict: approach-approach, approach-avoidance, avoidance-avoidance, and multiple approach-avoidance conflict.

Change can also be a major stressor. Divorce, illness in the family, unemployment, and moving to a new city are just a few examples of changes that create social, psychological, financial, and physical demands to which people must adapt and adjust.

Measuring Stressors

Attention to change was the keystone in a pioneering effort to find a standard way of measuring the stress in a person's life. Working from the assumption that *all* change, positive or negative, is stressful, Thomas Holmes and Richard Rahe developed in 1967 the Social Readjustment Rating Scale (SRRS). They asked a large number of people to rate a list of change-related stressors in terms of *life change units* (*LCUs*), the amount of change and demand for adjustment the stressor introduces into a person's life. Getting married, the point against which raters were told to compare all other stressors, was rated as slightly more stressful than losing one's job. Table 13.1 shows the forty-three items on the SRRS and their LCU ratings.

You can use the SRRS to measure the stressors in your own life by adding the LCUs associated with each item you have experienced within the past year. If your score strikes you as being high, don't be surprised. College students routinely face numerous stressors having to do with everything from course work to social life.

T H I N K I N G   C R I T I C A L L Y

Can Physical or Psychological Problems Be Predicted by Life Events Scales?

What am I being asked to believe or accept?
Some psychologists argue that people with relatively high scores on check lists like the SRRS are especially vulnerable to psychological problems and to illnesses ranging from colds to cancer.

What evidence is available to support the assertion?
There is a great deal of research showing that people who experience the most stressors—as measured by the SRRS and other life change scales—are the most likely to suffer physical illness, mental disorder, or other problems (Dohrenwend & Dohrenwend, 1978; Rowlison & Felner, 1988). One study found, for example, that physical illness was associated with SRRS scores under 200 only 37 percent of the time, but appeared 79 percent of the time when scores were above 300 (Holmes & Masuda, 1974).

Are there alternative ways of interpreting the evidence?
The meaning of scores on scales like the SRRS is debatable. For one thing, the scale is dominated by items involving undesirable changes, not just change *per se*. Second, much of the evidence for the link between negative life events and disorder comes from retrospective research. That is, people who *already* displayed physical or mental disorders reported that they experienced one or more major stressors just before their disorders appeared (Barrett, 1979; Rahe et al., 1974). This kind of evidence has several weaknesses. Perhaps current problems caused these people to recall the recent past as more stressful than it was. Perhaps some items on the SRRS (such as "personal injury or illness" or "revision of personal habits") are actually measuring current or long-term disorders, not identifying independent predictors of later disorder. Or perhaps reported stressful events (such as divorce) are the *result* of long-standing problems, not the cause (Cohen, 1987).

Table 13.1
The Social Readjustment Ratir
Scale (SRRS)

Each event in the SRRS has a life change unit (LCU) value associate(with it. People with a higher total LCUs may experience more stress-related problems, but stress media tors, such as social support and coping skills, also shape the effect of stressors.

Rank	Event	LCU Value
1	Death of spouse	100
2	Divorce	73
3	Marital separation	65
4	Jail term	63
5	Death of close family member	63
6	Personal injury or illness	53
7	Marriage	50
8	Fired at work	47
9	Marital reconciliation	45
10	Retirement	45
11	Change in health of family member	44
12	Pregnancy	40
13	Sex difficulties	39
14	Gain of new family member	39
15	Business readjustment	39
16	Change in financial state	38
17	Death of close friend	37
18	Change to different line of work	36
19	Change in number of arguments with spouse	35
20	Mortgage over $10,000	31
21	Foreclosure of mortgage or loan	30
22	Change in responsibilities at work	29
23	Son or daughter leaving home	29
24	Trouble with in-laws	29
25	Outstanding personal achievement	28
26	Wife begins or stops work	26
27	Begin or end school	26
28	Change in living conditions	25
29	Revision of personal habits	24
30	Trouble with boss	23
31	Change in work hours or conditions	20
32	Change in residence	20
33	Change in schools	20
34	Change in recreation	19
35	Change in church activities	19
36	Change in social activities	18
37	Mortgage or loan less than $10,000	17
38	Change in sleeping habits	16
39	Change in number of family get-togethers	15
40	Change in eating habits	15
41	Vacation	13
42	Christmas	12
43	Minor violations of the law	11

Source: Holmes & Rahe, 1967.

Further, evidence for a statistical relationship between SRRS scores and various forms of disorder does not necessarily translate to an equivalent risk for everyone who completes the scale. Even in prospective studies, where people's reports of current stressors are used to identify those who will show problems later, the correlation between stressful events and various disorders is usually too low (only around +.30) to allow accurate predictions about individuals (DePue & Monroe, 1986; Dohrenwend & Dohrenwend, 1984; Rabkin & Struening, 1976).

Indeed, the observed stress-disorder link may be due to factors other than life events alone. Two possibilities stand out. First, disorders may be related not to life events themselves but to people's *appraisal* of events as negative and threatening. Second, the appearance of problems may owe much to "daily hassles," including the physical discomforts of living in a noisy, overcrowded neighborhood, working at an unsatisfying job, or contending with urban commuting (Delongis, Folkman & Lazarus, 1988; Lazarus, 1985). If you have ever had a day when everything seemed to go wrong, you can understand the contribution of daily hassles to a person's total stress load.

What additional evidence would help to evaluate the alternatives?
Data on the impact of daily hassles (which are not measured by life events scales) would help clarify the relationship between various kinds of stressful events and disorder. One group of researchers (DeLongis, Folkman & Lazarus, 1988; Kanner et al., 1981) has already developed questionnaires to assess both daily hassles and the uplifts people experience (see Table 13.2). So far, research with scales like these suggests that predictions about the severity of disorder may be improved when based on hassles (but not on uplifts) as well as major stressors (Brantley et al., 1988; DeLongis, Folkman & Lazarus, 1988; Holahan, Holahan & Belk, 1984; Rowlison & Felner, 1988).

However, psychologists are still far from being able to identify with confidence the relative contributions of major life events and daily hassles to physical and mental disorder in a given individual. Their task is difficult partly because, as shown in Figure 13.1, numerous individual differences mediate, and thus cloud, the relationship between stressful events and stress reactions. Much more information will be needed about these mediating influences before accurate predictions about individuals will be possible.

What conclusions are most reasonable?
Close analysis of the link between life events and disorder provides reasons for skepticism about the utility of the SRRS and its variants (DePue & Monroe, 1986; Schroeder & Costa, 1984). This analysis suggests that predicting the likely impact of stress is far more difficult than just adding up scores on a check list. ■

Table 13.2
Daily Hassles and Uplifts

Here are some items from a recently revised version of the Daily Hassles and Uplifts Scale. The respondent is asked to make bedtime ratings (on 0–4 scales) of the degree to which each item was a hassle or an uplift that day. Ratings over several days or weeks can give a picture of people's stressors and pleasures that is more detailed than scales like the SRRS and may allow for a better understanding of the role of daily hassles in stress-related disorders.

How Much of a Hassle Was This Item for You Today?		How Much of an Uplift Was This Item for You Today?
0 1 2 3 4	Your child(ren)	0 1 2 3 4
0 1 2 3 4	Time with family	0 1 2 3 4
0 1 2 3 4	Sex	0 1 2 3 4
0 1 2 3 4	Fellow workers	0 1 2 3 4
0 1 2 3 4	Your workload	0 1 2 3 4
0 1 2 3 4	Meeting deadlines	0 1 2 3 4
0 1 2 3 4	Having enough money	0 1 2 3 4
0 1 2 3 4	Your physical appearance	0 1 2 3 4
0 1 2 3 4	The weather	0 1 2 3 4
0 1 2 3 4	Your neighborhood	0 1 2 3 4
0 1 2 3 4	Cooking	0 1 2 3 4
0 1 2 3 4	Home entertainment	0 1 2 3 4
0 1 2 3 4	Amount of free time	0 1 2 3 4

Source: Folkman & Lazarus, 1988.

Stress Responses

Stress reactions can be physical, psychological, or behavioral. For the sake of clarity, we will discuss each type of response separately, but all three types of stress reactions often occur together, especially as stressors become more intense. For example, Marlene's responses to the stress of her bus ride were physical (dizziness), psychological (depression), and behavioral (irritability). Furthermore, a stress response in one dimension can act as a stimulus setting off a stress response in another dimension (see Figure 13.2). For example, a physical stress reaction, such as mild chest pains following a family crisis, may lead to such psychological and behavioral stress responses as worrying about a heart attack and reluctance to have sex.

Physical Stress Responses

Linkages: How does stress affect the body? (a link to Biological Aspects of Psychology)

Anyone who has experienced a near accident or some other sudden, very frightening event knows that the physical responses to stress include rapid breathing, increased heartbeat, sweating, and, a little later, general shakiness, especially in the muscles of the arms and legs. These reactions are all part of a general pattern, or *syndrome*, known as the *fight-or-flight syndrome*. Recall from Chapter 12, on emotion, that this syndrome, created by the sympathetic branch of the autonomic nervous system, prepares the body to face or to flee an immediate threat.

When the danger is past, the fight-or-flight responses subside. However, when stressors are longer-lasting, these responses are only the beginning of a longer sequence of bodily reactions. Careful observation of animals and humans exposed to infections, radiation, temperature extremes, and other extended stressors led Hans Selye (pronounced ''sell-yay'') to suggest that this longer sequence of physical responses occurs in a consistent and very general pattern, which is triggered by the effort to adapt to any stressor. Selye called this sequence the **general adaptation syndrome**, or **GAS** (Selye, 1956, 1976).

Figure 13.2
Stress Responses
The three main kinds of stress responses can occur in reaction to outside stressors or to one another. For example, suppose your instructor suddenly announces that a major paper will be due in two weeks (an environmental stressor). If your psychological response involves becoming worried about the assignment, that worry might act as an internal stress stimulus, perhaps causing such behavioral stress responses as insomnia, which in turn creates physical stress due to lack of sleep. The psychological response to the loss of sleep might include an inability to concentrate, thus slowing down work on the paper (a behavioral effect) and prompting increased worry. In other words, to some extent, stress can arise from within, not just from the outside world.

The General Adaptation Syndrome   There are three stages in the GAS, as Figure 13.3 shows. The first stage is the **alarm reaction**, which involves some

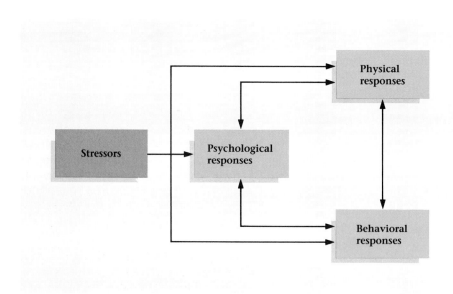

Figure 13.3
The General Adaptation Syndrome

Hans Selye's research suggested that physical reactions to stress occur in three phases: the alarm reaction, the stage of resistance, and the stage of exhaustion. During the alarm reaction, the body's resistance temporarily drops below its normal, ongoing level as it absorbs the initial impact of the stressor. However, the resistance soon increases dramatically, leveling off in the resistance stage, but ultimately declining if the exhaustion stage is reached. More recent approaches suggest that this sequence of events is not always as consistent and predictable as Selye suggested.

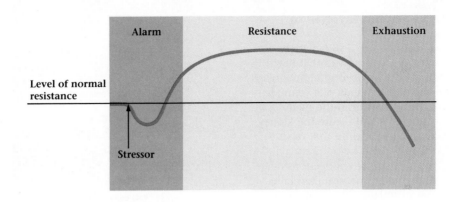

Source: Adapted from Selye, 1974.

version of the fight-or-flight syndrome. In the face of a mild stressor such as a hot room, the reaction may simply involve changes in heart rate, respiration, and perspiration that help the body regulate its temperature. More severe stressors prompt more dramatic alarm reactions, rapidly mobilizing the body's adaptive energy, much as a burglar alarm alerts the police and mobilizes them to take action (Selye, 1956).

If the stressor persists, the stage of **resistance** begins. Here, signs of the initial alarm reaction diminish, but the body settles in to resist the stressor on a long-term basis. The drain on adaptive energy is slower during the resistance stage than it was during the alarm reaction; in fact, there may be few outward signs that anything is wrong. But the body is working very hard, just as if it were in a tug-of-war, pulling steadily against an opponent of equal strength. Organs such as the adrenal glands, the thymus, the liver, and the kidneys release substances that increase blood pressure, fight inflammation, enhance muscle tension, increase blood sugar, and promote all the physical changes needed to cope with stressors (see Figure 13.4). Among these substances are *catecholamines*, especially adrenaline and noradrenaline, and *corticosteroids*, such as cortisol. The overall effect is to generate emergency energy. The more stressors there are (especially if new ones appear before recovery from the last one can take place) and the longer they last, the longer people need to expend resources in an effort to resist them.

The continued campaign of biochemical resistance is costly. It slowly but surely uses up the body's reserves of adaptive energy until, just as a slowly leaking tire eventually goes flat, the capacity to resist is gone. The body enters the third GAS stage, known as **exhaustion**. In extreme cases, such as prolonged exposure to freezing temperatures, the result is death. More commonly, the exhaustion stage is associated with signs of physical wear and tear, especially in organ systems that were weak in the first place or heavily involved in the resistance process. For example, if catecholamines and corticosteroids, which help fight stressors during the resistance stage, remain at high levels for an extended time, they can promote illnesses ranging from heart disease, high blood pressure, and arthritis to colds and flu (Anderson, 1989; Matthews et al., 1986). Selye called illnesses that are caused or promoted by stressors **diseases of adaptation.**

Beyond Selye's Model   Selye's model has been very influential, but it has also been criticized. At least in the case of humans, Selye overemphasized the role of fixed biological processes in determining stress responses and under-

Figure 13.4
Organ Systems Involved in the GAS

Stressors produce a wide variety of physiological responses that begin in the brain and spread to many organs throughout the body. For example, catecholamines from the medulla of the adrenal glands cause the kidneys to release a substance that raises blood pressure. The pituitary gland triggers release of endogenous opiates, the body's natural pain-killers. It also stimulates release of cortico-steroids, which help resist stress but, as we describe later, also tend to suppress the immune system, making the body more vulnerable to infection.

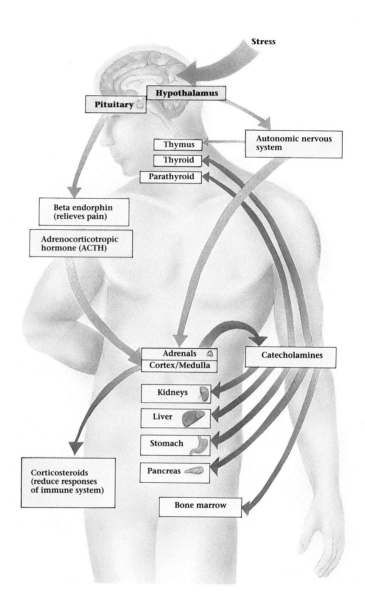

estimated the role of psychological factors such as emotional state or the way a person thinks about stressors (Appley & Trumbull, 1986; Lazarus & Folkman, 1984). For example, the alarm reaction may not be as general and automatic as Selye described, and specific responses later in the GAS can vary from person to person.

Criticisms of Selye's model led to the development of *psychobiological models* that emphasize the importance of psychological as well as biological variables in regulating and producing stress responses (DePue & Monroe, 1986; Mason, 1975; G. Schwartz, 1982; Smith & Anderson, 1986). According to psychobiological models, psychological variables, such as how a person thinks about a stressor, shape the impact of that stressor. For example, a given stressor will have a more negative impact if the person thinks about it as an uncontrollable threat rather than as a controllable challenge (Ganellen & Blaney, 1984; Rhodewalt & Zone, 1989). Furthermore, threat, conflict, frustration, and other psychological stressors can stimulate some of the same responses as physical danger (Frankenhaeuser et al., 1971; Rozanski et al., 1988).

Psychological Stress Responses

When people describe stress, they are more likely to say, "I got confused and felt angry and frustrated!" than "My heart rate increased and my blood pressure went up." In other words, when people describe stress, they are likely to mention changes in how they think or feel. These changes in emotion and cognition make up the second major category of stress responses: psychological stress responses.

Linkages: What emotions are tied to stress? (a link to Emotion)

Emotional Stress Responses   Physical responses to life's stressors are usually accompanied by emotional responses. If someone shows a gun and demands your money, you will no doubt experience the GAS alarm reaction, but you will also feel some strong emotion, probably anxiety, maybe anger. In fact, it is hard to imagine feeling anxiety, anger, or depression in the absence of a stressor.

Emotional stress responses usually occur in relation to clearly identifiable situations, such as lack of job security, marital conflict, or the constant pressure of daily hassles. In most cases, emotional stress reactions subside soon after the stressors are gone. However, if stressors continue for a long time or come in a tight sequence, emotional stress reactions may also continue, and the consequences can be serious. When people do not have a chance to recover their emotional equilibrium, they commonly report feeling tense or anxious more and more of the time. Increasingly intense feelings of fatigue, depression, and helplessness may also appear, as the long battle against stressors continues.

Sometimes, constant emotional arousal becomes so routine that the person can no longer pinpoint why it is there. The result may be a pattern called **generalized anxiety disorder** (or **free-floating anxiety**), in which the person is at a loss to explain his or her constant feelings of tension and anxiety. In other cases, as mentioned in Chapter 12, there may be occasional, sudden attacks of panic. We describe stress-related emotional disorders and ways to treat them in Chapters 15 and 16.

Linkages: Emotional stress responses can be severe, but they normally subside with time. However, people facing numerous stressful events in quick succession may experience negative emotional reactions for months or even years. These reactions can sometimes be so severe or long-lasting as to be considered major depression, generalized anxiety disorder, or other stress-related mental disorders discussed in Chapter 15.

Cognitive Stress Responses Reductions in the ability to concentrate, to think clearly, or to remember accurately are typical cognitive stress responses. As discussed later in this chapter, these problems usually occur as stressors elevate arousal above a person's optimal level.

One of the most common cognitive stress responses is **catastrophizing**, which means dwelling on and overemphasizing the potential consequences of negative events (Sarason et al., 1986). For example, during examinations, test-anxious college students are likely to say to themselves, "I'm falling behind" or "Everyone else is doing better than I am" (Sarason, 1978, 1984). These reactions are especially likely in people of moderate ability or those most uncertain about how well they will do (Defares, Grossman & de Swart, 1983; Spielberger, 1979). Catastrophizing can not only interfere directly with smooth cognitive functioning but also intensify emotional and physiological arousal, which in turn adds to the total stress response and further hampers performance (Darke, 1988; Geen, 1985; Sarason, 1984). Thus, cognitive reactions to stressors can themselves create additional stress responses, so that preoccupation with thoughts about failure may help bring about failure.

Other cognitive reactions to stress minimize the impact of stressors, at least temporarily. For example, some people automatically and often unknowingly respond to stressors with denial, repression, intellectualization, displacement, projection, and other cognitive strategies that Freud called defense mechanisms. **Defense mechanisms** are habitual psychological responses that help protect people from anxiety and other negative emotions accompanying stress. Table 13.3 contains several illustrations; additional examples are discussed in Chapter 14, on personality.

Defense mechanisms may cushion the emotional impact of stress, but they do little or nothing to eliminate the source of stress. For example, denying to yourself that a recent bad grade bothers you may make you feel better, but it will not improve your study habits. If you are facing a short-lived crisis, a natural disaster, or some other stressor you can do little about, defense mechanisms may work well. However, serious problems can result if you rely on defense mechanisms all the time and if they prevent you from recognizing and acting on stressors that can be changed (Moos & Schaefer, 1984). For example, according to one study, male heart attack victims who initially denied the reality or seriousness of their condition were less distressed, had shorter hospital stays, and showed fewer symptoms than those who focused on the gravity of their condition. However, those who continued to employ denial during the year after their release tended to have more subsequent heart problems, apparently because this defense allowed them to ignore doctors' orders about smoking, diet, and exercise (Levine et al., 1987).

In short, physical and emotional stress reactions provide signals that something is wrong, but cognitive reactions can jam those signals, stopping a person from developing strategies to cope with or eliminate sources of stress. Fortunately, many people routinely display rational and constructive cognitive reactions.

Behavioral Stress Responses

Clues about people's physical and emotional stress reactions come from *behavioral stress responses*; that is, from changes in how people look, act, or talk. Strained facial expressions, a shaky voice, tremors or spasms and jumpiness are common behavioral indicators of physiological stress responses. Posture can also convey information about stress, a fact used by skilled interviewers.

Table 13.3
Psychological Defenses Against Stress

These and other defense mechanisms are sometimes helpful in dealing temporarily with stressors. But overreliance on defense mechanisms usually leads to trouble in the long run, mainly because these mechanisms do nothing to eliminate sources of stress.

Denial	A man is severely overworked. He is not getting enough sleep, is eating poorly, and, though aware of being physically and mentally exhausted, tells his wife and coworkers, "Everything is fine. I'm too strong to be bothered by a little hard work."
Repression	A soldier finds it impossible to remember anything about the day his friend was killed by a sniper.
Rationalization	A father's hostility toward his son is expressed through frequent spankings, but explained away by claiming that the discipline is for the child's own good.
Intellectualization	A college student anxious about having fallen hopelessly behind in her reading spends most of her time discussing in cold, philosophical terms the inherent meaninglessness of grades and achievement.
Displacement	A business executive under constant stress brought on by fierce competition from other companies routinely blames her stomach ulcer and her irritability not on her own competitiveness but on "aggravation" caused by the incompetence of her employees.
Projection	A professor fails to perceive his own stress-related problems, claiming instead that the stress reactions of several colleagues have created such a tense atmosphere that it is impossible to get any work done.

Figure 13.5
One Behavioral Response to Stress

Deterioration of handwriting is one of many behavioral signs of stress. On the top is a sample of President Richard Nixon's signature when all was well in his administration. On the bottom, you can see what happened to his handwriting during the stress of the Watergate investigations that ultimately forced him from office.

When stress raises arousal above a person's optimal level, physical coordination, behavioral skills, and other aspects of behavior may be disrupted (Baumeister, 1984). Figure 13.5 shows one example. Even more obvious behavioral stress responses appear as people attempt to escape or avoid stressors. Some people quit their jobs, drop out of school, or even attempt suicide. Ten thousand college students attempt suicide every year, in part because of difficulty in coping with stressors such as academic requirements, financial problems, and relationship problems. Unfortunately, as discussed in the chapter on learning, escape and avoidance tactics deprive people of the opportunity to learn more adaptive ways of coping with stressful environments, including college.

Aggression is another common behavioral response to stressors. The angry words and, sometimes, flying fists that occur between shoppers at a crowded sale or motorists in a traffic jam testify to the role of frustration, conflict, and other stressors in triggering aggressive behavior. All too often, this aggressiveness is directed at members of one's own family (Hepworth & West, 1988; MacEwan & Barling, 1988). However, stressors alone are probably not responsible for all domestic violence. For example, violent behavior toward family members is particularly likely in those who not only face numerous stressors but whose learning history includes exposure to aggressive stress reactions in childhood, often as victims of abuse by their parents (Seltzer & Kalmuss, 1988;

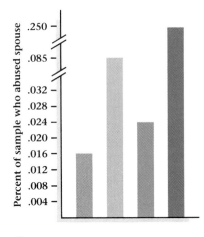

Moderate stress

Moderate stress plus exposure to family violence in childhood

High stress

High stress plus exposure to family violence in childhood

Figure 13.6
Stress and Violence
Many researchers have found that unemployment, inadequate pay, job dissatisfaction, and other stressors are associated with increases in the rate and severity of domestic violence (Mason & Blankenship, 1987; Ponzetti, Cate & Koval, 1982). One aspect of this relationship was examined in an interview study of 1,436 married people (about half female); the graph illustrates the findings. Though the vast majority of these married people did not abuse their spouses, the more stressors they faced, the more likely they were to be physically aggressive. Aggression was especially likely among those who, as children, saw their own parents react to stressors with violence toward one another or toward them (Seltzer & Kalmuss, 1988).

see Figure 13.6). Aggressive responses are also more likely when people try to blunt the impact of stressors with alcohol or drugs (O'Leary et al., 1989). Indeed, as discussed in Chapter 18, stressors are just one of many factors that underlie human aggression.

HIGHLIGHT

Burnout and Posttraumatic Stress Disorder

Physical, psychological, and behavioral stress responses sometimes appear together in patterns known as burnout and posttraumatic stress disorder. **Burnout** is a gradually intensifying pattern of physical, psychological, and behavioral dysfunction in response to a continuous flow of stressors (Farber, 1983; Rice, 1987; Riggar, 1985). Burnout typically begins with normal reactions to the conflict, frustration, and pressure of one's job (especially such high-stress jobs as police work or air-traffic control), but these reactions eventually become so severe as to impair functioning at work. The stress reactions can become so general that the person may appear to have developed a new personality, on and off the job. Previously reliable workers or once-attentive spouses may become indifferent, disengaged, impulsive, or accident prone. They may miss work frequently, oversleep, perform their jobs poorly, and become irritable, suspicious, withdrawn, depressed, and unwilling to talk about stress or anything else.

Because their problem develops gradually, people who suffer from burnout frequently fail to seek assistance. Attempts by family and friends to help may be met with aggressiveness, especially if alcohol or drugs are involved. College students sometimes display stress reactions similar to burnout from the pressure of heavy course loads, part-time jobs, constant deadlines, and a competitive atmosphere.

A different pattern of severe stress reactions is illustrated by the case of Mary, a thirty-three-year-old nurse who was raped at knifepoint by an intruder in her apartment (Spitzer et al., 1983). In the weeks following the attack, she became afraid of being alone and was preoccupied with the attack and with thoughts that it could happen again. She had additional locks installed on doors and windows but had such difficulty concentrating that she could not immediately return to work. She was repelled by the thought of sex and stated that she did not want to have sex for a long time.

Mary suffered from **posttraumatic stress disorder**, a pattern of adverse reactions following a traumatic event. Among the characteristic reactions are anxiety, irritability, jumpiness, inability to concentrate or work productively, sexual dysfunction, a lack of feeling (known as *emotional numbness*), and difficulty in getting along with others. The most common feature of posttraumatic stress disorder is re-experiencing the original trauma through nightmares or vivid memories. In rare cases, disturbing waking recollections, known as *flashbacks*, occur, in which the person behaves for minutes, hours, or days as if the trauma were occurring again. People who survive events in which others perished or who feel blame for others' deaths may also experience severe guilt or depression; some of the engineers who tried unsuccessfully to halt the disastrous launch of the space shuttle *Challenger* apparently suffered such reactions.

These problems may occur immediately, or they may be delayed; they may be temporary or continuing. The most severe and long-lasting difficulties usually appear as the result of experiences in military combat and prisoner-of-war camps. Indeed, approximately 15 percent of American veter-

Burnout on the job is especially likely when people face unrelenting pressure brought on by a heavy workload and the need to make split-second, life-and-death decisions. Air-traffic control typifies such occupations, but burnout is also a problem in law enforcement, medicine, nursing, and many other fields.

ans had such difficulties after they returned from the war in Vietnam (Kulka et al., 1988; Stretch, 1985). Some individuals who display posttraumatic stress disorders require professional help; others seem to recover without it. For most, improvement takes time; for nearly all, the support of family and friends is vital to recovery (Solomon, Mikulincer & Avitzur, 1988). ■

Interactions Between People and Stressors

In July 1988 the U.S.S. *Vincennes*, a naval cruiser, was assigned to protect commercial shipping near the coast of Iran. The crew had never before been in combat. They faced extreme heat as well as attacks from Iranian gunboats. These conditions apparently produced a pattern of stress responses that caused key crew members to misread radar signals from an ascending Iranian passenger plane as those of an attacking warplane. In the heat of the moment, no one noticed computer information that showed that the target aircraft was ascending, not attacking. The *Vincennes* crew shot the passenger plane down, killing all 290 persons aboard (Bales, 1988).

Would a different crew have acted differently? That will never be known. But it is known that there are individual differences in stress responses; one individual can survive, even thrive, under the same circumstances that lead another to break down, give up, and burn out. What determines how much and what kind of impact stressors will have? Research suggests that the answer lies in the *interaction* of particular stressors and particular people. In the sections that follow, we review some of the characteristics of people and stressors that moderate or intensify stress responses.

Predictability Predictable stressors often have less impact than those that are unpredictable (Cohen, 1980; Lazarus & Folkman, 1984), especially when the stressors are intense and occur for relatively short periods (Abbott, Schoen & Badia, 1984). For example, rats given a reliable warning signal every time they are to receive a shock show less severe physiological responses and more normal eating and drinking habits than animals receiving no warnings

Stress responses do not always cease when the stressors that created them are gone. A pattern of lingering problems known as posttraumatic stress disorder is especially likely following such catastrophic events as military combat or rape.

(Weinberg & Levine, 1980; Weiss, 1970). Humans also seem to be less stressed by shocks they know are coming (Badia, Suter & Lewis, 1967). In one study, men and women whose spouses had died suddenly displayed more immediate disbelief, anxiety, and depression than those who had weeks or months to prepare for the loss (Parkes & Brown, 1972).

This is not to say that predictability provides total protection against stressors. Laboratory research with animals has shown that predictable stressors, even if relatively mild, can be more damaging than unpredictable ones if they occur over long periods of time (Abbott, Schoen & Badia, 1984).

Knowing that a particular stressor *might* occur but being uncertain as to whether it will also tends to increase the impact of the stressor. For example, wives of American men missing in action in the Vietnam War showed poorer physical and emotional health than those who knew that their spouses had been killed in action or were being held as prisoners of war (Hunter, 1979). Similarly, uncertainty about whether their disease will return elevates anxiety among patients treated for cancer (Cohen & Lazarus, 1979).

Control   Stressors usually have less impact if people can exert some control over them (Rodin, 1986a). In one experiment, college students working on math problems showed far less psychological distress and physiological arousal if they could control the rate at which the problems appeared on a computer screen than if the problems appeared on a fixed, uncontrollable schedule (Bandura et al., 1988). Another study found that, when other risk factors were held constant, executives in high-stress jobs that allow them to control stress (for example, by determining their own schedules) had lower heart attack rates than waiters, cashiers, and cooks who had less control over the demands of their jobs (Karasek & Theorell, 1990).

Simply believing that a stressor is controllable, whether it is or not, can also reduce its impact (Cohen, 1980). For example, in one study some subjects were told that the duration of the shock they were to receive could be reduced from six seconds to three seconds if they responded quickly enough to a warning light (Geer, Davison & Gatchel, 1970). Other subjects received no such instructions. In fact, everyone received three-second shocks regardless of what they did, but those who thought they had control gave milder physiological responses than the others. Similarly, college students with high confidence in their ability to cope with a painful stressor showed significantly greater pain tolerance than those who felt less competent at pain control (Bandura et al., 1987). Numerous other studies suggest that people who feel in control of events experience those events as less negative and stressful and are less prone to psychological and physical disorders than those who feel less in control (e.g., Fleming, Baum & Weiss, 1987; Rhodewalt & Zone, 1989; Rodin & Salovey, 1989). Indeed, as discussed in Chapter 14, control appears to be an important component of stress-resistant, or "hardy," personalities.

On the other hand, people who do not think they have control over negative events appear especially prone to develop various physical and psychological problems. They often develop feelings of helplessness and hopelessness that may promote depression or other mental disorders. In one study on women undergoing tests for cervical cancer, researchers correctly predicted 74 percent of the malignancies just by knowing which subjects tended to react helplessly to recent stressors (Schmale & Iker, 1966). Other studies suggest that helplessness is related to lower survival rates among breast cancer patients (Jensen, 1987; Rodin & Salovey, 1989).

How Stressors Are Interpreted   The effects of perceived control on responses to stress are just part of a more general relationship between cognition—how people think about stressors—and the impact of stressors. As discussed in Chapter 5, perceptions of the world depend on which things people attend to and how they interpret them. A person might see a bright light as "glaring" or "glowing" and a broad smile as "warm" or "phony." Similarly, in Chapter 12, we noted that emotional reactions can depend on whether people think of events as dangerous or merely interesting. A given stressor, be it a hot elevator or a deskful of work, usually has more impact on those who perceive it as threatening or potentially harmful than on those who view it as stimulating or challenging. Some theorists, such as Richard Lazarus (1966; Lazarus & Folkman, 1984), go so far as to argue that unless a person interprets something as stressful, there will be no stress response.

Of course, the influence of cognitive responses weakens somewhat as stressors become more extreme: a bomb going off next to you will probably not be any less stressful if you think of it as fireworks. Still, even the impact of natural disasters or major stressors such as divorce may be less severe for those who think of them as challenges to be overcome rather than as the end of the world. One member of a divorcing couple might be devastated by feelings of failure, whereas the other might be invigorated by the prospect of beginning a new life.

Evidence for the effects of cognition on stress responses comes from both laboratory experiments and surveys. In a classic experiment, Lazarus and his colleagues showed three groups of students a film containing graphic scenes of bloody industrial accidents (Lazarus et al., 1965). Figure 13.7 shows the results. The intensity of students' physiological arousal during the film depended on how they had been instructed to think about it; those told to detach themselves mentally were the least affected. Similarly, noise-related distress among people living near airports appears to have more to do with

Figure 13.7
Cognition and Stress
When subjects were given different instructions about what to think about during a stressful film that showed industrial accidents, there were clear differences in physiological arousal during the film, as measured by sweat-gland activity. Those who were instructed to remain detached from the bloody scenes (the intellectualizers) or to think of them as unreal (the denial group) were less upset than those in an unprepared control group. These results provide one of many demonstrations that how people think about stressors can affect their responses to those stressors.

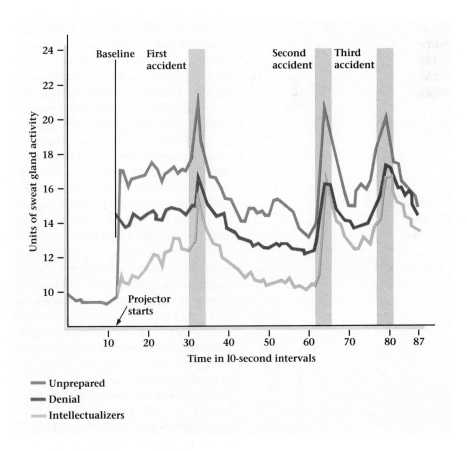

Source: Adapted from Lazarus et al., 1965.

how they evaluate the airport (for example, as a nuisance or as a source of employment) than with how much noise they must endure (Tracor, Inc., 1971). And college students who perceive the close proximity of others as undesirable report more distress in a crowded dormitory than those in the same dorm who perceive the presence of many others as enjoyable; in fact, those who enjoy high-density dorms may be distressed if the population falls too low (Miller & Nardini, 1977; Miller, Rossbach & Munson, 1981).

Several habitual cognitive patterns appear either to insulate people from the ill effects of stress or leave them especially vulnerable to those effects. Final conclusions are not yet possible, but numerous studies suggest that, in the long run, people suffer fewer stress-related problems when they

- focus attention on stressful events;
- perceive those events as temporary, nondisastrous challenges for which they take no blame;
- feel optimistic about overcoming the stressors.

Stress-related problems tend to be more common among people who persist at mentally evading stressors; perceive them as long-term, catastrophic threats that they brought on themselves; and are pessimistic about their ability to overcome the stressors (e.g., Bandura, 1989; Kobasa, Maddi & Zola, 1983; Miller, Brody & Summerton, 1988; Peterson, Seligman & Vaillant, 1988; Scheier & Carver, 1987). In fact, this research suggests that individual differences in how stressors are perceived combine with emotional and other factors to create the "disease-prone" or "stress-resistant" personalities described in Chapter 14 (Eysenck, 1988; Friedman & Booth-Kewley, 1987; Kobasa, 1982; Levy et al., 1987; McClelland, 1989; Watson & Pennebaker, 1989).

Social Support If you have ever appreciated the comforting presence of a good friend during troubled times or had to endure a bad experience on your own, you can probably vouch for the importance of social support in tempering the impact of stressful events. Social support consists of resources provided by other persons; friends and social contacts on whom you can depend for support form your **social support network** (Cohen & Syme, 1985; Gottlieb, 1981). The support may take many forms, including giving assistance in dealing with stressors (such as helping with car trouble, money problems, or other daily hassles) and buffering the impact of stressors by providing companionship, ideas for effective coping, and reassurance that one is cared about and valued and that everything will eventually be all right (Cohen & Wills, 1985; Rook, 1987; Sarason & Sarason, 1985; Schaefer, Coyne & Lazarus, 1982). Thus, even when social support cannot eliminate stressors, it can help people to feel less anxious, more optimistic, more capable of control, and more willing to try new ways of dealing with stressors.

The stress-reducing effects of social support have been documented in a wide range of research (House, Landis & Umberson, 1988; Thoits, 1986). For example, Andrew Billings and Rudolph Moos (1984, 1985) found that depression over major life stresses (divorce, unemployment, illness, or family conflict) was less severe among people who had more supportive social networks. In a pair of studies on undergraduate and graduate students, those with the least adequate social support networks suffered more emotional distress and were more vulnerable to upper respiratory infections during times of high academic stress than classmates who were part of a supportive network (Goplerud, 1980; Jemmott & Magloire, 1988). Indeed, one team of researchers concluded that having inadequate social support is as dangerous as smoking cigarettes or engaging in other unhealthy behaviors because it nearly doubles a person's risk of dying from disease, suicide, or other causes (House, Landis & Umberson, 1988).

The AIDS memorial quilt provides a tangible reminder of the important role of social support in helping people to cope with stressors of all kinds. People usually adjust better to their own illness, the death of a loved one, a divorce, or other crises if they have supportive friends and family around them (Holahan & Moos, 1987; Vachon, et al., 1980.)

But perhaps you noticed a problem here. The quality of social support may influence a person's ability to cope with stress, but the relationship may also work the other way around: people's ability to cope may determine the quality of social support they receive (Billings & Moos, 1981; Dunkel-Schetter, Folkman & Lazarus, 1987). For example, people who complain endlessly about stressors but never try to do anything about them may discourage social support, while those with an optimistic, action-oriented approach may attract reliable support.

In other words, the relationship between social support and the impact of stressors is not simple. Further, having too much support or support of the wrong kind can be as bad as not having enough. When friends and family overprotect a person, he or she may put less energy into coping efforts. Overly protective family support has been associated with increased disability and a tendency not to return to work after an accident or illness (Garrity, 1973; Hyman, 1971; Wortman, 1984). Similarly, tragic results may come from support for maladaptive responses, such as ignoring the early symptoms of a serious disease or eating an unhealthy diet (Kaplan & Hartwell, 1987; Pilisuk, Boylan & Acredolo, 1987). Further, if the efforts of a social support network become annoying, disruptive, or interfering, they may increase stress and intensify psychological problems (Pagel, Erdley & Becker, 1987).

Coping Skills Having adequate stress-coping skills is important for other reasons as well. Just as a football player in a sturdy helmet and protective pads is far less likely to be hurt in a game than someone wearing a T-shirt and cutoffs, people who are better equipped to cope with stress usually suffer fewer ill effects (Aldwin & Revenson, 1987). The numerous ways in which people cope with stressors have been categorized as *appraisal-focused*—thinking about stressors as challenges rather than threats, say; *problem-focused*—trying to alter or eliminate a source of stress by seeking help or planning strategies for handling money problems, for example; or *emotion-focused*—e.g., controlling negative emotions through calming thoughts or emotional detachment (Folkman & Lazarus, 1985; Moos & Billings, 1982). Other, more detailed classification systems include more specific coping methods, such as venting emotions, turning to religion, escaping via drugs, and the like (Carver, Scheier & Weintraub, 1989; Folkman et al., 1986; Rohde et al., 1990; Stone, Helder & Schneider, 1988). Some of these methods will be mentioned in our later discussion of how to cope with stress.

In Review: Stress Responses and Stress Mediators

Responses and Mediators	Examples
Responses	
Physical	Fight-or-flight syndrome (increased heart rate, respiration, and muscle tension, sweating, pupillary dilation); release of adrenaline, cortisol, and other chemicals. Eventual breakdown of organ systems involved in prolonged resistance to stressors.
Psychological	Anger, anxiety, depression, and other emotional states (sometimes leading to continuous anxiety or panic attacks); inability to concentrate or think logically; catastrophic thinking; use or overuse of defense mechanisms.
Behavioral	Aggression and escape/avoidance tactics (including suicide); disruptions in skilled performance.
Mediators	
Predictability	A tornado that strikes without warning may have a more devastating emotional impact than a long-predicted hurricane.
Control	Repairing a disabled spacecraft may be less stressful for the astronauts doing the work than for their loved ones on Earth, who can do nothing to help.
Interpretation	Thinking of a difficult new job as a challenge will create less discomfort than focusing on the likelihood of failure.
Social support	Having no one to talk to about a rape or other trauma may amplify the negative impact of the experience.
Coping skills	Having no effective way to relax after a hard day may prolong tension and other stress responses.

This review of factors that can alter the impact of stressors should make it obvious that what is stressful for a given individual is not determined simply by predispositions, coping styles, or situations. (See "In Review: Stress Responses and Stress Mediators.") What seems most important are interactions between the person and the situation, the mixture of each individual's resources and the specific characteristics of the situations encountered.

Stress, Illness, and Health

Several studies mentioned so far have suggested that stress plays a role in the appearance of physical illness. Those studies are part of a much larger body of research that has shed light not only on the stress-illness relationship but also on how people can use this knowledge to preserve their health.

Stress-Related Illness

The Type A behavior pattern involves far more than just working hard. Type A individuals are more interested in their achievements in the world of work than in social relationships. They often display selfishness, a strong fear of failure, and considerable hostility toward those whom they feel stand in the way of their success (Wright, 1988). The Type A pattern has been detected in people as young as eleven, and general predispositions for Type A behavior may appear much earlier (MacEvoy, et al., 1988; Matthews & Siegel, 1983.) However, the pattern usually emerges most clearly in adolescence or early adulthood (Steinberger, 1986; Wright, 1988).

Linkages: How might stress cause illness? (a link to Biological Aspects of Psychology)

During the 1940s and 1950s, work on the relationship between stress and illness focused on the role of psychological factors in Selye's diseases of adaptation. Particular attention was directed at bronchial asthma, high blood pressure, migraine headaches, stomach ulcers, arthritis, and other disorders associated with overarousal of the autonomic nervous system. Official classifications of mental disorders began to include *psychosomatic* or *psychophysiological* disorders; that is, physical problems that can clearly be brought on by psychological factors, such as frustration or conflict. Research now suggests that stressors and stress responses can set the stage for, worsen, or perhaps even cause almost any kind of physical illness, not just those that had been considered psychosomatic (Gatchel, Baum & Krantz, 1989).

One example is Alzheimer's disease, which causes severe memory loss. Some evidence suggests that the degeneration of the brain in Alzheimer's disease is worsened when cortisol is released during stress (Landfield, Baskin & Pitler, 1981; Sapolsky, Krey & McEwen, 1985). Specifically, it appears that too much cortisol can make some neurons in the hippocampus—an area important for normal memory—more likely to die prematurely (DeLeon et al., 1988).

Stress responses have also been linked to coronary heart disease. The discovery of this relationship began years ago, when two cardiologists, Meyer Friedman and Ray Rosenman (1959, 1974) noticed that the front edges of their waiting room chairs were being worn out especially fast. It was as if patients with heart disease were always on the edge of their seats. Interviews revealed that, indeed, many of the patients displayed a pattern of behavior that Friedman and Rosenman ultimately called Type A. People who display the **Type A** pattern tend to be impatient, intensely competitive, aggressive, hostile, and nonstop workers. They constantly attempt to do more and more in less and less time. They need to control events and tend to become very upset if they feel they cannot do so (Glass, 1977). While complaining bitterly about the amount of work they have to do, they also appear to crave constant evidence of their superior achievement. They seek out the most challenging and stressful work situations, thereby prompting supervisors and coworkers to channel even more work their way (Feather & Volkmer, 1988; Kirmeyer & Biggers, 1988; Smith & Anderson, 1986; Strube et al., 1987).

Apparently, it was no accident that a disproportionate number of Type A's appeared in a cardiology office. People who display the Type A pattern are more than twice as likely to suffer heart disease than their **Type B** peers, who are more relaxed and easygoing (Matthews, 1982; Rosenman et al., 1975; Siegel, 1984). The link between Type A behavior and heart disease is not always strong or consistent, however (Dimsdale, 1988; Matthews, 1988; Ragland & Brand, 1988; Suls & Wan, 1989). Not all Type A's are at equal risk. Some researchers suggest that it is not the Type A pattern as a whole that predicts heart disease but only certain elements of the pattern. The "toxic" components of the Type A pattern seem to be hostility, anger, cynicism, and time urgency, combined with the tendency to bottle up emotional expression and to ignore early symptoms of cardiac problems (Carver, Coleman & Glass, 1976; Dembroski & Williams, 1989; Matthews, 1988; Wright, 1988).

The precise mechanism underlying the relationship between Type A and illness is not clear (Friedman & Booth-Kewley, 1988). According to one theory, the physical stress responses of some Type A's include both constriction of peripheral blood vessels and increasing heart rate. Like a driver who damages a car by simultaneously flooring the accelerator and applying the brakes, these "hot reactors" may create excessive wear and tear on the arteries in the heart (Contrada, 1989; Elliot & Buell, 1983). There is even more evidence to support the theory that the more or less constant emotional stress responses of Type A's are accompanied by surges of hormones (particularly the catecholamines adrenaline and noradrenaline) into the bloodstream, which lead to increased fatty deposits in the arteries and, in turn, to heart disease (Dembroski & Williams, 1989). It has even been suggested that these hormone surges become—like salivation in Pavlov's dogs—classically conditioned responses to stress cues such as the sight of a classroom or workplace (Wright, 1988). The "toxic" components of the Type A pattern may also increase the risk of infections and other illnesses in addition to heart disease (Lazarus & Folkman, 1984; Suls & Sanders, 1988). The key to this relationship appears to lie in the physiological reactions to stress and their effects on the immune system.

HIGHLIGHT

Stress, Health, and the Immune System

The role of physiological stress responses in reducing the body's ability to fight disease was demonstrated more than a century ago. On March 19, 1878, at a seminar before the Academie de Médécine de Paris, Louis Pasteur showed his distinguished audience three chickens. One healthy bird, the control chicken, had been raised normally. A second bird had been intentionally infected with bacteria but given no other treatment; it was also healthy. The third chicken Pasteur presented was dead. It had been infected with the same bacteria as the second bird, but it had also been physically stressed by being exposed to cold temperatures (Kelley, 1985); as a result, the bacteria killed it.

The search conducted since Pasteur's time has greatly expanded our knowledge about how stressors affect the body's reaction to disease. **Psychoneuroimmunology** is the field that examines the interaction of psychological and physiological processes that affect the body's ability to defend itself against disease. The **immune system** is the body's first line of defense against invading substances and microorganisms. Impaired functioning of the immune system increases vulnerability to colds, mononucleosis, and many other infections (Jemmott & Locke, 1984; Jemmott & Magloire, 1988; Tecoma & Huey, 1985).

The mechanisms by which the nervous system affects the immune system are far from understood, but there is evidence for both endocrine and direct neural influences (Dunn, 1989). As mentioned earlier, when the body responds to physical or psychological stressors, cortisol and other corticosteroid hormones are released from the adrenal cortex. These hormones can suppress the responsiveness of the immune system, thus leaving the body more vulnerable to infection (Jessop, West & Sobotka, 1989; see Figure 13.4). Adrenaline secreted from the adrenal medulla under stress can also suppress immune cells, as do endogenous opiates (which also ease pain). There are also direct neural connections from the autonomic nervous system to cells of the immune system. This link can enhance or suppress immune functioning in different circumstances, the nature of which are still being studied (Dunn, 1989).

Thus, the "toxic" elements of the Type A pattern may be linked with disease partly because they bring excessive or prolonged secretion of catecholamines and corticosteroids, which ultimately weakens the body's immune system. There is even some evidence that stress-related suppression of the immune system may create vulnerability to certain forms of cancer (Cooper, 1985; Cox, 1984; Justice, 1985; Kiecolt-Glaser & Glaser, 1987).

Among the cells that form the army of the immune system are *T-cells,* which attack virally infected cells; *B-cells,* which form antibodies against foreign substances; and *natural killer cells,* which kill invaders like tumor cells and virally infected cells. Here, a patrolling immune system cell sends out an extension known as a *pseudopod* to engulf and destroy a bacterial cell before alerting more defenders.

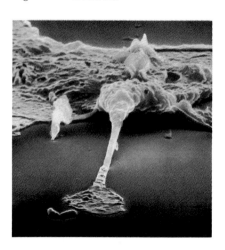

Source: Lennart Nilsson © Boehringer Ingelheim International GMBH.

"Mrs. Davis, I think I have to slow down."

Source: Drawing by Weber; © 1990 The New Yorker Magazine, Inc.

The effects of stress on the immune system and on health are not straightforward, however. For example, the stress of crowded living conditions increases chickens' susceptibility to some diseases but reduces their susceptibility to others (Gross & Colmano, 1969). Still, two characteristics of physical stress reactions in general also apply to the effect of stressors on the immune system.

First, psychological as well as physical stressors can affect the immune system. For example, husbands of women who died of cancer have shown diminished immune function for several months during bereavement (Schleifer et al., 1983). Among students, immune system activity has been found to be significantly lower during finals than during the period before or after exams (Jemmott & Magloire, 1988; Kiecolt-Glaser et al., 1984).

Second, psychological variables help regulate the impact of a stressor. More specifically, the effect of a stressor on the immune system depends on how the organism *copes* with it. For example, in several studies, rats were given mild but distressing shock to the toes, which they either could or could not escape by pressing a bar in the cage. Even though animals in both conditions experienced the same amount of shock, those unable to cope with it through bar pressing showed impaired functioning of the immune system (Laudenslager et al., 1983). In humans, people whose coping style includes self-blame when stressors occur have been found to show greater immune impairment than those who are less hard on themselves (Peterson, Seligman & Vaillant, 1988).

Research on stress-mediating factors that might dampen the impact of stressors on the immune system has focused largely on the benefits of social support (Cohen & Hoberman, 1983; Cohen & Wills, 1985; House, Landis & Umberson, 1988). For example, immune system functioning among students who can get emotional help from friends during stress appears better than among those with less adequate social support (Jemmott & Magloire, 1988). Social support may also help speed healing. Richard Lucas (1975) found faster recovery from surgery among patients who received extra attention and reassurance from the medical staff. Indeed, there is general evidence that people with better social support networks live longer than those with less support (Berkman & Syme, 1979).

No one knows exactly how social support dampens the physical impact of stressors. One possibility is that members of a helpful social support network provide encouragement to eat right, exercise, and engage in other healthy behaviors (House, Robbins & Metzner, 1982). There is also evidence that, in animals as well as humans, social contact with familiar members of one's species can modulate cardiac functioning and inhibit the potentially harmful excess secretion of catecholamines and cortisol (Bovard, 1985; Lynch, 1979). Finally, James Pennebaker (1985) has suggested that social support helps prevent illness mainly by providing the person under stress with an opportunity to express pent-up thoughts and emotions. Keeping important things to oneself, says Pennebaker, is itself a form of stress (Pennebaker, Colder & Sharp, 1990). In the laboratory, for example, subjects who were asked to try to deceive an experimenter displayed elevated physiological arousal (Pennebaker & Chew, 1985; Waid & Orne, 1981). Further, the spouses of suicide or accidental death victims who do not or cannot confide their feelings to others are most likely to develop physical illnesses during the year following the death (Pennebaker & O'Heeron, 1984). Future research in psychoneuroimmunology promises to reveal vital links in the complex chain of mental and physical events that determine whether people become ill or stay healthy. ■

Health Psychology

Research on stress and illness has done much to focus attention on how social, environmental, and behavioral factors affect health. This work fits nicely with evidence gathered during the 1970s that certain behaviors increase the risk of illness. Survey studies showed, for example, that smoking cigarettes, eating a high-cholesterol or high-salt diet, and getting too little exercise were important risk factors for heart disease, stroke, cancer, emphysema, and other serious illnesses. In one decade-long study in Alameda County, California, the death rate for men who did not smoke, drank alcohol in moderation, regularly slept seven or eight hours a night, ate breakfast, kept their weight within normal limits, and got regular exercise was almost four times lower than for those who followed three or fewer of these practices (Wiley & Camacho, 1980).

The 1970s were also a time of increased recognition that people's knowledge of illness and their reaction to illness can have a lot to do with its impact. Those who pay attention to their bodies (through regular checkups, for example), seek medical attention if symptoms appear, and carefully follow instructions about taking medication are more likely to remain healthy or to have serious illnesses treated early enough to make cure and rehabilitation possible.

Overall, it has been estimated that 50 to 70 percent of deaths from America's leading killers (including heart disease, cancer, stroke, auto accidents, diabetes, and cirrhosis of the liver) are attributable to unhealthy behavior patterns (Hamburg, Elliot & Parron, 1982; Lawrence, 1989). Recognizing that people have far more power than once imagined to prevent illness and preserve health, health-related professionals are now working together to find ways to use behavioral science to aid in the prevention, detection, and treatment of physical disease (Schwartz & Weiss, 1978). This broad-based movement, focused on how behavior and illness are linked, has become known as **behavioral**

medicine, and the subfield in which psychologists work to promote health, prevent illness, and conduct research on both has been labeled **health psychology** (Gatchel, Baum & Krantz, 1989; Matarazzo, 1980; Seeman, 1989).

Health psychologists teach patients to think pleasant thoughts and to use regulated breathing to ease the discomfort of painful medical tests; to prepare themselves mentally for the stress of heart surgery, thus speeding recovery; and to reduce the frequency of headaches through progressive relaxation or other special training. They also organize smoking-cessation clinics, weight-control and exercise programs, public education campaigns about high blood pressure, and similar efforts to alter behaviors that promote illness (Gebhardt & Crump, 1990).

One of the most important efforts in health psychology today is to prevent the spread of Acquired Immune Deficiency Syndrome (AIDS). Some researchers estimate that AIDS will soon affect 270,000 people in the United States and 50 to 100 million worldwide (Kelly & St. Lawrence, 1988). To help stem this epidemic, some health psychologists are working on public information campaigns that disseminate information about how AIDS is transmitted and how people can protect themselves. The phrasing and content of this information is shaped by research in social psychology, discussed in Chapter 17, on how to get people to accept and act on, rather than shut out, fear-provoking health messages. Health psychologists are also fighting AIDS by offering programs to help people practice safer sex (such as by using condoms) and to learn the cognitive and social communication skills needed to refuse to engage in high-risk sexual activities (Coates, 1990; Kelly et al., 1989; Roffman et al., 1988). They also help people infected with the AIDS virus to deal with stress stemming from the disease or from uncertainty about the future (Gatchel, Baum & Krantz, 1989). This work is vital because the immune-impairing effects of stress may hasten the progress of AIDS (Coates et al., 1987).

Health psychology is a rapidly growing field that offers many career opportunities. In the following section on coping with stress, we give further examples of research and treatment programs related to health psychology.

Coping with Stress

Linkages: How can people be helped to cope with stress? (a link to Treatment of Psychological Disorders)

Just as people with extra money in the bank can weather a financial crisis, those with stress-coping skills may escape even the harmful effects of intense stress. Like family money, the ability to handle stress appears to come naturally to some people, but coping can also be learned. In this section we briefly review the basic components of an effective stress-coping plan, some specific coping methods, and some programs designed to help people who face severe stressors.

A Plan for Coping

The first step in learning to cope with stress is to make a systematic assessment of the problem. This assessment involves (1) identifying sources of stress, which means listing events and situations that contain conflict, change, and other stressors; and (2) noting the physical effects of stress, such as headaches, lack of concentration, or excessive drinking. This survey helps establish the degree to which stress is disrupting your life.

Once you have pinpointed the sources and effects of stress, select an appropriate goal. Should you try to eliminate stressors or to alter your response to them? Knowing the difference between changeable and unchangeable stressors is important. If your current major has become a source of severe stress, you might change your major, but simply refusing to take stressful exams would not be wise. Stress-related problems appear especially prevalent among people who either exhaust themselves trying to change stressors that cannot be changed or who pass up opportunities to change those that can (Folkman, 1984). One example comes from a study of people who lived near the Three Mile Island nuclear reactor when the accident occurred there. Those who acted as if they could alter the consequences of the accident reported more symptoms of psychological stress than those who focused on accepting their situation (Collins, Baum & Singer, 1983).

Assessment and goal setting are just the first steps in a stress-management program. The entire sequence is laid out in Table 13.4.

Methods of Coping

No one method of coping with stressors is universally successful. For example, denying the existence of an uncontrollable stressor may be fine in the short run but may lead to problems if no other coping method is used (Suls & Fletcher, 1985). Similarly, people who rely exclusively on an active problem-solving approach may handle controllable stressors but find themselves nearly helpless in the face of uncontrollable ones (Rodin & Salovey, 1989). Fortunately, most people maintain a varied arsenal of coping methods.

The individuals most successful at stress management may be those best able to adjust their coping methods to the demands of changing situations and differing stressors (Carver, Scheier & Weintraub, 1989; Costa & McCrae, 1989; Folkman et al., 1986; House, Umberson & Landis, 1988). In a study of student nurses, for example, those who felt most in control of stressors reported taking direct action to alter changeable stressors while tending to accept or just not think about those that they saw as unchangeable. Those who felt less in control took less direct action and engaged in more inefficient, often wishful, thinking and denial—regardless of whether the stressors were changeable (Parkes, 1984). Similar results have been reported in other studies (e.g., Carver, Scheier & Weintraub, 1989; Folkman & Lazarus, 1980).

Table 13.4
Stages in Coping with Stress

Most successful stress-coping programs move systematically through several stages and aim to remove stressors that can be changed and reduce stress responses to stressors that remain (Silver & Wortman, 1980).

Stage	Task
1. Assessment	Identify the sources and effects of stress.
2. Goal setting	List the stressors and stress responses to be addressed.
	Designate which stressors are and are not changeable.
3. Planning	List the specific steps to be taken to cope with stress.
4. Action	Implement stress-coping plans.
5. Evaluation	Determine the changes in stressors and stress responses that have occurred as a result of stress-coping methods.
6. Adjustment	Alter coping methods to improve results, if necessary.

Like stress responses, strategies for coping with stress can be cognitive, behavioral, or physical. Together, these strategies can help reduce or eliminate stressors and minimize the intensity of stress responses.

Cognitive Coping Strategies   Cognitive methods involve changing how people interpret stressors. *Cognitive coping strategies* help people think more calmly, rationally, and constructively in the face of stress.

For example, students with heavy course loads, conflicts with parents, and numerous daily hassles may experience anxiety, confusion, discouragement, lack of motivation, and the desire to run away from it all through excessive involvement in anything from movies to drugs. Frightening, catastrophic thoughts students have about these stressors (e.g., "What if I fail?") can amplify maladaptive stress responses to the point that the failure they fear does indeed occur. Cognitive coping strategies replace catastrophic thinking with thoughts in which stressors are viewed as challenges rather than threats to self-esteem (Ellis & Bernard, 1985). This substitution process is often called **cognitive restructuring** (Lazarus, 1971; Meichenbaum, 1977). It can be done by practicing constructive thoughts such as "All I can do is the best I can." Coping by "talking to yourself" also allows a person to focus on constructive work rather than on fruitless worry and may generate a more hopeful emotional state. Cognitive coping does not eliminate stressors, but it can make them less threatening and disruptive. Thus, an overburdened student will still feel the pressure of college and will still want to succeed, but the prospect of failure will seem less horrible and the need for perfection less pressing.

Behavioral Coping Strategies   Even though people learn to think more calmly about deadlines and other stressors, they may have too many stressors occurring too close together and no plan for dealing with them. This is where behavioral coping methods come in. If you rearrange your world in ways that minimize the impact of stressors, you are using *behavioral coping strategies*.

Time management is one form of behavioral coping. For example, you might keep track of your time for a week and start a *time-management plan*. As shown on the left side of Table 13.5, the first step is to set out a schedule that shows how time is now typically spent. This initial schedule demonstrates that time is limited and pinpoints where time is and is not being used efficiently. It can also help identify all that needs to be done and how much time is available for each activity. Sometimes, a schedule like this makes it clear that some activities have to go. Or it may lead to other behavioral coping methods, such as following a more disciplined schedule or enrolling in a course to make study skills more efficient. Time management can also help control catastrophizing thoughts by providing visual reassurance that there is enough time for everything and a plan for handling it all.

Behavioral methods of coping with stress also involve paying attention to the total load of stressors and acting to keep it within manageable limits. Suppose you have a full course load, a part-time job, and a busy social life. Perhaps you are a single parent. You are often tired but manage to handle everything reasonably well. Now a professor offers you an unpaid research job that will increase your stress load, possibly beyond your ability to cope with it. Should you accept the job? As discussed in Chapter 11, on motivation, conflicts—especially approach-avoidance conflicts like this one—prompt some people to make almost any decision impulsively, just to have it over with. But there is a better way of coping with the stress of the conflict. By listing and examining the pros and cons and the potential costs and benefits of each course of action, you can analyze the problem carefully and rationally, then reach a decision based on that analysis.

Table 13.5
Time-Management Planning

A time-management plan aims to lessen stress by allocating time more efficiently. A complete plan would include schedules for each day of the week, with adjustments for special occasions and exam periods.

A Typical Day Now		Plan for a Time-Managed Day	
Time	*Activity*	*Time*	*Activity*
8:00 A.M.	Sleep		
8:30 A.M.	Continue sleeping	6:30–7:15 A.M.	Exercise
		7:15 A.M.	Shower; dress
9:00 A.M.	Shower; dress	8:00–8:45 A.M.	Breakfast; read paper; review class notes
9:50 A.M.	Leave for second class of the day		
10:00 A.M.–Noon	Classes	9:00 A.M.–Noon	Classes
Noon–1:55 P.M.	Lunch; talk with friends	Noon–1:00 P.M.	Lunch; talk with friends
2:00–4:00 P.M.	Classes	1:00–2:00 P.M.	Do assigned readings
4:00–6:00 P.M.	Library job	2:00–4:00 P.M.	Classes
6:00–7:30 P.M.	Dinner; talk with friends	4:00–6:00 P.M.	Library job
		6:00–7:00 P.M.	Dinner; talk with friends
7:30–9:00 P.M.	Study	7:00–11:00 P.M.	Study
9:00–Midnight	Drink with friends at campus bar	11:00 P.M.–Midnight	Watch TV with friends

Behavioral and cognitive skills often interact closely. Thinking calmly makes it easier to develop and use sensible plans for behavioral coping. When behavioral coping eliminates or minimizes stressors, people find it easier to think and feel better about themselves.

Physical Coping Strategies   People also cope with stress by directly altering their physical responses before, during, or after stressors occur. The most common *physical coping strategy* is the use of drugs.

Chemical coping methods are appropriate in some cases, as when prescribed sedation helps parents endure the temporary shock that follows the death of a child. However, drugs provide only temporary relief from stress. Using short-term methods to deal with long-term stressors such as unemployment or marital discord can lead to continued use of drugs and thus to addiction, physical illness, debt, and other problems. Moreover, when people depend on drugs to help them face stress, they often attribute any success to the drug, not to their own skill. This loss of perceived control over stressors may make the stressors even more threatening and disruptive. Finally, the same drug effects that blunt stress responses may also interfere with the ability to apply cognitive and behavioral coping strategies.

Nonchemical methods of reducing physical stress reactions include progressive relaxation training, physical exercise, biofeedback, and meditation (described in Chapter 6), among others. These procedures lead to a pleasant state of reduced physiological arousal (Carrington, 1984; Tarler-Benlolo, 1978). People can learn to use them at will, either to combat stressors as they occur or to calm down afterward. We will describe just two examples.

In **biofeedback training**, special equipment records stress-related physiological activity, such as heart rate, blood pressure, and muscle tension. The equipment continuously feeds this information to a person in the form of a

Exercise is an important physical strategy for coping with stress. It improves physical fitness and reduces the threat of coronary heart disease and other stress-related illnesses. There is also some evidence that physical exercise can reduce anxiety and depression for periods ranging from thirty minutes to several hours (Long, 1985; Sime, 1984).

changing tone or meter reading. With practice, some people can develop mental strategies that control these physiological processes and then use these strategies to reduce some stress responses in everyday situations (Budzynski & Stoyva, 1984). Whether biofeedback can have significant and enduring effects on severe stress-related problems such as high blood pressure and migraine headache is less certain (Gatchel, Baum & Krantz, 1989).

Progressive relaxation training is one of the most popular physical methods for coping with stress. Edmund Jacobson developed progressive relaxation techniques during the 1930s as a way of reducing tension in muscles that are under voluntary control, thus leading to reductions in heart rate and blood pressure and creating calmness (Jacobson, 1938; Paul, 1969b). Today, progressive relaxation training is learned by tensing a group of muscles (such as the hand and lower arm) for a few seconds, then releasing the tension and focusing on the resulting feelings of relaxation. This procedure is repeated at least once for each of sixteen muscle groups throughout the body (Bernstein & Borkovec, 1973). The basic procedures are learned and practiced while reclining comfortably in a quiet, dimly lit room. Once some skill at relaxation is developed, it can be used to calm down anywhere and anytime, often without lying down (Blanchard & Andrasik, 1985; Wolpe, 1982). ("In Review: Methods for Coping with Stress" summarizes our discussion of stress-coping methods. See p. 529.)

Some Stress-Coping Programs

Sometimes stressors and stress reactions are too intense, surprising, or otherwise overwhelming for people to handle without the help of mental health professionals. Psychologists and others involved in mental health care offer special stress-coping programs that give information, support, and training in coping skills (Ivancevich et al., 1990). When people develop these skills, they are more likely to be able to handle the next set of stressors on their own. Here we describe briefly a few stress-management programs.

Changing Type A Behavior We noted earlier that people who display certain "toxic" components of the Type A pattern—particularly anger, hostility, cynicism, and a sense of time urgency—may be especially vulnerable to coronary heart disease. Researchers have developed programs to reduce the health risks faced by Type A individuals by altering their frantic lifestyles and the intensity of their stress reactions.

In one study, the goal was to prevent second heart attacks in Type A individuals who had already had one (Friedman et al., 1986). Over a thousand of these heart attack patients received either (1) routine post-heart-attack counseling (such as advice about diet and exercise); (2) routine counseling plus a Type A modification program; or (3) no treatment. The modification program included relaxation training, group discussion of the reasons for Type A behavior and its dangers, making changes (such as saying no to overtime assignments) designed to reduce stressors, and slowing the pace of life by eating more slowly and taking time out to do nothing. After five years, recurrence of heart attacks was significantly lower among people who received the counseling plus Type A modification program than among groups that received either the routine counseling or no treatment (see Figure 13.8).

Similar programs have altered the behavior of healthy Type A people (Levenkron et al., 1983; Roskies et al., 1986), but it is not yet known whether the interventions actually prevent first heart attacks. Thus, more research is needed to evaluate the value of stress-management programs for healthy Type

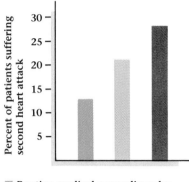

■ Routine medical counseling plus
   Type A modification program

░ Routine medical counseling alone

■ No counseling

Source: Friedman, et al., 1986.

Figure 13.8
Results of a Stress-Management Program
Friedman et al. (1986) found that Type A heart attack victims were significantly less likely to suffer second attacks if they received help in altering their Type A behavior in addition to routine medical counseling. This finding bodes especially well for these people's health because there is evidence that even Type A heart patients who receive no such help are already less likely to die of recurring heart attacks than Type B heart attack patients (Ragland & Brand, 1988). The reasons for this difference in long-term survival rates are not entirely clear. One possibility is that heart attacks in Type A's are brought on more by the intensity of their stress reactions than by an overall deterioration in their hearts (Brackett & Powell, 1988; Matthews, 1988). Thus, the hearts of Type A's may be in better condition after an attack than the hearts of Type B's. Whatever the case, the success of Friedman's program underscores the importance of stress-coping programs in cardiac rehabilitation.

A's. Such research is difficult, however, because these people are usually unwilling to take time out to learn to slow down (Wright, 1988). Whoever the subjects are, future programs are likely to focus on reducing hostility and other "toxic" elements of the Type A pattern.

Illness, Surgery, and Noxious Medical Procedures   Illness, surgery, and unpleasant medical procedures bring pain, lack of control, and other stressors. People who are the least prepared to deal with such stressors often become especially angry, anxious, and depressed (Cohen & Lazarus, 1979; Gatchel, Baum & Krantz, 1989). They also tend to experience more pain, need more medication, recover more slowly, and, at least among heart attack patients, have a lower survival rate (Garrity, 1975; Melamed & Siegel, 1980; Scheier et al., 1989). To combat these problems, health psychologists have developed special stress-management programs for patients who face medical procedures or chronic illnesses such as cancer, heart disease, and asthma (Carey & Burish, 1988; Ludwick-Rosenthal & Neufeld, 1988; Peterson, 1989).

In one experiment, adult surgical patients were given relaxation training, information about surgical procedures and postoperative pain, or both (Wilson, 1981). Compared with a control group that received no special preparation, patients who received both treatments had less pain and pain medication, felt better emotionally, began walking sooner, and went home earlier. Studies like this underscore the importance of helping surgery patients to develop behavioral coping strategies to use before and after surgery (MacDonald & Kuiper, 1983).

Another study demonstrated that distraction can help children cope with the discomfort of cancer chemotherapy (Redd et al., 1987). Those in the experimental group were allowed to play attention-getting video games while receiving their anticancer drugs. They reported significantly less anxiety and nausea (a common side effect) than a no-distraction control group.

Dealing with Trauma   Building on research in stress management, psychologists and other mental health professionals have helped hospitals, government agencies, and community groups create programs designed to help people cope with the psychological aftermath of traumas. Sometimes, as when a major earthquake struck San Francisco in 1989, the impact is communitywide and requires dozens of counselors to help victims deal with the sudden loss of family or friends, and also with more subtle problems such as feelings of guilt over having survived. Smaller-scale efforts have helped the families of victims of terrorist bombings or mass murder.

Perhaps the most common and personalized programs are those offered to rape victims by hospitals, mental health clinics, or women's advocacy and support groups. These programs make it easier for the victim to report a rape (perhaps through a special hotline number). Female counselors may provide information, advice, and support while the victim is being examined at a hospital or questioned by police. Counseling sessions help victims to express and start coping with the anger, humiliation, fear, guilt, and other emotional stress responses stemming from the attack. They may also discuss strategies for coping with such problems as fear of being alone, aversion to sexual activity, or conflict with husbands or boyfriends (Peters, 1977). The staff also guides the most seriously disturbed individuals to seek more formal psychotherapeutic help.

Coping with Major Changes: Widowhood and Divorce   Special stress-management programs are widely available to help individuals deal with the breakup of a marriage or the death of a spouse. For example, Carol Barrett

In Review: Methods for Coping with Stress

Type of Coping Method	Examples
Cognitive	Thinking of stressors as challenges rather than as threats; avoiding perfectionism.
Behavioral	Implementing a time-management plan; using systematic problem-solving and decision-making methods; where possible, making life changes to eliminate stressors.
Physical	Progressive relaxation training, exercise, biofeedback, meditation.

(1978) offered widows in the Los Angeles area one of three experiences: a confidante group, which emphasized the development of social support through close personal friendships; a consciousness-raising group, which focused on discussing the social role of widows; and a self-help group, which discussed ways of dealing with loneliness, grief, financial difficulties, legal matters, social interaction with men, and other problems that widows typically face. Each group met for two hours a week for seven weeks. Measures of personality, attitudes, and behaviors were taken before and as long as fourteen weeks after the program. Compared with an untreated group, the women in all three groups tended to feel more in control of their lives and more optimistic about their health.

Valuable as stress-management programs can be, they are not cures for stress. Long-term success in the form of reduced stress responsiveness and improved coping skills usually comes only to those who also work on their own to practice and improve on what formal programs have to offer.

Linkages: Stress and Thinking

How does stress change the ability to solve problems and make decisions?

In January 1989, a fire broke out in the left engine of a twin-engine British Midlands Airways jetliner over central England. For reasons that are still not entirely clear, the pilot mistakenly shut down the plane's right engine, after which the plane crashed, killing 44 people. This incident and nuclear power plant accidents at Three Mile Island in Pennsylvania and Chernobyl in the Soviet Union—as well as the release of toxic gas that killed thousands around a chemical plant in Bopal, India—have all been due, in part at least, to human error (Reason, 1990). A common factor in most of these events was that the mental performance of the people responsible was disrupted by pressure, conflict, boredom, or other stressors.

The potentially fatal impact of stressors lies primarily in their ability to alter physiological arousal. As mentioned in Chapter 11, a moderate level of arousal may improve a person's ability to perform a task, but overarousal or underarousal can interfere with the efficient processing of information, and performance may suffer (see Figure 11.4). Thus, if boredom produces enough underarousal that inattention results, a railroad worker may fail to throw a crucial switch, causing a fatal collision.

When stressors increase arousal beyond an optimum level, the ability to perform cognitive tasks, including thinking and speaking coherently, may be disrupted.

BLOOM COUNTY   **by Berke Breathed**

Overarousal is also dangerous because performance of complex and difficult tasks—such as dealing with airborne emergencies—are the first to be disrupted as arousal increases above a moderate level. Why? One reason is that increased arousal strengthens the tendency to perform behaviors that are most *dominant*, the ones a person knows best. This reaction may aid performance of an easy, familiar task (like riding a bike), but on more difficult or unfamiliar tasks, the well-learned behaviors overarousal elicits may be inappropriate. Foreign tourists in Britain, for example, when overaroused by the frustration, pressure, and change of their first attempt to drive on the left side of the road, tend to revert to their old habit of entering the right-hand lane as they make right turns. This tendency causes numerous head-on collisions each year.

Overarousal created by stressors also impairs performance on difficult tasks by interfering in several ways with people's ability to think clearly about complex material. For one thing, it tends to narrow the range of attention. Stress-narrowed attention, in turn, may intensify many of the problems in problem solving discussed in Chapter 9. For example, it can accentuate the tendency to cling to *mental sets*, which are established, though possibly inefficient, approaches to problems. The consequent inability to scan a wide range of creative solutions may add to the time needed to make decisions, solve problems, or reason efficiently (Darke, 1988; Keinan, Friedland & Ben-Porath, 1987). More specifically, stress can intensify *functional fixedness*, which is the tendency to use objects for only one purpose. People in hotel fires, for example, sometimes die trapped in their rooms because it did not occur to them to use the telephone or a piece of furniture to break a window.

The disruption of thinking ability by stressors can also occur through a splitting of attention. When trying to perform complex mental tasks under time pressure, for example, some people tend be distracted by worry about how much time is left and the consequences of failure (Baumeister, 1984). It is difficult to perform well on demanding mental tasks when attention is split in this way. Thus, participants on "Jeopardy!" and other game shows, pressured by time and the eyes of millions of viewers, sometimes miss questions that seem ridiculously easy to those watching calmly at home.

Decision making may also suffer when people face stressors. People who normally consider carefully all aspects of a situation before making a decision may, under stress, act impulsively and sometimes foolishly (Keinan, Friedland & Ben-Porath, 1987). Couples whose dating relationships have been full of conflict may suddenly decide to break up and then, just as suddenly, get married. High-pressure salespeople try to take advantage of people's tendency to act impulsively when under the influence of stressors by creating artificially time-limited offers or by telling customers that others are waiting to buy the item they are considering (Cialdini, 1988).

The disruptive impact of stressors on cognitive functioning must be taken into account when assessing performance. The best candidate for a particular job may not make the best presentation under the stress of an interview. Similarly, if an intelligence test was taken under unusually stressful circumstances, one might legitimately be skeptical about the validity of a low score.

Research on the links among stress, thinking, and performance has helped alert decision makers to the importance of reducing the stress under which people perform complex tasks. For years, commercial pilots have been limited in the number of hours they may fly per day, and air-traffic controllers are encouraged to take breaks every two hours. But sometimes, as when an engine is on fire or a nuclear reactor malfunctions, extreme stress is inevitable. Under these circumstances, the goal must be to assure that people perform at peak efficiency and communicate and work together effectively. The Federal Aviation Administration, commercial airlines, and other organizations have instituted new research and training programs designed to increase the likelihood that people will cooperate effectively during a crisis, consider all their options, and pay attention to all information that might avert a tragedy (Adler, 1989).

Future Directions

Early conceptions of stress characterized stressors as fixed forces acting on people who display relatively automatic stress responses, much as a shelf might sag under the weight of heavy books. This perspective has been superseded by psychobiological models and other more complex approaches. These newer approaches view stress not just in terms of stressors and stress responses but as a process in which particular categories of stressors and particular people's thoughts, emotions, and coping efforts all play important roles in determining who will suffer stress-related problems (e.g., Hobfall, 1989).

In the future, this emphasis on person-situation combinations is likely to expand to focus on how people and situations reciprocally influence one another over time to determine stress and its impact. This trend is evident in research on how certain Type A individuals seek out high-stress situations to which they then react intensely. Similarly, research on coping and social support is turning toward questions such as how particular coping styles attract or repel support, thus buffering or amplifying stressors.

Viewing stress as a dynamic interaction over time will widen the scope of research in other ways as well. It has already increased the attention devoted to how individual differences, such as physical predispositions and cognitive styles, influence responses to stressors. Among the variables likely to receive attention are the desire for control over life events (Rodin, 1986b), the preference for continuous self-evaluation (Strube et al., 1987), and the tendency to be optimistic or pessimistic about negative events (Peterson, Seligman & Valliant, 1988). One recent study of heart bypass surgery patients showed, for example, that those with optimistic expectations about the future employed more adaptive coping strategies, recovered faster, returned to normal activities sooner, and attained a higher quality of life than those with pessimistic outlooks (Scheier et al., 1989). Future research will also focus on how cognitive styles such as optimism or pessimism develop and when. Finally, there is a clear need for more research on how differences in age, gender, and race influence stress responsiveness, coping, and vulnerability to stress-related disorders (Anderson, 1989; Rodin & Salovey, 1989).

Interest in individual differences is also evident in research on coping. We have mentioned research suggesting that people who cope by denying, minimizing, or otherwise avoiding confrontation of stressors are at greater long-term risk for stress-related illness and psychological distress than those whose coping is more active and direct (Holahan & Moos, 1987; 1990). More elaborate systems are being developed to measure exactly how people cope (Carver, Scheier & Weintraub, 1989; Endler & Parker, 1990; Rohde et al., 1990). Of interest as well will be questions about how coping skills develop and the degree to which they can be strengthened through modeling, formal training, and other means. There may also be research on adjusting environments to match individuals' coping styles. It has been suggested, for example, that hospitals should routinely assess patients' preferences for focusing on or avoiding stressors, and then adjust accordingly the information given to each patient about his or her illness (Miller, Brody & Summerton, 1988).

Current concepts of stress have helped to build bridges between psychology and other disciplines, from physiology to sociology. The field of psychoneuroimmunology is a case in point. Research that views stress from a broad, interdisciplinary perspective is likely to have sweeping implications for enhancing well-being, improving health, and prolonging life. As described at the beginning of this chapter, it has already stimulated research on ways to protect elderly people's weakened immune systems from the stress of feeling they have no control over their environment.

For a more detailed look at stress and stress management, consider taking courses in health psychology, behavioral medicine, stress and coping, or other stress-related topics. Most courses in abnormal psychology and some in personality also examine the relationships among stress, health, mental disorder, and individual characteristics.

Summary and Key Terms

What Is Stress?

The term *stress* refers in part to *stressors*, events and situations that place physical or psychological demands on people. The term is also used to refer to *stress reactions*. Most generally, however, stress is viewed as an ongoing, interactive process that takes place as people adjust to and cope with their environment.

Stressors

Major Psychological Stressors

Stressors may be physical or psychological. Major psychological stressors include frustration, pressure, boredom, trauma, conflict, and change.

Measuring Stressors

Stressors can be measured by tests like the SRRS and the Daily Hassles Scale, but scores on such tests provide only a partial picture of stress in a given individual's life.

Stress Responses

Responses to stressors can be physical, psychological, and behavioral. These stress responses can occur alone or in combination, and the appearance of one can often stimulate the others.

Physical Stress Responses

Physical stress responses include short-term changes in heart rate, respiration, muscle tension, and other processes associated with the fight-or-flight syndrome. These responses subside when the stressor does. Longer-lasting stressors bring on a more elaborate physical response pattern known as the *general adaptation syndrome*, or *GAS*, which has three stages: the *alarm reaction*, *resistance*, and *exhaustion*. The GAS helps people resist stress but, if present too long, can lead to physical illnesses, which Selye called *diseases of adaptation*.

Psychological Stress Responses

Psychological stress responses include emotional and cognitive reactions. Anxiety, anger, and depression are among the most common emotional stress reactions; *generalized anxiety disorder*, or *free-floating anxiety* may also result. Cognitive stress reactions include disruptions in the ability to think clearly, remember accurately, and solve problems efficiently. They can also include *catastrophizing* about stressors and utilizing various *defense mechanisms*. Severe psychological stress responses may ultimately become mental disorder.

Behavioral Stress Responses

Behavioral stress responses include specific changes in posture, coordination, and other actions, including facial expressions, tremors, or jumpiness, which reflect physical tension or emotional stress reactions. More global behavioral stress responses include everything from irritability and aggression to excessive escapism and suicide attempts. Certain patterns of behavioral response to severe, long-lasting stressors or to trauma have been identified as *burnout* and *posttraumatic stress disorder*.

Interactions Between People and Stressors

The key to understanding stress appears to lie in understanding how specific stressors interact with particular people. Stressors are likely to have greater impact if they occur without warning, are uncontrollable, or involve a continuous parade of daily problems. The people most likely to react strongly to a stressor are those who perceive stressors as uncontrollable threats; who have the least *social support* from a *social support network*; or who have few stress-coping skills.

Stress, Illness, and Health

Stress-Related Illness

Psychological as well as physical stressors can create illness, especially for people who live high-pressure, competitive, *Type A* lifestyles. These people are more likely to suffer heart disease than their *Type B* peers. *Psychoneuroimmunology* is the field that examines the interaction of psychological and physiological processes that affect the body's ability to defend itself against disease. One important physiological response to stress is suppression of the *immune system*.

Health Psychology

Recognition of the link between stress and illness, as well as the role of behaviors like smoking in raising the risk of illness, prompted the development of *behavioral medicine* and *health psychology*. Researchers in this field seek to understand how psychological factors are related to physical disease and to use behavioral sciences, such as psychology, to help people behave in ways that prevent or minimize disease and promote health.

Coping with Stress

A Plan for Coping

In order to cope with stress, a person must clearly recognize stressors, establish goals, and develop a systematic stress-management plan through the use of coping skills.

Methods of Coping

Coping is most successful when people have a range of stress-management methods available and choose the ones best suited to whatever stressors they face at the moment. Important coping skills include *cognitive restructuring*, acting to minimize the number or intensity of stressors, and using *biofeedback training*, *progressive relaxation training*, or other techniques for reducing the intensity of physical stress reactions.

Some Stress-Coping Programs

Formal stress-management programs have been developed to help people who are most vulnerable to stress-related illnesses or who face major stressors such as surgery, military combat, or rape. Training in the development of coping skills is a basic part of such programs.

OUTLINE

Personality

During World War II, the U.S. government needed spies, assassins, and other specialists for secret operations behind enemy lines. Candidates for these jobs were taken to special camps, where they were given physical and psychological tests. In one test a candidate was given just a few minutes to instruct and supervise two enlisted men—"Buster" and "Kippy"—in the construction of a five-foot, cube-shaped wooden frame. What the candidate did not know was that the men were psychologists whose job was to frustrate and enrage him. Buster and Kippy were so good at acting lazy, stupid, and hostile that the cube was never built in the allotted time.

Did the government think that its spies would someday need to build giant Tinker Toy cubes in Nazi Germany? No, but the government did need to assess how well a person could perform under dangerous and stressful working conditions. The test was supposed to measure candidates' skill, ingenuity, endurance, and resistance to stress. The testers assumed that if a candidate did well on the test, then these characteristics were part of his personality and would come to the fore when needed.

These assumptions reflect just one of several ways of looking at personality. In everyday conversation, you might use the word *personality* to mean "charm" ("Abercrombie has a lot of personality") or a person's most prominent characteristic ("She has a trusting personality") or a general cause of behavior ("He wouldn't have so many problems if he didn't have such a rotten personality"). Psychologists' definitions of the term are also varied. We will define **personality** as the enduring pattern of psychological and behavioral characteristics by which each person can be compared and contrasted with other people. This unique pattern of characteristics makes each person an individual.

When they study personality, psychologists look at a person's consistencies or inconsistencies and at similarities and differences among people. Whatever aspect of personality researchers address, they almost always find themselves working with variables and data from other areas of psychology (see the Linkages diagram). Indeed,

535

LINKAGES

Personality

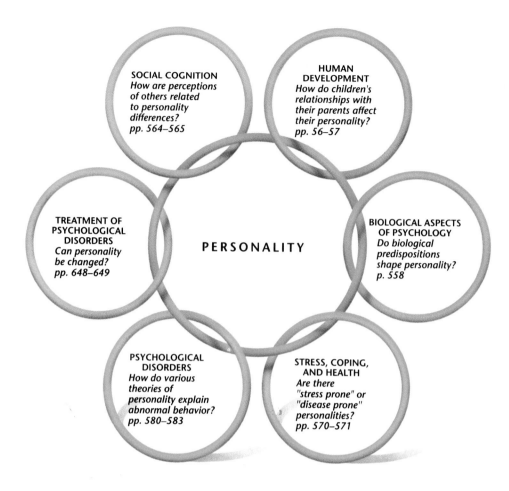

SOCIAL COGNITION
How are perceptions of others related to personality differences?
pp. 564–565

HUMAN DEVELOPMENT
How do children's relationships with their parents affect their personality?
pp. 56–57

TREATMENT OF PSYCHOLOGICAL DISORDERS
Can personality be changed?
pp. 648–649

PERSONALITY

BIOLOGICAL ASPECTS OF PSYCHOLOGY
Do biological predispositions shape personality?
p. 558

PSYCHOLOGICAL DISORDERS
How do various theories of personality explain abnormal behavior?
pp. 580–583

STRESS, COPING, AND HEALTH
Are there "stress prone" or "disease prone" personalities?
pp. 570–571

■ Look at the diagram above, which illustrates some of the relationships between the topic of this chapter, personality, and other chapter topics. The diagram shows just a sampling of the many linkages. (The page numbers indicate where the questions in the diagram are discussed.) In fact, you might think of personality as the coalescence in a particular individual of all the psychological, behavioral, and biological processes discussed in the other chapters of this book. Personality researchers focus their attention on how the coalescence takes place, on the resulting range of personalities, on the course of personality development over the life span, and on how personality influences and is influenced by the environment.

Much of our attention in this chapter is focused on attempts to create a general explanation for how this complicated process occurs. In exploring these efforts we revisit the general approaches to psychology introduced in Chapter 1. We also take a closer look at several issues outlined in Chapter 2, on human development, such as the impact of infants' relationships with their parents.

The theories of personality described in this chapter have been of enormous value in focusing research on likely causes of psychological disorders and in generating methods for treating those disorders. Thus, this chapter provides ideas that are applied in Chapters 15 and 16. ■

personality has been said to lie at the crossroads of all psychological research (Mischel, 1981). In this chapter we describe several approaches to the study of personality and some of the ways in which personality theory and research are being applied.

Studying Personality

Why does a person who is usually friendly sometimes get nasty? What makes one person consistently optimistic, whereas another is usually pessimistic? How much behavior is controlled by people's characteristics and how much by the situations they are in? How stable is personality over a person's lifetime? These are some of the questions personality theorists try to answer. To address these questions, they must have some way of assessing personality and some concepts to guide that assessment.

Methods of Assessing Personality

Suppose you were one of the psychologists choosing people for undercover work during World War II. How would you have judged whether a person was a good candidate? There are three basic tools for assessing personality: observations, interviews, and tests.

Observation allows direct assessment of many aspects of personality. How often does a specific behavior occur? How well is it performed? How consistent is a person's behavior in different situations? Observational methods can address questions such as these. Observation might involve watching a family during meals, monitoring schoolchildren in a playground, or asking people to keep track of every hostile remark made during the day. Psychologists have developed elaborate systems for coding and quantifying observations of people. Nonetheless, observation is a less popular method of assessment than interviews or tests.

Interviews provide a relatively natural way to gather information from the person's own point of view. They can be tailored to the intellectual level, emotional state, and special needs of the person being interviewed. Interviews can also be structured to gain information about important topics without spending much time on issues of less concern to the researcher.

Personality tests offer a more standardized and economical way of gathering information than either observation or interviews. To be useful, a personality test must meet certain standards of reliability and validity. As discussed in Chapter 10, on mental abilities, *reliability* refers to how stable or consistent the results of a test are, and *validity* reflects the degree to which a test measures what it is intended to measure. There are hundreds of tests intended to measure a vast array of personality characteristics. (Brief reviews of many of the best-known tests can be found in Anastasi, 1988; Mitchell, 1985; and Sweetland & Keyser, 1986.) One way to organize this assortment of tests is to classify them as *objective* or *projective*.

Objective Tests An **objective test** is a paper-and-pencil form containing specific questions ("Have you ever worried about your family without good reason?"), statements ("I think about sex more than most people"), or concepts ("My ideal self"). The respondent gives yes-no, true-false, or multiple-choice answers or ratings; these responses are sometimes called *self-reports*. Because of their standardized, written format, objective personality tests are less expensive and more efficient than other assessment methods. They can be

Figure 14.1
The MMPI: Clinical Scales and
Sample Profile

A score of 70 or more on any clinical scale means that the person's responses on that scale are more extreme than at least 95 percent of the normal population. The green line represents the profile of a person who tends to be anxious, depressed, and introverted; the red line suggests a seriously disturbed person with tendencies toward paranoia and bizarre thinking. There are many books available to guide MMPI interpretation (Dahlstrom, Lachar & Dahlstrom, 1986; Graham, 1987). Increasingly, MMPI scoring and analysis are done by computers (Butcher, 1987). In MMPI-2, a recent revision of the MMPI, a number of the original items are reworded or deleted; new items have been introduced, and new norms for interpreting the scores have been calculated (Butcher et al., 1989).

The clinical scales abbreviated in the figure are as follows:

1. Hypochondriasis (Hs)
   (concern with bodily functions and symptoms)
2. Depression (D)
   (pessimism, hopelessness, slowed thinking)
3. Hysteria (Hy)
   (use of physical or mental symptoms to avoid problems)
4. Psychopathic deviate (Pd)
   (disregard for social customs; emotional shallowness)
5. Maculinity/femininity (Mf)
   (interests associated with a particular sex)
6. Paranoia (Pa)
   (delusions, suspiciousness)
7. Psychasthenia (Pt)
   (worry, guilt, anxiety)
8. Schizophrenia (Sc)
   (bizarre thoughts and perceptions)
9. Hypomania (Ma)
   (overactivity, excitement, impulsiveness)
10. Social introversion (Si)
    (shy, insecure)

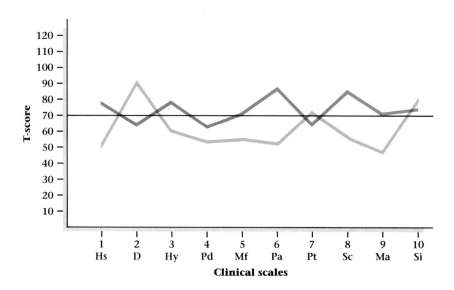

administered by nonprofessionals to many subjects at the same time. These tests can also be scored objectively, much like multiple-choice tests in the classroom. And, just as in the classroom, results from many people can be compared mathematically. For example, before interpreting your apparently high score on an objective test of anxiety, a psychologist would compare the score with *norms*, or average scores from others of your age and sex. Only if you were well above these averages would you be considered unusually anxious.

Some objective tests focus on one aspect of personality. Examples include the Multidimensional Anger Inventory (Siegel, 1986), the State-Trait Anxiety Inventory (Spielberger, 1983), and the Inventory of Interpersonal Problems (Horowitz et al., 1988). Other objective tests measure several personality characteristics in order to assess either the general functioning of "normal" people or the characteristics of people who are experiencing psychological problems.

The most widely used objective test for diagnosing psychological disorders is the *Minnesota Multiphasic Personality Inventory*, better known as the *MMPI*. It was developed during the 1930s at the University of Minnesota by Starke Hathaway and J. C. McKinley. They began by giving hundreds of true-false items to hundreds of people, including psychiatric patients. The 566 true-false items that became the MMPI were selected because people displaying different problems tended to answer them differently from one another as well as from nonpatients. For example, depressed persons tended to answer one group of items in the same general way, while schizophrenic patients answered a different group of items in a typical fashion. The groups of items are called *scales*. The MMPI contains ten *clinical scales*, which are described in Figure 14.1. The MMPI also provides four *validity scales*, which are item groups designed to detect whether respondents are distorting their answers, not understanding the items, or being uncooperative. Someone who responds "true" to items such as "I never get angry" or "Criticism doesn't bother me" may not be giving honest answers to the test as a whole.

Originally, the MMPI was interpreted on the basis of the highest clinical scale score. For example, a person whose highest score was on the depression scale might be diagnosed as depressed. However, research on the MMPI made psychologists aware that such diagnoses may not be valid (for example, ethnic, cultural, and racial factors can affect clinical scale scores; Dana, 1988), and they began to focus on the overall *profile* of scores formed when the scores for all scales are plotted, as shown in Figure 14.1. Today, interpretation of the MMPI concentrates on the profile formed by the highest two or three scales.

Another objective test frequently used for the assessment of psychological problems is the Millon Clinical Multiaxial Inventory, or MCMI (Millon, 1987). The MCMI, which consists of 175 true-false items, is designed to yield descriptions of personality and disorder that are compatible with the official system for classifying mental disorders in the United States. (This system is described in Chapter 15.) Like the MMPI, the MCMI can be scored and interpreted by computer.

The best-known objective tests for measuring a broad range of personality variables in normal people include the California Psychological Inventory, or CPI (Gough, 1987), the Sixteen Personality Factors Questionnaire, or 16 PF (Cattell & Eber, 1962), and the Personality Research Form, or PRF (Jackson, 1967). Like the MMPI, the PRF's items are grouped into scales, but the PRF scales are designed to measure several basic needs (see Table 14.1).

Table 14.1
Some Scales from the Personality Research Form

Notice the difference between these traits and the disordered characteristics measured by the MMPI in Figure 14.1. The PRF scales were derived from a list of psychological needs proposed by Henry Murray.

Scale	Description of High Scorer
Achievement	Aspires to accomplish difficult tasks; maintains high standards and is willing to work toward distant goals; responds positively to competition; willing to put forth effort to attain excellence.
Affiliation	Enjoys being with friends and people in general; accepts people readily; makes efforts to win friendships and maintain associations with people.
Autonomy	Tries to break away from restraints, confinement, or restrictions of any kind; enjoys being unattached, free, not tied to people, places, or obligations; may be rebellious when faced with restraints.
Change	Likes new and different experiences; dislikes routine and avoids it; may readily change opinions or values in different circumstances; adapts readily to changes in environment.
Dominance	Attempts to control environment, and to influence or direct other people; expresses opinions forcefully; enjoys the role of leader and may assume it spontaneously.
Endurance	Willing to work long hours; doesn't give up quickly on a problem; persevering, even in the face of great difficulty; patient and unrelenting in work habits.
Exhibition	Wants to be the center of attention; enjoys having an audience; engages in behavior which wins the notice of others; may enjoy being dramatic or witty.

Source: Jackson, 1974.

Figure 14.2
A Projective Test
Here is an inkblot similar to those included in the Rorschach test, which contains a set of ten patterns, some in color, others in black and white. The subject is asked to tell what the blot might be and then to explain why. What do you see? Most scoring methods pay attention to (1) what part of the blot the person responds to; (2) what particular features (such as small details or color) appear to determine each response; (3) the content of responses (for example, animals, knives, blood, maps, body parts); and (4) the popularity or commonness of the subject's responses compared to those of others who have taken the test. Several researchers have developed systems designed to guide the scoring and interpretation of Rorschach responses and to make the process more objective (Exner, 1985).

Projective Tests Unlike objective tests, **projective tests** contain relatively unstructured stimuli, such as inkblots, which can be perceived in many ways. Indeed, the idea behind projective tests is to provide stimuli that allow such a wide range of interpretations that responses reflect the individual's needs, fantasies, conflicts, thought patterns, and other aspects of personality. Some projective tests ask people to draw items (such as a house, a person, or a tree), to fill in the missing parts of incomplete pictures or sentences, or to say what they associate with a particular word.

In one widely used projective test, the *Thematic Apperception Test*, or *TAT*, the person looks at drawings and constructs a story about what is going on in the picture. (We described the TAT in the discussion of need achievement in Chapter 11, on motivation, but it is also used to assess personality more generally.) The test was developed by Henry Murray, who argued that personality develops as people find ways to meet their needs and that some needs are unconscious and can be measured only through projective methods. For example, if a person's stories about TAT pictures all contain a central character who feels abandoned and unloved, this might indicate that the person has a strong need for security and acceptance. Another well-known projective test, the *Rorschach*, asks people to say what they associate with a series of inkblots (see Figure 14.2).

Compared with the answers to objective tests, the stories, drawings, associations, and other responses to projective tests are difficult to translate into numerical scores. For many years, the only guidelines were long lists of scoring and interpretation rules provided by experts who had administered and analyzed hundreds of projective tests. Scoring and interpretation of projective tests could vary widely from one tester to the next. In an effort to reduce this subjectivity, some psychologists have developed more structured scoring systems for tests like the Rorschach (Exner, 1985).

In general, projective personality tests have lower reliability and validity than objective tests, which are themselves not always as reliable and valid as could be wished (Anastasi, 1988). Yet projective tests continue to be used. Why? Projective tests make it difficult for respondents to detect what is being measured and what the "best" answers would be. Projective testers argue, therefore, that their tests can measure aggressive and sexual impulses and other personality features that people might be reluctant to reveal. The ambiguous stimuli in projective tests may also capture how people respond to the uncertainty that they confront in real life. Psychologists can not only record people's responses to projective test stimuli but also observe signs of anxiety, enjoyment, hostility, or other responses to the testing situation. ("In Review: Personality Tests" summarizes the characteristics of objective and projective tests, along with some of their advantages and disadvantages.)

Using Personality Tests All tests, whether objective or projective, share certain potential drawbacks, especially if they are not administered, scored, interpreted, and used properly. For example, objective personality tests are often used to help select people for jobs, but although they may be capable of identifying mental disorder in job applicants (Butcher, 1979), they do not predict very well which individuals will be best at a particular job (Hunter & Hunter, 1984). Furthermore, some questions on personality tests strike many people as an invasion of privacy and irrelevant to their ability to do a job. Lawsuits against testing have been frequent in recent years. In fact, personality testing has been banned in the hiring of federal employees.

Problems may also arise when the results of a test are reported. A qualified person should be available to explain the scores. Otherwise, individuals may misunderstand the results and become distressed about what they believe are serious flaws in their personality.

In most situations, people have a legal right to review their own test results. Who else should have access to results? Many people worry that if their test results are kept in their personnel files, potential employers or others might review them and receive harmful impressions. Because these are serious concerns, the American Psychological Association has published ethical standards relating to procedures for the development, dissemination, and use of psychological tests (American Psychological Association, 1974, 1981). The goal is not only to improve the reliability and validity of tests but to assure that their results are used properly and fairly.

Systematic Approaches to Personality

Researchers in personality can approach their task from many different points of view, depending on their basic assumptions about people. For example, suppose your background is in anatomy (the study of physical structure), and you notice how bumpy the human skull is and how lumpy the brain is underneath it. You might theorize that those lumps and bumps mean something. Maybe a bump reflects a better-developed part of the brain and thus a stronger tendency to think in some particular way. With these assumptions as your guiding theory, you could study personality by investigating which part of the brain controls which behavior, emotion, or attitude. Your theory might allow you to describe people's personalities and even to make predictions about their behavior on the basis of skull examinations. How closely your descriptions and predictions actually correspond to a person's actions would provide a test of the validity of your theory and techniques. If the results were positive, you might try using your "lump-and-bump" method to detect criminals applying for jobs as bank guards or to match people in a dating service.

As it happens, a theory similar to this one was proposed by the eighteenth-century anatomist Franz Gall. He believed that each of thirty-five faculties (such as sense of humor or hostility) was localized in a specific part of the

Franz Gall, founder of phrenology, mapped out what he believed to be the physical location of each mental faculty and then used this map to translate skull examinations into personality sketches.

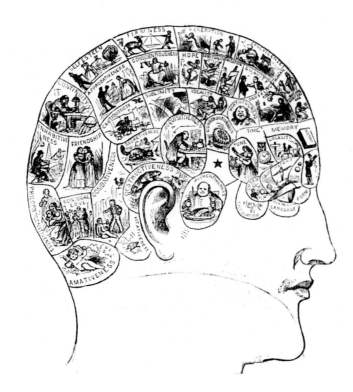

In Review: Personality Tests

Type of Test	Characteristics	Advantages	Disadvantages
Objective	Paper-and-pencil format; quantitatively scored	Efficiency, standardization	Subject to deliberate distortion
Projective	Unstructured stimuli create maximum freedom of response; scoring is subjective, though some objective methods exist	"Correct" answers not obvious; designed to tap unconscious impulses; flexible use	Reliability and validity lower than that of objective tests

brain. He called his theory of personality *phrenology*. When phrenology was subjected to scientific evaluation by other researchers, it proved inadequate and was rejected. However, it illustrates that all approaches to personality, even unsuccessful ones, contain several basic components:

1. A set of assumptions that forms a personality theory (in this case, phrenology).
2. Theory-guided decisions about where to look for evidence about personality. (Gall chose the brain.)
3. Ways of measuring or assessing personality. (Gall used physical examination of the skull.)
4. Special research methods to evaluate the personality theory. (Gall tried to relate bumps to behavior.)

Most approaches to personality also contain a fifth basic component: methods for helping people change, usually known as *psychotherapy*.

The sections that follow examine the four most prominent approaches to personality today: the psychodynamic, dispositional, behavioral, and phenomenological approaches.

The Psychodynamic Approach

Some people think personality is clearly reflected in behavior. A person with an "obnoxious personality," for example, shows it by acting obnoxiously. But is that all there is to personality? Not according to Sigmund Freud, who likened personality to an iceberg, with the tip visible but the bulk underwater.

As a physician during the 1890s, Freud specialized in treating "neurotic" disorders, such as blindness or paralysis, for which there was no physical cause. His patients did not appear to be faking, but their symptoms could often be made to disappear under hypnosis. Freud's experience with these cases led him to believe in *psychic determinism*, the idea that personality and behavior are determined more by psychological factors like resentment than by biological conditions or current life events. He proposed, further, that people may not know why they feel, think, or act the way they do, because

Linkages: Can behavior be motivated by needs and drives of which people are unaware? (a link to Motivation)

these activities are partly controlled by the *unconscious* part of the personality—the part of which people are not normally aware.

From these ideas Freud created the **psychodynamic approach** to personality, which holds that the interplay of unconscious psychological processes determines thoughts, feelings, and behavior. Understanding personality therefore requires exploring the unconscious, and Freud developed several methods for doing so. For example, through **free association**, which involves saying whatever comes to mind, Freud believed that thoughts, feelings, and impulses that are normally unconscious are disclosed. The nature and content of a person's dreams also provide data for personality assessment. These methods became part of Freud's theory of personality, his approach to research, and his therapy techniques, which are collectively known as **psychoanalysis**.

Freud assumed that people are born with basic instincts or needs—not only for food, water, and air but also for sex and aggression. He believed that needs for love, knowledge, security, and the like are derived from these more fundamental desires. Each person is faced with the task of figuring out how to meet his or her needs in a world that often frustrates these efforts. According to Freud, personality develops out of each person's struggle with this task and is reflected in how he or she goes about satisfying a range of needs.

The Structure of Personality

Figure 14.3 illustrates Freud's view of the structure of personality. He described personality as having three major components: the id, the ego, and the superego.

The **id** is a reservoir of unconscious energy, sometimes called psychic energy or **libido**, which includes the basic instincts, desires, and impulses with which all people are born. The id seeks immediate satisfaction, regardless of society's rules or the rights or feelings of others. In other words, the id operates on the **pleasure principle**, which guides people toward whatever feels good. Throwing a temper tantrum at your noisy neighbor's front door would reflect an id impulse.

As children grow, however, they learn that doing whatever they want is not always acceptable. Drawing with Mom's lipstick on the living room wall might be fun, but it might also lead to a scolding. As parents, teachers, and others place more restrictions on the expression of id impulses, a second part of the personality—the **ego** (or "self")—evolves from the id. The ego is responsible for organizing ways to get what a person wants in the world. It operates on the **reality principle**, making compromises between the unreasoning demands of the id and the practical constraints of the real world. The ego is the "executive" of the personality, because it tries to get needs met while protecting people from the harm that might result if they became aware of, let alone immediately acted out, their id impulses.

The more experience people have with the rules and morals of society, the more they tend to adopt them. As a result, children learn that certain behaviors are wrong and will even scold themselves for doing bad things. **Introjection** is the term Freud used for this process of *internalizing* parental and societal values into the personality. Introjected values, "shoulds" and "should nots," form the third component of personality: the **superego**. "Should nots," the things people come to believe are wrong, make up the part of superego known as the *conscience*. Pressure to conform to "shoulds," the ideal behaviors that people believe are right, comes from a second part of superego, known as the *ego ideal*. The superego might be thought of as operating on the *morality principle*, since violating either category of its rules results in guilt. The superego

Figure 14.3
Freud's Conception of the Personality Structure
This theoretical organization consists of the primitive, impulsive id; the stern, demanding superego (which includes the conscience); and the reality-oriented ego, which must work out compromises between internal demands and the limitations of the external world. Notice that parts of the personality are conscious, parts unconscious. Further, Freud recognized that between these levels is the preconscious—a region discussed in Chapter 6 as the location of memories and other material that are not usually in awareness but can be brought into consciousness with little or no effort.

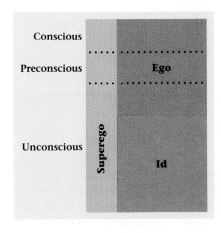

Source: Adapted from Liebert & Spiegler, 1987.

is just as relentless and unreasonable in its demands to be obeyed as the id is in its insistence that its needs be gratified.

Conflicts and Defenses

Basic needs (id), reason (ego), morality (superego), and the demands of the environment are often at odds. This inner turmoil is known as *intrapsychic* or *psychodynamic conflict* (see Table 14.2), which the ego must try to resolve. Freud believed that the number, nature, and outcome of intrapsychic conflicts shape each individual's personality and determine many aspects of behavior.

Most of what is in the unconscious, Freud said, is frightening or socially taboo; therefore, people try to keep this material out of awareness. They experience irrational, or *neurotic*, anxiety when unconscious impulses (such as the desire to harm a parent) threaten to reach consciousness. Neurotic anxiety might take the form of unreasonable precautions against getting dirty; this form of anxiety contrasts with *realistic anxiety*, which is felt in the face of a snarling dog or other real danger. *Moral anxiety* occurs in association with guilt over behavior that the superego has condemned.

One of the most important functions of the ego is to defend against neurotic anxiety and guilt. Often it does so by organizing realistic actions, as when a person seeks help because of impulses to abuse a child. However, the ego may also reduce anxiety or guilt by resorting to **defense mechanisms**, the unconscious psychological and behavioral tactics that protect a person from unpleasant emotions. Everyone uses defense mechanisms at one time or another, but overreliance on them can lead to problems.

To illustrate, suppose you find yourself physically attracted to your best friend's lover but find this impossible to admit, even to yourself. Your most primitive unconscious impulse might be to kill your friend, but becoming aware of this impulse would bring a flood of anxiety and guilt. To prevent this, your ego might employ repression. Unlike suppression, in which you

Table 14.2
Examples of Intrapsychic Conflicts

According to Freud, some of these conflicts may be wholly or partially conscious, but most of them tend to be unconscious.

Conflict	Example
Id vs. ego	Choosing between a small immediate reward and a larger reward that requires some waiting
Id vs. superego	Deciding whether to return the difference when you are overpaid or undercharged
Ego vs. superego	Choosing between telling a "white lie" and always telling the truth
Id and ego vs. superego	Deciding whether to retaliate against the attack of a weak opponent or to "turn the other cheek"
Id and superego vs. ego	Deciding, if you are a devout Roman Catholic, whether to use a contraceptive
Ego and superego vs. id	Choosing whether to steal something you want and cannot afford (the ego would presumably be increasingly involved as the probability of being apprehended increases)

Source: Liebert and Spiegler, 1987.

consciously deny certain feelings, **repression** unconsciously forces unacceptable impulses out of awareness, leaving you unaware that you had the taboo desires in the first place. Keeping strong feelings under wraps involves a distortion of reality that takes tremendous effort, like trying to hold an inflated beach ball under water.

Other ego defense mechanisms may help keep threatening material from surfacing or disguise it when it does. (We describe a few of these in Chapter 13, on stress; see Table 13.3.) Through **projection**, people attribute their own unacceptable desires to others. In our example, projection might make you fearful that others are out to steal your possessions (just as you want to "steal" from your friend). **Reaction formation** is a defense in which your behavior runs exactly opposite to your true feelings. Thus, you might develop an intense dislike for your friend's lover. In **displacement**, unacceptable impulses are diverted toward alternative targets. So you might express hostility toward people who remind you of your friend. **Intellectualization** helps a person minimize anxiety by viewing threatening issues in abstract terms. Thus, you might engage in endless talk about conflict-related topics such as platonic love, loyalty, or trust. **Rationalization** attempts to "explain away" unacceptable behavior. If you blurt out at a party how you really feel, you might later blame it on drunkenness. With **denial**, the most primitive defense, a person distorts reality simply by negating the truth. In our example, denial might lead you to repeatedly comment on your lack of romantic interest in the person you love. Finally, there is **sublimation**, the conversion of repressed yearnings into socially approved action. This defense might prompt you to throw yourself into hard physical labor or creative intellectual or artistic work.

Stages in Personality Development

Freud proposed that personality develops during childhood in several stages. These are called **psychosexual stages**, because at each stage a particular part of the body becomes the main source of pleasure. Freud said that failure to resolve the unique problems and conflicts of a stage can leave a person *fixated*; that is, overly attached to or unconsciously preoccupied with the pleasure area associated with that stage. Fixation occurs to some extent for everyone, he said, leaving each person with certain personality characteristics as adults.

The Oral Stage   A child's first year or so is called the **oral stage**, because the mouth is the center of pleasure. The infant uses its mouth to eat and to explore, mouthing everything from plastic toys to its own hands and feet. Personality problems occur when oral needs are either neglected or overindulged. Early weaning or greatly delayed weaning may leave a child overly attached to the bottle, the breast, and other forms of oral satisfaction. Fixation at the oral stage might produce adult characteristics such as talking too much, overeating, smoking, alcoholism, or using "biting" sarcasm. Desperate dependence on others is another possible sign of oral fixation.

The Anal Stage   The second psychosexual stage occurs during the second year, when the demand for toilet training clashes with the child's instinctual pleasure in having bowel movements at will. Because the focus of pleasure and conflict shifts from the mouth to the anus during this period, Freud called it the **anal stage**. It is at this stage that he believed the child's ego evolves to mediate parental demands for socially appropriate behavior. If toilet training is too harsh or is begun too early or too late, conflicts may result. Adults fixated at this stage might symbolically withhold feces by being stingy,

Freud called the first year or so of life the oral stage because, during this time, children use their mouths not only for eating, but for exploring their world. Children in the oral stage put into their mouths anything they can get their hands on.

extremely organized, stubborn, and perhaps excessively concerned with control, cleanliness, orderliness, or details. Or they might symbolically expel feces by being sloppy, disorganized, or impulsive.

The Phallic Stage   By the age of three or so and for about two years thereafter, the focus of pleasure shifts to the genital area. Emphasizing the psychosexual development of boys, Freud called this period the **phallic stage**. During this stage a boy's id impulses involve sexual desire for the mother and a desire to eliminate, even kill, the father, with whom the boy competes for the mother's affection. Freud called this constellation of impulses the **Oedipus complex**, because it parallels the plot of the Greek tragedy *Oedipus Rex*, in which Oedipus unknowingly kills his father and marries his mother. The boy's hostile fantasies about his father create a fear of retaliation called *castration anxiety*. The fear becomes so strong that the ego represses the incestuous desires. The boy then seeks to identify with his father, imitating him and, in the process, beginning to learn male gender-role behaviors.

According to Freud, the female child begins with a strong attachment to her mother. Freud believed the female child experiences *penis envy*. As she realizes that boys have penises and girls do not, she begins to hate her mother, perhaps blaming the mother for the missing anatomy and considering her inferior, and she transfers her love to her father. Because the girl must still avoid her mother's disapproval, she identifies with her mother, adopting female gender-role behaviors and subsequently choosing a male mate other than her father.

Freud believed that most people are fixated to some degree at the phallic stage. Extreme fear, aggression, or other difficulties with a boss, teacher, or other authority figure may reflect unresolved conflicts with the same-sex parent. Uncertainty about one's identity as a male or female, problems in maintaining a stable love relationship, and the appearance of disordered or socially disapproved sexual behavior may also stem from poorly resolved conflicts of the phallic stage, he said.

The Latency Period and the Genital Stage   As the phallic stage draws to a close, its conflicts are repressed or otherwise quieted by the ego. An interval of peace known as the **latency period** ensues, during which sexual impulses lie dormant and the child focuses on education and other matters. When children begin to mature physically during adolescence, sexual impulses reappear at the conscious level. The genitals again become the focus of pleasure, and the young person begins to seek relationships through which sexual impulses can be gratified. Thus begins what Freud called the **genital stage**, a period that spans the rest of life. The quality of relationships and the degree of fulfillment experienced during this stage are, according to Freud, tied directly to success in resolving conflicts during the earlier stages.

Variations on Freudian Personality Theory

Freud's ideas, especially the Oedipal theory, created controversy from the moment he presented them. Psychologists and psychiatrists raised issues such as: Are instinctual impulses as important as Freud maintained? Is adult personality entirely fixed by the experiences of the first six years of life? Do unconscious factors really determine most of human behavior? Believing that the answers to questions like these are ''no'' or ''not always,'' several theorists offered variations on Freud's ideas. Because their revisions preserved Freud's emphasis on the importance of psychological impulses and conflicts in personality and behavior, these individuals are sometimes called *neo-Freudians*.

Carl Jung's Analytic Psychology   Carl Jung (pronounced ''yoong'') believed that libido was not based just on sexual and aggressive instincts (1916). He saw it as a more general life force that includes an innate drive for the productive blending of basic impulses with real-world demands. Jung called this tendency toward growth-oriented resolution of conflicts the *transcendent function*.

Jung also believed that everyone has not only a personal unconscious (containing individually threatening memories and impulses) but also a **collective unconscious**, a kind of memory that stores all the images and ideas the human race has accumulated since its evolution from lower forms of life. Some of these images are called **archetypes**, because they consist of classic images or concepts. *Mother*, for instance, is an archetype; everyone is born with a shared readiness to see and react to certain people as mother figures. More ominous is the *shadow* archetype (similar to the id). It contains the most basic, ''darker'' instincts from prehuman centuries and, according to Jung, is embodied in notions like sin and the devil.

Jung did not identify specific stages in personality development. He suggested instead that people develop over time differing degrees of *introversion* (a tendency to reflect on one's own experiences) or *extraversion* (a tendency to focus on the social world) and differing tendencies to rely on specific psychological functions, such as thinking versus feeling. The combination of these tendencies, said Jung (1933), creates personalities that display distinctive and predictable patterns of behavior.

Alfred Adler's Individual Psychology   Alfred Adler (1927) emphasized the role of social urges in forming personality. Adler began with the assumption that each person is born helpless and dependent, which creates unpleasant feelings of inferiority. These negative feelings, combined with an innate desire to become a full-fledged member of the social world, provide the impetus for the development of personality. Adler referred to this process as *striving for superiority*, by which he meant a drive for fulfillment as a person, not just a desire to best others. If feelings of inferiority are intense, they drive a person to compensate for perceived inferiority. When the individual's personality revolves around trying to make up for some perceived deficit, the pattern is sometimes called an *inferiority complex.*

According to Adler, the ways each person tries to reach fulfillment constitute personality or, as he called it, **style of life.** Adler suggested that the style of life is directed not just by the unconscious but by what he called *guiding fictions,* which are conscious ideas, goals, and beliefs. These arise primarily from experiences within the family. For example, a child who is pampered and protected may believe that he or she is "special" and exempt from society's rules. This guiding fiction that "I'm special" is likely to lead to a selfish style of life, in which personal fulfillment comes at the expense of others. In contrast, "There is good in everyone" and "Tomorrow will be better than today" are guiding fictions that, whether true or not, are likely to create positive, upbeat styles of life.

Other Neo-Freudians   Other neo-Freudian theorists followed Adler's lead by focusing on how other people help shape an individual's personality. Erich Fromm (1941), Karen Horney (pronounced "horn-eye"; 1937), and Harry Stack Sullivan (1953) argued that once biological needs are met, the attempt to meet *social needs* (to feel protected, secure, and accepted, for example) is most influential in forming personality. The strategies people use to meet these needs, such as dominating other people or being dependent on them, become the personality. (Note the similarity to Adler's concept of a style of life.)

This emphasis on social factors in personality development is also reflected in the influential work of Erik H. Erikson (1963, 1968). In place of Freud's psychosexual stages, Erikson proposed eight **psychosocial stages,** in which the most important developments involve social crises. These stages were discussed in Chapter 2, on human development (see Table 2.2, p. 65).

The importance of social factors in personality is highlighted in a number of other psychodynamic theories that downplay the roles of instincts and the unconscious. *Ego psychologists,* including Freud's daughter, Anna, have described the ego as more than a mediator in conflicts among id, superego, and environment; in their view the ego begins to develop as a creative, adaptive force in its own right even before the anal stage (A. Freud, 1946; Fraiberg, 1987). It is responsible for language development, perception, attention, planning, learning, and many other psychological functions (Hartmann, 1939).

Object relations theorists such as Melanie Klein (1975), Otto Kernberg (1976), and Heinz Kohut (1984) focus on the early relationships between infants and their love objects, usually the mother and other primary caregivers. They study how primary caregivers provide protection, acceptance, and recognition and otherwise meet the infant's needs (Blatt & Lerner, 1983). These object relations have a significant impact on personality development. Ideally, development follows a sequence (discussed in Chapters 2 and 11) in which the child forms a secure early bond to the mother or other caregiver, tolerates gradual separation from the object of attachment, and finally develops the ability to relate to others as an independent, secure individual (Ainsworth, 1989). Distorted object relations can lead to inadequate self-esteem, difficulties in trusting or making commitments to others, or more serious mental disorders (Eagle, 1984).

Harry Stack Sullivan went so far as to say that "personality" is simply a name for each person's pattern of interpersonal behaviors. To understand personality he looked to the pattern of what a person did with others, said to others, and believed about others. For Sullivan, a person's self (the rough equivalent of Freud's ego) develops not to mediate unconscious conflict but to preserve feelings of security in an interpersonal world in which anxiety is the major threat. The self acts like a benevolent authority figure, guiding the development of personality, trying to maintain security with other people, seeking prestige, and protecting against anxiety through maneuvers similar to

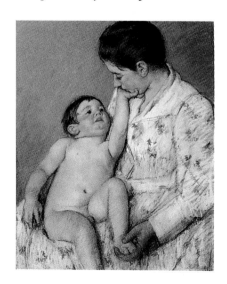

Object relations theorists focus on the relationships that form between babies and their first love objects (caregivers). The nature and quality of these relationships are seen as influencing both normal and abnormal personality development.

Figure 14.4
Leary's Interpersonal Circle
This model of interpersonal behavior contains two primary dimensions (Leary, 1957). The vertical dimension ranges from dominance to submission, the horizontal from love to hate. Each of the eight wedges represents a blend of power (dominance-submission) and affiliation (love-hate) in interpersonal behavior. The first word in the label, appearing in the outer ring of each wedge, describes a mild form of the behavior contained in that wedge; the second word refers to an extreme form of the behavior. The intensity of behavior increases from the center of the circle to the perimeter. For example, "guide, advise, teach" in its extreme form becomes "seeks respect compulsively, pedantic, dogmatic actions."

Freud's ego defense mechanisms. When anxiety becomes too severe, these manuevers become so extreme or so rigid that disturbed interpersonal relationships result. According to Sullivan, psychological disorders develop when disturbed interpersonal relationships become so taxing, cumbersome, or frustrating that constructive interactions with other people are not possible.

HIGHLIGHT

The Interpersonal Circle

Sullivan described the importance of interpersonal styles, but he left it to others to chart these styles and their relationship to one another. A major system for doing so was developed years ago by Timothy Leary and his associates (Leary, 1957). They organized styles of interpersonal behavior around a circle, called a *circumplex* (see Figure 14.4). In this model, all

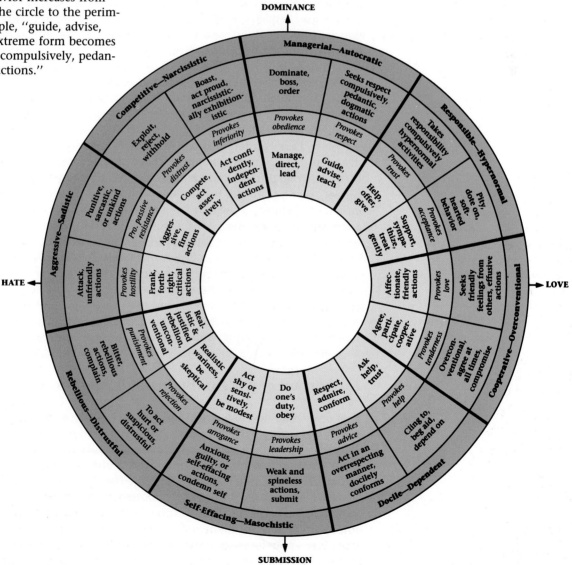

Source: Leary, 1957.

interpersonal behaviors are seen as blending degrees of power (dominance or submission) and of affiliation (love or hate). The result is eight styles of behavior, such as the competitive-narcissistic style and the docile-dependent style, arranged around the circle as shown in Figure 14.4.

The arrangement of the styles predicts, first of all, which behaviors are likely to appear together in the same person. Behaviors that appear next to each other in the circle are likely to occur together in an individual; behaviors appearing directly opposite each other are unlikely to appear in the same person. Thus, for example, a person who shows cooperative-overconventional behavior is more likely to also display docile-dependent behavior than to show self-effacing–masochistic behavior. A great deal of empirical research on Leary's system and similar models (Wiggins & Broughton, 1985) has supported the accuracy of their predictions.

The position of styles in the circle also yields predictions about interpersonal relationships. In fact, Leary viewed each of the eight categories in the circle as a set of learned manipulations for evoking desired behavior from others. People "pull" certain behaviors from others by deploying a typical interpersonal style. This "pulling" is compatible with Sullivan's notion that people adopt styles that protect their security and prevent anxiety. Thus, if you are insecure about your physical appearance, you might make self-effacing comments ("I look awful today") that "pull" reassuring statements from others. In general, the rule of *complementarity* applies: people tend to pull behavior from other people that is complementary to the behavior originally offered. Thus, dominant behavior tends to pull submissiveness from others, and vice versa. However, love usually evokes love and hate usually engenders hate.

Finally, Leary's interpersonal circle offers a way of viewing psychological disorders. Clinicians since Sullivan have argued that mental disorders should be understood as rigid and extreme patterns of interpersonal behavior (e.g. Kiesler, 1986). Consider the problems known as personality disorders (discussed in Chapter 15), which are long-standing interpersonal styles that either cause unhappiness for the person displaying them or for those forced to endure them. These problems can be seen as extreme, rigid examples of various wedges of Leary's interpersonal circle (Widiger & Frances, 1985; Wiggins & Pincus, 1989). For example, the dependent personality disorder is marked by pervasive submissiveness; the person is unable to make even simple decisions without advice and reassurance from others. The dependent personality seems to be "living in" the docile-dependent wedge, in which extremes of clingy submissiveness are encountered. ▪

Evaluation of the Psychodynamic Approach

Sigmund Freud developed the most comprehensive and influential personality theory ever proposed. His views influenced almost every aspect of modern Western thought, including psychology, medicine, literature, religion, sociology, and anthropology, and his ideas and techniques continue to be the basis for many practical applications. The most common application of psychodynamic concepts is in psychotherapy, which is the attempt to alleviate various forms of mental disorder through psychological means. Psychodynamic therapies (which are discussed in detail in Chapter 16) aim to help people make conscious previously unconscious aspects of personality so that they can resolve old conflicts. Furthermore, Freud's concepts generated methods of personality assessment such as psychodynamic interviews and projective tests (see Figure 14.5).

Source: Hammer, 1968.

**Figure 14.5
Interpretations Based on a
Draw-a-Person Test**
These drawings are by an eighteen-year-old male who had been caught stealing a television set. Using a psychodynamic approach, a psychologist interpreted the muscular figure as the young man's attempt to boast of masculine prowess, but also saw the muscles as overinflated into a "puffy softness," suggesting feelings of inadequacy. The drawing of the babylike figure was seen to reveal feelings of vulnerability, dependency, and a desire for affection. Appealing as these interpretations may be, the use of projective tests in personality assessment is not generally supported by research. In most cases, the results of projective tests have low predictive validity or add little information beyond what the psychologist might have inferred from other existing information.

Despite its broad acceptance and extraordinary influence, Freud's psychodynamic approach has several weaknesses. First, Freud's theory may reflect some important biases. He based his theory on observations of an unrepresentative sample of humankind: a small number of upper-class Viennese patients (mostly women), who not only had mental problems but were raised in a society that considered discussion of sex to be uncivilized. Moreover, Freud's focus on male psychosexual development and his bias toward male anatomy as something to be envied by women has caused male as well as female feminists to reject some or all of his ideas (Chesler, 1972). Further, his ideas may have been distorted by his refusal to believe his patients' accounts of sexual abuse by parents and other adults. He interpreted these stories as fantasies and wish fulfillment, not as memories, an interpretation that has become more questionable as the reality of child sexual abuse has become clearer (Masson, 1983).

Second, psychodynamic concepts such as id, ego, unconscious conflicts, and defense mechanisms are generally considered too vague to measure and test scientifically. For example, suppose a psychologist suspects that a man harbors strong, unconscious aggressive impulses. The suspicion would be confirmed if the man is often angry and hostile. But if he is unusually even-tempered, this calm could be seen as a defense against aggressive impulses. Occasional angry outbursts might be viewed as wavering ego control. In short, there is almost nothing the man can do that could not be interpreted as reflecting unconscious aggression.

Finally, Freud's belief that human beings are driven mainly by instinct and the unconscious ignores evidence that much human behavior goes beyond instinct gratification. The conscious drive to attain personal, social, and spiritual goals is also an important determinant of behavior, as is learning from others. Freud's emphasis on the importance of unconscious childhood conflicts in establishing adult behavior neglects the continuing role of learning and other environmental influences on behavior.

Ego psychologists and others who altered some of Freud's concepts and gave more attention to social influences have helped to divert some of these criticisms. So have attempts to investigate scientifically the existence and operation of psychodynamic constructs (Silverman & Weinberger, 1985). The results have not been generally accepted because of flaws in the research (Balay & Shevrin, 1988), but research on psychodynamic theory is becoming more sophisticated and reflects a willingness by psychodynamic therapists to subject their work to empirical testing (Wallerstein, 1989). Indeed, though the psychodynamic approach is less popular than it once was (Conway, 1988; Smith, 1982), there are many psychologists who continue to embrace psychodynamic ideas.

Still, the goal of measuring personality more precisely and the belief that psychodynamic theories underestimate the importance of learning principles or conscious intent have increased the popularity of other approaches, especially among young psychologists (Zook & Walton, 1989). We next describe some of these approaches, beginning with the dispositional approach.

The Dispositional Approach

If you were to ask a friend to describe the personality of someone you both know, he or she could probably do it without too much trouble. The personality sketch would probably be organized into a small number of descriptive categories. For example:

She is a truly caring *person, a real* extrovert. *She is* generous *with her time and she* works very hard *at everything she does. Yet, I think she also* lacks confidence. *She is* submissive *to other people's demands because she* needs to be accepted *by them.*

In other words, most people describe others by referring to the type of people they are ("extrovert"), to their most notable traits ("caring"; "lacks confidence"), or to their needs ("needs to be accepted"). Together, these statements describe a person's *dispositions*, the ways he or she usually thinks and behaves. This dispositional approach to personality is the oldest of the approaches we will consider.

The **dispositional approach** makes three basic assumptions.

1. Each person has stable, long-lasting dispositions to display certain behaviors, attitudes, and emotions. Thus, a basically gentle person tends to stay that way day after day, year after year.
2. These dispositions appear in diverse situations, and they explain why people act in predictable ways in many different settings. A person who is fiercely competitive at work will probably be competitive on the tennis court or at a party.
3. Each person has a different set of dispositions, or at least a set of dispositions of varying strengths, which assume a unique pattern. This creates an endless variety of human personalities.

Thus, the dispositional approach views personality as a combination of certain stable internal characteristics. For example, one variety of the dispositional approach assumes that people have unique mixtures of needs, which motivate them to think and behave as they do. The most prominent representative of this approach is Henry Murray, whose personality research began in the 1930s. Murray's list of needs included twelve biological needs, such as food, water, and air, and twenty-seven psychological needs, such as recognition and the need for achievement. Some of these needs were discussed in Chapter 11, on motivation (Murray, 1938, 1962). In the sections that follow we examine two other varieties of the dispositional approach.

Personality Types

When you hear someone say, "He's not my type," or "I'm not that type of person," you are hearing echoes of an age-old dream: to be able to classify people into a few basic kinds of personalities. The attempt to establish *types* of people goes back at least as far as Hippocrates, a physician of ancient Greece. He suggested that a certain *temperament*, or basic behavioral tendency, is associated with each of four bodily fluids, or *humors*: blood, phlegm, black bile, and yellow bile. Personality type, said Hippocrates, depends on how much of each humor a person has. The terms for these personality types— sanguine, phlegmatic, melancholic, and choleric—still survive.

Other dispositional theorists have tried to relate the appearance that people inherit to the type of personality they develop (Williams, 1967). This notion has great appeal. For example, look at Figure 14.6. Which of these men do you think is a photographer? an executive? a convicted rapist? a con artist? Most likely, you decided on the basis of some personal system that told you that certain types of people have a certain "look." (Check the bottom of page 554 to see how well you did.) Many people use a personal typing system to make assumptions about people on a first meeting (Warner & Sugarman, 1986); in Chapter 17, on social cognition, we discuss how this typing can influence attraction.

Figure 14.6
Types of Personality
What can you say about people's personalities by looking at them? Remarkably little, even though, as mentioned in Chapter 9, people tend to use representativeness heuristics to place others in personality types based on appearance. Thus, it might be tempting to assume that a small, tidy-looking person is more reliable or trustworthy than a big, slovenly one. Every year, well-dressed con artists exploit the trust engendered by mistaken type theories.

The study of the relationship between personality and the face or body is called *physiognomy* and goes back to Gall's phrenology. Modern physiognomy was promoted in the 1940s by William Sheldon, an American physician and psychologist, who believed that certain body builds were associated with different temperaments. However, research has not supported the validity of compressing human personality into a few types based on facial or bodily characteristics.

Personality Traits

A personality *type* is a discrete category. When people are typed, they belong to one class (male) or another (female). *Traits*, in contrast, are continuous qualities that individuals possess in different amounts. A person can possess a lot or a little of some trait or fall anywhere in between on a measure of that trait.

Many researchers have focused on traits as the building blocks of personality. They start with the assumption that each personality can be described in terms of how strong it is on various traits, such as hostility, dependency, sociability, and the like (see Figure 14.7). Thus, from the trait perspective, personality is like a fabric of many different-colored threads, some bright, some dull, some thick, some thin, which are never woven together in exactly the same way twice.

Allport's Trait Theory   Gordon Allport (1961) spent thirty years studying how traits combine to form the normal personality. He reported at least eighteen thousand traits. He also found that many of the labels for these traits refer to the same thing ("hostile," "nasty," and "mean" all convey a similar meaning), so that when people are asked to give a personality sketch, they can usually do the job using only about seven trait labels. Of course, for each person described those seven labels might be very different. Allport believed that such a set of labels represents a person's *central traits*, which are characteristics that organize and control behavior in many different situations. Central traits are roughly equivalent to the terms used in letters of recommendation ("reliable" or "distractible," for example) that are meant to convey what can be expected from a person most of the time (Liebert & Spiegler, 1982). Allport also found what he called *secondary traits*, which are traits that are more specific to certain situations and control far less behavior. "Hates salad bars" is an example of a secondary trait. In a few people, Allport found *cardinal traits*—dispositions that are so general and pervasive that they govern

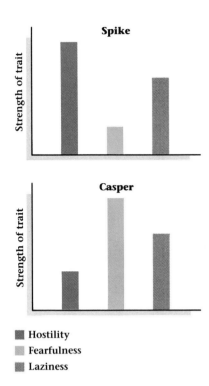

Figure 14.7
Two Personality Profiles
Personality traits can have different strengths in different people. In these examples, Spike and Casper can be said to have the same traits, but their behavior when insulted is likely to be quite different. Spike might return the insult in even harsher terms, whereas Casper would probably feel some anger but fail to express it for fear of retaliation.

virtually everything a person does. Albert Schweitzer and Mother Teresa, for example, illustrate the cardinal trait of humanitarianism.

In his research, Allport often took a *nomothetic* approach (which means carefully comparing many individuals in terms of the personality traits commonly found in most people to some degree). Still Allport never lost sight of the importance of studying the patterns of traits that appear in unique combination in an individual (the *idiographic* approach). His work in both areas provided an important part of the foundation for modern research on personality traits.

Factor-Analytic Methods Suppose that everyone has one hundred common traits, each of which appears in some strength in the personality. If you want to compare the personalities of two people, you would have to measure all hundred traits. It would be more convenient to know whether some of those hundred traits are correlated with others, so that if someone is strong on, say, optimism, that person is also going to be strong on happiness, friendliness, and hopefulness. If you knew these correlations, you could compare personalities by measuring just a few specific traits. It would be even better if, after identifying "trait clusters," you could determine *why* they appear together. Perhaps each cluster belongs to a more basic dimension of personality, so that a personality can be fully described by finding out a person's position on just a handful of basic dimensions. In fact, this strategy is followed by some personality researchers. Using a mathematical method known as *factor analysis*, they identify groups of traits that are correlated with one another but uncorrelated with other groups. They then give each group a label describing the basic personality dimension that underlies it. This, in essence, was the approach used by British psychologist Hans Eysenck.

Using factor analyses of the results of objective personality tests such as the Eysenck Personality Inventory, Eysenck concluded that any personality can be described by three basic factors (Eysenck, 1970, 1981):

Psychoticism. People high on psychoticism show such traits as cruelty, hostility, coldness, oddness, and rejection of social customs.

Introversion-extraversion. Extraverts are sociable and outgoing, enjoy parties and other social activities, take risks, and love excitement and change. Introverts tend to be quiet, thoughtful, and reserved, enjoying solitary pursuits and avoiding excitement and social involvement.

Emotionality-stability. At the one extreme of emotionality-stability are traits such as moodiness, restlessness, worry, anxiety, and other negative emotions. People at the opposite end of this scale are calm, even-tempered, relaxed, and emotionally stable.

Eysenck claimed that if it is known how people score on these dimensions, a number of their other key characteristics can be predicted. Figure 14.8 illustrates traits that, according to Eysenck, result from various combinations of introversion-extraversion and emotionality-stability. He also found that people with behavior disorders show characteristic scores on these two dimensions.

Eysenck argued that a person's position on these dimensions is determined largely by biological variables. In particular, he tied differences in extraversion-introversion to characteristic variations in cortical arousal. If a person inherits a nervous system with a low level of arousal, said Eysenck, he or she will be relatively insensitive to the effects of rewards and punishments, will therefore

---

* The men shown in Figure 14.6 are as follows (left to right): a photographer; Richard Speck, a convicted rapist and murderer; an executive; and Billy Sol Estes, a con artist. Photos (left to right) by Carol Palmer, UPI/Bettman Newsphotos, Steven Gyrina, and Wide World Photos.

Figure 14.8
Eysenck's Major Personality Dimensions

According to Eysenck, combining varying degrees of emotionality-stability and introversion-extraversion produces characteristic combinations of traits. For example, an introverted but stable person is likely to be controlled and reliable, whereas an introverted but emotional person is likely to be rigid and anxious. This figure also illustrates the rather amazing fact that the traits appearing in the four quadrants created by crossing Eysenck's two personality dimensions correspond roughly to Hippocrates' four temperaments. A third personality dimension, psychoticism, also plays a part in Eysenck's system.

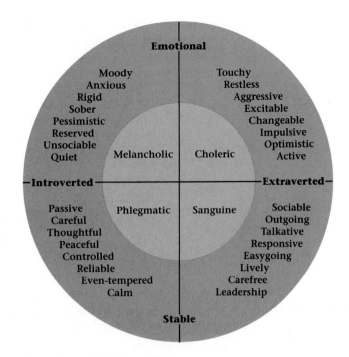

Source: Eysenck & Rachman, 1965.

Introversion-extraversion is one of the three dimensions that Hans Eysenck found within the structure of most people's personality. A relatively low level of arousal in extraverts, he argues, prompts them to seek the excitement and stimulation that introverts, with their already relatively high level of arousal, tend to avoid.

not develop conditioned responses very easily, and will not easily learn to play by the rules. As we discussed in the chapter on motivation, low levels of cortical arousal may lead a person constantly to look for excitement and change in order to increase arousal. In short, the person will be extraverted. In contrast, if a person inherits a sensitive, "overaroused" nervous system, Eysenck's theory predicts that he or she is likely to be strongly affected by rewards and punishments, develop conditioned responses easily, and avoid excessive stimulation; in other words, he or she will be an introvert.

Eysenck's analysis does have research support (Eysenck, 1982) and it remains influential, but it did not end the search for a few basic factors or traits that could describe human personality. More recently, dispositional theorists using factor analysis and other methods have begun to reach a consensus that five factors define the basic organization of human personality. Using these five factors, it may be possible to describe any personality and distinguish it from others. The components of this so-called *big five* model of personality are:

1. *Neuroticism* Persons scoring high on this factor are prone to feeling anxious in many situations. They are generally susceptible to experiencing other negative emotions like anger and depression, do not cope well with stress, and are likely to have unrealistic ideas about themselves.

2. *Extraversion* Extraverts typically like other people, prefer to be a part of social gatherings, and tend to be assertive, active, upbeat, and cheerful. Introverts, in this model, are not exactly the opposites of extraverts. Rather, they seem to lack extraverted qualities and therefore appear reserved, aloof or independent, and emotionally even-paced.

3. *Openness* Open persons have active imaginations, are sensitive to sights and sounds around them, are intellectually curious, and seem receptive to diverse "inner" and "outer" experiences. Openness is also correlated with a tendency to feel emotions keenly. Those low on openness tend to be conventional, down-to-earth, narrower in their interests, and unartistic.

4. *Agreeableness* This dimension describes whether a person has a positive or negative orientation toward others. Agreeable persons are eager to help

others and expect they will be treated with sympathy and cooperation. Cynicism, suspiciousness, and uncooperativeness characterize people low on this factor.

5. *Conscientiousness* High conscientiousness is reflected in a determined persistence to accomplish highly valued tasks. Conscientious persons are usually reliable; when they promise to do something, they do it. Conscientious people may also tend to be puritanical in their attitudes. Low scores on this factor are associated with laxness, aimlessness, and unreliability.

The NEO Personality Inventory, an objective personality test developed by Paul Costa and Robert McCrae (1989), yields scores on each of these five factors. (The name NEO is derived from neuroticism, extraversion, and openness—the three domains measured in the first edition of the test.) The NEO is available as a self-report questionnaire or as a rating scale to be completed by someone who knows the person being assessed (see Figure 14.9).

Figure 14.9
A Sample Summary of Results from the NEO Personality Inventory
In this example of the results a respondent might receive after taking the NEO, the five factors scored are, from the top row to the bottom row, neuroticism, extraversion, openness, agreeableness, and conscientiousness. The examiner marks one box in each row. Costa and McCrae (1989) argue that the NEO can be used to aid in the diagnosis of personality disorders and to understand how psychotherapy might affect different types of clients. For example, people who score high on the extraversion factor might prefer group to individual therapy, whereas introverts may do better in individual psychotherapy.

Compared with the responses of other people, your responses suggest that you can be described as:

☐ Sensitive, emotional, and prone to experience feelings that are upsetting.	☐ Generally calm and able to deal with stress, but you sometimes experience feelings of guilt, anger, or sadness.	☐ Secure, hardy, and generally relaxed even under stressful conditions.
☐ Extraverted, outgoing, active, and high-spirited. You prefer to be around people most of the time.	☐ Moderate in activity and enthusiasm. You enjoy the company of others but you also value privacy.	☐ Introverted, reserved, and serious. You prefer to be alone or with a few close friends.
☐ Open to new experiences. You have broad interests and are very imaginative.	☐ Practical but willing to consider new ways of doing things. You seek a balance between the old and the new.	☐ Down-to-earth, practical, traditional, and pretty much set in your ways.
☐ Compassionate, good-natured, and eager to cooperate and avoid conflict.	☐ Generally warm, trusting, and agreeable, but you can sometimes be stubborn and competitive.	☐ Hardheaded, skeptical, proud, and competitive. You tend to express your anger directly.
☐ Conscientious and well organized. You have high standards and always strive to achieve your goals.	☐ Dependable and moderately well organized. You generally have clear goals but are able to set your work aside.	☐ Easygoing, not very well organized, and sometimes careless. You prefer not to make plans.

Source: Reproduced by special permission of the publisher, Psychological Assessment Resources, Inc., Odessa, FL 33556, from the NEO Personality Inventory by Paul Costa and Robert McCrae. Copyright 1978, 1985, 1989 by PAR, Inc.

T H I N K I N G   C R I T I C A L L Y

Are Personality Traits Inherited?

If personality is made up of the "big five" factors or some other group of traits, where do they come from? One study described a pair of male twins who had been separated at five weeks of age and did not meet for thirty-nine years. Both men drove Chevrolets, chain-smoked the same brand of cigarettes, had divorced a woman named Linda, were remarried to a woman named Betty, had sons named James Allan, had dogs named Toy, enjoyed similar hobbies, and had served as sheriff's deputies (Tellegen et al., 1988).

What am I being asked to believe or accept?
Cases like this as well as dispositional theories such as Eysenck's have helped focus attention on the possibility that personality might be determined by biological factors and, more specifically, that psychological characteristics might be inherited (Goldsmith, 1983; Plomin, 1989). Anecdotal evidence of children who seem to "have" their parents' or grandparents' bad temper, generosity, or shyness also leads some to assert that personality is inherited.

What evidence is available to support the assertion?
Are personality traits themselves somehow passed on through genes? The evidence and the arguments regarding this assertion are much like those presented in Chapter 10 when we discussed the origins of differences in mental abilities. Resemblances among family members do provide an important source of evidence. Several studies have found moderate but significant correlations between children's personality test scores and those of their parents and siblings (Dixon & Johnson, 1980; Loehlin, Horn & Willerman, 1981; Scarr et al., 1981).

Are there alternative ways of interpreting the evidence?
Family resemblances could reflect inheritance or social influence. An obvious alternative interpretation of this evidence might be that parent-child similarities in personality come not from a child's genes but from the environment, especially from the modeling that parents and siblings provide. Children learn many rules, skills, and behaviors by watching those around them; perhaps they learn their personalities as well.

What additional evidence would help to evaluate the alternatives?
One way to evaluate the degree to which personality is inherited would be to study people in infancy, before the environment has had a chance to exert its influence. If the environment were entirely responsible for personality, newborn infants should be essentially alike. However, as discussed in Chapter 2, on human development, newborns do show differences in temperament—varying markedly in amount of activity, sensitivity to the environment, tendency to cry, and interest in new stimuli (Kagan, 1989; Korner, 1971). These differences suggest biological and perhaps genetic influences.

To evaluate the relative contributions of nature and nurture beyond infancy, psychologists have examined characteristics of adopted children. The influence of heredity in personality is supported if adopted children are more like their biological than their adoptive parents. If they are more like their adoptive family, a strong role for environmental factors in personality is suggested. Actually, adopted children's personalities do tend to resemble the personalities of their biological parents and siblings more than those of the families in which they are raised (Loehlin, Willerman & Horn, 1985; Scarr et al., 1981).

Further evidence for a genetic basis for human personality comes from studies in Europe and the United States that compared identical twins raised together, identical twins raised apart, nonidentical twins raised together, and nonidentical twins raised apart (Pedersen et al., 1988; Tellegen et al., 1988). They found that identical twins (who have the same genes) resemble each other more than do nonidentical twins (who have different genes) *regardless* of whether they are raised apart or together. In addition, whether identical twins are raised together or apart makes little difference; they still show consistent patterns of similarity in personality. Finally, research consistently shows that identical twins are more alike than nonidentical twins in their activity level, sociability, anxiety, emotionality, and helpfulness (Plomin, 1989). Other characteristics, such as aggression and distractibility, do not show as strong a genetic component (Plomin & Foch, 1980).

What conclusions are most reasonable?

Linkages: Do biological predispositions shape personality? (a link to Biological Aspects of Psychology)

Genetic influences do appear to contribute significantly to the variation in many personality traits. However, the influences of heredity and environment are so inextricably intertwined as to be inseparable (except theoretically, in statistical estimates). None of the research we have cited supports the existence of general "personality genes," nor is it likely that there are specific genes for each aspect of personality. It seems more likely that people inherit *general predispositions* toward certain levels of activity, forcefulness, emotionality, or sensation seeking, as well as toward left- or right-brain dominance and optimum arousal level (Eysenck, 1981; Kagan, Reznick & Snidman, 1988; Tellegen et al., 1987). These predispositions and physical features then interact with the environment to produce the specific features of personality. Thus, children who inherit a frail body may be especially likely targets for aggression by other children. These experiences might help create a tendency to avoid social interaction and thus encourage development of an introverted personality, characterized by self-consciousness and a preference for privacy. If the slender child has also inherited a predisposition toward social shyness or introversion, the development of the child's personality in this direction would be even more pronounced.

Thus, it appears that rather than inheriting specific personality traits, people inherit raw materials out of which personality is shaped by the world. However, further research is needed to determine which aspects of the environment are most important in shaping personality. In general, the *shared environment*—factors like socioeconomic status that equally affect all children in the same family—appear to have little influence on personality variation. By contrast, *nonshared environmental influences* appear to be very important in personality development (Plomin & Daniels, 1987). A child's place in the family birth order, differences in the way parents treat each of their children, and accidents and illnesses that alter a particular child's life or health are examples of nonshared factors that have a differential impact on each individual. ■

Evaluation of the Dispositional Approach

The dispositional approach to personality has gained wide acceptance among those who seek to explore and explain relatively stable patterns of thought and action on the basis of interacting genetic and environmental factors. This acceptance is embodied in the widespread use of objective personality tests, which are a mainstay of personality assessment. Today, it is rare that a psychologist would try to diagnose clients' psychological problems, predict

The dispositional approach to personality is highlighted in the courtroom, where defense attorneys try to show that their clients are not the type of people who could commit certain acts and where jurors are disqualified if they display traits suggesting that they might be unsympathetic to one side or the other. Though most people tend to think about other people in dispositional terms, critics of this approach to personality point out that it does not always result in accurate predictions of human behavior.

their potential for violent behavior or suicide, or judge their sanity for legal purposes without administering at least one established personality test, such as the MMPI. Indeed, psychologists from varying theoretical backgrounds use objective personality tests to measure individual differences related to job performance, resistance to stress, and improvement following psychological treatment.

Even attorneys sometimes apply dispositional concepts, in particular during the selection of juries (Nietzel & Dillehay, 1987). Actually, juries are "deselected," as lawyers reject individuals they feel might not be sympathetic to their case. Psychologists sometimes help by looking for clues to the traits of prospective jurors in their physical appearance, dress, or overt behavior. Does this use of the dispositional approach work? Most research indicates that the personalities of jurors who vote to acquit do not differ significantly from those voting to convict. And how do we know that a jury selected without the benefit of these methods would not have reached the same verdict? This use of the dispositional approach will remain controversial unless it is better supported in future research.

There are some problems and weaknesses associated with dispositional theories of personality. First, dispositional theories are better at describing people than at understanding them. You might say, for example, that Sally is nasty to others because she has a strong hostility trait, but other factors, such as how people treat her, could just as easily be responsible. It is important to go beyond merely inventing trait names to describe behavior. Some dispositional researchers, such as Eysenck, have tried to do so by isolating a few trait dimensions that can be used to predict how people will behave in a wide range of situations. It is in making such predictions that trait theory may be most useful (Epstein & O'Brien, 1985).

Second, the descriptions produced by dispositional approaches may not say much about a person that is unique. Consider how you might react to the following trait-oriented personality sketch:

You have a strong need for other people to like and admire you. You have a tendency to be critical of yourself. You have a great deal of unused capacity, which you have not turned to your advantage. . . . Disciplined and controlled on the outside, you tend to be worrisome and insecure inside. . . . At times you are extraverted, affable, and sociable; at other times, you are introverted, wary, and reserved. . . .

Does this description sound familiar? Does it describe anyone you know? Don't be surprised if it sounds like you. When psychology professors gave a longer version of this sketch to students who had just taken a personality test, nearly all of them said it was a "good" or even "excellent" description of their own personality (Ulrich, Stachnik & Stainton, 1963). At their worst, dispositional descriptions may be general enough to apply to most people, somewhat like the horoscopes printed each day in the newspapers.

Because dispositional theories of personality rely heavily on self-report personality tests to measure and validate traits and other characteristics, problems associated with these tests also raise questions about dispositional theories. Tests often yield different results depending on whether the test respondent was tired, giddy, or depressed. The testing situation itself may also affect responses. For example, hospitalized mental patients can fake responses depending on whether they wish to leave or to stay in the hospital (Braginsky, Grosse & Ring, 1966). These variations are especially troubling for dispositional theories because they suggest that test scores may not actually reflect traits that remain stable across time and situations (Kagan, 1988); they also fuel speculation that such traits may not exist.

The measurement of personality traits is a never-ending process of posing hypotheses about personality traits and then testing them empirically (Hogan & Nicholson, 1988). This process has revealed that some tests of some aspects of personality can be accurate descriptors of some of the people, some of the time. It is important to remember, however, that a person's responses to such tests are determined not by personality alone but also by the testing situation. The notion of personality as the product of person-situation interactions is an important one, to be discussed in the next section.

The Behavioral Approach

Linkages: How does the behavioral approach to psychology view personality? (a link to the World of Psychology)

According to the psychodynamic and dispositional approaches, outward behavior is a *sign* of inner personality. The **behavioral approach** instead views personality and behavior as basically the same thing. For behavioral theorists, *personality* is a label for the sum of a person's behavior patterns, of which any specific behavior is merely a *sample.*

Behaviorists assume that human behavior is determined mainly by what people have learned in life, especially by what they have learned by interacting with other people. The consistency of people's learning histories, not an inner personality structure, produces characteristic patterns of behavior. Successfully cheating on one test, for example, may encourage a person to do the same on other tests. According to the behavioral view, all behavior, normal and abnormal, develops through learning processes; even people with "disturbed" personalities *learned* to behave in problematic ways.

But what about the obvious inconsistencies in human behavior? People who are sociable in groups are sometimes awkward on a date; friendly men become wildly aggressive on a football field. Psychodynamic and dispositional theories explain these apparent inconsistencies by suggesting that different behaviors can reflect the same underlying trait, need, conflict, or defense. In contrast, the behavioral view explains these different behaviors by the concept of **situational specificity**. It says that in different situations, people are capable of many behaviors, not all of which are necessarily compatible or consistent. Yet all are genuine parts of a person's being; all are part of the endless interaction between behavioral tendencies and the situations of life.

By emphasizing the influence of situations on behavior, behaviorists challenge the importance of traitlike dispositions (Mischel, 1968). They hold that behavior is often specific to the situation and that traits are largely abstractions existing in the minds of observers rather than internal states that create consistency in different situations. Although behavior does show considerable traitlike stability across time and situations (Epstein & O'Brien, 1985; Mischel & Peake, 1983), some situations can overpower almost any personality trait. When situations are unambiguous and the consequences for inappropriate behavior are serious, people find their behavior controlled by the situation, not their dispositions. When approaching a stop sign, for example, all sorts of people stop in order to avoid having an accident or receiving a traffic ticket.

The behavioral approach can be traced back to the *radical behaviorism* of John B. Watson. As noted in Chapter 1, Watson (1924) used research on classical conditioning to support his claim that all human behavior, from mental disorder to scientific skill, is determined by learning. Today, behavioral theorists recognize that Watson's view was too extreme. However, they continue to emphasize the importance of environmental factors, and like Watson they are committed to studying objectively measurable behaviors, as assessed through careful observations, interviews, and special objective tests.

Today, there are two main versions of the behavioral model: the operant approach and the cognitive-behavioral approach. Each stresses different learning processes as the source of personality. The *operant approach* emphasizes the role of operant conditioning (discussed in Chapter 7), specifically the relationship between behavior and the rewards and punishments that follow it. The *cognitive-behavioral approach* (also known as *social-learning theory*) emphasizes classical as well as operant conditioning and includes learned thoughts, or cognitions, among the variables shaping personality.

The Operant Approach

Psychologist B. F. Skinner developed a behavioral approach that analyzes how observable behavior is learned in relation to observable environmental events. He referred to the interactions between behavior and the environment as *functional relationships*, and he sought to understand these relationships by using what he called the **functional analysis of behavior**.

Suppose a schoolboy causes trouble by hitting other children. Skinner would not speculate about the motivation or traits that might underlie such behavior. Instead, he would try to understand the behavior (and thus the child) by analyzing what stimuli preceded the responses and what consequences followed them. Careful observation may reveal that the aggression occurs mainly when a particular teacher is present to break up the fight. Perhaps the boy's aggression is being rewarded by the extra attention he gets from that teacher. This hypothesis could be evaluated by assigning another teacher to the child's class for a few days, then comparing the amount of aggressive behavior occurring on days when the original teacher was present, absent, and present again. Notice that functional analysis does not describe the boy's personality but summarizes what he finds rewarding (attention), what behaviors he is capable of (punching others), and what skills he lacks (for example, asking for attention in appropriate ways).

From Skinner's perspective, then, a "dependent" person is one who has been rewarded for dependence, and a "hostile" person has been reinforced for aggression. The same logic is applied to behavior disorders. Consider the mental patient who stares into space, refusing to speak. These behaviors might have begun in milder form, perhaps as responses to stress, but through inadvertent reinforcement by others, they became worse (Ayllon & Azrin, 1968; Ullmann & Krasner, 1975).

Cognitive Behavioral Approaches

Skinner focused on how the *external* environment determines personality through conditioning. But as discussed in the chapters on perception, thought, and stress, the *internal* environment—what people *think* about themselves and their lives—greatly affects how the outside world affects them. The importance of cognitive variables, along with classical and operant conditioning, is recognized in the *cognitive behavioral theories* of Julian Rotter, Albert Bandura, and Walter Mischel. In dealing with the aggressive schoolboy, for example, they might want to know not only what he has learned to do under particular circumstances, but also what he thinks about himself, his teacher, and his behavior.

Rotter's Expectancy Theory Rotter (1954) argued that learning creates cognitive expectancies that guide behavior. Specifically, he suggested that any

Linkages: As noted in Chapter 11, incentive theories of motivation emphasize the role of paychecks, good grades, and other desirable external goals in explaining a wide range of behavior, from physical labor to diligent studying. Incentives lie at the heart of Rotter's expectancy theory, a cognitive-behavioral theory of personality that views people's behavior as guided by learned expectations about the consequences of their actions and the perceived value of those consequences.

behavior is determined by (1) what the person expects to happen following the behavior, and (2) the value the person places on the outcome. For example, people might spend a lot of money on clothes to be worn at a job interview because (1) past learning leads them to expect that doing so will get them the job, and (2) they place a high value on having the job. Furthermore, Rotter hypothesized, people learn *general* ways of thinking about the world, especially about how life's rewards and punishments are controlled. Some people (*internals*) are likely to expect events to be controlled by their own efforts, whereas others (*externals*) tend to expect external forces over which they have no control to determine events.

Rotter developed a personality test, called the *Internal-External Locus of Control Scale*, or *I-E*, that measures the degree to which people expect events to be controlled by their own internal efforts or by external forces. Numerous studies have shown that people's scores on the test do correlate with differences in their behavior (Rotter, 1990). For example, internals do better at jobs in which they can set their own pace, whereas externals work better when a machine controls the pace (Eskew & Riche, 1982; see also Phares, 1973). Internals are also more health conscious than externals, more likely to seek medical treatment when they need it (Strickland, 1989), and generally less prone to stress-related illness. Indeed, as discussed at the end of this chapter, an internal locus of control is one aspect of the so-called stress-resistant, or *hardy*, personality.

Albert Bandura and Observational Learning Albert Bandura is perhaps best known for his work on *observational learning*, which means learning by watching others. As discussed in Chapter 7, people can learn by observing or hearing about the behavior of others and may then imitate these models (Bandura, 1986). They can learn even without reinforcement, and this learning depends on cognitive processes. As a result of observational learning, said Bandura, people (1) learn new behaviors, such as how to use a computer; (2) inhibit responses, as when a person does not try to open a door that someone else has found locked; (3) disinhibit responses, as when a person overcomes his or her reluctance to complain about bad restaurant service after hearing someone else do so; and (4) facilitate or prompt responses, as when one person's gift to a Salvation Army kettle influences others nearby to make donations.

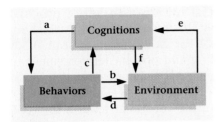

Figure 14.10
Reciprocal Determinism
Bandura suggests that the way people think, how people behave, and the nature of the environment are all determined by one another. For example, hostile thinking can lead to hostile behavior (line a), which in turn can intensify hostile thoughts (line c). At the same time, all that hostility is likely to offend others and create an environment of anger (line b), which calls forth even more negative thoughts and actions (lines d and e). These negative thoughts then alter perceptions, making the environment seem more threatening (line f).

Whatever behaviors are learned, they may in turn affect the environment, which may then affect cognitions, which may affect behavior, and so on. In short, according to Bandura (1978), overt behavior, cognitions, and the environment constantly influence one another, in what he called **reciprocal determinism** (see Figure 14.10).

One element in this web of influence is especially important in Bandura's view: the cognition called **self-efficacy**, which is the learned expectation of success, a person's belief that he or she can successfully perform a behavior regardless of past failures or current obstacles. According to Bandura, overt behavior is largely controlled by self-efficacy. The higher a person's self-efficacy regarding a particular situation, the greater his or her actual accomplishments in that situation will be. Thus, going to a party with the belief that you have the skills necessary to be a social success may create that success and blunt the impact of minor failures.

Self-efficacy interacts, according to Bandura, with expectancies about the outcome of behavior in general, and the result of this interplay helps to shape a person's psychological well-being (Bandura, 1982). Figure 14.11 shows how different interactions of these cognitions may produce different emotions and behaviors. If a person has little self-efficacy and also expects that nothing anyone does has much effect on the world, for example, apathy results. But if a person with low self-efficacy believes that other people do enjoy the benefits of their efforts, the result is self-disparagement and depression.

Mischel's Person-Situation Theory   Walter Mischel (1986) introduced an approach to personality based on a behaviorist version of dispositional concepts—what he calls *person variables*, which are identifiable characteristics that help differentiate people. The most important person variables, according to Mischel, are (1) competencies (the thoughts and actions the person can perform); (2) perceptions (how the person perceives the environment); (3) expectations (what the person expects to follow from various behaviors and what the person believes he or she is capable of doing); (4) subjective values (the person's ideals and goals); and (5) self-regulation and plans (the harshness of the person's standards for self-reward and plans for reaching goals).

According to Mischel, these person variables are responsible for differences in how each person handles new situations. When person variables dominate situational ones, the person behaves as he or she normally does. For example, a woman who expects that bad things do not happen to her would probably remain calm when a stranger appears at her door asking for directions. This calmness would be disrupted, however, if situational variables became dominant (as when the stranger pulls a knife and demands money). Mischel's formulation thus highlights the general cognitive-behavioral view that personality is a process, a continuously changing outcome of the interplay of a conscious, rational person and the world in which he or she lives.

Evaluation of the Behavioral Approach

The behavioral model holds several attractions. It is an objective and experimentally oriented approach. It defines its concepts operationally, relies on empirical data for its basic principles, and bases its applications on the results of empirical research. Its emphasis on learning engenders an optimistic attitude in its practitioners, who seem ready to tackle almost any problem.

As described in Chapter 16, for example, behavioral principles have guided the development of treatment methods for a wide range of psychological and behavioral disorders (Spiegler & Guevremont, in press). These principles have

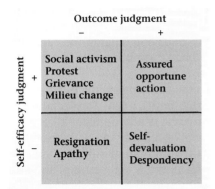

Source: Bandura, 1982.

Figure 14.11
Self-Efficacy, Outcome
Expectancies, and Psychological
Well-Being
According to Bandura, a person's
emotions and behavior reflect the
interaction of self-efficacy and outcome expectancies. Thus, a person
who has learned to believe that his
or her efforts lead to success (high
self-efficacy), but who perceives the
environment to be unresponsive to
those efforts, may become resentful
and socially active. Combining that
same level of self-efficacy with perceptions that the environment is responsive would lead, in this model,
to a person who is both active and
self-assured.

*Linkages: How are perceptions of oth-
ers related to personality differences?
(a link to Social Cognition)*

also been incorporated in many books that offer parents advice on child
rearing and methods for dealing with unruly children (Forehand & McMahon,
1981; Michelson et al., 1983; Patterson, 1982). For the most part, these methods
involve applying the principles of modeling and operant reinforcement to
create a stable, consistent home environment and to improve the behavioral
skills of young children. The goals are to have parents (1) show and tell a
child how to behave appropriately, (2) provide consistent rewards for good
behavior, and (3) either ignore or mildly reprimand misbehavior. A simple
example of such a program is illustrated in Figure 14.12.

Attractive as it may be, the behavioral approach has not escaped criticism.
It has been accused of reducing human beings to a set of acquired responses
derived from relationships with the environment. This view, critics say, is too
narrow, minimizes the importance of subjective experience, and tends to
exclude genetic, physiological, and other influences not based on learning. In
other words, behaviorists deal with an individual's behavior, but ignore the
individual.

Furthermore, the assessment methods used in the behavioral approach have
come under fire. To gather data about personality, behaviorists often conduct
interviews, ask people to keep a record of certain behaviors, or observe behavior
in simulated or actual social situations. These methods, critics argue, may be
no more reliable or valid than dispositional or psychodynamic methods, and
they may not be able to measure subtle cognitive variables.

Indeed, critics contend that the behavioral approach cannot deal adequately
with complex, internal problems. In the words of one observer, "Focusing on
visible behavior rather than inner states minimizes precisely those values,
feelings, fantasies, and motives which most distinguish and trouble human
life" (Korchin, 1976, p. 349). Even the theories of Rotter, Bandura, and Mischel
fail to satisfy critics on this point. The individual personality, the critics argue,
cannot be understood without focusing even more on nonbehavioral factors
such as perceptions, values, beliefs, expectancies, and intentions. These factors
are the focus of the phenomenological theories discussed next.

The Phenomenological Approach

Suppose you and a friend meet someone new at a party. Comparing notes
later, you discover a major discrepancy in your reactions. You thought the
new person was entertaining and humorous and showed a genuine interest
in others. Your friend saw the same person as a shallow, insincere individual,
who was hiding behind a humorous style and was merely pretending to be
interested. How can two people draw such opposite conclusions from the
same conversation? The phenomenological view holds that it was *not* the
same conversation. Just as each person sees something different in an inkblot,
each of you perceived a different reality, a different conversation, and a
different person.

This interpretation reflects the **phenomenological approach** to personality.
It holds that the specific ways each person perceives and interprets the world
make up personality and guide behavior. No one can understand another
person without somehow perceiving the world through that person's eyes. All
behavior, even if it looks bizarre, is meaningful to the person displaying it.
Proponents of this view believe that an individual's personal perception of
reality—not instincts, traits, or rewards—shapes his or her behavior from
moment to moment. This account of personality downplays the role of
instincts and the learning processes that humans and lower animals seem to

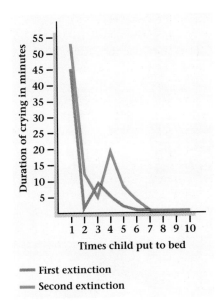

First extinction

Second extinction

Source: Adapted from Williams, 1959.

Figure 14.12
A Behavioral Program to
Control Crying
A child whose excessive bedtime crying had been inadvertently rewarded by parental attention was lovingly tucked in each night. Then all crying and other requests for attention were ignored. Based on the principle of extinction, this procedure not only reduced crying but created a more pleasant bedtime. The gray line shows the duration of crying on successive nights when the parents first used the extinction program. The pink line shows the results of a second extinction program that became necessary after the child's aunt rewarded his crying when the parents were away.

have in common. Instead, the phenomenological approach focuses on mental qualities that set humans apart: consciousness, self-awareness, creativity, planning, decision making, and responsibility. For this reason, the phenomenological approach is also called the *humanistic* view of personality.

This approach to personality has several roots, in philosophy as well as psychology. (In the language of philosophy, the mental experiencing of the world is called a *phenomenon*, and the study of how each person experiences reality is *phenomenology*.) The idea that each person experiences a unique version of reality derives from existential philosophers such as Kierkegaard and Sartre and from the work of the Gestalt psychologists. (As discussed in Chapter 5, the Gestalt psychologists emphasized that people are active participants in the process of perception.) The phenomenological approach also grew partly out of revisions of Freud's ideas—out of the work of Adler and Jung, who emphasized positive aspects of human nature, and of ego analysts, who highlighted the ego's direction of efforts toward growth.

Phenomenological theorists emphasize that each person actively constructs his or her own world. Humans are not merely passive carriers of traits, crucibles of intrapsychic conflict, or behavioral clay that is molded by learning. Instead, according to the phenomenological approach, the primary human motivator is an innate drive toward growth that prompts people to fulfill their unique and natural potential. Like the planted seed that naturally becomes a flower, people are inclined toward goodness, creativity, love, and joy.

George Kelly (1955), an experimental psychologist-turned-therapist, tried to blend some of these phenomenological concepts in a theory that also contained cognitive-behavioral features. Kelly emphasized that people's view of reality is important in guiding their behavior, but he suggested that this view is shaped by learned expectations. Expectations, said Kelly, form *personal constructs*, which are generalized ways of anticipating the world. According to Kelly, the nature of each person's unique constructs determines personality and influences behavior; personality development stems from the search for constructs that will allow people to predict and understand themselves and others. Perhaps because of its hybrid nature or its complexity, Kelly's theory received far less attention than the two more purely phenomenological theories of personality described in the following sections.

The Self Theory of Carl Rogers

The name of Carl Rogers is almost synonymous with the phenomenological approach (Rogers, 1942, 1951, 1961, 1970, 1980). Rogers assumed that each person responds as an organized whole to reality as he or she perceives it. He emphasized **self-actualization**, which he described as an innate tendency toward growth that motivates all human behavior. To Rogers, personality is the expression of each individual's self-actualizing tendency as it unfolds in that individual's uniquely perceived reality. If unimpeded, this process results in the full realization of the person's highest potential. If the process is thwarted, that potential may be dampened, and problems will appear.

To learn about personality, Rogers relied heavily on unstructured interviews in which interviewees decided what they wanted to talk about. Given sufficient freedom and encouragement, said Rogers, people eventually and spontaneously reveal whatever is important about their personalities.

The Concept of Self Central to Rogers's theory is the *self*, the part of experience that a person identifies as "I" or "me." According to Rogers, those who accurately experience the self—with all its preferences, abilities, fantasies,

What is reality? These people probably have differing perceptions of
how this accident happened and
who caused it. Their disagreement
reflects the phenomenological view
that each person's unique perceptions of the world shape personality
and guide behavior.

shortcomings, and desires—are on the road to self-actualization. The progress
of those whose experiences of the self become distorted, however, is likely to
be slowed or even stopped.

How can self-experiences become distorted? Rogers suggested that people
have a natural tendency to evaluate all experiences as positive if they enhance
self-actualization and as negative if they impede it. People also have a natural
tendency to seek positive experiences and avoid negative ones, simply on the
basis of their genuine, or organismic, reaction to them. A child would probably
say, "I like ice cream," because it tastes good, or "I hate cough syrup," because
it tastes bad. The child is aware of these self-experiences and is relaxed about
saying, essentially, "I like what feels good." In Rogers's terms, the child's
organismic experience and self-experience are consistent, or *congruent*.

Very early in life, however, children learn to need the approval of others,
which Rogers called *positive regard*. As a result, evaluations by parents, teachers,
and others begin to affect children's evaluations. When the evaluations by
others agree with a child's own evaluation (as when the pleasure of finger
painting is enhanced by a parent's approval), the child not only feels the
other's positive regard but also evaluates the self as "good" for having earned
approval. The result is a clearly identified and positively evaluated experience
of the self ("I like to paint") that the child gladly acknowledges. This self-
experience becomes part of the **self-concept**, which is the way one thinks of
oneself. Unfortunately, things do not always go so smoothly. If a pleasurable
self-experience is evaluated negatively by others, you must either do without
their positive regard or re-evaluate the experience. Rogers argued that because
positive regard from others allows a person to have positive self-regard, people
often choose to suppress their genuine feelings in order to get approval. Thus,
a little boy who is chided by his parents for enjoying dolls might adopt a
distorted self-experience ("I don't like dolls" or "Feeling good is bad").

In short, personality is shaped partly by the self-actualizing tendency and
partly by others' evaluations. In this way, people come to like what they are
"supposed" to like and to behave as they are "supposed" to behave. To an
extent, this process is adaptive, allowing people to get along in society.
However, it often requires that they stifle the self-actualizing tendency and
distort experience. Rogers argued that psychological discomfort, anxiety, or

According to Carl Rogers's self theory of personality, people who are clearly aware of their likes and dislikes, skills and shortcomings, will be more likely to become fulfilled, or self-actualized, than people who habitually alter their thoughts, feelings, and actions in an effort to please others. From the look on his face, this prize winner appears to be enjoying genuine satisfaction.

mental disorder can result when the feelings people let themselves experience or express are inconsistent, or *incongruent*, with their true feelings.

Conditions of Worth   Incongruence is likely when parents and teachers create **conditions of worth**, which means that they lead a child to believe that his or her worth as a person depends on displaying the "right" attitudes, behaviors, and values. Although conditions of worth are first set up by external pressure, they eventually become part of the person's internal makeup. (Notice the similarity between this idea and Freud's concept of superego.)

Conditions of worth are created whenever *people* are evaluated instead of their behavior. For example, parents who find their children smearing Jell-O on the kitchen floor are unlikely to say, "I love you, but I do not approve of this particular behavior." They are more likely to shout, "Bad boy!" or "Bad girl!" thus suggesting that the child can be loved and considered worthwhile only by being well behaved. As a result, the child's self-experience is not "I like smearing Jello-O, but Mom and Dad don't approve," but "Playing with Jell-O is bad, and I am bad if I like it, so I don't like it," or "I like it, so I must be bad." The child may eventually come to display very neat and tidy behaviors, which are not part of the real self, but of the ideal self dictated by the parents. Or the child may become quite naughty, in line with the new belief that he or she is "bad." Thus, from Rogers's perspective, rewards and punishments may shape or condition behavior, but their real importance for personality development lies in their potential for creating conditions of worth and, in turn, distorted self-perceptions and incongruence.

Cognitive psychologists have recently begun to explore self-perceptions or, as they call them, self-schemas. As discussed in Chapter 17, on social cognition, their findings tend to support Rogers's view that self-perception plays an important role in personality and that congruence may be important for psychological well-being.

Maslow's Humanistic Psychology

Like Rogers, Abraham Maslow (1954, 1962, 1971) saw personality as the expression of a basic human tendency toward growth and self-actualization. Maslow believed that self-actualization is not just a human capacity but a human need. In fact, as discussed in Chapter 11, on motivation, Maslow described it as the highest need in a *hierarchy of needs*. According to Maslow, people may be distracted from self-actualization by preoccupation with other needs.

Most people, said Maslow, are controlled by a **deficiency orientation**, a preoccupation with meeting perceived needs for material things. This orientation produces perceptions that life is a meaningless exercise in disappointment and boredom. People holding these perceptions are likely to behave in problematic ways. For example, in an attempt to satisfy the need for love and belongingness, people may focus on what love can give them (security), not on what they can give to another. According to Maslow, this deficiency orientation may lead a person to be jealous of a partner and to focus on what is missing; as a result, the person will never truly experience love and security.

In contrast, people with a **growth orientation** do not focus on what is missing but draw satisfaction from what they have, what they are, and what they can do. This orientation opens the door to what Maslow called *peak experiences*, in which one feels joy, even ecstasy, in the mere fact of being alive, being human, and knowing that one is utilizing one's fullest potential. ("In Review: Major Approaches to Personality" summarizes key features of the phenomenological approach, along with the other approaches we have described.)

According to Maslow's humanistic approach to personality, most people are preoccupied with what they do not have. The key to personal fulfillment, he argued, lies in focusing on what we *do* have, not only in terms of material possessions, but also in terms of skills and experiences.

Evaluation of the Phenomenological Approach

The phenomenological approach coincides with the way many people view themselves. It gives a central role to each person's immediate experience and emphasizes the uniqueness of each individual. It is an optimistic approach that places faith in a person's ability to fulfill his or her ultimate capacities.

The best-known applications of the phenomenological approach to personality are the client-centered therapy of Carl Rogers and the Gestalt therapy of Fritz Perls. These methods are discussed in Chapter 16. The phenomenological approach also inspired short-term group experiences such as sensitivity training, encounter groups, and personal growth groups. These experiences are designed to help "normal" people to become more aware of themselves and the way they relate to others, to begin breaking down the false fronts they use to protect their self-esteem, and to interact more genuinely with others.

For parents, the phenomenological approach offers programs designed to help them avoid creating conditions of worth while maximizing their children's potential. Most popular of these is a course called *Parent Effectiveness Training*, or *PET* (Gordon, 1970). Based on Rogers's self theory, the course helps parents learn to see their child as a human being with legitimate needs, feelings, and worth, not as a creature to be shaped, dominated, and controlled. It focuses on improving communication between parent and child and on resolving conflicts in a fashion that does not always create a winner and a loser. PET also helps parents to evaluate a child's behavior independently of the child's self. They are urged to make statements like "I don't want you to do that" or "I like to see you act that way," instead of giving judgments, such as "You are a good girl" or "You are a bad boy."

Despite these positive qualities, the phenomenological view has struck its critics as naive, romantic, and unrealistic. Are people all as inherently good and "growthful" as this approach suggests? The aggression and cruelty of which only humans appear capable calls this notion into question. Phenomenologists have also been chided for de-emphasizing the importance of inherited characteristics, biological processes, learning, situational influences, and unconscious motivation in shaping personality. Given the complexity of human motivation, the idea that everyone is directed only by an innate growth potential seems an oversimplification. So, too, is the phenomenological assumption that all human problems stem from blocked self-actualization; this view may lead to therapy in which everyone is treated basically the same.

The reliability and validity of phenomenological assessment methods have also been questioned. Rogers, for example, used a technique called the *Q-sort*. A person is given a large number of cards containing statements like "I am generally happy" or "I am overly suspicious." The task is to sort the statements into, say, ten categories ranging from "very uncharacteristic of me" to "very characteristic of me." This sorting is done twice, first on the basis of the person's real self and then on the basis of how he or she would like to be (the ideal self). If the two sortings are dissimilar, the person is revealing that his or her real and ideal self-concepts are not very close; there is little congruence. Repeated Q-sorts are used during therapy to chart changes in self-concept and reductions in incongruence. But does a person's Q-sort really represent his or her self-perceptions, or is it distorted by a desire to appear self-confident or "normal"?

Like the dispositional approach, phenomenological theories have been faulted for doing a better job of describing personality than explaining it. Saying that people behave as they do because of their perceptions, constructs, or actualizing tendencies does not deal with important underlying questions. Where does the actualizing tendency come from? How do perceptions develop? General notions that personality simply unfolds are unsatisfying to those interested in understanding personality development in more detail.

Finally, many phenomenological concepts, like many psychodynamic variables, are too vague to be tested empirically. Self-actualization and peak experience are two examples. Although phenomenologists like Rogers devoted years to systematic research on the relationship between people's self-perceptions and their behavior problems, and on the changes in self-perception that occur during therapy, many others actively avoid the scientific approach. They believe that people can understand themselves only through personal experience, not through experiments. This point of view has made the phenomenological approach unacceptable to those who favor experimental research as a means of learning about personality.

In Review: Major Approaches to Personality

Approach	Basic Assumptions About Behavior	Assessment Methods	Typical Research Methods
Psychodynamic	Determined by largely unconscious intrapsychic conflicts	Interviews and projective tests	Case reports
Dispositional	Determined by types, traits, or needs	Tests	Analysis of tests for basic personality dimensions
Behavioral	Determined by learning, cognitive factors, and specific situations	Interviews, objective tests, observations	Analysis of interactions between people and situations
Phenomenological	Determined by unique perception of reality	Interviews and tests	Studies of relationships between perceptions and behavior

Linkages: Personality, Stress, and Health

Are there "stress-prone" or "disease-prone" personalities?

The value of experimental research on personality has been highlighted by debates about the causes and effects of stress, which may include serious illness. In Chapter 13, on stress, we noted that some people overreact to stress; others suffer occasional symptoms but cope well with stress overall; and yet others seem to thrive on it. Research on personality has shed light on the reasons for these differences.

This research suggests, first of all, that certain characteristics may protect or buffer people from stress and subsequent sickness (Rodin & Salovey, 1989). The most carefully researched example of a psychological protector is the *hardy personality* (Kobasa, 1979, 1982). It was first described in the Chicago Stress Project, which gave personality tests to two groups of business executives who worked in stressful situations. One group showed many symptoms of illness; the other group, the "hardy" executives, showed few.

The scores of the hardy group revealed a personality with three characteristics: commitment, control, and challenge. *Commitment* refers to a strong involvement in personal values and goals; the hardy executives believed in what they were doing rather than merely going through the motions. *Control* involves belief in one's ability to exert control over or otherwise act to deal with problems; it is similar to Rotter's concept of an internal locus of control. Hardy executives preferred to confront, rather than shrink from, the world. And finally, hardy executives perceived stressful events as challenging opportunities, not as threats to their esteem, security, or independence.

Hardiness may also be related to high self-efficacy, or *dispositional optimism*, which is a persistent, long-term belief that most events will turn out well (Peterson, Seligman & Vaillant, 1988; Scheier & Carver, 1987). In fact, it appears that health and adjustment tend to be found in people who are a bit unrealistically positive about their self-efficacy, the world, or the future (Greenwald, 1980; Scheier & Carver, 1985; Taylor & Brown, 1988). Although there are limits to the truth of adages like "What I don't know won't hurt me," or "Ignorance is bliss," certain illusions seem to help people adjust to stress. Slightly exaggerated ideas of personal power, competence, and hopefulness, along with a tendency to blame bad outcomes on others while denying one's own faults, have often been linked with better physical and psychological conditions (Snyder & Higgins, 1988; Taylor & Brown, 1988).

Similarly, certain characteristics seem to make people especially vulnerable to illness. There does not appear to be a specific type of personality associated with each specific form of illness. However, various illnesses seem to be tied to negative feelings like cynicism, perceived helplessness, and frustrated attempts at control (McClelland, 1989). Preliminary findings indicate, for example, that a consistent pattern of depression, hostility, and anxiety is associated with increased risk of illnesses such as asthma, arthritis, ulcers, and headaches (Friedman & Booth-Kewley, 1987b). The relationship between the Type A behavior pattern described in Chapter 13 and physical disorders, particularly coronary heart disease, has been studied extensively (Friedman & Booth-Kewley, 1987a; Matthews, 1988; Suls & Sanders, 1988). Recall that the *toxic* components of the Type A pattern appear to be negative emotions like hostility, anger, and cynicism, especially in persons who have difficulty expressing negative feelings (Matthews, 1988). In contrast, Type A people who are fast moving, involved in their work, have an internal locus of control, and are emotionally expressive constitute a physically healthy group; these characteristics, which resemble the hardy personality, have been called the *charismatic Type A* pattern (Friedman & Booth-Kewley, 1987a).

How are personality factors linked to physical illness? One possibility is that personality does not increase susceptibility to illness; instead, personality

Not everyone in stressful jobs is equally vulnerable to stress-related problems. Among the characteristics that appear to protect people from the ill-effects of stressors are commitment to the task, a sense of control over events, optimism about the outcome of one's efforts, and a view of stressors as challenges rather than threats.

might be changed by illness. Perhaps anger and depression are reactions to being chronically sick. However, studies in which personality differences have been measured before assessment of changes in health indicate that those differences preceded the onset or worsening of illness in many cases (Matthews, 1988). In the chapter on stress we discussed other possible explanations for links between personality factors and physical illness. Certain characteristics have been associated with changes in physiological arousal, stress hormones, and the immune system—changes that in turn increase susceptibility to disease (Niaura et al., 1989; Stone et al., 1987). However, there are also data indicating that hardy persons react to stress with greater physiological responses than do those low in hardiness (Allred & Smith, 1989). Another possibility is that health practices create the link between personality and health. For example, hardy persons may maintain better diets, exercise more regularly, and not smoke because they believe these behaviors are important for good health (Wiebe & McCallum, 1986). Persons with long-standing, unexpressed negative emotions and pessimistic outlooks may not practice good health habits because they don't believe such habits matter.

In short, psychologists do not fully understand how links are forged between personality and illness. But personality seems to function like general eating habits: if you have a deficient diet, you run a greater risk for many types of illness.

Future Directions

There are many approaches to the concept of personality. In spite of differences among the approaches, there are also important similarities. All recognize that personality development begins in childhood and that much of personality develops through experience. All focus on the fundamental struggle each person faces in adapting to the world, even though they describe that adaptation differently, in terms of dealing with intrapsychic conflicts, developing traits, learning responses, or growing toward self-actualization. Finally, because thoughts can affect (and be affected by) behaviors and emotions, all approaches deal with cognitive processes in personality.

Progress toward a fuller understanding of human personality will probably come from an intelligent integration of the wisdom and research of more than one point of view. This trend toward the integration of diverse approaches is reflected in articles and books (Andrews, 1989; Messer & Winokur, 1986) and in the increasing eclecticism of personality research. Researchers are more concerned with examining specific variables and relationships than with trying to establish one approach as best.

This trend toward integration is also illustrated by the fact that the conflict over whether traits *or* situations are paramount subsided, if not disappeared, during the 1980s (Buss, 1989; Kenrick & Funder, 1988). Both dispositional and behavioral theorists recognize that it is the interaction between traits *and* situations that influences human behavior.

Future studies of consistency in personality will be aided by methods that have been developed for measuring consistency in a particular person in different situations or at different times (Lamiell, 1981; Lamiell & Trierweiler, 1986). That research is likely to focus on how consistency develops over a lifetime, how much of it is real, how much lies in the perceptions of those who observe it, and how much is determined by situational factors. Similarly, research on inconsistency will continue to explore questions such as how situations exert their influence and the degree to which a person's view of a situation changes its meaning and therefore its impact.

Individual differences will continue to be another burgeoning area of personality research. Specific variables most likely to be studied include how different people perceive and process information about themselves and their environment, what attributions they make about themselves and other people's behavior and personality, and how their emotions and thoughts interact to influence their attitudes and behavior.

If you want to learn more about personality and research in the area, consider taking a basic course in personality psychology and perhaps a laboratory in personality research methods.

Summary and Key Terms

Personality refers to the pattern of psychological and behavioral characteristics that distinguishes each person from everyone else.

Studying Personality

Methods of Assessing Personality

Personality is usually assessed through some combination of observations, interviews, and tests. Tests can be classified as either *objective* or *projective*. Objective personality tests are often used in an effort to identify people suited for certain kinds of jobs, but this use of personality tests does not usually work as well as employers might wish.

Systematic Approaches to Personality

The four main approaches to personality are the psychodynamic, the dispositional, the behavioral, and the phenomenological. Each approach contains basic assumptions and methods of measuring personality.

The Psychodynamic Approach

The *psychodynamic approach*, founded by Freud, assumes that personality is formed out of conflicts between basic needs and the demands of the real world. Most of these conflicts occur at an unconscious level, but their effects can be seen in everyday behavior.

The Structure of Personality

Freud believed that personality has three components—the *id*, which is a reservoir of *libido* and operates according to the *pleasure principle*; the *ego*, which operates according to the *reality principle*; and the *superego*.

Conflicts and Defenses

Id, ego, and superego are often in unconscious conflict. Various ego *defense mechanisms* keep these conflicts from becoming conscious. Key defense mechanisms are *denial*, *displacement*, *intellectualization*, *projection*, *rationalization*, *reaction formation*, *repression*, and *sublimation*.

Stages in Personality Development

Freud proposed that the focus of conflicts changes as the personality develops through *psychosexual stages*, which he identified as the *oral stage*, the *anal stage*, the *phallic stage*, the *latency period*, and the *genital stage*.

Variations on Freudian Personality Theory

Numerous psychodynamic theories have been based on Freud's original formulations. Prominent theorists include Jung, who argued that each person has both a personal and a *collective unconscious*, which stores *archetypes*; Adler, who held that a person's *style of life* constitutes personality; and Erikson, who proposed that personality develops through *psychosocial stages*, not psychosexual stages. These and other psychodynamic variations tend to downplay the role of instincts and the unconscious, emphasizing instead the importance of conscious processes, ego functions, and social and cultural factors.

Evaluation of the Psychodynamic Approach

The psychodynamic approach is reflected in many forms of psychotherapy. Critics fault the psychodynamic approach—especially Freud's orthodox version—for its lack of a scientific base, for the vagueness of its concepts, and for its view of humans as driven by instincts.

Other Key Terms in This Section: *free association, psychoanalysis, introjection, Oedipus complex*

The Dispositional Approach

The *dispositional approach* assumes that personality is made up of a set of stable internal characteristics that guide behavior. These characteristics have sometimes been described as personality types but more often as traits or needs.

Personality Types

For centuries, people have tried to place other people into a small number of personality types, but this effort has not been successful.

Personality Traits

Personality traits are seen by many as the building blocks out of which personality is created. These traits can appear at varying strengths in each person. Factor analysis of the results of personality tests is one method of isolating underlying personality dimensions. Recently, personality researchers have begun to agree on five such dimensions. Personality traits may be derived from inherited tendencies that provide the raw materials out of which experience molds each personality.

Evaluation of the Dispositional Approach

Dispositional theories have been criticized for being better at describing personality than at explaining it and for offering overly general descriptions of individuals. Problems associated with self-report tests of personality have also raised questions about dispositional theories.

The Behavioral Approach

The *behavioral approach* to personality assumes that personality is a label that summarizes a person's unique patterns of learned behaviors. It explains inconsistencies in behavior by the concept of *situational specificity*.

The Operant Approach

B. F. Skinner is the most prominent exponent of the operant approach to personality. He has argued that personality can be understood through the *functional analysis of behavior*, which examines how behavior has been rewarded or punished.

Cognitive-Behavioral Approaches

The cognitive-behavioral approach includes learned patterns of thinking among the factors shaping behavior and emphasizes the outcome of person-situation interactions. For example, Bandura highlighted the learned expectations he called *self-efficacy* and argued that *reciprocal determinism* characterizes the relationships among behavior, cognitions, and the environment. Mischel described how the varying importance of person variables and situation variables may account for consistencies and inconsistencies of behavior.

Evaluation of the Behavioral Approach

The behavioral approach has led to new forms of psychological treatment as well as suggestions for solving child-rearing problems. Critics of the behavioral approach see it as mechanistic and incapable of capturing what most psychologists mean by personality, including beliefs, intentions, and values.

The Phenomenological Approach

The *phenomenological approach*, which is also called the humanistic approach, is based on the assumption that personality is determined by the unique ways in which each individual views the world. These perceptions form a personal version of reality and guide behavior as people strive to reach their fullest human potential.

The Self Theory of Carl Rogers

Rogers believed that personality development is driven by an innate tendency toward *self-actualization* and shaped by social evaluations. He proposed that when people are free from *conditions of worth*, their personalities will be undistorted and free from psychological disorder.

Maslow's Humanistic Psychology

Maslow saw self-actualization as the highest need in a hierarchy of needs. Personality growth is optimized, he said, when people adopt a *growth orientation* rather than a *deficiency orientation*.

Evaluation of the Phenomenological Approach

Applications of the phenomenological approach include certain forms of psychotherapy, special group experiences designed to enhance personal growth, and Parent Effectiveness Training. Although the phenomenological approach has a large following, it has been faulted for being idealistic, for failing to explain personality development, and for being vague and unscientific.

Other Key Term in This Section: *self-concept*

O U T L I N E

Psychological Disorders

Mr. M., a thirty-two-year-old postal worker, lived comfortably and happily with his wife and their two children in a middle-class neighborhood. There was little warning of the day that Mr. M. suddenly told his wife that he was bursting with energy and ideas, that his job as a mail carrier was no longer fulfilling, and that he was wasting his talents. He stayed up most of that night writing furiously at his desk. The next morning he left for work at the usual time but returned in a couple of hours, his car crammed full of tropical fish equipment that he had bought after withdrawing all the funds from the family's savings account. He had also quit his job. Mr. M. explained that the previous night he had worked out a plan to modify existing equipment so "fish won't die anymore. We'll be millionaires." After unloading the car, Mr. M. began a door-to-door tour of his neighborhood in search of buyers for his "invention." Shortly thereafter, Mr. M. began receiving psychological treatment. The following conversation with his therapist illustrates some other aspects of his bizarre behavior and thought.

Therapist: Well, you seem pretty happy today.

Mr. M.: Happy! Happy! You certainly are a master of understatement, you rogue. (*Shouting, literally jumping out of his seat.*) Why I'm ecstatic. I'm leaving for the West Coast today, on my daughter's bicycle. Only 3,100 miles. That's nothing, you know. I could probably walk, but I want to get there by next week. And along the way I plan to contact a lot of people about investing in my fish equipment. I'll get to know more people that way—you know, Doc, "know" in the biblical sense. (*Leering at the therapist seductively.*) . . . (Adapted from Davison & Neale, 1990.)

At twenty-one, Mark complains that he feels "spaced out" and "creepy" much of the time. Unemployed, he lives with his parents and spends his time just watching TV or staring into space. He complains that he often feels he is outside himself, watching himself perform a script that someone else has written. Mark has had several jobs, but none lasted longer than a month. He was fired from

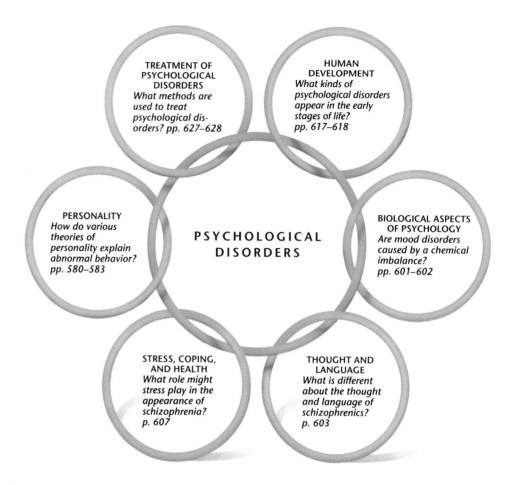

TREATMENT OF
PSYCHOLOGICAL
DISORDERS
*What methods are
used to treat
psychological dis-
orders? pp. 627–628*

HUMAN
DEVELOPMENT
*What kinds of
psychological disorders
appear in the early
stages of life?
pp. 617–618*

PERSONALITY
*How do various
theories of
personality explain
abnormal behavior?
pp. 580–583*

PSYCHOLOGICAL
DISORDERS

BIOLOGICAL ASPECTS
OF PSYCHOLOGY
*Are mood disorders
caused by a chemical
imbalance?
pp. 601–602*

STRESS, COPING,
AND HEALTH
*What role might
stress play in the
appearance of
schizophrenia?
p. 607*

THOUGHT AND
LANGUAGE
*What is different
about the thought
and language of
schizophrenics?
p. 603*

■ Look at the diagram above, which illustrates some of the relationships between the topic of this chapter, psychological disorders, and other chapter topics. Psychologists working to describe or explain psychological disorders rely heavily on concepts and data from other areas of psychology. In particular, the approaches to personality described in the previous chapter have been of enormous value in focusing research on likely causes of these disorders: psychodynamic conflicts, maladaptive learning experiences, blockages in the expression of potential, as well as genetic and biochemical problems are all possible triggers for disorder. In addition, the search for explanations has led researchers to examine whether stress may play a special role in the development of disorders.

These efforts to find the causes of disorders build on attempts to define more clearly just what disorder is and what problems constitute distinct disorders. Thus, whether psychologists are trying to explain disorders or treat them, their work involves perceiving and thinking about people and their problems. Research on information processing is shedding light on how limitations on these and other cognitive activities may affect attempts to classify and diagnose psychological disorders.

Remember that the questions shown in this diagram are only a sampling of the links between research in psychological disorders and other areas of psychology. The page numbers indicate where these questions are discussed. ■

his last job as a toy salesman after several customers complained that he spoke to them in vague terms and talked about irrelevant things. Mark is convinced that people dislike him, but he doesn't know why. He believes people change their seats on buses to avoid sitting next to him. He is unhappy and lonely, but he hasn't tried to re-establish what few friendships he once had. Mark has no definite plans for the future. He heard that one of his parent's friends was planning to open a chain of athletic shoe stores. Although he has no training in the retail business, he is "waiting" for an offer to manage one of these stores. (Adapted from Rosenhan & Seligman, 1989.)

Obviously, Mr. M. and Mark both have psychological problems. In fact, professionals diagnosed them as displaying some form of mental disorder, or psychopathology. **Psychopathology** involves patterns of thinking and behaving that are maladaptive, disruptive, or uncomfortable either for the person affected or for others. It is a social as well as a personal matter, and it has attracted the attention of psychologists in many subfields (see the Linkages diagram).

For centuries psychopathology has fascinated people, in part because its appearance is hard to predict. Sometime in their lives, most people encounter tragedy or trauma—a death, the loss of a job, a financial disaster—but somehow they adjust and go on. For some people, however, a single crisis can be psychologically shattering. Other individuals suffer mental disorders even though there is no apparent trauma.

Surveys have found that in any six-month period nearly 20 percent of the American population shows mild to severe mental disorder and that nearly one-third have experienced a disorder sometime in their lives (Meyers et al., 1984; Robins et al., 1984; see Figure 15.1). What determines who will "break down" and who will not? Is it a matter of will power, genetics, learned skills, sheer luck, or something else? We consider these questions in this chapter as we describe several major categories of psychopathology and some of their possible causes.

Figure 15.1
Mental Disorders in the American Population
A three-city survey of 9,543 people revealed that almost 1 in 5 displayed some form of mental disorder, either within the previous six months (Meyers et al., 1984) or at some time (Robins et al., 1984). Shown here are the estimated percentages of the population who exhibited some of the disorders described in this chapter. Note that the total percentage for all disorders is smaller than the total of the individual percentages, because some people had more than one disorder.

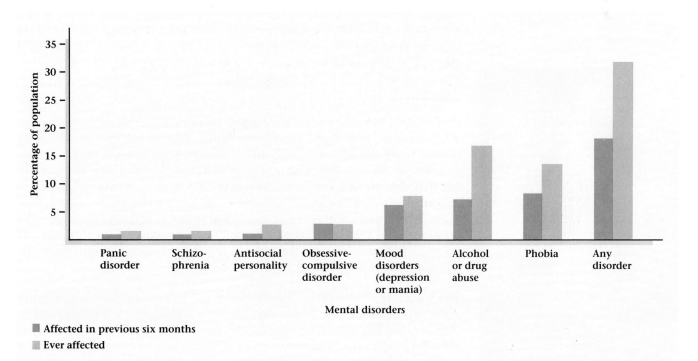

Affected in previous six months
Ever affected

Normality and Abnormality

Who decides what is maladaptive or abnormal? When is treatment required? In large measure, society shapes the answers to these questions. If you live in a tolerant society and do not upset other people too much, you can behave in unusual ways and still not be formally diagnosed or treated for psychopathology. For example, our collection of news clippings includes a story about a man in Long Beach, California who moved out of his apartment and left behind sixty thousand pounds of rocks, chunks of concrete, and slabs of cement neatly boxed and stacked in every room. And in Richmond, California, a woman regularly opened all her faucets, some connected to garden hoses hanging from trees, using more than twenty thousand gallons of water a day. In a less tolerant time or place these individuals might be taken into custody for treatment. We begin our exploration of psychopathology by considering some factors that determine what is considered normal and abnormal today.

What Is Abnormal?

Most people would agree that it is abnormal for a person to attempt suicide every time he or she is upset with the way a romantic partner is behaving. On the other hand, very few people would pin the "abnormal" label on someone who wears long-sleeved shirts in the summer. It is the vast range of behaviors between these extremes that causes debate over just what is normal and what is not. Here are three typical ways of defining what is abnormal.

The Statistical Approach   One straightforward way of deciding whether behavior is abnormal is to ask how common it is. From this perspective, whatever occurs frequently or is close to the behavior of the average person is considered normal. Thus, the *statistical approach* defines normal behavior by looking at what the average person does. Abnormality is then defined as deviance from whatever the greatest number of people, or the average person, does. For example, most people probably become angry with a coworker at some point over something the coworker has done, and occasional anger is not usually considered abnormal. If, however, a person acted angrily toward almost everyone, almost every day, you might label this behavior abnormal, in part because it represents a large departure from what is expected from the "average" person.

The statistical point of view provides an apparently clear criterion for abnormality, but it has some difficulties. As an example, recall from Chapter 10 that people who score significantly below average on IQ tests are often labeled "mentally retarded." Should a person with an unusually high IQ also be called abnormal? The statistical approach does not take into account the fact that some deviant behaviors, such as the ability to speak twelve languages, are valuable and desirable.

Another problem with the statistical view is that it equates normality with *conformity*. But nonconformists are often society's most creative thinkers. If everyone behaved the same, the research that led to computers, miracle drugs, and space travel might never have been done.

The Valuative Approach   An alternative to a statistical view of abnormality is the *valuative approach*: it says that behavior is abnormal if a person acts in ways that are not valued, no matter how many other people also behave that way. This criterion is sometimes called a "sociocultural" standard because it equates abnormality with violations of social rules and cultural norms. The

This woman is certainly dressed in an unusual way, but whether she will be labeled "abnormal" and perhaps given treatment depends on numerous factors, the most important of which is how abnormality is defined in her society.

valuative approach gets around the problem of calling geniuses and other valued nonconformists "abnormal." Valuative criteria mean that abnormality will be defined *relative* to prevailing standards. Unusual behavior might be ignored by this definition if it does not violate prevailing standards for living in a specific society.

But who determines the prevailing standards, the criteria for normality? If law or custom says that a behavior such as oral sex is wrong and therefore abnormal, but many people do it anyway, is that behavior really abnormal? If the answer is yes, very few people could be considered normal because there are so many ways of being abnormal and because most people probably display at least one of them. Furthermore, efforts to satisfy all valuative criteria may actually create anxiety and other stress-related problems.

A Practical Approach In reality, no one definition of abnormality is fully satisfactory. Therefore, both mental health professionals and the public use a combination of the statistical and valuative views. In this *practical approach*, judgments about abnormality and about who should receive treatment depend on (1) the *content* of behavior (what a person does and how it affects others), (2) the *context* of behavior (where and when the person does it), and (3) the subjective *consequences* of the behavior for the person (how much suffering and distress the person feels).

With regard to content, behavior is likely to be judged abnormal by society if it (1) is maladaptive or disabling, (2) appears bizarre or irrational, or (3) is unpredictable and uncontrolled (Rosenhan & Seligman, 1989). People will tolerate a considerable amount of bizarre and unpredictable behavior in themselves and others if the behavior is not frequent or disruptive enough to interfere with the conduct of everyday life. This *dysfunction* or *disability criterion* is probably the most fundamental aspect of judgments about the content of behavior, because actions that harm the well-being of an individual or a society usually demand strong interventions. From the practical viewpoint, behavior is unlikely to be formally considered abnormal if the person displaying it can get along from day to day and not cause others too much trouble. Thus, one successful businessman lined all his clothes with newspaper to protect himself against harmful radiation from alien spacecraft. Everyone at the office thought this was bizarre, but because he did his job efficiently, his behavior did not lead to formal diagnosis or treatment.

The second dimension of the practical approach relates to *context*—where and when behavior occurs. How would you feel if you were asked to enter an elevator and stare directly at another passenger during the ride? Or to tell jokes at a funeral? If you would hesitate, it is probably because you recognize that these actions would be inappropriate to the situation. Behaviors may be labeled abnormal if people use poor judgment about where they display them, thereby making observers uncomfortable. At the same time, the practical approach to abnormality says that people can perform all sorts of unconventional activities as long as they do not create discomfort and as long as they confine these activities to private places or to situations where everyone present approves.

The question of just what behaviors are approved in what situations is largely determined by the culture or subculture. What is normal in one culture may be abnormal in another. For example, on one Pacific island, social life is governed by hostility and suspicion. Gifts of food are assumed to be poisoned, and a poor crop is attributed to magical theft of nutrients from the soil. Anyone who is friendly is considered crazy (MacAndrew & Edgerton, 1969). Even within a culture, subcultural groups may use significantly different definitions of what is normal and abnormal. A street gang member who decides to concentrate on studying or doing other things considered normal by the dominant culture may be considered abnormal by other gang members.

The third dimension of the practical approach—the subjective *consequences* of the behavior—recognizes that even behavior that does not directly interfere with everyday functioning or disturb anyone else may cause the person to suffer. Subjective distress is not a necessary feature of abnormality. (Mr. M.'s behavior was considered abnormal in spite of his soaring enthusiasm about the tropical fish business.) However, when suffering is prolonged and unusually intense, it may be sufficient for a judgment of abnormality.

In summary, it is difficult to identify behaviors that are universally considered deviant or abnormal. The practical approach defines as *abnormal* statistically frequent or infrequent behavior that makes the person uncomfortable, that disables daily functioning, or that harms, significantly disrupts the lives, or violates the values of others.

Explaining Abnormal Behavior

Linkages: How do various theories of personality explain abnormal behavior? (a link to Personality)

Many explanations for abnormal behavior have been advanced over the centuries. At one time or another, each of three basic views has predominated. The earliest explanations were based on the **demonological model**, which claimed that abnormal behavior was the work of supernatural forces. A second viewpoint, espoused in ancient times and re-emphasized in present-day psychiatry, is the **medical model**, which is also known as the **biological model**. It explains abnormal behavior in terms of physical causes. The third perspective is the **psychological model**, which originated in the late nineteenth century. It holds that most abnormal behavior is the result of psychological disturbances such as personality conflicts, learned maladaptive habits, or distortions in how a person views the world.

Demonological and Medical Models   The demonological model was dominant until about the fourth century B.C. It was then that the Greek physician Hippocrates suggested a medical model of abnormality, in which behavior disorders, such as epilepsy and depression, were explained as physical diseases. Later Greek and Roman physicians expanded on or revised Hippocrates' views, giving birth to the notion of mental illness, or psychopathology.

During the Middle Ages (from about the fifth to about the fifteenth century A.D.), supernatural explanations of behavior disorders returned to prominence. A great deal of deviant behavior was tolerated and even encouraged if it was attributed to devotion to God. Thus, whipping oneself for one's sins was generally viewed as godly (Kroll, 1973). In the fourteenth and fifteenth centuries, disbelief in established religious doctrine (heresy) and other unusual behaviors were viewed as the work of the devil and his witches; heretics were burned at the stake. As the Middle Ages drew to a close, however, specialized hospitals, or *asylums*, for the insane began to appear throughout Europe. After the Middle Ages, medical doctors again took over responsibility for those considered mentally ill.

By 1850 almost every state in the United States had many state-run mental hospitals, each capable of housing thousands of patients. Medical research began to discover organic causes for some disorders. Physicians grew increasingly confident that it was only a matter of time before a physical cause would be found for all mental disorders. The search for organic causes proved difficult, however.

Even today, the medical model has yet to explain fully most behavior disorders. It remains influential, however, partly because there clearly *are*

Hogarth's eighteenth-century portrayal of "Bedlam," the colloquial name for St. Mary's of Bethlehem hospital in London. Most early mental hospitals were little more than prisons where the public could buy tickets to gawk at the patients, much as people go to the zoo today.

forms of abnormality that have a definite biological cause. These conditions are known as the **organic mental disorders**. They include disorders such as **dementia**, which is characterized by a loss of intellectual functions. Common symptoms include disturbances in memory, personality changes, and **delirium** (a clouded state of consciousness in which the person's thinking is confused and disjointed). In severe cases of dementia, such as Alzheimer's disease, the person may eventually become unable to recognize family members or to recall his or her name, address, or occupation. Learning new information also becomes difficult. Judgment is frequently affected; a formerly respectable person may suddenly begin propositioning strangers or committing petty crimes. Personal hygiene and appearance deteriorate, and the person may become very irritable or even paranoid. The most frequent causes of dementia are progressive deterioration of the brain as a result of aging, acute diseases (such as encephalitis or brain tumors) or head injury, and intoxication from alcohol or drugs.

The influence of the medical model is also bolstered by the way biological factors and psychological causes appear to interact to create many other mental disorders. These psychological causes are described by three major *psychological* models, which represent the psychodynamic, behavioral, and phenomenological perspectives described in Chapter 14, on personality.

Linkages: Can unconscious processes cause mental disorders? (a link to Consciousness)

The Psychodynamic Model   Late in the 1800s, Sigmund Freud began to challenge the strictly physical basis of the medical model. In the course of this challenge, Freud created the first psychological model of mental disorder. He described it as developing from psychological conflicts that begin early in childhood. This **psychodynamic model** views abnormal behavior as the result of unresolved, mostly unconscious clashes between instinctual desires and the demands of the environment and society. (These clashes are described in more detail in Chapter 14.)

Although Freud abandoned the search for *biological* factors underlying abnormal behavior, he still thought of it as an illness. Thus, while emphasizing psychological causation, his psychodynamic model shares numerous characteristics with the medical model. In both models, mental disorders feature problematic symptoms stemming from an underlying cause, which can be diagnosed, treated, and cured.

The psychodynamic model has generated many useful hypotheses about the causes and treatment of abnormal behavior, but critics point out that all disorders may not be rooted in unconscious conflicts. Further, the hidden nature of psychodynamic conflicts makes them difficult to measure objectively. Concern about these and other issues prompted the development of two other psychological models of abnormal behavior: the behavioral model and the phenomenological model.

The Behavioral Model   According to the **behavioral model**, most behavior disorders are caused by problematic learning experiences and current situations, not by biological imbalances or unconscious conflicts from the distant past (Bandura, 1969, 1986; Mischel, 1981; Skinner, 1953; Ullmann & Krasner, 1975). In fact, behavioral theorists argue that people learn maladaptive, abnormal behaviors just as they learn adaptive, normal behaviors. Just as you learned to enjoy your favorite food by discovering the rewards of its taste, a person who is terrified of crossing bridges probably learned this fear through negative experiences on a bridge. Thus, while biochemical or other physical factors might create predispositions for certain behaviors, the degree to which a person displays abnormal behavior mainly depends, say behaviorists, on how he or she *learns* to behave.

Behavioral theorists differ in the degree to which they focus exclusively on the interactions between overt behavior and the external environment. Some emphasize learned cognitive processes. This emphasis has generated a *cognitive-behavioral* model of disorder in which, for example, a person's depression might be seen as stemming not only from the loss of a job (an environmental event) but also from thoughts about low self-worth.

Behaviorists argue that, if abnormality is learned, behavior can be described as abnormal without labeling as abnormal the person displaying it. This approach makes it easier to focus attention on the person's strengths as well as problems. Also, society's deviants need not be seen as sick people, but as individuals who have learned specific maladaptive ways of thinking and behaving and who need help learning more adaptive thoughts and actions. Behaviorists refer to those they seek to help as *clients*, not patients, and they generally describe psychological problems as *behavior disorders* rather than as *mental illness*.

The Phenomenological Model   The third major psychological perspective is the **phenomenological model**. As discussed in Chapter 14, phenomenologists assume that human behavior is guided by the way each person perceives the world. If all goes well, each person naturally develops his or her unique potential. However, if self-actualization becomes blocked, psychological growth stops, and behavior disorder may appear as a signal of the problem. Growth is usually obstructed by a failure to be in touch with and express one's true feelings, some of which may be unacceptable to oneself or to others. When this happens, the person begins to distort his or her perceptions of reality. The greater the perceptual distortion and the less the emotional contact with one's feelings, the more serious the behavior disorder.

Like behavioral theorists, phenomenologists do not talk of "sick patients" but of disturbed clients. Further, abnormal behavior, no matter how unusual or seemingly irrational, is presumed to be a reasonable reaction to the world the client perceives.

An Integrated View: The Diathesis-Stress Model Today, the medical/biological, psychodynamic, behavioral, and phenomenological approaches represent the main views of psychopathology. Which of these four models is correct? All of them are valid and useful to some degree because they all provide a logical explanation for many behavior disorders, and they all have generated useful methods of treating those disorders (see Table 15.1). However, much research shows that no one model can fully account for all forms of abnormality; different disorders may be due to different types of causes, and a specific disorder may be traceable to more than one cause. This recognition has led to the **diathesis-stress model**, which combines physical factors (such as chemical imbalances), environmental factors (such as stress), and psychological factors into an integrated theory of causation.

The diathesis-stress model recognizes that each person inherits predispositions that leave him or her vulnerable to problems. The predisposition is called a **diathesis** (pronounced "die-a'-thesis"). Whether a predisposition leads to problematic behavior depends on what stressors a person confronts. Thus, a person may inherit a tendency toward sadness and depression, but expression of this tendency may appear only in stressful situations, such as a financial crisis. If no stressful situations occur, depression may not occur either. Similarly, as noted in Chapter 13, people who must deal with particular stressors may or may not show signs of psychopathology, depending on their ability to cope with those stressors. Later, we will describe how the diathesis-stress model, as well as the other approaches discussed here, are used to better understand specific types of psychological disorder.

**Table 15.1
Four Ways of Viewing Psychopathology**

Mr. A. is a forty-two-year-old man who lives with his wife and two teenage daughters in a large city on the West Coast. For over a year, he has been experiencing attacks of dizziness, accelerated heartbeat, and, most recently, fainting. These attacks come only when he is away from home or when his older daughter is there. The problem has become so severe that Mr. A. has had to take a leave of absence from his job. Here is a summary of how the four main approaches to psychopathology might view Mr. A.'s problems. The treatment methods are discussed in Chapter 16.

Approach	Possible Causes	Possible Treatment
Medical/biological	Organic disorder; perhaps overly reactive nervous system or biochemical imbalance, making Mr. A. vulnerable to stress.	Drugs
Psychodynamic	Unconscious conflicts, perhaps related to unacceptable impulses toward older daughter.	Talking therapy, aimed at gaining insight into and resolving conflicts.
Behavioral	Learned response to stress brought on by family and job responsibilities; symptoms rewarded by relief from duties.	Development of stress-coping techniques.
Phenomenological	Failure to recognize true feelings about family and job; perhaps feelings of wanting to be free are incongruent with his self-image and result in symptoms.	Therapy experiences designed to put Mr. A. in closer touch with his real feelings so that he can make some thoughtful decisions.

Classifying Abnormal Behavior

In spite of variations in what is called abnormal, there does seem to be a set of behavior patterns that roughly defines the range of most abnormality. It has long been the goal of those who study abnormal behavior to establish a system of classifying these patterns in order to understand and deal with them. *Psychodiagnosis* is the traditional medically oriented term for the process of classifying patients' mental disorders. Proponents of the behavioral and phenomenological models favor the term *assessment*, which they feel reflects their emphasis on describing clients in more detail than diagnostic labels can provide. Nevertheless, the dominant classification system is clearly label-oriented.

A Classification System: DSM-III-R In 1917 the American Psychiatric Association began publishing what has become the "official" diagnostic classification system, the *Diagnostic and Statistical Manual of Mental Disorders (DSM)*. In each of its editions, the DSM has included more categories. The revised third edition, DSM-III-R, was published in 1987 and contains over two hundred specific diagnostic labels.

DSM-III-R is basically a list of abnormal behavior patterns. Unlike the earlier DSM-I and DSM-II, it does not attempt to state the causes of all disorders (or directly endorse any particular theoretical model). Instead, DSM-III-R describes each disorder and provides criteria outlining what conditions must be present before making each diagnosis. The system allows for evaluations on five dimensions, or *axes*, which together provide a picture of a person's problems and their context. On Axis I there are sixteen major mental disorders (see Table 15.2). Axis II includes two additional types of disorder: developmental problems and personality disorders. (These are placed on a separate axis so that they are not overlooked when an Axis I problem attracts the most attention.) Any physical conditions that might be important in understanding a person's problems are listed on Axis III. On Axis IV the diagnostician rates (from 1 to 6) the amount of stress the person has faced in the past year. Finally, ratings (from 90 down to 1) of the person's psychological, social, and occupational functioning, currently and during the past year, appear on Axis V. Here is a sample DSM-III-R diagnosis.

Axis I   Major depression, single episode; alcohol dependence.

Axis II   Dependent personality disorder.

Axis III   Alcoholic cirrhosis of the liver.

Axis IV   Stressors: death of child. Severity: 6—catastrophic.

Axis V   Global assessment of functioning: currently, 50; highest in past year, 65.

Another notable feature of DSM-III-R is that two time-honored terms— neurosis and psychosis—no longer appear as major diagnostic categories. **Neurosis** referred to conditions in which some form of anxiety was the major characteristic. **Psychosis** included conditions involving more extreme problems that left the patient "out of touch with reality" or unable to function on a daily basis. The disorders once gathered under these headings in DSM-I and DSM-II now appear in various Axis I categories.

The Value of Psychodiagnosis David Tom, a Chinese immigrant, was in a hospital being treated for tuberculosis when a diagnostician failed to realize that he spoke an unusual Chinese dialect and labeled him psychotic. He was

Table 15.2
The Diagnostic and Statistical Manual (DSM) of the American Psychiatric Association

Axis I of the revised third edition (DSM-III-R) lists the major categories of mental disorders. Axis II contains personality disorders and problems in various areas of development.

Axis I (Major Mental Disorders)

1. *Disorders usually first evident in infancy, childhood, or adolescence* Problems such as hyperactivity, childhood fears, abnormal aggressiveness or other notable misconduct, failure to identify with one's own gender, frequent bedwetting or soiling, and other problems in normal social and behavioral development. Problems associated with eating too little (anorexia) or binge eating followed by self-induced vomiting (bulimia). These disorders are discussed in Chapter 11.

2. *Organic mental disorders* Problems caused by physical deterioration of the brain due to aging, disease, drugs or other chemicals, or other possibly unknown causes. These problems can appear as an inability to "think straight" (delirium) or as loss of memory and other intellectual functions (dementia).

3. *Psychoactive substance-use disorders* Psychological, behavioral, and physical problems caused by dependence on a variety of chemical substances, including alcohol, heroin, cocaine, amphetamines, hallucinogens, PCP, marijuana, and tobacco.

4. *Schizophrenia* Severe conditions characterized by abnormalities in thinking, perception, emotion, movement, and motivation that greatly interfere with daily functioning.

5. *Delusional (paranoid) disorders* Problems involving false beliefs (delusions) about such things as being loved by some high-status person, having inflated worth or power, or being persecuted, spied on, cheated on, followed, harassed, or kept from reaching important goals.

6. *Other psychotic disorders* Serious mental problems that are similar to but not as intense as schizophrenic or delusional (paranoid) disorders.

7. *Mood disorders* (also called *affective disorders*) Severe disturbances of mood, especially depression, overexcitement (mania), or alternating episodes of each extreme (as in bipolar disorder).

8. *Anxiety disorders* Specific fears (phobias), panic attacks, generalized feelings of dread, rituals of thought and action (obsessive-compulsive behavior) aimed at controlling anxiety, and problems caused by traumatic events, such as rape or military combat (see Chapter 12 for more on panic disorder and Chapter 13 for more on posttraumatic stress disorder).

9. *Somatoform disorders* Physical symptoms, such as paralysis and blindness, that are found to have no physical cause. Also, unusual preoccupation with physical health or with nonexistent or elusive physical problems (hypochondriasis).

10. *Dissociative disorders* Psychologically caused problems of consciousness and self-identification, including loss of memory (amnesia) or the development of more than one identity (multiple personality).

11. *Sexual disorders* Problems related to (a) finding sexual arousal through unusual objects or situations (like baby carriages or exposing oneself) or (b) unsatisfactory sexual activity (sexual dysfunction).

12. *Sleep disorders* Severe problems involving the sleep-wake cycle, especially an inability to sleep well at night or to stay awake during the day. (See Chapter 6.)

13. *Factitious disorders* False mental disorders, which are intentionally produced to satisfy some economic, psychological, or other need.

14. *Impulse control disorders* Compulsive gambling, stealing, or fire setting.

(Continued)

Table 15.2
The Diagnostic and Statistical
Manual (DSM) of the American
Psychiatric Association
(***Continued***)

15. *Adjustment disorders*   Failure to adjust to or deal well with such stressors as divorce, financial problems, family discord, or other unhappy life events.

16. *Psychological factors affecting physical condition*   True physical problems, such as headaches, high blood pressure, or ulcers that are caused or made worse by such psychological factors as anxiety (see Chapter 13, on stress).

Axis II (Developmental and Personality Disorders)

1. *Specific developmental disorders*   Mental retardation and autistic disorder (severe impairment in social and behavioral development), as well as other problems in the development of skill in reading, speaking, mathematics, or English.

2. *Personality disorders*   Individuals who may or may not receive an Axis I diagnosis but who show lifelong behavior patterns that are unsatisfactory to them or that disturb other people. The problematic features of their personality may involve unusual suspiciousness, unusual ways of thinking, self-centeredness, shyness, overdependency, excessive concern with neatness and detail, or overemotionality.

kept in mental institutions for more than thirty years. When the error was finally discovered in 1983, Tom was released, but his physical and mental condition had deteriorated so much during his hospital stay that he would spend the rest of his life in a group home for former mental patients.

The potential for misdiagnosis, and the biasing effects of diagnostic labels, were highlighted by a study in which David Rosenhan (1973) and nine associates presented themselves at ten psychiatric hospitals. Each person complained of the same faked symptoms: hearing a voice that said "dull," "empty," and "thud." Otherwise, they reported only truthful facts about their very normal lives. Yet all were admitted to the hospitals as patients, most with a diagnosis of schizophrenia, a serious disorder. Once in the hospital, these "patients" behaved normally and reported no voices or other symptoms. However, they were not detected as frauds by the staff (only by actual patients on the same wards). The staff interpreted even their normal actions (such as taking notes about their experiences) as symptoms that confirmed the original diagnoses. Why? Interpretations vary, but the main reason is probably that, as discussed in Chapter 5, on perception, people tend to see what they expect to see. Hospital staff expect to see deviance, thus making it more likely that whatever the volunteers said or did would be interpreted as deviant. In addition, because of the anchoring heuristic and the confirmation bias (discussed in Chapter 9, on thought), the diagnosticians tended to stick to their original hypothesis that the "patients" were mentally ill.

This research and the David Tom case illustrate some of the dangers of the diagnostic enterprise. Diagnostic labels (1) reflect an incomplete understanding of a person; (2) may be affected by personal opinions, expectations, and biases; and (3) do not always tell very much about a person. The dangers may be lessened by spending more time on each case and giving a descriptive summary of the person's background, problems, and potential strengths along with DSM-III-R labels. In practice, however, this may not be possible. Furthermore, many professionals want a shorthand, agreed-upon way of summarizing a person's problems. How good are those summary labels?

One major concern is *interrater reliability*, the degree to which different diagnosticians give the same label to the same person. Agreement has increased since DMS-III introduced specific criteria for àssigning each diagnosis. Recent studies indicate interjudge agreement as high as 83 percent on schizophrenia and mood disorder, and agreement for many other Axis I categories in the high 70s (Grove, 1987; Matarazzo, 1983). However, there are also instances of much lower reliability figures on Axis I, such as for anxiety disorders (Mannuzza et al., 1989), and reliability tends to be lower for diagnosis of the Axis II personality disorders (Mellsop et al. 1982) and childhood disorders (Bemporad & Schwab, 1986). In addition, agreement is usually easier to achieve in experiments than in everyday practice, since diagnosticians may not adhere closely to DSM-III-R criteria when they are facing time pressures and other demands. In one study at a New York psychiatric hospital, very different diagnoses were given to the same patients by different clinicians in as many as 75 percent of 131 randomly chosen cases (Lipton & Simon, 1985).

A second important question about psychodiagnosis concerns its *validity*; that is, do diagnostic labels give accurate information about the person? This is a difficult question because it is hard to find a fully acceptable standard for accuracy. Should the diagnosis be compared to the judgments of experts? Or should it be tested against the course of the patient's disorder? Despite these problems, there is evidence supporting the validity of some DSM-III criteria (Drake & Vaillant, 1985; Robins & Helzer, 1986), even though the validity for many categories remains too low. Of course, no shorthand label can specify exactly what each person's problems are or exactly how that person will behave in the future. All that can be reasonably expected of a diagnostic system is that it allows informative, general descriptions of the types of problems displayed by people who have been placed in different categories.

THINKING CRITICALLY

Is Psychodiagnosis Biased?

Some critics of psychodiagnosis have suggested that problems with the reliability and validity of DSM-III-R stem in part from bias in those who use it. Diagnosticians, like other people, hold expectations and stereotypes about certain groups of people, and these cognitive biases could color their judgments about how to label the behavior displayed by members of these groups.

What am I being asked to believe or accept?
The argument is that clinicians base their diagnoses partly on the gender or race or age of the client. Thus, it is alleged that a woman will be given a different, probably more severe, diagnosis than a man who presents similar symptoms, and that simply because they are members of a particular ethnic group, some people are diagnosed as suffering certain disorders more often than those in other groups.

Here, we focus on race as a possible biasing factor. Although there are also data about the effects of social class, gender, age, and even weight (Lopez, 1989), race is of special interest because it has been studied extensively and because there is evidence that it, along with social class, is an important variable in the development of mental illness. In contrast, gender has not been shown to be a major biasing factor even though it has also been studied a great deal.

What evidence is available to support the assertion?

Several facts suggest the possibility of racial bias in psychodiagnosis. African-American people receive the diagnosis of schizophrenia more frequently than Caucasians do (Manderscheid & Barrett, 1987). Further, relative to their presence in the general population, African-Americans are overrepresented in public mental health hospitals, where the most serious forms of disorder are seen, and underrepresented in private hospitals and outpatient clinics, where less severe problems are treated (Lindsey & Paul, 1989).

Are there alternative ways of interpreting the evidence?

Differences in diagnosis or in treatment patterns between racial groups do not automatically point to bias based on race. Perhaps there are real differences in psychological functioning associated with race. For example, if, on the average, African-Americans are exposed to more major stressors such as poverty and violence, they could be more vulnerable to more serious forms of mental disorder. Poverty, not diagnostic bias, could also be responsible for African-Americans seeking help more often at less expensive public hospitals rather than at more expensive private ones.

What additional evidence would help to evaluate the alternatives?

Do African-Americans actually display more signs of mental disorder, or do diagnosticians just perceive them as doing so? One way of approaching this question would be to conduct experiments in which diagnosticians assign labels to clients on the basis of case histories, test scores, and the like. Unknown to the diagnosticians, the cases would be selected so that pairs of clients show about the same objective amount of disorder, but one member of the pair is identified as Caucasian, the other as African-American. The existence of bias among the clinicians would be suggested if the African-American member of each pair more often received a diagnosis or a more severe diagnosis. However, studies like this have rarely been conducted in clinical settings.

A strategy that has been used with real clinical populations has clinicians conduct extensive, detailed interviews of patients and then reach a diagnosis and a judgment of the severity of the symptoms. These diagnoses and judgments are then statistically analyzed in equations that examine which variables predict the actual diagnoses the patients received when admitted to the hospital. If, after controlling for the type and severity of symptoms, a researcher discovers that African-Americans are still diagnosed with a certain disorder more often than Caucasians, evidence for bias is fairly strong. In studies that seek to control for the amount and severity of symptoms reported by African-American and Caucasian patients, African-Americans are indeed more frequently diagnosed as schizophrenic (Pavkov, Lewis & Lyons, 1989). In other words, there is evidence for racial bias, at least for some diagnoses.

What conclusions are most reasonable?

Just as DSM-III-R is imperfect, so are those who use it. Chapters 9 and 17, on thought and social cognition, discuss how cognitive biases and stereotypes shape human thought in matters large and small. No matter how precisely researchers specify the ideal criteria for assigning diagnostic labels, biases and stereotypes are likely to interfere with objectivity in applying those criteria. Recognizing the imperfections of the human information-processing system, clinical researchers seek the best ways to blend their judgments with those of computers that have been programmed to weigh and combine test scores and other information in an unbiased fashion (Nietzel, Bernstein & Milich, 1991). However, the discussion in Chapter 9 of the limitations of artificial intelligence suggests that humans will always play a role in diagnosis. As long as they do, some bias is likely to remain.

Bringing the effects of that bias to some irreducible minimum requires a better understanding of it. Bias does not necessarily reflect deliberate discrimination; it may be unintentional. For example, clinicians who have a racial or socioeconomic background that is different from that of their clients may not understand that a certain behavior reflects the clients' subculture, not mental illness. In short, reducing bias may require more than detecting and eliminating deliberate discrimination. Steven Lopez (1989) emphasizes the need to recognize and understand the limitations in information processing that affect clinicians. Thus, research on memory, problem solving, decision making, social attributions, and other aspects of cognition may turn out to be key ingredients in reducing bias in the diagnosis of behavior disorder. ■

A new version of DSM, to be called DSM-IV, is due to be published in about 1993. For now, DSM-III-R provides a convenient framework for our description of abnormality. We do not have the space to cover all the DSM-III-R categories, so we will sample several of the most prevalent, socially significant, or unusual examples of the major disorders on Axis I. In each instance, we will provide a general description, some clinical examples, and a brief discussion of possible causes of the disorder.

As you read, try not to catch "medical student's disease." Just as medical students often think they have the symptoms of every illness they read about, psychology students frequently worry that their behavior (or that of a relative or friend) signals some type of mental disorder. This is usually not the case; it is just that everyone has some problems, some of the time. It might be a good idea to review the criteria of the practical approach to abnormality and consider how frequently a problem occurs before deciding whether you or someone you know needs psychological help.

Anxiety Disorders

If you have ever been tense before an exam or a date or a visit to the dentist, you have a good idea of what anxiety feels like. Increased heart rate, sweating, rapid breathing, a dry mouth, and a sense of dread are common components of anxiety. Brief episodes of moderate anxiety are a normal part of life for most people. For others, anxiety is so intense, long standing, or disruptive that it is called an **anxiety disorder**.

Types of Anxiety Disorders

We discuss four types of anxiety disorders: phobia, generalized anxiety disorder, panic disorder, and obsessive-compulsive disorder.

Phobia   A strong, irrational fear of an object or situation that is not likely to be dangerous is called a **phobia**. The phobic person usually realizes that the fear makes no sense but cannot keep it from interfering with daily life. There are thousands of phobias, many of which have been given Greek names (see Table 15.3).

Table 15.3
Common Phobias

Some phobias are more familiar than others. Here is a sampling, along with their Greek names.

Name	Feared Stimulus
Acrophobia	Heights
Claustrophobia	Enclosed spaces
Hematophobia	Blood
Gephyrophobia	Crossing a bridge
Kenophobia	Empty rooms
Cynophobia	Dogs
Aerophobia	Flying
Entomophobia	Insects
Gamophobia	Marriage
Ophidiophobia	Snakes
Xenophobia	Strangers

DSM-III-R classifies phobias into simple, social, and agoraphobia subtypes. **Simple phobias** involve fear of specific situations or things, such as heights, darkness, animals, and air travel. Here is a case from one of the authors' files.

Mr. L. was a fifty-one-year-old office worker who became terrified whenever he had to drive over a bridge. For years, he avoided bridges by taking roundabout ways to and from work, and he refused to be a passenger in anyone else's car, lest they use a bridge. Even this very inconvenient adjustment was shattered when Mr. L. was transferred to a position requiring frequent automobile trips, many of which crossed bridges. He refused the transfer and was fired.

Social phobias involve persistent anxiety about being negatively evaluated by others or publicly embarrassed by doing something impulsive, outrageous, or humiliating. Fear of public speaking, "stage fright," and fear of eating or writing in front of others are examples.

Agoraphobia is a strong fear of being separated from a safe place like home or of being trapped in a place from which escape might be difficult. Attempts to leave home, especially alone, lead to increasing anxiety, nausea, dizziness, or fainting. Crowded public places like theaters or shopping malls are also upsetting because the person fears becoming helpless and incapacitated by some calamity. In severe cases, being alone at all, even at home, brings terror.

Like other phobias, agoraphobia is more often seen in women, many of whom are totally housebound by the time they seek help. Although agoraphobia occurs in less than 0.5 percent of the population, it is the phobia that most often brings people into treatment, mainly because it so severely disrupts everyday life (Chambliss & Goldstein, 1980).

Phobias can be very specific and unusual, which has provided grist for the humor mill, but the discomfort caused by severe phobias is no laughing matter.

THE FAR SIDE   By GARY LARSON

Luposlipaphobia: The fear of being pursued by timber wolves around a kitchen table while wearing socks on a newly waxed floor.

Source: The Far Side. Copyright 1985 Universal Press Syndicate. Reprinted by permission.

Generalized Anxiety Disorder   Excessive and long-lasting anxiety that is not focused on any particular object or situation marks **generalized anxiety disorder**. Because the problem occurs in virtually all situations and because the person cannot pinpoint its source, it is sometimes called *free-floating anxiety*. For weeks at a time, the person feels anxious and worried, sure that some disaster is imminent. The person becomes jumpy and irritable; sound sleep is impossible. Fatigue, inability to concentrate, and physiological signs of anxiety are also common.

Panic Disorder   For some people, anxiety takes the form of **panic disorder**, which we described in the Linkages section of Chapter 12, on emotion. People suffering from panic disorder experience terrifying *panic attacks* that come without warning or obvious cause and are marked by heart palpitations, pressure or pain in the chest, dizziness or unsteadiness, sweating, and faintness. Victims may come to worry constantly about having one of these unpredictable attacks and curtail activities to avoid possible embarrassment. In fact, panic attacks and agoraphobia tend to occur together. In many cases, agoraphobia develops after an initial panic attack (Breier, Charney & Heninger, 1986) as the person comes to fear having other attacks in places where help won't be available.

Obsessive-Compulsive Disorder Anxiety is also at the root of **obsessive-compulsive disorder**, in which the person is plagued by persistent, often upsetting thoughts that may motivate repetitive, uncontrollable behaviors that the person feels will neutralize the fears associated with those thoughts. If the person tries to interrupt the obsessive thoughts or cease the compulsive behavior, severe agitation and anxiety usually result. This pattern is very different from the occasional experience of having a repetitive thought going on "in the back of your mind" or rechecking to see that a door is locked. In obsessive-compulsive disorder, the thoughts and compulsions are constant intrusions that can severely impair daily activities.

Typical obsessive thoughts revolve around the possibility of harming someone or becoming infected. Compulsive behaviors often take the form of repetitive rituals, such as counting things or arranging objects "just so." Here is a rather severe case.

Marcia's symptoms began at a family Christmas party when she began to doubt whether she had correctly made the dessert. This doubt was accompanied by the fear that she might have harmed her children and guests, which soon spread to other areas. Marcia became unable to give her children vitamins for fear of making a mistake and injuring them, and she could not cook for fear that she would poison someone. She gave up driving the car, plagued by the thought that she might kill someone. She repeatedly checked locks, faucets, the fireplace, and her husband's tools as possible sources of danger. She began to bathe as often as six times a day, particularly if she happened to brush against something, such as

Linkages: Excessive hand washing is a classic feature of obsessive compulsive disorder. Though learning and environmental stress appear to play the major role in shaping and triggering this and other anxiety disorders, biological factors—including deficiencies in one of the neurotransmitters described in Chapter 3—may result in an oversensitive autonomic nervous system and a predisposition toward anxiety.

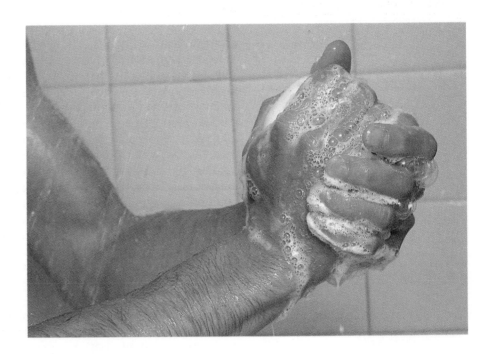

the garage door, that she saw as carrying germs. Her hands became swollen from repeated washings. (Based on Zax & Stricker, 1963, p. 171.)

Causes of Anxiety Disorders

As with all the forms of psychopathology we will consider, the exact cause of anxiety disorders is a matter of debate. All theoretical approaches offer explanations, but research suggests that the biological and behavioral models are particularly important (Rachman, 1989).

Biological Explanations The biological model suggests that anxiety disorders develop out of a predisposition to react with anxiety to a wide range of situations. The predisposition may be based on a deficiency, possibly inherited, of a particular neurotransmitter. The deficiency might create an autonomic nervous system that is oversensitive to stress. The possibility of inherited autonomic oversensitivity is supported by research showing that identical twins share anxiety disorders more often than other twins (Torgersen, 1983). More specifically, as mentioned in Chapter 12, panic attacks may result from an overreaction to lactic acid, a substance produced naturally when the body is under stress (Fishman & Sheehan, 1985). However, most researchers agree that biological predispositions are less critical than environmental stress and psychological factors in bringing about most anxiety disorders.

Behavioral Explanations In general, cognitive-behavioral explanations for anxiety disorders emphasize the role played by distortions in thinking. Persons suffering from an anxiety disorder may exaggerate the danger associated with certain stimuli and the number or severity of danger signals in their environment, thereby creating an unrealistic expectation that bad events are going to happen (Tomarken, Mineka & Cook, 1989). In addition, they tend to underestimate their own capacity for dealing with threatening events, resulting in anxiety and desperation when feared events do occur (Beck & Emery, 1985; Reiss & McNally, 1985; Telch et al., 1989).

The principles discussed in Chapter 7, on learning, have also generated explanations of anxiety disorders. For example, according to the behavioral model, obsessive-compulsive disorder might be a learned pattern that begins with a distressing thought. Those who are experiencing a lot of stress or who do not feel capable of dealing effectively with the topic of the thought may find it difficult to dismiss it. As it becomes more persistent, the thought engenders further anxiety. An action, such as hand washing, may relieve the anxiety and thus be strengthened through negative reinforcement. But such actions do nothing to eliminate the obsessive thoughts and so become compulsive, endlessly repeated rituals that keep the person trapped in a vicious circle of anxiety (Rachman & Hodgson, 1980).

According to behaviorists, phobias may be explained in part by classical conditioning. The object of the phobia becomes an aversive conditioned stimulus through association with a traumatic event (an unconditioned stimulus). Fear of dogs, for example, may result from an attack by a dog. Seeing or hearing about other people's bad experiences can produce the same result; most people who fear flying have never been in a plane crash. However, surveys of phobics indicate that direct conditioning is more common than observational learning as a pathway to phobia, especially in severe cases (Merckelbach et al., 1989; Ost, 1989). Once the fear is learned, avoidance of the feared object prevents the person from finding out that there is no need to be afraid. This cycle of avoidance helps explain why many fears do not simply extinguish, or disappear on their own.

H I G H L I G H T

Phobias and Preparedness

Some phobias are common, and others are rare. Why? If people are frightened by a snarling, chained dog, why don't they develop a fear of chains as well as of dogs? Given the number of times people are shocked trying to plug in lamps, why aren't there more electrical-outlet phobics?

The answer may be that people are *physiologically prepared* to learn certain fears, especially those that are self-protective, such as fear of heights or snakes (Seligman, 1971). This notion of preparedness has already been mentioned in Chapter 7, on learning. We discussed there how people are likely to develop taste aversions more quickly and easily than other associations. People and animals quickly learn to avoid a certain food after its taste has been associated with nausea, but they may never develop an aversion to bright lights or unusual sounds that are paired with nausea just as many times. Similarly, researchers have found it easier to create and harder to extinguish conditioned emotional reactions when the conditioned stimulus (for example, an angry face) "belongs" with the unconditioned stimulus (such as a loud scream) than when the two are unrelated—for example, a pretty landscape and a scream (Hamm, Vaitl & Lang, 1989). In other words, certain stimuli and certain responses appear to be especially easy to link.

Some laboratory evidence supports the notion that people are biologically prepared to learn certain phobias. A group of Swedish psychologists attempted to teach people to fear certain stimuli by associating the stimuli with electric shocks (Öhman, Dimberg & Öst, 1985; Öhman, Erixon & Lofberg, 1975). The subjects developed about equal conditioned anxiety reactions to slides of houses, human faces, and snakes. Later, however, when they were tested without shock, the reaction to snakes remained long after the houses and faces had failed to elicit a fear response. Thus, it may be that rare phobias are learned on the basis of specific classical conditioning; fear of, say, flash bulbs may stem from previous, particularly upsetting, startle reactions to them. Other, more common fears may develop because people are biologically prepared to react negatively to certain things.

Some research suggests that the preparedness effect may not be as special or as strong as once thought (Hugdahl & Johnson, 1989; McNally, 1987; Zafiropoulou & McPherson, 1986), but it remains an important phenomenon. Preparedness may stem from thousands of years of experience with poison, fire, heights, snakes, insects, and other objects and situations that were dangerous to our prehistoric ancestors. Those who quickly learned to avoid these things were more likely to survive than those who did not (De Silva, Rachman & Seligman, 1977). ■

Somatoform Disorders

Sometimes people show symptoms of a physical (somatic) disorder, even though there is no physical cause. Because these are psychological problems that take somatic form, they are called **somatoform disorders**. The classic example is **conversion disorder**, a condition in which a person appears to be, but is not, blind, deaf, paralyzed, insensitive to pain in various parts of the body, or even pregnant. In Freud's day, this disorder was called *hysteria*. Conversion disorders are rare, accounting for only about 2 percent of psychiatric diagnoses. Although they can occur at any point in life, they usually appear in adolescence or early adulthood.

Conversion disorders differ from true physical disabilities in several ways. First, they tend to appear when a person is under severe stress. Second, they often help reduce that stress. An opera singer, for example, may develop laryngitis just before a performance and thus avoid facing the audience; a person who has witnessed a horrible event may develop "blindness." Third, the person may show remarkably little concern about what is apparently a rather serious problem. Finally, the symptoms may be organically impossible, as Figure 15.2 illustrates.

Can people with a conversion disorder see and hear, even though they act as though they cannot? Experiments show that they can (Grosz & Zimmerman, 1970), but does this necessarily mean that the person is malingering or lying about the problem? No. Research on attention and consciousness suggests that people can use sensory input even when they are not consciously aware of doing so (Bargh, 1982; Nisbett & Wilson, 1977; Zajonc, 1980). The conversion process, while not destroying visual or auditory ability, may block the affected person from being aware of the information that his or her brain is still processing.

Another form of somatoform disorder is **hypochondriasis**, a strong, unjustified fear of heart disease, cancer, or illness in general, which is usually accompanied by reports of many vague symptoms. Hypochondriacs are always checking for symptoms of various diseases and remain preoccupied with their bodies.

Unlike hypochondriasis, in which the person misinterprets certain sensations as signs of sickness, persons displaying **somatoform pain disorder** complain of severe, often constant pain (commonly in the neck, chest, or back) for which no physical cause can be found. Nonetheless, the pain is felt as real and often develops after a physical trauma. The pain may become especially intense when the person faces stress, and it may prevent the person from engaging in certain activities (especially disliked activities).

Traditional explanations of somatoform disorders focus on conversion disorder. Freud believed that conversion disorder results when anxiety related to unconscious conflict is converted into physical symptoms. (This belief is,

Figure 15.2
Glove Anesthesia
In this conversion disorder, the person's insensitivity stops abruptly at the wrist (b). But if the nerves shown here (a) were actually impaired, part of the arm would also lose sensitivity. Other neurologically impossible symptoms seen in conversion disorder include sleepwalking at night on legs that are "paralyzed" during the day.

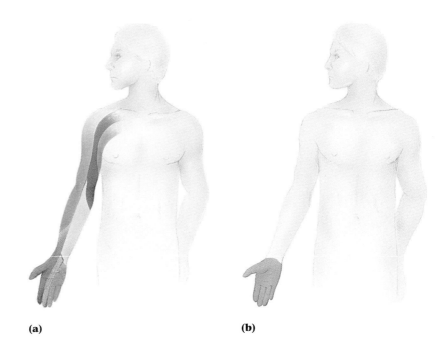

(a)   (b)

in fact, the source of the term.) In explaining somatoform disorders, behavioral as well as psychodynamic theorists point out that somatoform disorders can produce benefits by relieving sufferers of unpleasant responsibilities. Genetic factors do not seem important in somatoform disorders.

Dissociative Disorders

A sudden and usually temporary disruption in a person's memory, consciousness, or identity characterizes **dissociative disorders**. One example is the case of John, a thirty-year-old executive with a national computer manufacturing company. John was a meek person who was dependent on his wife for companionship and support. It came as a jolt when she announced that she was leaving him to live with his younger brother, an act she justified by saying, "This time I'm gonna try it before I buy it." John did not go to work the next day. In fact, nothing was heard from him for two weeks. Then he was arrested for public drunkenness and assault in a city more than three hundred miles from his home. The police discovered that during those two weeks John lived under another name at a flophouse hotel and made money by selling tickets at a pornographic movie theater. When he was interviewed, John did not know his real name or his real home, could not explain how he reached his present location, and could not remember much about the previous two weeks.

John's case illustrates the dissociative disorder known as **psychogenic fugue**, which is characterized by a sudden loss of memory and the assumption of a new identity in a new locale. Another dissociative disorder, **psychogenic amnesia**, also involves sudden memory loss. As in fugue, all identifying information may be forgotten, but the person does not leave home or create a new identity. These are rare conditions, but they tend to attract intense publicity because they are so perplexing.

The most famous, though also relatively rare, dissociative disorder is **multiple personality**, a condition in which a person has more than one identity, each of which speaks, acts, and writes in a very different way. Each personality seems to have its own memories, wishes, and (often conflicting) impulses. The different personalities even seem to show distinct biological characteristics. For example, heart rate and blood pressure differ from one personality to the next; among some women the different personalities are on different menstrual cycles. Some personalities may be aware of the existence of the others; some may not. Shifts among personalities are sudden, dramatic, and often stress related. Here is a famous case.

"Eve White" was a shy, reserved housewife and mother who began complaining of headaches and blackouts. It soon became obvious that during these blackouts she became "Eve Black," a hard-drinking, promiscuous member of the bar scene who was not very kind to her daughter. Since "Eve White" had no apparent knowledge of "Eve Black," she denied her husband's accusations of unfaithfulness and child neglect. Ultimately she was divorced. During psychiatric treatment, a third, far more balanced personality, known as "Jane," emerged and appeared to take over. This happy ending was marred in later years when Chris Sizemore, the real name of the patient in the "Eve" case, came forward to report on nineteen more personalities that had appeared in the twenty years since her therapy. (Sizemore & Pittillo, 1970.) *

---

* The report of this case, *The Three Faces of Eve*, became a Hollywood movie of the same name. The book and movie *Sybil* describe another celebrated case of multiple personality.

The apparently happy ending to the story of "Eve White's" multiple personality was marred when the real patient came forward to report on nineteen more personalities that had appeared during the twenty years since her therapy. Here, she shows paintings she completed while displaying some of these personalities. She apparently now maintains just one personality (Sizemore & Pittillo, 1970).

How do dissociative disorders develop? Psychodynamic theorists see massive repression of unwanted impulses or memories as the cause. The repression results in a "new person" who acts out impulses that would normally be unacceptable. Behavioral theorists focus on the fact that everyone is capable of behaving in very different ways depending on the circumstances (for example, boisterous in a bar, quiet and respectful in a church) and that, in rare cases, this variation can become so extreme that a person feels and is perceived by others as a "different person." Further, an individual may be rewarded for a sudden memory loss or unusual behavior by escaping stressful situations, responsibilities, or punishment for misdeeds.

Evaluating these general hypotheses has been difficult in part because of the rarity of dissociative disorders. However, cases of multiple personality have become more frequent recently. (Clinicians are either looking for it more carefully or the conditions leading to it are more prevalent.) The new data suggest three conclusions. First, many people showing multiple personality have experienced events that they would like to forget or otherwise avoid. The vast majority (some clinicians believe all) have suffered severe, unavoidable, persistent abuse in childhood. Second, most of them appear to be skilled at self-hypnosis, through which they can induce a trancelike state. Third, most found that they could escape the trauma of abuse at least temporarily by creating "new personalities" to deal with the stress (Bliss, 1980; Kluft, 1987).

Thus, recent data seem to indicate that sustained physical abuse may be a primary culprit in the development of multiple personality. Yet not all abused children display multiple personality, so researchers still have the task of understanding the specific combination of personal characteristics and environmental conditions that leads to this disorder. ("In Review: Anxiety, Somatoform, and Dissociative Disorders" presents a summary of our discussion of these topics.)

In Review: Anxiety, Somatoform, and Dissociative Disorders

Disorder	Subtypes	Major Symptoms
Anxiety disorders	Phobias	Intense, irrational fear of objectively nondangerous situations or things, leading to disruptions of behavior.
	Generalized anxiety disorder	Excessive anxiety not focused on a specific situation or object; free-floating anxiety.
	Panic disorder	Terrifying, repeated attacks of intense fear involving physical symptoms such as faintness, dizziness, and nausea.
	Obsessive-compulsive disorder	Persistent ideas or worries accompanied by ritualistic behaviors performed to neutralize the anxiety-driven thoughts.
Somatoform disorders	Conversion disorder	A loss of physical ability (e.g., sight, hearing) that is related to psychological factors.
	Hypochondriasis	Preoccupation with or belief that one has serious illness in the absence of any physical evidence.
	Somatoform pain disorder	Preoccupation with pain in the absence of physical reasons for the pain.
Dissociative disorders	Psychogenic fugue	Sudden, unexpected relocation with the assumption of a new identity and loss of memory of the past.
	Multiple personality disorder	Existence within same person of two or more distinct personalities, each with a unique way of thinking and behaving.

Mood Disorders

Everyone's feelings, or *affect*, tend to rise and fall from time to time. However, when people experience extremes of mood—wild elation or deep depression—for long periods, when they shift from one extreme to another, and especially when their moods are not consistent with the events around them, they are said to show a **mood disorder** (also known as *affective disorder*). We will describe two main types: depressive and bipolar disorders.

Depressive Disorders

Depression plays a central role in most mood disorders. It can range from occasional "down" periods to episodes severe enough to require hospitalization. A person suffering **major depression** feels sad and hopeless for weeks or months, often losing interest in all activities and taking pleasure in nothing. Feelings of inadequacy, worthlessness, or guilt are common. Everything, from conversation to bathing, is an unbearable, exhausting effort. Changes in eating habits resulting in weight loss or, sometimes, weight gain often accompany major depression, as does sleep disturbance or, less often, excessive sleeping. Problems in concentrating, making decisions, and thinking clearly are also common. In extreme cases, depressed people may express false beliefs, or **delusions**—worrying, for example, that the CIA is coming to punish them. Major depression may come on suddenly or gradually. It may consist of a single episode or, more commonly, an irregular, sometimes lifelong pattern of depressive periods. Here is one example of a case of major depression.

Mr. J. was a fifty-one-year-old industrial engineer. . . . Since the death of his wife five years earlier, he had been suffering from continuing episodes of depression marked by extreme social withdrawal and occasional thoughts of suicide. . . . He drank, and when thoroughly intoxicated would plead to his deceased wife for forgiveness. He lost all capacity for joy. . . . Once a gourmet, he now had no interest in food and good wine . . . [he] could barely manage to engage in small talk. . . . Appointments were missed and projects haphazardly started and left unfinished. (From Davison & Neale, 1990, p. 221.)

Most cases of depression do not become this severe. A far more common pattern is **dysthymia**, in which the person shows the sad mood, lack of interest, and loss of pleasure associated with major depression, but usually in a milder form and often spread out over a longer time. (The duration must be at least two years for the diagnosis of dysthymia to be made.) Mental and behavioral disruption may also be less severe. Most people exhibiting dysthymic disorder do not require hospitalization. However, some episodes may be extremely intense and can lead to suicide attempts.

HIGHLIGHT

Suicide and Depression

Virtually all of the factors related to depression are also associated with suicide. These include interpersonal crises, such as divorce; financial failure; sudden death in the family; intense feelings of frustration, anger, or self-hatred; and an absence of long-term or meaningful life goals (Farberow, Shneidman & Leonard, 1963; Paykel, Prusoff & Myers, 1975; Slater & DePue, 1981; Weissman, Fox & Klerman, 1973; Wekstein, 1979). Constant stress often leads to depression, so it is not surprising that those leading stress-filled lives show significantly higher suicide rates than the general population. Among students, the suicide rate increases dramatically at the beginning of each school year and at the end of each term (Klagsbrun, 1976). It also rises after the breakup of an engagement or other romantic relationship (Hendlin, 1975; Miller, 1975). About ten thousand college students try to kill themselves each year, and about one thousand succeed. This rate is much higher than the rate for the eighteen- to twenty-four-year-old noncollege population, but it is much lower than for the elderly (Blazer, Bacher & Manton, 1986).

Suicide attempts often reflect uncertainty about wanting to die. Only about 5 percent of all attempters appear truly intent on dying—they give little or no warning to others, and they choose quick and lethal methods such as shooting or hanging (Farberow & Litman, 1970). About 65 percent of attempters do not want to die but use the attempt to send a desperate "cry for help." Usually these individuals select relatively slow methods (nonlethal drug overdoses or minor wrist cuts, for example) and choose times and places that virtually guarantee that someone will save them. The remaining 30 percent are ambivalent; they face serious problems but still hope that things will improve. They usually try lethal but slow methods (such as a drug overdose) and let fate decide whether they will survive.

One myth about suicide is that people who talk about it will never try it. On the contrary, those who say they are thinking of suicide are much more likely to try suicide than the general population. In fact, according to Edwin Shneidman (1987), 80 percent of suicides are preceded by some kind of warning, whether direct ("I think I'm going to kill myself") or vague ("Sometimes I wonder if life is worth living"). However, not everyone who threatens suicide follows through. Knowing who will and who will not attempt suicide is difficult, but here are some useful guidelines (Shneidman, 1973, 1985, 1987):

1. People who attempt suicide tend to be in psychological pain, often stemming from an inability to meet needs ranging from basic physical necessities to love and esteem.
2. Suicide attempts are often associated with a tendency to seek instant escape from difficult problems. This behavioral style may stem from what George Kelly called personal constructs that limit one's perceptions of the world to black-and-white, either-or terms, with few options. Suicidal people see no option to pain but death.
3. Three times as many women attempt suicide as men, but because men tend to choose more lethal methods, three times as many men succeed. The gender difference in attempt rates reflects the fact that about twice as many women as men are diagnosed with major depression.
4. Males who are forty-five to sixty years old, divorced, with few family and friends, and living alone are especially likely to attempt suicide.
5. Previous suicide attempts suggest that future attempts are more likely, even when earlier attempts occurred years ago (Clark et al., 1989).
6. Suicide attempts among people prone to depression tend to occur either just after their energy returns following a bout of deep depression or while they are still depressed but in a desperate, agitated state.
7. Suicide is more likely when the person has not only talked about dying but developed a plan and given away possessions.

If you suspect that someone you know is thinking about suicide, encourage the person to contact a mental health professional or a crisis hotline. If the danger is imminent, make the contact yourself and ask for advice about how to respond. ■

Somewhere between 240,000 and 600,000 people attempt suicide every year in the United States and Canada; over 30,000 succeed (National Center for Health Statistics, 1988). Not all of these people are depressed, and not all depressed people attempt suicide, but the two problems are closely linked. Although the risk of suicide is about 1 percent during the year after a single depressive episode, it reaches about 15 percent during the lifetime of those who experience repeated episodes (Klerman, 1982). As a preventive measure, people who suffer major depression or intense episodes of dysthymia are often hospitalized.

Bipolar Disorder

The alternating appearance of two emotional extremes, or poles, characterizes **bipolar disorder**. We have already described one emotional pole: depression. The other is **mania**, which is an elated, very active emotional state. People in a manic state tend to be totally optimistic, boundlessly energetic, certain of having extraordinary powers and abilities, and bursting with all sorts of ideas. They become irritated with anyone who tries to reason with them or "slow them down." During manic episodes the person may make impulsive and unwise decisions (as in the case of Mr. M. described at the beginning of this chapter), spending their life savings on foolish schemes or giving away valuable possessions to total strangers.

In bipolar disorder, manic episodes may alternate every few days or weeks with periods of deep depression (sometimes, periods of relatively normal mood separate these extremes). This pattern has also been called *manic depression*. Compared with major depression, bipolar disorder is rare; it occurs in only about 1 percent of adults. Slightly more common is a pattern of less extreme mood swings known as *cyclothymia*.

Causes of Mood Disorders

Psychological Theories   Traditional psychodynamic theory suggests that depression is most likely among people with strong dependency needs. These needs, which develop from unconscious conflicts in the oral stage of development, leave the person vulnerable to exaggerated grief over interpersonal rejection or the death of a loved one. Because the lost loved one has been incorporated as part of the person's identity, anger and resentment over being abandoned are targeted against the self. Thus, the feelings of worthlessness and blame that are common in depression are meant for others, but they are turned inward. Other psychological theories about mood disorders are currently more influential than psychodynamic interpretations.

The behavioral model also recognizes that people become depressed when they lose important sources of reward. It goes on to suggest that the combination of loss (such as unemployment or the death of a spouse) and depressed mood often leads to a reduction in pleasant activities. This reduction may itself lead to more depression and to extra attention and sympathy from others, which can maintain the problem by reinforcing it (Lewinsohn, 1974).

Reinforcement is only part of the story, however. How people think about themselves, their world, and their future also seems important. Aaron Beck's (1967, 1987) cognitive theory of depression suggests that depressed people develop mental habits of (1) blaming themselves when things go wrong, (2) focusing on and exaggerating the dark side of events, and (3) jumping to overly generalized pessimistic conclusions. These cognitive habits, says Beck, are errors that lead to depressing thoughts and other symptoms of depression.

Depressed people do hold more negative beliefs about themselves and their lives than other people, but the exact significance of these beliefs is not yet clear (Barnett & Gotlieb, 1988). First of all, pessimistic beliefs may be a symptom of depression rather than a cause of it. Second, research indicates that the negative beliefs of depressed persons may not be errors at all; they may be very accurate (Snyder & Higgins, 1988; Taylor & Brown, 1988; see also the Linkages section in Chapter 14, on personality). In fact, their beliefs may be more accurate than those of nondepressed people, a difference that has been termed the "sadder-but-wiser" effect (Alloy & Abramson, 1979).

Mood disorders are scientifically puzzling and personally devastating. Tantalizing clues to the causes of these complex disorders have come from research on psychological and biological theories, but scientists are still left with many more questions than answers.

Another cognitive-behavioral theory of depression is based on *learned helplessness*, which we described in Chapter 7, on learning. When animals have no control over shock or other aversive events, they begin to appear depressed and become inactive. Interestingly, people who learn this temporary helplessness in the laboratory deal with laboratory tasks in ways similar to truly depressed individuals (Hiroto & Seligman, 1975; Klein & Seligman, 1976). Thus, lack of control over one's life, especially over its rewards and stressors, may be an important factor in depression. The extent to which women have less control over their lives may help explain why about twice as many women as men become depressed (Radloff, 1975).

Many people, however, have limited control; why aren't they all depressed? The way people tend to explain the world, their *attributional style*, may be key. Some researchers suggest that severe, long-lasting depression is far more likely among people who attribute their lack of control to a permanent, generalized lack of personal competence rather than to "the way things are" (Abramson, Seligman & Teasdale, 1978; Miller & Norman, 1979). Thus, people are prone to depression when they blame negative events on themselves and believe they will always be incapable of doing better.

Notice that this account of depression is analogous to diathesis-stress theory: a certain attributional style constitutes the predisposition (or diathesis) that makes a person vulnerable to depression (Peterson & Seligman, 1984). A new version of this attributional theory has proposed additional features, such as a general tendency to draw negative conclusions about oneself, that may be characteristic of the depressive style (Abramson, Metalsky & Alloy, in press).

Physiological Theories   When animals learn helplessness in the laboratory, they also show changes in the neurotransmitters norepinephrine and serotonin. As we discussed in Chapter 3, on biological aspects of psychology, these neurotransmitters are important in the regulation of moods. Can malfunctioning of these neurotransmitter systems explain mood disorders?

Some evidence on this question comes from studies of the effects of antidepressant drugs. Many drugs that relieve depression seem to work by almost immediately increasing the availability of norepinephrine and serotonin. However, changes in mood do not show up until a week or two after the treatment begins.

Comparisons between depressed and nondepressed people provide another source of evidence regarding the role of neurotransmitters. Compared with average people, depressed people probably have lower levels of norepinephrine or its chemical by-products (Bunney, Goodwin & Murphy, 1972; Crow et al., 1984). We say "probably" because some investigators have found evidence for *higher* levels of norepinephrine in depressed people (Gold et al., 1988). Studies of depressed people and their responses to antidepressant drugs suggest that although norepinephrine and serotonin systems are very probably malfunctioning in depression, the nature of the malfunction is not simple. One theory is that depression is due to a dysregulation of norepinephrine and serotonin, such that their levels and effects cannot be kept within the normal range (Siever & Davis, 1985). There is also the possibility that norepinephrine differences could be an effect rather than a cause of depression. In short, the exact relationship between the functioning of neurotransmitter systems and mood disorders has not yet been isolated.

Are there other physiological factors that might play a key role in mood disorders? One possibility is that depression might involve an abnormality in the biological systems that help people cope with stress. In particular, the control of the stress-related hormone cortisol is abnormal in about 70 percent of people diagnosed as major depressives (Carroll, 1982; Poland et al., 1987).

Linkages: Are mood disorders caused by a chemical imbalance? (a link to Biological Aspects of Psychology)

A synthetic hormone that normally suppresses the secretion of cortisol leads to *higher* levels of cortisol in depressed people.

In addition, the cyclical nature of many mood disorders suggests that abnormalities in biological rhythms might play a role in these disorders. People with bipolar disorder sometimes become depressed every six months, for example, regardless of whether life is going well or not. Depressed people also tend to have trouble sleeping; in most cases, they wake up abnormally early. Thus, depression may be a consequence of improper coordination among various biological cycles (Wehr et al., 1983). Depressed people may feel as they do because their biological clocks tell them that they are trying to function in the middle of the night. Resetting biological rhythms through methods such as sleep deprivation has relieved depression in some cases.

Whatever the primary physiological basis of mood disorders, there is evidence that it may be inherited; the evidence is especially strong for bipolar disorder. One review of research with twins found that if one member of a pair of identical twins developed bipolar disorder, 72 percent of the other members showed the same disorder; this happened in only 14 percent of nonidentical pairs (Allen, 1976). Other studies have found similar results (Egeland et al., 1987; Nurnberger & Gershon, 1984; Winder et al., 1986), though the search for the gene or genes responsible has recently bogged down (Barinaga, 1989). The children of parents who show major depression are more likely to develop depression themselves, but the evidence for inheritability of major depression is not as strong as for bipolar disorder (Andreasen et al., 1987).

This last fact raises a complicating possibility: there may be several types of depression, and each may be caused by different factors. The number and complexity of causal factors in mood disorders makes a diathesis-stress model—which recognizes the interaction of predispositions and life stresses—an especially appropriate guide for future research.

Schizophrenia

The following letter arrived in the mail a few years ago:

Dear Sir:

I want to buy a good book of Psychology without any bad topics of the mind such as suicide. Unfortunately, I recently purchased a William James Psychology Book. But I found something in it bad and the man was related to a very bad group of people in London. Therefore, I terrestrialize of want to possess one that teaches of all the good things of the mind. After all and before good is what victorizes and is preeminated and is naturally given and willed before any bad. So will you please teach me of the best author of Psychology to buy so I am not betrayed as I was before. Please correspond to very truly yours.

The author of this letter would probably be diagnosed as schizophrenic. Although commonly confused with multiple personality, schizophrenia is very different. **Schizophrenia** is a pattern of psychotic symptoms involving severely disturbed thinking, emotion, perception, and behavior; usually it seriously impairs the person's general functioning.

Schizophrenia constitutes one of the most serious and disabling of all mental disorders. It occurs in about 1 percent of the population, in about equal numbers of men and women, and tends to develop in adolescence or early adulthood. Schizophrenics usually require hospitalization, sometimes for weeks or months, sometimes for many years. At any specific time, this diagnostic group occupies about half the beds in mental hospitals. In the United States, about three or four million of these individuals are permanently unemployed and often unemployable.

Symptoms of Schizophrenia

Although the economic costs of schizophrenia run into billions of dollars (Gunderson & Mosher, 1975), the cost in human suffering is even greater.

Disorders of Thought   Schizophrenics display problems in both how they think and what they think. In fact, it was the apparent loosening of bonds among thoughts that prompted nineteenth-century psychiatrist Eugen Bleuler to coin the word *schizophrenia*, or "split mind" (see Neale, Oltmanns & Winters, 1983). (Contrary to popular belief, *schizophrenia* does not mean "split personality.") The *form* of the thought of schizophrenics is often incoherent. *Neologisms* ("new words" that have meaning only to the person speaking them) are common; *terrestrialize* is one of several examples in the letter at the beginning of this section. That letter also illustrates *loose associations*, the tendency for one thought to be logically unconnected, or only superficially connected, to the next. Sometimes the associations are based on double meanings or on the way words sound (*clang associations*). For example, "My true family name is Abel or A Bell. We descended from the clan of Abel, who originated the bell of rights, which we now call the bill of rights." In the most severe cases, thought becomes just a jumble of words known as *word salad*. For example, "Upon the advisability of held keeping, environment of the seabeach gathering, to the forest stream, reinstatement to be placed, poling the paddleboat, of the swamp morass, to the forest compensation of the dunce" (Lehman, 1967, p. 627).

The *content* of schizophrenic thinking is also disturbed. Often it includes a bewildering assortment of delusions. Delusions of persecution are among the most common. The person may think the Russian KGB is trying to harm him or her and may interpret everything from radio programs to people's gestures as part of the plot. Delusions that everything in the world is somehow related to oneself are called *ideas of reference*. Delusions of grandeur may also be present; one young schizophrenic was convinced that the president of United States was trying daily to contact him for advice. Other types of delusions include *thought broadcasting*, in which the person believes that his or her thoughts are being heard by others; *thought blocking* or *withdrawal*, which is the belief that someone is either preventing thoughts or "stealing" them as they appear; and *thought insertion*, which is the belief that other people's thoughts are appearing in one's mind. Some schizophrenics believe that, like a puppet, their behavior is being controlled by others.

Other Symptoms of Schizophrenia   Schizophrenics often report that they cannot focus their attention. They may feel overwhelmed as they try to attend to everything at once. Various perceptual disorders may appear. The person may feel detached from the real world; other people may seem to be flat cutouts. The body may feel like a machine, or parts of it may seem to be dead or rotting. About 75 percent of those diagnosed as schizophrenic report **hallucinations**, or false perceptions, usually of voices (Sartorius, Shapiro & Jablensky, 1974). These voices may sound like an overheard conversation or they may urge the person to do or not to do things; sometimes they comment on or narrate the person's actions.

Linkages: What is different about the thought and language of schizophrenics? (a link to Thought and Language)

Disordered thoughts and perceptions are often reflected in the artistic creations of schizophrenics. Here is one example from the collection of Hans Prinzhorn, a German psychiatrist who studied such paintings early in this century.

Unlike people suffering from mood disorders, schizophrenics usually do not experience extreme emotions. In fact, they may experience "flat" affect, showing little or no emotion even in the face of happy or sad events. Those who do display emotion often do so inappropriately—laughing while telling a sad story, crying for no apparent reason, or flying into a rage in response to a simple question. This lack of a coherent relationship between thoughts and feelings represents another way in which schizophrenia involves a kind of "split mind."

Some schizophrenics appear very agitated, ceaselessly moving their limbs, making facial grimaces, or pacing the floor in highly ritualistic sequences. Others become so withdrawn that they move very little.

Lack of motivation and social skills, deteriorating personal hygiene, and an inability to function day to day are other common characteristics of schizophrenia. Although these problems can develop suddenly, more often they appear gradually. They can become totally incapacitating.

The classic picture of the chronic schizophrenic includes lack of interest in anything, total preoccupation with an inner world (a condition known as *autism*), and loss of the sense of self. Not everyone labeled "schizophrenic" ends up this way, however.

Types of Schizophrenia

Especially during stupor, people who display catatonic schizophrenia may not speak, ignore all attempts at communication, and either become rigid or allow themselves to be put in virtually any posture.

DSM-III-R lists five subtypes of schizophrenia. A **residual schizophrenia** subtype is used for persons who have had a prior episode of schizophrenia but currently are not displaying active delusions, hallucinations, or overall disorganization of behavior. The other major subtypes are disorganized, catatonic, paranoid, and undifferentiated.

The main problems characterizing the **disorganized schizophrenia** subtype are jumbled and unrelated delusions and hallucinations. Speech may be incoherent. Strange facial grimaces and meaningless ritual movements are common. Affect is flat, though there may be inappropriate laughter or giggling. Personal hygiene is neglected, and the person may lose bowel and bladder control. Although many people think of this pattern when they think of schizophrenia, the disorganized type is rare, accounting for only about 5 percent of schizophrenia diagnoses.

The most significant characteristic of **catatonic schizophrenia** is disorder of movement. The individual alternates between total immobility or stupor and wild excitement. Especially during stupor, the person may not speak, ignoring all attempts at communication, and either become rigid or show a "waxy flexibility," which allows him or her to be "posed" in virtually any posture. About 8 percent of schizophrenics fall into this subtype.

About 40 percent of all schizophrenics appear in the **paranoid schizophrenia** subtype. Its most prominent features are delusions of persecution or grandeur accompanied by anxiety, anger, superiority, argumentativeness, or jealousy. Sometimes these feelings lead to violence. Compared with the other subtypes, paranoid schizophrenia tends to appear later in life, typically after the age of twenty-five or thirty, and there is much less impairment of affect and perception. In most cases, the person is able to complete an education, hold a job, and even have a family before problems become severe. Here is a description of one case:

Mr. S. was first admitted to the hospital at the age of forty-eight. Some weeks earlier, he had taken to sealing the cracks under doors and in window sashes with the metal from empty toothpaste tubes to "keep out radio waves" that were being directed at him by agents of "the Tsar Nicholas." He lost his job around this time because of similar behavior at work, but he attributed his dismissal to the machinations of enemies and unnamed fellow workers. On the hospital ward he was condescending to the other patients, demanding many privileges for himself and giving lengthy accounts of the importance attached to him by both the Russians and the White House. He spent many hours perusing newspapers to see if his movements were reported there. (Summarized from Maher, 1966, p. 308.)

Finally, as the name implies, **undifferentiated schizophrenia** is marked by patterns of disordered behavior, thought, and emotion that cannot be placed easily in any of the other subtypes. About 40 percent of diagnosed schizophrenics fall into this category.

The Search for Causes

There is probably more research on the causes of schizophrenia than on any other form of behavior disorder. One thing is certain: no single theory can adequately account for all forms of schizophrenia.

Linkages: Is schizophrenia caused by a chemical imbalance in the brain? (a link to Biological Aspects of Psychology)

Biological Factors   Schizophrenia may be due in part to problems in the brain, which, along with other causal factors, may be inherited (Faraone & Tsuang, 1985; Rosenthal, 1977; Sherrington et al., 1988). Schizophrenia does run in families (e.g., Kennedy et al., 1988). The children and siblings of schizophrenics are, overall, about ten times more likely than other people to develop schizophrenia. Identical twins share schizophrenia more often than nonidentical twins, and children of schizophrenics who are adopted by normal parents still display schizophrenia more often than the general population (Allen, Cohen & Pollin, 1972; Gottesman & Shields, 1972; Heston, 1966; Kety et al., 1975). Still, most people with schizophrenic relatives are not schizophrenic. What may be inherited is a *predisposition* toward schizophrenia.

Part of this predisposition may have to do with biochemistry. A great deal of research is examining the possibility that neurotransmitters, especially dopamine, play a role in causing or at least intensifying schizophrenic thought and behavior. The dopamine hypothesis came about in part because drugs that are used to treat schizophrenia blunt the action of dopamine in the brain. In fact, there is a high positive correlation between the effectiveness of these drugs and their ability to block dopamine receptors (Seeman & Lee, 1975). Some treated patients even show signs of Parkinsonism, a nervous disorder related to the presence of too little dopamine. Furthermore, as described in Chapter 6, heavy use of amphetamines is tied to both the stimulation of dopamine systems in the brain and schizophrenialike symptoms (Snyder, 1978). Indeed, giving amphetamines to schizophrenics makes their problems worse (Angrist, Lee & Gershon, 1974). It has thus been suggested that excess dopamine or oversensitivity to dopamine may be responsible either for some forms of schizophrenia or for the intensity of its symptoms (Davis, 1978; Meltzer & Stahl, 1976; Wong et al., 1986; see Figure 15.3).

Data from autopsies, x-rays, PET scans, and magnetic resonance images of the brain have spawned theories that suggest a relationship between schizophrenia and other brain abnormalities. Among these abnormalities are shrinking or deterioration of cells in the cerebral cortex or cerebellum; enlargement of the brain's fluid-filled ventricles (see Figure 15.4); disorganization of cells in the hippocampus (an area involved with the expression of emotion);

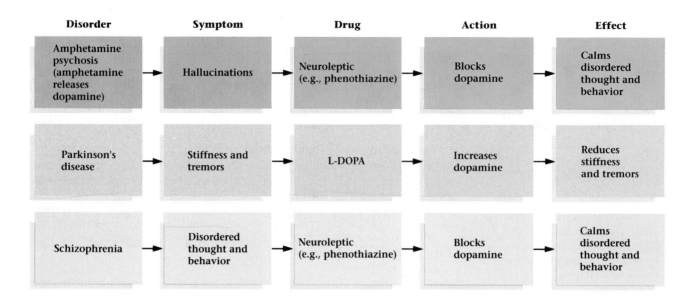

Disorder	Symptom	Drug	Action	Effect
Amphetamine psychosis (amphetamine releases dopamine) →	Hallucinations →	Neuroleptic (e.g., phenothiazine) →	Blocks dopamine →	Calms disordered thought and behavior
Parkinson's disease →	Stiffness and tremors →	L-DOPA →	Increases dopamine →	Reduces stiffness and tremors
Schizophrenia →	Disordered thought and behavior →	Neuroleptic (e.g., phenothiazine) →	Blocks dopamine →	Calms disordered thought and behavior

Source: Rosenhan & Seligman, 1989.

Figure 15.3
Evidence for the Dopamine Hypothesis of Schizophrenia
The results of numerous studies on the effects of dopamine-altering drugs suggest that, like Parkinson's disease and amphetamine psychosis, schizophrenia may be intimately related to dopamine levels in the brain.

reduced blood flow in certain parts of the brain, especially the frontal lobes (Buchsbaum et al., 1982; Weinberger, Berman & Zek, 1986); abnormalities in *brain lateralization*, the pattern of dominance of one cerebral hemisphere over the other, and in the way the hemispheres communicate with each other (Newlin, Carpenter & Golden, 1981); or other physical anomalies (Andreasen et al., 1982; Bruton et al., 1990; Golden et al., 1981; Silverton et al., 1988; Weinberger, Wagner & Wyatt, 1983).

Not all schizophrenics display such abnormalities—and some normal people do. But the relevance of brain disorders for schizophrenia is supported by evidence that the specific nature of the brain abnormality may be related to the person's symptoms. Some researchers have found that, among people labeled schizophrenic, those with abnormal brain structures tend to show passive or "negative" symptoms, such as reduced affect, apathy, and withdrawal; those with more normal-looking brains tend to show more active or "positive" symptoms, including hallucinations and delusions (Crow, 1980). Firm conclusions about the meaning of all of these correlations await further research.

Psychological Factors Psychodynamic theorists suggest that schizophrenic symptoms are generated by anxiety about expressing or becoming aware of unacceptable unconscious impulses. Psychoanalytic views of schizophrenia lack strong research support, however, and psychoanalytic treatments of schizophrenic patients have not been shown to be very effective (Mueser & Berenbaum, 1990; Stone, 1986).

Behavioral theories suggest that the problematic thoughts and behaviors of people labeled as schizophrenic reflect their learned, though maladaptive, way of trying to cope with anxiety (Mednick, 1958, 1970). Problems may also stem from patterns of reinforcement and punishment early in life: unfortunate learning experiences may have extinguished normal processes and inadvertently rewarded maladaptive behaviors and thoughts (Ullmann & Krasner, 1975). Though far from conclusive, evidence consistent with this view comes from studies showing that some schizophrenic behaviors can be reduced or

Figure 15.4
Brain Abnormalities in Schizophrenia
Here is a magnetic resonance imaging (MRI) comparison of the brain structure of a pair of identical twins, one of whom (on the right) has been diagnosed as schizophrenic. The schizophrenic twin was found to have greatly enlarged ventricals (fluid-filled cavities indicated by the arrows) and correspondingly less brain tissue, including in the hippocampal area (which is involved in memory and emotion). The same results were found in fourteen other identical twin pairs; the schizophrenic twin in some pairs also had smaller temporal lobes. No significant differences appeared between members of a seven-pair control group of normal identical twins. These results provide added support for the role of brain abnormalities in schizophrenia but, because identical twins have the same genetic heritage, suggest as well that these abnormalities may stem from nongenetic factors. What those factors might be is still unclear; viral infections during critical periods of brain development, head injury, and oxygen deprivation at birth are among the suggested possibilities.

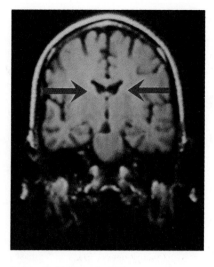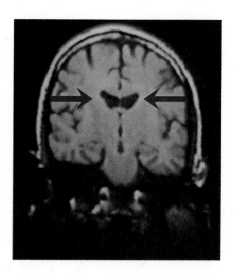

Source: Suddath et al., 1990.

Linkages: What role might stress play in the appearance of schizophrenia? (a link to Stress, Coping, and Health)

eliminated by ignoring them while systematically rewarding more adaptive alternatives (Paul & Lentz, 1977). Such *token-economy programs* are described in Chapter 16, on treatment.

On the assumption that the experiences that lead to schizophrenia occur in childhood, several theorists have looked for the psychological origins of the disorder in the families of schizophrenics. They have focused especially on the effects of conflict, coldness, and poor communication in the family. Even in a wildly disturbed family, however, only one child out of several may become schizophrenic. Further, the same conditions associated with schizophrenia in one person's family background may be associated with less severe disorders or no disorder at all in someone else's history. There is evidence for higher rates of relapse among recovered schizophrenics whose families show a chronically high level of emotional overinvolvement or *expressed emotion* (Leff, 1976), but so far, research has not supported the idea that family conditions cause schizophrenia. Indeed, faulty communication in the families of schizophrenics might be one of the *effects* of having a schizophrenic disrupt the family. Thus it is important to be cautious about invoking family theories of schizophrenia. The guilt and anguish of family members who feel blamed for their relative's devastation can, itself, be devastating (Johnson, 1989).

This discussion brings us back to the diathesis-stress approach, which presently seems the best theory to handle all the perspectives on the problem. ("In Review: Schizophrenia" summarizes these perspectives as well as the types and symptoms of schizophrenia.) This approach is embodied in the **vulnerability model** of schizophrenia (Cornblatt & Erlenmeyer-Kimling, 1985; Zubin & Spring, 1977). This model suggests that (1) different people have differing degrees of vulnerability to schizophrenia; (2) this vulnerability is partly genetic, but may not be entirely inherited; (3) the vulnerability may involve psychological components, such as a history of poor parenting, as well as biological components, such as a highly reactive autonomic nervous system. Thus, many different blendings of vulnerability and stress can lead to schizophrenia, as Figure 15.5 illustrates. Can knowledge of the particular blend in an individual allow accurate prediction about whether he or she will become schizophrenic (Mednick, Schulsinger & Griffith, 1981)? This is just one of the questions whose answers will ultimately strengthen the vulnerability model or lead in other directions.

In Review: Schizophrenia

Aspect	Key Features
Common symptoms	
Disorders of thought	Disturbed *content* involving delusions and disturbed *form*, such as loose associations, neologisms, and word salad.
Disorders of perception	Hallucinations or false perceptions; poorly focused attention.
Subtypes	
Disorganized	Unrelated delusions and hallucinations most prominent; flat affect; incoherence and disorganized behavior.
Catatonic	Disorders of movement most prominent, including stupor, bizarre postures, and excitement.
Paranoid	Delusions most prominent; later onset than other subtypes.
Undifferentiated	Psychotic symptoms that do not fit any of the other subtypes.
Proposed explanatory theories	
Biological	Genetics; excess dopamine; cell abnormalities; irregularities in brain structure.
Psychological	Learning and reinforcement of maladaptive behavior; family disturbance and impaired communication; unconscious conflicts and resulting anxiety.
Vulnerability (diathesis-stress)	A predisposition leaves the person *vulnerable* to schizophrenia, especially if significant stressors are encountered.

Figure 15.5
The Vulnerability Model of Schizophrenia
In this model, a person can cross the threshold into schizophrenia by having a strong predisposition for it and very little stress (point D); by having only a weak predisposition but a great deal of stress (point C); or any other sufficiently potent combination.

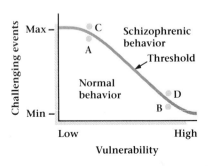

Source: Zubin & Spring, 1977.

Substance-Use Disorders

The use of alcohol and other psychoactive drugs has created major political, economic, social, and health problems worldwide—an ironic consequence of the long-standing tendency of many governments to approve of some drugs while condemning or even declaring "war" on others (Newcomb & Bentler, 1989). When people use psychoactive drugs for months or years in ways that harm themselves or others, they show what is called, in DSM-III-R, a **psychoactive substance-use disorder**. The substances involved most often are alcohol and other depressants, such as barbiturates and Quaaludes; opiates, such as heroin; stimulants, such as cocaine or amphetamines; and psychedelics, such as LSD.

As we discussed in Chapter 6, on consciousness, one effect of using some substances (including alcohol, heroin, and amphetamines) is **addiction**, a physical need for the substance. DSM-III-R calls addiction *dependence*. Usually, addiction is evident when the person begins to need more and more of a substance to achieve the desired state; this is called *building a tolerance*. When addicted people stop using the substance, they experience painful, often terrifying and potentially dangerous *withdrawal symptoms* as the body tries to readjust to a substance-free state. Even when use of a drug does not create physical addiction, some people may overuse, or *abuse*, it because it gives them self-confidence, enjoyment, or relief from tension. Thus, people can become *psychologically* dependent on psychoactive substances without becoming addicted to them. We described these drugs and their impact on consciousness in Chapter 6; here we are interested in the causes and broader consequences of their use.

Alcoholism

According to DSM-III-R, about 13 percent of American adults, or more than 20 million people, have developed *alcohol dependence or abuse*, a pattern of continuous or intermittent drinking that may lead to addiction and almost always causes severe social, physical, and other problems. Prolonged overuse of alcohol can result in life-threatening liver damage, vitamin deficiencies that can lead to an irreversible brain disorder called *Korsakoff's psychosis*, and a host of other physical ailments. Alcohol dependence or abuse, commonly referred to as **alcoholism**, has been implicated in half of all the traffic fatalities, homicides, and suicides that occur each year; alcoholism also figures prominently in rape and child abuse (Alcohol and Health Report, 1984; Mayer, 1983), as well as in elevated rates of hospitalization and absenteeism from work (Julien, 1988).

Alcoholism usually begins with social drinking, which graduates over a period of years into a different and far more problematic pattern, as Table 15.4 describes. In most cases, alcoholism stabilizes into one of three patterns identified decades ago by Elvin Jellinek (1960): (1) regular daily drinking of large amounts of alcohol, (2) regular heavy drinking on weekends only, or (3) binges of heavy drinking for weeks or months at a time, separated by long periods of sobriety. Addicted alcoholics continue to drink because they physically need alcohol. Not drinking can be painful and sometimes causes

Contrary to popular belief, only a small proportion of alcoholics are male "skid row bums"; the rest are found throughout the population, including an increasing proportion of women and teenagers.

Table 15.4
Social Drinking Versus Alcoholism

Social drinking patterns differ markedly from those of alcoholics, yet social drinking can easily evolve into alcoholism.

Social Drinkers	Alcoholics
Usually drink in moderation and can control the amount they consume.	Drink increasing quantities, often reaching an amazing capacity to drink more than other people. Sometimes drink until blacking out. May not remember events that occur while drinking.
Usually drink to enhance the pleasure of social situations.	Drink for the chemical effect, often to relieve tension or face problems; often drink alone, including in the morning to reduce hangover or to face the day.
Do not usually think about or talk about drinking in nondrinking situations.	Become preoccupied with getting their next drink, often sneaking drinks during working hours or at home.
Do not experience physical, social, or occupational problems caused by their drinking.	Suffer physical disorders, damaged social relationships, and impaired capacity to work because of drinking.

Linkages: What explanations for alcoholism do the psychodynamic and behavioral approaches suggest? (a link to the World of Psychology)

delirium tremens, or *DTs*, in which the alcoholic suffers confused thinking, frightening hallucinations, and gross disorientation.

Psychoanalytic theories suggest that alcoholism represents unfulfilled oral needs, but these theories have received almost no empirical support and are less influential than other approaches. One of these approaches is a behavioral theory that suggests that people learn to use alcohol because it helps them cope with stressors and reduce emotional stress reactions. Use becomes abuse, often addiction, if drinking is a person's main coping strategy. The stress-reduction theory of alcoholism has been supported by studies showing that alcohol can reduce animals' learned fear of a particular location and that animals in a stressful conflict situation will choose to drink alcohol if it is available (Conger, 1951; Freed, 1971). The stress-reducing effects of alcohol have also been shown in humans (Sher & Levenson, 1982), but not consistently (Steele & Josephs, 1988).

The importance of learning is also suggested by evidence that alcoholism is more common in ethnic and cultural groups (such as the Irish and English) where frequent drinking tends to be socially reinforced than in groups like the Jews, Italians, and Chinese, where all but moderate drinking tends to be discouraged (Frankel & Whitehead, 1981). Learning would also help explain why the prevalence of alcoholism is higher than average among people working as bartenders, cocktail servers, and in other jobs where alcohol is available and drinking is socially reinforced, even expected (Fillmore & Caetano, 1980). (It is also possible, however, that it was attraction to alcohol that led some of these people into such jobs in the first place.)

Alcoholism also appears to run in families, especially among males. The sons of alcoholics are more likely than others to become alcoholics themselves; if the sons are identical twins, both are at increased risk for alcoholism, even when they are raised apart (Goodwin, Crane & Guze, 1973). Data like these suggest that alcoholism may be due in part to an inherited predisposition of some kind, perhaps a greater ability to tolerate the short-term physical effects of alcohol (Goodwin, 1979; Schuckit, 1983). The possibility of a predisposition is also consistent with data showing that hyperactivity and antisocial behavior in childhood are reasonably good predictors of alcoholism in adults (e.g., Hechtman, Weiss & Perlman, 1984). Although it is easy to see how such a diathesis could interact with cultural traditions and other learning factors to create alcoholism, especially in those who have stressful lives, many alcoholics do not fit this neat picture. Tragically, the roots of alcoholism are still largely unknown.

Heroin and Cocaine Dependence

Like alcoholics, heroin addicts suffer many serious health problems, as a result of the drug itself and the poor eating and health habits it engenders. Further, the danger of death from an overdose, contaminated drugs, or AIDS (contracted through blood in shared needles) is always present.

Continued use or overdoses of cocaine can cause problems ranging from nausea and hyperactivity to paranoid thinking, sudden depressive "crashes," and even death. An estimated one million Americans have become dependent on cocaine, and millions more use it on occasion. The widespread availability of crack, a powerful and relatively cheap form of cocaine, has made it one of the most dangerous and addicting drugs in the country.

Although addiction to substances like heroin is largely a biological process brought about by the physical effects of the drugs, explaining why people first use dangerous drugs is more complicated. The causes of initial abuse are even less well established than the reasons for alcohol abuse, but the problem does not seem to be inherited. Psychological factors, such as the need to reduce stress, emulation of drug-using peers, thrill seeking, and social maladjustment, have all been proposed as causes. The desire to gain social status appears to be partially responsible for the increase in the use and abuse of cocaine in recent years. Research has not yet established why drugs become a problem for some people and not for others.

Sexual Disorders

There are two main categories of sexual disorders: **sexual dysfunction**, in which a person's desire for or ability to have satisfying sexual experiences is inhibited, and **paraphilias**, in which a person's sexual arousal is directed toward stimuli that are culturally or legally defined as inappropriate.

The most common sexual dysfunction for men is *erectile dysfunction* (once known as impotence), which is the inability to have or maintain an erection sufficient for intercourse. Most men experience erectile dysfunction at some point in their lives; it is considered a sexual dysfunction only if erectile difficulties occur consistently enough to interfere with sexual functioning and a partner's satisfaction. Psychological factors such as anxiety are considered the cause for as many as 95 percent of the cases of erectile dysfunction (Kaplan, 1974). Other possible causes include physical factors such as fatigue, diabetes, hypertension, and the side effects of medication or excessive use of alcohol or other drugs. Another common problem in men is *premature ejaculation*, or ejaculating sooner than they or their partner would like.

Infrequent orgasms or a lack of orgasms is probably the most frequent type of sexual dysfunction in women. Many nonorgasmic women have strong sexual desires and enjoy sexual contact, but psychological factors such as self-consciousness, a lack of self-confidence, or depression often contribute to their difficulties in experiencing an orgasm. Problems reaching orgasm are also often linked to basic difficulties in the emotional qualities of the romantic relationship.

People displaying paraphilias have recurrent sexual fantasies and strong sexual urges directed at either (1) nonhuman objects (such as women's shoes or purses), (2) children or other nonconsenting partners, or (3) the infliction of suffering or humiliation on themselves or their sexual partner. Paraphilias are usually found in males. Whether or not they act on their urges and fantasies, they are usually distressed by them. In many cases, they cannot become sexually aroused or reach orgasm without these stimuli or fantasies about them. The most common paraphilias are listed in Table 15.5.

Though relatively rare, paraphilias are of great concern, because by acting on these urges, people coerce or abuse others (especially children), invade other people's privacy, or display their sexuality in public places. From the practical perspective described at the beginning of this chapter, individuals who comfortably engage in paraphilia-driven sexual activities in private or with consenting partners might not be considered abnormal. However, the valuative perspective would consider paraphilias abnormal no matter how or where they appear.

Table 15.5
Some Paraphilias

According to DSM-III-R, in order to be diagnosed as a paraphilia, a person's distressing sexual fantasies or inappropriate sexual acts must have taken place repeatedly for at least six months.

Paraphilia	Definition
Pedophilia	Adult sexual gratification through sexual contact with children under the age of thirteen.
Exhibitionism	Achieving sexual arousal through exposing one's genitals to unsuspecting strangers in public.
Sexual sadism	Gaining sexual pleasure from inflicting real or simulated physical pain or psychological distress on another person. Beatings, bondage, and humiliation are often involved.
Sexual masochism	Gaining sexual pleasure from being the victim of the physical or psychological abuse described in sexual sadism.
Voyeurism	Achieving sexual arousal and orgasm by watching unsuspecting persons who are naked, undressing, or engaging in sexual activity. The voyeur often tries to look in the windows of private homes.
Fetishism	Using inanimate objects such as women's shoes, purses, and undergarments to achieve sexual arousal and gratification. The person may wear the items or merely use them as aids in masturbation.
Frotteurism	Achieving sexual arousal and orgasm from touching or rubbing against unsuspecting people in elevators, buses, or other (usually crowded) public places.

Personality Disorders

People labeled as having personality disorders are more disturbing than disturbed. **Personality disorders** are long-standing, inflexible ways of behaving that are not so much severe mental disorders as styles of life, which, from childhood or adolescence, create problems, usually for others (Millon, 1981). As mentioned in Chapter 14, some psychologists view personality disorders as interpersonal strategies or as the expression of extreme, rigid, and maladaptive personality traits (e.g., Widiger & Kelso, 1983).

The case of Mark described at the beginning of this chapter exemplifies **schizotypal personality disorder**, one of the twelve personality disorder subtypes listed on Axis II in DSM-III-R. The name suggests that the person displays some of the peculiarities seen in schizophrenia but is not disturbed enough to be diagnosed as schizophrenic. Another example is **narcissistic personality disorder**. Its main characteristics are an exaggerated sense of self-importance accompanied by a lack of empathy for others. People who earn this label act as though they deserve extraordinary privileges and consideration. They are often flamboyant, constantly need to be the center of attention, and tend to arrogantly overestimate their abilities and achievements. They commonly want to be seen with the "right people" but have few, if any, friends. They are filled with self-doubt, as evidenced by their extreme sensitivity to criticism and almost desperate need for compliments and admiration.

From the perspective of public welfare and safety, the most serious personality disorder is surely **antisocial personality**. It is marked by a long-term pattern of irresponsible, impulsive, unscrupulous, even criminal, behavior, beginning in childhood or early adolescence. In the nineteenth century, the pattern was called *moral insanity*, because such persons appeared to have no morals or common decency; later, people in this category were called *psychopaths* or *sociopaths*. The current "antisocial personality" label more accurately portrays them as troublesome, but not "insane" by the legal standards we will discuss shortly. Males outnumber females in this category three to one.

At their least troublesome, these people are a nuisance to others. They borrow money and fail to return it, they lie, and they "con" others into doing things for them. In fact, they are expert at taking advantage of the decency and trust of others to reach selfish goals. A hallmark of those displaying antisocial personality is a lack of remorse or guilt, whether they have wrecked a borrowed car or killed an innocent person. The following list of classic antisocial personality characteristics captures the essence of the disorder:

1. Considerable superficial charm
2. Average or above average intelligence
3. Absence of anxiety
4. Considerable poise, calmness, and verbal skill (a "good talker")
5. Unreliability; no sense of responsibility (often resulting in unemployment)
6. Untruthfulness and insincerity (often including criminal behavior)
7. Lack of guilt or shame
8. Complete self-centeredness, often accompanied by an inflated sense of self-worth
9. Absence of any real or deep feelings, including love
10. An impulsive, reckless, disorganized, and ultimately self-defeating lifestyle beginning in childhood that does not change in spite of repeated punishment (Cleckley, 1976; APA, 1987; Hare, 1980).

The senseless crime sprees documented in Truman Capote's *In Cold Blood* and Norman Mailer's *The Executioner's Song* represent the antisocial personality at its worst. At present there is no successful method for permanently altering the behavior of people displaying antisocial personality, but they seem to become less active and dangerous after the age of forty (Hare, McPherson & Forth, 1988).

What causes antisocial personality? There are numerous theories. Research on biological factors has found these people to be less sensitive than normals to electric shock and other punishments and to display an unusually low level of emotional arousal (Eysenck, 1960; Fenz, 1971; Newman & Kosson, 1986). These findings, along with the appearance of abnormal brain-wave patterns in some cases, have been used to account for the irresponsibility, impulsiveness, thrill seeking, and lack of anxiety and guilt associated with the disorder (Hare, 1970). From psychological and social perspectives, broken homes, rejection by parents, lack of good parental models, conflict-filled childhoods, and living in poverty have all been suggested as contributing to the problem. But all of these biological and psychosocial factors also appear in the backgrounds of people who do not develop antisocial personalities, so the causal picture is still cloudy.

Mental Illness in Society

As promised, we have reviewed some of the main forms of psychological disorders. Before concluding, it is important to put these disorders into perspective by considering two important social issues related to them.

Does Mental Illness Exist?

In the case of organic mental disorders, the concept of mental illness seems perfectly appropriate. But what about the majority of behavior disorders, for which no clear physical basis has been found? Should those who display such disorders be called ''sick'' too? Traditionalists in psychiatry and psychology say yes, either because a physical cause is suspected or because these disorders resemble physical illness. Critics, however, say no. The most prominent and vocal of these critics is psychiatrist Thomas Szasz (pronounced ''zaws''), who believes that the concept of mental illness is not only inappropriate but harmful.

Szasz prefers to think of the disorders listed in the DSM as ''problems in living.'' He first spelled out his view in an influential 1960 article called ''The Myth of Mental Illness'' and has repeated it since then (Szasz, 1974, 1987). Here is a summary of the arguments against the concept of mental illness presented by Szasz and like-minded critics (e.g., Ullmann & Krasner, 1969).

1. Calling a person ''sick'' when he or she has problems in living puts that person in the inferior, passive role of being a patient, a role in which the person may no longer be treated as a responsible adult.
2. When the concept of mental illness is applied, a kind of psychiatric tyranny may result, in which people who displease those in authority can be called sick and then either discredited or conveniently deposited in mental hospitals.
3. The role of ''patient'' inhibits people from trying to improve, because they are expected simply to follow a doctor's orders and wait for a cure.
4. Calling a disorder a ''mental illness'' implies that only medical doctors are qualified to deal with it. However, years of clinical experience has shown

Thomas Szasz and others see the concept of mental illness as encouraging the use of drugs and hospitalization to try solving problems in living that may have nothing to do with physical illness. This approach, they say, can result in an atmosphere of hopelessness while patients wait passively for a "cure."

that other professional helpers can play a beneficial role in treating behavior disorders.

5. A person who is called mentally ill bears a social stigma. Others may fear or avoid social contact, hesitate to offer a job, and in general fail to provide the support the person needs.

6. It is too easy to give up trying to help people if they are afflicted with a "mental illness" that has a poor prognosis.

Szasz's objections to the concept of mental illness stimulated a great deal of debate. They also prompted increasing recognition of the value of nonmedical concepts of abnormal behavior and (as described in Chapter 16) an expansion of the legal rights of those who receive treatment for mental disorder. However, conceiving of all abnormal behavior as merely "problems in living" creates some problems of its own. First, there is the question of evidence. Szasz essentially dismisses the potential significance of accumulated evidence for important biological and psychological factors that may contribute to many disorders (Monahan, 1988). Second, calling disorders "problems in living" risks trivializing the very real trauma and unhappiness suffered by many people who display abnormality. Finally, the argument that there is no such thing as mental illness may discourage some people from going to professionals who could help them. In other words, there is danger in replacing one extreme position ("all abnormality is illness") with another ("no abnormality is illness").

Behavior Disorder and Criminal Responsibility

One of the most important legal issues highlighted by the debate over Szasz's views is whether "mentally ill" people are responsible for their own behavior. If a person is "mentally ill," should he or she be prosecuted or punished for criminal behavior? Consider the following case:

Cheryl was barely twenty when she married Glen, a graduate student in biology. They moved into a large apartment complex near the university and within three years had two sons. Cheryl's friends had always been impressed by the attention and affection she showered on her boys; she seemed to be the ideal mother. She and Glen had serious marital problems, however, and she felt trapped and unhappy. One day Glen came home to find that Cheryl had stabbed both children to death. At her murder trial, she was found not guilty by reason of insanity and was placed in a state mental institution.

In most states the law says that mental illness, if severe enough, can protect some people from *prosecution* for a crime. People cannot be prosecuted unless they are both physically and mentally competent. If a defendant is found to be too mentally disturbed to understand the charges or to assist in the preparation of a defense, he or she can be declared incompetent to stand trial. In some cases, the defendant is declared incompetent but, after some time in a mental institution, recovers sufficiently to stand trial. In other cases, the court may decide that the defendant might never be competent to go to trial; then he or she is usually committed, in civil court, to a mental institution. This outcome happens infrequently, however, because competency to stand trial requires only minimal mental abilities. Furthermore, if drugs can produce temporary mental competence, the person will usually be required to go to trial.

In addition, severe mental illness can sometimes shield people from *punishment* for a crime even if they have been brought to trial; a person can be found not guilty by reason of insanity. The laws of most states hold that a person may be judged not guilty by reason of insanity if, at the time of the crime, mental illness prevented him or her from (1) understanding that the act was wrong, or (2) resisting the impulse to do wrong. The first criterion—understanding that an act was wrong—is known as the *McNaughton rule*. It stems from an 1843 English case in which a man named Daniel McNaughton, on hearing "instructions from God," tried to kill Prime Minister Robert Peel; he was found not guilty by reason of insanity and put in a mental institution for life. The second criterion is known as the *irresistible-impulse test*.

These two criteria are combined in a rule, now followed by most states, that was proposed in 1962; it holds that "a person is not responsible for criminal conduct if at the time of such conduct as a result of mental disease or defect he lacks substantial capacity either to appreciate the criminality (wrongfulness) of his conduct or to conform his conduct to the requirements of law" (American Law Institute, 1962, p. 66). This was Cheryl's defense, and the jury accepted it. In such cases, if the defendant is judged to be insane and a danger to self or to others at the time of the trial, he or she is usually required to receive treatment, typically through commitment to a hospital, until cured or no longer dangerous.

This rule has several problems. It was designed to protect the mentally ill, especially from being punished as criminals, but according to Szasz and other critics, there is no such thing as mental illness, so people should not be allowed to escape responsibility for their crimes. Whether one entirely agrees with Szasz or not, there are other significant problems with the insanity defense. First and most important, different experts often give conflicting testimony about the defendant's sanity at the time of the crime. (In Cheryl's case, one expert said she was sane; the other concluded she was insane.) The jury is left in the almost impossible position, as nonexperts, of deciding which expert to believe. Second, in some cases, a defendant found not guilty by reason of insanity can spend more time committed to a mental hospital than if he or she had been convicted of the crime and sentenced to prison. Although this does not happen often, it does illustrate how well-intentioned laws can sometimes produce a miscarriage of justice.

What can be done about these problems? Many reforms have been proposed and debated (Maeder, 1985; Rogers & Ewing, 1989; Smith & Meyer, 1987). Some reformers have suggested abolishing the insanity defense, but that appears unlikely. Three other, less extreme, reforms have been attempted. First, a new verdict of *guilty but mentally ill* can now be rendered in many states. This verdict allows the jury to conclude that although the defendant is guilty of the crime, he or she is also mentally ill. Defendants found guilty but mentally ill still serve a sentence but must also receive treatment while in prison or in a special institution. Mental health professionals have objected that this verdict is a political compromise that ensures neither proper treatment nor proper verdicts. A second type of reform was stimulated after John Hinckley was found not guilty by reason of insanity for the attempted murder of President Ronald Reagan. It is embodied in the Insanity Defense Reform Act, which eliminated (for federal courts) the irresistible-impulse criterion from the definition of insanity. Third, the federal courts and some states now require the *defendant* to prove that he or she was insane at the time of the crime, rather than requiring the prosecution to prove that the defendant was sane.

Clearly, no generally satisfactory solution for the dilemmas surrounding mental illness and criminal behavior has yet been found. Note, however, that the intensity of the arguments is disproportionately high given the frequency of the problem. The insanity plea is raised in only 1 to 2 percent of the cases that go to trial, and it is successful in only a tiny fraction of those cases.

Linkages: Psychological Disorders and Human Development

What kinds of psychological disorders appear in the early stages of life?

As we described in Chapter 2, childhood is a period of rapid physical, cognitive, emotional, and social changes. These changes and the stress associated with them can create or worsen disorders in children. Stress can do the same in adults, but childhood disorders are not just miniature versions of adult psychopathology. Because children's development is still incomplete and because their capacity to cope with stress is limited in important ways, children are often vulnerable to special types of disorders. Surveys consistently suggest that two broad categories encompass the majority of childhood behavior problems: externalizing and internalizing disorders (Quay, 1979).

The *externalizing*, or *undercontrolled*, category includes behaviors that are aversive to those in the child's environment. Lack of control, especially in boys, shows up in *conduct disorders* characterized by aggression, disobedience, destructiveness, and other obnoxious behaviors. Often these behaviors involve criminal activity. A genetic predisposition for conduct disorders is highly likely, but it is also clear that environmental and parenting factors influence the antisocial behavior of these children (Rutter & Giller, 1983).

Another kind of externalizing problem is *attention-deficit hyperactivity disorder (ADHD)*. This label is given to children who are impulsive and cannot concentrate on an activity as well as other children their age. Many of these children are *hyperactive*; they have great difficulty sitting still or otherwise controlling their physical activity. Their immaturity and astonishing ability to annoy and exhaust those around them creates numerous problems, especially at school (Henker & Whalen, 1989). Genetic predisposition, the occurrence of brain damage, dietary problems, poisoning, and ineffective parenting have all been proposed as possible causes of hyperactivity, but the role played by each of these factors is still uncertain (Marshall, 1989).

As many as 9 to 10 percent of elementary school boys and 2 to 3 percent of girls may be hyperactive (Ross & Ross, 1982). The problem often moderates or disappears by young adulthood, but some formerly hyperactive males continue to show problems in peer relationships and social adjustment (Milich & Landau, 1982; Weiss et al., 1985).

The second broad category of child behavior problems involves *internalizing*, or *overcontrol*. Children in this category experience internal distress, especially depression and anxiety, and may be socially withdrawn. In *separation anxiety disorder*, for example, the child constantly worries that he or she will be lost, kidnaped, or injured or that some harm may come to a parent (usually the mother). As a result, the child clings desperately to the parent and becomes upset or sick at the prospect of any separation.

A few childhood disorders do not fall in either the externalizing or internalizing category. An example is *autistic disorder*, a severe and puzzling condition, usually identified within the first thirty months of life. Autistic babies show no sign of attachment to their mothers, fathers, or anyone else. They do not smile, laugh, or make eye contact with their parents. They will not tolerate being held and cuddled; they prefer to remain in a world of their own. As years go by, they ignore others and instead rock themselves repetitively or play endlessly, it seems, with ashtrays, keys, or other inanimate objects. Language development is seriously disrupted in these children. Half never learn to speak at all. Autistic disorder is rare, occurring in fewer than five children per ten thousand births, but with few exceptions (Lovaas, 1987), it leads to a life of marginal adjustment, often within an institution.

Possible biological roots of autistic disorder include oversensitivity to stimulation (Zentall & Zentall, 1983) or abnormally high levels of natural opiates (discussed in Chapters 3 and 4), which may make autistic children less needful of comfort and other social interaction (Herman et al., 1986). Autistic children may also have problems with cell communication in the language areas of the brain (Minshew, Payton & Sclabassi, 1986). The specific causes of autistic disorder remain unknown, however.

Disorders of childhood differ from adult disorders not only because the patterns of behavior are distinct but also because their early onset renders childhood disorders especially capable of disrupting development. To take one example, children whose fear of school causes spotty attendance may not only fall behind academically but also fail to form the relationships with other children that promote normal social development. Some children may never make up for this deficit. For some, the long-term result may be adult forms of mental disorder.

Future Directions

There have been many ideas over the years about what constitutes abnormality. Even today the criteria for calling someone "crazy" differ from one culture or subculture to the next. During the last twenty-five years, mental health professionals have become increasingly aware that abnormality must be defined in relative terms, and they take a practical approach that examines the content, sociocultural context, and consequences of behavior before labeling it as abnormal. Future editions of the DSM are likely to continue the trend toward basing diagnoses on what a person does, where and when it is done, and who, if anyone, suffers.

The evolution of the DSM reflects another important trend: the development of increasingly specific criteria for diagnosing psychopathology. Each edition has specified more clearly the rules to be followed in placing people in various diagnostic categories. As the rules become clearer, the reliability of diagnoses is likely to increase even further.

Concerns remain over the validity of DSM diagnoses, especially for predicting behavior. A major goal of research on the validity of diagnostic categories involves studying whether members of a particular category share patterns of family history, genetic and biochemical factors, responses to specific treatments, and other characteristics. If shared patterns can be found, they may suggest theories about the causes and best treatments for a particular disorder.

Much of the research aimed at isolating factors that may be responsible for disorders reflects increasing attention to biological explanations. For example, some research suggests that anxiety disorders may be related to an overabundance of a molecule known as DBI (diazepam-binding inhibitor), which appears in areas of the brain involved with emotion and which heightens anxiety responses (Ferraro, Conti-Tronconi & Guidotti, 1986; Slobodyansky et al., 1989). In certain people, the nervous system seems especially capable of blocking incoming sensations, especially during stress-related emotional arousal; this blocking might be partially responsible for the appearance of conversion or other somatoform disorders. Abnormalities in areas of the brain involved in attention, perception, emotion, and thought may be related to some of the symptoms of schizophrenia (Suddath et al., 1990).

We expect that future research on the causes of mental disorders will have three characteristics. First, researchers will be looking for multiple rather than single causes for particular disorders. This trend is illustrated by the popularity of the diathesis-stress approach. This perspective leaves room for a variety of interacting factors—biological, psychological, environmental, and social—which, depending on their particular combination, may or may not produce abnormality. For example, exploration of the cognitive contributions to depression are increasingly concentrating not only on identifying specific cognitive patterns associated with depression (Strauman, 1989) but also how these patterns are related to other personality characteristics (Nietzel & Harris, in press) and how the patterns interact with negative life events (Mikulincer, 1988). Second, researchers will consider whether each category of mental disorder may contain subtypes and variants, each of which may have its own causal factors. This trend is exemplified by research suggesting that different biological factors may be associated with different subtypes of schizophrenia. Finally, because it now seems clear that no single perspective is capable of explaining mental disorders, we expect the future will see less dogmatism and more cooperation among researchers from many perspectives.

We have offered only a glimpse of the problems, issues, and theories that characterize the study of psychological disorders. For more detailed coverage, enroll in a course in abnormal psychology.

Summary and Key Terms

Mental disorder, or *psychopathology*, involves patterns of thinking and behaving that are maladaptive, disruptive, or distressing either for the person affected or for others.

Normality and Abnormality

Abnormal behavior is defined by the culture in which the behavior takes place.

What Is Abnormal?

Exactly what is abnormal can be defined by the *statistical approach*, in comparison to what most people do, or by the *valuative approach*, in relation to what society values. Each view has problems. A *practical approach* looks at the content, context, and consequences of behavior. From the practical perspective, abnormal behaviors make the person uncomfortable, disable daily functioning, or interfere substantially with the lives of others.

Explaining Abnormal Behavior

Abnormal behavior has been attributed, at one time or another, to the action of gods or the devil (the *demonological model*), to physical disease (the *medical* or *biological model*), or, in *psychological models*, to such factors as internal mental conflicts (the *psychodynamic model*), learned maladaptive behavior and thinking (the *behavioral model*), and a person's way of looking at the world (the *phenomenological model*). Because no one of these approaches is fully satisfactory, aspects of several models have been combined in the *diathesis-stress model*, which highlights the interactions among inherited predispositions, psychological characteristics, and the stresses of life.

Classifying Abnormal Behavior

The dominant system for classifying abnormal behavior is the *Diagnostic and Statistical Manual* (*DSM*) of the American Psychiatric Association. It includes sixteen major types of mental disorder, as well as a variety of less severe behavior problems. Even though it represents an improvement over previous diagnostic systems, some psychologists question the reliability, validity, and biased use of the DSM.

Other Key Terms in This Section: organic mental disorders, dementia, delirium, neurosis, psychosis.

Anxiety Disorders

Long-standing and disruptive patterns of fear characterize *anxiety disorders*.

Types of Anxiety Disorders

One major type of anxiety disorder involves *phobias*, which are specific fears; *simple phobia*, *social phobia*, and *agoraphobia* are the major kinds of phobias. Other anxiety disorders are *generalized anxiety disorder*, which involves nonspecific fears; *panic disorder*, with unpredictable attacks of intense anxiety; and *obsessive-compulsive disorder*, in which uncontrollable repetitive thoughts and ritualistic actions occur.

Causes of Anxiety Disorders

The biological and behavioral models provide the most influential explanations of anxiety disorders. Biological explanations suggest predispositions to show strong anxiety reactions in a wide range of situations; behavioral explanations emphasize the impact of learned anxiety responses and fear-enhancing thought patterns.

Somatoform Disorders

Somatoform disorders include *conversion disorder*, which involves physical problems that have no apparent physical cause; *hypochondriasis*, an unjustified concern over being ill; and *somatoform pain disorder*, in which pain is felt in the absence of a physical cause.

Dissociative Disorders

Dissociative disorders involve such rare conditions as *psychogenic fugue*, *psychogenic amnesia*, and *multiple personality*, in which a person suffers sudden memory loss or develops two or more separate identities. The experience of abuse in childhood may be a causal factor in multiple personality.

Mood Disorders

Mood disorders, or affective disorders, are quite common and involve extreme moods that may be inconsistent with events.

Depressive Disorders

Major depression is marked by feelings of inadequacy, worthlessness, and guilt; in extreme cases, *delusions* may also occur. More common is *dysthymia*, which includes similar but less severe symptoms persisting for a long period. Suicide is often related to these disorders.

Bipolar Disorder

Alternating feelings of depression and *mania* characterize *bipolar disorder*, which is also known as manic depression. Cyclothymia, which is a pattern of less extreme mood swings, is more common.

Causes of Mood Disorders

Mood disorders have been attributed to dependency needs, loss of significant sources of reward, pessimistic patterns of thinking about oneself, disruptions in neurotransmitter systems, and irregularities in daily biological rhythms. Some of these problems may be inherited, though their appearance may be determined by a diathesis-stress process.

Schizophrenia

Symptoms of Schizophrenia

Schizophrenia is perhaps the most severe and puzzling disorder of all. Among its symptoms are problems in thinking, perception (often including *hallucinations*), attention, emotion, movement, motivation, and daily functioning.

Types of Schizophrenia

Five subtypes of schizophrenia have been identified, including *residual*, *disorganized*, *catatonic*, *paranoid*, and *undifferentiated*.

The Search for Causes

The exact causes of schizophrenia are still unknown, but genetic factors, neurotransmitter problems, brain abnormalities, conflict-filled childhoods, and unfortunate learning experiences have all been implicated. The *vulnerability model* provides a promising framework for research into the causes.

Substance-Use Disorders

Psychoactive substance-use disorders such as *alcoholism* affect millions of people. *Addiction* and psychological dependence on these substances create disastrous personal and social problems.

Alcoholism

The physical addiction or psychological dependence associated with alcoholism causes physical illnesses and disruptions in social and occupational functioning and contributes heavily to accident and crime statistics. Genetic factors may create a predisposition for alcoholism, but learning, cultural traditions, and other nonbiological processes also seem important.

Heroin and Cocaine Dependence

Addiction to heroin and cocaine (especially crack) lead to serious physical and social problems, including the risk of death from overdoses. Stress reduction, imitation, thrill seeking, and social maladjustment may be more important causal factors than genetics, but the exact causes of initial use of these drugs are unknown.

Sexual Disorders

Sexual disorders include *sexual dysfunction*, which are problems in attaining sexual enjoyment, and *paraphilias*, which involve attraction to inappropriate stimuli, such as inanimate objects or children.

Personality Disorders

Personality disorders are long-term patterns of behavior that are not as severe as other mental disorders and are not always associated with personal discomfort, although they are disturbing to others. Examples include *schizotypal personality*, *narcissistic personality*, and *antisocial personality disorders*.

Mental Illness in Society

Does Mental Illness Exist?

Szasz has argued that mental illness is just a term for people's problems in living and that viewing these as illnesses deprives people of their rights. Szasz's critics suggest that his position is too extreme and may create new injustices, including depriving people of needed treatment.

Behavior Disorder and Criminal Responsibility

Szasz's arguments have fueled controversy over whether people identified as "mentally ill" should be protected from prosecution or punishment for crimes they may commit. Current rules do provide such protection for those who met legal criteria for insanity at the time of their crime, but difficulty in establishing defendants' mental state and other knotty problems have created dissatisfaction with those rules and prompted a number of reforms, including the "guilty but mentally ill" verdict.

Treatment of Psychological Disorders

Until recently, twenty-nine-year-old Lou S. had never had a serious problem in his life, and, as far as he knew, neither had anyone in his family. In the five years after earning a degree in chemistry from a prestigious university, Lou had landed a good job at a major engineering corporation, gotten married, and received two promotions. But Lou was troubled. He wasn't sleeping well, couldn't concentrate at work, and was drinking alcohol more and more frequently. Though he was living the American dream, Lou was depressed. He hadn't a clue why, and he didn't know what to do about it. He had long ago adopted his parents' view that anyone with psychological problems was just weak and that solving these problems was a private matter, to be handled without help. Lou told himself the depression would lift on its own so he refused to talk about his feelings, even to his wife, who encouraged him to do so. Instead, he accused her of nagging and not letting him be himself. He increased his drinking and started to see other women. Unfortunately, drinking and infidelity only made Lou feel worse about himself. He felt guilty and started to suspect that his wife no longer loved him. They argued more often and, at one point, Lou struck his wife. Then, while driving drunk on one of his nights out, Lou crashed into a bridge abutment. The coroner ruled his death an accident, but his wife still wonders if it was suicide. The tragedy in this case lies not only in the misery and the loss of life but also in the fact that they might have been prevented. Lou's prejudice against asking for help forced him to fall back on his own coping skills, which turned out to be inadequate.

About one of every ten people in the United States receives treatment for a psychological disorder at some time in his or her life (Klerman, 1983). Often, the problems involve the behavior disorders described in Chapter 15, but they may also be relatively mild, such as shyness or lack of self-confidence. In this chapter, we

LINKAGES

Treatment of

Psychological

Disorders

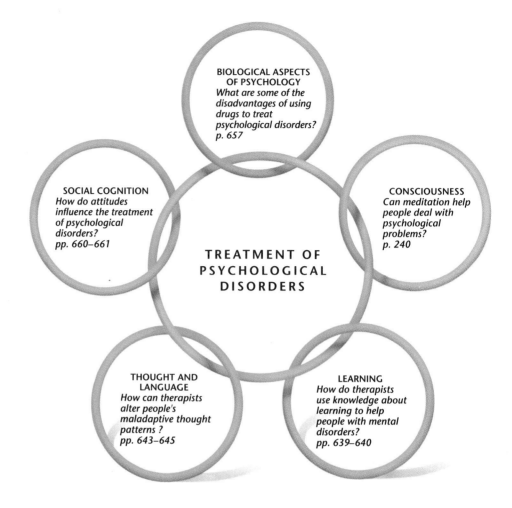

BIOLOGICAL ASPECTS
OF PSYCHOLOGY
*What are some of the
disadvantages of using
drugs to treat
psychological disorders?
p. 657*

SOCIAL COGNITION
*How do attitudes
influence the treatment
of psychological
disorders?
pp. 660–661*

CONSCIOUSNESS
*Can meditation help
people deal with
psychological
problems?
p. 240*

TREATMENT OF
PSYCHOLOGICAL
DISORDERS

THOUGHT AND
LANGUAGE
*How can therapists
alter people's
maladaptive thought
patterns ?
pp. 643–645*

LEARNING
*How do therapists
use knowledge about
learning to help
people with mental
disorders?
pp. 639–640*

■ Look at the diagram above, which illustrates some of the relationships between the topic of this chapter, the treatment of psychological disorders, and other chapter topics. There is today a variety of methods with proven value for reducing or eliminating psychological problems. Much of the basis for these methods lies in the theories of personality reviewed in Chapter 14. By spelling out proposed explanations for what can go wrong in the development of personality, those theories provided important general guidelines for treatment. For example, we will see in this chapter that the emphasis on learning found in behavioral theories of personality generated methods for teaching disturbed people how to think and act in more adaptive ways.

Modern methods of treatment also owe much to research in biological psychology, especially to research on the role of neurotransmitters in the brain. Recognition of the importance of biological processes has led to the development of drugs whose effects on neurotransmitters temporarily alleviate some symptoms of psychological disturbance.

These and other links—a sampling of which is shown in the diagram— are discussed in the text. The page numbers indicate where in the text each question is explored. ■

examine methods for treating and preventing a wide range of psychological disorders. The bases for most of these methods lie in the theories of personality and behavior disorder reviewed in Chapters 14 and 15. By spelling out proposed explanations for what can go wrong in the development of personality and behavior, those theories provide important guidelines for treatment (see the Linkages diagram).

After first examining some basic features of the treatment of psychological disorders, we discuss psychodynamic, phenomenological, and behavioral approaches to treatment. These rely mainly on **psychotherapy**, the treatment of psychological disorders through psychological methods, such as talking about problems and solutions and exploring new ways of thinking and acting. We then consider the biological approach to therapy, which depends mainly on drugs and other physical treatments. Although we discuss each of these approaches in a separate section, keep in mind that many of those who treat psychological problems do not adhere to only one set of methods. In fact, the majority of mental health professionals see themselves as *eclectic therapists* (Jensen, Bergin & Greaves, 1990); in other words, they might lean slightly toward one approach, but they borrow methods from other types of therapy (Zook & Walton, 1989). The eclectic therapist employs whatever combination of methods is likely to help a given client with a given problem (Garfield, 1982; Jensen, Bergin & Greaves, 1990; Wachtel, 1982).

Essentials of Therapy

Regardless of how it is done, psychotherapy boils down to one person trying to help another. All forms of therapy share certain basic features—not only with one another but also with efforts to treat the physically ill (Frank, 1973, 1978). These common features include

1. A *client* or patient who is suffering and seeks relief from a problem.
2. A *therapist* or helper who is socially accepted as capable of helping the client.

The image of therapy that comes quickest to many people's minds is of someone lying on a couch describing dreams to a bearded, pipe-smoking therapist who has a Viennese accent. To be sure, some therapy is done this way. But no single image can capture the many forms of modern treatment. It is offered to individuals, families, and groups in hospitals, community mental health centers, private clinics, and halfway houses (in which former hospital residents and other clients live while receiving therapy, supervision, and support). Treatment is also provided in prisons, military bases, drug and alcoholism treatment centers, and many other places.

3. A *theory* or rationale of the client's problems. In medicine, the theory involves germs, infections, and other biological processes. In psychology, the theory may involve psychodynamics, learning principles, interpersonal needs, or other psychological factors.

4. A set of *procedures* for dealing with the client's problems. The procedures usually grow out of the theory used. They may presume causes ranging from magic spells to infections and everything in between (Frank, 1973). Thus, the witch doctor combats the supernatural with special ceremonies and prayers, whereas the medical doctor treats infections with antibiotics. Later we review procedures used by mental health professionals.

5. A special social *relationship* between client and therapist. A positive working relationship is necessary for successful treatment. An atmosphere is created in which the client feels optimistic about solving problems, expects that the therapist's methods will help, and is motivated to work toward solutions. These characteristics mark all forms of healing to some extent. Even in medical treatment, where improvement usually depends mainly on drugs or surgery, patients' expectations can play an important role. You will see that some psychotherapists emphasize the relationship with the client much more than others.

Clients and Therapists

The people receiving psychotherapy may be classified into three categories. *Inpatients* are treated in a hospital or other residential institution; in public hospitals, many are older adult males from lower social class backgrounds. *Outpatients* receive psychotherapy while living in the community; they tend to be younger than the average inpatient, more often female than male, and typically come from the middle or upper classes. A final category is made up of people who come to therapy not because of major problems but to seek personal growth; they are usually young to middle-aged adults who have intellectual curiosity, financial resources, and leisure time.

Providers of psychological treatment are also a diverse group. **Psychiatrists** are medical doctors who complete special training in the treatment of mental disorders. **Psychologists** who do psychotherapy have completed a graduate program in clinical or counseling psychology, often followed by additional specialized training. Unlike psychiatrists, psychologists are not permitted to prescribe drugs. According to the American Psychological Association and the laws of most states, only those who hold a doctoral degree are officially recognized as clinical or counseling psychologists, but numerous individuals who have completed only a master's degree in these fields provide treatment services as well. *Psychiatric social workers* typically hold a master's degree from a school of social work and provide therapy in a hospital or clinic, though many also enter private practice. *Psychiatric nurses, occupational therapists*, and *recreational therapists* also provide therapy, most often as part of a hospital treatment team.

Interestingly, most people do not turn to any of these "official" agents for help—at least not at first (Cowen, 1982; Gurin, Veroff & Feld, 1960). They may go instead to a member of their family; to the clergy; to their physician, teacher, or lawyer; to their friends; to self-help groups (such as Alcoholics Anonymous); and even to their barber, beautician, or bartender. These helpers cannot offer formal treatment, but they aid a large number of distressed people. For example, as many as 6.25 million individuals, or 3.7 percent of all American adults, are estimated to participate in some type of self-help group or activity (Jacobs & Goodman, 1989). This number rivals the number of clients currently in psychotherapy and leads some clinicians to predict that self-help groups will become *the* major form of mental health treatment in the 1990s (Prochaska & Norcross, 1982).

Goals and Methods of Psychotherapy

Linkages: What methods are used to treat psychological disorders? (a link to Psychological Disorders)

Although there are similarities between the techniques of professional psychotherapists and those used by nonprofessional helpers and self-help groups (Winefield, 1987), formal psychotherapy is distinguished by a special set of goals and methods.

The general goal in treating psychological disorders is to help troubled people change their thinking and behavior so that they will be happier and more productive. In working with individuals, therapists translate this overall goal into more specific ones. They might aim to help their clients better understand their problems, to reduce emotional discomfort, to gain better control over a problem behavior, or to encourage the free expression of feelings. They might seek to provide new ideas or information about how to solve problems or to help their clients try new ways of thinking and behaving.

Psychological treatments work toward these goals in three main ways. First, therapists provide psychological support. They may offer a sympathetic ear and level-headed guidance in a crisis. Second, therapists may help clients eliminate troublesome behaviors and develop new and better ones. Finally, they may promote insight and self-exploration, helping clients to better understand motivations, emotions, perceptions, conflicts, and values. This requires clients to look beyond what is obvious and specific about themselves (such as being afraid of flying or having frequent arguments) and to consider what such problems might suggest about more subtle and general aspects of personality, such as a preoccupation with security or competitiveness.

The degree to which each of these general methods is used in a particular case depends on several factors. The problems, preferences, and financial circumstances of the client often shape the choice of method. In addition,

The methods used to treat psychological disorders are related to the presumed cause of the problems. In the days when gods or demons were blamed for behavior disorders, magical-religious practitioners tried to make the victim's body an uncomfortable place for an evil spirit. Here, an afflicted person's head is placed in an oven, supposedly resulting in the departure of numerous evil spirits.

the decision depends on the time available for treatment and the therapist's theoretical leanings and methodological preferences. There are more than a hundred specific methods of treatment (Corsini, 1981; Herink, 1980; Zeig, 1987).

H I G H L I G H T

Rules and Rights in the Therapeutic Relationship

Treatment of psychological disorders can be an intense emotional activity, and the relationship established with a therapist can profoundly affect the client's life. Professional ethics and common sense require the therapist to assure that this relationship does not harm the client. More specifically, the Ethical Standards of the American Psychological Association forbid a sexual relationship between therapist and client (APA, 1981, 1989) and require therapists, with a few exceptions, to keep everything a client says in therapy strictly confidential.

Confidentiality is one of the most important features of a successful therapeutic relationship, because it allows the client to disclose unpleasant or embarrassing feelings or events. Not many clients would reveal that they were hooked on cocaine or were having an extramarital affair if they thought the therapist would disclose these secrets to others. Professionals may consult with one another about a client, but each is required not to reveal information to outsiders (including members of the client's family) without the client's consent.

Professional rules about confidentiality are backed up in most states by laws recognizing that information revealed in therapy—like information given to a priest, a lawyer, or a physician—is privileged communication. This means that a therapist can refuse, even in court, to answer questions about a client or to provide personal notes or tape recordings from therapy sessions. However, under some special circumstances a therapist must violate confidentiality. Among these exceptions are cases in which (1) the client is so severely disturbed or suicidal that hospitalization is needed; (2) the client uses his or her mental condition and history of therapy as part of his or her defense in a civil or criminal trial; (3) the therapist must defend against the client's charge of malpractice; and (4) the therapist believes the client may commit a violent act against others.

This last condition poses a dilemma. Suppose a client says, "Someday I'm going to kill that brother of mine!" Should the therapist consider this a serious threat and warn the brother? In most cases, the danger is not real, but there have been tragic exceptions. A famous case occurred in 1969. A graduate student receiving therapy at the University of California at Berkeley revealed his intention to kill Tatiana Tarasoff, a young woman whom he had dated the previous year but who had since rejected him. The therapist took the threat seriously and consulted his supervisor and the campus police. It was decided that there was no real danger, so neither Tatiana nor her parents were warned. After terminating therapy, the client killed Ms. Tarasoff. Her parents sued the university, the campus police, and the therapist. The parents won their case, thus setting an important precedent and making therapists acutely aware of their legal responsibility to take reasonable steps to protect potential victims whenever a client makes a serious threat to harm a particular person.

Several states now have laws that specify when a therapist is liable for failing to take precautions to protect others from violent acts by the therapist's clients. However, accurately predicting violent behavior by specific individuals is extremely hard (Monahan, 1981). Thus, therapists sometimes have to make wrenchingly difficult decisions about whether to break confidentiality and call the police or warn a threatened person.

Besides confidentiality, people receiving treatment for psychological disorders have other legal rights. Perhaps most important, the mentally ill are protected from being casually and involuntarily committed to a mental hospital. According to decisions by federal courts throughout the 1970s and 1980s, a person threatened with commitment can expect written notice; an opportunity to prepare a defense with the help of an attorney; a court hearing, with a jury if desired; and the right to take the Fifth Amendment to avoid self-incrimination. Furthermore, before a person can be forcibly committed, the state must provide "clear and convincing" evidence that he or she is not only mentally ill but also poses an "imminent danger" to himself or herself or to others. Most states now require a periodic review of every committed person to determine whether he or she should be released. Commitment can no longer become an automatic life sentence. In addition, the person has the right to receive treatment while hospitalized. Finally, people have the right to refuse certain forms of treatment and to be subjected to as little restriction of their freedom as possible. (See Smith & Meyer, 1987 for thorough discussions of the rights both to receive and to refuse treatment.) If these conditions are not being met, the patient must be released.

Rules regarding hospitalized mental patients help protect them from abuse, neglect, coercion, and exploitation, but they create some difficulties as well. Staff members at mental health facilities worry that they might be sued if they keep patients unnecessarily confined or if they release a patient who then harms someone. Although noncriminal former mental patients are less dangerous than the general noncriminal population (Monahan, 1981), some do commit crimes—which are often well publicized. Thus the dilemma: to find a way to balance the legal rights of the individual patient against the legal rights of the public. ■

Psychodynamic Psychotherapy

The field of psychotherapy formally began with the work of Sigmund Freud. He established the psychodynamic approach to personality, which was described in Chapter 14. Central to this approach is the assumption that personality and behavior reflect the efforts of the ego to referee unconscious conflicts in dealing with the world. The key to helping troubled individuals, Freud thought, lay in helping them better understand unconscious conflicts. Freud's method of treatment, **psychoanalysis**, offers a set of psychological procedures for understanding unconscious conflicts and working through their effects. His one-to-one method of studying and treating people, his systematic search for relationships between an individual's life history and current problems, his emphasis on thoughts and emotions in treatment, and his focus on the client-therapist relationship reappear in almost all forms of psychotherapy. We will describe Freud's psychoanalytic methods first, then briefly consider some of the other treatments that are based on his psychodynamic approach.

Psychoanalytic Goals and Methods

Psychoanalysis developed mainly out of Freud's medical practice, which began in the late 1880s. He was puzzled by patients who suffered from hysterical ailments—blindness, paralysis, or other symptoms that have no physical cause. (As mentioned in Chapter 15, these are now called conversion disorders in DSM-III-R.) Freud tried to cure these patients through hypnotic suggestion, but he found it only partially and temporarily successful. Later, he and a colleague named Joseph Breuer began asking hypnotized patients to try recalling events that might have caused their symptoms. Breuer and Freud (1896) reported some success with this "talking cure." Eventually, Freud stopped using hypnosis and merely had the patient relax on a couch and report the memories that came to mind.

The results were surprising. Freud was struck by how many of his patients reported childhood memories of sexual abuse, usually by a parent or close relative. Either child abuse was rampant in Vienna at the time, or his patients' reports were distorted by psychological factors. Freud ultimately concluded that his patients' "memories" of childhood seduction might in fact reflect childhood fantasies (a conclusion that has recently come under attack, as discussed in Chapter 14, on personality). This reasoning shifted the focus of psychoanalytic therapy from efforts to recover lost memories to attempts to explore unconscious wishes and conflicts. His patients' hysterical symptoms, Freud concluded, developed out of conflicts based on unconscious wishes and fantasies.

From these beginnings, Freud created psychoanalysis. This method of treatment aims to help clients (1) gain insight by recognizing and dealing with unconscious thoughts and emotions, and (2) work through the many ways in which those unconscious elements affect everyday life. For example, a man might be hostile toward his boss, an older coworker, and all other "parent figures" in his life because he is unconsciously re-enacting childhood conflicts with an overprotective parent. The psychoanalyst would help the client recognize his hidden, pent-up anger toward the parent, experience it, and trace how this unconscious source of continuing anger and the defenses around it have been creating problems.

How does the therapist achieve these goals? Psychoanalytic treatment may require as many as three to five sessions per week for from two to fifteen years. Generally, the psychoanalyst aims to maintain a compassionate neutrality during treatment so that the client can, with the therapist's slow, patient guidance, develop insight into how past conflicts determine current problems. To provide this guidance the therapist uses several techniques.

Free Association   One technique is based on the idea that many clues to the unconscious lie in the constant stream of thoughts, feelings, memories, and images experienced by all people. These clues can be uncovered and understood if the client relaxes defenses and does not block the stream of consciousness. Thus, psychoanalysts use **free association**, a procedure in which the client relaxes, usually while lying on a couch, and reports everything that comes to mind as soon as it occurs, no matter how trivial, bizarre, or embarrassing it may seem.

Clues to the unconscious often come from the way thoughts are linked rather than the thoughts themselves. Consider this example from the free association of a middle-aged male.

My Dad called long distance last night. He seemed upset. . . . (Long silence.)
I almost fell asleep there for a minute. I used to do that a lot in college. Once I

woke up and saw the professor standing over me, shaking me, and the whole class was laughing.

Notice that after talking about his father, the client fell silent. When clients stop talking or claim that their minds are blank, the psychoanalyst may suspect that unconscious defense mechanisms are keeping threatening material out of consciousness. In this case, after having first thought about his father, the client remembered receiving punishment from an authority figure. This sequence might be a clue that unconscious conflicts with his father have not yet been resolved.

The Interpretation of Dreams   As discussed in Chapter 6, on consciousness, dreams may be a by-product of brain activity during sleep, but their content may also reflect the dreamer's emotional state or psychological concerns. Psychoanalysts believe that dreams express wishes, impulses, and fantasies that the dreamer's defenses keep unconscious during waking hours. Even in dreams, however, defenses usually disguise threatening material so that the dream does not frighten (and awaken) the dreamer. The analyst's task is to help the client search for the unconscious material contained in dreams.

As an example, suppose a woman reports the following dream: "I was sitting in a restaurant, having lasagna, when the president of the United States walked in and started a fistfight with my waiter." The client's description of a dream provides its *manifest content*. Manifest content often contains unimportant features and events from the day or reflects temporary needs. In this case, perhaps the dreamer had just seen the president on television or was hungry at bedtime. According to psychoanalytic theory, however, a dream also has *latent content*, which is its unconscious meaning, expressed by the dream's symbolism. How might a psychoanalyst probe the latent content of this dream? Perhaps the plate of lasagna represents an Italian friend, and the bout between president and waiter symbolizes the dreamer's conflict about wanting to be wealthy and powerful (the president) but also wanting to be of service to ("wait on") others. To uncover this content, the analyst may ask the client to free-associate to parts of the dream or may suggest an interpretation.

Dream analysis differs for each client. There are few, if any, universal dream symbols: giants do not always represent an angry father, water does not always represent birth, and long objects do not always represent penises.

The Analysis of Everyday Behavior   According to Freud (1914), human actions are never random; they are determined by a combination of conscious intentions and unconscious influences. Even apparently trivial behavior may hold important messages from the unconscious. For example, in the midst of the Watergate scandal that eventually drove him from office, former President Nixon made a speech to Congress in which he stated: "Join me in mounting a new effort to replace the discredited president." He meant to say "replace the discredited present welfare system." This *Freudian slip* revealed that the president might have had other things on his mind.

Lapses of memory may also be tied to unconscious defenses or impulses. Forgetting the content of a dream or the time of a therapy appointment might reflect a client's unconscious resistance to treatment.* Even accidents may be meaningful. Thus, the waiter who spills hot soup on an elderly male customer might be seen as acting out unconscious aggressive impulses against a father figure.

---

* It has been jokingly argued that you cannot win in psychoanalysis, because you are dependent if you show up early, resistant if you miss a session or show up late, and compulsive if you are right on time.

Giving Interpretations   By helping a client to understand the meaning of free associations, dreams, and everyday behavior, the psychoanalyst contributes greatly to the client's self-understanding. By asking questions, making comments, and suggesting interpretations, the therapist gradually leads the client to become aware of all aspects of his or her personality, including defenses and the unconscious material behind them. Here is an example of an analytic interpretation.

Client: I'm sorry to be late, but my brother-in-law called just as I was leaving. He told me my sister is sick again and asked if I had any extra cash to help with her medical bills. I said I did, but I don't know how I can help them and keep coming to see you. Sometimes, everything falls on me at once.

Therapist: You know, last session, we began to see that you have some very negative feelings toward your parents. That was difficult for you to accept. Today, you start off by saying that, through no fault of your own, you may not be able to continue therapy. Could it be that whenever you are threatened by what you are learning about yourself here, you use something beyond your control to divert our attention? I wonder, because you told me you used to get out of trouble this way as a child. When your parents got angry with you, you always blamed your mistakes on someone else who kept you from doing what you should. What do you think?

The basic strategy of the psychoanalyst is to construct increasingly accurate and empathic accounts of what has happened to the client (but has been "forgotten") and what is happening to the client (but is not understood). The analyst gradually shares these accounts with the client through interpretations.

Analysis of the Transference   Psychoanalysts believe that if they reveal nothing about themselves to a client, a transference relationship will develop. In **transference** the client unconsciously re-enacts, toward the therapist, many of the feelings, attitudes, reactions, and conflicts experienced in childhood with parents and other significant people. A "new edition" of the client's problems—a recapitulation of the childhood conflicts—appears in this transference. The transference may take many forms, including falling in love with the therapist, becoming dependent, or being hostile.

By analyzing the transference, the therapist helps the client resolve problems from the past that are dramatically illustrated in the present through the client-therapist relationship. Psychoanalysts believe the development of the transference allows clients to see clearly how old conflicts continue to haunt their lives. It also suggests ways in which these old conflicts can be laid to rest.

Variations on Psychoanalysis

Classical Freudian psychoanalysis is not as popular as it once was, partly because Freud's instinct-based personality theory has fallen into disfavor and partly because psychoanalysis is expensive and time consuming. Further, clients in analysis must be able to think clearly about abstract concepts. Thus, most children, as well as adults who lack verbal skills or display severe disorders, are not good candidates for classical psychoanalysis. These limitations of Freud's methods prompted other psychodynamic theorists to create variations on psychoanalytic treatment.

Many of the variations were developed by neo-Freudian therapists discussed in Chapter 14. Some focus less on the id, the unconscious, and the past than did Freud. They stress current problems and how the power of the client's ego can be harnessed to solve them. Examples of these variations include *ego*

To explore unconscious conflicts in children, some analytically oriented therapists use fantasy play with toys rather than traditional free association.

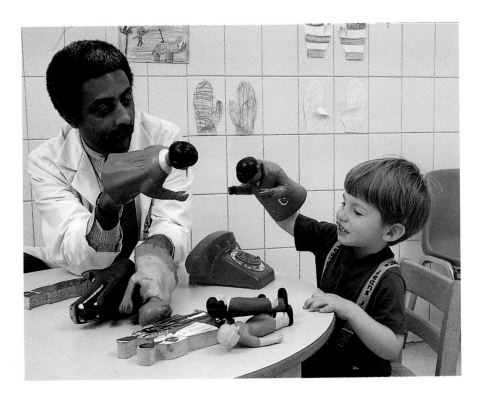

analysis (Hartmann, 1958; Klein, 1960), *interpersonal therapy* (Sullivan, 1954), *individual analysis* (Adler, 1963), and *object relations therapy* (Kohut, 1983). In these therapies, clients are helped to understand how their feelings of anxiety, insecurity, or inferiority originated and how they create disordered thoughts and problems in relating to others. Compared with the traditional analyst, these therapists are likely to be more active in providing encouragement and guidance. More than traditional Freudians, they also emphasize corrective emotional experiences arising from active support, emotional soothing, and direct reassurance of clients.

Other variations on psychoanalysis retain more of Freud's ideas but alter the format of treatment so that it is less intense, less expensive, and more appropriate for a broad range of people. For example, *psychoanalytically oriented psychotherapy* (Alexander, 1963), or *time-limited dynamic psychotherapy,* uses basic psychoanalytic methods, but flexibly (Davanloo, 1978; Sifneos, 1979; Strupp, 1989). Instead of lying on a couch, the client may sit facing the therapist and spend more time in conversation than in free association. Often the therapist is more active than a classical psychoanalyst in directing the client's attention to evidence of particular conflicts. The goal may range from giving psychological support to achieving basic changes in personality, and the therapy may be completed in fewer than thirty sessions. In some forms of psychodynamic treatment, clients may be seen in small groups rather than individually.

Reflections on Psychodynamic Therapy

Modern variants of psychoanalysis—with their de-emphasis of instincts, their focus on the client's potential for self-directed problem solving, and their greater use of reassurance and emotional supportiveness—have helped psychodynamic therapies retain their influence, even though the original psychoanalytic methods have lost considerable popularity (Jensen, Bergin &

Greaves, 1990). Although psychoanalysis requires verbal, reasonably affluent, adult clients with the patience and time for lengthy treatment, it remains a treatment that many clinicians believe is appropriate for some problems. Examples include problematic relationships involving excessive demands for independence or a strong yearning for dependence, as well as conflicts based on unreasonable demands for perfection or superior achievement.

Critics of psychodynamic therapies continue to point out that many of the concepts underlying these treatments—such as ego strength and defense mechanisms—are vague and difficult to measure. As a result, scientific evaluation of the effects of psychoanalytic treatment has lagged behind research on the outcome of other approaches. Further, many psychologists either ignore or remain uninformed about the considerable empirical research on psychoanalytic treatment that has been done (Fisher & Greenberg, 1977; Gill & Hoffman, 1982; Masling, 1982). Some of this research has shown, for example, that therapists' ability to be emotionally supportive of their clients may be more important in producing change than such psychoanalytic mainstays as interpretations or analysis of the transference (Wallerstein, 1989).

Phenomenological Psychotherapy

Until the 1940s, almost everyone doing psychotherapy used some form of psychoanalysis. Then an alternative came from therapists who had been trained in the psychodynamic tradition but adopted the phenomenological approach. As discussed in Chapters 14 and 15, *phenomenologists* emphasize the subjective interpretations that people place on events. Phenomenologists stress a psychology of choice more than of causation; they view humans as being capable of consciously controlling their actions and taking responsibility for their decisions. Many phenomenological therapists believe that human behavior is motivated by an innate drive toward growth and is guided from moment to moment by the way people perceive and interpret the world. Disordered behavior reflects a blockage of natural growth that is brought on by distorted perceptions or lack of awareness about feelings.

When the phenomenological approach was applied to psychotherapy, new treatments evolved. They operate on the following assumptions:

1. Treatment is a human encounter between equals, not a cure given by an expert. It is a way to help clients restart their natural growth and to feel and behave as they really are, not as someone has told them they should be.
2. Clients will improve on their own if the therapist creates the right conditions. These ideal conditions promote clients' awareness, acceptance, and expression of their feelings and perceptions. Thus, as in psychodynamic approaches, therapy promotes insight. Phenomenological therapy, however, seeks insight into current feelings and contemporary perceptions, not into unconscious childhood conflicts.
3. The best way to create these ideal conditions is to establish a relationship in which the client feels totally accepted and supported. The client's experience of this relationship, not any specific technique, brings beneficial changes.
4. Clients must remain responsible for choosing how they will think and behave.

There are many forms of phenomenological treatment. We will consider just two, those of Carl Rogers and Frederick S. Perls.

Client-Centered Therapy

Carl Rogers was trained in psychodynamic treatment methods during the 1930s, but he soon began to question their value. He especially disliked being a detached, expert observer who "figured out" the client. He became convinced that a less formal approach would be more effective for the client and more comfortable for the therapist. As a result, Rogers began using what he called *nondirective therapy*, which depends on the client's own drive toward growth or self-actualization. Rogers allowed his clients to decide what to talk about and when, without direction, judgment, or interpretation from the therapist. This approach is now called **client-centered therapy** or **person-centered therapy**, to emphasize the client's role. The foundation of Rogers's treatment is the creation of a relationship characterized by three important and inter-related attitudes: unconditional positive regard, empathy, and congruence.

Unconditional Positive Regard   The therapist must show **unconditional positive regard**, an attitude that says he or she cares about and accepts the client as a person and trusts the client's ability to change. To achieve this goal, the therapist listens to the client, without interrupting, and accepts what is said, without evaluating it. The therapist need not approve of everything the client says, but must accept it as a part of a valued person. The therapist must also trust clients to solve their own problems; therefore, the therapist does not give advice. Advice, said Rogers, carries the subtle message that clients are incompetent or inadequate, making them less confident and more dependent on help.

Empathy   The client-centered therapist is supposed to act not as an outsider who wants to pin a diagnostic label on the client but as someone who wants to appreciate how the world looks from the client's point of view. In other words, the client-centered therapist replaces an *external frame of reference*— looking at the client from the outside—with **empathy**, which involves an emotional understanding of what the client might be thinking and feeling.

Carl Rogers's client-centered therapy can be offered individually or in groups, where new interpersonal relationships can help clients continue their personal growth.

Empathic understanding requires an *internal frame of reference* shared with the client.

Empathy cannot be communicated just by saying, "I understand" or "I know just how you feel." Client-centered therapists convey empathy by showing that they are actively listening to the client. Like other skillful interviewers, they make eye contact with the client, nod in recognition as the client speaks, and give other signs of careful attention. They also use **reflection**, a special way of communicating the therapist's perceptions of what a client is saying and feeling; it shows that the therapist is actively listening and helps clients perceive their own thoughts and feelings. Here is an example.

Client: This has been such a bad day. I've felt ready to cry any minute and I'm not even sure what's wrong!

Therapist: You really do feel so bad. The tears just seem to well up inside, and it must be a little scary to not even know why you feel this way.

Notice that by paraphrasing what the client has said, the therapist reflected back not only the obvious feelings of sadness but also the subtle fear in the client's voice. Most clients respond to empathic reflection by elaborating on their feelings. In this example, the client went on to say, "It *is* scary, because I don't like to feel in the dark about myself. I have always prided myself on being in control."

By communicating the desire to listen and understand, the therapist can bring important material into the open without asking disruptive questions. In therapy, an empathic listener makes clients feel valued and worthy; thus, they are more likely to be confident and motivated to try solving their problems. Even in everyday situations, people who are thought of as easy to talk to tend to be "good listeners" who reflect back the important messages they hear from others.

Congruence   Sometimes called *genuineness,* **congruence** refers to a consistency between the way the therapist feels and the way he or she acts toward the client. The therapist's unconditional positive regard and empathy must be real, not manufactured. Experiencing the therapist's congruence allows the client to see that relationships can be built on openness and honesty. Ideally, this experience helps the client to try being more congruent in other relationships as well.

Here is an excerpt from client-centered therapy with a depressed young woman. It illustrates the three therapeutic attitudes just described.

Client: . . . I cannot be the kind of person I want to be. I guess maybe I haven't the guts or the strength to kill myself and if someone else would relieve me of the responsibility or I would be in an accident I, I . . . just don't want to live.

Therapist: At the present time things look so black that you can't see much point in living. [Note the use of empathic reflection and the absence of any criticism.]

Client: Yes. I wish I'd never started this therapy. I was happy when I was living in my dream world. There I could be the kind of person I wanted to be. But now there is such a wide, wide gap between my ideal and what I am. . . . [Notice how the client responds to reflection by giving more information.]

Therapist: It's really a tough struggle digging into this like you are and at times the shelter of your dream world looks more attractive and comfortable. [Reflection]

Client: My dream world or suicide. . . . So I don't see why I should waste your time—coming in twice a week—I'm not worth it—What do you think?

Therapist: It's up to you. . . . It isn't wasting my time. I'd be glad to see you whenever you come but it's how you feel about it. . . . [Note the congruence in stating an honest desire to see the client and the unconditional positive regard in trusting her capacity and responsibility for choice.]

Client: You're not going to suggest that I come in oftener? You're not alarmed and think I ought to come in every day until I get out of this?

Therapist: I believe you are able to make your own decision. I'll see you whenever you want to come. [Positive regard]

Client: (*Note of awe in her voice*) I don't believe you are alarmed about—I see—I may be afraid of myself but you aren't afraid for me. [She experiences the therapist's confidence in her.]

Therapist: You say you may be afraid of yourself and are wondering why I don't seem to be afraid for you? [Reflection]

Client: You have more confidence in me than I have. I'll see you next week . . . maybe. (Rogers, 1951, p. 49)

The client was right. At that point, the therapist did have more confidence in her than she had in herself. (She did not kill herself, by the way.) However, as successful client-centered therapy progresses, Rogers believed that clients become more self-confident, more aware of their feelings, more accepting of themselves, more comfortable and genuine with other people, more reliant on self-evaluation than on the judgments of others, and more effective and relaxed.

Gestalt Therapy

Another form of phenomenological treatment was developed by Frederick S. (Fritz) Perls, a European psychoanalyst who was also trained in Gestalt psychology. We noted in Chapter 5, on perception, that the term *Gestalt* ("organized whole") refers to perceptual principles through which people actively organize environmental stimuli into meaningful patterns. Similarly, Perls emphasized that the reality each person experiences depends on how he or she perceives the world (Perls, 1969, 1970; Perls, Hefferline & Goodman, 1951). He believed that psychological growth continues naturally as long as people remain clearly aware of their true feelings and act on them, not on other people's expectations. If people are blind to some aspects of themselves, their perceptions and behavior are not unified. Growth stops, and symptoms appear.

Like client-centered therapy, **Gestalt therapy** seeks to create conditions in which clients can become more unified, self-aware, and self-accepting. They then should be ready to grow again in their own unique, consciously guided directions. Very often, Gestalt therapy is offered in groups led by therapists who are much more active than Rogerians. Gestalt therapists use dramatic and direct methods as they prod clients to become aware of feelings and impulses that they have denied or disowned and to discard foreign feelings, ideas, and values.

Perls believed that when people talk about the past or the future, they are avoiding the present, escaping reality. Therefore, Gestalt therapists try to keep clients' attention focused on what they think and feel "here and now." They do this not by reflecting (as a Rogerian might) the client's desire to avoid dealing with the present but by pointing out the client's avoidance and

Gestalt therapists pay particular attention to clients' "body language," especially when it conflicts with what they are saying aloud. If this client had just said that she is enthusiastic about treatment, the therapist might wonder whether the client believed she should be enthusiastic but truly feels pessimistic.

insisting that it be stopped. Gestalt therapists pay particular attention to clients' "body language," especially when it conflicts with what they are saying. Here is a brief illustration.

Client: I wish I wasn't so nervous with people.

Therapist: Who are you nervous with?

Client: With everyone.

Therapist: With me, here, now?

Client: Yes, very.

Therapist: That's funny, because you don't look nervous to me.

Client: (*Suddenly clasping his hands*) Well, I am!

Therapist: What are you doing with your hands?

Client: Nothing, it's just a gesture.

Therapist: Do the gesture again (*Client reclasps his hands*) and again, harder (*Client clasps harder*). . . . [Exaggerating the gesture helps the client to be more aware of the feelings it conveys.] How does that feel?

Client: It feels kind of tight, constricted.

Therapist: Can you play that tightness? What would it say to you?

Client: OK, ah, I'm tight. I'm holding everything together. I'm keeping the lid on so you won't let too much out. [Now the client becomes aware that he fears self-disclosure and wants to keep the therapist at a distance.]

Gestalt therapists may also ask clients to engage in a kind of one-person drama involving imaginary dialogues, not only with people but even with inanimate objects or parts of their own personalities. Like a shy person who can be socially outgoing only while in a Halloween costume, clients often find these dialogues helpful in allowing them to get in touch with their feelings and express them. Similarly, instead of free-associating to a dream, clients are asked to give voice to its various parts in order to understand its significance.

Reflections on Phenomenological Therapy

Phenomenological therapies offer an optimistic, upbeat approach. They do not dwell on a client's problems but on psychological growth and ways to unleash each person's unique strengths and potential. In fact, Rogers's views have been criticized for ignoring the capacity for evil that seems to lurk within everyone. Nonetheless, phenomenological treatments are used for a wide variety of problems including, for example, doubts and insecurities associated with major setbacks or transitions such as divorce, loss of a job, illness, or death of a loved one. By helping clients create or discover meaning or value in even the worst events, the phenomenological therapist promotes the growth that is the main goal of treatment.

Even so, the problems with phenomenological theories mentioned in Chapter 14 have implications for phenomenological treatments. The approach provides idealistic goals but few specific procedures; many therapists find the notion of adopting certain attitudes or of facilitating growth too vague. Further, some problems may be so complex or severe that only a temporary feeling of well-being will occur unless the therapist provides concrete guidance or specific treatments. Finally, with the notable exception of Rogers, most phenomenological therapists have shown little interest in conducting scientific evaluations of their approach.

Behavior Therapies

Linkages: How do therapists use knowledge about learning to help people with mental disorders? (a link to Learning)

The psychodynamic and phenomenological approaches assume that if clients gain insight into underlying problems, the symptoms created by those problems will disappear more or less on their own. Behavior therapists emphasize a different kind of "insight." They try to help clients see their problems as learned behaviors that can be changed without searching for hidden meanings or unconscious causes.

Imagine that you have such a strong fear of speaking in public that you become ill when in front of an audience. You make up excuses to avoid having to speak, a strategy that eases anxiety for the moment but does nothing to solve the problem permanently. Could you reduce your fear without looking for unconscious causes? By helping you to understand the learning principles that maintain your fear and then to learn and practice new responses in feared situations, behavior therapy offers just such an alternative.

This approach is the logical outcome of the assumptions of the behavioral view. As discussed in Chapters 14 and 15, the behavioral approach sees learning as the basis of normal personality and of most behavior disorders. According to this perspective, disordered behavior and thinking are not symptoms of more general problems but samples of maladaptive thoughts and actions that the client has learned.

If previous learning experiences can produce problems in the way people behave and think, it is logical to suppose that new learning experiences might help solve these problems. Accordingly, **behavior therapy** (sometimes called **behavior modification**) uses the principles of learning discussed in Chapter 7 to change behavior. (You may find it helpful to look again at the reviews of these principles on pages 267 and 281.) Even if the learning that led to the problems began in childhood, behavior therapists focus on solving today's problems. For example, a man whose work suffers because of conflicts with coworkers might be encouraged to examine and alter how he presents ideas, gives and takes criticism, and offers rewards.

Behavior therapists begin by helping the client set specific goals. Usually, the goals involve eliminating undesirable behaviors and thoughts and developing new behaviors and thinking patterns. Some of the most notable features of behavior therapy include

1. Development of a good therapist-client relationship. As in other therapies, this relationship enhances clients' confidence that change is possible and makes it easier for clients to speak freely and to cooperate in the treatment.
2. Careful listing of the behaviors and thoughts to be changed. This assessment and the establishment of specific goals sometimes replaces the formal psychodiagnosis used in other approaches. Thus, instead of treating "depression" or "schizophrenia," behavior therapists work to change the thoughts, behaviors, and emotional reactions that cause people to be given these labels.
3. A therapist who acts as a kind of teacher/assistant by providing special learning-based treatments, giving "homework" assignments, and helping the client make specific plans for dealing with problems.
4. Continuous evaluation of the effects of therapy. The therapist and client may decide at any time to alter procedures that are not working.

Different versions of behavior therapy emphasize different types of learning, such as operant conditioning or classical conditioning, and somewhat different treatment targets. We will first describe behavioral techniques that emphasize direct changes in overt behavior, then discuss those, known as *cognitive behavior therapy,* that concentrate on modifying thinking patterns that accompany disturbed behavior.

Techniques for Modifying Behavior

Behavioral approaches to psychotherapy began when early researchers tried using classical conditioning and other learning principles to explain and change disordered human behavior (Kazdin, 1978). By 1970 behavior therapy had become firmly established as one of the most popular approaches to treatment.

Systematic Desensitization   One behavioral treatment often used to help clients deal with phobias and other irrational forms of anxiety was developed by Joseph Wolpe (1958). Called **systematic desensitization**, it is a method for reducing intense anxiety by having clients visualize a graduated series of anxiety-provoking stimuli while maintaining a state of relaxation. Wolpe believed that if clients can remain calm while experiencing gradually more intense versions of something they fear, the association that had been learned between anxiety and the feared object will be weakened, and the fear will disappear.

To bring this about, Wolpe first arranged for clients to do something incompatible with being afraid. Since it is hard to be tense and deeply relaxed at the same time, Wolpe used a technique called *progressive relaxation training* (described in Chapter 13) to prevent anxiety during desensitization. Next the client relaxes while imagining an item from an *anxiety hierarchy,* a sequence of increasingly fear-provoking situations; Table 16.1 presents an example. The client works through the hierarchy gradually, imagining a more difficult scene only after being able to tolerate the previous one without feeling any distress.

Table 16.1
Sample Desensitization Hierarchy

Desensitization hierarchies contain increasingly fear provoking stimuli, which the client visualizes while using relaxation techniques to remain calm.

Here are the first fifteen scenes from a hierarchy used with a client who feared flying.

1. You are reading the paper and notice an ad for an airline.
2. You are watching a television program that shows a group of people boarding a plane.
3. Your boss tells you that you need to make a business trip by air.
4. It is two weeks before your trip, and you ask your secretary to make airline reservations.
5. You are in your bedroom, packing a suitcase for your trip.
6. You are in the shower on the morning of your trip.
7. You are in a taxi on the way to the airport.
8. You are checking in for your flight and the agent says, "Would you like a window or aisle seat?
9. You are in the waiting lounge and hear an announcement that your flight is now ready for boarding.
10. You are in line, just about to board the airplane.
11. You are in your seat and hear the plane's engines start.
12. The plane begins to move as you hear the flight attendant say, "Be sure your seatbelts are securely fastened."
13. You look at the runway as the plane waits to take off.
14. You look out the window as the plane begins to roll down the runway.
15. You look out the window as the plane leaves the ground.

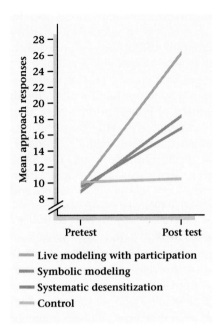

Mean approach responses

Pretest   Post test

— Live modeling with participation
— Symbolic modeling
— Systematic desensitization
— Control

Source: Bandura, Blanchard & Ritter, 1969.

Figure 16.1
Participant Modeling
One classic study compared the effects of systematic desensitization, participant modeling, symbolic modeling (watching filmed models), and no treatment (control) in the treatment of snake phobia. As the graph illustrates, all three behavioral methods produced more interaction with snakes than no treatment, but participant modeling was clearly the best; 92 percent of the subjects in that group were virtually free of any fear of harmless snakes.

Once clients can calmly imagine being in feared situations, they are better able to deal with those situations when they actually occur. Desensitization may be especially effective if the client can work on a hierarchy *in vivo,* or in real life (Speltz & Bernstein, 1979).

The exact reasons why systematic desensitization works are not entirely clear. Most clinicians believe that change occurs either through classical conditioning of a new, calmer conditioned response to the fear-provoking stimulus or through extinction, as the object or situation that had been a conditioned fear stimulus repeatedly occurs without being paired with pain or any other unconditioned stimulus.

Modeling Therapists often teach clients desirable behaviors by modeling those behaviors. In **modeling**, the client watches other people perform desired behaviors, thus vicariously learning some of the necessary skills without going through a lengthy trial-and-error process. For example, one therapist showed a twenty-four-year-old student with a severe spider phobia how to kill spiders with a fly swatter and had her practice this skill at home with rubber spiders (MacDonald & Bernstein, 1974). The combination of live modeling with gradual practice is called *participant modeling;* it is one of the most powerful treatments for fear (see Figure 16.1).

Modeling is also a major part of **assertiveness and social skills training**, a way of teaching clients how to interact with people more comfortably and effectively. Behavior therapists can help clients develop behaviors they lack—anything from helping college students make conversation on dates to rebuilding mental patients' ability to interact normally with people outside the hospital (Curran & Monti, 1982). In assertiveness training, the therapist helps clients learn and practice being more direct and expressive in social situations. (*Assertiveness* does not mean aggressiveness; it means clearly and directly expressing both positive and negative feelings and standing up for one's rights while respecting the rights of others; Alberti & Emmons, 1986.) Assertiveness training is often done in groups and involves a lot of modeling and role playing of specific social problems. For example, a client who feels afraid or silly about asking for a raise might perfect the skills needed by repeatedly role-playing the situation with the therapist or other members of a therapy group.

Positive Reinforcement Behavior therapists also use systematic **positive reinforcement**, or reward, to alter problematic behaviors ranging from nail-biting and childhood tantrums to juvenile delinquency, schizophrenia, and self-starvation. They follow the operant conditioning principles discussed in Chapter 7 to set up special contingencies, or relationships, between the client's behavior and its consequences. Here is one classic example.

Ann, a four-year-old preschooler, interacted well with teachers and other adults, but she was shy, silent, and withdrawn around other children (Allen et al., 1964). The psychologist working with the school noticed that Ann's teachers had been inadvertently rewarding her withdrawn behavior with lots of attention and coaxing. Thus, a program was set up in which the teachers were asked to give praise and attention only when Ann was at least standing or playing near another child. Later, they shaped Ann's behavior further by rewarding only genuine interaction with other children. Isolated play was always ignored. Ann soon began to spend most of her time with other children, instead of with adults, and continued to do so.

To improve the behavior of severely disturbed or mentally retarded clients in institutions, behavior therapists sometimes establish a **token economy,** a system of rewarding desirable behaviors with tokens, which are items such as poker chips that can be exchanged for snacks, access to television, or other rewards (Ayllon & Azrin, 1968; Kazdin & Bootzin, 1972). To set up a token economy, the staff (with the help of the client when possible) develops a list of target behaviors for each client, such as speaking clearly, playing cooperatively, or straightening up a bedroom. Next, a payment schedule is arranged; it states that the client receives a certain number of tokens immediately after displaying a certain amount of each target behavior. The staff also reinforces appropriate behaviors with praise, encouragement, and attention. Eventually, as improved behavior is supported by these social reinforcers (and the sense of pride and accomplishment they engender), clients can be "weaned" from the token economy. In fact, token economies are designed to shape and maintain patterns of behavior that will generalize beyond the institution.

Extinction Just as they can strengthen desirable behaviors, behavioral techniques can also weaken undesirable behaviors. Sometimes this is done through **extinction**, the process of removing the reinforcers that normally follow a particular response. If you have ever given up telephoning someone whose line is busy, you know how extinction works: when a behavior does not "pay off," people usually stop it. Though extinction changes behavior rather slowly, it has been a popular way of treating children and retarded or seriously disturbed adults, because it provides a gentle way to eliminate undesirable behaviors.

Another application of extinction is **flooding**, a procedure that keeps people in a feared but harmless situation, depriving them of their normally rewarding escape pattern. (Extinction methods are also called *forced-exposure techniques*.) Eventually, the client learns not to be afraid of the situation. For example, one person who feared riding on escalators was accompanied by her therapist on a twenty-seven-minute ride up and down the escalators of a department store. The client was at first very frightened. However, after staying in the situation until her anxiety subsided, she had no further trouble (Nisbett, 1973).

Linkages: Flooding is designed to extinguish severe anxiety by allowing it to occur without reinforcement. By the end of his airplane flight, this fearful client was far less anxious than he had been at the beginning. Like other behavioral treatments, flooding stems from the behavioral approach to personality described in Chapter 14. A fundamental assumption of that approach is that behavior disorders, like normal behaviors, are learned and can thus be "unlearned."

If undesirable behavior cannot be ignored or is being rewarded by onlookers (as when a child gets laughs by rapping on a classmate's head), the client may be placed in a boring place for a few minutes. This "time out" from positive reinforcement interrupts the reward process.

Linkages: How can therapists alter people's maladaptive thought patterns? (a link to Thought and Language)

Extinction techniques are often particularly effective when a client's fear is not focused on a specific stimulus. They have, for example, proven successful in the treatment of agoraphobia (Foa, Rothbaum & Kozak, 1989), which is the fear of being separated from home or other safe places.

Aversive Conditioning Many unwanted behaviors are so habitual and temporarily rewarding that they must be made less attractive if the client is to have any chance of learning alternatives; alcohol abuse is an example. The methods for doing this are known as **aversive conditioning**; they apply classical conditioning principles, associating physical or psychological discomfort with behaviors, thoughts, or situations the client wishes to stop or avoid. For example, alcoholics might be allowed to drink after taking a nausea-producing drug, so that the taste and smell of alcohol are associated with nausea rather than with the usual pleasurable feelings (Cannon & Baker, 1981). In some stop-smoking programs, smokers consume cigarettes very rapidly so that they will associate smoking with nausea and dizziness (Lichtenstein & Penner, 1977).

Aversive conditioning is unpleasant and uncomfortable, and often its effects are only temporary. Thus, many therapists avoid this method or use it only long enough to allow the client to learn alternative behaviors.

Punishment Sometimes the only way to eliminate a dangerous or disruptive behavior is to punish it with an unpleasant but not harmful stimulus, such as a shouted "No!" or a mild electric shock after the undesirable behavior occurs. Unlike aversive conditioning, in which the unpleasant stimulus occurs along with the behavior to be eliminated (a classical conditioning approach), **punishment** is an operant conditioning technique; it presents the unpleasant stimulus *after* the undesirable response occurs. (Though technically distinct, the two methods may overlap. Using mild shock to punish the act of drinking, for example, might also create a classically conditioned aversion as shock and the taste of alcohol are repeatedly paired.)

The careful use of therapeutic punishment is well illustrated in the case of a brain-damaged and hyperactive six-year-old girl who constantly endangered herself by climbing high on furniture, doorframes, trees, and even the side of her house. Her body bore numerous scars from several serious falls. Reinforcement for nonclimbing did not work, because when she was not climbing, she merely sat and rocked. Extinction was also ineffective. Finally, the child's parents were trained to administer mild electric shock with a hand-held wand while shouting "No!" whenever she was found climbing. This procedure worked. By eliminating climbing, it also created opportunities for the parents to reward other behaviors (Risley, 1968).

Cognitive Behavior Therapy

Psychodynamic and phenomenological therapists have long recognized that thought patterns may lead to depression, anger, or anxiety, even when there are no obvious reasons to feel those emotions. Behavior therapists have attacked these problems through methods known collectively as cognitive behavior therapy. In simplest terms, **cognitive behavior therapy** helps clients change the way they think as well as the way they behave. Instead of practicing new behaviors in assertiveness training, for example, some clients need to identify the habitual thoughts (such as "I shouldn't draw attention to myself") that get in the way of self-expression. Once the cognitive obstacles are brought to light, the therapist encourages the client to try new ways of thinking that will make it easier to behave more assertively or feel happier or more relaxed. The therapist may also help clients learn to say things to themselves that promote desirable behavior and prevent a relapse into undesirable behavior (Marlatt & Gordon, 1985).

Some methods of cognitive behavior therapy were developed by behavior therapists; others were borrowed from therapists who focus on cognitive processes but use techniques closely allied with the behavioral approach. One of these borrowed methods is **rational-emotive therapy (RET)**. Developed by Albert Ellis (1962, 1973; Ellis & Bernard, 1985), RET is based on the principle that anxiety, guilt, depression, and other psychological problems are not caused by frightening or upsetting events but by how people think about those events. Ellis says, for example, that you do not get upset because you fail a test but because you believe failure to be a disaster that indicates you are no good. RET aims first at identifying self-defeating, problem-causing thoughts. Among the most common of these thoughts are

1. I must be loved or approved by everyone.
2. I must be perfectly competent, adequate, and achieving to be worthwhile.
3. It is a terrible catastrophe when things are not as I want them to be.
4. Unhappiness is caused by outside forces over which I have no control.
5. There is always a right or a perfect solution to every problem, and it must be found or the results will be catastrophic.

After the client learns to recognize thoughts like these and see how they cause problems, the therapist uses modeling, encouragement, and logic to help the client replace these thoughts with more realistic and beneficial ones. Here is part of an RET session with a thirty-nine-year-old woman who suffered from panic attacks. She has just said it was "terrible" that she had a panic attack and passed out in a restaurant and that people "should be able to handle themselves!"

Therapist: . . . The reality is that . . . "shoulds" and "musts" are the rules that other people hand down to us, and we grow up accepting them as if they are the absolute truth, which they most assuredly aren't.

Client: You mean it is perfectly okay to, you know, pass out in a restaurant?

Therapist: Sure!

Client: But . . . I know I wouldn't like it to happen.

Therapist: I can certainly understand that. It would be unpleasant, awkward, inconvenient. But it is illogical to think that it would be terrible, or . . . that it somehow bears on your worth as a person. Thinking this way is also very self-defeating.

Client: What do you mean?

Therapist: Well, suppose one of your friends calls you up and invites you back to that restaurant. If you start telling yourself, "I might panic and pass out and people might make fun of me and that would be terrible," you are going to make yourself uptight. And you might find you are dreading going to the restaurant, and you probably won't enjoy the meal very much.

Client: Well, that is what usually happens.

Therapist: But it doesn't have to be that way. . . . The way you feel, your reaction . . . depends on what you choose to believe or think, or say to yourself. . . . (Masters et al., 1987)

Cognitive behavior therapists use many techniques related to RET to help clients learn to think in new, more adaptive ways. Techniques aimed at

Albert Ellis developed rational-emotive therapy (RET), a treatment method focused on helping clients alter the self-defeating thoughts that he sees as underlying disordered emotions and behavior. Many of Ellis's ideas have been incorporated into various forms of cognitive behavior therapy.

Aaron Beck's cognitive therapy aims at helping depressed clients identify and correct their tendency to dwell on their shortcomings and the negative events in their lives.

replacing upsetting thoughts with alternative thinking patterns are generally known as **cognitive restructuring** (Lazarus, 1971). These methods help clients learn calming thoughts to use in anxiety-provoking situations, such as tests or unpleasant conversations. These thoughts might take the form of "OK, stay calm, you can handle this if you just focus on the task and don't worry about being perfect" (Meichenbaum, 1977). These methods are sometimes expanded into **stress inoculation training**, in which the therapist asks the client to imagine being in a stressful situation so that he or she can practice new cognitive skills to reduce stress (Meichenbaum, 1985).

Especially with depressed clients, behavior therapists often use Aaron Beck's *cognitive therapy*, which contains another type of cognitive restructuring. Cognitive therapy helps clients see that depression occurs in part because they exaggerate the importance and frequency of negative events ("Nothing ever goes right!") and minimize the value of personal accomplishments ("Anyone could do that!"). The cognitive therapist helps clients identify logical inconsistencies and other errors in thinking that lead to depressive feelings. Clients are also given homework that helps them keep track of positive events and personal skills (Beck et al., 1979; Clark & Beck, 1989).

As mentioned in Chapter 15, however, depressed people's specific thoughts may not be in error; depression may be associated with a general cognitive style in which people attribute negative events to their own general and enduring incompetence rather than, say, bad luck or a temporary lack of effort (Peterson & Seligman, 1984). Accordingly, cognitive-behavior therapists also help depressed clients develop more optimistic ways of thinking and reduce their tendency to blame themselves for negative outcomes (Taylor, 1989).

Reflections on Behavior Therapies

Not all forms of behavior disorder can be treated through learning-based methods alone, but there is impressive evidence that behavior therapy methods can be very successful, particularly with certain disorders (Kazdin, 1984; Masters et al., 1987). The treatment of phobias and other anxiety disorders through desensitization and related techniques has been particularly successful, as has the use of cognitive therapy with depressed clients (Dobson, 1989). Behavioral reward systems for building new behaviors in adults and children also have an impressive record of success. Among mental patients who once did little more than sit and stare into space, token economy systems have dramatically improved personal grooming, social interaction, mealtime etiquette, and attendance at therapy sessions, while greatly reducing bizarre behaviors (Kazdin & Bootzin, 1972). More importantly, token systems have helped prepare even the most severely disturbed patients to live outside the mental hospital (Paul & Lentz, 1977). Token systems have also helped mentally retarded children and adults develop self-care, social, and vocational skills (Thompson & Grabowski, 1972), and they have reduced antisocial behavior in children and adolescents (Fixen et al., 1976; Kirigin et al., 1982). Furthermore, cognitive-behavioral techniques have been useful as part of behavioral treatments for overeating, drug abuse, cigarette smoking, troublesome sexual practices, and other problems of self-control (Freeman et al., 1989). Cognitive-behavioral techniques have proved as helpful in systematically dealing with clients' thoughts as other behavioral techniques have been with overt behaviors (Dush, Hirt & Schroeder, 1983; Miller & Berman, 1983).

Still, controversy surrounds behavior therapy. Punishment and aversive conditioning have been criticized as dehumanizing. In addition, skeptics argue that assertiveness training, social skills training, and cognitive-behavioral methods such as RET merely persuade clients to adopt the therapist's style of thinking and behaving. More generally, some critics view behavior therapy as too mechanical and too focused on overt behavior, which, they say, is only the symptom of deeper problems. They worry that treating symptoms without dealing with the underlying problems will lead to treatment failure or the appearance of new symptoms, through a process called *symptom substitution.*

In response to these criticisms, behavior therapists contend that they display just as much humanistic concern for their clients as other therapists. Regarding symptom substitution, behaviorists argue that overt behavior and maladaptive thoughts *are* the problems of greatest concern and that only if the therapist fails to detect an important aspect of these problems will treatment fail or create a new problem. Whether behavior therapy is superior or inferior to other forms of psychotherapy remains a hotly debated topic, as we discuss later in this chapter.

Group and Family Therapies

Much psychotherapy is conducted in individual interviews, but many therapists, regardless of their theoretical orientation, prefer to work with some clients in other formats. Often, this takes the form of group therapy or family therapy.

Group therapy is the simultaneous treatment of several clients under the leadership of a therapist who tries to facilitate helpful interactions among group members. There is no single theoretical approach to group therapy. Many groups are organized around one type of problem (such as alcoholism) or one type of client (such as adolescents or single parents). In most cases, six to twelve clients meet with their therapist at least once a week for about two hours. All group members agree to hold confidential everything that occurs within group sessions. Here is a brief excerpt from a session of group therapy.

Beth: After last week's session, I was very, very angry. I even thought I shouldn't be in this group any longer. I just feel like the claws are at me all the time.

Dora: I was feeling very worked up, too.

Fred: I just want to say one thing. That is, last week I felt the strangest tension and I couldn't decide whether it was me and I wanted to leave. Then I thought: This is ridiculous.

Beth: I almost . . . that is why I almost didn't want to come this week. I have got work to do and it is hard, and I don't need any extra tension in my life, especially this hounding that I have been getting for the past weeks.

Dora: Do you have any idea . . . do you realize why you have been getting all this? I give it to you because I am so irritated with you for not doing anything about your situation.

Beth: I get out and I do as much as I can. [*Pause*] Besides, I don't know that's the real reason for you and everyone else attacking me.

Dora: Well, if you don't believe me you can tell me what you think.

Beth: You're jealous of me.

Dora: Okay that's true, but don't put this into that category, because the reason I've been on you has got nothing to do with jealousy. . . .

Therapist: My question is, "When are you finally going to get better?"

Beth: When I stop letting the world control me. When I stop getting scared. When I start trusting myself a little bit more.

Therapist: What will you do in order to be that kind of a person?

Beth: Well, last week I deliberately put my movie script down and I rested when I felt like it. I walked outside and decided I was not going to punch myself out for this thing. (Verny, 1984)

As this excerpt illustrates, group therapy offers features not found in individual treatment (Yalom, 1985). First, group therapy allows the therapist to observe clients interacting with one another. Second, clients often feel less alone as they listen to the others and recognize that many people struggle with difficulties similar to or even more severe than their own. This recognition tends to raise each client's expectations for improvement, a factor important in all forms of treatment. Third, group members can bolster one another's self-confidence and self-acceptance as they come to trust and value one another and develop group cohesiveness. Fourth, clients learn from one another. They not only share ideas for solving problems but also give one another direct, honest feedback about how each member "comes across." In a sense, the group format allows each member to be both a client and a therapist. Finally, the group experience may make clients less guarded, more willing to share their feelings, and more sensitive to other people's needs, motives, and messages.

As its name implies, **family therapy** involves treatment of two or more individuals from the same family, one of whose problems make him or her the initially identified client. Family therapy developed from several sources: (1) the psychodynamic theory that psychological disorders are rooted in family conflicts; (2) clinical observations that successfully treated patients often relapse when they leave the hospital and return to their families; and (3) a recognition that few, if any, problems occur in a vacuum, and thus must be dealt with in the family setting in which they are maintained. As in group therapy, the family format gives the therapist an excellent view of how the

Family therapy—conducted here with a single parent and his children—initially focuses on the most troubled, or troublesome, individual. Eventually, however, the sessions explore the role each member plays in the problems of the "family system."

client interacts with others. It also provides a forum for discussing issues important to the family's life. Family therapy is based on the idea that the family is the "client" and that everyone in the family must take part in resolving family conflicts.

Whatever the problem, family therapy usually begins by encouraging the entire family to work on it. Because they are often in a crisis and highly motivated to help the most troubled person, family members usually accept this task readily (Haley, 1970). Soon, however, attention spreads from the identified client to the entire family, because most family therapists see the client as a part of a total "family system"; the client's disorder is believed to reflect the conflicts, communication problems, and other difficulties in the family as a whole (Goldenberg & Goldenberg, 1980; Haley, 1971; Minuchin, Rosman & Baker, 1978).

Indeed, the goal of family therapy is not just to alleviate the identified client's problems but to create harmony and balance within the family by helping each family member better understand the family's interactions and the problems they create (Gurman, Kniskern & Pinsoff, 1986). Virginia Satir (1967), a well-known practitioner of family therapy, offers the following example of how the family therapist tries to help parents and children communicate better with one another:

Mother: His pleasure is doing things he knows will get me up in the air. Every minute he's in the house . . . constantly.

Therapist: There's no pleasure to that, my dear.

Mother: Well, there is to him.

Therapist: No, you can't see his thoughts. You can't get inside his skin. All you can talk about is what you see and hear. You can say it *looks* as though it's for pleasure.

Mother: All right. Well, it looks as though, and that's just what it looks like constantly.

Therapist: He could be trying to keep your attention, you know. It is very important to Johnny what Mother thinks.

Evaluating Psychotherapy

Linkages: Can personality be changed? (a link to Personality)

Does psychotherapy work? If so, are some therapies better than others? In a sense psychotherapy must help clients because countless case reports and client testimonials tell of significant changes during and after psychotherapy. However, believing that therapy helps clients and demonstrating it scientifically are two very different things. In this section we examine whether psychotherapy helps people and which methods and which therapists are most effective.

In 1952 British psychologist Hans Eysenck reviewed several studies that compared the effects of traditional psychodynamic therapy with the results of routine medical care or no treatment for thousands of neurotic clients. To the surprise and dismay of many therapists, Eysenck (1952) concluded that traditional psychodynamic therapy did not increase clients' rates of improvement. In fact, he claimed that more untreated than treated clients recovered (72 percent versus about 66 percent). In the years that followed, Eysenck (1961, 1966) supported his conclusions with additional evidence. Meanwhile, critics looking at the same data argued that Eysenck was wrong (de Charms, Levy & Wertheimer, 1954; Luborsky, 1954, 1972). They accused Eysenck of ignoring several studies that supported the value of psychotherapy and of misinterpreting the data available to him. They pointed out that untreated clients may have been less disturbed in the first place than those in treatment; that untreated clients may have received informal treatment from their doctors; and that physicians who judged untreated clients' progress might have used more lenient criteria than the psychotherapists who rated their own clients.

The controversy over Eysenck's conclusions stimulated new and more sophisticated studies of the outcomes of many kinds of therapy. Surveys of this research have yielded consistently more optimistic results than Eysenck's. For example, psychotherapy clients did better than no-treatment controls in 20 of 33 studies reviewed by Lester Luborsky, Barton Singer, and Lise Luborsky (1975); the other 13 studies were interpreted as "ties." Other researchers have used a mathematical technique called *meta-analysis*, which involves quantifying the outcomes of different studies in the same way so that they can be compared and summarized. One meta-analysis examined 475 outcome studies and found that the average therapy client is better off after therapy than 80 percent of clients who do not receive therapy (Smith, Glass & Miller, 1980). Other meta-analyses have supported this assertion (Brown, 1987) and have resulted in the following additional conclusions about the effects of psychotherapy:

1. In general, better-designed studies yield larger estimates of the success of psychotherapy (Landman & Dawes, 1982).
2. Despite fears that the benefits of psychotherapy might be short-lived, the overall evidence is encouraging: client improvement is reasonably durable, at least as measured up to 18 months after the end of treatment (Nicholson & Berman, 1983).
3. Only a small percentage of clients (perhaps 10 percent) become worse after psychotherapy (Lambert, Shapiro & Bergin, 1986; Smith, Glass & Miller, 1980).

In short, the preponderance of research suggests that treatment is better than no treatment for the vast majority of clients. Still, two points must be remembered when considering the evidence for the benefits of psychotherapy.

First, the quality of research on its effectiveness is still quite variable. Critics of meta-analysis often argue, for example, that combining results from a mishmash of good, mediocre, and poor studies on the treatment of different problems with various techniques can be misleading (Brody, 1990; Strube, Gardner & Hartman, 1985; Paul, 1986; Wilson, 1985). Though the "average" client with the "average" problem may be helped by the "average" therapist using the "average" treatment, this may or may not be the case for a particular person working on a particular problem with a particular therapist in a particular way.

Second, the definition of "success" in therapy is far from clear. Some therapists look for changes in unconscious conflicts while others focus on alterations in overt behavior. In the outcome studies surveyed, a different set of observers using different standards might have made less optimistic judgments about the success of treatment (Strupp & Hadley, 1977). Further, the improvements reported, though statistically significant, are not necessarily clinically significant. *Clinically significant changes* are not only measurable, but also important for the person's life. For example, the reduction in scores on an anxiety test might be *statistically* significant in a group of treated clients, but if those clients do not feel noticeably less anxious in daily life, the change may not be clinically significant. The question of whether psychotherapy produces clinically significant changes is one that has, until recently, been largely neglected.

THINKING CRITICALLY

Are All Methods of Psychotherapy Equally Effective?

Although questions remain to be investigated, evidence for the benefits of psychotherapy provide encouragement for both clients and therapists. However, people considering therapy still need to know whether a particular form of treatment is likely to be especially beneficial. Our earlier discussions of specific methods of treatment suggested that some treatment techniques might be particularly useful in dealing with certain problems, but are any of the three main approaches to psychotherapy superior to the others overall? ("In Review: Approaches to Psychological Treatment" summarizes key features of these approaches.) Many therapists believe not only that psychotherapy in general "works" but also that their own particular brand of treatment is superior to others (e.g. Giles, 1990). Nonetheless, there is evidence suggesting that there are no significant differences in the overall effectiveness of the three main approaches to therapy (e.g., Stiles, Shapiro & Elliott, 1986). Is it really the case that, within broad limits, no matter what a therapist does, the outcome will be the same?

What am I being asked to believe or accept?

Some say that theoretical models of personality and abnormal behavior, and the specific treatment methods based on them, are irrelevant to the success of psychotherapy. This has been called the "Dodo Bird Verdict," after the *Alice in Wonderland* creature who, when called upon to judge who had won a race, answered, "Everybody has won and all must have prizes" (Luborsky et al., 1975).

What evidence is available to support the assertion?

Studies carefully comparing psychodynamic, behavioral, and phenomenological treatments in the same experiment have failed to show that one approach is notably superior to another, though all are superior to no treatment (Cross, Sheehan & Kahn, 1982; Olson et al., 1981; Sloane et al., 1975; Snyder & Wills, 1989). The traditional explanation for this effect is that almost all forms of therapy share common factors—including the empathy and support of the therapist, the hope and expectancy for improvement that therapy instills, the trust that develops between client and therapist, the discovery of new perspectives on problem solving—and that these factors override procedural and theoretical differences among treatments.

Indeed, the common effects of therapy could be due principally to the generally helpful human characteristics of many therapists (Lambert, 1989). There is evidence, for example, that certain people seem to be particularly effective in forming productive human relationships. Even without formal training, nonprofessionals can sometimes be as helpful as professional therapists because of personal qualities that are inspiring, healing, and soothing to others (Berman & Norton, 1985). People displaying these qualities have been dubbed SAUNAs—for Sensitive, Active, Unflappable, Nonpunitive, and Amoral, which means remaining nonjudgmental of others (Allen, 1977). That there are such people supports the notion that the techniques of a given approach to therapy may be less important in establishing its effectiveness than having practitioners using the approach who would be effective regardless of what methods they used.

Are there alternative ways of interpreting the evidence?

Critics of the Dodo Bird Verdict argue that the evidence for it is based on methods that may fail to detect genuine differences among methods. For example, consider again how the success of psychotherapy is measured. The client's condition before and after treatment is often determined through personality tests, interviews, or self-ratings. Behavioral theorists in particular argue that these assessments are too vague and global to capture specific and important changes in behavior and thus obscure potentially important differences among therapies (Rachman & Wilson, 1980).

It may also be that some specific techniques are more successful than others but that the usual grouping of therapies by theoretical orientation (psychodynamic, phenomenological, behavioral) rather than by specific procedures is inadequate to identify the crucial elements at work (Giles, 1990). This explanation, known as the *good moments* approach (Mahrer & Nadler, 1986), stresses specific events or interactions within therapy sessions (such as trying a new behavior with the therapist or disclosing a painful memory) that lead to positive changes (Marmar, 1990).

Finally, even if different therapies produce similar outcomes, it may not be because they share anything in common. Instead, several *different* mechanisms may be at work in various psychotherapies, all leading to essentially equal results. As an analogy, consider a student who cannot get along with a roommate. The student can try to solve this problem in several ways — moving from the dormitory, transferring to another university, talking with the dorm adviser, or discussing the conflicts with the roommate. Any of these strategies might be successful, but not because they shared some common "curative" ingredient. Likewise, it is possible that it is the therapist's skill in selecting and using a particular method at a particular point in therapy that determines how successful therapy will be (Lambert, DeJulio & Stein, 1978).

What additional evidence would help to evaluate the alternatives?
Continuing research on the "common factors," "good moments," and other hypotheses about the apparent equivalence of all therapy outcomes is obviously important. However, it is also important to consider whether the Dodo Bird Verdict may actually be the right answer to the wrong question about psychotherapy. Asking whether one treatment approach is superior to another presupposes that each approach (1) is consistent within itself and distinct from other approaches, and (2) has effects that can be evaluated separately from all potential confounding variables. These are questionable suppositions. For one thing, there are many versions of each approach; even in a careful treatment experiment, there can be subtle differences in the therapy received by different clients in the "same" treatment condition. As mentioned in relation to meta-analyses, combining results across many studies introduces even more variability in exactly what methods are actually being compared. Further, even if treatments were entirely distinct, it is difficult to know exactly what factors are responsible when clients improve (or do not improve); some combination of treatment methods, therapist and client characteristics, and client's problems is always involved in determining treatment outcome.

Accordingly, much more research is needed to determine if there are combinations of therapists, clients, and treatments that are ideally suited to remedying certain psychological problems (Talley, Strupp & Morey, 1990). These combinations have not yet been mapped out, but when differences do show up in meta-analyses or comparative studies, they tend to reveal a small to moderate advantage for behavioral and cognitive-behavioral methods, especially in the treatment of anxiety-related problems (Andrews & Harvey,

In Review: Approaches to Psychological Treatment

Dimension	Psychoanalytic	Phenomenological	Behavioral
Nature of the human being	Driven by sexual and aggressive instincts that create problems	Has free will, choice, and the capacity for self-determination and self-actualization	A product of social learning and conditioning; behaves on the basis of past experience
Therapist's role	Neutral; helps the client explore the meaning of free associations and other material from the unconscious	Facilitates the client's growth	Teacher/trainer who helps the client replace undesirable thoughts and behaviors with better ones; active, action oriented
Time frame	Emphasis on uncovering unresolved, unconscious conflicts from the distant past	Here and now; uses data of immediate experience	Current behavior and thoughts; may not need to know original causes in order to create changes
Goals	Psychosexual maturity through insight; strengthening of ego functions	Expanded awareness; fulfillment of potential; self-acceptance	Changes in thinking and behaving in particular classes of situations; better self-management
Typical methods	Free association, dream analysis, analysis of the transference, interpretations	Reflection-oriented interviews designed to communicate unconditional positive regard, empathy and congruence	Systematic desensitization, modeling, assertiveness and social skill training, positive reinforcement, aversive conditioning, punishment, extinction, cognitive restructuring

Source: Adapted from Goldenberg, 1983.

1981; Giles, 1983, 1990; Kazdin & Wilson, 1978; Lambert et al., 1986; Rachman & Wilson 1980; Searles, 1985).

More research is also needed on the degree to which the outcomes seen in therapy research are clinically, as opposed to just statistically, significant. One way to measure clinical significance is to compare treated clients to "normal" or nondisturbed persons in order to see how similar to the "normals" the clients have become. An example of this *normative comparison* is illustrated in Figure 16.2. If several treatments for a particular problem produce results that are equal statistically but are also equally trivial in clinical terms, perhaps the rational choice is not to choose any of them.

What conclusions are most reasonable?

This analysis suggests caution in drawing conclusions about the relative value of different approaches to therapy. Perhaps the most reasonable conclusion is that psychotherapy is usually a good bet. Even in light of apparently equivalent effects, however, the choice of a specific form of treatment, like the choice of a particular therapist, should not be made randomly. Careful consideration should be given to (1) what treatment approach, methods, and goals the client finds comfortable and appealing, and (2) information about the potential therapist's "track record" of clinically significant success with a particular method for treating problems like those of concern to the client. ■

Figure 16.2
Clinical Significance
The shaded area shows the typical range of deviant behavior per minute by "normal" boys in their homes. The solid line shows the average deviant behavior for a group of boys before, during, and after receiving treatment in the form of operant reinforcement for appropriate behavior. The boys' improvement was not only significant in comparison to their pretreatment baselines but also, as indicated by the shaded area, reflected a clinically significant change that placed them in the range of behavior seen in "normal" children.

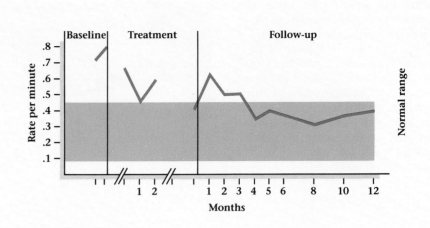

Source: Patterson, 1974.

Biological Treatments

Hippocrates, a physician of ancient Greece, was among the first to propose that psychological problems have physical causes. He prescribed rest, special diets, laxatives, and abstinence from alcohol or sex as treatments for psychological disorders. In the mental hospitals of Europe and America during the sixteenth through eighteenth centuries, "treatment" of psychological disorders consisted mainly of physical restraints, laxative purges, bleeding of "excess" blood, and induced vomiting. Cold baths, hunger, and other physical discomforts were also used in efforts to shock patients back to normality. Today, biological treatments for psychological problems are more sophisticated and include electroconvulsive therapy, psychosurgery, and psychoactive drugs.

Electroconvulsive Therapy

In the 1930s a Hungarian physician named Von Meduna suggested—incorrectly—that, since schizophrenia and epilepsy rarely occurred in the same person, epilepticlike seizures might combat schizophrenia. He began inducing convulsions in schizophrenics by using a drug called Metrazol. In 1938, Italian physicians Ugo Cerletti and Lucio Bini created seizures more easily by applying an electric current to schizophrenics' brains. During the next twenty years or so, a similar procedure became a routine treatment for schizophrenia, depression, and, sometimes, mania. Upon awakening after the shock-induced seizure, the patient typically remembered nothing about the events just preceding the shock and remained confused for varying periods of time. The treatment methods were relatively crude, and patients often received dozens, even hundreds, of shock treatments. Although many patients improved, the benefits were sometimes outweighed by negative side effects, including memory loss, speech disorders, and even some deaths (Breggin, 1979).

Today, the procedure of delivering an electric current to the brain to induce a convulsion is called **electroconvulsive therapy (ECT)**. It helps many patients overcome or reduce severe depression and the risk of suicide associated with it (Frankel, 1984; Scovern & Kilmann, 1980). However, contrary to Von Meduna's early claims, it is not an effective treatment for schizophrenia.

This crib was used in the nineteenth century to restrain unmanageable mental patients. The device was gentle compared with some of the methods endorsed in the late 1700s by Benjamin Rush, who is known as the "father" of American psychiatry. He advocated curing patients by frightening or disorienting them—for example, by placing them in a coffinlike box that was then briefly immersed in water.

No one knows for sure how ECT works, except that the convulsions, not the shock itself, are important. One possibility is that the convulsions somehow increase the amount of the neurotransmitter norepinephrine available at brain synapses (Chiodo & Antelman, 1980; Fink, 1979) and thereby alter mood. Another view is that the neurotransmitters that help the brain recover from the convulsion also reduce activity in areas of the brain associated with depression, thus relieving it (Sackeim, 1985). These are promising leads, but the answer is still in doubt (Sackeim, 1988).

ECT remains one of the most controversial methods of biological treatment. Critics argue that, too often, its effects are temporary and that it creates memory loss and other problems, including intense fear in patients and their families (Breggin, 1979; Palmer, 1981). Proponents perceive the benefits of the treatment outweighing the potential costs in most cases (Small, Small & Milstein, 1986). ECT is now given mainly to those whose depression is profound and fails to respond to antidepressant drugs, meaning that about 100,000 people a year receive ECT in the United States (Squire, 1987). This number is far smaller than during the 1940s and 1950s, but it appears to be increasing (Fink, 1988), perhaps in response to reviews of research that provide cautious encouragement for using ECT in combination with antidepressants in certain subtypes of depression (Janicak et al., 1985; NIMH, 1985).

To make electroconvulsive therapy (ECT) safer, patients today are given an anesthetic to make them unconscious before the shock is delivered and a muscle relaxant to prevent bone fractures during the convulsions. Also, the duration of shock is only about half a second, and a total of only about six to twelve shocks are given, one approximately every two days. Instead of passing current through both cerebral hemispheres (bilateral ECT), some doctors place both electrodes on the nondominant side of the patient's head. This unilateral ECT creates fewer undesirable side effects than bilateral ECT, but it is not clear whether it is as effective (Abrams et al., 1983; Daniel & Crovitz, 1983; Scovern & Kilmann, 1980; Weiner, 1984).

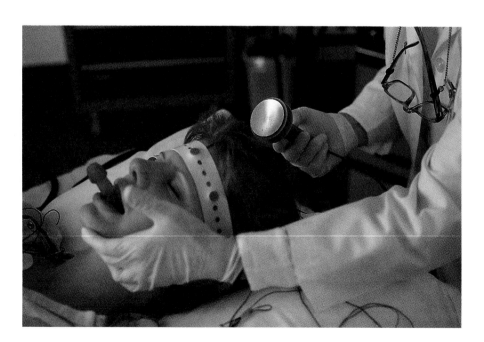

Psychosurgery

In ancient times, the desire to help severely troubled people apparently led to a form of surgery called *trephining*, in which a hole was made in the skull to allow evil spirits to escape. In the late 1930s a different theory led to **prefrontal lobotomy**, a procedure in which small holes were drilled in the skull and a sharp instrument was inserted and moved from side to side to destroy brain tissue (Freeman & Watts, 1942). The theory was that emotional reactions became exaggerated in disturbed people by neural processes in the frontal lobes and that the lobotomy disrupted these processes.

Lobotomy is one form of **psychosurgery**, a set of procedures in which parts of the brain are destroyed in an effort to alleviate psychological disorders (Valenstein, 1980). During the 1940s and 1950s psychosurgery was almost routine in the treatment of schizophrenia, depression, anxiety, aggressiveness, obsessive-compulsive disorder, and many other problems involving strong emotional responses (Valenstein, 1980). Unfortunately, brain surgery is risky and sometimes fatal, and its side effects and complications may be irreversible. The treatment was often too "successful." In some patients it produced uncharacteristic listlessness and a lack of any emotion; in other cases, patients became more emotional than before.

These and other problems prompted the Soviet Union to ban psychosurgery in 1951. Though still legal in the United States, these operations are done only as a last resort, when all less radical treatments have failed. Even then, modern psychosurgery involves destruction of only a tiny amount of brain tissue.

Psychoactive Drugs

The use of ECT and psychosurgery declined after the 1950s not only because of their side effects, complications, and general distastefulness, but also because they have been supplanted by psychoactive drugs. In Chapters 3 and 6, we described how psychoactive drugs affect neurotransmitter systems and consciousness. Here, we will describe how some of these drugs are used to combat anxiety disorders, depression, mania, and schizophrenia or to correct biological imbalances believed to be at the root of some mental disorders. Drugs used in the treatment of psychological disorders include antipsychotics, antidepressants, lithium, and anxiolytics (also known as tranquilizers or antianxiety drugs).

Antipsychotics In the 1940s, it was discovered that *reserpine*, a drug derived from the root of the snakeroot plant, seemed to act as an **antipsychotic** drug, alleviating mania, schizophrenia, and other severe forms of psychological disorder through the inhibition of certain chemical functions in the central nervous system. Unfortunately, reserpine also causes depression and lowers blood pressure. In the early 1950s, a synthetic antipsychotic drug was created. Known as chlorpromazine (and sold as Thorazine), it was the first of a group of *phenothiazines*, drugs that had effects on schizophrenic symptoms equal to those of reserpine but did not cause as many undesirable side effects. Their primary effect is to block the action of dopamine, a neurotransmitter that is thought to be involved in schizophrenia, as discussed in Chapter 15.

The phenothiazines created a revolution in the treatment of severe psychopathology. They reduce delusions, hallucinations, and other disturbed behavior. As a result, mental hospitals released thousands of patients and were able to avoid using padded cells, straitjackets, and other restraints that had been a standard feature of institutional treatment for centuries.

The phenothiazines, however, do have some problematic side effects. Because these drugs block dopamine receptors, early side effects include an inability to initiate certain movements and other symptoms similar to those of Parkinson's disease. After years of treatment, however, the dopamine receptors in movement systems compensate for the blockade by becoming more sensitive to dopamine. As a result of this adaptation, even more serious movement disorders may develop. One is called *tardive dyskinesia*, a syndrome marked by grotesque, uncontrollable, repetitive movements of the body and face. Uncontrollable movements of the face and tongue are especially prominent, and sometimes the person's arms or legs flail unpredictably. Tardive dyskinesia can be worse than the psychotic symptoms that prompted the drug treatment. There is one dopamine antagonist, *clozapine*, that does not cause movement disorders and appears to be even more effective in treating schizophrenia than more commonly used drugs (Meltzer, 1989). Unfortunately, clozapine has other side effects that are potentially fatal.

Antidepressants   Soon after antipsychotic drugs appeared, they were joined by medications designed to relieve depression. For years, the most common of these **antidepressants** were *monoamine oxidase* (or *MAO*) *inhibitors* and *tricyclics*. Of the two, tricyclics were used more frequently because they seem to work somewhat better, with fewer side effects. However, the even milder immediate side effects of a new drug called *fluoxetine* (sold as Prozac) has made it the most widely prescribed antidepressant in the United States. About 60 to 80 percent of the time, these drugs produce dramatic results, gradually lifting depression and allowing patients to return to a normal life, often with the help of continued medication, sometimes without it.

Antidepressants appear to work by increasing the amount of serotonin or norepinephrine available at brain synapses. (Prozac apparently does so by slowing reuptake of serotonin by the neurons that release it.) This idea is consistent with one neurotransmitter theory of depression mentioned in Chapter 15. However, it remains unclear why the rapid effect of these drugs on neurotransmitter levels is often not translated into improved mood for several weeks.

Lithium   Around 1970 the mineral salt *lithium* was found to be helpful not only in relieving depression but also in reducing and even preventing both the depression and the mania associated with bipolar disorder (Berger, 1978; Coppen, Metcalf & Wood, 1982). Lithium appears to control mania by reducing the norepinephrine available at brain synapses (the opposite of how some antidepressants work); why this also lifts depression is a mystery. The drug must be given carefully because an overdose can be harmful, even fatal. Many physicians prefer to deal with mania by using less toxic drugs, such as chlorpromazine or other antipsychotics.

Anxiolytics   In the 1950s **tranquilizers** such as meprobamate (sold as Miltown or Equanil), chlordiazepoxide (Librium), and diazepam (Valium) were introduced to treat anxiety. Today, these tranquilizers, now called **anxiolytics**, are the most widely prescribed and used of all legal drugs. Most people receiving these drugs are not hospitalized but experience anxiety or tension that interferes with their lives. Because anxiolytics are so good at producing calmness, many people come to depend on them just to get through the day. For some users, especially those on meprobamate, this calming effect may be accompanied by a lack of energy. Further, if the anxiolytic drugs are overused for long periods, psychological dependence on them can become addiction (Levenson, 1981).

Reflections on Biological Treatments

Linkages: What are some of the disadvantages of using drugs to treat psychological disorders? (a link to Biological Aspects of Psychology)

"In Review: Biological Treatments for Psychological Disorders" summarizes our discussion of biological treatment methods; our comments here focus on the most dominant of these, the psychoactive drugs. In spite of the widespread success of the "drug revolution" in the treatment of psychological disorders, enthusiasm about drugs is not universal. Critics point out three major limitations.

First, even if the origin of a disorder is physical, drugs may cover up the problem without permanently curing it. This masking effect is desirable in treating otherwise incurable physical conditions such as diabetes, but it may divert attention from potentially effective nondrug approaches to psychological problems. Anxiolytics, for example, do not teach people to cope with the source of their anxiety. Second, even beneficial drugs may be abused, resulting in physical or psychological dependence. Third, side effects present a problem. Some are merely annoying, such as the thirst and dry mouth produced by some antidepressants. Other side effects, like tardive dyskinesia, are far more serious. Furthermore, the long-term effects of drugs are not necessarily the same as the initial effects, and the final outcome may not be what was expected. Some delayed side effects appear only when it is too late to reverse them. (Concern over possibly serious delayed side effects of Prozac, for example, is now beginning to build.)

Yet research on psychoactive drugs holds the promise of creating both better medications and a fuller understanding of the origin and nature of some psychological disorders. For example, it has been discovered that the antidepressant clomipramine (sold as Anafranil) is quite effective in treating the symptoms of obsessive-compulsive disorder. This finding might lead to hypotheses about possible common features in the causes or effects of depression and obsessive-compulsive disorder. To find drugs that will relieve schizophrenia without affecting movement, or posing the dangers of clozapine, scientists will probably have to locate synapses that are defective in cases of schizophrenia but have a different receptor type than the synapses at which dopamine affects movement. Differentiating these neural circuits could produce not only a useful drug but also new information about schizophrenia (White & Wang, 1986). Similarly, as discussed in Chapter 6, on consciousness, research on anxiolytics promises to reveal information about the chemical aspects of anxiety.

In Review: Biological Treatments for Psychological Disorders

Method	Typical Disorders Treated	Possible Side Effects	Mechanism of Action
Electroconvulsive therapy (ECT)	Severe depression	Temporary confusion, memory loss, anxiety	Uncertain
Psychosurgery	Schizophrenia, severe depression	Listlessness, overemotionality	Uncertain
Psychoactive drugs	Anxiety disorders, depression, mania, schizophrenia	Variable, depending on drug used; movement disorders especially problematic	Alteration of various neurotransmitters in the brain

Obviously, drug treatments have limitations, and there are even greater limitations on our knowledge about them. Still, the benefits of antipsychotic and other drugs cannot be denied, and their use is likely to increase.

Community Psychology: From Treatment to Prevention

Assume psychologists knew exactly how to treat every psychological problem. Would there be enough professionals available to help everyone who needed it? Several authorities have argued that there are not and that there never will be (Albee, 1968). This view fostered the rise of **community psychology**, a movement that aims to minimize or prevent psychological disorders, not just treat them. This movement includes two main elements: community mental health programs and efforts to prevent disorders by altering the conditions that cause or aggravate them.

Components of Community Psychology

For the first half of this century, seriously disturbed people were given custodial care and medically oriented treatments in large state mental hospitals. Extended hospitalization isolated patients from their families and the larger community, often demoralizing them and making their condition worse (Ullmann & Krasner, 1975). Providing treatment outside a hospital, usually in the client's home community, was recognized as a more effective and less expensive approach (Kiesler & Sibulkin, 1987). Beginning in the late 1950s, this awareness, along with the availability of new drugs that reduced the need for physical restraints, fostered the release of many mental patients for treatment in their home communities. As a result of this *deinstitutionalization*, the number of patients in public mental hospitals dropped dramatically, and the treatment burden shifted to mental health professionals in local communities.

The *community mental health movement* arose in the 1960s as an attempt by the federal government to make treatment more accessible to people in need. To allow people to obtain low-cost mental health services without entering a hospital, plans were made for a nationwide network of community mental health centers. These centers were designed to provide outpatient therapy, short-term inpatient care, emergency services, and daytime programs for former hospital patients and others who need supervision but can live at home. The community mental health movement also aimed to make these services available to groups that had been neglected by the mental health system—the poor, ethnic and cultural minorities, and people with a need for multiple services.

A broader trend in community psychology involves the attempt to prevent psychological problems before they require treatment (Albee, 1985). Many psychological problems—especially those leading to child abuse, marital strife, failure in school, alcoholism, drug abuse, and suicide—occur in generation after generation. Trying to deal with these problems after they appear is like trying to rescue one person after another from a rushing river. Eventually, someone must go upstream and do something about whatever is causing all those people to fall in the river (Rappaport, 1977).

Some work by community psychologists involves *primary prevention*, which seeks to head off problems before they start (Caplan, 1964; Kessler & Albee, 1975). For example, unemployment, poverty, and overcrowded, substandard housing can create stress; and stress, as was noted in Chapters 13 and 15, is

Many community mental health centers provide mental health education as well as walk-in facilities or "hotlines" for people who are suicidal or in crises related to rape or domestic violence.

related to a variety of psychological disorders. Do something about social problems causing stress, say community psychologists, and you will reduce more stress and prevent more psychological problems than a battalion of psychotherapists could. To promote primary prevention, some community psychologists support political candidates or organize neighborhood residents to push for changes in the community. Most often, community psychologists act as consultants, working with schools and other community organizations to suggest ways of preventing psychological problems by teaching people new skills, by improving social and physical environments, and by easing transitions from one phase of life to another (Edelstein & Michelson, 1986; Felner & Adan, 1988; Rappaport, 1987; Zimmerman & Rappaport, 1988).

Less ambitious, but perhaps even more significant, are efforts at *secondary prevention*, which aim to detect psychological problems in their earliest stages and keep them from becoming worse. Examples include suicide prevention, programs that train teachers to identify early signs of child abuse, and Project Head Start, which helps preschoolers whose backgrounds decrease their chances of doing well in school.

Finally, efforts at *tertiary prevention* treat psychological disorders with an emphasis on minimizing their long-term effects and preventing their recurrence. The most prominent examples are programs designed to help emotionally disturbed or mentally retarded individuals develop the skills they need for semi-independent living in the community.

Reflections on Community Psychology

Community psychology is a laudable and ambitious enterprise, but it has been criticized on several counts. Primary prevention efforts have failed to reduce the prevalence of mental disorder significantly (Cowen, 1983; DeAngelis, 1989). And it has long been clear that community mental health centers often fail to deliver the broad range of services for which they were designed (President's Commission on Mental Health, 1978). Indeed, only about 20 percent of Americans with significant psychological disorders actually receive treatment. Among poor citizens (the economic group that displays the most serious forms of behavior disorder), only about 1 percent of those in need of help get it, or even try to get it (Shapiro et al., 1984).

These problems in providing services stem in part from the fact that only about half of the planned community mental health centers have opened—far less than the 1,500 envisioned in the 1960s. In addition, some mental health professionals oppose treating severely disturbed former patients as outpatients because of difficulty in coordinating and controlling their treatment. And some former patients who are homeless refuse to cooperate with community-based treatment. There are various reasons for this refusal, including mistrust of professionals, a desire for independence, and the confused thinking associated with some disorders. Whatever the reasons, the plight of former patients who are now homeless has led some observers to call for "reinstitutionalization," or the return of the most disordered clients to mental hospitals (Cordes, 1985). In light of data showing the negative effects of hospitalization (Kiesler, 1982), this could be an unfortunate step.

In spite of criticisms like these, the goal of reaching out to ever-widening circles of those in need and the ideal of prevention are sure to remain. There are indications that prevention of certain social-psychological problems—by helping people learn how to control stress, to develop new competencies, and to help one another—may be within reach (Rappaport, 1987). Prevention-oriented goals are also making their way into mainstream clinical psychology as clinicians become more interested in the promotion of physical and psychological health (Gatchel, Baum & Krantz, 1989). As research increases understanding of the causes and cures of psychological disorder, community psychology will become even more valuable.

Linkages: Psychological Treatment and Social Psychology

How do attitudes influence the treatment of psychological disorders?

We have seen that all therapists, regardless of theoretical orientation or procedural preferences, recognize that the relationship with their clients plays a role in the success of treatment. Indeed, they know that the treatment of psychological disorder is an inherently social undertaking (Frank, 1978). Accordingly, therapists are sensitive to and often make use of the principles of social cognition described in Chapter 17 to solidify the therapeutic relationship, enhance clients' involvement in treatment, and help bring about constructive change (Brehm & Smith, 1978; Snyder & Forsythe, 1990).

In particular, clients' attitudes may influence the outcome of treatment. As we discuss in Chapter 17, the components of an attitude include beliefs, feelings, and a tendency to behave in certain ways toward some attitude object. For example, a client's attitude about therapy might include the belief that it can work, positive feelings about entering treatment, and behavior that includes coming to treatment regularly.

If attitudes toward treatment in general, toward a particular therapist, or toward a certain drug engender client confidence and expectations for improvement, treatment may be enhanced. The same treatment might be less effective if accompanied by less positive attitudes (Wilkins, 1979).

The ability of positive attitudes to enhance the treatment of psychological disorders is one example of the *placebo effect*, which we discussed in Chapter 1. Though not fully understood, the placebo effect is not magical. In some cases, it reflects biological mechanisms. People's belief in the alleged painkilling value of an actually inert "drug," for example, can trigger the release of the body's own natural painkillers, as we described in Chapters 3 and 4. In other cases, the placebo effect occurs because beliefs can affect behavior. Clients who believe in the value of therapy or in the competence of a particular therapist are likely to be especially involved in treatment, focusing on the problems at hand, complying with treatment procedures, and working hard to resolve their difficulties. In other words, they behave in ways that give treatment every chance of success. Those who hold less favorable attitudes and expectations about treatment may tend to skip sessions, comply less with the therapist's methods and recommendations, and otherwise undermine the treatment process. Every year, many clients with very negative attitudes drop out of therapy prematurely, and many more refuse to begin treatment, even though it might have been helpful.

Therapists must take client attitudes into account when planning treatment. Demanding too much of a client who is not yet sure about staying in treatment may be a mistake. Some clients believe, incorrectly, that their only role is to listen to the therapist and passively wait for a cure. In such cases, treatment may begin with efforts to examine this belief and to promote greater client involvement in the therapy process. Some researchers have even developed brief "socialization" programs in which, for example, clients unfamiliar with the norms, or unspoken rules, about what is expected in therapy watch videotapes of other clients actively talking about and working on their problems with a therapist (Coleman & Kaplan, 1990; Heitler, 1976). If a client is skeptical about the value of therapy, a therapist might acknowledge and discuss the client's existing attitudes (perhaps beginning with "I realize that you don't

Clients' attitudes toward psychotherapy can sometimes be read on their faces, as well as in the degree to which they actively participate in the treatment process. Negative attitudes often create obstacles to improvement and thus may themselves become a topic of discussion in treatment.

have much faith in this''). As we discuss in the chapter on social cognition, two-sided messages are more effective than one-sided statements in changing the attitudes of skeptical audiences.

Once participating actively in therapy, the client's attitudes toward the process may become even more positive, not only because he or she is beginning to feel better, but also because, as described in Chapter 17, people tend to adjust their attitudes to match their behaviors. More positive attitudes may lead to a rising spiral of enhanced efforts at constructive change and further treatment gains.

Of course, if behavior always followed belief, much of therapy might involve little more than "selling" clients on treatment and letting them do the rest. But, as discussed in Chapter 17, even among people who are not plagued by psychological problems, the cognitive, affective, and behavioral components of their attitudes are not always in harmony; they may actually be in conflict. Therapists recognize, then, that clients who volunteer for treatment, and believe it will be helpful, may still not be particularly cooperative or hardworking in therapy. Often, these clients' behavior suggests that they want treatment to fail. Indeed, as we saw in Chapter 15, extreme discrepancies among the various components of people's attitudes can be a major part of their problems, and it may be just such discrepancies that the therapist must identify, bring to the client's attention, and try to correct. Awareness of the multifaceted aspects of attitudes in all people helps therapists not only to identify the links between normal and abnormal functioning, but also to remember that therapy, like other human relationships, is governed by the principles of social psychology.

There are many other examples of how social processes operate in treatment. As you read the next two chapters, ask yourself how some of the concepts described there — norms, reference groups, cognitive dissonance, self-perception theory, attribution, and the formation of relationships, for example — might come into play in the treatment of psychological disorders.

Future Directions

The treatment of psychological disorders relieves the suffering of thousands of clients each year. Yet the goal is always to do better. One of the most important and controversial issues in this field is how to choose methods that will be most effective for each client's problems.

Should each therapist continue using his or her favorite methods, regardless of what research might say, or should there be a research-based formula for matching treatments to problems? To help therapists decide, a task force of the American Psychiatric Association (1989) published *Treatments of Psychiatric Disorders*, a manual that suggests standards for the most appropriate treatments for different mental disorders. It contains general recommendations for treatment selection, includes a list of drugs (along with recommended dosages) suggested for use with specific problems, and discusses which aspects of a problem are more responsive to medication and which are more responsive to psychotherapy.

Reactions to this manual have been mixed. Many psychotherapists believe that treatment cannot yet be standardized because too little is known about what works best with given problems. Others object that the manual will retard the development of new therapies or restrict therapists' freedom to select treatments.

Indeed, future treatment efforts will probably continue to reflect eclecticism. There will also be continued emphasis on altering problematic thoughts as well as problematic behavior. The task of choosing methods of treatment may be facilitated by two research trends. First, through the intensive study of interactions between therapists and clients, researchers are seeking to learn how moment-to-moment changes in those interactions are related to specific beneficial events in therapy (Hill, 1990; Kadden et al., 1990). Second, researchers will continue to focus on which blend of methods is best for treating particular problems. Their efforts will include studies of how psychotherapy can best be combined with drug therapy. For example, anxiolytics, antidepressants, and other drugs once used primarily in the biological treatment of hospitalized patients or as an accompaniment to psychodynamic therapy are now being used more frequently in support of behavioral or other methods, particularly in difficult cases of agoraphobia, panic disorder, obesity, obsessive-compulsive disorder, and other problems (Craighead, 1984; Hersen et al., 1984; Klosko et al., 1990; Latimer, 1983; Stern, 1983; Turner, 1989; Zitrin, 1983).

Finally, psychologists will continue to work on answering the "ultimate question" in therapy outcome research: what treatment, by whom, is most effective for this individual with that specific problem, under which set of circumstances (Paul, 1969a)? Answering this question and determining how various treatments produce their effects will occupy researchers for many years to come (Stiles, Shapiro & Elliott, 1986; Talley, Strupp & Morey, 1990).

Several courses can help you learn more about the treatment of psychological disorders. In particular, we suggest that you take courses in psychotherapy, behavior modification, psychopharmacology, and community psychology.

Summary and Key Terms

Psychotherapy for psychological disorders is usually based on either psychodynamic, phenomenological, behavioral, or biological theories of personality and behavior disorder. Most therapists combine features of these approaches, in an eclectic approach.

Essentials of Therapy

All forms of treatment include (1) a client, (2) a therapist, (3) an underlying theory of behavior disorder, (4) a set of treatment procedures, which the underlying theory says should help, and (5) a special relationship between the client and therapist, which may make it easier for improvement to occur.

Clients and Therapists

Therapy may be offered to inpatients and outpatients in many different settings by *psychologists*, *psychiatrists*, and other mental health professionals.

Goals and Methods of Psychotherapy

The specific goal of treatment may be to help clients understand their problems, to reduce discomfort, to control problematic behavior, or to encourage the expression of feelings. To achieve the goals of treatment the therapist might seek to provide social support, to develop new ways of thinking and behaving, or to promote insight and self-exploration. Whatever the specific form of treatment, the client has, among other rights, the right to confidentiality.

Psychodynamic Psychotherapy

Psychodynamic psychotherapy began with Freud's *psychoanalysis* and seeks to help clients gain insight into unconscious conflicts and impulses and then to explore how those factors have created disorders.

Psychoanalytic Goals and Methods

Exploration of the unconscious is aided by the use of *free association*, dream interpretation, analysis of slips of the tongue and other everyday behaviors, and analysis of *transference*. The therapist often gives interpretations of what the client says and does, in order to help examine unconscious meanings.

Variations on Psychoanalysis

Some variations on psychoanalysis focus less on the id, the unconscious, and the past and more on helping clients to harness the ego to solve problems in the present. Other forms retain most of Freud's principles but use a more flexible format.

Reflections on Psychodynamic Therapy

Revisions of Freud's orthodox psychoanalytic treatment methods have helped make psychodynamic therapies attractive to many contemporary practitioners. Critics charge, however, that research support for specific psychodynamic methods is lacking.

Phenomenological Psychotherapy

Phenomenological psychotherapy helps clients to become more aware of discrepancies between their feelings and their behavior.

These discrepancies are seen to be at the root of behavior disorders and, according to the phenomenological approach, can be resolved by the client once they are brought to light in a good relationship with the therapist.

Client-Centered Therapy

Carl Rogers's *client-centered therapy*, also known as *person-centered therapy*, is the most prominent phenomenological method. Rogerian therapists help mainly by adopting attitudes toward the client that express *unconditional positive regard, empathy*, and *congruence*. These attitudes create a nonjudgmental atmosphere in which it is easier for the client to be honest with the therapist, with himself or herself, and with others. *Reflection* provides one way of creating this atmosphere.

Gestalt Therapy

Therapists employing the *Gestalt therapy* of Fritz Perls use more active techniques than Rogerian therapists, often confronting and challenging clients with evidence of their defensiveness, game playing, and other efforts to escape self-exploration.

Reflections on Phenomenological Therapy

Phenomenological treatment methods, with their focus on what is best in clients, have attracted a large following. However, critics see the theory underlying those methods as naive and incomplete, the methods themselves as too vague and passive, and most phenomenological therapists as unwilling to evaluate the approach scientifically.

Behavior Therapies

Behavior therapy, or *behavior modification*, applies laboratory-based principles of learning to eliminate undesirable patterns of thought and behavior and to strengthen more desirable alternatives.

Techniques for Modifying Behavior

Common behavioral treatments include *systematic desensitization, modeling*, and *assertiveness and social skills training*. More generally, behavioral therapists use *positive reinforcement* (sometimes in a *token economy*), techniques based on *extinction* (such as *flooding*), *aversive conditioning*, and *punishment* to strengthen desirable behaviors or weaken problematic behaviors.

Cognitive Behavior Therapy

Many behavior therapists also employ *cognitive behavior therapy* to help clients alter the way they think as well as how they behave. Among the specific cognitive-behavioral methods are *rational-emotive therapy (RET), cognitive restructuring, stress inoculation training*, and cognitive therapy.

Reflections on Behavior Therapies

Behavior therapies have racked up an impressive amount of evidence for their effectiveness, especially in relation to anxiety disorders and a number of other particular problems. Still, critics view the approach as dehumanizing, mechanical, and only superficially effective.

Group and Family Therapies

Therapists of all theoretical persuasions offer *group therapy* and *family therapy*. These forms of treatment take advantage of the group or family setting to enhance the effects of treatment.

Evaluating Psychotherapy

There is little agreement about exactly how to measure improvement following therapy and how best to design experiments that can assure that the improvement observed was actually due to the treatment itself and not to some other factor. One prominent outcome research method is *meta-analysis*. Most current observers conclude that clients who receive psychotherapy are better off than most clients who receive no treatment but that no single approach is uniformly better than all others for all clients and problems.

Biological Treatments

Biological treatment methods seek to relieve psychological disorder by physical rather than psychological means.

Electroconvulsive Therapy

Electroconvulsive therapy (ECT) involves passing an electric current through the patient's brain, usually in an effort to relieve severe depression.

Psychosurgery

Psychosurgery procedures such as *prefrontal lobotomy* are used as a last resort in an attempt to disrupt neural connections in the brain that are associated with mental disorder.

Psychoactive Drugs

Today the most prominent form of biological treatment involves psychoactive drugs, including those with *antipsychotic, antidepressant*, or *tranquilizing (anxiolytic)* effects.

Reflections on Biological Treatments

The most prominent form of modern biological treatment, psychoactive drugs, has proven impressively effective in many cases, but critics point out a number of undesirable side effects associated with these drugs, the risks of abuse, and the dangers of overreliance on chemical approaches to human problems that might have other solutions.

Community Psychology: From Treatment to Prevention

Concern about the effectiveness of psychotherapy and the realization that there will never be enough therapists to treat all who need help prompted the development of *community psychology*.

Components of Community Psychology

Community mental health programs and efforts to prevent mental disorders are the two main elements of the movement known as community psychology. Community mental health facilities provide the usual forms of treatment but also reach out, with professional and nonprofessional staff, to offer services to those who might not ordinarily ask for them. These services include crisis intervention, suicide prevention, community education, and day treatment for former mental patients.

Reflections on Community Psychology

Despite the efforts of community psychologists, the prevalence of mental disorders has not declined significantly, and many people still do not receive the mental health services they need.

O U T L I N E

Social Cognition

In 1989 an African-American man in New York City answered a newspaper ad for a used car. He was on his way to see the car when he wandered into a neighborhood that many of the residents considered "closed" to non-whites. He was soon attacked and killed by a group of Caucasian teenagers. His last moments were spent in terror and listening to racial slurs.

Why do such atrocities occur? People are not born hating all members of particular racial groups; they acquire these hostile feelings, usually through contact with prejudiced people. How this happens is one of the subjects examined by **social psychology**, the subspecialty concerned with all the ways a person's behavior and mental processes are influenced by other people. No aspect of life escapes this influence (see the Linkages diagram).

We begin our coverage of social psychology in this chapter by examining **social cognition**, the mental processes associated with how people perceive and react to other individuals and groups. In the process we examine how people form impressions of and become attracted to each other, how they form and change their attitudes, and how and why they use stereotypes to judge other people, sometimes in prejudiced ways. In the next chapter, we focus on patterns of group and interpersonal behavior such as conformity, aggression, and cooperation. Together, these chapters explore some of the complexities of how each person influences and is influenced by other people.

The Individual in a Social World

In Australia, an aboriginal tribe casts a spell of death on anyone who breaks the group's rules. From then on, no one mentions the offender, and no one pays the slightest attention to anything he or she does. After a short time, the rejected person sometimes dies, often by suicide. Experimenters skeptical about such reports created similar

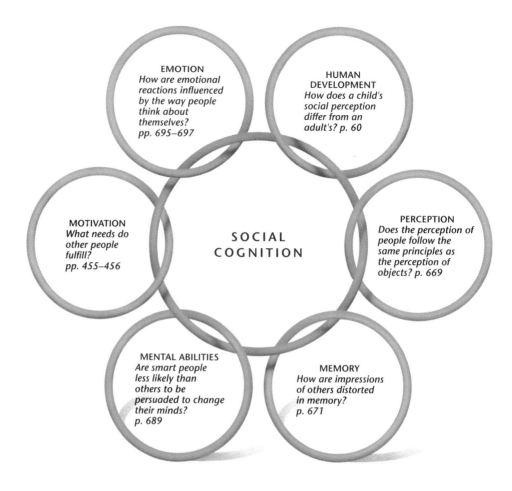

EMOTION
How are emotional reactions influenced by the way people think about themselves?
pp. 695–697

HUMAN DEVELOPMENT
How does a child's social perception differ from an adult's? p. 60

MOTIVATION
What needs do other people fulfill?
pp. 455–456

SOCIAL COGNITION

PERCEPTION
Does the perception of people follow the same principles as the perception of objects? p. 669

MENTAL ABILITIES
Are smart people less likely than others to be persuaded to change their minds?
p. 689

MEMORY
How are impressions of others distorted in memory?
p. 671

■ Look at the diagram above, which illustrates some of the relationships between the topic of this chapter, social cognition, and other chapter topics. (The page numbers indicate where the questions are discussed.) In previous chapters we discussed research into how people perceive, learn, remember, think, and feel. In this chapter we examine these same activities, but we look at how they occur when their objects are other people and at how other people influence these activities.

Basic principles discussed in Chapter 5, on perception, apply to social cognition as well. When you meet a new neighbor, for example, your first impression will reflect the influence of the top-down processing discussed in Chapter 5. Research on social cognition, however, provides a more detailed view of why your first impression is likely to be a lasting impression.

Similarly, cognitive biases and mental shortcuts, which were discussed in Chapter 9, on thought, also shape how people think about themselves and others. Studying these activities has produced an analysis of how people explain events, of how they account for their successes and failures. If you lose your temper with a friend, for example, are you likely to blame yourself, your friend, or the broken air conditioner? The factors affecting your choice are one of the topics explored by researchers in social cognition. Their findings have applications to many areas of psychology, because differences in how people make these choices help shape their feelings, their motivation, and their actions. ■

conditions on a military base. At first, the volunteer selected for social isolation tried desperately to elicit some response from other soldiers. When nothing he did resulted in attention, the man stopped talking and, later, stopped eating. He looked vaguely off into the distance and became oblivious to his surroundings. He walked around aimlessly, tripping over objects in his path. Alarmed, the researchers stopped the experiment (Ornstein, 1985).

These cases demonstrate the truth of the cliché that people are social beings. People fulfill many needs for one another, as demonstrated by studies discussed in Chapter 11, on motivation. In addition, intentionally or not, people influence one another in many other aspects of life. In this section we examine two of the most prominent examples of this influence: social comparison and social norms.

Social Comparison

People spend a good amount of time thinking about themselves, trying to evaluate their own perceptions, opinions, values, abilities, and so on. Decades ago, Leon Festinger (1954), one of the most influential theoreticians in social psychology, noted that self-evaluation involves two distinct types of questions: those that can be answered by taking a simple objective measurement and those that cannot. You can determine your height or weight, for example, by measuring it, but for other types of questions—about physical attractiveness, mental ability, or athletic prowess, for example—there are no objective criteria. In these cases, according to Festinger's theory of **social comparison**, people use other people as a basis of comparison. When you wonder how intelligent, insightful, interesting, or funny you are, you use *social* rather than objective criteria.

Whom do people use as a basis of comparison? Festinger said that people look to people who are similar to themselves. If you are curious about how good a golfer you are, you are likely to compare yourself not with a world-class golfer like Jack Nicklaus but with golfers of your own age, sex, and ability level (Gorenflo & Crano, 1989). The categories of people to which you see yourself as belonging and to which you habitually compare yourself are called **reference groups**.

Which reference groups you use can shape your satisfaction with life (Taylor, Buunk & Aspinwall, 1990). Consider the plight of people from a lower-class background who work their way up to a middle-class life. Along with new jobs and more responsibilities comes a higher income, but also new reference groups. As they begin to move up in an organization, they begin to associate with others who have an even higher standard of living. If they use these people as a basis for comparison, they begin to experience **relative deprivation**—the sense that, compared with those in the reference group, they are not doing well. Thus, moving from the lower to the middle or from the middle to the upper class is often an uncomfortable and frustrating experience (Crosby & Gonzalez-Intal, 1982). Similarly, when teenagers move from the relatively high status of being a senior in high school to the relatively low status of being a first-year college student, the sudden change in reference group and relative standing often creates disorientation, anxiety, and self-doubt, at least temporarily. Chronic use of extreme reference groups—such as the rich or famous—can create depression and anxiety for the average person (Taylor & Lobel, 1989). The cognitive-behavioral therapies described in Chapter 16 often help highly self-critical clients develop more positive self-evaluations by encouraging the use of more realistic reference groups.

Hare Krishnas and other fund raisers often give people a flower or other small gift before asking them for money. The donors' money is given not because of the gift's value—the gift is often discarded almost immediately—but apparently because of the reciprocity norm, which says that one good act deserves another.

Social Norms

Probably the most pervasive yet subtle way in which the social world influences people is through norms. **Norms** are learned, socially based rules that prescribe what people should or should not do in various situations. They are transmitted by parents, teachers, clergy, peers, and other agents of culture. Even when they cannot be verbalized explicitly (they are seldom written as laws), norms are so powerful that people often follow them automatically. At a movie, for example, norms tell you that you should get in line to buy a ticket rather than push people out of the way; they also give you the expectation that others will do the same. By telling people what is expected of them and others, norms make social situations less ambiguous and more comfortable.

One very powerful social norm is *reciprocity*, the tendency to respond to others as they have acted toward you (Cialdini, 1984). When an investigator sent Christmas cards to strangers, most responded with a card of their own; some even scribbled a personal note of good cheer (Kunz & Woolcott, 1976). During the 1970s, members of the Hare Krishna Society increased the society's revenues by trying a new strategy based on the reciprocity norm. Instead of simply asking people in public places for a donation, they first gave people a small gift, such as a flower. Then they asked for money but told people they could keep the flower whether or not they made a donation. This procedure was hugely successful (Cialdini, 1984).

Norms are neither universal nor unchanging (Kagitcibasi & Berry, 1989). In some Near Eastern cultures, people put their faces only inches away from the person they are talking with, displaying a norm that violates the greater distance Westerners usually observe. In certain American subcultures, youngsters are revered by peers for skill and daring at committing crimes. Social roles and status also affect which norms influence particular people in particular situations. Imagine yourself in a professor's office. The professor may lean back and put his or her feet up on the desk. If you put your feet on the professor's desk, however, you would be breaking a norm.

As we describe in the next chapter, very small groups of people—or even one influential person—can create norms powerful enough to produce con-

Linkages: The social norms that guide how people dress and what they should and should not do in various situations are a major aspect of the socialization process which, as described in Chapter 2 on development, begins in infancy. The process is the same the world over—parents, teachers, peers, religious leaders, and others communicate their culture's social norms to children—but differences in those norms result in quite different behaviors from culture to culture.

formity, compliance, and obedience. For now, we turn to an examination of how people come to perceive and judge the social world.

Social Perception

There is a story, perhaps apocryphal, about the president of a company who was having a lunch interview with a person being considered for an executive position. When the candidate salted his food without first tasting it, the president immediately decided not to hire him. The reason, he explained, was that the company would never hire a person who acted before collecting all relevant information. The candidate lost his chance because of the executive's **social perception**, which refers to the processes through which people interpret information about others, draw inferences about people, and develop mental representations of them. Social perception influences whether you see a person as hostile, friendly, repugnant, likable, or possibly lovable. It also helps to determine how you explain why people behave as they do.

First Impressions

Conventional wisdom says that first impressions of other people are very important, and research confirms their significance (Hamilton, 1988). First impressions are easily formed, difficult to change, and typically have a long-lasting influence on how one person reacts to another. How do people form impressions of people? And why are they so resistant to change?

Schemas The perception of people follows many of the same laws as the perception of objects, including the Gestalt principles discussed in Chapter 5. Consider Figure 17.1. As suggested by Gestalt principles, most people would not say that it is composed of eight separate straight lines; they are more likely to describe it as "a square with a notch in one side" (Woodworth & Schlosberg, 1954). Robert Woodworth suggested that this tendency is based on a **schema-plus-correction process**. A *schema* is a coherent, organized set of beliefs and expectations (Brewer & Nakamura, 1984; Rumelhart, 1984). In this case, the schema is "a square"; the correction is the notch. People use the schemas they already have to perceive and interpret new information.

The perception of people, like the perception of objects, involves the use of pre-existing schemas to integrate individual bits of information (Wyer & Srull, 1986). Your schema about grandmothers, for example, probably leads you to expect them to be elderly, sweet, gentle, kind, and conservative dressers. When you are introduced to a grandmother, you may perceive those characteristics that are a part of your schema of grandmothers, even if the particular grandmother you meet does not display them. Schemas allow you to skip the task of perceiving each element of a stimulus separately, to look instead at meaningful configurations, and to fill in missing information by using knowledge stored in long-term memory. It may take a very unusual grandmother (perhaps one who is forty-five years old, wears tight jeans, and rides a motorcycle) to focus your perceptions on her actual attributes (Fiske & Pavelchak, 1988).

Forming Impressions Schemas help create the tendency for people to infer a great deal about a person automatically, on the basis of limited information,

Figure 17.1
A Schema-Plus-Correction
People who see an object like this tend to use pre-existing knowledge, their schema of a square, and then correct or modify it in some way (here, with a notch). However, they will probably remember seeing only a square because, over time, people tend to forget corrections and remember only schemas.

Linkages: Does the perception of people follow the same principles as the perception of objects? (a link to Perception)

This particular grandmother probably does not fulfill your schema— your beliefs and expectations—of how grandmothers in general are supposed to look and act. Schemas help us to quickly categorize and respond appropriately to the people we meet, but they can also create narrowmindedness and, as we shall see later, prejudice.

and thus to form impressions quickly (Brewer, 1988). Suppose you attend a party where you are introduced to a woman who appears to be in her mid-thirties and is wearing a long black dress with a pearl necklace. You are told that she has just finished writing her third novel. After five minutes of conversation, you might infer that she is articulate, intelligent, educated, wealthy, witty, and much more interesting than anyone you have met during the past ten years. It is typical for people to take a few isolated bits of verbal and nonverbal behavior and infer from them all sorts of things about a person's life and personality. Some of them may be true, others not.

Two general tendencies influence whether a first impression is positive or negative. First, all else being equal, people tend to give others the benefit of the doubt and form positive impressions of them. In the absence of contradictory information, people assume that others are similar to themselves (Srull & Gaelick, 1983). Since most people tend to have a positive evaluation of themselves, they are predisposed toward liking other people as well.

The second principle is that negative information tends to carry more weight than positive information (Anderson, 1989). Why? People may act positively for any number of reasons: because they are nice, because they like you, because they are polite, or because they want to sell you insurance. However, it is assumed that negative acts come about only because the person is unfriendly or has some other undesirable characteristic. As a result, people are particularly attentive to negative acts and tend to weigh them heavily when forming impressions.

Lasting Impressions   In addition to being formed easily, first impressions tend to be difficult to change and thus to have a long-lasting influence (O'Sullivan & Durso, 1984). There are at least four reasons for the stability of first impressions.

First, as discussed in Chapter 9, on thought, people tend to be very confident, often overconfident, about their judgments. This confidence leads them to feel certain that they are correct and that they understand another person,

"*You are fair, compassionate, and intelligent, but you are perceived as biased, callous, and dumb.*"

Source: Drawing by Mankoff; © 1985 The New Yorker Magazine, Inc.

even when they have little objective information about that person (Fiske & Ruscher, 1989).

Second, people tend to interpret new information and events in ways that are consistent with an original impression. If you immediately like someone and he or she compliments you, you are likely to interpret the compliment as sincere praise. If, however, the compliment comes from someone you dislike, you will probably interpret it as insincere and begin looking for an ulterior motive. Similarly, self-assured behavior is interpreted as confidence among those one likes, but as arrogance or conceit among those one dislikes. In short, the meaning given to new social information is shaped by what is already known or believed about a person (Park, 1989).

Third, people remember their general impression or schema of another person better than any correction that is later added (Graesser & Nakamura, 1982). Imagine that you form an impression of someone as honest and friendly. One day you see the person receive too much change from a cashier and keep it. You may temporarily think of the person as someone who is basically honest but who occasionally commits a dishonest act. However, over time you will tend to forget the dishonest deed while vividly remembering your positive impression of the person as honest and friendly (Graesser et al., 1980). On the other hand, if you have a negative impression of someone, you will tend to forget positive things the person has done (Srull & Wyer, 1983).

Finally, people often act in ways that elicit from another person behavior that is consistent with their overall impression of that person (Snyder, 1984). This important tendency is worth a closer look.

Self-Fulfilling Prophecies Suppose you hear a man say something at a party that sounds boastful. This initial impression may prompt you to ask the man more about his accomplishments. As he lists them, you become convinced that he is boastful indeed (Jussim, 1989). Similarly, if the staff in a mental institution believes and acts as if patients diagnosed as schizophrenic are unable to bathe themselves, eat properly, and so on, those patients may become less and less likely to try to take care of themselves. In short, an initial impression, belief, or hypothesis can constitute a **self-fulfilling prophecy** (Merton, 1948), because it elicits behavior that ultimately confirms it (Wyer, Strack & Fuhrman, 1988).

The power of self-fulfilling prophecies was illustrated by one study in which men and women participated in a "get acquainted" conversation over an intercom system. Before the conversations took place, the men were shown photographs and told, falsely, that they were pictures of their partners. Some saw photographs of very attractive women, while others saw pictures that led them to believe their partner was somewhat unattractive. In fact, none of the photographs bore any relationship to the women's actual attractiveness. Independent judges listened to the ensuing conversations (but saw neither participant) and rated the women's behavior and personality. The women whom the men thought were attractive were judged as more articulate, lively, interesting, exciting, and fun to be with. Apparently, when the men thought their partners were physically attractive, they were more friendly and engaging themselves, and this behavior, in turn, elicited more positive reactions from the women. In contrast, men who thought their partners were unattractive behaved in a way that drew comparatively dull responses (Snyder, Tanke & Berscheid, 1977).

Self-fulfilling prophecies also help maintain judgments about groups. If you assume that members of a certain minority group are pushy or aggressive, for example, you might avoid them or act defensively around them. Faced with this behavior, members of the group might insist on being heard or become

Linkages: How are impressions of others distorted in memory? (a link to Memory)

As discussed in the chapter on mental abilities, a teacher's first impressions of a student's intelligence can create self-fulfilling prophecies. Teachers may inadvertently or consciously deprive children who impressed them as "dull" of the learning opportunities enjoyed by those who appeared "bright." This differential treatment may result in lowered academic performance, thus fulfilling the initial expectation.

frustrated and angry. These reactions fulfill the prophecy and perpetuate the impressions that created it (Messick & Mackie, 1989).

Explaining Behavior: Attribution

Impressions of others are only one aspect of social perception. Another important aspect is reflected in judgments about why people behave the way they do. Much as psychologists use the formal motivational theories described in Chapter 11, most people tend to rely on implicit theories to help explain the behavior they observe every day. To develop these theories, people often depend on their intuition. In this respect, then, everyone is an "intuitive psychologist."

Psychologists use the term **attribution** to describe the process people go through to explain the causes of behavior, including their own. As an example, suppose a friend failed to return borrowed lecture notes on time. You could attribute the behavior to many causes, from an unanticipated emergency to simple selfishness. Which of these alternatives you choose is important because it would help you to *understand* your friend's behavior, *predict* what will happen if your friend asks to borrow something in the future, and decide how to *control* the situation should it arise again. Similarly, whether a person attributes a spouse's nagging to stress-induced irritability or lack of love can influence whether that person seeks to work on the marriage or to dissolve it (Bradbury & Fincham, 1988).

People tend to attribute behavior in a particular situation either to mainly internal or mainly external causes. *Internal* causes are those that reflect characteristics of the person. *External* causes arise not from the person but from the situation. For example, if you attribute your friend's failure to return lecture notes to internal causes, you might decide your friend is inconsiderate, disorganized, lazy, or forgetful. If you look for mainly external causes, you might start worrying about the accident or sudden illness your friend must have suffered. Similarly, if you were to fail an exam, you could attribute the event mainly to internal or external causes. You might explain it by concluding that you're not very smart or that your schedule left you too little time to study. The attribution, in turn, might determine how much you study for the next exam or even whether you decide to stay in school. As discussed in Chapter 11, on motivation, there tend to be gender differences in the attributions people make in these kinds of situations. Partly as a result of the feedback they get from teachers, males are more likely than females to attribute failure to inadequate study time or other external causes; females tend to attribute failure to lack of ability (Burns & Seligman, 1989). These attributional differences may help males, and impair females, in maintaining self-confidence and persistence in the face of failure, especially in academic situations.

Criteria for Attributions   The decision to attribute behavior to internal or to external causes depends on three key characteristics of the behavior: consensus, consistency, and distinctiveness (Kelley, 1973). For example, suppose your father intensely dislikes your friend Ralph. Does the problem lie within your father? To decide how to explain the behavior, you would use these three criteria:

1. *Consensus* is the degree to which other people's behavior is similar to that of the person in question—in this case, your father. If everyone you know thinks Ralph is a twit, your father's behavior has a high degree of consensus, and you would attribute his reaction to something external to him,

Do Soviet leaders' statements about wanting peace with the United States reflect their inner feelings or merely a political situation in which it is wise to appear conciliatory, even while plotting world conquest. Social psychologists have found that the attributions that people make about the causes of behavior are systematically influenced by the consensus, consistency, and distinctiveness of the behavior.

something in the situation (probably something about Ralph). However, if everyone else thinks Ralph is the sweetest guy on the planet, your father's negative response would have low consensus, and you would probably attribute it to something about your father, such as his being a grouch.

2. *Consistency* is the degree to which the behavior occurs repeatedly in a particular situation. If your father sometimes warmly invites Ralph to dinner and sometimes throws him out of the house, the consistency of his behavior is low. This low consistency suggests that your father's behavior is attributable to the external situation—probably something that Ralph sometimes does. If the hostile behavior occurs every time Ralph is around, it has high consistency. But is your father's consistent behavior attributable to a stable internal cause (his consistent grouchiness) or to a stable external cause (a consistently jerky friend)? This question is difficult to determine without information about the third characteristic, distinctiveness.

3. *Distinctiveness* depends on the predictability of behavior in various situations. If your father is nasty to all your friends, no matter how they behave, his behavior toward Ralph has little distinctiveness. Low distinctiveness suggests that his reactions are attributable to his own internal characteristics. However, if he gets on famously with everyone you know except Ralph, your attribution about the cause of his behavior is likely to shift toward a cause that resides outside your father's personality, such as how Ralph acts.

In short, an internal attribution is most likely when there is low consensus, high consistency, and low distinctiveness. Thus, if you observe a coworker insulting customers (low consensus; most employees are polite to customers) every day (high consistency) no matter what the customers do (low distinctiveness), you would probably attribute this behavior to the coworker's personality rather than to the weather, the customers, or some other external cause. On the other hand, if you saw the same coworker on just one specific day (low consistency) being rude (low consensus) to one particular customer (high distinctiveness), you would be more likely to attribute the incident to the customer's behavior or some other external factor. External attributions are often made in response to other information patterns as well, as Figure 17.2 illustrates.

Figure 17.2
Causal Attributions
Here are the most common patterns of consensus, consistency, and distinctiveness that lead people to attribute other people's behavior to internal or external causes.

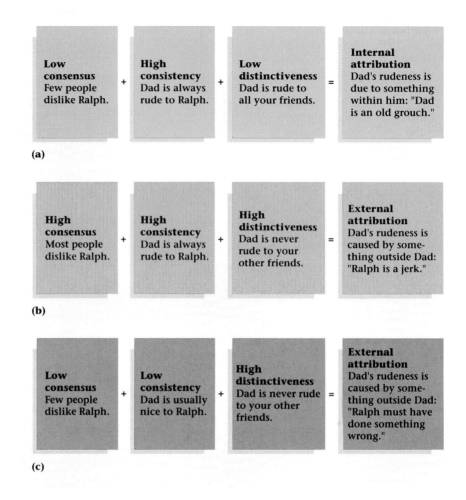

(a)

| Low consensus Few people dislike Ralph. | + | High consistency Dad is always rude to Ralph. | + | Low distinctiveness Dad is rude to all your friends. | = | Internal attribution Dad's rudeness is due to something within him: "Dad is an old grouch." |

(b)

| High consensus Most people dislike Ralph. | + | High consistency Dad is always rude to Ralph. | + | High distinctiveness Dad is never rude to your other friends. | = | External attribution Dad's rudeness is caused by something outside Dad: "Ralph is a jerk." |

(c)

| Low consensus Few people dislike Ralph. | + | Low consistency Dad is usually nice to Ralph. | + | High distinctiveness Dad is never rude to your other friends. | = | External attribution Dad's rudeness is caused by something outside Dad: "Ralph must have done something wrong." |

Attributional Biases Many experiments have supported the principles outlined in Figure 17.2 (Brown, 1986). These experiments suggest that for the most part, people are logical in the way they go about making causal attributions (Trope, 1989). However, people also have cognitive biases. These show up not only in the systematic problem-solving and decision-making errors described in Chapter 9, on thought, but also in inferences about the causes of people's actions. Psychological shortcuts sometimes create **attributional biases**, which are tendencies to systematically distort one's view of behavior.

One prominent example is called the **fundamental attribution error**, a general, widespread tendency to attribute the behavior of others to internal factors. Imagine that you see another student give an incorrect answer in class. You will probably attribute the behavior to an internal cause and infer that the person is not very smart. In doing so, however, you will fail to take into account many other factors (for example, lack of adequate study time) that might be relevant.

The fundamental attribution error has some significant consequences. For one thing, it may generate great confidence about impressions of other people. It also leads to underestimates of the variability in another's behavior created by external causes (Sande, Goethals & Radloff, 1988). Imagine a student who goes home every year at spring break to read and help around the house. The student's parents may believe this behavior occurs because the student is quiet, responsible, and serious. Because they make these internal attributions, they may not realize how differently their child acts at parties or football games or in other situations (Baxter & Goldberg, 1987). In general, people see other people in only a small set of social situations. This fact helps explain why dating is so fascinating (and sometimes frustrating). Only when you see other people in many settings does the true variability of their behavior become apparent.

More generally, the fundamental attribution error may also lead people to blame the victims of various unfortunate circumstances (Ryan, 1977). Unemployed workers are seen as lazy, homeless people are seen as irresponsible, and women who are raped are sometimes accused of having been seductive (Wyer, Bodenhausen & Gorman, 1985).

It is interesting that people usually avoid the fundamental attribution error when they explain their own behavior. In fact, there tends to be an **actor-observer bias**; that is, while attributing other people's behavior to internal causes, people are biased toward attributing their own behavior to *external* factors, especially when the behavior is inappropriate or involves failure. When you drive slowly and tentatively, it is because you are looking for a particular address (or Barney's Diner), not because you are a dimwitted ninny, like that slowpoke who crawled along in front of you yesterday.

The actor-observer bias results mainly from differences in the social information available when considering your own and others' behavior. When *you* are acting in a situation—giving a speech, perhaps—the stimuli that are most salient to you are likely to be external and situational, such as the temperature of the room and the size of the audience. Further, you have access to a great deal of information about other external factors, such as how much time you had to prepare your talk, the upsetting conversation you had this morning, or the speech course you took last term. Whatever the outcome of your efforts, you can easily attribute it to one or all of these external causes. But when you observe the behavior of someone else, the most salient stimulus in the situation is *that person*. Since you do not know what happened to the person last night, this morning, or last term, you are likely to attribute whatever he or she does to stable, internal characteristics.

Of course, people do not always attribute their own behavior to external forces. In fact, the degree to which they do so depends on whether the outcome is positive or negative. One group of researchers assessed introductory psychology students' attributions about their performance on a midterm examination (Smith & Ellsworth, 1987). Students who did well perceived the test as being fair and attributed their performance to their ability. Those students who performed poorly, however, believed that the test was picky and unfair, and they attributed their performance to an unreasonable instructor. The more unfair they perceived the test, the angrier they were with their instructor. These students were exhibiting the **self-serving bias**, the tendency to take credit for success (attributing it to one's personal characteristics or efforts) but to blame external causes for failure.

HIGHLIGHT

The Self-Protective Functions of Social Cognition

The self-serving bias occurs, in part, because people are motivated not to think about negative information. If you just failed an exam, it is painful to admit that it was fair. Moreover, to attribute failure to an internal characteristic is likely to be threatening to self-esteem. In fact, people are often motivated to think about things in a way that protects them from threatening conclusions, and there are many ways they accomplish this (Taylor & Brown, 1988).

In one study, students were asked to judge the likelihood that various events would happen to them compared with the likelihood that these events would happen to other students of the same age and sex. On the one hand, the students thought they were more likely than other students to like their first job, get a high starting salary, own their own home, travel to Europe, live past eighty, and have a mentally gifted child. On the other hand, they thought they were less likely than other students to develop a drinking problem, attempt suicide, get divorced, contract a venereal disease, get cancer, be sterile, or become involved in an automobile accident. Almost without exception, people believed positive events were more likely to happen to them and negative events were less likely to happen to them (Weinstein, 1980). This pattern of beliefs, called *unrealistic optimism*, has been found with respect to financial issues, health issues, freak accidents, and general happiness (Weinstein, 1989).

Why does everyone seem to think that he or she is better off than average? One reason is a feeling of *unique invulnerability* to negative events. Somehow people believe that a tragedy will never happen to them (Perloff & Fetzer, 1986). Most college women believe themselves much less likely than their peers to experience an unwanted pregnancy (Burger & Burns, 1988). Moreover, when they estimate their own risk of pregnancy, their judgments are unrelated to how often they have intercourse or what type of birth control they use, even though they realize that these factors shape the risk of pregnancy in other women (Whitley & Hern, 1990).

One mechanism that can create feelings of invulnerability is an *illusion of control* (Langer, 1989). In many situations, people believe they have some control over events that, in fact, they do not control. For example, people estimate their chances of winning a lottery as higher when they are able to pick their own ticket than when one is given to them (Langer, 1978).

When people *are* responsible for some outcome, they may use other methods of maintaining self-esteem (Baumgardner, Kaufman & Levy, 1989). When people anticipate a loss of self-esteem, they often adopt a *self-handicapping strategy* in which they arrange for failure to be attributed to an external cause (Baumgardner & Arkin, 1987). They may procrastinate, take drugs or alcohol, or not sleep—actions that make the cause of future performance ambiguous (Arkin & Baumgardner, 1985). These self-defeating actions can then be used to "explain" failure in a way that does not reflect internal characteristics (Basgall & Snyder, 1988). This strategy is used primarily when a person has succeeded in the past but doubts whether similar success can be maintained.

In the short run, each of the biases discussed in this chapter allows escape from something painful, but each can set the stage for a distorted view of reality, and, in the long run, can create problems. ("In Review: Some Biases in Social Perception" summarizes the common cognitive biases discussed here.) Though, as we discussed in Chapter 14, on personality, a certain amount of self-deception may help people deal with stress, overreliance on distortions of reality can, in the long term, complicate the task of coping with negative events. Feelings of invulnerability, illusions of control, and the defense mechanisms described in Chapter 13, on stress, may temporarily decrease anxiety, but they may also prevent people from taking rational steps necessary for long-term protection. Because people believe they are "hardy," they may not quit smoking; because they believe they live in a secure building, they may not lock their doors (Gollwitzer & Kinney, 1989). Self-handicapping strategies protect self-esteem in the short run, but in the long run they prevent achievements and eliminate the possibility of receiving useful information about one's strengths and weaknesses. ▪

In Review: Some Biases in Social Perception

Bias	Description
Importance of first impression	Ambiguous information is interpreted in line with a first impression, and the initial schema is recalled better and more vividly than any later correction to it. Actions based on this impression may elicit behavior that confirms it.
Fundamental attribution error	The general tendency to attribute the behavior of others to internal factors.
Actor-observer bias	The tendency for actors to attribute their own behavior to external causes and for observers to attribute the behavior of others to internal factors.
Self-serving bias	The tendency to attribute one's successes to internal factors and one's failures to external factors.
Unrealistic optimism	The tendency to assume that positive events are more likely and negative events are less likely to occur to oneself than to others.
Illusion of control	The general tendency to assume that one has control over events even when this is not true.

Interpersonal Attraction

Social perception obviously has a lot to do with how you think about and react to other people, including whether they attract or repel you. From childhood onward, people find that they like some people and dislike others. Why? Folklore says that "opposites attract," but it also says that "birds of a feather flock together." Like most instances of folk wisdom, each of these statements has some validity, but each needs to be qualified in important ways. To examine interpersonal attraction, we begin by looking at factors that lead to an initial attraction between people. We then examine how liking sometimes develops into an intimate relationship, how intimate relationships and love differ from other relationships, and what characteristics mark successful marriages.

Keys to Attraction

What is it that makes you like some people and not others? For attraction, as for the attribution of causes, characteristics of both the environment and the person play a role.

The Environment When thinking about why one person becomes attracted to another, it is easy to overlook the obvious. One of the most important determinants of attraction is simple physical proximity, or *propinquity*. In

In general, the more often people make contact with someone, the more they tend to like that person. This is one reason why next-door neighbors are much more likely to become friends than people who live farther from one another (Nahemow & Lawton, 1975).

Figure 17.3
Interpersonal Attraction and Attitudes
This graph shows the results of a study in which people first learned about the attitudes of another person. Their liking of the person was strongly influenced by the proportion of attitudes the person expressed that were similar to their own.

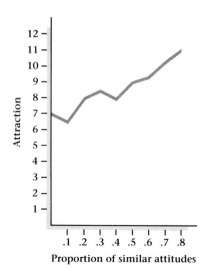

Source: Adapted from Byrne & Nelson, 1965.

apartment complexes, for example, many more friendships are formed among people who live on the same floor than among people who live on different floors (Nahemow & Lawton, 1975). Similarly, the likelihood that coworkers will form friendships increases when they have a lot of contact with each other (Segal, 1974).

Propinquity is important because it breeds familiarity (Moreland & Zajonc, 1982). As long as you are neutral or like a person even slightly at the beginning, you will tend to like the person more as you have additional contact (Bornstein, 1989). You will become more comfortable, less apprehensive, and feel as if you have a better understanding of the person.

The situation in which people first meet also influences attraction. The effect of the situation reflects the principles of conditioning discussed in Chapter 7, on learning. If you meet a stranger under comfortable physical conditions, you are much more likely to be attracted to that person than if the meeting occurs when you are hot or otherwise uncomfortable (Griffitt & Veitch, 1971). Similarly, receiving a reward in the presence of a stranger increases the chances that you will like that stranger (Lott & Lott, 1974). Association with rewards may generate attraction even if the other person is not responsible for providing the reward. In one study, an experimenter evaluated the creativity of a subject while another person watched. Compared with those who received a negative evaluation, subjects receiving a positive evaluation tended to like both the experimenter and the observer more, even though the observer did not provide the reinforcement (Griffitt & Guay, 1969). Thus, at least among people who are initially strangers, liking can occur because a person is associated with something pleasant.

Similarity of Attitudes People tend to like those whom they perceive as similar to themselves more than those whom they perceive as dissimilar (Grover & Brockner, 1989). In fact, there is a strong, direct relationship between the proportion of attitudes or opinions shared by two people and how much one likes the other, as Figure 17.3 illustrates. This is true of children, college students, adult workers, and senior citizens (Clore, 1975). One reason for this

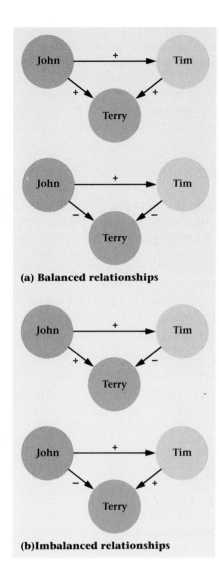

(a) Balanced relationships

(b)Imbalanced relationships

**Figure 17.4
Balanced and Imbalanced Relationships**
These are the most common balanced and imbalanced patterns of relationships among three people. The plus and minus signs refer to liking and disliking, respectively. Balanced relationships are comfortable and harmonious; imbalanced ones are often full of conflict and friction.

relationship is that people who share the same opinions confirm or validate one another's view of the world (Byrne, 1977).

Among the most influential similarities are attitudes toward people in the same social network. Imagine that John likes Tim. Then John meets Terry. John will be more attracted to Terry if Terry also likes Tim than if he does not. Now imagine a new scenario in which John dislikes Terry. Under these conditions, John will be more attracted to Tim if Tim also dislikes Terry. All else being equal, it appears that "the enemy of my enemy is my friend" (Aronson & Cope, 1968). In fact, when two people like one another, they seem to develop a norm by which they agree to like and dislike the same people (Jellison & Oliver, 1983).

More generally, people greatly prefer "balanced" over "imbalanced" relationships. As Figure 17.4 illustrates, if John likes Tim, the relationship is balanced as long as they agree on their evaluation of a third person, regardless of whether they like or dislike that person. However, the relationship will be imbalanced if John and Tim disagree on their evaluation of a third person.

Theorists once believed that the proportion of similar attitudes had a direct causal influence on how much two people like one another (Byrne, 1971). This view is oversimplified, however, because it describes a flow of causality in only one direction, from similar attitudes to increased attraction. When people interact for some time, *reciprocal causality* may occur: in other words, attraction may both affect and be affected by attitude similarity (Clark & Reis, 1988). Once you begin to develop a close bond with someone, your attitudes might become more similar to those of the other person, or you might change your perceptions of the other person's attitudes to make them more similar to your own. In one study, subjects were led to believe that another person either liked or disliked them (Curtis & Miller, 1986). When they thought the other person liked them, they saw that other person as warmer, friendlier, more open, a better listener, more trustworthy, and more similar to themselves. When they interacted with a person perceived as liking them, the subjects disclosed more personal information, asked more questions, and otherwise acted friendlier than if the person was said not to like them.

The original conception of attitude similarity also ignored the possible effect of dissimilar attitudes. Perhaps repulsion between people with dissimilar attitudes is more important than attraction between people with similar attitudes (Rosenbaum, 1986). If someone disagrees with you on even one or two important issues, you may develop an immediate and strong dislike for that person. Such disagreements *are* important (Byrne, Clove & Smeaton, 1986), but recent evidence indicates that even when dissimilar attitudes are taken into account, there is still a strong and direct relationship between the number of similar attitudes and the degree to which two people like each other (Smeaton, Byrne & Murnen, 1989).

Physical Attractiveness There is no doubt that physical attractiveness is an important factor in attraction, particularly in determining whether friendships are initiated (Maruyama & Miller, 1975). Even among members of the same sex, physical attractiveness is a key to popularity. This relationship is seen in grade school (Cavior & Dokecki, 1969) and continues among both male and female college students (Byrne, London & Reeves, 1968; Hatfield, 1986).

In the initial stages of a relationship, it appears that "more is better" as far as physical attractiveness is concerned. However, people who are dating steadily, engaged, or married tend to be very similar in their level of physical attractiveness (Curran & Lippold, 1975; Kalick, 1988; Price & Vanderberg, 1979). This phenomenon led to the **matching hypothesis** (Folkes, 1982), which states that a person is more likely to be romantically attracted to someone who is similar in physical attractiveness than to someone who is notably more or less attractive. Why? One reason is that people believe it is socially desirable to date and marry someone whose physical attractiveness is similar to their own (Greenberg & Cohen, 1982). This belief tends to mirror the values of society at large and seems to be based on the notion that marrying someone who is substantially more attractive reflects shallowness, whereas marrying someone substantially less attractive reflects low standards.

The Development of Intimate Relationships

Over time, people who are attracted to each other may become *interdependent*, which means that the thoughts, emotions, and behaviors of one person affect the thoughts, emotions, and behaviors of the other (Clark & Reis, 1988). Put another way, two people are interdependent to the degree that the events in one person's life affect both of them simultaneously. Interdependence is the defining characteristic of intimate relationships.

Intimate relationships usually develop slowly through a series of stages, as illustrated in Figure 17.5. One key in this evolution is *self-disclosure*, the revelation of fears, hopes, beliefs, weaknesses, and the like. Self-disclosure has

Figure 17.5
Development of Intimate Relationships
One person becomes aware of the other and begins forming an impression of that person during the awareness stage. In the surface contact stage two people begin interacting with one another directly. Since the two people have been strangers until this point, initial conversations are typically superficial. Intimacy begins when the relationship shows mutuality; that is, when people disclose information about their beliefs, preferences, goals, philosophies, and so on. The mutuality stage involves the disclosure of more and more intimate information and the development of an increasingly strong psychological bond.

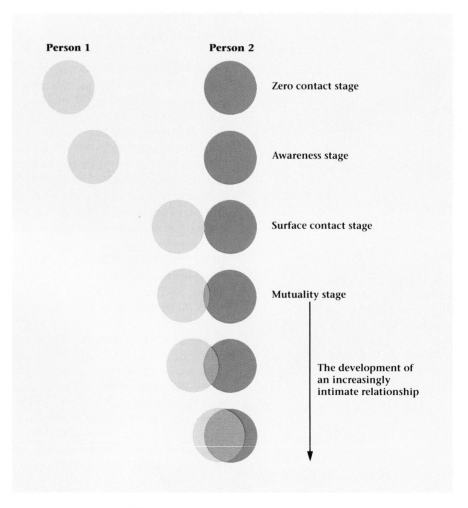

Source: Levinger & Snoek, 1972.

two independent dimensions: breadth and depth (Taylor & Altman, 1987). *Breadth* refers to the number of topics touched by self-disclosure. *Depth* refers to the amount of private information revealed about any topic. In the early stages of most relationships, one person offers self-disclosures with little depth or breadth. If the other person accepts the disclosures and reciprocates with other self-disclosures, the disclosures by both people gradually become deeper and broader. Sometimes one person temporarily backs away from the other (Levinger, 1988). Eventually, however, each person begins to care about and identify with the other and accepts some responsibility for what happens to that person.

Ideally, trust begins to develop as each person's self-disclosures are accepted by the other with understanding and caring (responses similar to Rogers's unconditional positive regard, discussed in Chapter 16, on treatment). This trust, in turn, makes the relationship more intimate, leads to further cycles of self-disclosure, greater trust, and deepening intimacy. Indeed, whether intimacy develops and deepens depends upon how each person responds to the other's disclosures and whether each offers new self-disclosures (Derlega et al., 1987). Rejected, neglected, and otherwise unreinforced disclosures tend to work against the development of intimacy.

If intimacy does develop, what are the key ingredients of the relationship? When people are asked to name these ingredients, the most common responses are *affection* and *emotional expressiveness* (Helgeson, Shaver & Dyer, 1987). Signs of affection are important because if one person perceives the other to be uninterested, further episodes of self-disclosure are unlikely and the person will begin to withdraw (Reis & Shaver, 1988). Emotional expressiveness is important because it enhances feelings of closeness and commitment to the relationship and because it is comforting to be able to express strong emotions. As noted in Chapter 13, being able to disclose strong feelings reduces stress and the risk of stress-related illness (Pennebaker & Beall, 1986).

Other key components of intimate relationships appear to be the *result* of intimacy (Clark & Reis, 1988). One is *support*, which refers in part to help with the daily hassles of life, such as giving a ride when the car breaks down, but also to psychological support, such as propping up a friend's confidence when things are not going well (Manne & Zautra, 1989). Two other frequently mentioned components of intimate relationships are *cohesiveness*, which refers to joint activities such as taking a vacation together, and *sexuality*.

Love and Marriage

Each year millions of people fall in love. (Millions of others wish they had.) There are approximately 1.5 million marriages in the United States each year, but also 1.2 million divorces. Psychologists have made considerable progress in understanding the experience of love and the institution of marriage, nearly all of it over the past ten years (Hendrick & Hendrick, 1989).

Analyzing Love   Most theorists agree that there are different types of love, each with its own set of characteristics (Sternberg & Barnes, 1988). One widely accepted view distinguishes between passionate love and companionate love (Hatfield, 1988). *Passionate love* is intense, arousing, and marked by both strong physical attraction and intense emotional attachment. Sexual feelings are very strong and thoughts of the other intrude on a person's awareness frequently. *Companionate love* is less arousing but psychologically more intimate. It is marked by mutual concern for the welfare of the other (Hendrick & Hendrick, 1986).

Though passion need never die, the basis for long-term intimate relationships tends to shift over the years from passionate love to companionate love, which is characterized by mutual self-disclosure, shared interests, and reciprocal caring.

Robert Sternberg (1988) has offered a more comprehensive analysis of love. According to his *triangular theory*, love has three basic components: *passion*, *intimacy*, and *commitment*. Variations in the strength of each component generate qualitatively different types of love, as Figure 17.6 illustrates. According to this analysis, passionate love (sometimes called "romantic love") involves passion and intimacy, but it lacks a meaningful degree of commitment to the other person. Companionate love is marked by a great deal of intimacy and commitment but little passion.

Another type of love distinguished by Sternberg is *fatuous love*, the type of love idealized in Hollywood movies. Two people meet, fall madly in love, and marry after a short, whirlwind romance. Fatuous love is based only on passion and commitment. When passion wilts, as it usually does, all that is left is commitment. But this commitment is likely to be superficial because intimacy has not been strongly developed. Thus, fatuous love is often short-lived.

According to Sternberg's model, the most complete and satisfying love is *consummate love*. It is the most complete because it includes a high level of all three components (passion, intimacy, and commitment). It is the most satisfying because the relationship is more likely to fulfill many of the needs of each partner. Consummate love is difficult to attain and may be even more difficult to maintain over time, but it is in many ways the ideal basis for marriage.

Strong and Weak Marriages   Psychologists have recently made considerable progress in understanding the most important factors involved in maintaining long-term relationships such as marriage (Hendrick, Hendrick & Adler, 1988). The level of self-disclosure in satisfying relationships tends to be reciprocal (Cohn & Strassberg, 1983); both men and women report the highest levels of marital satisfaction when mutual self-disclosure is high. In fact, the mutual sharing of interests, beliefs, opinions, and the like is often more important than sex (Sternberg & Grajek, 1984).

The perception that a relationship is equitable also enhances marital satisfaction (Hatfield et al., 1984). This perception is important because each partner's willingness to contribute to the relationship is fueled by the belief

Figure 17.6
Sternberg's Triangular Theory of Love
The three possible components of love are passion, intimacy, and commitment. Sternberg's four types of love reflect various combinations of these components.

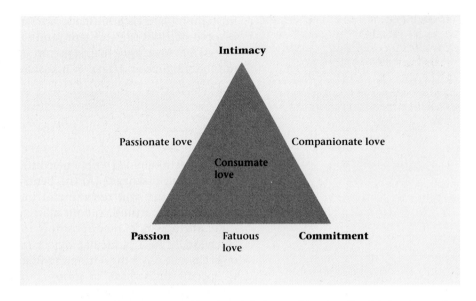

Source: Adapted from figure on p. 122 of Sternberg, R. J., "Triangulating Love," in R. J. Sternberg and M. L. Barnes, (eds.), *The Psychology of Love, 1988,* Yale University Press. Copyright © 1988 by Yale University Press. Reprinted by permission.

that the other will do the same. In other words, the partners develop trust (Clark, 1984). Partners in satisfying marriages trust the other person and are willing to take a long-term perspective. They are willing to make sacrifices because they trust that, in the long run, the other partner will reciprocate. Even specific violations of trust need not be fatal to a marriage if it is strong in other ways.

Marital satisfaction is also enhanced when the partners have complementary personality styles (Wiggins, Phillips & Trapnell, 1989). In this sense, opposites do attract. If one person tends to adopt a take-charge approach, he or she will interact best with a person who enjoys not having to make decisions, and vice versa. Similarly, a person who enjoys giving help will interact most comfortably with a partner who enjoys being helped.

Marital satisfaction also depends on the two people simply liking each other (Sternberg, 1987). Liking and respecting one's partner may be important in part because of their effect on how a couple handles anger (Berscheid, Snyder & Omoto, 1989). Conflict and anger are a part of all marriages, but dealing with them effectively is a hallmark of the most satisfying marriages (Repetti, 1989). In both happy and unhappy marriages, men tend to respond to anger from their spouse with anger of their own. But in happy marriages, the cycle of angry reactions is ultimately broken, usually by the wife, allowing the couple to deal with the problem at hand during moments of calm. In contrast, in unhappy marriages both husband and wife fall into a cycle in which they trade increasingly angry and hurtful remarks until communication breaks down (Gottman, 1979). When these episodes become frequent, couples begin to attribute any negative behavior of the spouse to an internal cause and any positive behavior to an external cause (Baucom, Sayers & Duhe, 1989). Thus, even if one spouse contributes significantly to the marriage, his or her efforts are dismissed by the other as insincere or unimportant.

Love and marriage are among the most cherished aspects of human existence. But they do not "just happen." People do sometimes experience "love at first sight" (Peele, 1988), and sometimes people feel an immediate closeness. Maintaining the long-term health of a relationship, however, requires work. Each person must occasionally make sacrifices, each must endure temporary frustrations, and each must adopt a long-range perspective and trust the other. Divorce statistics are constant reminders that marriage is difficult. But when successful, love and marriage can lead to the highest levels of personal fulfillment (Shaver, Hazan & Bradshaw, 1988).

Attitudes

The last section ended with a nice little sermon, but did it alter how you think or feel about marriage? Do the benefits of marriage seem worth the risks of divorce? Would you recommend marriage to others? These questions are related to your attitudes about marriage.

An **attitude** is a predisposition to respond cognitively, emotionally, or behaviorally to a particular object in a particular way (Rajecki, 1990). The object can be anything—from inanimate objects such as nuclear power plants, to specific individuals or groups, to actions such as having an abortion. Attitudes play an important role in guiding how people react to other people, what causes they support, what politicians they vote for, which brands they buy, and countless other daily decisions.

Components of Attitudes

Most theorists agree that an attitude has three components, as illustrated in Figure 17.7 (Breckler & Wiggins, 1989). The *cognitive* component is a set of beliefs, such as that whales are endangered and about to become extinct. The emotional, or *affective*, component consists of an evaluation: a like or dislike of the object of the attitude. Finally, the *behavioral* component involves a way of acting toward the attitude object. For example, if your attitude toward whales includes the belief that they are on the verge of extinction and the feeling that this state of affairs is very sad, you might donate money to the Save the Whales fund (McGuire, 1989).

If the cognitive, emotional, and behavioral components of attitudes were always in harmony, so that evaluations and actions always reflected what people believed, psychologists could measure all aspects of an attitude by measuring any one component. They could even predict how people would act toward an object by noting the beliefs and feelings they expressed (Ostrom, 1989). In fact, predicting a specific behavior on the basis of a person's attitude is difficult. For example, one survey revealed that more than half of American motorists believed that a speed limit of 55 mph saved lives and should be retained, but that most motorists regularly drove faster than 55 (Associated Press, 1986).

Discrepancies among components of an attitude appear for many reasons. First, there are always competing motives and competing attitudes (Rajecki, 1989). You might think about donating to the Save the Whales fund but then realize that your father's birthday is coming up. As a result, you might end up spending the money on a gift, even though the cognitive and affective components of your attitude toward whales remain positive. Second, an attitude can be expressed in many ways. One person might donate money, another might display a bumper sticker, another might fire off angry letters to members of Congress, and still another might picket whaling companies (Ronis, Yates & Kirscht, 1989). It is often difficult to predict what action a person will take. Third, because of social pressure in the form of norms, a person may suppress the behavioral aspects of an attitude while retaining the

Figure 17.7
Three Components of an Attitude
The three components of an attitude can be measured separately and through different assessment channels. For example, the cognitive component of an attitude is typically assessed through surveys, interviews, and other self-report methods. The affective component might be monitored by physiological recordings taken while a person watches a film about a topic relevant to the attitude. Measurement of the behavioral component could entail observing what a person does in relation to the attitude object.

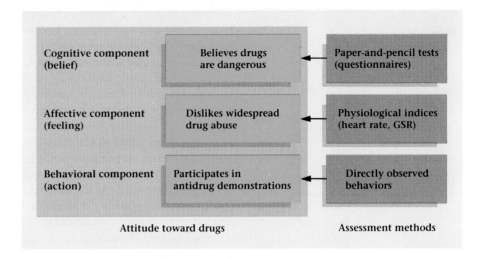

Source: Adapted from Kahn, 1984.

other components (Ajzen, 1989). Someone who believes that the rights of homosexuals should be protected might not campaign for this cause because doing so would upset friends who hold strong antihomosexual attitudes.

Does it matter to people if their behavior does not conform with their feelings or beliefs or if several attitudes are in conflict? What happens when the components of an attitude are inconsistent? Two theories—cognitive dissonance theory and self-perception theory—have suggested answers to these questions.

Cognitive Dissonance Theory The relationship between behavior and attitudes, and what occurs when they are inconsistent, was addressed by Leon Festinger's (1957) classic **cognitive dissonance theory.** This theory holds that people prefer their many cognitions, including those about their own behavior, to be consistent with one another. When their cognitions are inconsistent, or *dissonant*, people feel uneasy and are motivated to make them more consistent. If you hold the cognitions "I smoke" and "Smoking is bad," you should be motivated to reduce the resulting dissonance. One way to reduce dissonance is to alter the inconsistent cognition or attitude.

Festinger and Merrill Carlsmith (1959) conducted one of the earliest studies of dissonance. First they asked people to turn pegs on a board, a very dull task. Later some of these people were asked to persuade a waiting subject that the task was "exciting and fun." Some were told that they would be paid $1 to tell this lie; the rest were promised $20. After they had talked to the waiting subject, their attitudes toward the dull task were measured.

Figure 17.8 shows the results. It might seem reasonable that those who were paid $20 would like the dull task better than those paid just $1, but just the reverse occurred. Why? Festinger and Carlsmith (1959) argued that telling another person that a boring task is enjoyable will produce dissonance (between the thoughts "I think the task is boring" and "I am saying it is fun"). To reduce this dissonance, the people who were paid just $1 adopted a more favorable attitude toward the task, making their cognitions consistent: "I think the task is fun" and "I am saying it is fun." But if a person has adequate justification for the behavior, any dissonance will be automatically reduced simply by thinking about the justification. When subjects were paid $20, they had adequate justification for their behavior and so did not need to change their attitudes toward the task.

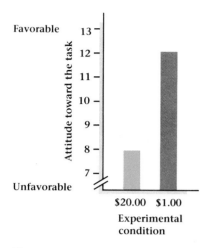

Source: Festinger & Carlsmith, 1959.

Figure 17.8
Cognitive Dissonance and
Attitude Change
People were paid by an experimenter to say that a boring task was
enjoyable. According to cognitive
dissonance theory, those paid $20
had clear justification for lying and
should have experienced little dissonance between what they said and
what they felt about the task; in fact,
their attitude toward the task did
not change very much. However,
subjects who received just $1 had
little justification to lie and could
reduce their dissonance mainly by
displaying a more positive attitude
toward the task, which they did.

Literally hundreds of other experiments have also found that people often
reduce dissonance by changing their attitudes (Aronson, 1988). In one of these
demonstrations, people were asked to eat fried grasshoppers (Zimbardo et al.,
1965). In some cases, the experimenter made this request in a very friendly
and apologetic way, explaining that the grasshoppers had been shipped
prematurely and had to be consumed before they spoiled. In other cases, the
experimenter was rude and unfriendly, complaining that the subjects were
late and were wasting his time. According to cognitive dissonance theory,
those who were asked to eat grasshoppers by the friendly experimenter could
easily justify their actions: "I don't like the idea of eating grasshoppers," but
"I'm eating them to please this nice person." Like the subjects who were paid
$20 to lie, these subjects did not change their attitude toward grasshoppers,
reporting them to be very distasteful. However, subjects approached by a rude
experimenter could only reduce the dissonance brought on by their agreement
to eat something distasteful by changing their attitude toward it. As expected
by dissonance theory, these subjects said the grasshoppers tasted good.

Self-Perception Theory Cognitive dissonance theory assumes that an
inconsistency among one's various thoughts results in a state of tension, but
Daryl Bem (1967) suggested an alternative that does not presuppose internal
tension. According to Bem's **self-perception theory**, situations often arise in
which people are not quite sure about their attitudes. When this happens,
Bem says, people look back to their behavior, consider it in light of the
circumstances, and then *infer* what their attitude about it must have been.
That is, you say, "If I did that under those circumstances, my attitude about
it must be this." This process requires no tension to drive it.

Consider again the grasshopper experiment. According to Bem, the subjects'
attitudes were determined not by dissonance reduction but by their inferences
about their actions. Subjects in the nice-experimenter condition may have
thought, "Well, if I ate grasshoppers, I must have done it because the experimenter was so nice about it, but they really tasted terrible." This kind of
thinking would leave these subjects' distaste for grasshoppers intact. Subjects
in the other condition may have thought, "I ate the grasshoppers, but that
experimenter was such a jerk that I never would have done it if they hadn't
tasted good."

Obviously, self-perception theory and cognitive dissonance theory often
make the same predictions. Indeed, both may be correct to some extent. There
is now clear evidence that cognitive dissonance creates an uncomfortable state
of arousal that people are motivated to reduce (Cooper & Fazio, 1984). However,
this is obviously not the only process that occurs. Researchers are trying to
discover the precise conditions under which cognitive dissonance theory and
self-perception theory are most applicable to understanding the relationships
among the cognitive, affective, and behavioral components of attitudes (Axsom,
1989).

Attitude Formation

People are not born with attitudes. From early childhood onward, however,
people continue to form attitudes about new objects. The advertising industry
certainly recognizes the possibility of forming attitudes. Advertisers spend
nearly $100 billion each year (Rossiter & Percy, 1987) to place their messages
virtually everywhere, from the inside of the New York Metropolitan Opera
program to the rear end of city buses. They do it because sales figures suggest
that it works. How are attitudes formed?

Virtually all of the principles discussed in Chapter 7, on learning, play a role in the formation of new attitudes. In childhood, modeling and other forms of social learning are especially important. Children learn from parents not only what objects *are* but what one should *believe* and *feel* about them and how one should *act* toward them. For example, children may learn from their parents' words not only that snakes are reptiles but also that snakes are slimy and should be feared and avoided. (This information, combined with observation of the parents' own reactions to snakes, can sometimes create a phobia in the child.) Thus, as the process of concept learning described in Chapter 9 proceeds, there appears to be a parallel process of learning attitudes about those concepts (Tourangeau & Rasinski, 1988). Some theorists view attitudes as complex knowledge structures that are stored in long-term memory and used just like any other information (Tourangeau et al., 1989).

Classical conditioning can also produce positive or negative attitudes (Calder & Gruder, 1989). Advertisers have found, for example, that people are more likely to form a positive attitude toward a product when it is repeatedly paired with enjoyable music (Gorn, 1982), soothing colors (Middlestadt, 1990), or other stimuli that elicit good feelings (Aaker & Stayman, 1989). Attitudes are also influenced by operant conditioning, as when parents reward a child for stating particular views or acting in particular ways.

Of course, attitudes are also formed on the basis of direct experience with objects. One interesting result of experience is the *mere exposure effect*. All else being equal, attitudes toward an object—a drink, a style of clothes, a politician, and so on—tend to become more positive as people are exposed to it more often (Zajonc & Markus, 1982). It is common, for example, for people to like a song only after they have heard it several times.

Attitude Change: The Role of Persuasive Communications

How many times has someone who disagrees with you about something tried to change your attitude about it? It happens all the time in relation to religion, politics, sports, fashion, and nearly everything else. Whether a communication succeeds in changing an attitude depends on a number of factors, including

In a political campaign, each candidate uses persuasive communications designed to strengthen the positive attitudes of supporters and to change the attitudes of those who are undecided, or even negative, about his or her candidacy. Ideally, positive attitudes will be translated into votes.

characteristics of (1) the communicator, (2) the message, and (3) the audience (Petty & Cacioppo, 1984).

The Communicator   Various characteristics of the communicator influence whether a message will change the audience's attitude:

1. Sources perceived as *credible*, or knowledgeable about the topic, are more effective at changing attitudes than are low-credibility sources (Cooper & Croyle, 1984).
2. Listeners are more likely to be persuaded if a communicator is perceived to be *trustworthy*. For this reason, people's attitudes are more likely to be influenced by a message that is accidentally overheard than by a presentation obviously intended to persuade (Walster & Festinger, 1962). To exploit this fact, advertisers often use testimonials from apparently unpaid consumers, who are supposedly unaware of being photographed.
3. As the *similarity* between the communicator and the audience increases, the communicator tends to be more effective in changing attitudes (Cialdini, Petty & Cacioppo, 1981). There appear to be two reasons for this effect. First, people perceive communicators who are similar to themselves to be more trustworthy than those who are less similar. Second, all else being equal, people tend to like others who are similar to themselves more than those who are perceived as dissimilar.

The Message   Imagine that your school is considering a 50 percent increase in tuition. Most of the administrators favor the proposal, but most of the students are against it. Suppose you wish to promote opposition to the proposal. What should you say to persuade people to your point of view?

Whether it is best to present one or two sides of an issue depends on the prior attitudes of the audience (Cialdini et al., 1981). Thus, if you are speaking to students, an already sympathetic audience, the most effective communication would contain only arguments against the tuition increase. This one-sided communication would bolster the audience's prior beliefs and reinforce its members' tendency to oppose the proposal. Contrary arguments can only sow the seeds of doubt. However, in talking to an audience that opposes your point of view, it is usually better to present both sides of the issue. In this way, you show respect for the audience's attitudes, recognize the validity of those attitudes, but also provide arguments for changing them. In short, a one-sided message is more effective when the audience is predisposed to the speaker's point of view; a two-sided message is more effective when the attitude of the audience is contrary to that of the speaker (McGuire, 1985).

The amount of attitude change is greatest when a persuasive message states explicit conclusions; for example, "It is therefore obvious that increasing tuition 50 percent will prevent many people from attending college." This principle applies with people of all intelligence levels (McGuire, 1969). But how mild or extreme should the conclusions be? If administrators favor a 50 percent increase in tuition and you favor no increase, would it be more effective to argue for a 40 percent increase, a 20 percent increase, or no increase?

An answer is suggested by a study in which students first rated the quality of several poems and then heard a message purportedly stating the "real" quality of the poems. Some students heard a message that supposedly came from a high-credibility source (a famous poet); others, from a low-credibility source (an uninformed undergraduate from an obscure school). When the students rated the poems again, their attitudes tended to change in the

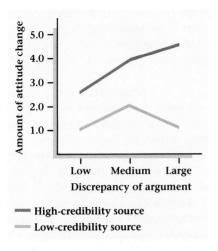

High-credibility source
Low-credibility source

Source: Aronson, Turner & Carlsmith, 1963.

Figure 17.9
Communicator Credibility and Persuasion
In general, highly credible sources produce more attitude change as the discrepancy between the speaker's arguments and the audience's attitudes increases. Low-credibility sources are most effective when arguing for moderate amounts of attitude change.

Linkages: Are smart people less likely than others to be persuaded to change their minds? (a link to Mental Abilities)

direction suggested by the message they had heard, and the amount of change was always greater for the high-credibility message (see Figure 17.9). However, the amount of change depended on both the credibility of the speaker and the amount of discrepancy between the speaker's message and the students' original ratings. For the high-credibility speaker, the greater the discrepancy between the message and the students' ratings, the larger the attitude change. For the low-credibility speaker, the most attitude change occurred when the discrepancy between the message and the students' original ratings was moderate (Aronson et al., 1963).

Sometimes communicators try to change attitudes by instilling fear in the audience. A health organization, for example, may suggest that you are likely to die prematurely if you do not eat a healthy diet. Can such **fear appeals** change attitudes? One of the first experiments to examine their influence was concerned with attitudes toward smoking. One group of subjects watched a movie in which the dangers of smoking were demonstrated with a smoking machine and charts of health data. A second group received the same information, but also saw an operation for the removal of a smoker's cancer-blackened lung. Compared with the first group, those in this high-fear condition were more upset, felt more likely to get lung cancer themselves, and were more eager to quit smoking (Leventhal, Watts & Pagano, 1967).

Fear appeals have limitations, however. Even when fear produces lasting effects on the *cognitive* component of an attitude, the effects on behavior often fade after several weeks or months (Rotfeld, 1989). More often than not, when fear has provoked efforts to quit smoking, people eventually start smoking again (Glasgow & Bernstein, 1981). Further, fear appeals are most effective when they are not *too* frightening and when they are accompanied by information about how to avoid the fearful consequences. If nothing but extremely frightening information is given, many people block out the message (Leventhal, 1970).

The Audience   Whoever is communicating, and whatever the message, some people in the audience change their attitudes and others do not (Cialdini et al., 1981). What factors are important in determining who changes and who does not?

One possibility is intelligence. Perhaps intelligent people, because they can better comprehend arguments, change their attitudes more easily than less intelligent people. Or perhaps intelligent people are better able to detect logical flaws in the arguments presented, are more likely to think of counter-arguments, and are therefore *less* likely to be persuaded to change their attitudes. In fact, research shows that both of these processes occur. Very intelligent people comprehend persuasive arguments better than less intelligent people, but they are also better able to refute them. As a result, there is no overall relationship between intelligence and susceptibility to persuasion (McGuire, 1985).

Susceptibility to persuasion does seem related to self-esteem, however. William McGuire (1969) suggested that individuals with low self-esteem are not confident about the correctness of their own attitudes and thus often change attitudes in response to persuasive messages. However, people with low self-esteem also tend to be inattentive and have little interest in the events that surround them. As a result, although individuals with low self-esteem are prone to accept the arguments of others, they seldom bother to think about or even pay attention to those arguments (see Figure 17.10a and b). Individuals high in self-esteem do pay attention to what others think, but they are so self-confident that they are seldom swayed. Consequently, both groups show little

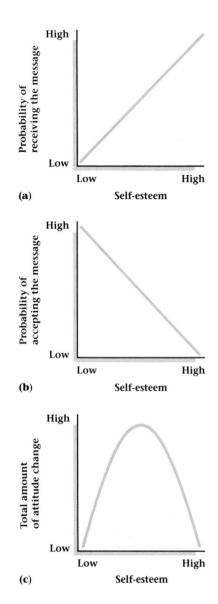

(a)

(b)

(c)

Source: Adapted from McGuire, 1968.

Figure 17.10
Self-Esteem and Attitude Change
People with high self-esteem pay attention to and understand a persuasive message but are usually so confident in their own beliefs that they reject it. Those with low self-esteem would be likely to accept the arguments presented, but because they seldom notice the message, they do not usually change their attitudes. People with moderate levels of self-esteem tend to show the greatest susceptibility to a persuasive message, because they not only notice and understand it but also tend to be uncertain of the correctness of their own beliefs.

attitude change (see Figure 17.10c). In contrast, those with moderate levels of self-esteem pay a reasonable amount of attention to what others say; they are also sufficiently unsure of their own attitudes to be persuaded. Thus, these individuals tend to change their attitudes the most (Gergen & Bauer, 1967; Nisbett & Gordon, 1967; Zellner, 1970).

Possibly the most important audience factor in attitude change is psychological involvement with the issue. High involvement leads people to think about the communication very carefully, and it can generate either more or less attitude change (Johnson & Eagly, 1989). When the topic of a communication pertains to beliefs and values that form part of a person's self-concept, involvement is high, but attitude change is unlikely because it would threaten the person's entire sense of self (Greenwald & Pratkanis, 1984). Thus, if you try to persuade a person who believes that abortion is murder to support its legality, the person's involvement is likely to be high, but so too is his or her resistance to change. However, high psychological involvement can enhance attitude change when a communication describes how to obtain a desirable outcome. In this case, as long as the position advocated in the communication is believable, attitude change is likely (Johnson & Eagly, 1989). Thus, an investment counselor touting the financial benefits of commodities futures may have a good chance of persuading a doubtful customer.

Reactance What if the combination of communicator, message, and audience does not favor attitude change? One obvious possibility is that some listeners will not change their attitudes, but the communicator may create an even less desirable outcome. Consider an experiment in which students heard arguments in favor of equal treatment for the Communist party of the United States (Worchel & Brehm, 1970). One group was given an extreme message, in which the speaker said, "You cannot believe otherwise" and "You have no choice but to believe this." Of these students, 50 percent accepted the arguments and changed their attitudes in the direction proposed; but 40 percent changed their attitudes in the direction *opposite* to that argued for. A control group received the same message, but without the two extreme statements. In this case, about 70 percent changed their attitudes in the direction suggested by the speaker and only 15 percent shifted in the opposite direction.

Such attitude reversal is important and pervasive. When people are told that they may not do something, they tend to become even more motivated to do it. When people are told that they may not have a particular object, they often go to extraordinary lengths to obtain it (Brehm, 1972). In one experiment, children were allowed to choose as a reward any brand of candy on display, except that the experimenter told some of the youngsters that they should *not* pick brand X (Hammock & Brehm, 1966). The result? Children who were told what not to do chose brand X much more often than those who were given a free choice.

According to one explanation of this reaction, when people perceive their freedom to be restricted, reactance occurs (Brehm, 1989). **Reactance** is a state of psychological arousal that motivates people to restore a lost sense of freedom by resisting, opposing, or contradicting whatever they feel caused the loss (Lessne & Venkatesan, 1989). For example, when the Coca-Cola Company told consumers that they would like its new Coke better than the old version, outrage erupted. When the company announced that the old version would no longer be available, over 40,000 people called the company headquarters to complain. Within two months, a company executive said, "Maybe we goofed." Coke Classic was brought back, and its sales rose (Ringold, 1988). ("In Review: Forming and Changing Attitudes" summarizes some of the major processes through which attitudes are formed and changed.)

In Review: Forming and Changing Attitudes

Type of Influence	Description
Other cognitions	When cognitions are inconsistent, they can lead to a change in attitude. For example, people who believe smoking is unhealthy and yet do so may come to think less negatively about smoking.
Behavior	Behaving in a manner that is inconsistent with an attitude can also lead to a change in the attitude, as when someone eats a new food that was initially thought to taste bad.
Modeling and conditioning	Attitudes are sometimes formed and changed through classical and operant conditioning processes or by observing the way others behave and speak about the attitude object.
Communicator	Attitudes are most likely to be changed when people hear arguments presented by a communicator who is perceived to be credible, trustworthy, and similar to themselves.
Message	When hearing a message that is inconsistent with their attitude, people are most likely to change their attitude when both sides of the issue are presented. Messages that arouse fear can also be effective if they include specific information about how to avoid the fearful consequences.
Audience	Attitude change is most likely among those with moderate levels of self-esteem. High personal involvement can also foster attitude change, but only if the prospect of change is not personally threatening.

Prejudice and Stereotypes

All of the principles underlying impression formation, attribution, attraction, and attitudes come together in the domain of prejudice and stereotypes. **Stereotypes** are impressions or schemas of entire groups of people. They are more powerful and more dangerous than individual impressions because they involve the false assumption that all members of a group share the same characteristics. Although the characteristics that make up the stereotype may be positive, they are usually negative. The most prevalent and powerful stereotypes focus on observable personal attributes, particularly race, gender, and age (Brewer, 1988).

Stereotyping often leads to **prejudice**, a positive or negative attitude toward an individual based simply on his or her membership in some group. *Prejudice* means literally "to prejudge." Like other attitudes, prejudice has cognitive, affective, and behavioral components. Indeed, stereotyped thinking is the cognitive component of prejudicial attitudes. The hatred, admiration, anger, and other feelings people have about stereotyped groups constitute the affective component. The behavioral component of prejudice often results in **discrimination**, which is differential treatment of individuals who belong to different groups.

Theories of Prejudice

Not all prejudice and stereotyping occur for the same reason (Stephan, 1985). We describe three of the most popular theories of prejudice. Each has empirical support and accounts for some, but not all, instances of stereotyping and prejudice.

Motivational Theories   One approach to prejudice looks at personality structure for an explanation. T. W. Adorno and his colleagues found that prejudice is most likely among people whose parents used punishment or harsh words to instill the belief that they must defer to and obey all those with a higher status than themselves (Adorno et al., 1950). This kind of upbringing was described in Chapter 2 as authoritarian parenting and, according to Adorno, encourages the development of a cluster of traits called the **authoritarian personality**. People with an authoritarian personality view the world as a strict social hierarchy. They feel they have the right to demand deference and cooperation from all those who have lower status. In order to know whom to obey and from whom to demand obedience, authoritarian people are motivated to identify other people's status in relation to themselves. This sets the stage for the development of negative stereotypes of those perceived as occupying a lower status, and for prejudice and discrimination against them.

One piece of evidence supporting the concept of the authoritarian personality is that people who are prejudiced against one group also tend to be prejudiced against other groups (Ehrlich, 1973). This pattern suggests that stereotypes and prejudices may serve some psychological need to derogate others. According to psychodynamic theorists, authoritarian personalities are probably using several defense mechanisms as well. For example, they may be displacing the hostility they originally felt toward their punitive parents onto the stereotyped group. They may also project their own fears and weaknesses onto the stereotyped group, and thereby convince themselves that the other group is indeed inferior.

Learning Theories   People often hold negative attitudes toward groups with whom they have had little or no contact. This can happen, for example, when a single negative experience with one member of a group creates negative feelings that generalize to the entire group. Further, just as social learning makes some people afraid to fly even though they have never been in a plane, there are people who have strong prejudices against African-Americans, Jews, Hispanics, or Native Americans, even though they have never interacted with even one member of the group in question. This fact supports a second approach to prejudice, which holds that prejudices, like other attitudes, are learned from personal experience and from the experiences reported by others.

This approach applies the principles of learning that we discussed in the context of attitude formation. It holds that children can learn stereotypes, prejudice, and discriminatory behaviors not from experiences with particular groups but from watching and listening to the words and deeds of parents, peers, and others (Karlins, Coffman & Walter, 1969). These influences are often reinforced by movies and television programs that portray ethnic or racial groups in ways that support common stereotypes.

Cognitive Theories A third approach to stereotyping and prejudice emphasizes the role of cognitive processes. It holds that stereotypes are inevitable responses to an extraordinarily complex social world (Fiske, 1989). There are so many people, so many situations in which one meets them, and so many possible behaviors that they might perform, that one cannot possibly attend to and remember them all. The most effective way to deal with this complexity is to group people into social categories. Just as people form categories for chairs, boats, shoes, and so on rather than remembering every detail about every object they have ever encountered, people also form categories for people. They create categories and mental lists of associated, often accurate, characteristics for teachers, athletes, strangers, politicians, criminals, and so on. These categories represent stereotypes.

How do people categorize other people? As we noted earlier, people often focus on age, gender, race, occupation, and other detectable distinctions (Brewer, 1988). They use these characteristics as the basis for creating ingroups and outgroups. An **ingroup** is any category of which people see themselves as a member. If you are African-American, African-Americans probably form your ingroup; if you are an African-American student, African-American students may form an even more specific ingroup. An **outgroup** is any group of which people do not see themselves as a member. People tend to see ingroup members as more physically attractive than outgroup members and assume that ingroup members have more desirable personality characteristics and engage in more socially accepted forms of behavior (Doise et al., 1972; Taylor & Jaggi, 1974). As might be expected, people tend to give preferential treatment to ingroup members (Turner & Oakes, 1989).

According to learning theory, negative attitudes about members of racial groups are based on negative personal experiences and/or the negative experiences and attitudes we hear about from others. As we shall see later, new and more positive experiences can alter these negative attitudes.

THINKING CRITICALLY

Does Contact with a Group Decrease Prejudice Against It?

One implication of learning theories of prejudice and stereotyping is that these phenomena are primarily due to ignorance about members of unfamiliar groups (Miller & Davidson-Podgorny, 1987). This conjecture has led to the **contact hypothesis**, which states that stereotypes and prejudices about a group will be reduced as contact with the group increases. A natural test for this hypothesis appeared during the 1960s and 1970s, when many schools across the United States became racially integrated for the first time.

What am I being asked to believe or accept?
The original formulation of the contact hypothesis was quite simple: As people have more and more contact with members of a group about which they hold a stereotype, they will realize that their stereotypes are untrue and change them. Through school desegregation, therefore, race relations should gradually improve, for several reasons (Stephan, 1985). First, and most important, each group would receive information that is inconsistent with the prior stereotype. Whites would observe that blacks act in ways that they had not expected, and blacks would see whites behave in ways they had not expected. Second, both blacks and whites would realize that they are more similar than they expected. They would slowly come to realize that they have the same hopes, desires, fears, and the like. Finally, each group would

Contact between members of different racial groups can reduce their prejudice toward one another. In one study of summer campers, children who had the most contact with members of another race showed much less prejudice at the end of camp than those with less contact (Eaton & Clore, 1975).

recognize that members of the other group are not all the same. Some blacks are introverted, others are extroverted; while some have a good sense of humor, others do not, and so on. The same is true of whites.

What evidence is available to support the assertion?

In fact, early results did not support the contact hypothesis. A few studies found a decrease in racial prejudice, but most found either no change or an increase in prejudice following desegregation. In one extensive study, for example, racial attitudes were measured both before and after school desegregation. Initially, both black and white children were relatively accepting of those from different racial backgrounds, but racial attitudes of both blacks and whites became much more negative once desegregation began (Rogers & Miller, 1981).

Negative results like these may mean that a hypothesis is overly simplistic or overly general, not utterly incorrect. Theorists recognized this possibility about the contact hypothesis and began to ask whether intergroup contact might lead to more positive racial attitudes for certain people or in certain situations. Perhaps intergroup contact would have more positive effects for younger children (whose learned prejudices have not had as much time to solidify) than for older children (who have had more "practice" at prejudice). Thus, even if young children have prior beliefs about children from other racial backgrounds, they may be more open to new experiences and may not display as much of the hatred and resentment that often goes with prejudice.

In fact, researchers found evidence for this interaction between contact and age. When first brought together in school, older children were very sensitive to existing intergroup differences in academic achievement, social interaction styles, athletic abilities, and the like. These perceived differences created considerable antagonism between blacks and whites (Miller, Rogers & Hennigan, 1983). Such problems were much less severe for children whose schooling began in an integrated environment and who thus watched one another develop from an early age.

In addition to age, however, the school environment shaped the effect of contact (Miller & Brewer, 1984). Intergroup contact reduced prejudice and stereotyping only under specific conditions (Cook, 1985). First, members of the two groups had to have roughly equal social and economic status. Second, the school situation had to foster cooperation and interdependence. When white and black students worked together on group projects and had to rely on one another's cooperation, racial attitudes toward one another improved. Third, the contact between group members had to occur on a one-on-one basis; it was only when one *individual* got to know another *individual* that the errors contained in stereotypes became apparent. Finally, it was important that members of each racial group were seen as typical and not unusual in any significant way. When these four conditions were met, racial attitudes among both whites and blacks became more positive. Unfortunately, in the vast majority of schools, these conditions were not met (Miller & Brewer, 1984).

Are there alternative ways of interpreting the evidence?

There are several problems with drawing conclusions about the contact hypothesis on the basis of observed consequences of different kinds of naturally occurring situations. For one thing, the situations in which the observations took place were not, by their very nature, under experimental control. So, for example, the fact that contact with other racial groups from a younger age is associated with less prejudice could be due to the early contact itself or to numerous uncontrolled factors, such as more liberal parental attitudes, growing up in a more racially tolerant era, having a particularly enlightened teacher, or the like. In short, perhaps the young children would have been less prejudiced than the older ones even without the contact.

What additional evidence would help to evaluate the alternatives?

Data from naturalistic observations must be supplemented by evidence from experimental studies aimed at determining more precisely if, when, and how intergroup contact leads to reductions in prejudice and stereotyping. So far, several experimentally created classroom situations have been tested for their effects on children's prejudice (Aronson, 1990). The most effective involve interracial cooperative learning, such as when each child is given a piece of a puzzle that the group must solve together (Slavin, 1985). Even with adults, friendly, cooperative contact in which two people work jointly toward a common goal tends to result in mutual respect and liking (Cook, 1984). Competition has the opposite effect.

What is it about cooperation and competition that produces these effects? One possibility is that competition creates anxiety and arousal. A competitor's actions, even when benign, are often attributed to self-serving ulterior motives, and negative attitudes toward the competitor often result, especially if he or she is very competent (Wilder & Shapiro, 1989). On the other hand, cooperative settings elicit empathic reactions. Successes lead to joint pride, and even mistakes or failures by the partner are often tolerated. In short, the other person is seen as someone who is similar to oneself, someone who tries hard and often succeeds, but also someone who sometimes makes mistakes (Lanzetta & Englis, 1989).

Additional studies like these, in the classroom and in the laboratory, will be valuable not only for evaluating the contact hypothesis but also as a guide to sculpting environments that foster greater tolerance and understanding.

What conclusions are most reasonable?

Based on the evidence available so far, it appears that stereotyping and prejudice are often based on ignorance born of unfamiliarity with other groups. It also appears that stereotyping and prejudice can be reduced through contact with members of the other group. However, contact alone is clearly not sufficient. Members of each group must perceive themselves to be of equal status, to be interdependent, and to share many of the same concerns. They must perceive others as individuals rather than merely as members of one group or another. When this is not the case (as in the apartheid system of South Africa), contact in the schools will help, but significant reductions in prejudice cannot be expected as long as there are obvious status differences in the larger society (Foster & Finchilescu, 1986). To the extent that racial differences in status and opportunity exist in America—and they do—contact can be only part of the solution to the problems of stereotyping, prejudice, and discrimination. ■

Linkages: Social Cognition and Emotion

How are emotional reactions influenced by the way people think about themselves?

Most of our discussion has focused on how people think about others. But people also spend considerable time thinking about themselves, how they will accomplish goals, how they appear to others, and so on. As noted in Chapter 12, on emotion, the way people interpret events and think about themselves has a strong impact on their emotional life.

The way we think about ourselves—our self-schema—can have a major impact on how we react emotionally. If, for example, we think of our value or competence in one situation as representing our value in all situations, then depression over a broken relationship, for example, might leave us feeling depressed about life in general. People who recognize that failure in one area does not mean they are utterly worthless may suffer less devastating emotional reactions to a particular unpleasant event.

In fact, people develop mental representations or schemas of themselves and modify these schemas over the course of their lifetime (Kihlstrom et al., 1988). The nature of these schemas differs from one person to another. Patricia Linville (1982) found that some people have a unified self-schema while others have a differentiated self-schema. People with a *unified self-schema* think of themselves as having more or less the same characteristics or attributes in every situation (at home, at a party, and so on) and in every role (as a student, friend, or romantic partner). People with a *differentiated self-schema* think of themselves as having different attributes when in different roles or situations.

These differences in the way people think about themselves have a strong impact on their emotional experiences (Linville, 1987). Imagine a student who fails an exam. No one is happy about such an experience. But those with a unified self-schema will have a much stronger emotional reaction to it because they will interpret failure in this one area as implying incompetence in all areas. After failing, they are likely to think less of themselves not only as a student but also as a romantic partner, as a son or daughter, and so on. People with a differentiated self-schema will be less likely to have this reaction. They may think less of themselves as a student, but failing an exam will have no implications for how they think of themselves as a friend, romantic partner, son, or daughter (Linville, 1985).

More recently, researchers have found that self-schemas contain information not only about what a person is (the *actual self*) but also about what a person wants to be (the *ideal self*) and what moral training tells a person he or she should be (the *ought self*). Emotional reactions resulting from discrepancies between the actual and ideal selves or between the actual and ought selves occur as early as the preschool years (Wells & Higgins, 1989). When people begin to think about the discrepancy between the actual self and the ideal self, they tend to experience emotions such as sadness, disappointment, and dissatisfaction with their lives (Higgins, 1987). In some cases, people begin to ruminate about such matters, and this produces symptoms of depression (Higgins, 1989). A discrepancy between the actual self and the ought self can produce emotions such as guilt, fear, and anxiety; ruminating about this discrepancy can produce physical and psychological agitation as well as the sympathetic nervous system arousal described in relation to emotion in Chapter

12. People often feel that they must do something to reduce the discrepancy, and they may try to do so by somehow punishing themselves (Higgins, 1989). Effective treatment of depression and anxiety disorders often requires analyzing why and how people think about such discrepancies (Baron, 1989; Pervin, 1989).

Future Directions

Social cognition is a dynamic and exciting aspect of social psychology. Each year new discoveries are reported, novel theories are proposed, and researchers examine the intricacies of social interaction at a finer level of detail. There is no doubt that this trend will continue.

One issue that cuts across all of the areas discussed in this chapter is the degree to which social cognition occurs automatically during social interactions. There are obviously cases in which this occurs, but there are also cases in which people think about events after the fact. Under what circumstances do people form impressions, become attracted to someone, or make attributions during the course of interactions, and when do they make such decisions only later, after thinking about them more carefully? There is no single answer to this question, but more and more research is showing that social thought is often spontaneous, automatic, and sometimes even beyond conscious control (Ostrom, 1990).

As an example, consider attributions. One group of researchers took advantage of the encoding specificity principle to study how and when attributions are made (Newman & Uleman, 1990). Recall from Chapter 8, on memory, that a retrieval cue is effective only when it taps into information that was originally encoded; this principle can be used to identify those situations in which people spontaneously make trait attributions (Bassili, 1989a). In one study, subjects read a series of statements such as "The secretary solves the mystery halfway through the book." After reading many sentences, the subjects were asked to recall them and were given certain retrieval cues to help. For the preceding sentence, the cue *smart* (a trait attribution) was much more effective than the cues *typewriter* or *detective* (both of which are semantically related to the topic of the sentence). This would happen only if subjects spontaneously inferred that the secretary must be smart when they first read the sentence. Interestingly, subjects had no recollection of having done this (Newman & Uleman, 1989). Such spontaneous attributions do not always occur, but they are very likely when one person is trying to form an impression of another (Bassili, 1989b).

Similarly, is stereotyping or prejudice a spontaneous reaction? Patricia Devine (1989a) has argued that many stereotypes are learned at a very early age and are known equally well by less prejudiced and more prejudiced individuals. In fact, if whites are asked to describe the common stereotype of a black, the responses of less and more prejudiced people are almost identical (Devine, 1989b). In many situations, whites automatically become aware of the stereotype when in the presence of a black. However, less prejudiced individuals make a strong distinction between their *knowledge* of the stereotype and their *personal beliefs*, and they think carefully about the difference between the two (Devine, 1989b). This leads them to treat particular blacks more as individuals and less as members of the stereotyped group. Because the stereotype is common and learned at an early age, however, it seems that whites cannot help but think about it—even if they do not believe it and show few signs of discrimination in their overt behavior.

Investigating how and what people think in their natural social environment is difficult, but researchers have shown enormous creativity in designing studies of these issues. If you are interested in learning more about them, consider taking an introductory social psychology course. Many psychology departments also offer more advanced courses in this subfield, including a course on attitudes.

Summary and Key Terms

Social psychology examines how a person's behavior and mental processes are influenced by other people. One aspect of this study is *social cognition*, the mental processes by which people perceive and react to others.

The Individual in a Social World

Social Comparison

When people have no objective criteria by which to judge themselves, they turn to *social comparison*, using others as criteria against which to judge themselves. Categories of people that are habitually used for social comparison are known as *reference groups*. Comparison to reference groups sometimes produces *relative deprivation*.

Social Norms

Social *norms* are learned rules of behavior that tell people what they should and should not do in various situations. Norms also lead people to develop expectations about how others will act. Reciprocity is an example of one norm with a widespread influence on everyday life.

Social Perception

Social perception guides impressions of others and interpretations of the reasons for their behavior.

First Impressions

First impressions are formed easily and quickly, in part because people use existing *schemas* when they perceive others. Often they apply a *schema-plus-correction process*. First impressions are difficult to change because people (1) are confident of their impressions of others, (2) tend to interpret new information so that it is consistent with the original impression, (3) tend to remember their general impression or schema better than any correction that is later added, and (4) often act in ways that elicit confirming information, a process known as a *self-fulfilling prophecy*.

Explaining Behavior: Attribution

Attribution is the process of explaining the causes of people's behavior, including one's own. People tend to attribute behavior to causes that are either internal or external to the actor. In general, people do this by applying three criteria to the behavior: consensus, consistency, and distinctiveness. Attributions are also shaped by *attributional biases*, which are tendencies to distort one's view of behavior systematically. The most common are the *fundamental attribution error*, the *actor-observer bias*, and the *self-serving bias*. In addition, people often protect themselves

from admitting something threatening (especially about themselves) through unrealistic optimism, a general illusion of control, and self-handicapping strategies.

Interpersonal Attraction

Keys to Attraction

Interpersonal attraction is a function of many variables. Propinquity is important because it allows for familiarity. The situation in which people first meet is important because positive or negative aspects of the situation tend to be associated with the other person. Obviously, characteristics of the other person are also important. Initially, attraction is strongest to those who are most physically attractive. But for long-term relationships, the *matching hypothesis* applies: people tend to choose others who have about the same level of physical attractiveness. Attraction is also greatest when two people share many similar attitudes.

The Development of Intimate Relationships

The defining characteristic of an intimate relationship is interdependence. The development of an intimate relationship is a slow process that depends primarily on increasingly deeper and broader levels of self-disclosure. The most important components of an intimate relationship are affection and emotional expressiveness; these often lead to feelings of support, cohesiveness, and sexuality.

Love and Marriage

Sternberg's triangular theory of love suggests that it is a function of three components: passion, intimacy, and commitment. Depending on the relative strengths of the three components, there are qualitatively different types of love, including passionate love, companionate love, fatuous love, and consumate love. Marital satisfaction is greatest when self-disclosure is high in both partners. It is also important that the two people perceive the relationship as being equitable and fair. This permits trust and creates a willingness for each person to make short-term sacrifices for the long-term viability of the relationship. Finally, simple liking and respect for each other are important because they allow people to deal effectively with conflict and anger.

Attitudes

Components of Attitudes

Most theorists agree that *attitudes* have three components: the cognitive, affective, and behavioral. However, the three components do not always fit together nicely, and it is often difficult to predict a specific behavior from what a person believes or feels about an object. *Cognitive dissonance theory* postulates that an inconsistency between or among cognitions (as in attitude-behavior discrepancies) creates a state of discomfort that often results in tension-reducing attitude change. *Self-perception theory* attempts to explain how attitudes can sometimes follow one's behavior rather than cause it.

Attitude Formation

Attitudes are often viewed as knowledge structures that are stored in long-term memory. Some attitudes are learned through modeling by parents or peers, others through classical conditioning or operant conditioning. Attitudes also appear to be subject to the mere exposure effect: all else being equal, people develop greater liking for a new object as they are exposed to it more often.

Attitude Change: The Role of Persuasive Communications

Attitude change is most likely when the source of a communication is perceived as credible, trustworthy, and similar to oneself. In general, a one-sided message is more effective when the audience is sympathetic to the speaker's point of view, while a two-sided message is more effective when the attitude of the audience is contrary to that of the speaker. Attitude change is also greatest when the speaker states explicit conclusions. *Fear appeals* can be highly effective—but only if they are not too frightening and are accompanied by specific guidelines for how to avoid the fearful consequences. Attitude change is greatest among individuals who have moderate levels of self-esteem. A high level of psychological involvement may encourage or discourage attitude change. If involvement is high because the communication shows how to obtain a desired outcome, attitude change is likely. Psychological *reactance* can lead people to change an attitude in the direction opposite to that advocated by the speaker.

Prejudice and Stereotypes

Stereotyping often leads to *prejudice* and *discrimination*.

Theories of Prejudice

One motivational theory suggests that prejudice and stereotyping are most common among people with an *authoritarian personality* because they feel a need to derogate others. Another approach notes that stereotypes, prejudice, and discriminatory behaviors can be learned from parents, peers, or the popular culture. This view has led to the *contact hypothesis*. It appears that intergroup contact can lead to a reduction of prejudice and more favorable attitudes toward the stereotyped group—but only if it occurs under specific conditions. Cognitive theories suggest that people categorize others into groups in order to reduce social complexity. The most common way to categorize is to place others into an *ingroup* or *outgroup*. Outgroup members are often discriminated against.

O U T L I N E

Interpersonal Behavior and Group Influences

Tom Penders, the men's basketball coach at the University of Texas, is an excellent social psychologist. After becoming frustrated with the team's lack of discipline, Penders introduced a new rule during the 1989–90 basketball season. Whenever a player missed a study hall without an excuse, a coach would call every player before dawn the next morning. All players would immediately go to the track. While the offending player stood in the middle and watched, all of his teammates would run laps as the sun rose. Penders felt that the punishment from teammates—or even the threat of such punishment—would be more effective than anything he himself could do to get the players to study. It looks as if he was correct: not one player missed a study hall without a valid excuse.

The previous chapter focused primarily on how people think about themselves and others. In this chapter we extend this analysis by examining how each person's behavior is influenced by others. This influence occurs in many ways (see the Linkages diagram), some of them direct and obvious and others quite subtle. To begin, we examine the tendency of people to act in ways that others suggest or demand.

Conformity and Compliance

Suppose you are with three friends. One says that Franklin Roosevelt was the greatest president in the history of the United States. You think that the greatest president was Abraham Lincoln, but before you can say anything, another friend agrees that it was Roosevelt, and then the other one does as well. What would you do? Disagree with all three? Maintain your opinion but keep quiet? Change your mind?

Individuals in almost any group—a family, a team, a government body—are likely to harbor differing attitudes and preferences. When people change their behavior or beliefs to match those of other members of a group, they are said to conform. **Conformity** occurs as a result of real

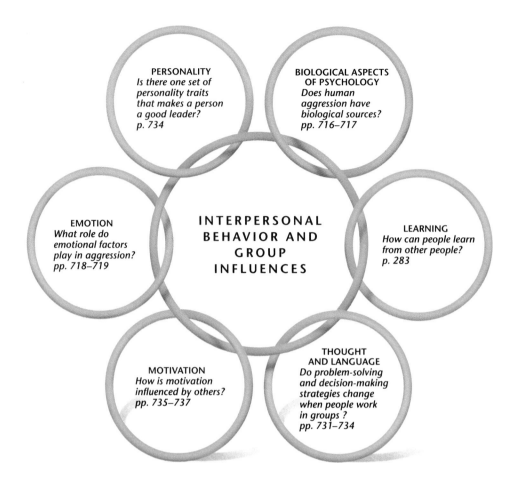

PERSONALITY
Is there one set of personality traits that makes a person a good leader?
p. 734

BIOLOGICAL ASPECTS OF PSYCHOLOGY
Does human aggression have biological sources?
pp. 716–717

EMOTION
What role do emotional factors play in aggression?
pp. 718–719

INTERPERSONAL BEHAVIOR AND GROUP INFLUENCES

LEARNING
How can people learn from other people?
p. 283

MOTIVATION
How is motivation influenced by others?
pp. 735–737

THOUGHT AND LANGUAGE
Do problem-solving and decision-making strategies change when people work in groups?
pp. 731–734

▪ Look at the diagram above, which illustrates some of the relationships between the topics of this chapter, interpersonal behavior and group processes, and other chapter topics. The diagram shows just a small sample of the linkages, since all the mental and behavioral processes discussed in previous chapters may be influenced by other people. In fact, research by social psychologists shows that the mere presence of other people can influence a person's motivation and performance.

Research by social psychologists goes beyond showing how other people affect an individual; it also explores patterns of behavior among people, such as aggression and altruism. To study these behaviors, social psychologists draw on research from virtually all other subfields of psychology. To examine aggression, for example, social psychologists have considered work ranging from the observations of ethologists to the theories of Freud. They have examined the role that might be played in aggression by biological factors, emotions, learning, and other processes. The page numbers in the diagram indicate where these and other linkages are discussed. ▪

or imagined, though *unspoken*, group pressure (Levine, 1989). When everyone around you stands up to applaud a performance you thought was mediocre, you may conform by standing as well. No one tells you to do this; the group's behavior simply creates a silent but influential pressure to follow suit. **Compliance**, in contrast, occurs when people adjust their behavior because of a direct request. If the last holdout for acquittal on a jury finally succumbs to the other jurors' browbeating, he or she has complied with overt social pressure.

The Role of Norms

Conformity and compliance are usually generated by a group's spoken or unspoken norms. As defined in Chapter 17, norms establish rules for behavior in given situations.

Muzafer Sherif (1937) managed to chart the formation of a group norm by taking advantage of a perceptual illusion called the *autokinetic phenomenon*. If you are placed in a completely dark room and shown a small, stationary point of light, the light will appear to move. (*Autokinetic* means "self-movement.") Some people tend to see a lot of movement and others report only a little. Each person's estimates of the apparent movement tend to stay within a small, characteristic range, such as from one to two inches or from five to six inches. Sherif put several people together in a dark room, switched on a point of light, and asked each person to report aloud how far the light had moved on repeated exposures. Eventually, the subjects' estimates tended to fall within a common *group* range; they had established a group norm. Even more important, when the individuals in the group were later tested alone, they continued to respond according to this norm.

The subjects in Sherif's experiment began by disagreeing with one another about an ambiguous situation and only slowly developed a group norm. Solomon Asch (1956) examined how people would respond when they were faced with a norm that already existed but that was obviously wrong. He showed subjects a standard line like the one in Figure 18.1(a); then they saw a display like that in Figure 18.1(b). Their task was to pick out the line in the display that was the same length as the line they had been shown first.

Each subject performed the task as part of a small group, but in reality all of the other participants were confederates of the experimenter. There were two conditions. In the control condition, the subject had to respond before any of the other participants. In the experimental condition, the subject did not respond until after the confederates did. The confederates chose the obviously correct response on six trials, but on the other twelve trials they all gave the same, obviously incorrect response. Thus, on twelve trials, each subject was confronted with a "social reality" created by the group norm that conflicted with the physical reality created by what the person could clearly see. Only 5 percent of the subjects in the control condition ever made a mistake on this easy perceptual task. However, among subjects who heard the confederates' responses before giving their own, about 70 percent made at least one error by conforming to the group norm.

Why Do People Conform?

Why did the people in Asch's experiment give so many incorrect responses when they were capable of near-perfect performance? One possibility, called

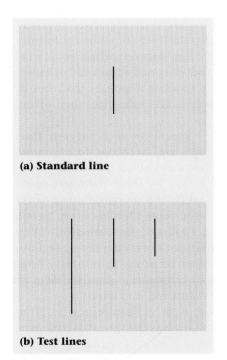

Figure 18.1
Types of Stimulus Lines Used in Experiments by Asch
Subjects in Asch's experiments saw a new set of lines on each of eighteen trials. Such experiments demonstrate that people often conform to the views of others in a group.

(a) Standard line

(b) Test lines

These worshipers at Mecca exemplify the power of religion and other social forces to produce conformity to group norms.

public conformity, is that they did not really change their minds. Instead, perhaps they gave an answer they did not believe simply because it was the socially desirable thing to do. Another possibility is called *private acceptance*: perhaps the subjects used the confederates' responses as legitimate evidence about reality, were convinced that their own perceptions were wrong, and so changed their minds. Morton Deutsch and Harold Gerard (1955) reasoned that if conformity disappeared when people gave their responses in private with complete anonymity, then Asch's findings must reflect public conformity, not private acceptance. In fact, conformity does decrease when people can respond anonymously instead of publicly, but it is not eliminated (Deutsch & Gerard, 1955). People sometimes publicly produce responses that they do not believe, but hearing other people's responses also influences their private beliefs (Moscovici, 1985).

Why do group norms wield such power? Recent research suggests three influential factors (Levine, 1989). First, people are motivated to be correct (Insko et al., 1985), and norms provide information about what is right and wrong. Second, people are motivated to be liked by other members of the group (Insko et al., 1983). Finally, norms guide the dispensation of social reinforcement and punishment (Levine, 1989). From childhood on, people learn that going along with group norms is good and earns rewards. (These positive outcomes presumably help compensate for not always saying or doing exactly what one pleases.) They also learn that breaking a norm may bring punishments ranging from scoldings for small violations to imprisonment for nonconformity with norms that have been translated into laws.

Consider what life would be like if there were no conformity to group norms—if, for example, no one paid attention to norms about taking turns when speaking, knocking before opening a closed door, or respecting people's rights to their own property. At best, life would be chaotic and unpredictable; at worst, the fabric of society would begin to disintegrate. At the same time, if everyone conformed all the time and in exactly the same way, the world might be a rather boring place, bereft of the variety, eccentricity, and even strangeness that makes human beings so fascinating. Thus, members of human social groups constantly search for the delicate balance that will assure group survival without squelching individuality (Goethals, 1986).

When Do People Conform?

Clearly, people do not always conform to group influence. In the Asch studies, for example, nearly 30 percent of the subjects did not go along with the confederates' obviously erroneous judgments. Countless experiments have probed the question of what combinations of people and circumstances do and do not lead to conformity.

Ambiguity of the Situation Ambiguity is very important in determining how much conformity will occur. When Asch (1956) varied his line-comparison task so that it became more difficult to be sure of the correct answer, conformity to incorrect group norms rose markedly. As the physical reality of a situation becomes less clear, people rely more and more on others' opinions (Shaw, Rothschild & Strickland, 1957), and conformity to a group norm becomes more likely.

You can demonstrate conformity on any street corner. First, create an ambiguous situation by having several people look up at the top of a building or high in the sky. When curious people ask what is going on, be sure everyone excitedly reports seeing something vague but interesting—perhaps a tiny, shiny object or a faint, mysterious light. (The hint of a flying saucer sighting is always helpful in such exercises.) In a situation like this, in which the alleged stimulus is fleeting or difficult to see, people are likely to perceive your group as providing valid information about the world. If you are especially successful, conforming newcomers will begin persuading other passers-by that there is something fascinating to be seen.

Unanimity and Size of the Majority If ambiguity contributes so much to conformity, why did so many of Asch's subjects conform to a judgment that was unambiguously wrong? The answer has to do with the unanimity of the group's judgment and the number of people expressing it.

Specifically, people experience great pressure to conform as long as the majority is unanimous. If even one other person in the group disagrees with the majority view, conformity drops greatly. For example, when Asch (1951) arranged for just one confederate to disagree with the others, the incidence of conformity was reduced to less than 10 percent. Once unanimity is broken, it becomes much easier to disagree with the majority, even if the other nonconformist does not agree with the person's own view (Nemeth & Chiles, 1988).

Conformity also depends on the size of the group. Asch (1955) examined this relationship by varying the number of confederates in the group from one to fifteen. The amount of conformity to incorrect norms grew as the number of people in the group increased, but most of the increase occurred as the size of the majority rose from one to about three or four members; further additions to the size of the majority had little effect. Other experimenters found different results, however. Under certain circumstances, conformity increased significantly as the size of the majority exceeded three or four (Gerard, Wilhelmy & Connolley, 1968; Milgram, Bickman & Berkowitz, 1969).

The key to these apparently contradictory results seems to lie in how people *perceive* the opinions of the majority (Wilder, 1977). In other words, the majority may have an actual size and a psychological size. The *psychological size* equals the number of members whose assessments are perceived as independent, reflecting each individual's carefully considered judgment. If everyone in a large group gives the same spoken answer to a question, one after the other, you might consider only the first three or four responses to be independent assessments. After that, you might perceive the rest of the people to be giving answers just to be compatible, and their answers may have little effect on you. Only the first few answers, which you perceive as independent, determine the psychological size of the majority. So, if subjects in Asch's original experiment believed that only the first three or four members were giving independent responses, the psychological size of the majority would remain at three or four, regardless of how many people were actually present. Conformity, therefore, would not increase with the actual size of the majority. If, however, the responses of all the other people are perceived to be independent, conformity increases steadily as the number of group members rises (Wilder, 1977).

Personal Characteristics   In general, people with high status in a group are less likely to conform than those with relatively low status (Buss et al., 1987). Attraction to a group also influences conformity. People are more likely to conform when they like the members of a group than when there is little or no attraction (Forsyth, 1983). Attraction may increase conformity because people tend to trust the judgment of those they like or because they want the approval of people to whom they are attracted. Conformity based on the desire for approval from attractive group members appears to be particularly likely among those with low self-esteem (Stang, 1972).

Another personal characteristic that may shape conformity is the degree to which people are concerned with being liked or with being correct. People who are preoccupied with being liked are likely to conform, particularly when they are also attracted to the others in the group. In contrast, people who are preoccupied with being right are less likely to conform, no matter how much or how little they are attracted to others in the group (Insko et al., 1985).

Inducing Compliance

The experiments just described involved conformity: the subjects experienced psychological pressure to conform to the views or actions of others, even though they were not specifically requested to do so. In contrast, *compliance* involves changing what you say or do because of a direct request from someone who has no authority over you.

How is compliance brought about? Many people believe that the direct approach is always best: if you want something, ask for it. But salespeople, political strategists, social psychologists, and other experts on the subject have learned that often the best way to get something is to ask for something else. This strategy usually takes one of three forms: the foot-in-the-door technique, the door-in-the-face procedure, or the low-ball approach.

The *foot-in-the-door technique* consists of beginning with small requests and working up to larger ones. Its name comes from an experiment in which homeowners in a wealthy California neighborhood were approached in one of two ways. In some cases, the experimenter claimed to represent a group concerned with reducing traffic accidents in the community and asked the homeowners if a large and unattractive "Drive Carefully" sign could be placed on their front lawn. Approximately 17 percent of the people approached in this way complied with the request. In the foot-in-the-door condition, home-owners were first asked only to sign a petition urging their legislators to work toward decreasing the number of accidents in the community. Several weeks later, a different experimenter asked these same people to place the "Drive

Carefully" sign on their lawn. In this case, 55 percent of the people complied (Freedman & Fraser, 1966).

Subsequent research has confirmed the compliance-inducing effect of preceding a large request with a much smaller one (Beaman et al., 1983). Why should this be so? First, people are usually far more likely to comply with a request whose cost in time, money, effort, or inconvenience is low rather than high. Second, complying with a small request makes people think of themselves as supporting and being committed to the source of the request. This occurs through the self-perception and cognitive dissonance processes discussed in Chapter 17 (e.g., "If I signed the petition, I must care enough about traffic safety to do something about it"). In the study just described, signing the petition constituted an explicit statement about concern for safe driving. When faced with the higher-cost request (displaying the sign), the subjects were likely to recall their previous action and to perceive their strong commitment to the safety issue. The likelihood of complying with the request was thus increased because doing so was consistent with these people's self-perceptions and past actions (Schwarzwald, Bizman & Raz, 1983).

People take advantage of the foot-in-the-door technique all the time. For example, some companies first ask prospective customers to respond to a mail survey about their product and then ask to visit to explain how it works (with no obligation, of course). Only then is the customer asked to buy the product. In some cases, the initial request requires only that the prospective customer accept a free gift. Agreeing to fill out the forms necessary to receive the gift constitutes the first, low level of compliance, to be followed, the company hopes, by compliance with a later request to buy something. Free gifts not only constitute a foot in the door but are likely to invoke the reciprocity norm discussed in Chapter 17: once they accept something, many people feel obligated to reciprocate by buying something.

The opposite approach, known as the *door-in-the-face procedure*, can also be effective in obtaining compliance (Cann, Sherman & Elkes, 1975). This strategy begins with a very large request that is likely to be denied. Then the person making the original request concedes that it was rather extreme and substitutes a lesser alternative, which is what the requester wanted in the first place. Because the new request now seems so modest in contrast with the first one, it is more likely to be granted.

Lech Walesa leading Poland's Solidarity Union's negotiating team. The door-in-the-face strategy for creating compliance is the heart and soul of most bargaining situations. In labor negotiations, both the company and the union usually begin by proposing wage and benefits packages that are obviously unacceptable to the other side. But neither side expects the initial proposal to be accepted; it is only the first and the most extreme request, compared to which later proposals will appear to be a compromise.

A third technique for "getting X by asking for Y" is called the *low-ball approach* (Cialdini et al., 1978). The first step is to obtain a verbal commitment from someone to do something. The second step is to show that only a higher-cost version of the initial request will do any good. Finally, that higher-cost request is made. The low-ball approach differs from the foot-in-the-door technique because the initial request is escalated after it is agreed to but before it can be fulfilled. For example, a student we know got a ride to campus every day in time for an 8:00 A.M. class from a friend whose first class was not until 10:00. She did it by first asking him if she could hitch a ride every day. Only after he had said yes did she tell him that she had to be picked up by 7:30. Apparently the low-ball approach works because once the initial request is granted, the person feels committed to help even if a later version of the request is larger (Burger & Petty, 1981).

Low-ball methods are often used in *bait-and-switch* sales schemes. For example, after a customer agrees to buy a microwave oven at a special sale price, the salesperson may come back from the storeroom to say that none of those models is left but that they do have another version that is even better, at a "slightly" higher price. Experts at this tactic use it so skillfully that customers may end up spending two or three times what they had planned.

Obedience

Compliance involves a change in behavior in response to a request. In contrast, **obedience** involves complying with an explicit *demand*, typically from an acknowledged authority figure. Many Nazi soldiers killed innocent people because they felt compelled to obey direct orders. And in 1978, in Guyana, South America, nearly one thousand members of a California-based organization called the People's Temple committed mass suicide when they obeyed an order from their leader, the Reverend Jim Jones, to drink poison.

Obedience in the Laboratory

In the 1960s Stanley Milgram realized that psychologists knew little about obedience and so developed a laboratory procedure to study it. Through an ad in local newspapers, he recruited forty male volunteers between the ages of twenty and fifty for his first experiment. Among the subjects were professionals, white-collar businessmen, and unskilled workers (Milgram, 1963).

Imagine you are one of the people who answered the ad. When you arrive for the experiment, you join a fifty-year-old gentleman who has also volunteered and has been scheduled for the same session. The experimenter explains that the purpose of the experiment is to examine the effects of punishment on learning. One of you—the "learner"—will try to learn a list of words; the other—the "teacher"—will help the learner remember the words by administering electric shock whenever he makes a mistake. Then the experimenter turns to you and asks you to draw one of two cards out of a hat. The one you draw says "TEACHER." You think to yourself that this must be your lucky day.

Now the learner is taken into another room and strapped into a chair, as shown in Figure 18.2. Electrodes are attached to his arms. You are shown a shock generator with thirty switches. The experimenter explains that the switch on the far left administers a very mild, 15-volt shock and that each succeeding switch increases the shock by 15 volts; the one on the far right delivers 450 volts. You also notice several labels on the shock generator. The far left section is labeled "Slight shock." Looking across the panel, you see "Moderate shock,"

On trial for his role in the Iran-Contra scandal, Marine colonel Oliver North argued that everything he did had been approved by his superiors and that he was doing his duty by following their orders. Obedience to legitimate authority provides the foundation of military discipline and is vital in civilian life as well, but legal and moral conflicts arise when obedience to a superior requires violating the law or abandoning personal standards.

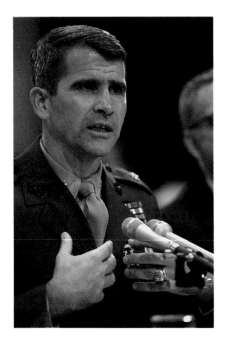

Figure 18.2
Studying Obedience in the Laboratory
In this photograph from Milgram's original experiment, a man is being strapped into a chair with electrodes on his arm. Although subjects in the experiment do not know it, the man is actually a confederate of the experimenter and receives no shock.

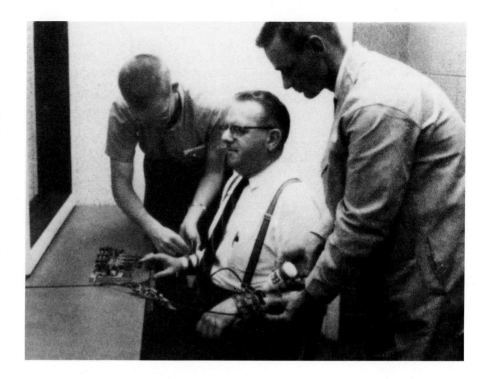

"Very strong shock," and, at the far right, "Danger—severe shock." The last two switches are ominously labeled "XXX." The experimenter explains that you, the teacher, will begin by reading a list of word pairs to the learner. Then you will go through the list again, presenting just one word of each pair; the learner should indicate which word went with it. After the first mistake, you are to throw the switch to deliver 15 volts of shock. Each time the learner makes a mistake, you are to increase the shock by 15 volts.

You begin, following the experimenter's instructions. But after the learner makes his fifth mistake and you throw the switch to give him 75 volts, you hear a loud moan. At 90 volts, the learner cries out in pain. At 150 volts, he screams and asks to be let out of the experiment. You look to the experimenter, who says, "Proceed with the next question."

What do you do? In fact, no shock was delivered in Milgram's experiments. The "learner" was always a confederate of the experimenter, and the moans and other signs of pain were an act. But you do not know that. What would you do in this situation? Suppose you continue and eventually deliver 180 volts. The learner screams that he cannot stand the pain any longer and starts banging on the wall. The experimenter looks at you and says, "You have no other choice; you must go on." Would you continue? Would you keep going even when the learner begged to be let out of the experiment and then fell silent? Would you administer 450 volts of potentially deadly shock to a perfect stranger who has done you no harm, just because an experimenter demands that you do so?

Figure 18.3 shows what the subjects in Milgram's experiment did. Not one subject stopped before 300 volts. Of the forty subjects in the experiment, twenty-six (or 65 percent) went all the way to the 450-volt level. The decision to continue was difficult and stressful for the subjects. Many protested repeatedly; but each time the experimenter told them to continue, they did so. Here is a partial transcript of what a typical subject said.

[After throwing the 180-volt switch]: *He can't stand it. I'm not going to kill that man in there. Do you hear him hollering? He's hollering. He can't stand it. What if something happens to him? I'm not going to get that man sick in there.*

Figure 18.3
Results of Milgram's Obedience Experiment

Note that 65 percent of the subjects tested gave the maximum amount of shock available. When Milgram asked a group of undergraduates how the subjects in the experiment would respond, they estimated that fewer than 2 percent would go all the way to 450 volts. He then asked a group of practicing psychiatrists, who gave similar predictions.

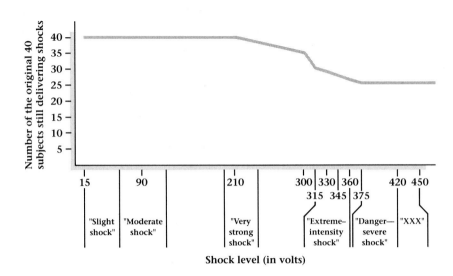

Source: Milgram, 1963.

He's hollering in there. Do you know what I mean? I mean, I refuse to take responsibility. He's getting hurt in there. He's in there hollering. Too many left here. Geez, if he gets them wrong. There are too many of them left. I mean, who is going to take responsibility if anything happens to that gentleman?

[After the experimenter accepts responsibility]: *All right . . .*

[After administering 240 volts]: *Oh no, you mean I've got to keep going up with the scale? No sir, I'm not going to kill that man. I'm not going to give him 450 volts.*

[After the experimenter says, "The experiment requires that you go on."]: *I know it does, but that man is hollering in there, sir.* (Milgram, 1974)

This subject administered shock up to 450 volts.

Factors Affecting Obedience

Milgram had not expected so many subjects to deliver such apparently intense shocks. Was there something about his procedure that produced such high levels of obedience? To find out, Milgram and other researchers varied the original procedure in numerous ways. The overall level of obedience to an authority figure was nearly always quite high, but the degree of obedience was affected by several characteristics of the situation and procedure.

Prestige   One possibility is that the status and legitimacy of the experimenter helped produce high levels of obedience in Milgram's original experiment. After all, that study was conducted at Yale University, and the newspaper ad had stated that the experimenter was a professor at Yale. To test the effects of status and prestige, Milgram rented a deserted office building in Bridgeport, Connecticut. He then placed an ad in the local newspaper that made no mention of Yale and instead said the research was sponsored by a private firm. In all other ways, the experimental procedure was identical to the original.

Under these less prestigious circumstances, the level of obedience dropped, but less than Milgram expected; 48 percent of the subjects continued to the maximum level of shock, compared with 65 percent in the original study. Milgram concluded that people were willing to do great harm to another even if the authority figure was not "particularly reputable or distinguished."

Proximity   In another variation on Milgram's original design, the extent of contact between the subject and the authority figure—the experimenter—was varied. For example, when the authority figure gave the instructions by phone, only 20 percent of the subjects gave the maximum shock; many other subjects lied, saying that they were continuing to administer higher levels of shock when they were not (Rada & Rogers, 1973). However, obedience remained quite high if the authority figure gave the instructions in person and then left the room (Rada & Rogers, 1973). In other words, the ability to obtain obedience apparently depended on some personal contact. Once the experimenter was established as an authority in the subject's mind, the contact did not need to be maintained. As proximity to the authority figure declined, however, obedience tended to drop as well.

Proximity between subject and victim also had an effect, as Figure 18.4 shows. As proximity to the victim increased, the level of obedience decreased substantially (Milgram, 1965). These results are consistent with the belief that it is easier for soldiers to follow orders to kill other people by high-altitude bombing than by, say, stabbing.

Presence of Others Who Disobey   These studies may lead you to wonder (as Milgram did) how the presence of other people might affect obedience. Milgram (1965) created a situation in which there were three teachers. Teacher 1 (who was a confederate of the experimenter) read the words to the learner. Teacher 2 (who was also a confederate) indicated whether the learner had made a correct or incorrect response. Then it was up to Teacher 3 (the actual subject) to deliver the shock when a mistake was made. At 150 volts, the learner began to complain bitterly that the shock was too painful. At this point, Teacher 1 (a confederate) refused to participate any longer and left the room. The experimenter asked him to come back, but he refused. The experimenter then instructed Teachers 2 and 3 to continue by themselves. The experiment continued for several more trials. However, at 210 volts, Teacher 2 said that the learner was suffering too much pain and also refused to participate. The experimenter then told Teacher 3 (the actual subject) to continue the procedure. In this case, only 10 percent of the subjects (compared with 65 percent in the original study) continued to deliver shock all the way up to 450 volts. Thus, as the research on conformity would suggest, it appears

Milgram's research suggested that the close proximity of an authority figure enhances obedience to authority. This principle is clearly employed in military organizations, where no member is ever far away from a source of authority in the form of a person of higher rank.

Figure 18.4
Obedience as a Function of Proximity to the Victim
The more feedback the subject received from the victim, the less shock he or she administered. In the remote condition, the subject and learner were in different rooms, and the subject could neither see nor hear the learner. In the voice feedback condition, the subject could hear the learner but not see him. In the proximity condition, subject and learner were in the same room, so that the learner could be seen and heard. In the touch proximity condition, the subject had to press the learner's hand onto a metal dish in order to administer the shock.

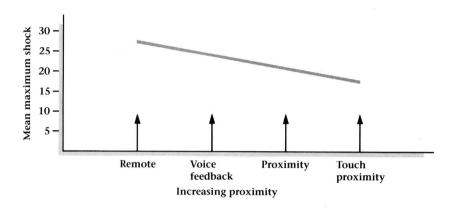

Source: Milgram, 1972.

Linkages: What ethical concerns limit studies of human obedience? (a link to the World of Psychology)

that the presence of others who disobey is the most powerful factor reducing subjects' obedience.

Evaluating Milgram's Studies

Nearly all social scientists agree that Milgram's studies were telling experiments. For the first time, here was evidence that a person did not have to be sadistic, or in any way "abnormal," to inflict pain—or even death—on another person (Miller, 1986). Given the right circumstances, it appeared that nearly everyone is capable of such acts. Nevertheless the meaning and ethics of Milgram's work continue to be debated (Ross, 1988).

Ethical Questions   Although the "learners" in Milgram's experiment suffered no pain, the subjects did. Milgram himself (1963) observed subjects "sweat, stutter, tremble, groan, bite their lips, and dig their fingernails into their flesh. Full-blown uncontrollable seizures were observed for three subjects" (p. 375). Furthermore, Milgram's subjects learned something about themselves that they really did not want to know: that they could be persuaded to inflict severe harm, possibly even death, on an innocent person.

Was it ethical for Milgram to inflict such burdens on his subjects? Milgram made several arguments in defense of his experiments. First, he noted that he expected nearly all of the subjects to stop at some point, certainly before they reached the "danger" level. Second, Milgram argued that his debriefing of the subjects prevented the experiment from doing any lasting harm. At the conclusion of the experiment, each subject was told that most people went all the way to the 450-volt level and that the learner did not experience any shock at all. Then the learner was brought into the room and interacted with the subject in a friendly fashion. Milgram claimed that this procedure helped the subjects understand that their behavior in the experiment was not unusual. Third, when Milgram later sent his subjects a questionnaire, 84 percent indicated they were glad that they had participated in the study. They felt that they had learned something important about themselves and that the experience had been worthwhile. Thus, Milgram argued, the experience was actually a positive one.

Ethical questions are difficult ones. The dialogue between Milgram and his critics has helped push investigators to consider further the ethical implications of their research. As we noted in the discussion of ethics in Chapter 1, psychologists have become increasingly sensitive to these issues. Today, committees evaluate proposals for experiments and are charged with protecting human subjects, balancing subjects' welfare against the gains that might result from an experiment. It is unlikely that these committees would approve Milgram's study if he proposed it today, and less controversial ways to study obedience are now being developed (Sackoff & Weinstein, 1988).

Questions of Meaning   Milgram's results were dramatic, but do they mean that most people are putty in the hands of authority figures? (For a summary of those results, plus the results of studies on conformity and compliance, see "In Review: Types of Social Influence.") Under the right circumstances, do people blindly follow inhumane orders from their leaders? Would you and your neighbors obey orders to incinerate people, as many Nazis and their collaborators did?

Some people interpret Milgram's data in just that fashion, and they may be right. However, drawing broad conclusions about human behavior in general

In Review: Types of Social Influence

Type	Definition	Key Findings
Conformity	A change in behavior or beliefs to match those of others in a group	In cases of ambiguity, people slowly develop a group norm and then adhere to it.
		Conformity occurs because people want to be right, because they want to be liked by others, and because conformity to group norms is usually reinforced.
		Conformity usually increases as the ambiguity of the situation, the psychological size of the majority, and the attractiveness of the group increases. Nonconformity is most likely among members who enjoy high status within the group.
Compliance	A change in behavior or beliefs because of a direct request	Compliance increases with the foot-in-the-door technique, which begins with a small request and works up to a larger one.
		The door-in-the-face procedure can also be used. After making a large request that is denied, the speaker substitutes a less extreme alternative that was desired all along.
		The low-ball approach also elicits compliance. A verbal commitment for something minor is first obtained; then the person claims that only a higher-cost version of the original request will suffice.
Obedience	A change in behavior to match an explicit demand, typically from an acknowledged authority figure	People may inflict great harm on others as long as an authority demands that they do so.
		Even when people obey orders to harm another person, they often agonize over the decision. The psychological stress involved can be extremely intense.
		People are most likely to disobey orders to harm another person when they have close proximity to the victim or see another person disobey.

on the basis of Milgram's results may be a mistake. The results of Milgram's experiments may, in large measure, reflect subjects' willingness to go along with an experimenter's charade, not obedience to dangerous demands. Martin Orne argued, for example, that many of Milgram's subjects must have realized that an experimenter would not actually endanger the life of another human being merely in order to study learning. Some subjects might also have noticed that, since the experimenter could have acted as the "teacher" himself, it must be their own behavior, not the learner's, that was under study (Orne & Holland, 1968).

If Orne is right, Milgram's ingenious research may have generated overly pessimistic conclusions about human beings. However, continuing news accounts of cruelty by people obeying the authority of military, terrorist, and cult leaders make it impossible to ignore Milgram's findings. Soldiers of every army in history, including U.S. soldiers, appear to have followed orders that resulted in inhumane acts against civilians as well as against enemy soldiers. Although many people routinely question and overtly oppose authority figures whenever they feel it is important to do so, most people do what authorities tell them to do, even when they have doubts.

The truth about the extent of human obedience and the circumstances under which it will be displayed remains to be discovered, but it may be less flattering than one might wish. We say this partly because much inhumanity occurs even without pressure for obedience. For example, a good deal of people's aggressiveness toward other people appears to come from within. In the next section, we consider human aggressiveness and some of the circumstances that influence its expression.

Aggression

Carl Panzram proclaimed with perverse pride that virtually his entire life was spent trying to figure out ways to make people suffer (Gaddis & Long, 1970). In the late 1920s he decided he would build a bomb designed to explode on contact and place it on a train track in the middle of a long tunnel. After the explosion, and before the passengers could escape from the train, Panzram planned to pump poisonous gas into the tunnel and, wearing a gas mask, go in and rob all of the bodies. He estimated that he could kill nearly four hundred people and collect up to $100,000, which he planned to use to finance additional acts of terrorism. Fortunately, Panzram's technical expertise was not sufficient to carry out his plans in full, but he did manage to kill twenty-five people before being caught, tried, and executed (Harrison, 1976).

Aggression occurs whenever an act is intended to harm another person (Krebs & Miller, 1985). It is easy to dismiss aggression as an aberration, something that is committed only by those who have some type of psychological disorder. Under the right circumstances, however, even the most peaceable person can lash out aggressively in anger. Over 70 percent of parents in the United States report that they have slapped their child in anger, and one-fifth of all parents have hit their children with objects such as sticks or leather belts. About one-third of husbands and wives have hit their spouse in anger, and life-threatening attacks with guns or knives occur in about 1 in 20 marriages (Straus et al., 1980). Violent crimes now occur at the rate of 1.5 million per year in the United States alone, including over 20,000 murders and 90,000 rapes (The World Almanac, 1988). Psychologists have long examined why human aggression is so prevalent and what circumstances make it more or less likely.

Why Are People Aggressive?

Aggression is a complex phenomenon, and theorists have attempted to explain it at several levels. Some theorists believe that evolution endowed each person with an instinctive predisposition toward aggressiveness. Others claim that parents, peers, and the culture at large teach people to aggress, and to do so in particular ways. Still others examine how brain abnormalities, hormones, and other physiological factors may set the stage for aggression. We will examine each of these views.

Instinct Theories Freud proposed that aggression is an instinctive biological urge that gradually builds and at some point must be released. Sometimes it is released in the form of physical or verbal abuse against another. Sometimes the aggressive impulse is turned inward and produces self-punitive actions, even suicide. Sometimes it can be released through socially acceptable activities, such as playing football, "beating" an opponent at chess, or "destroying" the enemy in a video arcade game. The best that can be hoped for, according to Freud, is that aggressive impulses will be channeled into socially acceptable forms.

Evidence for Freud's view that humans possess an aggressive instinct that presses for expression is scant. True, many people display aggressive behavior, but this behavior could be the product of learning rather than the expression of an instinct. In fact, in some societies, such as the Arapesh of New Guinea, aggression is rare, and peaceful coexistence and cooperation is the norm (Mead, 1963).

A slightly more complicated, milder version of an instinct theory of aggression comes from ethologists. As noted in Chapter 11, *ethologists* study the behavior of various species in their natural habitat. Many ethologists believe that all animals, including human beings, have an aggressive instinct. Unlike Freud, however, they suggest that for aggression to occur, an environmental stimulus, or **releaser**, must be present. Thus, ethological theory suggests that

Linkages: What motivates people to be aggressive? (a link to Motivation)

Playing football provides a socially acceptable channel through which people can express aggression and experience catharsis. According to psychoanalytic theory, catharsis can also occur vicariously, as when we watch other people display aggression in contact sports, violent films, and the like.

genetic factors create predispositions for aggression and that whenever aggressive impulses *and* a releaser are present an aggressive response is triggered (Lorenz, 1981).

The inherited nature of aggressive impulses is certainly apparent in the animal world. Among animals, aggressive behaviors tend to be ritualized, stereotyped, and triggered by specific stimuli. Furthermore, the same aggressive behaviors appear even if the animals have been raised in isolation and thus could not learn them from other animals (Flynn et al., 1970). In one study, the most aggressive members of a large group of mice were interbred; then the most aggressive of their offspring were also interbred. After this procedure had been followed for twenty-five generations, the resulting animals would immediately attack any mouse put in their cage. On the other hand, continuous inbreeding of the least aggressive members of the original group produced animals that were so nonaggressive that they would refuse to fight even when attacked (Lagerspetz, 1979).

Does the ethological theory describe human as well as animal behavior? Studies of twins reared together or apart do suggest that there may be a genetic component to aggression in humans (Rushton et al., 1986; Tellegen et al., 1988). However, the ethological theory of aggression has two major problems (Larsen, 1976). First, virtually all of the evidence comes from research with lower animals, where instincts of all kinds play a larger role than they do in humans (Lagerspetz & Lagerspetz, 1983). For this reason, many psychologists doubt whether the results apply to human beings. Second, the ethological theory does not account for the many specific forms that human aggression can take (Scott, 1983). People aggress with fists, guns, bombs, chemicals, knives, cars, insults, and any number of other weapons. Thus, even if an aggressive instinct sets the stage for aggression, the specific form it takes is often determined by learning (Kamin, 1986).

Biological Theories   Instinct theories suggest that the capacity for aggression is built into the human animal; biological theories seek to identify the biological structures or processes responsible for the expression of aggressive behavior. The search for these biological factors has focused on the nervous and endocrine systems.

Consider the case of Charles Whitman, a former altar boy and Eagle Scout, who was a student at the University of Texas when he began experiencing episodes of intense anxiety. He got into several fights, assaulted his wife, and, in conversations with several psychiatrists, revealed impulses toward extremely violent behavior. Shortly thereafter, he murdered his wife and his mother, then took a high-powered rifle with a telescopic sight to the top of a campus observation tower and for two hours shot at everyone he saw. He killed fourteen people and wounded two dozen more before the police killed him. An autopsy on Whitman revealed a tumor the size of a walnut in the area of the forebrain called the amygdala (see Figure 12.6). It is by no means true that all mass murderers have such tumors, but some people who exhibit sudden and extreme forms of aggression are suffering from some type of brain disorder (Mednick et al., 1984).

Numerous brain areas can influence aggression (Albert & Walsh, 1984). For example, lesions of the septum, the hypothalamus, and related areas in mice, rats, cats, dogs, and humans are followed by *defensive aggression*, which is heightened aggressive responsiveness to stimuli that are not ordinarily threatening. Stimulating different parts of the hypothalamus in cats produces two different types of aggression (Flynn et al., 1970): intense rage, in which the cats arch their backs, hiss violently, and attack anything that moves, or a

Linkages: Does human aggression have biological sources? (a link to Biological Aspects of Psychology)

slower, more gradual attack that resembles the normal predatory behavior of cats. When surgical lesions are made in the same hypothalamic regions in cats, aggressive behaviors often cease altogether. In most animal studies, lesions in the amygdala also decrease aggression. Indeed, small lesions in the human amygdala have been used to reduce aggression in people suffering from hyperaggressiveness brought on by epilepsy. Clearly, the brain has a strong influence in determining when aggression will occur.

Hormones also play a role. In both lower animals and humans, males tend to be more aggressive than females (Eagly & Steffen, 1986). This gender difference suggests that aggression may be related to differences in the amount of the masculine hormone *testosterone* present in each sex (Olweus, 1986). Experiments have shown that aggressive behavior increases or decreases dramatically with the amount of testosterone in an animal's body (Moyer, 1983), and violent criminals have been found to have abnormally high levels (Dabbs et al., 1987). In Norway, 224 men who had been convicted of aggressive sex crimes were castrated, which dramatically lowered their testosterone levels, their sex drive, and sexually related aggressiveness. But these men still behaved aggressively in situations unrelated to sex (Bremer, 1959). This result suggests that testosterone has its greatest and most durable influence, not through day-to-day effects, but through its impact on early brain development. In fact, artificial elevation in testosterone during prenatal development is associated with higher levels of aggression in adult humans (Reinisch, 1981).

Neurotransmitters may also play a role in aggression. In animals, aggressive behavior tends to be associated with high levels of adrenaline and nonadrenaline and low levels of serotonin. (These neurotransmitters are described in Chapter 3.) Conversely, when the level of adrenergic transmitters is low and serotonin is high, behavior tends to be far less aggressive (Whalen & Simon, 1984).

Learning Theories   In previous chapters we have described how cognitive-behavioral theorists emphasize the role of learned habits and thoughts in all aspects of human behavior. They recognize that biological and even instinctive factors set the stage for aggression, but they also say that most, if not all, aggressiveness can be best explained in terms of learning principles (Bandura, 1977; Zillmann, 1978b). Their research has documented two specific ways in which learning shapes aggressive behavior.

First, many aggressive responses are learned by watching others. The most obvious example is copycat crime, in which one person's well-publicized act of aggression (such as poisoning medicine in stores) is duplicated within days by other people. More generally, children learn and perform many novel aggressive responses that they see modeled by others (Bandura, 1983; Bandura, Ross & Ross, 1963). Bandura's "Bobo doll" experiments, which were described in Chapter 7, on learning, provided impressive demonstrations of the power of observational learning. Its significance is also highlighted by studies of the effects of televised violence, also discussed in Chapter 7. For example, the amount of violent content watched on television by eight-year-olds predicts aggressiveness in these children even ten years later (Centerwall, 1989; Eron, 1987). Because of individual differences in temperament, parental influences, and other factors, not everyone who sees aggression inevitably becomes aggressive. However, observational learning does play a significant role in the development and display of aggressive behavior (Berkowitz, 1984).

Second, the performance of aggressive acts depends greatly on the pattern of rewards and punishments a person has received. People become increasingly aggressive when they are positively reinforced for aggressiveness. Figure 18.5

Figure 18.5
Reinforcement and Aggression
In this experiment, people were asked to teach a person new material. They had the opportunity to administer electric shock as punishment for any errors that occurred. Some subjects were reinforced by the experimenter with praise when they delivered the shock. Other subjects were given no reinforcement for delivering shock. People who were reinforced for giving shock clearly became more aggressive over the course of the experiment.

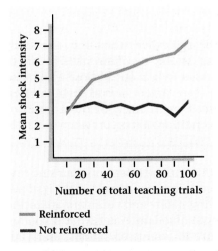

— Reinforced
— Not reinforced

Source: Geen & Stonner, 1971.

Learning to express aggression is especially easy for children living in war zones, where loaded weapons may serve as "toys" and where deadly aggressive acts are modeled almost daily.

illustrates one example. Other research indicates that people become less aggressive if they are punished for aggressive acts (Donnerstein & Donnerstein, 1976; Wilson & Rogers, 1975). In short, even if impulses toward aggression come partly from unlearned, biological sources, it appears that observing, practicing, and receiving rewards for aggression makes people more likely to behave aggressively when the right combination of impulse and opportunity occurs.

Clearly, human aggression has several possible sources. Sorting out the precise roles of instinct, physiology, and learning is difficult, and the task is complicated by emotional and environmental factors that can influence whether or not aggressive behavior occurs.

Emotional Factors in Aggression

Linkages: What role do emotional factors play in aggression? (a link to Emotion)

In general, people are more likely to be aggressive when they are both physiologically aroused and experiencing strong emotion such as anger (Berkowitz & Heimer, 1989). People tend either to lash out at those who make them angry or to displace their anger onto safe targets such as their children or dog. However, aggression can also be made more likely by other forms of emotional arousal, especially *frustration*, a condition that occurs when obstacles block the fulfillment of goals.

Frustration and Aggression　Suppose that a friend interrupts your studying for an exam by coming over unannounced to borrow a book. If things have been going well that day and you are feeling happy and confident about the exam, you are likely to be friendly and accommodating. But what if you are feeling frustrated? What if you are behind in your preparations, and your friend's visit represents the fifth interruption in the last hour? Under these emotional circumstances, you may react aggressively, perhaps berating your startled visitor for not calling ahead.

Your aggressiveness in this situation conforms to the behavior predicted by the **frustration-aggression hypothesis**, which was developed by John Dollard and his colleagues (Dollard et al., 1939). They proposed that "the occurrence of aggressive behavior always presupposes the existence of frustration, and contrawise . . . the existence of frustration always leads to some form of aggression" (p. 1). This hypothesis generated hundreds of experiments, many of which indicated that the hypothesis was too simple and too general. Frustration does not always produce aggression (Gentry, 1970). Sometimes it produces depression and withdrawal (Seligman, 1975). In addition, not all aggression is preceded by frustration. In many of the experiments described earlier, for example, the subjects were not frustrated, but they still made aggressive responses.

After many years of research, Leonard Berkowitz modified the frustration-aggression hypothesis in two ways. First, he suggested that frustration produces not aggression but a *readiness* to respond aggressively (Berkowitz, 1981). Once this readiness exists, cues in the environment that are associated with aggression will often lead a frustrated person to behave aggressively. Such cues could include objects such as guns or knives, television scenes of people arguing, and the like. Neither the frustration alone nor the cues alone are sufficient to set off aggression. When combined, however, they do. Support for this aspect of Berkowitz's theory has been quite strong (Geen & Donnerstein, 1983).

The second modification is that frustration creates a readiness to respond aggressively to the degree that it produces a negative emotion (Berkowitz, 1989). For example, unexpected failure at some task tends to create a more intense negative reaction than a failure that is expected (Berkowitz, 1988). For this reason, aggression is more likely to occur following an unexpected failure than after one that was expected. A number of experiments have supported this aspect of Berkowitz's theory as well. (See Finman & Berkowitz, 1989, for a review.)

Generalized Arousal Imagine you have just jogged two miles. You are hot, sweaty, and out of breath, but you are not angry. Still, the physiological arousal caused by jogging increases the probability that you will become aggressive if, say, a passer-by shouts an insult (Zillmann, 1983). Why? The answer lies in a phenomenon described in Chapter 12, on emotion: arousal from one experience may carry over to an independent situation, producing what is called *transferred excitation*. Thus, the physiological arousal caused by jogging may intensify your reaction to an insult (Sapolsky, 1984).

However, generalized arousal alone does not lead to aggression. It is most likely to produce aggression when the situation contains some reason, opportunity, or target for aggression (Zillmann, 1988). In one study, for example, people engaged in two minutes of vigorous exercise. Then they had the opportunity to deliver electric shock to another person. The exercise increased the level of shock delivered only if the subjects were first insulted (Zillmann, Katcher & Milavsky, 1972). Apparently, the arousal resulting from the exercise made aggression more likely; the insult "released" it. These findings are in keeping with the notion suggested by learning theorists (and by Berkowitz's revision of the frustration-aggression hypothesis) that aggression occurs not merely as a function of internal impulses *or* particular situations but as a result of the interaction of individual characteristics and particular environmental circumstances.

T H I N K I N G   C R I T I C A L L Y

Does Pornography

Cause Aggression?

In both men and women, sexual stimulation produces strong, generalized physiological arousal, especially in the sympathetic nervous system. Heart rate increases, adrenaline is released, breathing changes, and there is an experience of excitement and pleasure. If sexual arousal, like arousal in general, can make a person more likely to be aggressive (given a reason, target, and opportunity), then the question arises whether stimuli that create sexual excitation might be dangerous. In particular, does viewing pornographic material make people more likely to be aggressive? Over the years, numerous scholars concluded that there is no evidence for an overall relationship between any type of antisocial behavior and mere exposure to pornographic literature (Donnerstein, 1984). However, in 1986 the U.S. Attorney General's Commission on Pornography re-examined the question and after a year of study concluded that pornography is dangerous.

What am I being asked to believe or accept?
Specifically, the commission said that there is a causal link between viewing erotic material and several forms of antisocial behavior, including sexually related crimes.

What evidence is available to support the assertion?
The commission cited several types of evidence in support of its conclusion. First, there was the testimony of men convicted of sexually related crimes. Rapists, for example, are unusually heavy consumers of pornography, and they often say that they were aroused by erotic material immediately before committing a rape (Silbert & Pines, 1984). Similarly, child molesters often use pornography involving young children immediately before committing their crimes (Marshall, 1989).

In addition, the commission cited experimental evidence that men who are most aroused by aggressive themes in pornography are also the most potentially sexually aggressive. For example, compared with most men, convicted rapists become much more sexually aroused by scenes of rape and less aroused by scenes of mutually consenting sex (Abel et al., 1981).

Perhaps the most compelling evidence cited by the commission, however, came from transfer-of-excitation studies. In a typical study of this type, subjects are told that another subject in a separate room (actually a confederate of the experimenter) will be performing a learning task and that they are to administer an electric shock every time that the person makes a mistake. The subjects can vary the intensity of the shock (none actually reaches the confederate), but they are told that changing the intensity will not affect the speed of learning. So the shock intensity (and presumed pain) that they choose to administer is taken as an index of aggressive behavior. Some subjects watch a sexually explicit film before beginning the learning trials. The arousal created by the film appears to transfer into aggression, especially when the arousal is experienced in a negative way. For example, after watching a film in which several men have sex with the same woman, the subjects became aroused but tended to label the experience as somewhat unpleasant. In this condition, their aggressiveness during the learning experiment was greater than after watching no film at all (Donnerstein, 1984).

Are there alternative ways of interpreting the evidence?
The commission's interpretation of evidence was quickly criticized, on several counts. First, critics argued that some of the evidence should be given

little weight. In particular, how credible is the testimony of convicted sex offenders? It may reflect self-serving attempts to lay the blame for their crimes on pornography. At best, these reports provide correlational evidence, but they cannot establish that exposure to pornography causes aggression. Indeed, it may be that pornography partially *satisfies* sex offenders' aggressive impulses rather than creating them (Byrne & Kelley, 1989). Similarly, the fact that rapists are most aroused by rape-oriented material can show only that they prefer violence-oriented pornography, not that such material created their impulse to rape.

What about the evidence from transfer-of-excitation studies? To interpret these studies, you need to know that the pornography that led to increased aggression contained violence as well as sex; the sexual activity depicted was painful for or unwanted by the female. Thus, the subsequent increase in aggression could have been due either to transfer of sexual arousal *or* to the effects of observing violent behavior.

In fact, several careful experiments have found that even highly arousing sexual themes do not, in and of themselves, produce aggression. When men in transfer-of-excitation studies experience *pleasant* arousal by viewing a film depicting nudity or joyous, mutually consenting sexual activity, their subsequent aggression is actually less than when they viewed no film or a neutral film (Donnerstein et al., 1987). In short, the transfer-of-excitation studies might be interpreted as demonstrating not that sexually arousing material causes aggression but that portrayals of violence influence aggressiveness.

What additional evidence would help to evaluate the alternatives?
Two types of evidence are needed to understand more clearly the effects of pornography on aggression. First, since pornography can include sexual acts, aggressive acts, or both, the effects of each of these components must be more carefully examined. Second, factors affecting males' reactions to pornography, particularly pornography that involves violence, must be more clearly understood. Work has already begun on each of these fronts.

Aggressive themes—whether specifically paired with sexual activity or not—do appear to increase subsequent aggression (Linz et al., 1988). Research has focused on *aggressive pornography*, which contains sexual themes but also scenes of violence against women (Check & Guloien, 1989). In laboratory experiments, males often administer larger amounts of shock to females after viewing aggressive pornographic films as compared to neutral films. There is no parallel increase in aggression against other males, indicating that the films do not create a generalized increase in aggression but an increase in aggressiveness directed toward females (Zillmann & Weaver, 1989). Similarly, viewing aggressive pornography that depicts the *rape myth*—in which the victim of sexual violence appears to be aroused by the aggression—usually leads males to become less sympathetic toward the rape victim and more tolerant of aggressive acts toward women (Linz & Donnerstein, 1989). Sexually explicit films that contain no violence have no effects on attitudes toward rape (Linz et al., 1988).

In one study, 35 percent of all college men reported having been exposed to aggressive pornography within the past twelve months (Demare et al., 1988), and the figure may be even higher in the general population. Are all these men equally likely to become rapists? The evidence available so far suggests that the answer is no. Whether aggressive pornography alters men's behavior and attitudes toward women depends to some extent on the men. For example, compared to most men, convicted rapists report a much greater need to dominate and control women, and they show high levels of generalized anger toward women (Marshall, 1989). The men who appear most prone to acting out the scenes of violence against women that they see in aggressive pornography appear to be those who hold positive attitudes toward the domination of women and feel anger toward women in general (Malamuth, 1988).

What conclusions are most reasonable?

The attorney general's commission seemed to ignore numerous studies showing that the relationship between sexual arousal and aggression is neither consistent nor simple (Kelley et al., 1989). Analysis of this relationship reveals the importance of distinguishing between pornography in general and aggressive pornography in particular. The best evidence suggests that portrayals of violence—including aggressive pornography—affect attitudes toward aggression, and they may make sexual violence more likely in some viewers.

In general, however, the evidence offers no mandate for associating sexual arousal created by nonaggressive pornography with aggressive behavior. Indeed, for most people, sexual arousal and aggression remain quite separate. Even when the two are linked in particular people, there is evidence that the association is learned and can sometimes be changed. In one study, for example, sexually aggressive males underwent therapy in which they masturbated while viewing films of nonviolent, mutually enjoyable intercourse. They became sexually responsive to such scenes and less sexually responsive to depictions of violence (Abel et al., 1976). The use of nonaggressive erotic materials has also become a useful part of other, similar therapies (Kelley et al., 1989). ■

Environmental Influences on Aggression

Environmental psychology is the study of the relationship between people's physical environment and their behavior (Paulus & Nagar, 1989). For aggression, one particularly important aspect of the environment is the weather. As Figure 18.6 indicates, aggression and violence are most likely to occur during the hottest days of summer (Anderson, 1989). High temperatures are a source of stress, and, as discussed in Chapter 13, stress often leads people to become more aggressive.

Air pollution and noise are also sources of stress, and they, too, can influence whether a person displays aggression (Holahan, 1986). People tend to become more aggressive when breathing air that contains ethyl mercapton, a mildly unpleasant-smelling pollutant common in urban areas (Rotton et al., 1979). In addition, a study conducted in Dayton, Ohio, found that the frequency of aggressive family disturbances increased along with the ozone level in the air. Indoors, nonsmokers who inhale cigarette smoke commonly experience increases in irritability and anxiety (Jones, 1978). In laboratory studies, nonsmokers are more likely to become aggressive when breathing smoke-filled rather than clean air (Zillmann, Baron & Tamborini, 1981). Noise—usually defined as any unwanted sound (Kryter, 1970)—tends to make people irritable and more likely to display aggression, especially if the noise is unpredictable and irregular (Ward, 1974). Thus, laws that limit smoking in public places, that control air pollution outdoors, and that limit airport or other urban noise may help make the environment not only healthier but also less violent.

Living arrangements also influence aggressiveness. Compared with the tenants in high-rise apartment buildings, those in buildings with fewer floors are less likely to behave aggressively (Fisher, Bell & Baum, 1984). This difference

Figure 18.6
Effects of Temperature on Aggression
Research on police reports has revealed that rapes, assaults (in two studies), family disturbances, and violent uprisings such as street riots are most likely to occur during the hottest days of the year.

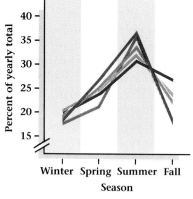

- Uprisings
- Family disturbances
- Assault
- Assault
- Rape

Source: Anderson, 1989.

appears to be due in part to how people feel when they are crowded. Crowding tends to create physiological arousal and to make people tense, uncomfortable, and more likely to report negative feelings (Epstein, Woolfolk & Lehrer, 1981). This arousal and tension can influence people to like one another less and to be more aggressive. One study of juvenile delinquents found that the number of behavior problems they displayed (including aggressiveness) was directly related to how crowded their living conditions had become (Ray et al., 1982). Studies of prisons have also found that as crowding increases so does the incidence of overt aggression (Paulus, 1988).

One result of this research is that psychologists are working with architects to develop settings that are psychologically comfortable. Psychologists have also become active in discussing the implications of environmental psychology for social policy (Craik, 1986). For example, because the architectural layout of prisons affects the physical health of the inmates (Schaeffer et al., 1988) as well as the incidence of violent aggression, a psychologically comfortable facility—although it may cost more to build—may speed rehabilitation and reduce the time and money needed to contend with aggressiveness, uncooperativeness, and damage stemming from violence (Wener et al., 1987). Environmental psychologists are increasingly active in debates about these facilities and their design (Gifford, 1987). This role is consistent with the approach of community psychology, which, as discussed in Chapter 16, emphasizes efforts to prevent or minimize human problems and represents yet another way in which psychological research is being applied to the promotion of human welfare.

The more empathic children are, the more inclined they are to be helpful (Zahn-Waxler, Friedman & Cummings, 1983). Even before their second birthday, empathic children begin to offer help to those who are hurt or crying by snuggling, patting, hugging, or offering food or even their own teddy bears.

Altruism and Helping Behavior

On a winter day several years ago, an airliner crashed into the ice-filled Potomac River in Washington, D.C. Many of the survivors were thrown, injured or unconscious, into the water and were in danger of drowning or freezing to death. A bystander named Lenny Skutnik dove into the river and helped several people to shore before exhaustion and the frigid temperatures nearly killed him. Skutnik acted as he did, not for money or any other material benefit, but simply to help other human beings.

Skutnik's actions provide a dramatic example of a common situation: people helping one another by doing everything from picking up dropped packages to donating kidneys. **Helping behavior** is defined as any act that is intended to benefit another person. Closely related to it is **altruism**, an unselfish concern with another's welfare (Batson, 1987). In the following sections we examine some of the reasons for altruism and helping and some of the conditions in which people are most likely to help others.

Why Do People Help?

The tendency to help others begins early, and it follows a predictable pattern. Around age six, children begin to help others as a form of self-punishment (Kenrick, 1989). They try to "make up" for a bad deed by doing a good deed. As they grow older, children use helping behavior to gain social approval, and their efforts at helping become more elaborate (Zahn-Waxler et al., 1982). Often they follow examples set by people around them; their helping behaviors are shaped by the norms established in their families and other reference groups. Further, children are praised and given other rewards for helpfulness, but scolded for selfishness. Eventually children come to believe that being helpful is good and that they are good when they are helpful. By the late teens, people often help others even when no one is watching and no one will know that they did so (Cialdini, 1981).

There are two major theories of why people help even when they cannot expect others to reward them for doing so. According to the **negative state relief model**, helping aids in eliminating negative moods and unpleasant feelings (Cialdini et al., 1987). Indeed, there is evidence that people in a bad mood are often most likely to help others (Carlson & Miller, 1987), and people usually report feeling much better after having helped someone (Millar et al., 1988). It appears that people learn to reward themselves after acts of good will by saying to themselves something like "I'm a good person for having done that." According to the negative state relief model, then, people help for essentially selfish reasons: to eliminate their own unpleasant emotional state or to make themselves feel good.

Linkages: Does empathy produce altruism? (a link to Emotion)

Of course, people do not have to be feeling bad in order to help others, and several studies suggest that truly unselfish forms of altruism also exist (Batson et al., 1989; Schroeder et al., 1988). The second major theory of helping, the **empathy-altruism model**, holds that unselfish helping can occur as a result of empathy with another person (Batson, 1987). Simply seeing another person's suffering or need can create *empathy*, which involves understanding or experiencing that person's emotional state (Eisenberg & Strayer, 1987). People are much more likely to help when they empathize with the other person (Eisenberg & Miller, 1987). Experiments have shown that people will help others even when their own personal distress is prolonged or increased. Thus, it appears that although people sometimes help others in order to reduce their own unpleasant emotional state, empathizing with another person can lead to unselfish helping.

H I G H L I G H T

Sociobiology

Because helping behavior and altruism are widespread and begin early in life, some observers see them as inborn (Crawford, Smith & Krebs, 1987). In his 1975 book *Sociobiology*, Edward O. Wilson proposed that altruism, cooperation, aggression, and other human and animal social behaviors that increase the chances of species survival are genetically encoded and passed from generation to generation. Today, those who endorse Wilson's point of view are called **sociobiologists**.

It is certainly consistent with Darwin's theory that survival-enhancing behaviors are passed on genetically. On the face of it, however, the assertion that altruism is inborn appears to make little evolutionary sense. In fact, one might expect that natural selection would be biased *against* individuals who help others at the risk of their own welfare. Yet people, like other animal species, do help one another, often at great personal risk. Some even die protecting their family or their home territory (Ridely & Dawkins, 1981). Why?

One sociobiological hypothesis holds that altruistic behavior is inherited because it protects not the individual but the individual's genes, which are shared to varying degrees with other members of the species. By helping or even dying for a cousin, a sibling, or, most of all, one's own child, the person increases the likelihood that at least some of his or her genetic characteristics will be passed on to the next generation through the beneficiary's reproduction (Knauft, 1989).

One of the fundamental reasons people give for helping others is that it makes them feel good; they experience satisfaction from giving aid or otherwise acting to benefit others rather than themselves.

Another proposal holds that people help because, in the long run, they are helping themselves (Caporael et al., 1989). Although there may be an immediate personal cost for helping others, doing so perpetuates a culture in which helping is the norm. This ensures that we ourselves will obtain help when we need it.

Some psychologists have found the sociobiological perspective useful for understanding why people cooperate with and help one another, for explaining why parents become attached to their infants and invest so much time and energy in caring for them, and for explaining why grandparents help with child care (Scarr, 1989). Nevertheless, the sociobiological approach is often faulted as a misguided view based on abstract theorizing, naive speculation, and unjustified extrapolation from animal studies rather than on solid human evidence (Kitcher, 1985).

Some critics are even harsher. They accuse sociobiologists of using scientific-sounding arguments to make unjust social arrangements sound like biological imperatives. Women's intense involvement in child rearing, for example, has been explained from a sociobiological perspective as stemming from the female's certainty that her own genes actually reside in her offspring. Men tend to be less involved, the theory goes, because the child's genes could have come from another man who, like themselves, seeks to perpetuate his genetic legacy by impregnating numerous women. This argument is used to justify promiscuity by men and discrimination against women, but it lacks supporting data from scientific studies of humans.

Any behavior—including helping—has many causes and can be explained at many levels. To say that there is a genetic contribution is part of the story, but it is not the whole story. Ultimately, any decision to help is based on a recognition that the other person needs help, on a weighing of the relative costs and benefits, on a judgment of whether one is capable of providing help, and so on. It is these more proximate causes that sociobiology has yet to address (Rushton, 1988).

Although sociobiology may predict the behavior of a species or a group, it does not appear to be very good at predicting the behavior of specific individuals (Tooby & Cosmides, 1989). Indeed, the question of how much heredity constrains variation in human social behavior is not answered by sociobiology. The work of developmental psychologists who test sociobiological explanations empirically will be of great value in learning more about the question. It is reasonable to expect that altruism and helping develop in an individual, as many other human behaviors do, through both inborn tendencies and environmental influences; that is, through both nature and nurture. ▪

When Are People Most Likely to Help?

Deeply rooted and well learned as they are, human altruism and helping behaviors are neither automatic nor invariable. This fact was dramatically demonstrated in New York City in 1964, when a woman named Kitty Genovese was repeatedly attacked and ultimately killed by a man with a knife, in full view and hearing of dozens of her neighbors. The tragic episode took more than thirty minutes to unfold, but no one physically intervened, and no one called the police until it was too late.

Public dismay and disbelief followed. Psychologists thought it unlikely that everyone in the neighborhood was callous and wondered whether something about the situation that night had deterred people from helping. Numerous studies of helping behavior followed; many of them led to important insights about the characteristics of situations that promote or inhibit helping. Among the most important characteristics of the situation are the clarity of the need for help, the attractiveness of the person in need, the familiarity of the situation, and the number of people available to help.

Is the Need Recognized?   The clarity of someone's need for help has a major impact on whether others provide help (Clark & Word, 1974). In one study, undergraduate students waiting alone in a campus building observed what appeared to be an accident involving a window washer. The man screamed as he and his ladder fell to the ground; then he began to clutch his ankle and groan in pain. All of the students looked out of the window to see what had happened, but only 29 percent of them did anything to help. Other students experienced the same situation, with one important difference: the man said he was hurt and needed help. In this case, more than 80 percent of the subjects came to his aid (Yakimovich & Saltz, 1971). Apparently, this one additional cue eliminated any ambiguity in the situation and led the vast majority of people to offer their help. In a similar experiment, 100 percent of the observers responded to a direct request for help (Clark & Word, 1972).

The Attractiveness of the Person in Need   People are much more likely to provide help to those they find attractive or likable than to others. In one study people with a large birthmark were less likely to receive help than those without such a mark (Piliavin, Piliavin & Rodin, 1975). Similarly, stranded motorists are more likely to receive help if they are dressed neatly than if their clothes are dirty and their hair is messy (Graf & Riddell, 1972; Morgan, 1973). Males are also more likely to help female rather than male motorists with car trouble (West, Whitney & Schnedler, 1975), and they are more likely to assist physically attractive than unattractive females (West & Brown, 1975).

Familiarity with the Surroundings   The probability that people will offer help also increases if they are in a familiar situation. This relationship was demonstrated in an experiment that set up an apparent emergency in a New York City subway station (where most of the observers were commuters who had come to the station many times) and in New York's LaGuardia Airport (where many of the travelers had never been before). A man with a bandaged leg and crutches hobbled along until he came upon a person sitting alone. Then he tripped, fell to the ground, and grasped his knee as if in pain (Latané & Darley, 1970). More than twice as many people helped in the subway station than in the airport. Further, habitual subway users were much more likely to help than those who used the subway infrequently.

The Presence of Others   The tendency to help is strongly influenced by the number of other people present. Somewhat surprisingly, however, the presence of others *inhibits* helping behavior (Miller & McFarland, 1987). This phenomenon was true in the Genovese case, and it has been demonstrated time and time again in everyday life—when a group of people watches but does nothing to stop a rape or a mugging—as well as in controlled experiments (Latané & Darley, 1968).

One explanation for this inhibiting effect is that each person thinks that someone else will help the victim. The tendency to deny any personal responsibility for responding when others are present is known as **diffusion of responsibility** (Mynatt & Sherman, 1975).

The degree to which the presence of other people will inhibit helping may depend on who those other people are. When they are strangers, perhaps poor communication inhibits helping. People have difficulty speaking to strangers, particularly in an emergency, and without speaking, it is difficult to know what the others intend to do. According to this logic, if people are with friends rather than strangers, they should be less embarrassed, more willing to discuss the problem, and thus more likely to help.

In one experiment designed to test this idea, a female experimenter led the subject to a room where he or she was to wait either alone, with a friend, with a stranger, or with a stranger who was a confederate of the experimenter (Latané & Rodin, 1969). The experimenter then stepped behind a curtain into an office. For nearly five minutes, she could be heard doing normal chores—opening and closing the drawers of her desk, shuffling papers, and so on. Then she could be heard climbing up on a chair. Soon there was a loud crash, and she screamed, "Oh, my God. . . . My foot, I . . . I can't move it. Oh, my ankle. . . . I can't get this . . . thing off me." Then the subject heard her groan and cry.

Would the subject go behind the curtain to help? Once again, as you can see in Figure 18.7, people were most likely to help if they were alone. When one other person was present, subjects were more likely both to communicate with one another and to offer help if they were friends than if they were strangers. When the stranger was the experimenter's confederate (who had been instructed not to help the woman in distress), virtually no subject offered to help. Other studies have confirmed that bystanders' tendency to help increases when they are coworkers, members of the same club, or know each other in some other way (Rutkowski, Gruder & Romer, 1983).

Conclusions   Whether helping and altruism are displayed depends on an interaction between the people involved and the situation. (See "In Review: Helping Behavior" for a summary of the major reasons why people help and the conditions under which they are most likely to do so.) Understanding the complexities underlying helping and altruism is of practical as well as theoretical importance. Indeed, the tendency to interpret emergency situations as emergencies and to take responsibility for doing something about them appears to be strengthened by an understanding of the social psychology of helping. For example, when confronted with a contrived emergency under

Figure 18.7
Helping in the Presence of Friends or Strangers
People are more likely to help when they are alone than in a group. However, diffusion of responsibility is lessened when the members of the group know one another.

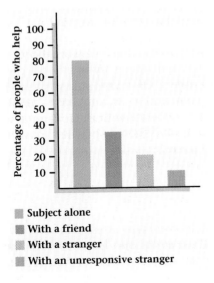

■ Subject alone
■ With a friend
■ With a stranger
■ With an unresponsive stranger

Source: Latané & Rodin, 1969.

In Review: Helping Behavior

Possible Reasons Why People Help	When People Are Most Likely to Help
Our genetic heritage predisposes people to help.	The need of the other person is recognized.
Helping eliminates negative moods and justifies positive self-reinforcement.	The other person is attractive.
Helping is triggered by empathy with those in need.	The potential helper is familiar with the surrounding environment.
Unselfish altruism.	Few others are present.
	The others present are friends or acquaintances of the potential helper.

circumstances unlikely to promote helping, students who had recently learned about diffusion of responsibility offered help nearly twice as often as those who had not received that information (Beaman et al., 1978). There is also a lesson here for the victims of mishaps. Especially if a number of people are present, it is important not only to ask for help but to tell a specific onlooker to take some specific action (e.g., "You, in the yellow shirt, please call an ambulance!").

Cooperation and Competition

Helping is one of the many ways in which people cooperate in order to accomplish their goals, but people also compete with others for limited resources. For example, several students can drive across the United States in three days by changing drivers every few hours; the trip could not be made so speedily by any one of them alone. When they arrive at their destination, however, these same students might all interview with a company that has only one job opening.

Cooperation is any type of behavior in which several people work together to attain a goal. **Competition** exists whenever individuals try to attain a goal for themselves while denying that goal to others. Of course, many activities fall somewhere between cooperation and competition or combine elements of both. For example, in team sports, people cooperate with their teammates but compete with members of the opposing team. When do people choose to cooperate, and when do they choose to compete?

The Prisoner's Dilemma

Suppose two people are separated immediately after being arrested for a serious crime. The district attorney believes they are guilty but does not have the evidence to convict them. Each prisoner can either confess or not. If they both refuse to confess, they will each be convicted of a minor offense and will be jailed for just one year. If they both confess, the district attorney will

Competition and cooperation are deeply interwoven components of human social behavior. Each of these farmers is competing with the others for maximum yields and profits, but when an accident or illness incapacitates one grower, neighbors usually pitch in to harvest the crop.

recommend a ten-year sentence. However, if one prisoner remains silent and one confesses, the district attorney will allow the confessing prisoner to go free, while the other will serve the maximum fifteen-year sentence.

Each prisoner faces a dilemma. Figure 18.8a outlines the possible outcomes. Obviously, the strategy that will guarantee the best *mutual* outcome—short sentences for both prisoners—is cooperation: both should remain silent. But the prisoner who remains silent runs the risk of receiving a very long sentence if the other prisoner confesses, and the prisoner who talks has the chance of gaining individually if the other prisoner does not talk. Thus, each prisoner has an incentive to compete for freedom by confessing. But if they *both* compete and confess, each will go to jail for longer than if nothing was said.

By setting up analogous situations in the laboratory, psychologists create what is called a **prisoner's dilemma game.** In a typical example, two people sit before separate control panels. Each subject has a red button and a black button, one of which is to be pushed on each of many trials. If, on a given trial, both subjects press their black buttons, each wins five dollars. If both press the red button, each loses five dollars. However, if player A presses the red button and player B presses the black button, A will win fifteen dollars and B will win nothing. Thus, pressing the black button is a cooperative response, allowing both players to gain; pressing the red button is a competitive response.

Figure 18.8b shows the possible outcomes for each trial. Over the course of the experiment, the combined winnings of the players are greatest if each presses the black button; that is, if they cooperate. By pressing the black button, however, one player becomes open to exploitation, because on any trial the other can take all the winnings and deny that person any gain by pressing the red button. Indeed, each player stands to benefit the most individually by pressing the red button occasionally.

What happens when people play the game? Overall, there is a strong tendency for people to exploit each other (Rosenbaum, 1980). People tend to respond competitively rather than cooperatively (Komorita, Sweeney & Kravitz, 1980) and find it difficult to resist the competitive choice on any given trial. This choice wins them more money on that trial, but in the long run they gain less than they would have gained through cooperation.

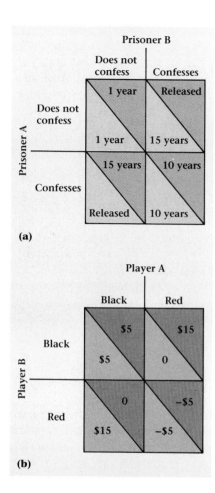

Figure 18.8
The Prisoner's Dilemma
In many cases, mutual cooperation is beneficial to two parties and mutual competition is harmful to both, but one party can exploit the cooperativeness of the other. The prisoner's dilemma provides a model for such situations. These diagrams show the potential payoffs in that situation and in the prisoner's dilemma game described in the text. Each player's payoff is a function of how both people respond.

The prisoner's dilemma game parallels numerous real-life dilemmas. When competing companies decide on their advertising budgets or when competing nations plan their military budgets, each side could save enormous sums if both sides would cut their budgets in half. But neither side is certain that the other will in fact cooperate. Fearing that the other side will instead spend enough to pull ahead, they continue to compete. (Even in the current climate of decreasing tension between the United States and the Soviet Union, there are those in both governments who warn against making cuts in defense spending that, if unmatched by the other power, could leave their side at a military disadvantage.)

If acting competitively leads to smaller rewards in the long run, then why do people persist in being competitive? There seem to be two reasons (Komorita, 1984). First, winning more than an opponent seems to be rewarding in itself. In the prisoner's dilemma game, many people want to outscore an opponent even if the result is that they win less money overall. Second, and more important, once several competitive responses are made, the competition seems to feed on itself. Each person becomes distrustful of the other, and cooperation becomes increasingly difficult. The more competitive one person acts, the more competitive the other becomes (Axelrod, 1984).

Fostering Cooperation

Is there any way to overcome the strong tendency to act competitively? Communication can make a difference (Bornstein et al., 1989). Usually, experimenters do not permit communication between the players in the prisoner's dilemma game. But in one study, the more visual and auditory communication was possible, the more cooperation occurred (Wichman, 1970). In another study, cooperation increased when one player communicated an intent to cooperate and then immediately followed it up with a cooperative response (Brickman, Becker & Castle, 1979).

Unfortunately, not all communication increases cooperation, just as not all contact reduces prejudice. If the communication takes the form of a threat, people apparently interpret the threat itself as a competitive response and are likely to respond competitively (van de Kragt et al., 1986). Furthermore, the communication must be relevant. In one study, cooperation increased only when people spoke openly about the game and how they would be rewarded for various responses. Specifically praising each other for past cooperation was most beneficial (Orbell et al., 1988).

People can also communicate implicitly, through the strategy they use. We have already noted that being competitive makes the other person less cooperative. It is possible to break this circle by adopting the *reformed sinner strategy*. This happens when one person initially responds very competitively but then consistently provides a cooperative response. Once the cooperative responses begin and are recognized as consistent, the other person usually reciprocates by cooperating (Axelrod, 1984).

Now imagine that one player consistently acts in a cooperative fashion no matter how the other person responds. This consistent cooperation has a powerful effect, especially if it occurs early in the game, before competitiveness has surfaced (Gruder & Duslak, 1973). The other person usually adopts the same strategy and begins cooperating as well. Sometimes, however, people view consistent cooperativeness as an invitation to exploit the other player (Hamner & Yukl, 1977). If a player is very competitive or doubts the cooperative player's motives, a cooperative strategy may lead to exploitation (McClintock & Liebrand, 1988).

Of all the strategies that can be used, the most simple also appears to be the most effective for producing long-term cooperation. This is to use basic learning principles and play *tit-for-tat*, rewarding cooperative responses with cooperation and punishing exploitation by generating exploitative strategies of one's own. Research indicates that cooperating after a cooperative response and competing after a competitive response produces a high degree of cooperation over time (McClintock & Liebrand, 1988). Apparently, the players learn that the only way to come out ahead is to cooperate.

Group Processes

Linkages: Do problem-solving and decision-making strategies change when people work in groups? (a link to Thought and Language)

How much should the city's teachers be paid next year? Is the defendant guilty or innocent? What was the cause of yesterday's plane crash? Many questions and problems like these are usually dealt with not by one person but by a group. In order for groups to make decisions, solve problems, or perform other tasks, they must cooperate. Often, however, there are competing factions in a group, some favoring one solution, others preferring a different approach. How does it all get resolved? How do groups reach their goals?

Decision Making in Groups

In Chapter 9 we described the rational processes, mental sets, and biases that influence an individual's efforts to make decisions. Those processes continue to operate when an individual becomes part of a group, but their influence on the decision is muted somewhat, since the interaction of the group also shapes the outcome.

Choosing an Option   Two of the most important factors affecting a group's decisions are (1) the prior opinions of its members, and (2) the order in which various options are considered. Each individual in a group has prior beliefs and attitudes. In principle, each person in the group should listen to the others, and the group should evaluate each argument on its merits and try to reach a consensus. In fact, people making decisions in a group often show a strong tendency to stick with their original beliefs. Thus, the ultimate decision a group makes is usually consistent with the view that most of its members held beforehand (Stasser et al., 1989).

Even though discussions rarely change people's opinions, they do shape a group's decision (Hastie, Penrod & Pennington, 1983). The discussions typically follow a consistent pattern (Hoffman, 1979). At first, various options are proposed and debated. This process continues until the group perceives that no member has strong objections to one option; that option becomes the minimally acceptable solution. At that point, the quality of the discussion changes dramatically (Hoffman, 1979). Rather than seriously considering subsequent options, the group immediately criticizes anything else that is proposed and begins arguing more and more strongly for the minimally acceptable solution. Thus, the first minimally acceptable solution that is offered is likely to survive as the group's decision (Hoffman & Maier, 1979).

One important implication of this process is that the order in which options are considered, rather than the quality of the options, can determine whether they will be adopted. Suppose that a group of friends is trying to decide which movie to rent at the video store. Fred and Ginger propose *Footlight Parade*, an old musical, but no one else wants to see a black-and-white film. Jason's

Linkages: Decisions made by groups reflect both the individual thinking, problem-solving, and decision-making skills and biases described in Chapter 9 and the impact of social forces such as conformity. Ironically, the give and take of group discussions usually do more to create workable outcomes than to substantially alter individual opinions.

nomination of *Friday the 13th, Part 62* is opposed by everyone with a weak stomach. Then Julie mentions *The Sound of Music*, a show that everyone is at least willing to see, even if they are not enthusiastic about it. This is the movie the group is likely to rent, even if someone later mentions a better one, because any ideas that come up after the minimally acceptable option is on the table are likely to meet harsh criticism (Moscovici, 1985). Why group members focus prematurely on one solution and close their minds to subsequent alternatives is not entirely clear.

Group Polarization   Group decisions are often either riskier *or* more conservative than the average group member might have made individually (Kaplan, 1987). For example, a committee charged with determining the appropriate punishment for a student might set a more severe penalty than most members, operating alone, would have chosen. On the other hand, when groups bet on horses, they are more conservative than individuals (Knox & Safford, 1976). This tendency for groups to make decisions that represent a shift toward one extreme or the other is called **group polarization**.

Two mechanisms apparently underlie group polarization. First, most arguments presented during the group discussion will favor the view of the majority, and most criticisms will be directed at the minority view. As a result, the new arguments each member hears are likely to favor what the majority believes. Thus, it will seem rational to those favoring the majority view—whether that view is risky or conservative—to adopt an even stronger version of it (Isenberg, 1986).

Second, the social comparison phenomenon described in Chapter 17 may contribute to polarization. Recall that people tend to perceive themselves in relation to those around them, especially to those in their reference groups. As a group begins to agree that a particular decision is desirable, a group norm is established, and members may try to establish themselves as being the most committed to that norm. (Indeed, various individuals may all claim to have proposed the accepted proposal or policy.) As the competition for most-committed group member continues, each individual may begin to advocate a more and more extreme position, and the group becomes polarized (Kaplan & Miller, 1987).

Groupthink Especially in small, close-knit groups, extreme decisions and policies reflect not only polarization but also a more general decision-making process called **groupthink**. Groupthink is a pattern of thinking that, over time, renders group members unable to evaluate options and decisions realistically (Janis, 1985). The decision of NASA to launch the space shuttle *Challenger* in 1986 appears to have been an example of groupthink. Although several engineers from outside of NASA expressed serious reservations about the design of the rocket and the wisdom of blasting off when temperatures were in the thirties, the small group responsible for launch control went ahead. The warnings were well-founded; *Challenger* exploded seventy-three seconds after liftoff, killing all aboard.

Groupthink is particularly likely under three conditions (Janis, 1985). The first is when group members making the decision feel very cohesive and isolated from outside forces. The second condition is the lack of an impartial leader. This condition appeared to play a crucial role in President Kennedy's decision to invade Cuba at the Bay of Pigs in 1961. Before the final decision was made, several advisers were told that the president had made up his mind and that it was time to "close ranks with the president." This created enormous pressures for conformity (McCauley, 1989). Finally, groupthink is likely when the group is influenced by intense stressors, especially time pressure.

When these conditions are met, groups tend to become very close-minded and to rationalize their decision as the only reasonable one. Other options are dismissed prematurely, and any dissenting voices are quickly suppressed. As a result, the group becomes more and more certain that the decision is correct and cannot possibly be wrong. To avoid groupthink, leaders must

President Nixon says goodbye after resigning his office. Many of the illegal or unwise tactics that forced the resignation appeared to be the result of *groupthink,* a distorted decision-making process to which Nixon and his closest advisors fell victim.

remain impartial and foster debate. Indeed, one of the most effective "anti-groupthink" methods is to arrange for one or more group members or outside experts to play "devil's advocate," challenging the group's emerging consensus and offering other perspectives and alternatives (Janis, 1985).

Group Leadership

Linkages: Is there one set of personality traits that makes a person a good leader? (a link to Personality)

Whether the goal is to make a decision, set a policy, solve a problem, or perform a task, groups usually engage in discussion. This process is usually facilitated by a *leader*—a person who organizes, summarizes, and moderates the discussion. A good leader can greatly aid a group in pursuing its tasks, and a poor one can impede a group's functioning. What makes a good leader?

Marvin Shaw (1981) reviewed thirty years of research on the personality of leaders and suggested that only three generalizations can be made. First, leaders tend to score very high on whatever skills are crucial to the group. Often they are intelligent, creative, and have good verbal skills. Second, leaders tend to have good social skills. They may have the ability to make others feel important, listened to, and cared for; they certainly can make others like them. Finally, leaders tend to be ambitious. They show initiative and self-confidence, and they enjoy being in a position of leadership.

Shaw also discovered that having these traits is not sufficient to ensure that a person will lead well. People who are effective leaders in one situation may not be effective in another (Hollander, 1985). It appears that there is no single type of good leader. Instead, good leadership depends on a person's traits, on the situation, and on the person's style of handling it.

Two main styles of leadership have been identified. The first style is **task-oriented** (Shaw, 1981). These leaders provide very close supervision, lead by giving directives, and generally discourage group discussion. Their style may not endear them to group members. Other leaders tend to adopt a **socio-emotional** style. They provide loose supervision, ask for members' ideas, and are generally concerned with subordinates' feelings (Shaw, 1981). They are usually well liked by the group, even when they must reprimand someone (Boyatzis, 1982).

The "best" leaders seem to be those whose style matches the circumstances and demands of the group's task (Sorrentino & Field, 1986). Task-oriented leaders are most effective when the group is working under time pressure, when the task is unstructured, and when it is unclear what needs to be done first and how the duties should be divided. People stranded in an elevator in a burning building, for example, need a task-oriented leader. On the other hand, socioemotional leaders are most effective when the task is structured and there are no severe time limitations (Chemers, 1987). These people would be particularly effective, for example, in managing an office in which the workers know their jobs well.

Management training programs have been designed to help leaders become more aware of leader-situation interactions (Ancona, 1987). High-level executives are trained to select lower-level leaders whose style matches the situation in which they will be operating (Leary et al., 1986). Research suggests that these programs can help leaders perform more efficiently (Hollander, 1985).

Deindividuation

Regardless of leaders, a fundamental tension usually exists within members of a group. Each member has powerful needs to feel unique and self-controlled but also to be part of a larger social entity (Maslach et al., 1985; Snyder & Fromkin, 1980). Most of the time people maintain a balance between these needs, conforming to group norms and demands in some situations and exerting their individuality in others. Sometimes, however, people appear to become part of the "herd." They experience **deindividuation**, a hypothesized psychological state in which a person becomes "submerged in the group" and loses the sense of individuality (Diener, 1979; Festinger, Pepitone & Newcomb, 1952).

When people experience deindividuation, their normal inhibitions are relaxed, and they often perform acts that they would not do otherwise. Fans at rock concerts and athletic events have trampled one another to death in their frenzy to get the best seats; normally mild-mannered adults have sometimes thrown rocks or fire bombs at police during political protests. Group leaders who understand how to create such situations can influence a group of people to do things they might not do as individuals. In the most perverted examples of this phenomenon, Adolf Hitler, Charles Manson, and the Reverend Jim Jones influenced groups of their followers to commit racial atrocities, ritual murders, and mass suicide.

Deindividuation appears to be caused by two factors (Prentice-Dunn & Rogers, 1989). First, normal cues to accountability are diminished. The person no longer thinks that he or she can be held personally accountable for what happens. This belief is fueled by the fact that so many people in the crowd are acting the same way. When accountability cues are diminished, people are much more likely to engage in deviant behavior. One psychology instructor asked his students what they would do if they were invisible for twenty-four hours. The most common responses described illegal activities such as robbing a bank (Dodd, 1985).

The second cause of deindividuation appears to involve a shift of attention away from internal thoughts and standards and toward the external environment (Prentice-Dunn & Rogers, 1989). The result appears to be heightened emotional arousal and an intense feeling of cohesiveness with other members of the group. Having members of the group wear unusual uniforms (such as Ku Klux Klan robes and hoods) or sing in unison fosters this shift of attention.

Deindividuation can produce desirable effects, as when a military unit completes a daring rescue by engaging, as a group, in dangerous activities that each individual might not perform alone (Diener, 1980). In general, however, the inhibitions that are released in deindividuation situations result in antisocial acts, and the emotional arousal that is generated makes such behavior difficult to stop once it has begun (Prentice-Dunn & Rogers, 1989). Deindividuation is another example of how, given the right circumstances, quite normal people can engage in destructive, even violent behavior.

Linkages: Motivation and Groups

How is motivation influenced by others?

In Chapter 11 we noted that social factors such as peer pressure, parental attitudes toward achievement, and the like often affect motivation. A person's current motivational state is also affected by the presence of other people. To illustrate, consider the very first experiment in social psychology, conducted by Norman Triplett in 1897.

Triplett noticed that bicyclists tended to race faster when a competitor was near than when all competitors were out of sight. Did just seeing one another remind the riders of the need to go faster to win? To test this possibility, Triplett arranged for bicyclists to complete a twenty-five-mile course under one of three conditions: riding alone and racing against the clock; riding with another cyclist, but not in competition; or competing directly with another rider. The cyclists went much faster when another rider was present than when they were simply racing against the clock, whether or not they were competing against the other person. Something about the *presence* of the other person, rather than competition, produced increased speed.

The term **social facilitation** describes circumstances in which the mere presence of other people improves performance. This improvement does not always occur, however. Other psychologists found evidence that the presence of other people sometimes *impairs* performance, a process known as **social interference**. For decades these results seemed contradictory; then Robert Zajonc (pronounced "zi-onze") suggested that they could both be explained by one process: arousal. The presence of other people, said Zajonc, increases a person's general level of arousal or motivation (Zajonc, 1965).

This idea is consistent with principles described in Chapter 13, on stress; the pressure of having other people watch you can act as a stressor that increases your arousal and, thus, makes you more error-prone. But how does increased arousal in the presence of others help to explain improved performance in such situations?

An answer is suggested by another point discussed in Chapter 13: increased arousal increases the tendency to perform those behaviors that are *most dominant*—the ones a person knows best—and this tendency may either help or hinder performance in a situation. When you are performing a familiar task such as riding a bike, increased arousal due to the presence of others should allow you to ride even faster than normal. However, when a task is unfamiliar, complex, or difficult, the best-learned responses may be detrimental. So when you try to perform a recently learned dance in the arousal-producing presence of others, old dance moves may appear, making your performance look awkward.

In other words, according to Zajonc, other people's presence can help or hinder performance depending on whether the most likely behavior in the situation is beneficial or harmful to that performance. Notice that this model is consistent with the effects of arousal described in the chapters on motivation and stress: increased arousal impairs performance on complex and difficult tasks more than on easy tasks.

What is there about the presence of others that leads to arousal? Recent evidence suggests two factors (Geen, 1989). First, people expect other people to evaluate their performance; therefore, they feel apprehensive about what others will think, whether those others are actually judging them or not (Guerin, 1986). The second way in which the presence of others may create arousal is by intensifying self-evaluation. Self-evaluation generally facilitates performance when the task is easy but impairs performance when the task is difficult (Jackson et al., 1988).

So far we have discussed situations in which an individual's motivation on a task is altered by the mere presence of others. If these other people are also working on the same task, however, their impact changes slightly. It is easy to identify and evaluate the performance of an individual in isolation, but when a group performs a task, it is not always possible to identify each individual's contributions. In such group situations, people often exert less effort than when performing alone, a phenomenon termed **social loafing** (Harkins & Szymanski, 1987). For example, when people are asked to clap as loudly as possible, they do better when alone than when they are part of a group (Kravitz & Martin, 1986). When individuals or groups are asked to solve intellectual puzzles, each person does better when performing alone than with others (Wedon & Gargano, 1988).

The winner of this competition could have been decided by comparing the times recorded as each contestant completed the course on his own. But because the presence of others often motivates improved performance, the winner's time will probably be faster when all the racers are on the track at once.

It should be noted that social loafing occurs only when people are able to "hide in the crowd"; that is, when their own individual level of performance cannot be identified. Anyone who has played in a large band or sung in a big chorus knows the temptation to "skip" the hardest or least familiar part of a piece, on the assumption that no one will know the difference. Under these conditions, one's level of arousal appears to decrease in the presence of others, as does apprehension over being negatively evaluated (Harkins, 1987). This tendency adds yet another twist to the topic of social motivation. When people can be lazy and exert less effort with no one knowing, they usually take advantage of the situation.

Social loafing can be seen in all sorts of groups, from volunteer committees to search parties. Concern over its effects is particularly high in business and industry, where social loafing can often reduce productivity. In order to maximize overall productivity, it is important for managers to develop ways of evaluating the efforts of every individual in a work group, not just the overall output of a team (Ilgen & Klein, 1989).

Future Directions

The influence of other people, individually and in groups, is diverse and multifaceted. You influence others, and they influence you. People help you and hurt you, cooperate with you and compete against you. Laboratory and field research in social psychology has helped to illuminate each of these processes and will continue to do so.

One recent trend in social psychology involves looking at how people perceive the rewards that accrue to them as individuals versus those that accrue to them as members of a group. In particular, attention has focused on **social dilemmas**, situations in which the option that is most rewarding for each individual will, if accepted by all, become catastrophic for everyone. It may be in a factory owner's self-interest to dump toxic sewage into a river. But if everyone does that, the environment will be destroyed and eventually become uninhabitable for everyone. Similarly, each individual will be financially better off by refusing to donate to the public broadcasting system. But if everyone refuses to donate, the programs on public broadcasting stations will not be available to anyone. If each individual makes a small sacrifice, everyone will experience a large benefit.

The same kinds of dilemmas exist in international relations. Consider, for example, the nuclear arms race. The United States and the Soviet Union are individually better able to defend themselves by stockpiling nuclear weapons, but if each country continues to do this, the stage is set for a nuclear war that will destroy both countries (Plous, 1988). Similarly, many smaller countries attempt to obtain nuclear bombs in an effort to enhance their own security. But as more countries develop and stockpile nuclear weapons, everyone's security becomes increasingly precarious (Kramer, 1989).

The psychological basis of the nuclear arms race (and preparations for biological and chemical warfare) is now undergoing intense study. Stockpiling appears to occur because of an escalation process in political decision making. Much as eyewitnesses, jurors, investors, and people in general tend to be overconfident about their judgments, politicians, too, may become overcommitted to prior decisions. As a result, they may feel a strong need to continually reassert and justify their support for the build-up of nuclear warheads, even during times of reduced East-West tensions (Staw & Ross, 1989). Another cause of escalation is the human tendency, discussed in Chapters 9 and 17, on thought and on social cognition, to interpret new data in a manner consistent with prior beliefs. Thus, nearly any action on the part of a country we believe to be an enemy is likely to be seen as aggressive and potentially threatening. This tendency makes the arms race very difficult to stop (Staw & Ross, 1989).

Psychologists have also discovered, however, that escalation in decision making can play a role in mutual cooperation, and herein lies hope for a solution to the arms race (Axelrod & Dion, 1988). As noted earlier, long-term cooperation *evolves* based on reciprocity. One side takes a small step that is then reciprocated by the other. Eventually, larger steps are taken and, as each side discovers that there are rewards in cooperating, the process proceeds more quickly and more intensely.

From a psychological perspective, then, the key to slowing or stopping international conflict seems to lie in shifting from escalating competition to even small steps toward cooperation. Psychologists are studying how to accelerate this cooperation. One way is to frame decisions differently. In the past, both the United States and the Soviet Union compared their own military strength to that of the other. Now each country is beginning to compare the cost of their security needs to the cost of other internal needs. The question is also being framed in terms of the mutual *benefits* of reducing the number of warheads on each side. Such reframing appears to be highly effective in accelerating the process of de-escalation (Kramer, 1989).

Social psychology highlights another factor that may be important to peace, namely the need to emphasize the similarity of the people on opposite sides of world conflicts (Gibbard, 1989). As we noted in the previous chapter, liking, cooperation, and mutual understanding are enhanced as people learn, through contact and other means, to perceive members of outgroups as more similar to themselves. In this respect, the numerous academic, cultural, commercial, and athletic exchange programs between the Soviet Union and the United States have had a dramatic psychological benefit. Although each side continues to see differences, it is clear that the citizens of both countries share many of the same hopes, dreams, and fears. This perception of similarity engenders liking and trust and sets the stage for further efforts at mutual cooperation.

One can anticipate that psychologists will continue studying the underpinnings of international cooperation. In fact, psychologists from numerous countries have formed an organization called Psychologists for Social Responsibility. Its members are dedicated to studying scientifically issues such as the arms race, as well as to providing workshops to foster international solutions to the social dilemmas that the people of the world must face and resolve together.

Summary and Key Terms

Conformity and Compliance

The Role of Norms

Norms establish the rules for what should and should not be done in a particular situation. They play an important role in *conformity* and *compliance*. People tend to follow the normative responses of others, and groups create their own norms when none already exist.

Why Do People Conform?

Evidence indicates that both public conformity and private acceptance occur. In other words, people sometimes publicly produce responses that they do not believe, but at other times the responses of others have a genuine impact on people's private beliefs. People conform because they want to be right, because they want to be liked, and because they are generally rewarded for doing so.

When Do People Conform?

People are most likely to conform when they have low status, the situation is ambiguous, and others in the group are unanimous in their evaluation. Also, conformity generally increases with increasing attraction to the group and with increased psychological size of the faction holding the majority view.

Inducing Compliance

Several techniques have been devised for inducing compliance. The most successful are the foot-in-the-door technique, the door-in-the-face procedure, and the low-ball approach.

Obedience

Obedience in the Laboratory

Milgram's research indicates that levels of *obedience* are high even when obeying an authority figure's commands results in pain and suffering for another person. Laboratory studies of obedience make it clear, however, that people experience considerable turmoil when inflicting pain on another person.

Factors Affecting Obedience

Obedience declines as the status of the authority figure declines, as the authority figure becomes more distant, as proximity to the victim increases, and when others are observed disobeying the authority figure.

Evaluating Milgram's Studies

Most scientists agree that Milgram's studies were informative, but because the subjects suffered such stress, his studies have been questioned on ethical grounds. Milgram was careful to debrief his subjects and have them later interact with the confederate in a friendly fashion. After the experiment, the vast majority of the subjects felt that the experience had been worthwhile.

Aggression

Why Are People Aggressive?

Aggression can occur for many reasons. Ethologists have argued that humans have a genetic predisposition to aggression that is triggered by environmental *releasers*. Learning is also known to play an important role, however, because people learn to aggress both from watching others and from being rewarded for being aggressive. Finally, some cases of aggression appear to be due to brain disorders or biochemical imbalances.

Emotional Factors in Aggression

A variety of emotional factors play a role in aggression. The *frustration-aggression hypothesis* suggests that frustration can lead to aggression, particularly if cues that invite or promote aggression are present. Arousal from sources completely unrelated to aggression, such as exercise, can also make aggressive responses more likely. This is particularly true when aggression is already a dominant response in that situation. There is no evidence that sexual arousal, in and of itself, produces aggression. However, exposure to aggressive pornography results in men becoming more accepting of aggressive acts toward women.

Environmental Influences on Aggression

Environmental factors such as high temperature, air pollution, noise, and crowding also appear to increase the likelihood of aggressive behavior, especially when people are already angry. Because of this, the results of research in *environmental psychology* are being used to design more psychologically comfortable places to live and work.

Altruism and Helping Behavior

Human behavior is also characterized by *altruism* and *helping behavior*.

Why Do People Help?

There are two major theories of why people help others. According to the *negative state relief model*, people help for essentially selfish reasons—to make themselves feel better and to eliminate negative moods and unpleasant feelings. There is also recent evidence, however, that people sometimes help even when their own distress is prolonged or increased. This finding has led to the *empathy-altruism model*, which suggests that some helping is truly unselfish and altruistic. *Sociobiologists* suggest that humans have a genetic predisposition to help.

When Are People Most Likely to Help?

People are most likely to help others when the need for help is clear, when the person who needs help is attractive, when the helpers are familiar with the surroundings, and when *diffusion of responsibility* is not created by the presence of others.

Cooperation and Competition

The Prisoner's Dilemma

When given a choice between *cooperation* and *competition*, people often compete with one another. This is true even when, as in the *prisoner's dilemma game*, they receive fewer rewards for competing than for cooperating.

Fostering Cooperation

Communication between competing parties generally leads to an increase in cooperation, especially if the communication is nonthreatening and relevant to the situation. One of the most effective strategies for producing long-term cooperation is playing tit-for-tat; that is, rewarding cooperative responses with cooperation and punishing exploitation by generating exploitive strategies of one's own.

Group Processes

Decision Making in Groups

People in groups have a strong tendency to stick to their original beliefs. Nevertheless, group decisions are often affected by the order in which various options are considered. In particular, there is a bias to adopt the first option that generates a minimally acceptable solution. Decisions made by groups are typically more extreme than the ones that individuals acting by themselves would make—a tendency known as *group polarization*. A pattern of thinking called *groupthink* is most likely to occur when a group is cohesive and feels isolated from outside forces, when it lacks a truly impartial leader, and when its decisions are made under the influence of stressors.

Group Leadership

There is no single personality type or behavioral style that always results in good leadership. *Task-oriented leaders* are most effective when the task is unstructured and the group is working under time pressure. *Socioemotional leaders* are most effective when the task is structured and there are no severe time limitations.

Deindividuation

Deindividuation is a hypothesized psychological state in which people temporarily lose their individuality in a group situation. As a result, their normal inhibitions are relaxed, and they may perform acts that they would not do otherwise. Deindividuation is most likely when normal accountability cues are diminished and attention is focused away from internal thoughts and toward the external environment.

Statistics in Psychological Research

Whether psychologists conduct experiments, field studies, case studies, naturalistic observations, or surveys, their investigations usually generate a large amount of **data:** numbers that represent their findings and provide the basis for their conclusions. In Chapter 1, we described how psychologists obtain their findings, and we discussed several factors vital to research design if that research is to yield meaningful data. No matter how well a study is designed, however, understanding and interpreting the results also depends on the adequacy of the researcher's *statistical analyses;* that is, on the methods used for summarizing and analyzing the data. In this appendix, we consider various *descriptive statistics* that psychologists use to describe and present their data. Then we discuss *inferential statistics,* the mathematical procedures used to draw conclusions from data and make inferences about what they mean.

Describing Data

To illustrate our discussion, consider a hypothetical experiment on the effects of incentives on performance. The experimenter presents a simple list of mathematics problems to two groups of subjects. Each group must solve the problems within a fixed time, but for each correct answer, the low-incentive group is paid ten cents, while the high-incentive group gets one dollar. The hypothesis to be tested is the **null hypothesis,** the assertion that the independent variable manipulated by the experimenter will have no effect on the dependent variable measured by the experimenter. In this case, the null hypothesis holds that the size of the incentive (the independent variable) will not affect performance on the mathematics task (the dependent variable).

Assume that the experimenter has obtained a random sample of subjects, assigned them randomly to the two groups, and done everything possible to avoid the confounds and other research problems discussed in Chapter 1. The experiment has been run, and the psychologist now has the data: a list of the number of correct answers reported by each subject in each group. Now comes the first task of statistical analysis: describing the data in a way that makes them easy to understand.

The Frequency Histogram

The simplest way to describe the data is to draw up something like Table A.1, in which all the numbers are simply listed. After examining the table, you might discern that the high-incentive group seems to have done better than the low-incentive group, but the difference is not immediately obvious. It might be even harder to see if there were more subjects and if the scores included three-digit numbers. A picture is worth a thousand words, so a more satisfactory way of presenting the same data is in a picturelike graphic known as a **frequency histogram** (see Figure A.1).

Construction of a histogram is simple. First, divide the scale for measuring the dependent variable (in this case, the number of correct solutions) into a number of categories, or "bins." The bins in our example are 1–2, 3–4, 5–6, 7–8, and 9–10. Next, sort the raw data into the appropriate bin. (For example, the score of a subject who had 5 correct answers would go into the 5–6 bin, a score of 8 would go into the 7–8 bin, and so on.) Finally, for each bin, count the number of scores in that bin and draw a bar up to the height of that number on the vertical axis of a graph. The set of bars makes up the frequency histogram.

Because we are interested in comparing the scores of two groups, there are separate histograms in Figure A.1: one for the high-incentive group and one for the low-incentive group. Now the difference between groups that was difficult to see in Table A.1 becomes clearly visible: more people in the high-incentive group obtained high scores than in the low-incentive group.

Histograms and other pictures of data are useful for visualizing and better understanding the "shape" of research data, but in order to analyze data statistically, the data making up these graphic presentations must be handled in other ways. For example, before we can tell whether two histograms are different statistically or just visually, the data they represent must be described in more precise mathematical terms.

Table A.1
A Simple Data Set

Here are the test scores obtained by thirteen subjects performing under low-incentive conditions and thirteen subjects performing under high-incentive conditions.

Low Incentive	High Incentive
4	6
6	4
2	10
7	10
6	7
8	10
3	6
5	7
2	5
3	9
5	9
9	3
5	8

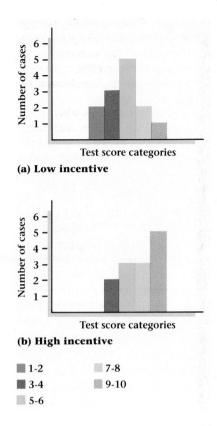

(a) Low incentive

(b) High incentive

■ 1-2   ■ 7-8
■ 3-4   ■ 9-10
■ 5-6

Figure A.1
Frequency Histogram
The height of each bar of a histogram represents the number of scores falling within each range of score values. The pattern formed by these bars gives a visual image of how research results are distributed.

Descriptive Statistics

The numbers that summarize a pool of data are called **descriptive statistics**. The four basic categories of descriptive statistics (1) measure the number of observations made; (2) summarize the typical value of a set of data; (3) summarize the spread, or variability, in a set of data; and (4) express the correlation between two sets of data.

N The easiest statistic to compute, abbreviated as N, simply describes the number of observations that make up the data set. In Table A.1, for example, $N = 13$ for each group, or 26 for the entire data set. Simple as it is, N plays a very important role in more sophisticated statistical analyses.

Measures of Central Tendency It is apparent in the histograms in Figure A.1 that there is a difference in the pattern of scores between the two groups. But how much of a difference? What is the typical value, the **central tendency**, that represents each group's performance? There are three measures that capture this typical value: the mode, the median, and the mean.

The **mode** is the value or score that occurs most frequently in the data. It is computed most easily by ordering the scores from lowest to highest, as has been done in Table A.2. The mode is 5 in the low-incentive group and 10 in the high-incentive group. Notice that these modes do indicate that the two groups are very different and that the mode of 5 does capture the flavor of the low-incentive group (it falls about in the middle). But, in the case of the high-incentive group, the mode (10) is actually an extreme score; it does not provide a value representative of the group as a whole. Thus, the mode can act like a microphone for a small but vocal minority, which, though speaking most frequently, does not represent the views of the majority.

Unlike the mode, the median takes all of the scores into account. The **median** is the halfway point in a set of data: half the scores fall above the median, half fall below it. To compute the median, arrange the scores from lowest to highest (as in Table A.2) and count the scores from lowest to highest until the halfway point is reached; that point is the median. If there is an even number of observations, so that the middle lies between two numbers, the median is the value halfway between those two numbers. Thus, if the

Table A.2
Measures of Central Tendency
Reordering the data in Table A.1 makes it easy to calculate the mean, median, and mode of the scores of subjects in the high- and low-incentive groups.

Low Incentive	High Incentive
2	3
2	4
3	5
3	6
4	6
5	7
Mode → ⑤ ← Median → ⑦	
5	8
6	9
6	9
7	10 ← Mode
8	10
9	10
Mean = 65/13 = 5	Mean = 94/13 = 7.23

midpoint is between 17 and 18, the median is 17.5. There are 13 scores in Table A.2; so the median is the seventh score, which is 5 for the low-incentive group and 7 for the high-incentive group.

The third measure of central tendency is the **mean**, which is the *arithmetic average*. When people talk about the "average" in everyday conversation, they are usually referring to the mean. To compute the mean, add the values of all the scores and divide by N (the total number of scores). For the scores in Table A.2, the mean for the low-incentive group is $65/13 = 5$, and for the high-incentive group, the mean is $94/13 = 7.23$.

Like the median (and unlike the mode), the mean reflects all the data to some degree, not just the most frequent data. Notice, however, that the mean reflects the *actual value* of all the scores, whereas the median gives each score equal weight, whatever its size. This difference can have a huge effect on how well the two statistics reflect the values of a particular set of data. Suppose, for example, that you collected data on the incomes of all fifty families in one small town and that the mean and the median incomes were the same: $20,000. A week later, a person moves to town with an annual income of $1 million. When you reanalyze the income data, the median will hardly change at all, because the millionaire just counts as one score added at the top of the list. However, when you compute the new mean, the actual *amount* of the millionaire's income is added to everyone else's income and divided by the old $N + 1$; as a result, the mean might double in value to $40,000. Because the mean is more representative than the median of the value of all the data, it is often preferred as a measure of central tendency. But sometimes, as in this example, the median may be better because it is less sensitive to extreme scores.

Measures of Variability   The **variability**, or spread, or dispersion of a set of data is often just as important as its central tendency. In the histograms in Figure A.1, for example, you can see that there is considerable variability in the low-incentive group; all five bins have at least one score in them. There is less variability in the high-incentive group; only four bins are represented. This variability can be quantified by measures known as the range and the standard deviation.

The **range** is simply the difference between the highest and the lowest value in the data set. For the data in Table A.2, the range for the low-incentive group is $9 - 2 = 7$; for the high-incentive group, the range is $10 - 3 = 7$. Like the median, the range does not reflect the values of all scores.

In contrast, the **standard deviation**, or **SD**, measures the average difference between each score and the mean of the data set. To see how the standard deviation is calculated, consider the data in Table A.3. The first step is to compute the mean of the set, in this case $20/5 = 4$. Second, calculate the difference, or *deviation* (D), of each score from the mean by subtracting the mean from each score, as in column 2 of Table A.3. Third, find the average of these deviations. However, if you calculated the average by finding the arithmetic mean, you would sum the deviations and find that the negative deviations exactly balance the positive ones, resulting in a mean difference of 0. Obviously there is more than zero variation around the mean in the data set. So, instead of employing the arithmetic mean, we compute the standard deviation by first squaring the deviations (which removes any negative values), summing these squared deviations, dividing by N, and then taking the square root of the result. These simple steps are outlined in more detail in Table A.3.

The standard deviation is a particularly important characteristic of any data set. For example, suppose you are a substitute teacher who comes to a new school hoping for an easy day's work. You are offered the choice of teaching

**Table A.3
Calculating the Standard Deviation**

The standard deviation of a set of scores reflects the average degree to which those scores differ from the mean of the set.

Raw Data	Difference from Mean = D		D²
2	2 − 4	= −2	4
2	2 − 4	= −2	4
3	3 − 4	= −1	1
4	4 − 4	= 0	0
9	9 − 4	= 5	25
Mean = 20/5 = 4			ΣD² = 34

$$\text{Standard deviation} = \sqrt{\frac{\Sigma D^2}{N}} = \sqrt{\frac{34}{5}} = \sqrt{6.8} = 2.6$$

Note: Σ means "the sum of."

one of two classes. In each, the students' mean IQ is 100. At first glance, there would appear to be no major difference between the classes' IQ scores. But it turns out that one class has an SD of 16; the SD of the other is 32. Since a higher standard deviation means more variability, the class with the SD of 32 is likely to be more difficult to teach because its students vary more in ability.

The Normal Distribution Now that we have described histograms and some descriptive statistics, we will reexamine how these methods of representing research data relate to some of the concepts discussed elsewhere in the book.

In most subareas in psychology, when researchers collect many measurements and plot their data in histograms, the pattern that results often resembles that shown for the low-incentive group in Figure A.1. That is, the majority of scores tend to fall in the middle of the distribution, with fewer and fewer occurring as one moves toward the extremes. As more and more data are collected, and as smaller and smaller bins are used (perhaps containing only one value each), the histograms tend to smooth out, until they resemble the bell-shaped curve known as the **normal distribution**, or *normal curve,* which is shown in Figure A.2a. When a distribution of scores follows a truly normal curve, its mean, median, and mode all have the same value. Furthermore, if the curve is normal, we can use its standard deviation to describe how any particular score stands in relation to the rest of the distribution.

IQ scores provide an example. They are distributed in a normal curve, with a mean, median, and mode of 100 and an SD of 16 (see Figure A.2b). In such a distribution, half of the population will have an IQ above 100, and half will be below 100. The shape of the true normal curve is such that 68 percent of the area under it lies within one standard deviation above and below the mean. In terms of IQ, this means that 68 percent of the population has an IQ somewhere between 84 (100 minus 16) and 116 (100 plus 16). Of the remaining 32 percent of the population, half falls more than 1 SD above the mean, and half falls more than 1 SD below the mean. Thus, 16 percent of the population has an IQ above 116, and 16 percent scores below 84.

The normal curve is also the basis for percentiles. A **percentile score** indicates the percentage of people or observations that fall below a given score in a normal distribution. In Figure A.2b, for example, the mean score (which is also the median) lies at a point below which 50 percent of the scores fall. Thus, the mean of a normal distribution is at the 50th percentile. What does this mean for IQ? If you score 1 SD above the mean, your score is at a point

Figure A.2
The Normal Distribution
Many kinds of research data approximate the symmetrical shape of the normal curve, in which most scores fall toward the center of the range.

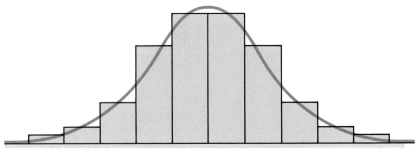

(a) Normal distribution, showing the smoothed approximation to the frequency histogram

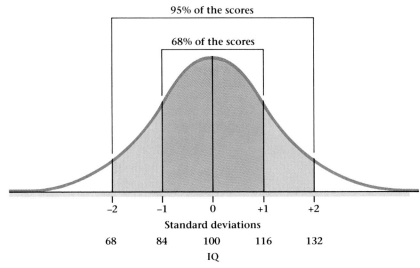

(b) The normal distribution of IQ

above which only 16 percent of the population falls. This means that 84 percent of the population (100 percent minus 16 percent) must be below that score; so this IQ score is at the 84th percentile. A score at 2 SDs above the mean is at the 97.5 percentile, because only 2.5 percent of the scores are above it in a normal distribution.

Scores may also be expressed in terms of their distance in standard deviations from the mean, producing what are called **standard scores.** A standard score of 1.5, for example, is 1.5 standard deviations from the mean.

Correlation Histograms and measures of central tendency and variability describe certain characteristics of one dependent variable at a time. However, psychologists are often concerned with describing the *relationship* between two variables. Measures of correlation are often used for this purpose. We discussed the interpretation of the *correlation coefficient* in Chapter 1; here we describe how to calculate it.

Recall that correlations are based on the relationship between two numbers associated with each subject or observation. The numbers may represent, say, a person's height and weight or the IQ of a parent and child. Table A.4 contains this kind of data for four subjects from our incentives study who took the test twice. (As you may recall from Chapter 10, the correlation between their scores

Table A.4
Calculating the Correlation Coefficient

Though it appears complex, calculation of the correlation coefficient is quite simple. The resulting r reflects the degree to which two sets of scores tend to be related, or to covary.

Subject	Test 1	Test 2	$(x - M_x)(y - M_y)$[b]
A	1	3	$(1 - 3)(3 - 4) = (-2)(-1) = +2$
B	1	3	$(1 - 3)(3 - 4) = (-2)(-1) = +2$
C	4	5	$(4 - 3)(5 - 4) = (1)(1) \quad = +1$
D	6	5	$(6 - 3)(5 - 4) = (3)(1) \quad = +3$
	[a]$M_x = 3$	$M_y = 4$	$\Sigma(x - M_x)(y - M_y) \qquad = +8$

[c] $\Sigma(x - M_x)^2 = 4 + 4 + 1 + 9 = 18$

[d] $\Sigma(y - M_y)^2 = 1 + 1 + 1 + 1 = 4$

[e] $r = \dfrac{\Sigma(x - M_x)(y - M_y)}{\sqrt{\Sigma(x - M_x)^2 \, \Sigma(y - M_y)^2}} = \dfrac{8}{\sqrt{18 \times 4}} = \dfrac{8}{\sqrt{72}} = \dfrac{8}{8.48} = +.94$

would be a measure of *test-retest reliability*.) The formula for computing the Pearson product-moment correlation, or r, is as follows:

$$r = \frac{\Sigma \, (x - M_x) \, (y - M_y)}{\sqrt{\Sigma \, (x - M_x)^2 \, \Sigma \, (y - M_y)^2}}$$

where:

x = each score on variable 1 (in this case, test 1)

y = each score on variable 2 (in this case, test 2)

M_x = the mean of the scores on variable 1

M_y = the mean of the scores on variable 2

The main function of the denominator in this formula is to ensure that the coefficient ranges from $+1.00$ to -1.00, no matter how large or small the values of the variables being correlated. The "action element" of this formula is the numerator. It is the result of multiplying the amounts by which each of two observations (x and y) differ from the means of their respective distributions (M_x and M_y). Notice that, if the two variables "go together" (so that, if one is large, the other is also large, and if one is small, the other is also small), then either both will tend to be above the mean of their distribution or both will tend to be below the mean of their distribution. When this is the case, $x - M_x$ and $y - M_y$ will both be positive, or they will both be negative. In either case, their product will always be positive, and the correlation coefficient will also be positive. If, on the other hand, the two variables go opposite to one another, such that, when one is large, the other is small, one of them is likely to be smaller than the mean of its distribution, so that either $x - M_x$ or $y - M_y$ will have a negative sign, and the other will have a positive sign. Multiplying these differences together will always result in a product with a negative sign, and r will be negative as well.

Now compute the correlation coefficient for the data presented in Table A.4. The first step (step a in the table) is to compute the mean (M) for each variable. M_x turns out to be 3 and M_y is 4. Next, calculate the numerator by finding the differences between each x and y value and its respective mean and by multiplying them (as in step b of Table A.4). Notice that, in this example, the differences in each pair have like signs, so the correlation coefficient will be positive. The next step is to calculate the terms in the denominator; in this case, as shown in steps c and d in Table A.4, they have values of 18 and 4. Finally, place all the terms in the formula and carry out the arithmetic (step e). The result in this case is an r of $+.94$, a high and positive correlation suggesting that performances on repeated tests are very closely related. A subject doing well the first time is very likely to do well again; a person doing poorly at first will probably do no better the second time.

Inferential Statistics

The descriptive statistics from the incentives experiment tell the experimenter that the performances of the high- and low-incentive groups differ. But there is some uncertainty. Is the difference large enough to be important? Does it represent a stable effect or a fluke? The researcher would like to have some *measure of confidence* that the difference between groups is genuine and reflects the effect of incentive on mental tasks in the real world, rather than the effect of the particular subjects used, the phase of the moon, or other random or uncontrolled factors. One way of determining confidence would be to run the experiment again with a new group of subjects. Confidence that incentives produced differences in performance would grow stronger if the same or a larger between-group difference occurs again. In reality, psychologists rarely have the opportunity to repeat, or *replicate*, their experiments in exactly the same way three or four times. But **inferential statistics** provide a measure of how likely it was that results came about by chance. They put a precise mathematical value on the confidence or probability that rerunning the same experiment would yield similar (or even stronger) results.

Differences Between Means: The *t* Test   One of the most important tools of inferential statistics is the *t* test. It allows the researcher to ask how likely it is that the difference between two means occurred by chance rather than as a function of the effect of the independent variable. When the *t* test or other inferential statistic says that the probability of chance effects is small enough (usually less than 5 percent), the results are said to be *statistically significant*. Conducting a *t* test of statistical significance requires the use of three descriptive statistics.

The first component of the *t* test is the size of the observed effect, the difference between the means. In the example shown in Table A.2, the difference between the means is $7.23 - 5 = 2.23$.

Second, the standard deviation of scores in each group must be known. If the scores in a group are quite variable, the standard deviation will be large, indicating that chance may have played a large role in producing the results. The next replication of the study might generate a very different set of group scores. If the scores in a group are all very similar, however, the standard deviation will be small, which suggests that the same result would probably occur for that group if the study were repeated. Thus, the *difference* between groups is more likely to be significant when each group's standard deviation is small.

Third, we need to take the sample size, N, into account. The larger the number of subjects or observations, the more likely it is that a given difference between means is significant. This is because, with larger samples, random factors within a group—the unusual performance of a few people who were sleepy or anxious or hostile, for example—are more likely to be canceled out by the majority, who better represent people in general. The same effect of sample size can be seen in coin tossing. If you toss a quarter five times, you might not be too surprised if heads comes up 80 percent of the time. If you get 80 percent heads after one hundred tosses, however, you might begin to suspect that this is probably not due to chance alone and that some other effect, perhaps some bias in the coin, is significant in producing the results.

To summarize, as the differences between the means get larger, as N increases, and as standard deviations get smaller, t increases. This increase in t raises the researcher's confidence in the significance of the difference between means.

Now we will calculate the t statistic and show how it is interpreted. The formula for t is:

$$t = \frac{M_1 - M_2}{\sqrt{\dfrac{(N_1 - 1)\, S_1^2 + (N_2 - 1)\, S_2^2}{N_1 + N_2 - 2}}}$$

where:

M_1 = mean of group 1

M_2 = mean of group 2

N_1 = number of scores or observations for group 1

N_2 = number of scores or observations for group 2

S_1 = standard deviation of group 1 scores

S_2 = standard deviation of group 2 scores

Despite appearances, this formula is quite simple. In the numerator is the difference between the two group means; t will get larger as this difference gets larger. The denominator contains an estimate of the standard deviation of the *differences* between group means; in other words, it suggests how much the difference between group means would vary if the experiment were repeated many times. Since this estimate is in the denominator, the value of t will get smaller as the standard deviation of group differences gets larger. For the data in Table A.2,

$$t = \frac{M_1 - M_2}{\sqrt{\dfrac{(N_1 - 1)\, S_1^2 + (N_2 - 1)\, S_2^2}{N_1 + N_2 - 2}}} = \frac{7.23 - 5}{\sqrt{\dfrac{(12)(5.09) + (12)(4.46)}{24}}}$$

$$= \frac{2.23}{\sqrt{4.78}} = 1.02 \text{ with 24 df}$$

To determine what a particular t means, we must use the value of N and a special statistical table called, appropriately enough, the t *table*. We have reproduced part of the t table in Table A.5.

Table A.5
The t Table

This table allows the researcher to determine whether an obtained t value is statistically significant. If the t value is larger than the one in the appropriate row in the .05 column, the difference between means that generated that t score is usually considered statistically significant.

df	*p* Value		
	.10 (10%)	**.05 (5%)**	**.01 (1%)**
4	1.53	2.13	3.75
9	1.38	1.83	2.82
14	1.34	1.76	2.62
19	1.33	1.73	2.54
22	1.32	1.71	2.50
24	1.32	1.71	2.49

First, find the computed value of *t* in the row corresponding to the **degrees of freedom,** or **df,** associated with the experiment. In this case, degrees of freedom are simply $N_1 + N_2 - 2$ (or two less than the total sample size or number of scores). Since our experiment had 13 subjects per group, df = 13 + 13 - 2 = 24. In the row for 24 df in Table A.5, you will find increasing values of *t* in each column. These columns correspond to decreasing *p* values, the probabilities that the difference between means occurred by chance. If an obtained *t* value is equal to or larger than one of the values in the *t* table (on the correct df line), then the difference between means that generated that *t* is said to be significant at the .10, .05, or .01 level of probability. Suppose, for example, that an obtained *t* (with 19 df) was 2.00. Looking along the 19 df row, you find that 2.00 is larger than the value in the .05 column. This allows you to say that the probability that the difference between means occurred by chance was no greater than .05, or 5 in 100. If the *t* had been greater than the value in the .01 column, the probability of a chance result would have been only .01, or 1 in 100.

The *t* value from our experiment was only 1.02, with 24 df. Because 1.02 is smaller than all the values in the 24 df row, the difference between the high- and low-incentive groups could have occurred by chance more than 10 times in 100. As noted earlier, when an obtained *t* is not large enough to exceed *t* table values at the .05 level or less, it is not usually considered statistically significant. Perhaps the difference between our incentive groups was not large enough, the group *N*s were not large enough, or the variance within the groups was too large.

Beyond the *t* Test   Many experiments in psychology are considerably more complex than simple comparisons between two groups. They often involve three or more experimental and control groups. Some experiments also include more than one independent variable. For example, suppose we had been interested not only in the effect of incentive size on performance, but also in the effect of problem difficulty. We might then create six groups whose subjects would perform easy or difficult problems with low, high, or very high incentives.

In an experiment like this, the results might be due to the incentive, the problem difficulty, or the combined effects (known as the *interaction*) of the two. Analyzing the size and source of these effects is typically accomplished through procedures known as *analysis of variance*. The details of analysis of variance are beyond the scope of this book, but the statistical significance of each effect is influenced by differences between means, standard deviation, and sample size in much the same way as described for the *t* test.

For more detailed information about how analysis of variance and other inferential statistics are used to understand and interpret the results of psychological research, consider taking courses in research methods and statistical or quantitative methods.

Summary and Key Terms

Psychological research generates large quantities of *data*. Statistics are methods for describing and drawing conclusions from data.

Describing Data

Frequency Histograms

Graphic representations such as *frequency histograms* provide visual descriptions of data, making the data easier to understand.

Descriptive Statistics

Numbers that summarize a pool of data are called *descriptive statistics*. The easiest statistic to compute is *n*, which gives the number of observations made. A set of scores can be described by giving two other types of descriptive statistic: a measure of *central tendency*, which describes the typical value of a set of data, and a measure of *variability*. Measures of central tendency include the *mean, median,* and *mode*; variability is typically measured by the *range* and by the *standard deviation.* Sets of data often follow a *normal distribution,* which means that most scores fall in the middle of the range, with fewer and fewer scores occurring as one moves toward the extremes. In a truly normal distribution the mean, median, and mode are identical. When a set of data shows a normal distribution, a data point can be cited in terms of *percentile scores,* which indicate the percentage of people or observations that fall below a certain score, and in terms of *standard scores,* which indicate the distance, in standard deviations, a score is located from the mean. Another type of descriptive statistic, a *correlation coefficient,* is used to measure the correlation between sets of scores.

Other Key Term in This Section: null hypothesis.

Inferential Statistics

Researchers use *inferential statistics* to quantify the probability that conducting the same experiment again would yield similar results.

Differences Between Means: The t Test

One inferential statistic, the *t test,* assesses the likelihood that differences between two means occurred by chance or reflect the effect of an independent variable. Performing a *t* test requires using the difference between the means of two sets of data, the standard deviation of scores in each set, and the number of observations or subjects. To interpret a *t* test, *degrees of freedom* must also be taken into account. When the *t* test indicates that the experimental results had a low probability of occurring by chance, the results are said to be statistically significant.

Beyond the t Test

When more than two groups must be compared, researchers typically rely on *analysis of variance* in order to interpret the results of an experiment.

Absolute threshold The minimum amount of stimulus energy that can be detected 50 percent of the time. (See also *internal noise* and *response bias.*) (*p. 177*)

Accessory structure A structure, such as the lens of the eye, that modifies a stimulus. In some sensory systems, this modification is the first step in sensation. (*p. 127*)

Accommodation (1) The ability of the lens to change its shape and bend light rays so that objects are in focus. (*p. 138*) (2) The process of modifying schemas as an infant tries out familiar schemas on objects that do not fit them. (*p. 45*)

Acetylcholine The neurotransmitter used by cholinergic neurons in the peripheral nervous system to control muscle contractions and in the central nervous system to control movement and memory. (*p. 108*)

Acoustic code A mental representation of information as a sequence of sounds. (*p. 302*)

Action potential An impulse that travels down an axon when the neuron becomes depolarized and sodium rushes into the cell. This kind of nerve communication is "all or none": the cell either fires at full strength or does not fire at all. (*p. 89*)

Active sleep (also called *REM sleep*) A stage of sleep during which the EEG resembles that of someone who is active and awake; the heart rate, respiration, blood pressure, and other physiological patterns are also very much like those occurring during the day. At the same time, the sleeper begins rapid eye movements beneath closed lids, and muscle tone decreases to the point of paralysis. (*p. 225*)

Actor-observer bias The tendency to attribute other people's behavior to internal causes while attributing our own behavior (especially our errors and failures) to external causes. (*p. 675*)

Acuity Visual resolution or clarity, which is greatest in the fovea because of its large concentration of cones. (*p. 140*)

Adaptation The process through which responsiveness to an unchanging stimulus decreases over time. (*p. 127*)

Adaptive reading A skill in which a reader speeds up and slows down according to the information content of the material and the level of comprehension that it requires. (*p. 208*)

Addiction Development of a physical need for a psychoactive drug. (*p. 608*)

Adrenal gland A part of the sympathetic nervous system that affects target organs by releasing adrenaline and noradrenaline into the bloodstream. The adrenal medulla facilitates com-

munication between the brain and various target organs; the adrenal cortex is involved in stress reactions. The release of adrenaline is responsible for the fight-or-flight syndrome. (See also *fight-or-flight syndrome.*) (*p. 474*)

Affective disorder See *mood disorder.*

Affirmation rule (also called *one-feature rule*) A rule that requires that an item must have one specific attribute to be classified as a member of a concept. (*p. 350*)

Age regression A phenomenon displayed by some hypnotized people that involves recalling and re-enacting behaviors from childhood. (*p. 235*)

Aggression An act that is intended to cause harm or damage to another person. (*p. 714*)

Agoraphobia A strong fear of being alone or away from the security of home. (*p. 590*)

Alarm reaction The first stage in the general adaptation syndrome, which involves some version of the fight-or-flight response. In the face of mild stressors the reaction may simply involve changes in heart rate, respiration, and perspiration that help the body regulate itself. More severe stressors prompt more dramatic alarm reactions, rapidly mobilizing the body's adaptive energy. (See also *exhaustion, fight-or-flight syndrome,* and *resistance.*) (*p. 506*)

Alcoholism A pattern of continuous or intermittent drinking that may lead to addiction and almost always causes severe social, physical, and other problems. (*p. 609*)

Algorithm A systematic procedure that cannot fail to produce a solution to a problem. It is not usually the most efficient way to produce a solution. (See also *heuristic.*) (*p. 355*)

Alpha wave Rhythmic brain waves that occur at a speed of about 8 to 12 cycles per second and are evident in stage 0, the stage preceding sleep, during which the person is relaxed, with eyes closed, but awake. (*p. 224*)

Altered state of consciousness (also called *alternate state of consciousness*) A condition that exists when quantitative and qualitative changes in mental processes are extensive enough that the person or objective observers notice significant differences in psychological and behavioral functioning. (*p. 223*)

Altruism An unselfish concern with another's welfare. (*p. 723*)

Amplitude The difference between the peak and the baseline of a waveform. (*p. 130*)

Analgesia The absence of the sensation of pain in the presence of a normally painful stimulus. The brain appears to use serotonin and endorphins to block painful stimuli. (*p. 160*)

Anal stage The second of Freud's psychosexual stages, usually occurring during the second year of life, in which the focus of pleasure and conflict shifts from the mouth to the anus. The demand for toilet training conflicts with the child's instinctual pleasure in having bowel movements at will. (*p. 545*)

Anchoring heuristic A shortcut in the thought process that involves adding new information to existing information to reach a judgment. (*p. 355*)

Androgens Masculine hormones that circulate in the bloodstream and regulate sexual motivation in both sexes. The principal androgen is testosterone, and relatively more androgens circulate in men than in women. (See also *testosterone*.) (*p. 447*)

Anorexia nervosa An eating disorder characterized by self-starvation and dramatic weight loss. (*p. 445*)

ANS See *autonomic nervous system*.

Anterograde amnesia A loss of memory for any event that occurs after a brain injury. (See also *retrograde amnesia*.) (*p. 326*)

Antidepressant A drug that relieves depression. (*p. 656*)

Antipsychotic A drug that alleviates the symptoms of schizophrenia or other severe forms of psychological disorder. (*p. 655*)

Antisocial personality A personality disorder involving a long-term, persistent pattern of impulsive, selfish, unscrupulous, even criminal behavior. (*p. 613*)

Anxiety disorder A condition in which intense feelings of apprehension are long-standing or disruptive. (See also *generalized anxiety disorder, panic disorder, phobia,* and *obsessive-compulsive disorder*.) (*p. 589*)

Anxiolytic A drug that reduces feelings of tension and anxiety. (*p. 244*)

Anxious insecure attachment A type of parent-child relationship in which the child is often upset when the mother leaves, but acts angry and rejects her efforts at contact when she returns. (*p. 54*)

Archetype According to Jung, a classic image or concept that is part of the collective unconscious. One archetype is the idea of mother; everyone is born with a kind of predisposition to see and react to certain people as mother figures. (*p. 547*)

Arousal A general level of activation that is reflected in several physiological systems and can be measured by electrical activity in the brain, heart action, muscle tension, and the state of many other organ systems. (*p. 437*)

Arousal theory A theory of motivation stating that people are motivated to behave in ways that maintain what is, for them, an optimal level of arousal. (*p. 438*)

Artificial concept Concepts that can be clearly defined by a set of rules or properties, so that each member of the concept has all of the defining properties and no nonmember does. (See also *natural concept*.) (*p. 349*)

Artificial intelligence The field that studies how to program computers to imitate the products of human perception, understanding, and thought. (*p. 365*)

Assertiveness and social skills training A set of methods for teaching clients who are anxious or unproductive in social situations how to interact with others more comfortably and effectively. (*p. 641*)

Assimilation The process of taking in new information about objects by trying out existing schemas on objects that fit those schemas. (*p. 44*)

Association cortex Those parts of the cerebral cortex that receive information from more than one sense or combine sensory and motor information to perform such complex cognitive tasks as associating words with images or abstract thought. (*p. 102*)

Attachment An affectionate, close, and enduring relationship with the single person with whom a baby has shared many experiences. (*p. 53*)

Attention The process of directing and focusing certain psychological resources, usually by voluntary control, to enhance information processing, performance, and mental experience. (*p. 202*)

Attitude A predisposition toward a particular cognitive, emotional, or behavioral reaction to an object, individual, group, situation, or action. (*p. 684*)

Attribution The process of explaining the causes of people's behavior, including one's own. (See also *attributional bias*.) (*p. 672*)

Attributional bias A tendency to distort one's view of behavior. (See also *fundamental attribution error*.) (*p. 674*)

Auditory nerve The bundle of axons that carries stimuli from the hair cells of the cochlea to the brain to facilitate hearing. (*p. 132*)

Authoritarian parent A firm, punitive, and unsympathetic parent who values obedience from the child and authority for himself or herself, does not encourage independence, is detached, and seldom praises the child. The result of this parenting style is often an unfriendly, distrustful, and withdrawn child. (*p. 56*)

Authoritarian personality The traits exhibited by people who view the world as a strict social hierarchy and feel they have the right to demand deference and cooperation from all those who have lower status. (*p. 692*)

Authoritative parent A parent who reasons with the child, encourages give and take, is firm but understanding, and gives the child more responsibility as he or she gets older. Children of this type of parent are usually friendly, cooperative, self-reliant, and socially responsible. (*p. 56*)

Autonomic nervous system (ANS) A subsystem of the peripheral nervous system that carries messages between the central nervous system and the heart, lungs, and other organs and glands in the body. The ANS regulates the activity of these organs and glands to meet varying demands placed upon the body and also provides information to the brain about that activity. (*p. 86*)

Availability heuristic A shortcut in the thought process that involves judging the frequency or probability of an event or hypothesis by how easily the hypothesis or examples of the event can be brought to mind. Thus, people tend to choose the hypothesis or alternative that is most mentally "available." (*p. 357*)

Average evoked potential A series of evoked brain potentials made in response to the same stimuli. The recording of average evoked potentials reflects the firing of large groups of neurons, within different regions of the brain, at different times during the sequence of information processing. The pattern of peaks provides information about mental chronometry that is more precise than overall reaction time. (See also *evoked potential*.) (*p. 346*)

Aversive conditioning A method for reducing unwanted behaviors by using classical conditioning principles to create a negative response to some stimulus. (*p. 643*)

Avoidance conditioning A type of learning in which an organism responds to a signal in a way that avoids exposure to an aversive stimulus. (*p. 276*)

Axon The fiber that carries signals from the body of a neuron out to where communication occurs with other neurons. Each neuron generally has only one axon leaving the cell body, but that one axon may have many branches. (*p. 88*)

Babblings Repetitions of syllables; the first sounds infants make that resemble speech. (*p. 377*)

Basilar membrane The floor of the fluid-filled duct that runs through the cochlea. Waves passing through the fluid in the duct move the basilar membrane, and this movement deforms hair cells that touch the membrane. (See also *cochlea*.) (*p. 132*)

Behavioral approach (also called *behavioral model*) Personality theories based on the assumption that human behavior is determined mainly by what a person has learned in life, especially by the rewards and punishments a person has experienced in interacting with other people. According to this approach, the consistency of people's learning histories, not an inner personality structure, produces characteristic behavior patterns. (*p. 7*)

Behavioral medicine A broad-based movement focused on how behavior and illness are linked. Medical doctors, psychologists, dentists, nurses, health educators, social workers, and other health-related professionals work together to find ways to use behavioral science to aid in the prevention, detection, treatment, and cure of physical disease. (*p. 522*)

Behavior modification See *behavior therapy*.

Behavior therapy (also called *behavior modification*) Treatments that use learning principles to change behavior by helping, often literally teaching, clients to act as well as to think differently. (*p. 639*)

Biased sample A group of research subjects selected from a population each of whose members did not have an equal chance of being chosen for study. (*p. 20*)

Binocular disparity A depth cue based on the difference between the two retinal images. It exists because each eye receives a slightly different view of the world. This difference, which decreases with distance, is measured by the brain, which combines the two images to create the perception of a single image located at a particular distance. (*p. 190*)

Biofeedback training Training methods whereby people can monitor and attempt to control normally unconscious physiological processes such as blood pressure, skin conductance, and muscle tension. (*p. 526*)

Biological approach See *biological model*.

Biological model A view in which behavior and behavior disorders are seen as the result of physical processes, especially those relating to the brain and to hormones and other chemicals. (*p. 580*)

Biological psychologist (also called *physiological psychologist*) A psychologist who analyzes the biological factors influencing behavior and mental processes. (*p. 4*)

Biological psychology (also called *physiological psychology*) The psychological specialty that researches the physical and chemical changes that cause and occur in response to behavior and mental processes. (*p. 83*)

Bipolar cells Cells through which a visual stimulus passes after going to the photoreceptor cells and before going to the ganglion cells. (*p. 141*)

Bipolar disorder A condition in which a person alternates between the two emotional extremes of depression and mania. (*p. 599*)

Bisexual People who engage in sexual activities with partners of both sexes. (*p. 450*)

Blind spot The point at which the axons from all of the ganglion cells converge and exit the eyeball. This exit point has no photoreceptors and is therefore insensitive to light. (*p. 148*)

Bottom-up processing Aspects of recognition that depend first on the information about the stimulus that comes "up" to the brain from the sensory receptors. (See also *top-down processing*.) (*p. 196*)

Brightness The overall intensity of all of the wavelengths that make up light. (*p. 144*)

Brown-Peterson procedure A method for determining how long unrehearsed information remains in short-term memory. It involves presenting a stimulus to individuals, preventing them from rehearsing it by having them perform a counting task, and then testing recall of the stimulus. (*p. 310*)

Bulimia An eating disorder that involves eating massive quantities of food and then eliminating the food by self-induced vomiting or strong laxatives. (*p. 445*)

Burnout A gradually intensifying pattern of physical, psychological, and behavioral dysfunctions in response to a continuous flow of stressors. (*p. 512*)

Cannon-Bard theory A theory of the experience of emotion in which the brain interprets an emotional situation through the thalamus, which sends sensory signals simultaneously to the cerebral cortex and the autonomic nervous system. The emotion becomes conscious in the cerebral cortex, and emotion is experienced with or without feedback about peripheral responses. (*p. 480*)

Case study A research method involving the intensive examination of some phenomenon in a particular individual, group, or situation. It is especially useful for studying complex or relatively rare phenomena. (*p. 18*)

Catastrophizing Dwelling on and overemphasizing the consequences of negative events; one of the most common cognitive stress responses. (*p. 510*)

Catatonic schizophrenia A type of schizophrenia characterized by a movement disorder in which the individual may alternate between total immobility or stupor (sometimes holding bizarre, uncomfortable poses for long periods) and wild excitement. (*p. 604*)

Central nervous system (CNS) The part of the nervous system encased in bone, including the brain and the spinal cord, whose primary function is to process information provided by the sensory systems and decide on an appropriate course of action for the motor system. (*p. 86*)

Central tendency The typical value in a set of data. (See also *mode, median,* and *mean.*) (*p. A–3*)

Cerebellum The part of the hindbrain whose function is to control finely coordinated movements and to store learned associations that involve movement, such as those movements required in dancing or athletics. (*p. 99*)

Cerebral cortex The outer surface of the cerebrum, consisting of two cerebral hemispheres. It is physically divided into four areas, called the frontal, parietal, occipital, and temporal lobes. It is divided functionally into the sensory cortex, the motor cortex, and the association cortex. (*p. 101*)

Cerebral hemisphere One-half, either right or left, of the round, almost spherical, outermost part of the cerebrum. (*p. 101*)

Cerebrum (also called the *telencephalon*) The largest part of the forebrain; it is divided into the right and left cerebral hemispheres and contains the striatum and the limbic system. (*p. 101*)

Characteristic frequency The frequency to which any given neuron in the auditory nerve is most sensitive. (*p. 134*)

Chromosome A long, thin structure in every biological cell that contains genetic information in the form of more than a thousand genes strung out like a chain. (*p. 38*)

Chunk Stimuli that are perceived as one unit or a meaningful grouping of information. Most people can hold five to nine (seven plus or minus two) chunks of information in short-term memory. (*p. 308*)

Circadian rhythm A cycle, such as waking and sleeping, that repeats about once a day. (*p. 229*)

Classical conditioning A procedure in which a neutral stimulus is paired with a stimulus that elicits a reflex or other response until the neutral stimulus alone comes to elicit a similar response. (*p. 259*)

Client-centered therapy (also called *person-centered therapy*) A type of therapy in which the client decides what to talk about and when, without direction, judgment, or interpretation from the therapist. This type of treatment is characterized by three important and interrelated therapist attitudes: unconditional positive regard, empathy, and congruence. (See also *congruence, empathy,* and *unconditional positive regard.*) (*p. 635*)

Clinical psychologist A psychologist who seeks to assess, understand, and correct abnormal behavior. (*p. 5*)

Closure A Gestalt grouping principle stating that people tend to fill in missing contours to form a complete object. (*p. 184*)

CNS See *central nervous system.*

Cochlea A fluid-filled spiral structure in the ear in which auditory transduction occurs. (*p. 132*)

Cognitive approach A way of looking at human behavior that emphasizes research on how the brain takes in information, creates perceptions, forms and retrieves memories, processes information, and generates integrated patterns of action. (*p. 8*)

Cognitive behavior therapy Treatment methods that help clients change the way they think as well as the way they behave. Cognitive obstacles are brought to light, and the therapist encourages the client to try new ways of thinking. (*p. 643*)

Cognitive dissonance theory A theory that proposes that uneasiness results when people's cognitions about themselves or the world are inconsistent with one another. Dissonance motivates people to take some action to make the cognitions consistent. (*p. 685*)

Cognitive map A mental representation, or picture, of the environment. (*p. 292*)

Cognitive psychologist A psychologist whose research focus is on analysis of the mental processes underlying judgment, decision making, problem solving, imagining, and other aspects of human thought or cognition. (*p. 3*)

Cognitive restructuring A therapy technique or process for coping with stress that involves replacing stress-provoking thoughts with more constructive thoughts in order to make stressors less threatening and disruptive. (*p. 525*)

Collective unconscious According to Jung, a kind of memory bank in which are stored all the images and ideas the human race has accumulated since its evolution from lower forms of life. (See also *archetype.*) (*p. 547*)

Common fate A Gestalt grouping principle stating that objects moving in the same direction and at the same speed are perceived as belonging together. (*p. 185*)

Community psychology A movement whose goal is to minimize or prevent psychological disorders through promoting changes in social systems and through community mental health programs designed to make treatment methods more accessible to the poor and others who are unserved or underserved by mental health professionals. (*p. 5*)

Competition Any type of behavior in which individuals try to attain a goal for themselves while denying that goal to others. (*p. 728*)

Complementary colors Colors that result in gray when lights of those two colors are mixed. Complementary colors are roughly opposite each other on the color circle. (*p. 146*)

Compliance Adjusting one's behavior to match that of a group because of directly expressed social influence. (*p. 703*)

Concept A class or category of objects, events, or ideas that have common properties. (See also *artificial concept* and *natural concept.*) (*p. 348*)

Concrete operations According to Piaget, the third stage of cognitive development, during which children can learn to count, measure, add, and subtract; their thinking is no longer dominated by visual appearances. (*p. 46*)

Conditioned stimulus (CS) In classical conditioning, the originally neutral stimulus that, through pairing with the unconditioned stimulus, comes to elicit a conditioned response. (*p. 259*)

Conditioned response (CR) In classical conditioning, the response that the conditioned stimulus elicits. (*p. 259*)

Conditions of worth According to Rogers, the feelings an individual experiences when the entire person, instead of a specific behavior, is evaluated. The person may feel that his or her worth as a person depends on displaying the right attitudes, behaviors, and values. (*p. 567*)

Cones Photoreceptors in the retina that use one of three varieties of iodopsin, a color-sensitive photopigment, to distinguish colors. (See also *rods.*) (*p. 139*)

Conformity Changing one's behavior or beliefs to match those of other group members, generally as a result of real or imagined, though unspoken, group pressure. (*p. 701*)

Confounding variable In an experiment, any factor that affects the dependent variable along with or instead of the independent variable. Confounding variables include random variables, the placebo effect, and experimenter bias. (*p. 21*)

Congruence In client-centered therapy, a consistency between the way therapists feel and the way they act toward the client; therapists' unconditional positive regard and empathy must be real, not manufactured. (*p. 636*)

Conjunctive rule A classification rule that requires that an item must have two or more specified attributes for it to be classified as a member of a concept. (*p. 350*)

Conscious level The level at which mental activities that we are aware of from moment to moment occur. (See also *preconscious level.*) (*p. 220*)

Consciousness The awareness of external stimuli and our own mental activity; also, mental processes of which we may be unaware. (*p. 215*)

Conservation The ability to recognize that the important properties of a substance, such as number, volume, or weight, remain constant despite changes in shape, length, or position. (*p. 46*)

Constructionist A view of perception taken by those who argue that the perceptual system uses fragments of sensory information to construct an image of reality. (See also *ecological view.*) (*p. 174*)

Contact hypothesis A hypothesis, based on learning theories of prejudice, that states that stereotypes and prejudices about a group should be reduced as contact (specifically, friendly contact, as equals) with that group increases. (*p. 693*)

Continuity A Gestalt grouping principle stating that sensations that appear to create a continuous form are perceived as belonging together. (*p. 184*)

Continuous reinforcement schedule In operant conditioning, a pattern in which a reinforcer is delivered every time a particular response occurs. (*p. 272*)

Control group In an experiment, the group that receives no treatment or provides some other base line against which to compare the performance or response of the experimental group. (*p. 20*)

Convergence (1) The receiving of information by one bipolar cell from many photoreceptors. Convergence allows bipolar cells to compare the amount of light on larger regions of the retina and increases the sensation of contrast. (*p. 142*) (2) A depth cue involving the rotation of the eyes to project the image of an object on each retina. The closer an object is, the more ''cross-eyed'' the viewer must become to achieve a focused image of it. (*p. 190*)

Convergent thinking The ability to apply the rules of logic and what one knows about the world in order to narrow down the number of possible solutions to a problem or perform some other complex cognitive task. (*p. 422*)

Conversion disorder A somatoform disorder in which a person appears to be, but actually is not, blind, deaf, paralyzed, insensitive to pain in various parts of the body, or even pregnant. (See also *somatoform disorder.*) (*p. 593*)

Cooperation Any type of behavior in which several people work together to attain a goal. (*p. 728*)

Cornea The curved, transparent, protective layer through which light rays enter the eye. (*p. 138*)

Corpus callosum A massive bundle of fibers that connects the right and left cerebral hemispheres and allows them to communicate with each other. Severing the corpus callosum causes difficulty in performing tasks that require information from both hemispheres, such as recognizing and naming objects. (*p. 104*)

Correlation In research, the degree to which one variable is related to another; the strength and direction of the relationship is measured by a correlation coefficient. Correlation does not guarantee causation. (*p. 12*)

Correlation coefficient A statistic, r, that summarizes the strength and direction of a relationship between two variables. Correlation coefficients vary from 0.00 to ±1.00. The plus or minus sign indicates the direction, positive or negative, of a relationship. An r of +1.00 or −1.00 indicates a perfect correlation, which means that if you know the value of one variable, you can predict with certainty the value of the other variable. (*p. 13*)

Creativity The capacity to produce original solutions or novel compositions. (*p. 421*)

Crisis of generativity A stage described by Erikson that occurs in people's thirties and is characterized by the desire to produce something lasting, usually through parenthood or job achievement. (*p. 74*)

Critical period An interval during which certain kinds of growth must occur if development is to proceed normally. (*p. 40*)

Cross-sectional study A research method in which data collected simultaneously from people of different ages are compared. (*p. 423*)

Crystallized intelligence The specific knowledge gained as a result of applying fluid intelligence. It produces verbal comprehension and skill at manipulating numbers. (See also *fluid intelligence.*) (*p. 414*)

Dark adaptation The increasing ability to see in the dark as time passes, due to the synthesis of more photopigments by the photoreceptors. (*p. 141*)

Data Numbers that represent research findings and provide the basis for research conclusions. (*p. A–1*)

Daydream An altered state of consciousness in which attention shifts away from external stimuli to dwell on internal events, sometimes in a fantasy-oriented, unrealistic way. (*p. 223*)

Decay theory A theory of forgetting stating that if people do not use information in long-term memory, it gradually fades until it is lost completely. (*p. 316*)

Decomposition A heuristic that consists of breaking a problem into smaller elements. (*p. 361*)

Deep structure An abstract representation of the relationships expressed in a sentence; the various underlying meanings of a given sentence. (*p. 372*)

Defense mechanism A psychological response that helps protect a person from anxiety and the other negative emotions accompanying stress; it does little or nothing to eliminate the source of stress. (*p. 510*)

Deficiency orientation According to Maslow, a preoccupation with meeting perceived needs for material things a person does not have that can lead to perceiving life as a meaningless exercise in disappointment and boredom. (*p. 567*)

Degrees of freedom The total sample size or number of scores in a data less the number of experimental groups. (*p. A–10*)

Deindividuation A hypothesized psychological state occurring in group members that results in loss of individuality and a tendency to do things not normally done when alone. (*p. 735*)

Delayed conditioning In classical conditioning, the most effective method of producing a strong conditioned response, which involves presenting the conditioned stimulus, leaving it on while presenting the unconditioned stimulus, and then terminating both at the same time. (*p. 260*)

Delirium An organic mental disorder that involves a clouded state of consciousness. The person has trouble "thinking straight," may be unable to focus on a conversation or other environmental events, and may appear confused. Symptoms may also include delusions, hallucinations, and disruption of the normal sleep-waking cycle. (*p. 581*)

Delta wave The slow (0.5 to 0.3 cycles per second), high-amplitude brain waves that usually first appear in stage 3 sleep. When delta waves occur more than 50 percent of the time, the person has entered stage 4, the deepest level of sleep and the one from which it is most difficult to be roused. (*p. 225*)

Delusion A false belief, such as those experienced by people suffering from schizophrenia or extreme depression. (*p. 598*)

Dementia An organic mental disorder that involves a loss of intellectual functions. It may occur alone or in combination with delirium. The most common symptoms involve loss of memory-related functions. (See also *delirium.*) (*p. 581*)

Demonological model An explanation of abnormal behavior as the work of the devil or other supernatural forces. (*p. 580*)

Dendrite In a neuron, the fiber that receives signals from the axons of other neurons and carries that signal to the cell body. A neuron can have up to several hundred dendrites. (*p. 88*)

Denial In psychodynamic theory, the most primitive defense mechanism. Denial distorts reality by leading a person to deny his or her impulses or refuse to recognize unpleasant events. (*p. 545*)

Deoxyribonucleic acid (DNA) The molecular structure of a gene that provides the genetic code. Each DNA molecule consists of two strands of sugar, phosphate, and nitrogen-containing molecules twisted around each other in a double spiral. (*p. 38*)

Dependent variable In an experiment, the factor affected by the independent variable. (*p. 20*)

Depressant A psychoactive drug that inhibits the functioning of the central nervous system. (*p. 242*)

Depth perception Perception of distance, one of the most important factors underlying size and shape constancy. Depth perception allows us to experience the world in three-dimensional depth, not as a two-dimensional movie. (*p. 187*)

Descriptive statistics Numbers that summarize a pool of research data. (*p. A–3*)

Developmental psychologist A psychologist who seeks to understand, describe, and explore how behavior and mental processes change over the course of a lifetime. (*p. 5*)

Developmental psychology The psychological specialty that documents the course of people's social, emotional, moral, and intellectual development over the life span and explores how development in different domains fits together, is affected by experience, and relates to other areas of psychology. (*p. 31*)

Diathesis An inherited predisposition that leaves a person vulnerable to problems. (*p. 583*)

Diathesis-stress model An integrative approach to psychological disorders that recognizes that each person inherits certain physical predispositions that leave him or her vulnerable to problems that may or may not appear, depending on what kinds of situations that person confronts. People who must deal with particular stressors may or may not develop psychopathology, depending on their predisposition and ability to cope with those stressors. (*p. 583*)

Dichotic listening task A task in which different messages are played into each ear. This type of task has been used to demonstrate the limitations of the capacity to divide attention. (*p. 203*)

Difference threshold See *Just-noticeable difference.*

Diffusion of responsibility The process through which a person tends not to take personal responsibility for helping someone in trouble when others are present. (*p. 727*)

Discrimination Differential treatment of various groups; the behavioral component of prejudice. (See also *prejudice.*) (*p. 692*)

Discriminative stimuli Stimuli that signal whether reinforcement is available if a certain response is made. (*p. 271*)

Diseases of adaptation Illnesses that are caused or promoted by stressors. (*p. 507*)

Disjunctive rule A classification rule that requires members of a concept to have one feature or another. (*p. 350*)

Disorganized schizophrenia A rare type of schizophrenia characterized by a variety of jumbled and unrelated delusions and hallucinations. The person may display incoherent speech, strange facial grimaces, and meaningless ritual movements and may neglect personal hygiene and lose bowel and bladder control. (*p. 604*)

Displacement In psychodynamic theory, a defense mechanism in which unacceptable impulses are diverted toward alternative targets. (*p. 545*)

Dispositional approach A personality theory based on the assumptions that 1) each person has stable, long-lasting dispositions to display certain behaviors, attitudes, and emotions; 2) these dispositions are general in that they appear in diverse situations; and 3) each person has a different set of dispositions, or at least a set of dispositions that assume a unique pattern. (*p. 552*)

Dissociation theory A theory that defines hypnosis as a condition in which people relax central control of mental processes and share some of that control with the hypnotist, who is allowed to determine what the person will experience and do. According to this theory, hypnosis is a socially agreed-upon opportunity to display one's ability to let mental functions become dissociated. (See also *role theory* and *state theory.*) (*p. 238*)

Dissociative disorder A rare condition that involves a sudden and usually temporary disruption in a person's memory, consciousness, or identity. (*p. 595*)

Divergent thinking The ability to think along many alternative paths to generate many different solutions to a problem. (*p. 421*)

DNA See *deoxyribonucleic acid.*

Dopamine A neurotransmitter used by dopaminergic neurons. In the substantia nigra, these neurons control movement. In the midbrain, dopaminergic neurons extend into the cerebral cortex to control movement and complex cognitive abilities. (*p. 109*)

Double-blind design A research design in which neither the experimenter nor the subjects know which is the experimental group and which is the control group. This design helps prevent experimenter bias (a confounding variable). (*p. 22*)

Dream A storylike sequence of images, sensations, and perception that lasts anywhere from several seconds to many minutes and occurs mainly during REM sleep (though it may take place at other times). (*p. 232*)

Drive In drive theory, a psychological state of arousal, created by an imbalance in homeostasis that prompts an organism to take action to restore the balance and, in the process, reduce the drive. (See also *need, primary drive,* and *secondary drive.*) (*p. 435*)

Drive reduction theory A theory of motivation stating that much motivation arises from constant imbalances in homeostasis. (See also *drive* and *homeostasis.*) (*p. 435*)

Dyslexia A condition in which a person who shows normal intelligence and full comprehension of spoken words has difficulty understanding written words. (*p. 208*)

Dysthymia A pattern of depression in which the person shows the sad mood, lack of interest, and loss of pleasure associated with major depression, but to a lesser degree. (See also *major depression.*) (*p. 598*)

Echo The mental representation of a sound in sensory memory. (*p. 307*)

Echoic memory The sensory register for auditory sensations. (*p. 307*)

Ecological view An approach to perception that states that humans and other species are so well adapted to their natural environment that many aspects of the world are perceived automatically and at the sensory level, without requiring higher-level analysis and inferences. (See also *constructionist.*) (*p. 174*)

ECT See *electroconvulsive therapy.*

EEG See *electroencephalogram.*

Ego In psychodynamic theory, that part of the personality that makes compromises and mediates conflicts between and among the demands of the id, the superego and the real world; the ego operates according to the reality principle. (See also *id* and *reality principle.*) (*p. 543*)

Eidetic memory A type of memory (commonly called photographic memory) that involves automatic, long-term, detailed, and vivid images of virtually everything a person has seen. About 5 percent of all school-age children have eidetic imagery, but almost no adults have it. (*p. 315*)

Elaborative rehearsal A memorization method that involves

thinking about how new information relates to information already stored in long-term memory. (*p. 313*)

Electroconvulsive therapy (ECT) A brief electric shock administered to the brain, usually to reduce profound depression that does not respond to drug treatments. (*p. 653*)

Electroencephalogram (EEG) A recording of the electrical signals produced by the nerve cells of the brain, obtained through electrodes attached to the surface of the skull. (*p. 94*)

Embryo The developing individual from the fourteenth day after fertilization until the third month after fertilization. (*p. 39*)

Emotion An experience that is felt as happening to the self, is generated, in part, by the cognitive appraisal of a situation, and is accompanied by both learned and reflexive physical responses. (*p. 472*)

Empathy In client-centered therapy, the therapist's attempt to appreciate how the world looks from the client's point of view. Empathy requires an internal perspective, a focus on what the client might be thinking and feeling. (*p. 635*)

Empathy-altruism model A theory that suggests that people help others because of empathy with their needs. (*p. 724*)

Encoding The process of putting information into a form that the memory system can accept and use; the process of constructing mental representations of physical stimuli. (*p. 302*)

Encoding specificity principle A retrieval principle stating that the ability of a cue to aid retrieval effectively depends on the degree to which it taps into information that was encoded at the time of the original learning. (*p. 319*)

Endocrine system A class of cells that form organs called glands and communicate with one another by secreting chemicals called hormones. (*p. 114*)

Endorphin One of a class of neurotransmitters that can bind to the same receptors that opiates, such as morphine and heroin, bind to and that produces the same behavioral effects of pain relief, euphoria, and, in high doses, sleep. (*p. 110*)

Environmental psychology The study of the effects of the general physical environment on people's behavior and mental processes. (*p. 722*)

EP See *evoked potential.*

Episodic memory A person's recall of a specific event that happened while he or she was present. (*p. 301*)

Escape conditioning A type of learning in which an organism learns to make a particular response in order to terminate an aversive stimulus. (*p. 276*)

Estradiol A feminine hormone; the main estrogen. (*p. 447*)

Estrogens Feminine hormones that circulate in the bloodstream of both men and women; relatively more estrogens circulate in women. One of the main estrogens is estradiol. (See also *estradiol, progesterone,* and *progestin.*) (*p. 447*)

Ethologist A scientist who studies animals in their natural environment to observe how environmental cues affect behavior. (*p. 19*)

Evoked potential (EP) A small, temporary change in EEG voltage that is evoked by some stimulus. One such change is the P300, a positive swing in electrical voltage that occurs about 300 milliseconds after a stimulus. It can be used to determine if a stimulus distracts a person's attention from a given task. (*p. 206*)

Exhaustion The last stage in the general adaptation syndrome, which occurs when resistance has depleted the body's adaptive energy and the capacity to resist is gone. The typical result of this stage is signs of physical wear and tear, especially in organs that were weak initially or heavily involved in the resistance process. Extreme cases can result in death. (See also *alarm stage* and *resistance*.) (*p. 507*)

Expected value The total benefit to be expected if a decision, though not always correct, were repeated several times. (*p. 368*)

Experiment A research method in which the researcher manipulates or controls one variable, the independent variable, and then observes its effect on another variable, the dependent variable. (*p. 20*)

Experimental group In an experiment, the group that receives the experimental treatment; its performance or response is compared with that of one or more control groups. (*p. 20*)

Experimental psychologist A psychologist who conducts experiments aimed at understanding learning, memory, perception, and other basic behavioral and mental processes. (*p. 2*)

Experimenter bias A confounding variable that occurs when an experimenter unintentionally encourages subjects to respond in a way that supports the hypothesis. (*p. 22*)

Expert system A computer program that helps people solve problems in a fairly restricted, specific area, such as the diagnosis of diseases. (*p. 363*)

Extinction The gradual disappearance of a conditioned response or operant behavior due to elimination of either the association between conditioned and unconditioned stimuli or of rewards for certain behaviors. (*p. 264*)

Factor analysis A statistical technique that involves computing correlations between large numbers of variables. Factor analysis is commonly used in the study of intelligence and intelligence tests. (*p. 414*)

Familial retardation Cases of mild retardation for which no environmental or genetic cause can be found. Most of the people in this group come from families in the lower socioeconomic classes and are more likely than those suffering from a genetic defect to have a relative who is also retarded. (*p. 418*)

Family therapy A type of treatment inspired by the psychodynamic theory that many psychological disorders are rooted in family conflicts. It involves two or more individuals from the same family, one of whose problems make him or her the initially identified client, although the family itself ultimately becomes the client. (*p. 647*)

Fear appeal A method of changing attitudes that involves instilling fear in the audience; it may produce lasting effects on the cognitive component of an attitude but does not usually have a lasting influence on behavior. (*p. 689*)

Feature analysis A view of recognition based on evidence that brain cells respond to specific features of stimuli. It holds that any stimulus can be described as a combination of features. (*p. 196*)

Feature detector A cell in the cortex that responds to a specific feature of an object. (*p. 150*)

Fechner's law A law stating that the perceived magnitude of a stimulus is the product of K (a constant fraction of the intensity of a stimulus for the particular sensory system involved) and the logarithm of the stimulus intensity. (See also *Stevens's power law* and *Weber's law*.) (*p. 181*)

Feedback system Arrangements in the central nervous system whereby information about the consequences of an action (such as muscle movement) goes back to the source of the action (the brain) for further adjustment, resulting in smoothly coordinated movement or other regulated processes. (*p. 99*)

Fetal alcohol syndrome A pattern of defects found in babies born to alcoholic women that includes physical malformations of the face and mental retardation. (*p. 40*)

Fetus The developing individual from the third month after conception until birth. (*p. 39*)

FI See *fixed interval schedule*.

Fiber tract Axons that travel together in bundles. They are also known as pathways. (*p. 93*)

Fight-or-flight syndrome The physical reactions initiated by the sympathetic nervous system that prepare the body to fight or to run from a threatening situation. These reactions include increased heart rate and blood pressure, rapid or irregular breathing, dilated pupils, perspiration, dry mouth, increased blood sugar, decreased gastrointestinal motility, and other changes. (See also *adrenal gland, alarm reaction,* and *sympathetic nervous system*.) (*p. 116*)

Figure That part of the visual field that has meaning, stands in front of the rest, and always seems to include the contours or borders that separate it from the relatively meaningless background. (See also *ground*.) (*p. 183*)

Fixed interval (FI) schedule In operant conditioning, a type of partial reinforcement schedule that provides reinforcement for the first response that occurs after some fixed time has passed since the last reward. (*p. 273*)

Fixed ratio (FR) schedule In operant conditioning, a type of partial reinforcement schedule that provides reinforcement following a fixed number of responses, regardless of how many responses have been made during that interval. (*p. 272*)

Flooding A procedure for reducing anxiety that involves keeping a person in a feared, but harmless, situation. Once deprived of his or her normally rewarding escape pattern, the client has no reason for continued anxiety. (*p. 642*)

Fluid intelligence The basic power of reasoning and problem solving. Fluid intelligence produces induction, deduction, reasoning, and understanding of relationships between different ideas. (See also *crystallized intelligence*.) (*p. 414*)

Forebrain The most highly developed part of the brain; it is responsible for the most complex aspects of behavior and mental life. (*p. 100*)

Formal operational period According to Piaget, the fourth stage in cognitive development, usually beginning around age eleven. It is characterized by the ability to engage in hypothetical thinking, including the imagining of logical consequences and the ability to think and reason about abstract concepts. (*p. 66*)

Fovea A region in the center of the retina where cones are highly concentrated. (*p. 140*)

FR See *fixed ratio schedule*.

Free association A psychoanalytic method that requires the client to report everything that comes to mind as soon as it occurs, no matter how trivial, senseless, or embarrassing it may seem. (*p. 543*)

Free-floating anxiety See *generalized anxiety disorder*. (*p. 509*)

Frequency The number of complete waveforms, or cycles, that pass by a given point in space every second. For sound waves, the unit of measure is called a hertz (Hz); one hertz is one cycle per second. (*p. 131*)

Frequency histogram A graphic presentation of data that consists of a set of bars each of which represents how frequently different values of variables occur in a data set. (*p. A–2*)

Frequency matching (also called the *volley theory*) A theory of hearing that explains how frequency is coded: the firing rate of a neuron matches the frequency of a sound wave. For example, one neuron might fire at every peak of a wave; so a 20 hertz sound could be coded by a neuron that fires twenty times per second. (*p. 135*)

Frustration-aggression hypothesis A proposition that the existence of frustration always leads to some form of aggressive behavior. (*p. 719*)

Functional analysis of behavior A method of understanding behavior (and thus the person) that involves analyzing exactly what responses occur under what conditions. This approach emphasizes the role of operant conditioning. (See also *operant conditioning*.) (*p. 561*)

Functional fixedness A tendency to think about familiar objects in familiar ways that may prevent using them in other, more creative ways. (*p. 358*)

Fundamental attribution error The tendency to be more aware of the influence of situational factors on one's own behavior than on the behavior of others. (*p. 674*)

GABA An inhibitory neurotransmitter that reduces the likelihood that the postsynaptic neuron will fire an action potential. GABA is used by neurons in widespread regions of the brain. (*p. 109*)

Ganglion cells The cells in the retina that generate action potentials. They're stimulated by bipolar cells; their axons extend out of the retina and travel to the brain. (*p. 143*)

GAS See *general adaptation syndrome*.

Gender role General patterns of work, appearance, and behavior that a society associates with being male or female. (*p. 60*)

Gene The biological instructions inherited from both parents and located on the chromosomes that provide the blueprint for physical development throughout the life span. (See also *deoxyribonucleic acid, dominant gene, genotype, phenotype*, and *recessive gene*.) (*p. 38*)

General adaptation syndrome (GAS) A consistent and very general pattern of responses triggered by the effort to adapt to any stressor. The syndrome consists of three stages: alarm reaction, resistance, and exhaustion. (See also *alarm reaction, exhaustion*, and *resistance*.) (*p. 506*)

Generalized anxiety disorder A condition that involves relatively mild but long-lasting anxiety that is not focused on any particular object or situation. (*p. 509*)

Genital stage The fifth and last of Freud's psychosexual stages, which begins during adolescence when the person begins to mature physically and sexual impulses begin to appear at the conscious level. The young person begins to seek out relationships through which sexual impulses can be gratified. This stage spans the rest of life. (*p. 547*)

Genotype The full set of genes, inherited from both parents, contained in twenty-three pairs of chromosomes. (*p. 38*)

Gestalt psychologists A group of psychologists who suggested, among other things, that there are six principles or properties behind the grouping of stimuli that lead the human perceptual system to "glue" raw sensations together in particular ways, organizing stimuli into a world of shapes and patterns. (See also *closure, continuity, orientation, proximity, similarity*, and *simplicity*.) (*p. 184*)

Gestalt therapy A form of treatment based on the assumption that clients' problems arise when people behave in accordance with other people's expectations rather than on their own true feelings. Gestalt therapy seeks to create conditions in which clients can become more unified, more self-aware, and more self-accepting. (*p. 637*)

G-factor A general intelligence factor that Charles Spearman postulated as accounting for positive correlations between people's scores on all sorts of mental ability tests. (*p. 413*)

Glutamate The major excitatory neurotransmitter in the central nervous system. (*p. 110*)

Gradient A continuous change across the visual field. (See also *movement gradient* and *textural gradient*.) (*p. 189*)

Grammar A set of rules for combining the symbols, such as words, used in a given language. (See also *language*.) (*p. 371*)

Ground The meaningless, contourless part of the visual field; the background. (See also *figure*.) (*p. 183*)

Group polarization The tendency for groups to make decisions that are more extreme than the decision an individual group member would make. (*p. 732*)

Group therapy Psychotherapy involving five to ten individuals. Clients can be observed interacting with one another; they can feel relieved and less alone as they listen to others who have similar difficulties, which tends to raise each client's hope and expectations for improvement; and they can learn from one another. (*p. 646*)

Groupthink A pattern of thinking that, over time, renders group members unable to evaluate realistically the wisdom of various options and decisions. (*p. 733*)

Growth orientation According to Maslow, drawing satisfaction from what is available in life, rather than focusing on what is missing. (*p. 567*)

Gustation The sense that detects chemicals in solutions that come into contact with receptors inside the mouth; the sense of taste. (*p. 153*)

Hallucination Perception of sights, sounds, or other stimuli that are not actually present. (*p. 603*)

Health psychology A field in which psychologists conduct and apply research aimed at promoting human health and preventing illness. (*p. 523*)

Helping behavior Any act that is intended to benefit another person. (*p. 723*)

Heterosexual Sexual motivation that is focused on members of the opposite sex. (*p. 450*)

Heuristic A mental shortcut or rule of thumb. (See also *anchoring heuristic, availability heuristic*, and *representativeness heuristic*.) (*p. 355*)

Higher-order conditioning The process of forming an association between a neutral stimulus and a conditioned (rather than unconditioned) stimulus. (*p. 265*)

Hindbrain An extension of the spinal cord contained inside the skull. Nuclei in the hindbrain, especially in the medulla, control blood pressure, heart rate, breathing, and other vital functions. (*p. 99*)

Hippocampus A limbic system structure that plays a major role in forming new memories. (*p. 101*)

Homeostasis The tendency for organisms to keep their physiological systems at a stable, steady level by constantly adjusting themselves in response to change. (*p. 99*)

Homosexual Sexual motivation that is focused on members of a person's own sex. (*p. 450*)

Hormone A chemical that is secreted by a gland into the bloodstream, which carries it throughout the body, enabling the gland to stimulate remote cells with which it has no direct connection. (*p. 115*)

Hue The essential "color," determined by the dominant wavelength of a light. Black, white, and gray are not considered hues because they have no predominant wavelength. (*p. 144*)

Humanistic approach See *phenomenological approach.*

Hypersomnia A sleeping problem characterized by sleeping longer than most people at night and by feeling tired and needing to take one or more naps during the daytime. (*p. 227*)

Hypnosis An altered state of consciousness brought on by special induction techniques and characterized by varying degrees of responsiveness to suggestions for changes in experience and behavior. (*p. 234*)

Hypochondriasis A strong, unjustified fear of physical illness. (*p. 594*)

Hypothalamus A structure in the forebrain that regulates hunger, thirst, and sex drives; it has many connections to and from the autonomic nervous system and to other parts of the brain. (*p. 101*)

Hypothesis In scientific research, a prediction stated as a specific, testable proposition about a phenomenon. (*p. 12*)

Icon A mental representation of a visual image that is retained for a brief time by the sensory register called iconic memory. (*p. 306*)

Iconic memory The sensory register that holds visual images, or icons, in sensory memory for about one second. (*p. 306*)

Id In psychodynamic theory, a personality component containing a reservoir of unconscious psychic energy (sometimes called libido) that includes the basic instincts, desires, and impulses with which all people are born. The id operates according to the pleasure principle, seeking immediate satisfaction, regardless of society's rules or the rights or feelings of others. (See also *pleasure principle.*) (*p. 543*)

Identity crisis A phase during which an adolescent attempts to develop an integrated image of himself or herself as a unique person by pulling together self-knowledge acquired during childhood. (*p. 66*)

Immediate memory span The maximum number of items a person can recall perfectly after one presentation of the items, usually six or seven items. (See also *chunk.*) (*p. 307*)

Immune system The body's first line of defense against invading substances and microorganisms. The immune system includes T-cells, which attack virally infected cells; B-cells, which form antibodies against foreign substances; and natural killer cells, which kill invaders like tumor cells and virally infected cells. (*p. 520*)

Incentive theory A theory of motivation stating that behavior is goal-directed; actions are directed toward attaining desirable stimuli, called positive incentives, and toward avoiding unwanted stimuli, called negative incentives. (*p. 439*)

Incubation A problem-solving technique that involves putting the problem aside for a while and turning to some other mental activity while the problem "incubates," perhaps at a subconscious level. (See also *subconscious level.*) (*p. 360*)

Inferential statistics A set of procedures that provides a measure of how likely it is that research results came about by chance. These procedures put a precise mathematical value on the confidence or probability that rerunning the same experiment would yield similar (or even stronger) results. (*p. A–8*)

Information processing The process of taking in, remembering or forgetting, and using, information. It is one model for understanding people's cognitive abilities. (*p. 48*)

Information-processing approach An approach to the study of intelligence that focuses on mental operations, such as attention and memory, that underlie intelligent behavior. (*p. 415*)

Information-processing system The procedures for receiving information, representing information with symbols, and manipulating those representations so that the brain can interpret and respond to the information. (*p. 343*)

Ingroup Any category of which people see themselves as a member. Characteristics such as age, sex, race, occupation, and other detectable distinctions form the basis of the categories. (See also *outgroup.*) (*p. 693*)

Insight In problem solving, a sudden understanding about what is required to produce a desired effect. (*p. 291*)

Insomnia The most common sleeping problem, in which a person feels tired during the day because of trouble falling asleep or staying asleep at night. (*p. 226*)

Instinct An innate, automatic disposition to respond in a particular way when confronted with a specific stimulus; instincts produce behavior over which an animal has no control. (*p. 434*)

Instrumental conditioning (also called *operant conditioning*) A process in which responses are learned that help produce some rewarding or desired effect. (*p. 267*)

Intellectualization In psychodynamic theory, a defense mechanism that minimizes anxiety by viewing threatening issues in cold, abstract terms. (*p. 545*)

Intelligence Those attributes that center around reasoning skills, knowledge of one's culture, and the ability to arrive at innovative solutions to problems. (*p. 391*)

Intelligence quotient An index of intelligence once calculated by dividing one's tested mental age by one's chronological age and multiplying by 100. Today, IQ is a number that reflects the degree to which a person's score on an intelligence test deviates from the average score of others in his or her age group. (*p. 396*)

Interference theory A theory stating that the forgetting of information in long-term memory is due to the influence of other learning. (See also *proactive interference, retroactive interference.*) (*p. 317*)

Intermittent reinforcement schedule See *partial reinforcement schedule.*

Internal noise The spontaneous, random firing of nerve cells that occurs because the nervous system is always active.

Variations in internal noise can cause absolute thresholds to vary. (*p. 177*)

Interposition A depth cue whereby closer objects block one's view of things farther away. (*p. 187*)

Intervening variable A variable that is not observed directly but that helps to account for a relationship between stimuli and responses. (*p. 433*)

Introjection In psychodynamic theory, the process of incorporating, or internalizing, parental and societal values into the personality. (*p. 543*)

IQ score See *intelligence quotient.*

IQ test A test designed to measure intelligence on an objective, standardized scale. (*p. 392*)

Iris The part of the eye that gives it its color and adjusts the amount of light entering it by constricting to reduce the size of the pupil or relaxing to enlarge it. (*p. 138*)

James-Lange theory A theory of the experience of emotion in which automatic, peripheral responses precede the experience of emotion. The conscious aspect of emotion arises later, when the brain observes these responses. (*p. 477*)

JND See *just-noticeable difference.*

Just-noticeable difference (JND) (also called *difference threshold*) The smallest detectable difference in stimulus energy. (See also *Weber's law.*) (*p. 180*)

Kinesthesia The sense that tells you where the parts of your body are with respect to one another. (*p. 164*)

Language Symbols and a set of rules for combining them that provides a vehicle for the mind's communication with itself and the most important means of communicating with others. (*p. 371*)

Latency period The fourth of Freud's psychosexual stages, usually beginning during the fifth year of life, in which sexual impulses lie dormant and the child focuses attention on education and other matters. (*p. 547*)

Latent learning Learning that is not demonstrated at the time it occurs. (*p. 292*)

Lateral geniculate nucleus (LGN) A region of the thalamus in which the axons from most of the ganglion cells in the retina finally end and form synapses. (*p. 148*)

Lateral inhibition The enhancement of the sensation of contrast that occurs when greater response to light in one photoreceptor cell suppresses the response of a neighboring cell.

Lateralization The tendency for one cerebral hemisphere to excel at a particular function or skill compared to the other hemisphere. (*p. 106*)

Law of effect A law stating that if a response made in the presence of a particular stimulus is followed by a reward, that same response is more likely to be made the next time the stimulus is encountered. Responses that are not rewarded are less likely to be performed again. (*p. 268*)

Learned helplessness A phenomenon that occurs when an organism has or believes that it has no control over its environment. The typical result of this situation or belief is to stop trying to exert control. (*p. 280*)

Learning Any relatively permanent change in an organism's behavior or mental processes that results from past experience. (*p. 257*)

Lens The part of the eye directly behind the pupil. Like the lens in a camera, the lens of the eye is curved so that it bends light rays, focusing them on the retina, at the back of the eye. (*p. 138*)

Levels-of-processing model A view stating that differences in how well something is remembered reflect the degree or depth to which incoming information is mentally processed. How long the information stays in memory depends on how elaborate the mental processing and encoding becomes. (*p. 325*)

LGN See *lateral geniculate nucleus.*

LH See *luteinizing hormone.*

Libido See *id.*

Light intensity A physical dimension of light waves that refers to how much energy the light contains; it determines the brightness of light. (See also *light wavelength.*) (*p. 137*)

Light wavelength A physical dimension of light waves that refers to their length. At a given intensity, different light wavelengths produce sensations of different colors. (See also *light intensity.*) (*p. 137*)

Limbic system A set of brain structures that play important roles in regulating emotion and memory. The limbic system is a "system" because its components have major interconnections and influence related functions. (*p. 101*)

Linear perspective A depth cue whereby the closer together two converging lines are, the greater the perceived distance. (*p. 188*)

Logic The mental procedures that yield a valid conclusion during the reasoning process. (See also *reasoning.*) (*p. 353*)

Longitudinal study A research method in which a group of people is repeatedly tested as they grow older. (*p. 423*)

Looming A motion cue involving a rapid expansion in the size of an image so that it fills the available space on the retina. People tend to perceive a looming object as an approaching stimulus, not as an expanding object viewed at a constant distance. (*p. 191*)

Loudness A psychological dimension of sound determined by the amplitude of a sound wave; waves with greater amplitude produce sensations of louder sounds. Loudness is described in units called decibels. (*p. 131*)

Lucid dreaming The awareness that a dream is a dream while it is happening. This phenomenon is evidence that sleep does not involve a total loss of consciousness or mental functioning. (*p. 234*)

Magnetic resonance imaging (MRI) A highly advanced technique that detects naturally occurring magnetic fields surrounding atoms in brain tissue to create exceptionally clear pictures of the structures of the brain. (*p. 95*)

Maintenance rehearsal Repeating information over and over to keep it active in short-term memory. This method is ineffective for encoding information into long-term memory. (See also *elaborative rehearsal.*) (*p. 312*)

Major depression A condition in which a person feels sad and hopeless for weeks or months, often losing interest in all activities and taking pleasure in nothing. Weight loss and lack of sleep or, in some cases, overeating and excessive sleeping are frequent accompaniments, as are problems in concentrating, making decisions, and thinking clearly. (*p. 597*)

Mania An elated, very active emotional state. (*p. 599*)

Matching hypothesis A hypothesis that people are most likely to be attracted to others who are similar to themselves in physical attractiveness. (*p. 679*)

Maturation Natural growth or change, triggered by biological factors, that unfolds in a fixed sequence relatively independent of the environment. (*p. 34*)

Mean A measure of central tendency that is the arithmetic average of the scores in a set of data; the sum of the values of all the scores divided by the total number of scores. (*p. A–4*)

Median A measure of central tendency that is the halfway point in a set of data: half the scores fall above the median, half fall below it. (*p. A–3*)

Medical model See *biological model*.

Meditation A set of techniques designed to create an altered state of consciousness characterized by inner peace, calmness, and tranquillity. (*p. 239*)

Medulla An area in the hindbrain that controls blood pressure, heart rate, breathing, and other vital functions through the use of reflexes and feedback systems. (*p. 99*)

Menopause The point in middle adulthood when a woman stops menstruating. (*p. 70*)

Mental ability A capacity to perform the higher mental processes of reasoning, remembering, understanding, problem solving, and decision making. (*p. 389*)

Mental chronometry The timing of mental events that allows researchers to infer what stages exist during cognition. (See also *average evoked potential, evoked potential,* and *information-processing system.*) (*p. 345*)

Mental model A cluster of propositions that represents people's understanding of how things work and guides their interaction with those things. (*p. 351*)

Mental set The tendency for old patterns of problem solving to persist, even when they might not be the most efficient method for solving a given problem. (*p. 358*)

Metacognition The knowledge of what strategies to apply, when to apply them, and how to deploy them in new situations so that new specific knowledge can be gained and different problems mastered. (*p. 419*)

Metamemory Knowledge about how one's own memory works. Metamemory involves understanding the abilities and weaknesses of one's own memory, knowing about different types of memory tasks, and knowing what types of strategies are most effective in remembering new information. (*p. 329*)

Midbrain A small structure that lies between the hindbrain and the forebrain. The midbrain relays information from the eyes, ears, and skin, and controls certain types of automatic behaviors in response to information received through those structures. (*p. 100*)

Midlife transition A point at around age forty when adults take stock of their lives, reappraise their priorities, and, sometimes, modify their lives and relationships. (*p. 74*)

Mnemonics Strategies for placing information in an organized context in order to remember it. Two powerful methods are the peg-word system and the method of loci. (*p. 330*)

Mode A measure of central tendency that is the value or score that occurs most frequently in a data set. (*p. A–3*)

Modeling A method of therapy in which desirable behaviors are demonstrated as a way of teaching them to clients. (*p. 641*)

Mood disorder (also called *affective disorder*) A condition in which a person experiences extremes of mood for long periods, shifts from one mood extreme to another, and experiences moods that are inconsistent with the happy or sad events around them. (*p. 597*)

Morpheme The smallest unit of language that has meaning. (See also *phoneme.*) (*p. 371*)

Motherese A type of speech that adults use when talking to language-learning children. It parallels children's own speech and is characterized by short sentences and concrete, basic nouns and active verbs—not pronouns, adjectives, conjunctions, or past tenses. Grammatically correct utterances are exaggerated, repeated, and enunciated clearly. (*p. 379*)

Motivation The influences that account for the initiation, direction, intensity, and persistence of behavior. (*p. 431*)

Motive A reason or purpose for behavior. (*p. 433*)

Motor cortex The part of the cerebral cortex whose neurons control voluntary movements in specific parts of the body. Some neurons control movement of the hand; others stimulate movement of the foot, the knee, the head, and so on. (*p. 102*)

Motor systems The parts of the nervous system that influence muscles and other organs to respond to the environment in some way. (*p. 85*)

Movement gradient The graduated difference in the apparent movement of objects across the visual field. Faster relative movement across the visual field indicates closer distance. (*p. 189*)

Multiple personality disorder The most famous and least commonly seen dissociative disorder, in which a person reports having more than one identity, and sometimes several, each of which speaks, acts, and writes in a very different way. (See also *dissociative disorder.*) (*p. 595*)

Myelin A fatty substance that wraps around some axons and increases the speed of action potentials. (*p. 89*)

Naloxone A drug that can block the effects of opiate drugs, such as heroin, as well as naturally occurring opiates called endorphins. (*p. 113*)

Narcissistic personality disorder A personality disorder characterized by an exaggerated sense of self-importance combined with self-doubt. (*p. 613*)

Narcolepsy A daytime sleep disorder in which a person switches abruptly and without warning from an active, often emotional waking state into several minutes of REM sleep. In most cases the muscle paralysis associated with REM causes the person to collapse on the spot and to remain briefly immobilized even after awakening. (*p. 227*)

Narcotic A psychoactive drug, such as opium, morphine, or heroin, that has the ability to produce both sleep-inducing and pain-relieving effects. (*p. 246*)

Natural concept Concepts that have no fixed set of defining features but instead share a set of characteristic features. Members of a natural concept need not possess all of the characteristic features. (*p. 349*)

Need In drive reduction theory, a biological requirement for well-being that is created by an imbalance in homeostasis. (See also *drive, primary drive,* and *secondary drive.*) (*p. 435*)

Need achievement A motive influenced by the degree to which a person establishes specific goals, cares about meeting those goals, and experiences feelings of satisfaction by doing so; it is often measured by the Thematic Apperception Test. (*p. 457*)

Negative reinforcer An unpleasant stimulus, such as pain. The removal of a negative reinforcer following some response is likely to strengthen the probability of that response recurring. The process of strengthening behavior by following it with the removal of a negative reinforcer is called negative reinforcement. (See also *positive reinforcer.*) (*p. 270*)

Negative state relief model A theory suggesting that people help others because doing so reduces their own negative moods and unpleasant feelings. (*p. 724*)

Nervous system A complex combination of cells whose primary function is to allow an organism to gain information about what is going on inside and outside the body and to respond appropriately. (*p. 85*)

Neuron The fundamental unit of the nervous system; a nerve cell. Neurons have the ability to communicate with one another. (*p. 87*)

Neurosis A condition in which a person is uncomfortable (usually anxious) but can still function. (*p. 584*)

Neurotransmitter A chemical that assists in the transfer of signals from the axon of one neuron (presynaptic cell) across the synapse to the receptors on the dendrite of another neuron (postsynaptic cell). (*p. 90*)

Neurotransmitter system A group of neurons that communicates by using the same neurotransmitter, such as acetylcholine or dopamine. (*p. 107*)

Nightmare A frightening, sometimes recurring dream that takes place during REM sleep. (*p. 228*)

Night terrors A rapid awakening from stage 4 to REM sleep, often accompanied by a horrific dream that causes the dreamer to sit up staring, let out a bloodcurdling scream, and abruptly awaken into a state of intense fear that may last up to thirty minutes. This phenomenon is especially common in children, but milder versions occur among adults. (*p. 228*)

Nonconscious level A segment of mental activity devoted to those processes that are totally inaccessible to conscious awareness, such as blood flowing through veins and arteries, the removal of impurities from the blood, and the measuring of blood sugar by the hypothalamus. (*p. 219*)

Norepinephrine The neurotransmitter found in both the central and the peripheral nervous systems that is used by neurons called adrenergic neurons to regulate sleep, learning, and mood. (*p. 108*)

Norm (1) A description of the frequency at which a particular score occurs, which allows scores to be compared statistically. (*p. 397*) (2) A learned, socially based rule that prescribes what people should or should not do in various situations. (*p. 668*)

Normal distribution A dispersion of scores such that the mean, median, and mode all have the same value. When a distribution has this property, the standard deviation can be used to describe how any particular score stands in relation to the rest of the distribution. (*p. A–5*)

Nuclei Collections of nerve cell bodies in the central nervous system. (*p. 93*)

Null hypothesis The assertion that the independent variable manipulated by the experimenter will have no effect on the dependent variable measured by the experimenter. (*p. A–1*)

Obedience A form of compliance in which people comply with a demand, rather than with a request, because they think they must or should do so; obedience can be thought of as submissive compliance. (See also *compliance.*) (*p. 708*)

Obesity A condition in which a person is severely overweight, often by as much as one hundred pounds. (*p. 444*)

Objective test A paper-and-pencil form containing clear, specific questions, statements, or concepts to which the respondent is asked to give yes-no, true-false, or multiple-choice answers. (*p. 537*)

Object permanence The knowledge, resulting from an ability to form mental representations of objects, that objects exist even when they are not in view. (*p. 45*)

Observational learning Learning how to perform new behaviors by watching the behavior of others. (*p. 283*)

Obsessive-compulsive disorder An anxiety disorder in which a person becomes obsessed with certain thoughts or images or feels a compulsion to do certain things. If the person tries to interrupt obsessive thinking or compulsions, severe agitation and anxiety usually result. (*p. 591*)

Oedipus complex According to psychodynamic theory, during the phallic stage, a boy's id impulses involve sexual desire for the mother and the desire to eliminate, even kill, the father, who is competition for the mother's affection. The hostile impulses create a fear of retaliation so strong that the ego represses the incestuous desires. Then the boy identifies with the father and begins to learn male sex-role behaviors. (See also *phallic stage.*) (*p. 546*)

Olfaction The sense that detects chemicals that are airborne, or volatile; the sense of smell. (*p. 153*)

Olfactory bulb The brain structure that receives messages regarding olfaction, or the sense of smell. (*p. 154*)

One-feature rule See *affirmation rule.*

One-word stage A stage of language development during which children build their vocabularies one word at a time, tend to use one word at a time, and tend to overextend the use of a single word. (*p. 378*)

Operant A response that has some effect on the world; it is a response that operates on the environment in some way. (See also *operant conditioning.*) (*p. 270*)

Operant conditioning A virtual synonym for instrumental conditioning; a process studied by B. F. Skinner in which an organism learns to respond to the environment in a way that helps produce some desired effect. Skinner's primary aim was to analyze how behavior is changed by its consequences. (*p. 269*)

Operational definition A statement of the operations or methods used to measure a variable. (*p. 12*)

Opponent-process theory (1) A theory of color vision stating that the visual elements sensitive to color are grouped into three pairs: a red-green element, a blue-yellow element, and a black-white element. Each element signals one color or the other—red or green, for example—but never both. (*p. 146*) (2) A theory of motivation based on the assumptions that, first, any reaction to a stimulus is automatically followed by an opposite reaction, called the opponent process; and that, second, after repeated exposure to the same stimulus, the initial reaction weakens, and the opponent process becomes stronger. (*p. 439*)

Optic chiasm Part of the bottom surface of the brain where half of the optic nerve fibers cross over to the opposite side of the brain; beyond the chiasm the fibers ascend into the brain itself. (*p. 148*)

Optic nerve A bundle of fibers composed of axons from ganglion cells that carries visual information to the brain. (*p. 148*)

Oral stage The first of Freud's psychosexual stages, occurring during the first year of life, in which the mouth is the center of pleasure. (*p. 545*)

Organic mental disorder Forms of abnormal behavior that have a clearly biological basis. (See also *delirium* and *dementia*.) (*p. 581*)

Orientation A Gestalt grouping principle stating that when basic features of stimuli have the same orientation (such as horizontal, vertical, or at an angle), people tend to group those stimuli together. (*p. 184*)

Otolith A small crystal in the fluid-filled vestibular sacs of the inner ear that, when shifted by gravity, stimulates nerve cells that inform the brain of the position of the head relative to the earth. (*p. 165*)

Outgroup Any group of which people do not see themselves as a member. (See also *ingroup*.) (*p. 693*)

Panic disorder Anxiety in the form of terrifying panic attacks that come without warning or obvious cause. These attacks last for a few minutes and are marked by heart palpitations, pressure or pain in the chest, dizziness or unsteadiness, sweating, and faintness. They may be accompanied by feeling detached from one's body or feeling that people and events are not real. The person may think he or she is about to die or "go crazy." (*p. 494*)

Papillae Structures that contain groups of taste receptors; the taste buds. (*p. 155*)

Parallel distributed processing (PDP) models An approach to understanding object recognition in which various elements of the object are thought to be simultaneously analyzed by a number of widely distributed but connected neural units in the brain. (*p. 198*)

Parallel search A theoretical retrieval process in which information in short-term memory is examined all at once. (See also *serial search*.) (*p. 312*)

Paranoid schizophrenia A type of schizophrenia characterized by delusions of persecution or grandeur accompanied by anxiety, anger, superiority, argumentativeness, or jealousy; these feelings sometimes lead to violence. (*p. 604*)

Paraphilia A sexual disorder in which a person's sexual interest is directed toward stimuli that are culturally or legally defined as inappropriate. (*p. 611*)

Parasympathetic nervous system The subsystem of the autonomic nervous system that typically influences activity related to the protection, nourishment, and growth of the body. (See also *autonomic nervous system*.) (*p. 473*)

Partial reinforcement extinction effect A phenomenon in which behaviors learned under a partial reinforcement schedule are far more difficult to extinguish than those learned on a continuous reinforcement schedule. Individuals on a partial reinforcement schedule usually are not immediately aware that their behavior is no longer being reinforced; they are used to not being rewarded for every response. However, individuals on a continuous reinforcement schedule are ac-

customed to being reinforced for each response and are more sensitive to the lack of reward. (*p. 273*)

Partial reinforcement schedule (also called *intermittent reinforcement schedule*) In operant conditioning, a pattern of reinforcement in which a reinforcer is administered only some of the time after a particular response occurs. (See also *fixed interval schedule, fixed ratio schedule, variable interval schedule,* and *variable ratio schedule*.) (*p. 272*)

Percentile score The percentage of people or observations that fall below a given score in a normal distribution. (*p. A-5*)

Perception The process through which people take raw sensations from the environment and interpret them, using knowledge, experience, and understanding of the world, so that the sensations become meaningful experiences. (*p. 171*)

Perceptual constancy The perception of objects as constant in size, shape, color, and other properties despite changes in their retinal image. (*p. 185*)

Performance scale Five subtests in the Wechsler scales that include tasks that require spatial ability and the ability to manipulate materials; these subtests provide a performance IQ. (See also *verbal scale*.) (*p. 395*)

Peripheral nervous system All of the nervous system that is not housed in bone. It has two main subsystems: the somatic nervous system and the autonomic nervous system. (*p. 86*)

Permissive parent A parent who gives his or her child complete freedom and whose discipline is lax. Children of this type of parent are often immature, dependent, and unhappy, lack self-reliance and self-control, and seek parental help for even the slightest problems. (*p. 56*)

Personality The pattern of psychological and behavioral characteristics by which each person can be compared and contrasted with other people; the unique pattern of characteristics that emerges from the blending of inherited and acquired tendencies to make each person an identifiable individual. (*p. 535*)

Personality disorder Long-standing, inflexible ways of behaving that are not so much severe mental disorders as styles of life, which, from childhood or adolescence, create problems, usually for others. (*p. 613*)

Person-centered therapy See *client-centered therapy*.

PET scanning Positron emission tomography; a technique that detects—and creates a visual image of—activity in various parts of the brain. (*p. 94*)

Phallic stage The third of Freud's psychosexual stages, lasting from approximately ages three to five, in which the focus of pleasure shifts to the genital area; the Oedipus complex occurs during this stage. (See also *Oedipus complex*.) (*p. 546*)

Phenomenological approach (also called *phenomenological model*) A view of personality based on the assumption that each personality is created out of each person's unique way of perceiving and interpreting the world. Proponents of this view believe that one's personal perception of reality shapes and controls behavior from moment to moment. (*p. 564*)

Phenotype How an individual looks and acts, which depends on how a person's inherited characteristics interact with the environment. (*p. 38*)

Pheromones Chemicals that are released by one animal and detected by another, and then shape that second animal's behavior or physiology. Often, though not always, the pheromone is detected by the olfactory system. (*p. 155*)

Phobia An anxiety disorder that involves a strong, irrational fear of an object or situation that does not objectively justify such a reaction. The phobic individual usually realizes that the fear makes no sense but cannot keep it from interfering with daily life. (*p. 266*)

Phoneme The smallest unit of sound that affects the meaning of speech. (See also *morpheme*.) (*p. 371*)

Photopigment A chemical contained in photoreceptors that responds to light and assists in changing light into neural activity. (*p. 139*)

Photoreceptor A nerve cell in the retina that codes light energy into neural activity. (See also *rods* and *cones*.) (*p. 139*)

Physiological psychologist See *biological psychologist*.

Physiological psychology See *biological psychology*.

Pinna The crumpled, oddly shaped part of the outer ear that collects sound waves. (*p. 132*)

Pitch How high or low a tone sounds; the psychological dimension determined by the frequency of sound waves. High-frequency waves are sensed as sounds of high pitch. (*p. 131*)

Placebo A physical or psychological treatment that contains no active ingredient but produces an effect because the person receiving it believes it will. In an experiment, the placebo effect (a confounding variable) occurs when the subject responds to the belief that the independent variable will have an effect, rather than to the actual effect of the independent variable. (*p. 22*)

Place theory (also called the *traveling wave theory*) A theory of hearing stating that hair cells at a particular place on the basilar membrane respond most to a particular frequency of sound. High-frequency sounds produce a wave that peaks soon after it starts down the basilar membrane. Lower-frequency sounds produce a wave that peaks farther along the basilar membrane. (*p. 134*)

Pleasure principle In psychodynamic theory, the operating principle of the id, which guides people toward whatever feels good. (See also *id*.) (*p. 543*)

Positive reinforcement See *positive reinforcer*.

Positive reinforcer A stimulus that strengthens a response if it follows that response. It is roughly equivalent to a reward. Presenting a positive reinforcer after a response is called positive reinforcement. (See also *negative reinforcer*.) (*p. 270*)

Posthypnotic amnesia The inability of hypnotic subjects to recall what happened during hypnosis. For some, recall fails even when they are told what went on. (*p. 235*)

Posthypnotic suggestion Instructions about experiences or behavior to take place after hypnosis has been terminated. (*p. 235*)

Postsynaptic potential The change in the membrane potential of a neuron that has received stimulation from another neuron. (*p. 91*)

Posttraumatic stress disorder A pattern of adverse and disruptive reactions following a traumatic event. One of its most common features is re-experiencing the original trauma through nightmares or vivid memories. (*p. 512*)

Preconscious level A segment of mental activity devoted to sensations and everything else that is not currently conscious, but of which people can easily become conscious at will. The amount of material at this level far surpasses what is present at the conscious level at any given moment. (See also *conscious level, nonconscious level, subconscious level,* and *unconscious level*.) (*p. 219*)

Predictive value The ability of a conditioned stimulus reliably to signal an unconditioned stimulus. Predictive value will be highest if the conditioned stimulus is presented every time the unconditioned stimulus is presented. (*p. 263*)

Prefrontal lobotomy A form of psychosurgery in which a sharp instrument is inserted into the brain and used to destroy brain tissue. (*p. 655*)

Prejudice A positive or negative attitude toward an entire group of people. (See also *discrimination*.) (*p. 691*)

Premenstrual syndrome (PMS) A monthly experience of depressed mood and irritability that occurs in some women. (*p. 117*)

Preoperational period According to Piaget, the second stage of cognitive development, during which children begin to understand, create, and use symbols to represent things that are not present. (*p. 45*)

Primacy effect A characteristic of recall in which recall for the first two or three items in a list is particularly good. (See also *recency effect*.) (*p. 326*)

Primary cortex See *primary auditory cortex* and *primary visual cortex*.

Primary auditory cortex The first cells in the cerebral cortex to receive information about sounds. This area is in the temporal lobe and is connected to areas of the brain involved in language perception and production. (*p. 135*)

Primary drive A drive that arises from basic biological needs. (See also *drive, need,* and *secondary drive*.) (*p. 436*)

Primary reinforcer Something that meets an organism's most basic needs, such as food, water, air, and moderate temperatures. A primary reinforcer does not depend on learning to exert its influence. (See also *secondary reinforcer*.) (*p. 274*)

Primary visual cortex An area in the occipital lobe, at the back of the brain, to which neurons in the lateral geniculate nucleus relay visual input. (*p. 149*)

Prisoner's dilemma game A research situation in which mutual cooperation guarantees the best mutual outcome; mixed cooperative and competitive responses by each person guarantee a favorable outcome for one person and an unfavorable outcome for the other; and mutual competition guarantees the worst mutual outcome. (*p. 729*)

Proactive interference A cause of forgetting in which previously learned information, now residing in long-term memory, interferes with the ability to remember new information. (See also *retroactive interference*.) (*p. 317*)

Procedural memory (also called *skill memory*) A type of memory that contains information about how to do things. (*p. 301*)

Progesterone A feminine hormone; the main progestin. (*p. 447*)

Progestins Feminine hormones that circulate in the bloodstream of both men and women; relatively more progestins circulate in women. One of the main progestins is progesterone. (See also *estradiol, estrogen,* and *progesterone*.) (*p. 447*)

Progressive relaxation training A procedure for learning to relax that involves tensing a group of muscles for a few seconds, then releasing that tension and focusing attention on the resulting feelings of relaxation; the procedure is repeated at least once for each of sixteen muscle groups throughout the body. Progressive relaxation training is a popular physiological method for coping with stress and an important part of systematic desensitization, a method for treating phobias. (*p. 527*)

Projection   In psychodynamic theory, a defense mechanism in which people see their own unacceptable desires in others instead of in themselves. (*p. 545*)

Projective test   Personality tests made up of relatively unstructured stimuli, such as inkblots, which can be perceived and responded to in many ways; particular responses are seen as reflecting the individual's needs, fantasies, conflicts, thought patterns, and other aspects of personality. (*p. 540*)

Proposition   The smallest unit of knowledge that can stand as a separate assertion, may be true or false, and may represent a relationship between a concept and a property of that concept or between two or more concepts. (*p. 350*)

Proprioceptive   The sensory systems that allow us to know about where we are and what each part of our body is doing. (See also *kinesthesia* and *vestibular sense*.) (*p. 164*)

Prototype   A member of a natural concept that possesses all or most of the characteristic features. (*p. 350*)

Proximity   A Gestalt grouping principle stating that the closer objects are to one another, the more likely they are to be perceived as belonging together. (*p. 184*)

Psychedelic   Psychoactive drugs, such as LSD, PCP, and marijuana, that alter consciousness by producing a temporary loss of contact with reality and changes in emotion, perception, and thought. (*p. 246*)

Psychiatrist   A medical doctor who has completed special training in the treatment of mental disorder. Psychiatrists can prescribe drugs. (*p. 626*)

Psychoactive drug   A chemical substance that acts on the brain to create some psychological effect. (*p. 111*)

Psychoactive substance-use disorder   A problem that involves use of psychoactive drugs for months or years in ways that harm the user or others. (*p. 608*)

Psychoanalysis   A method of psychotherapy that seeks to help clients gain insight by recognizing, understanding, and dealing with unconscious thoughts and emotions presumed to cause their problems and work through the many ways in which those unconscious causes appear in everyday behavior and social relationships. (*p. 629*)

Psychodynamic approach   (also called *psychodynamic model*) A view developed by Freud that emphasizes the interplay of unconscious mental processes in determining human thought, feelings, and behavior. (*p. 543*)

Psychogenic amnesia   A psychological disorder marked by a sudden loss of memory, which results in the inability to recall one's own name, occupation, or other identifying information. (*p. 595*)

Psychogenic fugue   A sudden loss of memory and the assumption of a new identity in a new locale. (*p. 595*)

Psychology   The science of behavior and mental processes. (*p. 1*)

Psychometric approach   A way of studying intelligence that emphasizes the analysis of the "products" of intelligence, especially scores on intelligence tests. (*p. 413*)

Psychoneuroimmunology   The field that examines the in-

teraction of psychological and physiological processes that affect the ability of the body to defend itself against disease. (*p. 520*)

Psychopathology   Patterns of thinking and behaving that are maladaptive, disruptive, or uncomfortable for the person affected or for those with whom he or she comes in contact. (*p. 577*)

Psychopharmacology   The study of psychoactive drugs and their effects. (*p. 111*)

Psychophysics   An area of research that focuses on the relationship between the physical characteristics of environmental stimuli and the conscious psychological experience those stimuli produce. Psychophysical researchers seek to understand how people make contact with and become conscious of the world. (*p. 176*)

Psychosexual stage   In psychodynamic theory, a period of personality development in which internal and external conflicts focus on particular issues. There are five stages during which pleasure is derived from different areas of the body. (See also *anal stage, genital stage, latency period, oral stage,* and *phallic stage*.) (*p. 545*)

Psychosis   A condition involving a loss of contact with reality or an inability to function on a daily basis. (*p. 584*)

Psychosocial stages   Eight stages of lifelong personality development, proposed by Erikson, that emphasize social crises as the most important determinants of personality. (*p. 548*)

Psychosurgery   Procedures that destroy various regions of the brain in an effort to alleviate psychological disorders; this surgery is done infrequently and only as a last resort. (*p. 655*)

Psychotherapy   The treatment of psychological disorders through psychological methods, such as analyzing problems, talking about possible solutions, and encouraging more adaptive ways of thinking and acting. (*p. 625*)

Puberty   The condition of being able for the first time to reproduce; it occurs during adolescence and is characterized by fuller breasts and rounder curves in females and by broad shoulders and narrow hips in males. Facial, underarm, and pubic hair grows. Voices deepen, and acne may appear. (*p. 62*)

Punishment   The presentation of an aversive stimulus or the removal of a pleasant stimulus; punishment decreases the frequency of the immediately preceding response. (*p. 277*)

Pupil   An opening in the eye, just behind the cornea, through which light passes. (The pupil appears black because there is no light source inside the eyeball and very little light is reflected out of the eye.) (*p. 138*)

Quantitative psychologist   A psychologist who uses mathematical methods to summarize and analyze data from all subfields of psychology. (*p. 5*)

Quiet sleep   (also called *slow-wave sleep*) Sleep stages 1 through 4, which are accompanied by slow, deep breathing; a calm, regular heartbeat; and reduced blood pressure. (*p. 225*)

Random sample   A group of research subjects selected from a population each of whose members had an equal chance of being chosen for study. (*p. 20*)

Random variable   In an experiment, a confounding variable in which an uncontrolled or uncontrollable factor affects the dependent variable along with or instead of the independent variable. Random variables can include factors such as differences in the subjects' backgrounds, personalities, and physical health, as well as differences in experimental conditions. (*p. 21*)

Range A measure of variability that is the difference between the highest and the lowest value in the data set. (*p. A–4*)

Rational-emotive therapy (RET) A treatment that involves identifying self-defeating, problem-causing thoughts that clients have learned and using modeling, encouragement, and logic to help the client replace these maladaptive thought patterns with more realistic and beneficial ones. (*p. 644*)

Rationalization In psychodynamic theory, a defense mechanism in which one attempts to "explain away" unacceptable behavior. (*p. 545*)

Reactance A state of psychological arousal that motivates people to restore a lost sense of freedom by resisting, opposing, or contradicting whatever they feel caused the loss. (*p. 690*)

Reaction formation In psychodynamic theory, a defense mechanism in which one's behavior runs exactly opposite to one's true feelings. (*p. 545*)

Reaction range A roughly defined area of genetically determined potential for mental ability within which environmental factors operate to increase or decrease a person's demonstrated mental ability. Reaction range is a theoretical concept, not a fixed set of boundaries on mental ability. (*p. 407*)

Reaction time The elapsed time between the presentation of a stimulus and an overt response to it. (*p. 345*)

Reality principle According to psychodynamic theory, the operating principle of the ego that involves, for example, compromises between the unreasoning demands of the id to do whatever feels good and the demands of the real world to do what is acceptable. (See also *ego.*) (*p. 543*)

Reasoning The process by which people evaluate and generate arguments and reach conclusions. (See also *logic.*) (*p. 353*)

Recency effect A characteristic of recall in which recall is particularly good for the last few items on a list. (See also *primacy effect.*) (*p. 326*)

Receptive field The portion of the world that affects a given neuron. For example, in the auditory system, one neuron might respond only to sounds of a particular pitch; that pitch is its receptive field. (*p. 143*)

Receptor (1) A site on the surface of the postsynaptic cell that allows only one type of neurotransmitter to fit into it and thus trigger the chemical response that may lead to an action potential. (*p. 91*) (2) A cell that is specialized to detect certain types of energy and convert it into neural activity. This conversion process is called transduction. (*p. 127*)

Receptor agonist A molecule, very similar to a neurotransmitter, that may occupy receptor sites for that neurotransmitter. Many drugs mimic neurotransmitters in this way. They fit snugly into the receptors and change a cell's membrane potential just as the neurotransmitter would. (*p. 112*)

Receptor antagonist A drug that is similar enough to a neurotransmitter to occupy its receptor sites on nerve cells, but not similar enough to fit snugly and change the cells' membrane potential. While it remains attached to the receptors, the drug competes with and blocks neurotransmitters from occupying and acting on the receptors. (*p. 112*)

Reciprocal determinism According to Bandura, the ways in which people's overt behaviors, cognitions, and the environment constantly influence one another. (*p. 563*)

Reconditioning The relearning of a conditioned response following extinction. Because reconditioning takes much less time than the original conditioning, some change in the organism must persist even after extinction. (*p. 265*)

Reduced clarity A depth cue whereby an object whose retinal image is unclear is perceived as being farther away. (*p. 189*)

Reference group A category of people to which people compare themselves. (*p. 667*)

Reflection Restating or paraphrasing what the client has said, which shows that the therapist is actively listening and helps make the client aware of the thoughts and feelings he or she is experiencing. (*p. 636*)

Reflexes Involuntary, unlearned reactions in the form of swift, automatic, and finely coordinated movements in response to external stimuli. Reflexes are organized completely within the spinal cord. (*p. 98*)

Refractory period A short rest period between action potentials; it is so short that a neuron can send action potentials down its axon at rates of up to one thousand per second. (*p. 89*)

Rehearsing Repeating information to oneself, which allows the information to be maintained in short-term memory indefinitely, as long as rehearsing continues. (See also *elaborative rehearsal* and *maintenance rehearsal.*) (*p. 310*)

Reinforcer A stimulus event that increases the probability that the response that immediately preceded it will occur again. (See also *positive reinforcer* and *negative reinforcer.*) (*p. 270*)

Relative deprivation The sense that a person is not doing as well as others in the same reference group. (*p. 667*)

Relative size A depth cue whereby larger objects are perceived as closer than smaller ones. (*p. 187*)

Reliability The degree to which a test can be repeated with the same results. Tests with high reliability yield scores that are less susceptible to insignificant or random changes in the test taker or the testing environment. (*p. 397*)

REM behavior disorder A sleep disorder in which a person fails to show the decreased muscle tone normally seen in REM sleep, thus allowing the sleeper to act out dreams, sometimes with dangerous results. (*p. 228*)

REM sleep See *active sleep.*

Representativeness heuristic A shortcut in the thought process that involves judging the probability that a hypothesis is true or that an example belongs to a certain class of items by first focusing on the similarities between the example and a larger class of events or items and then determining whether the particular example represents essential features of the larger class. (*p. 355*)

Repression In psychodynamic theory, a defense mechanism that involves unconsciously forcing unacceptable impulses out of awareness, leaving the person unaware that he or she had the taboo desires in the first place. (*p. 545*)

Residual schizophrenia The designation for persons who have displayed symptoms of schizophrenia in the past, but not in the present. (*p. 604*)

Resistance The second stage in the general adaptation syndrome, in which signs of the initial alarm reaction diminish while the body settles in to resist the stressor on a long-term basis. (See also *alarm reaction* and *exhaustion.*) (*p. 507*)

Response bias A person's willingness or reluctance to respond to a stimulus, which reflects motivation and expectancies. Response bias is a source of variation in absolute threshold. (*p. 177*)

Response criterion The internal rule a person uses to decide whether or not to report a stimulus; it reflects the person's motivation and expectations. (*p. 178*)

RET See *rational-emotive therapy.*

Reticular formation A network of nuclei and fibers threaded throughout the hindbrain and midbrain. This network alters the activity of the rest of the brain. (*p. 100*)

Retina The surface at the back of the eye onto which the lens focuses light rays. (*p. 138*)

Retrieval The process of recalling information stored in memory and bringing it into consciousness. (*p. 302*)

Retrieval cues Stimuli that allow people to recall things that were once forgotten and help them to recognize information stored in memory. (*p. 319*)

Retroactive interference A cause of forgetting in which new information placed in memory interferes with the ability to recall information already in memory. (*p. 317*)

Retrograde amnesia A loss of memory for events prior to some critical brain injury. Often, a person will be unable to remember anything that occurred in the months, or even years, before the injury. In most cases, the memories return gradually, but recovery is seldom complete. (See also *anterograde amnesia.*) (*p. 327*)

Rods Photoreceptors in the retina that allow sight even in dim light because their photopigment contains rhodopsin, a light-sensitive chemical. Rods cannot discriminate colors. (See also *cones.*) (*p. 139*)

Role theory A theory that states that hypnotized subjects act in accordance with a special social role, which demands compliance, and do not enter an altered state of consciousness. According to this theory, the procedures for inducing hypnosis provide a socially acceptable reason to follow the hypnotist's suggestions. (See also *dissociation theory* and *state theory.*) (*p. 236*)

Sampling The process of selecting subjects who are members of the population that the researcher wishes to study. (*p. 20*)

Saturation The purity of a color. A color is more pure, more saturated, if a single wavelength is relatively more intense—contains more energy—than other wavelengths. (*p. 144*)

Savings A method for measuring forgetting by computing the difference between the number of repetitions needed to learn, say, a list of words, and the number of repetitions needed to relearn it after some time has elapsed. (*p. 316*)

Schachter-Singer theory A theory of the experience of emotion in which the cognitive act of labeling originally undifferentiated physiological arousal constitutes the core of emotion. People may attribute physiological arousal to different emotions depending on the information that is available about the situation. (See also *attribution.*) (*p. 483*)

Schema A basic unit of knowledge; a generalization based on experience of the world. Schemas organize past experience and provide a framework for understanding future experience; a coherent, organized set of beliefs and expectations that can influence the perception of others and objects. (*p. 36*)

Schema-plus-correction process An impression to which a

change has been added. In social perception, the initial impression of a person is remembered better than is the change. (*p. 669*)

Schizophrenia A pattern of severely disturbed thinking, emotion, perception, and behavior that constitutes one of the most serious and disabling of all mental disorders. (*p. 602*)

Schizotypal personality disorder A pattern of emotional and behavior disorder that is similar to, but significantly less intense than, schizophrenia. (*p. 613*)

Script A mental representation of a familiar sequence of activity, usually involving people's behavior. (*p. 351*)

SD See *standard deviation.*

Secondary drive A stimulus that acquires the motivational properties of a primary drive through classical conditioning or other learning mechanisms. (See also *drive, need,* and *primary drive.*) (*p. 436*)

Secondary reinforcer A reward that people or animals learn to like. Secondary reinforcers gain their reinforcing properties through association with primary reinforcers. (*p. 275*)

Secure attachment A type of parent-child relationship in which an infant's urge to be close to the parent for comfort, contact, and conversation is balanced by an urge to explore the environment. (*p. 54*)

Self-actualization According to Rogers, an innate tendency toward growth that motivates all human behavior to seek the full realization of a person's highest potential. (*p. 565*)

Self-concept The way one thinks of oneself. (*p. 566*)

Self-efficacy According to Bandura, learned expectations about the probability of success in given situations; a person's expectation of success in a given situation may be enough to create that success and even to blunt the impact of minor failures. (*p. 563*)

Self-fulfilling prophecy An impression-formation process in which an initial impression elicits behavior in another that confirms the impression. (*p. 671*)

Self-perception theory A theory that holds that when people are unsure of their attitude in a situation, they consider their behavior in light of the circumstances and then infer what their attitude must have been. (*p. 686*)

Self-serving bias The cognitive tendency to attribute one's successes to internal characteristics while blaming one's failures on external causes. (*p. 675*)

Semantic code A mental representation of an experience by its general meaning. (*p. 302*)

Semantic memory A type of memory containing generalized knowledge of the world that does not involve memory of specific events. (*p. 301*)

Semantics In language, the rules that govern the meaning of words and sentences. (See also *syntax.*) (*p. 371*)

Semicircular canal An arc-shaped tube in the inner ear containing fluid that, when shifted by head movements, stimulates nerve cells that provide information to the brain about the rate and direction of those movements. (*p. 165*)

Sensation A message from a sense, which comprises the raw information that affects many kinds of behavior and mental processes. (*p. 125*)

Sense A system that translates data from outside the nervous system into neural activity, giving the nervous system, especially the brain, information about the world. (*p. 125*)

Sensitivity The ability to detect a stimulus; sensitivity is

influenced by neural noise, the intensity of the stimulus, and the capacity of the sensory system. (*p. 178*)

Sensorimotor period The first in Piaget's stages of cognitive development, when the infant's mental activity is confined to sensory perception and motor skills. (*p. 45*)

Sensory cortex The part of the cerebral cortex located in the parietal, occipital, and temporal lobes that receives stimulus information from the skin, eyes, and ears, respectively. (*p. 102*)

Sensory memory A type of memory that is very primitive and very brief, but lasts long enough to connect one impression to the next, so that people experience a smooth flow of information. (See also *sensory register.*) (*p. 304*)

Sensory register A memory system that holds incoming information long enough for it to be processed further. (See also *sensory memory.*) (*p. 304*)

Sensory systems The parts of the nervous system that provide information about the environment; the senses. (*p. 85*)

Serial search A theoretical retrieval process in which information in short-term memory is examined one piece at a time. (See also *parallel search.*) (*p. 312*)

Serotonin A neurotransmitter used by serotonergic neurons, which are located in the hindbrain and forebrain, to regulate sleep, mood, and pain sensation. (*p. 109*)

Set-point concept A theory of hunger and the regulation of eating based on studies of the hypothalamus. According to this theory, a homeostatic mechanism in the brain establishes a level, or set point, based on body weight or some related metabolic signal. Normal animals eat until their set point is reached, then stop until their brain senses a drop in desirable intake, at which time they eat again. (*p. 442*)

Sexual dysfunction Problems with sex that involve sexual motivation, arousal, or orgasmic response regardless of sexual orientation, including low sexual desire, erectile dysfunction, infrequent orgasms, lack of orgasms, retarded ejaculation, and premature ejaculation. (*p. 611*)

Sexual response cycle The pattern of arousal during and after sexual activity. (*p. 449*)

Shaping In operant conditioning, a procedure that involves reinforcing responses that come successively closer to the desired response. (See also *successive approximation.*) (*p. 272*)

Short-term memory (also called *working memory*) A stage of memory in which information can last less than half a minute unless rehearsed. (*p. 307*)

Signal-detection theory A formal mathematical model of what determines a person's report that a near-threshold stimulus has or has not occurred. (*p. 178*)

Similarity A Gestalt grouping principle stating that similar elements are perceived to be part of a group. (*p. 184*)

Simple phobia A strong irrational fear of specific things or situations, such as heights, darkness, animals, or air travel. (*p. 590*)

Simplicity A Gestalt grouping principle stating that people tend to group stimulus features in a way that provides the simplest interpretation of the world. (*p. 184*)

Situational specificity The concept that in different situations, people are capable of many different behaviors, not all of which are necessarily compatible or consistent. (*p. 560*)

Sleep apnea A sleep disorder in which people briefly but repeatedly stop breathing during the night. (*p. 228*)

Sleepwalking A phenomenon that starts primarily in non-REM sleep, especially in stage 4, and involves walking while one is asleep. It is most common during childhood. In the morning sleepwalkers usually have no memory of their travels. (*p. 228*)

Slow-wave sleep See *quiet sleep.*

Social clock Particular age ranges during which certain milestones that mark a person's progress through life, such as completing school, leaving home, and getting married, are expected to occur. (*p. 73*)

Social cognition Mental processes associated with people's perceptions of and reactions to other people. (*p. 665*)

Social comparison Using other people as a basis of comparison for evaluating oneself. (*p. 667*)

Social dilemma A situation in which the short-term decisions of individuals become irrational in combination and create long-term, clearly predictable damage for a group. (*p. 737*)

Social facilitation A phenomenon in which the mere presence of other people improves a person's performance on a given task. (*p. 736*)

Social interference The impairment of human performance by the presence of other people.

Socialization The process by which parents, teachers, and others teach children the skills and social norms necessary to be well-functioning members of society. (*p. 56*)

Social learning Learning that occurs based on experiences with others, for example, through processes known as vicarious conditioning and observational learning. (See also *observational learning* and *vicarious conditioning.*) (*p. 282*)

Social loafing Exerting less effort when performing a group task (in which one's contribution cannot be identified) than when performing the same task alone. (*p. 736*)

Social perception The processes through which people interpret information about others, draw inferences about them, and develop mental representations of them. (*p. 669*)

Social phobia A strong, irrational fear relating to social situations. Common examples include fear of being negatively evaluated by others or publicly embarrassed by doing something impulsive, outrageous, or humiliating. (*p. 590*)

Social psychologist A psychologist who studies how people influence one another's behavior and attitudes, especially in groups. (*p. 5*)

Social psychology The psychological subfield that explores the effects of the social world on the behavior and mental processes of individuals, pairs, and groups. (*p. 4*)

Social referencing A phenomenon in which other people's facial expressions, tone of voice, and bodily gestures serve as guidelines for how to proceed in uncertain situations. (*p. 490*)

Social support The material, emotional, psychological, and other resources provided by other people, especially during times of stress. (*p. 516*)

Social support network The friends and social contacts on whom one can depend for help and support. (*p. 516*)

Sociobiologist A proponent of the theory that human and animal social behaviors that increase the chances of species survival are genetically encoded and passed from generation to generation. (*p. 724*)

Socioemotional leadership A leadership style in which the leader provides loose supervision, asks for group members' ideas, and is generally concerned with subordinates' feelings. (*p. 734*)

Somatic nervous system The subsystem of the peripheral nervous system that transmits information from the senses to the central nervous system and carries signals from the CNS to the muscles that move the skeleton. (*p. 86*)

Somatic sense (also called *somatosensory system*) A sense that is spread throughout the body, not located in a specific organ. Somatic senses include touch, temperature, pain (the skin senses), and kinesthesia. (*p. 156*)

Somatoform disorder A psychological problem in which a person shows the symptoms of some physical (somatic) disorder, even though there is no physical cause. (See also *conversion disorder.*) (*p. 593*)

Somatoform pain disorder A pattern of complaints about severe pain, for which no physical cause can be found. (*p. 594*)

Somatosensory system See *somatic sense.*

Sound A repetitive fluctuation in the pressure of a medium like air. (*p. 130*)

Specific nerve energies A doctrine that states that stimulation of a particular sensory nerve provides codes for that one sense, no matter how the stimulation takes place. (*p. 128*)

Spinal cord The part of the central nervous system contained within the spinal column that receives signals from peripheral senses (such as touch and pain) and relays them to the brain. It also conveys messages from the brain to the rest of the body. (*p. 98*)

Spontaneous recovery The reappearance of the conditioned response after extinction and without further pairings of the conditioned and unconditioned stimuli. (*p. 265*)

Standard deviation (SD) A measure of variability that is the average difference between each score and the mean of the data set (*p. A–4*)

Standard score A value that indicates the distance, in standard deviations, between a given score and the mean of all the scores in a data set. (*p. A–6*)

Stanford-Binet A test for determining a person's intelligence quotient, or IQ. (*p. 392*)

State of consciousness The characteristics of consciousness at any particular moment—for example, what reaches awareness, what levels of mental activity are most prominent, and how efficiently a person is functioning. (*p. 222*)

State theory A theory that proposes that hypnosis does indeed create an altered state of consciousness. (See also *dissociation theory* and *role theory.*) (*p. 237*)

Statistical analysis The mathematical methods used to summarize and analyze research data. Some frequently used statistics include the mean, median, mode, standard deviation, correlation coefficient, and *t* test. (*p. 6*)

Statistically significant In statistical analysis, a term used to describe the results of an experiment when the outcome of a statistical test indicates that the probability of those results occurring by chance is small (less than 5 percent). (*p. 14*)

Stereotype An impression or schema of an entire group of people that involves the false assumption that all members of the group share the same characteristics. (*p. 691*)

Stevens's power law A law that generates accurate functions

relating energy to subjective intensity for almost any kind of stimulus. (*p. 181*)

Stimulant A psychoactive drug that has the ability to increase behavioral and mental activity. Amphetamines and cocaine do so primarily by augmenting the action of the neurotransmitters dopamine and norepinephrine. (*p. 244*)

Stimulus discrimination A process through which individuals learn to differentiate among similar stimuli and respond appropriately to each one. (See also *stimulus generalization.*) (*p. 264*)

Stimulus generalization A phenomenon in which a conditioned response is elicited by stimuli that are similar but not identical to the conditioned stimulus. The greater the similarity between a stimulus and the conditioned stimulus, the stronger the conditioned response will be. (*p. 264*)

Storage The process of maintaining information in the memory system over time. (*p. 302*)

Stress The process of adjusting to circumstances that disrupt, or threaten to disrupt, a person's equilibrium. (*p. 501*)

Stress inoculation training A treatment method in which the therapist asks clients to imagine being in some stressful situation so that they can practice using new cognitive skills under controlled conditions. (*p. 645*)

Stressor An event or situation to which people must adjust. (*p. 501*)

Stress reaction The physical, psychological, and behavioral responses people display in the face of stressors. (*p. 501*)

Striatum A structure within the forebrain that is involved in the smooth initiation of movement. (*p. 101*)

Style of life According to Adler, the ways in which each person goes about trying to reach personal and social fulfillment. (*p. 548*)

Subconscious level The term used by those who do not accept Freud's theory to designate the mental level at which important but normally inaccessible mental processes take place. (See also *unconscious level.*) (*p. 220*)

Sublimation In psychodynamic theory, a defense mechanism that involves converting repressed yearnings into socially approved action. (*p. 545*)

Substance-use disorder See *psychoactive substance-use disorder.*

Substantia nigra An area of the midbrain involved in the smooth initiation of movement. (*p. 100*)

Successive approximation In operant conditioning, responses that come successively closer to a desired response. (See also *shaping.*) (*p. 272*)

Superego According to psychodynamic theory, the component of personality that tells people what they should and should not do. Its two subdivisions are the conscience, which dictates what behaviors are wrong, and the ego ideal, which sets perfectionistic standards for desirable behaviors. (*p. 543*)

Surface structure The strings of words that people produce; the order in which words are arranged. (*p. 372*)

Survey A research method that involves giving people questionnaires or special interviews designed to obtain descriptions of their attitudes, beliefs, opinions, and intentions. (*p. 18*)

Susceptibility The degree to which people comply with and become involved in hypnosis and hypnotic suggestions. Susceptibility can be measured by tests such as the Stanford

Hypnotic Susceptibility Scales and the Harvard Group Scale of Hypnotic Susceptibility. (*p. 235*)

Syllogism In the reasoning process, an argument made up of two propositions, called premises, and a conclusion based on those premises. (See also *proposition*.) (*p. 353*)

Sympathetic nervous system The subsystem of the autonomic nervous system that usually prepares the organism for vigorous activity, including the fight-or-flight syndrome. (See also *autonomic nervous system* and *fight-or-flight syndrome*.) (*p. 473*)

Synapse The tiny gap between neurons across which the neurons communicate. (*p. 88*)

Syntax In language, the set of rules that govern the formation of phrases and sentences. (See also *semantics*.) (*p. 371*)

Systematic desensitization A behavioral method for reducing anxiety in which clients visualize increasingly threatening versions of feared stimuli while using relaxation methods to remain calm. (*p. 640*)

Task-oriented leadership A leadership style in which the leader provides close supervision, leads by giving directives, and generally discourages group discussion. (*p. 734*)

Telegraphic speech Utterances that are brief and to the point and that leave out any word not absolutely essential to the meaning the speaker wishes to convey; children's first sentences, consisting of two-word utterances. (*p. 378*)

Temperament An individual's basic, natural disposition; the beginning of an individual's identity or personality, which is evident from infancy. (*p. 52*)

Teratogen A harmful substance, such as alcohol and other drugs, that can invade a pregnant woman's womb and cause birth defects in her child. (*p. 40*)

Terminal drop A sharp decline in mental functioning that tends to occur in late adulthood, a few years or months before death. (*p. 76*)

Test A systematic procedure for observing behavior in a standard situation and describing it with the help of a numerical scale or a category system. (*p. 397*)

Testosterone A masculine hormone, the principal androgen. (See also *androgens*.) (*p. 447*)

Textural gradient A graduated change in the texture, or "grain," of the visual field, whereby changes in texture across the retinal image are perceived as changes in distance; objects with finer, less detailed textures are perceived as more distant. (*p. 189*)

Thalamus A structure in the forebrain that relays signals from the eyes and other sense organs to higher levels in the brain and plays an important role in processing and making sense out of this information. (*p. 101*)

Theory An integrated set of principles that can be used to explain, predict, and control certain phenomena. (In psychology, the phenomena are behaviors and mental processes.) (*p. 16*)

Thinking The manipulation of mental representations, performed in order to reason, understand a situation, solve a problem, make a decision, or reach some other goal. The manipulations can also be less goal-directed, such as in daydreaming. (*p. 348*)

Timbre The quality of sound that identifies it, so that, for example, a middle C played on the piano is clearly distin-

guishable from a middle C played on a trumpet. The timbre depends on the mixture of frequencies and amplitudes that make up the sound. (*p. 131*)

Token economy A system for improving the behavior of severely disturbed or mentally retarded clients in institutions that involves rewarding desirable behaviors with tokens that can be exchanged for snacks, field trips, access to television, or other privileges. (*p. 641*)

Top-down processing Those aspects of recognition that are guided by higher-level cognitive processes and psychological factors like expectations. (See also *bottom-up processing*.) (*p. 196*)

Topographical representation A map of each sense, contained in the primary cortex. Any two points that are next to each other in the stimulus will be represented next to each other in the brain. (*p. 129*)

Tranquilizer See *Anxiolytic*.

Transduction The second step in sensation, which is the process of converting incoming energy into neural activity through receptors. (*p. 127*)

Transference A phenomenon in which a client transfers to the therapist many of the feelings, attitudes, reactions, and conflicts experienced in childhood toward parents, siblings, and other significant people. (*p. 632*)

Transferred excitation The process of carrying over arousal from one experience to an independent situation, which is especially likely to occur when the arousal pattern from the nonemotional source is similar to the pattern associated with a particular emotion. (*p. 486*)

Trichromatic theory The theory postulated by Young and Helmholtz that there are three types of visual elements, each of which is most sensitive to different wavelengths, and that information from these three elements combines to produce the sensation of color. (*p. 145*)

Tympanic membrane A tightly stretched membrane (also known as the *eardrum*) in the middle ear that generates vibrations that match the sound waves striking it. (*p. 132*)

Type A A personality type characterized by nonstop working, intense competitiveness, aggressiveness, and impatience, accompanied by an especially strong need to control events. (See also *Type B*.) (*p. 519*)

Type B A personality type characterized by a more relaxed and easygoing attitude than that associated with the Type A personality. (See also *Type A*.) (*p. 519*)

Unconditional positive regard In client-centered therapy, the therapist's attitude that expresses caring for and acceptance of the client as a valued person. (*p. 635*)

Unconditioned response (UCR) In classical conditioning, the automatic or unlearned reaction to a stimulus. (See also *conditioned response*.) (*p. 259*)

Unconditioned stimulus (UCS) In classical conditioning, the stimulus that elicits a response without conditioning. (See also *conditioned stimulus*.) (*p. 259*)

Unconscious level A segment of mental activity proposed by Freud that contains sexual, aggressive, and other impulses, as well as once-conscious but unacceptable thoughts and feelings of which an individual is completely unaware. (See also *conscious level, nonconscious level, preconscious level,* and *subconscious level*.) (*p. 220*)

Undifferentiated schizophrenia Patterns of disordered thought, behavior, and emotions that are characteristic of schizophrenia but that cannot easily be placed in any specific schizophrenic subtype. (*p. 605*)

Utility In rational decision making, any subjective measure of value. (*p. 368*)

Validity The degree to which a test measures what it is supposed to measure. (*p. 398*)

Variability A measure of the dispersion of scores in a set of data. (See also *range* and *standard deviation*.) (*p. A–4*)

Variable In an experiment, any specific factor or characteristic that can vary. (*p. 12*)

Variable interval (VI) schedule In operant conditioning, a type of partial reinforcement schedule that provides reinforcement for the first response after some varying period of time. For example, in a VI 60 schedule the first response to occur after an average of one minute would be reinforced, but the actual time between reinforcements could vary from, say, 1 second to 120 seconds. (*p. 273*)

Variable ratio (VR) schedule A type of partial reinforcement schedule that provides reinforcement after a varying number of responses. For example, on a VR 30 schedule, a rat might sometimes be reinforced after ten bar presses, sometimes after fifty bar presses, but an average of thirty responses would occur before reinforcement is given. (*p. 272*)

Verbal scale Six subtests in the Wechsler scales that measure verbal skills as part of a measure of overall intelligence. (See also *performance scale*.) (*p. 394*)

Vestibular sense The proprioceptive sense that provides information about the position of the body in space and about its general movements. It is often thought of as the sense of balance. (*p. 164*)

VI See *variable interval schedule*.

Vicarious conditioning Learning the relationship between a response and its consequences (either reinforcement or punishment) or the association between a conditioned stimulus and a conditioned response by watching others. (*p. 282*)

Visible light Electromagnetic radiation that has a wavelength from about 400 nanometers to about 750 nanometers. (A nanometer is one-billionth of a meter.) (*p. 137*)

Visual code A mental representation of stimuli as pictures. (*p. 302*)

Visual dominance A phenomenon that occurs when information received by the visual system conflicts with information coming from other sensory modalities; the sense of vision normally overrides other sensory information and is perceived as accurate. Visual dominance is a major factor in people's ability to be fooled by certain illusions. (*p. 192*)

Volley theory See *frequency matching*.

Vulnerability model A view of schizophrenia that suggests that different people have differing degrees of vulnerability to schizophrenia; this vulnerability may not be entirely inherited; and it may involve psychological and biological components. (See also *diathesis* and *stress*.) (*p. 607*)

Waveform A graphic representation of sound or other energy. For sound, a waveform represents in two dimensions the wave that moves through the air in three dimensions. The point where the air is compressed the most is the peak of the graph. The lowest point, or trough, is where the air pressure is least compressed. (*p. 130*)

Wavelength The distance from one peak to the next in a waveform. (*p. 131*)

Weber's law A law stating that the smallest detectable difference in stimulus energy, the just-noticeable difference (JND), is a constant fraction, K, of the intensity of the stimulus, I. The constant varies for each sensory system and for different aspects of sensation within those systems. In algebraic terms, Weber's law is JND = KI. (See also *just-noticeable difference*.) (*p. 180*)

Word A unit of language composed of one or more morphemes. (See also *morpheme*.) (*p. 371*)

Working memory See *short-term memory*.

Aaker, D. A., & Stayman, D. M. (1989). What mediates the emotional response to advertising? The case of warmth. In P. Cafferata & A. Tybout (Eds.), *Cognitive and affective responses to advertising*. Lexington, MA: Lexington Books.

Abbott, B. B., Schoen, L. S., & Badia, P. (1984). Predictable and unpredictable shock: Behavioral measures of aversion and physiological measures of stress. *Psychological Bulletin, 96,* 45–71.

Abel, G. G., Blanchard, E. B., & Becker, J. V. (1976). Psychological treatment of rapists. In M. Walker & S. Brodsky (Eds.), *Sexual assault: The victim and the rapist*. Lexington, MA: Lexington Books.

Abel, G. G., Blanchard, E. B., & Barlow, D. H. (1981). Measurement of sexual arousal in several paraphilias: The effects of stimulus modality, instrumental set, and stimulus content on the objective. *Behavior Research and Therapy, 19,* 25–33.

Abeles, N. (1985). Proceedings of the American Psychological Association, 1985. *American Psychologist, 41,* 633–663.

Abraham, G. E. (1983). Nutritional factores in the etiology of the premenstrual tension syndromes. *Journal of Reproductive Medicine, 28,* 446–464.

Abraham, H. D., & Wolf, E. (1989). Visual function in past users of LSD: Psychophysical findings. *Journal of Abnormal Psychology, 97,* 443–447.

Abrams, R., Taylor, M., Faber, R., Ts'o, T., Williams, R., & Almy, G. (1983). Bilateral vs. unilateral electronconvulsive therapy: Efficacy and melancholia. *American Journal of Psychiatry, 140,* 463–465.

Abramson, L. Y., Seligman, M. E. P., & Teasdale, J. D. (1978). Learned helplessness in humans: Critique and reformulation. *Journal of Abnormal Psychology, 87,* 49–74.

Abramson, L. Y., Metalsky, G. I., & Alloy, L. B. (1989). Hopelessness depression: A theory-based subtype. *Psychological Review, 96,* 358–372.

Achenbach, T. M. (1982). *Developmental psychopathology* (2nd ed.). New York: Wiley.

Adam, K., & Oswald, I. (1977). Sleep is for tissue restoration. *Journal of the Royal College of Physicians, 11,* 376–388.

Adams, G. R., & Jones, R. M. (1983). Female adolescents' identity development: Age comparisons and perceived child-rearing experience. *Developmental Psychology, 19,* 249–256.

Adams, H. E., & Chioto, J. (1983). Sexual deviations. In H. E. Adams & P. B. Sutker (Eds.), *Comprehensive handbook of psychopathology*. New York: Plenum Press.

Adams, J. A. (1989). *Human factors engineering*. New York: Macmillan.

Ader, R., & Cohen, N. (1985). CNS–immune system interactions: Conditioning phenomena. *Behavior and Brain Sciences, 8,* 379–394.

Adler, A. (1963). *The practice and theory of individual psychology* (original work published 1927). Paterson, NJ: Littlefield Adams.

Adler, T. (1989, March). FAA establishes unit to study human error. *APA Monitor.*

Adorno, T. W., Frenkel-Brunswik, E., Levinson, D. J., & Sanford, R. N. (1950). *The authoritarian personality*. New York: Harper & Row.

Aiken, L. R. (1987). *Assessment of intellectual functioning*. Boston, MA: Allyn & Bacon.

Ainsworth, M. D. S. (1973). The development of infant-mother attachment. In B. M. Caldwell & H. N. Ricciuti (Eds.), *Review of child development research: Vol. 3*. Chicago: University of Chicago Press.

Ainsworth, M. D. S. (1989). Attachments beyond infancy. *American Psychologist, 44,* 709–716.

Aitchison, J. (1983). *The articulate mammal: An introduction to psycholinguistics* (2nd ed.). New York: Universe.

Ajzen, I. (1989). Attitude structure and behavior. In A. R. Pratkanis, S. J. Breckler, & A. G. Greenwald (Eds.), *Attitude structure and function*. Hillsdale, NJ: Lawrence Erlbaum Associates.

Alan Guttmacher Institute (1981). *Teenage pregnancy: The problem that hasn't gone away*. New York: Alan Guttmacher Institute.

Albee, G. (1968). Conceptual models and manpower requirements in psychology. *American Psychologist, 23,* 317–320.

Albee, G. (1985, February). The answer is prevention. *Psychology Today.*

Albert, D. J., & Walsh, M. L. (1984). Neural systems and the inhibitory modulation of agnostic behavior: A comparison of mammalian species. *Neuroscience and Biobehavioral Reviews, 8,* 5–24.

Alberti, R. E., & Emmons, M. L. (1986). *Your perfect right: A guide to assertive living* (5th ed.). San Luis Obispo, CA: Impact Publishers.

Alcohol and health: Report to the U.S. Congress. (1984). Rockville, MD: Department of Health and Human Services.

Aldwin, C. M., & Revenson, T. A. (1987). Does coping help? A reexamination of the relation between coping and mental health. *Journal of Personality and Social Psychology, 53,* 337–348.

Alexander, F. M. (1963). *Fundamentals of psychoanalysis*. New York: W. W. Norton.

Allen, G. J. (1977). *Understanding psychotherapy*. Champaign, IL: Research Press.

Allen, K. E., Hart, B. M., Buell, J. S., Harris, F. R., & Wolf, M. M. (1964). Effects of social reinforcement on isolate behavior of a nursery school child. In L. P. Ullmann & L. Krasner (Eds.), *Case studies in behavior modification*. New York: Holt, Rinehart and Winston.

Allen, M. G. (1976). Twin studies of affective illness. *Archives of General Psychiatry, 33,* 1476–1478.

Allen, M. G., Cohen, S., & Pollin, W. (1972). Schizophrenia in veteran twins: A diagnostic review. *American Journal of Psychiatry, 128,* 939–947.

Alloy, L. B., & Abramson, L. Y. (1979). Judgment of contingency in depressed and nondepressed students: Sadder but wiser? *Journal of Experimental Psychology: General, 108,* 441–485.

Allport, G. W. (1961). *Pattern and growth in personality.* New York: Holt, Rinehart & Winston.

Allred, K. D., & Smith, T. W. (1989). The hardy personality: Cognitive and physiological responses to evaluative threat. *Journal of Personality and Social Psychology, 56,* 257–266.

Amabile, T. (1989). *Growing up creative.* New York: Random House.

Amabile, T. M., Hennessey, B. A., & Grossman, B. S. (1986). Social influences on creativity: The effects of contracted-for reward. *Journal of Personality & Social Psychology, 50,* 14–23.

American Law Institute. (1962). *Model penal code: Proposed offical draft.* Philadelphia: Author.

American Psychiatric Association. (1989). *Treatments of psychiatric disorders.* Washington, DC: American Psychiatric Press.

American Psychological Association. (1974). *Standards for educational and psychological test and manuals.* Washington, DC: Author.

American Psychological Association. (1981). Ethical principles of psychologists. *American Psychologist, 36,* 633–638.

American Psychological Association. (1981/1989). Ethical principles of psychologists. *American Psychologist, 36,* 633–638. (Amended June 2, 1989)

American Psychological Association. (1984). *Behavioral research with animals.* Washington, DC: American Psychological Association.

American Psychological Association. (1987). *Casebook on ethical principles of psychologists.* Washington, DC: American Psychological Association.

American Psychological Association (1990). Ethical principles of psychologists (Amended June 2, 1989). *American Psychologist, 45,* 390–395.

Anastasi, A. (1971). Note on the concepts of creativity and intelligence. *Journal of Creative Behavior, 5,* 113–116.

Anastasi, A. (1982). *Psychological testing* (5th ed.). New York: Collier Macmillan.

Anastasi, A. (1988). *Psychological testing* (6th ed.). New York: Macmillan.

Ancona, D. G. (1987). Groups in organizations: Extending laboratory models. In C. Hendrick (Ed.), *Group processes and intergroup relations.* Newbury Park, CA: Sage.

Andersen, G. J. (1986). The perception of self motion: Psychological and computational approach. *Journal of Experimental Psychology: Perception & Human Performance, 11,* 122–132.

Anderson, C. A. (1989). Temperature and aggression: Ubiquitous effects of heat on occurrence of human violence. *Psychological Bulletin, 106,* 74–96.

Anderson, J. R. (1979). *Cognitive psychology.* New York: Academic Press.

Anderson, J. R. (1989). A rational analysis of human memory. In H. L. Roediger & F. I. M. Craik (Eds.), *Varieties of memory and consciousness.* Hillsdale, NJ: Lawrence Erlbaum Associates.

Anderson, N. B. (1989). Racial differences in stress-induced cardiovascular reactivity and hypertension: Current status and substantive issues. *Psychological Bulletin, 105,* 89–105.

Anderson, N. H. (1989). Functional memory and on-line attribution. In J. N. Bassili (Ed.), *On-line cognition in person perception.* Hillsdale, NJ: Lawrence Erlbaum Associates.

Anderson, R. C., Reynolds, R. E., Schallert, D. L., & Goetz, E. T. (1977). Frameworks for comprehending discourse. *American Educational Research Journal, 14,* 367–382.

Anderson, T. H. (1978). *Another look at the self-questioning study technique* (Technical Ed. Rep. No. 6). Champaign: University of Illinois, Center for the Study of Reading.

Andreasen, N. C., Olson, S. A., Dennert, J. W., & Smith, M. R. (1982). Ventricular enlargement in schizophrenia: Relationship to positive and negative symptoms. *American Journal of Psychiatry, 139,* 297–302.

Andreasen, N. C., Rice, J., Endicott, J., Coryell, W., Grove, W. W., & Reich, T. (1987). Familial rates of affective disorder. *Archives of General Psychiatry, 44,* 461–472.

Andrews, G., & Harvey, R. (1981). Does psychotherapy benefit neurotic patients? *Archives of General Psychiatry, 138,* 1203–1208.

Andrews, J. D. W. (1989). Integrating vision of reality: Interpersonal diagnosis and the existential vision. *American Psychologist, 44,* 803–817.

Angoff, W. H. (1989). The nature-nurture debate, aptitudes, and group differences. *American Psychologist, 43,* 713–720.

Angrist, B., Lee, H. K., & Gershon, S. (1974). The antagonism of amphetamine-induced symptomatology by a neuroleptic. *American Journal of Psychiatry, 131,* 817–819.

Anshel, M. W., & Wrisberg, C. A. (1988). The effect of arousal and focused attention on warmup decrement. *Journal of Sport Behavior, 11,* 18–31.

Appley, M. H., & Trumbull, R. (Eds.) (1986). *Dynamics of stress: Physiological, psychological, and social perspectives.* New York: Plenum Press.

Archambault, C. M., Czyzewski, D., Cordua y Cruz, G. D., Foreyt, F. P., & Mariotto, M. J. (1989). Effects of weight cycling in female rats. *Physiology and Behavior, 46,* 417–421.

Arenberg, D. (1982). Changes with age in problem solving. In F. I. M. Craik & S. Trehub (Eds.), *Aging and cognitive processes* (pp. 221–236). New York: Plenum.

Arkin, R. M., & Baumgardner, A. H. (1985). Self-handicapping. In J. H. Harvey & G. Weary (Eds.), *Attribution: Basic issues and applications.* New York: Academic Press.

Arlin, P. K. (1980, June). *Adolescent and adult thought: A search for structures.* Paper presented at the meeting of the Jean Piaget Society, Philadelphia, PA.

Arnheim, R. (1969). *Visual thinking.* Berkeley: University of California Press.

Aronoff, J., Barclay, A. M., & Stevenson, L. A. (1988). The recognition of threatening stimuli. *Journal of Personality and Social Psychology, 54,* 647–655.

Aronson, E. (1988). *The social animal* (5th ed.). San Francisco: Freeman.

Aronson, E. (1990). Applying social psychology to desegregation and energy conservation. *Personality and Social Psychology Bulletin, 16,* 118–132.

Aronson, E., & Cope, V. (1968). My enemy's enemy is my friend. *Journal of Personality and Social Psychology, 8,* 8–12.

Aronson, E., Brewer, M., & Carlsmith, J. M. (1963). Experimentation in social psychology. In G. Lindzey & E. Aronson (Eds.), *The handbook of social psychology: Vol. 1* (3rd ed.). New York: Random House.

Aronson, E., Turner, J. A., & Carlsmith, J. M. (1963). Communicator credibility and communication discrepancy as a determinant of opinion change. *Journal of Abnormal and Social Psychology, 67,* 31–36.

Asch, S. E. (1951). Effects of group pressure upon the modification and distortion of judgments. In H. Guetzkow (Ed.), *Groups, leadership, and men.* Pittsburgh: Carnegie Press.

Asch, S. E. (1955). Opinions and social pressure. *Scientific American, 193,* 31–35.

Asch, S. E. (1956). Studies of independence and conformity: A minority of one against a unanimous majority. *Psychological Monographs, 70,* 1–70.

Aserinsky, E., & Kleitman, N. (1953). Regularly occurring periods of eye motility and concomitant phenomena during sleep. *Science, 118,* 273.

Ashcraft, M. H. (1989). *Human memory and cognition.* Glenview, IL: Scott Foresman

Ashmead, D. H., & Perlmutter, M. (1980). Infant memory in everyday life. In M. Perlmutter (Ed.), *New directions in child development: Children's memory.* San Francisco: Jossey-Bass.

Aslin, R. N., Pisoni, D. B., & Jusczyk, P. W. (1983). Auditory development and speech perception in infancy. In P. H. Mussen (Ed.), *Handbook of child psychology: Vol. 2.* New York: Wiley.

Associated Press. (1984). *Man sets wife afire after watching TV movie.*

Associated Press. (1986). *Media general poll.*

Associated Press (1989, August 20). Think you have a great memory? Forget it. *Chicago Tribune,* sec. 2, p. 1.

Atkinson, J. W., & Birch, D. (1978). *Introduction to motivation* (2nd ed.). New York: D. Van Nostrand.

Atkinson, J. W., & Raynor, J. O. (1974). *Personality, motivation, and achievment.* Washington, DC: Hemisphere.

Atkinson, R. C., & Shiffrin, R. M. (1968). Human memory: A proposed system and its control processes. In K. Spence (Ed.), *The psychology of learning and motivation: Vol. 2.* New York: Academic Press.

Averill, J. S. (1980). On the paucity of positive emotions. In K. R. Blankstein, P. Pliner, & J. Polivy (Eds.), *Advances in the study of communication and affect: Vol. 6. Assessment and modification of emotional behavior.* New York: Plenum Press.

Axelrod, R. (1984). *The evolution of cooperation.* New York: Basic Books.

Axelrod, R., & Dion, D. (1988). The further evolution of cooperation. *Science, 242,* 1385–1390.

Axsom, D. (1989). Cognitive dissonance and behavior change in psychotherapy. *Journal of Experimental Social Psychology, 25,* 234–252.

Ayllon, T., & Azrin, N. H. (1968). *The token economy: A motivational system for therapy and rehabilitation.* New York: Appleton-Century-Crofts.

Babad, E., Bernieri, F., & Rosenthal, R. (1989). Nonverbal communication and leakage in the behavior of biased and unbiased teachers. *Journal of Personality and Social Psychology, 56,* 89-94.

Bach, S., & Klein, G. S. (1957). The effects of prolonged subliminal exposure of words. *American Psychologist, 12,* 397–398.

Backstrom, T., & Carstensen, H. (1974). Estrogen and progesterone in plasma in relation to premenstrual tension. *Journal of Steroid Biochemistry, 5,* 257–260.

Baddeley, A. (1982). *Your memory: A user's guide.* New York: Macmillan.

Bahrick, H. P. (1984). Semantic memory content in permastore: Fifty years of memory for Spanish learned in school. *Journal of Experimental Psychology: General, 113,* 1–29.

Bahrick, H. P., & Boucher, B. (1968). Retention of visual and verbal codes of the same stimuli. *Journal of Experimental Psychology, 78,* 417–422.

Baker, T. B., & Tiffany, S. T. (1985). Morphine tolerance as habituation. *Psychological Review, 92,* 78–108.

Balay, J., & Shevrin, H. (1988). The subliminal psychodynamic activation method: A critical review. *American Psychologist, 43,* 161–174.

Bales, J. (1988, December). *Vincennes:* Findings could have helped avert tragedy, scientists tell Hill panel. *APA Monitor,* pp. 10–11.

Balota, D. A. (1983). Automatic semantic activation and episodic memory encoding. *Journal of Verbal Learning and Verbal Behavior, 22,* 88–104.

Bandura, A. (1965). Influence of a model's reinforcement contingencies on the acquisition of imitative responses. *Journal of Personality and Social Psychology, 1,* 589–595.

Bandura, A. (1969). *Principles of behavior modification.* New York: Holt, Rinehart and Winston.

Bandura, A. (1977). *Social learning theory* (original work published 1971). Englewood Cliffs, NJ: Prentice-Hall.

Bandura, A. (1978). The self system in reciprocal determinism. *American Psychologist, 33,* 344–358.

Bandura, A. (1982a). The assessment and predictive generality of self-percepts of efficacy. *Journal of Behavior Therapy and Experimental Psychiatry, 13,* 195–199.

Bandura, A. (1982b). Self-efficacy mechanism in human agency. *American Psychologist, 37,* 122–147.

Bandura, A. (1983). Psychological measurement of aggression. In R. G. Green and C. I. Donnerstein (Eds.). *Aggression: Theoretical and empirical reviews* (Vol. 1). New York: Academic Press.

Bandura, A. (1986). *Social foundations of thought and action: A social cognitive theory.* Englewood Cliffs, NJ: Prentice-Hall.

Bandura, A. (1989). Self-efficacy mechanism in physiological activation and health-promoting behavior. In J. Madden IV, S. Matthysse, & J. Barchas (Eds.), *Adaptation, learning, and affect.* New York: Raven Press.

Bandura, A., Blanchard, E. B., & Ritter, B. (1969). The relative efficacy of desensitization and modeling approaches for inducing behavioral, affective, and attitudinal changes. *Journal of Personality and Social Psychology, 13,* 173–199.

Bandura, A., Cioffi, D., Taylor, C. B., & Brouillard, M. E. (1988). Perceived self-efficacy in coping with cognitive stressors and opioid activation. *Journal of Personality and Social Psychology, 55,* 479–488.

Bandura, A., Ross, D., & Ross, S. A. (1963). Imitation of film-mediated aggressive models. *Journal of Abnormal and Social Psychology, 66,* 3–11.

Bandura, A., O'Leary, A., Taylor, C. B., Gauthier, J., & Gossard, D. (1987). Perceived self-efficacy and pain control: Opioid and non-opioid mechanisms. *Journal of Personality and Social Psychology, 53,* 563–571.

Bank, S., & Kahn, M. D. (1975). Sisterhood-brotherhood is powerful: Sibling subsystems and family therapy. *Family Process, 14,* 311–337.

Banks, M. S., & Salapatek, P. (1983). Infant visual perception. In P. H. Mussen (Ed.), *Handbook of child psychology: Vol. 2. Infancy and developmental psychobiology.* New York: Wiley.

Barbaro, N. M. (1988). Studies of PAG/PVG stimulation for pain relief in humans. *Progress in Brain Research, 77,* 165–173.

Barber, T. X. (1969). *Hypnosis: A scientific approach.* New York: Van Nostrand Reinhold.

Barclay, J. R., Bransford, J. D., Franks, J. J., McCarrell, N. S., & Nitsch, K. (1974). Comprehension and semantic flexibility. *Journal of Verbal Learning and Verbal Behavior, 13,* 471–481.

Barenboim, C. (1981). The development of person perception in childhood and adolescence: From behavioral comparisons to psychological constructs to psychological comparisons. *Child Development, 52,* 129–144.

Bargh, J. A. (1982). Attention and automaticity in the processing of self-relevant information. *Journal of Personality and Social Psychology, 43,* 425–436.

Barinaga, M. (1989). Manic depression gene put in limbo. *Science, 246,* 886-887.

Barnett, B. J. (1989). Information processing components and knowledge representation: An individual differences approach to modeling pilot judgment. *Proceedings of the 33rd Annual Meeting of the Human Factors Society.* Santa Monica, CA: Human Factors Society.

Barnett, P. A., & Gotlieb, I. H. (1988). Psychosocial functioning and depression: Distinguishing among antecedents, concomitants, and consequences. *Psychological Bulletin, 104,* 97–126.

Baron, J. (1989). Why a theory of social intelligence needs a theory of character. In R. S. Wyer & T. K. Srull (Eds.), *Advances in social cognition: Vol. 2. Social intelligence and cognitive assessments of personality.* Hillsdale, NJ: Lawrence Erlbaum Associates.

Barrett, C. J. (1978). Effectiveness of widows' groups in facilitating change. *Journal of Consulting and Clinical Psychology, 46,* 20–31.

Barrett, J. E. (Ed.). (1979). *Stress and mental disorder.* New York: Raven.

Barron, F., & Harrington, D. M. (1981). Creativity, intelligence, and personality. *Annual Review of Psychology, 52,* 439–476.

Bartoshuk, L. M., Gentile, R. L., Moskowitz, H. R., & Meiselman, H. L. (1974). Sweet taste induced by miracle fruit (Synsephalum dulcificum). *Physiology and Behavior, 12,* 449–456.

Bartus, R. T., Dean, R. L., III, Beer, B., and Lippa, A. S. (1982). The cholinergic hypothesis of geriatric memory dysfunction. *Science, 217,* 408–417.

Basgall, J. A., & Snyder, C. R. (1988). Excuses in waiting: External locus of control and reactions to success-failure feedback. *Journal of Personality and Social Psychology, 54,* 656–662.

Bassili, J. N. (1989a). Trait encoding in behavior identification and dispositional inference. *Personality and Social Psychology Bulletin, 15,* 285–296.

Bassili, J. N. (1989b). Traits as action categories versus traits as person attributes in social cognition. In J. N. Bassili (Ed.), *On-line cognition in person perception.* Hillsdale, NJ: Lawrence Erlbaum Associates.

Bates, E. (1976). *Language and context: The acquisition of pragmatics.* New York: Academic Press.

Bates, J. E. (1980). The concept of difficult temperament. *Merrill-Palmer Quarterly, 25,* 299–319.

Batson, C. D. (1987). Prosocial motivation: Is it ever truly altruistic? In L. Berkowitz (Ed.), *Advances in experimental social psychology* (Vol. 20). Orlando, FL: Academic Press.

Batson, C. D., Batson, J. G., Griffitt, C. A., Barrientos, S., Brandt, J. R., Sprengelmeyer, P., & Bayly, M. J. (1989). Negative-state relief and the empathy-altuism hypothesis. *Journal of Personality and Social Psychology, 56,* 922–933.

Baucom, D. H., Sayers, S. L., & Duhe, A. (1989). Attributional style and attributional patterns among married couples. *Journal of Personality and Social Psychology, 56,* 596–607.

Baumeister, R. F. (1984). Choking under pressure: Self-consciousness and paradoxical effects of incentives on skillful performance. *Journal of Personality and Social Psychology, 46(3),* 610–620.

Baumeister, R. F. (1989). Social intelligence and the construction of meaning in life. In R. S. Wyer & T. K. Srull (Eds.), *Advances in social cognition: Vol. 2. Social intelligence and cognitive assessments of personality.* Hillsdale, NJ: Lawrence Erlbaum Associates.

Baumgardner, A. H., & Arkin, R. M. (1987). Coping with the prospect of social disapproval: Strategies and sequelae. In C. R. Snyder & C. Ford (Eds.), *Clinical and social psychological perspectives on negative life events.* New York: Plenum.

Baumgardner, A. H., Kaufman, C. M., & Levy, P. E. (1989). Regulating affect interpersonally: When low self-esteem leads to greater enhancement. *Journal of Personality and Social Psychology, 56,* 907–921.

Baumrind, D. (1975). Early socialization and adolescent competence. In S. E. Dragastin & G. H. Elder (Eds.), *Adolescence in the life cycle.* New York: Wiley.

Baxter, L.R., et al. (1985). *Archives of General Psychiatry, 42.*

Baxter, T. L., & Goldberg, L. R. (1987). Perceived behavioral consistency underlying trait attributions to oneself and another: An extension of the actor-observer effect. *Personality and Social Psychology Bulletin, 13,* 437–447.

Beaman, A. L., Barnes, P. J., Klentz, B., & McQuirk, B. (1978). Increasing helping rates through information dissemination: Teaching pays. *Personality and Social Psychology Bulletin, 4,* 406–411.

Beaman, A. L., Cole, C. M., Preston, M., Klentz, B., & Steblay, N. M. (1983). Fifteen years of foot-in-the-door research: A meta-analysis. *Personality and Social Psychology Bulletin, 9,* 181–196.

Beatty, J. (1982). Task evoked pupillary responses, processing load, and the structure of processing resources. *Psychological Bulletin, 91,* 276–292.

Beatty, W. W. (1985). Assessing remote memory for space: The Fargo Map Test. *Journal of Experimental and Clinical Neuropsychology, 7,* 640.

Beatty, W. W., & Spangenberger, M. (1988). Persistence of geographic memories in adults. *Bulletin of the Psychonomic Society, 26,* 104–105.

Beck, A. J., & Shipley, B. E. (1989). *Special report: Recidivism of prisoners released in 1983.* Washington, DC: U.S. Department of Justice, Bureau of Justice Statistics.

Beck, A. T. (1967). *Depression: Clinical, experimental and theoretical aspects.* New York: Harper & Row.

Beck, A. T. (1987). Cognitive model of depression. *Journal of Cognitive Psychotherapy, 1,* 2–27.

Beck, A. T., & Emery, G. (1985). *Anxiety disorders and phobias: A cognitive perspective.* New York: Basic Books.

Beck, A. T., Rush, A. J., Shaw, B. F., & Emery, G. (1979). *Cognitive therapy of depression.* New York: Guilford Press.

Beck, J. (1966). Perceptual grouping produced by changes in orientation and shape. *Science, 154,* 538–563.

Bell, A., Weinberg, M. S., & Hammersmith, S. K. (1983). *Sexual preference development in men and women.* Bloomington: Indiana University Press.

Bell, B. E., & Loftus, E. F. (1989). Trivial persuasion in the courtroom: The power of (a few) minor details. *Journal of Personality and Social Psychology, 56,* 669–679.

Bell, R. R., & Bell, P. L. (1972). Sexual satisfaction among married women. *Medical Aspects of Human Sexuality, 6,* 136–144.

Belli, R.F. (1989). Influences of misleading postevent information: Misinformation interference and acceptance. *Journal of Experimental Psychology: General, 118,* 72-85.

Belmont, J. M., & Butterfield, E. C. (1971). Learning strategies as determinants of memory deficiencies. *Cognitive Psychology, 2,* 411–420.

Belsky, J. (1988). The "effects" of infant day care reconsidered. *Early Childhood Research Quarterly, 3,* 235–272.

Bem, D. J. (1967). Self-perception: An alternative interpretation of cognitive dissonance phenomena. *Psychological Review, 74,* 183–200.

Bem, D. J., & Allen, A. (1974). On predicting some of the people some of the time: The search for cross-situational consistencies in behavior. *Psychological Review, 81,* 506–520.

Bem, S. L. (1987). Masculinity and femininity exist only in the mind of the perceiver. In J. M. Reinisch, L. A. Rosenbaum, & S. A. Sanders (Eds.), *Masculinity/femininity: Basic perspectives.* New York: Oxford University Press.

Bemis, K. M. (1978). Current approaches to the etiology and treatment of anorexia nervosa. *Psychological Bulletin, 85,* 593–617.

Bemporad, J. R., & Schwab, M. E. (1986). The DSM-III and clinical child psychiatry. In T. Millon & G. L. Klerman (Eds.), *Contemporary directions in psychopathology: Toward the DSM-IV* (pp. 135–150). New York: Guilford Press.

Bennett, H. L., Giannini, J. A., & Davis, H. S. (1985). Nonverbal response to intraoperational conversation. *British Journal of Anaesthesia, 57,* 174–179.

Benson, H. (1975). *The relaxation response.* New York: Morrow.

Bergen, R. S., & Dweck, C. S. (1989). The functions of personality theories. In R. S. Wyer & T. K. Srull (Eds.), *Advances in social cognition: Vol. 2: Social intelligence and cognitive assessments of personality.* Hillsdale, NJ: Lawrence Erlbaum Associates.

Berger, P. A. (1978). Medical treatment of mental illness. *Science, 200,* 974–981.

Berkman, L., & Syme, S. L. (1979). Social networks, host resistance, and mortality: A nine-year follow-up study of Alameda County residents. *American Journal of Epidemiology, 109,* 186–204.

Berkowitz, B. (1965). Changes in intellect with age: IV. Changes in achievement and survival in older people. *Journal of Genetic Psychology, 107,* 3–14.

Berkowitz, L. (1981). Aversive conditions as stimuli for aggression. In L. Berkowitz (Ed.), *Advances in experimental social psychology: Vol. 15.* New York: Academic Press.

Berkowitz, L. (1984). Some effects of thought on anti- and prosocial influences of media events: A cognitive-neoassociation analysis. *Psychological Bulletin, 95,* 410–427.

Berkowitz, L. (1988). Frustrations, appraisals, and aversively stimulated aggression. *Aggressive Behavior, 14*, 3–11.

Berkowitz, L. (1989). Frustration-aggression hypothesis: Examination and reformulation. *Psychological Bulletin, 106*, 59–73.

Berkowitz, L., & Heimer, K. (1989). On the construction of the anger experience: Aversive events and negative priming in the formation of feelings. In L. Berkowitz (Ed.), *Advances in experimental social psychology* (Vol. 22). New York: Academic Press.

Berkun, M. M. (1964). Performance decrement under psychological stress. *Human Factors, 6*, 21–30.

Berlyne, D. E. (1960). *Conflict, arousal, and curiosity.* New York: McGraw-Hill.

Berman, J. S., & Norton, N. C. (1985). Does professional training make a therapist more effective? *Psychological Bulletin, 98*, 401–407.

Bernard, L. L. (1924). *Instinct.* New York: Holt, Rinehart & Winston.

Berndt, T. J. (1978a, August). *Children's conceptions of friendship and the behavior expected of friends.* Paper presented at the annual meeting of the American Psychological Association, Toronto, Ontario.

Berndt, T. J. (1978b, August). *Developmental changes on conformity to parents and peers.* Paper presented at the annual meeting of the American Psychological Association, Toronto, Ontario.

Berndt, T. J., & Hawkins, J. A. (1987). *The contribution of supportive friendships to adjustment after the transition to junior high school.* Unpublished manuscript, Department of Psychological Sciences, Purdue University.

Bernstein, D. A. (1970). The modification of smoking behavior: A search for effective variables. *Behaviour Research and Therapy, 8*, 133–146.

Bernstein, D. A., & Borkovec, T. D. (1973). *Progressive relaxation training: A manual for the helping professions.* Champaign, IL: Research Press.

Bernstein, I. H., Bissonnette, V., Vyas, A., & Barclay, P. (1989). Semantic priming: Subliminal perception or context? *Perception and Psychophysics, 45*, 153–161.

Bernstein, I. L. (1978). Learned taste aversions in children receiving chemotherapy. *Science, 200*, 1302–1303.

Berscheid, E., Snyder, M., & Omoto, A. M. (1989). Issues in studying close relationships: Conceptualizing and measuring closeness. In C. Hendrick (Ed.), *Review of personality and social psychology* (Vol. 10). Newbury Park, CA: Sage.

Best, C. T., & Queen, H. F. (1989). Baby, it's in your smile: Right hemiface bias in infant emotional expressions. *Developmental Psychology 25*, 264–276.

Best, J. B. (1989). *Cognitive psychology.* St. Paul, MN: West Publishing Co.

Bexton, W. H. (1953). *Some effects of perceptual isolation in human beings.* Unpublished doctoral dissertation, McGill University, Montreal.

Bexton, W. H., Heron, W., & Scott, T. H. (1954). Effects of decreased ariation in the sensory environment. *Canadian Journal of Psychology, 8*, 70–76.

Bharucha, J. J. (1984). Anchoring effects in music: The resolution of dissonance. *Cognitive Psychology, 16*, 485–518.

Biederman, I. (1987). Recognition by components. *Psychological Review, 94*, 115–147.

Biederman, I., Mezzanotte, R. J., Rabinowitz, J. C., Franeolin, C. M., & Plude, D. (1981). Detecting the unexpected in photo-interpretation. *Human Factors, 23*, 153–163.

Bijou, S. W., & Baer, P. M. (1961). *Child development: Vol. 1. A systematic and empirical theory.* New York: Appleton-Century-Crofts.

Billings, A. G., & Moos, R. H. (1981). The role of coping responses and social resources in attentuating the impact of stressful life events. *Journal of Behavioral Medicine, 4*, 139–157.

Billings, A. G., & Moos, R. H. (1984). Coping, stress, and social resources among adults with unipolar depression. *Journal of Personality and Social Psychology, 46(4)*, 877–891.

Billings, A. G., & Moos, R. H. (1985). Life stressors and social resources affect posttreatment outcomes among depressed patients. *Journal of Abnormal Psychology, 94(2)*, 140–153.

Binet, A., & Simon, T. (1905). Méthodes nouvelles pour le diagnostic du niveau intellectuel des anormaux. *L'Année Psychologique, 11*, 191–244.

Black, J., Carroll, J., & McGuigan, S. (1987). What kind of minimal instruction manual is the most effective? In J. Carroll & P. Tanner (Eds.), *Human factors in computing systems and graphic interface.* Toronto, Canada: Computer-Human Interaction and Graphics Interface.

Blakemore, C., & Van Slayters, R. C. (1974). Reversal of the physiological effects of monocular deprivation in kittens: Further evidence for a sensitive period. *Journal of Physiology, 206*, 419–436.

Blanchard, E. B., & Andrasik, F. (1985). *Management of chronic headaches: A psychological approach.* New York: Pergamon Press.

Blatt, S. J., & Lerner, H. (1983). Psychodynamic perspectives on personality theory. In M. Hersen, A. E. Kazdin, & A. S. Bellack (Eds.), *The clinical psychology handbook* (pp. 61–68). New York: Pergamon Press.

Blazer, D. G., Bacher, J. R., & Manton, K. G. (1986). Suicide in late life: Review and commentary. *Journal of the American Geriatrics Society, 34*, 519–525.

Bliss, E. L. (1980). Multiple personalities: Report of fourteen cases with implications for schizophrenia and hysteria. *Archives of General Psychiatry, 37*, 1388–1397.

Block, J. (1971). *Lives through time.* Berkeley: Bancroft Books.

Block, J. H. (1980). Another look at sex differentiation in the socialization behavior of mothers and fathers. In F. Denmark & J. Sherman (Eds.), *Psychology of women: Future directions of research.* New York: Psychological Dimensions.

Block, J. H. (1983). Differential premises arising from differential socialization of the sexes: Some conjectures. *Child Development, 54*, 1335–1354.

Block, V., Hennevin, E., & LeConte, P. (1977). Interaction between post-trial reticular stimulation and subsequent paradoxical sleep in memory consolidation processes. In R. R. Drucker-Colin & J. L. McGlaugh (Eds.), *Neurobiology of sleep and memory.* New York: Academic Press.

Blum, K., Noble, E., Sheridan, P., Montgomery, A., Ritchie, T., Jagadeeswaran, P., Nogami, H., Briggs, A., & Cohn, J. (1990). Allelic association of human dopamine D_2 receptor gene in alcoholism. *Journal of the American Medical Association, 263*, 2055–2060.

Blurton-Jones, N. (1972). Categories of child-child interaction. In N. Blurton-Jones (Ed.), *Ethological studies of child behaviour.* Cambridge: Cambridge University Press.

Bolles, R. C. (1975). *Theory of motivation* (2nd ed.). New York: Harper & Row.

Bonica, J. (1984). Interview quoted in C. Wallis, Unlocking pain's secrets. *Time*, pp. 58–66.

Bonnet, M. H., & Arand, D. L. (1989). Sleep loss in aging. *Clinics in Geriatric Medicine, 5*, 405–420.

Booth, D. A. (1980). Acquired behavior controlling energy intake and output. In A. J. Stunkard (Ed.), *Obesity.* Philadelphia: W. B. Saunders.

Bootzin, R. R., & Nicassio, P. M. (1978). Behavioral treatments for insomnia. In M. Herson, R. Eisler, & P. M. Miller (Eds.), *Progress in behavior modification: Vol. 6.* New York: Academic Press.

Boring, E. G. (1923). Intelligence as the tests test it. *New Republic, 35*, 35–37.

Boring, E. G. (1930). A new ambiguous figure. *American Journal of Psychology, 42,* 444–445.

Borkowski, J. G., Weyhing, R. S., & Turner, L. A. (1986). Attributional retraining and the teaching of strategies. *Exceptional Children, 53,* 130–137.

Bornstein, G., Rapoport, A., Kerpel, L., & Katz, T. (1989). Within- and between-group communication in intergroup competition for public goods. *Journal of Experimental Social Psychology, 25,* 422–436.

Bornstein, R. F. (1989). Exposure and affect: Overview and meta-analysis of research, 1968–1987. *Psychological Bulletin, 106,* 265–289.

Botwinick, J. (1966). Cautiousness in advanced age. *Journal of Gerontology, 21,* 347–353.

Botwinick, J. (1977). Intellectual abilities. In J. E. Birren & K. W. Schaie (Eds.), *Handbook of the psychology of aging.* New York: Van Nostrand Reinhold.

Bourne, L. E. (1967) Learning and utilization of conceptual rules. In B. Kleinmuntz (Ed.), *Concepts and the structure of memory.* New York: Wiley.

Bovard, E. W. (1985). *Brain mechanisms in effects of social support on viability.* In R. B. Williams (Ed.), *Perspectives on behavioral medicine.* New York: Academic Press.

Bower, G. H. (1970). Organizational factors in memory. *Cognitive Psychology, 1,* 18–46.

Bower, G. H. (1973). How to . . . uh . . . remember! *Psychology Today,* pp. 62–67.

Bower, G. H. (1975). Cognitive psychology: An introduction. In W. K. Estes (Ed.), *Handbook of learning and cognitive processes: Vol. 1.* Hillsdale, NJ: Lawrence Erlbaum Associates.

Bower, G. H. (1981). Mood and memory. *American Psychologist, 36,* 129–148.

Bower, G. H., Gilligan, S. G., & Monteiro, K. P. (1981). Selectivity of learning caused by affective states. *Journal of Experimental Psychology: General, 110,* 451–473.

Bower, T. G. R., & Wishart, J. G. (1972). The effects of motor skill on object permanence. *Cognition, 1,* 165–172.

Bowerman, C. E., & Kinch, J. W. (1956). Changes in family and peer orientation of children between the fourth and tenth grades. *Social Forces, 37,* 206–211.

Bowlby, J. (1989). *A secure base: Parent-child attachment and healthy human development.* New York: Basic Books.

Boyatzis, R. E. (1982). *The competent manager.* New York: Wiley.

Bozarth, M. A., & Wise, R. A. (1985). Toxicity associated with long-term intravenous heroin and cocaine self-administration in the rat. *Journal of the American Medical Association, 254,* 81–83.

Bradbury, T. N., & Fincham, F. D. (1988). Individual difference variables in close relationships: A contextual model of marriage as an integrative framework. *Journal of Personality and Social Psychology, 54,* 713–721.

Bradley-Johnson, S., Graham, D. P., & Johnson, C. M. (1986). Token reinforcement on WISC-R performance for white, low-socioeconomic, upper and lower elementary-school-age students. *Journal of School Psychology, 24,* 73–79.

Braginsky, B. M., Grosse, M., & Ring, K. (1966). Controlling outcomes through impression management: An experimental study of the manipulative tactics of mental patients. *Journal of Consulting Psychology, 30,* 295–300.

Bransford, J. D., & Johnson, M. K. (1972). Contextual prerequisites for understanding: Some investigations of comprehension and recall. *Journal of Verbal Learning and Verbal Behavior, 11,* 717–726.

Bransford, J. D., Nitsch, K. E., & Franks, J. J. (1977). Schooling and the facilitation of knowing. In R. C. Anderson, R. J. Spiro, & W. E. Montague (Eds.), *Schooling and the acquisition of knowledge.* Hillsdale, NJ: Lawrence Erlbaum Associates.

Brantigan, T. A., Brantigan, C. O., & Joseph, N. H. (1978). Beta blockage and musical performance. *Lancet, 896,* ii.

Brantley, P. J., Dietz, L. S., McKnight, G. T., Jones, G. N., & Tulley, R. (1988). Convergence between daily stress inventory and endocrine measures of stress. *Journal of Consulting and Clinical Psychology, 56,* 549–551.

Braunstein, M. (1990). Structure from motion. In J. Elkind, S. Card, J. Hochberg, & B. Huey (Eds.), *Human performance models for computer-aided engineering.* Orlando, FL: Academic Press.

Brazelton, T. B., & Tronick, E. (1983). Preverbal communication between mothers and infants. In W. Damon (Ed.), *Social and personality development.* New York: W. W. Norton.

Breckler, S. J., & Wiggins, E. C. (1989). On defining attitude and attiude theory: Once more with feeling. In A. R. Pratkanis, S. J. Breckler, & A. G. Greenwald (Eds.), *Attitude structure and function.* Hillsdale, NJ: Lawrence Erlbaum Associates.

Breggin, P. R. (1979). *Electroshock: Its brain-disabling effects.* New York: Halsted Press.

Brehm, J. (1972). *Responses to loss of freedom: A theory of psychological reactance.* Morristown, NJ: General Learning Press.

Brehm, J. W. (1989). Psychological reactance: Theory and applications. *Advances in Consumer Research, 16,* 72–75.

Brehm, J. W., & Self, E. A. (1989). The intensity of motivation. *Annual Review of Psychology, 40,* 109–131.

Brehm, S. S., & Smith, T. W. (1986). Social psychological approaches to psychotherapy and behavior change. In S. L. Garfield & A. E. Bergin (Eds.), *Handbook of psychotherapy and behavior change* (3rd ed.). New York: Wiley.

Brehmer, B. (1981). Models of diagnostic judgment. In J. Rasmussen & W. Rouse (Eds.), *Human detection and diagnosis of systems failures.* New York: Plenum Press.

Breier, A., Chaney, D.S., & Heninger, G. R. (1986). Agoraphobia with panic attacks: Development, diagnostic stability and course of illness. *Archives of General Psychiatry, 43,* 1029–1036.

Breland, K., & Breland, M. (1966). *Animal behavior.* New York: Macmillan.

Bremer, J. (1959). *Asexualization.* New York: Macmillan.

Breuer, J., & Freud, S. (1966). *Studies on hysteria* (original work published 1896) New York: Avon.

Brewer, M. B. (1988). A dual process model of impression formation. In T. K. Srull & R. S. Wyer (Eds.), *Advances in social cognition: Vol. 1. A dual process model of impression formation.* Hillsdale, NJ: Lawrence Erlbaum Associates.

Brewer, W. F., & Nakamura, G. V. (1984). The nature and functions of schemas. In R. S. Wyer & T. K. Srull (Eds.), *Handbook of social cognition: Vol. 1.* Hillsdale, NJ: Lawrence Erlbaum Associates.

Brewer, W. F., & Pani, J. R. (1984). The structure of human memory. In G. H. Bower (Ed.), *The psychology of learning and motivation: Vol. 17.* New York: Academic Press.

Brewer, W. F., & Treyens, J. C. (1981). Role of schemata in memory for places. *Cognitive Psychology, 13,* 207–230.

Brickman, P., Becker, L. J., & Castle, S. (1979). Making trust easier and harder through two forms of sequential interaction. *Journal of Personality and Social Psychology, 37,* 515–521.

Brigham, C. C. (1923). *A study of American intelligence.* Princeton, NJ: Princeton University Press.

Brody, E. B., & Brody, N. (1976). *Intelligence: Nature, determinants, and consequences.* New York: Academic Press.

Brody, J. E. (1983, December 13). Divorce's stress exacts long-term health toll. *New York Times,* p. 17

Brody, N. (1990). Behavior therapy versus placebo: Comment on Bowers and Clum's meta-analysis. *Psychological Bulletin, 107,* 106–109.

Brooks-Gunn, J. (1988). Antecedents and consequences of variations in girls' maturational timing. *Journal of Adolescent Health Care, 9(5),* 1–9.

Brooks-Gunn, J., & Furstenberg, F. F. (1989). Adolescent sexual behavior. *American Psychologist, 44,* 249–257.

Brown, A. L. (1975). The development of memory: Knowing, knowing about knowing, and knowing how to know it. In H. W. Reese (Ed.), *Advances in child development and behavior: Vol. 10.* New York: Academic Press.

Brown, H., Adams, R. G., & Kellam, S. G. (1981). A longitudinal study of teenage motherhood and symptoms of distress: Woodlawn Community Epidemiological Project. In R. Simmons (Ed.), *Research in community and mental health: Vol. 2.* Greenwich, CT: JAI Press.

Brown, J. (1958). Some tests of the decay theory of immediate memory. *Quarterly Journal of Experimental Psychology, 10,* 12–21.

Brown, J. (1987). A review of meta-analyses conducted on psychotherapy outcome research. *Clinical Psychology Review, 7,* 1–23.

Brown, J. D., & McGill, K. L. (1989). The cost of good fortune: When positive life events produce negative health consequences. *Journal of Personality and Social Psychology, 57,* 1103–1110.

Brown, R. (1986). *Social psychology: The second edition.* New York: The Free Press.

Brown, R., & Kulik, J. (1977). Flashbulb memories. *Cognition, 5,* 73–99.

Brown, R., & McNeill, D. (1966). The "tip-of-the-tongue" phenomenon. *Journal of Verbal Learning and Verbal Behavior, 5,* 325–337.

Brown, R. A. (1973). *First language.* Cambridge: Harvard University Press.

Brownell, K. D., Greenwood, M. R. C., Stellar, E., & Shrager, E. E. (1986). The effects of repeated cycles of weight loss and regain in rats. *Physiology and Behavior, 38,* 459–464.

Brundin, P., Nilsson, O. G., Gage, F. H., & Bjorkland, A. (1985). Cyclosporin A increases survival of cross-species intrastriatal grafts of embryonic dopamone-containing neurons. *Brain Research, 60,* 204–208.

Bruner, J. (1964). The course of cognitive growth. *American Psychologist, 19,* 1–55.

Bruton, C. J., Crow, T. J., Frith, C. D., Johnstone, E. C., Owens, D. G. C., & Roberts, G. W. (1990). Schizophrenia and the brain: A prospective cliniconeuropathological study. *Psychological Medicine, 20,* 285–304.

Bryan, J. H. (1975). Children's cooperation and helping behaviors. In E. M. Hetherington (Ed.), *Review of child development research: Vol. 5.* Chicago: University of Chicago Press.

Bryan, J. H., & Luria, Z. (1978). Sex-role learning: A test of the selective attention hypothesis. *Child Development, 49,* 13–23.

Bryant, J., Carveth, R. A., & Brown, D. (1981). Television viewing and anxiety: An experimental examination. *Journal of Communication, 31,* 106–119.

Bryant, R. A., & McConkey, K. M. (1989). Hypnotic blindness: A behavioral and experiential analysis. *Journal of Abnormal Psychology, 98,* 71–77.

Buchsbaum, M. S., Ingvar, D. H., Kessler, R., Waters, R. N., Cappelletti, J., van Kammen, D. P., King, A. C., Johnson, J. L., Manning, R. G., Flynn, R. W., Mann, L. S., Bunney, W. E., & Sokoloff, L. (1982). Cerebral glucography with positron tomography: Use in normal subjects and patients with schizophrenia. *Archives of General Psychiatry, 39,* 251–259.

Budzynski, T. H., & Stoyva, J. M. (1984). Biofeedback methods in the treatment of anxiety and stress. In R. L. Woolfolk & P. M. Lehrer (Eds.), *Principles and practice of stress management.* New York: Guilford Press.

Bunney, W. E., Jr., Goodwin, F. K., & Murphy, D. L. (1972). The "switch process" in manic-depressive illness: 3. Theoretical implications. *Archives of General Psychiatry, 27,* 312–317.

Burchfield, S. R. (1979). The stress response: A new perspective. *Psychosomatic Medicine, 41,* 661–672.

Burger, J. M., & Burns, L. (1988). The illusion of unique invulnerability and the use of effective contraception. *Personality and Social Psychology Bulletin, 14,* 264–270.

Burger, J. M., & Petty, R. E. (1981). The low-ball compliance

technique: Task or person commitment? *Journal of Personality and Social Psychology, 40,* 492–500.

Burns, M. O., & Seligman, M. E. P. (1989). Explanatory style across the life span: Evidence for stability over 52 years. *Journal of Personality and Social Psychology, 56,* 471–477.

Buss, A. H. (1989). Personality as traits. *American Psychologist, 44,* 1378–1388.

Buss, D. M. (1981). Predicting parent-child interactions from children's activity level. *Developmental Psychology, 17,* 59–65.

Buss, D. M., Gomes, M., Higgins, D. S., & Lauterbach, K. (1987). Tactics of manipulation. *Journal of Personality and Social Psychology, 52,* 1219–1229.

Butcher, J. N. (1979). Use of the MMPI in personnel selection. In J. N. Butcher (Ed.), *New developments in the use of the MMPI.* Minneapolis: University of Minnesota Press.

Butcher, J. N. (Ed.). (1987). *Computerized psychological assessment: A practitioner's guide.* New York: Basic Books.

Butcher, J. N., & Hatcher, C. (1988). The neglected entity in air disaster planning: Psychological services. *American Psychologist, 43,* 724–729.

Butcher, J. N., Dahlstrom, W. G., Graham, J. R., Tellegen, A., & Kaemmer, B. (1989). *Manual for administration and scoring of the MMPI-2.* Minneapolis: University of Minnesota Press.

Butler, R. N. (1963). The life review: An interpretation of reminiscence in the aged. *Psychiatry, 26,* 65–76.

Butler, R. N. (1975). *Why survive? Being old in America.* New York: Harper & Row.

Byrne, D. (1971). *The attraction paradigm.* New York: Academic Press.

Byrne, D. (1977). Social psychology and the study of sexual behavior. *Personality and Social Psychology Bulletin, 3,* 3–30.

Byrne, D., & Kelley, K. (1989). Basing legislative action on research data: Prejudice, prudence, and empirical limitations. In D. Zillmann & J. Bryant (Eds.), *Pornography: Research advances and policy considerations.* Hillsdale, NJ: Lawrence Erlbaum Associates.

Byrne, D., & Nelson, D. (1965). Attraction as a linear function of proportion of positive reinforcements. *Journal of Personality and Social Psychology, 1,* 659–663.

Byrne, D., Clore, G. L., & Smeaton, G. (1986). The attraction hypothesis: Do similar attitudes affect anything? *Journal of Personality and Social Psychology, 51,* 1167–1170.

Byrne, D., London, O., & Reeves, K. (1968). The effects of physical attractiveness, sex, and attitude similarity on interpersonal attraction. *Journal of Personality, 36,* 259–271.

Cabanac, M. (1971). The physiological role of pleasure. *Science, 173,* 1103–1107.

Calder, B. J., & Gruder, C. L. (1989). Emotional advertising appeals. In P. Cafferata & A. Tybout (Eds.), *Cognitive and affective responses to advertising.* Lexington, MA: Lexington Books.

Campbell, B. A., & Kraeling, D. (1953). Response strength as a function of drive level and amount of drive reduction. *Journal of Experimental Psychology, 45,* 97–101.

Campione, J. C., Brown, A. L., & Ferrara, R. A. (1982). Mental retardation and intelligence. In R. J. Sternberg (Ed.), *Handbook of human intelligence.* Cambridge: Cambridge University Press.

Campos, J., Langer, A., & Krowitz, A. (1970). Cardiac responses on the visual cliff in prelocomotor human infants. *Science, 170,* 196–197.

Camras, L. A. (1977). Facial expressions used by children in a conflict situation. *Child Development, 48,* 1431–1435.

Cann, A., Sherman, S. J., & Elkes, R. (1975). Effects of initial request size and timing of a second request on compliance: The foot-in-the-door and the door-in-the-face. *Journal of Personality and Social Psychology, 32,* 774–782.

Cannon, D. S., & Baker, T. B. (1981). Emetic and electric shock alcohol aversion therapy: Assessment of conditioning. *Journal of Consulting and Clinical Psychology, 49,* 20–33.

Cannon, W. B. (1927). The James-Lange theory of emotions: A

critical examination and an alternative. *American Journal of Psychology, 39,* 106–124.

Cannon, W. B., & Washburn, A. L. (1912). An explanation of hunger. *American Journal of Physiology, 29,* 444–454.

Cantor, N., & Kihlstrom, J. F. (1989). Social intelligence and cognitive assessments of personality. In R. S. Wyer & T. K. Srull (Eds.), *Advances in social cognition: Vol. 2: Social intelligence and cognitive assessments of personality.* Hillsdale, NJ: Lawrence Erlbaum Associates.

Cantor, N., & Langston, C. A. (1989). Ups and downs of life tasks in a life transition. In L.A. Pervin (Ed.), *Goal concepts in personality and social psychology.* Hillsdale, NJ: Lawrence Erlbaum Associates.

Caplan, G. (1964). *Principles of preventive psychiatry.* New York: Basic Books.

Caporael, L. R., Dawes, R. M., Orbell, J. M., & van de Kragt, A. J. C. (1989). Selfishness examined: Cooperation in the absence of egoistic incentives. *Behavioral and Brain Sciences, 12,* 683–739.

Capron, C., & Duyme, M. (1989). Assessment of effects of socio-economic status on IQ in a full cross-fostering study. *Nature, 340,* 552–553.

Carey, M. P., & Burish, T. G. (1988). Etiology and treatment of the psychological side effects associated with cancer chemotherapy: A critical review and discussion. *Psychological Bulletin, 104,* 307–325.

Cargan, L., & Melko, M. (1982). *Singles: Myths and realities.* Beverly Hills, CA: Sage.

Carlson, C. R., & Masters, J. C. (1986). Inoculation by emotion: Effects of positive emotional states on children's reactions to social comparison. *Developmental Psychology, 22,* 760–765.

Carlson, J. S., Jensen, C. M., & Widaman, K. F. (1983). Reaction time, intelligence and attention. *Intelligence, 7,* 329–344.

Carlson, M., & Miller, N. (1987). Explanation of the relation between negative mood and helping. *Psychological Bulletin, 102,* 91–108.

Carmichael, L. L., Hogan, H. P., & Walter, A. A. (1932). An experimental study of the effect of language on the reproduction of visually perceived form. *Journal of Experimental Psychology, 15,* 73–86.

Carrington, P. (1984). Modern forms of meditation. In R. L. Woolfolk & P. M. Lehrer (Eds.), *Principles and practice of stress management.* New York: Guilford Press.

Carrington, P. (1986). Meditation as an access to altered states of consciousness. In B. B. Wolman & M. Ullman (Eds.), *Handbook of states of consciousness.* New York: Van Nostrand Reinhold.

Carroll, J. B. (1982). The measurement of intelligence. In R. J. Sternberg (Ed.), *Handbook of human intelligence.* Cambridge: Cambridge University Press.

Carroll, J. M., & Carrithers, C. (1984). Blocking learner error states in a training-wheels system. *Human Factors, 26,* 377–390.

Carson, R. C., Butcher, J. N., & Coleman, J. C. (1988). *Abnormal psychology and modern life* (8th ed.). Glenview, IL: Scott Foresman.

Cartwright, R. D. (1978). *A primer on sleep and dreaming.* Reading, MA: Addison-Wesley.

Cartwright, R. D., Lloyd, S., Knight, S., & Trenholme, I. (1984). Broken dreams: A study of the effects of divorce and depression on dream content. *Psychiatry, 47,* 251–259.

Carver, C., Coleman, A., & Glass, D. (1976). The coronary-prone behavior pattern and suppression of fatigue on a treadmill task. *Journal of Personality and Social Psychology, 33,* 460–466.

Carver, C. S., Scheier, M. F., & Weintraub, J. K. (1989). Assessing coping strategies: A theoretically based approach. *Journal of Personality and Social Psychology, 56,* 267–283.

Casper, R. C., Eckhert, E. D., Halmi, K. A., Goldberg, S. C., & Davis, J. M. (1980). Bulimia: Its incidence and clinical importance in patients with anorexia nervosa. *Archives of General Psychiatry, 37,* 1030–1035.

Caspi, A., Elder, G. H., & Bem, D. J. (1988). Moving away from the world: Life-course patterns of shy children. *Developmental Psychology, 24,* 824–831.

Cattell, R. B. (1971). *Abilities: Their structure, growth and action.* Boston: Houghton Mifflin.

Cattell, R. B., & Eber, H. W. (1962). *Manual for forms A and B of the Sixteen Personality Factor Questionnaire.* Champaign, IL: Institute for Personality and Ability Testing.

Cavanaugh, J. C. (1988). The place of awareness in memory development across adulthood. In L. W. Poon, D. C. Rubin, & B. A. Wilson (Eds.), *Everyday cognition in adulthood and later life.* Cambridge: Cambridge University Press.

Cavior, N., & Dokecki, P. R. (1969). *Physical attractiveness and popularity among fifth-grade boys.* Paper presented at the annual convention of the Southwestern Psychological Association.

Ceci, S. J., & Liker, J. K. (1986). A day at the races: A study of IQ, expertise and cognitive complexity. *Journal of Experimental Psychology: General, 115,* 255–266.

Centerwell, B. S. (1989). Exposure to television as a cause of violence. In G. Comstock (Ed.), *Public communication and behavior* (Vol. 2). San Diego: Academic Press.

Cerf, C. (1984). *The experts speak.* New York: Pantheon.

Cermak, L. S. (1989) Synergistic ecphory and the amnesic patient. In H. L. Roediger & F. I. M. Craik (Eds.), *Varieties of memory and consciousness.* Hillsdale, NJ: Erlbaum.

Chaiken, A. L., Sigler, E., & Derlega, V. J. (1974). Nonverbal mediators of teacher expectancy effects. *Journal of Personality and Social Psychology, 30,* 144–149.

Chambliss, D., & Goldstein, A. (1980). The treatment of agoraphobia. In A. Goldstein & E. Poa (Eds.), *Handbook of behavioral interventions.* New York: Wiley.

Chance, P. (1988, April). Knock wood. *Psychology Today.*

Chapanis, A., Parrish, R., Ockman, R. B., & Weeks, G. D. (1977). Studies in interactive communications: II. *Human Factors, 19,* 101–126.

Chapman, C. R., Benedetti, C., Colpitts, Y. H., & Gerlach, R. (1983). Naloxone fails to reverse pain threshold elevated by acupuncture: Acupuncture analgesia reconsidered. *Pain, 16,* 13–31.

Chase, G. (1986). Visual information processing. In K. Boff, L. Kaufman, & J. Thomas (Eds.), *Handbook of perception and human performance* (Vol. 2). New York: Wiley.

Chase, W. G., & Ericsson, K. A. (1979, November). *A mnemonic system for digit span: One year later.* Paper presented at the meeting of the Psychonomic Society, Phoenix, AZ.

Chase, W. G., & Ericsson, K. A. (1981). Skilled memory. In J. R. Anderson (Ed.), *Cognitive skills and their acquisition.* Hillsdale, NJ: Lawrence Erlbaum Associates.

Check, J. V. P., & Guloien, T. H. (1989). Reported proclivity for coercive sex following repeated exposure to sexually violent pornography, nonviolent dehumanizing pornography, and erotica. In D. Zillmann & J. Bryant (Eds.), *Pornography: Research advances and policy considerations.* Hillsdale, NJ: Lawrence Erlbaum Associates.

Chemers, M. M. (1987). Leadership processes: Intrapersonal, interpersonal, and societal influences. In C. Hendrick (Ed.), *Group processes.* Newbury Park, CA: Sage.

Cherry, C. (1953). Some experiments on the reception of speech with one and two ears. *Journal of the Acoustical Society of America, 25,* 975–979.

Chesler, P. (1972). *Women and madness.* New York: Doubleday.

Chesnic, M., Menyuk, P., Liebergott, J., Ferrier, L., & Strand, K. (1983, April). *Who leads whom?* Paper presented at the meeting of the Society for Research in Child Development, Detroit, MI.

Chi, M. T., Feltovitch, P. J., & Glaser, R. (1981). Representation of physics knowledge by novices and experts. *Cognitive Science, 5,* 121–152.

Chi, M. T. H., Glaser, R., & Farr, M. J. (Eds). (1988). *The nature of expertise.* Hillsdale, NJ: Lawrence Erlbaum Associates.

Chignell, B., & Peterson, J. G. (1988). Strategic issues in knowledge engineering. *Human Factors, 30,* 381–394.

Chiodo, L. A., & Antelman, S. M. (1980). Electroconvulsive shock: Progressive dopamine autoreceptor subsensitivity independent of repeated treatment. *Science, 210,* 799–801.

Chomsky, N. (1957). Syntactic structures. The Hague: Mouton.

Chorover, L. (1965). Discussion of the effects of electroconvulsive shock on performance and memory. In D. P. Kimble (Ed.), *The anatomy of memory.* Palo Alto, CA: Science & Behavior Books.

Christenssen-Szalanski, J. J., & Bushyhead, J. B. (1981). Physicians' use of probabilistic information in a real clinical setting. *Journal of Experimental Psychology: Human Perception and Performance, 7,* 928–936.

Christianson, S. (1989). Flashbulb memories: Special, but not so special. *Memory & Cognition, 17,* 435–443.

Chugani, H. T., & Phelps, M. E. (1986). Maturational changes in cerebral function in infants determined by 18FDG positron emission tomography. *Science, 231,* 840–843.

Chwalisz, K., Diener, E., & Gallagher, D. (1988). Autonomic arousal feedback and emotional experience: Evidence from the spinal cord injured. *Journal of Personality and Social Psychology, 54,* 820–828.

Cialdini, R. B. (1984). *Influence: The new psychology of modern persuasion.* New York: Quill.

Cialdini, R. B. (1988). *Influence: Science and practice.* Glenview, IL: Scott Foresman.

Cialdini, R. B., Baumann, D. J., & Kenrick, D. T. (1981). Insights from sadness: A three-step model of the development of altruism as hedonism. *Developmental Review, 1,* 207–223.

Cialdini, R. B., Cacioppo, J. T., Bassett, R., & Miller, J. A. (1978). Low-ball procedure for producing compliance: Commitment then cost. *Journal of Personality and Social Psychology, 36,* 463–476.

Cialdini, R. B., Petty, R. E., & Cacioppo, J. T. (1981). Attitude and attitude change. *Annual Review of Psychology, 32,* 357–404.

Cialdini, R. B., Schaller, M., Houlihan, D., Arps, K., Fultz, J., & Beaman, A. L. (1987). Empathy-based helping: Is it selflessly or selfishly motivated? *Journal of Personality and Social Psychology, 52,* 749–758.

Clark, D. A., & Beck, A. T. (1989). Cognitive theory and therapy of anxiety and depression. In P. C. Kendall & D. Watson (Eds.), *Anxiety and depression: Distinctive and overlapping features* (pp. 379–412). New York: Academic Press.

Clark, D. C., Gibbons, R. D., Fawcett, J., & Scheftner, W. A. (1989). What is the mechanism by which suicide attempts predispose to later suicide attempts? A mathematical model. *Journal of Abnormal Psychology, 98,* 42–49.

Clark, E. (1978). Strategies for communicating. *Child Development, 49,* 953–959.

Clark, H., & Clark, E. (1977). *Psychology and language: An introduction to psycholinguistics.* New York: Harcourt Brace Jovanovich.

Clark, M. S. (1984). Record keeping in two kinds of relationships. *Journal of Personality and Social Psychology, 47,* 549–557.

Clark, M. S., & Isen, A. M. (1982). Toward understanding the relationship between feeling states and social behavior. In A. H. Hastorf & A. M. Isen (Eds.), *Cognitive social psychology.* New York: Elsevier.

Clark, M. S., & Reis, H. T. (1988). Interpersonal processes in close relationships. *Annual Review of Psychology, 39,* 609–672.

Clark, R. D., & Word, L. E. (1972). Why don't bystanders help? Because of ambiguity? *Journal of Personality and Social Psychology, 24,* 392–400.

Clark, R. D., & Word, L. E. (1974). Where is the apathetic bystander? Situational characteristics of the emergency. *Journal of Personality and Social Psychology, 29,* 279–287.

Clarke, A. M., & Clarke, A. D. B. (1976a). Some continued experiments. In A. M. Clarke & A. D. B. Clarke (Eds.), *Early experience: Myth and evidence.* New York: Free Press.

Clarke, A. M., & Clarke, A. D. B. (Eds.). (1976b). *Early experience: Myth and evidence.* London: Open Books.

Clarke-Stewart, K. A. (1973). Interactions between mothers and their young children: Characteristics and consequences. *Monographs of the Society for Research in Child Development, 38* (6-7, Serial No. 153).

Clarke-Stewart, K. A. (1978). And daddy makes three: The father's impact on mother and young child. *Child Development, 49,* 466–478.

Clarke-Stewart, K. A. (1980). The father's contribution to child development. In F. A. Pedersen (Ed.), *The father-infant relationship: Observational studies in a family context.* New York: Praeger Special Studies.

Clarke-Stewart, K. A. (1988a). Parents' effects on children's development: A decade of progress? *Journal of Applied Developmental Psychology, 9,* 41–84.

Clarke-Stewart, K. A. (1988b). What does research say about the effects of day care? In L. J. Schweinhart & L. de Pietro (Eds.), *Shaping the future for early childhood programs* (pp. 23–27). Ypsilanti, MI: High/Scope Press.

Clarke-Stewart, K. A. (1989a). Infant day care: Maligned or malignant? *American Psychologist, 44,* 266–273.

Clarke-Stewart, K. A. (1989b). Risks for children when parents divorce. *NEA Today: Issues '89,* Vol. 7(6).

Clarke-Stewart, K. A., & Fein, G. G. (1983). Early childhood programs. In P. H. Mussen (Ed.), *Handbook of child psychology: Vol. 2. Infancy and developmental psychobiology.* New York: Wiley.

Clarke-Stewart, K. A., & Hevey, C. M. (1981). Longitudinal relations in repeated observations of mother-child interaction from 1 to 2-1/2 years. *Developmental Psychology, 17,* 127–145.

Clausen, J., Sersen, E., & Lidsky, A. (1974). Variability of sleep measures in normal subjects. *Psychophysiology, 11,* 509–516.

Cleary, T. A., Humphreys, L. G., Kendrick, S. A., & Wesman, A. (1975). Educational use of tests with disadvantaged students. *American Psychologist, 30,* 15–41.

Cleckley, H. (1976). *The mask of sanity* (5th ed.). St. Louis: Mosby.

Clemant, C., & Falmagne, R. C. (1986). Logical reasoning, world knowledge, and mental imagery. *Memory and Cognition, 14,* 299–307.

Clifford, B. R., & Hollin, C. R. (1981). Effects of the type of incident and number of perpetrators on eyewitness testimony. *Journal of Applied Psychology, 67,* 364–370.

Cline, V. B., Croft, R. G., & Courrier, S. (1973). Desensitization of children to television violence. *Journal of Personality and Social Psychology, 27,* 360–365.

Clore, G. L. (1975). *Interpersonal attraction: An overview.* Morristown, NJ: General Learning Press.

Coates, T. J. (1990). Strategies for modifying sexual behavior for primary and secondary prevention of HIV disease. *Journal of Consulting and Clinical Psychology, 58,* 57–69.

Coates, T. J., & Thoreson, C. E. (1977). *How to sleep better.* Englewood Cliffs, NJ: Prentice-Hall.

Coates, R. A., Soskoline, C. L., Calzavara, L., Read, S. E., Fanning, M. M., Shephard, F. A., Klein, M. M., & Johnson, J. K. (1987). The reliability of sexual histories in AIDS-related research: Evaluation of an interview administered questionnaire. *Canadian Journal of Public Health, 77,* 343–348.

Cohen, F., & Lazarus, R. S. (1979). Coping with the stresses of illness. In G. C. Stone, F. Cohen, & N. E. Adler (Eds.), *Health psychology: A handbook.* San Francisco: Jossey-Bass.

Cohen, G. (1989). *Memory in the real world.* Hillsdale, NJ: Lawrence Erlbaum Associates.

Cohen, L. (Ed.) (1987). *Research on stressful life events: Theoretical and methodological issues.* Beverly Hills, CA: Sage.

Cohen, N., & Ader, R. (1988). Immunomodulation by classical conditioning. *Advances in Biochemical Psychopharmacology, 44,* 199–202.

Cohen, N. J., McCloskey, M., & Wible, C. B. (1988). There is still no case for a flashbulb-memory mechanism: Reply to Schmidt and Bohannon. *Journal of Experimental Psychology: General, 117,* 336–338.

Cohen, S. (1980). Aftereffects of stress on human performance and social behavior. A review of research and theory. *Psychological Bulletin, 88,* 82–108.

Cohen, S., & Hoberman, H. M. (1983). Positive events and social supports as buffers of life change stress. *Journal of Applied Social Psychology, 13,* 99–125.

Cohen, S., & Syme, S. L. (1985). Issues in the study and application of social support. In S. Cohen & S.L. Syme (Eds.), *Social support and health.* New York: Academic Press.

Cohen, S., & Wills, T. A. (1985). Stress, social support, and the buffering hypothesis. *Psychological Bulletin, 98,* 310–357.

Cohn, J., & Tronick, E. Z. (1989). Specificity of infants' response to mothers' affective behavior. *Journal of the American Academy of Child and Adolescent Psychiatry, 28,* 242–248.

Cohn, J. F., & Tronick, E. Z. (1983). Three-month-old infants' reaction to simulated maternal depression. *Child Development, 54,* 185–193.

Cohn, N. B., & Strassberg, D. S. (1983). Self-disclosure reciprocity among preadolescents. *Personality and Social Psychology Bulletin, 9,* 97–102.

Coile, D. C., & Miller, N. E. (1984). How radical animal activists try to mislead humane people. *American Psychologist, 39,* 700–701.

Colby, A., Kohlberg, L., Gibbs, J., & Lieberman, M. (1983). A longitudinal study of moral judgment. *Monographs of the Society for Reserach in Child Development, 48* (1, Serial No. 200).

Coleman, D. J., & Kaplan, M. S. (1990). Effects of pretherapy videotape preparation on child therapy outcomes. *Professional Psychology: Research and Practice, 21,* 199–203.

Coles, M. (1989) Modern mind-brain reading: Psychophysiology, physiology & cognition. *Psychophysiology, 26,* 251–269.

Colletta, N. D. (1979). Support systems after divorce: Incidence and impact. *Journal of Marriage and the Family, 41,* 837–846.

Collins, D. L., Baum, A., & Singer, J. E. (1983). Coping with chronic stress at Three Mile Island: Psychological and biochemical evidence. *Health Psychology, 2,* 149–166.

Colombo, M., D'Amato, M. R., Rodman, H. R., & Gross, C. G. (1990). Auditory association cortex lesions impair auditory short-term memory in monkeys. *Science, 247,* 336–338.

Commission of Inquiry into the Non-medical Use of Drugs. (1970, 1972, 1973). *Interim Report.* Ottawa: Queen's Printer for Canada.

Condry, J., & Condry, S. (1976). Sex differences: A study in the eye of the beholder. *Child Development, 47,* 812–819.

Condry, J., & Siman, M. L. (1974). Characteristics of peer adult-oriented children. *Journal of Marriage and the Family, 36,* 543–554.

Conger, J. J. (1951). The effects of alcohol on conflict behavior in the albino rat. *Quarterly Journal of Studies on Alcohol, 12,* 1–29.

Connelly, J. C. (1980). Alcoholism as indirect self-destructive behavior. In N. L. Farberow (Ed.), *The many faces of suicide: Indirect self-destructive behavior.* New York: McGraw-Hill.

Conrad, R. (1964). Acoustic confusions in immediate memory. *British Journal of Psychology, 55,* 75–84.

Contrada, R. J. (1989). Type A behavior, personality hardiness, and cardiovascular responses to stress. *Journal of Personality and Social Psychology, 57,* 895–903.

Conway, J. B. (1988). Differences among clinical psychologists: Scientists, practitioners, and scientist-practitioners. *Professional Psychology: Research and Practice, 19,* 642–655.

Cook, S. W. (1984). The 1954 social science statement and school desegregation: A reply to Gerard. *American Psychologist, 39,* 819–832.

Cook, S. W. (1985). Experimenting on social issues: The case of school desegregation. *American Psychologist, 40,* 452–460.

Cooper, C. L. (1985). *Psychosocial stress and cancer.* New York: Wiley.

Cooper, G. D., Adams, H. B, & Scott, J. C. (1988). Studies in REST: I. Reduced environmental stimulation therapy (REST) and reduced alcohol consumption. *Journal of Substance Abuse Treatment, 5,* 61–68.

Cooper, H. (1979). Pygmalion grows up: A model for teacher expectation communication and performance influence. *Review of Educational Research, 49,* 389–410.

Cooper, J., & Croyle, R. T. (1984). Attitudes and attitude change. *Annual Review of Psychology, 35,* 395–426.

Cooper, J., & Fazio, R. (1984). A new look at dissonance theory. In L. Berkowitz (Ed.), *Advances in experimental social psychology* (Vol. 17). Orlando: Academic Press.

Coppen, A., Metcalf, M., & Wood, K. (1982). Lithium. In E. S. Paykel (Ed.), *Handbook of affective disorders.* New York: Guilford Press.

Corby, N., & Solnick, R. L. (1980). Psychosocial and physiological influences on sexuality in the older adult. In J. E. Birren & R. B. Sloane (Eds.), *Handbook of mental health and aging* (pp. 893–921). Englewood Cliffs, NJ: Prentice-Hall.

Cordes, C. (1985, April). A step back. *APA Monitor,* 12–14.

Coren, S., & Girgus, J. (1978). *Seeing is deceiving: The psychology of visual illusions.* Hillsdale, NJ: Lawrence Erlbaum Associates.

Cornblatt, B., & Erlenmeyer-Kimling, L. E. (1985). Global attentional deviance in children at risk for schizophrenia: Specificity and predictive validity. *Journal of Abnormal Psychology, 94,* 470–486.

Corsini, R. (Ed.). (1981). *Handbook of innovative psychology.* New York: Wiley.

Corwin, J. T., & Cotanche, D. A. (1988). Regeneration of sensory hair cells after acoustic trauma. *Science, 240,* 1772–1774.

Costa, P. T., Jr., & McCrae, R. R. (1988). Personality in adulthood: A six-year longitudinal study of self-reports and spouse ratings on the NEO personality inventory. *Journal of Personality and Social Psychology, 54,* 853–863.

Costa, P. T., Jr. & McCrae, R. R. (1989). Personality, stress, and coping: Some lessons from a decade of research. In K. S. Markides & C. L. Cooper (Eds.), *Aging, stress, social support, and health.* New York: Wiley.

Cotman, C. W., Monaghan, D. T., & Ganong, A. H. (1988). Excitatory amino acid neurotransmission: NMDA receptors and Hebb-type synaptic plasticity. Annual Review of *Neuroscience 11,* 61–80.

Cowan, N. (1988). Evolving concepts of memory storage, selective attention, and their mutual constraints within the human information-processing system. *Psychological Bulletin, 104,* 163–191.

Cowan, W. M. (1979). The development of the brain. *Scientific American, 241,* 112–133.

Cowen, E. L. (1982). Help is where you find it: Four informal helping groups. *American Psychologist, 37,* 385–395.

Cowen, E. L. (1983). Primary prevention: Past, present, and future. In R. D. Felner, L. A. Jason, J. N. Moritsugu, & S. S. Faber (Eds.), *Preventive psychology: Theory, research and practice.* New York: Pergamon Press.

Cowen, G., & Sharp, D. (1988). Neural nets and artificial intelligence. In S. R. Graubard (Ed.), *The artificial intelligence debate.* Cambridge, MA: MIT Press.

Cowles, J. T. (1937). Food-tokens as incentives for learning by chimpanzees. *Comparative Psychology Monographs* 14(5, Serial No. 71).

Cox, T. (1984). Stress: A psychophysiological approach to cancer. In C. L. Cooper (Ed.), *Psychosocial stress and cancer.* New York: Wiley.

Coyle, J. T., Price, D. L., & DeLong, M. R. (1983). Alzheimer's disease: A disorder of cortical cholinergic innervation. *Science, 219,* 1184–1190.

Craighead, L. W. (1984). Sequencing of behavior therapy and pharmacotherapy for obesity. *Journal of Consulting and Clinical Psychology, 52,* 190–199.

Craik, F. I. M., & Lockhart, R. S. (1972). Levels of processing: A framework for memory research. *Journal of Verbal Learning and Verbal Behavior, 11,* 671–684.

Craik, F. I. M., & Rabinowitz, J. C. (1984). Age differences in the acquisition and use of verbal information. In H. Bouma & D. G. Bouwhuis (Eds.), *Attention and performance: Vol. 10.* Hillsdale, NJ: Lawrence Erlbaum Associates.

Craik, K. H. (1986). Psychological perspectives on technology as societal option, source of hazard, and generator of environmental impacts. In V. Covello & J. Mumpower (Eds.), *Technology assessment, environmental impact assessment, and risk analysis.* New York: Springer-Verlag.

Crandall, C. S. (1988). Social contagion of binge eating. *Journal of Personality and Social Psychology, 55,* 588–598.

Crawford, C., Smith, M., & Krebs, D. (Eds.). (1987). *Sociobiology and psychology: Ideas, issues, and applications.* Hillsdale, NJ: Lawrence Erlbaum Associates.

Crick, F., & Mitchison, G. (1983). The function of dream sleep. *Nature, 304,* 111–114.

Cronbach, L. J. (1975). Five decades of public controversy over mental testing. *American Psychologist, 30,* 1–14.

Cronbach, L. J. (1970). *Essentials of psychological testing* (3rd ed.). New York: Harper & Row.

Crosby, F., & Gonzalez-Intal, A. M. (1982). Relative deprivation and equity theories: A comparative analysis of approaches to felt injustice. In R. Folger (Ed.), *The sense of injustice: Social psychological perspectives.* New York: Plenum Press.

Cross, D. G., Sheehan, O. W., & Kahn, J. A. (1982). Short- and long-term follow-up of clients receiving insight-oriented therapy and behavior therapy. *Journal of Consulting and Clinical Psychology, 50,* 103–112.

Crow, T. J. (1980). Molecular pathology of schizophrenia: More than one disease process? *British Medical Journal, 280,* 66–68.

Crow, T. J., Ball, Bloom, S. R., Brown, R., Bruton, C. J., Colter, N., Frith, C. D., Johnstone, E. C., Owens, D. G. C., & Roberts, G. W. (1989). Schizophrenia as an anomaly of development of cerebral asymmetry: A postmortem study and a proposal concerning the genetic basis of the disease. *Archives of General Psychiatry, 46,* 1145-1150.

Crow, T. J., Cross, A. J., Cooper, S. J., Deakin, J. F., Ferrier, I. N., Johnson, J. A., Joseph, M. H., Owen, F., Poulter, M., Lofthouse, R., et al. (1984). Neurotransmitter receptors and monoamine metabolites in the brains of patients with Alzheimer-type dementia and depression, and suicides. *Neuropharmacology, 12,* 1561–1569.

Crowder, R. G. (1989). Modularity and dissociations in memory systems. In H. L. Roediger & F. I. M. Craik (Eds.), *Varieties of memory and consciousness.* Hillsdale, NJ: Lawrence Erlbaum Associates.

Csikszentmihalyi, M., & Larson, R. (1984). *Being adolescent: Conflict and growth in the teenage years.* New York: Basic Books.

Curcio, C. A., Sloan, D. R., Jr., Packer, O., Hendrickson, A. E., & Kalina, R. E. (1987). Distribution of cones in human and monkey retina: Individual variability and radial asymmetry. *Science, 236,* 579–582.

Curran, J. P., & Lippold, S. (1975). The effects of physical attraction and attitude similarity on attraction in dating dyads. *Journal of Personality, 43,* 528–539.

Curran, J. P., & Monti, P. M. (1982). *Social skills training: A practical handbook for assessment and treatment.* New York: Guilford Press.

Curtis, R. C., & Miller, K. (1986). Believing another likes or dislikes you: Behaviors making the beliefs come true. *Journal of Personality and Social Psychology, 51,* 284–290.

Curtiss, S. (1977). *Genie: A psycholinguistic study of a modern-day wild child.* New York: Academic Press.

Cutting, J. (1987). Perception and information. *Annual Review of Psychology, 38,* 61–90.

Czeisler, C. A. (1988). *Final report on the Philadelhia Police Department shift rescheduling program.* Boston: Center for Design of Industrial Schedules.

Czeisler, C. A., Johnson, M. P., Duffy, J. F., Brown, E. N., Ronda, J. M., & Kronauer, R. E. (1990). Exposure to bright light and darkness to treat physiologic maladaptation to night work. *New England Journal of Medicine, 322,* 1253–1259.

Czeisler, C. A., Kronauer, R. E., Allan, J. S., Duffy, J. F., Jewett, M. E., Brown, E. N., & Ronda, J. M. (1989). Bright light induction of strong (Type 0) resetting of the human circadian pacemaker. *Science, 244,* 1328–1333.

Dabbs, J. M., Jr., Frady, R. L., Caur, T. S., & Besch, N. F. (1987). Saliva testosterone and criminal violence in young prison inmates. *Psychosomatic Medicine, 49,* 174–182.

Dahlstrom, W. G., Lachar, D., & Dahlstrom, L. E. (1986). *MMPI patterns of American minorities.* Minneapolis: University of Minnesota Press.

Dale, P. S. (1976). *Language and the development of structure and function.* New York: Holt, Rinehart and Winston.

Damon, W., & Hart, D. (1982). The development of self-understanding from infancy through adolescence. *Child Development, 53,* 841–864.

Dana, R. H. (1988). Culturally diverse groups and MMPI interpretation. *Professional Psychology: Research and Practice, 19,* 490–495.

Daniel, W. F., & Crovitz, H. F. (1983). Acute memory impairment following electroconvulsive therapy: 1. Effects of electrical stimulus and number of treatments. *Acta Psychiatrica Scandinavica, 67,* 57–68.

Darke, S. (1988). Effects of anxiety on inferential reasoning task performance. *Journal of Personality and Social Psychology, 55,* 499–505.

Darley, C. F., Tinklenberg, J. R., Hollister, L. E., & Atkinson, R. C. (1973a). Marijuana and retrieval from short-term memory. *Psychopharmacologica, 29,* 231–238.

Darley, C. F., Tinklenberg, J. R., Roth, W. T., Hollister, L. E., & Atkinson, R. C. (1973b). Influence of marijuana on storage and retrieval processes in memory. *Memory and Cognition, 1,* 196–200.

Davanloo, J. (Ed.). (1978). *Basic principles and techniques in short-term dynamic psychotherapy.* New York: Spectrum.

Davidson, A. D. (1979, Spring). Coping with stress reactions in rescue workers: A program that worked. *Police Stress.*

Davidson, J. M., Camargo, C. A., & Smith, E. R. (1979). Effects of androgen on sexual behavior in hypogonadal men. *Journal of Clinical Endocrinological Metabolism, 48,* 955–958.

Davidson, J. M., Kwan, M., & Greenleaf, W. J. (1982). Hormonal replacement and sexuality in men. *Clinics in Endocrinology and Metabolism, 11,* 599–623.

Davidson, R. J. (1984). Affect, cognition, and hemispheric specialization. In C. E. Izard, J. Kagan, & R. B. Zajonc (Eds.), *Emotions, cognition, and behavior.* Cambridge: Cambridge University Press.

Davidson, R. J., Ekman, P., Saron, C., Senulis, J., & Friesen, W. V. (1990). Approach-withdrawal and cerebral asymmetry: Emotional expression and brain physiology: I. *Journal of Personality and Social Psychology, 58,* 330–341.

Davis, J. D., Gallagher, R. J., Ladove, R. F., & Turansky, A. J. (1989). Inhibition of food intake by a humoral factor. *Journal of Comparative and Physiological Psychology, 67,* 407–414.

Davis, J. M. (1978). Dopamine theory of schizophrenia: A two-factor theory. In L. C. Wynne, R. L. Cromwell, & S. Matthysse (Eds.), *The nature of schizophrenia: New approaches to research and treatment* (pp. 105–115). New York: Wiley.

Davis, K. B., (1929). *Factors in the sex life of twenty-two hundred women.* New York: Harper & Brothers.

Davis, R. (1986). Assessing the eating disorders. *The Clinical Psychologist, 39,* 33–36.

Davis, R. A., & Moore, C. C. (1935). Methods of measuring retention. *Journal of General Psychology, 12,* 144–155.

Davison, G. C., & Neale, J. M. (1990). *Abnormal psychology* (5th ed.). New York: Wiley.

Dawes, R., Faust, D., & Meehl, P. E. (1989). Clinical versus actuarial judgment. *Science, 243,* 1668–1674.

de Charms, R., & Moeller, G. H. (1962). Values expressed in American children's readers: 1800–1950. *Journal of Abnormal and Social Psychology, 64,* 136–142.

de Charms, R., Levy, J., & Wertheimer, M. (1954). A note on attempted evaluations of psychotherapy. *Journal of Clinical Psychology, 10,* 233–235.

De Robertis, E., Pena, C., Paladini, C., & Medina, J. H. (1988). New developments on the search for the endogenous ligand(s) of central benzodiazepine receptors. *Neurochemistry International, 13,* 1–11.

De Silva, P., Rachman, S., & Seligman, M. E. P. (1977). Prepared phobias and obsessions: Therapeutic outcome. *Behaviour Research and Therapy, 15,* 65–77.

DeAngelis, T. (1989, November). NIMH fails to reach its prevention goals. *APA Monitor,* p. 29.

Deci, E. L. (1980). *The psychology of self-determination.* Lexington, MA: D. C. Heath.

Deci, E. L., Connell, J. P., & Ryan, M. (1987). *Self-determination in a work organization.* Unpublished manuscript, University of Rochester, Rochester, NY.

Defares, P. B., Grossman, P., & de Swart, H. C. G. (1983). Test anxiety, cognitive primitivation, and hyperventilation. In H. M. van der Ploeg, R. Schwarzer, & C. D. Sprilberger (Eds.), *Advances in test anxiety research: Vol. 2.* Hillsdale, NJ: Lawrence Erlbaum Associates.

Deikman, A. J. (1982). The observing self. Boston: Beacon Press.

DeLeon, M. J., McRae, T., Tsai, J. R., George, A. E., Marcus, D. L., Freeman, M., Wolf, A. P., & McEwen, B. S. (1988). Abnormal cortisol response in Alzheimer's disease linked to hippocampal atrophy. *The Lancet, 2(8607),* 391–392.

Dellas, M., & Gaier, E. C. (1970). Identification of creativity: The individual. *Psychological Bulletin, 73,* 55–73.

DeLongis, A., Folkman, S., & Lazarus, R. S. (1988). The impact of daily stress on health and mood: Psychological and social resources as mediators. *Journal of Personality and Social Psychology, 54,* 486–495.

Demare, D., Briere, J., & Lips, H. M. (1988). Violent pornography and self-reported likelihood of sexual aggression. *Journal of Research in Personality, 22,* 140–153.

Dember, W. N., Earl, R. W., & Paradise, N. (1957). Response by rats to differential stimulus complexity. *Journal of Comparative and Physiological Psychology, 50,* 514–518.

Dembroski, T. M., & Williams, R. B. (1989). Definition and assessment of coronary-prone behavior. In N. Schneiderman, P. Kaufmann, & S. M. Wiess (Eds.), *Handbook of research methods in cardiovascular behavioral medicine.* New York: Plenum.

Dement, W. (1960). The effect of dream deprivation. *Science, 131,* 1705–1707.

Dement, W., & Kleitman, N. (1957). Cyclic variations in EEG during sleep and their relation to eye movements, body motility and dreaming. *Electroencephalography and Clinical Neurophysiology, 9,* 673–690.

Dempster, F. N. (1988). The spacing effect: A case study in the failure to apply the results of psychological research. *American Psychologist, 43,* 627–634.

Dennerstein, L., Spencer, G. C., Gotts, G., Brown, J. B., Smith, M. A., & Burrows, G. D. (1985). Progesterone and the premenstrual syndrome: a double-blind crossover trial. *British Medical Journal, 290,* 1617–1621.

Dennis, W. (1960). Causes of retardation among institutional children: Iran. *Journal of Genetic Psychology, 96,* 47–59.

Dennis, W. (1973). *Children of the creche.* New York: Appleton-Century-Crofts.

Denton, G. (1980). The influence of visual pattern on perceived speed. *Perception, 9,* 393–402.

DePue, R. A., & Monroe, S. M. (1986). Conceptualization and measurement of human disorder in life stress research: The problem of chronic disturbance. *Psychological Bulletin, 99,* 36–51.

Derlega, V. J., Winstead, B. A., Wong, P. T. P., & Greenspan, M. (1987). Self-disclosure and relationship development: An attributional analysis. In M. E. Roloff & G. R. Miller (Eds.), *Interpersonal processes: New directions in communication research.* Newbury Park, CA: Sage.

DeStefano, L. (1986). *Personal communication.* University of Illinois.

Deutsch, J. A., Young, W. G., & Kalogeris, T. J. (1978). The stomach signals satiety. *Science, 201,* 165–167.

Deutsch, M., & Gerard, H. B. (1955). A study of normative and informative social influences on individual judgments. *Journal of Abnormal and Social Psychology, 51,* 629–636.

Devine, P. G. (1989a). Automatic and controlled processes in prejudice: The role of stereotypes and personal beliefs. In A. R. Pratkanis, S. J. Breckler & A. G. Greenwald (Eds.), *Attitude structure and function.* Hillsdale, NJ: Lawrence Erlbaum Associates.

Devine, P. G. (1989b). Stereotypes and prejudice: Their automatic and controlled components. *Journal of Personality and Social Psychology, 56,* 5–18.

Dickinson, A., & Mackintosh, N. J. (1978). Classical conditioning in animals. *Annual Review of Psychology, 29,* 587–612.

Diener, E. (1979). Deindividuation, self-awareness, and disinhibition. *Journal of Personality and Social Psychology, 37,* 1160–1171.

Diener, E. (1980). Deindividuation: The absence of self-awareness and self-regulation in group members. In P.B. Paulus (Ed.), *The psychology of group influence.* Hillsdale, NJ: Lawrence Erlbaum Associates.

DiLollo, V., Hanson, D., & McIntyre, J. S. (1983). Initial stages of visual information processing in dyslexia. *Journal of Experimental Psychology: Human Perception and Performance, 9,* 923–935.

Dimsdale, J. E. (1988). A perspective on type A behavior and coronary disease. *New England Journal of Medicine, 318,* 110–112.

DiPietro, J. A. (1981). Rough and tumble play: A function of gender. *Developmental Psychology, 17,* 50–58.

Dixon, L. K., & Johnson, R. C. (1980). *The roots of individuality.* Monterey, CA: Brooks/Cole.

Dobson, K. S. (1989). A meta-analysis of the efficacy of cognitive therapy for depression. *Journal of Consulting and Clinical Psychology, 57,* 414–419.

Dodd, D. K. (1985). Robbers in the classroom: A deindividuation exercise. *Teaching of Psychology, 12,* 89–91.

Dohrenwend, B. S., & Dohrenwend, B. P. (1978). Some issues in research on stressful life events. *Journal of Nervous and Mental Disease, 166,* 7–15.

Dohrenwend, B. S., & Dohrenwend, B. P. (1984). Life stress and illness: Fomulations of the issues. In B. S. Dohrenwend & B. P.

Dohrenwend (Eds.), *Stressful life events and their contexts.* New Brunswick, NJ: Rutgers University Press.

Doise, W., Csepeli, G., Cann, H. D., Gouge, C., Larson, K., & Ostell, A. (1972). An experimental investigation into the formation of intergroup representations. *European Journal of Social Psychology, 2,* 202–204.

Dollard, J., Doob, L., Miller, N., Mowrer, O. H., & Sears, R. R. (1939). *Frustration and aggression.* New Haven: Yale University Press.

Donaldson, M., & Balfour, G. (1968). Less is more: A study of language comprehension in children. *British Journal of Psychology, 59,* 461–471.

Donchin, E. (1981). Surprise! . . . Surprise? *Psychophysiology, 18,* 493–513.

Donchin, E., Kramer, A. F., & Wickens, C. D. (1986). Applications of brain event-related potentials to problems in engineering psychology. In M. G. H. Coles, E. Donchin, & S. Porges (Eds.), *Psychophysiology: Systems, processes, and applications* (pp. 702–718). New York: Guilford Press.

Donlon, T. F. (Ed.). (1984). *College board technical handbook for the SAT.* New York: College Entrance Examination Board.

Donnerstein, E. (1984). Aggression. In A. S. Kahn (Ed.), *Social psychology.* Dubuque, IA: William C. Brown.

Donnerstein, E. (1984). Pornography: Its effects on violence against women. In N. M. Malamuth & E. Donnerstein (Eds.), *Pornography and sexual aggression.* New York: Academic Press.

Donnerstein, E., & Donnerstein, M. (1976). Research in the control of interracial aggression. In R. G. Geen & E. C. O'Neal (Eds.), *Perspectives on aggression.* New York: Academic Press.

Donnerstein, E., Linz, D., & Penrod, S. (1987). *The question of pornography.* New York: Free Press.

Donovan, W. L., Leavitt, L. A., & Balling, J. D. (1978). Maternal physiological response to infant signals. *Psychophysiology, 15,* 68–74.

Dore, J. (1978). Conditions for the acquisition of speech acts. In I. Markova (Ed.), *The social context of language.* New York: Wiley.

Doty, R. L. (1981). Olfactory communication in humans. *Chemical Senses, 6,* 351–376.

Dowson, D. I., Lewith, G. T., & Machin, D. (1985). The effects of acupuncture versus placebo in the treatment of headache. *Pain, 21,* 35–42.

Drake, R. E., & Vaillant, G. E. (1985). A validity study of Axis II of DSM-III. *American Journal of Psychiatry, 142,* 553–558.

Dreyfus, H., & Dreyfus, S. (1986). Why computers may never think like people. *Technology Review, 89,* 41–61.

Dreyfus, H. L., & Dreyfus, S. E. (1987). *Mind over machine.* New York: The Free Press.

Dreyfus, H. L., & Dreyfus, S. E. (1988). Making a mind versus modeling the brain: Intelligence back at a branchpoint. In S. R. Graubard (Ed.), *The artificial intelligence debate.* Cambridge, MA: MIT Press.

Drucker-Colin, R. R., & McGaugh, J. L. (Eds.) (1977). *Neurobiology of sleep and memory.* San Diego: Academic Press.

Druckman, D., & Swets, J. A. (1988). *Enhancing human performance: Issues, theories, and techniques.* Washington, DC: National Academy Press.

Dubow, E. F., Huesmann, L. R., & Eron, L. D. (1987). Childhood correlates of adult ego development. *Child Development, 58,* 859–869.

Duke, P. M., Carlsmith, J. M., Jennings, D., Martin, J. A., Dornbusch, S. M., Gross, R. T., & Siegel-Gorelick, B. (1982). Educational correlates of early and late sexual maturation in adolescence. *Journal of Pediatrics, 100,* 633–637.

Dunkel-Schetter, C., Folkman, S., & Lazarus, R. S. (1987). Correlates of social support receipt. *Journal of Personality and Social Psychology, 53,* 71–80.

Dunn, A. J. (1989). Psychoneuroimmunology for the psychoneuroendocrinologist: A review of animal studies of nervous system–immune system interactions. *Psychoneuroendocrinology, 14,* 251–274.

Duplessis, Y. (1979). Current directions in European parapsychology. In W. G. Roll (Ed.), *Research in parapsychology* (1979). Metuchen, NJ: Scarecrow Press.

Dusek, J. B., & Flaherty, J. F. (1981). The development of the self-concept during the adolescent years. *Monographs of the Society for Research in Child Development, 46* (4, Serial No. 191).

Dush, D. M., Hirt, M. L., & Schroeder, H. (1983). Self-statement modification with adults: A meta-analysis. *Psychological Bulletin, 94,* 408–422.

Dutton, D. G., & Aron, A. P. (1974). Some evidence for heightened sexual attraction under conditions of high anxiety. *Journal of Personality and Social Psychology, 30,* 510–517.

Dweck, C. S., & Gilliard, D. (1975). Expectancy statements as determinants of reactions to failure: Sex differences in persistence and expectancy change. *Journal of Personality and Social Psychology, 32,* 1077–1084.

Dweck, C. S., & Licht, B. G. (1980). Learned helplessness and intellectual achievement. In M. E. P. Seligman & J. Garber (Eds.), *Human helplessness: Theory and application.* New York: Academic Press.

Dweck, C. S., & Repucci, N. D. (1973). Learned helplessness and reinforcement responsibility in children. *Journal of Personality and Social Psychology, 25,* 109–116.

Dweck, C. S., Davidson, W., Nelson, S., & Enna, B. (1978). Sex differences in learned helplessness: II. The contingencies of evaluative feedback in the classroom, and III. *An experimental analysis. Developmental Psychology, 14,* 268–276.

Eagle, M. (1984). *Recent developments in psychoanalysis: A critical evaluation.* New York: McGraw-Hill.

Eagly, A. H., & Steffen, V. J. (1986). Gender and aggressive behavior: A meta-analytic review of the social psychology literature. *Psychological Bulletin, 100,* 309–330.

Easterbrook, J. A. (1959). The effect of emotion on cue utilization and the organization of behavior. *Psychological Review, 66,* 183–207.

Eaton, W. O., & Clore, G. L. (1975). Interracial imitation at a summer camp. *Journal of Personality and Social Psychology, 32,* 1099–1105.

Ebbinghaus, H. (1885). *Memory: A contribution to experimental psychology* (H. A. Roger & C. E. Bussenius, Trans., 1913). New York: Columbia University Press.

Eberts, R., & MacMillan, A. C. (1985). Misperception of small cars. In R. Eberts & C. Eberts (Eds.), *Trends in ergonomics/human factors III.* Amsterdam: Elsevier.

Eckert, E. D., Bouchard, T. J., Bohlen, J., & Heston, L. L. (1986). Homosexuality in monozygotic twins reared apart. *British Journal of Psychiatry, 148,* 421–425.

Edelstein, B. A., & Michelson, L. (Eds.) (1986). *Handbook of prevention.* New York & London: Plenum Press.

Educational Testing Service (1987). *ETS sensitivity review process.* Princeton, NJ: ETS.

Edwards, A. E., & Acker, L. E. (1972). A demonstration of the long-term retention of a conditioned GSR. *Psychosomatic Science, 26,* 27–28.

Edwards, W. (1987). Decision making. In G. Salvendy (Ed.), *Handbook of human factors.* New York: Wiley.

Edwards, W., Lindman, H., & Phillips, L. D. (1965). Emerging technologies for making decisions, In T. M. Newcomb (Ed.), *New directions in psychology II.* New York: Holt, Rinehart and Winston.

Egeland, B., Jacobvitz, D., & Sroufe, L. A. (1988). Breaking the cycle of abuse. *Child Development, 59,* 1080–1088.

Egeland, J. A., Gerhard, D. S., Pauls, D. L., Sussex, J. N., Kidd, K. K.,

Allen, C. R., Hostetter, A. M., & Housman, D. E. (1987). Bipolar affective disorders linked to DNA markers on chromosome II. *Nature, 325,* 783–787.

Ehrlich, H. J. (1973). *The social psychology of prejudice.* New York: Wiley.

Ehrlichman, H. & Halpern, J.N. (1988). Affect and memory: Effects of pleasant and unpleasant odors on retrieval of happy and unhappy memories. *Journal of Personality and Social Psychology, 55,* 769-779.

Eich, E. (1989). Theoretical issues in state dependent memory. In H. L. Roediger & F. I. M. Craik (Eds.), *Varieties of memory and consciousness.* Hillsdale, NJ: Lawrence Erlbaum Associates.

Eich, E., & Metcalfe, J. (1989). Mood dependent memory for internal versus external events. *Journal of Experimental Psychology: Learning, Memory, and Cognition, 15,* 443–455.

Eich, J. E., Weingartner, H., Stillman, R. C., & Gillin, J. C. (1975). State dependent accessibility of retrieval cues in the retention of a categorized list. *Journal of Verbal Learning and Verbal Behavior, 14,* 408–417.

Eichorn, D. H., Clausen, J. A., Haan, N., Honzik, M. P., & Mussen, P. H. (1981). *Present and past in middle life.* New York: Academic Press.

Eikelboom, R., & Stewart, J. (1982). Conditioning of drug-induced physiological responses. *Psychological Review, 89,* 507–528.

Eisenberg, N., & Miller, P. A. (1987). The relation of empathy to prosocial and unrelated behaviors. *Psychological Bulletin, 101,* 91–119.

Eisenberg, N., & Strayer, J. (1987). Critical issues in the study of empathy. In N. Eisenberg & J. Strayer (Eds.), *Empathy and its development.* Cambridge, Eng., Cambridge University Press.

Eisner, J., Roberts, W., Heymsfield, S., & Yager, J. (1985). Anorexia nervosa and sudden death. *Annals of Internal Medicine, 102,* 49–52.

Ekman, P. (1980). Biological and cultural contributions to body and facial movement in the expression of emotions. In A. Rorty (Ed.), *Explaining emotions.* Berkeley: University of California Press.

Ekman, P. (1984). Expression and the nature of emotion. In K. Sherer & P. Ekman (Eds.), *Approaches to emotion.* Hillsdale, NJ: Lawrence Erlbaum Associates.

Ekman, P., & Friesen, W. V. (1986). A new pan-cultural facial expression of emotion. *Motivation and Emotion, 10,* 159–168.

Ekman, P., Davidson, R. J., & Friesen, W. V. (1990). The Duchenne smile: Emotional expression and brain physiology II. *Journal of Personality and Social Psychology, 58,* 342–353.

Ekman, P., Friesen, W. V., & Ellsworth, P. (1972). *Emotion in the human face: Guidelines for research and a review of findings.* New York: Pergamon Press.

Ekman, P., Friesen, W. V., & O'Sullivan, M. (1988). Smiles when lying. *Journal of Personality and Social Psychology, 54,* 414–420.

Ekman, P., Levenson, R. W., & Friesen, W. V. (1983). Autonomic nervous system activity distinguishes among emotions. *Science, 221,* 1208–1210.

Elashoff, J. D. (1979). Box scores are for baseball. *Brain and Behavioral Sciences, 3,* 392.

Elliot, R. S., & Buell, J. C. (1983). The role of the central nervous system in sudden cardiac death. In T.M. Dembroski, T. Schmidt, & G. Blunchen (Eds.), *Biobehavioral bases of coronary-prone behavior.* New York: Karger.

Elliott, E. S., & Dweck, C. S. (1988). Goals: An approach to motivation and achievement. *Journal of Personality and Social Psychology, 54,* 5–12.

Ellis, A. (1962). *Reason and emotion in psychotherapy.* New York: Lyle Stuart.

Ellis, A. (1973). Rational-emotive therapy. In R. Corsini (Ed.), *Current psychotherapies.* Itasca, IL: Peacock.

Ellis, A., & Bernard, M. E. (1985). *Clinical applications of rational-emotive therapy.* New York: Plenum Press.

Ellis, H. C., & Ashbrook, P. W. (1988). Resource allocation model of the effects of depressed mood states on memory. In K. Fiedler & J. Forgas (Eds.), *Affect, cognition, and social behavior.* Toronto: Hogrefe.

Ellis, H. C., & Hunt, R. R. (1983). *Fundamentals of human memory and cognition* (3rd ed.). Dubuque, IA: William C. Brown.

Ellis, H. C., & Hunt, R. R. (1989). *Fundamentals of human memory and cognition* (4th ed.). Dubuque, IA: William C. Brown.

Ellis, L., & Ames, M. A. (1987). Neurohormonal functioning and sexual orientation: A theory of homosexuality-heterosexuality. *Psychological Bulletin, 101,* 233–258.

Elton, D., Burrows, G. D., & Stanley, G. V. (1980). Chronic pain and hypnosis. In G. D. Burrows & L. Dennerstein (Eds.), *Handbook of hypnosis and psychosomatic medicine.* Amsterdam: Elsevier.

Emmons, R. A., & King, L. A. (1988). Conflict among personal strivings: Immediate and long-term implications for psychological and physical well-being. *Journal of Personality and Social Psychology, 54,* 1040–1048.

Emmons, R. A., & King, L. A. (1989). Personal striving differentiation and affective reactivity. *Journal of Personality and Social Psychology, 56,* 478–484.

Endler, N. S., & Parker, J. D. A. (1990). Multidimensional assessment of coping: A critical evaluation. *Journal of Personality and Social Psychology, 58,* 844–854.

Engen, T. (1987). Remembering odors and their names. *American Scientist, 75,* 497–502.

Enright, R. D., Lapsley, D. K., & Levy, V. M., Jr. (1983). Moral education strategies. In M. Pressley & J. R. Levin (Eds.), *Cognitive strategy research: Educational application.* New York: Springer-Verlag.

Epstein, S., & O'Brien, E. J. (1985). The person-situation debate in historical and current perspective. *Psychological Bulletin, 98,* 513–537.

Epstein, W. (1961). The influence of syntactical structure on learning. *American Journal of Psychology, 74,* 80–85.

Epstein, Y. M., Woolfolk, R. L., & Lehrer, P. M. (1981). Physiological, cognitive, and nonverbal responses to repeated experiences of crowding. *Journal of Applied Social Psychology, 11,* 1–13.

Erdelyi, M. H. (1985). *Psychoanalysis: Freud's cognitive psychology.* San Francisco: W. H. Freeman.

Erdelyi, M. H., & Goldberg, B. (1979). Let's not sweep repression under the rug: Toward a cognitive psychology of repression. In J. F. Kihlstrom & F. J. Evans (Eds.), *Functional disorders of memory.* Hillsdale, NJ: Lawrence Erlbaum Associates.

Ericsson, K. A., & Polson, P. G. (1988). An experimental analysis of the mechanisms of a memory skill. *Journal of Experimental Psychology: Learning, Memory, and Cognition, 14,* 305–316.

Ericsson, K. A., Chase, W. G., & Faloon, S. (1980). Acquisition of a memory skill. *Science, 208,* 1181–1182.

Eriksen, C., & Yeh, Y. Y. (1985). Allocation of attention in the visual field. *Journal of Experimental Psychology: Human Perception & Performance, 11,* 583–597.

Erikson, E. H. (1963). *Childhood and society.* New York: W. W. Norton.

Erikson, E. H. (1968). *Identity: Youth and crisis.* New York: W. W. Norton.

Eron, L. D. (1987). The development of aggressive behavior from the perspective of a developing behaviorism. *American Psychologist, 42,* 435–442.

Eron, L. D., Huesmann, R., Brice, P., Fischer, P., & Mermelstein, R. (1983). Age trends in the development of aggression, sex typing, and related television habits. *Developmental Psychology, 19,* 71–77.

Eskew, R. T., & Riche, C. V. (1982). Pacing and locus of control in quality control inspection. *Human Factors, 24,* 411–415.

Evans, C. (1983). *Landscapes of the night: How and why we dream.* New York: Viking Press.

Evans, D. A., Fundenstein, H. H., Albert, M. S., Scherr, P. A., Cook, N. R., Chown, M. J., Hebert, L. E., Hennekens, C. H., & Taylor, J. O. (1989). Prevalence of Alzheimer's disease in a community population of older persons: Higher than previously reported. *Journal of the American Medical Association, 262,* 2551–2556.

Evans, J., Barsten, J., & Pollard, P. (1983). On the conflict between logic and belief in syllogistic reasoning. *Memory and Cognition, 11,* 295–306.

Evans, P. (1989). *Motivation and emotion.* New York: Routledge.

Exner, J. E. (1985). *The Rorschach: A comprehensive system* (Vol. 1, 2nd ed.). New York: Wiley.

Eysenck, H. J. (1952). The effects of psychotherapy: An evaluation. *Journal of Consulting Psychology, 16,* 319–324.

Eysenck, H. J. (1960). *Behavior therapy and the neuroses.* London: Pergamon Press.

Eysenck, H. J. (1961). The effects of psychotherapy. In H. J. Eysenck (Ed.), *Handbook of abnormal psychology.* New York: Basic Books.

Eysenck, H. J. (1966). *The effects of psychotherapy.* New York: International Science Press.

Eysenck, H. J. (1970). *The structure of human personality* (3rd ed.). London: Methuen.

Eysenck, H. J. (1980). *The causes and effects of smoking.* Beverly Hills, CA: Sage.

Eysenck, H. J. (Ed.). (1981). *A model for personality.* New York: Springer-Verlag.

Eysenck, H. J. (1982). Development of a theory. In C. D. Spielberger (Ed.), *Personality, genetics, and behavior.* New York: Praeger.

Eysenck, H. J. (1987). Speed of information processing, reaction time, and the theory of intelligence. In P. A. Vernon (Ed.), *Speed of information-processing and intelligence* (pp. 21–67). Norwood, NJ: Ablex.

Eysenck, H. J. (1988, December). Health's character. *Psychology Today,* pp. 27–35.

Eysenck, H. J., & Eysenck, M. W. (1985). *Personality and individual differences.* New York: Plenum.

Fabricius, W. V., & Wellman, H. M. (1983). Children's understanding of retrieval cue utilization. *Developmental Psychology, 19,* 15–21.

Facchinetti, F., Centini, G., Parrini, D., Petroglia, F., D'Antona, N., Cosmi, E. V., & Genazzani, A. R. (1982). Opioid plasma levels during labor. *Gynecology & Obstetrics Investigations, 13,* 155–163.

Facchinetti, F., Martignoni, E., Petraglia, F., Sances, M. G., Nappi, G., & Genazzani, A. R. (1987). Premenstrual fall of plasma beta-endorphin in patients with premenstrual syndrome. *Fertility and Sterility, 47,* 570–573.

Faden, A. I., Demediuk, P., Panter, S. S., & Vink, R. (1989). The role of excitatory amino acids and NMDA receptors in traumatic brain injury. *Science, 244,* 798–800.

Fairburn, C. (1981). A cognitive behavioral approach to the treatment of bulimia. *Psychological Medicine, 11,* 707–711.

Faraone, S. V., & Tsuang, M. T. (1985). Quantitative models of the genetic transmission of schizophrenia. *Psychological Bulletin, 98,* 41–66.

Farber, B. (Ed.). (1983). *Stress and burnout in human service professions.* New York: Pergamon Press.

Farberow, N. L., & Litman, R. E. (1958–1970). *A comprehensive suicide prevention program* (Unpublished final report DHEW NIMH Grants No. MH 14946 & MH 00128). Los Angeles, CA: Suicide Prevention Center.

Farberow, N. L., Shneidman, E. S., & Leonard, C. (1963, February 25). Suicide among general medical and surgical hospital patients with malignant neoplasms. (Medical Bulletin MB-9, pp. 1–11). Washington, DC: Veterans Administration, Department of Medicine and Surgery.

Farley, F. (1986, May). The big T in personality. *Psychology Today.*

Farley, J., & Alkon, D. L. (1985). Cellular mechanisms of learning, memory, and information storage. *Annual Review of Psychology, 36,* 419–494.

Farwell, L. A., & Donchin, E. (1989). Detection of guilty knowledge with ERPs. *Society for Psychophysiology Abstracts, 26,* S8.

Feather, N. T., & Volkmer, R. E. (1988). Preference for situations involving effort, time pressure, and feedback in relation to Type A behavior, locus of control, and test anxiety. *Journal of Personality and Social Psychology, 55,* 266–271.

Fechter, L. D., Young, J. S., Carlisle, L. (1988). Potentiation of noise induced threshold shifts and hair cell loss by carbon monoxide. *Hearing Research, 34,* 1, 39–48.

Feingold, A. (1988). Cognitive gender differences are disappearing. *American Psychologist, 43,* 95–103.

Felner, R. D., & Adan, A. M. (1988). The school transitional environment project: An ecological intervention and evaluation. In R. H. Price (Ed.), *Fourteen ounces of prevention: A casebook for practitioners.* Washington, DC: American Psychological Association.

Fenz, W. D. (1971). Heart rate responses to a stressor: A comparison between primary and secondary psychopaths and normal controls. *Journal of Experimental Research in Personality, 5,* 7–13.

Fernald, A. (1981, April). *Four-month-olds prefer to listen to "motherese."* Paper presented at the meeting of the Society for Research in Child Development, Boston, MA.

Ferraro, P., Conti-Tronconi, B., & Guidotti, A. (1986). DBI, an anxiogenic neuropeptide found in human brain. *Advances in Biochemistry and Psychopharmacology, 41,* 177–185.

Festinger, L. (1954). A theory of social comparison processes. *Human Relations, 7,* 117–140.

Festinger, L. (1957). *A theory of cognitive dissonance.* Evanston, IL: Row, Petersen.

Festinger, L., & Carlsmith, J. M. (1959). Cognitive consequences of forced compliance. *Journal of Abnormal and Social Psychology, 58,* 203–210.

Festinger, L., Pepitone, A., & Newcomb, T. M. (1952). Some consequences of deindividuation in a group. *Journal of Abnormal and Social Psychology, 47,* 383–389.

Feuerstein, R. (1980). *Instrumental enrichment: An intervention program for cognitive modifiability.* Baltimore: University Park Press.

Fiandaca, M. S., Kordower, J. H., Hansen, J. T., Jiao, S. S., & Gash, D. M. (1988). Adrenal medullary autografts into the basal ganglia of cebus monkeys: Injury-induced regeneration. *Experimental Neurology, 102,* 76–91.

Field, T., Woodson, R., Cohen, D., Garcia, R., & Greenberg, R. (1983). Discrimination and imitation of facial expressions by term and preterm neonates. *Infant Behavior and Development, 6,* 485–490.

Fillenbaum, S. (1974). Pragmatic normalization: Further results for some conjunctive and disjunctive sentences. *Journal of Experimental Psychology, 103,* 913–921.

Fillmore, K. M., & Caetano, R. (1980, May 22). *Epidemiology of occupational alcoholism.* Paper presented at the National Institute on Alcohol Abuse and Alcoholism's Workshop on Alcoholism in the Workplace, Reston, VA.

Fine, T. H., & Turner, J. W. (1982). The effect of brief restricted environmental stimulation therapy in the treatment of essential hypertension. *Behaviour Research and Therapy, 20,* 567–570.

Finer, B. (1980). Hypnosis and anaesthesia. In G. D. Burrows & L. Dennerstein (Eds.), *Handbook of hypnosis and psychosomatic medicine.* Amsterdam: Elsevier.

Fink, M. (1979). *Convulsive therapy: Therapy and practice.* New York: Raven.

Fink, M. (1988). The use of ECT in the United States. *American Journal of Psychiatry, 145,* 133–134.

Finman, R., & Berkowitz, L. (1989). Some factors influencing the effects of depressed mood on anger and overt hostility toward another. *Journal of Research in Personality, 23,* 70–84.

Finn, P. R., Zeitouni, N. C., & Pihl, R. O. (1990). Effects of alcohol on psychophysiological hyperreactivity to nonaversive stimuli in men at high risk for alcoholism. *Journal of Abnormal Psychology, 99,* 79–85.

Fiore, J., Becker, J., & Coppel, D. (1983). Social network interactions: A buffer or a stress. *American Journal of Community Psychology, 11,* 423–439.

Firestein, S., & Werblin, F. (1989). Odor-induced membrane currents in vertebrate-olfactory receptor neurons. *Science, 244,* 79–82.

Fischer, E., Haines, R., & Price, T. (1980). *Cognitive issues in head up displays.* (NASA Technical Paper 1711). Washington, DC: NASA.

Fischoff, B. (1977). Perceived informativeness of facts. *Journal of Experimental Psychology: Human perception and performance, 3,* 349–358.

Fischoff, B. (1982). Debiasing. In D. Kahneman, P. Slovic, & A. Tversky (Eds.), *Judgment under uncertainty: Heuristics and biases.* New York: Cambridge University Press.

Fischoff, B., & MacGregor, D. (1982). Subjective confidence in forecasts. *Journal of Forecasting, 1,* 155–172.

Fischoff, B., & Slovic, P. (1980). A little learning . . . Confidence in multicue judgment tasks. In R. Nickerson (Ed.), *Attention and performance: VIII.* Hillsdale, NJ: Lawrence Erlbaum Associates.

Fischoff, B., Slovic, P., & Lichtenstein, S. (1977). Knowing with certainty: The appropriateness of extreme confidence. *Journal of Experimental Psychology: Human Perception and Performance, 3,* 552–564.

Fisher, J. D., Bell, P. A., & Baum, A. (1984). *Environmental psychology* (2nd ed.). New York: Holt, Rinehart and Winston.

Fisher, S., & Greenberg, R. P. (1977). *The scientific credibility of Freud's theories and therapy.* New York: Basic Books.

Fishman, S. M., & Sheehan, D. V. (1985, April). Anxiety and panic: Their cause and treatment. *Psychology Today,* pp. 26–32.

Fiske, D. W., & Maddi, S. R. (1961). *Functions of varied experience.* Homewood, IL: Dorsey Press.

Fiske, M. (1980). Tasks and crises of the second half of life: The interrelationship of commitment, coping, and adaptation. In J. E. Birren & R. B. Sloane (Eds.), *Handbook of mental health and aging.* Englewood Cliffs, NJ: Prentice-Hall.

Fiske, S. T. (1989). Examining the role of intent: Toward understanding its role in stereotyping and prejudice. In J. S. Uleman & J. A. Bargh (Eds.), *Unintended thought.* New York: Guilford Press.

Fiske, S. T., & Pavelchak, M. A. (1986). Category-based versus piecemeal-based affective responses: Developments in schema-triggered affect. In R. M. Sorrentino & E. T. Higgins (Eds.), *Handbook of motivation and cognition.* New York: Guilford Press.

Fiske, S. T., & Ruscher, J. B. (1989). On-line processes in category-based and individuating impressions: Some basic principles and methodological reflections. In J. N. Bassili (Ed.), *On-line cognition in person perception.* Hillsdale, NJ: Lawrence Erlbaum Associates.

Fitch, N., Becker, R., & Heller, A. (1988). The inheritance of Alzheimer's disease: A new interpretation. *Annals of Neurology, 23,* 14–19.

Fixen, D. L., Phillips, E. L., Phillips, E. A., & Wolf, M. M. (1976). The teaching-family model of group home treatment. In W. E. Craighead, A. E. Kazdin, & M. J. Mahoney (Eds.), *Behavior modification: Principles, issues, and applications.* Boston: Houghton Mifflin.

Flaherty, C. F., Uzwiak, A. J., Levine, J., Smith, M., Hall, P., & Schuler, R. (1980). Apparent hyperglycemic and hypoglycemic conditional responses with exogenous insulin as the unconditioned stimulus. *Animal Learning and Behavior, 8,* 382–386.

Flavell, J. H. (1985). *Cognitive development* (2nd ed.). Englewood Cliffs, NJ: Prentice-Hall.

Flavell, J. H., & Wellman, H. M. (1977). Metamemory. In R. V. Kail & J. W. Hagen (Eds.), *Perspectives on the development of memory and cognition.* Hillsdale, NJ: Lawrence Erlbaum Associates.

Flavell, J. H., Beach, D. H., & Chinsky, J. M. (1966). Spontaneous verbal rehearsal in a memory task as a function of age. *Child Development, 37,* 283–299.

Flavell, J. H., Friedrichs, A. G., & Hoyt, J. D. (1970). Developmental changes in memorization processes. *Cognitive Psychology, 1,* 324–340.

Fleming, I., Baum, A., & Weiss, L. (1987). Social density and perceived control as mediators of crowding stress in high density residential neighborhoods. *Journal of Personality and Social Psychology, 52,* 899–906.

Flynn, J., Vanegas, H., Foote, W., & Edwards, S. (1970). Neural mechanisms involved in a cat's attack on a rat. In M. Whelan, R. F. Thompson, M. Verzeano, & N. Weinberger (Eds.), *The neural control of behavior.* New York: Academic Press.

Foa, E. B., Rothbaum, B. O., & Kozak, M. J. (1989). Behavioral treatments for anxiety and depression. In P. C. Kendall & D. Watson (Eds.), *Anxiety and depression: Distinctive and overlapping features* (pp. 413–454). San Diego: CA: Academic Press.

Fodor, J. A., Bever, T. G., & Garrett, M. F. (1974). *The Psychology of Language.* New York: McGraw-Hill.

Foenander, G., & Burrows, G. D. (1980). Phenomena of hypnosis: 1. Age regression. In G. D. Burrows & L. Dennerstein (Eds.), *Handbook of hypnosis and psychosomatic medicine.* Amsterdam: Elsevier.

Folkes, V. S. (1982). Communicating the reasons for social rejection. *Journal of Experimental Social Psychology, 18,* 235–252.

Folkman, S. (1984). Personal control and stress and coping processes: A theoretical analysis. *Journal of Personality and Social Psychology, 46,* 839–852.

Folkman, S., & Lazarus, R. S. (1980). An analysis of coping in a middle-aged community sample. *Journal of Health and Social Behavior, 21,* 219–239.

Folkman, S., & Lazarus, R. S. (1985). If it changes, it must be a process: A study of emotion and coping during three stages of a college examination. *Journal of Personality and Social Psychology, 48,* 150–170.

Folkman, S., Lazarus, R. S., Gruen, R. J., & DeLongis, A. (1986). Appraisal, coping, health status, and psychological symptoms. *Journal of Personality and Social Psychology, 50,* 571–579.

Ford, C. E., Wright, R. A., & Haythornthwaite, J. (1985). Task performance and magnitude of goal valence. *Journal of Research in Personality, 19,* 253–260.

Ford, D. E., & Kamerow, D. B. (1989). Epidemiologic study of sleep disturbances and psychiatric disorders: An opportunity for prevention? *Journal of the American Medical Association, 262,* 1479–1484.

Forehand, R., & McMahon, R. J. (1981). *Helping the non-compliant child: A clinician's guide to parent training.* New York: Guilford.

Foreyt, J. P., & Kondo, A. T. (1984). Advances in behavioral treatment of obesity. In M. Hersen, R. M. Eisler, & P. M. Miller (Eds.), *Progress in behavior modification: Vol. 16.* New York: Academic Press.

Forsyth, D. R. (1983). *An introduction to group dynamics.* Monterey, CA: Brooks/Cole.

Foster, D., & Finchilescu, G. (1986). Contact in a "non-contact" society: The case of South Africa. In M. Hewstone & R. Brown (Eds.), *Contact and conflict in intergroup encounters.* New York: Blackwell.

Foulkes, D., & Fleisher, S. (1975). Mental activity in relaxed wakefulness. *Journal of Abnormal Psychology, 84,* 66–75.

Fozard, J., Wolf, E., Bell, B., Farland, R., & Podolsky, S. (1977). Visual perception and communication. In J. Birren & K. Schaie (Eds.), *Handbook of the psychology of aging.* New York: Van Nostrand Reinhold.

Fozard, J. L. (1980). The time for remembering. In L. W. Poon (Ed.), *Aging in the 1980s: Psychological issues.* Washington, DC: American Psychological Association.

Fraiberg, S. (1987). Pathological defenses in infancy. In L. Fraiberg

(Ed.), *Selected writings of Selma Fraiberg.* Columbus, OH: Ohio State University Press.

Frank, G. (1976). Measures of intelligence and critical thinking. In I. B. Weiner (Ed.), *Clinical methods in psychology.* New York: Wiley.

Frank, J. S. (1973). *Persuasion and healing* (rev. ed.). Baltimore: Johns Hopkins University Press.

Frank, J. S. (1978). *Psychotherapy and the human predicament.* New York: Schocken Books.

Frankel, B. G., & Whitehead, P. C. (1981). *Drinking and damage: Theoretical advantages and implications for prevention* (Monograph 14). New Brunswick, NJ: Rutgers Center of Alcohol Studies.

Frankel, F. H. (1984). Electroconvulsive therapies. In T. B. Karasu (Ed.), *The psychiatric therapies.* Washington, DC: American Psychological Association.

Frankenberg, W. K., & Dodds, J. B. (1967). The Denver developmental screening test. *Journal of Pediatrics, 71,* 181–191.

Frankenhaeuser, M., Nordheden, B., Myrsten, A., & Post, B. (1971). Psychophysiological reactions to understimulation and overstimulation. *Acta Psychologica, 35,* 298–308.

Frankmann, S. P., & Green, B. G. (1987). Differential effects of cooling on the intensity of taste. *Annals of the New York Academy of Science, 510,* 300–303.

Frase, L. T. (1975). Prose processing. In G. H. Bower (Ed.), *The psychology of learning and motivation: Vol. 9.* New York: Academic Press.

Fredericksen, N. (1986). Toward a broader conception of human intelligence. *American Psychologist, 41,* 445–452.

Freed, E. X. (1971). Anxiety and conflict: Role of drug-dependent learning in the rat. *Quarterly Journal of Studies on Alcohol, 32,* 13–29.

Freedman, J. L. (1988). Television violence and aggression: What the evidence shows. In S. Oskamp (Ed.), *Television as a social issue.* Newbury Park, CA: Sage.

Freedman, J. L., & Fraser, S. C. (1966). Compliance without pressure: The foot-in-the-door technique. *Journal of Personality and Social Psychology, 4,* 195–202.

Freeman, A., Simon, K. M., Beutler, L. E., & Arkowitz, H. (1989). *Comprehensive handbook of cognitive therapy.* New York: Plenum.

Freeman, W., & Watts, J. W. (1942). *Psychosurgery.* Springfield, IL: Charles C. Thomas.

Fremgen, A., & Fay, D. (1980). Overextensions in production and comprehension: A methodological clarification. *Journal of Child Language, 7,* 205–211.

Freud, A. (1946). *The ego and the mechanisms of defense.* New York: International Universities Press.

Freud, S. (1900). The interpretation of dreams. In J. Strachey (Ed.), *The standard edition of the complete psychological works of Sigmund Freud: Vol. 8.* London: Hogarth Press.

Freud, S. (1914). *The psychopathology of everyday life.* New York: Macmillan.

Frezza, M., Di Padova, C., Pozzato, G., Terpin, M., Baraona, E., & Lieber, C. S. (1990). High blood alcohol levels in women: The role of decreased gastric alcohol dehydrogenase activity and first-pass metabolism. *New England Journal of Medicine, 322,* 95–99.

Friedman, H. S., & Booth-Kewley, S. (1987a). The "disease-prone personality": A meta-analytic view of the construct. *American Psychologist, 42,* 539–555.

Friedman, H. S., & Booth-Kewley, S. (1987b). Personality, Type A behavior, and coronary heart disease: The role of emotional expression. *Journal of Personality and Social Psychology, 53,* 783–792.

Friedman, H. S., & Booth-Kewley, S. (1988). Validity of the Type A construct: A reprise. *Psychological Bulletin, 104,* 381–384.

Friedman, M., & Rosenman, R. H. (1959). Association of specific overt behavior patterns with blood and cardiovascular findings: Blood cholesterol level, blood clotting time, incidence of arcus senilis, and clinical coronary artery disease. *Journal of the American Medical Association, 169,* 1286–1296.

Friedman, M., & Rosenman, R. H. (1974). *Type A behavior and your heart.* New York: Knopf.

Friedman, M., Thoresen, C., Gill, J., Ulmer, D., Powell, L., Price, V., Brown, B., Thompson, L., Rabin, D., Breall, W., Bourg, E., Levy, R., & Dixon, T. (1986). Alteration of type A behavior and its effects on cardiac recurrences in post myocardial infarction patients: Summary results of the recurrent coronary prevention project. *American Heart Journal, 112,* 653–665.

Friedman, M. I., & Stricker, E. M. (1976). The physiological psychology of hunger: A physiological perspective. *Psychological Review, 83,* 409–431.

Friedmann, T. (1989). Progress toward human gene therapy. *Science, 244,* 1275–1281.

Frisch, H. L. (1977). Sex stereotypes in adult-infant play. *Child Development, 48,* 1671–1675.

Frodi, A. M., Lamb, M. E., Leavitt, L. A., & Donovan, W. L. (1978). Fathers' and mothers' responses to infant smiles and cries. *Infant Behavior and Development, 1,* 187–198.

Fromm, E. (1941). *Escape from freedom.* New York: Rinehart.

Furstenberg, F. F. (1982). Conjugal succession: Reentering marriage after divorce. In P. B. Baltes & O. G. Brim, Jr. (Eds.), *Life-span development and behavior: Vol. 4* (pp. 107–146). New York: Academic Press.

Furstenberg, F. F., Brooks-Gunn, J., & Chase-Lansdale, L. (1989). Teenaged pregnancy and childbearing. *American Psychologist, 44,* 313–320.

Furth, H. (1964). Research with the deaf: Implications for language and cognition. *Psychological Bulletin, 62,* 145–164.

Gaddis, T. E., & Long, J. O. (1970). *Killer: A journal of murder.* New York: Macmillan.

Gagnon, J. H., & Simon, W. (1973). *Sexual conduct: The social sources of human sexuality.* Chicago: Aldine.

Galin, D. (1974). Implications for psychiatry of left and right cerebral specialization. *Archives of General Psychiatry, 31,* 572–583.

Gallup, G. G., McClure, M. K., Hill, S. D., & Bundy, R. A. (1971). Capacity for self-recognition in differentially reared chimpanzees. *Psychological Record, 21,* 69–74.

Ganchrow, J. R., Steiner, J. E., & Daher, M. (1983). Neonatal facial expressions in response to different qualities and intensities of gustatory stimuli. *Infant Behavior and Development, 6,* 189–200.

Ganellen, R. J., & Blaney, P. H. (1984). Hardiness and social support as moderators of the effects of life stress. *Journal of Personality and Social Psychology, 47,* 156–163.

Garcia, J., & Koelling, R. A. (1966). Relation of cue to consequences in avoidance learning. *Psychonomic Science, 4,* 123–124.

Garcia, J., Hankins, W. G., & Rusiniak, K. W. (1974). Behavioral regulation of the milieu interne in man and rat. *Science, 185,* 824–831.

Garcia, J., Kimeldorf, D. J., Hunt, E. L., & Davies, B. P. (1956). Food and water consumption of rats during exposure to gamma radiation. *Radiation Research, 4,* 33–41.

Garcia, J., Rusiniak, K. W., & Brett, L. P. (1977). Conditioning food-illness aversions in wild animals: Caveat Canonici. In H. Davis & H. M. B. Hurwitz (Eds.), *Operant-Pavlovian interactions.* Hillsdale, NJ: Lawrence Erlbaum Associates.

Garcia Coll, C. T., Oh, W., & Hoffman, J. The social ecology: Early parenting of Caucasian American mothers. *Child Development, 58,* 955–963.

Gardner, H. (1983). *Frames of mind: The theory of multiple intelligences.* New York: Basic Books.

Gardner, R. A., & Gardner, B. T. (1978). Comparative psychology and language acquisition. *Annals of the New York Academy of Science, 309,* 37–76.

Garfield, S. L. (1982). Eclecticism and integration in psychotherapy. *Behavior Therapy, 13,* 610–623.

Garfinkel, P. E., Moldofsky, H., & Garner, D. M. (1980). The heterogeneity of anorexia nervosa. *Archives of General Psychiatry, 37,* 1036–1040.

Garmezy, N. (1988, April). *From adult schizophrenia to children resilient under stress.* Paper presented at the annual meeting of the Midwestern Psychological Association, Chicago, IL.

Garrity, T. F. (1973). Vocational adjustment after first myocardial infarction: Comparative assessment of several variables suggested in the literature. *Social Science and Medicine, 7,* 705–717.

Garrity, T. F. (1975). Morbidity, mortality, and rehabilitation. In W. D. Gentry & R. B. Williams, Jr. (Eds.), *Psychological aspects of myocardial infarction and coronary care.* St. Louis: Mosby.

Garvey, C. (1975). Requests and responses in children's speech. *Journal of Child Language, 2,* 41–63.

Gatchel, R. J., Baum, A., & Krantz, D. S. (1989). *An introduction to health psychology* (2nd ed.). New York: Random House.

Gawin, F. H., & Ellinwood, E. H., Jr. (1988). Cocaine and other stimulants: Actions, abuse, and treatment. *New England Journal of Medicine, 318,* 1173–1182.

Gazzaniga, M. S. (1989). Organization of the human brain. *Science, 245,* 947–952.

Gazzaniga, M. S., & LeDoux, J. E. (1978). *The integrated mind.* New York: Plenum Press.

Gebhardt, D. L., & Crump, C. E. (1990). Employee fitness and wellness programs in the workplace. *American Psychologist, 45,* 262–272.

Geen, R. G. (1985). Test anxiety and visual vigilance. *Journal of Personality and Social Psychology, 49,* 963–970.

Geen, R. G. (1989). Alternative conceptions of social facilitation. In P. B. Paulus (Ed.), *Psychology of group influence* (2nd ed.). Hillsdale, NJ: Lawrence Erlbaum Associates.

Geen, R. G., & Donnerstein, E. I. (Eds.). (1983). *Aggression: Theoretical and empirical reviews.* New York: Academic Press.

Geen, R. G., Beatty, W. W., & Arkin, R. M. (1984). *Human motivation.* Boston: Allyn & Bacon.

Geer, J. H., Davison, G. C., & Gatchel, R. I. (1970). Reduction of stress in humans through nonveridical perceived control of aversive stimulation. *Journal of Personality and Social Psychology, 16,* 731–738.

Gellhorn, E., & Loofbourrow, G. N. (1963). *Emotions and emotional disorders.* New York: Harper & Row.

Gelman, R. (1969). Conservation acquisition: A problem of learning to attend to relevant attributes. *Journal of Experimental Child Psychology, 7,* 167–187.

Gentner, D., & Stevens, A. L. (1983). *Mental models.* Hillsdale, NJ: Lawrence Erlbaum Associates.

Gentry, W. D. (1970). Effects of frustration, attack, and prior aggressive training on overt aggression and vascular processes. *Journal of Personality and Social Psychology, 16,* 718–725.

Gerard, H. B., Wilhelmy, R. A., & Connolley, E. S. (1968). Conformity and group size. *Journal of Personality and Social Psychology, 8,* 79–82.

Gerbner, G., Gross, L., Morgan, M., & Signorielli, N. (1986). Living with television: The dynamics of the cultivation process. In J. Bryant & D. Zillmann (Eds.), *Perspectives on media effects.* Hillsdale, NJ: Lawrence Erlbaum Associates.

Gergen, K. J., & Bauer, R. A. (1967). Interactive effects of self-esteem and task difficulty on social conformity. *Journal of Personality and Social Psychology, 6,* 16–21.

Gerschman, J. A., Reade, P. C., & Burrows, G. D. (1980). Hypnosis and dentistry. In G. D. Burrows & L. Dennerstein (Eds.), *Handbook of hypnosis and psychosomatic medicine.* Amsterdam: Elsevier.

Geschwind, N. (1979). Specializations of the human brain. *Scientific American, 241,* 180–199.

Gewirtz, J. L. (1972). *Attachment and dependency.* Washington, DC: Winston.

Gfeller, J. D., Lynn, S. J., & Pribble, W. E. (1987). Enhancing hypnotic susceptibility: Interpersonal and rapport factors. *Journal of Personality and Social Psychology, 52,* 595–596.

Ghiselli, E. E. (1973). The validity of aptitude tests in personnel selection. *Personnel Psychology, 26,* 461–477.

Gibbard, A. (1989). Selfish genes and ingroup altruism. *Behavioral and Brain Sciences, 12,* 706–707.

Gibson, E. J., & Walk, R. D. (1960). The visual cliff. *Scientific American, 202,* 64–71.

Gibson, J. J. (1979). *The ecological approach to visual perception.* Boston: Houghton Mifflin.

Gifford, R. (1987). *Environmental psychology: Principles and practice.* Boston: Allyn & Bacon.

Gil, D. G. (Ed.). (1979). *Child abuse and violence.* New York: AMS Press.

Gilbert, E., & DeBlassie, R. (1984). Anorexia nervosa: Adolescent starvation by choice. *Adolescence, 19,* 840–846.

Gilbert, R. M. (1984). Caffeine consumption. In G. A. Spiller (Ed.), *The methylxanthine beverages and foods: Chemistry, consumption, and health effects.* New York: Liss.

Giles, T. R. (1983). Probable superiority of behavioral interventions: II. Empirical status of the equivalence of therapies hypothesis. *Journal of Behavior Therapy & Experimental Psychiatry, 14,* 189–196.

Giles, T. R. (1990). Bias against behavior therapy in outcome reviews: Who speaks for the patient? *The Behavior Therapist, 13,* 86–90.

Gill, M. M., & Brenman, M. (1959). *Hypnosis and related states.* New York: International Universities Press.

Gill, M. M., & Hoffman, I. Z. (1982). A method of studying the analysis of aspects of the patient's experience of the relationship in psychoanalysis and psychotherapy. *Journal of the American Psychoanalytic Association, 30,* 137–167.

Gillette, M. U. (1986). The suprachiasmatic nuclei: Circadian phase-shifts induced at the time of hypothalamic slice preparation are preserved in vitro. *Brain Research, 379,* 176–181.

Gilligan, C. (1982). *In a different voice: Psychological theory and women's development.* Cambridge: Harvard University Press.

Gilligan, C., & Wiggins, G. (1987). The origins of morality in early childhood relationships. In J. Kagan & S. Lamb (Eds.), *The emergence of morality.* Chicago: University of Chicago Press.

Gilman, A. G., Goodman, L. S., Rall, T. W., & Murad, F. (1985). *Goodman and Gilman's the pharmacological basis of therapeutics* (7th ed.). New York: Macmillan.

Glanzer, M., & Cunitz, A. (1966). Two storage mechanisms in free recall. *Journal of Verbal Learning and Verbal Behavior, 5,* 351–360.

Glaser, R. (1990). The reemergence of learning theory within instructional research. *American Psychologist, 45,* 29–39.

Glaser, R., & Bassok, M. (1989). Learning theory and the study of instruction. *Annual Review of Psychology, 40,* 631–666.

Glasgow, R. E., & Bernstein, D. A. (1981). Behavioral treatment of smoking behavior. In L. A. Bradley & C. K. Prokop (Eds.), *Medical Psychology: A New Perspective.* New York: Academic Press.

Glass, D. C. (1977). *Behavior patterns, stress, and coronary disease.* Hillsdale, NJ: Lawrence Erlbaum Associates.

Gleitman, L. R., Newport, E. L., & Gleitman, H. (1984). The current status of the motherese hypothesis. *Journal of Child Language, 11,* 43–79.

Glenn, S. M., & Cunningham, C. C. (1983). What do babies listen to most? A developmental study of auditory preferences in non-handicapped infants and infants with Down's syndrome. *Developmental Psychology, 19,* 332–337.

Glick, P. C. (1980). Remarriage: Some recent changes and variations. *Journal of Family Issues, 1,* 455–478.

Gnepp, J. (1983). Children's social sensitivity: Inferring emotions from conflicting cues. *Developmental Psychology, 19,* 805–814.

Goddard, H. H. (1917). Mental tests and the immigrant. *Journal of Delinquency, 2,* 243–277.

Godden, D. R., & Baddeley, A. D. (1975). Context-dependent memory in two natural environments: On land and underwater. *British Journal of Psychology, 66,* 325–331.

Goelet, P., Castellucci, V. F., Schacher, S. & Kandel, E. R. (1986). The long and the short of long-term memory—A molecular framework. *Nature, 322,* 419–422.

Goethals, G. R. (1986). Fabricating and ignoring social reality: Self-serving estimates of consensus. In J. M. Olson, C. P. Herman, & M. P. Zanna (Eds.), *Relative deprivation and social comparison.* Hillsdale, NJ: Lawrence Erlbaum Associates.

Gold, P. W., Goodwin, F. K., & Chrousos, G. P. (1988). Clinical and biochemical manifestations of depression: relation to the neurobiology of stress. *New England Journal of Medicine, 319,* 348–353.

Goldberger, L. (1982). Sensory deprivation and overload. In L. Goldberger & S. Breznitz (Eds.), *Handbook of stress: Theoretical and clinical aspects.* New York: Free Press.

Golden, C. J., Moses, J. A., Fishburne, F. J., Engum, E., Lewis, G. P., Wisniewski, A. M., Conley, F. K., Berg, R. A., & Graber, B. (1981). Cross-validation of the Luria-Nebraska Neuropsychological Battery for the presence, lateralization, and location of brain damage. *Journal of Consulting Clinical Psychology, 50,* 87–95.

Goldenberg, H. (1983). *Contemporary clinical psychology* (2nd ed.). Monterey, CA: Brooks/Cole.

Goldenberg, I., & Goldenberg, H. (1980). *Family therapy: An overview.* Monterey, CA: Brooks/Cole.

Goldfoot, D. A. (1977). Sociosexual behaviors of nonhuman primates during development and maturity: Social and hormonal relationships. In A. M. Schrier (Ed.), *Behavioral primatology: Advances in research and theory: Vol. 1.* Hillsdale, NJ: Lawrence Erlbaum Associates.

Goldin-Meadow, S., & Feldman, H. (1977). The development of language-like communication without a language model. *Science, 197,* 401–403.

Goldman, R. D., & Widawski, M. H. (1976). A within subjects technique for comparing college grading standards. *Educational Psychology Measurement, 36,* 381–390.

Goldman-Rakic, P. S. (1987). Development of cortical circuitry and cognitive function. *Child Development, 58,* 601–622.

Goldsmith, H. H. (1983). Genetic influences on personality from infancy to adulthood. *Child Development, 54,* 331–355.

Goldstein, M. J., Kant, H. S., Judd, L., Rice, C., & Green, R. (1971). Experience with pornography: Rapists, pedophiles, homosexuals, transsexuals, and controls. *Archives of Sexual Behavior, 1,* 1–15.

Goleman, D. (1986, April 8). Studies point to the power of nonverbal signals. *New York Times.*

Gollwitzer, P. M., & Kinney, R. F. (1989). Effects of deliberative and implemental mind-sets on illusion of control. *Journal of Personality and Social Psychology, 56,* 531–542.

Goodenough, F. L. (1932). Expression of the emotions in a blind-deaf child. *Journal of Abnormal and Social Psychology, 27,* 328–333.

Goodwin, D. W. (1979). Alcoholism and heredity: A review and hypothesis. *Archives of General Psychiatry, 36,* 57–61.

Goodwin, D. W., Crane, J. B., & Guze, S. B. (1973). Alcoholic "blackouts": A review and clinical study of 100 alcoholics. *American Journal of Psychiatry, 26,* 191–198.

Gopher, D., Weil, M., & Siegal, D. (1989). Practice under changing priorities: an approach to the training of complex skills. *Acta Psychologica, 1571,* 147–177.

Goplerud, E. N. (1980). Social support and stress during the first year of graduate school. *Professional Psychology, 11,* 283–290.

Gordon, N. P., Cleary, P. D., Parker, C. E., & Czeisler, C. A. (1986). The prevalence and health impact of shiftwork. *American Journal of Public Health, 76,* 1225–1228.

Gordon, T. (1970). *Parent effectiveness training: The no-lose program for raising responsible children.* New York: Wyden.

Gore, S. (1978). The effect of social support in moderating the health consequences of unemployment. *Journal of Health and Social Behavior, 19,* 157–165.

Gorenflo, D. W., & Crano, W. D. (1989). Judgmental subjectivity/objectivity and locus of choice in social comparison. *Journal of Personality and Social Psychology, 57,* 605–614.

Gorman, J. M., Liebowitz, M. R., Fyer, A. J., & Stein, J. (1989). A neuroanatomical hypothesis for panic disorder. *American Journal of Psychiatry, 146,* 148–161.

Gorman, M. E. (1986). How the possibility of error affects falsification on a task that models scientific problem solving. *British Journal of Psychology, 77,* 85–96.

Gorn, G. J. (1982). The effects of music in advertising on choice behavior: A classical conditioning approach. *Journal of Marketing, 46,* 94–101.

Gottfredson, L. S., & Crouse, J. (1986). Validity versus utility of mental tests: Example of the SAT. *Journal of Vocational Behavior, 29,* 363–378.

Gottlieb, A. (1988). *Blood magic.* Berkeley: University of California Press.

Gottlieb, B. H. (Ed.). (1981). *Social networks and social support.* Beverly Hills, CA: Sage.

Gottman, J. M. (1979). *Marital interaction: Experimental investigation.* New York: Academic Press.

Gough, H. (1987). *California Psychological Inventory: Administrator's guide.* Palo Alto, CA: Consulting Psychologists Press.

Gould, S. J. (1983). *The mismeasure of man.* New York: W. W. Norton.

Graesser, A. C., & Nakamura, G. V. (1982). The impact of a schema on comprehension and memory. In G. H. Bower (Ed.), *The psychology of learning and motivation: Vol. 16.* New York: Academic Press.

Graesser, A. C., Woll, S. B., Kowalski, D. J., & Smith, D. A. (1980). Memory for typical and atypical actions in scripted activities. *Journal of Experimental Psychology: Human Learning and Memory, 6,* 503–515.

Graf, R. C., & Riddell, L. C. (1972). Helping behavior as a function of interpersonal perception. *Journal of Social Psychology, 86,* 227–231.

Graham, C., & Evans, F. J. (1977). Hypnotizability and the deployment of waking attention. *Journal of Abnormal Psychology, 86,* 631–638.

Graham, J. R. (1987). *The MMPI: A practical guide* (2nd ed.). New York: Oxford University Press.

Granneman, J., & Friedman, M. J. (1980). Hepatic modulation of insulin-induced gastric acid secretion and EMG activity in rats. *American Journal of Physiology, 238,* 346–352.

Graubard, S. R. (Ed.) (1988). *The artificial intelligence debate.* Cambridge, MA: MIT Press.

Green, D. M., & Swets, J. A. (1965). *Signal detection theory and psychophysics.* New York: Wiley.

Green, E. J., Greenough, W. T., & Schlumpf, B. E. (1983). Effects of complex or isolated environments on cortical dendrites of middle-aged rats. *Brain Research, 264 (2),* 233–240.

Green, R. (1987). *The "sissy boy syndrome" and the development of homosexuality.* New Haven: Yale University Press.

Greenberg, J., & Cohen, R. L. (Eds.). (1982). *Equity and justice in social behavior.* New York: Academic Press.

Greenberg, L. (1986). Change process research. *Journal of Consulting and Clinical Psychology, 54,* 4–9.

Greene, B. (1985, January 15). Less violence would be a big hit on TV. *Chicago Tribune.*

Greeno, J. G., Riley, M. S., & Gelman, R. (1984). Conceptual competence and children's counting. *Cognitive Psychology, 16,* 94–143.

Greenough, W. T. (1985). The possible role of experience-dependent synaptogenesis, or synapses on demand, in the memory process. In N. M. Weinberger, J. L. McGaugh, & G. Lynch (Eds.), *Memory systems of the brain*. New York: The Guilford Press.

Greenough, W. T., Black, J. E., & Wallace, C. S. (1987). Experience and brain development. *Child Development, 58*, 539–559.

Greenwald, A. (1980). The totalitarian ego: Fabrication and revision of personal history. *American Psychologist, 35*, 603–618.

Greenwald, A. G., & Pratkanis, A. R. (1984). The self. In R. S. Wyer & T. K. Srull (Eds.), *Handbook of social cognition* (Vol. 3). Hillsdale, NJ: Lawrence Erlbaum Associates.

Greer, L. D. (1980). *Children's comprehension of formal features with masculine and feminine connotations*. Unpublished master's thesis, Department of Human Development, University of Kansas, Lawrence, KS.

Gregory, R. L. (1968). Visual illusions. *Scientific American, 219*, 66–67.

Gregory, R. L. (1973). *Eye and brain* (2nd ed.). New York: McGraw Hill.

Griffiths, R. R., & Woodson, P. P. (1988). Caffeine physical dependence: A review of human and laboratory animal studies. *Psychopharmacology, 94*, 437–451.

Griffitt, W., & Veitch, R. (1971). Hot and crowded: Influence of population density and temperature on interpersonal affective behavior. *Journal of Personality and Social Psychology, 17*, 92–98.

Griffitt, W. B., & Guay, P. (1969). "Object" evaluation and conditioned affect. *Journal of Experimental Research in Personality, 4*, 1–8.

Gross, W. B., & Colmano, G. (1969). The effect of social isolation on resistance to some infectious diseases. *Poultry Science, 48*, 514–520.

Grosz, H. I., & Zimmerman, J. (1970). A second detailed case study of functional blindness: Further demonstration of the contribution of objective psychological data. *Behavior Therapy, 1*, 115–123.

Grove, H. (1987). The reliability of psychiatric diagnosis. In C. G. Last & M. Hersen (Eds.), *Issues in diagnostic research* (pp. 99–119). New York: Plenum.

Grover, S. L., & Brockner, J. (1989). Empathy and the relationship between attitudinal similarity and attraction. *Journal of Research in Personality, 23*, 469–479.

Gruder, C. L., & Duslak, R. J. (1973). Elicitation of cooperation by retaliatory and nonretaliatory strategies in a mixed motive game. *Journal of Conflict Resolution, 17*, 162–174.

Guerin, B. (1986). Mere presence effects in humans: A review. *Journal of Experimental Social Psychology, 22*, 38–77.

Guerin, D., & Gottfried, A. W. (1986). Infant temperament as a predictor of preschool behavior problems. *Infant Behavior and Development, 9*, 152. (Special issue: abstracts of papers presented at the Fifth International Conference on Infant Studies.)

Guilford, J. P. (1959). Traits of creativity. In H. H. Anderson (Ed.), *Creativity and its cultivation*. New York: Harper & Row.

Guilford, J. P., & Hoepfner, R. (1971). *The analysis of intelligence*. New York: McGraw-Hill.

Gunderson, J. G., & Mosher, L. R. (1975). The cost of schizophrenia. *American Journal of Psychiatry, 132*, 901–905.

Gurin, G., Veroff, J., & Feld, S. (1960). *Americans view their mental health: A nationwide survey*. New York: Basic Books.

Gurman, A. S., Kniskern, D. P., & Pinsof, W. M. (1986). Research on marital and family therapies. In S. L. Garfield & A. E. Bergin (Eds.), *Handbook of psychotherapy and behavior change* (3rd ed.), pp. 565–624. New York: Wiley.

Guroff, G. (1980). *Molecular neurobiology*. New York: Marcel Dekker.

Gustavson, C. R., Garcia, J., Hawkins, W. G., & Rusiniak, K. W. (1974). Coyote predation control by aversive conditioning. *Science, 184*, 581–583.

Gwirtsman, H. E., & Germer, R. H. (1981). Abnormalities of dexamethasone suppression test and urinary MHPG in anorexia nervosa. *American Journal of Psychiatry, 138*, 650–653.

Ha, H., Tan, E. C., Fukunaga, H., & Aochi, O. (1981). Naloxone reversal of acupuncture analgesia in the monkey. *Experimental Neurology, 73*, 298–303.

Haan, N., Aerts, E., & Cooper, B. A. B. (1985). *On moral grounds: The search for practical morality*. New York: New York University Press.

Haber, R. N. (1979). Twenty years of haunting eidetic imagery: Where's the ghost? *The Behavioral and Brain Sciences, 2*, 583–629.

Halbreich, U., Endicott, J., Goldstein, S., & Nee J. (1986). Premenstrual changes and changes in gonadal hormones. *Acta Psychiatrica Scandinavia, 74*, 576–586.

Haley, J. (1970). Family therapy. *International Journal of Psychiatry, 9*, 233–242.

Haley, J. (1971). Family therapy: A radical change. In J. Haley (Ed.), *Changing families: A family therapy reader*. New York: Grune & Stratton.

Hamburg, D. A., Elliot, G. R., & Parron, D. L. (1982). *Health and behavior: Frontiers of research in the biobehavioral sciences*. Washington, DC: National Academy Press.

Hamilton, D. L. (1988). Understanding impression formation: What has memory research contributed? In P. R. Solomon, G. R. Goethals, C. M. Kelley, & B. Stephens (Eds.), *Memory: An interdisciplinary approach*. New York: Springer-Verlag.

Hamilton, P. (1989). *The interaction of depressed mothers and their 3-month-old infants*. Unpublished doctoral dissertation, Boston University.

Hamm, A. O., Vaitl, D., & Lang, P. J. (1989). Fear conditioning, meaning, and belongingness: A selective association analysis. *Journal of Abnormal Psychology, 98*, 395–406.

Hammarback, S., Damber, J. E., & Backstrom, T. (1989). Relationship between symptom severity and hormone changes in women with premenstrual syndrome. *Journal of Clinical Endocrinology and Metabolism, 68*, 125–130.

Hammock, T., & Brehm, J. W. (1966). The attractiveness of choice alternatives when freedom to choose is eliminated by a social agent. *Journal of Personality, 34*, 546–554.

Hamner, W. C., & Yukl, G. A. (1977). The effectiveness of different offer strategies in bargaining. In D. Druckman, (Ed.), *Negotiations: Social-psychological perspectives*. London: Sage.

Hansel, C. E. M. (1966). *ESP: A scientific evaluation*. New York: Scribner.

Hanson, J. W. (1977). Unpublished manuscript.

Hardaway, R. A. (1990). Subliminally activated symbiotic fantasies: Facts and artifacts. *Psychological Bulletin, 107*, 177–195.

Hardimann, P. T., Dufresne, R., & Mestre, J. (1989). The relation between problem categorization and problem solving among experts and novices. *Memory and Cognition, 17*, 627–638.

Hare, R. D. (1970). *Psychopathy: Theory and research*. New York: Wiley.

Hare, R. D. (1980). A research scale for the assessment of psychopathy in criminal populations. *Personality and Individual Differences, 1*, 111–119.

Hare, R. D., McPherson, L. M., & Forth, A. E. (1988). Male psychopaths and their criminal careers. *Journal of Consulting and Clinical Psychology, 56*, 710–714.

Hari, R., & Lounasmaa, O. V. (1989). Recording and interpretation of cerebral magnetic fields. *Science, 244*, 432–436.

Harkins, S. G. (1987). Social loafing and social facilitation. *Journal of Experimental Social Psychology, 23*, 1–18.

Harkins, S. G., & Szymanski, K. (1987). Social loafing and social facilitation: New wine in old bottles. In C. Hendrick (Ed.), *Group processes and intergroup relations*. Newbury Park, CA: Sage.

Harlow, H. F. (1958). The nature of love. *American Psychologist, 13*, 673–685.

Harlow, H. F., Harlow, M. K., & Suomi, S. J. (1971). From thought to therapy: Lessons from a private library. *American Scientist, 59,* 538–549.

Harris, J. E., & Morris, P. E. (Eds.) (1984). *Everyday memories, actions, and absent-mindedness.* New York: Academic Press.

Harris, P. L. (1974). Perseverative search at a visibly empty place by young infants. *Journal of Experimental Child Psychology, 18,* 535–542.

Harris, R. J., Sardarpoor-Bascom, F., & Meyer, T. (1989). The role of cultural knowledge in distorting recall for stories. *Bulletin of the Psychonomic Society, 27,* 9–10.

Harrison, A. A. (1976). *Individuals and groups.* Monterey, CA: Brooks/Cole.

Hart, J., Jr., Berndt, R. S., & Caramazza, A. (1985). Category-specific naming deficit following cerebral infarction. *Nature, 316,* 439–440.

Hart, J. T. (1965). Memory and the feeling-of-knowing experience. *Journal of Educational Psychology, 56,* 208–216.

Hart, J. T. (1967). Second-try recall, recognition, and the memory-monitoring process. *Journal of Educational Psychology, 58,* 193–197.

Hart, S. N., & Brassard, M. A. (1987). A major threat to children's health: psychological maltreatment. *American Psychologist, 42,* 160–165.

Harter, S., & Zigler, E. (1974). The assessment of effectance motivation in normal and retarded children. *Developmental Psychology, 10,* 169–180.

Hartman, B. K., Cozzari, C., Berod, A., Kalmbach, S. J., & Faris, P. L. (1986). Central cholinergic innervation of the locus coeruleus. *Society for Neuroscience Abstracts, 12,* 770.

Hartmann, E., Baekeland, F., & Zwilling, G. (1972). Psychological differences between long and short sleepers. *Archives of General Psychiatry, 26,* 463–468.

Hartmann, H. (1939). Psychoanalysis and the concept of health. *International Journal of Psychoanalysis, 20,* 308–321.

Hartmann, H. (1958). *Ego psychology and the problem of adaptation.* New York: International Universities Press.

Hastie, R., Penrod, S. D., & Pennington, N. (1983). *Inside the jury.* Cambridge: Harvard University Press.

Hatfield, E. (1986). *Mirror, mirror: The importance of looks in everyday life.* Albany: State University of New York Press.

Hatfield, E. (1988). Passionate and companionate love. In R. J. Sternberg & M. L. Barnes (Eds.), *The psychology of love.* New Haven: Yale University Press.

Hatfield, E., Traupman, J., Sprecher, S., Utne, M., & Hay, T. (1984). Equity and intimate relations. In W. Ickes (Ed.), *Compatible and incompatible relationships.* New York: Springer-Verlag.

Hatfield, G., & Epstein, W. (1985). The status of the minimum principle in the theoretical analysis of visual perception. *Psychological Bulletin, 97,* 155–186.

Haviland, S. E., & Clark, H. H. (1974). What's new? Acquiring new information as a process in comprehension. *Journal of Verbal Learning and Verbal Behavior, 13,* 512–521.

Hawkins, F. (1987). *Human factors in flight.* Brookfield, VT: Gower.

Hayes, J. R. M. (1952). *Memory span for several vocabularies as a function of vocabulary size.* Massachusetts Institute of Technology Acoustic Laboratory Progress Report. Cambridge: MIT.

Hayslip, B., & Sterns, H. L. (1979). Age differences in relationships between crystallized and fluid intelligences and problem solving. *Journal of Gerontology, 14,* 404–414.

He, L. F. (1987). Involvement of endogenous opioid peptides in acupuncture analgesia. *Pain, 31,* 99–121.

Hearold, S. (1986). A synthesis of 1043 effects of television on social behavior. In G. Comstock (Ed.), *Public communication and behavior.* New York: Academic Press.

Heath, L., Kruttschnitt, C., & Ward, D. (1986). Television and violent criminal behavior: Beyond the Bobo doll. *Violence and Victims, 1,* 177–190.

Hebb, D.O. (1949). *The organization of behavior.* New York: Wiley.

Hebb, D. O. (1955). Drives and the C.N.S. (conceptual nervous system). *Psychological Review, 62,* 243–254.

Hebb, D. O. (1978, November). On watching myself get old. *Psychology Today,* pp. 15–23.

Hechtman, L., Weiss, G., & Perlman, T. (1984). Hyperactives as young adults: Past and current substance abuse and antisocial behavior. *American Journal of Orthopsychiatry, 54,* 415–425.

Heider, E. (1972). Universals of color naming and memory. *Journal of Experimental Psychology, 93,* 10–20.

Heitler, J. B. (1976). Preparatory techniques in initiating expressive psychotherapy with lower-class, unsophisticated patients. *Psychological Bulletin, 83,* 339–352.

Helgeson, V. S., Shaver, P., & Dyer, M. (1987). Prototypes of intimacy and distance in same-sex and opposite-sex relationships. *Journal of Social and Personal Relationships, 4,* 195–233.

Helson, R., & Moane, G. (1987). Personality change in women from college to midlife. *Journal of Personality and Social Psychology, 53,* 176–186.

Hendlin, H. (1975). Student suicide: Death as a life-style. *Journal of Nervous and Mental Disease, 160,* 204–219.

Hendrick, C., & Hendrick, S. (1986). A theory and method of love. *Journal of Personality and Social Psychology, 50,* 392–402.

Hendrick, C., & Hendrick, S. (1989). Research on love: Does it measure up? *Journal of Personality and Social Psychology, 56,* 784–794.

Hendrick, S., Hendrick, C., & Adler, N. L. (1988). Romantic relationships: Love, satisfaction, and staying together. *Journal of Personality and Social Psychology, 54,* 980–988.

Henig, R. M. (1988, August). How a body ages. *The Washingtonian,* pp. 59–65.

Henker, B., & Whalen, C. K. (1989). Hyperactivity and attention deficits. *American Psychologist, 44,* 216–223.

Hepworth, J. T., & West, S. G. (1988). Lynchings and the economy: A time-series reanalysis of Hovland and Sears (1940). *Journal of Personality and Social Psychology, 55,* 239–247.

Herink, R. (Ed.) (1980). *The psychotherapy handbook: The A to Z guide to more than 250 different therapies in use today.* New York: New American Library.

Herman, B. H., Hammock, M. K., Arthur-Smith, A., Egan, J., Chatoor, I., Zelnik, N., Carradine, M., Appelgate, K., Boecks, R., & Sharp, S. D. (1986, November). Role of opioid peptides in autism: Effects of acute administration of naltrexone. *Society for Neuroscience Abstracts, 12.*

Herman, C. P., & Polivy, J. (1975). Anxiety, restraint, and eating behavior. *Journal of Abnormal Psychology, 84,* 666–672.

Herman, J. H., & Roffwarg, H. P. (1983). Modifying oculomotor activity in awake subjects increases the amplitude of eye movement during REM sleep. *Science, 220,* 1074–1076.

Heron, W. (1957). The pathology of boredom. *Scientific American, 196,* 52–56.

Herrnstein, R. J. (1989, May). IQ and falling birth rates. *Atlantic Monthly,* pp. 72–76.

Hersen, M., Bellack, A. S., Himmelhoch, J. M., & Thase, M. E. (1984). *Behavior Therapy, 15,* 21–40.

Herzberg, F. (1966). *Work and the nature of man.* New York: Crowell.

Herzberg, F. (1968). One more time: How do you motivate employees? *Harvard Business Review, 46,* 53–62.

Herzog, D. B. (1982). Bulimia: The secretive syndrome. *Psychosomatics, 22,* 481–487.

Heston, L. L. (1966). Psychiatric disorders in foster home reared children of schizophrenic mothers. *British Journal of Psychiatry, 112,* 819–825.

Higgins, E. T. (1987). Self-discrepancy: A theory relating self and affect. *Psychological Review, 94,* 319–340.

Higgins, E. T. (1989). Knowledge accessibility and activation: Subjectivity and suffering from unconscious sources. In J. S. Uleman & J. A. Bargh (Eds.), *Unintended thought.* New York: Guilford Press.

Hilgard, E. R. (1965). *Hypnotic susceptibility.* New York: Harcourt, Brace and World.

Hilgard, E. R. (1977). *Divided consciousness: Multiple controls in human thought and action.* New York: Wiley.

Hilgard, E. R. (1979). *Personality and hypnosis: A study of imaginative involvement.* Chicago: University of Chicago Press.

Hilgard, E. R. (1980). Consciousness in contemporary psychology. *Annual Review of Psychology, 31,* 1–26.

Hilgard, E. R. (1982). Hypnotic susceptibility and implications for measurement. *International Journal of Clinical and Experimental Hypnosis, 30,* 394–403.

Hilgard, E. R., Morgan, A. H., & MacDonald, H. (1975). Pain and dissociation in the cold pressor test: A study of "hidden reports" through automatic key-pressing and automatic talking. *Journal of Abnormal Psychology, 84,* 280–289.

Hill, B. (1968). *Gates of horn and ivory.* New York: Taplinger.

Hill, C. E. (1990). Exploratory in-session process research in individual psychotherapy: A review. *Journal of Consulting and Clinical Psychology, 58,* 288–294.

Hill, D. L., & Przekop, P. R., Jr. (1988). Influences of dietary sodium on functional taste receptor development: A sensitive period. *Science, 241,* 1826–1828.

Hill, D. L., Mistretta, C. M., & Bradley, R. M. (1986). Effects of dietary NaCl deprivation during early development on behavioral and neurophysiological taste responses. *Behavioral Neuroscience, 100,* 390–398.

Hill, W. F. (1982). *Principles of learning.* Palo Alto, CA: Mayfield.

Hilton, H. (1986). *The executive memory guide.* New York: Simon & Schuster.

Hinton, J. (1967). *Dying.* Harmondsworth, UK: Penguin.

Hintzman, D. L. (1986). Schema abstraction in a multiple trace memory model. *Psychological Review, 93,* 411–428.

Hintzman, D. L. (1988). Judgments of frequency and recognition memory in a multiple-trace memory model. *Psychological Review, 95,* 528–551.

Hiroto, D. S., & Seligman, M. E. P. (1975). Generality of learned helplessness in man. *Journal of Personality and Social Psychology, 31,* 311–327.

Hirsch, J., & Knittle, J. L. (1970). Cellularity of obese and nonobese human adipose tissue. *Federation of American Societies for Experimental Biology: Federation Proceedings, 29,* 1516–1521.

Hirsch-Pasek, K., Treiman, R., & Schneiderman, M. (1984). Brown and Hanlon revisited: Mothers' sensitivity to ungrammatical forms. *Journal of Child Language, 11,* 81–88.

Hirtle, S. C., & Jonides, J. (1985). Evidence of hierarchies in cognitive maps. *Memory and Cognition, 13,* 208–217.

Hobfall, S. E. (1989). Conservation of resources: A new attempt at conceptualizing stress. *American Psychologist, 44,* 513–524.

Hochberg, J. E., & McAlister, E. (1955). Relative size versus familiar size in the perception of represented depth. *American Journal of Psychology, 68,* 294–296.

Hockey, G. R. (1984). Varieties of attentional state: The effects of environment. In R. Paraduraman & R. Davies (Eds.), *Varieties of attention.* New York: Academic Press.

Hockey, R. (1986). Changes in operator efficiency as a function of environmental stress. In K. Boff, L. Kaufman, & J. Thomas (Eds.), *Handbook of Perception and Human Performance.* New York: Wiley.

Hoffman, C., & Hurst, N. (1990). Gender stereotypes: Perception or rationalization? *Journal of Personality and Social Psychology, 58,* 197–208.

Hoffman, L. R. (Ed.). (1979). *The group problem solving process: Studies of a valence model.* New York: Praeger.

Hoffman, L. R., & Maier, N. R. F. (1979). Valence in the adoption of solutions by problem-solving groups: Concept, method, and results. In L. R. Hoffman (Ed.), *The group problem solving process: Studies of a valence model.* New York: Praeger.

Hoffman, M. L. (1970). Moral development. In P. H. Mussen (Ed.), *Carmichael's manual of child psychology: Vol. 2.* New York: Wiley.

Hoffman, M. L. (1977). Sex differences in empathy and related behaviors. *Psychological Bulletin, 84,* 712–722.

Hogan, R., & Nicholson, R. A. (1988). The meaning of personality test scores. *American Psychologist, 43,* 621–626.

Holahan, C. J. (1986). Environmental psychology. *Annual Review of Psychology, 37,* 381–407.

Holahan, C. J., & Moos, R. H. (1987). Personality, coping, and family resources in stress resistance: A longitudinal analysis. *Journal of Personality and Social Psychology, 51,* 389–395.

Holahan, C. J., & Moos, R. H. (1990). Life stressors, resistance factors, and improved psychological functioning: An extension of the stress resistance paradigm. *Journal of Personality and Social Psychology, 58,* 909–917.

Holahan, C. K., Holahan, C. J., & Belk, S. S. (1984). Adjustment in aging: The role of life stress, hassles, and self-efficacy. *Health Psychology, 3,* 315–328.

Holding, D. H. (1976). An approximate transfer surface. *Journal of Motor Behavior, 8,* 1–9.

Holding, D.H. (Ed.). (1989) *Human skills* (2nd ed.). New York: John Wiley & Sons.

Holender, D. (1986). Semantic activation without conscious identification. *Behavioral and Brain Sciences, 9,* 1–66.

Hollander, E. P. (1985). Leadership and power. In G. Lindzey & E. Aronson (Eds.), *The handbook of social psychology: Vol. 2.* (3rd ed.). New York: Random House.

Holmes, D. S. (1984). Meditation and somatic arousal reduction: A review of the experimental evidence. *American Psychologist, 39,* 1–10.

Holmes, T. H., & Masuda, M. (1974). Life change and illness susceptibility. In B. S. Dohrenwend and B. P. Dohrenwend (Eds.), *Stressful life events: Their nature and effects.* New York: John Wiley & Sons.

Holway, A. H., & Boring, E. G. (1941). Determinants of apparent visual size with distance variant. *American Journal of Psychology, 54,* 21–37.

Horn, J. L. (1979). The rise and fall of human abilities. *Journal of Research and Development in Education, 12,* 59-78.

Horney, K. (1937). *Neurotic personality of our times.* New York: W. W. Norton.

Horner, M. S. (1970). Femininity and successful achievement: A basic inconsistency. In J. M. Bardwicks (Ed.), *Feminine personality and conflict.* Monterey, CA: Brooks/Cole.

Horowitz, A. V., & Horowitz, V. A. (1975). *The effects of task-specific instructions on the picture memory of children in recall and recognition tasks.* Paper presented at the Society for Research in Child Development, Denver, CO.

Horowitz, L. M., Rosenberg, S. E., Baer, B. A., Ureno, G., & Villasenor, V. S. (1988). The inventory of interpersonal problems: Psychometric properties and clinical applications. *Journal of Consulting and Clinical Psychology, 56,* 885–892.

Hosch, H. M., & Cooper, D. S. (1982). Victimization as a determinant of eyewitness accuracy. *Journal of Applied Psychology, 67,* 649–652.

House, J. S., Landis, K. R., & Umberson, D. (1988). Social relationships and health. *Science, 241,* 540–545.

House, J. S., Robbins, C., & Metzner, H. L. (1982). The association of social relationships and activities with mortality: Prospective evidence from the Tecumseh community health study. *American Journal of Epidemiology, 116,* 123–140.

House, J. S., Umberson, D., & Landis, K. R. (1988). Structures and processes of social support. *Annual Review of Sociology, 14,* 293–318.

Houston, B. K., & Snyder, C. R. (Eds.). (1987). *Type A behavior pattern: Current trends and future directions.* New York: Wiley.

Howard, D. V. (1983). *Cognitive psychology.* New York: Macmillan.

Howe, M. J. A. (1970). Using students' notes to examine the role of the individual learner in acquiring meaningful subject matter. *Journal of Educational Research, 64,* 61–63.

Hoyer, W. J., & Plude, D. J. (1980). Attentional and perceptual processes in the study of cognitive aging. In L. W. Poon (Ed.), *Aging in the 1980s: Psychological issues.* Washington, DC: American Psychological Association.

Hsu, L. K. G. (1980). Outcome of anorexia nervosa: A review of the literature (1954 to 1978). *Archives of General Psychiatry, 37,* 1041–1046.

Hubel, D. H., & Wiesel, T. N. (1979). Brain mechanisms of vision. *Scientific American, 241,* 150–162.

Hudspeth, A. J. (1983). The hair cells of the inner ear. *Scientific American, 248,* 54–64.

Huesmann, L. R., Laperspetz, K., & Eron, L. D. (1984). Intervening variables in the TV violence-aggression relation: Evidence from two countries. *Developmental Psychology, 20,* 746–775.

Hugdahl, K., & Johnsen, B. H. (1989). Preparedness and electrodermal fear-conditioning: Ontogenetic vs. phylogenetic explanations. *Behaviour Research and Therapy, 27,* 269–278.

Hull, C. L. (1943). *Principles of behavior.* New York: Appleton-Century-Crofts.

Hull, C. L. (1951). *Essentials of behavior.* New Haven: Yale University Press.

Humphreys, L. G. (1984). General intelligence. In C. R. Reynolds & R. T. Brown (Eds.), *Perspectives on bias in mental testing.* New York: Plenum Press.

Humphreys, L. G. (1988). Trends in levels of academic achievement of blacks and other minorities. *Intelligence, 12,* 231–260.

Humphreys, L. G., & Davey, T. C. (1988). Continuity in intellectual growth from 12 months to 9 years. *Intelligence, 12,* 183–197.

Humphreys, M. S., Bain, J. D., & Pike, R. (1989). Different ways to cue a coherent memory system: A theory for episodic, semantic, and procedural tasks. *Psychological Review, 96,* 208–233.

Hunt, E. (1987). The next word on verbal ability. In P. A. Vernon (Ed.), *Speed of information-processing and intelligence* (pp. 347–392). Norwood, NJ: Ablex.

Hunt, E. (1983). On the nature of intelligence. *Science, 219,* 141–146.

Hunt, C. B. (1980). Intelligence as an information processing concept. *British Journal of Psychology, 71,* 449–474.

Hunt, E., & Lansman, M. (1983). Individual differences in intelligence. In R. Sternberg (Ed.), *Advances in the psychology of human intelligence.* Hillsdale, NJ: Lawrence Erlbaum Associates.

Hunt, M. (1982). *The universe within.* New York: Simon & Schuster.

Hunt, R., & Rouse, W. B. (1981). Problem solving skills of maintenance trainees in diagnosing faults in simulated power plants. *Human Factors, 23,* 317–328.

Hunter, E. J. (1979). *Combat casualties who remain at home.* Paper presented at Western Regional Conference of the Inter University Seminar, "Technology in Combat." Naval Postgraduate School, Monterey, CA.

Hunter, F. T., & Youniss, J. (1982). Changes in functions of three relations during adolescence. *Developmental Psychology, 18,* 806–811.

Hunter, J. E. (1986). Cognitive ability, cognitive aptitudes, job knowledge, and job performance. *Journal of Vocational Behavior, 29,* 340–362.

Hunter, J. E., & Hunter, R. F. (1984). Validity and utility of alternative predictors of job performance. *Psychological Bulletin, 96,* 72–98.

Hunter, M. A., & Ames, E. W. (1988). A multifactor model of infants' preferences for novel and familiar stimuli. In C. Rovee-Collier & L. P. Lipsitt (Eds.), *Advances in infancy research: Vol. 5* (pp. 69–91). Norwood, NJ: Ablex.

Hurst, R., & Hurst, L. (1982). *Pilot error.* London: Granada.

Huston, A. C. (1983). Sex-typing. In P. H. Mussen (Ed.), *Handbook of child psychology: Vol. 4* (4th ed.). New York: Wiley.

Huston, A. C., & Wright, J. C. (1989). The forms of television and the child viewer. In G. Comstock (Ed.), *Public communication and behavior* (Vol. 2). San Diego: Academic Press.

Huttenlocher, J. (1974). The origins of language comprehension. In R. L. Solso (Ed.), *Theories in cognitive psychology.* Hillsdale, NJ: Lawrence Erlbaum Associates.

Huttenlocher, P. R. (1979). Synaptic density in human frontal cortex: Developmental changes and effects of aging. *Brain Research, 163,* 195–205.

Hyde, J. S., & Phillis, D. E. (1979). Androgyny across the life span. *Developmental Psychology, 15,* 334–336.

Hyde, J. S., Fennema, E., & Lamon, S. J. (1990). Gender differences in mathematics performance: A meta-analysis. *Psychological Bulletin, 107,* 139–155.

Hyman, H., & Barmack, J. E. (1954). Special review: Sexual behavior in the human female. *Psychological Bulletin, 51,* 418–427.

Hyman, M. D. (1971). Disability and patients' perceptions of preferential treatment: Some preliminary findings. *Journal of Chronic Diseases, 24,* 329–342.

Ilgen, D. R., & Klein, H. J. (1989). Organizational behavior. *Annual Review of Psychology, 40,* 327–351.

Insko, C. A., Drenan, S., Solomon, M. R., Smith, R., & Wade, T. J. (1983). Conformity as a function of the consistency of positive self-evaluation with being liked and being right. *Journal of Experimental Social Psychology, 19,* 341–358.

Insko, C. A., Smith, R. H., Alicke, M. D., Wade, J., & Taylor, S. (1985). Conformity and group size: The concern with being right and the concern with being liked. *Personality and Social Psychology Bulletin, 11,* 41–50.

Isabella, R. A., Belsky, J., & von Eye, A. (1989). Origins of infant-mother attachment: An examination of interactional synchrony during the infant's first year. *Developmental Psychology, 25,* 12–21.

Isenberg, D. J. (1986). Group polarization: A critical review and meta-analysis. *Journal of Personality and Social Psychology, 50,* 1141–1151.

Istomina, Z. M. (1975). The development of voluntary memory in pre-school age children. *Soviet Psychology, 13,* 5–64.

Ivancevich, J. M., Matteson, M. T., Freedman, S. M., & Phillips, J. S. (1990). Worksite stress management interventions. *American Psychologist, 45,* 252–261.

Izard, C. E. (1971). *The face of emotion.* New York: Appleton-Century-Crofts, New York.

Izard, C. E. (1977). *Human emotions.* New York: Plenum Press.

Izard, C. E. (1990). Facial expressions and the regulation of emotions. *Journal of Personality and Social Psychology, 58,* 487–498.

Jacklin, C. N. (1989). Female and male: Issues of gender. *American Psychologist, 44,* 127–133.

Jackson, D. N. (1967). *Personality Research Form manual.* Goshen, NY: Research Psychologists Press.

Jackson, J. M., Buglione, S. A., & Glenwick, D. S. (1988). Major league baseball performance as a function of being traded: A drive theory analysis. *Personality and Social Psychology Bulletin, 14,* 46–56.

Jacobs, B. L. (1987). How hallucinogenic drugs work. *American Scientist, 75,* 386–392.

Jacobs, M. K., & Goodman, G. (1989). Psychology and self-help groups: Predictions on a partnership. *American Psychologist, 44,* 536–545.

Jacobson, A., Kales, J., & Kales, A. (1969). Clinical and electrophysiological correlates of sleep disorders in children. In A. Kales (Ed.), *Sleep: Physiology and pathology.* Philadelphia: J. B. Lippincott.

Jacobson, E. (1938). *Progressive relaxation.* Chicago: University of Chicago Press.

Jacoby, T., & Padgett, T. (1989, August 7). Waking up the jury box. *Newsweek,* p. 51.

Jaffe, J. H. (1975). Drug addiction and drug abuse. In L. S. Goodman & A. Gilman (Eds.), *The pharmacological basis of therapeutics* (5th ed.). New York: Macmillan.

James, W. (1890). *Principles of psychology.* New York: Holt.

James, W. (1892). *Psychology: Briefer course.* New York: Holt.

Jamison, K. R. (1984). Manic-depressive illness and accomplishment: Creativity, leadership, and social class. In F. K. Goodwin & K. R. Jamison (Eds.), *Manic-depressive illness.* New York: Oxford University Press.

Janicak, P. C., Davis, J. M., Gibbons, R. D., Ericksen, S., Chang, S., & Gallagher, P. (1985). Efficacy of ECT: A meta-analysis. *American Journal of Psychiatry, 142,* 297–302.

Janis, I. L. (1985). Sources of error in strategic decision making. In J. M. Pennings (Ed.), *Organizational strategy and change.* San Francisco: Jossey-Bass.

Jann, M. W. (1988). Buspirone: An update on a unique anxiolytic agent. *Pharmacotherapy, 8,* 100–116.

Janowitz, H. D. (1967). Role of gastrointestinal tract in the regulation of food intake. In C. F. Code (Ed.), *Handbook of physiology: Alimentary canal 1.* Washington, DC: American Physiological Society.

Janowitz, H. D., & Grossman, M. I. (1949). Some factors affecting the food intake of normal dogs and dogs with esophagostomy and gastric fistula. *American Journal of Physiology, 159,* 143–148.

Janowitz, H. D., & Grossman, M. I. (1951). Effect of prefeeding, alcohol and bitters on food intake of dogs. *American Journal of Physiology, 164,* 182–186.

Jellinek, E. M. (1960). *The disease concept of alcoholism.* New Haven: Hillhouse Press.

Jellison, J. M., & Oliver, D. F. (1983). Attitude similarity and attraction: An impression management approach. *Personality and Social Psychology Bulletin, 9,* 111–115.

Jemmott, J. B., III, & Magloire, K. (1988). Academic stress, social support, and secretory immunoglobulin A. *Journal of Personality and Social Psychology, 55,* 803–810.

Jemmott, J. B., & Locke, S. E. (1984). Psychosocial factors, immunologic mediation, and human susceptibility to infectious diseases: How much do we know? *Psychological Bulletin, 95,* 78–108.

Jenkins, J. G., & Dallenbach, K. M. (1924). Oblivescence during sleep and waking. *American Journal of Psychology, 35,* 605–612.

Jensen, A. R. (1969). How much can we boost IQ and scholastic achievement? *Harvard Educational Review, 39,* 1–123.

Jensen, J. P., Bergin, A. E., & Greaves, D. W. (1990). The meaning of eclecticism: New survey and analysis of components. *Professional Psychology: Research and Practice, 21,* 124–130.

Jensen, M. R. (1987). Psychological factors predicting the course of breast cancer. *Journal of Personality, 55,* 317–342.

Jeremy, R. J., & Hans, S. L. (1985) . Behavior of neonates exposed in utero to methadone as assessed on the Brazelton Scale. *Infant Behavior and Development, 8,* 323–336.

Jessop, J. J., West, G. L., & Sobotka, T. J. (1989). Immunomodulatory effects of footshock in the rat. *Journal of Immunology, 25,* 241–249.

Johansson, G., Hofsten, C. V., & Jansson, G. (1980). Event perception. *Annual Review of Psychology, 31,* 27–63.

Johnson, B. T., & Eagly, A. H. (1989). Effects of involvement on persuasion: A meta-analysis. *Psychological Bulletin, 106,* 290–314.

Johnson, D. L. (1989). Schizophrenia as a brain disease. *American Psychologist, 44,* 553–555.

Johnson, J. S., & Newport, E. L. (1989). Critical period effects in second language learning. *Cognitive Psychology, 21,* 60–99.

Johnson, M. K., & Hasher, L. (1987). Human learning and memory. *Annual Review of Psychology, 38,* 631–668.

Johnson-Laird, P. N. (1983). *Mental models.* Cambridge: Harvard University Press.

Johnson-Laird, P. N., & Steedman, M. (1978). The psychology of syllogisms, *Cognitive Psychology, 10,* 64–99.

Johnston, L. D., O'Malley, P. M., & Bachman, J. G. (1987). *National trends in drug use and related factors among American high school students and young adults, 1975–1986.* Rockville, MD: National Institute on Drug Abuse.

Johnston, L. D., O'Malley, P. M., & Bachman, J. G. (1989). *Drug use, drinking, and smoking: National survey results from high school, college, and young adult populations, 1975–1988.* Rockville, MD: National Institute on Drug Abuse.

Jones, D. M. (1989). Culture and testing. *American Psychologist, 44,* 360–366.

Jones, G. V. (1989). Back to Woodworth: Role of interlopers in the tip-of-the-tongue phenomenon. *Memory and Cognition, 17,* 69–76.

Jones, J. W. (1978). Adverse emotional reactions of nonsmokers to secondary cigarette smoke. *Environmental Psychology and Nonverbal Behavior, 3,* 125–127.

Jones, L. V., & Appelbaum, M. I. (1989). Psychometric methods, *Annual Review of Psychology, 40,* 23–44.

Jones, M. C. (1957). The later careers of boys who were early or late maturing. *Child Development, 28,* 113–128.

Jones, R. T. (1984). The pharmacology of cocaine. In J. Grabowski (Ed.), *Cocaine: Pharmacology, effects, and treatment of abuse.* Rockville, MD: National Institute on Drug Abuse.

Jordan, H. A. (1969). Voluntary intragastric feeding: Oral and gastric contributions to food intake and hunger in man. *Journal of Comparative and Physiological Psychology, 68,* 498–506.

Jordan, T. G., Grallo, R., Deutch, M., & Deutch, C. P. (1985). Long-term effects of enrichment: A 20-year perspective on persistence and change. *American Journal of Community Psychology, 13,* 393–414.

Josephson, W. L. (1987). Television violence and children's aggression: Testing the priming, social script, and disinhibition predictions. *Journal of Personality and Social Psychology, 53,* 882–890.

Julien, R. M. (1988). *A primer of drug action* (5th ed.). San Francisco: W. H. Freeman.

Jung, C. G. (1916). *Analytical psychology.* New York: Moffat.

Jung, C. G. (1933). *Psychological types.* New York: Harcourt, Brace and World.

Jussim, L. (1989). Teacher expectations: Self-fulfilling prophecies, perceptual biases, and accuracy. *Journal of Personality and Social Psychology, 57,* 469–480.

Justice, A. (1985). Review of the effects of stress on cancer in laboratory animals: Importance of time of stress application and type of tumor. *Psychological Bulletin, 98,* 108–138.

Kadden, R. M., Cooney, N. L., Getter, H., & Litt, M. D. (1990). Matching alcoholics to coping skills or interactional therapies: Posttreatment results. *Journal of Consulting and Clinical Psychology, 57,* 698–704.

Kagan, J. (1984). *The nature of the child.* New York: Basic Books.

Kagan, J. (1988). The meanings of personality predicates. *American Psychologist, 43,* 614–620.

Kagan, J. (1989). Temperamental contributions to social behavior. *American Psychologist, 44,* 668–674.

Kagan, J., Kearsley, R. B., & Zelazo, P. R. (1978). *Infancy: Its place in human development.* Cambridge: Harvard University Press.

Kagan, J., Reznick, J. S., & Snidman, N. (1988). Biological bases of childhood shyness. *Science, 240,* 167–171.

Kagan, J., Reznick, J. S., Snidman, N., Gibbons, J., & Johnson, M. O. (1988). Childhood derivatives of inhibition and lack of inhibition to the unfamiliar. *Child Development, 59,* 1580–1589.

Kagitcibasi, C., & Berry, J. W. (1989). Cross-cultural psychology: Current research and trends. *Annual Review of Psychology, 40,* 493–531.

Kahn, A. S. (1984). *Social psychology.* Dubuque, IA: William C. Brown.

Kahneman, D., & Tversky, A. (1984). Choices values and frames. *American Psychologist, 39,* 341–356.

Kahneman, D., Beatty, J., & Pollack, I. (1967). Perceptual deficits during a mental task. *Science, 157,* 218–219.

Kahneman, D., Slovic, P., & Tversky, A. (Eds.). (1982). *Judgment under uncertainty: Heuristics and biases.* New York: Cambridge University Press.

Kalick, S. M. (1988). Physical attractiveness as a status cue. *Journal of Experimental Social Psychology, 24,* 469–489.

Kalish, H. I. (1981). *From behavioral science to behavior modification.* New York: McGraw-Hill.

Kamin, L. J. (1969). Predictability, surprise, attention and conditioning. In B. A. Campbell & R. M. Church (Eds.), *Punishment and aversive behavior.* New York: Appleton-Century-Crofts.

Kamin, L. J. (1986). Is there crime in the genes? The answer may depend on who chooses what evidence. *Scientific American, 254,* 22–27.

Kandel, D. B., Davies, M., Karus, D., & Yamaguchi, K. (1986). The consequences in young adulthood of adolescent drug involvement: An overview. *Archives of General Psychiatry, 43,* 746–754.

Kandel, E. (1976). *Cellular basis of behavior.* San Francisco: Freeman.

Kanner, A. D., Coyne, J. C., Schaefer, C., & Lazarus, R. S. (1981). Comparison of two modes of stress measurement: Daily hassles and uplifts versus major life events. *Journal of Behavioral Medicine, 4,* 1–39.

Kaplan, H. S. (1974). *The new sex therapy.* New York: Brunner/Mazel.

Kaplan, M. F. (1987). The influencing process in group decision making. In C. Hendrick (Ed.), *Group processes.* Newbury Park, CA: Sage.

Kaplan, M. F., & Miller, C. E. (1987). Group decision making and normative vs. informational influence: Effects of type of issue and assigned decision rule. *Journal of Personality and Social Psychology, 53,* 306–313.

Kaplan, R. M., & Hartwell, S. L. (1987). Differential effects of social support and social network on physiological and social outcomes in men and women with Type II diabetes mellitus. *Health Psychology, 6,* 387–398.

Karasek, R., & Theorell, T. (1990). *Healthy work: Job stress, productivity, and the reconstruction of working life.* New York: Basic Books.

Karlins, M., Coffman, T. L., & Walter, G. (1969). On the fading of social stereotypes: Studies in three generations of college students. *Journal of Personality and Social Psychology, 13,* 1–16.

Kastenbaum, R. (1965). Wine and fellowship in aging: An exploratory action program. *Journal of Human Relations, 13,* 266–275.

Kastenbaum, R., Kastenbaum, B. K., & Morris, J. (1989). Strengths and preferences of the terminally ill: Data from the National Hospice Demonstration Study.

Kato, S., Wakasa, Y., & Yanagita, T. (1987). Relationship between minimum reinforcing doses and injection speed in cocaine and pentobarbital self-administration in crab-eating monkeys. *Pharmacology, Biochemistry, & Behavior, 28,* 407–410.

Katzell, R. A., & Thompson, D. E. (1990). Work motivation: Theory and practice. *American Psychologist, 45,* 144–153.

Kauffman, J. M., Gerber, M. M., & Semmel, M. I. (1988). Arguable assumptions underlying the regular education initiative. *Journal of Learning Disabilities, 21,* 6–11.

Kaufman, A. S., & Kaufman, N. L. (1983). *Kaufman assessment battery for children.* Circle Pines, MN: American Guidance Services.

Kaufman, L., & Rock, I. (1962). The moon illusion. *Science, 136,* 953–961.

Kaufman, R., Maland, J., & Yonas, A. (1981). Sensitivity of 5- and 7-month-old infants to pictorial depth information. *Journal of Experimental Child Psychology, 32,* 162–168.

Kavanaugh, R. D., & Jirkovsky, A. M. (1982). Parental speech to young children: A longitudinal analysis. *Merrill-Palmer Quarterly, 28,* 297–311.

Kazdin, A. E. (1978). Evaluating the generality of findings in analogue therapy research. *Journal of Consulting and Clinical Psychology, 46,* 673–686.

Kazdin, A. E. (1984). *Behavior modification in applied settings* (3rd ed.). Homewood, IL: Dorsey Press.

Kazdin, A. E., & Bootzin, R. R. (1972). The token economy: An evaluative review. *Journal of Applied Behavior Analysis, 5,* 343–372.

Kazdin, A. E., & Wilson, G. T. (1978). *Evaluation of behavior therapy: Issues, evidence, and research strategies.* Cambridge: Ballinger.

Keane, T. M., Lisman, S. A., & Kreutzer, J. (1980). Alcoholic beverages and their placebos: An empirical evaluation of expectancies. *Addictive Behavior, 4,* 313–328.

Keele, S. W. (1973). *Attention and human performance.* Pacific Palisades, CA: Goodyear.

Keeney, T. J., Cannizzo, S. R., & Flavell, J. H. (1967). Spontaneous and induced verbal rehearsal in a recall task. *Child Development, 38,* 953–966.

Keesey, R. E. (1980). A set-point analysis of the regulation of body weight. In A. J. Stunkard (Ed.), *Obesity.* Philadelphia: W. B. Saunders.

Keesey, R. E., & Powley, T. L. (1975). Hypothalamic regulation of body weight. *American Scientist, 63,* 558–565.

Keesey, R. E., & Powley, T. L. (1986). The regulation of body weight. *Annual Review of Psychology, 37,* 109–133.

Keinan, G., Friedland, N., & Ben-Porath, Y. (1987). Decision making under stress: Scanning of alternatives under physical threat. *Acta Psychologica, 64,* 219–228.

Keller, A., Ford, L. H., & Meacham, J. A. (1978). Dimensions of self-concept in preschool children. *Developmental Psychology, 14,* 483–489.

Kelley, H. H. (1973). The processes of causal attribution. *American Psychologist, 28,* 107–128.

Kelley, J. A., St. Lawrence, J. S., Hood, H. V., & Brasfield, T. L. (1989). Behavioral intervention to reduce AIDS risk activities. *Journal of Consulting and Clinical Psychology, 57,* 60–67.

Kelley, K., Dawson, L., & Musialowski, D. M. (1989). Three faces of sexual explicitness: The good, the bad, and the useful. In D. Zillmann & J. Bryant (Eds.), *Pornography: Research advances and policy considerations.* Hillsdale, NJ: Sage.

Kelley, K. W. (1985). Immunological consequences of changing environmental stimuli. In G. P. Moberg (Ed.), *Animal stress.* Bethesda, MD: American Physiological Society.

Kellogg, R. T. (1988). Attentional overload and writing performance: Effects of rough draft and outline strategies. *Journal of Experimental Psychology: Learning, Memory, and Cognition, 14,* 355–365.

Kelly, D. H., & Burbeck, C. A. (1984). Critical problems in spatial vision (review). *Critical Reviews in Biomedical Engineering, 10, 2,* 125–177.

Kelly, G. A. (1955). *The psychology of personal contructs.* New York: W. W. Norton.

Kelly, J. A., & St. Lawrence, J. S. (1988). AIDS prevention and treatment: Psychology's role in the health crisis. *Clinical Psychology Review, 8,* 255–284.

Kempe, H. C., & Helfer, R. E. (Eds.) (1972). *Helping the battered child and his family.* Philadelphia: Lippincott.

Kendler, K. S., Heath, A., Martin, M. G., & Eaves, L. J. (1986). Symptoms of anxiety and depression in a volunteer twin population: The etiologic role of genetic and environmental factors. *Archives of General Psychiatry 43,* 213–221.

Kennedy, J. L., Giuffra, L. A., Moises, H. W., Cavalli-Sforza, L. L., Pakstis, A. J., Kidd, J. R., Castiglione, C. M., Sjogren, B., Wetterm-berg, L., & Kidd, K. K. (1988). Evidence against linkage of schiz-ophrenia to markers on chromosome 5 in northern Swedish pedigree. *Nature, 336,* 167–170.

Kenrick, D. T. (1989). Selflessness examined: Is avoiding tar and feathers nonegoistic? *Behavioral and Brain Sciences, 12,* 711–712.

Kenrick, D. T., & Funder, D. C. (1988). Profiting from controversy: Lessons from the person-situation debate. *American Psychologist, 43,* 23–34.

Kernberg, O. (1976). *Object relations theory and clinical psychoanalysis.* New York: Jason Aronsen.

Kernis, M. H., Brockner, J., & Frankel, B. J. (1989). Self-esteem and reactions to failure: The mediating role of overgeneralization. *Journal of Personality and Social Psychology, 57,* 707–714.

Kessler, M., & Albee, G. W. (1975). Primary prevention. *Annual Review of Psychology, 26,* 557–591.

Kessler, R. C., Downey, G., Milavsky, J. R., & Stipp, H. (1988). Clustering of teenage suicides after television news stories about suicides: A reconsideration. *American Journal of Psychiatry, 145,* 1379–1383.

Kety, S. S., Rosenthal, D., Wender, P. H., Schulsinger, F., & Jacobson, B. (1975). Mental illness in the biological and adoptive families of adopted individuals who have become schizophrenic: A prelim-inary report based on psychiatric interviews. In R. R. Fieve, D. Rosenthal, & H. Brill (Eds.), *Genetic research in psychiatry.* Balti-more: Johns Hopkins University Press.

Keys, A., Brozek, J., Henschel, A., Mickelson, O., & Taylor, H. (1950). *The biology of human starvation.* Minneapolis: University of Min-nesota Press.

Kiecolt-Glaser, J. K., & Glaser, R. (1987). Psychosocial moderators of immune function. *Annals of Behavioral Medicine, 9,* 16–20.

Kiecolt-Glaser, J. K., Garner, W., Speicher, C. E., Penn, G. M., Holliday, J., & Glaser, R. (1984). Psychosocial modifiers of im-munocompetence in medical students. *Psychosomatic Medicine, 46,* 7–14.

Kiesler, C. A. (1982). Mental hospitals and alternative care: Nonin-stitutionalization as potential public policy for mental patients. *American Psychologist, 37,* 349–360.

Kiesler, C. A., & Sibulkin, A. E. (1989). *Mental hospitalization: Myths and facts about a national crisis.* Newbury Park, CA: Sage.

Kiesler, D. J. (1986). The 1982 interpersonal circle: An analysis of DSM-III personality disorders. In T. Millon & G. L. Klerman (Eds.), *Contemporary directions in psychopathology: Towards the DSM-IV.* New York: Guilford.

Kihlstrom, J. F. (1987). The cognitive unconscious. *Science, 237,* 1445–1452.

Kihlstrom, J. F., Cantor, N., Albright, J. S., Chew, B. R., Klein, S. B., & Niedenthal, P. M. (1988). Information processing and the study of the self. In L. Berkowitz (Ed.), *Advances in experimental social psychology* (Vol. 19). New York: Academic Press.

Kinney, H. C., & Filiano, J. J. (1988). Brainstem research in sudden infant death syndrome. *Pediatrician, 15,* 240–250.

Kinsey, A. C., Pomeroy, W. R., & Martin, C. E. (1948). *Sexual behavior in the human male.* Philadelphia: W. B. Saunders.

Kinsey, A. C., Pomeroy, W. R., Martin, C. E., & Gebhard, P. H. (1953). *Sexual behavior in the human female.* Philadelphia: W. B. Saunders.

Kintsch, W., & Bates, E. (1977). Recognition memory for statements from a classroom lecture. *Journal of Experimental Psychology: Human Learning and Memory, 3,* 150–159.

Kirigin, K. A., Braukmann, C. J., Atwater, J. D., & Wolf, M. M. (1982). An evaluation of teaching-family (Achievement Place) group

homes for juvenile offenders. *Journal of Applied Behavior Analysis, 15,* 1–16.

Kirmeyer, S. L., & Biggers, K. (1988). Environmental demand and demand engendering behavior: An observational analysis of the type A pattern. *Journal of Personality and Social Psychology, 54,* 997–1005.

Kitcher, P. (1985). *Vaulting ambition: Sociobiology and the quest for human nature.* Cambridge: MIT Press.

Klagsbrun, F. (1976). *Too young to die: Youth and suicide.* Boston: Houghton Mifflin.

Klatzky, R. L. (1980). *Human memory: Structures and processes* (2nd ed.). San Francisco: W. H. Freeman.

Klein, D. C., & Seligman, M. E. P. (1976). Reversal of performance deficits and perceptual deficits in learned helplessness and de-pression. *Journal of Abnormal Psychology, 85,* 11–26.

Klein, G.A. (1990). Recognition-primed decisions. In W. R. Rouse (Ed.), *Advances in man machine systems research.* Greenwich, CT: JAI Press.

Klein, M. (1960). *The psychoanalysis of children.* New York: Grove Press.

Klein, M. (1975). *The writings of Melanie Klein: Vol. 3.* London: Hogarth Press.

Klein, S. B., Loftus, J., & Burton, H. A. (1989). Two self-reference effects: The importance of distinguishing between self-descrip-tiveness judgments and autobiographical retrieval in self-referent coding. *Journal of Personality and Social Psychology, 56,* 853–865.

Klerman, G. L. (1982). *Practical issues in the treatment of depression and mania.* In E. S. Paykel (Ed.), Handbook of affective disorders. New York: Guilford Press.

Klerman, G. L. (1983). The efficacy of psychotherapy as a basis for public policy. *American Psychologist, 38,* 929–934.

Kline, D. W., & Szafran, J. (1975). Age differences in backward monoptic masking. *Journal of Gerontology, 30,* 307–311.

Klosko, J. S., Barlow, D. H., Tassinari, R., & Cerny, J. A. (1990). A comparison of alprazolam and behavior therapy in treatment of panic disorder. *Journal of Consulting and Clinical Psychology, 58,* 77–84.

Kluft, R. P. (1987). An update on multiple personality disorder. *Hospital and Community Psychiatry, 38,* 363–373.

Knauft, B. M. (1989). Sociality versus self-interest in human evolu-tion. *Behavioral and Brain Sciences, 12,* 712–713.

Knittle, J.L., Tinners, K., Ginsberg-Fellner, F., Brown, R. E., & Katz, D. P. (1979). The growth of adipose tissue in children and adolescents. *Journal of Clinical Investigation, 63,* 239–241.

Knoll, J., Dallo, J., & Yen, T. T. (1989). Striatal dopamine, sexual activity and lifespan. Longevity of rats treated with (-)deprenyl. *Life Sciences, 45,* 525–531.

Knox, R. E., & Safford, R. K. (1976). Group caution at the racetrack. *Journal of Experimental Social Psychology, 12,* 317–324.

Kobasa, S. C. (1979). Stressful life events, personality, and health: An inquiry into hardiness. *Journal of Personality and Social Psy-chology, 37,* 1–11.

Kobasa, S. C. (1982). The hardy personality: Toward a social psy-chology of stress and health. In G. S. Sanders & J. Suls (Eds.), *Social Psychology of Health and Illness.* Hillsdale, NJ: Lawrence Erlbaum Associates.

Kobasa, S. C., Maddi, S. R., & Kahn, S. (1982). Hardiness and health: a prospective study. *Journal of Personality and Social Psychology, 42,* 168–177.

Kobasa, S. C., Maddi, S. R., & Zola, M. A. (1983). Type A and hardiness. *Journal of Behavioral Medicine, 6,* 41–51.

Kochanek, T. (1986). Background factors in child abuse and neglect. *The Brown University Child Behavior and Development Letter, 2,* 12, 1–3.

Koeske, R. D. (1987). Premenstrual emotionality: Is biology destiny?

In M. R. Walsh (Ed.), *The psychology of women*. New Haven: Yale University Press.

Koestner, R., Zuckerman, M., & Koestner, J. (1989). Attributional focus of praise and children's intrinsic motivation: The moderating role of gender. *Personality and Social Psychology Bulletin, 15,* 61–72.

Kofta, M., & Sedek, G. (1989). Repeated failure: A source of helplessness or a factor irrelevant to its emergence? *Journal of Experimental Psychology: General, 118,* 3–12.

Kohlberg, L. (1966). A cognitive-developmental analysis of children's sex role concepts and attitudes. In E. E. Maccoby (Ed.), *The development of sex differences*. Stanford, CA: Stanford University Press.

Kohlberg, L., & Gilligan, C. (1971). The adolescent as a philosopher: The discovery of the self in a postconventional world. *Daedalus, 100,* 1051–1086.

Kohn, M. L. (1977). *Class and conformity: A study in values* (2nd ed.). Chicago: University of Chicago Press.

Kohut, H. (1983). Selected problems of self-psychological theory. In J. D. Lichtenberg & S. Kaplan (Eds.), *Reflections on self psychology* (pp. 387–416). Hillsdale, NJ: Lawrence Erlbaum Associates.

Kohut, H. (1984). Selected problems of self-psychological theory. In J. D. Lichtenberg & S. Kaplan (Eds.), *Reflections on self psychology* (pp. 387–416). Hillsdale, NJ: Lawrence Erlbaum Associates.

Kolata, G. (1985). Why do people get fat? *Science, 227,* 1327–1328.

Komorita, S. S. (1984). Coalition bargaining. In L. Berkowitz (Ed.), *Advances in experimental social psychology: Vol. 18.* New York: Academic Press.

Komorita, S. S., Sweeney, J., & Kravitz, D. A. (1980). Cooperative choice in the N-person dilemma situation. *Journal of Personality and Social Psychology, 38,* 504–516.

Koob, G. F., & Bloom, F. E. (1988). Cellular and molecular mechanisms of drug dependence. *Science, 242,* 715–723.

Korchin, S. J. (1976). *Modern clinical psychology: Principles of intervention in the clinic and community*. New York: Basic Books.

Korner, A. F. (1971). Individual differences at birth: Implications for early experience and later development. *American Journal of Orthopsychiatry, 41(4).*

Kosslyn, S. (1976). Can imagery be distinguished from other forms of internal representation? Evidence from studies of information retrieval times. *Memory and Cognition, 4,* 291–297.

Kosslyn, S. (1983). *Ghosts in the mind's machine*. New York: Norton.

Kosslyn, S. M. (1988). Aspects of a cognitive neuroscience of mental imagery. *Science, 240,* 1621–1626.

Kozel, N. J., Grider, R. A., & Adams, E. H. (1982). National surveillance of cocaine use and related health consequences. *Morbidity and Mortality Weekly Report, 20,* 265–273.

Kraft, C. (1978). A psychophysical approach to air safety: Simulator studies of visual illusions in night approaches. In H. L. Pick, H. W. Leibowitz, J. E. Singer, A. Steinschneider, & H. W. Stevenson (Eds.), *Psychology: From research to practice*. New York: Plenum Press.

Kramer, R. M. (1989). Windows of vulnerability or cognitive illusions? Cognitive processes and the nuclear arms race. *Journal of Experimental Social Psychology, 25,* 79–100.

Kravitz, D. A., & Martin, B. (1986). Ringelmann rediscovered: The original article. *Journal of Personality and Social Psychology, 50,* 936–941.

Krebs, D. L., & Miller, D. T. (1985). Altruism and aggression. In G. Lindzey & E. Aronson (Eds.), *Handbook of social psychology*, Vol. 2 (3rd ed.). New York: Random House.

Krebs, R. L. (1967). *Some relations between moral judgment, attention, and resistance to temptation*. Unpublished doctoral dissertation, University of Chicago, Chicago, IL.

Krech, D. (1978). Quoted in M. C. Diamond, The aging brain: Some enlightening and optimistic results. *American Scientist, 66,* 66–71.

Kriger, S. F., & Kroes, W. H. (1972). Child-rearing attitudes of Chinese, Jewish, and Protestant mothers. *Journal of Social Psychology, 86,* 205–210.

Kristeller, J. L., Schwartz, G. E., & Black, H. (1982). The use of restricted environmental stimulation therapy (REST) in the treatment of essential hypertension: Two case studies. *Behaviour Research and Therapy, 20,* 561–566.

Kroll, J. (1973). A reappraisal of psychiatry in the middle ages. *Archives of General Psychiatry, 26,* 276–283.

Krosnick, J. A., & Judd, C. M. (1982). Transitions in social influence at adolescence: Who induces cigarette smoking? *Developmental Psychology, 18,* 359–368.

Kryter, K. D. (1970). *The effects of noise on man*. New York: Academic Press.

Kuhn, D., Nash, S. C., & Brucken, L. (1978). Sex role concepts of two- and three-year-olds. *Child Development, 49,* 445–451.

Kulka, R. A., Schlenger, W. E., Fairbank, J. A., Hough, R. L., Jordan, B. K., Marmar, C. R., & Weiss, D. S. (1988). *Contractual report of findings from the national Vietnam veterans readjustment study: Vol. 1.* Research Triangle Park, NC: Research Triangle Institute.

Kunst-Wilson, W. R., & Zajonc, R. B. (1980). Affective discrimination of stimuli that cannot be recognized. *Science, 207,* 557–558.

Kunz, P. R., & Woolcott, M. (1976). Season's greetings: From my status to yours. *Social Science Research, 5,* 269–278.

Kutas, M., & Van Petten, C. (1988). Event-related brain potential studies of language. In P. K. Ackles, J. R. Jennings, & M. G. H. Coles (Eds.), *Advances in psychophysiology* (Vol. 3). Greenwich, CT: JAI Press.

Laberge, S. P., Nagel, L. E., Dement, W. C., & Zarcone, V. P. (1981). Lucid dreaming verified by volitional communication during REM sleep. *Perceptual and Motor Skills, 52,* 727–732.

Labouvie-Vief, G. (1982). Discontinuities in development from childhood. In T. M. Field, A. Huston, H. C. Quay, L. Troll, & G. E. Finley (Eds.), *Review of human development*. New York: Wiley.

Lacks, P., Bertelson, A. D., Sugerman, J., & Kunkel, J. (1983). The treatment of sleep-maintenance insomnia with stimulus-control techniques. *Behaviour Research and Therapy, 21,* 291–295.

Lagerspetz, K. M. J., & Lagerspetz, K. Y. H. (1983). Genes and aggression. In E. C. Simmel, M. E. Hahn, & J. K. Walters (Eds.), *Aggressive behavior: Genetic and neural approaches*. Hillsdale, NJ: Lawrence Erlbaum Associates.

Laird, J. D. (1984). The real role of facial response in the experience of emotion: A reply to Tourangeau and Ellsworth, and others. *Journal of Personality and Social Psychology, 29,* 909–917.

Lamal, P. A. (1989). Attending to parapsychology. *Teaching of Psychology, 16,* 28–30.

Lamb, M. E. (1976). Parent-infant interaction in 8-month-olds. *Child Psychiatry and Human Development, 7,* 56–63.

Lamb, M. E. (1977). Father-infant and mother-infant interaction in the first year of life. *Child Development, 48,* 167–181.

Lambert, M. J. (1989). The individual therapist's contribution to psychotherapy process and outcome. *Clinical Psychology Review, 9,* 469–486.

Lambert, M. J., DeJulio, S. S., & Stein, D. M. (1978). Therapist interpersonal skills: Process, outcome, methodological considerations and recommendations for future research. *Psychological Bulletin, 85,* 467–489.

Lambert, M. J., Shapiro, D. A., & Bergin, A. E. (1986). The effectiveness of psychotherapy. In S. L. Garfield & A. E. Bergin (Eds.), *Handbook of psychotherapy and behavior change* (3rd ed.). New York: Wiley.

Lambert, W. W., Solomon, R. L. C., & Watson, P. D. (1949). Reinforcement and extinction as factors in size estimation. *Journal of Experimental Psychology, 39,* 637–641.

Lamiell, J. T. (1981). Toward an idiothetic psychology of personality. *American Psychologist, 36,* 276–289.

Lamiell, J. T., & Trierweiler, S. J. (1986). Personality measurement and intuitive personality judgments from an idiothetic point of view. *Clinical Psychology Review, 6,* 471–491.

Landers, S. (1989a, March). Colleges urged not to disclose average scores. *APA Monitor,* p. 12.

Landers, S. (1989b, April). NY: Scholarship awards are ruled discriminatory. *APA Monitor,* p. 14.

Landfield, P. W., Baskin, R. K., & Pitler, T. A. (1981). Brain aging correlates: retardation by hormonal-pharmacological treatments. *Science, 214,* 581–584.

Landman, J. T., & Dawes, R. M. (1982). Psychotherapy outcome: Smith and Glass' conclusions stand up under scrutiny. *American Psychologist, 36,* 937–952.

Lang, P. J., & Melamed, B. G. (1969). Avoidance conditioning therapy of an infant with chronic ruminative vomiting. *Journal of Abnormal Psychology, 74,* 1–8.

Langer, E. (1978). Rethinking the role of thought in social interaction. In J. H. Harvey, W. J. Ickes, & R. F. Kidd (Eds.), *New directions in attribution research* (Vol. 2). Hillsdale, NJ: Lawrence Erlbaum Associates.

Langer, E. (1989). *Mindfulness.* Reading, MA: Addison-Wesley.

Langlois, J. H., & Downs, A. C. (1980). Mothers, fathers, and peers as socialization agents of sex-typed play behavior in young children. *Child Development, 51,* 1237–1247.

Lanzetta, J. T., & Englis, B. G. (1989). Expectations of cooperation and competition and their effects on observer's vicarious emotional responses. *Journal of Personality and Social Psychology, 56,* 543–554.

Larkin, J., McDermott, J., Simon, D., & Simon, H. (1981). Expert and novice performance in solving physics problems. *Science, 208,* 1335–1342.

Larsen, K. S. (1976). Aggression: Myths and models. Chicago: Nelson-Hall.

Larson, G. E., & Saccuzzo, D. P. (1989). Cognitive correlates of general intelligence: Toward a process theory of g. *Intelligence, 13,* 5–32.

Lashley, K. S. (1929). *Brain mechanisms and intelligence.* Chicago: University of Chicago Press.

Latané, B., & Darley, J. M. (1968). Group inhibition of bystander intervention in emergencies. *Journal of Personality and Social Psychology, 10,* 215–221.

Latané, B., & Darley, J. (1970). *The unresponsive bystander: Why doesn't he help?* New York: Appleton-Century-Crofts.

Latané, B., & Rodin, J. (1969). A lady in distress: Inhibiting effects of friends and strangers on bystander intervention. *Journal of Experimental Social Psychology, 5,* 189–202.

Latimer, P. R. (1983). Antidepressants and behavior therapy in agoraphobia and obsessive-compulsive disorders: A commentary. *Journal of Behavior Therapy and Experimental Psychiatry, 14,* 25–27.

Laudenslager, M. L., Ryan, S. M., Drugan, R. C., Hyson, R. L., & Maier, S. F. (1983). Coping and immunosuppression: Inescapable but not escapable shock suppresses lymphocyte proliferation. *Science, 221,* 568–570.

Lawrence, R. (1989). *Guide to clinical preventive services.* Report of the U.S. Preventive Services Task Force. Baltimore: Williams & Wilkins.

Lawshe, C. H. (1975). A quantitative approach to content validity. *Personnel Psychology, 28,* 563–575.

Lazar, I., Darlington, R. B., Murray, H. W., & Snipper, A. S. (1982). Lasting effects of early education: A report from the consortium for longitudinal studies. *Monograph of Society for Research in Child Development, 47* (195, Serial No. 2-3).

Lazarus, A. A. (1971). *Behavior therapy and beyond.* New York: McGraw-Hill.

Lazarus, R. S. (1966). *Psychological stress and the coping process.* New York: McGraw-Hill.

Lazarus, R. S. (1985). Puzzles in the study of daily hassles. *Journal of Behavioral Medicine, 7,* 375–389.

Lazarus, R. S., & Folkman, S. (1984). *Stress, appraisal, and coping.* New York: Springer.

Lazarus, R. S., Opton, E. M., Nomikos, M. S., & Rankin, M. O. (1965). The principle of short-circuiting of threat: Further evidence. *Journal of Personality, 33,* 622–635.

Leary, M. R., Robertson, R. B., Barnes, B. D., & Miller, R. S. (1986). Self-presentations of small group leaders: Effects of role requirements and leadership orientation. *Journal of Personality and Social Psychology, 51,* 742–748.

Leary, T. (1957). *Interpersonal diagnosis of personality: A functional theory and methodology for personality evaluation.* New York: Ronald Press.

Leask, J., Haber, R. N., & Haber, R. B. (1969). Eidetic imagery in children: II. Longitudinal and experimental results. *Psychonomic Monograph Supplements, 3*(3, Whole No. 35).

Lederhouse, R. (1982). Territorial defense and lek behavior of the black swallowtail butterfly, *Papilio polyxenes. Behavioral Ecology and Sociobiology, 10,* 109–118.

LeDoux, J. E., Romanski, L., & Xagoraris, A. (1989). Indelibility of subcortical emotional memories. *Journal of Cognitive Neuroscience, 1,* 238–243.

Leeper, R. (1935). A study of a neglected portion of the field of learning: The development of sensory organization. *Journal of Genetic Psychology, 46,* 41–75.

Leff, J. P. (1976). Schizophrenia and sensitivity to the family environment. *Schizophrenia Bulletin, 2,* 566–574.

Lehman, D. R., Ellard, J. H., & Wortman, C. B. (1986). Social support for the bereaved: Recipients' and providers' perspectives on what is helpful. *Journal of Consulting and Clinical Psychology, 54,* 438–446.

Lehman, H. C. (1968). The creative production rates of present versus past generations of scientists. In B. L. Neugarten (Ed.), *Middle age and aging.* Chicago: University of Chicago Press.

Lehman, H. E. (1967). Schizophrenia: IV. Clinical features. In A. M. Freedman, H. I. Kaplan, & H. S. Kaplan (Eds.), *Comprehensive textbook of psychiatry.* Baltimore: Williams & Wilkins.

Leibowitz, H. W., & Pick, H. (1972). Cross cultural and educational aspects of the Ponzo perspective illusion. *Perception & Psychophysics, 12,* 430–432.

Leibowitz, H. W., Brislin, R., Perlmutter, L., & Hennessy, R. (1969). Ponzo perspective illusion as a manifestation of space perception. *Science, 166,* 1174–1176.

Lelwica, M., & Haviland, J. (1983, April). Ten-week-old infants' reactions to mothers' emotional expressions. Paper presented at the biennial meeting of the Society for Research in Child Development, Detroit.

LeMagnen, J. (1971). Advances in studies on the physiological control and regulation of food intake. In E. Stellar & J. M. Sprague (Eds.), *Progress in physiological psychology: Vol. 4.* New York: Academic Press.

Lenneberg, E. H. (1967). *Biological foundations of language.* New York: Wiley.

Lerner, R. M. (1984). *On the nature of human plasticity.* New York: Cambridge University Press.

Lesgold, A. M. (1984). Acquiring expertise. In J. R. Anderson & S. M. Kosslyn (Eds.), *Tutorials in learning and memory.* San Francisco: W. H. Freeman.

Lessne, G., & Venkatesan, M. (1989). Reactance theory in consumer research: The past, present, and future. *Advances in Consumer Research, 16,* 76–78.

Levenkron, J. C., Cohen, J. D., Mueller, H. S., & Fisher, E. B. (1983). Modifying the Type A coronary-prone behavior pattern. *Journal of Consulting and Clinical Psychology, 51(2),* 192–204.

Levenson, A. H. (1981). *Basic psychopharmacology.* New York: Springer.

Levenson, R. W., Ekman, P., & Friesen, W. V. (in press). Voluntary facial action generates emotion-specific autonomic nervous system activity. *Psychophysiology.*

Leventhal, H. (1970). Findings and theory in the study of fear communications. In L. Berkowitz (Ed.), *Advances in experimental social psychology: Vol. 5.* New York: Academic Press.

Leventhal, H., & Tomarken, A. J. (1986). Emotion: Today's problems. *Annual Review of Psychology, 37,* 565–610.

Leventhal, H., Watts, J. C., & Pagano, F. (1967). Effects of fear and instructions on how to cope with danger. *Journal of Personality and Social Psychology, 6,* 313–321.

Levin, D. N., Xiaoping, H., Tan, K. K., Galhotra, S., Pelizzari, C. A., Chen, G. T. Y., Beck, R. N., Chen, C. T., Cooper, M. D., Mullen, J. F., Hekmatpanah, & Spire, J. P. (Sept. 1989). The brain: Integrated three-dimensional display of MR and PET images. *Radiology, 786.*

Levine, J., Warrenburg, S., Kerns, R., Schwartz, G., Delaney, R., Fontana, A., Gradman, A., Smith, S., Scott, A., & Cascione, R. (1987). The role of denial in recovery from coronary heart disease. *Psychosomatic Medicine, 49,* 109–117.

Levine, J. D., Gordon, N. C., & Fields, H. L. (1979). Naloxone dose dependently produces analgesia and hyperalgesia in postoperative pain. *Nature, 278,* 740–741.

Levine, J. M. (1989). Reaction to opinion deviance in small groups. In P. B. Paulus (Ed.), *Psychology of group influence* (2nd ed.). Hillsdale, NJ: Lawrence Erlbaum Associates.

Levine, M. (1966). Hypothesis behavior by humans during discrimination learning. *Journal of Experimental Psychology, 71,* 331–338.

Levine, M. (1988). *Effective problem solving.* Englewood Cliffs, NJ: Prentice-Hall.

Levinger, G. (1988). Can we picture love? In R. J. Sternberg & M. L. Barnes (Eds.), *The psychology of love.* New Haven: Yale University Press.

Levinger, G., & Moles, O. C. (1979). *Divorce and separation: Context, causes, and consequences.* New York: Basic Books.

Levinger, G., & Snoek, J. D. (1972). *Attraction in relationship: A new look at interpersonal attraction.* Morristown, NJ: General Learning Press.

Levinson, D. J., Darrow, C. N., Klein, E. B., Levinson, M. H., & McKee, B. (1978). *The seasons of a man's life.* New York: Knopf.

Levy, S., Herberman, R., Lippman, M., & d'Angelo, T. (1987). Correlation of stress factors with sustained depression of natural killer cell activity and predicted prognosis in patients with breast cancer. *Journal of Clinical Oncology, 5,* 348–353.

Lewin, I. (1983). The psychological theory of dreams in the Bible. *Journal of Psychology and Judaism, 7,* 73–88.

Lewin, K. (1936). *Principles of topological psychology.* New York: McGraw-Hill.

Lewinsohn, P. H. (1974). A behavioral approach to depression. In R. J. Friedman & M. M. Katz (Eds.), *The psychology of depression: Contemporary theory and research.* Washington, DC: Winston-Wiley.

Lewinsohn, P. M., & Rosenbaum, M. (1987). Recall of parental behavior by acute depressives, remitted depressives, and nondepressives. *Journal of Personality and Social Psychology, 52,* 611–619.

Lewontin, R. (1976). Race and intelligence. In N. J. Block & G. Dworkin (Eds.), *The IQ controversy: Critical readings.* New York: Pantheon.

Leyens, J. P., Camino, L., Parke, R. D., & Berkowitz, L. (1975). The effects of movie violence on aggression in a field setting as a function of group dominance and cohesion. *Journal of Personality and Social Psychology, 32,* 346–360.

Lichstein, K. L., & Fischer, S. M. (1985). Insomnia. In M. Hersen & A. S. Bellak (Eds.), *Handbook of clinical behaviour therapy with adults.* New York: Plenum.

Licht, B. G., & Dweck, C. S. (1984). Determinants of academic achievement: The interaction of children's achievement orientations with skill area. *Developmental Psychology, 20,* 628–636.

Lichtenstein E., & Penner, M. P. (1977). Long-term effects of rapid smoking treatment for dependent cigarette smokers. *Addictive Behaviors, 2,* 109–112.

Liddell, H. (1950). Some specific factors that modify tolerance for environmental stress. In H. G. Wolff, S. G. Wolff, & C. C. Hare (Eds.), *Life stress and bodily disease.* Baltimore: Williams & Wilkins.

Lieberman, M. A., & Tobin, S. (1983). *The experience of old age.* New York: Basic Books.

Liebert, R. M., & Spiegler, M. D. (1982). *Personality: Strategies and issues* (4th ed.). Homewood, IL: Dorsey.

Liebert, R. M., & Sprafkin, J. (1988). *The Early Window.* (3rd ed.). New York: Pergamon.

Lindsay, D. S., & Johnson, M. K. (1989). The eyewitness suggestibility effect and memory of source. *Memory & Cognition, 17,* 349–358.

Lindsay, P. H., & Norman, D. A. (1977). *Human information processing* (2nd ed.). New York: Academic Press.

Lindsey, K. P., & Paul, G. L. (1989). Involuntary commitments to public mental institutions: Issues involving the overrepresentation of blacks and assessment of relevant functioning. *Psychological Bulletin, 106,* 171–183.

Lindvall, O., Brundin, P., Widner, H., Rehncrona, S., Gustavii, B., Frackowiak, R., Leenders, K. L., Sawle, G., Rothwell, J. C., Marsden, C. D., & Bjorklund, A. (1990) Grafts of fetal dopamine neurons survive and improve motor function in Parkinson's disease. *Science, 247,* 574–577.

Lintern, G., & Gopher, D. (1978) Adaptive training of perceptual-motor skills. Issues, results and future directions. *International Journal of Man-Machine Studies, 10,* 521–551.

Linville, P. W. (1982). Affective consequences of complexity regarding the self and others. In M. S. Clark & S. T. Fiske (Eds.), *Affect and cognition.* Hillsdale, NJ: Lawrence Erlbaum Associates.

Linville, P. W. (1985). Self-complexity and affective extremity: Don't put all of your eggs in one cognitive basket. *Social Cognition, 3,* 94–120.

Linville, P. W. (1987). Self-complexity as a cognitive buffer against stress-related illness and depression. *Journal of Personality and Social Psychology, 52,* 663–676.

Linz, D., & Donnerstein, E. (1989). The effects of counter-information on the acceptance of rape myths. In D. Zillmann & J. Bryant (Eds.), *Pornography: Research advances and policy considerations.* Hillsdale, NJ: Lawrence Erlbaum Associates.

Linz, D. G., Donnerstein, E., & Penrod, S. (1988). Effects of long-term exposure to violent and sexually degrading depictions of women. *Journal of Personality and Social Psychology, 55,* 758–768.

Lipton, A. A., & Simon, F. S. (1985). Psychiatric diagnosis in a state hospital: Manhattan State revisited. *Hospital Community Psychiatry, 36,* 368–373.

Lisak, D. & Roth, S. (1988). Motivational factors in nonincarcerated sexually aggressive men. *Journal of Personality and Social Psychology, 55,* 795–802.

Littman, M. S. (1989). *Poverty in the United States, 1987.* Washington, DC: U.S. Department of Commerce, Bureau of the Census.

Livingstone, M., & Hubel, D. (1988). Segregation of form, color, movement, and depth: Anatomy, physiology, and perception. *Science, 240,* 740–749.

Loeb, G. E. (1989). Neural prosthetic interfaces with the nervous system. *Trends in Neuroscience, 12,* 195–201.

Loehlin, J. C. (1989). Partitioning environmental and genetic contributions to behavioral development. *American Psychologist, 44,* 1285–1292.

Loehlin, J. C., Horn, J. M., & Willerman, L. (1981). Personality resemblance in adoptive families. *Behavior Genetics, 11,* 309–330.

Loehlin, J. C., Willerman, L., & Horn, J. M. (1985). Personality resemblances in adoptive families when the children are late-adolescent or adult. *Journal of Personality and Social Psychology, 48,* 376–392.

Loftus, E. F. (1979). *Eyewitness testimony.* Cambridge: Harvard University Press.

Loftus, G. R., & Hogden, J. (1988). Picture perception: Information extraction and phenomenological appearance. In G. H. Bower (Ed.), *The psychology of learning and motivation, vol. 22.* San Diego, CA: Academic Press.

Loftus, E. F. (1984). Eyewitness on trial. In B. D. Sales & A. Alwork (Eds.), *With liberty and justice for all.* Englewood Cliffs, NJ: Prentice-Hall.

Loftus, E. F., & Hoffman, H. G. (1989). Misinformation and memory: The creation of new memories. *Journal of Experimental Psychology: General, 118,* 100–104.

Loftus, E. F., & Loftus, G. R. (1980). On the permanence of stored information in the human brain. *American Psychologist, 35,* 409–420.

Loftus, G. R. (1983). The continuing persistence of the icon. *The Behavioral and Brain Sciences, 6,* 28.

Loftus, G. R. (1985). On worthwhile icons: Reply to DiLollo and Haber. *Journal of Experimental Psychology: Human Perception and Performance, 11,* 384–388.

Loftus, G. R., & Hanna, A. M. (1989). The phenomenology of spatial integration: Data and models. *Cognitive Psychology, 21,* 363–397.

Logothetis, N. K., & Schall, J. D. (1989). Neuronal correlates of subjective visual perception. *Science, 245,* 761–763.

Logue, A. W. (1986). *The psychology of eating and drinking.* New York: W. H. Freeman.

Long, B. C. (1985). Stress-management interventions: A 15-month follow-up of aerobic conditioning and stress inoculation training. *Cognitive Therapy and Research, 9,* 471–478.

Long, G. M., & Beaton, R. J. (1982). The case for peripheral persistence: Effects of target and background luminance on a partial-report task. *Journal of Experimental Psychology: Human Perception and Performance, 8,* 383–391.

Long, P. (1986, January). Medical mesmerism. *Psychology Today.*

Loomis, A. L., Harvey, E. N., & Hobart, G. A. (1937). Cerebral states during sleep as studied by human brain potentials. *Journal of Experimental Psychology, 21,* 127–144.

Lopes, L. L. (1982). *Procedural debiasing* (Tech. Rep. WHIPP 15). Madison: University of Wisconsin, Human Information Processing Program.

Lopez, S. R. (1989). Patient variable biases in clinical judgment: Conceptual overview and methodological considerations. *Psychological Bulletin, 106,* 184–203.

Lorenz, K. (1981). *Foundations of ethology.* New York: Springer-Verlag.

Lott, A. J., & Lott, B. E. (1974). The role of reward in the formation of positive interpersonal attitudes. In T. L. Houston (Ed.), *Foundations of interpersonal attraction.* New York: Academic Press.

Lovaas, O. I. (1987). Behavioral treatment and normal educational and intellectual functioning in young autistic children. *Journal of Consulting and Clinical Psychology, 55,* 3–9.

Luborsky, L. (1954). A note on Eysenck's article, "The effects of psychotherapy: An evaluation." *British Journal of Psychology, 45,* 129–131.

Luborsky, L. (1972). Another reply to Eysenck. *Psychological Bulletin, 78,* 406–408.

Luborsky, L., Singer, B., & Luborsky, L. (1975). Comparative studies of psychotherapies: Is it true that everyone has won and all must have prizes? *Archives of General Psychiatry, 32,* 995–1008.

Lucas, R. (1975). The affective and medical aspects of different preoperative interventions with heart surgery patients. *Dissertation Abstracts International, 36,* 5763B.

Luce, G. G. (1971). *Body time.* New York: Random House.

Luce, S., & Hoge, R. (1978). Relations among teacher ratings, pupil-teacher interactions, and academic achievement: A test of teacher expectancy hypothesis. *American Educational Research Journal, 15,* 489–500.

Luchins, A. S. (1942). Mechanization in problem solving: The effect of Einstellung. *Psychological Monographs, 54*(6, Whole No. 248).

Ludwick-Rosenthal, R., & Neufeld, R. W. (1988). Stress management during noxious medical procedures: An evaluative review of outcome studies. *Psychological Bulletin, 104,* 326–342.

Ludwig, A. M. (1969). Altered states of consciousness. In C. T. Tart (Ed.), *Altered states of consciousness.* New York: Wiley.

Luria, Z., & Rubin, J. Z. (1974). The eye of the beholder: Parents' views on sex of newborns. *American Journal of Orthopsychiatry, 44,* 512–519.

Lykken, D. T. (1979). The detection of deception. *Psychological Bulletin, 86,* 47–53.

Lynch, J. J. (1979). *The broken heart.* New York: Basic Books.

Lynch, K. (1960). *The image of the city.* Cambridge MA: MIT Press.

Lynn, D. B., & Cross, A. D. (1974). Parent preference of preschool children. *Journal of Marriage and the Family, 36,* 555–559.

Lynn, S. J., & Rhue, J. W. (1986). The fantasy-prone person: Hypnosis, imagination, and creativity. *Journal of Personality and Social Psychology, 51,* 404–408.

Lynn, S. J., & Rhue, J. W. (1988). Fantasy proneness: Hypnosis, developmental antecedents, and psychopathology. *American Psychologist, 43,* 35–44.

Lynn, S. J., Weekes, J. R., & Milano, M. J. (1989). Reality versus suggestion: Pseudomemory in hypnotizable and simulating subjects. *Journal of Abnormal Psychology, 98,* 137–144.

Lytton, H. (1987, April). Direction of effects in child socialization with particular reference to conduct disorder. Paper presented at the meeting of the Society for Research in Child Development, Baltimore.

MacAndrew, C., & Edgerton, R. B. (1969). *Drunken comportment.* Chicago: Aldine.

Maccoby, E. E., & Feldman, S. S. (1972). Mother-attachment and stranger-reactions in the third year of life. *Monographs of the Society for Research in Child Development, 37*(1, Serial No. 146).

Maccoby, E. E., & Jacklin, C. N. (1974). *The psychology of sex differences.* Stanford, CA: Stanford University Press.

MacDonald, M., & Bernstein, D. A. (1974). Treatment of a spider phobia with in vivo and imaginal desensitization. *Journal of Behavior Therapy and Experimental Psychiatry, 5,* 47–52.

MacDonald, M. R., & Kuiper, N. A. (1983). Cognitive-behavioral preparations for surgery: Some theoretical and methodological concerns. *Clinical Psychology Review, 3,* 27–39.

Mace, W. M., & Turvey, M. T. (1983). The implications of occlusion for perceiving persistence. *The Behavioral and Brain Sciences, 6,* 29–31.

MacEvoy, B., Lambert, W. W., Karlberg, P., Karlberg, J., Klackenberg-Larsson, & Klackenberg, G. (1988). Early affective antecedants of adult type A behavior. *Journal of Personality and Social Psychology, 54,* 108–116.

MacEwan, K. E., & Barling, J. (1988). Multiple stressors, violence in the family of origin, and marital aggression: A longitudinal investigation. *Journal of Family Violence, 3,* 73–87.

MacKenzie, B. (1984). Explaining race differences in IQ: The logic, the methodology, and the evidence. *American Psychologist, 39,* 1214–1233.

MacLeod, C. M. (1988). Forgotten but not gone: Savings for pictures and words in long-term memory. *Journal of Experimental Psychology: Learning, Memory, and Cognition, 14,* 195–212.

Madni, A. (1988). The role of human factors in expert system design and acceptance. *Human Factors, 30,* 395–414.

Madrazo, I., Drucker-Colin, R., Diaz, V., Martinez-Mata, J., Torres, C., & Becerril, J. J. (1987). Open microsurgical autograft of adrenal medulla to the right caudate nucleus in two patients with intractable Parkinson's disease. *New England Journal of Medicine, 316,* 831–834.

Maeder, T. (1985). *Crime and madness.* New York: Harper & Row.

Magos, A. L., Brincat, M., & Studd, J. W. W. (1986). Treatment of the premenstrual syndrome by subcutaneous oestradiol implants and cyclical oral norethisterone: placebo controlled study. *British Medical Journal, 292,* 1629–1633.

Maher, B. A. (1966). *Principles of psychopathology: An experimental approach.* New York: McGraw-Hill.

Mahler, M. S., Pine, F., & Bergman, A., (1975). *The psychological birth of the human infant.* New York: Basic Books.

Mahrer, A. R., & Nadler, W. P. (1986). Good moments in psychotherapy: A preliminary review, a list, and some promising research avenues. *Journal of Consulting and Clinical Psychology, 54,* 10–15.

Main, M., & George, C. (1985). Responses of abused and disadvantaged toddlers to distress in agemates: A study in the day care setting. *Developmental Psychology, 21,* 407–412.

Main, M., & Goldwyn, R. (1984). Predicting rejection of her infant from mother's representation of her own experience: Implications for the abused-abusing intergenerational cycle. *Child Abuse & Neglect, The International Journal, 8,* 203–217.

Majewska, M. D., Harrison, N. L., Schwartz, R. D., Barker, J. L., & Paul, S. M. (1986). Steroid hormone metabolites are barbiturate-like modulators of the GABA receptor. *Science, 232,* 1004–1007.

Malamuth, N. M. (1988). Predicting laboratory aggression against female and male targets: Implications for sexual aggression. *Journal of Research in Personality, 22,* 474–495.

Malatesta, C. Z., & Izard, C. E. (1984). The ontogenesis of human social signals: From biological imperative to symbol utilization. In N. A. Fox & R. J. Davidson (Eds.), *The psychobiology of affective development* (pp. 161–206). Hilsdale NJ: Lawrence Erlbaum Associates.

Manderscheid, R., & Barrett, S. (1987) (Eds.), *Mental health, United States, 1987* (National Institute of Mental Health, DHHS Pub. No. ADM 87-1518). Washington, DC: U.S. Government Printing Office.

Mane, A., Adams, J. A., & Donchin, E. (1989). Adaptive and part-whole training in the acquisition of a complex perceptual-motor skill. *Acta Psychologica, 71,* 179–196.

Manis, F., Keating, D. P., & Morrison, F. J. (1980). Developmental differences in the allocation of processing capacity. *Journal of Experimental Child Psychology, 29,* 156–159.

Manne, S. L., & Zautra, A. J. (1989). Spouse criticism and support: Their association with coping and psychological adjustment among women with rheumatoid arthritis. *Journal of Personality and Social Psychology, 56,* 608–617.

Mannuzza, S., Martin, L. Y., & Gallops, M. S. (1989). Reliability of anxiety assessment. *Archives of General Psychiatry, 46,* 1093–1101.

Marantz, S. A., & Mansfield, A. F. (1977). Maternal employment and the development of sex-role stereotyping in five- to eleven-year-old girls. *Child Development, 48,* 668–673.

Marcel, A. J. (1983). Conscious and unconscious perception: Experiments on visual masking and word recognition. *Cognitive Psychology, 15,* 197–237.

Marini, Z., & Case, R. (1989). Parallels in the development of preschoolers' knowledge about their physical and social worlds. *Merrill-Palmer Quarterly, 35,* 63–88.

Marino, J., Gwynn, M. I., & Spanos, N. P. (1989). Cognitive mediators in the reduction of pain: The role of expectancy, strategy use, and self-presentation. *Journal of Abnormal Psychology, 98,* 256–262.

Marks, L. E., & Miller, G. A. (1964). The role of semantic and syntactic constraints in the memorization of English sentences. *Journal of Verbal Learning and Verbal Behavior, 3,* 1–5.

Marlatt, G. A., & Rohsenow, D. J. (1980). Cognitive processes in alcohol use: Expectancy and the balanced placebo design. In N.

K. Mello (Ed.), *Advances in substance abuse: Behavioral and biological research.* Greenwich, CT: JAI Press.

Marlatt, G. A., & Gordon, J. R. (1985). *Relapse prevention.* New York: Guilford Press.

Marlatt, G. A., Baer, J. S., Donovan, D. M., & Kivlahan, D. R. (1988). Addictive behaviors: Etiology and treatment. *Annual Review of Psychology, 39,* 223–252.

Marmar, C. R. (1990). Psychotherapy process research: Progress, dilemmas, and future directions. *Journal of Consulting and Clinical Psychology, 58,* 265–272.

Marr, D. (1982). *Vision.* New York: W. H. Freeman & Co.

Marsh, H. W. (1989). Sex differences in the development of verbal and mathmematics constructs: The high school and beyond study. *American Educational Research Journal, 26,* 191–225.

Marshall, G. D., & Zimbardo, P. G. (1979). Affective consequences of inadequately explained arousal. *Journal of Personality and Social Psychology, 37,* 970–985.

Marshall, P. (1990). Attention deficit disorder and allergy: A neurochemical model of the relation between the illnesses. *Psychological Bulletin, 106,* 434–446.

Marshall, S. L. A. (1947). *Men against fire.* New York: Morrow.

Marshall, W. L. (1989). Pornography and sex offenders. In D. Zillmann & J. Bryant (Eds.), *Pornography: Research advances and policy considerations.* Hillsdale, NJ: Lawrence Erlbaum Associates.

Martin, G. (1989). Voice control: Review and data. *International Journal of Man-Machine Systems, 30,* 355–375.

Martindale, C. (1981). *Cognition and consciousness.* Homewood, IL: Dorsey Press.

Maruyama, G., & Miller, N. (1975). *Physical attractiveness and classroom acceptance* (Research Report 75-2). Los Angeles: University of Southern California, Social Science Research Institute.

Maslach, C. (1979). Negative emotional biasing of unexplained arousal. *Journal of Personality and Social Psychology, 37,* 953–969.

Maslach, C., Stapp, J., & Santee, R.T. (1985). Individuation: Conceptual analysis and assessment. *Journal of Personality and Social Psychology, 49,* 729–738.

Masling, J. (Ed.) (1982). *Empirical studies of psychoanalytical theories* (Vol. 1). Hillsdale, NJ: Lawrence Erlbaum Associates.

Maslow, A. H. (1954). *Motivation and personality.* New York: Harper.

Maslow, A. H. (1962). *Toward a psychology of being.* Princeton, NJ: Van Nostrand.

Maslow, A. H. (1970). *Motivation and personality* (2nd ed.). New York: Harper & Row.

Maslow, A. H. (1971). *The farther reaches of human nature.* New York: McGraw-Hill.

Mason, A., & Blankenship, V. (1987). Power and affiliation motivation, stress, and abuse in intimate relationships. *Journal of Personality and Social Psychology, 52,* 203–210.

Mason, J. W. (1975). A historical view of the stress field. *Journal of Human Stress, I,* 22–36.

Mason, R. T., Fales, H. M., Jones, T. H., Pannell, L. K., Chinn, J. W., & Crews, D. (1989). Sex pheromones in snakes. *Science, 245,* 290–293.

Massaro, D. W. (1989). Testing between the TRACE model and the fuzzy logical model of speech perception. *Cognitive Psychology, 21,* 398–421.

Masson, J. M. (1983). *Assault on the truth: Freud's suppression of the seduction theory.* New York: Farrar, Straus, & Giroux.

Masters, J. C., Burish, T. G., Hollon, S. D., & Rimm, D. C. (1987). *Behavior therapy: Techniques and empirical findings* (3rd ed.). San Diego: Harcourt Brace Jovanovich.

Matarazzo, J. D. (1980). Behavioral health and behavioral medicine: Frontiers for a new health psychology. *American Psychologist, 35,* 807–817.

Matarazzo, J. D. (1983). The reliability of psychiatric and psychological diagnosis. *Clinical Psychology Review, 3,* 103–145.

Mathies, H. (1989). Neurobiological aspects of learning and memory. *Annual Review of Psychology, 40,* 381–404.

Matlin, M. W. (1987). *Sensation and perception* (2nd ed.). Boston: Allyn & Bacon.

Matthews, K., Weiss, S., Detre, T., Dembrowski, T., Falkner, B., Manuck, S., & Williams, R. (1986) (Eds.), *Handbook of stress reactivity and cardiovascular disease.* New York: Wiley.

Matthews, K. A. (1982). Psychological perspectives on the Type-A behavior pattern. *Psychological Bulletin, 91,* 293–323.

Matthews, K. A. (1988). Coronary heart disease and type A behaviors: Update on and alternative to the Booth-Kewley and Friedman (1987) quantitative review. *Psychological Bulletin, 104,* 373–380.

Matthews, K. A., & Siegel, J. M. (1983). Type A behaviors for children, social comparison, and standards for self-evaluation. *Developmental Psychology, 19,* 135–140.

Maurer, D., & Vogel, V. H. (1973). *Narcotics and narcotic addiction.* Springfield, IL: Charles C. Thomas.

Mayer & Price. (1982). A physiological and psychological analysis of pain: A potential model of motivation. In D. W. Pfaff (Ed.), *The physiological mechanisms of motivation.*

Mayer, J. (1975). Obesity during childhood. In M. Winick (Ed.), *Childhood obesity.* New York: Wiley.

Mayer, R. E. (1983). *Thinking, problem solving, and cognition.* San Francisco: W. H. Freeman.

Mayer, W. (1983). Alcohol abuse and alcoholism: The psychologist's role in prevention, research, and treatment. *American Psychologist, 38,* 1116–1121.

McCann, T., & Sheehan, P. W. (1988). Hypnotically induced pseudomemories—Sampling their conditions among hypnotizable subjects. *Journal of Personality and Social Psychology, 54,* 339–346.

McCarley, R. W. (1987). REM sleep generation: Intracellular studies of pontine reticular neurons. *Neuroscience, 22,* 387.

McCarthy, G., & Donchin, E. (1979). Event-related potentials: Manifestations of cognitive activity. In F. Hoffmeister & C. Muller (Eds.), *Bayer symposium: VIII. Brain function in old age.* New York: Springer.

McCauley, C. (1989). The nature of social influence in groupthink: Compliance and internalization. *Journal of Personality and Social Psychology, 57,* 250–260.

McClelland, D. C. (1958). Risk-taking in children with high and low need for achievement. In J. W. Atkinson (Ed.), *Motives in fantasy, action, and society.* Princeton, NJ: Van Nostrand.

McClelland, D. C. (1985). *Human motivation.* Glenview, IL: Scott, Foresman.

McClelland, D. C. (1989). Motivational factors in health and disease. *American Psychologist, 44,* 675–683.

McClintock, C. G., & Liebrand, W. B. G. (1988). Role of interdependence structure, individual value orientation, and another's strategy in social decision making: A transformational analysis. *Journal of Personality and Social Psychology, 55,* 396–409.

McCloskey, D. I. (1978). Kinesthetic sensibility. *Physiological Reviews, 58,* 763.

McCloskey, M. (1983). Naive theories of motion. In D. Gentner & K. Stevens (Eds.), *Mental models.* Hillsdale, NJ: Lawrence Erlbaum Associates.

McCloskey, M., Wible, C. G., & Cohen, N. J. (1988). Is there a special flashbulb-memory mechanism? *Journal of Experimental Psychology: General, 117,* 171–181.

McConkie, G. W., Kerr, P. W., Reddix, M. D., & Zola, D. (1988). Eye movement control during reading: I. The location of the intitial eye fixations on words. *Vision Research, 28,* 1107–1118.

McCormick, D. A., & Thompson, R. F. (1984). Cerebellum essential involvement in the classically conditioned eyelid response. *Science, 223,* 296–299.

McCrae, R. R., & Costa, P. T., Jr. (1982). Aging, the life course, and models of personality. In T. M. Field, A. Huston, H. C. Quay, L. Troll, & G. E. Finley (Eds.), *Review of human development.* New York: Wiley-Interscience.

McDougall, W. (1904). The sensations excited by a single momentary stimulation of the eye. *British Journal of Psychology, 1,* 78–113.

McDougall, W. (1908). *An introduction to social psychology.* London: Methuen.

McFarland, C., Ross, M., DeCourville, N. (1989). Women's theories of menstruation and biases in recall of menstrual symptoms. *Journal of Personality and Social Psychology, 57,* 522–531.

McGarvey, R. (1989, February). Recording success. *USAIR Magazine,* pp. 94–102.

McGrady, A., Turner, J. W., Fine, T. H., Higgins, J. T. (1987). Effects of biobehaviorally-assisted relaxation training on blood pressure, plasma renin, cortisol, and aldosterone levels in borderline essential hypertension. *Clinical Biofeedback and Health: An International Journal, 10,* 16–25.

McGuire, W. J. (1968). Personality and susceptibility to social influence. In E. F. Borgatta & W. W. Lambert (Eds.), *Handbook of personality theory and research.* Chicago: Rand McNally.

McGuire, W. J. (1969). The nature of attitudes and attitude change. In G. Lindzey & E. Aronson (Eds.), *The handbook of social psychology: Vol. 3.* (2nd ed.). Reading, MA: Addison-Wesley.

McGuire, W. J. (1985). Attitudes and attitude change. In G. Linzey & E. Aronson (Eds.), *The handbook of social psychology: Vol. 2.* (3rd ed.). New York: Random House.

McGuire, W. J. (1989). The structure of individual attitudes and attitude systems. In A. R. Pratkanis, S. J. Breckler, & A. G. Greenwald (Eds.), *Attitude structure and function.* Hillsdale, NJ: Lawrence Erlbaum Associates.

McKenna, R. J. (1972). Some effects of anxiety level and food cues on the eating behavior of obese and normal subjects: A comparison of the Schachterian and psychosomatic conceptions. *Journal of Personality and Social Psychology, 22,* 311–319.

McNally, R. J. (1987). Preparedness and phobias: A review. *Psychological Bulletin, 101,* 283–303.

McNeil, T. F., & Persson-Blennow, I. (1988). Stability of temperament characteristics in childhood. *American Journal of Orthopsychiatry, 58,* 622–626.

Mead, M. (1963). *Sex and temperament in three primitive societies.* New York: William Morrow.

Mednick, S. A. (1958). A learning theory approach to research in schizophrenia. *Psychological Bulletin, 55,* 316–327.

Mednick, S. A. (1970). Breakdown in individuals at high-risk for schizophrenia: Possible predispositional perinatal factors. *Mental Hygiene, 54,* 50–63.

Mednick, S. A., Gabrielli, W. F., & Hutchings, B. (1984). Genetic influences in criminal convictions: Evidence from adoption court. *Science, 224,* 891–894.

Mednick, S. A., Schulsinger, F., & Griffith, J. (1981). Children of schizophrenic mothers: The Danish high-risk study. In F. Schulsinger, S. A. Mednick, & J. Knop (Eds.), *Longitudinal research: Methods and uses in behavioral science.* Hingham, MA.: Martinus Nijhoff.

Mehle, T. (1982). Hypothesis generation in an automobile malfunction inference task. *Acta Psychologica, 52,* 87–116.

Meichenbaum, D. (1977). *Cognitive behavior modification: An integrative approach.* New York: Plenum Press.

Meichenbaum, D. (1985). *Stress-inoculation training.* New York: Pergamon Press.

Melamed, B. G., & Siegel, L. J. (1980). *Behavioral medicine.* New York: Springer.

Mello, N. K., Mendelson, J. H., Bree, M. P., & Lukas, S. E. (1989). Buprenorphine suppresses cocaine self-administration by rhesus monkeys. *Science, 245,* 859–862.

Mellsop, G., Varghese, F., Joshua, S., & Hicks, A. (1982). The reliability of Axis II of DSM-III. *American Journal of Psychiatry, 139,* 1360–1361.

Meltzer, H. Y. (1989). Duration of a clozapine trial in neuroleptic-resistant schizophrenic. *Archives of General Psychiatry, 46,* 668.

Meltzer, H. Y., & Stahl, S. M. (1976). The dopamine hypothesis of schizophrenia: A review. *Schizophrenia Bulletin, 2,* 19–76.

Meltzoff, A. N. (1988). Imitation of televised models by infants. *Child Development, 59,* 1221–1229.

Melzack, R., & Wall, P. D. (1965). Pain mechanisms: A new theory. *Science, 150,* 971–979.

Merckelbach, H., de Ruiter, C., van den Hout, M. A., & Hoekstra, R. (1989). Conditioning experiences and phobias. *Behaviour Research & Therapy, 27,* 657–662.

Merritt, J. O. (1979). None in a million: Results of mass screening for eidetic ability using objective tests published in newspapers and magazines. *The Behavioral and Brain Sciences, 2,* 612.

Merton, R. (1948). The self-fulfilling prophecy. *Antioch Review, 8,* 193–210.

Merzenich, M. M., & Kass, J. H. (1980). Principles of organization of sensory-perceptual systems in mammals. In J. M. Sprague & A. N. Epstein (Eds.), *Progress in psychobiology and physiological psychology: Vol. 9.* New York: Academic Press.

Messer, S. B., & Winokur, M. (1986). Eclecticism and the shifting visions of reality in three systems of psychotherapy. *International Journal of Eclectic Psychotherapy, 5,* 115–124.

Messick, D. M., & Mackie, D. M. (1989). Intergroup relations. *Annual Review of Psychology, 40,* 45–81.

Messick, S. (1980). *The effectiveness of coaching for the SAT: A review of and reanalysis of research from the fifties to the FTC.* Princeton, NJ: Educational Testing Services.

Messick, S., & Jungeblut, A. (1981). Time and method in coaching for the SAT. *Psychological Bulletin, 89,* 191–216.

Meuser, K. T., & Berenbaum, H. (1990). Psychodynamic treatment of schizophrenia: Is there a future? *Psychological Medicine, 20,* 253–262.

Meyer, R. G. (1975). A behavioral treatment of sleepwalking associated with test anxiety. *Journal of Behavior Therapy and Experimental Psychiatry, 6,* 167–168.

Meyer, R. G., & Hardaway-Osborne, Y. V. (1982). *Case studies in abnormal behavior.* Boston: Allyn & Bacon.

Meyers, J. K., Weissman, M. M., Tischler, G. L., Holzer, C. E., Leaf, P. J., Orvaschel, H., Anthony, J. C., Boyd, J. H., Burke, J. D., Jr., Kramer, M., & Stoltzman, R. (1984). Six-month prevalence of psychiatric disorders in three communities. *Archives of General Psychiatry, 41,* 959–967.

Michelson, L., Sugai, D. P., Wood, R. P., & Kazdin, A. E. (1983). *Social skills assessment and training with children.* New York: Plenum.

Middlestadt, S. E. (1990). The effect of background and ambient color on product attitudes and beliefs. *Advances in Consumer Research, 17,* pp. 244–249.

Mikulincer, M. (1988). Reactance and helplessness following exposure to unsolvable problems: The effects of attributional style. *Journal of Personality and Social Psychology, 54,* 679–686.

Milgram, S. (1963). Behavioral study of obedience. *Journal of Abnormal and Social Psychology, 67,* 371–378.

Milgram, S. (1965). Some conditions of obedience and disobedience to authority. *Human Relations, 18,* 57–76.

Milgram, S. (1974). *Obedience to authority.* New York: Harper & Row.

Milgram, S., & Jodelet, D. (1976). Psychological maps of Paris. In H. M. Proshansky, W. H. Itelson, & L. G. Revlin (Eds.), *Environmental Psychology.* New York: Holt, Rinehart and Winston.

Milgram, S., Bickman, L., & Berkowitz, L. (1969). Note on the drawing power of crowds of different size. *Journal of Personality and Social Psychology, 13,* 79–82.

Milich, R., & Landau, S. (1982). Socialization and peer relations in hyperactive children. In K. D. Gadow & I. Bailer (Eds.), *Advances in learning and behavioral disabilities: A research annual* (Vol. 1, pp. 283–339). Greenwich, CT: JAI Press.

Millar, M. G., Millar, K. U., & Tesser, A. (1988). The effects of helping and focus of attention on mood states. *Personality and Social Psychology Bulletin, 14,* 536–543.

Miller, A. G. (1986). *The obedience experiments: A case study of controversy in social science.* New York: Praeger.

Miller, D. B., & Olson, D. (1978). *Typology of marital interaction and contextual characteristics: Cluster analysis of the I. M. C.* Unpublished paper available from D. Olson, Minnesota Family Study Center, University of Minnesota.

Miller, D. T., & McFarland, C. (1987). Pluralistic ignorance: When similarity is interpreted as dissimilarity. *Journal of Personality and Social Psychology, 53,* 298–305.

Miller, G. A. (1956). The magical number seven, plus or minus two: Some limits on our capacity to process information. *Psychological Review, 63,* 81–97.

Miller, G. A., Heise, G. A., & Lichten, W. (1951). The intelligibility of speech as a function of the text and the test materials. *Journal of Experimental Psychology, 329–335.*

Miller, I. W., & Norman, W. H. (1979). Learned helplessness in humans: A review and attribution model. *Psychological Bulletin, 86,* 93–118.

Miller, J. P. (1975). Suicide and adolescence. *Adolescence, 10(37),* 11–24.

Miller, N., & Brewer, M. (Eds.). (1984). *Groups in contact: The psychology of desegregation.* New York: Academic Press.

Miller, N., & Davidson-Podgorny, G. (1987). Theoretical models of intergroup relations and the use of cooperative teams as an intervention for desegregated settings. In C. Hendrick (Ed.), *Group processes and intergroup relations.* Newbury Park, CA: Sage.

Miller, N., Rogers, M., & Hennigan, K. (1983). Increasing interracial acceptance: Using cooperative games in desegregated elementary schools. In L. Bickman (Ed.), *Applied social psychology annual* (Vol. 4). Beverly Hills: Sage.

Miller, N. E. (1959). Liberalization of basic S-R concepts: Extensions to conflict behavior, motivation, and social learning. In S. Koch (Ed.), *Psychology: A study of science: Vol. 2.* New York: McGraw-Hill.

Miller, N. E., Bailey, C. U., & Stevenson, J. A. F. (1930). Decreased hunger but increased food intake resulting from hypothalmic lesions. *Science, 112,* 256–259.

Miller, R. C., & Berman, J. S. (1983). The efficacy of cognitive-behavior therapies: A quantitative review of the research evidence. *Psychological Bulletin, 94,* 39–53.

Miller, S., & Nardini, R. M. (1977). Individual differences in the perception of crowding. *Environmental Psychology and Nonverbal Behavior, 2,* 3–13.

Miller, S., Rossbach, J., & Munson, R. (1981). Social density and affiliative tendency as determinants of dormitory residential outcomes. *Journal of Applied Social Psychology, 11,* 356–365.

Miller, S. M., Brody, D. S., & Summerton, J. (1988). *Journal of Personality and Social Psychology, 54,* 142–148.

Miller-Jones, D. (1989). Culture and testing. *American Psychologist, 44,* 360–366.

Millon, T. (1981). Disorders of personality. *DSMIII: Axis II.* New York: Wiley.

Millon, T. (1987). *Millon Clinical Multiaxial Inventory-II.* Minneapolis: National Computer Systems.

Milner, B. R. (1966). Amnesia following operation on temporal lobes. In C. W. M. Whitty & O. L. Zangwill (Eds.), *Amnesia.* London: Butterworth.

Mineka, S., & Hendersen, R. W. (1985). Controllability and predictability in acquired motivation. *Annual Review of Psychology, 36,* 495–529.

Minimi, H., & Dallenbach, K. M. (1946). The effect of activity upon learning and retention in the cockroach. *American Journal of Psychology, 59,* 1–58.

Minshew, N. J., Payton, J. B., & Sclabassi, R. J. (1986). Cortical neurophysiologic abnormalities in autism. *Neurology, 36* (Suppl. 1), 194.

Minuchin, S., Rosman, B. L., & Baker, L. (1978). *Psychosomatic families: Anorexia nervosa in context.* Cambridge, MA: Harvard University Press.

Mischel, W. (1968). *Personality and assessment.* New York: Wiley.

Mischel, W. (1981). *Introduction to personality* (3rd ed.). New York: Holt, Rinehart, & Winston.

Mischel, W. (1984). Convergences and challenges in the search for consistency. *American Psychologist, 39,* 351–364.

Mischel, W. (1986). *Introduction to personality* (4th ed.). New York: Holt, Rinehart, & Winston.

Mischel, W., & Peake, P. K. (1983). Some facets of consistency: Replies to Epstein, Funder, and Bem. *Psychological Review, 90,* 394–402.

Mishkin, M., & Appenzeller, T. (1987). The anatomy of memory. *Scientific American, 256,* 80–89.

Mitchell, J. V. (Ed.). (1985). *The ninth mental measurements yearbook.* Lincoln, NE: Buros Institute of Mental Measurements.

Mogenson, G. J. (1976). Neural mechanisms of hunger: Current status and future prospects. In D. Novin, W. Wyrwicka, & G. Bray (Eds.), *Hunger: Basic mechanisms and clinical applications.* New York: Raven.

Monahan, J. (1981). *Predicting violent behavior: An assessment of clinical techniques.* Beverly Hills, CA: Sage.

Monahan, J. (1988). Risk assessment of violence among the mentally disordered: Generating useful knowledge. *International Journal of Law and Psychiatry, 11,* 249.

Money, J. (1987). Human sexology and psychoneuroendocrinology. In D. Crews (Ed.), *Psychobiology of reproductive behavior: An evolutionary perspective.* Englewood Cliffs, NJ: Prentice-Hall.

Money, J. (1987). Sin, sickness, or status? Homosexuality, gender identity, and psychoneuroendocrinology. *American Psychologist, 42,* 384–399.

Money, J., Schwartz, M., & Lewis, V. G. (1984). Adult erotosexual status and fetal hormonal masculinization and demasculinization: 46,XX congential virilizing adrenal hyperplasia and 46,XY androgen-insensitivity syndrome compared. *Psychoneuroendocrinology, 9,* 405–414.

Monk, T. H., Moline, M. L., & Graeber, R. C. (1988). Inducing jet lag in the laboratory patterns of adjustment to an acute shift in routine. *Aviation and Space Environmental Medicine, 59,* 703–710.

Montemayor, R. (1983). Parents and adolescents in conflict: All families some of the time and some families most of the time. *Journal of Early Adolescence, 3,* 83–103.

Montgomery, K. C. (1953). Exploratory behavior as a function of "similarity" of stimulation situations. *Journal of Comparative and Physiological Psychology, 46,* 129–133.

Moore, R. Y., & Bloom, F. E. (1979). Central catecholamine neuron systems: Anatomy and physiology of the norepinephrine and epinephrine systems. *Annual Review of Neuroscience, 2,* 113–168.

Moore-Ede, M. C., Sulzman, F. M., & Fuller, C. A. (1982). *The clocks that time us.* Cambridge: Harvard University Press.

Moos, R. H., & Billings, A. G. (1982). Conceptualizing and measuring coping resources and processes. In L. Goldberger & S. Breznitz (Eds.), *Handbook of stress.* New York: Macmillan.

Moos, R. H., & Schaefer, J. (1984). The crisis of physical illness: An overview and conceptual approach. In R. H. Moos (Ed.), *Coping with physical illness: New perspectives.* New York: Plenum Press.

Morawitz, D. (1989). Behavioral self-help treatment for insomnia: A contolled evaluation. *Behavior Therapy, 20,* 365–379.

Moray, N. (1960). Attention in dichotic listening: Affective cues and influence of instructions. *Quarterly Journal of Experimental Psychology, 11,* 56–60.

Moreland, R. L., & Zajonc, R. B. (1982). Exposure effects in person perception. *Journal of Experimental Social Psychology, 18,* 395–415.

Morgan, C. D., & Murray, H. A. (1935). A method for investigating fantasy: The thematic apperception test. *Archives of Neurology and Psychiatry, 34,* 289–306.

Morgan, W. G. (1973). Situational specificity in altruistic behavior. *Representative Research in Social Psychology, 4,* 56–66.

Morrison, F., Holmes, D. L., & Haith, M. M. (1974). A developmental study of the effects of familiarity on short term visual memory. *Journal of Experimental Child Psychology, 18,* 412–425.

Mortimer, R. G., Goldsteen, K., Armstrong, R. W., & Macrina, D. (1988). *Effects of enforcement, incentives, and publicity on seat belt use in Illinois.* University of Illinois, Dept. of Health & Safety Studies, Final Report to Illinois Dept. of Transportation (Safety Research Report #88-11).

Moscovici, S. (1985). Social influence and conformity. In G. Lindzey & E. Aronson (Eds.), *The handbook of social psychology: Vol. 2.* (3rd ed.). New York: Random House.

Moss, H. A., & Susman, E. J. (1980). Longitudinal study of personality development. In O. G. Brim & J. Kagan (Eds.), *Constancy and change in human development.* Cambridge, MA: Harvard University Press.

Mowrer, O. H., & Ullman, A. D. (1945). Time as a determinant in integrative learning. *Psychological Review, 52,* 61–90.

Moyer, K. E. (1983). The physiology of motivation: Aggression as a model. In C. J. Scheier & A. M. Rogers (Eds.), *G. Stanley Hall Lecture Series: Vol. 3.* Washington, DC: American Psychological Association.

Mueller, D., Edwards, D. W., & Yarvis, R. M. (1977). Stressful life events and psychiatric symptomatology: Change or undesirability? *Journal of Health and Social Behavior, 18,* 307–316.

Mueller, E. (1972). The maintenance of verbal exchanges between young children. *Child Development, 43,* 930–938.

Mueller, E. (1989). Toddlers' peer relations: Shared meaning and semantics. In W. Damon (Ed.), *Child development today and tomorrow* (pp. 312–331). San Francisco: Jossey-Bass.

Mueller, E., & Lucas, T. (1975). A developmental analysis of peer interaction among toddlers. In M. Lewis & L. A. Rosenblum (Eds.), *Friendship and peer relations.* New York: Wiley-Interscience.

Mueller, E., & Vandell, D. (1979). Infant-infant interaction. In J. D. Osofsky (Ed.), *Handbook of infant development.* New York: Wiley.

Murray, H. A. (1938). *Explorations in personality.* New York: Oxford University Press.

Murray, H. A. (1962). *Explorations in personality.* New York: Science Editions.

Murstein, B. I. (1980). Mate selection in the 1970s. *Journal of Marriage and the Family, 42,* 777–792.

Musick, J. (1987, September 14). Press conference concerning the Ounce of Prevention Project, Chicago, IL.

Mussen, P. H., & Eisenberg-Berg, N. (1977). *The roots of caring.* New York: W. H. Freeman.

Myers, A. K., & Miller, N. E. (1954). Failure to find a learned drive based on hunger: Evidence for learning motivated by "exploration." *Journal of Comparative and Physiological Psychology, 47,* 428–436.

Myers, J. L., O'Brien, E. J., Balota, D. A., & Toyofuku, M. L. (1984). Memory search without interference: The role of integration. *Cognitive Psychology, 16,* 217–242.

Myles-Worsley, M., Johnston, W. A., & Simons, M. A. (1989). The influence of expertise on x-ray image processing. *Journal of*

Experimental Psychology: Learning, Memory, and Cognition, 14, 553–557.

Mynatt, C., & Sherman, S. J. (1975). Responsibility attribution in groups and individuals: A direct test of the diffusion of responsibility hypothesis. *Journal of Personality and Social Psychology, 32,* 1111–1118.

Nagel, D. (1988) Human error in aircraft operations. In E. Wiener & D. Nagel (Eds.), *Human factors in aviation.* San Diego: Academic Press.

Nahemow, L., & Lawton, M. P. (1975). Similarity and propinquity in friendship formation. *Journal of Personality and Social Psychology, 32,* 205–213.

Nash, M., Drake, S., Wiley, S., Khalsa, S., & Lynn, S. (1986). Accuracy of recall by hypnotically age-regressed subjects. *Journal of Abnormal Psychology, 95,* 298–300.

Nathans, J. E., Thomas, D., & Hogness, D. (1986). Molecular genetics of human color vision: The genes encoding blue, green, and red pigments. *Science, 232,* 193–202.

National Academy of Sciences. (1982). *Marijuana and health.* Washington, DC: National Academy Press.

National Center for Health Statistics (1988). Advance report of final mortality statistics, 1986. *NCHS Monthly Vital Statistics Report, 37,* (Suppl. 6).

National Commission on Marijuana and Drug Abuse, Raymond P. Shafer, Chair. (1972). *Marijuana: A signal of misunderstanding.* New York: New American Library.

National Institute of Mental Health (1985). *Electroconvulsive therapy: Consensus development conference statement.* Bethesda, MD: U.S. Department of Health and Human Services.

Navon, D., & Gopher, D. (1979). On the economy of the human processing system. *Psychological Review, 86,* 254–255.

Neale, J. M., Oltmanns, T. F., & Winters, K. C. (1983). Recent developments in the assessment and conceptualization of schizophrenia. *Behavioral Assessment, 5,* 33–54.

Neisser, U., & Becklan, R. (1975). Selective looking: Attention to visually specified events. *Cognitive Psychology, 7,* 480–494.

Nelson, K. E., Denninger, M. M., Bonvillian, J. D., Kaplan, B. J., & Baker, N. (1983). Maternal input adjustments and nonadjustments as related to children's linguistic advances and to language acquisition theories. In A. D. Pellegrini & T. D. Yawkey (Eds.), *The development of oral and written languages: Readings in developmental and applied linguistics.* Norwood, NJ: Ablex.

Nelson, T. O., & Leonesio, R. J. (1988). Allocation of self-paced study time and the "labor-in-vain effect." *Journal of Experimental Psychology: Learning, Memory, and Cognition, 14,* 676–686.

Nelson, T. O., & Narens, L. (1980). A new technique for investigating the feeling of knowing. *Acta Psychologica, 46,* 69–80.

Nelson, T. O., Leoneslo, R. J., Shimamura, A. P., Landwehr, R. F., & Narens, L. (1982). Overlearning and the feeling of knowing. *Journal of Experimental Psychology: Learning, Memory, and Cognition, 8,* 279–288.

Nemeth, C., & Chiles, C. (1988). Modelling courage: The role of dissent in fostering independence. *European Journal of Social Psychology, 18,* 275–280.

Neugarten, B. L. (1968). Adult personality: Toward a psychology of the life cycle. In B. L. Neugarten (Ed.), *Middle age and aging.* Chicago: University of Chicago Press.

Neugarten, B. L. (1977). Personality and aging. In J. E. Birren & K. W. Schaie (Eds.), *Handbook of the psychology of aging.* New York: Van Nostrand Reinhold.

Neugarten, B. L., & Neugarten, D. A. (1987). The changing meanings of age. *Psychology Today,* pp. 29–33.

Neugarten, B. L., Havighurst, D. J., & Tobin, S. S. (1968). Personality and patterns of aging. In B. L. Neugarten (Ed.), *Middle age and aging.* Chicago: University of Chicago Press.

Nevin, A., & Thousand, J. (1986). What the research says about limiting or avoiding referrals to special education. *Teacher Education and Special Education, 9,* 149–161.

Newcomb, M. D., & Bentler, P. M. (1989). Substance use and abuse among children and teenagers. *American Psychologist, 44,* 242–248.

Newell, A., & Simon, H. A. (1972). *Human problem solving.* Englewood Cliffs, NJ : Prentice-Hall.

Newlin, D. B., Carpenter, B., & Golden, C. J. (1981). Hemispheric asymmetries in schizophrenia. *Biological Psychiatry, 16,* 561–582.

Newman, J. P., & Kosson, D. S. (1986). Passive avoidance learning in psychopathic and nonpsychopathic offenders. *Journal of Abnormal Psychology, 95,* 252–256.

Newman, L. S., & Uleman, J. S. (1989). Spontaneous trait inference. In J. S. Uleman & J. A. Bargh (Eds.), *Unintended thought.* New York: Guilford Press.

Newman, L. S., & Uleman, J. S. (1990). Assimilation and contrast effects in spontaneous trait inference. *Personality and Social Psychology Bulletin, 16,* 224–240.

Niaura, R., Herbert, P., Petrie, C., McMahan, N., & Somerville, L. (1989). *Repressive coping and blood lipids: Gender and age effects.* Paper presented at the Tenth Annual Meeting of the Society of Behavioral Medicine, San Francisco.

Nichols, R. (1978). Twin studies of ability, personality, and interests. *Homo, 29,* 158–173.

Nicholson, R. A., & Berman, J. S. (1983). Is follow-up necessary in evaluating psychotherapy? *Psychological Bulletin, 93,* 261–278.

Nickerson, R. A., & Adams, M. J. (1979). Long-term memory for a common object. *Cognitive Psychology, 11,* 287–307.

Nietzel, M. T., & Dillehay, R. C. (1987). *Psychological consultation in the courtroom.* New York: Pergamon.

Nietzel, M. T., & Harris, M. (in press). Relationship of dependency and achievement/autonomy to depression. *Clinical Psychology Review.*

Nietzel, M. T., Bernstein, D. A., & Milich, R. (1991). *Introduction to clinical psychology* (3rd ed.). Englewood Cliffs, NJ: Prentice-Hall.

Nietzel, M. T., Guthrie, P. R., & Susman, D. T. (1990). Utilization of community and social support resources. In F. H. Kanfer & A. P. Goldstein (Eds.), *Helping people change* (4th ed.). New York: Pergamon Press.

Nilsson, L. (1989). Classification of human memory. In H. L. Roediger & F. I. M. Craik (Eds.), *Varieties of memory and consciousness.* Hillsdale, NJ: Lawrence Erlbaum Associates.

Nisbet, E. B. (1973). An escalator phobia overcome in one session of flooding in vivo. *Journal of Behavior Therapy and Experimental Psychiatry, 4,* 405–406.

Nisbett, R. E. (1972). Hunger, obesity, and the ventromedial hypothalamus. *Psychological Review, 79,* 433–453.

Nisbett, R. E., & Gordon, A. (1967). Self-esteem and susceptibility to social influence. *Journal of Personality and Social Psychology, 5,* 268–276.

Nisbett, R. E., & Wilson, T. D. (1977). Telling more than we can know: Verbal reports on mental processes. *Psychological Review, 84,* 231–259.

Norman, D. (1987). Categorization of action slips. *Psychological Review, 88,* 1–15.

Norman, D. A. (1988). *The psychology of everyday things.* New York: Basic Books.

Nottebohm, F. (1985). Neuronal replacement in adulthood. *Annals of the New York Academy of Science, 457,* 143–161.

Novick, L. R. (1988). Analogical transfer, problem similarity, and expertise. *Journal of Experimental Psychology: Learning, Memory, and Cognition, 14,* 510–520.

Nurnberger, J. I., & Gershon, E. S. (1984). Genetics of affective disorders. In R. M. Post & J. C. Ballenger (Eds.), *Neurobiology of mood disorders*. Baltimore: Williams & Wilkins.

O'Leary, K. D., Barling, J., Arias, I., Rosenbaum, A., Malone, J., Tyree, A. (1989). Prevalence and stability of physical aggression between spouses: A longitudinal analysis. *Journal of Consulting and Clinical Psychology, 57,* 263–268.

O'Sullivan, C. S., & Durso, F. T. (1984). The effect of schema incongruent information on memory for stereotypical attributes. *Journal of Personality and Social Psychology, 47,* 55–70.

Offenbach, S. I. (1974). A developmental study of hypothesis testing and cue selection strategies. *Developmental Psychology, 10,* 484–490.

Office of Technology Assessment (1988). *Safe skies for tomorrow.* Washington, DC: U.S. Government Printing Office.

Öhman, A., Dimberg, U., & Öst, L. G. (1985). Animal and social phobias: A laboratory model. In S. Reiss & R. R. Bootzin (Eds.), *Theoretical issues in behavior therapy.* Orlando, FL: Academic Press.

Öhman, A., Erixon, G., & Lofberg, I. (1975). Phobias and preparedness: Phobic versus neutral picture as conditioned stimuli for human autonomic responses. *Journal of Abnormal Psychology, 84,* 41–45.

Olds, J. (1973). Commentary on positive reinforcement produced by electrical stimulation of septal areas and other regions of rat brain. In E. S. Valenstein (Ed.), *Brain stimulation and motivation: Research and commentary.* Glenview, IL: Scott, Foresman.

Olds, J., & Milner, P. (1954). Positive reinforcement produced by electrical stimulation of septal areas and other regions of the rat brain. *Journal of Comparative and Physiological Psychology, 47,* 419–427.

Olds, M. E., & Fobes, J. L. (1981). The central basis of motivation: Intracranial self stimulus studies. *Annual Review of Psychology, 32,* 523–574.

Olney, J. W., Labruyere, J., & Price, M. T. (1989). Pathological changes induced in cerebrocortical neurons by phencyclidine and related drugs. *Science, 244,* 1360–1362.

Olpe, H. R., Steinmann, M. W., & Jones, R. S. G. (1985). Electrophysiological perspectives on locus coeruleus: Its role in cognitive versus vegetative functions. *Physiological Psychology, 13,* 179–187.

Olsen, K. M. (1969). *Social class and age-group differences in the timing of family status changes: A study of age-norms in American society.* Unpublished doctoral dissertation, University of Chicago, Chicago, IL.

Olson, G. M., & Sherman, T. (1983). Attention, learning, and memory in infants. In P. H. Mussen (Ed.), *Handbook of child psychology: Vol. 2. Infancy and developmental psychobiology.* New York: Wiley.

Olson, R. K., & Attneave, F. (1970). What variables produce stimulus grouping? *American Psychologist, 83,* 1–21.

Olson, R. P., Ganley, R., Devine, V. T., & Dorsey, G. C., Jr. (1981). Long-term effects of behavioral versus insight-oriented therapy with inpatient alcoholics. *Journal of Consulting and Clinical Psychology, 49,* 866–877.

Olweus, D. (1986). Aggression and hormones: Behavioral relationships with testosterone and adrenaline. In D. Olweus, J. Block, & M. Radke-Yarrow (Eds.), *Development of antisocial and prosocial behaviors.* Orlando, FL: Academic Press.

Orbell, J. M., van de Kragt, A. J. C., & Dawes, R. M. (1988). Explaining discussion-induced cooperation. *Journal of Personality and Social Psychology, 54,* 811–819.

Orne, M. T. (1970). Hypnosis, motivation and the ecological validity of the psychological experiment. In W. J. Arnold & M. M. Page (Eds.), *Nebraska symposium on motivation.* Lincoln: University of Nebraska Press.

Orne, M. T. (1977). The construct of hypnosis: Implications of definition for research and practice. In W. E. Edmonston, Jr. (Ed.), Conceptual and investigative approaches to hypnosis and hyp-

notic phenomena. *Annals of the New York Academy of Sciences, 296,* 14–33.

Orne, M. T. (1979). The use and misuse of hypnosis in court. *International Journal of Clinical and Experimental Hypnosis, 14,* 311–341.

Orne, M. T. (1980). On the construct of hypnosis: How its definition affects research and its clinical application. In G. D. Burrows & L. Dennerstein (Eds.), *Handbook of hypnosis and psychosomatic medicine.* Amsterdam: Elsevier.

Orne, M. T., & Evans, F. J. (1965). Social control in the psychological experiment: Antisocial behavior and hypnosis. *Journal of Personality and Social Psychology, 1,* 189–200.

Orne, M. T., & Holland, C. H. (1968). On the ecological validity of laboratory deceptions. *International Journal of Psychiatry, 6,* 282–293.

Orne, M. T., Sheehan, P. W., & Evans, F. J. (1968). Occurrence of posthypnotic behavior outside the experimental setting. *Journal of Personality and Social Psychology, 9,* 189–196.

Ornstein, R. (1985). *Psychology: The study of human experience.* San Diego: Harcourt Brace Jovanovich.

Ornstein, R. E. (1977). *The psychology of consciousness* (2nd ed.). New York: Harcourt Brace Jovanovich.

Ortega, K. A. (1989). Problem solving: Expert/novice differences. *Human Factors Society Bulletin, 32,* 1–5.

Ortony, A., Clore, G. L., & Collins, A. (1988). *The cognitive structure of emotions.* Cambridge, Eng.: Cambridge University Press.

Ory, J. (1986). *College, department, and course grade distribution for fall semester, 1985* (Research Memorandum No. 222). Champaign: University of Illinois, Office of Instructional Resources.

Öst, L. G. (1985). Ways of acquiring phobias and outcome of behavioral treatments. *Behaviour Research and Therapy, 23,* 683–689.

Oster, H. (1981). "Recognition" of emotional expression in infancy? In M. E. Lamb & L. R. Sherrod (Eds.), *Infant social cognition.* Hillsdale, NJ: Lawrence Erlbaum Associates.

Ostrom, T. M. (1989). Interdependence of attitude theory and measurement. In A. R. Pratkanis, S. J. Breckler, & A. G. Greenwald (Eds.), *Attitude structure and function.* Hillsdale, NJ: Lawrence Erlbaum Associates.

Ostrom, T. M. (1990). The maturing of social cognition. In T. K. Srull & R. S. Wyer (Eds.), *Advances in social cognition: Vol. 3. Content and process specificity in the effects of prior experiences.* Hillsdale, NJ: Lawrence Erlbaum Associates.

Otis, L. S. (1984). The adverse effects of meditation. In D. H. Shapiro & R. N. Walsh (Eds.), *Meditation: Classical and contemporary perspectives.* New York: Aldine.

Ottati, V. C., Riggle, E. J., Wyer, R. S., Schwarz, N., & Kuklinski, J. (1989). Cognitive and affective bases of opinion survey responses. *Journal of Personality and Social Psychology, 57,* 404–415.

Overton, D. A. (1984). State dependent learning and drug discriminations. In L. L. Iverson, S. D. Iverson, & S. H. Snyder (Eds.), *Handbook of psychopharmacology* (Vol. 18). New York: Plenum Press.

Pachella, R. (1974). The use of reaction time measures in information processing research. In B. H. Kantowitz (Ed.), *Human information processing.* Hillsdale, NJ: Lawrence Erlbaum Associates.

Pagel, M. D., Erdley, W. W., & Becker, J. (1987). Social networks: We get by with (and in spite of) a little help from our friends. *Journal of Personality and Social Psychology, 53,* 793–804.

Paivio, A. (1986). *Mental representations: A dual coding approach.* New York: Oxford University Press.

Palmer, F. H., & Anderson, L. W. (1979). Long term gains from early intervention: Findings from longitudinal studies. In E. Zigler & J. Valentine (Eds.), *Project Head Start: A legacy of the war on poverty.* New York: Free Press.

Palmer, R. L. (Ed.) (1981). *Electroconvulsive therapy: An appraisal.* New York: Oxford University Press.

Palmer, S. E. (1975). The effects of contextual scenes on the identification of objects. *Memory and Cognition, 3,* 519–526.

Park, B. (1989). Trait attributions as on-line organizers in person impressions. In J. N. Bassili (Ed.), *On-line cognition in person impression.* Hillsdale, NJ: Lawrence Erlbaum Associates.

Parker, J. G., & Asher, S. R. (1987). Peer relations and later adjustment: Are low-accepted children "at risk"? *Psychological Bulletin, 102,* 358–389.

Parkes, C. M., & Brown, R. (1972). Health after bereavement: A controlled study of young Boston widows and widowers. *Psychosomatic Medicine, 34,* 449–461.

Parkes, J. D., & Lock, C. B. (1989). Genetic factors in sleep disorders. *Journal of Neurology, Neurosurgery, and Psychiatry,* June (Supplement), 101–108.

Parkes, K. R. (1984). Locus of control, cognitive appraisal, and coping in stressful episodes. *Journal of Personality and Social Psychology, 46,* (3), 655–668.

Parke, R. D., Berkowitz, L., Leyens, J. P., West, S. G., & Sebastian, R. J. (1977). Some effects of violent and nonviolent movies on the behavior of juvenile delinquents. In L. Berkowitz (Ed.), *Advances in experimental social psychology: Vol. 10.* New York: Academic Press.

Parten, M. B. (1932). Social participation among preschool children. *Journal of Abnormal and Social Psychology, 27,* 243–269.

Parten, M. B. (1971). Social play among preschool children. In R. E. Herron & B. Sutton-Smith (Eds.), *Child's play.* New York: Wiley. (Reprinted from *Journal of Abnormal and Social Psychology,* 1933, *28,* 136–147)

Patrick, C. J., Craig, K. D., & Prkachin, K. M. (1986). Observer judgments of pain: Facial action determinants. *Journal of Personality and Social Psychology, 50,* 1291–1298.

Patterson, F. G. (1978). The gestures of a gorilla: Language acquisition in another pongid. *Brain and Language, 5,* 72–97.

Patterson, G. R. (1974). Intervention for boys with conduct problems: Multiple settings, treatments, and criteria. *Journal of Consulting and Clinical Psychology, 42,* 471–481.

Patterson, G. R. (1982). *Coercive family process.* Eugene, OR: Castalia Press.

Pattie, F. A. (1935). A report of attempts to produce uniocular blindness by hypnotic suggestion. *British Journal of Medical Psychiatry, 15,* 230–241.

Paul, G. L. (1969a). Behavior modification research: Design and tactics. In C. M. Franks (Ed.), *Behavior therapy: Appraisal and status* (pp. 29–62). New York: McGraw-Hill.

Paul, G. L. (1969b). Physiological effects of relaxation training and hypnotic suggestion. *Journal of Abnormal Psychology, 74,* 425–437.

Paul, G. L. (1986). Can pregnancy be a placebo effect? Terminology, designs, and conclusions in the study of psychosocial and pharmacological treatments of behavior disorders. *Journal of Behavior Therapy and Experimental Psychiatry, 17,* 61–82.

Paul, G. L., & Lentz, R. J. (1977). *Psychosocial treatment of chronic mental patients: Milieu versus social learning programs.* Cambridge: Harvard University Press.

Paulus, P. B. (1988). *Prison crowding: A psychological perspective.* New York: Springer-Verlag.

Paulus, P. B., & Nagar, D. (1989). Environmental influences on groups. In P. B. Paulus (Ed.), *Psychology of group influence* (2nd ed.). Hillsdale, NJ: Lawrence Erlbaum Associates.

Pavlov, I. P. (1927). *Conditioned reflexes* (G. V. Anrep, Trans.). London: Oxford University Press.

Pavlov, T. W., Lewis, D. A., & Lyons, J. S. (1989). Psychiatric diagnosis and racial bias: An empirical investigation. *Professional Psychology: Research and Practice, 20,* 364–368.

Paykel, E. S., Prusoff, B. A., & Myers, J. K. (1975). Suicide attempts and recent life events. *Archives of General Psychiatry, 32,* 327–333.

Peck, J. W. (1978). Rats defend different body weights depending on palatability and accessibility of their food. *Journal of Comparative and Physiological Psychology, 92,* 555–570.

Pedersen, D., & Wheeler, J. (1983). The Muller-Lyer illusion among Navajos. *Journal of Social Psychology, 121,* 3–6.

Pedersen, N. L., Plomin, R., McClearn, G. E., & Friberg, L. (1988). Neuroticism, extraversion, and related traits in adult twins reared apart and reared together. *Journal of Personality and Social Psychology, 55,* 950–957.

Peele, S. (1988). Fools for love: The romantic ideal, psychological theory, and addictive love. In R. J. Sternberg & M. L. Barnes (Eds.), *The psychology of love.* New Haven: Yale University Press.

Pennebaker, J. W. (1985). Traumatic experience and psychosomatic disease: Exploring the roles of behavioural inhibition, obsession, and confiding. *Canadian Psychology, 26,* 82–95.

Pennebaker, J. W., & Beall, S. K. (1986). Confronting a traumatic event: Toward an understanding of inhibition and disease. *Journal of Abnormal Psychology, 95,* 274–281.

Pennebaker, J. W., & Chew, C. H. (1985). Deception, electrodermal activity, and inhibition of behavior. *Journal of Personality and Social Psychology, 49,* 1427–1433.

Pennebaker, J. W., & O'Heeron, R. C. (1984). Confiding in others and illness rate among spouses of suicide and accidental death victims. *Journal of Abnormal Psychology, 93,* 473–476.

Pennebaker, J. W., Colder, M., & Sharp, L. K. (1990). Accelerating the coping process. *Journal of Personality and Social Psychology, 58,* 528–537.

Peper, R. J., & Mayer, R. E. (1978). Note taking as a generative activity. *Journal of Educational Psychology, 70,* 514–522.

Perloff, L. S., & Fetzer, B. K. (1986). Self-other judgments and perceived vulnerability to victimization. *Journal of Personality and Social Psychology, 50,* 502–511.

Perls, F. S. (1969). *Gestalt therapy verbatim.* Lafayette, CA: Real People Press.

Perls, F. S. (1970). Four lectures. In J. Fagan & I. L. Shepherd (Eds.), *Gestalt therapy now* (pp. 14–38). Palo Alto, CA: Science and Behavior Books.

Perls, F. S., Hefferline, R. F., & Goodman, P. (1951). *Gestalt therapy.* New York: Julian Press.

Perper, T. (1985). *Sex signals: The biology of love.* Philadelphia: ISI Press.

Pervin, L. A. (1989). Psychodynamic-systems reflections on a social-intelligence model of personality. In R. S. Wyer & T. K. Srull (Eds.), *Advances in social cognition: Vol. 2. Social intelligence and cognitive assessments of personality.* Hillsdale, NJ: Lawrence Erlbaum Associates.

Peters, J. J. (1977). The Philadelphia rape victim project. In D. Chappell, R. Geiss, & G. Geis (Eds.), *Forcible rape: The crime, the victim, and the offenders.* New York: Columbia University Press.

Peterson, A. C. (1987, September). Those gangly years. *Psychology Today,* pp. 28–34.

Peterson, C., & Seligman, M. E. P. (1984). Causal explanations as a risk factor for depression: Theory and evidence. *Psychological Review, 91,* 347–374.

Peterson, C., Seligman, M. E. P., & Vaillant, G. E. (1988). Pessimistic explanatory style is a risk factor for physical illness: A thirty-five-year longitudinal study. *Journal of Personality and Social Psychology, 55,* 23–27.

Peterson, L. (1989). Special series: Coping with medical illness and medical procedures. *Journal of Consulting and Clinical Psychology, 57,* 331–332.

Peterson, L. R., & Peterson, M. J. (1959). Short-term retention of individual verbal items. *Journal of Experimental Psychology, 58,* 193–198.

Petri, H. L. (1986). *Motivation: Theory and research* (2nd ed.). Belmont, CA: Wadsworth.

Petty, R. E., & Cacioppo, J. T. (1981). *Attitudes and persuasion: Classic and contemporary approaches.* Dubuque, IA: William C. Brown.

Phares, E. J. (1973). *Locus of control: A personality determinant of behavior.* Morristown, NJ: General Learning Press.

Phelps, M. E., & Mazziotta, J. C. (1985). Positron emission tomography: Human brain function and biochemistry. *Science, 228,* 799–809.

Phoenix, C. H., Goy, R. W., Gerall, A. A., & Young, W. C. (1959). Organizing action of prenatally administered testosterone propionate on the tissue mediating mating behavior in the female guinea pig. *Endocrinology, 65,* 369–382.

Piaget, J. (1952). *The origins of intelligence in children.* New York: International Universities Press.

Piliavin, I. M., Piliavin, J. A., & Rodin, J. (1975). Costs, diffusion, and the stigmatized victim. *Journal of Personality and Social Psychology, 32,* 429–438.

Pilisuk, M., Boylan, R., & Acredolo, C. (1987). Social support, life stress, and subsequent medical care utilization. *Health Psychology, 6,* 273–288.

Pillemer, D. B., Goldsmith, L. R., Panter, A. T., & White, S. H. (1988). Very long-term memories of the first year in college. *Journal of Experimental Psychology: Learning, Memory, and Cognition, 14,* 709–715.

Platt, S. A., & Sanislow, C. A. (1988). Norm-of-reaction: Definition and misinterpretation of animal research. *Journal of Comparative Psychology, 102,* 254–261.

Plomin, R. (1989). Environment and genes: Determinants of behavior. *American Psychologist, 44,* 105-111.

Plomin, R., & Daniels, D. (1987). Why are children in the same family so different from each other? *Behavioral and Brain Sciences, 10,* 1–16.

Plomin, R., & Foch, T. T. (1980). A twin study of objectively assessed personality in childhood. *Journal of Personality and Social Psychology, 39,* 680–688.

Plous, S. (1988). Modeling the nuclear arms race as a perceptual dilemma. *Philosophy and Public Affairs, 17,* 44–53.

Poeck, K. (1969). Pathophysiology of emotional disorders associated with brain damage. In P. J. Vinken & G. W. Bruyn (Eds.), *Handbook of clinical neurology: Vol. 3.* New York: American Elsevier.

Poggio, T, Gamble, E. B., & Little, J. J. (1988). Parallel integration of vision modules. *Science, 242,* 436–440.

Poincaré, H. (1913). Mathematical creation. In G. H. Halstead (Trans.), *The foundations of science.* New York: Science Press.

Poland, R. E., Rubin, R. T., Lesser, I. M., Lane, L. A., & Hart, P. J. (1987). Neuroendocrine aspects of primary endogenous depression. *Archives of General Psychiatry, 44,* 790–796.

Pollack, I. (1953). The assimilation of sequentially coded information. *American Journal of Psychology, 66,* 421–435.

Pollard-Gott, L. (1983). Emergence of thematic concepts in repeated listening to music. *Cognitive Psychology, 15,* 66–94.

Polya, G. (1957). *How to solve it.* Garden City, NY: Anchor.

Ponzetti, J. J., Cate, R. M., & Koval, J. E. (1982). Violence between couples: Profiling the male abuser. *The Personnel and Guidance Journal, 61,* 222–224.

Poon, L. W., & Fozard, J. L. (1978). Speed of retrieval from long-term memory in relation to age, familiarity, and datedness of information. *Journal of Gerontology, 33,* 711–717.

Pope, H. G., & Katz, D. L. (1988). Affective and psychotic symptoms associated with anabolic steroid use. *American Journal of Psychiatry, 145,* 487–490.

Poppel, E. (1988). *Mindworks: Time and conscious experience.* Orlando: Harcourt Brace Jovanovich.

Porter, R. H., Cernich, J. M., & McLaughlin, F. J. (1983). Maternal recognition of neonates through olfactory cues. *Physiology and Behavior, 30,* 151–154.

Posner, M., Petersen, S., Fox, P., & Raichle, M. E. (1988). Localization of cognitive operation in the human brain. *Science, 240,* 1627–1631.

Posner, M. I. (1978). *Chronometric explorations of the mind.* Hillsdale, NJ: Lawrence Erlbaum Associates.

Posner, M. I., Nissen, M. J., & Klein, R. (1976). Visual dominance: An information processing account of its origins and significance. *Psychological Review, 83,* 157–171.

Power, T. G., & Parke, R. D. (1983). Patterns of mother and father play with their 8-month-old infant: A multiple analysis approach. *Infant Behavior and Development, 6,* 453–459.

Powers, D. E. (1986). Relations of test item characteristics to test preparation/test practice effects: A quantitative summary. *Psychological Bulletin, 100,* 67–77.

Powley, T. L., & Keesey, R. E. (1970). Relationship of body weight to the lateral hypothalamic syndrome. *Journal of Comparative and Physiological Psychology, 70,* 25–36.

Premack, D. (1965). Reinforcement theory. In D. Levine (Ed.), *Nebraska symposium on motivation.* Lincoln: University of Nebraska Press.

Premack, D. (1971). Language in chimpanzees? *Science, 172,* 808–822.

Prentice-Dunn, S., & Rogers, R. W. (1989). Deindividuation and the self-regulation of behavior. In P. B. Paulus (Ed.), *Psychology of group influence* (2nd ed.). Hillsdale, NJ: Lawrence Erlbaum Associates.

President's Commission on Mental Health. (1978). *Report to the President.* Washington, DC: Superintendent of Documents, U.S. Government Printing Office.

Price, R. A., & Vanderberg, S. G. (1979). Matching for physical attractiveness in married couples. *Personality and Social Psychology Bulletin, 5,* 398–400.

Pritchard, W. S. (1981). The psychophysiology of P300. *Psychological Bulletin, 89,* 506–540.

Prochaska, J. O., & Norcross, J. C. (1982). The future of psychotherapy: A Delphi poll. *Professional Psychology, 13,* 620–627.

Provence, S., & Lipton, R. C. (1962). *Infants in institutions.* New York: International Universities Press.

Putallaz, M., & Gottman, J. (1981). An interactional model of children's entry into peer groups. *Child Development, 52,* 986–994.

Pyle, R. L., Mitchell, J. E., & Eckert, E. D. (1981). Bulimia: A report of 34 cases. *Journal of Clinical Psychiatry, 42,* 60–64.

Quartermain, D., Kissileff, H., Shapiro, R., & Miller, N. E. (1971). Suppression of food intake with intragastric loading: Relation to natural feeding cycle. *Science, 173,* 941–943.

Quattrochi, J. J., Mamelak, A. N., Madison, R. D., Macklis, J. D., & Hobson, J. A. (1989). Map inputs to REM sleep induction sites with carbachol-fluorescent microspheres. *Science, 245,* 984–986.

Quay, H. C. (1979). Classification. In H. C. Quay & J. S. Werry (Eds.), *Psychopathological disorders of childhood* (2nd ed.). New York: Wiley.

Rabbitt, P. (1977). Changes in problem solving ability in old age. In J. E. Birren & K. W. Schaie (Eds.), *Handbook of the psychology of aging.* New York: Van Nostrand Reinhold.

Rabkin, J. G., & Struening, E. L. (1976). Life events, stress, and illness. *Science, 194,* 1013–1020.

Rachman, S. (1989). *Fear and courage* (2nd ed.). New York: Freeman.

Rachman, S. J., & Hodgson, R. J. (1980). *Obsessions and compulsions.* Englewood Cliffs, NJ: Prentice-Hall.

Rachman, S. J., & Wilson, G. T. (1980). *The effects of psychological therapy* (2nd ed.). New York: Pergamon Press.

Rada, J. B., & Rogers, R. W. (1973). *Obedience to authority: Presence of authority and command strength.* Paper presented at the annual convention of the Southeastern Psychological Association.

Rader, N., Spiro, D. J., & Firestone, P. B. (1979). Performance on a stage IV object permanence task with standard and nonstandard covers. *Child Development, 50,* 908–910.

Radloff, L. (1975). Sex differences in depression: The effects of occupation and marital status. *Sex Roles, 1,* 249–265.

Ragland, D. R., & Brand, R. J. (1988). Type A behavior and mortality from coronary heart disease. *New England Journal of Medicine, 318,* 65–69.

Rahe, R., Romo, M., Bennett, L., & Siltanen, P. (1974). Recent life changes, myocardial infarction, and abrupt coronary death: Studies in Helsinki. *Archives of Internal Medicine, 133,* 221–228.

Rajecki, D. W. (1990). *Attitudes: Themes and advances* (2nd ed.). Sunderland, MA: Sinauer Associates.

Rakic, P., & Yaklovlev P. I. (1968). Development of the corpus callosum and the cavum septi in man. *Journal of Comparative Neurology, 132,* 45–72.

Raloff, J. (1985). A sweet taste of success to drink in. *Science News, 127,* 262.

Ramachandran, V. S. (1988, August). Perceiving shape from shading. *Scientific American,* pp. 76–83.

Rappaport, J. (1977). *Community psychology: Values, research and action.* New York: Holt, Rinehart and Winston.

Rappaport, J. (1987). Terms of empowerment/exemplars of prevention: Toward a theory for community psychology. *American Journal of Community Psychology, 15,* 117–148.

Raschke, H. J. (1977). The role of social participation in postseparation and postdivorce adjustment. *Journal of Divorce, 1,* 129–140.

Raskin, D. C., & Podlesny, J. A. (1979). Truth and deception: A reply to Lykken. *Psychological Bulletin, 86,* 54–59.

Rasmussen, J. (1981). Models of mental strategies in process control. In J. Rasmussen & W. Rouse (Eds.), *Human detection and diagnosis of system failures.* New York: Plenum Press.

Ratcliff, R., & McKoon, G. (1989). Memory models, text processing, and cue-dependent retrieval. In H. L. Roediger & F. I. M. Craik (Eds.), *Varieties of memory and consciousness.* Hillsdale, NJ: Lawrence Erlbaum Associates.

Ray, D. W., Wandersman, A., Ellisor, J., & Huntington, D. E. (1982). The effects of high density in a juvenile correctional institution. *Basic and Applied Social Psychology, 3,* 95–108.

Raynor, J. O. (1970). Relationships between achievement-related motives, future orientation, and academic performance. *Journal of Personality and Social Psychology, 15,* 28–33.

Reason, J. (1989). *Human Error.* Cambridge, Eng.: Cambridge University Press.

Reason, J. (1990). *Human error.* Cambridge, Eng.: Cambridge University Press.

Rechtschaffen, A., Gilliland, M. A., Bergmann, B. M., & Winter, J. B. (1983). Physiological correlates of prolonged sleep deprivaton in rats. *Science, 221,* 180–184.

Redd, W. H. (1984). Psychological intervention to control cancer chemotherapy side effects. *Postgraduate Medicine, 75,* 105–113.

Redd, W. H., Jacobsen, P. B., Die-Trill, M., Dermatis, H., McEvoy, M., & Holland, J. C. (1987). Cognitive/attentional distraction in the control of conditioned nausea in pediatric cancer patients receiving chemotherapy. *Journal of Consulting and Clinical Psychology, 55,* 391–395.

Reder, L. M., & Anderson, J. R. (1980). A partial resolution of the paradox of interference: The role of integrating knowledge. *Cognitive Psychology, 12,* 447–472.

Reed, T. (1980). Challenging some "common wisdom" on drug abuse. *International Journal of the Addictions, 15,* 359–373.

Reedy, M. N. (1983). Personality and aging. In D. S. Woodruff & J. E. Birren (Eds.), *Aging: Scientific perspectives and social issues* (2nd ed.). Monterey, CA: Brooks/Cole.

Reedy, M. N., Birren, J. E., & Schaie, K. W. (1981). Age and sex differences in satisfying love relationships across the adult life span. *Human Development, 24,* 52–56.

Regan, D., Kaufman, L., & Lincoln, J. (1986). Motion in depth and visual acceleration. In K. Boff, L. Kaufman, & J. Thomas (Eds.), *Handbook of Perception and Human Performance.* New York: Wiley.

Reiman, E. M., Fusselman, M. J., Fox, P. T., & Raichle, M. E. (1989). Neuroanatomical correlates of anticipatory anxiety. *Science, 243,* 1071–1074.

Reiman, E. M., Raichle, M. E., Butler, F. K., Herscovitch, P., & Robins, E. (1984). A focal brain abnormality in panic disorder, a severe form of anxiety. *Nature, 310,* 683-685.

Reinisch, J. M. (1981). Prenatal exposure to synthetic progestins increases potential for aggression in humans. *Science, 211,* 1171–1173.

Reis, H. T., & Shaver, P. (1988). Intimacy as an interpersonal process. In S. Duck (Ed.), *Handbook of personal relationships.* Chichester, UK: Wiley.

Reisberg, D., Heuer, F., McLean, J., & O'Shaughnessy, M. (1988). The quantity, not the quality of affect predits memory vividness. *Bulletin of the Psychonomic Society, 26,* 100–103.

Reisenzein, R. (1983). The Schachter theory of emotion: Two decades later. *Psychological Bulletin, 94,* 239–264.

Reisman, J. M. (1976). *A history of clinical psychology.* New York: Irvington.

Reiss, S., & McNally, R. J. (1985). The expectancy model of fear. In S. Reiss & R. R. Bootzin (Eds.), *Theoretical issues in behavior therapy.* New York: Academic Press.

Reitman, J. S. (1971). Mechanisms of forgetting in short-term memory. *Cognitive Psychology, 2,* 185–195.

Reitman, J. S. (1974). Without surreptitious rehearsal, information in short-term memory decays. *Journal of Verbal Learning and Verbal Behavior, 13,* 365–377.

Repetti, R. L. (1989). Effects of daily workload on subsequent behavior during marital interaction: The roles of social withdrawal and spouse support. *Journal of Personality and Social Psychology, 57,* 651–659.

Rescorla, L. A. (1981). Category development in early language. *Journal of Child Language, 8,* 225–238.

Rescorla, R. (1988). Pavlovian conditioning: It's not what you think it is. *American Psychologist, 43,* 151–159.

Rescorla, R. A. (1968). Probability of shock in the presence and absence of CS in fear conditioning. *Journal of Comparative and Physiological Psychology, 66,* 1–5.

Revusky, S. H. (1971). The role of interference in association over a delay. In W. K. Honig & P. H. R. James (Eds.), *Animal memory.* New York: Academic Press.

Revusky, S. H. (1977). The concurrent interference approach to delay learning. In L. M. Barker, M. R. Best, & M. Domjan (Eds.), *Learning mechanisms in food selection.* Waco, TX: Baylor University Press.

Reynolds, D. V. (1969). Surgery in the rat during electrical analgesia induced by focal brain stimulation. *Science, 164,* 444–445.

Rheingold, H. L., & Eckerman, C. O. (1971). Departures from the mother. In H. R. Schaffer (Ed.), *The origins of human social relations.* London: Academic Press.

Rhodewalt, F., & Zone, J. B. (1989). Appraisal of life change, depression, and illness in hardy and nonhardy women. *Journal of Personality and Social Psychology, 56,* 81–88.

Rholes, W. S., & Ruble, D. N. (1984). Children's understanding of dispositional characteristics of others. *Child Development, 55,* 550–560.

Rice, P. L. (1987). *Stress and health: Principles and practice for coping and wellness.* Pacific Grove, CA: Brooks/Cole.

Richardson, P. H., & Vincent, C. A. (1986). Acupuncture for the treatment of pain: A review of evaluative research. *Pain, 24,* 15–40.

Rickards, J. P. (1976). Interaction of position and conceptual level of adjunct questions in immediate and delayed retention of text. *Journal of Educational Psychology, 68,* 210–217.

Ridley, M., & Dawkins, R. (1981). The natural selection of altruism. In J. P. Rushton & R. M. Sorrentino (Eds.), *Altruism and helping behavior.* Hillsdale, NJ: Lawrence Erlbaum Associates.

Riegel, K. F. (1975). Toward a dialectical theory of development. *Human Development, 18,* 50–64.

Riese, M. L. (1986). Temperament stability between the neonatal period and 24 months in full-term and preterm infants. *Infant Behavior and Development, 9,* 305. (Special issue: abstracts of papers presented at the Fifth International Conference on Infant Studies.)

Riggar, T. F. (1985). *Stress burnout: An annotated bibliography.* Carbondale: Southern Illnois University Press.

Riggio, R. E. (1989). *Introduction to industrial/organizational psychology.* Glenview, IL: Scott Foresman.

Riggle, (1989). (See Ottati, et al., 1989.)

Ringold, D. J. (1988). Consumer response to product withdrawal: The reformulation of Coca-Cola. *Psychology & Marketing, 5,* 189–210.

Rinn, W. E. (1984). The neuropsychology of facial expression: A review of the neurological and psychological mechanisms for producing facial expressions. *Psychological Bulletin, 95,* 52–77.

Risley, T. R. (1968). The effects and side effects of punishing the autistic behaviors of a deviant child. *Journal of Applied Behavior Analysis, 1,* 21–34.

Robertson, J., & Robertson, J. (1971). Young children in brief separation: A fresh look. *Psychoanalytic Study of the Child, 26,* 264–315.

Robins, L. N., & Helzer, J. E. (1986). Diagnosis and clinical assessment: The current state of psychiatric diagnosis. *Annual Review of Psychology, 37,* 409–432.

Robins, L. N., Helzer, J. E., Weissman, M. M., Orvaschel, H., Gruenberg, E., Burke, J. D., Jr., & Regier, D. A. (1984). Lifetime prevalence of specific psychiatric disorders in three sites. *Archives of General Psychiatry, 41,* 949–958.

Rock, I. (1975). *An introduction to perception.* New York: Macmillan.

Rock, I. (1978). *An introduction to perception.* New York: Macmillan.

Rock, I. (1983). *The logic of perception.* Cambridge, MA: MIT Press.

Rodgers, J. L., & Rowe, D. C. (1988). Influence of siblings on adolescent sexual behavior. *Developmental Psychology, 24,* 722–728.

Rodin, J. (1973). Effects of distraction on the performance of obese and normal subjects. *Journal of Comparative and Physiological Psychology, 83,* 68–78.

Rodin, J. (1980). Current status of the internal-external hypothesis of obesity: What went wrong? *American Psychologist, 36,* 361–372.

Rodin, J. (1986a). Aging and health: Effects of the sense of control. *Science, 233,* 1271–1276.

Rodin, J. (1986b). Health, control, and aging. In M. Baltes & P. Baltes (Eds.), *Aging and control.* Hillsdale, NJ: Lawrence Erlbaum Associates.

Rodin, J., & Langer, E. J. (1977). Long-term effects of a control-relevant intervention with the institutionalized aged. *Journal of Personality and Social Psychology, 35,* 879–902.

Rodin, J., & Salovey, P. (1989). Health psychology. *Annual Review of Psychology, 40,* 533–580.

Rodin, J., Bartoshuk, L., Peterson, C., & Shank, D. (1990). Bulimia and taste: Possible interactions. *Journal of Abnormal Psychology, 99,* 32–39.

Roffman, R. A., Gilchrist, L. D., Stephens, R. S., & Kirham, M. A. (1988, November). *Relapse prevention with gay or bisexual males at risk of AIDS due to engaging in unsafe sexual behavior.* Paper presented at the annual meetings of the Association for the Advancement of Behavior Therapy, New York.

Roffwarg, H. P., Muzio, J. N., & Dement, W. C. (1966). Ontogenetic development of the human sleep-dream cycle. *Science, 152,* 604–619.

Rogers, C. R. (1951). *Client-centered therapy.* Boston: Houghton Mifflin.

Rogers, C. R. (1961). *On becoming a person.* Boston: Houghton Mifflin.

Rogers, C. R. (1970). *Carl Rogers on encounter groups.* New York: Harper & Row.

Rogers, C. R. (1980). *A way of being.* Boston: Houghton Mifflin.

Rogers, J., Madamba, S. G., Staunton, D. A., & Siggins, G. R. (1986). Ethanol increases single unit activity in the inferior olivary nucleus. *Brain Research, 385,* 253–262.

Rogers, M., & Miller, N. (1981). *The effect of school setting on cross-racial interaction.* Paper presented at the Annual Meeting of the American Psychological Association, Montreal.

Rogers, R., & Ewing, P. (1989). Ultimate opinion proscriptions: A cosmetic fix and a plea for empiricism. *Law and Human Behavior, 13,* 357–374.

Rohde, P., Lawinsohn, P. M., Tilson, M., & Seeley, J. R. (1990). Dimensionality of coping and its relation to depression. *Journal of Personality and Social Psychology, 58,* 499–511.

Ronis, D. L., Yates, J. F., & Kirscht, J. P. (1989). Attitudes, decisions, and habits as determinants of repeated behavior. In A. R. Pratkanis, S. J. Breckler, & A. G. Greenwald (Eds.), *Attitude structure and function.* Hillsdale, NJ: Lawrence Erlbaum Associates.

Rook, K. S. (1987). Social support versus companionship: Effects on life stress, loneliness, and evaluations by others. *Journal of Personality and Social Psychology, 52,* 1132–1137.

Rosch, E. (1975). Cognitive representations of semantic categories. *Journal of Experimental Psychology: General, 104,* 192–223.

Rosch, E., Mervis, C. B., Gray, W. D., Johnson, D. M., & Boyes-Braem, P. (1976). Basic objects in natural categories. *Cognitive Psychology, 8,* 382–439.

Rose, S. A., Feldman, J. F., & Wallace, I. F. (1988). Individual differences in infants' information processing: Reliability, stability, and prediction. *Child Development, 59,* 1177–1197.

Rosen, B. C., & D'Andrade, R. (1959). The psychosocial origins of achievement motivation. *Sociometry, 22,* 188–218.

Rosenbaum, M. E. (1980). Cooperation and competition. In P. B. Paulus (Ed.), *The psychology of group influence.* Hillsdale, NJ: Lawrence Erlbaum Associates.

Rosenbaum, M. E. (1986). The repulsion hypothesis: On the non-development of relationships. *Journal of Personality and Social Psychology, 51,* 1156–1166.

Rosenbaun, D. L., & Seligman, M. E. (1989). *Abnormal psychology* (2nd ed.). New York: Norton.

Rosenberg, M. B., Friedmann, T., Robertson, R. C., Tuszynski, M., Wolff, J. A., Breakefield, X. O., & Gage, F. H. (1988). Grafting genetically modified cells to the damaged brain: Restorative effects of NGF expression. *Science, 242,* 1575–1578.

Rosenhan, D. L. (1973). On being sane in insane places. *Science, 179,* 250–258.

Rosenhan, D. L. & Seligman, M.E.P. (1989). *Abnormal psychology.* (2nd ed.) New York: Norton.

Rosenman, R. H., Brand, R. J., Jenkins, D., Friedman, M., Straus, R., & Wurm, M. (1975). Coronary heart disease in the Western Collaborative Group study: Final follow-up experience of 8½ years. *Journal of the American Medical Association, 233,* 872–877.

Rosenthal, D. (1977). Searches for the mode of genetic transmission in schizophrenia: Reflections and loose ends. *Schizophrenia Bulletin, 3,* 268–276.

Rosenthal, R. R., & Jacobson, L. (1968). *Pygmalion in the classroom.* New York: Holt, Rinehart and Winston.

Rosenzweig, M. R., Bennett, E. L., & Diamond, M. C. (1972). Brain changes in response to experiences. *Scientific American, 226,* 22–39.

Roskies, E., Seraganian, P., Oseasohn, R., Hanley, J. A., Collu, R., Martin, N., & Smilga, C. (1986). The Montreal type A intervention project: Major findings. *Health Psychology, 5,* 45–69.

Ross, B. H. (1984). Reminders and their effects in learning a cognitive skill. *Cognitive Psychology, 16,* 371–416.

Ross, D. M., & Ross, S. A. (1982). *Hyperactivity: Current issues, research, and theory.* New York: Wiley & Sons.

Ross, L. D. (1988). Situationist perspectives on the obedience experiments. *Contemporary Psychology, 33,* 101–104.

Ross, M. (1989). Relation of implicit theories to the construction of personal histories. *Psychological Review, 96,* 341–357.

Ross, S. M., & Ross, L. E. (1971). Comparison of trace and delay classical eyelid conditioning as a function of interstimulus interval. *Journal of Experimental Psychology, 91,* 165–167.

Rossiter, J. R., & Percy, L. (1987). *Advertising and promotion management.* New York: McGraw-Hill.

Rotfeld, H. J. (1989). Fear appeals and persuasion: Assumptions and errors in advertising research. In J. H. Leigh & C. R. Martin (Eds.), *Current issues and research in advertising.* Ann Arbor: University of Michigan Press.

Rotter, J. B. (1954). *Social learning and clinical psychology.* Englewood Cliffs, NJ: Prentice-Hall.

Rotter, J. B. (1990). Internal versus external control of reinforcement: A case history of a variable. *American Psychologist, 45,* 489–493.

Rotton, J., Frey, J., Barry, T., Mulligan, M., & Fitzpatrick, M. (1979). The air pollution experience and physical aggression. *Journal of Applied Social Psychology, 9,* 397–412.

Rouéché, B. (1986, December 8) Cinnabar. *The New Yorker.*

Rouse, W. B., & Morris, N. M. (1986). On looking into the black box: Prospects and limits in the search for mental models. *Psychological Bulletin, 100,* 349–363.

Rowlison, R. T., & Felner, R. D. (1988). Major life events, hassles, and adaptation in adolescence: Confounding in the conceptualization and measurement of life stress and adjustment revisited. *Journal of Personality and Social Psychology, 55,* 432–444.

Rozanski, A., Bairey, C. N., Krantz, D. S., Friedman, J., Resser, K. J., Morell, M., Hilton-Chalfen, S., Hestrin, L., Bietendorf, J., & Berman, D. S. (1988). Mental stress and the induction of silent myocardial ischemia in patients with coronary artery disease. *The New England Journal of Mecicine, 318,* 1005–1012.

Rozin, P. (1982). "Taste-smell confusions" and the duality of the olfactory sense. *Perception and Psychophysics, 31,* 397–401.

Rubin, E. (1915). *Synsoplevede figure.* Copenhagen: Gyldendalske.

Rubinow, D. R., & Roy-Byrne P. (1984). Premenstrual syndromes: Overview from a methodological perspective. *American Journal of Psychiatry, 141,* 163–172.

Rubinow, D. R., Roy-Byrne, P., Hoban, M. C., Grover, G. N., Stambler, N., & Post, R. M. (1988). Premenstrual mood changes: Characteristic patterns in women with and without premenstrual syndrome. *Journal of Affective Disorders, 10,* 85–90.

Rubinstein, T., & Mason, A. F. (1979, November). The accident that shouldn't have happened: An analysis of Three Mile Island. *IEEE Spectrum,* 37–57.

Ruble, D. N. (1977). Premenstrual symptoms: a reinterpretation. *Science, 197,* 291–292.

Ruble, D. N., Fleming, A. S., Hackel, L. S., & Stangor, C. (1988). Changes in the marital relationship during the transition to first time motherhood: Effects of violated expectations concerning division of household labor. *Journal of Personality and Social Psychology, 55,* 78–87.

Ruehlman, L. S., & Wolchik, S. A. (1988). Personal goals and interpersonal support and hindrance as factors in psychological distress and well-being. *Journal of Personality and Social Psychology, 55,* 293–301.

Rumbaugh, D. M. (Ed.). (1977). *Language learning by a chimpanzee: The Lana project.* New York: Academic Press.

Rumelhart, D. E. (1984). Schemata and the cognitive system. In R. S. Wyer & T. K. Srull (Eds.), *Handbook of social cognition: Vol. 1.* Hillsdale, NJ: Lawrence Erlbaum Associates.

Rumelhart, D. E., McClelland, J. L. & the PDP Research Group, (1986). *Parallel distributed processing: Vol. 1. Foundations.* Cambridge, MA: MIT Press.

Rundus, D. (1971). Analysis of rehearsal processes in free recall. *Journal of Experimental Psychology, 89,* 63–77.

Rushton, J. P. (1988). Epigenic rules in moral development: Distal-proximal approaches to altruism and aggression. *Aggressive Behavior, 14,* 35–50.

Rushton, J. P., Fulker, D. W., Neale, M. C., Nias, D. K. B., & Eysenck, H. J. (1986). Altruism and aggression: The heritability of individual differences. *Journal of Personality and Social Psychology, 50,* 1192–1198.

Russek, M. (1971). Hepatic receptors and the neurophysiological mechanisms controlling feeding behavior. In S. Ehrenpreis (Ed.), *Neurosciences research: Vol. 4.* New York: Academic Press.

Russell, M. J. (1976). Human olfactory communication. *Nature, 260,* 520–522.

Russell, M. J., Dark, K. A., Cummins, R. W., Ellman, G., Callaway, E., & Peeke, H. V. S. (1984). Learned histamine release. *Science, 225,* 733–734.

Rutkowski, G. K., Gruder, C. L., & Romer, D. (1983). Group cohesiveness, social norms, and bystander intervention. *Journal of Personality and Social Psychology, 44,* 545–552.

Rutter, M., & Giller, H. (1984). *Juvenile delinquency: Trends and perspectives.* New York: Guilford.

Ryan, W. (1977). *Blaming the victim.* New York: Vintage Books.

Rynders, J., & Horrobin, J. (1980). Educational provisions for young children with Down's syndrome. In J. Gottlieb (Ed.), *Educating mentally retarded persons in the mainstream* (pp. 109–147). Baltimore: University Park Press.

Sachs, J. (1967). Recognition memory for syntactic and semantic aspects of connected discourse. *Perception and Psychophysics, 2,* 437–442.

Sackeim, H. A. (1985, June). The case for ECT. *Psychology Today,* pp. 36–40.

Sackeim, H. A. (1988). Mechanisms of action of electroconvulsive therapy. In A. J. Frances & R. E. Hales (Eds.), *Annual Review of Psychiatry* (Vol. 7). Washington, DC: American Psychiatric Press.

Sackeim, H. A., Gur, R. C. J., & Saucy, M. C. (1978). Emotions are expressed more intensely on the left side of the face. *Science 202,* 434–436.

Sackoff, J., & Weinstein, L. (1988). The effects of potential self-inflicted harm on obedience to an authority figure. *Bulletin of the Psychonomic Society, 26,* 347–348.

Sacks, O. (1985). *The man who mistook his wife for a hat.* New York: Summit Books.

Saghir, M. T., & Robins, E. (1973). *Male and female homosexuality: A comprehensive investigation.* Baltimore: Williams & Wilkins.

Sajwaj, T., Libet, J., & Agras, S. (1974). Lemon-juice therapy: The control of life-threatening rumination in a six-month infant. *Journal of Applied Behavioral Analysis, 7,* 557–563.

Sakitt, B., & Long, G. M. (1979). Spare the rod and spoil the icon. *Journal of Experimental Psychology: Human Perception and Performance, 5,* 19–30.

Salthouse, J. A. (1985). *A theory of cognitive aging.* Amsterdam: North Holland.

Sampson, H. A., & Jolie, P. L. (1984). Increased plasma histamine concentrations after food challenges in children with atopic dermatitis. *The New England Journal of Medicine, 311,* 372–376.

Sande, G. N., Goethals, G. R., & Radloff, C. E. (1988). Perceiving one's own traits and others': The multifaceted self. *Journal of Personality and Social Psychology, 54,* 13–20.

Sanderson, W. C., Rapee, R. M., & Barlow, D. H. (1989). The influence of an illusion of control on panic attacks induced via inhalation of 5.5% carbon dioxide-enriched air. *Archives of General Psychiatry 46*, 157–162.

Sapolsky, B. S. (1984). Arousal, affect, and the aggression-moderating effect of erotica. In N. M. Malamuth & E. I. Donnerstein (Eds.), *Pornography and sexual aggression.* New York: Academic Press.

Sapolsky, R. M., Krey, L. C., & McEwen, B. S. (1985). Prolonged glucocorticoid exposure reduces hippocampal neurin number: Implications for aging. *Journal of Neuroscience, 5,* 1222–1227.

Sarason, I. G. (1978). The test anxiety scale concept and research. In C. D. Spielberger & I. G. Sarason (Eds.), *Stress and anxiety: Vol. 5* (pp. 193–216). Washington, DC: Hemisphere.

Sarason, I. G. (1984). Stress, anxiety, and cognitive interference: Reactions to tests. *Journal of Personality and Social Psychology, 46(4),* 929–938.

Sarason, I. G., & Sarason, B. R. (Eds.). (1985). *Social support: Theory, research and applications.* The Hague: Martinus Nijhof.

Sarason, I. G., Sarason, B. R., Keefe, D. E., Hayes, B. E., & Shearin, E. N. (1986). Cognitive interference: Situational determinants and traitlike characteristics. *Journal of Personality and Social Psychology, 51,* 215–226.

Sarbin, T. R. (1950). Contributions to role-taking theory: I. Hypnotic behavior. *Psychological Review, 57,* 255–270.

Sarnoff, C. (1976). *Latency.* New York: Aronson.

Sartorius, N., Shapiro, R., & Jablensky, A. (1974). The international pilot study of schizophrenia. *Schizophrenia Bulletin, 1,* 21–35.

Satir, V. (1967). *Conjoint family therapy* (rev. ed.). Palo Alto, CA: Science and Behavior Books.

Saufley, W. H., Otaka, S. R., & Bavaresco, J. L. (1985). Context effects: Classroom tests and context independence. *Memory and Cognition, 13,* 522–528.

Savage-Rumbaugh, E. S., Pate, J. L., Lawson, J., Smith, S. T., & Rosenbaum, S. (1983). Can a chimpanzee make a statement? *Journal of Experimental Psychology: General, 112,* 469–487.

Savin-Williams, R. C., & Demo, D. H. (1984). Developmental change and stability in adolescent self-concept. *Developmental Psychology, 20,* 1100–1110.

Scarr, S. (1989). Sociobiology: The psychology of sex, violence, and oppression. *Contemporary Psychology, 34,* 440–443.

Scarr, S., & Carter-Saltzman, L. (1982). Genetics and intelligence. In R. Sternberg (Ed.), *Handbook of human intelligence.* Cambridge: Cambridge University Press.

Scarr, S., & Weinberg, R. A. (1976). IQ test performance of black children adopted by white families. *American Psychologist, 31,* 726–739.

Scarr, S., Webber, P. L., Weinberg, R. A., & Wittig, M. A. (1981). Personality resemblance among adolescents and their parents in biologically related and adoptive families. *Journal of Personality and Social Psychology, 40,* 885–898.

Schachter, S. (1959). *The psychology of affiliation.* Stanford, CA: Stanford University Press.

Schachter, S. (1971). Some extraordinary facts about obese humans and rats. *American Psychologist, 26,* 129–144.

Schachter, S., & Friedman, L. N. (1974). The effects of work and cue prominence on eating behavior. In S. Schachter & J. Rodin (Eds.), *Obese humans and rats.* Potomac, MD: Lawrence Erlbaum Associates.

Schachter, S., & Singer, J. (1962). Cognitive, social and physiological determinants of emotional state. *Psychological Review, 69,* 379–399.

Schachter, S., & Rodin, J. (Eds.). (1974). *Obese humans and rats.* Potomac, MD: Lawrence Erlbaum Associates.

Schaefer, C., Coyne, J. C., & Lazarus, R. S. (1982). The health-related functions of social support. *Journal of Behavioral Medicine, 4,* 381–406.

Schaefer, J., Sykes, R., Rowley, R., & Baek, S. (1988, November). *Slow country music and drinking.* Paper presented at the 87th

annual meetings of the American Anthropological Association, Phoenix, AZ.

Schaeffer, M. A., Baum, A., Paulus, P. B., & Gaes, G. G. (1988). Architecturally mediated effects of social density in prison. *Environment and Behavior, 20,* 3–19.

Schafer, R., & Murphy, G. (1943). The role of autism in a figure-ground relationship. *Journal of Experimental Psychology, 32,* 335–343.

Schaffer, C. E., Davidson, R. J., & Saron, C. (1983). Frontal and parietal EEG asymmetry in depressed and non-depressed subjects. *Biological Psychiatry, 18,* 753–762.

Schaie, K. W. (1979). The primary mental abilities in adulthood: An exploration in the development of psychometric intelligence. In P. B. Baltes & O. G. Brim, Jr. (Eds.), *Life-span development and behavior: Vol. 2.* New York: Academic Press.

Schaie, K. W., & Labouvie-Vief, G. (1974). Generational versus ontogenetic components of change in adult cognitive behavior. *Developmental Psychology, 10,* 305–320.

Scheerer, M., Rothmann, R., & Goldstein, K. (1945). *A case of "idiot savant": An experimental study of personality organization.* Psychol. Monognomics, 58 (4).

Scheier, M. F., & Carver, C. S. (1985). Optimism, coping, and health: Assessment and implications of generalized outcome expectancies. *Journal of Personality, 4,* 219–247.

Scheier, M. F., & Carver, C. S. (1987). Dispositional optimism and physical well-being: The influence of generalized outcome expectancies on health. *Journal of Personality, 55,* 169–210.

Scheier, M. F., Matthews, K. A., Owens, J. F., Magovern, G. J., Lefebvre, R. C., Abbott, R. A., & Carver, C. S. (1989). Dispositional optimism and recovery from coronary artery bypass surgery: The beneficial effects on physical and psychological well-being. *Journal of Personality and Social Psychology, 57,* 1024–1040.

Schenck, C. H., Bundlie, S. R., Patterson, A. L., & Mahowald, M. W. (1987). Rapid eye movement sleep behavior disorder: A treatable parasomnia affecting older adults. *Journal of the American Medical Association, 257,* 1786–1789.

Schick, R. R., Yaksh, T. L., & Go, V. L. W. (1986). An intragastric meal releases the putative satiety factor cholecystokinin from hypothalamic neurons in cats. *Brain Research, 370,* 349–353.

Schiff, M., Duyme, M., Dumaret, A., Stewart, J., Tomkiewicz, S., & Feingold, J. (1978). Intellectual status of working class children adopted early into upper-middle class families. *Science, 200,* 1503–1504.

Schleifer, S. J., Keller, S. E., Camerino, M., Thornton, J. C., & Stein, M. (1983). Suppression of lymphocyte stimulation following bereavement. *Journal of the American Medical Association, 250,* 374–377.

Schlesier-Stroop, B. (1984). Bulimia: A review of the literature. *Psychological Bulletin, 95,* 247–257.

Schlossberg, N. K. (1987, May). Taking the mystery out of change. *Psychology Today,* pp. 74–75.

Schmale, A. H., & Iker, H. P. (1966). The effect of hopelessness and the development of cancer. *Psychosomatic Medicine, 28,* 714–721.

Schmidt, S. R., & Bohannon, J. N. (1988). In defense of the flashbulb-memory hypothesis: A comment on McCloskey, Wible, and Cohen (1988). *Journal of Experimental Psychology: General, 117,* 332–335.

Schnapf, J. L., & Baylor, D. A. (1987). How photoreceptor cells respond to light. *Scientific American, 256,* 40–47.

Schnapf, J. L., Kraft, T. W., & Baylor, D. A. (1987). Spectral sensitivity of human cone photoreceptors. *Nature, 325,* 439–441.

Schneider, B. (1985). Organizational behavior. *Annual Review of Psychology, 36,* 573–611.

Schneider, W. (1984). Developmental trends in the metamemory-behavior relationship. In D. L. Forrest-Pressley, G. E. MacKinnon,

& P. G. Waller (Eds.), *Metacognition, cognition, and human performance.* New York: Academic Press.

Schneider, W., & Detweiler, M. (1988). The role of practice in dual-task performance: Toward workload modeling in a connectionist/control architecture. *Human Factors, 30,* 539–566.

Schoenfeld, H. H. (1979). Explicit heuristic training as a variable in problem solving performance. *Journal for Research in Mathematical Education, 10,* 173–187.

Schroeder, D. A., Dovidio, J. F., Sibicky, M. E., Matthews, L. L., & Allen, J. L. (1988). Empathic concern and helping behavior: Egoism or altruism? *Journal of Experimental Social Psychology, 24,* 333–353.

Schroeder, D. H., & Costa, P. T. (1984). Influence of life event stress on physical illness: Substantive effects or methodological flaws? *Journal of Personality and Social Psychology, 46,* 853–863.

Schuckit, M. A. (1983). The genetics of alcoholism. In B. Tabakoff, P. B. Sutker, & C. L. Randall (Eds.), *Medical and social aspects of alcohol use.* New York: Plenum Press.

Schuckit, M. A., & Gold, E. (1988). Serum prolactin levels in sons of alcoholics and control subjects. *American Journal of Psychiatry, 144,* 854–859.

Schulz, R. (1978). *The psychology of death, dying, and bereavement.* Reading, MA: Addison-Wesley.

Schum, D. (1975). The weighing of testimony of judicial proceedings from sources having reduced credibility. *Human Factors, 17,* 172–203.

Schwartz, G. E. (1982). Testing the biopsychosocial model: The ultimate challenge facing behavioral medicine. *Journal of Consulting and Clinical Psychology, 50,* 6.

Schwartz, G. E., & Weiss, S. M. (1978). Behavioral medicine revisited: An amended definition. *Journal of Behavioral Medicine, 1,* 249–252.

Schwartz, J. T. (1988). The new connectionism: Developing relationships between neuroscience and artificial intelligence. In S. R. Graubard (Ed.), *The artificial intelligence debate.* Cambridge, MA: MIT Press.

Schwartz, R. M. (1982). Cognitive-behavior modification: A conceptual review. *Clinical Psychology Review, 2,* 267–293.

Schwartz, S., & Griffin, T. (1986). *Medical thinking: The psychology of medical judgment and decision-making.* New York: Springer-Verlag.

Schwarzwald, J., Bizman, A., & Raz, M. (1983). The foot-in-the-door paradigm: Effects of second request size on donation probability and donor generosity. *Personality and Social Psychology Bulletin, 9,* 443–450.

Schwitzgebel, R. L., & Schwitzgebel, R. K. (1980). *Law and psychological practice.* New York: Wiley.

Scott, J. P. (1983). A systems approach to research on aggressive behavior. In E. C. Simmel, M. E. Hahn, & J. K. Walters (Eds.), *Aggressive behavior: Genetic and neural approaches.* Hillsdale, NJ: Lawrence Erlbaum Associates.

Scovern, A. W., & Kilmann, P. R. (1980). Status of electroconvulsive therapy: Review of the outcome literature. *Psychological Bulletin, 87,* 260–303.

Seab, J. P., Jagust, W. J., Wong, S. T. S., Roos, M. S., Reed, B. R., & Budinger, T. F. (1988). Quantitative NMR measurements of hippocampal atrophy in Alzheimer's disease. *Magnetic Resonance in Medicine, 8,* 200–208.

Searles, J. S. (1985). A methodological and empirical critique of psychotherapy outcome meta-analysis. *Behaviour Research and Therapy, 23,* 453–463.

Sears, R. R. (1972). Attachment, dependency, and frustration. In J. L. Gewirtz (Ed.), *Attachment and dependency.* Washington, DC: Winston.

Secord, D., & Peevers, B. (1974). The development and attribution of person concepts. In T. Mischel (Ed.), *Understanding other persons.* Oxford: Blackwell.

Secretary of Health and Human Services. (1987). *Sixth special report to the U.S. Congress on alcohol and health* (DHHS Publication No. 87-1519). Rockville, MD: U.S. Department of Health and Human Services.

Secretary of Health, Education, and Welfare. (1980). *Marijuana and health.* Washington, DC: U.S. Government Printing Office.

Seeman, J. (1989). Toward a model of positive health. *American Psychologist, 44,* 1099–1109.

Seeman, P., & Lee, T. (1975). Antipsychotic drugs: Direct correlation between clinical potency and presynaptic action on dopamine neurons. *Science, 188,* 1217–1219.

Segal, M., & Bloom, F. E. (1976). The action of norepinephrine in the rat hippocampus: III. Hippocampal cellular responses to locus coeruleus stimulation in the awake rat. *Brain Research, 107,* 499–511.

Segal, M. W. (1974). Alphabet and attraction: An unobtrusive measure of the effect of propinquity in a field setting. *Journal of Personality and Social Psychology, 30,* 654–657.

Seifer, R., & Sameroff, A. (1989, January). Paper on the Rochester Longitudinal Study presented at the annual convention of the American Association for the Advancement of Science, San Francisco.

Seitz, V., Apfel, N. H., & Rosenbaum, L. (1981). Projects Head Start and Follow Through: A longitudinal evaluation of adolescents. In M. J. Begam, H. Garber, & H. C. Haywood (Eds.), *Prevention of retarded development in psychosocially disadvantaged children.* Baltimore: University Park Press.

Sejnowski, T. J., & Rosenberg, C. R. (1987). Parallel networks that learn to pronounce English text. *Journal of Complex Systems, 1,* 145–168.

Sejnowski, T. J., Koch, C., & Churchland, P. S. (1988). Computational neuroscience. *Science, 241,* 1299–1306.

Seligman, M. E. P. (1970). On the generality of the laws of learning. *Psychological Review, 77,* 406–418.

Seligman, M. E. P. (1971). Phobias and preparedness. *Behavior Therapy, 2,* 307–320.

Seligman, M. E. P. (1975). *Helplessness: On depression, development, and death.* San Francisco: W. H. Freeman.

Seligman, M. E. P., & Maier, S. F. (1967). Failure to escape traumatic shock. *Journal of Experimental Psychology, 74,* 1–9.

Seligman, M. E. P., Klein, D. C., & Miller, W. R. (1976). Depression. In H. Leitenberg (Ed.), *Handbook of behavior modification and behavior therapy.* Englewood Cliffs, NJ: Prentice-Hall.

Selman, R. L. (1980). *The growth of interpersonal understanding: Developmental and clinical analyses.* New York: Academic Press.

Selman, R. L. (1981). The child as a friendship philosopher. In S. R. Asher & J. M. Gottman (Eds.), *The development of children's friendships.* New York: Cambridge University Press.

Selman, R. L., Schorin, M. Z., Stone, C. R., & Phelps, E. (1983). A naturalistic study of children's social understanding. *Developmental Psychology, 19,* 82–102.

Seltzer, J. A., & Kalmuss, D. (1988). Socialization and stress explanations for spouse abuse. *Social Forces, 67,* 473–491.

Selye, H. (1956). *The stress of life.* New York: McGraw-Hill.

Selye, H. (1976). *The stress of life* (2nd ed.). New York: McGraw-Hill.

Shaffer, L. H. (1975). Multiple attention in continuous verbal tasks. In S. Dornic (Ed.), *Attention and performance: Vol. V.* New York: Academic Press.

Shank, R., & Abelson, R. (1977). *Scripts, plans, goals, and understanding.* Hillsdale, NJ: Lawrence Erlbaum Associates.

Shapiro, D. H. (1980). *Meditation: Self regulation strategy and altered state of consciousness.* New York: Aldine.

Shapiro, D. H., & Giber, D. (1978). Meditation and psychotherapeutic effects: Self regulation strategy and altered states of consciousness. *Archives of General Psychiatry, 35,* 294–302.

Shapiro, D. H., & Walsh, R. N. (Eds.). (1984). *Meditation: Classical and contemporary perspectives.* New York: Aldine.

Shapiro, S., Skinner, E. A., Kessler, L. G., Von Korff, M., German, P. S., Tischler, G. L., Leaf, P. J., Beham, L., Cottler, L., & Legler, D. A. (1984). Utilization of health and mental health services. *Archives of General Psychiatry, 41,* 971–978.

Shaver, P., Hazan, C., & Bradshaw, D. (1988). Love as attachment: The integration of three behavioral systems. In R. J. Sternberg & M. L. Barnes (Eds.), *The psychology of love.* New Haven: Yale University Press.

Shaw, M. E. (1981). *Group dynamics: The psychology of small group behavior* (3rd ed.). New York: McGraw-Hill.

Shaw, M. E., Rothschild, G. H., & Strickland, J. F. (1957). Decision processes in communication nets. *Journal of Abnormal and Social Psychology, 54,* 323–330.

Sheehy, G. (1977). *Passages: Predictable crises of adult life.* New York: Bantam.

Shepard, C., Kohut, J. J., & Sweet, R. (1989). *News of the weird.* New York: New American Library.

Shepard, R. & Metzler, J. (1971). Mental rotation of three dimensional objects. *Science, 171,* 701–703.

Shepherd-Look, D. L. (1982). Sex differentiation and the development of sex roles. In B. B. Wolman & G. Stricker (Eds.), *Handbook of developmental psychology.* Englewood Cliffs, NJ: Prentice-Hall.

Sher, K. J., & Levenson, R. W. (1982). Risk for alcoholism and individual differences in the stress-response-dampening effects of alcohol. *Journal of Abnormal Psychology, 91,* 350–367.

Sherif, M. (1937). An experimental approach to the study of attitudes. *Sociometry, 1,* 90–98.

Sherrington, R., Brynjolfsson, J., Petursson H., Potter, M., Dudleston, K., Barraclough, B., Wasmuth, J., Dobbs, M., & Gurling, H. (1988). Localization of a susceptibility locus for schizophrenia on chromosome 5. *Nature, 336,* 164–167.

Sherwin, B. B. (1988). Affective changes with estrogen and androgen replacement therapy in surgically menopausal women. *Journal of Affective Disorders, 14,* 177–187.

Sherwin, B. B., Gelfand, M. M., & Brender, W. (1985). Androgen enhances sexual motivation in females: A prospective crossover study of sex steroid administration in the surgical menopause. *Psychosomatic Medicine, 47,* 339–351.

Sherwin, R., & Sherry, C. (1985). Campus sexual norms and dating relationships: A trend analysis. *Journal of Sex Research, 21,* 258–274.

Shiffrin, R. M. (1973). Information persistence in short-term memory. *Journal of Experimental Psychology, 100,* 39–49.

Shimamura, A. P., & Squire, L. R. (1988). Long-term memory in amnesia: Cued recall, recognition memory, and confidence ratings. *Journal of Experimental Psychology: Learning, Memory, and Cognition, 14,* 763–770.

Shneidman, E. S. (1973). Suicide. In *Encyclopedia Britannica.* Chicago: Encyclopedia Britannica.

Shneidman, E. S. (1985). *Definition of suicide.* New York: Harper & Row.

Shneidman, E. S. (1987, March). At the point of no return. *Psychology Today.*

Shor, R. E., & Orne, M. T. (1963). Norms on the Harvard group scale of hypnotic susceptibility, Form A. *International Journal of Clinical and Experimental Hypnosis, 11,* 39–47.

Shortcliffe, E. H. (1983). Medical consultation systems: Designing for doctors. In M. E. Sime & M. J. Coombs (Eds.), *Designing for human computer communication.* New York: Academic Press.

Shugan, S. M. (1980). The cost of thinking. *Journal of Consumer Research, 7,* 99–111.

Siegel, J. M., (1984). Type A behavior: Epidemiologic foundations and public health implications. *Annual Review of Public Health, 5,* 343–367.

Siegel, J. M. (1986). The Multidimensional Anger Inventory. *Journal of Personality and Social Psychology, 51,* 191–200.

Siegel, J. M., & Rogawski, M. A. (1988). A function for REM sleep: Regulation of noradrenergic receptor sensitivity. *Brain Research Review, 13,* 213–233.

Siegel, L. S., McCabe, A. E., Brand, J., & Matthews, J. (1978). Evidence for the understanding of class inclusion in preschool children: Linguistic factors and training effects. *Child Development, 49,* 688–693.

Siegel, S. (1984). Pavlovian conditioning and heroin overdose: Reports by overdose victims. *Bulletin of the Psychonomic Society, 22,* 428–430.

Siegel, S., & Ellsworth, D. W. (1986). Pavlovian conditioning and death from apparent overdose of medically prescribed morphine: A case report. *Bulletin of the Psychonomic Society, 24,* 278–280.

Siever, L. J., & Davis, K. L. (1985). Overview: Toward a dysregulation hypothesis of depression. *American Journal of Psychiatry, 142,* 1017–1031.

Sifneos, P. (1979). *Short-term dynamic psychotherapy: Evaluating and technique.* New York: Plenum Press.

Sigman, M., Cohen, S., Beckwith, L., & Parmelee, A. (1986). Infant attention in relation to intellectual abilities in childhood. *Developmental Psychology, 6,* 788–792.

Silbert, M. H., & Pines, A. M. (1984). Pornography and sexual abuse of women. *Sex Roles, 10,* 857–868.

Silver, R. L., & Wortman, C. B. (1980). Coping with undesirable life events. In J. Garber & M. E. P. Seligman (Eds.), *Human helplessness: Theory and applications* (pp. 279–340). New York: Academic Press.

Silverman, L. H. (1983). Subliminal psychodynamic activation method: Overview and comprehensive listing of studies. In J. Masling (Ed.), *Empirical studies in psychoanalysis* (Vol. 1). Hillsdale, NJ: Lawrence Erlbaum Associates.

Silverman, L. H., & Weinberger, J. (1985). Mommy and I are one: Implications for psychotherapy. *American Psychologist, 40,* 1296–1308.

Silverton, L., Mednick, S. A., Schulsinger, F., Parnas, J., & Harrington, M. E. (1988). Genetic risk for schizophrenia, birthweight, and cerebral ventricular enlargement. *Journal of Abnormal Psychology, 97,* 496–498.

Silviera, J. M. (1971). *Incubation: The effect of interruption timing and length on problem solution and quality of problem processing.* Unpublished doctoral dissertation. University of Oregon, Eugene.

Sime, W. E. (1984). Psychological benefits of exercise training in the healthy individual. In J. D. Matarazzo, S. M. Weiss, J. A. Herd, N. Miller, & S. M. Weiss (Eds.), *Behavioral health: A handbook of health enhancement and disease prevention.* New York: Wiley.

Simmons, R. G., Rosenberg, F., & Rosenberg, M. (1973). Disturbance in the self-image at adolescence. *American Sociological Review, 38,* 553–568.

Simon, H. A. (1974). How big is a chunk? *Science, 183,* 482–488.

Simons, C. (1987, December). A long-distance ticket to life. *Smithsonian,* pp. 44–52.

Singer, J. (1976). *The inner world of daydreaming.* New York: Harper & Row.

Singley, M. K., & Anderson, J. R. (1989). *The transfer of cognitive skill.* Cambridge, MA: Harvard University Press.

Sizemore, C. C., & Pittillo, E. S. (1970). *I'm Eve.* New York: Doubleday.

Skinner, B. F. (1953). *Science and human behavior.* New York: Macmillan.

Skinner, B. F. (1961). *Cumulative record* (3rd ed.). Englewood Cliffs, NJ: Prentice-Hall.

Slaby, R. G., & Frey, K. S. (1975). Development of gender constancy and selective attention to same-sex models. *Child Development, 46,* 849–856.

Slamecka, N. J., & McElree, B. (1983). Normal forgetting of verbal lists as a function of their degree of learning. *Journal of Experimental Psychology: Learning, Memory, and Cognition, 9,* 384–397.

Slater, J., & DePue, R. A. (1981). The contribution of environmental events and social support to serious suicide attempts in primary depressive disorder. *Journal of Abnormal Psychology, 90,* 17–35.

Slavin, R. E. (1985). Cooperative learning: Applying contact theory in desegregated schools. *Journal of Social Issues, 41,* 45–62.

Sloane, R. B., Staples, F. R., Cristol, A. H., Yorkston, N. J., & Whipple, K. (1975). *Psychotherapy versus behavior therapy.* Cambridge: Harvard University Press.

Slobodyansky, E., Guidotti, A., Wambebe, C., Berkovich, A., & Costa, E. (1989). Isolation and characterization of a rat brain triakonta-tetraneuropeptide, a posttranslational product of diazepam binding inhibitor: Specific action at the Ro 5-4864 recognition site. *Journal of Neurochemistry, 53,* 1276–1284.

Slovic, P. (1984). *Facts versus fears: Understanding perceived risk.* In science and public policy seminar sponsored by the Federation of Behavioral and Psychological and Cognitive Sciences, Washington, DC.

Small, I. F., Small, J. G., & Milstein, V. (1986). Electroconvulsive therapy. In P. A. Berger & H. K. H. Brodie (Eds.), *American handbook of psychiatry: Biological psychiatry* (2nd ed., Vol. 8). New York: Basic Books.

Smeaton, G., Byrne, D., & Murnen, S. K. (1989). The repulsion hypothesis revisited: Similarity irrelevance or dissimilarity bias? *Journal of Personality and Social Psychology, 56,* 54–59.

Smith, A. C., III, & Kleinman, S. (1989). Managing emotions in medical school: Students' contacts with the living and the dead. *Social Psychology Quarterly, 52,* 56–69.

Smith, C. A. (1989). Dimensions of appraisal and physiological response in emotion. *Journal of Personality and Social Psychology, 56,* 339–353.

Smith, C. A., & Ellsworth, P. C. (1987). Patterns of appraisal and emotion related to taking an exam. *Journal of Personality and Social Psychology, 52,* 475–488.

Smith, D. (1982). Trends in counseling and psychotherapy. *American Psychologist, 37,* 802–809.

Smith, G. F., & Dorfman, D. D. (1975). The effect of stimulus uncertainty on the relationship between frequency of exposure and liking. *Journal of Personality and Social Psychology, 31,* 150–155.

Smith, J. C. (1975). Meditation as psychotherapy: A review of the literature. *Psychological Bulletin, 82,* 558–564.

Smith, M. L., Glass, G. V., & Miller, T. I. (1980). *The benefits of psychotherapy.* Baltimore: Johns Hopkins University Press.

Smith, P. K., & Connolly, K. (1972). Patterns of play and social interaction in preschool children. In N. Blurton Jones (Ed.), *Ethological studies of child behaviour.* Cambridge: Cambridge University Press.

Smith, S., & Freedman, D. G. (1983, April). *Mother-toddler interaction and maternal perception of child temperament in two ethnic groups: Chinese-American and European-American.* Paper presented at the meeting of the Society for Research in Child Development, Detroit, MI.

Smith, S. L. (1975). Mood in the menstrual cycle. In E. J. Sacher (Ed.), *Topics in psychoendocrinology.* New York: Grune & Stratton.

Smith, S. M., Brown, H. O., Toman, J. E. P., & Goodman, L. S. (1947). The lack of cerebral effects of d-tubocurarine. *Anesthesiology, 8,* 1–14.

Smith, S. M., Glenberg, A. M., & Bjork, R. A. (1978). Environmental context and human memory. *Memory and Cognition, 6,* 342–355.

Smith, S. M., Vela, E., & Williamson, J. E. (1988). Shallow input processing does not induce environmental context-dependent recognition. *Bulletin of the Psychonomic Society, 26,* 537–540.

Smith, S. R., & Meyer, R. G. (1987). *Law, behavior, and mental health: Policy and practice.* New York: New York University Press.

Smith, T. W., & Anderson, N. B. (1986). Models of personality and disease: An interactional approach to type A behavior and cardiovascular risk. *Journal of Personality and Social Psychology, 50,* 1166–1173.

Smith, T. W., Allred, K. D., Morrison, C. A., & Carlson, S. D. (1989). Cardiovascular reactivity and interpersonal influence: Active coping in a social context. *Journal of Personality and Social Psychology, 56,* 209–218.

Snarey, J. (1987). A question of morality. *Psychological Bulletin, 97,* 202–232.

Snow, R. E., & Yallow, E. (1982). Education and intelligence. In R. Sternberg (Ed.), *Handbook of human intelligence.* Cambridge: Cambridge University Press.

Snowdon, C. T. (1969). Motivation, regulation, and the control of meal parameters with oral and intragastric feeding. *Journal of Comparative and Physiological Psychology, 69,* 91–100.

Snyder, C. R., & Forsythe, D. R. (Eds.). (1990). *Handbook of social clinical psychology: The health perspective.* New York: Pergamon Press.

Snyder, C. R., & Fromkin, H. L. (1980). *Uniqueness: The human pursuit of difference.* New York: Plenum.

Snyder, C. R., & Higgins, R. L. (1988). Excuses: Their effective role in the negotiation of reality. *American Psychologist, 104,* 23–35.

Snyder, D. K., & Wills, R. M. (1989). Behavioral versus insight-oriented marital therapy: Effects on individual and interspousal functioning. *Journal of Consulting and Clinical Psychology, 57,* 39–46.

Snyder, M. (1984). When belief creates reality. In L. Berkowitz (Ed.), *Advances in experimental social psychology* (Vol. 18). New York: Academic Press.

Snyder, M., Tanke, E. D., & Berscheid, E. (1977). Social perception and interpersonal behavior: On the self-fulfilling nature of social stereotypes. *Journal of Personality and Social Psychology, 35,* 656–666.

Snyder, S. H. (1978). Dopamine and schizophrenia. In L. C. Wynne, R. L. Cromwell, & S. Matthysse (Eds.), *The nature of schizophrenia: New approaches to research and treatment* (pp. 87–94). New York: Wiley.

Snyderman, M., & Herrnstein, R. J. (1983). Intelligence tests and the Immigration Act of 1924. *American Psychologist, 38,* 986–995.

Sokoloff, L. (1981). Localization of functional activity in the central nervous system by measurement of glucose utilization with radioactive deoxyglucose. *Journal of Cerebral Blood Flow & Metabolism, 1,* 7–36.

Soloman, Z., Mikulincer, M., & Avitzur, E. (1988). Coping, loss of control, social support, and combat-related posttraumatic stress disorder: A prospective study. *Journal of Personality and Social Psychology, 55,* 279–285.

Solomon, R. L. (1980). The opponent-process theory of acquired motivation: The costs of pleasure and the benefits of pain. *American Psychologist, 35,* 691–712.

Solomon, R. L., & Corbit, J. D. (1974). An opponent-process theory of motivation: I. Temporal dynamics of affect. *Psychological Review, 81,* 119–145.

Solomon, R. L., Kamin, L. J., & Wynne, L. C. (1953). Traumatic avoidance learning: The outcomes of several extinction procedures with dogs. *Journal of Abnormal and Social Psychology, 48,* 291–302.

Solso, R. L. (1988). *Cognitive psychology.* Newton, MA: Allyn & Bacon.

Sorce, J., Emde, R., & Frank, M. (1982). Maternal referencing in normal and Down's syndrome infants: A longitudinal study. In R. Emde & R. Harmon (Eds.), *The development of attachment and affiliative systems.* New York: Plenum Press.

Sorce, J., Emde, R., Campos, J., & Klinnert, M. (1981, April). *Maternal emotional signaling: Its effect on the visual cliff behavior of one-year-olds.* Paper presented at the meetings of the Society for Research in Child Development, Boston, MA.

Sorrentino, R. M., & Field, N. (1986). Emergent leadership over time: The functional value of positive motivation. *Journal of Personality and Social Psychology, 50,* 1091–1099.

Spanier, G. B., & Lewis, R. A. (1980). Marital quality: A review of the seventies. *Journal of Marriage and the Family, 42,* 825–839.

Spanos, N. P., Lush, N. I., & Gwynn, M. I. (1989). Cognitive skill-training enhancement of hypnotizability: Generalization effects and trance logic responding. *Journal of Personality and Social Psychology, 56,* 795–804.

Spearman, C. (1927). *The abilities of man.* London: Macmillan.

Spelke, E. S. (1982). Perceptual knowledge of objects in infancy. In J. Mehler, M. Garrett, & E. Walker (Eds.), *Perspectives on mental representation.* Hillsdale, NJ: Lawrence Erlbaum Associates.

Spelke, E. S., van Hofsten, C., & Kestenbaum, R. (1989) . Object perception in infancy: Interaction of spatial and kinetic information for object boundaries. *Developmental Psychology, 25,* 185–196.

Speltz, M. L., & Bernstein, D. A. (1979). The use of participant modeling for claustrophobia: A case report. *Journal of Behavior Therapy and Experimental Psychiatry, 10,* 251–255.

Spence, M. J., & DeCasper, A. J. (1982, March). *Human fetuses perceive maternal speech.* Paper presented at the meeting of the International Conference on Infant Studies, Austin, TX.

Sperling, G. (1960). The information available in brief visual presentations. *Psychological Monographs, 74,* 1–29.

Sperry, R. W. (1968). Hemisphere deconnection and unity in conscious awareness. *American Psychologist, 23,* 723–733.

Sperry, R. W. (1974). Lateral specialization in the surgically separated hemispheres. In F. O. Schmitt & F. G. Wordon (Eds.), *The neurosciences third study program.* Cambridge: MIT Press.

Spiegel, D., Bloom, J. R., Kraemer, H. C., & Gottheil, E. (1989, October 14). Effect of psychosocial treatment on survival of patients with metastatic breast cancer. *The Lancet 2* (8668), 888–891.

Spiegler, M. D., & Guevremont, D. C. (in press). *Contemporary behavior therapy.* Pacific Grove, CA: Brooks/Cole.

Spielberger, C. (1979). *Understanding stress and anxiety.* New York: Harper & Row.

Spielberger, C. D. (1983). *State-Trait Anxiety Inventory (Form Y) manual.* Palo Alto, CA: Consulting Psychologists Press.

Spitzer, R. L., Severino, S. K., Williams, J. B., & Parry, B. L. (1989). Late luteal phase dysphoric disorder and DSM-III-R. *American Journal of Psychiatry, 146,* 892–897.

Spitzer, R. L., Skodol, A. E., Gibbon, M., & Williams, J. B. W. (1983). *Psychopathology: A casebook.* New York: McGraw-Hill.

Springer, S. P., & Deutsch, G. (1989). *Left brain, right brain.* San Francisco: W. H. Freeman.

Squire, L. R. (1986). Mechanisms of memory. *Science, 232,* 1612–1619.

Squire, S. (1987, November 22). Shock therapy's return to respectability. *New York Times Magazine,* pp. 78–89.

Squires, K. C., Donchin, E., Herning, R. I., & McCarthy, G. (1977). On the influence of task relevance and stimulus probability on event-related-potential components. *Electroencephalography and Clinical Neurophysiology, 42,* 1–14.

Squires, R. F., & Braestrup, C. (1977). Benzodiazepine receptors in rat brain. *Nature, 266,* 732–734.

Srull, T. K., & Gaelick, L. (1983). General principles and individual differences in the self as a habitual reference point: An examination of self-other judgements of similarity. *Social Cognition, 2,* 108–121.

Srull, T. K., & Wyer, R. S. (1983). The role of control processes and structural constraints in models of memory and social judgement. *Journal of Experimental Social Psychology, 19,* 497–521.

Staddon, J. E. R., & Ettinger, R. H. (1989). *Learning: An introduction to the principles of adaptive behavior.* San Diego: Harcourt Brace Jovanovich.

Standing, L., Conezio, J., & Haber, R. N. (1970). Perception and memory for pictures: Single-trial learning of 2500 visual stimuli. *Psychonomic Science, 19,* 73–74.

Stang, D. J. (1972). Conformity, ability and self-esteem. *Representative Research in Social Psychology, 3,* 97–103.

Stanislaw, H., & Rice, F. J. (1988). Correlation between sexual desire and menstrual cycle characteristics. *Archives of Sexual Behavior, 17,* 499–508.

Stankov, L. (1983). Attention and intelligence. *Journal of Educational Psychology, 75,* 471–490.

Stanley, G., & Hall, R. (1973). Short term visual information processing in dyslexics. *Child Development, 44,* 841–844.

Stasser, G., Kerr, N. L., & Davis, J. H. (1989). Influence processes and consensus models in decision-making in groups. In P. B. Paulus (Ed.), *Psychology of group influence* (2nd ed.). Hillsdale, NJ: Lawrence Erlbaum Associates.

Staw, B. M., & Ross, J. (1989). Understanding behavior in escalation situations. *Science, 246,* 216–220.

Stearns, C. Z., & Stearns, P. N. (1986). *Anger: The struggle for emotional control in America's history.* Chicago: University of Chicago Press.

Steele, C. M. (1986, January). What happens when you drink too much? *Psychology Today.*

Steele, C. M., & Josephs, R. A. (1988). Drinking your troubles away II: An attention-allocation model of alcohol's effects on psychological stress. *Journal of Abnormal Psychology, 97,* 196–205.

Steinberger, L. (1986). Stability (and instability) of type A behavior from childhood to young adulthood. *Developmental Psychology, 22,* 393–402.

Stephan, W. G. (1985). Intergroup relations. In G. Lindzey & E. Aronson (Eds.), *Handbook of social psychology,* Vol. 2 (3rd ed.). New York: Random House.

Stephens, J. H., & Kamp, M. (1962). On some aspects of hysteria: A clinical study. *Journal of Nervous and Mental Disease, 134,* 305–315.

Stern, R. (1983). Antidepressant drugs in the treatment of obsessive-compulsive disorders. *Journal of Behavior Therapy and Experimental Psychiatry, 14,* 19–23.

Sternberg, R. J. (1982). Reasoning, problem solving and intelligence. In R. J. Sternberg (Ed.), *Handbook of human intelligence.* Cambridge: Cambridge University Press.

Sternberg, R. J. (1985). *Beyond IQ: A triarchic theory of human intelligence.* Cambridge, MA: Cambridge University Press.

Sternberg R. J. (1987). Liking versus loving: A comparative evaluation of theories. *Psychological Bulletin, 102,* 331–345.

Sternberg, R. J. (1988). *The triarchic mind.* New York: Cambridge Press.

Sternberg, R. J. (1988). Triangulating love. In R. J. Sternberg & M. L. Barnes (Eds.), *The psychology of love.* New Haven: Yale University Press.

Sternberg, R. J., & Barnes, M. L. (Eds.). (1988). *The psychology of love.* New Haven: Yale University Press.

Sternberg, R. J., & Detterman, D. (1986). *What is intelligence?* Norwood, NJ: Ablex.

Sternberg, R. J., & Gastel, J. (1989). Coping with novelty in human intelligence: An empirical investigation. *Intelligence, 13,* 187–197.

Sternberg, R. J., & Grajeck, S. (1984). The nature of love. *Journal of Personality and Social Psychology, 47,* 312–329.

Sternberg, S. (1966). High-speed scanning in human memory. *Science, 153,* 652–654.

Sternberg, S. (1969). Mental processes revealed by reaction time experiments. *American Scientist, 57,* 421–457.

Sternglanz, S. H., & Serbin, L. A. (1974). Sex-role stereotyping in children's television programs. *Developmental Psychology, 10,* 710–715.

Stevens, A., & Coupe, P. (1978). Distortions in judged spatial relations. *Cognitive Psychology, 10,* 422–437.

Stevens, J. C., & Hooper, J. E. (1982). How skin and object temperature influence touch sensation. *Perception and Psychophysics, 32,* 282–285.

Stevens, S. S. (1957). On the psychophysical law. *Psychological Review, 64,* 153–181.

Stewart, A. J. (1989). Social intelligence and adaptation to life changes. In R. S. Wyer & T. K. Srull (Eds.), *Advances in social cognition: Vol. 2: Social intelligence and cognitive assessments of personality*. Hillsdale, NJ: Lawrence Erlbaum Associates.

Stewart, A. L., & Brook, R. H. (1983). Effects of being overweight. *American Journal of Public Health, 73*, 171–178.

Stigler, J. W. (1984). "Mental abacus": The effect of abacus training on Chinese children's mental calculation. *Cognitive Psychology, 16*, 145–176.

Stiles, W. B., Shapiro, D. A., & Elliott, R. (1986). "Are all psychotherapies equivalent?" *American Psychologist, 41*, 165–180.

Stokes, A. F., Wickens, C. D., & Kite, K. (1990). *Display technology: Human factors concepts*. Warrendale, PA: Society of Automotive Engineers, Inc.

Stone, A. A., Cox, D. S., Valdimarsdottir, H., Jandorf, N., & Neale, J. M. (1987). Evidence that secretory IgA antibody is associated with daily mood. *Journal of Personality & Social Psychology, 52*, 988–993.

Stone, A. A., Helder, L., & Schneider, M. S. (1988). Coping with stressful events: Coping dimensions and issues. In L. H. Cohen (Ed.), *Research on stressful life events: Theoretical and methodological issues*. New York: Sage.

Stone, M. H. (1986). Exploratory psychotherapy in schizophrenia-spectrum patients: A reevaluation in the light of long-term follow-up of schizophrenic and borderline patients. *Bulletin of the Menninger Clinic, 50*, 287–306.

Storms, M. D. (1980). Theories of sexual orientation. *Journal of Personality and Social Psychology, 38*, 783–792.

Storms, M. D. (1981). A theory of erotic orientation development. *Psychological Review, 88*, 340–353.

Strauman, T. J. (1989). Self-discrepancies in clinical depression and social phobia: Cognitive structures that underlie emotional disorders? *Journal of Abnormal Psychology, 98*, 14–22.

Straus, M. A., Gelles, R. J., & Steinmetz, S. K. (1980). *Behind closed doors*. Garden City, NY: Anchor Books.

Strayer, D. L., Wickens, C. D., & Braune, R. (1987). Adult age differences in the speed and capacity of information processing: 2. An electrophysiological approach. *Psychology and Aging, 2*, 99–110.

Streissguth, A. P., Barr, H. M., Sampson, P. D., Darby, B. L., & Martin, D. C. (1989). IQ at age 4 in relation to maternal alcohol use and smoking during pregnancy. *Developmental Psychology, 25*, 3–11.

Stretch, J. D. (1985). Posttraumatic stress disorder among U.S. Army Reserve Vietnam and Vietnam-era veterans. *Journal of Consulting and Clinical Psychology, 53*, 935.

Streufert, S. (1986). *Complexity, managers and organizations*. Orlando, FL: Academic Press.

Strickland, B. R. (1989). Internal-external control expectancies: From contingency to creativity. *American Psychologist, 44*, 1–12.

Stroop, J. R. (1935). Studies of interference in serial verbal reactions. *Journal of Experimental Psychology, 18*, 643–662.

Strube, M. J., Boland, S. M., Manfredo, P. A., & Abdulrahman, A. (1987). Type A behavior pattern and the self-evaluation of abilities: Empirical tests of the self-appraisal model. *Journal of Personality and Social Psychology, 52*, 956–974.

Strube, M. J., Gardner, W., & Hartmann, D. P. (1985). Limitations, liabilities, and obstacles in reviews of the literature: The current status of meta-analysis. *Clinical Psychology Review, 5*, 63–78.

Strupp, H. H. (1989). Psychotherapy: Can the practitioner learn from the researcher? *American Psychologist, 44*, 717–724.

Strupp, H. H., & Hadley, S. W. (1977). A tripartite model of mental health and therapeutic outcomes. *American Psychologist, 32*, 187–196.

Suberi, M., & McKeever, W. F. (1977). Differential right hemispheric memory storage of emotional and non-emotional faces. *Neuropsychologia, 15*, 757–768.

Suddath, R. L., Christison, G. W., Torrey, E. F., Casanova, M. F., & Weinberger, D. R. (1990). Anatomical abnormalities in the brains of monopsychotic twins discordant for schizophrenia. *New England Journal of Medicine, 322*, 789–794.

Suedfeld, P. (1980). *Restricted environmental stimulation: Research and clinical applications*. New York: Wiley.

Suedfeld, P., & Baker-Brown, G. (1986). Restricted environmental stimulation therapy and aversion conditioning in smoking cessation: Active and placebo effects. *Behaviour Research & Therapy, 24*, 421–428.

Suedfeld, P., Roy, C., & Landon, P. B. (1982). Restricted environmental stimulation therapy in the treatment of essential hypertension. *Behaviour Research and Therapy, 20*, 553–560.

Sulin, R. A., & Dooling, D. J. (1974). Intrusion of a thematic idea in retention of prose. *Journal of Experimental Psychology, 103*, 255–262.

Sullivan, H. S. (1953). *The interpersonal theory of psychiatry*. New York: W. W. Norton.

Sullivan, H. S. (1954). *The psychiatric interview*. New York: W. W. Norton.

Sullivan, J. W., & Horowitz, F. D. (1983). The effects of intonation on infant attention: The role of the rising intonation contour. *Journal of Child Language, 10*, 521–534.

Sullivan, K., & Sullivan, A. (1980). Adolescent-parent separation. *Developmental Psychology, 10*, 93–99.

Suls, J., & Fletcher, B. (1985). The relative efficacy of avoidant and nonavoidant coping strategies: A meta-analysis. *Health Psychology, 4*, 249–288.

Suls, J., & Sanders, G. (1988). Type A behavior as a general risk factor for physical disorder. *Journal of Behavioral Medicine, 11*, 201–225.

Suls, J., & Wan, C. K. (1989). The relation between type A behavior and chronic emotional distress: A meta-analysis. *Journal of Personality and Social Psychology, 57*, 505–512.

Suzdak, P. D., Glowa, J. R., Crawley, J. N., Schwartz, R. D., Skolnick, P., & Paul, S. M. (1986). A selective imidazobenzodiazepine antagonist of ethanol in the rat. *Science, 234*, 1243–1247.

Swaab, D. F., & Fliers, E. (1985). A sexually dimorphic nucleus in the human brain. *Science, 228*, 1112–1115.

Swanson, L. W. (1976). The locus coeruleus: A cytoarchitectonic, Golgi, and immunohistochemical study in the albino rat. *Brain Research, 110*, 39–56.

Sweetland, R. C., & Keyser, D. J. (Eds.). (1986). *Tests: A complete reference for assessments in psychology, education, and assessment*. Kansas City, MO: Test Corporation of America.

Sweller, J., & Gee, W. (1978). Einstellung: The sequence effect and hypothesis theory. *Journal of Experimental Psychology: Human Learning and Memory, 4*, 513–526.

Swets, J., & Druckman, D. (1988). *Enhancing human performance*. Washington, DC: National Academy of Sciences Press.

Swift, D. W., & Freeman, M. H. (1986, July). Application of head up displays to ears. *Displays*, pp. 107–110.

Szasz, T. S. (Ed.). (1974). *The age of madness: The history of involuntary hospitalization*. New York: Jason Aronson.

Szasz, T. S. (1987). *Insanity: The idea and its consequences*. New York: Wiley.

Szmukler, G. I., & Russell, G. F. M. (1986). Outcome and prognosis of anorexia nervosa. In K. D. Brownell & J. P. Foreyt (Eds.), *Handbook of eating disorders*. New York: Basic Books.

Talley, P. F., Strupp, H. H., & Morey, L. C. (1990). Matchmaking in psychotherapy: Patient-therapist dimensions and their impact on outcome. *Journal of Consulting and Clinical Psychology, 58*, 182–188.

Tanner, C. M. (1989). The role of environmental toxins in the etiology of Parkinson's disease. *Trends in Neurosciences, 12*, 49–54.

Tarler-Benlolo, L. (1978). The role of relaxation in biofeedback training: A critical review of the literature. *Psychological Bulletin, 85*, 727–755.

Tarpy, R. M., & Sawabini, F. L. (1974). Reinforcement delay: A selective review of the last decade. *Psychological Bulletin, 81,* 984–987.

Taylor, D. A., & Altman, I. (1987). Communication in interpersonal relationships: Social penetration processes. In M. Roloff & G. Miller (Eds.), *Exploration in interpersonal communication* (2nd ed.). Beverly Hills: Sage.

Taylor, D. M., & Jaggi, V. (1974). Ethnocentrism and causal attribution in a South Indian context. *Journal of Cross-Cultural Psychology, 5,* 162–171.

Taylor J. W. (1979). Plasma progesterone, oestradiol 17 beta and premenstrual symptoms. *Acta Psychiatrica Scandinavica, 60,* 76–86.

Taylor, S. E. (1989). *Positive illusions: Creative self-deception and the healthy mind.* New York: Basic Books.

Taylor, S. E., & Brown, J. D. (1988). Illusion and well-being: A social psychological perspective on mental health. *Psychological Bulletin, 103,* 193–210.

Taylor, S. E., & Lobel, M. (1989). Social comparison activity under threat: Downward evaluation and upward contacts. *Psychological Review, 96,* 569–575.

Taylor, S. E., Buunk, B. P., & Aspinwall, L. G. (1990). Social comparison, stress, and coping. *Personality and Social Psychology Bulletin, 16,* 74–89.

Tecoma, E. S., & Huey, L. Y. (1985). Psychic distress and the immune response. *Life Sciences, 36,* 1799–1812.

Teitelbaum, P. (1957). Random and food-directed activity in hyperphagic and normal rats. *Journal of Comparative and Physiological Psychology, 50,* 486–490.

Teitelbaum, P. (1961). Disturbances in feeding and drinking behavior after hypothalamic lesions. In M. R. Jones (Ed.), *Nebraska symposium on motivation.* Lincoln: University of Nebraska Press.

Telch, M. J., Brouillard, M., Telch, C. F., Agras, W. S., & Taylor, C. B. (1989). Role of cognitive appraisal in panic-related avoidance. *Behaviour Research & Therapy, 27,* 373–383.

Tellegen, A., Lykken, D. T., Bouchard, T. J., Wilcox, K. J., Segal, N. L., & Rich, S. (1988). Personality similarity in twins reared apart and together. *Journal of Personality and Social Psychology, 54,* 1031–1039.

Terenius, L. (1988). Significance of opioid peptides and other potential markers of neuropeptide systems in cerebrospinal fluid. *Progress in Brain Research, 77,* 419–429.

Terkel, J., & Rosenblatt, J. S. (1972). Humoral factors underlying maternal behavior of parturition: Cross transfusion between freely moving rats. *Journal of Comparative and Physiological Psychology, 80,* 365–371.

Terman, L. M. (1916). *The measurement of intelligence.* Boston: Houghton Mifflin.

Terman, L. M. (1948). Kinsey's "Sexual behavior in the human male": Some comments and criticisms. *Psychological Bulletin, 45,* 443–459.

Terman, L. M., & Oden, M. (1959). *The gifted group at midlife.* Stanford, CA: Stanford University Press.

Terman, L. M., & Oden, M. H. (1947). *The gifted child grows up: Volume 4. Genetic studies of genius.* Stanford, CA: Stanford University Press.

Terrace, H. S., Petitto, L. A., Sanders, D. L. & Berer, J. G. (1979). Can an ape create a sentence? *Science, 206,* 891–902.

Tetrud, J. W., & Langston, J. W. (1989). The effect of deprenyl (selegiline) on the natural history of Parkinson's disease. *Science, 245,* 519–522.

Thoits, P. A. (1986). Social support as coping assistance. *Journal of Personality and Social Psychology, 54,* 416–423.

Thomae, H. (1980). Personality and adjustment to aging. In J. E. Birren & R. B. Sloane (Eds.), *Handbook of mental health and aging.* Englewood Cliffs, NJ: Prentice-Hall.

Thomas, A., & Chess, S. (1977). *Temperament and development.* New York: Brunner/Mazel.

Thomas, E. L., & Robinson, H. A. (1972). *Improving reading in every class: A sourcebook for teachers.* Boston: Allyn & Bacon.

Thompson, C. P., & Cowan, T. (1986). Flashbulb memories: A nicer interpretation of a Neisser recollection. *Cognition, 22,* 199–200.

Thompson, S. K. (1975). Gender labels and early sex role development. *Child Development, 46,* 339–347.

Thompson, T., & Grabowski, J. (Eds.). (1972). *Behavior modification of the mentally retarded.* New York: Oxford University Press.

Thorndike, E. L. (1898). Animal intelligence: An experimental study of the associative processes in animals. *Psychological Monographs, 2*(Whole No. 8).

Thorndike, R. L., Hagan, E., & Sattler, J. (1986). *Stanford-Binet* (4th ed.). Chicago: Riverside.

Tinbergen, N. (1989). *The study of instinct.* Oxford: Clarendon.

Tolman, E. C., & Honzik, C. H. (1930). Introduction and removal of reward and maze performance in rats. *University of California Publication in Psychology, 4,* 257–275.

Tomarken, A. J., Mineka, S., & Cook, M. (1989). Fear-relevant selective associations and covariation bias. *Journal of Abnormal Psychology, 98,* 381–394.

Tooby, J., & Cosmides, L. (1989). Evolutionary psychologists need to distinguish between the evolutionary process, ancestral selection pressures, and psychological mechanisms. *Behavioral and Brain Sciences, 12,* 724–725.

Torgersen, S. (1983). Genetic factors in anxiety disorders. *Archives of General Psychiatry, 40,* 1085–1089.

Tourangeau, R., & Rasinski, K. A. (1988). Cognitive processes underlying context effects in attitude measurement. *Psychological Bulletin, 103,* 299–314.

Tourangeau, R., Rasinski, K. A., Bradburn, N., & D'Andrade, R. (1989). Belief accessibility and context effects in attitude measurement. *Journal of Experimental Social Psychology, 25,* 401–421.

Trabasso, T., & Bower, G. H. (1968). *Attention in learning.* New York: Wiley.

Tracor, Inc. (1971). *Community reaction to aircraft noise: Vol. 1* (NASA Report CR-1761). Washington, DC: National Aeronautics and Space Administration.

Tranel, D., & Damasio, A. R. (1985). Knowledge without awareness: An autonomic index of facial recognition by prosopagnosics. *Science, 228,* 1453–1454.

Treffert, D. A. (1988). The idiot savant: A review of the syndrome. *American Journal of Psychiatry, 145,* 563–572.

Treisman, P. U. (1985). *A study of the mathematics performance of black students at the University of California, Berkeley.* Unpublished manuscript.

Tronick, E. Z. (1989). Emotions and emotional communication in infants. *American Psychologist, 44,* 112–119.

Trope, Y. (1989). The multiple roles of context in dispositional judgment. In J.N. Bassili (Ed.), *On-line cognition in person perception.* Hillsdale, NJ: Lawrence Erlbaum Associates.

Trujillo, C. M. (1986). A comparative evaluation of classroom interactions between professors and minority and non-minority college students. *American Educational Research Journal, 23,* 629–642.

Tsang, P. S., & Wickens, C. D. (1988). The structural constraints and strategic control of resource allocation. *Human Performance, 1,* 45–72.

Tulving, E. (1972). Episodic and semantic memory. In E. Tulving & W. Donaldson (Eds.), *Organization of memory.* New York: Academic Press.

Tulving, E. (1974). Cue-dependent forgetting. *American Scientist, 62,* 74–82.

Tulving, E. (1979). Relation between encoding specificity and levels of processing. In L. S. Cermak & F. I. M. Craik (Eds.), *Levels of processing in human memory.* Hillsdale, NJ: Lawrence Erlbaum Associates.

Tulving, E. (1982). *Elements of episodic memory.* New York: Oxford University Press.

Tulving, E. (1985). How many memory systems are there? *American Psychologist, 40,* 385–398.

Tulving, E., & Psotka, J. (1971). Retroactive inhibition in free recall: Inaccessibility of information available in the memory store. *Journal of Experimental Psychology, 87,* 1–8.

Tulving, E., & Schacter, D. L. (1990). Priming and human memory systems. *Science, 247,* 301–306.

Tulving, E., & Thomson, D. M. (1973). Encoding specificity and retrieval processes in episodic memory. *Psychological Review, 80,* 352–373.

Turiel, E. (1966). An experimental test of the sequentiality of developmental stages in the child's moral judgments. *Journal of Personality and Social Psychology, 3,* 611–618.

Turk, D. C. (1978). Cognitive behavioral techniques in the management of pain. In P. J. Foreyt & D. P. Pathjen (Eds.), *Cognitive behavior therapy: Research and applications.* New York: Plenum Press.

Turkington, C. (1987). Special talents. *Psychology Today,* pp. 42–46.

Turkkan, J. S. (1989). Classical conditioning: The new hegemony. *Behavioral & Brain Sciences, 12,* 121–179.

Turner, A. M., & Greenough, W. T. (1985). Differential rearing effects on rat visual cortex synapses: I. Synaptic and neuronal density and synapses per neuron. *Brain Research, 329,* 195–203.

Turner, J. C., & Oakes, P. J. (1989). Self-categorization theory and social influence. In P. B. Paulus (Ed.), *Psychology of group influence* (2nd ed.). Hillsdale, NJ: Lawrence Erlbaum Associates.

Turnstall, O., Gudjonsson, G., Eysenck, H., & Haward, L. (1982). Professional issues arising from psychological evidence presented in court. *Bulletin of the British Psychological Society, 35,* 329–331.

Tversky, A. (1972). Elimination by aspects: A theory of choice. *Psychological Review, 79,* 281–299.

Tversky, A., & Kahneman, D. (1974). Judgment under uncertainty: Heuristics and biases. *Science, 185,* 1124–1131.

Tversky, A., & Kahneman, D. (1981). The framing of decisions and the psychology of choice. *Science, 211,* 453–458.

Tversky, B., & Tuchin, M. (1989). A reconciliation of the evidence on eyewitness testimony: Comments on McCloskey and Zaragoza. *Journal of Experimental Psychology: General, 118,* 86–91.

Tyler, S., & Elliott, C. D. (1988). Cognitive profiles of groups of poor readers and dyslexic children on British ability scales. *British Journal of Psychology, 79,* 493–508.

Udry, J. R., Billy, J. O. G., Morris, N. M., Groff, T. R., & Raj, M. H. (1985). Serum androgenic hormones motivate sexual behavior in adolescent boys. *Fertility and Sterility, 43,* 90–94.

Ullmann, L., & Krasner, L. (1975). *A psychological approach to abnormal behavior* (2nd ed.). Englewood Cliffs, NJ: Prentice-Hall.

Ulrich, R. E., Stachnik, T. J., & Stainton, N. R. (1963). Student acceptance of generalized personality interpretations. *Psychological Reports, 13,* 831–834.

U. S. Congress. (1983). *Scientific validity of polygraph testing: A research review and evaluation* (Technical Memorandum OTA-TM-H-15). Washington, DC: U. S. Congress, Office of Technology Assessment.

U. S. Department of Commerce. (1986). *Statistical Abstract* (106th ed.). Washington, DC: U. S. Government Printing Office.

Vachon, M. L. S. Lyall, W. A. L., Rogers, J., Freeman-Letofsky, K., & Freeman, S. J. J. (1980). A controlled study of self-help intervention for widows. *American Journal of Psychiatry, 137,* 1380–1384.

Vaillant, G. E. (1977). *Adaptation to life: How the best and brightest came of age.* Boston: Little, Brown.

Valenstein, E. S. (Ed.). (1980). *The psychosurgery debate.* San Francisco: W. H. Freeman.

Van Buskirk, R. L., & Erickson, R. P. (1977). Odorant responses in taste neurons of the rat NTS. *Brain Research, 135,* 287–303.

van de Kragt, A. J. C., Orbell, J. M., Dawes, R. M., Braver, S., & Wilson, L. (1986). Doing well and doing good as ways of resolving social dilemmas. In H. Wilkie, D. Messick, & C. Rutte (Eds.), *Experimental social dilemmas.* Frankfurt: Verlag Peter Lang.

Van Dyke, C., & Byck, R. (1982). Cocaine. *Scientific American, 246,* 128–141.

Vane, J. (1972). Intelligence and achievement test results of kindergarten children in England, Ireland and the United States. *Journal of Clinical Psychology, 29,* 191–193.

Vernon, P. A. (1983). Speed of information processing and general intelligence. *Intelligence, 7,* 53–70.

Vernon, P. A. (1987a). New developments in reaction time research. In P. A. Vernon (Ed.), *Speed of information-processing and intelligence* (pp. 1–20). Norwood, NJ: Ablex.

Vernon, P. A. (Ed.). (1987b). *Speed of information-processing and intelligence.* Norwood, NJ: Ablex.

Verny, T. R. (1984). *Inside groups: A practical guide to encounter groups and group therapy.* New York: McGraw-Hill.

Vincent, C. A., & Richardson, P. H. (1986). The evaluation of therapeutic acupuncture: Concepts and methods. *Pain, 24,* 1–13.

Vincent, J. P., Kartalovski, B., Geneste, P., Kamenka, J. M., & Lazdunski, M. (1979). Interaction of phencyclidine ("angel dust") with a specific receptor in rat brain membranes. *Proceedings of the National Academy of Sciences, 76,* 4678–4682.

Vitiello, M. V., Carlin, A. S., Becker, J., Bradley, B., & Dutton, J. (1989). The effect of subliminal oedipal and competitive stimulation on dart throwing: Another miss. *Journal of Abnormal Psychology, 98,* 54–56.

Vokey, J. R., & Read, J. D. (1985). Subliminal messages: Between the devil and the media. *American Psychologist, 40,* 1231–1239.

Volkmar, F. R., & Greenough, W. T. (1972). Rearing complexity affects branching of dendrites in the visual cortex of the rat. *Science, 176,* 1445–1447.

Von Wright, J. M., Anderson, K., & Stenman, U. (1975). *Generalization of conditioned GSRs in dichotic listening.*

Vuchinich, R. E., & Sobell, M. B. (1978). Empirical separation of physiological and expected effects of alcohol on complex perceptual motor performance. *Psychopharmacology, 60,* 81–85.

Waagenaar, W. A. (1989). *Paradoxes of gambling behavior.* Hillsdale, NJ: Lawrence Erlbaum Associates.

Wachs, T. D., & Gruen, C. E. (1982). *Early experience and human development.* New York: Plenum Press.

Wachtel, P. L. (1967). Conceptions of broad and narrow attention. *Psychological Bulletin, 68,* 417–419.

Wachtel, P. L. (1982). *Psychoanalysis and behavior therapy.* New York: Basic Books.

Wade, C. (1988, April). *Thinking critically about critical thinking in psychology.* Paper presented at the annual meeting of the Western Psychological Association, San Francisco, CA.

Wagner, H. L., MacDonald, C. J., & Manstead, A. S. R. (1986). Communication of individual emotions by spontaneous facial expressions. *Journal of Personality and Social Psychology, 50,* 737–743.

Waid, W. M., & Orne, M. T. (1981). Cognitive, social, and personality processes in the physiological detection of deception. In L. Berkowitz (Ed.), *Advances in experimental social psychology: Vol. 14.* New York: Academic Press.

Wainer, H. (1988). How accurately can we assess changes in minority performance on the SAT? *American Psychologist, 43,* 774–778.

Walberg, H. J. (1987). Studies show curricula efficiency can be attained. *NASSP Bulletin, 71,* 15–21.

Waldrop, M. M. (1984). Computer vision. *Science, 224,* 1225–1227.

Walker, L. J. (1982). The sequentiality of Kohlberg's stages of moral development. *Child Development, 53,* 1330–1336.

Walker, L. J. (1989). A longitudinal study of moral reasoning. *Child Development, 60,* 157–166.

Walker-Andrews, A. (1988). Infants' perception of the affordances of expressive behaviors. In C. Rovee-Collier & L. P. Lipsitt (Eds.), *Advances in infancy research: Vol. 5* (pp. 173–221). Ablex.

Wall, P. D., & Cronly-Dillon, J. R. (1960). Pain, itch and vibration. *AMA Archives of Neurology, 2,* 365–375.

Wallace, R. K., & Benson, H. (1972). The physiology of meditation. *Scientific American, 226,* 84–90.

Wallerstein, R. S. (1989). The psychotherapy research project of the Menninger Foundation: An overview. *Journal of Consulting and Clinical Psychology, 57,* 195–205.

Wallman, J., Gottlieb, M. D., Rajaram, V., & Fugate-Wentzek, L. A. (1987). Local retinal regions control local eye growth and myopia. *Science, 237,* 73–76.

Walster, E., & Festinger, L. (1962). The effectiveness of "overheard" persuasive communications. *Journal of Abnormal and Social Psychology, 65,* 395–402.

Waltz, D. L. (1988). The prospects for building truly intelligent machines. In S. R. Graubard (Ed.), *The artificial intelligence debate.* Cambridge, MA: MIT Press.

Ward, W. D. (1974). *Proceedings of the international congress on noise as a public health problem.* Washington, DC: U. S. Government Printing Office.

Warden, C. J. (1931). *Animal motivation: Experimental studies on the albino rat.* New York: Columbia University Press.

Warm, J. S. (Ed.). (1984). *Sustained attention in human performance.* London: Wiley.

Warner, R. A., & Sugarman, D. B. (1986). Attributions of personality based on physical appearance, speech, and handwriting. *Journal of Personality and Social Psychology, 50,* 792–799.

Waterman, A. S. (1982). Identity development from adolescence to adulthood: An extension of theory and a review of research. *Developmental Psychology, 18,* 341–358.

Watkins, B. (1989, June 14). Many campuses now challenging minority students to excel in math and science. *Chronicle of Higher Education,* pp. A13–A16.

Watkins, L. R., & Mayer, D. J. (1982). Organization of endogenous opiate and nonopiate pain control systems. *Science, 216,* 1185–1192.

Watkins, M. J. (1989). Willful and nonwillful determinants of memory. In H. L. Roediger & F. I. M. Craik (Eds.), *Varieties of memory and consciousness.* Hillsdale, NJ: Lawrence Erlbaum Associates.

Watson, D., & Pennebaker, J. W. (1989). Health complaints, stress, and distress: Exploring the role of negative affectivity. *Psychological Review, 96,* 234–254.

Watson, J. B. (1913). Psychology as a behaviorist views it. *Psychological Review, 20,* 158–177.

Watson, J. B. (1924). *Behaviorism.* New York: W. W. Norton.

Watson, J. B. (1930). *Behaviorism* (rev. ed.). New York: Norton.

Watson, M. W. (1981). The development of social roles: A sequence of social-cognitive development. *New Directions for Child Development, 12,* 33–41.

Webb, W. B. (1968). *Sleep: An experimental approach.* New York: Macmillan.

Webb, W. B. (1975). *Sleep: The gentle tyrant.* Englewood Cliffs, NJ: Prentice-Hall.

Wechsler, D. (1949). *The Wechsler Intelligence Scale for children.* New York: Psychological Corporation.

Wedon, E., & Gargano, G. M. (1988). Cognitive loafing: The effects of accountability and shared responsibility on cognitive effort. *Personality and Social Psychology Bulletin, 14,* 159–171.

Wehr, T. A., Sack, D., Rosenthal, N., Duncan, W., & Gillian, J. C. (1983). Circadian rhythm disturbances in manic-depressive illness. *Federation Prac., 42,* 2809–2814.

Weinberger, D. A., Schwartz, G. E., & Davidson, R. J. (1979). Low anxious, high anxious and repressive coping styles: Psychometric patterns and behavioral and physiological responses to stress. *Journal of Abnormal Psychology, 88,* 369–380.

Weinberger, D. R. (1988). Schizophrenia and the frontal lobe. *Trends in Neurosciences, 11,* 367–370.

Weinberger, D. R., Berman, K. F., & Zec, R. F. (1986). Physiologic dysfunction of dorsolateral prefrontal cortex in schizophrenia, I. Regional cerebral blood flow evidence. *Archives of General Psychiatry, 43* (2), 114–124.

Weinberger, D. R., Wagner, R. L., & Wyatt, R. J. (1983). Neuropathological studies of schizophrenia: A selective review. *Schizophrenia Bulletin, 9,* 193–212.

Weinberg, J., & Levine, S. (1980). Psychobiology of coping in animals: The effects of predictability. In S. Levine & H. Ursin (Eds.), *Coping and health.* New York: Plenum.

Weinberg, R. A. (1989). Intelligence and IQ: Landmark issues and great debates. *American Psychologist, 44,* 98–104.

Weiner, B. (1972). *Theories of motivation.* Chicago: Rand McNally.

Weiner, B. (1980). *Human motivation.* New York: Holt, Rinehart and Winston.

Weiner, R. D. (1984). Does electroconvulsive therapy cause brain damage? *The Behavioral and Brain Sciences, 7,* 1–53.

Weinstein, N. D. (1980). Unrealistic optimism about future life events. *Journal of Personality and Social Psychology, 39,* 806–820.

Weinstein, N. D. (1989). Effects of personal experience on self-protective behavior. *Psychological Bulletin, 105,* 31–50.

Weiss, G., Hechtman, L., Milroy, T., & Perlman, T. (1985). Psychiatric status of hyperactives as adults: A controlled prospective 15-year follow-up of 63 hyperactive children. *Journal of American Academy of Child Psychiatry, 24,* 211–220.

Weiss, J. M. (1970). Somatic effects of predictable and unpredictable shock. *Psychosomatic Medicine, 32,* 397–409.

Weiss, V. (1986). From memory span and mental speed toward the quantum mechanics of intelligence. *Journal of Personality and Individual Differences, 7,* 737–749.

Weissman, M. M., Fox, K., & Klerman, G. L. (1973). Hostility and depression associated with suicide attempts. *American Journal of Psychiatry, 103,* 450–455.

Weitzenhoffer, A. M., & Hilgard, E. R. (1962). *Stanford hypnotic susceptibility scale, Form C.* Palo Alto, CA: Consulting Psychologists Press.

Wekstein, L. (1979). *Handbook of suicidology: Principles, problems, and practice.* New York: Brunner/Mazel.

Wells, G. L., & Leippe, M. R. (1981). How do triers of fact infer the accuracy of eyewitness identification? *Journal of Applied Psychology, 67,* 682–687.

Wells, R. S., & Higgins, E. T. (1989). Inferring emotions from multiple cues: Revealing age-related differences in "how" without differences in "can." *Journal of Personality, 57,* 747–771.

Wener, R., Frazier, W., & Farbstein, J. (1987, June). Building better jails. *Psychology Today.*

West, S. G., & Brown, T. J. (1975). Physical attractiveness, the severity of the emergency and helping: A field experiment and interpersonal simulation. *Journal of Experimental Social Psychology, 11,* 531–538.

West, S. G., & Graziano, W. G. (1989). Long-term stability and change in personality: An introduction. *Journal of Personality, 57,* 175–193.

West, S. G., Whitney, G., & Schnedler, R. (1975). Helping a motorist in distress: The effects of sex, race, and neighborhood. *Journal of Personality and Social Psychology, 31,* 691–698.

Wexley, K. N., & Yukl, G. A. (1984). *Organizational behavior and personnel psychology.* Homewood, IL: Richard D. Irwin.

Whalen, R., & Simon, N. G. (1984). Biological motivation. *Annual Review of Psychology, 35,* 257–276.

Whimbey, A. (1976). *Intelligence can be taught*. New York: Bantam.

White, F. J., & Wang, R. Y. (1986). Electrophysiological evidence for the existence of both D-1 and D-2 dopamine receptors in the rat nucleus accumbens. *Journal of Neuroscience, 6*, 274–280.

White, G. L., Fishbein, S., & Rutstein, J. (1981). Passionate love and the misattribution of arousal. *Journal of Personality and Social Psychology, 41*, 56–62.

Whitehouse, P. J., Struble, R. G., Hedreen, J. C., Clark, A. W., White, C. L., Parhad, I. M., & Price, D. L. (1983). Neuroanatomical evidence for a cholinergic deficit in Alzheimer's disease. *Psychopharmacology Bulletin, 19*, 437–440.

Whitley, B. E., & Hern, A. L. (unpublished manuscript). Perceptions of vulnerability to pregnancy and the use of effective contraception.

Whorf, B. L. (1956). *Language, thought and reality*. Cambridge and New York: MIT Press and Wiley.

Wichman, H. (1970). Effects of isolation and communication on cooperation in a two-person game. *Journal of Personality and Social Psychology, 16*, 114–120.

Wickens, C. D. (1989). Attention. In D. Holding (Ed.), *Human skills*. New York: Wiley.

Wickens, C. D. (1991). *Engineering psychology and human performance* (2nd ed.). New York: Harper Collins.

Wickens, C. D., Aretz, A., & Harwood, K. (1989). Frame of reference for electronic maps. In R. Jenson (Ed.), *Proceedings, 5th international symposium on aviation psychology*. Columbus, OH: Ohio State University.

Wickens, C. D., Heffley, E., Kramer, A., & Donchin, E. (1980). The event related brain potential as an index of attention allocation in visual displays. In *Proceedings, 24th Annual Meeting of the Human Factors Society*. Santa Monica: Human Factors.

Wickens, D. D. (1938). Transference of conditioned excitation and conditioned inhibition from one muscle group to the antagonistic muscle group. *Journal of Experimental Psychology, 22*, 101–123.

Wickens, D. D. (1972). Characteristics of word encoding. In A. W. Melton & E. Martin (Eds.), *Coding processes in human memory*. Washington, DC: Winston.

Wickens, D. D. (1973). Some characteristics of word encoding. *Memory and Cognition, 1*, 485–490.

Wickless, C., & Kirsch, I. (1990). Effects of verbal and experiential expectancy manipulations on hypnotic susceptibility. *Journal of Personality and Social Psychology, 57*, 762–768.

Wickramasekera, I. (1985). A conditioned response model of the placebo effect: Predictions from the model. In L. White, B. Tursky, & G. E. Schwartz, (Eds.), *Placebo: Theory, research, and mechanisms*. New York: Guilford Press.

Widiger, T. A., & Frances, A. (1985). The DSM-III personality disorders: Perspectives from psychology. *Archives of General Psychiatry, 42*, 615–623.

Widiger, T. A., & Kelso, K. (1983). Psychodiagnosis of Axis II. *Clinical Psychology Review, 3*, 491–510.

Widom, C. S. (1989). Does violence beget violence? A critical examination of the literature. *Psychological Bulletin, 106*, 3–28.

Wiebe, D. J., & McCallum, D. M. (1986). Health practices and hardiness as mediators in the stress-illness relationship. *Health Psychology, 5*, 425–438.

Wiener, E., & Nagel, D. (1988). *Human factors in aviation*. Orlando, FL: Academic Press.

Wiener, E. L. (1977). Controlled flight into terrain accidents. *Human Factors, 19*, 171–180.

Wiesenfeld, A. R., & Klorman, R. (1978). The mother's psychophysiological reactions to contrasting affective expressions by her own and an unfamiliar infant. *Developmental Psychology, 14*, 294–304.

Wiggins, J. S., & Broughton, R. (1985). The interpersonal circle: A structural model for the integration of personality research. In R. Hogan & W. C. Jones (Eds.), *Perspective in personality: Theory, measurement, and interpersonal dynamics* (Vol. 1). Greenwich, CT: JAI Press.

Wiggins, J. S., & Pincus, A. L. (1989). Conceptions of personality disorders and dimensions of personality. *Psychological Assessment: A Journal of Consulting and Clinical Psychology, 1*, 305–316.

Wiggins, J. S., Phillips, N., & Trapnell, P. (1989). Circular reasoning about interpersonal behavior: Evidence concerning some untested assumptions underlying diagnostic classification. *Journal of Personality and Social Psychology, 56*, 296–305.

Wightman, D. C., & Lintern, G. (1985). Part task training of tracking in manual control. *Human Factors, 27*, 267–283.

Wilder, D. A. (1977). Perception in groups, size of opposition, and social influence. *Journal of Experimental Social Psychology, 13*, 253–268.

Wilder, D. A., & Shapiro, P. N. (1989). Role of competition-induced anxiety in limiting the beneficial impact of positive behavior by an outgroup member. *Journal of Personality and Social Psychology, 56*, 60–69.

Wiley, J. A., & Camacho, T. C. (1980). Life-style and future health: Evidence from the Alameda County study. *Preventive Medicine, 9*, 1–21.

Wilkins, W. (1979). Expectations in therapy research: Discriminating among heterogeneous nonspecifics. *Journal of Consulting and Clinical Psychology, 47*, 837–845.

Wilkinson, A. C. (1984). Children's partial knowledge of the cognitive skill of counting. *Cognitive Psychology, 16*, 28–64.

Williams, C. D. (1959). Elimination of tantrum behavior by extinction procedures. *Journal of Personality and Social Psychology, 59*, 269.

Williams, D. E., & Page, M. M. (1989). A multi-dimensional measure of Maslow's hierarchy of needs. *Journal of Research in Personality, 23*, 192–213.

Williams, R. C. (1985). *College, department, and course grade distribution for fall semester, 1984 (Research Memorandum No. 222)*. Champaign: University of Illinois, Office of Instructional Resources.

Williams, R. J. (1967). The biological approach to the study of personality. In T. Million (Ed.), *Theories of psychopathology*. Philadelphia: W. B. Saunders.

Willis, W. D., Jr. (1988). Dorsal horn neurophysiology of pain. *Annals of the New York Academy of Science, 531*, 76–89.

Wilson, B. A. (1987). *Rehabilitation of memory*. New York: Guilford Press.

Wilson, E. O. (1975). *Sociobiology: The new synthesis*. Cambridge, MA: Harvard University Press.

Wilson, G. T. (1984). *Weight control treatments*. In J. D. Matarazzo, S. M. Weiss, J. H. Herd, & N. E. Miller (Eds.) *Behavioral health: A handbook of health enhancement and disease prevention*. New York: Wiley.

Wilson, G. T. (1985). Limitations of meta-analysis in the evaluation of the effects of psychological therapy. *Clinical Psychology Review, 5*, 35–47.

Wilson, J. F. (1981). Behavioral preparation for surgery: Benefit or harm? *Journal of Behavioral Medicine, 4*, 79–102.

Wilson, L., & Rogers, R. W. (1975). The fire this time: Effects of race of target, insult and potential retaliation in black aggression. *Journal of Personality and Social Psychology, 32*, 857–864.

Wilson, M. A., Dwyer, K. D., & Roy, E. J. (1989). Direct effects of ovarian hormones on antidepressant binding sites. *Brain Research Bulletin, 22*, 181–185.

Wilson, S. C., & Barber, T. X. (1978). The creative imagination scale as a measure of hypnotic responsiveness: Applications to experimental and clinical hypnosis. *The American Journal of Clinical Hypnosis, 20*, 235–249.

Winder, P. H., Kety, S. S., Rosenthal, D., Schulsinger, F., Ortmann, J., & Lunde, I. (1986). Psychiatric disorders in biological and adoptive families of adopted individuals with affective disorders. *Archives of General Psychiatry, 43,* 923–929.

Winefield, H. R. (1987). Psychotherapy and social support: Parallels and differences in the helping process. *Clinical Psychology Review, 7,* 631–644.

Winterbottom, M. R. (1953). *The relation of childhood training in independence to achievement motivation.* Unpublished doctoral dissertation, University of Michigan, Ann Arbor.

Winton, W. M. (1987). Do introductory textbooks present the Yerkes-Dodson law correctly? *American Psychologist, 42,* 202–203.

Wise, R. A. (1978). Catecholamine theories of reward: A critical review. *Brain Research, 152,* 215–247.

Wise, R. A. (1988). The neurobiology of craving: Implications for the understanding and treatment of addiction. *Journal of Abnormal Psychology, 97,* 118–132.

Wise, R. A., & Rompre, P. P. (1989). Brain dopamine and reward. *Annual Review of Psychology, 40,* 191–225.

Wish, M., Deutsch, M., & Kaplan, S. J. (1976). Perceived dimensions of interpersonal relations. *Journal of Personality and Social Psychology, 33,* 409–420.

Wissler, C. (1901). The correlation of mental and physical traits. *Psychological Monographs, 3,* 1–62.

Wolpe, J. (1958). *Psychotherapy by reciprocal inhibition.* Stanford, CA: Stanford University Press.

Wolpe, J. (1982). *The practice of behavior therapy* (3rd ed.). New York: Pergamon Press.

Wong, B. Y. L. (1986). Metacognition and special education: A review of a view. *The Journal of Special Education, 20,* 9–29.

Wong, D. F., Wagner, H. N., Tune, L. E., Dannals, R. F., Pearlson, G. D., Links, J. M., Tamminga, C. A., Broussolle, E. P., Ravert, H. T., Wilson, A. A., Toung, J. K. T., Malat, J., Williams, J. A., O'Tuama, L. A., Snyder, S. H., Kuhar, M. J., & Gjedde, A. (1986). Positron emission tomography reveals elevated D$_2$ dopamine receptors in drug-naive schizophrenics. *Science, 234,* 1558–1563.

Wood, J. V. (1989). Theory and research concerning social comparisons of personal attributes. *Psychological Bulletin, 106,* 231–248.

Woodhead, M. (1988). When psychology informs public policy: The case of early childhood intervention. *American Psychologist, 43,* 443–454.

Woods, D. D., O'Brien, J. F., & Hanes, L. F. (1987). Human factors challenges in process control: The case of nuclear power plants. In G. Salvendy (Ed.), *Handbook of human factors* (pp. 1724–1770). New York: Wiley.

Woodworth, R. S., & Schlosberg, H. (1954). *Experimental psychology.* New York: Holt.

Woody, E. Z., Costanzo, P. R., Liefer, H., & Conger, J. (1981). The effects of taste and caloric perceptions on the eating behavior of restrained and unrestrained subjects. *Cognitive Therapy and Research, 5,* 381–390.

Woolfolk, R. L., & McNulty, T. F. (1983). Relaxation treatment for insomnia: A component analysis. *Journal of Consulting and Clinical Psychology, 4,* 495–503.

Worchel, S., & Brehm, J. W. (1970). Effects of threats to attitudinal freedom as a function of agreement with the communicator. *Journal of Personality and Social Psychology, 14,* 18–22.

The World Alamanac. (1988). New York: Pharos Books.

Wortman, C. B. (1984). Social support and the cancer patient: Conceptual and methodological issues. *Cancer, 53,* 2339–2360.

Wright, L. (1988). The type A behavior pattern and coronary artery disease: Quest for the active ingredients and the elusive mechanism. *American Psychologist, 43,* 2–14.

Wurtman, R. J., & Wurtman, J. J. (1989). Carbohydrates and depression. *Scientific American, 260,* 68–75.

Wyer, R. S., & Srull, T. K. (1986). Human cognition in its social context. *Psychological Review, 93,* 322–359.

Wyer, R. S., Bodenhausen, G. V., & Gorman, T. F. (1985). Cognitive mediators to rape. *Journal of Personality and Social Psychology, 48,* 324–338.

Wyer, R. S., Strack, F., & Fuhrman, R. W. (1988). Erwerb von Informationen uber Personen: Einflusse von Aufgabenstellung und personlichen Erwartungen. *Zeitschrift fur experimentelle und angewandte Psychologie, 35,* 657–688.

Yakimovich, D., & Saltz, E. (1971). Helping behavior: The cry for help. *Psychonomic Science, 23,* 427–428.

Yalom, I. D. (1985). *The theory and practice of group psychotherapy* (3rd ed.). New York: Basic Books.

Yerkes, R. M. (Ed.). (1921). Psychological examining in the U.S. Army. *Memoirs of the National Academy of Sciences,* No. 15.

Yesavage, J. A., Leirer, V. O., Denari, M., & Hollister, L. E. (1985). Carry-over effects of marijuana intoxication on aircraft pilot performance: A preliminary report. *American Journal of Psychiatry, 142,* 1325–1329.

Young, F. A., Leary, G. A., Baldwin, W. R., West, D. C., Box, R. A., Harris, E., & Johnson, C. (1969). The transmission of refractive errors within Eskimo families. *American Journal of Optometry, 46,* 676–685.

Young, M. (1966). Problem solving performance in two age groups. *Journal of Gerontology, 21,* 505–509.

Young, M. (1971). Age and sex differences in problem solving. *Journal of Gerontology, 26,* 331–336.

Youtz, R. P. (1968). Can fingers "see" color? *Psychology Today.*

Zafiropoulou, M., & McPherson, F. M. (1986). "Preparedness" and the severity and outcome of clinical phobias. *Behavior Research and Therapy, 24,* 221–222.

Zahn-Waxler, C., Iannotti, R., & Chapman, M. (1982). Peers and prosocial development. In K. H. Rubin & H. S. Ross (Eds.), *Peer relationships and social skills in childhood.* New York: Springer-Verlag.

Zajonc, R. B. (1965). Social facilitation. *Science, 149,* 269–274.

Zajonc, R. B. (1980). Feeling and thinking: Preferences need no inferences. *American Psychologist, 35,* 151–175.

Zajonc, R. B., & Markus, H. (1982). Affective and cognitive factors in preferences. *Journal of Consumer Research, 9,* 123–131.

Zaragoza, M. S., & Koshmider, J. W. (1989). Misled subjects may know more than their performance implies. *Journal of Experimental Psychology: Learning, Memory, and Cognition, 15,* 246–255.

Zarski, J. J. (1984). Hassles and health: A replication. *Health Psychology, 3,* 243–251.

Zautra, A. J., & Reich, J. W. (1983). Life events and the perceptions of life quality: Developments in a two-factor approach. *Journal of Community Psychology, 11,* 121–132.

Zax, M., & Stricker, G. (1963). *Patterns of psychopathology.* New York: Macmillan.

Zeig, J. K. (Ed.) (1987). *The evolution of psychotherapy.* New York: Bruner Mazel.

Zellner, M. (1970). Self-esteem, reception, and influenceability. *Journal of Personality and Social Psychology, 15,* 87–93.

Zentall, S. S., & Zentall, T. R. (1983). Optimal stimulation: A model of disordered activity and performance in normal and deviant children. *Psychological Bulletin, 94,* 446–471.

Zigler, E., & Seitz, V. (1982). Social policy and intelligence. In R. J. Sternberg (Ed.), *Handbook of human intelligence.* Cambridge: Cambridge University Press.

Zillmann, D. (1978a). Attribution and misattribution of excitatory reactions. In J. H. Harvey, W. J. Ickes, & R. F. Kidd (Eds.), *New directions in attribution research: Vol. 2.* Hillsdale, NJ: Lawrence Erlbaum Associates.

Zillmann, D. (1978b). *Hostility and aggression.* Hillsdale, NJ: Lawrence Erlbaum Associates.

Zillmann, D. (1983). Arousal and aggression. In R. Geen & E.

Donnerstein (Eds.), *Aggression: Theoretical and empirical reviews.* New York: Academic Press.

Zillmann, D. (1984). *Connections between sex and aggression.* Hillsdale, NJ: Lawrence Erlbaum Associates.

Zillmann, D. (1988). Cognition-excitation interdependencies in aggressive behavior. *Aggressive Behavior, 14,* 51–64.

Zillmann, D., & Weaver, J. B. (1989). Pornography and men's sexual callousness toward women. In D. Zillmann & J. Bryant (Eds.), *Pornography: Research advances and policy considerations.* Hillsdale, NJ: Lawrence Erlbaum Associates.

Zillmann, D., Baron, R. A., & Tamborini, R. (1981). Social costs of smoking: Effects of tobacco smoke on hostile behavior. *Journal of Applied Social Psychology, 11,* 548–561.

Zillmann, D., Katcher, A. H., & Milavsky, B. (1972). Excitation transfer from physical exercise to subsequent aggressive behavior. *Journal of Experimental Social Psychology, 8,* 247–259.

Zimbardo, P. G., Weisenberg, M., Firestone, I., & Levy, B. (1965). Communicator effectiveness in producing public conformity and private attitude change. *Journal of Personality, 33,* 233–255.

Zimmerman, B. J., & Schunk, D. H. (1989). *Self-regulated learning and academic achievement.* New York: Springer-Verlag.

Zimmerman, M., & Rappaport, J. (1988). Citizen participation, perceived control and psychological empowerment. *American Journal of Community Psychology, 16,* 725–750.

Zinberg, N. E. (1974). *High states: A beginning study.* Washington, DC: Drug Abuse Council.

Zirkel, S., & Cantor, N. (1990). Personal construal of life tasks: Those who struggle for independence. *Journal of Personality and Social Psychology, 58,* 172–185.

Zitrin, C. M. (1983). Differential treatment of phobias: Use of imipramine for panic attacks. *Journal of Behavior Therapy and Experimental Psychiatry, 14,* 11–18.

Zoller, C. L., Workman, J. S., & Kroll, N. E. A. (1989). The bizarre mnemonic: The effect of retention interval and mode of presentation. *Bulletin of the Psychonomic Society, 27,* 215–218.

Zook II, A., & Walton, J. M. (1989). Theoretical orientations and work settings of clinical and counseling psychologists: A current perspective. *Professional Psychology: Research and Practice, 20,* 23–31.

Zubek, J. P. (Ed.). (1969). *Sensory deprivation: Fifteen years of research.* New York: Appleton-Century-Crofts.

Zubin, J., & Spring, B. (1977). Vulnerability—A new view of schizophrenia. *Journal of Abnormal Psychology, 86,* 103–126.

Zuckerman, M. (1979). *Sensation seeking: Beyond the optimal level of arousal.* Hillsdale, NJ: Lawrence Erlbaum Associates.

Zuckerman, M. (1984). Sensation seeking: A comparative approach to a human approach. *The Behavioral and Brain Sciences, 7,* 413–471.

C R E D I T S

Table of Contents: **p. vii:** © Peter Wiegel/Transglobe Agency, Hamburg. **p. viii:** D.N. Levin, H. Xiaoping, K.K. Tan, S. Galhotra, C. A. Pelizzari, G. T. Y. Chen, R. N. Beck, C-T Chen, M.D. Cooper, J.F. Muller, J. Hekmatpanah, and J. P. Spire (1989). The brain: Integrated three-dimensional display of MR and PET images. *Radiology, 172,* 783–789. **p. viii:** © Mike Surowiak/TSW-Click/Chicago. **p. ix:** © Charles Harbutt/Actuality, Inc. **p. x:** © Jerry Howard/Positive Images. **p. x:** © Dan McCoy/Rainbow. **p. xi:** © Erika Stone. **p. xi:** © John Eastcott/Yva Momatiuk/The Image Works. **p. xii:** © Warren Garst/Tom Stack & Associates. **p. xii:** © 1985 Christopher Morris/Black Star. **p. xiii:** © H. W. Silvester/Photo Researchers, Inc. **p. xiii:** © Michael Heron/Monkmeyer Press Photos. **p. xiv:** © Catherine Karnow/Woodfin Camp & Associates.

Chapter 1: **p. 2:** (*top*) Historical Pictures Service. (*bottom*) Bettmann Archive. **p. 4:** © Yoav/Phototake. **p. 6:** (*top*) © Raoul Hackel/Stock, Boston. (*bottom*) Courtesy, National Library of Medicine, Bethesda, MD. **p. 7:** (*top*) Bettmann Archive. (*bottom*) Courtesy, B. F. Skinner. **p. 8:** Courtesy, the Carl Rogers Memorial Library. **p. 9:** Michael Heron/Monkmeyer Press. **p. 10:** *Table 1.2* Adapted from Howard, A., Pion, G. M., Gottfredson, G. D., Flattau, P. E., Oskamp, S., Pfafflin, S. M., Bray, D. W., & Burstein, A. G. (1986). "The Changing Face of American Psychology: A Report from the Committee on Employment and Human Resources." *American Psychologist, 41,* 1311–1327. Copyright 1986 by The American Psychological Association. Adapted by permission. **p. 11:** © Peter Wiegel/Transglobe Agency, Hamburg. **p. 13:** Four by Five/Superstock. **p. 16:** © 1982 Phil Huber/Black Star. **p. 18:** © Ellis Herwig/The Picture Cube. **p. 19:** © Thomas McAvoy, Life Magazine, © 1955 Time, Inc. **p. 20:** © Charles Harbutt/Actuality, Inc. **p. 26:** © Don Smetzer/TSW-Click/Chicago.

Chapter 2: **p. 33:** © Elizabeth Crews. **p. 36:** Courtesy, Dr. Benjamin Harris. **p. 37:** © Michael Weisbrot & Family. **p. 40:** © Camera M. D. Studios, 1973. **p. 42:** *Figure 2.4* © Elizabeth Crews. **p. 46:** © Yves De Braine/Black Star. **p. 49:** © Michael Weisbrot & Family. **p. 51:** © Elizabeth Crews/Stock, Boston. **p. 52:** *Figure 2.6* Copyright Paul Ekman 1975. Ekman, P. & Friesen, W. V. *Unmasking the Face,* reprint edition. Palo Alto, Ca: Consulting Psychologists Press, 1984. **p. 56:** © Michael Hayman/Photo Researchers, Inc. **p. 58:** Tom Rosenthal/Su-

perstock. **p. 60:** © Wanstall/The Image Works. **p. 63:** © Bob Daemmrich/The Image Works. **p. 62:** *Figure 2.7* Adapted from "Standards from birth to maturity for height, weight, height velocity: British children" by Tanner, J. M., Whitehouse, R. H., and Takaishi, M. *Archives of Diseases in Childhood,* 1966, *41,* 454–471. Reprinted by permission. **p. 69:** United Nations Photo 149,525/Milton Grant. **p. 73:** *Figure 2.8* From *The Seasons of Man's Life* by Daniel J. Levinson et al. Copyright © 1978 by Daniel J. Levinson. Reprinted by permission of Alfred A. Knopf, Inc. **p. 74:** © Bob Daemmrich. **p. 77:** LLR/Research. Photo by Joyce Kitchell.

Chapter 3: **p. 90:** *Figure 3.5* Micrograph produced by John E. Heuser of Washington University School of Medicine, St. Louis, Mo. **p. 94:** (*top*) By permission of the Brain Tissue Resource Center, Ralph Lowell Laboratories, McLean Hospital. (*bottom*) © Fred McConnaughey/Photo Researchers, Inc. **p. 95:** *Figure 3.10* L. R. Baxter et al., Archives of General Psychiatry, 1985, vol. 42, p. 444. Copyright 1985, American Medical Association. **p. 96:** *Figure 3.11* J. P. Seab et al. (1988) "Magnetic Resonance in Medicine" 8, 200–208, Copyright 1988, Academic Press. (*bottom*) The Far Side. Copyright 1986 Universal Press Syndicate. Reprinted with Permission. All rights reserved. **p. 97:** *Figure 3.12* D. N. Levin, H. Xiaoping, K. K. Tan, S. Galhotra, C. A. Pelizzari, G. T. Y. Chen, R. N. Beck, C-T. Chen, M. D. Cooper, J. F. Mullan, J. Hekmatpanah and J-P. Spire (1989). *The Brain:* integrated three-dimensional display of MR and PET images. *Radiology,* 172: 783–789. By permission of the author. **p. 104:** *Figure 3.17* Reprinted with permission of Macmillan Publishing Company, a Division of Macmillan, Inc. from *The Cerebral Cortex of Man* by Wilder Penfield and Theodore Rasmussen. Copyright 1950 Macmillan Publishing Company; copyright renewed © 1978 Theodore Rasmussen. **p. 107:** *Figure 3.20* Drs. J. C. Mazziota and M. E. Phelps, UCLA School of Medicine. **p. 111:** © Peter Chapman. **p. 119:** *Figure 3.25* J. L. Conel, *The Postnatal Development of the Human Cerebral Cortex,* Vols. I, VIII, Harvard University Press, 1939, 1967. Reprinted by permission.

Chapter 4: **p. 131:** (*top*) © Dana Fineman/Sygma. (*bottom*) *Table 4.1* M. W. Levine and J. M. Shefner, *Fundamentals of Sensation and Perception,* 1981. Reprinted by permission of M. W. Levine. **p. 132:** *Figure 4.3* Part a from *Speech and Hearing* (revised ed.), by Harvey Fletcher, D. Van Nostrand Company,

Inc., 1952. Part b reprinted by permission of John Wiley and Sons, Inc. From E. G. Boring et al., *Foundations of Psychology.* Copyright © 1948 by John Wiley and Sons, Inc. **p. 133:** Courtesy of Annie Roy. **p. 136:** Scanning electron micrographs by Robert E. Preston, Courtesy of Professor J. E. Hawkins, Kresge Hearing Research Institute, University of Michigan. **p. 137:** © Michael Wernen/Transglobe Agency, Hamburg. **p. 140:** © 1984 Barney Nelson/Black Star. **p. 145:** Kurschner/ Bavaria Bildagentur GMBH. **p.146:** © 1987 Peter L. Chapman. All rights reserved. **p. 148:** *Figure 4.21* Dvorine Color Vision Test. Copyright © 1944, 1953, 1958 by The Psychological Corporation. Reproduced by permission. All rights reserved. **p. 151:** *Figure 4.24* From Hubel, D. H., and Wiesel, T. N., 1962, 1965; redrawn by Kuffler, S. W. and Nicholls, A., 1976, *From Neuron to Brain,* Sinauer Associates, Inc. Reprinted by permission. **p. 152:** From *Fundamentals of Sensation and Perception* by M. W. Levine and J. M. Shefner, Addison Wesley, 1981. **p. 155:** The Far Side. Copyright 1988 Universal Press Syndicate. Reprinted with Permission. All rights reserved. **p. 156:** © Charles Kennard/Stock, Boston. **p. 158:** © Globe Press/ Bavaria Bildagentur GMBH. **p. 160:** Courtesy of The Daily Illini, cartoon by Eric Smelroth © 1987. **p. 161:** UPI/Bettmann Newsphotos. **p. 164:** © Bruce Curtis/Peter Arnold, Inc.

Chapter 5: p. 175: *Figure 5.3* © Charles Harbutt/Actuality, Inc. **p. 176:** *Table 5.1* Galanter, E. (1962). "Contemporary psychophysics." In R. Brown (Ed.) *New directions in psychology.* New York: Holt, Rinehart & Winston. **p. 181:** © Alan Carey/The Image Works. **p. 183:** © Will Barnet, Collection, Mr. & Mrs. Lee M. Oser, Jr. **p. 185:** *Figure 5.11* © Bob Daemmrich. **p. 186:** © Jim Anderson/Woodfin Camp & Associates. All rights reserved. **p. 187:** *Figure 5.13* AP/Wide World Photos. **p. 188:** Muschenetz/Bavaria Bildagentur GMBH. **p. 194:** *Figure 5.20* From Margaret W. Matlin, *Sensation and Perception,* Second Edition. Copyright © 1988 by Allyn and Bacon. Reprinted with permission. **p. 197:** Ronald C. James. **p. 198:** Ronald C. James. **p. 200:** *Figure 5.26* Rumelhart, D. E. and McClelland, J. L. (1986). *Parallel Distributing Processing Vol. 1: Foundations.* Cambridge, MA: MIT Press. Copyright © 1986 by the Massachusetts Institute of Technology. Reprinted by permission. *Figure 5.27* "Context and Recognition." From *Human Factors,* Vol. 23, No. 2, 1981. Copyright 1981 by The Human Factors Society, Inc., and reprinted by permission. **p. 203:** © Frank Siteman/The Picture Cube. **p. 205:** © Allan Tannenbaum/ Sygma. **p. 207:** © Mike Surowiak/TSW-Click/Chicago. **p. 209:** *Figure 5.32* © Enrico Ferorelli. *Figure 5.33* From Kaufmann, R., Maland, J., and Yonas, A. "A sensitivity of 5 and 7 month old infants to pictorial depth information." *Journal of Experimental Child Psychology,* 1981, *32,* 162–168. Reprinted by permission.

Chapter 6: p. 219: *(top) Figure 6.2* From *Mindworks: Time and Conscious Experience* by E. Poppel, Tom Artin translator, copyright © 1985 by Deutsche Verlags-Anstalt GmbH, Stuttgart, copyright © 1988 by Harcourt Brace Jovanovich. Reprinted by permission of Harcourt Brace Jovanovich. *(bottom)* © Bob Daemmrich/Stock, Boston. **p. 220:** Copyright © 1986, Washington Post Writers Group. **p. 224:** © Grant LeDuc/Monkmeyer Press Photo. **p. 225:** *Figure 6.3* Reprinted with permission of Macmillan Publishing Company from *Sleep: An Experimental Approach* by Wilse B. Webb. Copyright © 1968 by Macmillan Publishing Company. **p. 226:** *Figure 6.4* Adapted

from Cartwright, *A Primer of Sleep and Dreaming.* Reading, Mass.: Addison-Wesley, 1978. Reprinted by permission of the author. **p. 227:** *Figure 6.5* From "Ontogenetic Development of the Human Sleep Dream Cycle," H. P. Roffwarg et al. *Science,* Vol. 152, #3722, p. 606, April 29, 1966. Copyright 1966 by the AAAS. Reprinted with permission of The American Association for the Advancement of Science. **p. 230:** © Barbara Alper/Stock, Boston. **p. 232:** *Figure 6.8* Adapted from V. Block et al., "Interaction between post-trial reticular stimulation and subsequent paradoxical sleep in memory consolidation processes." In R. R. Drucker-Colin and J. L. McGaugh (Eds.), *Neurobiology of sleep and memory.* Copyright (c) 1977 by Academic Press, Inc. With permission of Academic Press. **p. 233:** Thomas Hart Benton. "The Engineer's Dream", oil and tempera. Memphis Brooks Museum of Art, Eugenia Buxton Whitnel Fund 75.1. **p. 235:** *Figure 6.9* From *Hypnotic Susceptibility* by Ernest R. Hilgard, copyright © 1965 Harcourt Brace Jovanovich, Inc. Reprinted by permission of the author. **p. 236:** © Tom Creek/Stock, Boston. **p. 237:** *Figure 6.10* From Pattie, F. A. "A report of attempts to produce uniocular blindness by hypnotic suggestion," *British Journal of Medical Psychology,* 1935, *15,* 236, Figure 1. Reprinted by permission. **p. 238:** *Figure 6.11* From *Divided Consciousness: Multiple Controls in Human Thought and Action* by E. R. Hilgard. Copyright © 1977 John Wiley and Sons, Inc. Reprinted by permission of John Wiley and Sons, Inc. **p. 242:** *Figure 6.12* From "Effects of Alcohol on Aggression in Males," A. R. Lang, D. J. Goeckner, V. J. Adesso & G. A. Marlett, *Journal of Abnormal Psychology,* #84, pp. 508–516. Copyright 1975 by the American Psychological Association. Adapted by permission. **p. 243:** *(top) Figure 6.13* Kolata, G. (1986). "New drug counters alcohol intoxication" *Science,* 234, 1198–1199. Photo by Jules Asher at NIMH. **p. 245:** © Arlene Collins/Monkmeyer Press Photo. **p. 246:** © Barbara Alper/Stock, Boston. **p. 248:** © Richard Hutchings/Photo Researchers, Inc. **p. 250:** © Positive Images.

Chapter 7: p. 261: © Thomas Kitchin/Tom Stack & Associates. **p. 262:** © 1982 David Burnett/Contact Press/Woodfin Camp & Associates. All rights reserved. **p. 266:** © Jerry Howard/ Positive Images. **p. 269:** *Figure 7.8* Courtesy Pfizer, Inc.; Courtesy of Peter J. Urcuioli. **p. 270:** © Rick Smolan/Stock, Boston. **p. 271:** Figure 7.10 © Frank Lotz Miller/Black Star. **p. 272:** © Charles Harbutt/Actuality, Inc. **p. 274:** Figure 7.11 Adapted from "Teaching Machines" by B. F. Skinner. Copyright © 1961 by Scientific American, Inc. All rights reserved. **p. 275:** © Michal Heron 1981/Woodfin Camp & Associates. All rights reserved. **p. 277:** *Figure 7.12* From *The Psychology of Learning and Memory.* By Douglas L. Hintzman. Copyright © 1978 by W. H. Freeman and Company. Reprinted with permission. **p. 278:** *Figure 7.13* Lang, P. and Melamed, B. "Case report: Avoidance conditioning of an infant with chronic ruminative vomiting." *Journal of Abnormal Psychology,* 74, 1–8. Copyright © 1969 by the American Psychological Association, Reprinted by permission of author. **p. 280:** © Stacky Pick/Stock, Boston. **p. 283:** *Figure 7.14* Courtesy Albert Bandura, Stanford University. **p. 290:** *Figure 7.17* Yerkes Regional Primate Research Center of Emory University. **p. 291:** *Figure 7.18* Kohler, W. 1976. *The Mentality of Apes.* London: Routledge and Kegan Paul Pic. **p. 293:** © Barbara Filet/TSW-Click/ Chicago.

Chapter 8: p. 301: © Carol Palmer. **p. 303:** © Elizabeth Crew. **p. 305:** *Figure 8.3* From "Contextual Prerequisites for Understanding: Some Investigations of Comprehension and Recall" by Bransford and Johnson, *Journal of Verbal Learning and Verbal Behavior, 61,* pp. 717–726, 1972. With permission of Academic Press. **p. 306:** *Figure 8.4* From *Human Memory: The Processing of Information* by G. R. Loftus and E. F. Loftus, 1976, Hillsdale, NJ: Lawrence Erlbaum Associates, Inc. Copyright 1976 by Lawrence Erlbaum Associates, Inc. Reprinted by permission. **p. 307:** *Figure 8.6* From "Some Temporal Characteristics of Visual Pattern Perception" by Ericksen and Collins, *Journal of Experimental Psychology, 74,* pp. 476–484. Copyright © 1967 by the American Psychological Association. Adapted by permission. **p. 308:** (*top*) *Figure 8.7* Reprinted with permission of Macmillan Publishing Company from *Cognitive Psychology* by Darlene V. Howard. Copyright © 1983 by Darlene V. Howard. (*bottom*) © Michael Weisbrot and Family. **p. 309:** © Owen Franken/Stock, Boston. **p. 310:** (*top*) *Figure 8.8* From "Short-Term Retention of Individual Verbal Items" by Peterson and Peterson, *Journal of Experimental Psychology, 58,* pp. 193–198. (*bottom*) © Michael Weisbrot and Family. **p. 311:** *Figure 8.9* From "Some Characteristics of Word Encoding" by Delos Wickens. *Memory and Cognition, 1,* pp. 485–490. Copyright 1973 Psychonomic Society Publications. Reprinted by permission. **p. 312:** *Figure 8.10* From "High Speed Scanning in Human Memory" by S. Sternberg, *Science,* Vol. 153., #3736, pp. 652–654, August 5, 1966. Copyright 1966 by the American Association for the Advancement of Science. Reprinted by permission. **p. 313:** Drawing by Lorenz; © 1988 The New Yorker Magazine, Inc. **p. 314:** *Figure 8.12* From "Long-term memory for a common object" by R. S. Nickerson and M. J. Adams. *Cognitive Psychology,* 1979, *11,* 287–307. Reprinted by permission. **p. 319:** *Figure 8.14* From Minimi, H., and Dallenbach, K. M. (1946). "The Effect of Activity Upon Learning and Retention in the Cockroach." *American Journal of Psychology, 59,* 1–58. Copyright 1946 by the Board of Trustees of the University of Illinois. Reprinted by permission. **p. 320:** *Figure 8.15* From "Retroactive Inhibition in Free Recall: Inaccessibility of Information Available in the Memory Store" by Tulving and Psotka. *Journal of Experimental Psychology, 87,* pp. 1–8, 1971. Copyright © 1971 by the American Psychological Association. Adapted by permission. **p. 321:** © J. Patrick Forden/Sygma. **p. 322:** Doonesbury. Copyright 1986 G. B. Trudeau. Reprinted with permission of Universal Press Syndicate. All rights reserved. **p. 327:** *Figure 8.19* From "Two Storage Mechanisms in Free Recall," by M. Glanzer and A. R. Cunitz. In *Journal of Verbal Learning and Verbal Behavior,* 1966, *5,* 351–360. Copyright © 1966 by Academic Press, Inc. Reprinted by permission. **p. 328:** © Bob Clay/Jeroboam, Inc. **p. 329:** (*left*) © 1989 Grant LeDuc/Monkmeyer Press Photo. (*right*) © John Let/Stock, Boston. **p. 331:** *Figure 8.20* Reprinted with permission from *Psychology Today Magazine.* Copyright © 1973 (PT Partners, L.P.).

Chapter 9: p. 345: © Dan McCoy/Rainbow. **p. 349:** (*left*) © Robert Eckert/EKM/Nepenthe. (*right*) AP/Wide World Photos. **p. 352:** *Figure 9.6* From "Mental Rotation of Three-Dimensional Objects," R. Shepard et al., *Science,* Vol. 171, #3972, pp. 701–703, figure on page 702, 19 February 1971. Copyright 1971 by the American Association for the Advancement of

Science. Reprinted by permission. **p. 354:** © Christopher Morris/Black Star. **p. 360:** © Jill Cannelfax/EKM-Nepenthe. **p. 364:** © Louie Psihoyos/Matrix. **p. 369:** © Sygma. **p. 374:** *Figure 9.13* From *Cognitive Psychology and Information Processing* (p. 513, figure 13.4) by R. Lachman, J. L. Lachman & E. C. Butterfield, 1979, Hillsdale, NJ: Lawrence Erlbaum Associates. Copyright 1979 by Lawrence Erlbaum Associates. Reprinted by permission. **p. 375:** (*top*) © Laimute Druskis/Jeroboam, Inc. (*bottom*) © Andy Levin 1986. All rights reserved/Photo Researchers, Inc. **p. 377:** © Erika Stone. **p. 381:** Professor H. S. Terrace, Columbia University. **p. 384:** © Eva Momatiuk & John Eastcott 1978/Woodfin Camp & Associates. All rights reserved.

Chapter 10: p. 393: *Table 10.1* Michael T. Nietzel/Douglas A. Bernstein, *Introduction to Clinical Psychology,* 2/e, © 1987, p. 133. Reprinted by permission of Prentice-Hall, Inc., Englewood Cliffs, New Jersey. **p. 394:** © 1987 Ray Stott/The Image Works. **p. 395:** *Figure 10.1* Wechsler Intelligence Scale for Children-Revised. Copyright © 1974 by The Psychological Corporation. Reproduced by permission. All rights reserved. **p. 398:** © Carol Palmer. **p. 399:** © Joseph Szabo/Photo Researchers, Inc. **p. 401:** © Topham/The Image Works. **p. 402:** *Figure 10.3* Robert L. Williams, *Black Intelligence Test of Cultural Homogeneity,* 1972. Reprinted by permission of the author. **p. 404:** *Figure 10.4* From the *Dynamic Assessment of Retarded Performers* by Reuven Feuerstein. Copyright © 1979 by Scott, Foresman and Company. Reprinted by permission of the author. **p. 406:** (*top*) © Leo Cullum 1987. (*bottom*) *Figure 10.5* From "Familial Studies of Intelligence: A Review," T. Bouchard et al., *Science,* Vol. 212, #4498, pp. 1055–9, 29 May 1981. Copyright 1981 by the American Association for the Advancement of Science. Reprinted by permission. **p. 408:** © Elizabeth Crews. **p. 409:** Three Lions/Superstock. **p. 411:** © Brent Jones. **p. 415:** "Jeopardy!" photo courtesy of Merv Griffin Enterprises. **p. 416:** *Figure 10.7* From the *Raven Standard Progressive Matrices.* Reprinted by permission of J. C. Raven Limited. **p. 418:** Pam Price/Stock, Boston. **p. 420:** Drawing by McCallister; © 1990 The New Yorker Magazine, Inc. **p. 421:** © Martin Rogers 1985/Stock, Boston. **p. 425:** © William Strode 1987/Woodfin Camp & Associates.

Chapter 11: p. 435: © Frans Lanting/Photo Researchers, Inc. **p. 437:** (*top*) *Figure 11.3* Fred Sponholtz. (*bottom*) © Michael Collier/Stock, Boston. **p. 438:** *Figure 11.4* From D. Hebb, "Drives and the CNS," *Psychological Review,* 62, 243–253, 1955. **p. 440:** *Figure 11.5* From R. L. Solomon and J. D. Corbit, "An Opponent-Process Theory of Motivation: I. Temporal Dynamics of Affect," *Psychological Review,* 81, 119–145, 1974. Copyright (c) 1974 by the American Psychological Association. Adapted by permission. **p. 443:** Courtesy of Neal Miller, Rockefeller University. **p. 445:** From "The Control of Eating Behavior in an Anorexic by Operant Techniques," by Arthur J. Bachrach, William J. Erwin, and Jay P. Mohr, in *Case Studies in Behavior Modification,* edited by Leonard P. Ullman and Leonard Krasner. © 1965 by Holt, Rinehart & Winston. **p. 447:** © Henley and Savage/TSW-Click/Chicago. **p. 449:** Figure 11.8 Adapted from W. H. Masters and V. E. Johnson, *Human Sexual Response,* p. 5 (Boston: Little, Brown and Company, 1966). Reprinted by permission. **p. 452:** © Peter L. Chapman. **p. 453:** (*top*) *Figure 11.9* Harlow Primate Laboratory, University of Wisconsin. (*bottom*) *Figure 11.10* Harlow Primate Laboratory, University of Wisconsin. **p. 453:** Harlow Primate Laboratory, University of Wisconsin. **p. 454:** *Figure 11.11* From *Animal Motivation: Experimental Studies on the Albino Rat*, by C. J. Warden, copyright 1931 Columbia University Press, New York. Used by permission. **p. 455:** (*left*) © Jane Scherr/Jeroboam, Inc. (*right*) © Warren Garst/Tom Stack & Associates. **p. 456:** © 1985 Gary Sigman/Black Star. **p. 457:** (*top*) AP/Wide World Photos. (*bottom*) *Figure 11.12* Reprinted by permission of the publishers from Henry A. Murray, *Thematic Apperception Test*, Cambridge, Mass.: Harvard University Press, copyright © 1943 by the president and fellows of Harvard College, © 1971 by Henry A. Murray. **p. 461:** © William Strode/Woodfin Camp & Associates. **p. 462:** *Figure 11.13* Adapted from A. H. Maslow (1943), A theory of human motivation, *Psychological Review, 50,* 370–396. **p. 464:** © Glasheen Graphics.

Chapter 12: p. 474: © John Eastcott/Yva Momatiuk/The Image Works. **p. 479:** *Figure 12.4* Copyright, Paul Ekman, 1983. Photos of actor Tom Harrison, from Ekman, P., Levenson, R. W. and Friesen, W. V. "Autonomic nervous system distinguishes among emotions," *Science,* 1983, *221.* **p. 478:** *Figure 12.3* From "Voluntary Facial Action Generates Emotion-Specific Autonomic Nervous System Activity," by R. W. Levenson, P. Ekman, and W. V. Friesen, *Psychophysiology,* 1990, *27,* 363–384. Copyright 1990, The Society for Psychophysiological Research. Reprinted with permission of the author and the publisher from Levenson, Ekman, and Friesen, 1990. **p. 483:** © Rick Mansfield/The Image Works. **p. 485:** © Michael McGovern/The Picture Cube. **p. 488:** (*left*) © Jonathan Blair/Woodfin Camp & Associates. (*center*) © Karen Sherlock/Third Coast Stock Source. (*right*) © Eastcott/Momatiuk/Woodfin Camp & Associates. All rights reserved. **p. 489:** *Figure 12.8* From "The recognition of threatening facial stimuli" by Aronoff, J., Barclay, A. M., and Stevenson, L. A., 1988, *Journal of Personality and Social Psychology, 54,* pp. 647–655. Copyright 1988 by the American Psychological Association. Reprinted by permission. **p. 490:** © Copyright Paul Ekman, 1972 P. Ekman "Universals and cultural differences in facial expressions of emotion," in J. Cole (Ed.), Nebraska Symposium on Motivation, 1971, Vol. 19, Lincoln: University of Nebraska Press, 1972. **p. 491:** *Figure 12.9* From *The Neurological Examination* 4th ed., by R. N. Dejong. New York: Lippincott/Harper & Row, 1979. **p. 492:** *Figure 12.10* From "Pathophysiology of emotional disorders associated with brain damage" by K. Poeck, in P. J. Vinken and G. W. Bruyn (Eds) *Handbook of Clinical Neurology,* Vol. 3. New York: American Elsevier, 1969. **p. 493:** (*top*) *Figure 12.11* © Bill Aron 1989/Jeroboam, Inc. (*bottom*) From "Baby, it's in your smile: Right hemiface bias in infant emotional expressions," by C. T. Best and H. F. Queen (1989) *Developmental Psychology,* 25, 264–276. Copyright 1989 by the American Psychological Association. Reprinted by permission. **p. 495:** *Figure 12.12* Reprinted with permission from *Psychology Today Magazine.* Copyright © 1985 (PT Partners, L.P.).

Chapter 13: p. 502: © Jack Prelutsky/Stock, Boston. **p. 504:** *Table 13.1* Reprinted with permission from *Journal of Psychosomatic Research,* Vol. 11, T. H. Holmes and R. H. Rahe, "The Social Readjustment Scale," copyright 1967, Pergamon Press.

p. 505: *Table 13.2* From Delongis, A., Folkman, S., & Lazarus, R. S. (1988). "The Impact of Daily Stress on Health and Mood: Psychological and Social Resources as Mediators." *Journal of Personality and Social Psychology, 54,* 486–495. Copyright 1988 by the American Psychological Association. Reprinted by permission. **p. 507:** *Figure 13.3* From *Stress Without Distress* by Hans Selye, M. D. Copyright © 1974 by Hans Selye, M. D. Reprinted by permission of Harper & Row, Publishers, Inc. **p. 508:** *Figure 13.4* Artwork of the Organ System by Michael James Wright from *The New York Times,* May 24, 1983. Copyright (c) 1983 by The New York Times Company. Reprinted by permission. **p. 509:** © David Burnett/Stock, Boston. **p. 513:** (*top*) © Charles Feil/Stock, Boston. (*bottom*) © 1985 Christopher Morris/Black Star. **p. 515:** *Figure 13.7* Adapted from Lazarus, Opton, Nornikos, and Rankin, *Journal of Personality, 33* (4). Copyright © 1965 by Duke University Press. Reprinted by permission. **p. 517:** © Laimute Druskis 1988/Photo Researchers, Inc. **p. 519:** © Grant LeDuc/Monkmeyer Press Photo. **p. 520:** Lennart Nilsson © Boehringer Ingelheim International GMBH. **p. 521:** Drawing by Weber; © 1990 The New Yorker Magazine, Inc. **p. 527:** © 1988 Grant LeDuc/Monkmeyer Press Photo. **p. 528:** *Figure 13.8* From J. D. Levenkron et al., "Modifying the Type A Coronary Prone Behavior Pattern." *Journal of Consulting and Clinical Psychology,* Vol. 51, #2, pp. 192–204. Copyright 1983 by the American Psychological Association. Adapted by permission. **p. 530:** © 1984, Washington Post Writers Group, reprinted with permission.

Chapter 14: p. 539: *Table 14.1* Material taken from the *Personality Research Form Manual, Second Edition.* Copyright 1989, Douglas N. Jackson. Reproduced with permission of Sigma Assessment Systems, Inc., Research Psychologists Press Division, Port Huron, MI. **p. 540:** *Figure 14.2* © Carol Palmer. **p. 541:** Bettmann Archive. **p. 543:** *Figure 14.3* Adapted from *Personality: Strategies and Issues,* 6th edition, by R. M. Liebert and M. D. Spiegler. Copyright © 1990 by Wadsworth, Inc. Reprinted by permission of Brooks/Cole Publishing Company, Pacific Grove, CA 93950. **p. 544:** *Table 14.2* Robert M. Liebert and Michael D. Spiegler, *Personality: Strategies and Issues,* Chicago, IL, The Dorsey Press, © 1987, p. 95. Reprinted by permission. **p. 546:** © H. W. Silvester/Photo Researchers, Inc. **p. 548:** From the collection of the New Britain Museum of American Art, Connecticut, Harriet Russell Stanley Fund. Photo by E. Irving Blomstrann. **p. 549:** *Figure 14.4* Leary, T. (1957). *Interpersonal Diagnosis of Personality: A Functional Theory and Methodology for Personality Evaluation.* New York: Ronald Press Co. Reprinted by permission of the author. **p. 551:** *Figure 14.5* Emanuel F. Hammer, Ph.D., "Projective Drawings," in Rabin, ed., *Projective Techniques in Personality Assessment,* pp. 375–376. Copyright © 1968 by Springer Publishing Company, Inc., New York. Used by permission. **p. 553:** *Figure 14.6* (*a*) © Palmer & Brilliant; (*b*) UPI/Bettman Newsphotos; (*c*) © Steven Gyurina; (*d*) AP/Wide World Photos. **p. 555:** (*top*) *Figure 14.8* Eysenck, H. J., Rachman, S.: "The Causes and Cures of Neurosis: An Introduction to Modern Behavior Therapy Based on Learning Theory and the Principle of Conditioning." 1965. EDITS. Reprinted by permission. (*bottom*) Photograph by Bill Brandt: "East End Girl, Dancing the Lambeth Walk. Copyright Mrs. Noya Brandt. Courtesy: Edwynn Houk Gallery,

Inc., Chicago. **p. 556**: *Figure 14.9* Reproduced by special permission of the publisher, Psychological Assessment Resources, Inc., Odessa, FL 33556, from the NEO Personality Inventory by Paul Costa and Robert McCrae. Copyright 1978, 1985, 1989 by PAR, Inc. **p. 559**: © Jim Pickerell 1986/TSW-Click/Chicago. **p. 562**: © Scott J. Witte 1986/Third Coast Stock Source. **p. 564**: *Figure 14.11* From "The Assessment and Predictive Generality of Self-Percepts of Efficacy" by A. Bandura, 1982, *Journal of Behavior Therapy and Experimental Psychiatry, 13*, pp. 195–199. Copyright 1982 by the American Psychological Association. Reprinted by permission. **p. 565**: *Figure 14.12* From C. D. Williams, 1959, "The Elimination of Tantrum Behavior by Extinction Procedures," *Journal of Abnormal and Social Psychology, 59*, p. 269. **p. 566**: © Mark Reinstein/Gamma-Liaison. **p. 567**: © Bob Daemmrich/The Image Works. **p. 568**: © Julie Houch/TSW-Click/Chicago. **p. 571**: © Robert Frerck/TSW-Click/Chicago.

Chapter 15: p. 578: © Carol Palmer/The Picture Cube. **p. 581**: Culver Pictures, Inc. **p. 585**: *Table 15.2* Reprinted with permission from the *Diagnostic and Statistical Manual of Mental Disorders, Third Edition, Revised.* Copyright 1987, American Psychiatric Association. **p. 590**: The Far Side. Copyright 1985 Universal Press Syndicate. Reprinted by permission. All rights reserved. **p. 591**: © Frank Siteman/Stock, Boston. **p. 596**: "I'm Eve" by Chris Sizemore and Ellen Sain Pittilo. Copyright © 1977 by Chris Costner Sizemore. Reprinted by permission of Doubleday & Company, Inc. **p. 599**: © Miro Vintoniv/Stock, Boston. **p. 600**: © Joel Gordon, 1978. **p. 603**: Courtesy of the Prinzhorn-Collection. Photograph by Manfred Zentsch. **p. 604**: © Grunnitus/Monkmeyer Press Photo. **p. 606**: *Figure 15.3* Reproduced from *Abnormal Psychology*, Second Edition, by David L. Rosenhan and Martin E. P. Seligman, by permission of W. W. Norton & Company, Inc. Copyright © 1989, 1984 by W. W. Norton & Company, Inc. **p. 607**: *Figure 15.4* Office of Scientific Information, National Institute of Mental Health. **p. 608**: *Figure 15.5* From J. Zubin and B. Spring, 1977. "A New View of Schizophrenia," *Journal of Abnormal Psychology, 86*, pp. 103–126. Copyright 1977 by the American Psychological Association. Adapted by permission. **p. 609**: © Larry Mulvehill/Photo Researchers, Inc. **p. 615**: © Eric A. Roth/The Picture Cube. **p. 618**: © Peeter Vilms/Jeroboam, Inc.

Chapter 16: p. 625: © W. S. Silver/The Picture Cube. **p. 627**: Historical Pictures Service. **p. 633**: © Michal Heron/Monkmeyer Press Photos. **p. 635**: © Jim Pickerell/Black Star. **p. 638**: © Michael Weisbrot and Family. **p. 641**: *Figure 16.1* From Bandura, Blanchard, Ritter: *Journal of Personality and Social Psychology*, 1969, *13*, 173–199. Copyright 1969 by the American Psychological Association. Adapted by permission. **p. 642**: © Rick Friedman 1985/Black Star. **p. 643**: © Michael Hayman/Stock, Boston. **p. 644**: Courtesy, Albert Ellis, Institute for Rational Emotive Therapy. **p. 645**: Courtesy, Dr. Aaron T. Beck. **p. 647**: © Ann Chwatsky/Jeroboam, Inc. **p. 653**: *Figure 16.2* From G. R. Patterson, "Intervention for Boys with Conduct Problems: Multiple Settings, Treatments, and Criteria," *Journal of Consulting and Clinical Psychology*, 1974, *42*, 471–81. Copyright 1974 by the American Psychological Association. Reprinted by permission. **p. 654**: (*top*) Historical Pictures Service. (*bottom*) © Will McIntyre/Photo Researchers, Inc.

p. 659: © Alan Carey/The Image Works. **p. 661**: © Bohdan Hrynewych/Stock, Boston.

Chapter 17: p. 668: (*top*) © Frank Siteman/Picture Cube. (*bottom left*) © 1984 Robert Azzi/Woodfin Camp & Associates. (*bottom right*) © Homer Sykes 1984/Woodfin Camp & Associates. **p. 670**: Drawing by Mankoff; © 1985 The New Yorker Magazine, Inc. **p. 671**: © Andrew Holbrooke 1988/Black Star. **p. 672**: © Janice Fullman/The Picture Cube. **p. 673**: UPI/Bettmann Newsphotos. **p. 678**: (*top*) © George Goodwin/Monkmeyer Press Photo. (*bottom*) *Figure 17.3* From D. Byrne and D. Nelson, "Attraction as a Linear Function of Proportion of Positive Reinforcements," *Journal of Personality and Social Psychology, 1*, 659–663. Copyright 1965 by the American Psychological Association. Adapted by permission. **p. 680**: *Figure 17.5* Copyright © George Levinger and J. Diedrick Snoek, 1972. *Attraction in Relationship: A New Look at Interpersonal Attraction.* Morristown, NJ: General Learning Press, 1972. **p. 682**: © Catherine Karnow/Woodfin Camp & Associates. **p. 683**: *Figure 17.6* Adapted from figure on p. 122 of Sternberg, R. J., "Triangulating Love," in R. J. Sternberg and M. L. Barnes, (Eds.), *The Psychology of Love*, 1988, Yale University Press. Copyright © 1988 by Yale University Press. Reprinted by permission. **p. 685**: *Figure 17.7* Adapted with permission from Kahn, Arnold S., *Social Psychology*, © 1984 Wm. C. Brown Publishers, Dubuque, Iowa. All rights reserved. **p. 685**: *Figure 17.8* From L. Festinger and J. M. Carlsmith, "Cognitive Consequences of Forced Compliance," *Journal of Abnormal and Social Psychology, 58*, 203–210. **p. 686**: *Figure 17.9* From E. Aronson, J. A. Turner, and J. M. Carlsmith: "Communicator Credibility and Communicator Discrepancy as a Determinant of Opinion Change." *Journal of Abnormal and Social Psychology, 67*, 31–36. Copyright 1963 by the American Psychological Association. Adapted by permission. **p. 687**: © Ira Wyman/Sygma. **p. 689**: *Figure 17.10* From W. J. McGuire, 1968, "Personality and Susceptibility to Social Influence" in E. F. Borgatta and W. W. Lambert: *Handbook of Personality Theory and Research.* Reprinted by permission of the author. **p. 692**: © Alice Kandell/Photo Researchers, Inc. **p. 693**: © George Mars Cassidy/The Picture Cube. **p. 696**: © Paula M. Lerner/The Picture Cube.

Chapter 18: p. 704: © Nabeel Turner/TSW–Click/Chicago. **p. 703**: *Figure 18.1* From "Opinions and Social Pressure" by Solomon E. Asch. Illustration on p. 32 by Sara Love. Copyright © 1955 by Scientific American, Inc. All rights reserved. **p. 707**: © Kok/Gamma Liaison. **p. 708**: © Wally McNamee 1987/Woodfin Camp & Associates. **p. 709**: Figure 18.2 © 1965 by Stanley Milgram, from the film *Obedience*, distributed by the New York University Film Division and the Pennsylvania State University, PCP. By permission of the Estate of Stanley Milgram. **p. 710**: *Figure 18.3* Courtesy of Alexandra Milgram. From S. Milgram, "Behavioral Study of Obedience," *Journal of Abnormal and Social Psychology, 67*, 371–378. Copyright 1963 by the American Psychological Association. Adapted by permission of the publisher and literary executor. **p. 711**: © Thomas Hopker/Woodfin Camp & Associates. **p. 712**: *Figure 18.4* Stanley Milgram, "Some Conditions of Obedience and Disobedience to Authority." *Human Relations*, Vol. 18, No. 1, 1965, p. 63. Copyright © 1972 by Stanley Milgram. Reprinted by permission of Alexandra Milgram, literary executor.